Philosophers and Physiologists Important for the History of Psychology

Thomas Hobbes (1588–1679)

John Locke

John Locke (1632–1704)

George Berkeley (1685–1753)

Locke publishes *Essay Concerning Human Understanding* (1690)

David Hartley (1705–1757) Julien de La Mettrie (1709–1751)

David Hume (1711–1776)

Immanuel Kant (1724–1804)

Johann Wolfgang von Goethe (1749–1832)

Franz Joseph Gall (1758–1828)

Georg Friedrich Hegel (1770–1831) James Mill (1773–1836)

Charles Bell (1774–1842) Johann Friedrich Herbart (1776–1841)

François Magendie (1783–1855) Arthur Schopenhauer (1788–1860)

Pierre Flourens (1794–1867) Ernst Weber (1795–1878)

Auguste Comte (1798–1857)

Gustav Fechner (1801–1887) John Stuart Mill (1806–1873)

Charles Darwin (1809–1882) Alexander Bain (1818–1903)

Hermann Helmholtz (1821–1894) Francis Galton (1822–1911)

Pierre Paul Broca (1824–1880)

Ewald Hering (1834–1918)

Gustav Fritsch (1838–1927) Eduard Hitzig (1838–1907)

Camillo Golgi (1843–1926)

Carl Wernicke (1848–1905)

Santiago Ramón y Cajal (1852–1934)

Charles Sherrington (1857–1952)

Fechner publishes *Elements of Psychophysics* (1860)

Otto Loewi (1873–1961)

Wilder Penfield (1891–1976)

Representative Historical Events

1600 Giordano Bruno burned as a heretic

James I dies

1650 Descartes dies

Newton publishes *Principia Mathematica*

1700 Frederick the Great is born

Handel flourishes

1750 J. S. Bach dies

Josiah Wedgwood founds pottery works

American Revolution begins

French Revolution begins

1800 Goethe and Napoleon meet

Mississippi becomes a state

Texas becomes a state

1850 Phineas P. Gage's accident

Karl Marx flourishes

Darwin publishes *Origin of Species* (1859)

Babe Ruth is born

1900

Charles Darwin

Connections in the History and Systems of PSYCHOLOGY

Connections in the History and Systems of PSYCHOLOGY

THIRD EDITION

B. Michael Thorne
Mississippi State University

Tracy B. Henley
Texas A&M University–Commerce

Houghton Mifflin Company
Boston   New York

To Wanda, my wife and life companion, and to my children, Dean and Erin—B. M. T.

To Robert Alexander Henley—T. B. H.

Publisher: Charles Hartford

Senior Sponsoring Editor: Kerry T. Baruth

Development Editor: Caryn Yilmaz

Associate Project Editor: Shelley Dickerson

Marketing Manager: Jane Potter

Senior Manufacturing Coordinator: Priscilla J. Bailey

Cover images:

1. Plato and Aristotle, detail from the fresco *The School of Athens* by Raphael (1483–1520). Stanza della Segnatura, Vatican Palace/Scala/Art Resource, NY.
2. B. F. Skinner in his laboratory. Photograph, B. F. Skinner Foundation.
3. Galton Anthropometric Laboratory, opened 1884. Photograph, © The Grant Museum of Zoology and Comparative Anatomy, University College, London, UK.
4. Title page, René Descartes, *Les Meditations.* Rare Book Room, Cambridge University Library, Cambridge, UK.
5. Mock-up title page, Charles Darwin, *The Origin of Species.* American Philosophical Society, Philadelphia, PA.

Text credits: Ch. 7: Excerpts from Boring, E. G. (1927). "Edward Bradford Titchener: 1867–1927." *The American Journal of Psychology, 38,* 488–506; Ch. 10: Excerpt from letter by Dr. B. F. Skinner is reprinted with permission of the B. F. Skinner Foundation, Morgantown, WV; Ch. 10: Ross, D. (1972). *G. Stanley Hall: The Psychologist as Prophet.* Copyright © 1972 D. Ross. Reprinted by permission of the University of Chicago Press; Ch. 12: Excerpts from Hannush, M. J. (1987). "John B. Watson Remembered: An Interview with James B. Watson." *Journal of the History of the Behavioral Sciences, 23,* 137–152. Reprinted by permission of the author; Ch. 12: Excerpts from Watson, J. B. (1936). John Broadus Watson. In C. Murchison (Ed.), *A History of Psychology in Autobiography* (Vol. 3, pp. 271–281). Worcester, MA: Clark University Press. Reprinted by permission of Clark University Press; Ch. 15: From "In Memory of Sigmund Freud," by W. H. Auden, as appeared in *Collected Poems* by W. H. Auden. Reprinted by permission of the publisher, Faber and Faber, Ltd.; Ch. 18: From Turing, A. M. (1950). "Computing Machinery and the Mind." *Mind, 59,* 433–460. Reprinted by permission of Oxford University Press.

Printed in the U.S.A.

Library of Congress Control Number: 2003110170

ISBN: 0-618-41512-2

123456789–MV–08 07 06 05 04

Brief Contents

Contents

Preface

Most students close their undergraduate careers—and open their graduate ones—with a course about the history of their field. With this in mind, we set out to write a book for such a course in psychology. In writing this book, we were guided by three goals: (1) to make the work scholarly and comprehensive; (2) to incorporate as many pedagogical aids as possible; and (3) to make the subject interesting and entertaining, consistent with current, accurate, and comprehensive scholarship.

NEW FOR THIS EDITION

In our revision, we have been guided by the same three goals. For example, in our efforts to keep the book as scholarly and comprehensive as possible, we have incorporated information from more than 185 new references; 153 of these are dated 1990 or later, with more than 100 dated from 2000 and beyond. In addition to updating and expanding the reference list, **key changes** for this edition are as follows:

- New photographs and figures have been added to the already exceptional illustrations in the book.
- Birth and death dates have been added to the photographs where appropriate.
- To enhance the usefulness of the book as a reference, for each name boldfaced in the text, the page number on which the fullest biographical information appears is boldfaced in the Name Index.
- The emphasis in earlier editions on the schools of psychology has been drastically reduced.
- A timeline of important psychological and historical events has been added to the inside front and back covers.

Important chapter-by-chapter changes include:

- **Chapter 1: Introduction.** The chapter now concludes with a discussion of psychology as a science and how changes in the philosophy of science have affected the science of psychology. The second edition's discussion of Goddard and the Kallikaks has been replaced by the investigation of Clever Hans from Chapter 8 in the second edition, which illustrates the success of the early use of the scientific method to solve the mystery of an apparent horse genius.
- **Chapter 2: Precursors to Psychology in Ancient Greece.** The section entitled "Other Schools of Thought," which covers Skepticism, Cynicism, Stoicism, and Epicureanism, has been moved to Chapter 3.
- **Chapter 3: The Roman Period and the Middle Ages.** Chapter 3 in the second edition, which covered the Roman period and the Middle Ages, as well as the philosophers of the early Renaissance, has been divided into two chapters for this edition. As the title indicates, Chapter 3 now covers the Roman period and the Middle Ages. The discussion of Jesus, Mohammed, and the Crusades

has been increased, and the coverage of "scholasticism" has been amplified.

- **Chapter 4: The Renaissance and Early Modern Philosophers.** This is the second half of the previous edition's Chapter 3. Julien de La Mettrie, whose philosophy can be seen as a step beyond that of Descartes, has been moved from the next chapter to this one. The concept of "humanism" is more fully introduced.
- **Chapter 5: Empiricism, Associationism, Positivism, and Common-Sense Psychology.** The term "empiricism" is more extensively defined in the chapter's introduction. There is now additional discussion of Jeremy Bentham and utilitarianism, as well as of John Stuart Mill's subdivision of psychology, which he called "ethology." Further distinction has been made between the positivisms of Comte and Mach.
- **Chapter 6: Continental Philosophies: Rationalism, Romanticism, and Existentialism.** The introduction of existentialism has been moved to this chapter from the second edition's Chapter 15, with an increase in both the biography and ideas of existentialism's founders, Kierkegaard and Nietzsche. The introduction to romanticism also has been amplified.
- **Chapter 7: Physiological Influences on the Development of Psychology.** The coverage of psychophysics (Weber and Fechner) has been moved back to this chapter from its second edition position in the following chapter. The discussion of Roger Sperry's split-brain research, previously linked with Fechner, is now in Chapter 16's section on neuroscience. Additions have been made to the discussions of Helmholtz, Fritsch and Hitzig, and Cajal.
- **Chapter 8: The Origins of Modern Scientific Psychology in Germany.** This is a combination of the second edition's Chapters 7 and 8, without psychophysics. Specifically, Wundt's German contemporaries (Brentano, Stumpf, Husserl, Ebbinghaus, G. E. Müller, and Külpe) are now included with Wundt. There is expanded discussion of why psychology arose out of the German university system. In order to condense the chapter, cuts were made in the discussion of Titchener's psychology and Ebbinghaus's methodology, and the discussion of Stumpf's investigation of Clever Hans has been moved to Chapter 1.
- **Chapter 9: Darwin's Influence.** As part of the deemphasis on the schools of psychology, this chapter's title has been changed from "British Forerunners of Functionalism" to "Darwin's Influence." The term "uniformitarianism" has been redefined for clarity, and the section on correlation and regression has been expanded.
- **Chapter 10: Early American Psychology.** The title change from "American Forerunners of Functionalism" to "Early American Psychology" represents a further deemphasis of the schools of psychology. The Titchener-Münsterberg comparison has been removed as a separate subheading, and the material in the comparison has been reduced substantially.
- **Chapter 11: Functionalism.** There are no major changes, but the manuscript has been streamlined in places to make room for reference additions.
- **Chapter 12: Animal Psychology and Early Behaviorism.** Lashley, and all related material, has been moved to Chapter 16.
- **Chapter 13: Neobehaviorism.** The conclusions section has been lengthened to note that behaviorism, loosely defined, may not have been "killed" by the cognition revolution, and, in fact, may be the force that best unifies modern psychology.
- **Chapter 14: Gestalt Psychology.** Coverage of Harry Harlow's explanation for insight learning has been increased. A diagram of Lewin's life space concepts has been added.
- **Chapter 15: Psychoanalysis.** Much of the coverage of Kierkegaard and Nietzsche has been moved to Chapter 6. Adler and Jung's discussion has been moved to this chapter from Chapter 16 in the second edition. Discussion of the specifics of Freud's theory and of the ideas of the neo-Freudians has been dramatically tightened.
- **Chapter 16: Mind and Brain: Clinical Psychology Meets Neuroscience.** The title change from "Clinical Psychology Beyond Psychoanalysis" reflects the new emphasis on clinical psychology and neuroscience (clinical and experimental). The coverage of clinical psychology in the first half of the chapter is the same as in the second edition, without Adler and Jung. New for this edition, the neuroscience section collects the material on

Lashley and associates from Chapter 12, adds Sperry from the second edition's Chapter 7, and provides expanded coverage of A. R. Luria.

- **Chapter 17: Applied Psychology.** The material on Goddard and the Kallikaks in Chapter 1 of the second edition has been returned to this chapter. In the discussion of the study of gender differences, there is now an examination of why interest in women's issues waned in the 1920s and was reawakened in the 1960s and 1970s.
- **Chapter 18: The Cognitive "Revolution."** Although there are no major changes, the manuscript has been streamlined in places to make room for reference additions.

RETAINED IN THIS EDITION

Because students (and their instructors) like to learn about people—their lives and their ideas—we have made our biographical information as three-dimensional as possible. For example, from our book, readers can get a sense of William James as a person, that he agonized over a career and suffered from depression before finding his true calling in teaching, that he had a lifelong interest in the paranormal, in addition to the standard facts that he lived from 1842 to 1910 and wrote what may be psychology's most famous book. We have also introduced information that reveals the struggle of women early in the history of American psychology, including the efforts of pioneers such as Mary Calkins, Milicent Shinn, and Margaret Floy Washburn. This, and the special coverage we have given to minorities in the history of psychology, reflects our awareness of two important facts: First, women and minorities have made historically significant contributions to psychology; and, second, the discipline of psychology has long been attractive to women and minorities.

In addition to providing rich biographical coverage, our book is about connections—emphasized even in the title, *Connections in the History and Systems of Psychology*. We have been struck by the fascinating and substantive connections that permeate the history of psychology, and we have made such connections an integrating feature of this book. All too often students leave their history of psychology courses without a sense of who was contemporary with whom, who influenced whom, and whose ideas affected which system of psychology, thereby missing out on the overarching themes in the history of our field.

In Chapter 1, we talk about how historical facts are often biased by the filters through which they pass (e.g., historians and/or the people involved). It is undoubtedly true that we have "filtered" this survey of the history of psychology. You do not have to be an ardent behaviorist to appreciate that the social and educational contexts from which we emerge shape our thoughts and actions. Likewise, some historians clearly endorse a certain view of the history of science: that it must be thematic, that it is paradigmatic, that it often is socially constructed, and so on. Although we are aware of many such theories, we have attempted to favor none of them.

TEXT ORGANIZATION

In keeping with our efforts to deemphasize the "great schools" of psychology, the book is no longer explicitly divided into three sections. Following an introductory chapter, we cover psychology's philosophical and physiological antecedents in Chapters 2 through 7. Our philosophical coverage begins in Chapter 2 with the ancient Greeks, emphasizing the main currents of thought during the "Golden Age" of Greece (e.g., of the philosophers Socrates, Plato, and Aristotle).

Next, we explore the development of philosophy and science through the Roman period, the Middle Ages, and into the Renaissance in Chapters 3 and 4. In Chapter 4, we highlight Descartes as a major transitional figure leading toward the modern era. Instructors wishing to emphasize psychology's "modern" history can use Chapter 4 as a convenient starting point.

From Descartes and his immediate successors on the Continent (e.g., Spinoza and Leibniz), we examine the major philosophical antecedents to the beginning of psychology as a separate discipline. Particularly emphasized are the British empiricists and associationists (e.g., Locke, Berkeley, Hume, and James and John Stuart Mill), the French empiricists (e.g., Condillac and Cabanis), and the Continental rationalists (e.g., Kant, Hegel, and Herbart). The influences from positivism and romanticism are also detailed.

Chapter 7 surveys the effects on psychology from physiology through the 19th century. The chapter ends with a description of Weber and Fechner's psychophysics, which some historians of psychology (e.g., Boring) have suggested as the beginning of scientific psychology.

Chapter 8 examines the work of Wundt, his students, and contemporaries. Wundt is generally considered the originator of psychology as a separate scientific discipline. In addition to covering Wundt's voluntarism and Titchener's structuralism, the chapter includes individuals who offered a phenomenological alternative to Wundt's view of psychology, including Brentano, Stumpf, Külpe, and G. E. Müller.

Next, we examine the antecedents and founding of functionalism, the system that developed in opposition to voluntarism and structuralism. Because evolution was central to the thinking of the functionalists, we begin by focusing on Darwin and his cousin Galton. We cover extensively American anticipators such as James, Hall, and Cattell, and the founders and developers of the school—Dewey, Angell, Carr, Woodworth, and Thorndike—conclude the chapters devoted to the formation of American functional psychology.

The study of animal behavior (e.g., by Romanes, C. Lloyd Morgan, Thorndike, and Yerkes), Russian objective psychology—culminating with Pavlov—and the pragmatic approach of Watson are highlighted in our examination of behaviorism's founding. Reflecting behaviorism's belief in the importance of the environment for the development of behavior, we focus on learning theory in the contributions of neobehaviorists such as Guthrie, Tolman, Hull, and Skinner.

After behaviorism, Chapters 14 and 15 survey the two remaining systems of psychology that developed during the early history of psychology as a science: Gestalt psychology and psychoanalysis. Chapter 16 looks at the development of clinical psychology and modern neuropsychology, whereas Chapter 17 examines the history of several areas of applied psychology (i.e., intelligence testing, psychometrics, social psychology, and industrial psychology).

Focusing on the cognitive "revolution," the book's final chapter looks at early contributors (e.g., Bartlett, Vygotsky, and Piaget) and explores the work of such contemporaries as Chomsky, Bruner, Miller, and Neisser. Some of the topics of interest are memory, categorization, reasoning, and artificial intelligence.

PEDAGOGICAL FEATURES: DRAWING CONNECTIONS

To stimulate reader interest and to help students draw thematic and biographical connections, this book incorporates a number of special features.

- **Extensive and carefully selected illustrations.** We have consciously tried to include photos and illustrations whenever appropriate to bring history to life. Several of the pictures are rare and show the individuals at younger ages than typically seen in histories of psychology.
- **Chapter outlines.** Each chapter begins with an outline of the chapter's major topics, giving the reader an overview of the chapter's contents.
- **Chronologies.** The timelines that open each chapter are designed to orient the reader to the period of history discussed in the chapter. They show when the chapter's major characters lived within the context of major world events, and help illustrate the connections—some substantive, others merely fascinating coincidence—among people, ideas, and the times.
- **Connections questions.** To further aid the reader's development of connections in the material, we have supplied several questions that draw together many related concepts at the end of each chapter. These questions can serve as critical thinking exercises.
- **Chapter summaries.** Good summaries help reinforce the information the reader has been exposed to in the chapter. In writing the summaries, we have tried to present enough information to refresh and help organize the reader's learning without inviting laziness.
- **Annotated suggested readings.** For the reader whose interest has been piqued by our presenta-

tion, a brief, annotated list of suggested readings accompanies each chapter. We have chosen articles and books that are particularly readable examples of the work of key individuals in each chapter.
- **Key terms and glossary.** Throughout the book, we have highlighted key names and terms by boldfacing them. All boldfaced names and terms appear in a comprehensive glossary at the end of the book.
- **Ancillary material.** The book's major ancillary is a combination Instructor's Resource Manual (IRM) and Test Bank. The IRM offers chapter-by-chapter suggestions for teaching the history and systems course, including classroom discussion ideas. The Test Bank supplies both multiple-choice and essay questions.

ACKNOWLEDGMENTS

At each stage of development, certain individuals played facilitating roles in this project. At Houghton Mifflin, Kerry Baruth served as the Senior Sponsoring Editor for this edition. In addition, we have been aided immensely by Editorial Assistant Caryn Yilmaz and Project Editors Shelley Dickerson and Nancy Benjamin. We would also like to thank Dr. George Windholz at the University of North Carolina at Charlotte for his efforts at securing for us reprints of his many fine articles on Pavlov. At Mississippi State University, our department head, Steve Klein, continues to help us in myriad ways. We also wish to acknowledge several of our colleagues who helped us get the third edition off to a good start:

A. Jerry Bruce, Sam Houston State University
Robert B. Cameron, Fairmont State College
Marc A. Linberg, Marshall University
Jonathan Raskin, State University of New York at New Paltz
Warren R. Street, Central Washington University
Susana Urbina, University of North Florida

We owe an enormous debt as well to the colleagues listed below for their thoughtful reviews of the first- and second-edition manuscripts as they were being developed:

Tom Allaway, Algoma University College
Gira Bhatt, Camosun College
C. George Boeree, Shippensburg University
Charles L. Brewer, Furman University
A. Jerry Bruce, Sam Houston State University
Gerald S. Clack, Loyola University New Orleans
Rebecca L. Van Cleave, Carson-Newman College
Philip W. Compton, Ohio Northern University
George M. Diekhoff, Midwestern State University
Wallace E. Dixon, Heidleberg College
Charles E. Early, Roanoke College
Michael L. Epstein, Rider University
Kathleen M. Galleher, St. Mary's University of Minnesota
Harvey J. Ginsburg, Southwest Texas State University
Bruce B. Henderson, Western Carolina University
Stephen Hoyer, Pittsburg State University
Deborah Johnson, University of Southern Maine
William Klipec, Drake University
Donald McBurney, University of Pittsburgh
Robert J. Presbie, State University of New York, New Paltz
Tom Randall, Rhode Island College
John P. Rickards, University of Connecticut, Storrs
Michael J. Scavio, California State University, Fullerton
David J. Schneider, Rice University
Ronald D. Taylor, University of Kentucky
W. Scott Terry, The University of North Carolina at Charlotte
Phil D. Wann, Missouri Western State College
Catherine M. Wehlburg, Stephens College
David Zehr, Plymouth State College

B. Michael Thorne
Tracy B. Henley

Connections in the History and Systems of PSYCHOLOGY

Introduction

CHAPTER 1

How are the years 1879 and a small room in a university dining hall connected to the founding of psychology as a separate science? What famous person in psychology's history wrote a serious work on the spiritual life of plants? In what way are the sights a German psychologist saw out his train window as he rode along the Rhine River in 1910 connected to the development of Gestalt psychology? What is the connection between Phineas P. Gage's accident in which a metal rod was blown through his head and our present-day conviction that the brain is the organ of the mind?

If you are thinking that a list of questions is an odd way to begin a textbook, you are right. But hold on—we have more questions that might pique your interest in psychology's history.

Can you connect a young Harvard graduate student's prohibited mind-reading experiments in children, his aborted study of learning in chickens, and his cat puzzle boxes with one of psychology's most enduring and important "laws"? What woman was the only student in the class that first used William James's (1890) now-classic *Principles of Psychology* as a textbook? Why do you think she was the only student in the class? Whose novel—*Walden Two*—popularized the behaviorist approach to learning and social engineering?

As you might imagine, there are literally thousands of additional questions we might ask, but a textbook devoted solely to questions would not be very informative. Because all of these questions are answered in this book, you have interesting reading ahead.

OUTLINE

WHY STUDY THE HISTORY OF PSYCHOLOGY?

As Harvard historian, philosopher, and poet George Santayana (Chapter 10) said, "Those who do not know history are doomed to repeat it." In other words, if we examine the mistakes of our predecessors, perhaps we can avoid making the same or similar ones. But, first, we have to know about the mistakes themselves.

For example, structuralism (Chapter 8), an approach that sought to discover the contents or elements of consciousness by using introspective analysis, is today generally considered one of psychology's digressions. Still, it was important both because it revealed introspection as a technique *not* to pursue in the way Edward Bradford Titchener, structuralism's founder, had chosen to pursue it, and because it gave more flexible systems like functionalism (Chapter 11) and Gestalt psychology (Chapter 14) something to oppose. Scientific movements begin out of such competition (Boring, 1929).

Another reason a course in the history of psychology is important involves connections. Too often psychology students have little conception of how the modern ideas they are exposed to evolved, or even how the ideas are related. If there is one thing about psychology that we can say with assurance, it is that the field is incredibly diverse. History is one course that cuts across the subfields of our science, ties them together, and allows you to see the evolution of ideas within them. You begin your study with a course of broad scope—introductory psychology—and we believe that near the end of your coursework you should have a similar integrative experience. By synthesizing psychology's disparate elements, by tracing the progression of ideas and scientific developments, a history course provides the breadth needed to complete your training. In this book, we will examine topics in cognition, sensation and perception, physiological psychology, learning, intelligence testing, psychoanalysis, social psychology, developmental psychology, and other areas. We will discuss all of these areas from the unifying perspective of history.

A course in the history of psychology helps students gain perspective on the world and their place in it. In this way, the course can be a major part of the psychology student's liberal arts education (Fuchs & Viney, 2002). In addition, an overview of the history of psychology can help students develop a more critical view of all the new techniques and ideas they will encounter in a career as a psychologist. By revealing the great ideas and accomplishments of people in the past, a history course should also give students a sense of humility.

Yet another reason the study of the history of psychology is important is because it introduces (or reintroduces) the student to the terminology of psychology and to the rich meaning behind each term. For example, what does it mean to be a behaviorist or a Gestaltist or a logical positivist? The answer in each case can be found in the study of the history of psychology.

Of course, little justification is necessary when a topic is as fascinating as the history of psychology (Baker, 2002). Like so many famous figures through the ages, most of the people who made psychology what it is had one thing in common—they were not dull. In fact, they were often "characters" with interesting lives, amazing accomplishments, and sometimes incredible insights. We hope that our treatment of psychology's important people and their ideas will stimulate you to pursue further the study of psychology's history.

THOUGHTS ABOUT HISTORY

Unfortunately for the students of history and the writers of history textbooks, history's "facts" are often elusive and frequently cannot be verified. An event occurs and may or may not be recorded, and even when it is registered, the record may be distorted by the recorder's perspective. To illustrate this biasing effect, Albert Hastorf and Hadley Cantril (1954) conducted an important study of perspective. Their work followed that season's Dartmouth-Princeton football game. Both schools' newspapers devoted much space for several weeks after the game to the events surrounding the injury to the Princeton quarterback. The Princeton paper discussed Dartmouth's *clear* strategy of dispatching the quarterback early in the game, whereas the Dartmouth paper reported only a roughly fought, fair contest with unfortunate, but accidental, injuries. Which paper was right?

Hastorf and Cantril (1954) showed students at both schools clips of the game film and asked them questions, some designed to determine which fouls, if any, were "flagrant." Not surprisingly, students from the two schools reported seeing different things. Think of the last televised football game you watched. If you supported a particular team and there was a controversial play, your perception of the play probably favored your team. The same thing is true of many historical facts—they were recorded by people with perspectives that probably influenced their perceptions.

As one example, much of what the modern world knows of the psychology of Wilhelm Wundt (Chapter 8), the man usually credited with founding psychology as a science in 1879, comes from the writings of one of psychology's most famous historians, **Edwin Garrigues Boring** (1886–1968). Was Boring's treatment of Wundt completely unbiased? Probably not.

Boring (1950) dedicated his classic work, *A History of Experimental Psychology,* to his mentor, Edward Bradford Titchener (Chapter 8). Titchener received his Ph.D. under Wundt and modeled his psychology after what he perceived to be the most important aspects of his teacher's system. Actually,

Titchener adopted only a part of Wundt's system and downplayed or ignored much of the rest. Influenced by Titchener, Boring perpetuated this restricted view of Wundt, which has only recently been revised (e.g., Blumenthal, 1979; Danziger, 1979; Leahey, 1981).

Our point here is not to criticize unduly Boring's most important work but, rather, to recognize some of the sources of bias that can infect any historian's efforts. One nearly ubiquitous form is called the **presentist bias,** which is the tendency to discuss and analyze past ideas, people, and events in terms of the present. For example, if we refer to a past psychologist (e.g., Titchener) as someone who treated his female students less seriously than their male counterparts, we are imposing our present sensitivities on a bygone era. We are forgetting that during most of our history such bias against women (or religions or ethnic groups) was the cultural norm, and the person we are describing was probably just reflecting the milieu in which he or she lived.

Also, any history textbook will reflect the idiosyncrasies of its author(s). That is, the authors decide to include and emphasize certain events, ideas, topics, and people and to ignore or deemphasize others. A classic work by a philosopher of science, **Thomas Kuhn** (1922–1996), suggested one reason for this phenomenon of history.

Kuhn (1970) wrote that once a particular theory has become widely accepted, the theory's proponents exercise a certain degree of power. By controlling the journals that publish current research, they are able to downplay competing theories. Proponents of the dominant theory may also write the textbooks (including history texts) for that generation. An analysis of psychology textbooks shows omissions and emphases in keeping with the theoretical leanings of the writer(s) (Henley, Johnson, Herzog, & Jones, 1989). Historical segments in some textbooks suggest that past theories were steppingstones to the modern "correct" way of thinking. However, Kuhn contended that there is little evidence for this stepwise ideal and that such depictions of history's progress are often fictions intended to lend credibility to existing ideas.

We admit our own agendas in selecting material for this text. We are biased in favor of the famous (and infamous) people important in psychology's history. We are biased in favor of interesting and colorful material, although we have provided appropriate coverage of other less interesting, but undeniably important, facts in the history of our field. We are biased in favor of people and events that seem relevant to contemporary American psychology, although we appreciate that many parallel insights arose in Asia. We are somewhat biased in favor of the ***Zeitgeist*** (spirit of the times) theory of history, and this is why our title begins with the word *Connections.* In other words, we believe that discoveries, new ideas, and inventions do not arise in a vacuum and that it is important to place them in historical perspective. Our effort to provide historical context is evident in the chronologies at the beginning of each chapter following this one and in the Connections Questions posed after every chapter. Still, despite our bias in favor of the *Zeitgeist* theory, the text is primarily organized around people.

Archives of the History of American Psychology–The University of Akron.

Edwin G. Boring (1886–1968), early in his career

Boring (1950) argued for the *Zeitgeist,* or, as he sometimes called it, the naturalistic theory of history, as opposed to the personalistic, or great person, view. Are important historical contributions the sole property of great minds, or do great minds make such contributions because of their cultural and intellectual contexts? For example, was Wundt the founder of psychology as a separate scientific discipline because of his genius, or would psychology have arisen as a science in the late 19th century even if Wundt had decided to remain a politician?

There is much evidence to support the idea that the latter part of the 19th century was the right time for the birth of scientific psychology. For example, Franz Brentano (Chapter 8), Wundt's contemporary, had a competing system based on his *Psychologie vom empirischen Standpunkte* (*Psychology From an Empirical Standpoint*), which was published in 1874, the same year Wundt finished publishing his work calling for a separate science of psychology, *Grundzüge der physiologischen Psychologie* (*Principles of Physiological Psychology*).

Further evidence for the *Zeitgeist* theory comes from discovery multiples, which are independent contributions occurring at nearly the same time. For example, calculus was developed (ca. 1675) independently by Gottfried Wilhelm von Leibniz and Sir Isaac Newton (both Chapter 4). And Charles Darwin (Chapter 9) was stimulated to publish his theory of evolution in 1859 by a paper sent to him the year before by Alfred Russel Wallace (Chapter 9), a young naturalist. In a letter to a friend dated June 18, 1858, the day on which Wallace's paper arrived, Darwin wrote: "[I]f Wallace had my MS. sketch written out in 1842, he could not have made a better short abstract! Even his terms now stand as heads of my chapters" (Darwin, 1898, p. 473).

Additional evidence for the naturalistic theory of history comes from ideas that had to be "rediscovered" because the intellectual climate was not right for their acceptance. For example, consider the use of systematic desensitization as a method for removing pathological fears. In systematic desensitization, the treated person is gradually exposed in a nonthreatening context either to ideas of the feared object or to the feared object itself. John Locke (1693/1964; Chapter 5) gave instructions for the removal of "vain terrors" in children that sound remarkably like the method "discovered" by Joseph Wolpe (Chapter 5) in 1958 and actually used by Mary Cover Jones (and reported by John Watson, 1928/1972; Chapter 12) in removing a child's fears of white, furry animals.

According to Boring (1950), "You get the personalistic view when you ignore the [antecedents] of the great man, and you get the naturalistic view back again when you ask what made the great man great" (p. 4). We will ask what made the great person great in our review of the history of psychology. That is, we will explore wherever possible the "connections" between one person's great idea and the ideas of his or her predecessors and contemporaries. Note that what Boring and others called the "great man" view we are calling the "great person" approach. We strongly believe that women have also shaped the history of psychology. Wherever possible, we will discuss the contributions of women who have often been omitted in earlier treatments of psychology's history.

Another problem in writing about history is that historical facts are not like scientific facts; we cannot verify them experimentally. All we have to go on are the writings of observers at the time or the later writings of people who got their "evidence" by word of mouth, from people's memories of the events. Sometimes the observers were the people themselves—that is, the writings are autobiographical.

Although getting the words directly from the source would seem to be ideal, there are several reasons why autobiographical material might be distorted. For example, most people write autobiographies long after the events have taken place. Human memory is notoriously fallible and often changes over time.

Events and sequences of events are often remembered as being more orderly than they really were. That is, an autobiographer may inadvertently "clean up" certain memories to make the narrative of his or her life history more cohesive. Modern cognitive psychologists (Chapter 18) have studied autobiographical memories, including our tendency to "reconstruct," as opposed to "re-view," the information we remember. These reconstructions can change our memory based on events in the present or during the intervening period.

Although these effects have long been known (e.g., Bartlett, 1932), modern research is particularly illuminating. For example, Ulric Neisser's (1982) book, *Memory Observed,* presents work that shows this influence in everyday events. In one study, subjects were asked to recall whether they saw broken glass in a film of an automobile accident. Subjects who were asked if they saw glass after the two cars "smashed" said yes 32% of the time, whereas subjects who were asked if they saw glass after the two cars "hit" said yes only 14% of the time. Actually, there was no broken glass in the film (see Loftus & Palmer, 1974, for the complete study).

In addition, much of what we remember relates to us. Because we have a set of beliefs about ourselves, our memory of autobiographical events tends to conform to our self-perceptions, even when they conflict with what actually happened. One well-documented example of this phenomenon involves John Dean—a major player in the 1972 Watergate scandal, which eventually led to the resignation of President Richard Nixon. Comparison of Dean's testimony to subsequently recovered tape recordings revealed that, although his memory was remarkable in many ways, it was also systematically distorted to present Dean as more important than he really was. Neisser (1982) argued convincingly that Dean's strong self-image contaminated and reorganized his recall of the events in which he participated. According to Neisser's research, then, we tend to remember information in ways that support our self-image. Furthermore, we may unconsciously reorganize information to make it consistent with beliefs about how we should have acted in a given situation.

It is also possible for autobiographical material to present events in a more negative light than they deserve. For example, G. Stanley Hall's autobiography (Hall, 1923; Chapter 10) perhaps reflects in its bitterness the author's age and health. Similarly, we know that Wundt's autobiography contained several factual errors (Hilgard, 1987), and to hear John Watson (1936)—one of the central figures of American behaviorism (Chapter 12)—tell it, it is a miracle he ever finished college.

So, historical facts may become distorted by the people involved, and sometimes this may even be recognized at the time the autobiography is written. For example, pharmacologist Otto Loewi (Chapter 7) wrote at the beginning of an autobiographical sketch: "An advantage of autobiography may be that its author reports more competently than others on his inner experience and its effects; yet, even so, fiction may come into play because a retrospective report may not always truly reflect the past as it happened" (Loewi, 1960, p. 3).

Recognizing the limitations of biographical and autobiographical material, Innes (1969) suggested that biographies and autobiographies should contain extensive details about the subject's family life and social background. This level of detail may be necessary for future historians to examine the effects of the early environment on a person's subsequent life and thought. Although we could not include as much biographical detail on major individuals as you would find in dedicated biographies, we have tried to present enough information to give you at least the flavor of the life and times of the individual.

Of course, factual inaccuracies sometimes enter our story of the history of psychology without being introduced in either biographies or autobiographies. Even worse, such inaccuracies become remarkably hard to dislodge once they have taken root (Burton, 2001). For example, the illusion in which a circle ringed by smaller circles appears larger than the same-sized circle surrounded by larger circles is often called the Titchener illusion, or sometimes the Ebbinghaus/Titchener illusion, as though the two men discovered it independently. Burton's analysis of the historical evidence indicates that Ebbinghaus created the illusion and that the first mistaken attribution to Titchener came nearly 60 years after the illusion's introduction. Unfortunately, this mistaken attribution has persisted despite a number of efforts to set the record straight, including one by E. G. Boring (1961), Titchener's student and propagandist. It remains to be seen whether Burton's attempt will be any more successful than Boring's.

Before leaving our "thoughts about history," we should temper our discussion of the difficulties of verifying the truth of historical facts by noting that the answer to much of the problem lies in the use of multiple sources and methods. For example, although much of Watson's (1936) autobiographical essay is negative in tone, we can assess the truth of what he wrote by examining archival material that may be available, by studying the excellent Watson biographies, by reading other contemporary writings by Watson and others, and so forth. In other words, even though any given source may be biased or otherwise inaccurate, the historian often does not have to depend on a single source of information. The list of references at the end of this book illustrates the myriad sources available for the student in search of history.

For further discussion of some of the issues involved in writing about the history of psychology, see Hilgard, Leary, and McGuire (1991). In addition to E. G. Boring, any list of noteworthy historians of psychology would include **Robert I. Watson** (1909–1980) and **Ernest R. Hilgard** (1904–2001). Among other contributions, Watson implemented the first doctoral degree program in the history of psychology in the United States at the University of New Hampshire in 1967, helped plan the Archives of the History of American Psychology, and aided in launching the *Journal of the History of the Behavioral Sciences,* an invaluable source of information on the history of psychology and other behavioral sciences (Ross, 1981). Another invaluable resource for the psychological historian began in 1998, the APA journal *History of Psychology*, edited by Michael M. Sokal.

Perhaps Hilgard's most important contribution to the field was his monumental *Psychology in America: A Historical Survey* (Hilgard, 1987). For his many contributions to psychology in such disparate areas as conditioning and learning, the teaching of introductory psychology, and hypnosis, Hilgard received honors such as the presidency of the American Psychological Association (1949), the APA's 1969 Distinguished Scientific Contribution Award, and the APA's 1994 award for Outstanding Lifetime Achievement in Psychology (Leary, 2002).

In this section, we have discussed some of the many factors that influence written historical accounts, such as presentism, *Zeitgeist* theory, self-serving bias, the reconstructive nature of memory, self-deprecation, and confirmation by multiple sources. These are just a few aspects of **historiography**, the field devoted to the study of how historical events are reported in writing, to the methodology of historians. Professional historians are well aware of the principles of historiography, whereas most histories of psychology have been written by psychologists, persons with an interest and background in psychology who are less mindful of these principles. Boring's (1950) *A History of Experimental Psychology* is a good example of this "old history" of psychology. Of course, most of the current textbooks in the history and systems of psychology were produced, not by professional historians, but by psychologists interested in the history of their discipline. This characterization also includes the present textbook and its authors.

Since about 1970, a "new history," as Laurel Furumoto (1989) has dubbed it, has arisen. This approach to the history of psychology involves people specifically trained to be historians of psychology, who do focused research using original source material. At the present time, this new history has not been widely incorporated either into textbooks or into history and systems courses (Hogan, Goshtashpour, Laufer, & Haswell, 1998; Samelson, 1999).

WHERE DO WE START?

Although Lapointe (1970) traced the term *psychology* to Melanchthon in 1540, he later concluded, "there is no evidence for the often-repeated claim that Melanchthon is the author of the term" (Lapointe, 1972, p. 331). Other research, including Lapointe's own, points to a slightly earlier origin. Specifically, both Brožek (1999) and Ungerer and Bringmann (1997) cited the lost work of Marcus Marulus (Marulić in Croatian), *Psichiologia*, published in about 1520. More recently, Vande Kemp (2002) has traced the origin of the term *psychology* from the philosophical-theological tradition, along with changes in its meaning. She, too, acknowledged Marulus's first use of the word.

Of course, the Greek root *psyche* is clearly much older. So, where should we start our history of psychology? We could start with the 1879 founding of psychology's first experimental laboratory by Wilhelm Wundt or with the 1816 publication of Johann Friedrich Herbart's *Lehrbuch zur Psychologie* (*Textbook of Psychology*), which is often considered the first textbook in psychology.

Perhaps we should journey back further to the time of René Descartes (Chapter 4), the 17th-century philosopher/mathematician associated with the period that historians consider the beginning of the "modern era." In the work of the ancient Greeks, we find the antecedents of many contemporary ideas, as we will illustrate in Chapter 2. But why start with the Greeks? After all, we can imagine prehistoric people studying the behavior of predatory and prey animals. In that sense, prehistoric people were the first comparative psychologists. In addition, early men and women undoubtedly studied the behavior of their fellows, making them all psychologists of a sort.

In fact, Cambridge ethologist Nicholas Humphrey (1983) suggested that modern humans should perhaps be known as *Homo psychologicus* rather than *Homo sapiens.* Humphrey argues that what makes humans different from other animals is their ability to decipher what other humans must be feeling and thinking both by studying their behavior and by imagining what it would be like to be in their position. Indeed, Humphrey believes that consciousness evolved specifically for the capacity to "do psychology."

But prehistoric is, after all, *pre*historic. We obviously cannot begin our look at the history of psychology before recorded history began. Still, the idea that humans have always been interested in psychological topics is nicely captured in Hermann Ebbinghaus's famous quotation from his *Abriss der Psychologie* (*A Summary of Psychology*): "Psychology has a long past, but only a short history" (Ebbinghaus, 1910, p. 9). The "long past" referred to thought about psychological topics throughout recorded history, whereas "short history" recognized the founding of psychology as a distinct scientific discipline in the latter half of the 19th century. Ebbinghaus's own history ended in 1909 with his death from pneumonia at the age of 59 (Chapter 8).

As we hinted above, we will begin our look at psychology's history with the ancient Greeks. Many of them were concerned with questions and topics that are still debated by modern psychologists. Some of the questions they tried to answer were: What are the senses, and how do they work? What (and where) is the mind, and how is it related to the body? What are the principles of human learning and memory? Are there chemical (humoral) causes for human behavior? What are the relative contributions of nature (heredity) and nurture (the environment) to behavior? The next section describes some of these ancient questions and recurring issues in greater detail.

SOME OF PSYCHOLOGY'S RECURRING ISSUES

In the history of psychology, some of the many issues that have surfaced repeatedly and have led to much debate are the **mind-body problem,** reductionism versus nonreductionism, and the **nature-nurture controversy.** Each of these issues has a rich history and, in some modern guise, remains with us today.

The Mind-Body Problem

Some philosophers have suggested that people have both a body and a mind; others have contended that there is only body or only mind. If there is both a body and a mind, are they connected or are they separate? The issue has often had religious overtones—in some languages the words for mind and soul are the same. Because the body is obviously mortal, a belief in immortality requires a soul (mind). The various "solutions" to the mind-body problem generally fall into two categories: monism and dualism.

Monism assumes only one underlying reality, either mind or body, but not both. The major forms of monism are materialism and mentalism. **Materialism** assumes that the only underlying reality is physical; there is only body. Critics say that the materialists have lost their minds. From ancient times, Democritus (ca. 400 B.C.E.; Chapter 2) exemplifies this position, and the claim that all thought and action can be reduced to the electrochemical activity of the brain is a more recent example. **Mentalism** (also called **immaterialism** or **subjective idealism**) is a version of monism that holds that reality ultimately exists in the mind. In the absence of a perceiving mind, the physical world is irrelevant (or perhaps does not exist). Although this position can be traced to antiquity, modern versions are often based on the writings of the philosopher George Berkeley (ca. 1710; Chapter 5). Other mentalists want to maintain a primary role for the mind but also acknowledge the brain's importance, which makes them dualists of one sort or another.

Dualism is the mind-body position that says that both mind and body exist. The major forms of dualism are interactionism and parallelism. **Interactionism** is the position that mind and body are separate, but they interact. Mind can influence body and vice versa, according to this solution's chief proponent, René Descartes (ca. 1640). **Parallelism**, or **psychophysical parallelism**, is the view that mind and body are separate entities that do not interact. They appear to interact because they are perfectly constructed and are set into motion at the same time, like two perfect clocks started simultaneously that would always have the same time even though they have no effect on each other. Psychophysical parallelism was the position taken by Gottfried Wilhelm von Leibniz (ca. 1695).

Double aspectism is the mind-body solution that holds that mind and body are just two aspects of the same thing, like the obverse and reverse of a coin. From this definition, you can probably see the difficulty in classifying the solution. Mind and body both exist simultaneously; they are inseparable without interacting. This position was originally proposed by Baruch Spinoza (ca. 1665; Chapter 4).

Probably the most interesting of the many other mind-body positions is epiphenomenalism. Closely related to materialism, **epiphenomenalism** holds that the brain's activity produces mind as a sort of byproduct. The mind does not influence the brain or behavior any more than the noise of a car's engine influences the way it runs. The origin of epiphenomenalism is often attributed to Thomas Hobbes (Chapter 5), and a variety of contemporary versions are popular today.

Now that we have briefly surveyed some of the major mind-body positions, consider where *you* stand on the issue. If you are at all religious, it is likely that you subscribe to some form of dualism, believing that your ultimate self (soul) is nonphysical and thus beyond the bounds of sciences such as physics, chemistry, or physiology. If this is your belief, you are in good company, as dualism "is the most common theory of mind in the public at large" (Churchland, 1984, p. 7)—even though it would be possible to reconcile most religions with other mind-body explanations.

Modern neuroscientists are more likely to favor one of the many forms of materialism, such as reductive materialism, in which mental states are synonymous with physical states of the brain. However, materialism is by no means the only possibility among neuroscientists; indeed, toward the end of his life, Nobel Prize–winning biopsychologist Roger Sperry (Chapter 16) appeared to espouse an interactive dualism. Sperry (1994) noted that the "emergent whole [of consciousness] constantly exerts downward control over its parts. . . . In the new view . . . things are doubly determined, not only from lower levels upward, but also from above downward" (p. 11).

As you can see, the mind-body issue has both a long history and contemporary relevance, and the positions we have presented by no means exhaust the possibilities. A good source for additional reading is Paul Churchland's (1984) *Matter and Consciousness*, which is further described in the list of suggested readings at the end of the chapter. In fact, so many different views exist, and so much time has been devoted to their discussion, that some philosophers (e.g., Ryle, 1949; Wittgenstein, 1953) have wondered whether the whole mind-body issue is simply a "bad" question.

Gilbert Ryle (Chapter 18) called the mind "the ghost in the machine," and in an attempt to provide a fresh perspective on the nature of mind, he suggested that we reflect on how we talk and think about the mind and psychological phenomena in general. In this vein, Ryle's discussion of the **category mistake** became the centerpiece of his 1949 book, *The Concept of Mind.* Ryle related the following story to illustrate a category mistake—a story that, by analogy, illustrates how the mind-body problem may have been misconceived.

> A foreigner visiting Oxford or Cambridge for the first time is shown a number of colleges, libraries, playing fields, museums, scientific departments and administrative offices. He then asks "But where is the University? I have seen where the members of the Colleges live, where the Registrar works, where the scientists experiment and the rest. But I have not yet seen the University in which reside and work the members of your University." It has then to be explained to him that the University is not another collateral institution, some ulterior counterpart to the colleges, laboratories and offices which he has seen. The University is just the way in which all that he has already seen is organized. (p. 16)

In other words, Ryle (1949) was suggesting that the mind and body are not at the same "level" of analysis, just as the University and the physical buildings at Oxford are not at the same level, even though philosophers and psychologists have long spoken and theorized about the mind and the body as if they exist on the same plane.

Reductionism Versus Nonreductionism

The main idea of **reductionism** is to look for increasingly more biological, chemical, and physical explanations of psychological phenomena, whereas **nonreductionism** asserts that psychological phenomena should stand on their own, without the need for biological or biochemical explanations. For example, suppose a rat learns a maze. A nonreductionist would say the rat's behavior can be explained in terms of stimuli in the maze, the responses the animal makes to the stimuli, the presence or absence of rewards, and so forth. By contrast, a reductionist would look for the brain areas and transmitter substances involved in the activity or even for genetic causes underlying the behavior. Physiological psychologists are reductionists, and many of them would argue that psychology is just a branch of biology. By contrast, the Gestalt psychologists tended toward nonreductionism, believing that behavior should be studied as intact, meaningful wholes and rejecting the search for simpler, more elemental explanations.

The Nature-Nurture Controversy

Three of the many other terms related to this longstanding issue are *nativism-empiricism, heredity-environment,* and *innate-learned.* The basic question is, How much of behavior is instinctive, programmed, or unlearned, and how much is learned or acquired through experience with the environment?

Actually, the most extreme positions have been taken by **nurturists**, people who argued for the learning side of the issue. For example, John Locke viewed the mind as "white paper" on which experience writes. John Watson and other behaviorists were also outspoken proponents of the nurture idea.

By contrast, **nativists** have usually taken less extreme positions in the discussion, often accepting that much of behavior is indeed learned while pointing to fundamental elements and organizing principles that seem innate. For instance, René Descartes believed that most of the mind's ideas come from experience, but he also thought that some ideas are so clear and perfect that they have to be innate, put there by God. Examples included unity, infinity, the geometrical axioms, and God himself. Others of interest to psychology who are generally classified as nativists include Socrates and Plato (Chapter 2), Leibniz, Kant (Chapter 6), and such relatively recent psychologists as William McDougall (Chapter 12), Eleanor Gibson (Chapter 13), and the Gestalt psychologists.

The genesis of intelligence in the individual, whether it is primarily inherited or a function of the environment, is an ongoing contemporary illustration of the nature-nurture controversy. Sir Francis Galton, Charles Darwin's cousin, was an early proponent of the inheritance of intelligence, as were the first American psychologists, men such as James McKeen Cattell and G. Stanley Hall. On the nurture side of the argument are the behaviorists, such as John Watson and B. F. Skinner. More recently, we find the extremes of the controversy represented by researchers such as Arthur Jensen (nature) and Leon

Kamin (nurture). We will have more to say about the nature-nurture issue in intelligence in Chapter 17.

All of these issues, and many more, such as the nomothetic-idiographic distinction, have been important in the history of psychology and especially in its philosophical past. **Nomothetic** refers to the study of large groups in order to determine general tendencies of human nature, whereas **idiographic** involves the study of individuals in order to uncover differences between people. We see this distinction between the psychologies of Wundt student Edward Bradford Titchener (nomothetic) and James Mark Baldwin (idiographic), as well as others. For a longer list of important issues in the history of psychology, see Chapter 21 in Hilgard's (1987) *Psychology in America: A Historical Survey.*

Even today, psychologists can be characterized by their stances on the debates we have introduced here. Particularly in the first part of this book—because of its focus on psychology's philosophical antecedents—we will make explicit connections between theorists and these thematic issues. To a lesser extent, we will continue to make such connections in the remainder of the book. As you learn more about where thinkers of the past have stood on the different issues, you may want to consider your own positions on them.

ORGANIZATION OF THE BOOK

In organizing our history of psychology textbook, we might have taken a strictly chronological approach, beginning at some time in the distant past, such as 460 B.C.E., perhaps, because that was about the time that the Greek philosopher Anaxagoras (Chapter 2) introduced the concept of *nous*, or mind. From this beginning, we would have worked our way first by centuries and then by decades until we came to the present day. In taking a strictly chronological approach, however, we would probably have missed history's patterns.

Our approach is in fact *roughly* chronological, emphasizing the contributions of important people in the history of philosophy, psychology, and science in general. We will begin with the ancient Greeks, and our organization after the beginnings of scientific psychology will focus on psychology's major systems and schools. Although the terms *system* and *school* are often used interchangeably, a distinction can be made. A **system** refers to a collection of ideas defining what is psychological and the methods that will be used to study the psychological, whereas a **school** consists of the people who more or less agree with the system. Recently, Dewsbury (2002a) has suggested a subdivision of a school, which he calls a **family**. He uses the term to refer to psychologists sharing a common developmental influence, whose later work, no matter how diverse, somehow reflects this developmental influence. Dewsbury illustrates the concept by considering the careers of five men who worked with renowned physiological psychologist Karl Lashley at the University of Chicago. Their later work often reflected their experiences with Lashley.

As psychology matured, its systems and schools became so diffuse that today they no longer exist. Accordingly, after discussing the last of the schools, we will examine more recent history in the context of important topics in the 21st century. One theme throughout the history of psychology is the discipline's effort to become or to be a science.

ABOUT PSYCHOLOGY AND SCIENCE

From our chapter-opening question, you can infer that the founding of psychology as a separate science occurred in 1879. Without quibbling about the date and place, did psychology truly become a science in the latter half of the 19th century? What makes something a science, and does psychology conform to the requirements? Further, how does the history of science intersect with the history of psychology?

At your college or university, the psychology department may be in a College of Arts and Sciences, along with departments of biological sciences, chemistry, physics, foreign languages, English, sociology, among others. Where does psychology lie? Is it an art or a science? As it turns out, it is a bit of both.

What Makes Something a Science?

For our purposes, we will define a scientific discipline as one that uses objective observations to develop and test theories. By objective, we mean observations that are unbiased, impersonal, independent of the thoughts and feelings of the observer. From this definition, and common sense, an approach like the one Isaac Newton took in creating modern physics becomes the model for science.

Speaking broadly, we can divide the academic disciplines into those that use empirical observations, in the sense that they rely exclusively on objective experiences, and those that use more subjective types of data. Similarly, we can distinguish between academic disciplines that focus on building and testing theories, such as genetics or physics, and disciplines that have other primary objectives, such as teaching us how to do something (e.g., architecture, accounting, engineering, computer programming) or simply describing past and present beliefs and accomplishments (e.g., history, philosophy). Thus, courses such as marine biology and organic chemistry, which rely on objective observations to develop and test theories, can be grouped among the sciences, whereas courses such as technical writing, folk dancing, and Native American religions, which do not employ objective observation for building and testing theories, are not considered sciences.

Despite the simplicity of our definition of science, it still fails to categorize all fields of inquiry neatly. In fact, there are at least two problems with it: First, many academic disciplines use a variety of methods, some scientific and some unscientific. For example, a historian who develops her understanding of marriage in the 18th-century American South through a study of surviving period documents may be doing excellent research without performing any objective observations or building or testing a theory. Her goal may be just to organize and describe the information that exists. That same historian could use the scientific method to study marriage in the contemporary rural South, using census data, direct observation, and interviews to test the theory that little has changed in the institution in the last 200 years.

The second problem is related to the first: Many academic disciplines are multifaceted, with some scientific and some nonscientific divisions. For example, as we noted earlier, the field of psychology itself is extremely diverse, containing such subfields as behavioral neuroscience, developmental psychology, learning psychology, cognitive psychology, social psychology, clinical psychology, industrial psychology, and so on. Because of this diversity, some psychologists may be more "scientific" than others, in the sense that they are more likely to use the scientific method in their work. Thus, from outside the field, the behavioral neuroscientist is likely to be viewed as a scientist, whereas the practicing clinical psychologist may be seen as an artist practicing his or her craft, or as an applied psychologist using certain tools to improve a person's condition.

In fact, this difference in the perception of scientific and applied psychology has sometimes created tensions within the discipline itself and certainly has created confusion in the public's understanding of psychology (Stanovich, 2001). Nevertheless, one popular ideal remains that of the psychological scientist conducting research that has direct application to the "real world." For example, a school psychologist may conduct research that helps to improve the quality of classroom instruction, or a cognitive psychologist may do studies that ultimately lead to a safer and more effective airplane cockpit.

The use of multiple methods and the multifaceted nature of many disciplines, especially in the social sciences, makes them harder to classify than fields such as physics or poetry. Perhaps we should just accept the idea that our definition of science illuminates two ends of a continuum of science and nonscience. The question that still remains is, Where does psychology lie on this continuum?

Is Psychology a Science?

To the extent that psychology uses objective observations to develop and test theories, we can safely call it a science. Looking at psychology more closely, we have observed that not all of psychology's many divisions are equally scientific. For the most part, however, the history of psychology is the story of researchers who trusted in the utility of the scientific method. Various forms of "applied psychology," which may be better understood as an art, or as engineering, are relatively modern features of the discipline. Thus, for the most part, we will focus here on the development of scientific psychology, and the story of psychology's struggles to get its phenomena to yield to scientific investigation will be a recurrent theme.

Intersections Between Science and Psychology

Not all cultures value science equally. For example, printing and primitive rocketry are considered two of the most important scientific accomplishments of the European Middle Ages, but both had been discovered far earlier by the Chinese, who used them almost exclusively for entertainment. Like many of Western civilization's ideals, the pursuit of science is part of the legacy we inherited from the ancient Greeks. Although we acknowledge Thales as the "first philosopher" in Chapter 2, we could just as easily have called him the first scientist, as he was one of the first persons we know of to popularize the idea that through science humans could predict and control nature.

Also mentioned in Chapter 2, the followers of Pythagoras can be viewed as a cult of rational science, and over time the Pythagoreans learned they could use mathematics to model nature. One of the giants of the ancient world, Aristotle combined formal logic with natural observation to become a clear forerunner of the modern "scientific method." In addition, the rise of rational medicine in the ancient Greek world illustrates how a scientific approach displaced prevailing folk wisdom and mysticism. Unfortunately, the history of science does not show a smooth progression, and the Greek scientific accomplishments were virtually lost to Western civilization by the heyday of the Roman Empire.

Above all, the Romans were fiercely pragmatic. They readily understood the importance of roads and bridges, sanitation, and fresh water, and even today there are remnants of Roman roads from North Africa to England. The Roman aqueduct remains one of the most impressive feats of engineering in history. Because of their love of the practical, however, the Romans were skeptical about both science and philosophy. After all, in the absence of an immediate application, of what use were they?

In Chapter 3, we will show that this inherent Roman skepticism evolved into an even greater mistrust of science with the rise of Christianity. Early Church luminaries such as St. Augustine and St. Jerome preached messages often perceived as unscientific, and through much of the medieval period, science was essentially lost to Western civilization.

Fortunately, during this same period, extensions of Greek science flourished in the Arabic world. By the late Middle Ages, Islamic philosophy and science was being taught in the fledgling European universities. This renewed interest in the wisdom of the ancients became an important element of the Renaissance, which reinstated science as one of Western civilization's core ideals. At the end of Chapter 3, we will take a closer look at the important figures in Renaissance science, such as Galileo Galilei, Francis Bacon, and Isaac Newton.

In the early modern era (Chapters 4–6), many of our contemporary ideas about both science and psychology were first expressed. During this period, psychology as we know it was originally conceived as an outgrowth of empirical and rational philosophy, and science displaced religion (or the state) as the ultimate authority on worldly matters. This new appreciation of science is usually seen as the product of positivism, a philosophy of science first developed by Auguste Comte and subsequently refined by Ernst Mach and others. **Positivism** advocated a science based on observable facts and their logical relations to each other. We will explore positivism and its relation to psychology in Chapter 5.

By the 18th century, the study of the mind was generally accepted as a viable academic discipline. Still, some of its greatest proponents, such as Immanuel Kant, did not believe psychology could ever be a true science. In its simplest form, the problem was that sciences are based on objective observations, and the mind is not directly observable, so how could psychology ever become a science? As we will see in Chapter 7, psychology began to emerge as a science when questions about the mind became coupled with studies of the brain and the nervous system. For example,

Gustav Fechner's psychophysical investigations of the mind-body interface showed definitively that one could scientifically investigate the mind.

Despite Fechner's claim as the founder of psychology as a science, historians of psychology generally select Wilhelm Wundt and the year 1879 as the beginning of psychology as a separate scientific discipline. Grounded in the empirical tradition, Wundt's conception of psychology was radically scientific. Although some of Wundt's own students (e.g., Edward Bradford Titchener) and many of his contemporaries (e.g., Franz Brentano, William James) questioned Wundt's understanding of psychology as a science, they accepted his emphasis on making psychology as scientific as possible. Despite his many and varied disagreements with Wundt, James's appreciation of the need to make psychology a science at Harvard led him to hire a Wundt-trained psychologist, Hugo Münsterberg, as director of the Harvard laboratory.

The desire to make psychology as scientific as possible was the genesis of the American system of behaviorism (Chapters 12 and 13). In "Psychology as the Behaviorist Views It," Watson (1913) used science first as a weapon to bludgeon competing systems and then as a tool to articulate a plan for a new psychology based on the objective observation of behavior.

In the decades following Watson's "manifesto," other prominent behavioral theorists such as Clark Hull and B. F. Skinner used a revised positivistic understanding of science to forge their own approaches to psychology. Although different behaviorists held conflicting views on specific topics, such as whether they should employ unseen variables (for example, Hull and Edward Tolman used such unseen mechanisms as intervening variables and hypothetical constructs, whereas Skinner did not), this was the age of operationism in psychology. Operationism was brought to psychology from physics by Harvard psychologist S. S. Stevens. According to **operationism**, or **logical positivism**, to be truly scientific, psychologists should only study things that they could define operationally—that is, in terms of the operations used to measure them. As an example, an operational definition of hunger, a concept that could not be observed directly and was thus not scientific according to the earlier positivism, might be the number of hours since an animal had last eaten or the amount of food consumed at a meal.

So positivism as a philosophy of science became logical positivism in order to give unobservable, but meaningful, concepts an objective basis through operationism. Another step in the evolution of the philosophy of science is typically associated with Austrian philosopher of science **Karl Popper** (1902–1994) and his **principle of falsifiability**, which states that a scientific theory has the capability of being falsified or refuted. According to Popper, the dividing line between a science and a nonscience is that truly scientific theories are framed in such a way that they can be refuted by a false instance. That is, a truly scientific theory can never be verified conclusively, but it can be falsified if a prediction based on it proves untrue.

According to Popper, psychoanalysis is a good illustration of a nonscientific theory because it can never be falsified; any set of behaviors can always be reconciled with the theory. Scientific theories, by contrast, make predictions that risk overturning the theories. Appropriately enough, these are called **risky predictions**.

Introduced earlier in the chapter, Thomas Kuhn (1970) had much to say about theoretical development in science. According to Kuhn, a science begins with a period of agreement about what it is, what it will study, and the methods it will use. At this point, the science has only one model, or paradigm, and is in what Kuhn called a period of "normal" science.

This so-called normal period inevitably comes to an end when the paradigm encounters an event that cannot be reconciled with it. This anomalous event causes a period of instability in the discipline, in which the field's older scientists try to modify and retain their theory, whereas the younger researchers clamor for competing theories and a new paradigm for the discipline.

Eventually, a new paradigm emerges victorious—there is a paradigm shift, in other words. The science then enters another normal period during which the new theory prospers. This period lasts until a new anomalous event occurs, and a new revolution in the science begins. In Chapter 18, we will apply this Kuhnian model to the current cognitive "revolution."

Work in the philosophy of science has continued since Kuhn's efforts. For example, Paul Feyerabend (1975), Imre Lakatos (1978), and Larry Laudan (1977) have each modified and extended Kuhn's ideas into more refined criticisms of positivism. These works have often focused on debunking the "ideal" of science as a purely objective and methodologically consistent enterprise, showing instead that social forces and practical concerns make science a far more "human," and hence "messy," affair.

How Is Psychology Perceived by the Public?

To this point, we have told you that psychology as a separate discipline began with an emphasis on being a science, and the discipline's approach to science has been affected by changes in the philosophy of science. Has psychology succeeded in its quest to be a science? How well has it sold itself to the public as science that can offer solutions to the problems of living?

One partial answer to this question comes from an analysis of commentaries on psychology published in the *New York Times*, arguably the foremost newspaper in America. Dennis (2002) examined nearly 200 commentaries on psychology published in the *Times* between 1904 and 1947. Up until World War I, the *Times*'s coverage focused on the work of Hugo Münsterberg, Harvard's laboratory director, which was seen as having real world applicability. Psychology's positive glow, as seen in the *Times*'s commentaries, carried into the early 1920s. When psychology's efforts in such areas as intelligence testing, childrearing, and psychoanalysis failed to fulfill their initial promise, however, the *Times*'s commentaries turned sharply critical. From the late 1920s through the 1940s, solutions offered by the science of psychology appeared to fare little better than, and sometimes not as well as, common sense.

Of course, the history of psychology as a science has nearly doubled in length since the commentaries that Dennis (2002) analyzed were published. Obviously, we need a similar analysis of the commentaries (since 1947) in order to understand the way psychology as a useful science has been viewed in the more recent past and today.

Benjamin, Campbell, Luttrell, Bryant, and Holtz (1997) provided another view of how early psychology was portrayed to the public through an examination of entries in American encyclopedias from 1880 to 1940. Benjamin et al. found that the description of psychology in encyclopedia entries lagged behind what was really happening in the field. For example, as the foremost school of psychology at the time, behaviorism should have dominated the 1940 entries, but this was not the case. The entries were not up to date because they were written by psychologists trained in an earlier period when psychology was still closely tied to philosophy.

Again, for our purposes, Benjamin et al.'s (1997) analysis has the same problem we saw with Dennis's (2002): It ends too soon. We can, however, surmise that the problem with out-of-date entries Benjamin et al. observed has and will continue to be a difficulty in encyclopedia entries. Psychologists on the cutting edge of their science are likely to be too engaged in conducting research, writing grant proposals, and training young researchers to invest their time in writing encyclopedia entries. Thus, that task has typically fallen to individuals past their prime as psychological researchers, whose knowledge of the current science of psychology is likely to be somewhat out of date.

We will end this introduction to the history of psychology by recounting one of early psychology's great successes in the application of the scientific method to resolve an apparently insoluble problem: the secret of *der kluge Hans* (**Clever Hans**), the wonder horse.

Exposing Clever Hans

Owned by Herr von Osten, a former mathematics teacher, Clever Hans appeared to be a horse genius. Hans was actually Hans II, Hans I having died

Archives of the History of American Psychology–The University of Akron.

Testing Clever Hans

Herr von Osten is the gentleman with a full beard wearing a long coat and a light-colored hat.

before attaining the abilities of his successor (Candland, 1993). Hans had apparently been taught to perform mathematical calculations, to read and spell, to identify musical tones, and to identify the interrelationships among tones. Hans answered questions by tapping his hoof or by pointing his head toward an appropriate card or object. The horse's apparent intelligence was considered important support for the continuity of mental ability stressed by Darwin's theory of evolution.

As Director of the Berlin Psychological Institute, Carl Stumpf served on a commission that investigated Hans's abilities. In September 1904, the commission concluded that in all likelihood Hans was not being intentionally aided by von Osten. Additionally, the commission could not determine any unintentional cueing, and Stumpf selected his student **Oskar Pfungst** (1874–1932) to assist in further investigating Hans. Pfungst himself was assisted by Erich von Hornbostel as "recording secretary" (Bringmann & Abresch, 1997). The experiments Pfungst conducted represent "the first application of sophisticated methods to the study of animal behaviour . . . and read, even now, like a textbook illustration of how to apply experimental methods to a psychological problem" (Boakes, 1984, p. 78).

After determining that Hans could correctly answer questions asked by people other than his owner, Pfungst then had a questioner present items to Hans for which the questioner either knew or did not know the answer. Pfungst found that Hans correctly answered the questions over 90% of the time in the "tester-with-knowledge" condition but no more than 10% of the time if the tester did not know the answer. Somehow a tester who knew the answer was giving Hans that information. Pfungst's "tester-without-knowledge" condition possibly represents the first use of something like a double-blind procedure to control for experimenter effects.

Obviously, Hans was responding to some kind of signal from his questioner, but what was it? Pfungst began his search for the cue by testing the horse's vision. When blinders were applied to prevent Hans from seeing a questioner standing to his side, "Hans would always make the most strenuous efforts to get a view of the questioner, and . . . would rave and tear at the lines whenever the attempt was made to tie him" (Pfungst, 1911/1965, pp. 42–43). Although the test was difficult to conduct, the result was unequivocal: Hans was almost always correct in his response if the questioner stood in front of him, where Hans could see him, and nearly always wrong when the questioner stood to the side. So, Hans was using visual cues to get the answer, but, again, what exactly were the cues?

With "keen eyes and iron patience" (Stumpf, 1930, p. 407), Pfungst discovered that questioner head movement was the key.

> As soon as [Mr. von Osten] had given a problem to the horse, he, involuntarily, bent his head and trunk slightly forward and the horse would then put his right foot forward and begin to tap, without, however, returning it each time to its original position. As soon as the desired number of taps was given, the questioner would make a slight upward jerk of the head. Thereupon the horse would immediately swing his foot in a wide circle, bringing it back to its original position. (Pfungst, 1911/1965, p. 47)

Other movements that would cue Hans to stop tapping included slight motions of the eyebrows and even dilation of the nostrils.

Using his findings, Pfungst was able to demonstrate the same phenomenon in the laboratory with himself as the horse. Including a young psychology student named Kurt Koffka (Chapter 14), subjects were asked to think of a number and Pfungst then tapped it out with his hand, stopping when he saw the kind of signal Hans had responded to. Many of the subjects saw the test as an effective demonstration of mind reading.

Although Pfungst did not fully appreciate them, the study of Clever Hans demonstrated a number of important learning phenomena. At first, von Osten rewarded Hans for each correct response, but as the horse became more proficient, he was rewarded for a gradually decreasing proportion of successful responses. This anticipates B. F. Skinner's (Chapter 13) partial-reinforcement work by several decades.

Pfungst's laboratory modeling of Hans's behavior enabled Pfungst to demonstrate what has since been called "conditioning without awareness." Pfungst told a subject to think of "left" or "right" in any order, and Pfungst would try to indicate the subject's thought by lowering his arm if the thought was "right" or raising it if the thought was "left." After several trials, Pfungst found that the subject began to raise his eyes when thinking "left" and to lower them when thinking "right," apparently having learned to anticipate Pfungst's arm movements.

> Afterwards the people taking part in these experiments reported that they had simply tried to imagine the objects; they claimed that they never thought about the related arm movement of the experimenter and were completely unaware of the changes that had occurred in their own behavior. (Boakes, 1984, p. 80)

Hans's owner was apparently blameless in the episode, believing unconditionally in his horse's reasoning ability. He was deeply disturbed by Pfungst's findings and died within a few months of the publication of *Clever Hans* (*The Horse of Mr. von Osten*) by Pfungst (1911/1965). Ironically, Pfungst's fine research was not even rewarded with a degree (Candland, 1993).

CONCLUSIONS

In this introductory chapter, we have tried to stimulate your interest. We have also given you some thoughts on history in general and the history of psychology in particular. Because we have introduced important terms and ideas, you will find a summary at the end of the chapter (and in other chapters) to underscore the material covered. In addition, we mentioned several important people (Wundt, Ebbinghaus, Descartes, etc.), and we will have much more to say about them later.

At this point we might ask, Is the history of psychology about ideas, events, or people? For us, it is about all three. Although it is possible to write a history of psychology that emphasizes ideas while deemphasizing the lives and historical times of the people with the ideas, we feel that such a history misses both what is important for understanding the context in which the ideas arose and what makes the historical figures real to the reader. We have tried to strike a balance, sketching the lives and times of the most important figures in psychology's history while covering their major ideas in some depth.

We have provided a glossary of terms and names at the end of the book that includes all the boldfaced items from this and the remaining chapters. Finally, in case we have you hooked on the history of psychology, we have included a set of suggested readings about some of the more interesting topics and people we have discussed in this chapter.

SUMMARY

Why Study the History of Psychology?

Reasons to study the history of psychology include the idea that people who do not know history are likely to repeat the mistakes of the past, the fact that a history course can integrate many of the disparate elements in psychology, and the idea that the history of psychology is interesting.

Thoughts About History

History's "facts" are often elusive and hard to verify. One reason for this is that historians are often biased reporters. Autobiographies may be biased as well, either because of a person's faulty memory or because the person, consciously or unconsciously, makes the story different than it actually was.

This text somewhat favors the *Zeitgeist,* or spirit of the times, theory of history in contrast to the great person viewpoint, although the book will contain much information on psychology's "great people," as well. Although the truth about the lives and ideas of people important for psychology is sometimes difficult to verify, the answer to much of the problem lies in using multiple sources and methods in historical research.

Where Do We Start?

Candidates for where to start our look at psychology include Wundt's 1879 founding of psychology's first experimental laboratory and Herbart's first textbook of psychology. However, remembering Ebbinghaus's famous statement, "Psychology has a long past, but only a short history," we will begin with the ancient Greeks because they tried to answer many questions still with us today.

Some of Psychology's Recurring Issues

Some of psychology's recurring issues are the mind-body problem, reductionism versus nonreductionism, and the nature-nurture controversy. We will revisit these issues in many places in the book.

The main positions taken on the mind-body problem are monism—there is only one underlying reality, either mind (mentalism) or body (materialism)—and dualism. Dualism is the mind-body solution that says that both mind and body exist. The mind and the body either interact (interactionism) or do not interact (psychophysical parallelism). Double aspectism is the solution that holds that mind and body are two aspects of the same thing, like the two sides of a coin. Epiphenomenalism is a mind-body position that holds that the brain's activity produces mind as a byproduct.

Reductionists look for increasingly elemental explanations for psychological phenomena, whereas nonreductionists believe that psychological phenomena can stand on their own, without the need for more elemental explanations. The nature-nurture controversy is concerned with the extent to which behavior patterns are instinctive or inherited (nature) or are learned through interaction with the environment (nurture).

Organization of the Book

The organization of this text is roughly chronological, looking at psychology's development from the Greeks through the major systems or schools of psychology. A psychological system is a collection of ideas defining what is psychological and the methods used to study it, whereas a school consists of the people who display allegiance to the system.

We defined a scientific discipline as one using objective observations to develop and test theories. Because of its great diversity of subdivisions and methods, psychology is difficult to categorize on a scientific/nonscientific continuum. Some areas within psychology, however, definitely use objective observations to develop and test theories, so we can safely conclude that they are scientific.

In tracing the intersections between science and psychology, we noted that positivism stressed a science based on observable facts and their logical relations to each other. Based on this approach to science, scientific psychology began to emerge with Gustav Fechner's psychophysical investigations of the mind-body connection. Nevertheless, Wilhelm Wundt's founding of a psychological laboratory in 1879 is usually cited as the true beginning of psychology as a science.

In the 20th century, a new approach to the philosophy of science called logical positivism, or operationism, took hold first in physics and later in psychology. Operationism advocated that psychologists study only phenomena that could be defined by the operations used to measure them. Further evolution in the philosophy of science includes Karl Popper's principle of falsifiability and Thomas Kuhn's discussion of theoretical development in science. Popper's principle notes that a scientific theory has the capability of being falsified; because they do not have this capability, areas in psychology such as psychoanalysis are considered nonscientific. Based on newspaper commentaries, psychology, at least in its early period, failed to present a good case for being worthwhile science.

Exposing Clever Hans

The study and debunking of *der kluge Hans* (Clever Hans) as a horse genius is a story of the triumph of the use of the scientific method by early psychologists. Using careful experimental methodology, Oscar Pfungst studied Hans and found the horse had been trained to respond to almost imperceptible signals from its owner. Using his knowledge of the signals, Pfungst was able to demonstrate Hans-like phenomena in the laboratory with himself as the "horse." Pfungst's study of Clever Hans anticipated several learning phenomena discovered years later.

KEY NAMES AND TERMS

Edwin Garrigues Boring (p. 4)
category mistake (p. 10)
Clever Hans (p. 16)
double aspectism (p. 10)
dualism (p. 10)
epiphenomenalism (p. 10)
family (p. 12)
Ernest R. Hilgard (p. 8)
historiography (p. 8)
idiographic (p. 12)
immaterialism (p. 10)
interactionism (p. 10)
Thomas Kuhn (p. 5)
logical positivism (p. 15)
materialism (p. 9)
mentalism (p. 10)
mind-body problem (p. 9)
monism (p. 9)
nativists (p. 11)
nature-nurture controversy (p. 9)
nomothetic (p. 12)
nonreductionism (p. 11)
nurturists (p. 11)
operationism (p. 15)
parallelism (p. 10)
Oscar Pfungst (p. 17)
Karl Popper (p. 15)
positivism (p. 14)
presentist bias (p. 5)
principle of falsifiability (p. 15)
psychophysical parallelism (p. 10)
reductionism (p. 11)
risky predictions (p. 15)
school (p. 12)
subjective idealism (p. 10)
system (p. 12)
Robert I. Watson (p. 8)
Zeitgeist (p. 5)

SUGGESTED READINGS

Churchland, P. (1984). *Matter and consciousness.* Cambridge, MA: MIT Press. This is an extremely readable book with excellent coverage of the mind-body problem and many other issues related to "philosophical" psychology.

Hilgard, E. R., Leary, D. E., & McGuire, G. R. (1991). The history of psychology: A survey and critical assessment. *Annual Review of Psychology, 42,* 79–107. This is a fine overview of the approaches to the study of psychology's history and of the outstanding people who have studied that history.

Kuhn, T. (1970). *The structure of scientific revolutions* (Rev. ed.). Chicago: University of Chicago Press. This is the classic work on the nature of science. It is also a good starting point if you are interested in the topic, and we will revisit it in Chapter 18.

Neisser, U. (1982). *Memory observed.* San Francisco: Freeman. Although somewhat dated, this anthology contains many of the finest works pertaining to the psychology of memory. Original studies on reconstructive memory, in addition to other fascinating topics, can be found in *Memory Observed.*

Pfungst, O. (1965). *Clever Hans (The horse of Mr. von Osten).* New York: Holt, Rinehart and Winston, Inc. (Original work published 1911) This is the report of Pfungst's efforts to discover and test the cues Hans used to answer questions put to him. There are introductions by Robert Rosenthal and Carl Stumpf, as well as supplements giving the reports from the commissions organized to study Hans and a detailing of von Osten's teaching methods.

Ryle, G. (1949). *The concept of mind.* London: Hutchinson. Considered a classic in "philosophical behaviorism," this philosophy textbook offers much of value to theoretical psychology.

Precursors to Psychology in Ancient Greece

CHAPTER 2

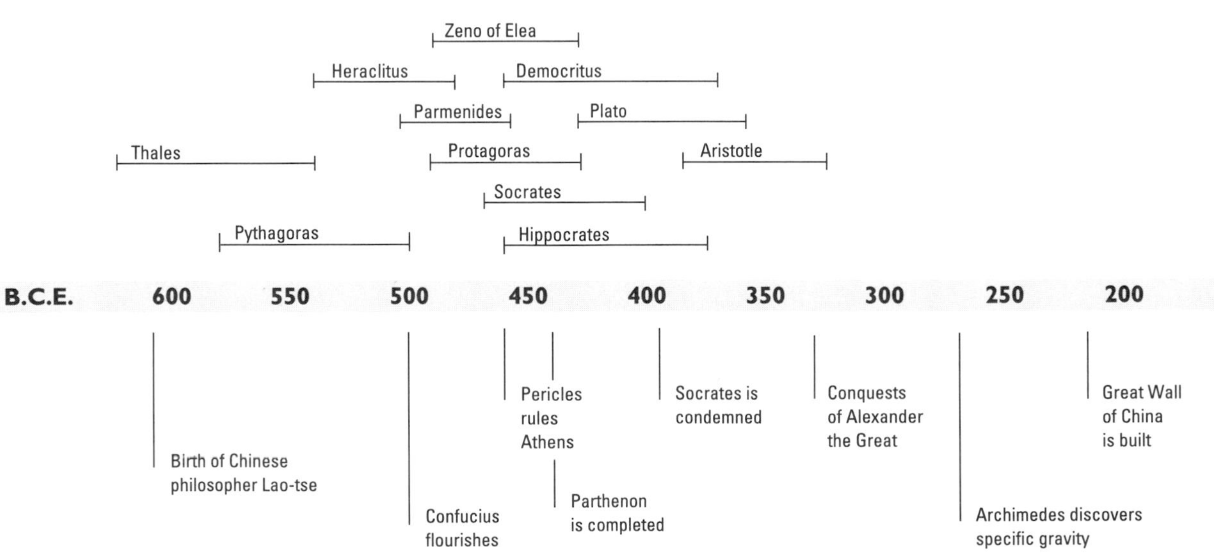

OUTLINE

The Golden Age of Greece

Philosophy in the Golden Age

- Pythagoras and the Pythagoreans
- Heraclitus
- Parmenides
- Zeno's Paradoxes
- Democritus
- The Sophists
- Protagoras
- Socrates
- Plato
- Aristotle

Medicine in the Golden Age and Beyond

- Alcmaeon
- Hippocrates
- Galen

Conclusions

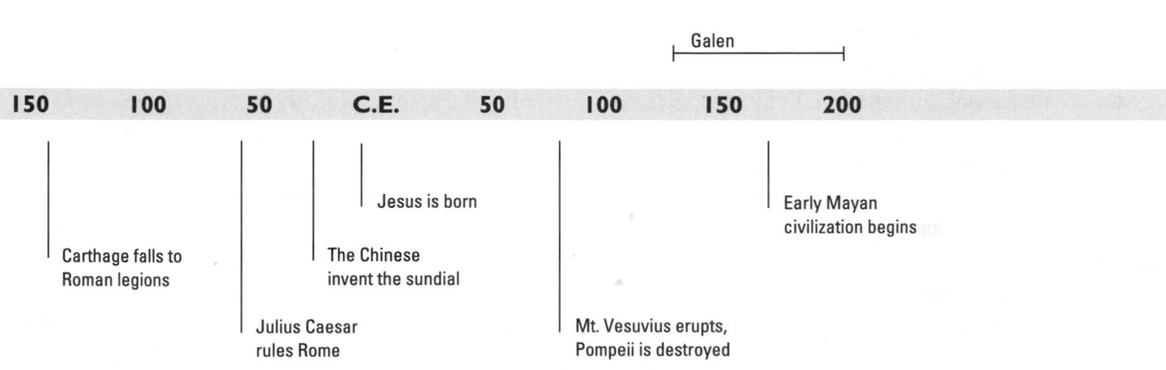

THE GOLDEN AGE OF GREECE

Although some historians of psychology devote little or no attention to ancient philosophers and physiologists, there are important reasons why we have put them first. For example, scholars in many disciplines (e.g., physics, physiology, philosophy) recognize the pre-Socratic Greeks as the authors of the oldest body of ideas clearly related to philosophy and science. Although older sources exist and may even be of interest to psychology (e.g., Laver, 1972), for the most part they concern religious, accounting, or political matters.

A more substantive reason—which connects ancient philosophy and physiology with modern psychology—is that the basic categories, questions, and foundations for subsequent Western thought are first articulated in the work of the Greeks. For example, many have observed (e.g., Lakoff, 1987) that the basic categories that organize thinking in the Western world (i.e., distinctions such as living and dead, plant and animal, real and imaginary) are not recognized by all cultures. Such distinctions at the heart of modern Western science originated in the speculations of the pre-Socratic philosophers.

In Chapter 1, we noted that the history of psychology, particularly the earlier philosophical history, can be viewed in terms of several key issues. In contemporary terms, the issues are the mind-body problem, the nature-nurture controversy, and so forth. Virtually all of these issues were first considered by the ancient Greeks, and an outline of the answers adopted by modern philosophers and scientists can often be found in their writings.

Of particular interest to us in psychology, some of the first speculations about such topics as motivation, learning, sensation and perception, and personality can be found in the teachings of the ancients. We encourage you to look for what might be recognizable as truly psychological material in our survey of the classical contributions to philosophy and in our review of the early advances in physiology and medicine.

Often considered the "first" Greek philosopher, **Thales** (ca. 624–545 B.C.E.) nicely illustrates the search for knowledge that became philosophy and science. Thales proposed the first natural (as opposed to supernatural) explanation for the universe, with his belief that water is the essence of all things. Thales used mathematics to predict a solar eclipse, which earned him popular acclaim and demonstrated that a knowledge of nature brought power over the environment. This search for knowledge soon blossomed in the period called the **Golden Age of Greece**. Figure 2.1 shows a map of ancient Greece and its outposts.

Historian Will Durant (1939) considered the century and a half between the birth of the ruler Pericles (ca. 490 B.C.E.) and the death of Aristotle (322 B.C.E.) the most memorable period in the history of the world.

Born of distinguished parents, **Pericles** (ca. 490–429 B.C.E.) was carefully educated. He heard the lectures of the philosopher Zeno of Elea (discussed later) and studied with the philosopher **Anaxagoras** (ca. 500–428 B.C.E.), who was prosecuted for arguing that the sun was a red-hot mass of rock at a time when the sun was a god to many. Under Pericles' rule, Athens enjoyed the privileges of both democracy and a benign dictatorship.

Sparta, Athens's chief rival, was in disarray from internal problems and natural disasters. Because the struggle between Greece and Persia flared up periodically, for their protection the Greek cities organized the Delian Confederacy under Athenian leadership (477 B.C.E.). Through its sea power, Athens soon dominated its allies, and the Confederacy became the Athenian Empire.

PHILOSOPHY IN THE GOLDEN AGE

Greek philosophy reached its zenith in the age of Pericles, and "in Periclean Athens the 'dear delight' of philosophy captured the imagination of the educated classes; . . . philosophers were lionized, and clever arguments were applauded like sturdy blows at the Olympic games" (Durant, 1939, p. 349). One important philosophical debate contrasted materialism and idealism. As we noted in Chapter 1, materialism is the belief that matter is the only reality and that the universe, including thoughts and feelings, can be explained only in terms of matter.

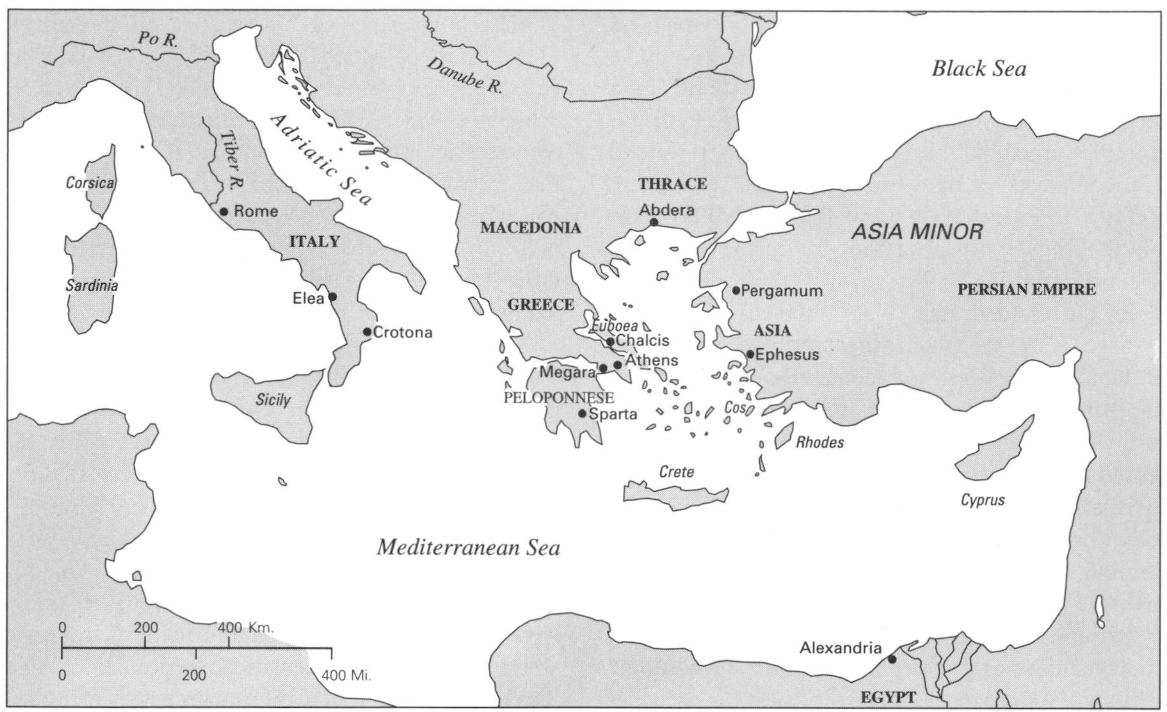

FIGURE 2.1 Map of ancient Greece and its outposts
Although this map does not correspond to any specific date, it is representative of Greece's Golden Age.

By contrast, **idealism** (immaterialism, mentalism) is the view that ideas are the ultimate reality (hence idea-lism) and it is impossible to know whether reality exists apart from the mind. In many ways, the materialism-idealism debate is the foundation for the tension between empirical and rational conceptions of psychology explored in Chapter 8.

Pythagoras and the Pythagoreans

In the 6th century B.C.E., **Pythagoras** (ca. 580–500 B.C.E.) founded a mystical cult society in which philosophy and mathematics constituted a lifestyle aimed at salvation. His life is shrouded by myth and legend, and we know of him through the writings of other Greeks.

After much travel, Pythagoras settled in Crotona, a Greek colony in southern Italy, where he founded a successful school that operated on the principle of equality of the sexes. Trained in philosophy, literature, and domestic skills, "Pythagorean women" were honored as the epitome of Greek femininity.

Pythagoras believed the soul was immortal, undergoing reincarnation in different forms of animal life (transmigration of the soul). Hence, meat eating was prohibited, and there were additional rules of abstinence, including the mysterious dictum "Do not eat beans." To be freed from the cycle of rebirth, the Pythagoreans believed the soul had to be purified, which was best achieved through studying science and mathematics. The chain of transmigration could be ended only by living a completely virtuous life, which Pythagoras apparently tried to do.

Pythagoras is associated with mathematical discoveries—most importantly, the relation between music and numbers (e.g., modern-day octaves and scales) and the Pythagorean theorem (the square of the hypotenuse of a right triangle is equal to the sum of the squares of the other two sides). In fact, Pythagoras believed that the explanation for everything could be found through numbers and their relations. In a remarkable break with their predecessors, the Pythagoreans "assumed that the book of nature . . . is written in the language of mathematics" (Allen, 1966, p. 6), and it is no exaggeration to say that the Pythagoreans laid the foundations of present-day mathematics and scientific inquiry.

In the Golden Age, Plato was enamored with Pythagoras and took from him such things as his scorn of democracy, his love of geometry, and his ideas of the nature and destiny of the soul. Additionally, early "scientific" physicians such as Alcmaeon (discussed later) are believed to have been influenced by Pythagoras. Historians often credit Pythagoras with founding both science and philosophy in Western civilization. Indeed, the word *philosophy* may have been his creation: "He rejected the term *sophia*, or wisdom, as pretentious, and described his own pursuit of understanding as *philosophia*—the love of wisdom" (Durant, 1939, p. 164).

Heraclitus

Born in Ephesus of an aristocratic family, **Heraclitus** (ca. 540–480 B.C.E.) was a younger contemporary of Pythagoras. Heraclitus was known in antiquity by such unflattering terms as "the obscure" and "the riddler" because of his tendency to express himself obliquely. To illustrate Heraclitus's impenetrability in his own time, the playwright Euripides purportedly gave a copy of Heraclitus's work to Socrates and later asked Socrates' opinion of it. Socrates replied, "What I understand is excellent, as is no doubt the part I don't understand. But it takes a Delian [inhabitant of Delos] diver to get to the bottom of it" (from Diogenes Laertius; MacLennan, 1995).

Heraclitus's fascination with change led to his most famous statement, which is often paraphrased: "You can never step into the same river twice." That is, because the river continuously flows, the water you enter a second time will not be the same water you stepped into originally. (In psychology, no two experiences can ever be identical because knowledge of the first will influence perception of the second.)

Heraclitus expressed his reliance on the senses: "The things of which there is seeing and hearing and perception, these do I prefer" (Kirk, Raven, & Schofield, 1983, p. 188). But Heraclitus also said, "Evil witnesses are eyes and ears for men, if they have souls that do not understand their language" (p. 188), by which he meant that understanding requires the ability to interpret sensory information correctly. For understanding to occur, sensory information must be tempered with *logos*, or reason.

The concept of *logos* was extremely important in ancient Greek philosophy. The word was derived from the expression "to say," and its most fundamental meaning was "saying" or "speaking" in the sense of giving a reason or providing an explanation. However, the term also meant to calculate a ratio—the basis of Pythagorean mathematics and religion—or to show the true form of a thing. For the Pythagoreans, these seemingly different meanings were really identical: To explain something was to be able to provide a mathematical account of it. This idea is a part of much modern science, including some areas of psychology, where the most convincing explanation for a phenomenon is thought to be provided by a mathematical model.

With his focus on change, Heraclitus provided an image of the world not easily captured by mathematical or rational structures. Thus, MacLennan (1995) suggested that in Heraclitus we see the birth of a different explanatory tradition that can be traced through history to modern chaos theory. **Chaos theory** holds that complex systems (e.g., behavioral phenomena) create unpredictability (chaos) and that random events (hence, chaotic) have an order of their own.

Heraclitus believed that the essence of all things was fire, because fire is ever-changing. Fire is either going down through progressive condensation into moisture, water, and earth or going up from earth to water to moisture to fire. Everything is constantly "becoming," changing between pairs of opposites such as night and day and life and death. For Heraclitus there was unity in opposites. In fact, Heraclitus considered strife from the tension of opposites necessary for development. Each member of an opposing pair was necessary for the existence of its opposite.

In sum, Heraclitus's philosophy contained three major principles: fire, constant change, and the unity of opposites. These principles have been incorporated into subsequent philosophies. For example, the divinity of fire is invoked in the Christian final conflagration; the idea of struggle and change as necessary for development reappears in the writings of Charles Darwin and Herbert Spencer (both in Chapter 9) and Friedrich Nietzsche (Chapter 6); and the unity of opposites can be seen in Hegel's writings (Chapter 6).

Parmenides

Parmenides (ca. 504–456 B.C.E.) was born in Elea, a Greek city on the Italian coast. In his youth, he studied with a Pythagorean, but there is little evidence for strict Pythagorean ideas in the thought of the mature Parmenides.

The purpose of Parmenides' work was to show that belief in the reality of the physical world of change and plurality is mistaken. Instead, Parmenides proposed an indestructible, static, ungenerated, spherical One. Whereas Heraclitus said all things change, Parmenides said all things are one and never change.

In rejecting change, Parmenides argued that there is no state of nonbeing from which something can arise. If something "comes to be," then it must "not have been," but Parmenides argued that this state of "nonbeing" was impossible. "How could it come to be? For if it came into being, it is not. . . . Thus coming to be [change] is extinguished and perishing [is] unheard of" (Kirk et al., 1983, p. 250). That is, something neither can be generated (come to be) nor can it perish.

Change assumes that something changes from nonbeing to being or from being to being, and Parmenides argued against this assumption. If something arises from being, then it already is, and there is no change. If something arises from nonbeing, then the assumption is that nonbeing is something. Parmenides considered this assumption a contradiction because every something has being, and if something has being, then it cannot be "nonbeing."

Although Parmenides believed that he had demonstrated logically that change does not exist, he recognized that things appear to be in a state of flux. His answer lay in the distinction between appearances and reality: Reality is the basis of truth, whereas appearances from sensory experience can result in no more than opinion. Opinions based on sensation must yield to reason, which tells us that if there is a single substance comprising everything, then movement or change cannot occur.

Thus, for Parmenides our experience is invalid. The way of truth is knowledge from the gods, and the way of seeming is what comes through our senses. Parmenides' position is obvious—given the choice, he would select truth, or reason, rather than the appearances of the senses.

Parmenides' method for seeking truth was extreme **rationalism,** or the use of reason. Thought implanted by the gods contains truth. Any object of thought must exist because we have thought of it, and we cannot think of nothing. In the philosopher's words: "What is there to be said and thought must needs be: for it is there for being, but nothing is not" (Kirk et al., 1983, p. 247). That is, if you can think of something and speak of it, then it must exist. Parmenides denied the existence of nothingness, arguing that because thoughts must be of something, then nothingness (the void) cannot exist.

Parmenides' differentiation of appearance and reality, of opinion and knowledge, became the basis for Platonism. His objections to plurality and change inspired Plato's belief that the sensory world is a lower form of reality than the world known through reason. Parmenides' chief defender was Zeno.

Zeno's Paradoxes

Little is known about **Zeno of Elea** (ca. 490–430 B.C.E.) other than that he was a follower of Parmenides. According to one account, Zeno and Parmenides traveled together to Athens, where Socrates met them, but this is contradicted by Diogenes Laertius, who noted that Zeno so loved Elea that he never left the city. Zeno's end is equally mysterious, and the reported details of his attempted overthrow of a tyrant at Elea, and of his capture, torture, and murder, vary greatly.

Parmenides believed the senses give information about appearances and not about reality, and Zeno proved this to his satisfaction in his millet seed example (millet is a cereal grass with tiny seeds):

The fall of a single millet seed to the ground makes no sound; empty a half-bushel of seeds, and there will be a sound. Our senses have fooled us, because either the single falling seed made a sound or the many falling made no sound. Zeno concluded that it was more profitable to seek the truth through reason than to use sensory information.

To defend Parmenides against critics who argued for change and plurality, Zeno composed several paradoxes, of which nine have survived. One paradox describes a runner traversing a racecourse. According to the Pythagoreans, the distance around a racecourse is divisible into units. Suppose the distance is 400 meters. The 400 meters can be divided in half, the first half divided in half, and so on, *ad infinitum.* In other words, there is an infinity of units into which the racecourse can be divided, and this infinite number of units must be traveled by a runner in a finite amount of time, which Zeno argued was impossible. Thus, he reasoned, there is no motion.

One answer to Zeno's paradox is that time itself can be divided infinitely, so the time to travel the racecourse is infinite in its divisibility, just as is the distance. Given this assumption, the paradox disappears. Still, Zeno's paradoxes have been revived as serious philosophical issues in modern times by Lewis Carroll, the pseudonym of mathematician Charles Dodgson (1832–1898), who wrote *Alice's Adventures in Wonderland;* by Nobel laureate Bertrand Russell (Chapter 13), the famous philosopher and mathematician; and by cognitive scientist Douglas Hofstadter (1979) in the Pulitzer Prize–winning book, *Gödel, Escher, Bach: An Eternal Golden Braid.*

To refute Parmenides' theory of the unchanging, motionless, indivisible One, Leucippus developed the philosophy of **atomism**—the idea that the universe is made of tiny, indivisible particles (atoms, from the Greek *atomos,* meaning indivisible). His theory was developed in greater detail by his pupil and associate, Democritus.

Democritus

Democritus (ca. 460–370 B.C.E.) was born in Abdera, a town in northeast Greece. He received a large inheritance, much of which he spent in travel. Although Democritus was a prolific writer, few of his works have survived. He is best known for his theory that there were only atoms and the void.

Unlike many of the ancient Greeks, Democritus believed that the senses can be trusted, for all practical purposes. Sensations are caused by atoms leaving an object and contacting our sense organs. However, the object qualities in the outside world that can be perceived directly are weight (heavy or light) and texture (hard or soft); all other qualities represent the interaction of our atoms with the atoms we receive from the object. These other qualities (e.g., taste, color) are secondary qualities, or qualities that depend on a perceiver. Thus, sensory experience is relative to the individual. (The analysis of secondary qualities was central to early modern philosophers such as John Locke and George Berkeley [Chapter 5].) In a frequently quoted passage, Democritus wrote that "By convention sweet is sweet, bitter is bitter, hot is hot, cold is cold, color is color; but in truth there are only atoms and the void." He also believed that all sensations are reducible to touch, because the atoms emitted by objects are interpreted as having contacted or touched the body atoms of the perceiver.

The atoms comprising the world differ in size, shape, and weight, with mind atoms being tiny, round, and smooth, like the atoms of fire. The mind atoms receive an image (*eidolon*) of the object being sensed, but in storage the *eidola* rub against each other and are altered, resulting in errors in our memory.

Democritus is sometimes labeled a materialist because he believed that all matter, including the soul, was made of the same atomic material. Additionally, because Democritus believed that the behavior of atoms is lawful and determines both physical and mental events, he has been called a **determinist**. Determinism is the belief that all events are determined by prior causes, and we will encounter such determinists as John Watson (Chapter 12) and B. F. Skinner (Chapter 13), who believed in environmental determinism, whereas Sigmund Freud (Chapter 15) embraced a psychological determinism. On the issue of reductionism versus nonreductionism, Democritus was clearly a reductionist, because he believed that everything on the observable level could be explained by the interaction of things (atoms) at a more fundamental level. Finally, on the nature-nurture issue, Democritus has been labeled a nurturist because he believed that the mind's contents come from the *eidola* received by the senses.

In Democritus's naturalistic, deterministic theory, there was no need for a deity as a prime mover, and Democritus thought that bodily atoms assumed some other form with a person's death. Without spiritual survival, there was no higher state to which humans might aspire—hence, no absolute standard of action. Despite this, Democritus believed the mind or soul atoms were the body's noblest part, and a wise person would free himself or herself from bodily passions, superstition, and ignorance to seek through contemplation such happiness as was humanly possible. For Democritus, happiness came not from things but from culture. Sensual pleasure is only briefly satisfying, and no pleasure outweighs the gaining of knowledge. Thus, Democritus counseled a life of moderation, good cheer, and serenity of the soul. Presumably taking his own advice, he lived to either 90 or 109, depending on the source. Democritus supposedly attributed his longevity to eating honey daily and bathing with oil.

In the atomists we find much of relevance for modern science: in their conception of a universe consisting of elemental particles, in their distinction between primary and secondary qualities, and in their insistence on determinism. Note, however, that their beliefs were based not on scientific inquiry but, rather, on their efforts to challenge Parmenides and Zeno's rationalistic position.

The Sophists

The Greek philosophers to this point were searching for a general principle or principles to explain the universe. For Heraclitus, the principle was change, whereas for Parmenides and Zeno it was the lack of change. Parmenides denied the existence of empty space and thus of movement, because movement can occur only when an object occupies a void. To counter Parmenides' argument for a static universe, Democritus conceived a universe consisting of atoms and the void (empty space). Lack of agreement on a universal principle prompted the Sophists and Socrates to focus on issues more relevant to human behavior—that is, on the study of people.

The **Sophists** (from *sophistes,* which means "wise man") were traveling teachers who played an important role in educating young men aspiring to leadership positions in Periclean Athens. Under Pericles, aristocracy was replaced with democracy, which meant that free citizens became eligible for public office. However, the old style of education had not prepared men for the changing conditions of political life. Without a university system, the Sophists were needed to teach logic, science, philosophy, and particularly rhetoric, or persuasive speaking.

At first the Sophists enjoyed a favorable reputation, but it soon became clear that the art of persuasion could be used both for good and for ill. "Rhetoric aims at persuasion, not truth, and the popular charge that the Sophists undertook to make the weak argument stronger and the strong argument weak was quite correct" (Allen, 1966, p. 18). Today, *sophistry* is defined as the use of misleading but clever arguments.

The Sophists' reputation was further tarnished by the justified claim that they took young men from good families and taught them to analyze skeptically their ancestors' religion and ethics. The Sophists' *skepticism* is the philosophical position that absolute knowledge is impossible and that inquiry must be a process of doubting in order to obtain even relative knowledge.

In addition, far from being disinterested thinkers, some of the Sophists levied high fees for their teaching, which meant that only the wealthy could profit from it. The relatively poor Socrates could afford only the Sophists' "short course."

Protagoras

Protagoras was among the most famous of the Sophists, and we will consider his ideas in order to illustrate Sophist thought. Born in Abdera, **Protagoras** (ca. 490–420 B.C.E.) was an older contemporary of Democritus and during his lifetime was better known and more influential than the younger man. Protagoras was also a frequent visitor to Athens and a friend of Pericles.

Most of our knowledge of Protagoras comes from Plato's dialogues—discussions of Plato's ideas and thoughts written as conversations between two people—one of which is named for Protagoras. Although Plato generally despised the Sophists, his treatment of Protagoras was respectful. In fact, in Plato's account of an exchange with Socrates, Protagoras makes the superior showing, appearing more the gentlemanly philosopher, whereas Socrates appears more the Sophist.

Unlike Parmenides, Protagoras accepted sensation as the source of knowledge, refusing to theorize any higher reality. Truth, goodness, and beauty are relative to the individual. This is the main point of Protagoras's famous saying: "Man is the measure of all things, of the things that are, that they are, and of the things that are not, that they are not" (Stumpf, 1989, p. 32). Protagoras did accept one thing as true, however—that there are no ultimate truths. Protagoras's philosophical position is called **relativism**, which is the theory that conceptions of truth and moral values are not absolute but are relative to their possessors.

Protagoras concluded that knowledge is relative to each person, which makes it impossible to discover the "true" nature of anything. Thus, Protagoras's approach could not readily be used to build a system of knowledge, because each person would perceive things differently. However, such ideas remain a part of contemporary psychology, as reflected in various movements in social psychology (Chapter 17).

Protagoras also believed moral judgments are relative, and there is no absolute code all humans should adopt. Laws and moral rules are based on convention, not on nature. Yet despite his belief in a moral relativism, Protagoras taught that the state makes the laws, and that we should conform to them in order to have a peaceful, orderly society.

Protagoras also took a relativistic approach to religion, saying that it was impossible for anyone to know with certainty about the existence and nature of the gods. Because of this statement, the Athenian Assembly banished Protagoras and ordered his works burned in the marketplace. It is said that he fled for Sicily but drowned on the way.

Although Protagoras himself supported the rule of law by convention, his teaching of cultural relativity led many to conclude that no behavior is absolutely right or wrong. Socrates' mission was to expose the fallacies in the Sophists' reasoning and to reestablish some concept of truth and a basis for moral judgments.

Socrates

Paradoxically, although Socrates was one of the Sophists' most constant critics, many Athenians considered him a Sophist because his approach—unrelenting analysis of a subject—was similar to that of the Sophists. The difference was that Socrates sought fundamental concepts of truth and goodness, whereas the Sophists believed there were no absolute truths. Also, Socrates refused pay for his instruction, although he did occasionally accept help from his wealthy friends.

Except for military service, Athenian-born **Socrates** (469–399 B.C.E.) spent nearly his whole life within the city's walls. Although he wrote nothing and did not found a school, Socrates is considered one of the greatest philosophers, his pivotal influence illustrated by the frequent classification of all earlier Greek philosophers as pre-Socratic. We know about him from three sources—Plato, Aristophanes, and Xenophon—each undoubtedly biased in his own way.

The comic playwright Aristophanes portrayed Socrates as a professional Sophist in *The Clouds,* whereas Xenophon, abandoning philosophy for the military, described his revered teacher as a practical figure—like Xenophon himself. But Plato is the source of most of our knowledge of Socrates, through dialogues that have preserved Socrates' memory.

In the early dialogues, Socrates was often the leading figure, and some feel that Plato described the historical Socrates and that all the ideas expressed in Plato's dialogues really came from his teacher. On the other hand, Aristotle attributed to Socrates the universal definitions and inductive arguments—that is, the method—and attributed to Plato the development of some of the particulars, such as the theory of Forms. The **theory of Forms** holds that there are universal Ideas, or Forms, that underlie what we know through our senses and that these Forms can be realized only through rational, deductive, logical means. The most widely accepted view is that Plato's early dialogues portray Socrates' philosophical activities, whereas the later dialogues express Plato's views.

Socrates' father was a sculptor, and his mother was a midwife. At Socrates' birth, Pericles was a young man, and Euripides and Sophocles were boys who

Socrates (469–399 B.C.E.)

later wrote great tragic plays that Socrates may have seen. The building of the Parthenon occurred during his lifetime, which spanned Greece's Golden Age.

Socrates distinguished himself in three military campaigns by bravery, physical endurance, and indifference to climate and alcohol. According to one source, Socrates was walleyed, snub-nosed, and bald in later life, with a walk like a duck (Allen, 1966), which may explain why he was portrayed in *The Clouds* as a strutting waterfowl.

Socrates was forced by what he called his *daimon,* or inner guiding spirit, to examine the moral attitudes of his contemporaries. To overcome the Sophists' relativism and skepticism, Socrates sought a foundation on which to build knowledge, which he found in the *psyche,* or soul. For Socrates, the soul was the human capacity for intelligence and character. A person's aim should be to make the soul as good as possible, in keeping with knowledge of true moral values. Before Socrates, Apollo's motto, "Know Thyself," inscribed on the entrance to the temple at Delphi, was interpreted to mean that a person should know and stay in his or her place in society. Socrates interpreted the words more literally, believing that human happiness comes from spiritual perfection, which requires self-knowledge. Only with self-knowledge can a person know good from evil, and for Socrates, "the unexamined life is not worth living."

Like the Sophists, Socrates used **dialectic**, or logical argumentation, to uncover an issue's truth. Unlike the Sophists, who often used dialectic simply to train orators, Socrates used it to achieve creative ideas of goodness and truth. The "Socratic method" began with Socrates asking someone to define something like beauty, truth, or justice. He would then point out contradictions and problems in the definitions, claiming all the while to be as ignorant as the person questioned. By correcting a person's incomplete or inaccurate notions, Socrates believed he could tease out the truth. In one demonstration of the method's power, Socrates coaxed the Pythagorean theorem from an ignorant lad.

A person cannot be taught virtue, although facts about virtue, what people in the past have thought, can be taught. In order to truly understand virtue, a person must "discover" it for himself or herself, and this was the point of the Socratic method. Personal discovery produces insight, which can never be taken away. When Socrates said "virtue is knowledge" (or "knowledge is virtue"), he meant that virtue is self-knowledge, knowledge of the soul's nature and of the true goal in life and how to achieve it.

Socrates distinguished between two objects of thought, the particular (e.g., a beautiful flower) and the general or universal (e.g., the Idea of Beauty), which are related to the distinction between appearances and reality, respectively. Only by a rigorous process of definition does the mind grasp the distinction between the particular and the general, and the goal of the process is to uncover the clear and fixed concepts that Socrates sought.

The end of the 5th century B.C.E. brought upheaval in Athens, and many Athenians longed for a return to the old order of things. Socrates had spent his adult life questioning the old concepts and was brought to trial on the charges of not worshipping the State's gods and of corrupting youth.

Convicted, Socrates was permitted to suggest his own punishment. When he proposed that Athens should reward him by according him "public maintenance in the prytaneum," his arrogance led to a death sentence. Still, his friends could have arranged for Socrates' escape; but having examined escape dialectically, he chose instead to drink the poison hemlock.

Although Socrates' enemies removed him from Athenian life, they could not remove his influence. The dialectic technique was passed on through Plato to Aristotle, who developed it into a system of logic that survives unchanged today. Through his pupils, Socrates' many ideas—for example, the importance of self-knowledge, the notion that personal discovery produces insight, the distinction between the particular and the general—form the backbone of most later Western philosophies.

Plato

A year after Pericles' death, **Plato** (427–347 B.C.E.) was born into an aristocratic Athenian family. He was named Aristocles, meaning "best and renowned," and later acquired the nickname Plato because of his broad shoulders. True to his original name, Plato excelled in virtually every field from philosophy to sports and, at 20, considered careers either as a poet or as a politician before succumbing to Socrates and philosophy. As a philosopher, Plato's influence has been so great that English mathematician and philosopher Alfred North Whitehead (1861–1947) once characterized the history of Western philosophy as but a series of "footnotes to Plato."

After Socrates' death, Plato and other Socratic disciples found refuge with the philosopher Euclides at Megara. From there, Plato traveled in Greece, Egypt, southern Italy—where he probably studied with Pythagoreans—and Sicily before returning to Athens in about 387 B.C.E. With financial aid from friends, Plato founded the **Academy** in a grove of trees (the grove of *Akademos,* a figure in Greek legend) outside Athens. Plato directed the Academy for the rest of his life, and it survived over 900 years before being closed by the Christian emperor Justinian in 529 C.E.

The Academy's chief subjects were philosophy and mathematics, the latter considered so important that the warning "Let no one without geometry enter here" was inscribed over the portal. Although knowing geometry may have been required for admission, the inscription probably reflected the Pythagorean belief in the primacy of mathematics in all understanding.

Plato's writings consist primarily of some 30 dialogues customarily categorized as early, middle, and late. In most of the early dialogues (e.g., the *Laches* and the *Apology*), Socrates, the main character, engages in dialectics with his fellow Greeks to ascertain the definition of different moral virtues. In the *Apology,* Socrates defends himself against the charges for which he was sentenced to die.

The middle dialogues (e.g., the *Phaedo* and the *Republic*) show Socrates expressing more positive, systematic views, which some modern scholars assume to be Plato's. In these dialogues, we find Plato's theory of knowledge as recollection, the theory of Forms, and his ideas on the soul's immortality. The *Republic* describes Plato's famous political utopia.

Less literary than the earlier dialogues, the third group is a series of sophisticated criticisms of the metaphysical and logical assumptions of doctrines from the middle group. Examples include the *Parmenides* and the *Laws.*

Theory of Forms

For Plato, there were two worlds—a world of Knowledge and a world of Opinion—Parmenides' "Way of Truth" and "Way of Seeming," respectively. The world of Knowledge contains the **Forms,** or Ideas, which are the universals known only through reason. By contrast, the world of Opinion contains the changing particulars of the material world conveyed to us by our senses. Because the senses are inaccurate, the body actually hinders us in acquiring knowledge of the Forms.

To Plato, the relation between the two worlds is one of imitation. The particulars are to the universals as the shadows of objects are to the objects that cast them. To illustrate this analogy, in Book VII of the Republic, Plato presented his famous parable of men in a cave or den. It begins with Socrates saying:

> Behold! human beings living in an underground den, which has a mouth open towards the light and reaching all along the den; here they have been from their childhood, and have their legs and necks chained so that they cannot move, and can only see before them, being prevented by the chains from turning round their heads. Above and behind them a fire is blazing at a distance, and between the fire and the prisoners there is a raised way; and you will see, if you look, a low wall built along the way, like the screen which marionette players have in front of them, over which they show the puppets. (Plato, *Republic*; Loomis, 1942, p. 398)

Along the raised way, walking men carry various objects, which project shadows onto the cave wall before the chained people. To the chained people, "the truth would be literally nothing but the shadows of the images" (Plato, *Republic;* Loomis, 1942, p. 399). For Plato, the flickering shadows on the cave's wall are like our sensations, providing us with unreliable images of a reality we can know only from reasoning.

It is a reality we have known before, because our souls originally resided in purity and bliss in the throng of human souls that God distributed among the stars. Attracted to the earth, each soul is joined to a body for a lifetime. During this earthly life, the soul has reminders of the world of true Being and perfect Form in which it once dwelled. Learning to understand and appreciate the perfect Forms is a matter of **anamnesis**, or recollection of information we already possess. Note that Plato's belief that Truth and Knowledge are present in the soul before birth is an extreme nature position that lays the foundation for other philosophers such as Kant (Chapter 6) and for psychologists such as Eleanor Gibson (Chapter 13).

Education's purpose is to lead people from the cave into the world of light, to turn them from the world of appearance to the world of reality. Once a person has left the cave and achieved a higher knowledge of reality, the person must not be permitted to stay in the world of contemplation. Instead, the educated person should return to the cave to participate in the life of the prisoners.

Unlike most of his contemporaries, Plato did not limit education to men, and women were admitted into the Academy. In the *Republic,* he noted that many women are superior to men in many things. For example, they may have greater musical skills and be better at curing disease. Thus, Plato concluded that girls and boys should receive the same education. In earlier writings, Plato appealed for female political participation, and "as far as we know, Plato was the first to argue seriously that women should share as equals with men in the public life of the state" (Loomis, 1942, p. 17).

Plato's Tripartite Soul

As Plato described it in the *Republic,* the soul has three parts (hence **tripartite soul**): reason, spirit, and appetite. Reason is the rational part of the soul, whereas spirit and appetite are the irrational parts. The rational part comes from the same receptacle as the World Soul, which means it originally has a clear vision of the Forms. Because the soul's irrational part is created by the gods who form the body, it has a tendency to pull the soul toward the earth and away from heaven's purity. The conflicting natures of the rational and irrational parts of the soul are beautifully illustrated in the *Phaedrus* by the image of a charioteer (reason) driving two horses: a well-trained thoroughbred (spirit) and a wild brute (appetite). We see Plato's rational and irrational parts of the soul echoed over 2,000 years later in Sigmund Freud's ego and id—the rational and irrational parts of the mind, respectively.

For Plato, bodily stimulation enables the irrational part of the soul to overcome its rational counterpart. This leads to the search for pleasure and the exaggeration of such drives as hunger and sex. Because of the susceptibility of the spirit and appetites of the soul to the body's influences, the soul's harmony is disturbed and reason is prevented from recalling the truth it once knew. By exposing the soul to many sensations, the body is responsible for ignorance, imprudence, and lust.

Morality comes when the soul's lost inner harmony is reestablished. Reason must regain control over the irrational. Whereas the Sophists had taught that a culture could define the good life however it wished, Plato taught that virtue is grounded in the nature of the soul. Virtue is attained when each of the soul's parts performs the function for which it was created, and this requires reason to keep the spirit and the appetites in check. Success in reasoning's function produces the virtue of wisdom.

By the same token, the appetites and the spirit have their functions to play in the good life. When the appetites are restrained, avoiding the excesses that would defeat the sovereignty of reason, the virtue of temperance results. The virtue of courage is produced when the spirit is restrained. When each of the soul's parts is fulfilling its particular function, the result is the virtue of justice. Justice reflects a person's achievement of inner harmony, which comes only when all of the soul's parts are performing their special functions.

Plato's Contributions

Plato gave us some fundamental rules of logical reasoning, although logic itself was systematized by Aristotle. In Plato's dialogues, Socrates insists on defining terms, on distinguishing between mere opinion and true knowledge, and on differentiating words from the objects they represent. Plato's Forms are also related to contemporary use of the term *concept* to refer to something abstracted from physical reality. We will encounter the modern study of concepts in our discussion of cognitive psychology (Chapter 18).

Plato was the father of all idealistic philosophers who see behind the visible, inconstant world an invisible world of order, intelligence, and purpose striving to reveal itself. He was also the forerunner of many rationalists who have argued for innate knowledge—for example, Descartes (Chapter 4), Leibniz (Chapter 4), and Kant.

Aristotle

Unlike Socrates and Plato, **Aristotle** (384–322 B.C.E.) was born not in Athens but in Stagira, a Greek colony in Macedonia, which was a country north of Greece. Aristotle's father was the court physician to Amyntas II, Macedonia's ruler, the father of Philip, and Alexander the Great's grandfather. As a boy, Aristotle was undoubtedly exposed by his father to the biological sciences, and, indeed, Aristotle's most abundant observations were in biology.

In 368 B.C.E., Aristotle traveled to Athens to study under Plato at the Academy. It is believed that he stayed at the Academy, first as a student and later as a teacher, until Plato died in 347 B.C.E. Next, Aristotle went to the court of Hermeias—a former Academy pupil—where, in 344 B.C.E., he married Pythias, Hermeias's niece and adopted daughter. After Pythias's death, Aristotle began a lasting but never legalized relation with Herpyllis, with whom he had a son, Nicomachus. One of Aristotle's most popular works, the *Nicomachean Ethics,* was named after the boy. Tradition holds that Nicomachus collected and edited the notes that became the *Ethics* from a set of Aristotle's lectures.

In 343 B.C.E., Philip invited Aristotle to be the teacher of his 13-year-old son Alexander, who later became the conqueror known as Alexander the Great. Aristotle taught the lad until Alexander took the throne upon his father's assassination.

Returning to Athens, Aristotle founded the **Lyceum,** named for its proximity to buildings devoted to *Apollo Lyceus* (God of Shepherds). The Lyceum's students were called "peripatics," which means "to walk about," perhaps because of Aristotle's tendency to pace while lecturing, or because of the type of open-air porch (*peripaté*) on which he often lectured. Like the Academy, the Lyceum survived until closed by the emperor Justinian.

With Alexander's death in 323, a wave of anti-Macedonian feeling swept Athens, and Aristotle was accused of impiety. He fled Athens to settle on a Greek island in the Aegean and died a year later.

Aristotle's writings can be divided into two main groups: the 27 nonsurviving dialogues for which Aristotle was known in antiquity, and treatises based on Aristotle's lecture notes, which were unknown outside the Lyceum until published in the 1st century B.C.E. The surviving writings are extraordinary in their range and originality, including discussions of logic, physics and metaphysics, astronomy, biology and physiology, psychology, ethics, art, language, and

"School of Athens" by Raphael; ©Bettmann/CORBIS.

Plato (427–347 B.C.E.) and Aristotle (384–322 B.C.E.)

politics. They profoundly influenced medieval Islamic philosophy and Christian philosophy (Chapter 3).

Aristotle and Plato Compared

In some ways the thought of Aristotle was the opposite of that of his former teacher. Plato was more of a rationalist, believing that reality could be known only through reason and that the role of perception is merely to remind us of what we already know. By contrast, Aristotle was more like an empiricist who believed that perception is a direct avenue to reality and that all concepts are derived from sense experience.

Plato was an idealist who taught that reality consists not of what we can know through our senses but, rather, of the transcendent Forms. Aristotle believed the world to be a blend of the material and the ideal. The material world, an object of opinion for Plato, was an object of knowledge for Aristotle.

Plato relied on **deductive reasoning**—that is, reasoning from a known principle to an unknown. In addition to deduction, Aristotle applied **inductive reasoning,** or reasoning from the particular to the general. Thus, Aristotle sometimes used experience and observation to test deduced principles, and at other times he arrived at general principles inductively, through the prior application of observation. Note that reasoning from induction can lead only to probable truth, as any future observation may negate the theory achieved inductively. Unlike Plato, Aristotle was always ready to modify his theories if observation showed them to be incorrect.

Although Plato and Aristotle disagreed on many important points, they both opposed Democritus, who held that the universe could be explained in purely mechanical terms. Both Plato and Aristotle believed that God, Aristotle's Unmoved Mover, exists independently of material form.

Aristotle and the Scientific Method

In the *Organon* (Greek for "tool" or "instrument"), Aristotle systematically demonstrated the reasoning process that leads to sure knowledge—namely, the **syllogism**. Beginning with a fundamental, unarguable, general statement, additional statements about particular instances follow of necessity. If all A are B, and C is an example of A, then C must be B. Aristotle's standard example is: All men (A) are mortal (B). Because Socrates (C) is a man (A), then Socrates (C) is mortal (B). Syllogistic reasoning as an avenue to knowledge became something of an obsession among Western philosophers after Aristotle's rediscovery in the later Middle Ages (Chapter 3).

In syllogistic or deductive reasoning, the basic statement from which we are reasoning must be both correct and comprehensive. Lack of either condition may invalidate the conclusions, but if the initial premises are true, then a valid conclusion necessarily follows.

Aristotle also systematized inductive argument, a second form of reasoning that can lead to valid conclusions. If many observations all point to the same general conclusion, then the conclusion may well be correct. For example, every morning we have observed that the sun rises in the east and sets in the west. From this, we may conclude that the sun *always* rises in the east and sets in the west. Still, we must remain vigilant to the exception that will negate the principle, and we must not be too hasty in drawing conclusions. With inductive reasoning, there is always the danger that sweeping conclusions may be drawn from limited data, and Aristotle himself was often guilty of this type of error.

In *Metaphysics* (meaning "after physics"), Aristotle began his search for the fundamental principles of the universe with a review of the theories of previous Greek thinkers. He rejected all of the earlier theories as being insufficiently analytical. They had failed to incorporate the four basic **causes:** material, formal, efficient, and final. To understand anything completely, we must know its four causes.

The *material cause* answers the question, Of what is a thing made? For example, a statue's material cause is the marble from which it is chiselled. Aristotle criticized many of the earlier philosophers for being content with simply naming the material(s) making up an object and for not recognizing that there was more to causation. The *formal cause* answers the question, What is it? When we say an object is a statue of Aphrodite, we have identified its form, the pattern its material has assumed. The *efficient cause* answers the question, By whom or by what is the object made? We say the efficient cause of the statue is the sculptor, wielding his hammer and chisel. The *final cause* answers the question, What is the purpose or end for which the object was made? A statue's final cause may be to satisfy the sculptor's creative urges, to provide something the sculptor can sell to put food on the table, or to please its viewers.

By noting and emphasizing final cause, Aristotle revealed his belief in **teleology,** the idea that everything is directed toward a definite end and a final purpose. An acorn has the potential to become an oak tree, and its **entelechy,** its built-in goal or function, keeps it moving toward its appropriate end. Aristotle believed in the priority of actuality over potentiality. Although a girl is potentially a woman, before a girl could exist with that potentiality, there first had to be an actual woman.

To explain the constantly changing world of potential striving toward an end that perishes, Aristotle assumed the existence of a pure actuality that was above the world of potential, or dying things. Thus, he postulated a Being of pure actuality, motionless because change is a kind of motion. This was the Unmoved Mover, which Aristotle considered more scientifically than theologically. The Unmoved Mover was the final cause toward which everything strives.

Aristotle did not think of the Unmoved Mover as a conscious entity prescribing purposes or goals for the world. Instead he conceived of It as the unconscious principle of motion inherent in the universe. Later Christian philosophers, particularly St. Thomas Aquinas (Chapter 3), equated Aristotle's Unmoved Mover with the God of Christianity.

Aristotle's Biology

Aristotle made many contributions in biology. For example, he was the first to construct a rational classification scheme for the animal kingdom, dividing it into *anaima* and *enaima*—bloodless and blooded—animals. These divisions correspond approximately to our invertebrates and vertebrates, respectively. Aristotle separated animals with blood into fishes, amphibians, birds, and mammals.

Aristotle's theory of analogous organs demonstrated his recognition of the interrelations of animals throughout the animal kingdom. Thus, he saw a bird's feather as the analogue of a fish's scale and a nail as the analogue of a claw. Aristotle at times even approached the concept of evolution:

> Nature proceeds little by little from things lifeless to animal life in such a way that it is impossible to determine the exact line of demarcation. . . . Thus, next after lifeless things in the upward scale comes the genus of plants, relatively lifeless as compared with animals, but alive as compared with corporeal objects. There is in plants a continuous scale of ascent towards the animal. There are certain objects in the sea concerning which one would be at a loss to determine whether they be animal or vegetable.

> . . . In regard to sensibility, some animals give no sign of it, others indicate it obscurely. . . . And so throughout the animal scale there is a graduated differentiation. (Aristotle, *History of Animals;* Durant, 1939, p. 530)

Aristotle's conception of the world of nature consisting of a hierarchy from the simplest entity to the most complex creature was a powerful influence on later European thinking. Charles Darwin found the principle of natural selection foreshadowed in Aristotle's *Physicae Auscultationes*:

> Wheresoever, therefore, all things together (that is all the parts of one whole) happened like as if they were made for the sake of something, these were preserved, having been appropriately constituted by an internal spontaneity; and whatsoever things were not thus constituted, perished, and still perish. (Aristotle, *Physicae Auscultationes*; Appleman, 1979, p. 19)

To further acknowledge Aristotle's influence, Darwin wrote: "Linnaeus and Cuvier have been my two gods, . . . but they were mere schoolboys compared to old Aristotle" (Loomis, 1943, p. xxvii).

Aristotle's notion that animals might be arranged on a graded scale of complexity led many later scholars to accept the idea that animals could be ranked on a continuous dimension known as the *scala naturae,* or Great Chain of Being (Lovejoy, 1936). At the bottom were animals like sponges that were essentially formless, whereas humans were at the top of the scale. The phylogenetic scale is a modern version of this natural scale, and it has been suggested that many comparative psychologists and other psychologists who study animals (e.g., neuroanatomists, physiologists) have mistakenly relied too heavily on the Aristotle-inspired scale (Hodos & Campbell, 1969). The result was a lack of theory in comparative psychology.

In addition to Aristotle's sometimes brilliant observations and suggestions, there are many errors in the *History of Animals,* some simply amusing (e.g., the only diseases from which elephants suffer are runny nose and flatulence) and others of more consequence. One of the latter was his conclusion that the heart was the source of the blood and the seat of sensations, emotions, intelligence, and, most importantly, the *psyche.*

Aristotle's Psychology

Although *psyche* means "soul," Aristotle meant it as a vital principle that differentiates the living and the nonliving. All living things possess ***psyche,*** but there are different grades: vegetative (or nutritive), sensitive, and rational. Plants have only a vegetative *psyche,* which allows them to take in matter, grow, and reproduce, whereas animals and humans also have a sensitive *psyche* that allows them to sense and to perceive their environments. In addition to the five traditional senses—vision, audition, olfaction, gustation, and touch—Aristotle proposed a common sense that assimilates the information from the other senses. The sensitive *psyche* also allows the qualities sensed to continue after the object sensed is no longer present. In other words, it is responsible for memory and imagination. Only humans possess a rational *psyche,* which permits thinking and reasoning.

Several observations led Aristotle to put *psyche* in the heart. First, he knew that diseases of the heart are fatal, and *psyche* is present only in the living. Also, feelings such as anger and fear produce changes experienced as sensations in the chest. Aristotle further observed that the heart is the first organ formed in the embryonic chicken, and its beating signals life. Finally, Aristotle rejected the brain as the organ of the *psyche,* because cerebral tissue is insensitive to direct stimulation. For Aristotle, the brain probably cooled the blood. Aristotle was not alone in making this mistake: "Twenty-five centuries before Aristotle, Egyptians, too, identified the heart with psychological activity, and . . . they also treated the brain, insofar as they noted it at all, as a more or less useless substance" (Laver, 1972, p. 181).

Because one definition Aristotle gave the *psyche* was that it was a substance with the capacity to receive knowledge, what is the source of this knowledge? Unlike Plato, who held that knowledge was already present from the time the soul dwelled among the Forms, Aristotle believed that sensation preceded thought and that mind without thought

Aristotle Contemplating the Bust of Homer

was like a blank slate. The blank slate metaphor will reappear in the work of the British empiricists (especially John Locke) and in that of all the psychologists who have taken the nurture position on the nature-nurture issue.

According to Tigner and Tigner (2000), Aristotle conceived a theory of intelligence that resembles Robert Sternberg's contemporary theory. Both are triarchic models, with Aristotle dividing intelligence into theoretical, practical, and productive intelligence. The corresponding concepts from Sternberg's work are analytical, practical, and creative intelligence. By theoretical, Aristotle meant the ability to know or understand the world's truths; in Rembrandt's painting *Aristotle Contemplating the Bust of Homer*, the figure of Aristotle himself illustrates the ancient master of theoretical knowledge. Productive intelligence refers to artistic ability, broadly defined, and Rembrandt used the image of Homer to show productive intelligence. Practical intelligence enables its possessor to do or accomplish something, to "get something done"; Aristotle's pupil Alexander the Great represented this form of intelligence. In a brief response to Tigner and Tigner, Sternberg (2000) noted that their article shows one more reason why it is so important for students of psychology to study the history of their field: Information from the past, even the distant past, can inform our contemporary thought about such things as the nature of intelligence.

For Aristotle, humans were the only animals with thought, even though other animals have sensations that produce images (mental representations created by sensations that outlast the sensations) that may become memories (the retention of the mental representations). Remembering is the recalling of some previously created image, and Aristotle explicitly stated that memory does not take place without an image.

Aristotle also held that thought requires images: "Now we have already discussed imagination [the formation of images] in the treatise *On the Soul* and we concluded there that thought is impossible without an image" (Aristotle, *Parva Naturalia;* Sahakian, 1968, p. 11). Similarly, the founder of scientific psychology, Wilhelm Wundt, and his student, Edward Bradford Titchener (both Chapter 8), considered "imageless" thought impossible. Wundt's and Titchener's adherence to Aristotelian dogma created controversy in the late 19th and early 20th centuries with members of the Würzburg School (Chapter 8) and others who believed thought sometimes occurs without images.

Remembering is a spontaneous reproduction of past experiences, whereas recall involves an active search that attempts to recover previous perceptions. In describing recall, Aristotle touched on principles that have been incorporated into the doctrine of association held by most learning theorists in modern times (Chapter 13). Aristotle's **principles of association** are similarity, contrast, and contiguity. That is, the recall of an object or event tends to evoke the memory of ones like it (similar to it), ones opposite to it (contrasted to it), or ones that occurred at the same time or place (contiguous to it) in the original learning.

Aristotle named additional factors important in recollection that have been incorporated into modern learning theory (see Maniou-Vakali, 1974). For example, he recognized that repetition improves our ability to recall something. Also, Aristotle noted that some things are easier to remember than others;

some experiences are better remembered after one or a few repetitions than others often experienced. In addition to the many psychological reasons for this phenomenon—for example, meaningfulness, strong emotional coloring—it fits nicely with modern ideas on biological predispositions and constraints on learning (e.g., Timberlake & Lucas, 1989) as well as with some less modern but historically significant ideas (see Thorndike, Chapter 12).

Dreaming is related to the same processes involved in remembering and recollection. Images created from sensations retained by the mind are aroused during sleep and become the dream. Note that Aristotle recognized the similarity between dreams during sleep and hallucinations produced by illness in the waking state. "So much is clear on this subject that the same agency which in disease produces illusion while we are awake, also produces the condition of illusion in sleep" (Aristotle, *Parva Naturalia;* Sahakian, 1968, p. 13).

Aristotle was the first to recognize psychological **catharsis** (from the Greek *katharsis,* which means purification), although the term had been used earlier by the physician Hippocrates (for whom it meant the evacuation of morbid humors) and by Plato (in reference to the purification of the soul by philosophy). Aristotle believed that tragic drama allows the viewer to purify or purge negative emotions, through the process of identification with the tragic hero. Sigmund Freud made catharsis a basic component of psychoanalysis.

Aristotle's Influence

Aristotle dared much and failed at times, but even with all his errors, he is truly the forerunner of the "scientific method." He gave us advanced logic (an empirical approach to knowledge in contrast to Plato's extreme rationalism), and many of his observations anticipated more modern conceptions (e.g., evolution, principles of association, the mind as a blank slate). Aristotle also wrote about many other things that have undoubtedly influenced modern psychology directly or indirectly. For example, his writings on art and tragedy shaped the structure of Shakespeare's plays, and the idea of his "lost work" on comedy has served to advance one modern linguistic theory—semiotics, the study of signs and sign systems (Eco, 1983).

Even with all his accomplishments, it can be argued that Aristotle had a negative influence on science for several hundred years (although it was not his fault). Scholars in the Middle Ages considered Aristotle's Unmoved Mover evidence that he was a divinely inspired monotheist, making his writings the final authority on worldly matters. And because Aristotle's monotheism indicated his divine inspiration, there was no need to continue scientific exploration. Scholars should concentrate on spiritual matters.

Eventually, Renaissance scientists such as Copernicus, Galileo, Newton, and Harvey (all Chapter 4) challenged Aristotle on so many points that his monopoly on scientific thought expired. However, "few philosophers of the remote past, if any, are so conspicuously alive in the range of questions they provoke and in the resourcefulness of the arguments they offer" (Nussbaum, 1998, p. 74).

MEDICINE IN THE GOLDEN AGE AND BEYOND

Both in the distant past and in recent times, psychology arose from philosophy and physiology. After our examination of philosophy in the Golden Age, we now turn to physiology and medicine in the same period. We will begin with Alcmaeon, an important precursor to Hippocrates, considered by many the most famous physician of all time. Hippocrates lived during Greece's Golden Age, and his development of rational medicine—medicine based on reason rather than religion—was anticipated by Alcmaeon.

Alcmaeon

At the time of **Alcmaeon** (ca. 500 B.C.E.), Greek medicine was largely tied to religion. Treatment occurred in the temples of Asclepius (the Greek god of medicine), where the priests subjected patients to ritual and suggestion, extracted large sums of money, and probably cured patients whose symptoms were largely psychological and those for whom rest was needed. A harmless snake was often used to treat patients in the temples of Asclepius, as the early Greeks revered the serpent as a creature blessed with the earth's healing powers. Also, because the snake sheds its skin and then appears renewed, it became for the Greeks a symbol of eternal life. Today, the snake wrapped around the staff of Asclepius is one of the symbols of the medical profession (Finger, 2000).

Alcmaeon was one of the first recorded anatomists. In his animal dissections he located the optic nerves and discovered the eustachian tubes connecting the throat with the middle ears. Unlike some, Alcmaeon believed the brain was the organ of thought. Following the Pythagoreans, Alcmaeon considered health a matter of harmonious balance of such opposites as dry/wet, hot/cold, and bitter/sweet, with disease resulting from an imbalance. Although Alcmaeon has been called the founder of Greek medicine, his is a relatively late name in a long line of secular physicians originating before recorded history.

Hippocrates

The son of a physician, **Hippocrates** (ca. 460–377 B.C.E.) was born on Cos, an island in the Aegean Sea, off the southwest coast of present-day Turkey. Although Hippocrates is often called the father of medicine and there are literally dozens of treatises penned under his name, most of these works were almost certainly written by Hippocrates' followers.

Unlike some, Hippocrates considered the brain the organ of the mind, and in one of the Hippocratic works, *On Injuries of the Head*, the author made the correct association between wounds on one side of the head and seizures and paralysis on the other side of the body (Finger, 2000). In *On the Sacred Disease*, Hippocrates broke with his contemporaries, who thought epilepsy was caused by the gods stealing a victim's mind. Instead, Hippocrates attributed the disorder to natural causes and in particular to an imbalance in the four humors.

The four **humors** (bodily fluids) of Hippocrates were black bile, yellow bile, blood, and phlegm, which Hippocrates thought were distilled from the four basic elements posited by the poet and philosopher Empedocles (ca. 490–430 B.C.E.): earth, air, fire, and water, respectively. Humoral imbalance resulted in disease, whereas balance was essential to health. Naturalistic treatments were used to restore humoral balance, and Hippocrates prescribed such remedies as purgatives, bloodletting, exercise, and special diets. As Magner (1992) noted, "In a fundamental sense, *dietetics* was the basis of the art of healing. According to Hippocrates, human beings could not consume the rough food suitable for other animals; thus, the first cook was the first physician" (p. 68, italics in the original).

Hippocrates described the symptoms of numerous mental disorders, including phobias, postpartum depression (depression after childbirth), and hysteria (a physical disorder without organ pathology). Believing that hysteria occurred only in women, Hippocrates attributed it to the "wandering uterus." For example, Hippocrates thought hysterical blindness was produced when the uterus lodged behind the eyes. Thus, he prescribed marriage and pregnancy to restore the uterus to its normal location. Hippocrates' notion that hysteria (a somatoform disorder in current terminology) was exclusively a disorder of women held until challenged in modern times by Freud and others.

Probably Hippocrates' greatest contribution was his continuing fight to free medicine from philosophical and religious influences. Although he occasionally prescribed prayer, Hippocrates insisted that theology per se had no place in medicine. Remnants of Hippocratic treatment can be seen even in relatively modern times—bleeding was widely practiced until at least the middle of the 19th century—and George Washington's death may have been hastened by excessive bloodletting.

Galen

We know of Hippocrates in part through **Galen** (ca. 130–200 C.E.). Galen was born in Pergamum, where he discovered philosophy at 14, remaining always under its spell despite turning to medicine at 17. Galen served for a time as a surgeon in the

National Library of Medicine, Washington, D.C.

Galen (130–200 C.E.) contemplates a human skeleton, whose perfection confirms Galen's belief in a divine purpose in nature

Pergamum school for gladiators, which probably exposed him to internal human anatomy. His extensive travels took him eventually to Rome, where he practiced until his success in exposing the dishonesty of many Roman physicians resulted in his having to flee the city temporarily. There may have been another reason for Galen's unpopularity in Rome, however. As Finger (2000) put it, "Some of the sniping he endured was probably due to professional jealousy, but much was the result of his gigantic ego and abrasive disposition" (p. 41). Although Galen's name derives from a Greek word meaning "peaceful" or "gentle," apparently Galen was anything but peaceful and gentle.

Living some 600 years after Hippocrates, Galen was strongly influenced by Hippocratic medicine and by Aristotle's biology. Like Hippocrates, Galen believed the brain was the organ of the mind, opposing Aristotle's notion that the mind was located in the heart. Drawing on the writings of his predecessors, especially Hippocrates, and on his own experiments, Galen produced some 500 volumes, of which over 100 have survived. These volumes cover all branches of medicine and many areas of philosophy.

Roman law forbade human dissection, so Galen dissected and vivisected animals, sometimes generalizing too readily to humans (Sarton, 1954). (Vivisection is dissection performed on the living.) From his investigations, Galen can be said to have founded experimental neurology. He recognized 7 of the 12 pairs of cranial nerves, demonstrated that injuries to one side of the brain resulted in functional impairment on the opposite side of the body, and distinguished between motor and sensory nerves, a distinction lost until finally reestablished in the 19th century (Chapter 7). In addition, Galen named such neural structures as the corpus callosum, the pineal and pituitary glands, and the ventricles. He believed that the ventricles serve as the reservoir for **animal spirits**, the mysterious substance that many Greeks felt distinguished the living from the dead.

Galen incorporated Hippocrates' humoral theory into a personality theory in which the predominance of each humor is associated with a particular temperament. For example, Galen believed that an excess of blood is related to being cheerful or sanguine (from the Latin *sanguineus,* meaning blood). Excessive black bile makes a person melancholic or sad, whereas too much yellow bile gives a person a choleric or fiery temperament. Finally, an excess of phlegm produces a sluggish or dull individual—that is, one who is phlegmatic. Jackson (1969) has suggested that Galen's personality theory "provided the conceptual framework for a physiological psychology" (p. 369). Further evidence for Galen's status as an early physiological psychologist is that "he seems to have repeatedly insisted that mental states . . . were reflections of physiological states" (p. 371), a thoroughly modern point of view. In fact, if we translate the term *humors* into *neurotransmitters,* Galen's humoral theory of temperament becomes compatible with current theories of the biochemical basis of conditions such as depression and schizophrenia. In addition, Galen's four-factor temperament theory is compatible with several contemporary models of personality (Merenda, 1987).

Galen rejected the mechanistic interpretations of biology held by atomists such as Democritus. In his studies, Galen was struck by the beauty and functional utility of the body's parts, which he believed showed purpose in the body's design. For Galen, purpose in the origin, structure, and function of organs revealed divine influence in the workings of the universe. Early Christians were as impressed with Galen's monotheism as they were with Aristotle's, and until the Renaissance, Galen was the unquestioned authority in physiology. Galen became "an Aristotle for medieval medicine" (Durant, 1944, p. 507) and, according to Magner (1992), was "known as the Medical Pope of the Middle Ages" (p. 88).

CONCLUSIONS

Our survey of the philosophical traditions of the ancient Greeks has been designed to lay the foundation for Chapter 3's look at philosophy (and psychology) from the time of the Roman Empire to the Renaissance. Granted, important work in philosophy also occurred in places other than the city-states of ancient Greece. For example, Egypt and Babylon were known for their rich philosophical traditions, and precursors of psychology can be seen in ancient Egypt (Laver, 1972). Alexandria, Egypt, in particular, was home to important thinkers, including the anatomists Herophilus and Erasistratus. Erasistratus is sometimes said to have been the first to distinguish between motor and sensory nerves and to have been the first to do *in vivo* work on the nervous system. However, historical events like the development of key trade routes, the spread of certain religions, and the ravages of wars made the philosophical systems of Periclean Greece and not Assyria (or elsewhere) of direct importance for modern psychology.

The Golden Age of Greece was a time in which medicine, philosophy, and science flourished, and it is possible for us to see connections from the Golden Age to the 21st century. Examples include the struggle begun by Alcmaeon and Hippocrates to develop medicine as a rational science, the debate between materialism and idealism, and the belief, begun by Pythagoras, that to know a thing is to be able to capture it mathematically. In addition, we see the origins of some of the most fundamental concepts of modern science (e.g., atomic theory) in the writings of the ancient Greeks.

Socrates, Plato's mentor, is still considered by some to be the most impressive thinker of all time. Although he was not a scientist, his ideas and methods provided the foundation for productive inquiry. We will see that the writings of Plato and Aristotle shaped the scientific and intellectual pursuits of Western civilization for centuries. Aristotelian thought, especially on biological and physical science, became dogma after its rediscovery in the medieval period and provided a system for the scientists and philosophers of the Renaissance to attack. Still, a variety of concepts from both Plato and Aristotle can be seen in more modern psychology (e.g., mental representations, catharsis, principles of association).

Clearly, medicine, philosophy, and science did not end with the decline of the Greek city-states. As we will see in Chapter 3, several schools (e.g., Stoicism, Cynicism) emerged and were popular during the Roman era.

SUMMARY

The Golden Age of Greece

The period between the birth of Pericles and the death of Aristotle is sometimes called the Golden Age of Greece. During much of this time, Athens flourished under democratic rule.

Philosophy in the Golden Age

The philosophical positions of materialism and idealism were debated during Greece's Golden Age. An idealist, Plato was the end of a line of development beginning with Pythagoras and Parmenides, whereas Democritus was a materialist. Plato also took much from the work of Pythagoras, who is strongly associated with mathematical discoveries, particularly of the relations between music and numbers.

Heraclitus's fascination with change can be linked to modern chaos theory. Parmenides rejected Heraclitus's idea of change, which he explained by distinguishing appearances from reality. Appearances we know from sensory experience; reality we know from reason. Parmenides' extreme rationalism became the basis for Platonism. By composing several paradoxes to show that change and movement are impossible, Zeno of Elea defended Parmenides.

In order to refute Parmenides' theory of the unchanging One, Democritus developed atomism, a theory maintaining that the universe consists of atoms (tiny, indivisible particles) and the void. Democritus held that all the qualities of objects we experience, except for weight and texture, are secondary qualities. He has been called a materialist, a determinist, a reductionist, and a nurturist.

The Sophists taught young men logic, science, philosophy, and rhetoric. Protagoras accepted sensation as the source of knowledge, refusing to theorize a higher reality. One of the greatest of the ancient philosophers, Socrates was sometimes accused of being a Sophist because of his "Socratic method" of logical argumentation to achieve creative ideas of concepts like beauty and truth. Socratic suggestions such as the importance of self-knowledge and the distinction between the general and the particular formed the foundation of most later Western philosophies.

Socrates' pupil Plato founded the Academy. Like Parmenides, Plato believed in a world of Knowledge (containing the Forms, or Ideas) and a world of Opinion. Learning to understand the Forms requires the recollection of knowledge we already possess, and Plato believed that knowledge is in the soul before birth. Plato's tripartite soul consisted of reason, spirit, and appetite.

Plato's student Aristotle founded a rival school—the Lyceum. Whereas Plato was a rationalist, Aristotle was more of an empiricist who sought knowledge through the senses. In addition to Plato's deductive reasoning, Aristotle used the inductive method. Aristotle discovered the reasoning form called the syllogism and wrote about four basic causes: material, formal, efficient, and final.

Aristotle's belief that animals might be arranged on a hierarchy of complexity led to the *scala naturae.* For Aristotle, all living things possessed *psyche,* but there were three different grades: vegetative, sensitive, and rational. Aristotle placed the mind in the heart, held that the mind without thought was like a blank slate, suggested three principles of association for recall, and recognized catharsis.

Medicine in the Golden Age and Beyond

Alcmaeon and Hippocrates practiced rational medicine rather than medicine tied to religion. Alcmaeon discovered the eustachian tubes and considered the brain the organ of thought. Hippocrates attributed epilepsy to natural causes and described the symptoms of several mental disorders. He believed that an imbalance in the four humors caused disease. Galen incorporated humoral theory into a personality theory and wrote extensively on the brain's ventricles, considering them the reservoir for animal spirits. Because of his monotheism, the early Christians made Galen the unquestioned authority in physiology.

CONNECTIONS QUESTIONS

1. How might Greece's political system in the Age of Pericles be connected with the rise of the Sophists?
2. Why is the debate between the ideas of Heraclitus and those of Parmenides of importance to psychology?
3. Contrast and compare Plato and Aristotle across as many dimensions as you can.
4. Locate as many connections as you can between the thought of the ancient Greek physicians and philosophers and that of the psychologists in the 19th, 20th, and 21st centuries.
5. Should the history of psychology begin with the Greeks? Some point earlier? Later? Why?
6. What connections might you draw between Galen and modern neurotransmitter research?

KEY NAMES AND TERMS

Academy (p. 32)
Alcmaeon (p. 39)
anamnesis (p. 33)
Anaxagoras (p. 24)
animal spirits (p. 41)
Aristotle (p. 34)
atomism (p. 28)
catharsis (p. 39)
causes (p. 36)
chaos theory (p. 26)
deductive reasoning (p. 35)
Democritus (p. 28)
determinist (p. 28)
dialectic (p. 31)
entelechy (p. 36)
Forms (p. 32)
Galen (p. 40)
Golden Age of Greece (p. 24)
Heraclitus (p. 26)
Hippocrates (p. 40)
humors (p. 40)
idealism (p. 25)
inductive reasoning (p. 35)
Lyceum (p. 34)
Parmenides (p. 27)
Pericles (p. 24)
Plato (p. 32)
principles of association (p. 38)
Protagoras (p. 29)
psyche (p. 37)
Pythagoras (p. 25)
rationalism (p. 27)
relativism (p. 30)
Socrates (p. 30)
Sophists (p. 29)
syllogism (p. 35)
teleology (p. 36)
Thales (p. 24)
theory of Forms (p. 30)
tripartite soul (p. 33)
Zeno of Elea (p. 27)

SUGGESTED READINGS

Allen, R. E. (Ed.) (1966). *Greek philosophy: Thales to Aristotle.* New York: Macmillan. This commonly used reader has short original passages by classical Greek philosophers, including Plato and Aristotle. In addition, there is a brief introduction that contains biographical information for the major Greek philosophers.

Durant, W. (1939). *The life of Greece.* New York: Simon and Schuster. This is the second volume in a monumental 10-volume work by Will and Ariel Durant. Like all the volumes, *The Life of Greece* is highly readable and extensively referenced. Although modern historians question elements of Durant's work, it remains a delightful introduction.

Kirk, G. S., Raven, J. E., & Schofield, M. (Eds.) (1983). *The Presocratic philosophers* (2nd ed.). Cambridge: Cambridge University Press. This is one of the standard texts for the study of pre-Socratic philosophy. It provides detailed coverage of all the pre-Socratics, including several we did not examine in this chapter.

Sahakian, W. S. (Ed.) (1968). *History of psychology: A source book in systematic psychology.* Itasca, IL: F. E. Peacock Publishers, Inc. Sahakian's book contains brief excerpts from the writings of most of the major Greek philosophers, including passages from Democritus, Socrates and Plato, and Aristotle. A variety of other volumes like Sahakian's book can be found, each providing an economical introduction to many original works.

Books of readings from Plato and Aristotle are always in print. A good starting place for Plato would be one of the dialogues such as *Meno* or the *Republic.* One of Aristotle's most popular and readable works is the *Nicomachean Ethics,* which should be readily available.

The Roman Period and the Middle Ages

CHAPTER 3

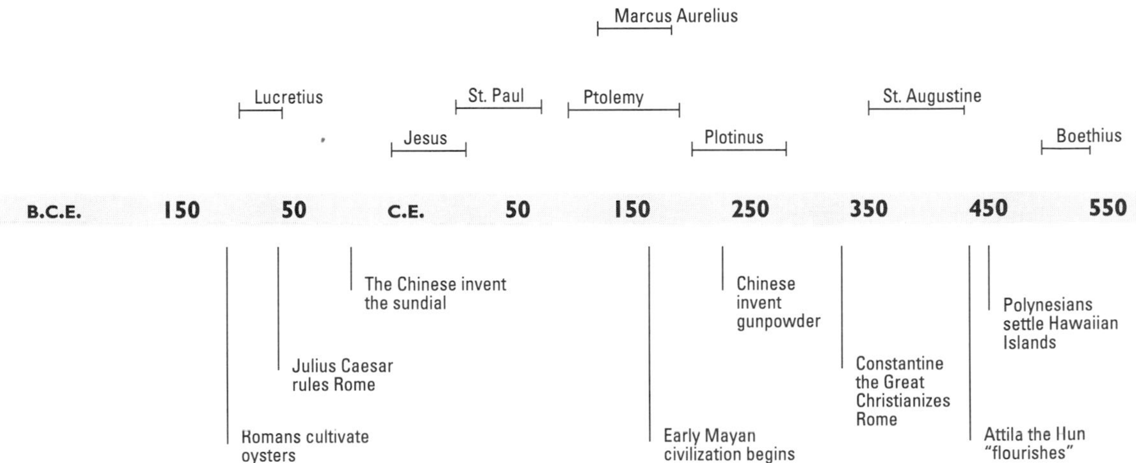

OUTLINE

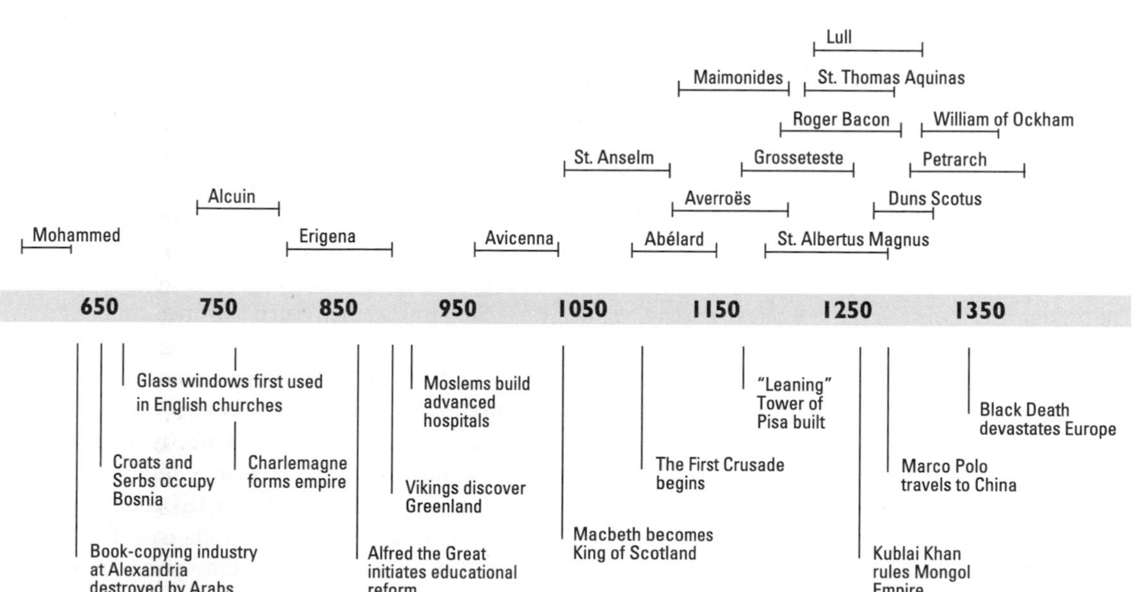

Lull
Maimonides
St. Thomas Aquinas
Roger Bacon
William of Ockham
St. Anselm
Grosseteste
Petrarch
Alcuin
Averroës
Duns Scotus
Mohammed
Erigena
Avicenna
Abélard
St. Albertus Magnus
650
750
850
950
1050
1150
1250
1350
Glass windows first used in English churches
Moslems build advanced hospitals
"Leaning" Tower of Pisa built
Black Death devastates Europe
Croats and Serbs occupy Bosnia
Charlemagne forms empire
The First Crusade begins
Marco Polo travels to China
Vikings discover Greenland
Macbeth becomes King of Scotland
Book-copying industry at Alexandria destroyed by Arabs
Alfred the Great initiates educational reform
Kublai Khan rules Mongol Empire

PHILOSOPHICAL AND THEOLOGICAL THOUGHT DURING THE ROMAN PERIOD

Greece's Golden Age did not end simply because Aristotle died. Its decline really began earlier with Athens' defeat in the Peloponnesian War by Sparta and its allies (with help from the Persians). This 404 B.C.E. defeat led to a dismantling of the Athenian Empire and to the installation in Athens of a Spartan-backed puppet regime. After a year of terror, the Thirty Tyrants were overthrown and democracy was reestablished, but Athens did not recover its former glory.

Just as Greece's Golden Age did not end with Aristotle's death, neither did Greek philosophy. After Aristotle, **Theophrastus** (ca. 372–286 B.C.E.) became the head of the Lyceum. Theophrastus tended to be more empirical than Aristotle, with a special interest in botany, where his contributions have led many to label him the founder of plant science. In a work on the senses and sensation, Theophrastus described in detail the observable processes of the mind, which he placed in the brain, unlike Aristotle. Theophrastus described such processes as sensation and perception, pain and pleasure, and emotions in a work that some consider an early discussion of physiological psychology (e.g., Stratton, 1917).

In addition to the work at the Lyceum, several other schools flourished in the Greco-Roman period, including Skepticism, Cynicism, Epicureanism, and Stoicism.

Skepticism

Skepticism was founded by **Pyrrho** (ca. 365–270 B.C.E.), who traveled in Persia and India with Alexander the Great. Like Socrates, Pyrrho wrote nothing, yet had a great effect on his students and contemporaries. Pyrrho's version of **Skepticism** held that we are never in a position to have definitive beliefs about anything, including Skepticism itself. The only way to avoid believing in something that may be false is to not believe in anything. This does not mean you should disregard the rules of society, however. It just means you should not believe there is any rational basis for such rules.

Cynicism

The school of **Cynicism** was cofounded by **Antisthenes** (ca. 455–360 B.C.E.) and his pupil **Diogenes** (ca. 410–320 B.C.E.). Antisthenes was one of the people with Socrates when he died. Together, Diogenes and Antisthenes taught a back-to-nature life free from society's conventions. Diogenes became famous for his disregard of creature comforts and social niceties. According to legend, when Alexander the Great asked what he, Alexander, could do for Diogenes, the Cynic replied, "You could move out of the sun and not cast a shadow on me." Supposedly Diogenes lived in a barrel, "like a dog," thereby earning the title *kynikos*, which means "like a dog." From *kynikos* came *cynic*.

The Cynics both dropped out of society and attacked its precepts, seeing in society only hypocrisy, envy, greed, and hate. Another story tells of Diogenes wandering the streets of Athens by day carrying a lamp, searching for an honest man. Much of Cynicism was incorporated into Stoicism, but, unlike the Cynics, the Stoics did not reject society's comforts.

Stoicism

Zeno of Citium (ca. 333–262 B.C.E.) founded Stoicism, named for the *Stoa Poikile* (painted colonnade, or porch) in which Zeno began his school. The chief themes of **Stoicism**—that the world functions according to a master plan and whatever happens is just part of the plan—were developed by Zeno's successor, Cleänthes of Assos. Because life's events cannot be changed, it is best just to accept them. Acceptance is aided by a detached or indifferent attitude—by being stoic.

Stoicism gained such diverse adherents as the philosopher Seneca, the slave (and later, noted teacher) Epictetus, and the Roman emperor **Marcus Aurelius** (121–180 C.E.). Marcus Aurelius was one of the best of the Roman emperors, and his *Meditations* reveal his innermost thoughts and are a delight to read. Being stoic was particularly adaptive under the Roman Empire, which emphasized fidelity to law and order. As the Roman Empire began to crumble, however, people sought other answers concerning how to cope with life. As we will see, many found the answer in the new religion of Christianity.

Epicureanism

Epicureanism, the philosophy of **Epicurus** (ca. 341–270 B.C.E.), can be traced back to the atomism of Democritus. Like Democritus, Epicurus rejected the idea of an afterlife or of supernatural influences. In fact, Epicurus's disciple **Lucretius** (ca. 99–55 B.C.E.) proudly called Epicurus the "destroyer of religion."

Today, the term *epicure* describes a person who is especially fond of luxury and sensuous pleasure, although this was not the life Epicurus endorsed. Epicurus refined **hedonism**—the search for pleasure and the avoidance of pain—by looking for pleasure in serenity and freedom from fear, not from sensuality, which he recognized was often followed by pain. For example, overindulgence in alcohol usually leads to a hangover. True pleasure, the absence of pain and anxiety, is to be found in simplicity and moderation.

Although the schools of thought we have just discussed—Skepticism, Cynicism, Stoicism, and Epicureanism—had a significant impact during the Roman period, the greatest influence on modern psychology during this period came from religious writers such as St. Paul. Before the Roman Empire fell, Christianity and what we call Western thought became virtually synonymous. Much of our folk wisdom about human behavior, whether we realize it or not, comes from Pauline writings on the life and teachings of Jesus Christ.

THE RISE OF CHRISTIANITY

Although he is mentioned in the writings of such historians of antiquity as Josephus, Suetonius, and Tacitus, much of what we know of the life of Jesus comes from the Gospels according to Saints Matthew, Mark, Luke, and John. Joshua ben Joseph, or **Jesus**, which is the Greek equivalent, lived from approximately 4 B.C.E. (Matthew tells us he was born just before the death of Herod the Great, the ruler of Palestine) until his crucifixion in about 30 C.E. Actually, the biography in the Gospels accounts for only about 50 days in the life of Jesus, and much of that comes near the end of his life.

In the three centuries following the death of Jesus, the decline in the power of Rome coincided with an increased acceptance of Christianity. Exploited by their rulers and the ruling class, common people lived in poverty and misery. Under such conditions, it made sense to focus on a spiritual life that held the promise of something better in the hereafter.

At first, Christianity was confined to a minor Jewish sect—Christ being a Jew—and it was largely through St. Paul's efforts that the Christian community became established. **Paul** (originally Saul; 10–64 C.E.) was born in Tarsus, a city now in southern Turkey, then part of the Roman Empire. Paul trained as a rabbi in Jerusalem, even though there was a respected "university" in Tarsus, where he may have begun his classical education. He was probably executed by the Roman Emperor Nero.

Paul was extremely knowledgeable about Jewish theology and Greek philosophy, which he combined with Christ's teachings to provide much of the actual theology that became Christianity's foundation. Much of what Paul wrote in his letters to individuals and to numerous early Christian churches was practical advice about daily matters and does not concern us here.

Paul considered the human body evil and the spirit (or soul) divine, and, in fact, many writers have suggested that Western civilization's notion of the body as "dirty," particularly the sexual body, can be traced to Paul. The rational mind is caught between the body and the spirit, sometimes serving one and sometimes serving the other. Like Plato, Paul saw the body as the major source of our problems, and he saw faith in God rather than the use of reason as the solution to the conflict. As we will see throughout this chapter, from the time of St. Paul on, Christianity exerted a major force on Western philosophy.

Plotinus

Plotinus (ca. 205–270) was a Neoplatonist philosopher who greatly influenced early Christian thought. Probably born in Egypt of Roman parentage, he received a Greek education and studied in Alexandria under Ammonius Saccas, the founder of Neoplatonic philosophy. Beginning in Alexandria, **Neoplatonism** tried to combine Plato's views with ethical concepts from Christianity, Judaism, and Near Eastern mysticism.

Although Plato's ideas became part of early Church doctrine, Aristotle was considered the master philosopher (Stagner, 1988). One explanation for why Plato's ideas were accepted without giving him credit is that he was too closely associated with Socrates, who was considered an extreme skeptic who questioned everything. Also, because much of Aristotle's work had been lost by the time of the Roman Empire, the incompatibility of his views and Plato's was not widely recognized.

Despite his acceptance of much of Plato's philosophy, Plotinus's opinion of sensory experience was less negative than Plato's. For Plotinus, although there was much of beauty in the sensory world, it was less perfect than the spiritual world. Because the spiritual world was the early Christians' chief concern, it was a short journey for some from Neoplatonism to Christianity. Thus, through the Church, Neoplatonism became the dominant European philosophy for generations, bridging the gap between ancient and medieval thought.

Philosophical Library, New York.

St. Augustine (354–430) reading St. Paul's Epistles

St. Augustine

The most influential Christian scholar following St. Paul, **St. Augustine** of Hippo (354–430) was born in Tagaste, part of the Roman province of Numidia, which is in North Africa. According to Copleston (1950), the "African Doctor . . . came of a pagan father, Patricius, and a Christian mother, St. Monica" (p. 55). Augustine's mother introduced him to Christianity at an early age, and at 16 his father sent him to Carthage to study rhetoric and law. In Carthage, Augustine read Cicero's *Hortensius* and wrote of it that "I was inflamed by such a love of philosophy." In addition, he took a mistress, later remarking: "Give me chastity and continency, but not yet." His mistress gave him a son.

In 383, Augustine traveled to Rome and a year later went to Milan to teach rhetoric. In 387, Augustine and his son were baptized by St. Ambrose. Augustine returned to Africa and became Bishop of Hippo in 396. Augustine died in 430, as the Vandals besieged Hippo.

Like Descartes (Chapter 4) over a thousand years later, Augustine sought one certain aspect of human experience, and, like Descartes, he found it in the fact that he doubted. For Augustine, this proved the validity of inner experience, which could be studied through **introspection** (literally "to look within"). Introspection in some form has been a major method in psychology since St. Augustine's time.

We can see other similarities in the thinking of Augustine and Descartes, for example, regarding the difference between humans and animals: Both Augustine and later Descartes believed that humans have a soul and animals do not. Also like Descartes, Augustine believed the soul influences the body and vice versa, arguing that an excess of bile makes a person irritable, and external events can make a person irritable and thereby increase the production of bile (Murray, 1983).

Augustine's *Confessions* (ca. 400) is both a spiritual autobiography and an original work of philosophy considered a classic of world literature. Wills (1999) argued that the title *Confessions* is misleading, preferring *The Testimony* instead. Wills's point is that Augustine "was not particularly interested in giving us literal details of his biography" (p. xx), that much of what he wrote in *Confessions* is not to be taken literally. However, "once we . . . understand his theological language, previously unsuspected information about his life . . . can be retrieved" (p. xx), which is what Wills has done in his biography of St. Augustine.

St. Augustine also wrote about such psychological matters as free will, reason, and memory. Augustine believed our freedom to choose explains evil in the world. People choose evil, thereby denying themselves an afterlife. During life, incorrect choices lead to guilt, which, along with feelings of virtue for having chosen correctly, operates as an internal control over behavior.

Augustine considered extensively the nature of human knowledge, including scientific knowledge. Using Thales (Chapter 2) as his prototypical scientist, Augustine was not totally sympathetic to "knowledge" unconnected with religion. For Augustine, reason without faith was possible, but necessarily incomplete. Humans have an ultimate spiritual destiny, and the human condition cannot be understood unless viewed from the standpoint of the Christian faith. In fact, Augustine believed the world must be considered from this perspective, which meant that science and philosophy not in the service of theology were suspect (St. Augustine, 412–427/1931).

Augustine's influence set the tone of Christian thinking for the next millennium and may have been important in the pervasive distrust in science characteristic of the Christian Church. In fact,

> his influence did not end with the Middle Ages. Throughout the Reformation, appeals to Augustine's authority were commonplace on all sides. His theory of illumination [the idea that God's intercession—"light of eternal reason"—is necessary for us to recognize the eternal, immutable truths] lives on in Malebranche. . . . His approach to the problem of evil and to human free will is still widely held today. His force was and is still felt not just in philosophy but also in theology, popular religion, and political thought. . . . (Spade, 1994, pp. 57–58)

CHRISTIANITY, ISLAM, AND JEWISH PHILOSOPHY OF THE MEDIEVAL ERA

The **Middle Ages** are often said to have begun with the collapse of the Roman Empire around 500 and to have lasted until the Renaissance, which began about 1500. Historians have suggested that the Middle Ages arose from the fusion of three different traditions: the Roman Empire, Christianity, and the German "barbarians." In fact, the idea of a "middle age" was the creation of Renaissance thinkers such as Giovanni Andrea, who coined the phrase in the 15th century, and Georg Horn, whose *Arca Noae* (1666) established the idea of three historical "ages." These writers were eager to distinguish their "Modern World" from the recent past—the Middle Age—as well as to compare it with antiquity (the "Ancient World," or the "Age of Antiquity").

The Medieval period—part of which is sometimes called the Dark Age because of the relative lack of philosophical and scientific development during these years—gave birth to the Europe we recognize today. This was a turbulent period marked by hostilities of often epic proportions as nation states rose and fell.

Beginning in the late 11th century and lasting through most of the 13th century, the **Crusades** were a series of wars sanctioned by the pope. The various campaigns differed greatly in their aims, with motivations ranging from the desire to recover the Holy Lands, particularly Jerusalem, from the Muslims to the urge to acquire more land and expand trade. The outcomes of the campaigns also varied considerably and can be summarized as follows: The First Crusade (1096–1099) captured Jerusalem and established kingdoms on the Syrian coast. The Second Crusade (1147–1149) failed completely, as did the Third Crusade (1189–1192), which tried to recapture Jerusalem after its fall in 1187. Initially directed against Egypt, the Fourth Crusade (1202–1204) was diverted by the Venetians in order to loot and plunder Constantinople. As a result, the entire crusade movement was discredited, although not discontinued, as Crusades Five through Eight captured and lost various cities in what is today the Middle East. There was even a so-called Children's Crusade, during which thousands of youth journeyed across Europe on their way to the Holy Lands; many were sold into slavery or died of hunger and disease along the way. For our purposes, the most important aspect of the strife of the Crusades is that it exposed Western Europeans to both "lost" classical knowledge, which had been preserved and studied in the Arab world, and to a new world of previously unknown Islamic (and Judaic) scholarship.

The Early Middle Ages

We begin with the primarily Aristotelian writings of **Anicius Manlius Severinus Boethius** (ca. 480–524). Boethius's most famous work was *The Consolation of Philosophy*, written while the author was in prison awaiting execution. Boethius had been an important political figure whose goals included translating the Greek classics into Latin and reforming education. During his lifetime, the state of Roman science and philosophy was low, with virtually none of Plato or Aristotle's works available. Although Boethius's plans for educational reform were cut short, he was responsible for much of the Greek wisdom that survived into the medieval period. For the next millennium, the *Consolation* was probably the most widely read book after the Bible. Boethius is important because he connects later medieval scholarship with the classical Greek philosophies.

Alcuin (ca. 735–804) was another beacon of learning during the early Middle Ages. A monk, Alcuin was born and educated at York before being invited to the court of Charlemagne (742–814), King of the Franks. There, he became Charlemagne's principal advisor. Under Charlemagne's direction, Alcuin founded the Palatine school in the capital at Aachen (now a German city). The Palatine school may have been the conceptual model for the University of Paris.

Alcuin's impact on education during the Carolingian Empire (Charlemagne's empire) is undisputed. He may also have been involved in scientific information exchanges with Islamic philosophers, medical information exchanges with Jewish scholars, and the initial introduction of Arabic numerals into Western civilization (perhaps to facilitate computations in astrology and astronomy, as Roman numerals are tedious for advanced calculations).

John Scotus Erigena (ca. 810–877) was another key thinker of the early medieval period. Erigena was born in "Scotia" (now Ireland); *Eriugena* means "born of the peoples of Erin," and Erin is another name for Ireland (Wippel & Wolter, 1969). Like Alcuin under Charlemagne, Erigena was the master of the Palatine school under Charles the Bald. In his major writings, Erigena attempted to fuse Neoplatonism with Christian doctrines and to reconcile faith and reason. He is also considered to have anticipated aspects of both Hegelian rationalism (Chapter 6) and scholasticism (discussed later in this chapter). Supposedly, Erigena's students killed him with their writing pens, for the "sin of trying to make them think."

Although the period from the Roman Empire until the Renaissance was dominated by religious thought, not all of it was Christian. Next, we will consider Islamic and Jewish contributions.

Islamic Philosophy

At a time when most of the wisdom of the ancient Greeks was lost to Europe, the Arabs were able to make great advances in philosophy, medicine, and science by building directly on the classical works, particularly Aristotle's. In the Arab world, Islam was the predominant religion, arising from the teachings of Mohammed (Muhammad).

Mohammed

Mohammed (ca. 570–632) was born in Mecca, the Islamic holy city in Saudi Arabia. His original name was Ubu'l Kassim, and he was the son of Abdallâh. Orphaned at 6, Mohammed was raised by relatives and trained to be a merchant like his father. At 24, he was employed by a rich widow, whom he eventually married and by whom he had six children.

At about the age of 40, Mohammed began to receive revelations from Allah (God) that he recorded in the Qur'an, or Koran. Allah's commandments to Mohammed included the destruction of idols at the shrine in Mecca and the transfer of wealth from the rich to the poor. Although Mohammed had some support in his home city, it was not nearly enough, and he and his small band of supporters were forced to migrate (the Hegira) to a nearby town, Yathrib, which is now known as Medina, "the city of the prophet."

By 629, Mohammed took control of Mecca, and by 630, he and his followers had gained control over all of Arabia. In 632, Mohammed made his last pilgrimage to Mecca. He died shortly after his return to Medina, and his tomb in the mosque there is revered throughout the Islamic world. Within 100 years of Mohammed's death, the Muslim sphere of influence was larger than the Roman Empire at its height.

Although there were many well-known Arabic philosophers, we will focus on Avicenna and Averroës. A Persian, Avicenna represents the "Eastern" tradition, whereas Averroës is more "Western," having lived and worked in Cordova, Spain. Both men were Muslims and wrote in Arabic, but neither was an Arab, illustrating the Islamic world's scope. Both were important for Western philosophy because they preserved and transmitted the teachings of Aristotle and other Greek thinkers and because they wrote interpretations of the Greeks that led to controversy (and ultimately to change) in medieval philosophy.

National Library of Medicine, Washington, D.C.

Avicenna (980–1037)

Avicenna

Born in what is now Turkistan, a region of Central Asia, **Avicenna** (Arabic name, ibn Sina; 980–1037) was precocious, memorizing the Koran by age 10 and becoming a practicing physician at 16. Centering on Aristotle, Avicenna's philosophy also contained original elements and Neoplatonic influences. Much of Avicenna's work involved making Aristotle compatible with the prevailing theology. For example, based in part on Aristotle's ideas, Avicenna sought to explain human intellectual activity by distinguishing between the possible intellect and the Agent Intellect. God creates a single effect called an *Intelligence,* which, in turn, creates subordinate Intelligences. The final Intelligence—the Agent Intellect—creates the minds (souls) of humans.

However, humans initially have only a possible intellect, in the sense of a potential. Although the human intellect has the potential to know, it is not created with knowledge, which reflects Aristotle's nurture position on the nature-nurture issue. The intellect's acquisition of knowledge requires the bodily senses, the power to retain images in memory, and the ability to discover the essence of things through abstraction.

Because he was a physician, Avicenna's writings were quite influential. According to Alexander and Selesnick (1966). *The Canon* was an attempt to combine Aristotle's philosophy with Hippocrates' and Galen's observations and speculation. Thus, like Galen's work, *The Canon* contains both outstanding medical writing and much that has been discredited subsequently.

Of particular interest for psychology, Avicenna wrote about treating mental disorders. For example, when a patient claimed to be a cow, Avicenna told the patient he had sent for a butcher to slaughter him. After first having the patient tied hand and foot, Avicenna declared the man too lean to be butchered and decided he would have to be fattened for slaughter. The patient began eating vigorously, soon lost his delusion, and was cured.

Although he tended to accept most Aristotelian ideas, Avicenna rejected Aristotle's theory concerning the transmission of odors, which held that odor did not require the movement of any substance. Plato, by contrast, apparently thought odors were transmitted by odorous vapors or fumes. In rejecting the Aristotelian approach, Avicenna was on the wrong side of medieval history, as Aristotle's thinking prevailed in the Middle Ages, only to be overturned by Plato's approach in the modern era (Kemp, 1996, 1997).

Once discovered, Avicenna's work interested Christian scholars. For example, in the 13th century, Siger de Brabant at the University of Paris came under suspicion for teaching Arabic "psychology." Christian theologian St. Bonaventura thought that Arabic psychology, as taught by Siger de Brabant, threatened personal individuality, although Avicenna had not intended this interpretation. The problem for Christian writers was that the Agent Intellect, and not God, enlightened the human intellect. Although Siger de Brabant was eventually acquitted by the Inquisitor, he was apparently murdered by his secretary while being held for surveillance.

Philosophical Library, New York.

Averroës (1126–1198)

Averroës

Like Avicenna, **Averroës** (1126–1198) was a prodigious scholar. In his home town of Cordova, Spain, he studied philosophy, mathematics, theology, law, and medicine. Although he served first as a judge and later as a physician, he spent the bulk of his time writing commentaries, becoming known in the Middle Ages as "The Commentator" (Stumpf, 1989).

Averroës thought Aristotle was the greatest of all philosophers and considered him a model of human perfection. Although he generally started from the same Aristotelian source, Averroës did not always agree with Avicenna. For example, Averroës did not believe that humans have possible intellects separate from the Agent Intellect. He also denied the doctrine of immortality and had little respect for theology, which explains why many pre-Renaissance Christian theologians found his teachings heretical. Averroës's primary importance came from his belief that philosophy and theology could be independent, another foreshadowing of scholasticism, the major intellectual movement of the late Middle Ages.

In summary, we can say that Averroës left a dual legacy: On the one hand, he was primarily responsible for bringing Aristotle's work to the attention of scholars in the Western world. On the other hand, he added to and modified Aristotle's teachings, "with the result that 'Averroism'—seen by Christians as bad for being both Islamic and based on the pagan Aristotle—was severely attacked by the Church in the early thirteenth century" (Murray, 1983, p. 51).

In addition to Averroës and Avicenna, various other Arabic thinkers were eventually discovered by the West. Some, such as **al-Kindi** (ca. 800–870), were similar to what we would now label physiological psychologists. Sometimes called the "philosopher of the Arabs," al-Kindi was a tutor at the court in Baghdad who wrote extensively, although many of his works have been lost. Like many other Arabs, al-Kindi was particularly interested in vision, which he believed "would prove to be the key to the discovery of nature's most fundamental secrets" (Magner, 1992, p. 146).

Jewish Philosophy

Jews were treated inconsistently in Europe. Sometimes their knowledge (often medical) brought fame and fortune, whereas at other times they were persecuted as pagans. Like Arabic thought, Jewish philosophy was more advanced than Christian scholarship throughout the Middle Ages.

Maimonides

Of the Jewish thinkers from this era, **Maimonides,** or Moses Ben Maimon (1135–1204), was the most influential. He was born at nearly the same time and in the same place (Cordova, Spain) as Averroës. Maimonides emigrated from Spain to Morocco and then to Egypt, where he practiced medicine. In his medical writings, he anticipated modern ideas of bodily afflictions caused by both psychological factors and allergies.

In *The Guide of the Perplexed*, his most important work, Maimonides intended to harmonize Judaism with philosophical thought. Although he consulted an enormous array of literature, his *Guide* was dominated by Aristotelian thought. Despite this influence, he managed to include some rather distinctive ideas. For example, Maimonides believed there was no basic conflict between faith and reason, between theology and science; for him, the two were different forms of knowledge and thus not at odds with each other. In addition, he considered the doctrine of the creation of the world a matter of religious belief, as something for which philosophical proof was necessarily indecisive. Thomas Aquinas (discussed later), who was greatly influenced by Maimonides, adopted the same view of creation and concluded that the religious approach should take precedence, because it does not conflict with rational thought. Maimonides also anticipated three of the proofs Aquinas developed for the existence of God. It is through Aquinas that many of Maimonides's insights were transmitted to later *Thomists* (followers of *Thom*as Aquinas).

CHRISTIAN PHILOSOPHY IN THE LATER MIDDLE AGES

Gradually Western scholars (often monks) became familiar with Greek and Roman thought, often through reading Jewish and Islamic writers (Knowles, 1988). In turn, a renewed interest in philosophy and science emerged to become the foundation for the Renaissance. In the Augustinian tradition, some of these scholars were skeptical of science or philosophy that did not serve theology. This skepticism has often been misinterpreted as an anti-intellectualism, and many of the most gifted thinkers of the Middle Ages—such as St. Peter Damian (1007–1072)—have been erroneously portrayed as mindlessly against philosophy and science. In fact, at issue was the place of, and not the use of, this newly acquired wisdom. Several generations were required to clarify the relation between reason and faith, and St. Anselm was one of the important early contributors.

St. Anselm

Born into a noble family, **St. Anselm** (1033–1109) became a Benedictine monk against his father's wishes. He eventually became the Archbishop of Canterbury, a position he held until his death. Anselm believed strongly that dialectics and other rational aspects of formal philosophy were important to theologians. His belief in the value of reason for understanding God directly conflicts with the Christian tradition emphasizing acceptance on faith.

Anselm is important for **scholasticism**, a system of thought and a method that dominated the Middle Ages. The central aim of the *schoolmen*, as the adherents of scholasticism were called, was to join faith to

Philosophical Library, New York.

Anselm (1033–1109), the Archbishop of Canterbury

reason, to use logical deduction to account for traditional theological teachings. The system was primarily a fusion of the philosophies of Plato and particularly Aristotle with Christian theology.

St. Anselm is perhaps best known for his **ontological argument** for God's existence, which begins with the statement that God is "that than which nothing greater can be thought." If God did not exist, then something greater than He could be thought; thus, God must exist. Anselm's ontological argument was used by Descartes and others.

Peter Abélard

Peter Abélard (1079–1142) was perhaps the most brilliant of the Western philosophers between Aristotle and Descartes, but not the most saintly. The eldest son of a noble Brittany family, Abélard sought intellectual debate, forsaking a military career for the love of "dialectical disputation" (Wippel & Wolter, 1969). He studied first under a nominalist, then under a realist. **Nominalists** believed that universals exist in name only, that words like *goodness* and *beauty* are merely labels allowing the categorization of objects with similar traits. By contrast, **realists** believed there are universals like *goodness* and *beauty* that are independent of specific examples and have a real existence not unlike Plato's Forms.

Abélard's school endorsed "moderate realism" in the nominalist-realist debate. His position was that there is a reality behind the universals, whose ground is the way similar things strike our minds. Although this is an objective ground for the universals, it is not something real in the sense of a thing, as the "exaggerated" realists contended. Abélard also rejected the strict nominalist view that the universal is just a subjective ideal for which there is no objective basis.

Abélard's moderate position on universals conquered the extremes of realism and nominalism, and the next major treatment of universals came with William of Ockham nearly 2 centuries later. Although he was sometimes critical of Aristotle, Abélard was also one of the persons most responsible for the high esteem in which the Greek master was held by the Church for centuries. Additionally, some of Abélard's Aristotelian reflections are directly important for psychology. For example, Abélard held that the act of thinking and the content of thought are distinct from each other. The importance of this point for understanding the nature of human thought was still being considered as recently as the late 19th century by William James (Chapter 10).

Abélard became the most celebrated teacher in Paris, and his particular dialectical techniques are said to have revolutionized the teaching of theology. However, Abélard's reputation for publicly debating and often ridiculing other well-known teachers and church figures proved costly. First, there was his love affair with Héloïse, the 17-year-old niece of the canon Fulbert, with whom Abélard was lodging. Although the couple was secretly married after Héloïse gave birth to Abélard's son, her relatives broke into

Peter Abélard (1079–1142) installs Héloïse as the abbess of the Convent of the Paraclete

Abélard's bedroom one night and castrated him. When two of Abélard's assailants were captured, they lost their genitals *and* their eyes, which shows that some sympathized with Abélard. Still, Abélard's career in the Church was tarnished. "He felt a certain unpoetic justice in his fall: he had been maimed in the flesh that had sinned, and had been betrayed by the man whom he had betrayed" (Durant, 1950, p. 938).

Near the end of his life, St. Bernard accused him of heresy, arranged for his condemnation, and thwarted his attempts at a papal appeal. Banned from teaching, Abélard was condemned to live in bitter silence at the Cluny monastery. At his death, Héloïse had Abélard's remains interred at the monastic school he founded and then gave to her and a sisterhood. When Héloïse died in 1164, she was placed in the same tomb. Their remains were taken to Paris in 1800, and in 1817 the two historic lovers were buried in the same sepulchre.

St. Thomas Aquinas

Born in the castle of Roccasecca (in Italy), **St. Thomas Aquinas** (1225–1274) was educated by the Benedictines of Monte-Cassino and at the University of Naples. When he entered the Dominican order in 1243, his brothers kidnapped him and imprisoned him in the family castle for 2 years. Escaping to Cologne, Aquinas became a pupil of **St. Albertus Magnus** (ca. 1193–1280), the era's major Aristotelian scholar.

At Naples, Aquinas read Aristotle and probably Avicenna, Averroës, and Maimonides, becoming such an Aristotelian devotee that it is not clear if it makes sense to talk about a separate Thomistic psychology. Aquinas's main contribution was to reintroduce the West to Aristotle's psychology through Christianity's filter.

Aquinas also championed the view that reason and faith are compatible, arguing that all true paths should lead to the same result. Therefore, faith and reason could be considered independently, and a philosophy separate from theology was suggested for the first time in almost 1,000 years in the Christian world. Aquinas himself continued to blend faith and reason in good scholastic fashion.

Aquinas wrote about such psychological matters as the relation between the soul (mind) and the body, in some ways anticipating Descartes' mind-body interactionism; "faculties" (rational, sensitive, nutritive, etc.); and the *agens intellectus* (Avicenna's Agent Intellect), or the part of us concerned with understanding, judgment, and reason. Like the good Aristotelian he was, Aquinas accepted the mind as a *tabula rasa* and concluded that the mind's knowledge accumulates through sensory input. In Chapter 5, we will see this echoed in the empiricist's creed: There is nothing in the mind that was not first in the senses. In summarizing the influence of Aquinas, Murray (1983) wrote, ". . . his role was less that of an explorer and more that of a

St. Thomas Aquinas (1225–1274)

synthesizer, one who pulled together all existing knowledge into a Christian edifice structured on Aristotelian logic" (p. 53).

Aquinas was a unifying force for theology and philosophy in the 13th century. The reactions to his work by two Franciscan friars associated with Oxford, England, John Duns Scotus and William of Ockham, led to the dissolution of Aquinas's synthesis.

John Duns Scotus

Called the Subtle Doctor in his day, **John Duns Scotus** (ca. 1265–1308) was born in Scotland at the Duns estate, near the present town of Duns. He was educated and taught at Oxford, Paris, possibly Cambridge, and Cologne, where he died. So successful was his teaching at Oxford that "the numerous foreign students could not be accommodated in the town, and . . . he taught at Paris with even greater success" (Runes, 1959, p. 133). After his untimely death, however, his enemies burned his books and disparaged his name to the point that his followers, originally known as Dunsmen, became Duncemen and eventually Dunces, a term first applied to any opponent of education and later to any stupid person. Why was Duns Scotus the subject of such derision after his death?

In short, Duns Scotus made the mistake of criticizing both Aristotle and Aquinas. Whereas Aquinas argued for the supremacy of reason, Duns Scotus argued for the supremacy of the will in God, a view that became known as *voluntarism.* For Duns Scotus, if God's will were subordinate to reason, then it would appear that God is limited, which cannot be. Thus, God's will must be absolutely free. One consequence of this argument is that God's moral rules are good because God willed them to be good, not because His wisdom recognized them as such. It follows, then, that one cannot comprehend morality from a rational standpoint, only from the perspective of acceptance on faith. In the latter part of the 19th century, Wilhelm Wundt, considered the creator of a separate science of psychology, used the term *voluntarism* in a similar sense to describe his system (Chapter 8).

William of Ockham

William of Ockham (ca. 1285–1349) was born in the town of Ockham, near present-day London. Ockham studied at Oxford as an "inceptor," or beginner, and never attained a higher position because of his controversial views. Pope John XXII summoned Ockham to answer charges of heresy, and he was excommunicated. Fleeing to Bavaria, Ockham died in Munich, probably from the Black Death.

Ockham is known for having rejected more central assumptions of the Church and of philosophy than anyone else of his time. In the struggle to find universals, Ockham held that universality can be attributed only to terms, not to things, which is the nominalist position.

In psychology, Ockham is best known for **Ockham's razor**. Ockham believed that arguments should have their extraneous assumptions shaved away, a point sometimes called the *Law of Parsimony*, which holds that of two equally plausible explanations, the simplest—usually the one with the fewest assumptions—is preferred. Ockham chose the nominalist position because it did not require him to assume that universals have an independent reality. That is, nominalism required fewer assumptions than realism. Ockham's razor also tended to negate Aquinas's synthesis of philosophy and theology, and it should not surprise us that Ockham's political activities contributed to the modern political notion of the separation of church and state.

According to Kemp (1998), Ockham also applied his razor in challenging the widely held belief in the Middle Ages about mental representations of perceived objects. Such representations were often described in terms of the "wax tablet metaphor," which probably first appeared in Plato's writings. Specifically, medieval writers such as Augustine and Avicenna believed that the perception of external reality led to a more or less enduring impression of that reality on the mind of the perceiver, similar to the seal of a ring when impressed into a block of wax. This impression on a physical surface was called either a *form* or *species* in medieval writings. Ockham argued that it was unnecessary to assume people form an internal representation of external objects or scenes, and thus rejected the prevailing belief in mental representations of the wax-tablet variety. In the late 19th century, C. Lloyd Morgan (Chapter 12) applied a principle like Ockham's razor to explanations of animal behavior.

MEDIEVAL SCIENCE BEFORE THE RENAISSANCE

Although pre-Renaissance scientific achievement was limited, a few names deserve mention. For example, British philosopher **Adelard of Bath** traveled to Syria in the 12th century in search of science. As Southern (1986) noted, "He did not seek to fill gaps in a body of knowledge already almost complete: he sought to revive old and forgotten sciences" (p. 87). To this end, Adelard translated Euclid's *Elements*, as well as Arabic works in astronomy and mathematics. He can be considered the first of a series of English scholars known, not as mere disciples of Aristotle, but as popularizers of other Greek, Arabic, or even local and contemporary masters.

Robert Grosseteste (ca. 1175–1253) was the first chancellor of Oxford University, and a catalog of his works includes treatises on sound, motion, and color—all topics of interest to psychology (Southern, 1986). **Roger Bacon** (ca. 1214–1292) studied at Oxford and Paris and gained a reputation for knowledge that led some to call him *Doctor mirabilis* (wonderful doctor). His interest in nature's secrets aroused the suspicions of his fellow Franciscans, and Bacon was denounced as a sorcerer and imprisoned for 10 years with neither books nor scientific instruments. Bacon's name is associated with inventions like the magnifying glass and gunpowder and with speculations on lighter-than-air flying machines, telescopes, and microscopes. Despite his confinement and the Franciscans' censorship, Bacon managed to publish important works on mathematics, philosophy, and logic.

Raymond (or Ramon) **Lull** (ca. 1232–1315), a Spanish theologian and mystic known as *Doctor Illuminatus* (enlightened doctor) because of his great learning, was perhaps the only person of this period to have been more ambitious than Roger Bacon. Born in Majorca, Lull led a dissolute life as a soldier and troubadour poet in his youth. In 1266, he became an ascetic and began a crusade to convert the Muslims to Christianity. Toward this end, he presented a system for acquiring knowledge and solving all possible problems by manipulating fundamental ideas using Aristotelian logic. Like Leibniz several hundred years later, Lull assumed a kind of logical atomism—in other words, that elementary concepts exist from which all knowledge is constructed. He aimed to build a device "programmed" with the atomic concepts and logical rules of reasoning and then to let the machine generate all knowledge. Some modern commentators (MacLennan, 1995; Moody, 1967) have suggested that Lull was the father of computer programming. Lull also designed and constructed machines to present pairs of God's attributes to infidels who "were

Philosophical Library, New York.

Raymond Lull (ca. 1232–1315)
(Doctor Illuminatus)

supposed to be brought to the True Faith by the revelations" (Glymour, Ford, & Hayes, 1995, p. 7).

An adversary of Averroës, Lull lectured against Averroës's principles at the University of Paris. Afterward, he returned to Algeria to continue his mission to convert Muslims. Tradition holds that Lull, twice banished from Algeria, was stoned to death on his third mission.

UNIVERSITIES IN THE MIDDLE AGES

In Chapter 2, we noted Plato's Academy and Aristotle's Lyceum, both closed by the Emperor Justinian in 529. And in the first century C.E., St. Paul probably studied at a university in Tarsus, then part of the Roman Empire. These early universities, however, were not universities as we think of them today; indeed, we should probably look to the later Middle Ages for the first true universities.

The first European universities were Italy's University of Bologna (founded in 1119) and the University of Paris (whose founding date is controversial). Oxford University also began in the 12th century, its development hastened by the exclusion of Englishmen from the University of Paris in 1167. Other early universities were started at Cambridge (1284) in England, at Toulouse (1229) and Orléans (1309) in France, and at Lisbon (1290) in Portugal.

Many of the early universities originally followed a curriculum suggested by Boethius and established by Alcuin at the Palatine. This curriculum consisted of an arts course—actually, the study of the seven liberal arts (arithmetic, geometry, astronomy, music, grammar, rhetoric, and dialectic) plus natural philosophy or science, ethics, and metaphysics—and advanced courses in law, medicine, and theology. After becoming truly important in the 13th century, universities became a powerful intellectual force during the Renaissance, both for preserving and spreading knowledge and for producing it.

CONCLUSIONS

Historically, the more than 1,300 years from Christ's birth to the beginning of the Renaissance encompass the decline of the Roman Empire and the millennium of the Middle Ages. In science, the period takes us from the ancients' superstition and speculation to the inventions (e.g., magnifying glass, gunpowder) and speculation of Roger Bacon and Raymond Lull.

In philosophy, there is the decline and resurgence of the philosophies of the ancient Greeks and their synthesis with theology, which we can see in the writings of St. Paul, Plotinus, and St. Augustine. The decline of the Roman Empire ushered in a period during which interest in and knowledge of classical, secular philosophy was lost in the West. St. Anselm and other scholastics reawakened interest in the philosophers of ancient Greece, Islamic philosophers such as Avicenna and Averroës and events such as the Crusades further facilitated the West's rediscovery of Aristotle. Even St. Aquinas's efforts to reconcile Christianity and Aristotle were anticipated by Maimonides.

The Church's acceptance of Aristotelian ideas had far-reaching implications for Western philosophy and science. One implication, derived from Aristotle's system of formal logic and particularly from the syllogism, was that with the correct initial premise, all knowledge could be determined. This idea is particularly evident in the work of Lull described in this chapter and philosophers such as Descartes and Leibniz discussed in Chapter 4.

Although the acceptance of Aristotelian logic was beneficial for science, the Church's unquestioning adoption of Aristotle's theory of the universe had a more negative impact. The Inquisition frequently handicapped progress in science. In time, concern with human interests rather than with the natural world fostered the movement away from Aristotelianism that became the Renaissance. We will begin with this movement in Chapter 4.

SUMMARY

Philosophical and Theological Thought During the Roman Period

In addition to continuing work at the Lyceum, several schools flourished in the Greco-Roman period, including Skepticism, founded by Pyrrho; Cynicism, founded by Antisthenes and Diogenes; Epicureanism, founded by Epicurus and mostly known through the efforts of Lucretius; and Stoicism, founded by Zeno of Citium and popularized by Marcus Aurelius. After the crucifixion of Jesus, St. Paul was largely responsible for the establishment of the Christian community through which he continues to exert an influence on science and on thoughts about human behavior. Plotinus established Neoplatonism, a school combining Plato, Christian and Judaic religious concepts, and Near Eastern mysticism.

St. Augustine was not totally sympathetic to knowledge unconnected with religion, and this negative attitude became part of the Christian Church's distrust of science. For Augustine, consciousness could be studied by looking within (introspection). We can see a number of similarities in the thinking of St. Augustine and Descartes.

Christianity, Islam, and Jewish Philosophy of the Medieval Era

For our purposes, the main effect of the series of pope-sanctioned wars called the Crusades was that they exposed Western Europeans to both classical knowledge and a world of Islamic and Judaic scholarship.

An Aristotelian scholar, Boethius aimed to reform education. His reform plans were cut short by his execution.

Under Charlemagne's direction, Alcuin founded the Palatine school. Erigena—who attempted to fuse Neoplatonism with Christian doctrines—directed the Palatine school under Charles the Bald.

Avicenna and Averroës were Islamic philosophers whose work centered on Aristotle. Avicenna's philosophy also contained novel elements, including the distinction between the possible intellect and the Agent Intellect. Averroës disagreed with Avicenna's distinction and had little respect for theology. Another Arabic philosopher, al-Kindi, was particularly interested in vision. Seeking to harmonize Judaism with Aristotle, Maimonides was the era's most influential Jewish thinker.

Christian Philosophy in the Later Middle Ages

St. Anselm is often considered the founder of scholasticism, a system of thought in the Middle Ages that used logical deduction to account for theological teachings. Anselm is also remembered for the ontological argument for God's existence. Peter Abélard took a moderate position in the nominalist-realist debate, which was the argument between people who believed that universals exist in reality (realists) and those who thought that universals exist in name only (nominalists). St. Thomas Aquinas sought the synthesis of Aristotle with Christianity and argued that faith and reason are not incompatible. He also concluded that the mind's knowledge accumulates through sensory input.

The philosophy of John Duns Scotus was a reaction against both Augustine and Aquinas, and his argument for the will's supremacy in God was called voluntarism. William of Ockham is best known for Ockham's razor, which argues for taking the explanation of a phenomenon requiring the fewest assumptions.

Medieval Science Before the Renaissance

Highlights of science in this period include Roger Bacon's inventions of such things as the magnifying glass and gunpowder and his speculations about flying machines, telescopes, and microscopes. Raymond Lull conceived of a machine that would generate all knowledge.

Universities in the Middle Ages

Universities at Bologna, Paris, and Oxford were founded in the 12th century. Other important early universities were at Cambridge in England, Toulouse and Orléans in France, and Lisbon in Portugal. Many of the early universities followed the curriculum that Alcuin established at the Palatine.

CONNECTIONS QUESTIONS

1. In what sense is medieval thought an attempt to connect and reconcile faith and reason?
2. What connections can you make between the philosophers of the ancient world (e.g., Plato, Aristotle) and medieval thought?
3. How would you connect the first universities to the one you attend?
4. What connections can you see between Christian, Jewish, and Islamic scholars in the Middle Ages?
5. How do the Middle Ages connect the ancient world with our "modern" world?

KEY NAMES AND TERMS

Peter Abélard (p. 56)
Adelard of Bath (p. 59)
Alcuin (p. 52)
al-Kindi (p. 55)
Antisthenes (p. 48)
Marcus Aurelius (p. 48)
Averroës (p. 54)
Avicenna (p. 53)
Roger Bacon (p. 59)
Anicius Manlius Severinus Boethius (p. 52)
Crusades (p. 51)
Cynicism (p. 48)
Diogenes (p. 48)
Epicureanism (p. 49)
Epicurus (p. 49)
John Scotus Erigena (p. 52)
Robert Grosseteste (p. 59)
hedonism (p. 49)
introspection (p. 50)
Jesus (p. 49)
Lucretius (p. 49)
Raymond Lull (p. 59)
Maimonides (p. 55)
Middle Ages (p. 51)
Mohammed (p. 52)
Neoplatonism (p. 49)
nominalist (p. 56)
Ockham's razor (p. 58)
ontological argument (p. 56)
Paul (p. 49)
Plotinus (p. 49)
Pyrrho (p. 48)
realist (p. 56)
scholasticism (p. 55)
John Duns Scotus (p. 58)
Skepticism (p. 48)
St. Anselm (p. 55)
St. Thomas Aquinas (p. 57)
St. Augustine (p. 50)
St. Albertus Magnus (p. 57)
Stoicism (p. 48)
St. Paul (p. 49)
Theophrastus (p. 48)
William of Ockham (p. 58)
Zeno of Citium (p. 48)

SUGGESTED READINGS

Augustine (1963). *Confessions.* New York: New American Library. (Original work published 400) Available in many different editions, St. Augustine's *Confessions* is an autobiographical account of the man's fascinating life and times.

Kemp, S. (1996). *Cognitive psychology in the Middle Ages.* Westport, CT: Greenwood Press. Less restrictive than the title suggests, this book was written by Simon Kemp, who is the foremost authority on psychology in the Middle Ages. This slender volume covers most of the connections between medieval thought and scientific psychology.

Saunders, J. L. (Ed.) (1966). *Greek and Roman philosophy after Aristotle.* New York: The Free Press. This is a nice anthology containing short selections by the Cynics, Stoics, and so on. You will be surprised to see that much of the wisdom of these schools remains with us today.

Wills, G. (1999). *St. Augustine.* New York: Lipper/Viking. This highly readable, brief biography of Augustine explores the very human individual behind the saint.

Wippel, J. F., & Wolter, A. B. (1969). *Medieval philosophy.* New York: Free Press. This is a standard textbook on medieval philosophy. The book contains excerpts from the writings of most of the philosophers and theologians covered in the first half of this chapter.

The Renaissance and Early Modern Philosophers

CHAPTER 4

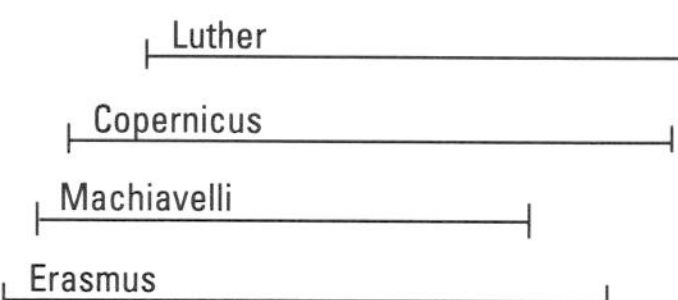

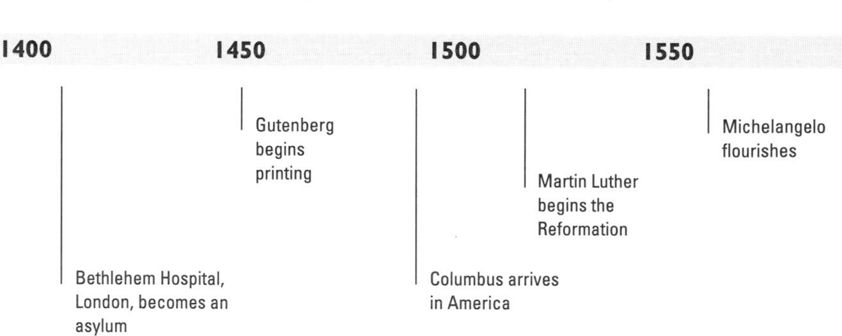

OUTLINE

The Renaissance

- Renaissance Humanism
- Renaissance Science

The Early Modern Philosophers

- René Descartes
- Julien Offray de La Mettrie
- Baruch Spinoza
- Gottfried Wilhelm von Leibniz

Conclusions

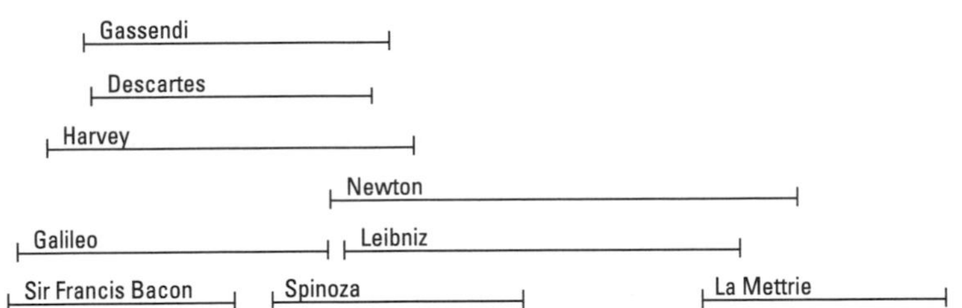

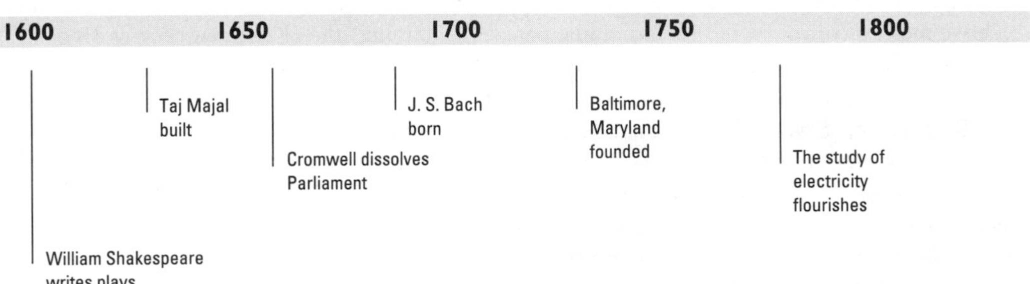

THE RENAISSANCE

Although there were other renaissances (e.g., the 8th- and 9th-century Carolingian Empire, the 12th-century foundation of the first true universities), when we speak of the Renaissance (literally "rebirth"), we mean the revival of classical art, architecture, literature, and learning that originated in Italy and spread throughout Europe from the 14th through the 16th centuries. Contemporaneous with this revival and contributing to it were such things as the discovery of America, the religious Reformation, and astronomical discoveries. Developed earlier, the universities became a powerful intellectual force during the Renaissance, both for preserving and spreading knowledge and for producing it.

Perhaps more than any other development, the rise of printing fueled the intellectual flowering of the Renaissance. Scholars who had previously spent their time copying manuscripts were now free to create new ones. Similarly, the slow progression of knowledge that resulted from a limited number of hand-copied books was over. Soon, anyone with a desire to read Aristotle could readily locate a copy of something the Greek master had written. Note that the inventor of printing—usually considered to be either **Johannes Gutenberg** (1400–1468) or **Laurens Janszoon Coster** (ca. 1370–1440)—actually reinvented printing, as the art of printing from a single block was known in China by the 6th century C.E., and moveable type was in use by the 11th century.

Renaissance Humanism

Major changes in the social order produced the *Zeitgeist* that fostered and encouraged the Renaissance scientific achievements. For example, **humanism,** by which we mean a concern with the individual person as a part of the world of nature, as part of the here and now, is considered a primary factor contributing to the Renaissance. Several themes characterized this new focus on human interests, including curiosity about human abilities and accomplishments; a desire to make religion more individualistic and less ceremonial; historical interest, particularly in the leading Greek and Roman poets, philosophers, and politicians; and opposition to the blind support of Aristotle as the authority on secular science. We see evidence of Renaissance humanism reflected in the era's art, with an emphasis on nontheological human figures; in the period's science, with its focus on humanity's problems; and in the music of the day, which is becoming more secular than sacred.

Early people whose work embodied one or more of humanism's themes include Petrarch, Juan Luis Vives, and Giovanni Pico. **Petrarch** (1304–1374), or Francesco Petrarca, was an Italian poet and scholar whose writings arguably signal the beginning of the Renaissance. Petrarch wrote in opposition to Averroës's reliance on Aristotle, a philosopher Petrarch found suspect. Petrarch's opposition to scholasticism and to religious authority aided challenges to Aristotelian scientific dogma.

Spaniard **Juan Luis Vives** (1492–1540) is important for his views on education and for his three-volume work on psychology and the scientific method, *De anima et Vita* (1538). Vives applied a biomedical approach to fields such as education and psychology. For example, in psychology, Vives relied on Hippocratic humoral explanations for mental phenomena rather than using scholastic arguments about the nature and essence of the soul and its faculties. For emphasizing the physiological aspects of the life processes, Vives deserves consideration as "The Father of Modern Psychology" (Clements, 1967).

Italian philosopher and humanist **Giovanni Pico della Mirandola** (1463–1494) emphasized individualism. Although Pico's range of influence was broad, his work on human dignity was his most enduring contribution. Pico's philosophical works included an attempted reconciliation of Platonic and Aristotelian doctrines and a document on free will.

Another major social change leading to and sustaining the Renaissance involved **Martin Luther** (1483–1546), the German founder of the Protestant Reformation. Although most of Luther's actions were motivated by disgust over conditions within the Catholic Church, humanism's themes are apparent in his works. For example, Luther argued that Aristotle's assimilation was a major cause of the Church's decline, and he also sought a more personalized and less ritualistic religion. Clearly the Reformation changed Western society, in part by challenging the pope's authority as well as Aristotelian dogma. Both challenges fueled the *Zeitgeist* that produced psychology's most immediate philosophic antecedents.

Desiderius Erasmus (1466–1536) was another early Renaissance social philosopher. Ordained a priest in 1492, Erasmus was already turning from scholasticism toward humanism. Among other things, he tried to dispel the myth of better life through alchemy (chemistry of the Middle Ages whose principal aims were to discover the potion for eternal youth and to change base metals into gold). He sided with neither Catholics nor Protestants in their conflicts and managed to become an enemy of both sides. Without approving of Luther's theology, Erasmus defended him for the sake of freedom of conscience and helped save Luther's life at the beginning of the latter's challenge of the Catholic Church.

Niccolò Machiavelli (1469–1527) achieved the "honor" of having his name become a word, *Machiavellian,* which refers to the use of deceit and duplicity to achieve goals. It also refers to a psychological construct (e.g., Christie & Geis, 1960; Wilson, Near, & Miller, 1996). Machiavelli's reputation rests largely on *The Prince,* published 5 years after his death. His torture by the Medici (a banking family that ruled Florence and funded much of the artistic Renaissance) gave Machiavelli firsthand experience of human cruelty. *The Prince* is basically a handbook for rulers; its main theme is that "the ends justify the means."

Machiavelli wrote other works—for example, *Discourses*—that are less cynical than *The Prince.* In *Discourses,* Machiavelli presented an analysis of republican government in which he praised democracy. Machiavelli's admirers lauded his realism about human nature, whereas his more numerous and vocal critics saw him as dangerously amoral. Interestingly, Machiavelli's disciples were sometimes Machiavellian in their public pronouncements about him. For example, King Frederick II of Prussia (1712–1786) wrote a book opposing Machiavelli at the same time that he practiced Machiavelli's ideas. Machiavelli's views contributed to an image of human nature that has remained part of psychology in some form ever since.

Renaissance Science

At the beginning of the Renaissance, ancient and conventional wisdom began to be questioned, and much was found to be wrong. This era marks the birth of many ideas central to modern science, and we will survey briefly some key contributions that provided an important foundation for all subsequent sciences, including psychology. One change in our way of thinking about ourselves, the universe, and our place in the universe came with the publication by **Nicolas Copernicus** (1473–1543), modern astronomy's Polish founder, of a heliocentric (sun-centered) view of the universe. Before Copernicus, Ptolemy's (ca. 90–168) geocentric (earth-centered) view prevailed, because it agreed with the theological idea of humans' central place in creation. Thus, Copernicus's *On the Revolutions of the Celestial Spheres* received a hostile reception in 1543. Tradition holds that Copernicus delayed publication and first saw the book on his deathbed.

Italian philosopher **Giordano Bruno** (1548–1600) extended the Copernican system to include an infinity of suns like ours, with each circled by planets possibly inhabited by sentient beings. Bruno traveled widely in Europe, lecturing about a pantheistic philosophy in which God animated all creation. Arrested by the Inquisition, Bruno was burned at the stake in Rome after an 8-year trial. Although the Renaissance favored change, there was resistance to ideas too different from long-held beliefs.

Another scientist who ran afoul of the Inquisition was Italian astronomer, mathematician, and natural scientist **Galileo Galilei** (1564–1642). Having perfected the refracting telescope invented in Holland, Galileo used it to make observations that convinced him Copernicus's theory was correct. In 1632, Galileo published a work supporting the Copernican system and was called before the Inquisition. He was tried, convicted, and forced to abjure (recant) his teachings. Under house arrest near Florence, Galileo continued his studies while gradually losing his sight and hearing. Galileo's final discovery was the moon's monthly and annual oscillations, made just before he became totally blind.

In addition, Galileo did work directly relevant to psychology. For example, he believed that subjective

Nimatallah/Art Resource, NY.

Galileo Galilei (1564–1642)

properties such as color, smell, and taste do not have the same reality as physical properties of objects such as shape and motion and that the subjective qualities reside in the observer rather than in the object observed. Galileo called the qualities inherent in matter (e.g., shape, quantity, and motion) **primary qualities,** whereas **secondary qualities** (e.g., color, smell, and taste) arise when the primary qualities contact an observer's sensory apparatus. Galileo's distinction was accepted by many later theorists, including Descartes and Newton, some of the British empiricists, and the first psychologists.

Tycho Brahe (1564–1601), a Dane, and the German astronomer **Johann Kepler** (1571–1630), who went to Prague as Brahe's assistant and succeeded him in 1601, made further astronomical discoveries. At 14, Brahe witnessed a partial solar eclipse and became obsessed with astronomy. The greatest of the pretelescope astronomers, Brahe was brilliant but hot-tempered; at 19, he lost most of his nose in a duel and wore a fake silver nose thereafter. Kepler made discoveries in optics, physics, and geometry and proposed laws of planetary motion that formed the basis for Isaac Newton's later discoveries.

Galileo's contemporary, Englishman **Sir Francis Bacon** (1561–1626) made no signal discoveries, but his promotion of experimentation for understanding nature gives him an important place in the history of science. Abandoning the deductive logic of his predecessors, Bacon stressed the need to be continually on guard for evidence that might refute a previously held belief. For Bacon, truth came not from authority but from experience. Almost singlehandedly, he created the inductive scientific method. As we will see, B. F. Skinner (Chapter 13) discovered Bacon early and became an ardent proponent of the inductive approach to the science of psychology. Unfortunately, Bacon's experiment on the effects of cold on meat preservation may have contributed to his death.

Bacon is perhaps best known for his discussion of **Idols,** or preconceived notions that contaminate reasoning. For example, based on Plato's cave allegory, Bacon's Idols of the Cave refer to limitations placed on the untrained mind by experience (e.g., by books read, by intellectual authorities accepted). Idols of the Tribe are biases that an individual brings to any experience. Idols of the Market Place are biases resulting from carelessly created language, which can weaken knowledge. Finally, Idols of the Theater are the "grand systematic dogmas" we endorse—such as the principles of science—out of custom, gullibility, and laziness.

Another Englishman, **William Harvey** (1578–1657), experimentally studied blood's circulation and proved conclusively that the heart was simply a pump. Thus, Harvey demonstrated that the scientific method could be used to study a biological system as precisely as physical systems are studied by physicists, paving the way for experimental biology.

Sir Isaac Newton (1642–1727) was an English physicist and mathematician and one of the greatest scientists of all time. His most important discoveries include the law of gravitation, the idea that white light is a mixture of all colors, and calculus. Newton constructed the first reflecting telescope, and his 1687 publication, *Philosophiae*

Philosophical Library, New York.

Isaac Newton (1642–1727) studying a beam of light

naturalis principia mathematica (*Mathematical Principles of Natural Philosophy*), inspired John Locke (Chapter 5) to write a work of great importance for psychology (*An Essay Concerning Human Understanding*). In 1995, a special issue of *The Journal of Mind and Behavior* (Vol. 16, No. 1) explored Newton's monumental impact on science, including his influence on psychology.

Newton also was involved in several controversies, including one with Gottfried Leibniz (discussed later) over the discovery of calculus. Some of Newton's irascible behavior may have resulted from mercury poisoning (Broad, 1981); before 1693, he had been involved in alchemical experiments often pursued until late at night, and sometimes he fell asleep next to bubbling retorts. During his "madness," Newton wrote many strange letters to his friends, accusing Locke in one letter of trying to embroil him with women. Further evidence for Newton's mercury poisoning comes from samples of his hair, which have been found to contain elevated mercury concentrations.

THE EARLY MODERN PHILOSOPHERS

As you can see from our survey of social and scientific changes, Western Europe was awash with new ideas and creative personalities. Added to this ferment was danger from the Church, which sought to protect its influence over the spiritual realm and all other aspects of the lives of its faithful. However, no matter how repressive the Church tried to be, there were always people willing to risk everything to defend their perception of the truth. We have noted some who ran afoul of the Inquisition: Copernicus, who delayed publishing his heretical views of the universe; Bruno, who was burned at the stake for supporting Copernicus and going beyond him; Galileo, who was forced to recant his views; and Luther, who was nearly killed before he could begin the Reformation. Against this backdrop of scientific and social change appeared a man who altered philosophy forever, the individual whom historians of philosophy and psychology most frequently cite as marking the onset of the modern period—René Descartes.

René Descartes

His mother died within a few days of his birth, the victim of the tuberculosis she bequeathed to her son. **René Descartes** (1596–1650) himself was so weak that the attending physician had no hope for his survival. In fact, if a nurse had not nourished and warmed him with her body, Descartes would soon have followed his mother.

Descartes was born near Tours, France, in a town now called La Haye-Descartes. His father was a wealthy lawyer who willed his son an annual income that gave Descartes the freedom to live without having to work. In 1604, Descartes entered the Jesuit College of La Flèche, where his teachers recognized his delicate health and mental precocity and allowed him to stay in bed beyond normal rising hours. Descartes spent the time devouring books and developed a lasting admiration for the Jesuits.

At 17, Descartes went to Paris and from Paris to the University of Poitiers, where he graduated with degrees in civil and canon law. Next, he enlisted in

Archives of the History of American Psychology–The University of Akron.

René Descartes (1596–1650)

the army of Prince Maurice of Nassau. Descartes continued his studies, particularly in mathematics, through various military campaigns. On November 10, 1619, he had three visions or dreams in which a divine spirit revealed a new philosophy. This experience led Descartes to formulate analytic geometry and to pursue the application of mathematical methodology to philosophy. He conceived of a system of true knowledge modeled on mathematics and supported by rationalism, the use of reason to develop knowledge.

Returning to France in 1622, Descartes took care of financial matters, and then set off again on his travels. In 1628, he settled in Holland, where he spent most of the remainder of his life. Although he moved more than 20 times during the next 2 decades, probably to conceal himself, Descartes was usually near either a university or a library.

In 1649, 23-year-old Queen Christina of Sweden invited Descartes to her court to teach her philosophy. Christina was friends with many academics, including Giles Ménage (1613–1692), known for his *History of Women Philosophers* and for his commentary on Diogenes Läertius's *Lives of the Greek Philosophers.* Despite his misgivings, Descartes sailed from Amsterdam to Stockholm on the warship the queen had sent. Descartes found that Christina wanted her instruction at 5 A.M., 3 days a week, in the depths of the Scandinavian winter. He had spent a lifetime as a late riser, and under the queen's regimen he developed a cold, then pneumonia. Soon thereafter, on February 11, Descartes died, having received the last rites of the Catholic Church. His final words are said to have been, "*ça mon âme, il faut partir*" ("so my soul, a time for parting").

The fate of Descartes' body is both grisly and ironic. Buried in Stockholm, his corpse was exhumed 16 years later for return to France. In an apparent show of disrespect, Sweden's French ambassador cut off Descartes' right forefinger as a souvenir. When the coffin for his remains was found to be too short, his head was removed to be shipped back to France separately. Descartes' body was subsequently buried in Paris with a fitting ceremony, but his head was stolen by an army captain and took 150 years to reach Paris, where it has apparently been in the *Academie des Sciences* ever since (Boakes, 1984). Ironically, Descartes, whose head is perhaps permanently separated from his body, was the author of the mind-body problem.

Descartes' Method

In *Discours de la Méthode* (*Discourse on Method,* 1637), Descartes began by rejecting all dogma and authority, particularly that of Aristotle. He would doubt everything, refusing to accept anything as true unless he was certain of it. But how could he be sure of the existence of anything? Could he be certain of the reality of objects because he sensed them? Unlike Aristotle and Francis Bacon, Descartes put little weight on sensory experience and experimentation for gathering knowledge. Like Plato, Descartes relied mainly on reasoning.

Descartes sought first an idea so clear and distinct to his mind that its truth was unquestionable. He could then progress from this starting point through the orderly use of intuition and deduction. By intuition, Descartes meant a vision so clear it could not be doubted; by deduction, he meant making all possible inferences from facts of which he was sure.

Descartes' search for something absolutely certain led him to perhaps philosophy's most famous statement: *Je pense, donc je suis* in French; *Cogito ergo sum* in Latin. "I think, therefore I am." Like many ideas we will encounter, this one was not original with its author; St. Augustine had used a similar argument, and Descartes had probably read his work.

Cogito ergo sum asserts the existence of the thinker, but this thinking thing is not the body, and Descartes still had doubts about the existence of his body and of anything else beyond his thinking. How could he proceed from the certainty of his existence as a thinking thing? First, Descartes asked himself what made the statement *Cogito ergo sum* true and certain, concluding that he could safely assume the truth of things he conceived clearly and distinctly. Descartes now had to prove the existence of God and that God is not a deceiver. If God were a deceiver, then even clear and distinct ideas could be false.

Descartes decided that the ideas that passed through his mind originated either from within, from his mind's invention, or from without. Because he was a finite, imperfect being, his conception of God as a perfect Being could only have come from an outside source—that is, from God. Further, because experience teaches us that deception comes from some defect, God, a perfect being, cannot be a deceiver.

Next, Descartes argued for the reality of the physical world and of his bodily self. We all experience moving about, making contact with objects, and receiving sense impressions, and these experiences imply a body, which Descartes called "an extended substance." Our belief that these experiences come from contact with something real must come from God, because God would be deceitful if the experiences were produced by objects without physical reality. As God is not deceitful, we must accept the reality of corporeal objects.

At this point, Descartes believed he had proved the existence of God, the self, and things. Descartes argued for a duality of substances in nature; there were thinking things (the mind; *l'âme,* the French word Descartes used, means either mind or soul) and extended things (the body). This distinction leads to Descartes' **mind-body dualism.**

Mind-Body Dualism

For Descartes, the mind is unextended, free, and without substance. Its ideas have no length, width, weight, or any other material quality. The mind is distinct from the body and surely survives the body's death (here the word *soul* is more appropriate). Only humans have mind.

By contrast, the body is extended, is limited, has substance, and operates by mechanical principles. For Descartes, the mechanical statues in the gardens of the palace at St. Germain were analogous to the operations of human and animal bodies. The automatons operated by hydraulic pressure so that when a visitor stepped on a pressure plate in a walkway, water coursing through pipes caused the statues to move. Adopting Galen's ideas (Chapter 2), Descartes envisioned human and animal bodies animated by fluids in tubes (nerves) connected to empty bladders (muscles).

As further evidence for a mind-body dualism, Descartes adopted Galileo's distinction for dealing with the separation of physics and psychology, which was the distinction between primary and secondary qualities. Secondary qualities (sensations) exist only in mind, whereas bodies exist only in shape (extension) and motion.

Descartes' denial of mind to animals was important, as acceptance of a human-animal continuity could lead to the idea that hedonism is the only rational basis for human conduct. If animals can attain Heaven with little virtuous behavior, there is no reason for humans to be good in order to achieve the same end. Also, if animals are just automata—an idea that antedated Descartes (Bandrés & Llavona, 1992)—then animal dissections are like dismantling a piece of machinery. Descartes, who performed many dissections and vivisections, argued that although vivisection might appear to be painful to an animal, this is not the case because the animal has no mind and is not conscious in the way we are.

Descartes realized that many of the human body's activities (e.g., respiration, digestion, and circulation) are as mechanical and automatic as the activities of animals or machines. But the mind can influence the body and vice versa. Although the body is primarily responsible for physical sensations and perceptions, the mind knows about them, and its thinking can be affected by this knowledge. As an example of body affecting mind, recall how your thoughts focused on bodily sensations the last time you were ill. And the mind's influence on the body is evident in the act of will that enables you to keep your arm still when receiving an injection. Thus, Descartes believed in mind-body interaction, but the interaction was problematic for his strict dualism. Interaction requires contact, which necessitates an extended mind. Of course, Descartes recognized that the mind was unextended and lacking in substance; hence, the mind-body "problem."

Descartes chose the brain's **pineal gland** as the point of interaction between the mind (soul) and the body. In *Passions of the Soul,* Descartes wrote:

> Although the soul is joined to the whole body, there is . . . a certain part in which it exercises its functions more particularly than in all the others; and . . . it seems as though . . . the part of the body in which the soul exercises its functions immediately is in nowise the heart, nor the whole of the brain, but merely the most inward of all its parts . . . a certain very small gland [the pineal or *conarium*] which is situated in the middle of its substance and so suspended above the duct whereby the animal spirits in its anterior cavities have communication with those in the posterior, that the slightest movements which take place in it may alter very greatly the course of these spirits; and reciprocally that the smallest changes which occur in the course of the spirits may do much to change the movements of this gland. (Descartes; Wilson, 1969, p. 362)

Why the pineal gland? Our sense organs are paired, but our thoughts of an object are unitary, which means that somewhere in the mind the dual sensory messages are combined into one thought. Descartes chose the pineal gland because of its singular nature and its central location in the brain. In addition, he thought the gland had such mobility that little force would be required for its movement. Descartes rejected another of the brain's singular structures, the better-known pituitary gland, for a number of reasons. First and foremost, the pituitary was not considered a part of the brain in the 17th century, and Descartes believed the "seat of the soul" had to be in the brain. Also, there was little disagreement about the function of the pituitary in Descartes' day: It was considered a waste-disposal area (Finger, 2000).

The pineal is not, as psychological historian Robert I. Watson (1971) wrote, "a vestigial organ of no functional significance whatsoever" (p. 239). Indeed, the pineal hormone melatonin provides a signal of the changing length of days in mammals, with less melatonin released on longer days. In seasonal breeders, the melatonin signal determines reproductive readiness through its effects on the gonads (Goldman, 1999). Although it has been suggested that changes in melatonin production are related to the onset of puberty in humans, "it is not yet clear that these correlations are functionally related" (Luboshitzky & Lavie, 1999, p. 355).

Innate and Derived Ideas

For Descartes, ideas that come to mind with certainty and inevitability are **innate ideas** and do not come from experience. Self, Descartes' first principle, is an example of an idea he considered innate, along with God, space, time, motion, and certain geometrical axioms.

Descartes did not mean that the innate ideas are completely formed and always present in every person. Instead, they represent a potentiality of thought that can be brought forth by experience. Unfortunately, errors in sensory experiences may prevent innate ideas from appearing. Descartes' concept of innate ideas is reminiscent of Plato's (Chapter 2) Forms—innate universals known only through reasoning—and Plato also believed that sensory information (the body) could hinder the development of knowledge already in the mind.

In addition, Descartes recognized **derived ideas** that come from environmental experiences and are stored in memory through an alteration of the nervous system. He proposed that a new experience forces animal spirits through a particular set of the brain's pores, which leaves an imprint analogous to the holes left in linen cloth through which a set of needles has passed. When the experience is repeated, the partially open pores more easily allow the animal spirits to pass. A "memory trace" has been created through a change in the brain. Substitute *synapses* and *nerve impulses* for *pores* and *animal spirits,* and Descartes' idea about memory formation sounds remarkably modern.

Descartes' Influence

Descartes made further contributions related to psychology, and overall his influence has been enormous. For example, he was the first to describe the retinal image, which is a tiny, inverted model of the scene external to the eye projected by the lens onto the retina. Descartes scraped off the back outer covering of a bull's eye, inserted the eye into an opening bored in a shutter, and described the image he saw on the back of the eyeball (Boring, 1950).

Descartes was also the first to describe reflex action. For him, sensory stimulation causes tiny fibers in the hollow nerves to open specific brain pores, which release animal spirits into the appropriate muscles for movement. A particular movement follows predictably from specific sensory stimulation, a conception anticipating the idea of reflex action. Descartes differentiated two kinds of reflexive responses: The first accounted for automatic and immediate responses, the kind we call reflexes; the second was a learned reaction in which the response becomes associated with the stimulus in some unspecified way.

Descartes' conception of the reflex as a stimulus-response process occurring through the nervous system became crucial for psychology. The reflex action concept and the view of animals as automatons influenced the development of both animal and physiological psychology.

The late Renaissance fostered a new world view, illustrated through Galileo's conception of the universe as a giant machine in which lawful explanations are possible. Descartes' work was compatible with the new world image, because he saw the human body as a machine capable of affecting and being affected by the mind. Descartes perceived human behavior as lawful and ultimately explainable, and, most importantly, he localized the mind-body interaction in the brain.

Because Descartes believed ideas exist in the mind before sensory experience, he is a nativist according to Chapter 1's discussion of the nature-nurture dichotomy. Descartes' nativism is important for stimulating opposition in the British empiricists (e.g., Locke and Berkeley, Chapter 5) and others.

On the mind-body issue, Descartes is classified as an interactive dualist, because he believed both mind and body exist independently but interact. However, a review of correspondence in 1643 between Descartes and Princess Elizabeth, later queen of Bohemia, suggests that Descartes' status as a dualist depends on the Cartesian work being considered (Tibbetts, 1973). *Passions of the Soul* provides the classical statement of psychophysical dualism, whereas Descartes' letters indicate a muddled picture. The problem with Descartes' dualism, which Elizabeth addressed in her letters, lay in explaining how the immaterial mind interacts with the material body. Another French philosopher, Pierre Gassendi (discussed later), was also aware of this difficulty.

Descartes used a rationalistic, deductive approach to generate knowledge, which others replaced with an experimental, inductive approach. One of Descartes' most important successors, John Locke, admired Descartes' mechanistic approach to the physical world but rejected rationalism in order to establish the empiricist tradition in psychology.

Descartes' lasting and widespread influence occurred in part because, like Galileo, he wrote in his native tongue rather than in the Latin used in most scholarly books of the period. Unlike Galileo, Descartes avoided trouble with the Inquisition primarily by putting many of his thoughts into manuscripts published after his death. Still, at one point he was attacked by clergy in Holland, who managed to get his books banned from universities because they were considered subversive. The irony is that Descartes was sincere in his religious faith. Hearing of Galileo's condemnation by the Inquisition in 1633, Descartes set aside writings in which he had planned to combine all his scientific work and wrote to a friend, "on no account will I publish anything . . . that might displease the Church" (Fischer, 1887, p. 231).

As we indicated in Chapter 1's discussion of mind-body positions, Descartes' belief in an immaterial mind (soul) and a material body is widely accepted by the so-called person in the street. In fact, this separation of body and mind is what Damasio (1994) called "Descartes' error," in his book of the same title. According to Damasio, Descartes' initial statement—I think, therefore I am—

> illustrates precisely the opposite of what I believe to be true about the origins of mind and about the relation between mind and body. It suggests that thinking, and awareness of thinking, are the real substrates of being. . . .
>
> Yet long before the dawn of humanity, beings were beings. At some point in evolution, an elementary consciousness began. With that elementary consciousness came a simple mind; with greater complexity of mind came the possibility of thinking. . . . For us then, in the beginning it was being, and only later it was thinking. . . . We are, and then we think, and we think only inasmuch as we are, since thinking is indeed caused by the structures and operations of being. (p. 248)

As you can see, Descartes' thought and arguments still have the power to stimulate discussion nearly $3^1/_2$ centuries after his death.

Pierre Gassendi

One of Descartes' earliest and most ardent critics was French philosopher and scientist **Pierre Gassendi** (1592–1655). Born in Provence, Gassendi was so bright that at age 16 he was appointed a teacher of rhetoric, and at 25 he became professor of philosophy at the University of Aix. In 1645, Gassendi became professor of mathematics at the Collège Royal in Paris, where his friends included Kepler and Galileo.

Without his moderate conduct and religious faithfulness, Gassendi's beliefs in Copernican astronomy, the atomism of Democritus, and Epicurean moral philosophy might have caused him problems with the Inquisition. However, he combined his materialism with a belief in the God of the Bible, asserting that atoms were created and given an initial push by God, but from then on everything continued by its own laws. Gassendi considered the greatest pleasures to be mental, and he strongly advocated the experimental approach to science.

Like Descartes, Gassendi opposed the teachings of Aristotle. Yet despite this similarity between the two, he also criticized Descartes. He began his criticism by asserting that the unextended, immaterial mind could neither influence nor be influenced by the extended, material body. Only the physical can influence the physical. Further, Gassendi noted that anything that moves exists, which made him wonder why Descartes had to struggle to conclude that his thinking proved his existence. Continuing, Gassendi challenged Descartes' notion that animals are purely mechanical and only humans have mind. If movement proves existence, then why do humans need mind to move when, according to Descartes, animals do not? For Gassendi, the mind's operations come from the workings of the brain, and a separate, immaterial mind is not needed to explain our behavior.

We can see Gassendi's influence in the writings of another French philosopher, Julien de La Mettrie, who took the step beyond Descartes to argue, like Gassendi, against the idea of an immaterial mind that only humans possess. Unlike Gassendi, however, La Mettrie did not display the sort of moderate conduct and religious faithfulness that would have prevented him from running afoul of the Church.

Julien Offray de La Mettrie

Julien Offray de La Mettrie (1709–1751) was born on Christmas Day in St. Malo, a seaport in Brittany, France. Rather than becoming a priest, as his father wanted, in 1725 La Mettrie became a doctor. In 1733 he went to Leyden to study under the famous Dutch physiologist Hermann Boerhaave (1668–1738). A year later La Mettrie published a translation of Boerhaave's *Aphrodisiacus,* adding to it his own work on venereal diseases. After publishing a treatise on vertigo, La Mettrie was criticized for his presumption in publishing his own thoughts so early in his career.

In 1742 La Mettrie went to Paris, where he met the Duke of Gramont. La Mettrie accompanied the Duke to war as the physician to his guards. At a siege, La Mettrie had an attack of fever, about which La Mettrie's eulogizer, Frederick the Great of Prussia, wrote:

> For a philosopher an illness is a school of physiology; [La Mettrie] believed that he could clearly see that thought is but a consequence of the organization of the machine, and that the disturbance of the springs has considerable influence on that part of us which the metaphysicians call soul. (La Mettrie, 1748/1912, p. 6)

In 1745 La Mettrie published *The Natural History of the Soul*, which expressed his materialistic philosophy. In it La Mettrie formulated his belief in the similarity of animals and humans. For him there was as much evidence for the capacity of feeling in animals as there was in people.

Spurred by the outcry over *The Natural History of the Soul*, La Mettrie fled France for Holland's more liberal climate. With the publication of *Man a Machine*, Calvinists, Catholics, and Lutherans forgot their dividing issues and united in their outrage. La Mettrie fled to Prussia, where Frederick the Great gave him a pension and membership in the Berlin Academy of Sciences.

La Mettrie's first theme in *Man a Machine* was his view of the direct relation between physical factors and mental states. For La Mettrie, Descartes' dualism came from a lack of evidence from clinical medicine. From his fever La Mettrie had observed that bodily changes can have profound effects on the mind, and he concluded, "the diverse states of the [mind] are always correlative with those of the body" (La Mettrie, 1748/1912, p. 97).

The book's second major theme is the continuity of intelligence in the animal kingdom, which argues against a discontinuity between humans and their closest relatives, the great apes. Animals have varying capacities to learn, and La Mettrie (1748/1912, p. 100) asked: "[W]ould it be absolutely impossible to teach the ape a language?" La Mettrie thought it would be possible and sketched a plan for an ape's education that he believed would produce "a perfect man, a little gentleman, with as much matter or muscle as we have, for thinking and profiting by his education" (p. 103).

Is it possible to teach language to an ape? The first modern attempts to teach chimpanzees to talk were failures (e.g., Hayes, 1951), and later efforts avoided the lack of chimp vocal ability by requiring the animals to use nonverbal expression. For example, Gardner and Gardner (1969) trained a chimp to use over 130 different signs from American Sign Language. However, many believe that language-taught apes have not become La Mettrie's "perfect men" (e.g., Terrace, 1979). After 5 years of attempts to teach a chimp sign language, Terrace concluded that the ape could imitate his trainers but was unable to acquire grammar rules and could not spontaneously generate sentences.

National Library of Medicine, Washington, D.C.

Julien Offray de La Mettrie (1709–1751)

Research by Sue Savage-Rumbaugh and her colleagues (e.g., Savage-Rumbaugh, Murphy, Sevcik, Brakke, Williams, & Rumbaugh, 1993) is better controlled than earlier work, and the experimenters claim their pigmy chimp has used keyboard symbols to solve problems creatively and to describe future actions, which he then performed. Earlier critics of ape language, Herbert Terrace and MIT linguist Noam Chomsky (Chapter 18), are not disarmed by the new research, however. In fact, Chomsky "ridicules the notion that any species would have a capacity highly advantageous to survival but not use it until a researcher taught them to" (Gibbons, 1991, p. 1562). We still have no definitive answer to La Mettrie's question, but it appears unlikely that an ape can learn human language (Thorne, 1997).

Man a Machine's third theme concerns morality. La Mettrie wrote, "Some say that there is in man a natural law, a knowledge of good and evil, which has never been imprinted on the heart of animals" (La Mettrie, 1748/1912, p. 114). Disagreeing, La Mettrie first argued from examples that animals possess natural law. Conversely, if we deny animals the knowledge of good and evil, then we must also deny it in people, for humans are "not moulded from a costlier clay; nature has used but one dough, and has merely varied the leaven" (p. 117).

"Nature has created us all solely to be happy," La Mettrie (1748/1912, p. 121) wrote. Many believe that La Mettrie's death—supposedly from indigestion after overindulging in a meal of pheasant and truffles—illustrates the proper reward for unbridled hedonism. In public, Frederick the Great claimed La Mettrie died from a fever that first deprived him of his intelligence. "It seems that the disease, knowing with whom it had to deal, was clever enough to attack his brain first, so that it would more surely confound him" (p. 9). In private, Frederick admitted the truth of popular legend. La Mettrie died on November 11, 1751, not quite 42 years old.

La Mettrie's Influence

According to Boakes (1984), La Mettrie's writings and the circumstances of his death combined to give him "a monstrous reputation" (p. 92), which meant that his works were never cited, even by the late 18th-century writers he influenced. His ideas on the importance of an individual's environment undoubtedly influenced the author of the *Declaration of Independence* in 1776. Thomas Jefferson's appeal to self-evident truths harkens back to Descartes, but the ideas that all people are created equal and that one of our inalienable rights is the pursuit of happiness bear La Mettrie's imprint.

La Mettrie's discussion of animal continuity in *Man a Machine* anticipated many claims of the English evolutionists a century later. In addition, La Mettrie's conviction that training could convert an ape into a perfect little person and that human behavior can be understood mechanically dovetails nicely with American behaviorism. With his rejection of Descartes' mind-body problem by focusing on the body, La Mettrie's ideas were important for the journey from spiritualism toward materialism and physiological interpretations of mind.

Despite contemporary critics like Gassendi, Descartes' philosophy continued to influence the thinkers of the Renaissance and beyond. Another challenge to Cartesian dualism came from Baruch Spinoza, a man who adopted some of Descartes' methods, using them to deduce a mind-body solution even less acceptable to the Church than Descartes'.

Baruch Spinoza

Baruch (or Benedictus; Baruch is Hebrew for "blessed," which in Latin is Benedictus) **Spinoza** (1632–1677) was born in Amsterdam, where his Jewish family had moved from Spain to escape religious persecution. Spinoza's mother died when he was 6, bequeathing him the same consumption (tuberculosis) from which she suffered. (Recall Descartes had a similar inheritance.) To support himself, Spinoza ground and polished lenses for microscopes, telescopes, and eyeglasses.

At 23, Spinoza was excommunicated from the synagogue and ostracized from the local Jewish community for revealing doubts about his religious teachings. "[N]o one was to speak or write to him, or do him any service, or read his writings, or come within the space of four cubits' [approximately 20 in. or 50 cm] distance from him" (Durant & Durant, 1963, pp. 622–623).

Before his ostracism, Spinoza had been a brilliant student. In fact, his teachers "were exasperated at the defection of their most promising pupil, and endeavoured to retain him in their communion by the offer of a yearly pension of 1,000 florins" (Elwes, 1883/1951, p. xii). Spinoza rejected the offer. As testimony to his brilliance, Elwes detailed the languages Spinoza had mastered as follows: He had

> gained a knowledge of French, Italian, and German; Spanish, Portuguese, and Hebrew were almost his native tongues, but curiously enough . . . he wrote Dutch with difficulty. Latin was not included in the Jewish curriculum . . . , but Spinoza, feeling probably that it was the key to much of the world's best knowledge, set himself to learn it . . . (p. xi)

Like Descartes, Spinoza valued privacy. In 1660, he moved to the village of Rijnsburg, where he wrote several minor works and Book I of his posthumously published *Ethic Demonstrated in Geometrical Order* or, more simply, the *Ethics.* Next, Spinoza moved to a town near The Hague, the capital of the Netherlands, where he continued grinding lenses and working on the *Ethics.* In 1670, Spinoza moved to The Hague, living his last 6 years in a single room on the top floor of a private home. In 1673, he was offered a philosophy professorship at the University of Heidelberg, where he was to have the freedom to philosophize, as long as he did not say anything to disturb established religion, but he graciously declined.

The great mathematician/philosopher Leibniz visited Spinoza in 1676 (the two had begun a correspondence in 1671 [Nadler, 1999]), but Spinoza was in an advanced state of consumption, probably aggravated by the glass dust he had breathed for years. He died in February 1677, and through the efforts of friends and admirers, the *Ethics* and several other of his works were published toward the end of the year.

Baruch Spinoza (1632–1677)

Spinoza's Philosophy

Like Descartes, Spinoza thought he could achieve knowledge of reality using the method of geometry. That is, he would begin by developing clear and distinct principles from which he would deduce all knowledge (recall Raymond Lull). Again, the approach was rationalistic and deduction-based rather than empirical and inductive as in Francis Bacon's case.

In contrast to Descartes' relatively simple system, Spinoza's contained some 250 axioms and theorems. Like Descartes, Spinoza believed that clear and distinct ideas were true. However, instead of starting with the idea of self, Spinoza began with God, because, for him, God must precede everything else.

Spinoza's approach to God is **pantheism,** the belief that God is everything. He equated God with Nature, as shown in his Latin phrase *Deus sive Natura* (God or Nature). Spinoza concluded that the ultimate nature of reality is a single substance (God or Nature) with an infinity of attributes. We can know of only two attributes of substance: thought (mind) and extension (body). For Descartes, this meant that there were two substances, mind and body, which interacted, but the problem was that the unextended mind should not be able to affect the extended body. This was no problem for Spinoza, however, who saw the mind and the body as two different ways of expressing the activity of a single substance. There is no separation of the mind and the body, because they are just different aspects of the same thing—God. God is both infinite thought and infinite extension. Mind and body do not interact because they are one with God, which is everything. Spinoza's mind-body solution is called **double aspectism.** An illustrative analogy is that mind and body are like two sides of a coin.

In Spinoza's universe, everything is determined. Our feeling of having freedom of will is an illusion caused by our ignorance of prior causes, which determine all our actions, mental and physical. There is a unity of Nature, and the human species is part of it.

According to Spinoza, there are three levels of knowledge, and by refining our understanding of things, we can ascend from imagination, to reason, and finally to intuition. At the imagination level, ideas come from sensations and are concrete and specific, although they are inadequate and do not give us true knowledge. At the reason level, we have scientific knowledge. At this level, we can deal with abstract ideas rather than being confined to particular ideas from our sensations. Here, knowledge is adequate and true. Finally, at the intuition level, we become increasingly aware of Nature and of our place in it. Our knowledge at the first level is seen from a new perspective. Where we first saw bodies disconnectedly, we now see them as part of Nature's grand scheme.

Although our behavior is determined, Spinoza believed that morality comes with improving our knowledge by moving from the imagination level to the intuition level. Only through knowledge can we achieve happiness, for it is only through knowledge that we gain freedom from our passions. Our passions enslave us when they are attached to temporary things and when we do not understand them. Greater understanding brings better control. The kind of knowledge that frees us from our passions necessarily leads to the knowledge and intellectual love of God, which is not the love of God as a divine person but more like the pleasure from understanding a mathematical formula. Spinoza conceded that his way to morality was difficult.

Spinoza's Influence

Like the Stoics, Spinoza believed in a strict determinism, both of psychological and physiological events. His **psychic determinism**—behavior is determined by mental causes—came 300 years before Sigmund Freud's (Chapter 15), and Spinoza is often considered a forerunner of psychoanalysis, because Freud certainly knew of Spinoza's works.

Spinoza's work was at first condemned as atheistic and subversive because he equated God and nature, and between "1650 and 1680 there were some fifty edicts, by church authorities, against the reading or circulation of the philosopher's works" (Durant & Durant, 1963, p. 631). However, Spinoza's reputation improved, and he is now considered, along with Descartes and Leibniz, one of the 17th century's great rationalist thinkers. In fact, Bernard (1972) argued that because of his influence on relatively modern people (e.g., Freud, Fechner, Wundt), "modern [scientific] psychology owes a far greater historical debt to Spinoza than to Descartes" (p. 215). Many of the same individuals were similarly influenced by one of Spinoza's acquaintances—Gottfried Wilhelm von Leibniz.

Gottfried Wilhelm von Leibniz

The son of a University of Leipzig professor, **Gottfried Wilhelm von Leibniz** (1646–1716) was born in Leipzig, Germany. The precocious Leibniz read Latin at 8 and Greek at 12, and by then he had read most of the classics in Latin. At 15 he entered the University of Leipzig, and at 20 he applied for the doctorate in law. Instead of waiting a year because of his youth, he went to a smaller university at Altdorf, Switzerland, where he earned his degree in 6 months. Leibniz's dissertation so impressed university authorities that he was offered a professorship, which he declined.

After a year in Nuremberg, Leibniz moved to western Germany, where he became legal advisor to the Elector of Mainz (a German prince authorized to vote to elect the Pope). At Mainz, Leibniz revised and systematically organized laws, worked to unify the Christian religions, and absorbed the philosophy, mathematics, and science of the day.

In 1672, Leibniz went to Paris, where he met **Nicolas Malebranche** (1638–1715), a French philosopher who adopted Descartes' dualism but explained mind-body interaction as the intervention of God. Malebranche's position is called **occasionalism,** because our need to act becomes the *occasion* for divine intervention. Leibniz also met Christiaan Huygens (1629–1693), a noted Dutch physicist who led him into higher mathematics, and Leibniz began work leading to his discovery of the infinitesimal (integral) calculus.

On a trip to England in 1673, Leibniz showed Royal Society members a mathematical calculating machine, which so impressed them that they made him one of the first non-British members. By 1676, Leibniz had discovered both the differential calculus and the infinitesimal calculus. Leibniz published his two discoveries in 1684 and 1686, unaware that Isaac Newton had made the same observations earlier. Because Newton did not publish his work until

1692, a quarrel over priority erupted. Although Newton was the earlier inventor, Leibniz's notation system proved superior, and we use it today.

Following the death of the Elector of Mainz, Leibniz accepted a position as court councilor to the House of Hanover (a political entity in northern Germany). On his way back to Germany, Leibniz stopped in Amsterdam, meeting both Spinoza and Anton van Leeuwenhoek (1632–1723), the modern microscope's inventor. The microorganisms Leibniz saw in van Leeuwenhoek's microscope undoubtedly influenced his conception of a creation composed of living, organic units.

In 1685, Leibniz was assigned to write a history of the House of Hanover. Fortunately, Leibniz's historian duties did not occupy all of his time, and he continued his voluminous correspondence with people all over the Continent. In his lifetime, Leibniz made original contributions in mathematics, optics, mechanics, statistics, logic, and probability theory; he wrote on history, law, and political theory, and his philosophy was the foundation of 18th-century rationalism.

Despite his accomplishments, Leibniz's enthusiasms were so many that he rarely finished anything, and it was left to future generations to organize his notes, correspondence, and unpublished manuscripts. Considered almost a clown because of his jet-black wig and his taste in clothes, Leibniz was ridiculed during his lifetime. His overly optimistic philosophy (e.g., this is the best of all possible worlds) made him the model for the asinine philosopher Pangloss in Voltaire's satirical short story *Candide.*

In 1714, Leibniz's patron became England's George I. Because of his priority squabble with Newton, Leibniz was ordered to stay in Hanover and finish the family history. When Leibniz died 2 years later, no one of importance attended his funeral, and his death was unmarked by the society he founded (the Society of the Sciences at Berlin, which became the Prussian Academy).

Monads

Leibniz was dissatisfied with the mind-body solutions of both Descartes and Spinoza, although he felt a closer affinity to the latter. In fact, according to

National Library of Medicine, Washington, D.C.

Gottfried Wilhelm von Leibniz (1646–1716)

philosopher/mathematician Bertrand Russell (1937), "Leibniz fell into Spinozism whenever he allowed himself to be logical; in his published works, accordingly, he took care to be illogical" (p. vii). As we have noted, the main problem with Descartes' mind-body solution is that it does not explain the immaterial mind's interaction with the material body. Spinoza's solution was to have only one substance, with both mind and body attributes. Leibniz rejected Spinoza's pantheism equating God, humans, and nature, because Leibniz wanted to keep the three separate. Instead, Leibniz adopted Spinoza's single-substance theory, but his single substance was so extraordinary he was able to use it to speak of God's transcendence, the individuality of people, and the reality of freedom and purpose.

Looking through van Leeuwenhoek's microscope, Leibniz had seen microorganisms forming a world within a world. Because everything we see can be divided into smaller parts, surely all substances are merely collections of simple substances.

Leibniz called these simple substances **monads**, a word that comes from the Greek *monas,* meaning "a unit." In Chapter 2, we noted that Democritus believed all things are composed of indivisible atoms. Atoms and monads differ in that atoms are extended and have substance, whereas monads are force or energy. Also, atoms are lifeless particles, whereas monads are alive and active, with differing degrees of perceptual ability. Monads are unextended, uncreatable, indestructible, immutable, and independent of each other. Leibniz saw the world as an infinite collection of monads.

In this collection, monads are arranged hierarchically by the clarity and distinctiveness of their consciousness. First, there is a supreme monad, God, from which all other monads are created. All-knowing, the supreme monad is revealed to varying degrees by its creations, the finite monads.

As the conscious souls of humans, rational monads are closest to God in the clarity and completeness of their consciousness. Rational monads have the capability for simple perception and also for apperception, by which Leibniz meant reasoning ability and self consciousness. The rational monads of human beings are both conscious and aware of their consciousness.

Sentient monads make up the souls of nonhuman organisms, providing their possessors with simple perceptual ability and memory, but denying them the self-consciousness and reasoning ability of rational monads. Finally, simple monads are the components of both organic and inorganic matter, reacting to the world unconsciously.

Pre-Established Harmony. Although independent, the monads act according to a pre-established harmony. For example, although it may appear that the human mind's rational monads and the body's sentient and simple monads interact, this is not true. Their apparent interaction comes from their parallel and harmonious courses, established by the supreme monad. Leibniz used the metaphor of perfectly constructed clocks started simultaneously, which all keep the same time, but do so independently. For Leibniz, the pre-established harmony of all things was another proof of God's existence. Leibniz's mind-body solution is called **psychophysical parallelism.**

The world's harmony convinced Leibniz God had created the best of all possible worlds. Leibniz recognized the world's disorder and evil but considered the world compatible with a benevolent God, reasoning that if God made his creation perfect, then it would be God. Therefore, creation must be imperfect, and evil is an absence of perfection, not something God created. Furthermore, Leibniz assumed that God constructed the best possible imperfect world.

Levels of Consciousness. Because all substance is made of monads, there are different degrees or levels of consciousness in any substance. The levels range from clear and distinct apperceptions through perceptions that never reach consciousness. Leibniz called these latter perceptions ***petite perceptions,*** and an example is the sound of Zeno's single millet seed (Chapter 2). This noise is too faint to be registered, but the sound of a half-bushel of falling millet seeds reaches consciousness and is apperceived.

Leibniz's Influence

Leibniz's degrees of consciousness, and thus unconscious ideas, have influenced later psychological thought. For example, Freud made levels of consciousness a major psychoanalytic concept. Leibniz's influence is also apparent in Ernst Weber and Gustav Fechner's just noticeable differences (Chapter 7), in Franz Brentano's act psychology (Chapter 8), and in Wilhelm Wundt's concept of apperception (Chapter 8).

Like the Pythagoreans, Leibniz imagined that all knowledge could be represented mathematically. Building on Lull and, more importantly, on English churchman and scientist John Wilkins (1614–1672), Leibniz saw the possibility of computing all knowledge from a device "programmed" with fundamental concepts. Leibniz envisioned the day when "no discussion between two philosophers will be any longer necessary. . . . It will rather be enough for them to . . . say . . . "Calculemus!" (Let us calculate!) (Leibniz, as cited in Bochenski, 1961, p. 275). Leibniz's mathematical calculator, which he called the Stepped Reckoner (Glymour et al., 1995), improved on mathematician, physicist, and psychological philosopher **Blaise Pascal's** (1623–1662) earlier machine. Although Leibniz's device could multiply and divide, it could not compute or handle extremely large numbers (MacLennan, 1995). This work establishes Leibniz's claim as a forerunner of cognitive science (Chapter 18).

One of Leibniz's most important works for psychology was *New Essays on Human Understanding,* an essay critical of John Locke's *Essay Concerning Human Understanding.* We will discuss Locke's *Essay* and Leibniz's *New Essays* in the next chapter.

CONCLUSIONS

The growing importance of the universities, the discovery of the New World, the development of printing, the religious Reformation, and scientific and astronomical discoveries combined to create the intellectual climate that fostered the Renaissance. Also important was a focus on the concerns of humans as part of the world of nature. All of these factors created the atmosphere that led to a significant divergence in philosophical thinking from the ancient Greeks. The first philosopher to attempt a complete break with the philosophies of the past was René Descartes, who is often considered the first modern philosopher.

Descartes' solution to the mind-body problem, mind-body interactionism, created a problem of its own: explaining how the immaterial mind interacts with the material body. To solve Descartes' problem, Gassendi and La Mettrie argued for a materialistic monism, whereas Leibniz developed a noninteractive dualism we call psychophysical parallelism. Spinoza attempted to solve the problem by envisioning mind and body as merely two parts of the same whole—God.

Descartes' method, rationalism, began as a philosophical tradition before Plato, was carried to new heights by Descartes, and was further refined by Spinoza and Leibniz. In the next chapter, we will contrast rationalism with British empiricism, a system that owes much to Sir Francis Bacon's promotion of experimentation for understanding nature.

SUMMARY

Renaissance Humanism

Focusing on human interests rather than on religion or the natural world, early humanists included Juan Luis Vives, Petrarch, and Pico. Distrusting Aristotle, Petrarch wrote mostly in opposition to Averroës. Petrarch's opposition to scholasticism and to religious authority helped later challenges to Aristotelian dogma.

Giovanni Pico's contribution was an attempted reconciliation of Platonic and Aristotelian doctrines. Martin Luther began the Protestant Reformation in opposition to conditions he saw in the Catholic Church. Drawn to humanism, Desiderius Erasmus reacted against scholasticism and defended Luther early in Luther's challenge to the Catholic Church.

The term *Machiavellian* comes from the name of Niccolò Machiavelli, author of *The Prince,* which is mainly a handbook for rulers who believe "the ends justify the means."

Renaissance Science

Nicolas Copernicus replaced the earth-centered idea of the universe with a sun-centered view. For defending the Copernican system, Giordano Bruno was burned at the stake by the Inquisition. Galileo made many astronomical discoveries and distinguished between primary and secondary qualities of objects. Johann Kepler, Tycho Brahe's assistant and successor, proposed laws of planetary motion fundamental to some of Isaac Newton's work.

Sir Francis Bacon promoted experimentation for understanding nature, and William Harvey used experimentation to show that the heart was a pump. Physicist and mathematician Newton conceived the law of gravitation, discovered that white light is a mixture of all colors, invented calculus, and constructed the first reflecting telescope.

The Early Modern Philosophers

Descartes began his new philosophy by searching for an idea of which he was certain, which he found summarized in *Cogito ergo sum* (I think, therefore I am). From this beginning, Descartes conceived a mind-body dualism in which the mind is unextended and lacks substance, whereas the body is extended and has substance. Descartes believed that the body operates mechanically and that animals have body but not mind. For Descartes, there were both innate and derived ideas. One of Descartes' early critics, Pierre Gassendi tried to reconcile an atomic materialism with Christian doctrine. A nonbeliever, Julien de La Mettrie took the obvious step beyond Descartes, concluding that there was no more evidence for rationality (mind, soul) in humans than in animals. Humans, he wrote, are "not moulded from a costlier clay."

Spinoza's philosophy equated God with Nature and concluded that the ultimate nature of reality is a single substance (God) with an infinity of attributes. Spinoza saw the mind and the body as two sides of the same coin; his mind-body solution is called double aspectism.

To solve the mind-body problem, Leibniz invented the monad, an unextended, uncreatable, indestructible, immutable substance. Although independent, monads appear to act in concert because of a pre-established harmony, a mind-body solution called psychophysical parallelism. Because all substance is made of monads and monads vary in consciousness, there are different levels of consciousness in any substance.

CONNECTIONS QUESTIONS

1. What connections can you make between Renaissance scientific advances in areas such as astronomy and the rise of philosophical psychology?
2. In constructing his theory of mind and body, what connections with the past did Descartes make or break?
3. What are some of the connections between the religion and philosophy of the central characters discussed in this chapter (Descartes, Spinoza, Leibniz, and so on)?
4. What was the major criticism of Descartes' solution to the mind-body problem, and how did Spinoza and Leibniz attempt to resolve it?

KEY NAMES AND TERMS

Sir Francis Bacon (p. 68)
Tycho Brahe (p. 68)
Giordano Bruno (p. 67)
Nicolas Copernicus (p. 67)
Laurens Janszoon Coster (p. 66)
derived ideas (p. 72)
René Descartes (p. 69)
double aspectism (p. 77)
Desiderius Erasmus (p. 67)
Galileo Galilei (p. 67)
Pierre Gassendi (p. 74)
Johannes Gutenberg (p. 66)
William Harvey (p. 68)
humanism (p. 66)
Idols (p. 68)
innate ideas (p. 72)
Johann Kepler (p. 68)
Julien Offray de La Mettrie (p. 74)
Gottfried Wilhelm von Leibniz (p. 78)
Martin Luther (p. 66)
Niccolò Machiavelli (p. 67)
Nicolas Malebranche (p. 78)
mind-body dualism (p. 71)
Giovanni Pico della Mirandola (p. 66)
monads (p. 80)
Sir Isaac Newton (p. 68)
occasionalism (p. 78)
pantheism (p. 77)
Blaise Pascal (p. 80)
petite perceptions (p. 80)
Petrarch (p. 66)
pineal gland (p. 72)
primary qualities (p. 68)
psychic determinism (p. 78)
psychophysical parallelism (p. 80)
secondary qualities (p. 68)
Baruch Spinoza (p. 76)
Juan Luis Vives (p. 66)

SUGGESTED READINGS

Boakes, R. (1984). *From Darwin to behaviourism: Psychology and the minds of animals.* New York: Cambridge. This book is out of print, but it may be in your library. Boakes's work has excellent pictures of the people discussed and fascinating accounts of their lives (recall his account of the treatment of Descartes' body). The psychological insights are important, as well.

Descartes, R. (1956). *Discourse on method* (L. J. Lafleur, Trans.). Indianapolis: Bobbs-Merrill. (Original work published 1637) This work is available in many different editions and should be read by anyone wishing to explore Descartes in his own words.

La Mettrie, J. O. d. (1912). *Man a machine* (M. W. Calkins, Trans.). La Salle, IL: Open Court. (Original work published 1748) As you read this book, keep in mind that it was extremely controversial at the time it was published, and the outcry against it forced La Mettrie to flee to the more liberal atmosphere of Prussia and its ruler, Frederick the Great. How would its theme of continuity in the animal kingdom be viewed by a biologist today? By a religious fundamentalist?

Machiavelli, N. (1891). *Il principe.* Oxford: The Clarendon Press. (Original work published 1532) Machiavelli's *The Prince* is available in many different contemporary editions. A delight to read, *The Prince* is a timeless treatise on human nature.

Wilson, M. D. (Ed.) (1969). *The essential Descartes.* New York: Mentor Books. This small book is representative of the many works on Descartes. Such works can be found in bookstores selling used books, usually in the philosophy section. It contains a broad sampling of Descartes' writings, including some of his correspondence with Princess Elizabeth, later queen of Bohemia.

Empiricism, Associationism, Positivism, and Common-Sense Psychology

CHAPTER 5

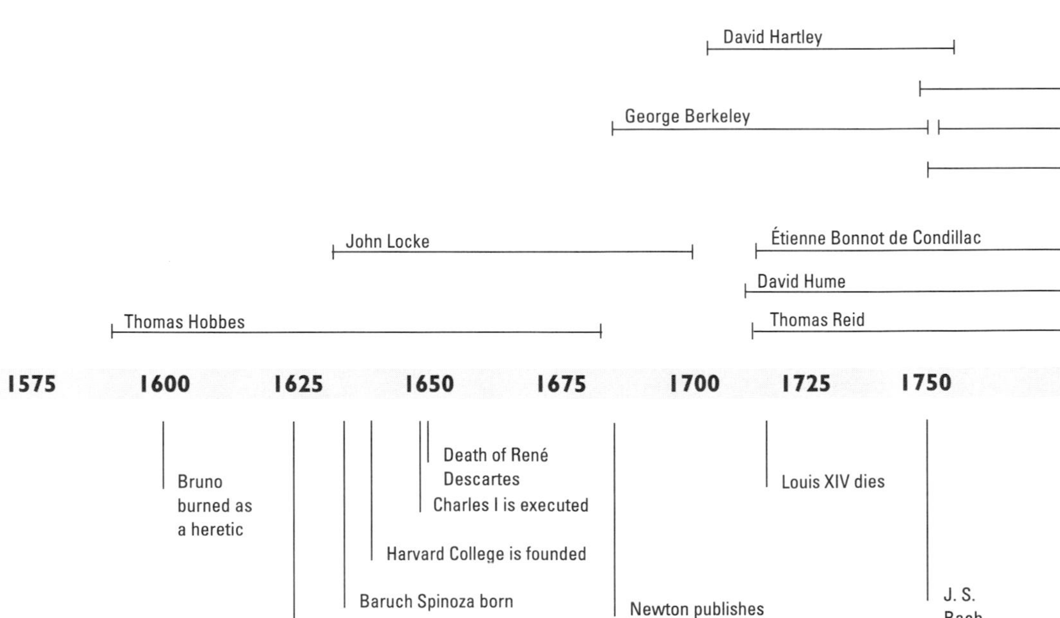

OUTLINE

British Empiricism
- Thomas Hobbes
- John Locke
- George Berkeley
- David Hume

British Associationism
- David Hartley
- James Mill and John Stuart Mill
- Alexander Bain

French Empiricism
- Étienne Bonnot de Condillac
- Pierre Jean Georges Cabanis

Positivism
- Auguste Comte
- Ernst Mach

The Scottish School
- Thomas Reid

Conclusions

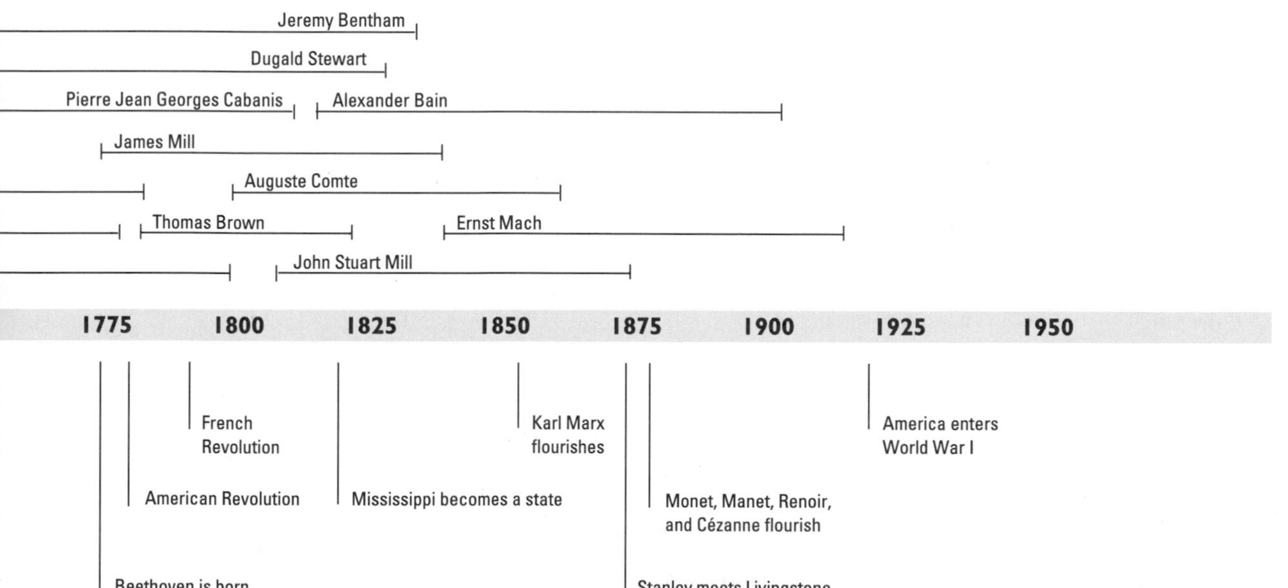

After the Renaissance, so many important events happened concurrently but at different locations that a chronological approach is less desirable than it was in Chapters 2, 3, and 4. For this reason, historians of philosophy and psychology often use a standard set of spatial-topical categories—for example, British empiricism, British associationism, and the Scottish School—to cover the period from the late 1600s through the early 1800s.

Bear in mind that these categories are the invention of historians, and the actual people may have considered themselves in very different relation to their predecessors, contemporaries, and successors than we arrange them today. For example, David Hume is usually considered a British empiricist, even though he was Scottish by birth and could be seen as the first of the associationists. Also, grouping people thematically is sometimes misleading chronologically. For example, British associationism is generally presented before either French empiricism or the Scottish School, although it does not predate either. Fortunately, the chronological timeline should help you see who was contemporary with whom.

As we indicated in Chapter 4, once Renaissance thinkers broke away from the restraints of medieval dogma, knowledge grew rapidly. Descartes, Spinoza, and Leibniz developed systems that were not merely modifications of Plato or Aristotle but new rationalistic approaches. We will explore Continental rationalism after Leibniz in the next chapter, but here the theme is **empiricism**—the search for knowledge through experience rather than through reasoning and the theory that all knowledge comes from sensory experience. Robinson (1995) defined empiricism more precisely as follows:

> Empiricism . . . is an overarching philosophy that confers epistemological [epistemology is the study of the origin, nature, methods, and limits of knowledge] authority on direct experience. It takes the evidence of sense as constituting the primary data of all knowledge. It stipulates that knowledge cannot exist unless this evidence has first been gathered, that all subsequent intellectual processes must use this evidence and only this evidence in framing valid propositions about the real world. (p. 152)

From this definition, we see that knowledge begins with sensory information, or, as the British empiricists were fond of saying: "There is nothing in the intellect that wasn't first in the senses." But we should not infer from this that sensory information constitutes all knowledge. As Robinson indicates, for the empiricist, intellectual processes use the sensory information to develop subsequent ideas about the real world.

We will begin with the British philosophers who used the empirical approach advocated by Isaac Newton and Francis Bacon. Just as Newton had attempted to explain the universe by using a few basic observed principles, the British empiricists aimed to do the same for the mind, thereby laying experimental psychology's foundation.

Experimental psychology's foundation also benefited from positivism. Although developments in quantum physics have challenged elements of positivism as a philosophy of science, many of positivism's basic principles for theory development and evaluation are firmly established as part of psychology's experimental method. For better or worse, Comte's vision of science (discussed later) as a more fundamental basis for social change than religion is with us today. To illustrate, ask yourself this question: If a televangelist and a perceptual researcher both announce that playing too many video games will make you go blind, which one are you more likely to believe?

BRITISH EMPIRICISM

Note that the British empiricists were not empirical in the modern sense of the term. In contemporary psychology, *empirical* is often used to indicate formal observations and controlled experiments. The British empiricists were philosophers who used their everyday experiences to obtain principles from which they logically (and rationally) deduced systems. In addition, we do not intend to imply that the use of *rationalism* and *empiricism* are mutually exclusive. Rationalists such as Descartes also used their experiences in developing their systems, just as the empiricists used a great deal of reasoning. We begin with Thomas Hobbes, who numbered among his friends Francis Bacon, Galileo, and Gassendi.

Thomas Hobbes

Thomas Hobbes was born prematurely on April 5, 1588, his birth supposedly hastened by news of the approaching Spanish Armada. Although Hobbes often attributed his natural timidity to this early exit from the womb, as the most conspicuous heretic of his age he may have inherited a combative streak. An Anglican vicar in the southern England town of Malmesbury, Hobbes's father got into a fight at his church and then disappeared, leaving his children's care to a prosperous brother.

At 20, Hobbes graduated from Oxford and became a private tutor to William Cavendish, who became the second Earl of Devonshire. Hobbes's association with the Cavendish family enabled him to travel and meet important people; it also protected him from the criticism that invariably followed his publications.

Hobbes served briefly as Francis Bacon's secretary, an experience perhaps leading to his empirical philosophy. A visit to Galileo in 1636 may have reinforced Hobbes's desire to describe the universe mechanically. Hobbes's political theory was influenced by the conflict between King Charles I and Parliament that sent Hobbes fleeing to the Continent in 1640. As a published defender of an absolute monarchy, Hobbes felt threatened as the struggle progressed into civil war. Victory went to Oliver Cromwell (1599–1658), and Charles I was executed in 1649. Hobbes served 2 years as the mathematics tutor to the exiled Prince of Wales, who became Charles II.

In 1651, Hobbes published *Leviathan or The Matter, Form and Power of A Commonwealth, Ecclesiastical and Civil,* which led to an outcry in France that forced him to reconcile with Cromwell and return to England, where he again secured the Earl of Devonshire's protection. As *Leviathan* became more widely read, Hobbes was besieged by critics, and in 1666 Parliament considered a motion to burn him as a heretic. Hobbes's clerical enemies blamed him for the Plague and the Great Fire of London (1665–1666), which they saw as God's wrath against England for harboring such an outspoken atheist. Newly restored King Charles II came to his aid, gave Hobbes a pension, had his portrait painted, and welcomed him to court.

Thomas Hobbes (1588–1679)

A sickly youth, Hobbes was healthy in old age, playing tennis until he was 75. On December 4, 1679, at 91, Hobbes died after receiving the Sacrament as an Anglican. Given his reputation as an atheist, this is ironic, although deathbed conversions are not uncommon.

Hobbes's Philosophy

At 40, Hobbes happened upon a copy of Greek mathematician Euclid's *Elements.* Hobbes fell in love with the structure of geometry, in which interconnected propositions issue from basic definitions and axioms. Like Descartes and Spinoza (Chapter 4), Hobbes sought to combine philosophy and mathematics.

Hobbes's theory of humans and society was a mechanical model whose main ingredients were bodies and motion. The idea of a world of bodies in motion may have come from Galileo or from William Harvey, who discovered the circulation of blood. Because he did not believe in incorporeal beings, Hobbes denied the reality of spirit, or God, if the terms were used to imply beings without bodies. He considered the theologians' view of God as an incorporeal substance a contradiction in terms.

Although Hobbes was somewhat inconsistent in his writings, he most often viewed consciousness as simply an epiphenomenon, or byproduct, of the brain's activity. That is, Hobbes thought mental processes were caused by motions in the brain.

Anticipating Locke, Hobbes saw all knowledge as arising from sensation: "For there is no conception in a man's mind, which hath not at first, totally, or by parts, been begotten upon the organs of Sense" (Hobbes, 1651/1914, p. 3). Thus, Hobbes rejected Descartes' belief in innate ideas for a psychological empiricism in which all knowledge comes from sensory experience.

Additionally, there is imagination, which here means the formation of an image. In Hobbes's materialistic explanation, imagination "is nothing but *decaying sense* . . ." (Hobbes, 1651/1914, p. 5, italics in the original), the retention of an object's image when the object is removed. Memory is the expression of the decay of the sense experience when it is old and fading. Hobbes concluded that imagination and memory are just different names for the same thing.

For Hobbes, thought was a sequence of imaginations or memories, determined by laws of the association of ideas. He used contiguity to explain how one thought leads to another. Memories, imaginations, and sense experiences occurring together are associated with each other, with the result that one can call up the other. Also, free will did not exist for Hobbes. There is an unbroken chain of causes and effects, and if we could see the connections, we would understand that "voluntary" behavior is actually determined.

Hobbes's mechanical model readily explained dreams. Whereas waking imaginations proceed from external motions (e.g., the contact of an object with a sensory receptor) to internal motions (imaginations), dreams proceed from internal motions in the brain outward. The fantastic nature of dreams occurs because there is no external sensation to provide a reference point.

Hobbes's political beliefs stemmed from his pessimistic view of "human nature," which he saw as basically aggressive and selfish. Without a strong form of government, human life is "solitary, poore, nasty, brutish, and short" (Hobbes, 1651/1914, p. 65). Enlightened selfishness leads to a "social contract," in which people cede the right of aggression to an absolute ruler. "Leviathan" was Hobbes's name for this omnipotent state.

Summarizing Hobbes

In general, we can describe Hobbes's positions with the labels we used for Democritus (Chapter 2). Thus, Hobbes was a *determinist* who believed that all events are set by prior causes. He was a *materialist* because he believed that all existence consists of bodies in motion, and he did not believe in incorporeal substances. And he was a *reductionist* because he thought that observable events could be explained on a more basic level, and that all could ultimately be explained by the interaction and motion of bodies. His development of reductionism is perhaps his most important contribution for modern psychology. Like Democritus, Hobbes was a *nurturist* who rejected innate ideas for the belief that the mind's contents come from sensory experience—a belief that earned him the *empiricist* label. Hobbes, again like Democritus and particularly like Galileo, held that the object qualities we experience reside not in the objects but in ourselves. Qualities such as taste and odor are secondary qualities, in other words.

Hobbes was among the first to apply empirical methods to questions of human nature. From Hobbes's speculations, Locke developed a more careful and orderly system in *An Essay Concerning Human Understanding.* Hobbes's materialism also strongly influenced later thought, particularly that of Julien de La Mettrie (Chapter 4). We can conclude that Hobbes anticipated many subsequent empirical and materialistic images of mind that remain vital to psychology.

John Locke

John Locke (1632–1704) was born in Wrington in the southwest England county of Somerset. Locke's father was the attorney for a local Parliament member, who sponsored Locke for admission to London's Westminster School. In Locke's second year at school, King Charles I was executed in nearby Whitehall Palace yard. Although Locke probably did not see the execution, it undoubtedly influenced his philosophy.

At 20, Locke entered Oxford as a scholarship student. Studying medicine, he rejected the approach rooted in the classical Greek and Latin texts for the observational, experimental approach taught and practiced by scientists such as Thomas Willis (1621–1675). Willis was a pioneer in brain anatomy and one of the founders of the Royal Society in 1662. A circuit of blood vessels at the brain's base is called the circle of Willis in his honor.

Locke also interacted with Robert Boyle (1627–1691), a scientist central to chemistry's modernization. From Boyle, Locke learned how to approach problems empirically. Boyle also gave Locke the familiar distinction between primary and secondary qualities. Later we will see the influence of Newton's *Principia* on Locke's most famous work. Newton had taken an atomistic, reductionistic approach to understanding the universe, and Locke adopted a similar approach for the mind.

After receiving a bachelor's and a master's degree from Oxford, Locke stayed on as a don. Because he had not taken the medical courses in the classical vein, Locke never received a medical degree. However, he did enjoy some success as a physician, because of a chance encounter with Sir Anthony Ashley Cooper (1621–1683). Lord Ashley had a liver cyst; when it became inflamed, Locke inserted a drainage tube through an abdominal incision. Ashley lived the rest of his life with the tube in place.

Ashley became the first Earl of Shaftesbury and was much involved in British politics until 1681. Locke, more of a trusted advisor and friend than a physician to Ashley, shared in the earl's success and found his political philosophy molded in the process.

National Library of Medicine, Washington, D.C.

John Locke (1632–1704)

In 1679, the earl encountered difficulties over the royal succession. Charles II had no legitimate offspring, his brother James was a Catholic, and Shaftesbury and his supporters feared a Catholic king who might owe primary allegiance to the pope. Although Shaftesbury steered a bill through Parliament disqualifying Catholics from the succession, Charles II stood his ground, and the battle was joined. Locke wrote papers supporting his patron's cause, including drafts of *Two Treatises of Government.*

Briefly imprisoned, Shaftesbury fled to Holland, and Locke prudently followed in 1684. Assuming an alias and moving frequently, Locke finished *An Essay Concerning Human Understanding* and *Two Treatises.* In 1689, William III and his wife, Mary II, replaced James II as the monarchs of Great Britain and Ireland. Locke returned to England, and the *Essay* and *Two Treatises* were published in 1690, making Locke the most renowned philosopher of his day.

After 1691, Locke lived mainly at Oates Manor in Essex with Sir Francis Masham and his wife. He spent his time writing and rewriting until he died in 1704, while listening to Lady Masham reading Psalms.

An Essay Concerning Human Understanding

Ideas: The Mind's Contents. Locke's impetus for the *Essay* came in 1670, when a philosophical discussion with several friends bogged down. Locke decided to investigate the more general question of the origin and nature of human abilities.

Locke concluded that our knowledge is restricted to ideas. These were not Plato's innate universals (Chapter 2) but, rather, ideas generated from experience. There are no innate ideas, as Descartes and others would have us believe.

> Let us then suppose the mind to be, as we say, white paper, void of all characters, without any ideas; how comes it to be furnished? . . . To this I answer, in one word, from *experience*. . . . Our observation employed either about external sensible objects, or about the internal operations of our minds perceived and reflected on by ourselves, is that which supplies our understandings with all the materials of thinking. (Locke, 1690/1964, pp. 89–90, italics in the original)

People who argued for innate ideas often pointed to such universal principles as "it is impossible for the same thing to be and not to be." Even if such ideas are universal—which Locke doubted because children and the retarded do not have them—they do not have to be innate. Locke considered the innateness doctrine unnecessary, because he could explain the presence of "universal" ideas with an empirical description of their source in experience.

Sensation and Reflection. For Locke, the two sources of ideas from experience are sensation and reflection. By **sensation**, Locke meant the impressions passively received from our sense organs and transmitted to our minds. These impressions constitute **simple ideas**, because they cannot be divided further. For example, from a rose we receive a color sensation, an odor sensation, and a feeling of texture if we touch the petals. Although the rose is a combination of qualities, for us the qualities are simple ideas because each enters through a separate sense. Simple ideas have their origin in sensations and also in reflection.

Locke said that **reflection** is the "perception of the operations of our own minds within us, as it is employed about the ideas it has got" (Locke, 1690/1964, p. 90). That is, additional ideas are created by the mind's operations, working on previously received sensations. The mind's operations comprising reflection are "*perception, thinking, doubting, believing, reasoning, knowing, willing,* and all the different actings of our own minds . . ." (Locke, 1690/1964, p. 90, italics in the original). Ideas created by reflection cannot be innate, because reflection must initially use ideas that have entered the mind through the senses.

In addition to simple ideas from the senses, the mind can use its operations to create other simple ideas. For example, a simple idea created by reflecting on sensations received from a flower might be the idea of pleasure. Locke wrote that pleasure or pain is involved in almost all of our ideas, whether they are ideas of sensation or of reflection.

Whereas simple ideas are received passively by the mind, **complex ideas** are created by combining simple ideas of both kinds. Several simple ideas of sensation, such as the color and smell of a flower, might combine with a simple idea of reflection (e.g., pleasure) to give the complex idea of a rose.

Although Locke is credited with coining the phrase "the association of ideas," it was not added to the *Essay* until the fourth edition. In the chapter on "associations," Locke does not refer either to Aristotle (Chapter 2) or to Hobbes, and he does not formulate any "laws of association." He argued that experience can cause ideas to be linked in an infinite variety of combinations and that associations formed "accidentally" can be just as compelling as more "natural" associations. For example, a child repeatedly told not to talk to strangers may associate strangers and danger just as strongly as roundness and yellowness are associated with lemons.

Interestingly, Locke considered the association of ideas important for creating pathological aversions. For example, he clearly described what we call **conditioned taste aversion** (e.g., Garcia, Hankins, & Rusiniak, 1974; see also Chapter 12) in the following:

> A grown person surfeiting with honey no sooner hears the name of it, but his fancy immediately carries sickness and qualms to his stomach, and he cannot bear the very idea of it; other ideas of dislike, and sickness, and vomiting, presently accompany it, and he is disturbed. . . . (Locke, 1690/1964, p. 252)

Perception. Locke wrote that perception "is the first faculty of the mind exercised about our ideas . . ." and that "it is the first and simplest idea we have from reflection, and is by some called thinking in general" (Locke, 1690/1964, p. 119). Locke also speculated on the form our perceptions would take if, as adults, we suddenly gained use of a sense we had previously lacked.

Locke quoted a letter from Irish scientist **William Molyneux** (or Molineux, as Locke spelled it; 1656–1696) in which Molyneux speculated that a person born blind who gained sight as an adult would be unable to make distinctions visually that the person had learned to make with other senses. Agreeing, Locke predicted that the person would be unable to identify objects visually that had been known previously only by touch, because visual perception of an object such as a cube depends on visual sensations creating the appropriate ideas in the mind. Without these ideas, the person would not be able to recognize the object by sight.

The answer as to whether Locke and Molyneux were right is not clear-cut. Several people born blind who gained sight through surgery (e.g., cataract removal) have been studied, and many of the cases have supported Locke and Molyneux's position. Often these people could see little at first and were unable to name the simplest objects or shapes. Many required lengthy training before there was useful vision, suggesting that visual ideas are necessary before there can be visual perceptions. However, "some did see quite well almost immediately, particularly those who were intelligent and active, and who had received a good education while blind" (Gregory, 1966, p. 193). Gregory concluded it is "extremely difficult, if not entirely impossible, to use these cases to answer Molyneux's question" (p. 198). An adult learning to use vision is not at all like an infant undergoing initial learning. For one thing, the adult has a vast store of knowledge from other senses.

Primary and Secondary Qualities. Like Galileo, Descartes, Boyle, and others before him, Locke differentiated between primary and secondary qualities of objects. Locke's primary qualities included solidity, extension, figure, and mobility. Secondary qualities are "qualities which in truth are nothing in the objects themselves but powers to produce various sensations in us . . ." (Locke, 1690/1964, p. 112). Examples include color, sound, taste, smell, and temperature, which Locke demonstrated with three bowls. Fill the bowl on the left with cold water, the one on the right with hot water, and the one in the middle with lukewarm water. Place your right hand in the hot water and your left hand in the cold water. Your right hand feels hot and your left hand cold, just as you would expect. Next, place both hands into the middle bowl. Now, your left hand feels warm and your right hand feels cool even though both hands are in the same water, which Locke believed demonstrated that the sensation of temperature comes from experience (i.e., is a secondary quality).

Actually, if sensation is understood to be the *warming* or *cooling* of the skin, then Locke's demonstration could be of a primary quality. Because the empiricists did not see relations or change as sensations, they missed truths that William James (Chapter 10) and later the Gestaltists (Chapter 14) could see. The empiricists' problem may have been they were not empirical enough. They adhered to their beliefs in the primacy of sensation rather than allowing themselves to be convinced by the evidence from their experiences. Nevertheless, Locke's demonstration successfully made his intended point.

By differentiating primary and secondary qualities, Locke was trying to distinguish appearance from reality, a distinction reflecting Newton's influence. Newton explained the appearance of white, for example, by the motions of tiny, invisible particles. Reality is found not in the secondary quality of whiteness but in the movement of the tiny particles themselves. Although the secondary qualities are just appearance, there is something real behind them (particles in motion), and Locke called this underlying reality *substance.* Locke could not precisely describe substance, writing, "if anyone will examine himself concerning his notion of pure substance in general, he will find he has no other idea of it at all, but only a supposition of he knows not what *support* of such qualities which are capable of producing simple ideas in us" (Locke, 1690/1964, p. 185, italics in the original). Locke considered substance the explanation for sensation.

Degrees of Knowledge. Because he could not describe substance, Locke was led to consider the extent and validity of our knowledge. First, he defined knowledge as "nothing but *the perception of the connexion and agreement, or disagreement and repugnancy, of any of our ideas*" (Locke, 1690/1964, p. 320, italics in the original). In some cases, the mind immediately perceives the agreement or disagreement of two ideas, and Locke called this *intuitive knowledge.* "Thus the mind perceives that white is not black, that a circle is not a triangle. . . . Such kinds of truths the mind perceives at the first sight of the ideas together by bare intuition" (Locke, 1690/1964, pp. 325–326).

Next, the mind again perceives the agreement or disagreement between ideas, but not immediately. Instead, the agreement or disagreement occurs through the intervention of one or more other ideas, and Locke called this *demonstrative knowledge.* An example is proving propositions in geometry.

According to Locke (1690/1964), whatever falls short of intuitive or demonstrative knowledge is "but *faith* or *opinion,* but not knowledge . . ." (p. 330). However, there is another kind of knowledge, *sensitive knowledge,* or knowledge of things received through our senses. Sensitive knowledge is less precise and verifiable than intuitive and demonstrative knowledge, which makes it difficult to be sure that things exist. Locke wrote: "of the *real actual existence of things,* we have an intuitive knowledge of *our own existence,* and a demonstrative knowledge of the existence of a *God:* of the existence of *anything else,* we have no other but a sensitive knowledge; which extends not beyond the objects present to our senses" (Locke, 1690/1964, pp. 340–341, italics in the original).

Leibniz's Critique of the Essay

In 1696, Leibniz wrote a 7-page review of Locke's *Essay,* known to him at the time only from an abstract. When Leibniz learned that Locke had "misunderstood" his criticisms, he began to elaborate them. By the time Locke died in 1704, Leibniz's critique was nearly 600 pages long. Having no wish to argue with a dead man, Leibniz did not finish his commentary, which was published in 1765, nearly 50 years after Leibniz died.

Considered Leibniz's (1765/1949) greatest work, *New Essays on Human Understanding* begins with a summary of the author's psychology, followed by a Socratic dialogue between fictional characters representing Locke's and Leibniz's views. After praising Locke's *Essay* as "one of the most beautiful and esteemed works of this period" (p. 41), Leibniz posed the question central to his criticism, which is

> whether the [mind] in itself is entirely empty as the tablets upon which as yet nothing has been written (*tabula rasa*) according to Aristotle, and the author of the Essay, and whether all that is traced thereon comes solely from the senses and from experience; or whether the [mind] contains originally the principles of many ideas and doctrines which external objects merely call up on occasion, as I believe with Plato. . . . (Leibnitz, 1765/1949, pp. 42–43)

In other words, is the mind empty, with all its contents coming from experience à la Aristotle and Locke, or does the mind contain innate "ideas and doctrines" à la Plato and Leibniz? Note that Locke compared the mind at birth to "white paper," not to a *tabula rasa* (clean slate or erased tablet), as a passage in Aristotle was translated (see also Petryszak, 1981).

Leibniz may have been attacking a "straw man" by interpreting Locke's *Essay* as implying there is nothing in the mind that did not enter through the senses. As we noted, Locke identified the second source of the mind's ideas as reflection, "the perception of the operations of our own minds" (Locke, 1690/1964, p. 90). Because the operations (e.g., perception, thinking, doubting, reasoning, etc.) antedate experience, they are innate. Thus, at least some of Leibniz's criticisms were of a Locke of Leibniz's construction.

To the empiricist creed "there is nothing in the intellect that was not first in the senses," Leibniz (1765/1949, p. 111) added "except the intellect itself." Leibniz then wrote: "the [mind] comprises being, substance, unity, identity, cause, *perception, reason,* and many other notions which the senses cannot give" (p. 111, italics added). Leibniz's innate additions to the mind's contents included Locke's operations. Decades later, Immanuel Kant (Chapter 6) offered a similar rationalist critique of David Hume's empirical philosophy (discussed later).

Locke and the Education of Children

Although he never married, Locke presented his views on childrearing to Edward and Mary Clarke (Locke's cousin) in letters written while he was in Holland. The Clarkes had asked for advice on educating their son, and Locke responded, later using the letters as the basis for *Some Thoughts Concerning Education* (1693).

Not surprisingly, Locke stressed the importance of early education. Although he conceded that some small number of people are constitutionally superior, he wrote:

> Examples of this Kind are but few, and I think I may say, that of all the Men we meet with, Nine Parts of Ten are what they are, Good or Evil, useful or not, by their Education. 'Tis that which makes the great Difference in Mankind. The little, and almost insensible Impressions on our tender Infancies, have very important and lasting Consequences" (Locke, 1705; Axtell, 1968, p. 114)

John B. Watson (Chapter 12) would certainly have agreed.

Locke's letters covered a wide array of educational topics, including passages on reward and punishment, dancing, manners, obstinacy, and so forth. Much of Locke's advice is antiquated from our perspective (e.g., he recommended bathing a child's feet nightly in cold water and giving the child leaky shoes to toughen the youngster against diseases that could follow wet feet), but some of his advice sounds remarkably modern. For example, in a passage that might have come from a current chapter on treating a phobia with behavior therapy, Locke used a fear of frogs to detail a method we call **systematic desensitization** and usually attribute to **Joseph Wolpe** (1915–1997).

> Your Child shrieks, and runs away at the sight of a Frog; Let another catch it, and lay it down at a good distance from him: At first accustom him to look upon it; When he can do that, then to come nearer to it, and see it leap without Emotion; then to touch it lightly when it is held fast in another's hand; and so on, till he can come to handle it as confidently as a Butter-fly, or a Sparrow. By the same way any other vain Terrors may be remov'd; if Care be taken, that you go not too fast, and push not the Child on to a new degree of assurance, till he be thoroughly confirm'd in the former. (Locke, 1705; Axtell, 1968, p. 223)

Locke's nurture emphasis is echoed in many of John B. Watson's writings, and Mary Cover Jones, working with Watson, used Locke's method for removing "vain Terrors" to treat a fear of animals in a child (see Chapter 12).

Locke and Politics

During Locke's life, the monarchy was first in power, then out of power after a civil war, and finally restored to power. Hobbes's response was to argue for an absolute monarchy because of his low opinion of the natural state of humans. By contrast, Locke favored a constitutional monarchy in *Two Treatises of Government.* His social contract theory defended the natural rights of individuals, justified constitutional law, and called for majority rule.

Further, Locke wrote that if the ruling body violated the natural rights of the governed, the people had the right to overthrow the government. The leaders of both the American Revolution (1776) and the French Revolution (1789) used Locke's writings to defend their actions. Locke's natural rights of the people became the American Constitution's Bill of Rights, and our Declaration of Independence owes much to Locke's political writings. In addition, Locke's political writings were used as justification in his own time for the "Glorious Revolution" of 1689.

Locke's Influence

Locke's *Essay* is often said to mark British empiricism's beginning as an organized system. George Berkeley and David Hume were profoundly influenced by the *Essay*, as were 18th-century French philosophers, especially Étienne Bonnot de Condillac (discussed later). We can say that Locke's philosophy dominated the 18th century just as Descartes' did the 17th.

Locke's view of a relatively passive mind largely populated with sensory experiences, as well as his understanding of how perception gives rise to conception, is the basis of many subsequent psychological theories. For example, in Chapters 12 and 13 we will see Locke's influence in the more recent emphasis on conditioning and learning for behavior. In addition, although he did not develop it, Locke's phrase "association of ideas" led to the school of British associationism (discussed later).

Next we will discuss George Berkeley, who took Locke's distinction between primary and secondary qualities to its logical conclusion.

George Berkeley

By courtesy of the National Portrait Gallery, London.

George Berkeley (1685–1753)

George Berkeley, or Bishop Berkeley of Cloyne, was born at Dysert Castle in County Kilkenny, Ireland, on March 12, 1685. Although Berkeley never ventured farther west than Rhode Island, the American town of Berkeley, California, is named after him.

At 15, Berkeley entered Dublin's Trinity College, and he stayed there as student, fellow, and tutor until 1713. After traveling abroad, Berkeley returned in 1721 to Trinity College, where he earned further degrees and in 1723 was appointed Hebrew Lecturer. By 1724, Berkeley was obsessed with founding a college in the New World (i.e., the Bermudas) to promote religion among American Indians. With the promise of money from Parliament to start St. Paul's College, in 1728, newly married, Berkeley sailed for America, arriving in Newport, Rhode Island, in 1729. When the promised funding did not appear, Berkeley returned to England in 1731. Berkeley was so impressed by what he found in America that he helped establish the University of Pennsylvania, contributed land and books to Yale, donated books to Harvard, and wrote a poem containing the famous line "Westward the course of empire takes its way."

In 1734, Berkeley was appointed Bishop of Cloyne. On Sunday evening, January 14, 1753, Berkeley died from a "palsy in the heart" while listening to his wife read a sermon. His death went unnoticed until his daughter, handing him a cup of tea, discovered that his body was cold and his joints were stiff.

Berkeley's Contributions

Virtually all of Berkeley's accomplishments for psychology are contained in his three most important books: *An Essay Towards a New Theory of Vision* (1709), *A Treatise Concerning the Principles of Human Knowledge* (1710), and *Three Dialogues Between Hylas and Philonous* (1713). (The similarity between the titles of the first two books and Locke's *An Essay Concerning Human Understanding* is not accidental.) *An Essay Towards a New Theory of Vision* was triggered by Locke's quoting in his *Essay* a letter from William Molyneux (who, not coincidentally, was a tutor at Trinity College, Dublin) predicting that a blind man gaining sight would have to learn to recognize objects visually. Although Berkeley agreed that experience is necessary for visual perception, his analysis of depth perception and the judgment of distances took a different tangent from Locke's. Locke assumed that visually recognized objects really exist; there must be substance in order for objects to have primary qualities. Further, when we see an object at a distance from ourselves, although we do not directly experience the object and the distance, both are really there.

For Berkeley, our perceptions of distance *and objects* are mental constructs.

> It is, I think, agreed by all, that *distance* of itself, and immediately, cannot be seen. For *distance* being a line directed end-wise to the eye, it projects only one point [to] the eye. Which point remains invariably the same, whether the distance be longer or shorter. (Berkeley, 1709/1837, p. 86, italics in the original)

Because we do not see distance directly, we acquire through experience with distance cues the ability to tell that some objects are farther from us than others. In *New Theory of Vision,* Berkeley clearly described three cues to distance perception, although he did not apply our modern names to them. In **interposition,** near objects hide or partially hide more distant objects. Berkeley (1709/1837) wrote: "when I perceive a great number of intermediate *objects,* such as houses, fields, rivers, and the like, which I have experienced to take up a considerable space, I thence form a judgment . . . that the *object* I see beyond them is at a great distance" (p. 86, italics in the original).

The **relative size** cue occurs when two objects of the same size are at different distances from the observer and the near object appears larger than the more distant object. According to Berkeley (1709/1837), "when an *object* appears faint and small, which at a near distance I have experienced to make a vigorous and large appearance, I instantly conclude it to be far off" (p. 86, italics in the original).

Convergence is the inward rotation of our eyes to keep an approaching object in focus. Berkeley's description was explicit:

> when we look at a near *object* with both eyes, according as it approaches or recedes from us, we alter the disposition of our eyes, by lessening or widening the interval between the *pupils.* This . . . turn of the eyes is attended with a sensation, which seems to me to be that which in this case brings the *idea* of greater or lesser distance into the mind. (Berkeley, 1709/1837, pp. 87–88, italics in the original)

Thus, we have extensive experience associating visual cues with objects at different distances from us, and Berkeley recognized the principle of association, without specifically naming it.

> Not that there is any natural or necessary connexion between the sensation we perceive by the turn of the eyes, and greater or lesser distance; but because the mind has by constant *experience* found the different sensations corresponding to the different dispositions of the eyes, to be attended each with a different degree of distance in the *object:* there has grown an habitual or customary connexion between those two sorts of *ideas.* (Berkeley, 1709/1837, p. 88, italics in the original)

This "habitual or customary connexion" between ideas is formed by experience, through their frequent association.

After *New Theory of Vision,* Berkeley published *A Treatise Concerning the Principles of Human Knowledge* when he was only 25. *Principles,* too, was triggered by Locke's *Essay.* If all ideas come from sensations and our knowledge of the world depends on our perception, then Berkeley drew the obvious conclusion: *esse est percipi*—to be, is to be perceived. In one of the most famous passages in philosophy, Berkeley wrote:

> Some truths there are so near and obvious to the mind that a man need only open his eyes to see them. Such I take this important one to be, to wit, that all the choir of heaven and furniture of the earth, in a word all those bodies which compose the mighty frame of the world, have not any subsistence without a mind, that their being is to be perceived or known. . . . (Berkeley, 1710/1837, p. 9)

Berkeley's idea that the world exists only in being perceived was obvious to *his* mind, but it was less obvious to others. In one famous criticism, James Boswell (1740–1795) challenged Samuel Johnson (1709–1784) to refute Berkeley as they were leaving church. Dr. Johnson kicked a large stone, saying, "I refute it thus." Johnson's point was that his pain from kicking the rock proved its existence. If Berkeley had been present, he would have told Johnson that Johnson's idea of the rock included the associated ideas of solidity and heaviness, both of which would produce the sensation of pain when he kicked the rock.

Although he had written that objects exist in being perceived, Berkeley did not deny the ultimate reality of objects. For him, the world depended for its permanence on God's infinite mind. Like Locke, Berkeley believed that the sensations we receive from an object come from a real object. Unlike Locke, Berkeley thought the object's ultimate reality occurred because it was perceived by the "ultimate Perceiver."

Berkeley did not need Locke's distinction between primary and secondary qualities. For him, all object qualities were secondary because their existence depends on their being perceived. He wrote, "it is evident from what we have already shewn, that extension, figure and motion are only ideas existing in the mind . . ." (Berkeley, 1710/1837, p. 9). That is, we cannot think of an object's size, shape, or motion independently of our perception of it. These "primary" qualities are just as much ideas in our minds as Locke's secondary qualities. Therefore, objects are the sum of their perceived qualities, which is why Berkeley argued that to be is to be perceived.

Berkeley's Influence

Berkeley's mind-body position has been variously called mentalism, immaterialism, and subjective idealism. Immaterialism is perhaps most appropriate because Berkeley's aim in much of his writing was to crush the materialism that he saw as the "main pillar and support of scepticism, so likewise upon the same foundation have been raised all the impious schemes of Atheism and irreligion" (Berkeley, 1710/1837, p. 25).

However, although he believed he had demolished materialism with his prescription *esse est percipi,* Berkeley did not want to destroy the science of his day, which depended heavily on the concept and study of matter. Rather, he wanted to rid science, particularly physics, of such metaphysical notions as force and gravity, which are used as though they refer to an underlying material substance. Sensed qualities are all that can be shown to exist, and we know about them through experience, which is all we have to go on (empiricism).

Thus, Berkeley's lasting influence came from his strict empirical approach to knowledge, not from his idealism or immaterialism. Although Berkeley sought to destroy skepticism, some felt his writings had the opposite effect. For example, David Hume (1748/1955) wrote:

> indeed most of the writings of [Berkeley] form the best lessons of scepticism, which are to be found either among the ancient or modern philosophers. . . . But that all his arguments, though otherwise intended, are, in reality, merely sceptical, appears from this, that *they admit of no answer and produce no conviction.* Their only effect is to cause that momentary amazement and irresolution and confusion, which is the result of scepticism. (p. 163, italics in the original)

As a summary of Berkeley's accomplishments, we find Durant and Durant's (1963) comment delightful: "No man ever surpassed him in proving the unreality of the real. In his effort to restore religious belief, and to exorcise the Hobbesian materialism that was infecting England, [Berkeley] turned philosophy outside in . . ." (p. 597).

David Hume

David Hume was born on April 26, 1711, in Edinburgh, Scotland. Although he came from a good family, the Humes were not wealthy, and, as the younger son, Hume received a meager inheritance. Hume's family planned for him to study law, but he was more interested in philosophy. He studied at the University of Edinburgh but did not graduate.

In 1734, Hume briefly tried the life of commerce but soon realized that this was not for him. He went to France to pursue his studies in a country retreat, perhaps fleeing from Agnes Galbraith's charge that he was the father of the child she carried, and there he established his life's plan: "I resolved to make a very rigid frugality supply my deficiency of fortune, to maintain unimpaired my independence, and to regard every object as contemptible except the improvement of my talents in literature" (Hume, 1776/1955, p. 4).

Hume's literary talents needed improving. His first and most important work, *A Treatise of Human Nature,* published anonymously in 1739–1740, "fell *deadborn from the press*" (Hume, 1776/1955, p. 4, italics in the original). A simplified version published as *An Inquiry* (or *Enquiry*) *Concerning Human Understanding* (1748) was at least initially no more successful. (Again, note the title's similarity to Locke's *Essay.*) Although other writings received a more gratifying response, Hume's atheism prevented him from attaining two professorships he sought.

In 1745, Hume served as the tutor to an insane nobleman, a position from which he gained appointments that improved his economic situation. In 1752, Hume became the keeper of the library of the Faculty of Advocates in Edinburgh. Although the position paid little, it provided access to a large library and stimulated Hume to write a history of England. Unfortunately, the first volume of Hume's history was not well received: "I was assailed by one cry of reproach, disapprobation, and even detestation . . . and after the first ebullitions of . . . fury were over, what was still more mortifying, the book seemed to sink into oblivion" (Hume, 1776/ 1955, p. 7).

David Hume (1711–1776)

As secretary to an ambassador in Paris from 1763 to 1765, Hume was generally treated royally. In fact, the ambassador was amazed to find his secretary more celebrated than he. Hume was much admired and became a favored guest both in Paris and later in London, where he served briefly as undersecretary of state for the Northern Department. Before returning to London from France, Hume befriended Jean-Jacques Rousseau (Chapter 6). Rousseau accompanied Hume back to England, but Rousseau's developing paranoia led him to provoke a quarrel with Hume and flee back to France.

In 1768, Hume returned to Edinburgh to stay. In the spring of 1775, he was "struck with a disorder in my bowels, which at first gave me no alarm, but has since, as I apprehend it, become mortal and incurable" (Hume, 1776/1955, p. 10). Hume died on August 25, 1776, and a large crowd attended his funeral despite a heavy downpour.

Hume's Psychology

Although we can find relevant ideas for modern psychology in the writings of Locke, Descartes, and even Plato and Aristotle, they were clearly philosophers, not psychologists. Hume was also a philosopher, but a portion of his work is distinctively psychological, and several authors (e.g., Bricke, 1974; Miller, 1971) have traced psychology's roots as an independent science to Hume. Either directly, or indirectly through late British empiricism's influence on psychology's more recognized founders (Wundt, Chapter 8; James, Chapter 10), Hume's contributions represent an important milestone in the history of psychology.

Impressions and Ideas. Hume began by accepting the empiricism of Locke and Berkeley: All the mind's contents come from experience through **impressions**, by which Hume (1748/1955) meant "all our more lively perceptions, when we hear, or see, or feel, or love, or hate, or desire, or will" (p. 27). Hume called the second class of the mind's perceptions ideas, which are faint copies of impressions.

Because he believed there were no ideas without impressions, Hume also predicted that a man born blind and gaining sight would have to develop visual ideas through experience. Like Locke, he distinguished between simple and complex ideas, and impressions, too, could be either simple or complex. Simple impressions or ideas cannot be further subdivided, whereas complex impressions or ideas can be broken down further. For example, the impression or idea of an apple is a compound of simple impressions or ideas, which include the apple's color, odor, taste, shape, and so forth.

Although there must be a prior impression for every idea, not every idea reflects a corresponding impression. For example, we may imagine a horse with wings, although we have never seen such a thing. We have seen creatures with wings, and we have seen horses, and when we have an idea of a flying horse, it is through our mind's association of ideas.

Association of Ideas. Hume (1748/1955) was explicit about the principles of **association of ideas:** "To me there appear to be only three principles of connections among ideas, namely, *Resemblance, Contiguity* in time or place, and *Cause* or *Effect*" (p. 32, italics in the original). To illustrate the three principles, Hume wrote:

> A picture naturally leads our thoughts to the original [resemblance]. The mention of one apartment in a building naturally introduces an inquiry . . . concerning the others [contiguity]; and if we think of a wound, we can scarcely forbear reflecting on the pain which follows it [cause and effect]. (Hume, 1748/1955, p. 32)

Causality. Hume's thinking about **causality,** or cause and effect, was both original and influential: He considered cause an idea that could not be shown to have objective reality.

> When we look about us toward external objects and consider the operation of causes, we are never able, in a single instance, to discover any power or necessary connection . . . which binds the effect to the cause and renders the one an infallible consequence of the other. We only find that the one does actually in fact follow the other. The impulse of one billiard ball is attended with motion in the second. This is the whole that appears to the *outward* senses. The mind feels no sentiment or *inward* impression from this succession of objects; consequently, there is not, in any single particular instance of cause and effect, anything which can suggest the idea of power or necessary connection. (Hume, 1748/1955, pp. 74–75, italics in the original)

We infer that event A causes event B when we have experienced the two events many times in temporal sequence. The idea of a "necessary connection" between the events occurs in our minds, not in the conjunction of the two events. Thus, causality is a habit of the mind that comes from frequent repetitions of A followed by B. Hume did not deny causality, as some have said; rather, he denied that reason is capable of apprehending it.

When objects or events have been constantly observed to be conjoined, we immediately infer the existence of one when we experience the other. According to Hume, "habit" is the principle by which this connection of objects or events is formed. He saw habit "as the ultimate principle which we can assign all of our conclusions from experience" (Hume, 1748/1955, p. 57).

Note that Hume saw habit, not reasoning, as the ultimate principle allowing us to draw inferences from our experiences. This is equally true for animals, which,

> as well as men, learn many things from experience and infer that the same events will always follow from the same causes. . . . This is still more evident from the effects of discipline and education on animals, who by the proper application of rewards and punishments may be taught any course of action the most contrary to their natural instincts and propensities. (Hume, 1748/1955, pp. 112–113)

We will see this idea echoed nearly 150 years later in Edward Lee Thorndike's law of effect (Chapter 12).

The Mind and External Reality. For Locke, our experience of objects comes from sensations, and he assumed that the objects have substance. Berkeley argued that things exist in being perceived, and the "ultimate Perceiver" gives the universe its apparent permanence. Hume went one step further, contending that mind consists only of impressions and their associations, and there is no "ultimate Perceiver" to give things independent existence. Hume wrote, "nothing can ever be present to the mind but an image or perception, and . . . the senses are only the inlets through which these images are conveyed, without being able to produce any immediate intercourse between the mind and the object" (Hume, 1748/1955, pp. 160–161).

If our knowledge of external reality comes from our impressions, which are merely copies of external objects, how can we prove that our perceptions are caused by external objects? First, Hume suggested experience: "But here experience is and must be entirely silent. The mind has never anything present to it but the perceptions, and cannot possibly reach any experience of their connection with objects" (Hume, 1748/1955, p. 162).

The "veracity of the Supreme Being" will not work either. If "his veracity were at all concerned in this matter, our senses would be entirely infallible, because it is not possible that he can ever deceive" (Hume, 1748/1955, p. 162). In a related matter, Hume agreed with Berkeley that there are only secondary qualities. For Hume, Locke's primary quality of extension "is entirely acquired from the senses of sight and feeling" (p. 163).

In the end, there is no rational or experiential proof of the existence of external things. Instead, we form a belief in the independent existence of certain things through our awareness of the constancy and coherence of our impressions. For example, if you look at the room you are now in and then shut your eyes, when you reopen them you will receive the same impressions you received before. This constancy aids your belief in external reality without proving its existence.

Hume's Influence

One of Hume's most important contributions was that he provided a focus for the attacks of his successors. As we noted, Hume took the step beyond Berkeley's conclusion that God validated the world's existence. The skeptic Hume concluded that we have direct knowledge only of the mind's processes. This conclusion led him to doubt the existence of the self, God, and the external world and also led other philosophers to try to show the error of Hume's ways. A fellow Scot, Thomas Reid (discussed later) may have been stimulated to philosophical activities by Hume's skepticism, and, on the Continent, Hume awakened Immanuel Kant from his "dogmatic slumber" with his discussion of causality.

Hume's belief in the importance of association and his specification of the major principles, resemblance (similarity) and contiguity, have been crucial for psychology. Although he initially listed cause and effect as an associative principle, he came to see it as contiguity with a feeling of a necessary connection between two events or objects. He saw habit as the ultimate principle allowing us to generalize from our experiences and believed this principle was equally at work in animals. By recognizing the similarity in the mental lives of animals and people, Hume provided an argument for a comparative approach a century before Darwin (Chapter 9).

For Hume, there had to be a prior impression before there could be an idea, and he believed any idea could be traced back to the impression(s) giving rise to it. Ideas with no basis in our experience should be discarded, and this included ideas of divinity and metaphysics. As he expressed it:

> When we run over libraries, persuaded of these principles, what havoc must we make? If we take in our hand any volume—of divinity or school metaphysics, for instance—let us ask, Does it contain any abstract reasoning concerning quantity or number? No. Does it contain any experimental reasoning concerning matter of fact and existence? No. Commit it then to the flames, for it can contain nothing but sophistry and illusion. (Hume, 1748/1955, p. 173)

BRITISH ASSOCIATIONISM

The British empiricists—Hobbes, Locke, Berkeley, and Hume—rejected the Cartesian belief in innate ideas that could be deduced by rational means, assuming instead that the mind's ideas originate in sensory experience. The empiricists incorporated in their theories conceptions of the "association of ideas," a phrase Locke introduced in his *Essay*. However, none of the empiricists elevated the association of ideas to a doctrine, although Hume came close. Beginning with David Hartley, the remaining key British empiricists are also called British associationists because they formalized the association of ideas. Derived from empiricism, **associationism** includes formal rules for the mind's association of ideas.

David Hartley

David Hartley (1705–1757) was born in Halifax, a city in Yorkshire, England. A minister's son, Hartley initially planned to be a minister himself, but his objection to an article dealing with eternal damnation prevented him from signing a document necessary for Church of England membership. Blocked from becoming a cleric, Hartley studied medicine at Cambridge and became a successful physician.

In his spare time, Hartley worked for 18 years on *Observations on Man, His Frame, His Duty and His Expectations,* which was published in 1749 (see Webb, 1988, for a discussion of the development of *Observations*). Newton and Locke were two major influences on Hartley's thinking, and *Observations* represents the fusion of Locke's association of ideas and Newton's theory of vibrations. Although Hume's *Treatise* was published before *Observations,* Hartley began his work nearly a decade before Hume's publication, and Hartley was probably not directly influenced by Hume.

Hartley's Psychology

Hartley adopted Newton's notion of solid nerves in which tiny particles vibrate in response to sensory events (Smith, 1987). The vibrations produce miniature vibrations **(vibratiuncles)** in the brain's "medullary particles." Hartley considered vibratiuncles the physical manifestation of ideas. Whereas Hume said ideas were faint copies of impressions (mainly sensations), Hartley said that the vibratiuncles were tiny representations of the sensory vibrations in the nerves. Thus, Hartley's work can be seen as Hume (and as Smith suggests, Newton) translated to the physiological level.

Following Newton, Hartley noted that the vibratiuncles continue briefly after the triggering sensation has been withdrawn. A **positive afterimage** illustrates this property, which Hartley (1749/1966) called Proposition 3—"*The Sensations remain in the Mind for a short time after the sensible Objects are removed*" (p. 9, italics in the original). To illustrate, Hartley wrote of briefly continuing to perceive a candle flame after a person has closed his or her eyes.

Thus, ideas (vibratiuncles) are faint copies of sensations and the two—ideas and sensations—are associated through contiguity, which Hartley said could be either synchronous (simultaneous) or successive. Ideas, too, can be associated through contiguity, and a particular sensation may arouse a sequence of ideas with which it has been frequently paired. For example, Proposition 10 states,

> *Any Sensations A, B, C, &c. by being associated with one another a sufficient Number of Times, get such a Power over the corresponding Ideas a, b, c, &c. that any one of the Sensations A, when impressed alone, shall be able to excite in the Mind, b, c, &c. the Ideas of the rest.* (Hartley, 1749/1966, p. 65, italics in the original)

David Hartley (1705–1757)

Hartley applied his vibration and association doctrines to psychological topics, such as words and associated ideas, emotions and motivation (Mischel, 1966), memory, and imagination. For Hartley, association was the basis of mental compounding, and simple ideas associated together become combinations of ideas and eventually one complex idea. In fact, if enough simple ideas coalesce into a complex idea, each simple idea may no longer be discernible, a notion that foreshadows John Stuart Mill's mental chemistry (discussed later).

Hartley's Influence

According to Webb (1988), Hartley was the first to study psychological phenomena (mind) as a natural science, he was the forerunner of physiological psychology as a recognized subdiscipline, and he was the father of British associationism as a long-standing psychological theory. To name the process by which ideas and sensations are joined, Hartley chose a chapter title from Locke's *Essay:* "Of the association of ideas." However, the impetus for Hartley's thinking about association probably came from the Reverend John Gay's writings about association as the basis of morality.

Along with contiguity as the condition for the association of ideas, Hartley recognized the necessity of repetition, although he did not name or formalize it as a principle. We will see the importance of repetition in Ebbinghaus's memory research (Chapter 8) and in Thorndike's law of exercise (Chapter 12).

Hartley unequivocally stressed the brain's importance for mental activity, a fact we take for granted but one that needed frequent repetition in the 18th and 19th centuries. To illustrate how Hartley connected brain activity with mental functions, he wrote the following about memory and its susceptibility to neural insult: "Memory depends entirely or chiefly on the State of the Brain. For Disease, Concussions of the Brain, spirituous Liquors, and some Poisons, impair or destroy it; and it generally returns again with the Return of Health. . . . (Hartley, 1749/1966, p. 374).

Hartley also influenced individuals better known for their nonpsychological contributions. For example, Joseph Priestly (1733–1804), the chemist who discovered oxygen, published an abridged version of Hartley's *Observations* in 1775 that included three essays of Priestly's own. The English poet and philosopher **Samuel Taylor Coleridge** (1772–1834) was so impressed with Hartley's *Observations* that he named his first son David Hartley. Two years later, however, Coleridge's enthusiasm for Hartley's mechanical psychology had waned, and he named his second son Berkeley. Interestingly, Coleridge's critical self-examination of such problems as opium addiction anticipated modern research in psychopathology.

Hartley and Hume were contemporaries, and throughout the 18th century Hartley was at least as influential as Hume. In the introduction to a modern edition of Hartley's *Observations,* Huguelet (1966, p. xii) observed that the "true heir of Hartley's philosophy was the Utilitarian James Mill . . . , who employed the *Observations on Man* as the basis of his . . . *Analysis of the Phenomena of the Human Mind* (1829)."

James Mill and John Stuart Mill

James Mill

James Mill (1773–1836) was a shoemaker's son from Scotland. Sir John Stuart, a Baron of the Exchequer in Scotland, noticed Mill's brilliance and Mill attended the University of Edinburgh on a scholarship begun by Lady Jane Stuart and friends for educating young men to be Scottish Church ministers.

Licensed as a preacher in 1798, Mill never secured a congregation because people did not understand his sermons. He moved to London in 1802 and supported himself for the next 17 years through journalism and editorial work.

James Mill got married in 1805, and the following year a son, John Stuart, named for Mill's benefactor, was born. In John Stuart Mill's autobiography, there is no mention of his mother, although in an early draft he indirectly referred to her as someone whom his father "had not, and never could have supposed that he had, the inducements of kindred intellect, tastes, or pursuits" (J. S. Mill, 1873/1969, p. 4). Although James Mill and his wife were not kindred spirits, they eventually had nine children. Ironically, James Mill was an early proponent of birth control (Mazlish, 1975).

Hulton Archive.

James Mill (1773–1836)

In 1806, James Mill began writing *History of British India.* Published in 1817, it was an immediate success. In 1819, James Mill achieved financial security by taking a post at the East India Company, where he remained until his death.

Both James and John Stuart Mill were followers of **Jeremy Bentham** (1748–1832), a pioneer of **Utilitarianism.** The Utilitarian social movement taught that the goal of all behavior and legislation should be to achieve the "greatest good for the greatest number." Attracted by its simplicity and appeal to common sense, several generations of educated Englishmen were strongly influenced by Bentham's philosophy of Utilitarianism.

Bentham was extremely precocious, studying Latin grammar at 4, entering Queen's College in Oxford at 12, and earning his bachelor's degree at 15. At that point, he was admitted to Lincoln's Inn to study for a legal career, in accordance with his father's wishes. Bentham earned a master's degree at the age of 18 but decided against a career in law, opting instead for a literary career.

Bentham's orientation to philosophy was provided by the empiricists Locke and particularly Hume. We will see the central principle of his philosophy of utility—hedonism, or the search for pleasure, and the avoidance of pain—reflected in the work of the last of the British empiricists we will consider: Alexander Bain. In his *Introduction to the Principles of Morals and Legislation,* published in 1789, Bentham began by paying homage to the twin forces in human (and animal) nature: pleasure and pain. From them, he derived his principle of utility, which approves or disapproves of each of our actions based on whether the action either increases or diminishes happiness.

Further, Bentham developed a sort of hedonic calculus, which was an attempt to calculate mathematically how much pleasure or pain a particular action would produce. One difficulty with Bentham's pleasure–pain calculus, as pointed out later by John Stuart Mill, was that it focused exclusively on the quantitative aspects of pleasure, equating all actions that produced the same amount of pleasure. Thus, for Bentham, playing a game of cards would be equivalent to writing great poetry, if both actions led to the same amount of pleasure. Mill, on the other hand, noted that pleasures differ in quality as well as quantity, and he considered intellectual pleasures and other "higher" pleasures (e.g., of imagination and of moral sentiments) to have a greater value than pleasures of "mere sensation."

Bentham and James Mill took leading roles in founding University College, London, where Bentham's stuffed and clothed body, with his preserved head between his feet, remains on permanent display, as stipulated in his will.

Jeremy Bentham (1748–1832)

The Psychology of James Mill

In *Analysis of the Phenomena of the Human Mind* (1829), James Mill followed Hartley (and Hume with slightly different terminology) in making sensations and ideas the mind's basic elements. To Aristotle's five senses—vision, audition, olfaction, gustation, and touch—Mill added muscular sensations (e.g., feelings of contraction and relaxation), sensations of disorganization in any body part (e.g., itching, burning), and sensations from the alimentary canal (e.g., feelings in the stomach caused by seasickness). These sensations are the primary elements of consciousness, and ideas are copies of sensations that remain in the mind after the source of a sensation is removed. Unlike Hume, Mill did not think ideas are necessarily weaker than sensations.

In "The Association of Ideas," Mill gave the rules by which ideas are associated in the mind. In one passage, he used his "train of thought" to illustrate how sensations call forth ideas that trigger other ideas, and so on.

> If our senses are awake, we are continually receiving sensations. . . . After sensations, ideas are perpetually excited of sensations formerly received; after those ideas, other ideas: and during the whole of our lives, a series of those two states of consciousness, called sensations, and ideas, is constantly going on. I see a horse: that is a sensation. Immediately I think of his master: that is an idea. The idea of his master makes me think of his office; he is a minister of state: that is another idea. The idea of a minister of state makes me think of public affairs; and I am led into a train of political ideas; when I am summoned to dinner. This is a new sensation. . . . (Mill, 1869/1967, p. 70)

According to Mill, the strength of associations may vary because of vividness and frequency. The more vivid the paired ideas, the stronger will be their association. Similarly, the association between frequently paired ideas will tend to be stronger than that between ideas that occur together infrequently. Mill considered frequency the most important of the two determinants of an association's strength. Vividness and frequency can be found today in most theories of conception and categorization (e.g., Barsalou, 1985). The strength of associations can be seen in their permanence, certainty, and facility. More permanent associations are stronger than less permanent ones; more certain (i.e., more correct) associations are stronger; and easily formed associations are stronger.

Mill also believed that all associations occur from contiguity alone. Of causation, Mill (1869/1967) wrote: "Causation, the second of Mr. Hume's principles, is the same [as] contiguity in time, or the order of succession. Causation is only a name for the order established between an antecedent and a consequent . . ." (p. 110). Mill also reduced resemblance to contiguity. That is, we classify alike things together, not necessarily because of their similarity, but because they frequently have been grouped together in our experience. "When we see a tree, we generally see more trees than one; . . . a man, more men than one. From this observation, I think, we may refer resemblance to the law of frequency . . ." (p. 111).

Like Hartley, Mill wrote that contiguity could occur either from successive pairings of ideas or from ideas occurring synchronously. To illustrate, the words you are reading are associated successively, but the books in your bookcase are associated synchronously. Mill thought that many more sensations and ideas were received successively than synchronously.

Mill also distinguished simple ideas from complex ideas, which are combinations of simple and/or complex ideas. The uniting of two complex ideas, through association, Mill said that Hartley had called a **duplex idea.** In a footnote to the revised edition of his father's work, John Stuart Mill wrote: "I have been unable to trace in Hartley the expression here ascribed to him. In every passage that I can discover, the name [Hartley] gives to a combination of two or more complex ideas is that of a *decomplex* idea" (Mill, 1869/1967, p. 115, italics in the original).

Finally, in a frequently quoted passage, Mill carried the mental compounding model to its logical extreme:

> Brick is one complex idea, mortar is another complex idea; these ideas with ideas of position and quantity, compose my idea of a wall. My idea of a plank is a complex idea, my idea of a rafter is a complex idea, my idea of a nail is a complex idea. These, united with the same ideas of position and quantity, compose my duplex idea of a floor. In the same manner my complex idea of glass, and wood, and others, compose my duplex idea of a window; and these duplex ideas, united together, compose my idea of a house, which is made up of various duplex ideas. How many complex, or duplex ideas, are all united in the idea of furniture? . . . How many more in the idea called Every Thing? (Mill, 1869/1967, pp. 115–116)

Although it may be reasonable to conclude that the idea of everything comprises all the ideas of things, there is little reason to believe that a consciousness could simultaneously contain a limitless number of ideas. Thus, the passive association of ideas reached its peak in James Mill's mental compounding model. In the process, the model's flaws were exposed, and John Stuart Mill revised his father's views.

John Stuart Mill

Like his intellectual predecessors, James Mill took an extreme nurture approach, and, accordingly, he structured his firstborn son's experience to contain as many intellectual ideas as possible. The result was in one sense a triumph—John Stuart Mill (1873/1969) described himself as someone who "started . . . with an advantage of a quarter of a century over my contemporaries" (p. 20)—and in other ways a failure. John Stuart Mill suffered several episodes of depression, attributing them to his father's efforts: "My education, which was wholly his work, had been conducted without any regard to the possibility of its ending in [depression]; and I saw no use in giving him the pain of thinking that his plans had failed, when the failure was probably irremediable" (p. 82).

Following his father's and Jeremy Bentham's plan for his education, perhaps based on the French empiricist Claude Helvetius's (1715–1771) philosophy, **John Stuart Mill** (1806–1873) learned Greek when he was 3, committing to memory lists of Greek words and their English meanings that his father had written out for him on cards. Note that this feat indicates that Mill already knew how to read English. By the time he was 8, Mill had read a variety of classical Greek works, including Plato's first six dialogues and the writings of several Greek historians. Perhaps wistfully, he wrote, "Of children's books, any more than of playthings, I had scarcely any . . ." (Mill, 1873/ 1969, p. 7).

At 8, Mill learned Latin, teaching it to a younger sister as he progressed. At this time, he became

National Portrait Gallery, London.

John Stuart Mill (1806–1873) in old age

responsible for educating his siblings, a task he disliked because he was held accountable for them. Mill's reading continued in Greek, Latin, and English, and he also studied mathematics and science. One important book for his education was his father's *History of British India.* During the year before the book was published, when Mill was no more than 11 or 12, he read the manuscript while his father corrected the page proofs.

John Stuart Mill's education with his father as "headmaster" essentially ended at the age of 14, when the boy went to stay with Jeremy Bentham's brother's family in France. Before he left, John Stuart Mill's father told him that he would discover he had been taught many things his contemporaries did not know and that he would be complimented on his great knowledge. However, John Stuart Mill should take this as testimony to his father's efforts, not to how bright or learned he was.

Was John Stuart Mill (1873/1969) being disingenuous when he wrote, "in all these natural gifts [e.g., quick apprehension, an accurate and retentive memory] I am rather below than above par" (pp. 19–20)? Although John Stuart Mill was obviously extremely intelligent—one estimate put his IQ at 190, the highest IQ of any of 300 "geniuses" (Cox, 1926)—he seems to have attributed his accomplishments almost solely to his father's efforts. In his autobiography, Mill explained that his father persistently prevented him from hearing himself praised by others. "If I thought anything about myself, it was that I was rather backward in my studies, since I always found myself so, in comparison with what my father expected from me" (p. 21).

John Stuart Mill was particularly deficient in his emotions, which he insightfully attributed to the influence of both his parents. Mill (1873/1969) wrote of his father: "The element which was chiefly deficient in his [emotional] relation to his children, was that of tenderness" (p. 32). In a passage edited from the final document, he noted, "a really warm hearted mother, would in the first place have made my father a totally different being, and in the second would have made the children grow up loving and being loved. . . . [T]o make herself loved . . . required qualities which she unfortunately did not possess" (p. 33).

Still, John Stuart Mill was able to love at least one person, Harriet Taylor, whom he met in 1830. Mill was 25, and Harriet Taylor was 23, married, with two children. For slightly more than 2 decades, Mill maintained a Platonic but close relationship with Mrs. Taylor, who sometimes lived apart from her husband. In 1851, 2 years after she was widowed, Harriet Taylor became Harriet Mill. She died just 7 years later.

Outwardly impervious to their contemporaries' opinions, both Mill and Harriet Taylor suffered various ailments, at least some of which were probably psychosomatic. Harriet Taylor Mill was only 50 when she died.

The Psychology of John Stuart Mill

In 1843, John Stuart Mill published his most important work for psychology—*A System of Logic Ratiocinative and Inductive, Being a Connected View of the Principles of Evidence and the Methods of Scientific Investigation. A System of Logic,* as it is usually known, went through eight editions in Mill's lifetime.

In the book, Mill considered whether a science of human nature is possible. Although Auguste Comte (discussed later), whom Mill supported for a time (see Heyd, 1989), denied the possibility, Mill argued for it in a chapter titled "That There Is, or May Be, a Science of Human Nature." Mill (1884) wrote, "Any facts are fitted . . . to be a subject of science" (p. 552) and that included psychology's facts. Mill recognized that psychology did not have the exactness of a science such as astronomy, "but there is no reason that it should not be as much a science as . . . Astronomy was when its calculations had only mastered the main phenomena . . ." (pp. 553–554).

Like the earlier British empiricists and associationists, John Stuart Mill divided the mind's contents into impressions and ideas. But unlike his father, Mill returned to Hume's distinction between impressions and ideas, in which ideas are necessarily weaker than the impressions giving rise to them.

To Hume's similarity and contiguity, Mill added intensity. "The third law [of association] is, that greater intensity in either or both of the impressions, is equivalent, in rendering them excitable by one another, to a greater frequency of conjunction" (Mill, 1884, p. 557). By intensity, Mill meant the vividness his father had mentioned as a factor affecting an association's strength.

John Stuart Mill's major addition to psychology was the idea of a **mental chemistry.** Using the rules of the association of ideas, James Mill had devised mental compounding, in which all the elements of a complex idea still exist, although they may have disappeared through associative coalescence. The idea thus formed might appear to be a simple idea, but James Mill believed it still consisted of all the simple ideas comprising it, even though breaking it into its components would be difficult.

John Stuart Mill extended his father's analysis of the combining of ideas as follows:

> [T]he laws of the phenomena of mind are sometimes analogous to mechanical, but sometimes also to chemical laws . . . so it appears to me that the Complex Idea, formed by the blending together of several simpler ones, should, when it really appears simple, (that is, when the separate elements are not consciously distinguishable in it,) be said to *result from,* or *be generated by,* the simple ideas, not to *consist* of them. . . . These therefore are cases of mental chemistry, in which it is proper to say that the simple ideas generate, rather than that they compose, the complex ones. (J. S. Mill, 1884, p. 558, italics in the original)

Thus, for John Stuart Mill the whole idea was sometimes the sum of its parts, as his father had written, but sometimes it was an idea *generated* by its simple components, not consisting of them.

Mill's Science of Character Formation

John Stuart Mill did not stop with a science of psychology; he also envisioned a subdivision of psychology he called *ethology,* which would be the science of the formation of character. Note that Mill was not using the term *ethology* (Chapter 12) in the sense we use it today—as the science that studies animal behavior in relation to the animal's natural environment. Mill's ethology would study character formation, or how the environment shapes differences in individual humans. As he put it, "Every individual is surrounded by circumstances different from those of every other individual . . . and none of these differences are without their influence in forming a different type of character" (Mill, 1884, p. 564).

Mill did not believe in a universal human character, but he did think there were universal laws for the formation of character. He did not think the laws could be determined experimentally, however. The appropriate experiment would require

> a number of human beings to bring up and educate from infancy to mature age; and . . . it would be necessary to know and record every sensation or [impression] received by the young pupil from a period long before it could speak. . . . It is not only impossible to do this completely, but even to do so much of it as should constitute a tolerable approximation. (Mill, 1884, p. 565)

Because of the impossibility of direct experimentation or even of "simple observation" for determining the laws of character formation, Mill concluded that his ethology would be of necessity a deductive science, "a system of corollaries from Psychology, the experimental science" (Mill, 1884, p. 569). In the eighth edition of his *System of Logic*, Mill admitted that little had been done to develop such a science. From what we know of the early life of John Stuart Mill, it is entirely possible that his interest in a science of human character formation was a direct result of the strange circumstances that had led to his own character development.

The Influence of the Mills

James Mill's mental compounding through the laws of association is considered the culmination of British associationism and a psychological dead end. His son's mental chemistry, however, was an important concept we will see reflected in the writings of William James and the Gestalt psychologists. John Stuart Mill's support of the possibility of a science of psychology may have influenced Wundt, who established psychology as a separate scientific discipline shortly after Mill's death.

The final British associationist was a friend of John Stuart Mill, assisted in Mill's revision of his father's *Analysis of the Phenomena of the Human Mind*, wrote biographies of both Mills, has been called the first true psychologist, and brought British associationism to a climax.

Alexander Bain

Like James Mill, whom he greatly admired, **Alexander Bain** (1818–1903) was Scottish. He was born in Aberdeen, the son of a weaver. Bain was perhaps as precocious as John Stuart Mill but without Mill's educational advantages. He worked at the loom to pay for an irregular education and often had to borrow books to increase his knowledge. By 17, Bain had taught himself geometry, algebra, trigonometry, and Newtonian calculus. He had studied astronomy, natural philosophy, and Hume and was learning Latin from Newton's *Principia* and an English translation. Bain was fortunate to have been born in perhaps the only country at the time where someone poor, but intellectually gifted, could go to a university fairly easily. Bain entered Marischal College, where he shared with another student the school's highest honors upon graduation.

Alexander Bain (1818–1903)

For the next 20 years, Bain supported himself in London and Scotland with freelance writing. Attempts to secure a university position were rebuffed because of his youthful radicalism and because he never became a church member; instead he became an agnostic (Macmillan, 2000). Finally, in 1860 he was appointed Professor of Logic at the University of Aberdeen, where he remained for the rest of his life. His appointment was aided by the publication of his two most important works: *The Senses and the Intellect* (1855) and *The Emotions and the Will* (1859).

Bain's Psychology

A systematic treatise on psychology, Bain's two books were published separately because the first volume failed to find a ready market. Despite their initial lack of success, Bain spent much of his last 40 years revising the works that became the standard British psychological text.

Like Hartley, Bain linked psychology with physiological processes. Unlike Hartley, Bain used physiological processes that were as real as contemporary knowledge could make them rather than being based on speculative Newtonian physiology. For Bain, mental and bodily events occurred in parallel, without a causal relation between them. However, contrary to the opinion of some, Bain did not originate psychophysical parallelism, a distinction we attributed to Leibniz in Chapter 4.

One of Bain's most original contributions to psychology was his discussion of the origin and development of voluntary behavior. Bain combined the effects of pleasure and pain (hedonic effects) with spontaneous behavior to produce what is formalized in Thorndike's law of effect. It was probably significant for Bain's development that his friend John Stuart Mill applied his "greatest happiness principle" to politics and to personal morals. Mill derived the principle by adapting the criterion of utility originated by his father and Jeremy Bentham.

Bain's linkage of spontaneous behavior with the "greatest happiness principle" apparently stemmed from observations he made on the behavior of lambs during their first few hours of life. Initial movements produce only chance contact with the mother. However, these contacts lead to more directed behavior, and in less than 24 hours, at the sight of its mother, the lamb approaches her, finds the teat, and begins to feed. An association has been made between a particular stimulus (i.e., the sight of the mother's teat) and the movements needed to reach it. Bain provided other examples of this "trial and error" behavior to suggest that the process "was the universal means by which voluntary control over spontaneous activity is first achieved" (Boakes, 1984, p. 9). He was unable to suggest a physiological basis for the process, writing:

> I cannot descend deeper into the . . . cerebral organization than to state . . . that when pain co-exists with an accidental alleviating movement, or when pleasure co-exists with a pleasure-sustaining movement, such movements become subject to the control of the respective feelings which they occur in company with. . . . Turn it over as we may on every side, some such ultimate connexion between the two great primary manifestations of our nature—pleasure and pain, with active instrumentality—must be assumed as the basis of our ability to work out ends. (Bain, 1859, p. 349)

Bain's statement contains all the elements of the law of effect, the idea that successful behaviors tend to be repeated whereas unsuccessful behaviors drop out. We can trace a connection between Bain and Thorndike through C. Lloyd Morgan (Chapter 12), a British comparative psychologist whom Bain influenced. In 1896, Morgan lectured at Harvard on his learning studies with chickens. A graduate student at Harvard, Thorndike soon began his own studies on the intelligence of chickens and other animals, which led to his 1898 statement of the law of effect.

Bain's Influence

In 1876, Bain founded the journal ***Mind***, which, despite its philosophical bent, may be considered the first journal of psychology. Bain chose **George Croom Robertson** (1842–1892), a former student of his, to be the journal's first editor. Robertson proved to be an exceptional editor; when he retired because of illness, he received a gold watch and a signed letter of gratitude for his services from 74 *Mind* contributors. Although *Mind* was not a journal of experimental findings, this was caused by the lack of such research in England at the time, as Robertson was steadfast in his efforts to promote "scientific psychology" (King, 2000).

As we will see, the beginning of experimental psychology occurred in Germany, and the first modern experimental psychology journal was started by Wundt 7 years after *Mind* appeared. *Mind* remains a respected vehicle for essays in the philosophy of psychology and the philosophy of mind.

Some authorities consider Alexander Bain the first true psychologist, although the same claim could be made about others, such as Hume, Hartley, and James Mill. Boakes (1984) suggested that Bain is the first psychologist because he devoted almost his entire career to the study of mind and behavioral phenomena.

Although Descartes and Hartley both presented neurological explanations for actions, their explanatory mechanisms were fanciful. Because Bain applied known physiological mechanisms in his explanations, he is also often considered the first physiological psychologist (see Macmillan, 2000).

In Bain's interest in and explanations for voluntary behavior, we see much that probably influenced behaviorism's founders. His work signals the end of philosophical associationism, the armchair associationism of Hartley, the Mills, and Bain himself. After Bain—whose most important publications for psychology came in the 1850s—we will see the growth of the experimental approach to psychology.

FRENCH EMPIRICISM

In France, as in England, some philosophers sought to explain the mind as Newton had explained the universe, through the use of a few basic elements and principles. As we noted in Chapter 4, in Descartes' mind-body dualism, people had minds as well as bodies, but animals were mechanical, without a mind (or soul), and thus effectively separated from humans. Several of Descartes' French successors were impressed with his belief in the mechanical actions of animals and thought a mechanistic explanation for animal actions might generalize to human behavior as well. That is, perhaps humans are merely automata or machines. The idea of man as a machine particularly appealed to Julien Offray de La Mettrie, whose life and work we covered in Chapter 4.

In Chapter 4, we briefly discussed French philosopher and scientist Pierre Gassendi, one of Descartes' most ardent critics. As we indicated, Gassendi opposed Descartes' interactive dualism by arguing that an immaterial mind cannot influence or be influenced by a material body. Further, Gassendi argued that the mind's operations originate from the workings of the brain and that humans are just matter that is potentially as understandable as anything else in the universe. Gassendi's materialistic or physical monism was similar to that endorsed in antiquity by Democritus. We saw Gassendi's influence in La Mettrie's writings, and we will also see it in the mechanistic empiricism of Condillac.

Étienne Bonnot de Condillac

Étienne Bonnot (1715–1780) was a French Jesuit priest who became the Abbot of Condillac; hence, **Étienne Bonnot de Condillac**. Condillac was a friend of French social philosopher Jean-Jacques Rousseau, and although he did not read English, he greatly admired John Locke. As a priest, Condillac probably would not have read La Mettrie, although his work is sufficiently reminiscent of La Mettrie's to suggest its author was familiar with the latter's mechanistic writings.

At first, Condillac's writings on reflection and sensation as the sources of knowledge basically parroted Locke in French. Later, Condillac's work assumed a more mechanistic tone, and he argued in *Treatise on Sensation* (1754) that logically only sensation could be a source of knowledge. In *Treatise*, Condillac asked readers to picture a marble statue, internally organized like themselves, but with a mind free of ideas. The *sentient statue* has only the sense of smell and can distinguish pleasure from pain. From this, Condillac tried to show that all forms of thought could be derived from sensations alone. With four other senses, the statue would develop a complex mind.

In short, Condillac suggested that the higher mental processes used in Locke's reflection originated from sensation. Condillac also rejected instinct as an innate process blind to experience, instead advocating an extreme nurture position that better fits our modern "blank slate" conception of Locke's empiricism than Locke himself fits it.

Like La Mettrie, Condillac held that the study of animals should be useful in understanding humans because the same mechanisms and processes give rise to sensation and knowledge in both. Thus, Condillac can be seen as further departing from Descartes' philosophical disinterest in animals and moving toward empirical psychology's wide use of animals to explore general principles of learning and motivation.

By the late 18th century, aided by Cartesian critics such as Nicholas de Malebranche and Pierre Gassendi (both Chapter 4), Condillac's mechanistic empiricism had replaced Descartes' rationalistic philosophy in French schools. Condillac also influenced other important Continental empiricists and mechanists, such as **Charles Étienne Bonnet**

Étienne Bonnot de Condillac (1715–1780)

(1720–1793), a Swiss empiricist impressed by the sentient statue's logic. Bonnet was a naturalist until failing eyesight forced him to abandon insect experimentation for philosophy. Trained in biology, Bonnet added physiology to Condillac's statue. Condillac also influenced **Antoine Destutt de Tracy** (1754–1836), a French mechanist who believed that mental phenomena were mechanistically caused by biological phenomena. For him, understanding how sensations led to knowledge required understanding how the brain received and processed sensory experience. However, Destutt de Tracy's contemporary, Pierre Cabanis, was the premier French mechanist.

Pierre Jean Georges Cabanis

Pierre Jean Georges Cabanis (1757–1808) was such an indifferent student that his father sent him to Paris to fend for himself. There, he read the classics and more contemporary writings by Descartes, La Mettrie, Condillac, Locke, and Goethe (Chapter 6). Adding Hippocrates and Galen to his reading, Cabanis became a doctor and was briefly the personal physician to Mirabeau (1749–1791), a leader of the French Revolution. Cabanis was a member of the Committee of Five Hundred, the revolutionary ruling body of France, before becoming a professor of medicine at the University of Paris in 1799.

Although Cabanis is considered primarily a mechanist and empiricist, his writings contain elements of **vitalism,** the notion that life is caused by a principle distinct from chemical and physical forces. A move toward **panpsychism,** the idea that mind or soul pervades everything, is also evident in Cabanis' work. However, Cabanis is best known for his views on the biological basis of mental events.

Cabanis' mind-body interest apparently began when he was asked to determine whether guillotine victims were still conscious after being beheaded. Despite reports of eye movements in disembodied heads and of headless bodies standing and moving around, Cabanis concluded that neither the heads nor the bodies were conscious. The brain was necessary for consciousness, and the movements were just reflex actions.

For Cabanis, the brain was the organ designed to produce thought, just as the stomach and intestines perform digestion. Expressing a modern view of the relation between mental events and brain processes, he suggested that mental events *are* brain processes. This view led to the 19th-century interest in the localization of mental functions in specific brain areas (Chapter 7) and also to the eventual reconceptualization of mental abnormality as "mental illness." Among the many candidates for the title of the first physiological psychologist (e.g., Descartes, Hartley, Bain), Cabanis fits this label as well as any and better than most.

A contemporary of Cabanis, **François-Pierre Maine de Biran** (1766–1824) was, like Cabanis, part vitalist philosopher and part physiologist. He advocated a type of "experimental psychology," which, nevertheless, was quite different from that of Wundt. Maine de Biran eventually drifted from experimental psychology toward a Cartesian spiritualism (i.e., toward an interest in a soul separate from the body and deserving of study). Freud was probably influenced by Maine de Biran's belief that much of importance in life is not experienced consciously.

Two other French empiricists are noteworthy: Hippolyte Taine and Théodule Ribot. **Hippolyte Adolphe Taine** (1828–1893) is sometimes called the French Bain. Taine's 1875 work, *On Intelligence*, was reportedly used by William James at Harvard. Taine's similarities to Bain include a belief in psychophysical parallelism and associationism and an interest in the physiology of mental events. Although Taine's academic position was in aesthetics, he strongly influenced the development of French empirical psychology.

Taine's 1876 journal article on children's language acquisition stimulated the interest of the journal's publisher, **Théodule Armand Ribot** (1839–1916), in child development. Ribot is generally considered by historians to have founded French scientific psychology through his books on 19th-century British and German psychology, his chair at the *Collège de France*, and his assistance in organizing the first laboratory of experimental psychology in France (Nicolas & Murray, 1999). Nicolas and Charvillat (2001) have described the context in which the teaching of psychology as an autonomous subject began in France and have reproduced Ribot's first psychology lecture at the *Collège de France* in 1888. Ribot also helped organize the First International Congress of Psychology, which was held in 1889 with Ribot as president. His journal, *Revue Philosophique*, was the French equivalent of Bain's *Mind* (Hilgard, 1987).

POSITIVISM

British empiricists and French mechanists shared the belief that knowledge comes from experience. By Wundt's time (i.e., the latter part of the 19th century), empiricism's focus on experience had begun to shape the understanding of science itself. One approach to science was based only on empirical observation—on observable scientific facts and their logical relations to each other. Called **positivism,** this system originated with the ideas of Auguste Comte.

Auguste Comte

Auguste Marie François Xavier Comte (1798–1857) was born at Montpellier, in southern France. Benjamin Franklin (1706–1790), whom Comte called the modern Socrates, was the idol of his youth. The France of Comte's boyhood had just endured the Revolution, and it was a time of political upheaval. This instability influenced Comte's main philosophical goal, which was the total reorganization of society in accordance with science.

Comte's personal life also was filled with turmoil and upheaval. Twice he was committed to an insane asylum, once following a brief, unhappy marriage and attempted suicide, and again after the death of the love of his life, Clotilde de Vaux.

Comte's major work, *Cours de Philosophie Positive* (*Course of Positive Philosophy*), was published in several volumes between 1830 and 1842. The work won Comte a number of adherents, including John Stuart Mill, who for a time helped Comte financially. After de Vaux's death, Comte alienated many of his admirers with his efforts to establish his positive philosophy as a religion. In his Religion of Humanity, Comte exalted the human being as an object of worship. As one wag put it, his religion had all the trappings of the Catholic Church (e.g., a priesthood, sacraments, saints, etc.) without the Christianity. Comte himself was the High Priest.

Although Comte is credited with originating positive philosophy, or positivism, the ideas were part of the *Zeitgeist,* according to John Stuart Mill. Positivism can be understood as a movement that rejects the notion of an ultimate goal or purpose to nature, just as it rejects the idea of secret causes of things (it is antimetaphysical). Positivism seeks to replace not only religion, but philosophy itself, with science. Seeking explanations of phenomena at progressively more basic levels, it is reductionistic and aims to formulate the laws of science as the laws of constant relations among phenomena. Positivism's facts are to be gathered through empirical, objective observations.

Comte's philosophical approach stemmed from his **Law of Three Stages.** First comes the *theological stage,* in which phenomena are explained by the

Stock Montage.

Auguste Comte (1798–1857)

dictates of some deity. Thought next moves to the *metaphysical stage,* in which divine concepts are replaced by impersonal abstractions. For example, in astronomy's metaphysical stage, stars were thought to move in circles because the circle was considered the most perfect geometric shape. The third stage is the *positivistic,* or *scientific stage,* which Comte said implies experiment, observation, and the explanation of phenomena through the laws of natural cause and effect.

Before Comte began to propagandize his Religion of Humanity, he sought to establish a science of society whose goal was to serve humanity. He called this science sociology and placed it at the apex of the sciences, which, in order of decreasing generality and increasing complexity, were mathematics, astronomy, physics, chemistry, biology, and sociology. Comte intentionally omitted psychology because he did not think a science of the mind was possible, particularly if that science used introspection as its principal method (Wilson, 1991). According to Comte,

> the mind may observe all phenomena but its own. . . . In order to observe, your intellect must pause from activity; yet it is this very activity that you want to observe. If you cannot effect the pause, you cannot observe: if you do effect it, there is nothing to observe. (Comte; Commins & Linscott, 1954, p. 234)

John B. Watson (Chapter 12) similarly criticized introspection in 1913, and the success that Watson and later behaviorists earned by emphasizing the observation of behavior owed much to positivism.

Comte's later writings were strongly influenced by his brief love affair with Clotilde de Vaux. Stressing the intellect as a reforming force in his early writings, he placed feelings above intellect after 1845. Still, he considered the aim of human effort to be the improvement of the human condition. Comte believed that the altruistic nature of people was an established fact. The phrenologist Franz Joseph Gall (Chapter 7) claimed there was a benevolence organ in the human brain, and Comte believed in phrenology.

We can see Comte as a member of the list of thinkers concerned with scientific method, empiricism, objectivism, and the acceptance only of absolutely certain facts. This list begins with Francis Bacon (Chapter 4) and Thomas Hobbes and includes most of the empiricists and associationists. In some ways, this early positivism can be seen as culminating in the writings of another English psychological philosopher, Herbert Spencer (Chapter 9). The list also suggests why Comte's positivist movement gained more adherents in England than it did in France. Another version of positivism arose in Germany—Ernst Mach's.

Ernst Mach

Ernst Mach (1838–1916) was born in Turas, Moravia, then part of Austria. Mach studied at Vienna, became professor of mathematics at Graz for 3 years, physics professor at Prague for 28 of his most productive years, and then professor of physics at Vienna.

Although he was a physicist, Mach published many observations relevant for psychology, including work on visual space perception (see Banks, 2001), the perception of bodily rotation, and a theory of hearing. His most important work for psychology was published in 1886, *Analyse der Empfindungen (Analysis of Sensations)*, although there were other contributions (Arens, 1985).

In *Analysis*, Mach established what has been called early modern positivism or, sometimes, Machian positivism. The purpose of Machian positivism was to establish a set of basic rules that would ensure the integrity of science. The main idea is that sensations are the basic data of science. That is, science is public and observational, and the data of observation are sensory experiences. Positivism under Mach was evolving into a set of guidelines for the proper conduct of legitimate science.

One major difference in the positivisms of Comte and Mach lay in the type of evidence each man was willing to investigate. Mach accepted Hume's assertion that we never experience the physical world directly, that all we can know of the external world is the evidence of our senses. Thus, Mach was willing to place equal importance on psychic and physical facts. Comte, by contrast, accepted only physical events as worthy of investigation, and, as we have noted, rejected a science of psychology based on introspection. Mach saw data from the observation of consciousness as legitimate, thereby justifying introspection.

Independently, **Richard Avenarius** (1843–1896) expressed similar ideas about the proper conduct of science, worked out in careful detail. According to Boring (1950), Zürich philosophy professor Avenarius "was as difficult, uninspiring and involved a thinker as Mach was simple, dramatic and clear" (p. 395). Furthermore, Avenarius's books "were even more difficult to write than to read, for they broke Avenarius's health and he died not long after their publication" (p. 396). Still, Avenarius was admired by Titchener (Chapter 8), who organized his conception of structural psychology in accordance with positivistic principles.

Somewhat after Mach and Avenarius, Rudolf Carnap (Chapter 13), **Moritz Schlick** (1882–1936), and other members of the **Vienna Circle** continued positivism's refinement through a systematic investigation of the logic of science. Known as **logical positivism,** Carnap and Schlick's movement rejected most traditional metaphysics as giving meaningless solutions to pseudoproblems. In psychology, both modern and logical positivism set the stage for behaviorism. As we will see in Chapters 12 and 13, the objective approach to science required by positivism favored behaviorism's takeover of psychology, and Watson was simply part of that movement (Mackenzie, 1972).

A common goal of all positivistic philosophies has been to make science primary. Because of this, Comte, "modern" positivism, and logical positivism are three connected, but different, attempts to bolster the nature and status of science. In turn, the alliance of positivism and behaviorism greatly enhanced psychology's standing as a scientific discipline.

Ernst Mach (1838–1916)

THE SCOTTISH SCHOOL

As we noted earlier, David Hume took the logical step beyond Berkeley's philosophical position. Berkeley had written that things exist in being perceived and that the very permanence of the external world validates God's existence. As a nonbeliever, Hume could not invoke God's infinite mind to explain the apparent permanence of reality, which led him to conclude that we have direct knowledge only of the mind's processes, a knowledge that does not permit us to be certain of anything.

In Hume's native Scotland, a number of philosophers felt that Hume and British empiricism had gone too far down the path of skepticism. It was time to return to a grounding in reality, to the certainty of knowledge. Stimulated by Hume into philosophical activity, Thomas Reid was the first member of what became known as the Scottish School, although Hume's skepticism may not have been the only force behind the school's development (see Robinson, 1989). Reid's school is called the **Scottish School** because its major members were all professors at Scottish universities.

Philosophical Library, New York.

Thomas Reid (1710 1796)

Thomas Reid

Thomas Reid (1710–1796) was born into an important and well-educated Scottish family in Strachen, near Aberdeen. He came from a long line of Presbyterian ministers, and like many of them, he combined religious and academic pursuits (Brooks, 1976). Reid spent much of his life and career affiliated with the University of Aberdeen, from which he graduated at 16. He worked there as a librarian, a minister, and a professor before he took Glasgow's chair of moral philosophy in 1764. (A "chair" is normally the pinnacle rank of academia.)

Reid's connection to Hume was not limited to a common Scottish ancestry or vocation (both were librarians for a time). Although he admitted the soundness of Hume's logic, Reid disagreed with Hume's thesis that the mind knows only its own processes and can only infer the existence of anything outside itself. This premise offended common sense, and Reid's position is called either "common-sense" psychology or the Scottish School of moral philosophy ("moral philosophy" was the name given to psychological theory until almost the 20th century). Note that Aristotle (Chapter 2) used the term *common sense* to refer to a sense beyond the traditional five that integrates or assimilates information from the other senses.

Reid replaced the empiricist's view of the mind as a passive collection of ideas with a faculty-based, action-oriented psychology (e.g., Brooks, 1976). For Reid, the mind was an entity containing a variety of active powers or faculties. He identified 24 such powers (e.g., self-preservation, hunger) and 6 intellectual powers (e.g., judgment, memory, perception). The phrenologist Franz Joseph Gall (Chapter 7) took the faculties that he localized in brain areas from Reid and his followers. Reid himself "provided neither a physiological explanation for the operation of the faculties nor offered any suggestions regarding their physiological location" (Brooks, p. 71). Reid's approach is sometimes called **faculty psychology.**

We can see in Reid many connections to subsequent philosophical and psychological positions. For example, in repudiating Hume's skepticism, Reid adopted a common-sense method involving an analysis of ordinary language. Reid's approach is similar to modern-day ordinary-language philosophy (e.g., Wittgenstein, 1953; Chapter 18). Reid's view of perceptual acts as contacting real objects also heralds Franz Brentano's act psychology (Chapter 8). Reid assumed that many of the mind's faculties are innate, and we find his nativism in Gestalt psychology and in the writings of a host of early American psychologists.

The Scottish common-sense doctrine was well received by early American psychologists (Chapter 10). This was particularly true at Princeton, where the president, James McCosh, wrote a textbook that provided competition for William James's *Principles of Psychology.* Reid's chief popularizer was his student, Dugald Stewart.

Dugald Stewart (1753–1828) was born, reared, and educated in Edinburgh, where his father was Professor of Mathematics. Stewart also studied in Glasgow under Reid and for 35 years was Professor of Moral Philosophy at Edinburgh. Scottish philosophers with ties to this chair shaped and influenced early psychology in America.

As Reid's chief interpreter, Stewart lectured at Edinburgh to classes filled with people seeking intellectual expansion. In addition to popularizing Reid's faculty psychology, Stewart is known for two of his students: James Mill and **Thomas Brown** (1778–1820). Brown eventually claimed Stewart's Edinburgh chair, where he produced a compromise between Scottish common-sense psychology and British associationism. To avoid the Scottish aversion to associationism that had developed because of its connection with Hume's atheistic skepticism, Brown named his principle for the connection of ideas *suggestion.* His primary laws of suggestion were resemblance, contrast, and nearness in time and space, which you may recognize as the principles (similarity, contrast, contiguity) Aristotle described as important for the recall of an event.

As we noted, Reid's solution to the doubt Hume had cast on the reality of external objects was to appeal to a common-sense notion of external validity. It makes common sense for us to trust the impressions we receive from the external world. Brown argued that our belief that external objects exist comes from the felt resistance of muscular exertion. The smell of a rose is initially pure sensation, but when the smell accompanies muscular effort to move the flower, the sensations come to suggest resistance, implying that we have perceived a real object. Brown's theory of perception directly anticipated that of Lotze (Chapter 6).

In his lectures, Brown also talked about a *mental chemistry,* using the term to refer to the outcome of a psychological combination that no longer resembled its components. Somewhat later, John Stuart Mill further developed, and is recognized for, the mental chemistry idea.

Because of Brown's compromises with associationism, it is difficult to know whether to include him with the Scottish School or to classify him as a British associationist whose work slightly preceded that of the Mills. Further, Mills (1987) established connections between Brown and the French empiricists Condillac and Destutt de Tracy. Perhaps because he stayed in Scotland and was so closely associated with Stewart, he is generally considered part of the Scottish School.

CONCLUSIONS

Beginning with Hobbes, we see the unification of themes that provided the groundwork for empirical psychology. These themes—determinism, materialism, reductionism, and a nurturist approach to the origin of ideas—were not original with empiricism. However, against the backdrop of scientists such as Galileo and Newton, Hobbes's appropriated themes presaged a new era for psychology.

Locke, Berkeley, and Hume built on Hobbes's themes and reshaped them into British empiricism. Although each of the British empiricists held unique views about the nature of mind and humans, two features of their work emerged to spark later traditions: the association of ideas and a strong nurturist philosophy.

Although associationist overtures can be found in Hobbes and Locke, Hume is the transitional figure between the *philosophy* of British empiricism and the *psychology* of the British associationists Hartley, the Mills, and Bain. We can characterize British associationism as an early form of "modern" psychology because of the clear influence the associationists had on such later empirical psychologists as James and Wundt.

The strong nurturist viewpoint of the British empiricists—that all the mind's ideas come through experience with the external world—was the second feature that figured prominently in other traditions. As we have seen, the nurturist idea spread to France where it was pushed to logical extremes in the works of La Mettrie and Condillac. In fact, Condillac's sentient statue illustrates two of the fundamental propositions of empiricism: the primacy of sense data and the passive reception of such data by the mind. This period witnessed the waning of Descartes' influence on French thought and the rise of French psychology through Cabanis, Taine, and Ribot. As is true of the British, we now more clearly recognize as psychological the theorists with interests in physiology and association.

Psychology as a science owes an enormous debt to positivism, which traces its roots to Auguste Comte. Positivism matured into an important philosophy of science under Mach and Avenarius and stood as the gatekeeper of all the sciences from physics to psychology by the time of the Vienna Circle. By establishing the ground rules for proper science during an era in which science rose from hobby to religion, positivism's gatekeeping function cannot be overestimated. In psychology, behaviorism under Watson, Skinner, and Hull allied itself with positivistic conceptions of science in order to flourish.

French empiricism (mechanism or materialism) and British associationism were not the only products of British empiricism. There was also the Scottish School under the direction of Reid, Stewart, and Brown. The Scottish School advocated faculty psychology, a view that in modern dress continues to be a viable alternative as a theory of mind (see Fodor, 1983).

Many of the people covered in this chapter were contemporaries, both of each other and of the "Continentals" we will cover in the next chapter. This chapter, in conjunction with the next, lays out the empiricism-rationalism debate along which many subsequent issues in psychology can be mapped.

SUMMARY

The chapter's main theme is empiricism—the search for knowledge through experience rather than through reasoning. The British empiricists (Hobbes, Locke, Berkeley, and Hume) sought to explain the mind through a few basic, observed principles.

British Empiricism

Thomas Hobbes sought the union of philosophy and geometry. He rejected Descartes' belief in innate ideas for the belief that sensations produce all the mind's ideas, which are linked by contiguity. Like Democritus, Hobbes was a determinist, a materialist, a reductionist, a nurturist, and an empiricist.

In *An Essay Concerning Human Understanding,* John Locke described the mind as initially like "white paper," devoid of ideas. Experience provides sensations and reflection (the operations of the mind on the ideas from sensation). Simple ideas cannot be further divided, and complex ideas are a combination of simple ideas. Locke distinguished primary and secondary qualities of objects and believed there is substance behind secondary qualities.

Leibniz objected to Locke's characterization of the mind at birth as "white paper." To the empiricist creed "There is nothing in the intellect that was not first in the senses" Leibniz added "except the intellect itself." However, Leibniz may have attacked a Locke who never existed.

George Berkeley gave an empiricist account of the development of visual depth perception in *An Essay Towards a New Theory of Vision.* In *A Treatise Concerning the Principles of Human Knowledge,* Berkeley concluded that "to be, is to be perceived," and he attributed the ultimate reality of objects to God's infinite mind. Only secondary qualities existed for Berkeley, whose mind-body position has been called mentalism, immaterialism, or subjective idealism.

David Hume accepted Locke's and Berkeley's empiricism, dividing the mind's contents into impressions (lively perceptions) and ideas (faint copies of impressions). Hume explicitly named the principles of the association of ideas: resemblance and contiguity. He attributed causality to a habit of the mind rather than to a "necessary connection" between events.

British Associationism

The British associationists elevated the association concept to a doctrine. David Hartley founded associationism with *Observations on Man, His Frame, His Duty and His Expectations.* Because of his medical background, Hartley gave associationist ideas a physiological basis, and his work can be seen as Hume translated to the physiological level.

James Mill took passive associationism to its logical conclusion. Ideas are copies of sensations; through contiguity, simple ideas unite to become complex ideas and the union of complex ideas produces duplex ideas. James Mill's son, John Stuart Mill, added mental chemistry—an idea is generated by its simple components rather than consisting of them—to mental compounding.

Alexander Bain's *The Senses and the Intellect* and *The Emotions and the Will* became the standard British psychological texts for nearly 50 years. Bain's linkage of spontaneous behavior with the "greatest happiness principle" anticipated Thorndike's law of effect. Bain's journal *Mind* can be considered the world's first journal of psychology.

French Empiricism

Like their British counterparts, French empiricists sought to explain the mind through the use of basic components and principles. The French empiricists thought it might be possible to generalize a mechanical explanation of animal behavior to the behavior of humans.

In *Treatise on Sensation,* Étienne Bonnot de Condillac created a "sentient statue," with only one sense (smell) and the ability to distinguish pleasure from pain. From this, Condillac tried to show that all forms of thought could be derived from sensations alone. Charles Étienne Bonnet added physiology to Condillac's statue, and Antoine Destutt de Tracy believed that mental phenomena were caused by biological phenomena.

Pierre Jean Georges Cabanis concluded that the brain is necessary for consciousness and that mental events are brain processes. Cabanis's contemporary, François-Pierre Maine de Biran, advocated an introspective method he called "experimental psychology."

Hippolyte Adolphe Taine is sometimes called the French Bain because of similarities in the two men. One of Taine's papers stimulated Théodule Armand Ribot's interest in child development.

Positivism

Originated by Auguste Comte, positivism is a philosophical system based only on empirical observation—that is, on observable scientific facts and their interrelations. For Comte, the development of each field of thought moved through three stages: the theological stage, the metaphysical stage, and the positivistic or scientific stage. Comte did not think a science of the mind using introspection was possible.

Physicist Ernst Mach worked on visual space perception and audition, and his *Analysis of Sensations* established Machian positivism, whose central idea is that sensations are the basic data of all science. Independently, Richard Avenarius expressed similar ideas. Later, Rudolf Carnap and Moritz Schlick developed logical positivism, a movement that rejected most traditional metaphysics and aided the rise of behaviorism.

The Scottish School

Thomas Reid, Dugald Stewart, and Thomas Brown, professors at Scottish universities, comprised the common-sense or Scottish School of psychology. Reid was stimulated by Hume's empirical skepticism to found a common-sense psychology in which the mind was seen as an entity containing 24 active powers and 6 intellectual powers. Stewart popularized Reid's faculty psychology and is perhaps best known for his students, James Mill and Thomas Brown. Brown compromised common-sense psychology with British associationism, calling his mechanism for combining the mind's elements suggestion rather than association.

CONNECTIONS QUESTIONS

1. How many different connections can you make between Aristotle's ideas and the ideas of the various philosophers discussed in this chapter?
2. How does the mind-body problem connect to empiricism?
3. What connections can you make between the empirical psychologists and contemporary psychological theory?
4. In what ways did political events connect to philosophical psychology during this period?
5. How is positivism connected to psychology?

KEY NAMES AND TERMS

association of ideas (p. 98)
associationism (p. 100)
Richard Avenarius (p. 113)
Alexander Bain (p. 107)
Jeremy Bentham (p. 102)
George Berkeley (p. 94)
Charles Étienne Bonnet (p. 109)
Thomas Brown (p. 115)
Pierre Jean Georges Cabanis (p. 110)
causality (p. 98)
Samuel Taylor Coleridge (p. 101)
complex ideas (p. 90)
Auguste Marie François Xavier Comte (p. 111)
Étienne Bonnot de Condillac (p. 109)
conditioned taste aversion (p. 91)
convergence (p. 95)
duplex idea (p. 104)
empiricism (p. 86)
faculty psychology (p. 115)
David Hartley (p. 100)
Thomas Hobbes (p. 87)
David Hume (p. 97)
impressions (p. 98)
interposition (p. 95)
Law of Three Stages (p. 111)
John Locke (p. 89)
logical positivism (p. 113)
Ernst Mach (p. 112)
François-Pierre Maine de Biran (p. 110)
mental chemistry (p. 106)
James Mill (p. 102)
John Stuart Mill (p. 104)
Mind (p. 108)
William Molyneux (p. 91)
panpsychism (p. 110)
positive afterimage (p. 100)
positivism (p. 111)
reflection (p. 90)
Thomas Reid (p. 114)
relative size (p. 95)
Théodule Armand Ribot (p. 111)
George Croom Robertson (p. 108)
Moritz Schlick (p. 113)
Scottish School (p. 114)
sensation (p. 90)
simple ideas (p. 90)
Dugald Stewart (p. 115)
systematic desensitization (p. 93)
Hippolyte Adolphe Taine (p. 111)
Antoine Destutt de Tracy (p. 110)
Utilitarianism (p. 102)
vibratiuncles (p. 100)
Vienna Circle (p. 113)
vitalism (p. 110)
Joseph Wolpe (p. 93)

SUGGESTED READINGS

Comte, A. (1954). The positive philosophy. In S. Commins & R. N. Linscott (Eds.), *Man & the universe: The philosophers of science* (pp. 223–241). New York: Pocket Books, Inc. In addition to the reading from Comte, this little paperback contains readings from Copernicus, Francis Bacon, Descartes, Darwin, Freud, and Albert Einstein, as well as others. Most anthologies on the philosophy of science will include a selection from Comte.

Hartley, D. (1966). *Observations on man, his frame, his duty, and his expectations.* Gainesville, FL: Scholars' Facsimiles & Reprints. (Original work published 1749)

Hobbes, T. (1914). *Leviathan.* London: J.M. Dent & Sons Ltd. (Original work published 1651)

Hume, D. (1955). *An inquiry concerning human understanding.* Indianapolis, IN: Bobbs-Merrill. (Original work published 1748; "My own life," a brief autobiographical sketch, was originally published 1776)

Leibnitz, G. W. (1949). *New essays concerning human understanding.* (A. G. Langley, Trans.). La Salle, IL: Open Court. (Original work published 1765)

Locke, J. (1964). *An essay concerning human understanding.* New York: New American Library. (Original work published 1690)

Mill, J. (1967). *Analysis of the phenomena of the human mind* (2nd ed.). New York: Augustus M. Kelley, Publishers. (Original work published 1869) It is frequently rewarding to read the original writings of famous historical figures, and several original works cited in this chapter are listed here. Although specific editions have been given, there are often other reprints available. If you have access to used-book bookstores, you may be able to find inexpensive paperback editions of the above in the philosophy section.

Mazlish, B. (1975). *James and John Stuart Mill.* New York: Basic Books. This book of "psychohistory" recounts the incredibly complex relations between one of history's most famous father-son pairs.

Mill, J. S. (1969). *Autobiography.* Boston: Houghton Mifflin. (Original work published 1873) This remarkable document details Mill's unusual education, his mental crisis, and his special love, Harriet Taylor.

Continental Philosophies: Rationalism, Romanticism, and Existentialism

CHAPTER 6

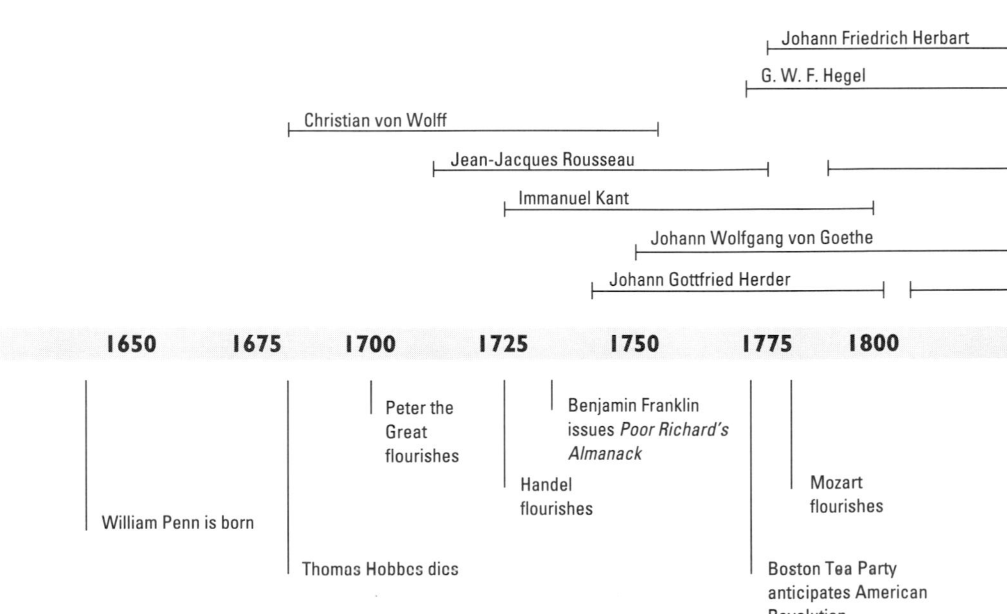

OUTLINE

Rationalism

- Immanuel Kant
- Georg Wilhelm Friedrich Hegel
- Johann Friedrich Herbart and Rudolf Hermann Lotze

Romanticism

- Johann Gottfried Herder
- Jean-Jacques Rousseau
- Johann Wolfgang von Goethe
- Arthur Schopenhauer

Existentialism

- Sören Aabye Kierkegaard
- Friedrich Wilhelm Nietzsche

Conclusions

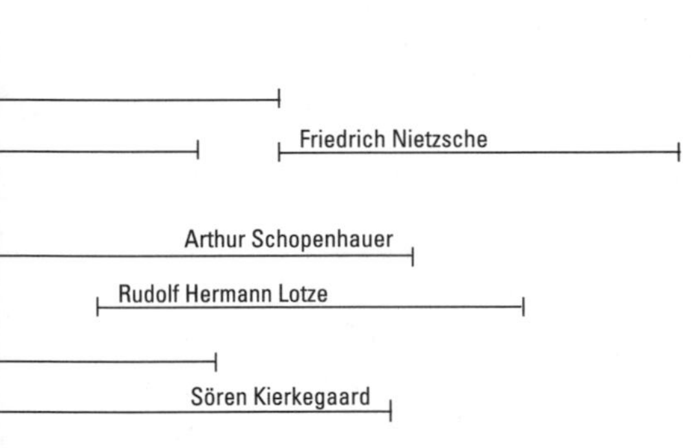

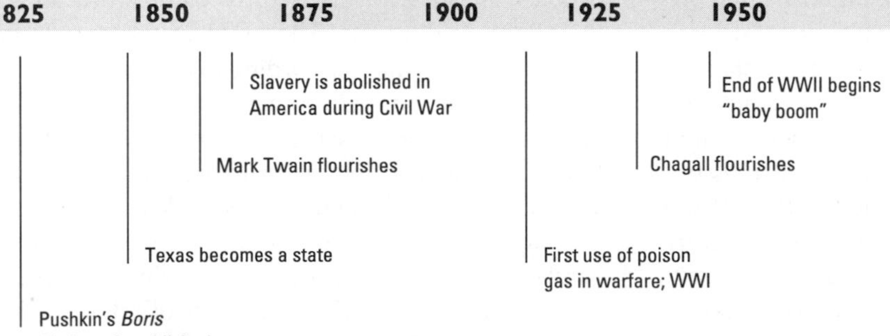

In this chapter, the main themes will be Continental (mainly German) **rationalism** (the use of reason to develop knowledge), romanticism (an emphasis on the whole person and particularly on personal feelings), and existentialism (which stresses the individual's isolation and freedom of choice). All of these philosophical systems were an important part of the 19th-century *Zeitgeist* and remain active today. In fact, with the rise of cognitive psychology (Chapter 18), rationalism is perhaps a greater influence on psychology than ever before.

Romanticism, too, is still found on college campuses, although more often in departments of English and philosophy than in psychology. We will look at the origins of existentialism here and examine its influence on clinical psychology in Chapter 16.

RATIONALISM

Rationalism matured as a philosophical system in Germany in the period just before the birth of psychology as a formal academic discipline. Many historians draw close connections between German rationalism and the rise of psychology (e.g., Boring, 1950; Leary, 1978), and rationalism's legacy remains a central part of psychology today. At the end of Chapter 5, we reviewed some of the elements of empiricism that were important for psychology—for example, the passive mind, the primacy of experience. Other psychologists, with roots in rationalism, have held that the mind actively structures sensory experience into meaningful perceptions and have tended to favor more nativist explanations for psychological processes.

The empirical-rational debate is still active in philosophy, where empiricism and rationalism represent competing views on the origin of knowledge. Similarly, in psychology, where the terms stand as shorthand for nurturist, passive-mind, behavioral (empirical) views in contrast to nativist, active-mind, cognitive (rational) views, the debate is still an issue.

In Chapter 5, we examined the reaction of one German philosopher (Leibniz) to Locke's empiricism, and we will begin our look at rationalism with a review of the response of a later German rationalist (Kant) to a later British empiricist (Hume).

Immanuel Kant

Immanuel Kant (1724–1804) was born in the university town of Königsberg, Prussia, and lived there all his life except for a brief period of tutoring in a nearby village. Kant entered the University of Königsberg in 1740, eventually earning his doctoral degree in 1755. He lectured at the university for 15 years as a *Privatdozent* (private teacher), all his pay coming from his students' fees. During this time, he was twice denied promotion, and he remained so poor that he never married.

In 1770, Kant assumed the chair of logic and metaphysics at the university. [A German professorship (or chair) includes a permanent salary that is continued in full even in retirement.] At about this time, he was awakened by Hume from his "dogmatic slumbers" and began work on the book that brought him his greatest acclaim as a philosopher, the *Critique of Pure Reason,* published in 1781. After 1781, students flocked to his classes, young philosophers made pilgrimages to Königsberg to see Kant, and he continually had to change restaurants for his midday meal because the public came to watch him eat.

As a teacher with many years' experience, Kant wrote a textbook of pedagogy. This book, he often said, contained many good principles of teaching—none of which he had ever actually applied. In addition, he believed in devoting most of his efforts to students of average ability, as the dunces were beyond help and the geniuses could fend for themselves (Durant, 1961).

It is a testament to the importance of its ideas that Kant's master work brought him such great fame, as "no one has ever found the *Critique of Pure Reason* an easy book" (Lindsay, 1934, p. ix). In fact, Kant was both a popular lecturer and an excellent teacher, and people familiar with his lectures complained about the *Critique*'s difficulty. The problem was that Kant structured the *Critique* according to the classifications of formal logic, but within these limits, he wrote like he lectured. "This is the explanation of the combination . . . of a rigid logical structure and a free and almost careless argumentation about details" (p. xi).

Despite his fame, the diminutive Kant (he was barely 5 feet tall) led a life of regularity and order. When Kant left his house for a stroll along "The Philosopher's Walk," his neighbors knew it was pre-

Immanuel Kant (1724–1804)

cisely 3:30 P.M. Kant walked in every season, sunshine or rain, although if rain threatened, his servant could be seen walking behind, a large umbrella under his arm. Never healthy, Kant attributed his survival to his regimen. One of his favorite principles was to breathe only through his nose, particularly when outdoors. During the cool seasons, Kant allowed no one to talk to him during his walks, considering silence preferable to a cold.

Kant resigned his university chair in 1797 and entered a long period of physical decline. He was buried in the Königsberg cathedral, although he had cared little for organized religion and had attended church only when his academic responsibilities required it. Over his grave were inscribed his words: "The starry heavens above me; the moral law within me."

Critique of Pure Reason

Before reading Hume—probably *An Inquiry Concerning Human Understanding,* which appeared in German in 1755—Kant spent time familiarizing himself with and elaborating on the work of **Christian von Wolff** (1679–1754). Wolff was a pupil of Leibniz and twice a professor at the University of Halle, the first time on Leibniz's recommendation. Wolff is an important transitional figure in the development of German psychological philosophy. As several historians have noted (e.g., Leary, 1982), he was an early German proponent of faculty psychology, and he identified empirical psychology and rational psychology as distinct approaches in content and method. Elements of his distinction remain with us today as part of the "empiricism versus rationalism" debate. The term *psychology* gained stature through its frequent use by Wolff in *Psychologia Empirica* and in *Psychologia Rationalis* (Boring, 1966). Another of Wolff's contributions was his influence on Kant, who considered him the greatest of the dogmatic philosophers, or philosophers who were relatively inflexible proponents of rationalism.

Thus, two systems of thought influenced Kant: rationalism à la Descartes, Spinoza, Leibniz, and particularly Wolff and empiricism à la Locke, Berkeley, and particularly Hume. Kant believed that both systems gave a biased view of knowledge, and he aimed for their synthesis.

Empiricism sought knowledge through sensory information and a posteriori reasoning (reasoning based on experience; inductive, empirical reasoning), whereas rationalism used a priori reasoning (reasoning based on theory rather than on experience; deductive reasoning). Both traditions viewed the mind as passive, containing either ready-made (innate) ideas for further analysis, according to the rationalists, or no ideas at all, according to the empiricists, who saw ideas as originating from sense impressions through experience with the outside world.

Kant aimed for a Copernican-type revolution of mind and knowledge. When Copernicus (Chapter 4) realized he could not explain the movements of the planets and stars by describing them as revolving around an observer on Earth—that is, by identifying Earth as the center of the universe—he shifted to the idea that the observer revolves relative to the heavenly bodies. Analogously, if the mind's knowledge of objects does not exist a priori and passive sensory experience cannot account for all knowledge of objects and their relations (as in Hume's cause-effect dilemma), then Kant's answer lies in having the mind's structure and capacities mold experience. This, Kant believed, is accomplished through certain fundamental categories of thought.

As we noted previously, Hume's exposition of causality stimulated Kant. Hume had argued that because all our knowledge comes from experience, and we never experience causality, we cannot use our present experience to predict future events. "Causality" is just an idea that comes from our habit of associating events because we experience them together. Without causality, we can never conclude that event A causes resulting event B (i.e., there can be no guaranteed inductive inferences). Because science is built up from inductive inference, Hume in effect was saying there could be no certain scientific knowledge. Impressed by the scientific advances in his day, Kant thought he needed to rescue science from Hume's skepticism by salvaging causality from the humble status of uncertain conjecture to which Hume had banished it.

To rescue causality, Kant made it part of the mind's inherent structure. That is, he accepted and then bypassed Hume's argument that we can never directly experience cause-effect relations. The problem that followed in Hume's argument stemmed from the basic empiricist assumption that all knowledge comes from sensations. "There can be no doubt that all our knowledge begins with experience," Kant wrote. "But though all our knowledge *begins* with experience, it does not follow that it all arises *out of* experience" (Kant, 1787/1929, p. 41, italics added).

Knowledge of causality (and certain other knowledge, as well) must exist for us before experience and must not arise from experience. Consider the following: We are willing to accept the proposition that every change must have a cause. Yet, the truth of this proposition can never be verified by our experience, because we will never experience *every* change. Because it is always finite, experience can never give us knowledge about the universality of propositions.

Kant agreed with the British empiricists that sensations precede knowledge. However, as soon as we have sensations, they are molded by the mind's structure, which is a priori—that is, before the sensations. The mind for Kant was not a passive entity shaped by experience but, rather, an active agent, coordinating sensations into perceptions and perceptions into knowledge, changing our many experiences into the unity of thought.

Sensations are things like a taste on the tongue, a sound in the ear, a touch on the skin, that the mind takes and classifies according to its inherent forms of "intuition" (perception), which are the forms of space and time. That is, the mind attributes a set of sensations to some object *here* or to some object *there,* to an object that is *now* before us or to one that *was* before us or *will be* before us. Perceptions are sensations that pass through the mind's categories of space and time.

Perceptions become knowledge through their transformation by the mind's inherent forms of conception. Like the space and time forms, the forms of conception are independent of experience. Kant called them **categories of thought,** and they included reality, totality, cause and effect, and existence and nonexistence. Kant believed that we have 12 such innate categories of thought that shape our experiences. Because these categories are part of the mind's structure, they permit us to conceptualize totality, for example, even though we can never experience *all* of anything. Similarly, because cause and effect are categories of the mind, we are willing to believe that one event causes another even though we never directly experience causality. Finally, it makes no sense for the mind initially to be a "blank slate," because without a priori knowledge of space and time, how could sensations themselves be sensibly organized?

Thus, for Kant our experience of the outside world, which he called the **noumenal world,** is always filtered through the structure of our minds to give us the **phenomenal world,** our inner world. The noumenal world consists of "things-in-themselves," which we can never experience directly. Our phenomenal world is created by the intuitions and conceptions (the categories) of our minds. Most modern cognitive psychologists adhere to Kant's distinction between the noumenal and phenomenal worlds and thus study the nature and structure of the mental representations we form through experience, which in turn direct our behaviors.

Kant's categories of thought can be seen as analogous, in some ways, to the faculties of the Scottish

School (Chapter 5), and, in fact, Kant was attracted to Reid's faculty psychology. However, Kant's categories did not have any particular location in the mind or brain and thus were incompatible with the faculty psychology of the phrenologists (Chapter 7).

Just as Kant sought to rescue causality (and science) with his categories of thought, he also sought to rescue morality from Utilitarianism (Chapter 5). Kant believed that moral knowledge was based on a priori judgments just as was scientific knowledge. Kant called his supreme a priori principle of morality the **categorical imperative,** which is categorical in the sense of applying to all rational beings and imperative because it is the principle according to which we should act. Basically, the categorical imperative is that a person should act in such a way that the rule behind his or her actions could serve as a universal law for all to follow. Although the categorical imperative is innate, humans can choose whether to act in accordance with it (we have free will, in other words). Kant's axiomatic (rule-based) approach to ethical matters still represents the major alternative to Utilitarianism's "greatest good for the greatest number" principle.

Kant's Influence

Kant saw the mind not as a passive recipient of sensations like the empiricists had thought, but as an active contributor to the experience of the world. The immediate objects of perception depend both on sensations *and* on perceptual apparatus, which orders and structures sensations into intelligible unities. In Chapter 14 we will show that Gestalt psychology was indebted to Kant—specifically, to his conception of perception and cognitive structure. Kant's influence is also evident in the work of James J. and Eleanor Gibson (Chapter 13), and through the Gestaltists and the Gibsons, it flavors much of cognitive psychology.

Kant's more immediate influence was on the German physiologists we will cover in Chapter 7, as they considered the implications of the law of specific nerve energies, which held that each nerve imparts its own particular quality to the sensations it receives. The idea of specific nerve energies is analogous to Kant's predispositions in the mind, which impart their particular qualities on the information the mind receives.

Kant did not think the study of the mind and its organizing properties—psychology—would ever acquire the status of a true science. Among his objections was the belief that mental phenomena could neither be manipulated experimentally nor described mathematically. One 19th-century German who was undeterred by Kant's conjectures was Gustav Fechner, who was 3 years old when Kant died. Fechner aimed to develop a mathematical equation to express the relation between physical stimuli and the mental experience of the stimuli; we will review his work in Chapter 7.

The generation of German philosophers following Kant can be viewed as his "disciples." Thus, the work of Hegel, Herbart, Fichte, and Schopenhauer—all post-Kantian philosophers discussed later—began with or passed through a period of Kantian commentary and extension. With this in mind, it is difficult to overestimate Kant's influence on later philosophy and psychology. The subject of psychology interested Kant throughout his life (Gouaux, 1972), and it is fair to say that he, "more than any other philosopher of the eighteenth century, has profoundly influenced that science since his time" (Buchner, 1897, p. 14).

Georg Wilhelm Friedrich Hegel

Born in Stuttgart, Germany, **Georg Wilhelm Friedrich Hegel** (1770–1831) was educated at Tübingen University, where he studied theology. Deciding against the clergy, Hegel became a private tutor first in Berne, Switzerland, and then in Frankfurt-am-Main. In 1801, Hegel went to the University of Jena, but his academic career there ended when the university was closed in 1806 following Napoleon's defeat of the Prussian troops at Jena. Shortly after this event, Hegel published his first great work—*Phänomenologie des Geistes* (*The Phenomenology of Mind*). According to Lavine (1984), *Phenomenology* "is one of the great works of genius that Western civilization has produced—but it is difficult, conceptually and stylistically, and in some parts almost impossible to penetrate" (p. 202). Given the obscurity of his style and the wealth of

Stock Montage.

Georg Wilhelm Friedrich Hegel (1770–1831)

ideas he embraced, it is easy to see why so many different people after Hegel found relevance for their positions in his writings.

Hegel temporarily served as a newspaper editor at Bamberg before becoming headmaster of the gymnasium at Nuremberg (1808–1816). In 1816, Hegel ascended to the chair in philosophy at the University of Heidelberg, mainly on the strength of his publication of *Wissenschaft der Logik* (*Science of Logic*) in two volumes in 1812 and 1816. In this work, Hegel set forth his famous dialectic, which we will discuss later.

In 1817, Hegel produced a compilation of his complete system of philosophy, *Encyclopädie der philosophischen Wissenschaften in Grundrisse* (*Encyclopedia of the Philosophical Sciences, Comprising Logic, Philosophy of Nature and of Mind*). Hegel's work led to his elevation in 1818 to Europe's most prestigious academic position—the chair in philosophy at the University of Berlin—where he remained until his death from cholera in 1831.

Following Kant, Hegel accepted the categories of thought, but with a twist: Hegel objectified Kant's concepts of the mind. That is, for Hegel, the categories exist independently of any individual's thought, which is not all that strange if you consider that most of us assume naively that concepts like time and space are "out there" in the world and not "in here" in our minds. For Hegel, the categories have their being in the Absolute. Like Spinoza (Chapter 4), who saw God in everything and everything in God, Hegel saw the universe as an interconnected unity, which he called the Absolute (God).

Unlike psychologists, who tend to focus on the individual, Hegel's system typically dealt with larger units, such as nations and populations. His interest in psychology centered on the nature of *Geist,* the German word for mind or spirit we encountered in *Zeitgeist,* or spirit of the times. Although Hegel's "macroscopic focus" on large units served Darwin and Marx well in their understanding of species and society, respectively, this element of Hegel's philosophy alienated others, such as Kierkegaard.

Evolution was central to Hegel's philosophy, and everything, including humanity, is evolving toward the Absolute. Hegel's mechanism for evolution was **dialectical movement,** in which every condition (thought, thing) leads inexorably to its opposite, and from the conflict of opposites a new, higher whole emerges. Hegel called the initial condition the *thesis,* its opposite the *antithesis,* and the emerging whole the *synthesis.* Each synthesis becomes the thesis in a progression toward the Absolute. Dialectical movement is illustrated in Figure 6.1 in the development of theories by the ancient Greeks. Thus, Heraclitus believed that all is change (thesis), which led Parmenides to propose that nothing changes (antithesis). Plato's view that some things change (world of opinion) but some things are constant (world of knowledge) can be viewed as a synthesis of Heraclitus and Parmenides.

Hegel's dialectical process can be seen clearly throughout Sigmund Freud's works. For example, the instinctual id can be interpreted as thesis, the superego (conscience) as antithesis, and the ego, which tries to reconcile the id-superego conflict, as synthesis. Hegel's influence is also evident in the works of Freud's one-time associates Alfred Adler and Carl Jung (both Chapter 15), especially in their

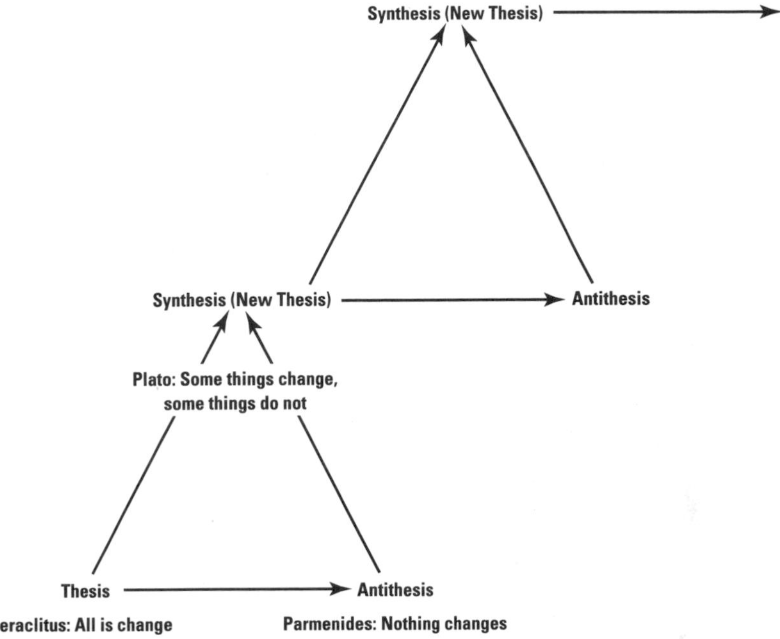

FIGURE 6.1 Dialectical movement

ideas about inferiority/superiority and the collective unconscious, respectively.

Sören Kierkegaard and Karl Marx (1818–1883) were educated in the German university system at the height of Hegel's influence. Although each became a major philosopher—Kierkegaard as the founder of existentialism and Marx through the social and economic philosophy for communism—both were importantly influenced by Hegel. Kierkegaard's existentialism, with its emphasis on the experience of individuals, emerged in response to Hegel's system that highlighted abstract concepts such as "nation," "people," and "spirit." By contrast, Marx developed a materialistic version of Hegel that Marx said "turned Hegel on his head," and his economic theory can be seen as an extension of Hegel's dialectical reasoning into economics.

Existentially oriented psychologists such as Carl Rogers and Abraham Maslow (both Chapter 16), with interests in alienation and self-actualization, demonstrate a Hegelian influence. Other suggested Hegelian influences include a connection with Gustav Fechner's psychophysics (Chapter 7), with Jean Piaget's work on ontogeny (Chapter 18), and with Thomas Kuhn's concept of scientific revolutions (Chapters 1 and 18).

The evolutionary focus in Hegel undoubtedly was part of the *Zeitgeist* that influenced Darwin (Chapter 9), and a connection exists between Hegel and several of the major figures of American psychology. G. Stanley Hall's (Chapter 10) initial interest in psychology as well as many elements of John Dewey's (Chapter 11) functionalism were closely connected to Hegelian ideas. In fact, along with members of the Scottish School (Chapter 5), Hegel was embraced by American psychological textbooks until the end of the 19th century.

Johann Friedrich Herbart and Rudolf Hermann Lotze

Conventional wisdom assigns the "founding" of modern psychology to either Gustav Fechner (Chapter 7), Wilhelm Wundt (Chapter 8), or William James (Chapter 10), and a strong case can be made for each man. However, most historians

Johann Friedrich Herbart (1776–1841)

of psychology like to note an earlier figure who seems pivotal in the transition from either physiology or philosophy (or both) to psychology, someone other than the "big three" whose contributions seem crucial to the founding of modern psychology. Although some of the figures in Chapter 5 (e.g., Alexander Bain) are sometimes assigned such a pivotal role, Johann Friedrich Herbart and Rudolf Hermann Lotze are two German thinkers more often accorded the distinction.

Johann Friedrich Herbart

Johann Friedrich Herbart (1776–1841) was born in Oldenburg, Germany. Because of an accident in infancy, he was a frail child who was educated at home by his mother until the age of 12. At 16, Herbart became profoundly impressed by Kant, who, in 1792, was at the height of his power and influence. Two years later, Herbart entered the university at Jena to study under one of Kant's disciples, the philosopher Johann Gottlieb Fichte (1762–1814). (Note that Hegel succeeded Fichte at Berlin.)

After 3 years, Herbart left Jena to become a private tutor in Switzerland. While there, he developed a lifelong interest in education per se, and before leaving, he visited Johann Heinrich Pestalozzi (1746–1827), the famous Swiss educational reformer. Because of Herbart's later research on pedagogy, Boring (1950) called him "the 'father' of scientific pedagogy" (p. 250). With a pedagogy grounded in psychology, Herbart is considered the founder of educational psychology by many authorities.

Next, Herbart spent 3 years in Bremen before enrolling at the University of Göttingen. After receiving his doctoral degree in philosophy, Herbart was invited to remain at Göttingen, which he did until 1809. There, Herbart's interests shifted from Kant to Leibniz (Chapter 4), and the influence of Leibniz's mathematics and his monadology is obvious in Herbart's psychological writings.

Herbart left Göttingen to fill Kant's philosophy chair at Königsberg, a position that attests to his stature among other German philosopher-psychologists of the day. He remained at Königsberg for almost 25 years before returning to Göttingen, and he remained in the chair at Göttingen until his death in 1841. Three years after Herbart's death, Lotze assumed the chair.

As primarily a rationalist philosopher, Herbart had clear ideas about psychology. One of his claims to the status of the first psychologist is that he was the first person to write a textbook on psychology as a so-named and independent discipline (*Lehrbuch zur Psychologie* or *Textbook of Psychology,* published in 1816). Herbart conceived of psychology not as "moral philosophy," but as a separate science. However, like Kant, he saw psychology as a science that was not conducive to experimentation. "What Herbart gave to psychology was status. He took it out of both philosophy and physiology and sent it forth with a mission of its own" (Boring, 1950, p. 252).

Today, it is hard to imagine a science that is not conducive to experimentation. Although Herbart thought of psychology as *empirical,* it was empirical in the sense of being grounded in experience. Only through later positivist conceptions (e.g., Mach;

Chapter 5) would *empirical* come to be nearly synonymous with *experimental.*

Herbart also thought of psychology as being mathematical and developed a mathematical theory analogous to Newton's model of the movement of heavenly bodies. In Newton's model of the universe, mathematical equations described such movement, whereas in Herbart's version of the mind, formulas described the movement of *Vorstellungen*, or mental ideas (Boudewijnse, Murray, & Bandomir, 1999). According to Boudewijnse et al., Herbart developed his mathematical approach to psychology in the context of scientific literature that valued mathematics in all the sciences. In modern times, this literature began with Descartes' work and was transmitted to Herbart through Newton's and Kant's writings.

In the period immediately following Herbart's presentation of his mathematical approach to psychology in 1824, it was widely taught and positively valued by several people, including Hermann Ebbinghaus (Boudewijnse, Murray, & Bandomir, 2001). Herbart's approach was opposed by Fechner and Wundt, however, both of whom advocated the creation of psychology as an empirical, not rational, science. Thus, after about 1850, Herbart's approach was largely ignored. According to Boudewijnse et al., the reasons for the theory's dismissal include the lack of experimentation by Herbart, a misrepresentation of the theory by Wundt, and the lack of an English translation of the book in which Herbart presented the theory. Boudewijnse et al. concluded that Herbart's mathematical approach deserves reconsideration in the 21st century.

Although historical developments have shown that Herbart's approach was not the only possible mathematical psychology, "it was the first to be recognized as a viable alternative; and it inspired the further evolution of mathematical psychology" (Leary, 1980, p. 159). As we will see in Chapter 7, Fechner successfully united Herbart's use of mathematics with an experimental approach to sensory phenomena.

Herbart's influence on Fechner also included his conception of the **threshold,** or **limen of consciousness.** By threshold of consciousness, Herbart meant a limit that an idea had to surpass to become conscious. In this, he was influenced by Leibniz, whose monads had different levels of consciousness, with *petite perceptions* never reaching consciousness. For Leibniz, perceptions that reached consciousness were apperceived, and Herbart also used the concept of apperception, referring to the **apperceptive mass** as a group of compatible ideas that forms in consciousness—it is what you are attending to at any moment in time. In order for an unconscious idea to enter the apperceptive mass, it must be compatible with the ideas already there. Otherwise, it will be prevented from entering the mass by being repressed.

Herbart's conception of ideas striving to enter consciousness but being prevented through repression became a central feature of Freud's psychoanalysis. Herbart also influenced Wundt's thinking, but perhaps Herbart's greatest effect came through Wundt's attempts to disprove Herbart's belief that psychology could not be an experimental science.

Herbart's writing also anticipated themes and concepts central to Gestalt psychology (Chapter 14), and Heider (1970) suggested that Herbart's ideas were overlooked until the Gestaltists embraced them, because the time was not right for them. "It took Wertheimer [Gestalt psychology's founder] to teach us to understand Herbart's remarks on perception as it took Freud to give meaning to what Herbart said about repression and other phenomena. There are probably still many insightful passages in Herbart . . . with which the spirit of the times will eventually catch up" (p. 139).

As we indicated, Herbart was interested in education, or pedagogy. In fact, Herbart's renown in educational circles was such that a movement bearing his name, Herbartianism, was quite influential in America at the beginning of the 20th century (Boudewijnse et al., 2001). This movement died shortly thereafter, however, probably because educators began to focus on experimental data from the classroom and on the work of psychologists such as Edward Lee Thorndike (Chapters 11 and 12).

As an educator, one of Herbart's suggestions was that material to be learned is best learned when it is first previewed, then presented, and finally, reviewed. Herbart also observed that relating or connecting new information to older, more familiar information is important to learning. Take another look at the organization of each chapter in this book, and we think you will find we have applied Herbart's principles.

You might also reflect on the good lecturers you have had. Did they use the "Tell them what you are going to tell them, tell them, and then tell them what you told them" approach? Did they connect new material to things with which you were already familiar, such as experiences you may have had or previous course material?

Rudolf Hermann Lotze

Rudolf Hermann Lotze (1817–1881) was born in Bautzen, Sacony (a former kingdom in southern Germany), the son of a military physician. Shortly before his 17th birthday, Lotze entered the University of Leipzig, where he earned doctorates in both medicine and philosophy in 1838 (Meischner-Metge & Meischner, 1997). Although trained primarily as a physician, he was always interested in philosophy and the arts, and his first publication after his dissertation was a book of poems.

At Leipzig, Lotze had contact with both Ernst Weber and Gustav Fechner, and Boring (1950) described him as a "silent listener in Fechner's circle" (p. 263). After a year of "private practice," Lotze returned to Leipzig, where he had simultaneous appointments in both the medical and philosophy faculties.

Rudolf Hermann Lotze (1817–1881)

In 1844, Lotze went to Göttingen to fill the chair in philosophy opened by Herbart's death. Lotze retained the chair for more than 35 years, and it passed to his student, G. E. Müller (Chapter 7). In 1852, Lotze produced his magnum opus, *Medicinische Psychologie oder Physiologie der Seele* (*Medical Psychology or Physiology of the Soul*), in which the phrase *physiological psychology* first appeared. In 1881, Lotze was persuaded by Hermann von Helmholtz (Chapter 7) and others to accept the chair of philosophy at Berlin. Three months later, Lotze died of pneumonia.

In large part, Lotze's influence on the development of psychology came through his students and friends. For example, his student, G. E. Müller, who succeeded him at Göttingen, did much to further experimental psychology. Another student, Carl Stumpf (Chapter 8), developed a laboratory at the University of Berlin to rival Wundt's Leipzig laboratory. And Lotze helped Franz Brentano (Chapter 8), philosopher, psychologist, and important countervoice to Wundt, to gain a position at the University of Vienna during one of Brentano's periods of difficulty with the Catholic Church.

Lotze's major direct contribution to psychology came in his theory of space perception. In some ways, Lotze's theory continued the empirical tradition from Thomas Brown (Chapter 5), while rejecting the Kantian approach, which considered space perception inherent in the mind. Actually, Lotze's theory also had nativist elements (i.e., he believed that the mind possesses the tendency to arrange its sensory contents spatially), but the space perception that develops comes from experience with nonspatial input.

To illustrate Lotze's theory, consider the development of space perception through tactual sensations. According to Lotze, every tactual sensation produces a **local sign,** or "sensory address," which for touch is a pattern of intensities that varies according to where the touches occur on the body. For example, a touch on the arm produces a different pattern than a touch on the leg, which provides a different pattern than a touch on the back, and so on. Similarly, a touch at one point on the arm results in a different pattern than a touch at another point on the arm. In general, local signs are stimulation patterns that convey some sense of location. In Lotze's theory, the conscious perception of space develops from experience and movement. Movement changes the place of stimulation by an object, which correspondingly changes the local signs. Because the mind has the tendency to arrange its inputs spatially, the movement-produced changes in local signs create the perception of space. We will encounter Lotze's empirical version of space perception again when we discuss Carl Stumpf, who used Lotze's theory as the starting point for his own nativist theory, and when we consider the Helmholtz-Hering debate (empiricist-nativist, respectively) in Chapter 7.

Psychology's Founder Reconsidered

We began this section by suggesting that either Herbart or Lotze can be considered pivotal to the founding of psychology. In some respects, both men remind us of William James, another leading candidate for the title of first psychologist. Like James, Lotze was the mentor of students who distinguished themselves in psychology (e.g., Carl Stumpf, G.E. Müller). Also like James, Lotze was part-physician and part-philosopher in his interests and training. Like James, Lotze was not a psychologist, yet was essential to psychology (see Henley & Thorne, 1992).

Comparing Herbart and James, we note that Herbart contributed the first textbook in psychology, whereas William James's (1890) *Principles of Psychology* is widely credited with being the greatest textbook in the history of psychology. Like Herbart's, James's conception of empiricism did not lead to the type of scientific research that would be the hallmark of experimental psychology (e.g., Johnson & Henley, 1990; Robinson, 1993). In short, although we too are tempted by Lotze and Herbart (and William James), we will honor Wundt as the first true psychologist in the modern sense of that term. In Chapter 8 we will examine the reasons for Wundt's signal place in the history of psychology.

As we saw in our discussion of positivism (Chapter 5) and rationalism in the 19th century, science was in the air, and a positivistic version of psychology was about to be born. In addition to the empiricist-rationalist debate we examined at the beginning of this chapter, there were other competing ideas concerning the scope and nature of psychology. For example, the pioneer Belgian psychologist Desiré Mercier (1851–1926) advocated a return to Aristotle and scholasticism. More enduringly, romanticism was another Continental movement influencing art, literature, music, philosophy, and psychology in the late 18th and 19th centuries.

ROMANTICISM

Romanticism in philosophy was a reaction against both empiricism and rationalism. For the romantics, the empiricists diminished humans either as unemotional machines, or as beings in which the emotions were developed through hedonism—the search for pleasure and the avoidance of pain. Rational thought, for the romantics, often produced equally unappealing conceptions of human nature as under the control of abstract forces. In addition, the rationalists often considered human emotions and emotional experiences more destructive than beneficial, particularly if they were not rationally constrained.

The romantics rejected the Newtonian view of the world as a mechanical system acting in accordance with mathematical laws in favor of a more organic conception, best comprehended and appreciated through a sort of poetic intuition. Humans are not coldly calculating creatures, but beings motivated by chaotic passions. So, the romantics thought it was necessary to consider the whole person, particularly the person's feelings. Romanticism's foundation lay in the views of Johann Gottfried Herder.

Johann Gottfried Herder

Johann Gottfried Herder (1744–1803) was a German critic and poet, born in East Prussia. He studied at Königsberg, where he became a disciple of Kant. In his later years, Herder opposed Kant, particularly the

Johann Gottfried Herder (1744–1803)

idea of a "depraved nature" in humans because of "original sin."

By contrast to Kant, Herder was entranced with unsophisticated human nature. For example, his love for the music of the people led him to collect folksongs, which he published. Herder saw adoration of the historical past as a means to refresh the sentiments of modern society and stressed the importance of the historical method for understanding humankind.

In his reverence for history and a belief in the historical method's importance, Herder was anticipated by a man with remarkably similar views, although Herder's were formed independently. Herder's forerunner was **Giambattista Vico** (1668–1744), who died the year Herder was born. Born in Naples, Italy, Vico was a philosopher and historian. In Vico's major work, *Scienza Nuova* (*The New Science,* 1725), he distinguished between historical and scientific explanations, rejected the idea of an unchanging human nature, and argued that recurring historical developments can be understood only by studying the changes in human nature as expressed through language, myth, and culture.

Herder influenced Wundt in his focus on the study of cultures, language, and myth. Wundt's monumental *Völkerpsychologie* (*Cultural Psychology*) was the study of such things as language, myths, and social customs through historical records and literature. In addition, Wundt saw the new science of psychology as lying somewhere between the social sciences (*Geisteswissenschaften*) and the natural or physical sciences (*Naturwissenschaften*), which also were distinguished by Herder.

Herder, who considered change, growth, and development of fundamental importance to his world view, also in some ways anticipated evolutionary theory. However, he is perhaps best remembered for his influence on Goethe, whom he met in Strassburg in 1770, and for the development of German romanticism. Although Herder laid much of the groundwork for romanticism in philosophy, we must look to a man with a "delicate and neurotic nature . . ." (Durant, 1961, p. 259) for a complete understanding of romanticism.

Jean-Jacques Rousseau

Jean-Jacques Rousseau (1712–1778) was born in Geneva, Switzerland. His mother died at his birth, and his father, a violent and dissipated man, abandoned him to the care of relatives in 1722. As a consequence, Rousseau had little early family life and less formal education. At 16, he fled to Italy and Savoy (part of the former empire of Sardinia), where he lived with and eventually became the lover of Baronne Louise de Warens. In 1741, Rousseau was replaced in her affections by a wigmaker, and he moved to Paris, where he thrived. In Paris, he began an "association" with an illiterate servant, Thérèse le Vasseur, by whom he fathered five children, all consigned to a foundling home. Ironically, Rousseau is well known for his influential essay on the education of children.

In 1755, Rousseau published *Discours sur l'Origine et les Fondements de l'Inégalité Parmi les Hommes* (*Discourse on the Origin and Foundations of Inequality Amongst Men*), in which he stressed the natural goodness of humans and society's corrupting influence. Recall that Hobbes's view of human nature was exactly the opposite. Hobbes saw the natural condition of humans as a state of mutual warfare and believed that enlightened selfishness would lead people to form a "social contract" giving the right of aggression to an absolute ruler.

In 1762, Rousseau published his masterpiece, *Du Contrat Social* (*The Social Contract*), in which he discussed the social contract that exists wherever there is a legitimate government. Under Rousseau's social contract, all people modify their conduct to be in accord with the freedom of others, surrendering their rights to the collective "general will." Individuals thereby lose individual liberty and a right to everything, but they gain civil liberty and property rights. *Du Contrat Social,* with its slogan "Liberty, Equality, Fraternity," became the bible of the French Revolution, which began a decade after Rousseau's death. The slogan still graces French coins.

Also in 1762, Rousseau published *Émile,* an essay on education, written as a novel. [Excerpts can be found in more contemporary works, such as Archer (1964).] In *Émile,* Rousseau included the "Confession of Faith of the Savoyard Vicar," whose central argument was that reason is against belief in God and immortality, but feeling strongly favors such belief. Hence, it is better to trust feeling than to yield to the despair of skepticism.

Émile greatly affected the educationists of the time, particularly Pestalozzi, who, as we noted, influenced Herbart. Kant, too, was profoundly influenced by *Émile,* omitting his daily walk in order to finish it. *Émile* so inflamed the political and religious establishment that Rousseau was forced to flee to Switzerland and then to England at Hume's invitation, as we noted in Chapter 5. While working on his autobiographical *Confessions,* Rousseau became seriously unstable, provoking fights with his friends, particularly Hume. He returned to France in 1767, where he eked out a living copying music, something he had done before he became famous. He finished writing his *Confessions* and several other works, while continuing to decline emotionally. Rousseau died suddenly in Ermenonville in 1778, arousing suspicions that he had committed suicide. His remains were later transferred to Paris, where they rest alongside Voltaire's in the Panthéon.

To summarize, Rousseau's writings began the romantic movement by stressing the importance of feelings and deemphasizing reason, suggesting a new direction for education, and profoundly influencing subsequent philosophies. After the inauguration of romanticism through Rousseau's writings, German romanticism was exemplified by the work of a man of towering intellect—Johann Wolfgang von Goethe.

Jean-Jacques Rousseau (1712–1778)

Johann Wolfgang von Goethe

Johann Wolfgang von Goethe (1749–1832) was born in Frankfurt-am-Main. Privately educated by his father, he studied reluctantly for a law profession until a love affair stimulated him to write his first two plays. Following an illness, he returned to the study of law at Strassburg, where he came under Herder's influence. For example, Herder introduced him to Shakespeare's work (Eiermann, 1997–1999).

In 1771, Goethe returned to Frankfurt and became a newspaper critic. He began work on his most famous literary masterpiece, *Faust,* which was eventually published in two parts in 1808 and 1832. An earlier

Philosophical Library, New York.

Johann Wolfgang von Goethe (1749–1832)

triumph came with the publication of *Leiden des jungen Werthers* (*The Sorrows of Young Werther,* 1774), which is the tale of a young man in a hopeless love affair. *Werther* solves the problem of dissonant obligations by nobly committing suicide; Goethe's powerful writing actually triggered a number of suicides.

With age, Goethe increasingly disapproved of the German romanticism that he had crystallized. He particularly disliked the romantics' enthusiasm for the French Revolution, which he satirized in several works. In addition, he disliked what he considered the German romantics' disregard for style, and he attempted to correct this problem by example.

Goethe apparently lived life to the fullest, spurred on by the desire to explore whatever can be explored, to inquire as far as possible, and not to give up too quickly. He died at Weimar, a town in central Germany, where he is buried in a ducal vault near his friend, Friedrich Schiller (1759–1805). Schiller was a dramatist, poet, and historian who, in the last decade of his life, conducted an intense literary rivalry with Goethe.

Goethe influenced psychology in a number of ways. For example, both Sigmund Freud and Carl Jung (Chapter 15) acknowledged a debt to him. Freud indicated that Goethe's essay on nature and Darwin's evolutionary theory were in part responsible for his decision to go into medicine. Aspects of Freud's libido (psychic energy) theory are also traceable to Goethe.

Apparently, modern behavior therapy owes an unrecognized debt to Goethe. As a 20-year-old law student, Goethe developed an aversion to loud sounds and fears of heights and dark places, all of which he treated with what we call implosive therapy. For example, to treat his fear of heights, he forced himself to climb to the highest part of a church tower, repeating this procedure until he was no longer afraid. And to treat his aversion to loud sounds, he voluntarily exposed himself to the following: "In the evening when they beat the tattoo, I went near the multitude of drums, the powerful rolling and beating of which might have made one's heart burst in one's bosom" (Goethe, 1848–1849; cited in Bringmann, Voss, & Balance, 1997, p. 35). Similar methods were successfully used on his other symptoms (Bringmann, Krichev, & Balance, 1970; Bringmann et al.).

Goethe's influence came through his scientific pursuits as well. Unlike many of the romantics, Goethe was also a scientist, and he made contributions in such diverse fields as anatomy, mineralogy, meteorology, botany, zoology, and optics. Although many of his observations were excellent, Goethe unwisely attempted to refute Newton's then-prevailing theory of color vision (ca. 1810), finding it impossible to think of white light as a mixture of all colors. In this respect, Newton was right and Goethe was wrong, but Goethe's methodology was important for psychology. Goethe believed in exact observation of phenomena, and his desire to study intact, meaningful experiences rather than fragmented, artificial ones led to refinements in phenomenology, an important element of Gestalt psychology.

Helmholtz, the famous German physiologist, knew of Goethe's phenomenological approach to the study of vision. Unfortunately, by focusing on Goethe's errors of observation (e.g., his erroneous conclusion about white light), Helmholtz overlooked valid observations (e.g., the prominence of red-green and blue-yellow color pairs) that led to the development of an alternative theory of color vision to his own.

Goethe's observations on vision also stimulated research by other scientists, particularly **Jan Purkinje** (1787–1869). Purkinje was the Czechoslovakian physiologist after whom the Purkinje shift is named. The Purkinje shift refers to a change from cone vision to rod vision in twilight (such that objects appear to lose their color). In fact, it was at dawn rather than at twilight when Purkinje made the observation leading to his reporting of the phenomenon (Zusne, 1989), which means that he observed the complementary process of a shift from rod vision to cone vision (Brožek, 1989; Brožek & Hoskovec, 1997). As Brožek further noted,

> the phenomenon described by Purkinje in a few lines, all but incidentally, came to represent to "psychologists in the street" the sum total of what they know about a man who fell in love with psychology at the age of 19 yr.; published innovative contributions to the knowledge of vision at the age of 36 and 38; offered to medical students lectures on general and physiological psychology when between the ages of 40 and 55; raised questions about the significance of the available information on visual perception for anatomy, physiology, physics, art, and crafts at the age of 73; and, in his late seventies, in the handwritten "Psychological fragments," had interesting things to say on the past and future of scientific psychology. . . . (pp. 821–822)

Following Goethe, Purkinje promoted the phenomenological tradition in psychology, and Boring (1950) cited the Purkinje phenomenon as the "sort of basic fact which phenomenology can yield" (p. 20).

The description of the phenomenon we call the Purkinje shift did not originate with Jan Purkinje, according to Wade and Brožek (2001). Earlier accounts of the change in spectral sensitivity can be found in Aristotle and Leonardo da Vinci, and particularly in the writings of a Bavarian artist named Mathias Klotz. Klotz published his work on color vision theory in 1806 and 1816, well before Purkinje's account in 1825. Wade and Brožek reported that Purkinje's account of the phenomenon was more explicit than those of his predecessors, however.

In addition to Purkinje, Goethe interested his friend Arthur Schopenhauer in color vision.

Arthur Schopenhauer

Arthur Schopenhauer (1788–1860) was born in Danzig, a seaport in Poland. His family was historically wealthy and well-connected, as illustrated by the fact that when Russia's Peter the Great and the Empress Catherine visited Danzig, they stayed in Schopenhauer's great-grandfather's house. Schopenhauer's father was a banker, and his mother was one of the period's leading novelists. The young Schopenhauer accompanied his parents in their travels throughout Europe, and the experience broadened his horizons but interrupted the continuity of his early education. However, Schopenhauer was so intelligent he was able to compensate quickly for his lack of systematic study.

Educated to become a merchant, Schopenhauer soon showed a strong interest in philosophy. After his father's apparent suicide, the 17-year-old was on his own. He and his mother were temperamentally opposites: She was optimistic and pleasure-loving, whereas he was pessimistic and distrustful. Goethe exacerbated problems between them by telling the mother that her boy would become famous. Schopenhauer's mother was irritated because she had never heard of two geniuses in the same family. "Finally, in some culminating quarrel, the mother pushed the son and rival down the stairs; whereupon [Schopenhauer] bitterly informed her that she would be known to posterity only through him" (Durant, 1961, p. 303). He never saw his mother again, and his prophetic curse has largely been realized.

In 1809, Schopenhauer embarked on a university education. Although his doctoral dissertation at the University of Jena was published in 1813 and received praise from Goethe, it attracted little attention and few copies were sold. Undeterred, Schopenhauer immediately began writing what became his masterpiece, and everything he did after it can be seen as merely commentaries on *Die Welt als Wille und Vorstellung* (*The World as Will and Representation,* 1819). Again, the world was not ready for Schopenhauer's message, and 16 years after its publication, the author learned that most of the edition had been sold as waste paper.

Arthur Schopenhauer (1788–1860) and "friend"

In 1822, Schopenhauer had the chance to present his philosophy at the University of Berlin. Like his publications, this attempt to gain recognition for his ideas was unsuccessful. In part, Schopenhauer defeated himself by scheduling his lectures opposite Hegel's, with the result that he found himself lecturing to an empty classroom. Schopenhauer resigned and sought revenge through bitterly negative comments about Hegel in his later publications. For example, in the preface to the second edition of *The World as Will and Representation,* Schopenhauer (1844/1969) wrote: "How could minds strained and ruined in the freshness of youth by the nonsense of Hegelism still be capable of following Kant's profound investigations?" (p. xxiv).

Perhaps Schopenhauer also considered it poetic justice that he fled Berlin at the onset of a cholera epidemic in 1831 and never returned, but Hegel returned too soon and became a victim. Schopenhauer lived the remainder of his life in Frankfurt, his only companion a poodle, which the townspeople dubbed "Young Schopenhauer."

In the mid-19th century, disillusioned with efforts to achieve lasting peace and stability, Europeans eventually embraced Schopenhauer's dark philosophy. Fame at last found the great pessimist, and on his 70th birthday in 1858, Schopenhauer received congratulations from every continent. He died 2 years later.

Schopenhauer's philosophy was inspired by Plato, Kant, and Goethe, as well as by the ancient Indian philosophy known as the *Vedas* (sacred literature of Hinduism). *The World as Will and Representation* begins with the statement: "The world is my representation" [or, as it is sometimes translated, "The world is my idea"]. By this, Schopenhauer was conveying his acceptance of Kant's position that the world is known to us only through our sensations and ideas. The world presents itself to us as an object to a subject, and as subjects we know only the world of our perception. The world of objects is but representation or idea, completely determined by the subject. Thus, the world is my (or your, or Schopenhauer's) idea. Note the similarity to Berkeley's (Chapter 5) subjective idealism—to be, is to be perceived.

Schopenhauer also accepted Kant's belief that the human mind organizes its inputs according to certain a priori categories. Having accepted rationalistic idealism, Schopenhauer vigorously attacked materialism, the philosophical doctrine that matter is the only reality and that everything can be explained as matter. When we know matter only through mind, through ideas, how can we explain mind as matter? Schopenhauer wrote that "the materialist was like Baron von Münchausen [1720–1797, the German soldier who told tall tales of his exploits], who, when swimming in water on horseback, drew his horse up by his legs, and himself by his upturned pigtail" (Schopenhauer, 1844/1969, p. 27). In Schopenhauer's opinion, von Münchausen's feat was as stupendous as the materialists' attempt to explain living phenomena by physical and chemical forces.

Thus, the world is idea, and the world is also **will,** which is the central theme of Schopenhauer's philosophy. By *will,* Schopenhauer meant something more like Freud's *libido,* or driving force behind human action, than he did *decision making* or *choice.* Here is a major disagreement between Kant and Schopenhauer: Kant had said we can never directly know the noumenal world, the world outside ourselves, the world of "things-in-themselves." But Schopenhauer thought there was one exception to the notion that we are always on the outside of things, and that is the knowledge each of us has of his or her own "willing." Although we ordinarily think of our bodily actions as the product of willing, Schopenhauer saw willing and action as the same thing: The body's actions are merely the "act of the will objectified." What we know of ourselves is that we belong to the inner nature of what is to be known. We are the "thing-in-itself," and the thing-in-itself is will. Thus, the essence of each of us is will. Further, will is the inner nature of everything, of the world, and we arrive at the conclusion with which this paragraph began: The world is will.

Note that the will is in everything, not just in rational beings. It is in animals and even in inanimate objects. In fact, there is only one will, and each thing is just a specific example of it. The driving impulse of all nature is will, and this endless striving is the "will to live," whose enemy is death. But the will can defeat death through the ultimate martyrdom of reproduction. Like a modern evolutionary biologist, for Schopenhauer the only purpose of the will to live is to continue the cycle of life.

Remember that Schopenhauer was the ultimate philosopher of pessimism. Thinking like the merchant he was almost trained to be, Schopenhauer equated life to a business whose proceeds did not come close to covering its cost. There can be no true happiness because happiness is only a temporary respite from pain. Pain results from desires, most of which go unfulfilled.

For Schopenhauer, there were at least two avenues of potential escape from the will's dictates: asceticism and aesthetics. Like the Epicureans and the Stoics (both Chapter 3), Schopenhauer understood that self-control and avoiding worldly temptations were one route to psychological health. By being ascetics and practicing abstinence and self-denial, we can thwart the will as much as possible and come close to freeing ourselves from it. Of course, death is the ultimate freedom from the will, and the only reason suicide is not more often practiced is that it is the opposite of the will to survive.

Another way to at least partially escape the will's dictates is through aesthetics (i.e., through the contemplation of artistic beauty). When we examine a work of art, we become knowing, as opposed to willing, people. What we see is the universal element in a painting. If we happen to study a painting of a person, we may see the painting as the representation of some element of humanity we all share. This view is close to Plato's concept of the Idea (or Form).

In the end, we cannot win. With the beginning of our greater understanding and wisdom, the body begins its inevitable decay. Eventually, we meet death, which has been playing with us as a cat plays with a mouse.

Schopenhauer's pessimism was pervasive, and it came in part from the romantic movement, with its emphasis on feelings rather than rationality or experience. During this period, in a letter to Sir Horace Mann, Horace Walpole aptly wrote, "This world is a comedy to those who think, a tragedy to those who feel" (Henry, 1955, p. 524).

Possibly Schopenhauer's greatest influence on psychology can be seen in Freud's writings. Schopenhauer's concept of will as a blind driving force is similar to the Freudian id. In addition, Schopenhauer wrote of repression of unwanted thoughts into the unconscious and of the resistance that occurs with any attempt to retrieve the repressed thoughts. Freud credited Schopenhauer with being the first to discover these unconscious processes, although Freud contended he had discovered them independently.

Wundt, scientific psychology's founder, also shows Schopenhauer's influence in his psychology of consciousness. Like Kant and Schopenhauer, Wundt stressed the mind's ability to organize its elements. Schopenhauer's philosophy clearly influenced many existential philosophers.

EXISTENTIALISM

We introduced romanticism as a reaction against empiricism and rationalism, and the same can be said of existentialism. **Existentialism** is a philosophy stressing the individual's isolation in a hostile universe, and it emphasizes the individual's freedom of choice and responsibility for the consequences of actions chosen. Here, we will discuss existential philosophy's founders, Sören Kierkegaard and Friedrich Nietzsche. Nietzsche, in particular, is often seen as a transitional figure between romanticism and existentialism.

Two themes perhaps best capture existential philosophy's appeal for psychology. The first is that subjective meaning, rather than a third-person account of brain or behavior, should be psychology's central focus. This theme was, and still is, embraced by many psychologists and can be found clearly in the work of William James (Chapter 10) and Sigmund Freud (Chapter 15), among others.

Existential philosophy's second major theme is that humans have the freedom to make choices and in turn must take responsibility for their choices. For Kierkegaard and Nietzsche, this meant resisting the tendency to consider God or society responsible for failures and successes instead of accepting them as the result of freely chosen actions. In contemporary psychology, this theme means resisting reductionistic and deterministic accounts of human behavior that attribute human actions either to biology or to the environment.

Sören Aabye Kierkegaard

Poet, philosopher, theologian, and psychologist **Sören Aabye Kierkegaard** (1813–1855) was born in Copenhagen, Denmark, the youngest of seven children of Michael Pederson Kierkegaard and his second wife, Anne Lund Kierkegaard. Kierkegaard was greatly influenced by his father, who had earned enough of a fortune by the age of 40 to retire from business to a life of leisure. Unfortunately for the young Kierkegaard, his father suffered from recurring bouts of depression, a tendency he passed on to his son. Michael Kierkegaard also had a dim view of life and a preoccupation with spiritual concerns. In keeping with his depressive and somber tendencies, the elder Kierkegaard's Christianity emphasized the pain and suffering of Christ. Thus, even as a child, Kierkegaard was exposed to the idea that he would have to suffer and accept scorn for trying to reveal the truth, just as Christ had been tortured and derided.

At the University of Copenhagen, Kierkegaard began to study theology, although he quickly found himself more interested in philosophy and literature. Kierkegaard was educated at the height of Hegel's popularity in Germany and Denmark, and at first he was strongly attracted to Hegel. Later, many of his ideas came from his dissatisfaction with Hegel's system. Indeed, Kierkegaard came to view Hegel as "comic" because in trying to capture the structure of reality, Hegel had lost sight of the most important element—personal existence.

Periodically suffering from depression and mental anguish, Kierkegaard was particularly disturbed by his father's death in 1838. Soon after this, in 1840, he became engaged to Regine Olsen, an 18-year-old woman he had known for at least a year. No sooner had Regine accepted his proposal, however, than he began having second thoughts, eventually concluding it would be wrong to saddle Regine with his depressive mental state.

After the definitive breakup late in 1841, Kierkegaard traveled to Berlin, where he began to write feverishly. As a result of this literary activity, Kierkegaard published six books in 1843, the first of which is entitled *Either/Or*.

In *Either/Or*, Kierkegaard presented two ways of life, calling one the aesthetic and the other the ethical. Kierkegaard used the world *aesthetic* to describe a stage or plane of existence in which an individual lives on the sensory level. This is someone whose main purpose in life is to achieve sensory pleasure. Life on the aesthetic plane leads to despair, because the individual realizes there is (or ought to be) something more. This "something more" makes itself felt as a sense of dread, and Kierkegaard later wrote two books on the twin themes of dread and despair: *The Concept of Dread* (1844) and *The Sickness Unto Death* (1849). Kierkegaard's "dread" is similar to what modern clinical psychologists call anxiety, whereas his "sickness unto death" corresponds with what we call depression.

Of course, some individuals who live on the aesthetic plane may respond to the sense of dread by moving to a higher level, the *ethical* plane. In this stage, the individual accepts rules of conduct that reason develops. As an illustration of the differences in the stages, the aesthetic individual yields to impulse

From Sören Kierkegaard, Fear and Trembling *(New York: Penguin USA, 1985).*

Sören Kierkegaard (1813–1855), drawn by his cousin Christian Kierkegaard in 1840

whenever there is a sexual attraction, whereas the ethical individual recognizes and accepts the obligations of fidelity to remain loyal to the partner.

There is a higher plane than the ethical one, however, and at some point the person on the ethical plane realizes something is still missing, which is a relationship with God. Kierkegaard referred to this third plane as the *religious* stage. Whereas one can reach the ethical stage through a conscious choice or commitment to upholding the moral law, one can attain the religious stage only through a "leap of faith." Because the relationship between God and the individual is a unique and subjective experience, there is no objective knowledge about it that the individual can use to reveal how to achieve it. This is why one can only achieve the relationship through an act of faith.

During his life, Kierkegaard achieved some popularity through his writings. In both philosophy and theology, his stature has continued to grow, but interest in his poetry and psychology has waxed and waned in the time since his death (Nordentoft, 1972). We will briefly revisit Kierkegaard's importance for the origins of modern clinical psychology in Chapter 15.

Friedrich Wilhelm Nietzsche

Born in the small German town of Röcken, which is located in rural farmland southwest of Leipzig, **Friedrich Wilhelm Nietzsche** (1844–1900) was the son of a Lutheran minister, who died when Nietzsche was just 4 years old. Six months later, Nietzsche's younger brother died, leaving Nietzsche in an all-female environment consisting of his mother, his paternal grandmother, two paternal aunts, and his younger sister.

From age 14 to age 19, Nietzsche lived and studied in an excellent boarding school, Schulpforta, and following his graduation he entered the University of Bonn. At first, Nietzsche studied theology and philology, which he later defined as the art of reading slowly, but soon concentrated on the latter. Nietzsche followed one of his teachers to the University of Leipzig, where his scholarship was so exceptional that he was offered a faculty position in philology, today defined as the scientific analysis of written records and literary texts, at the University of Basel before he had obtained a Ph.D. at Leipzig. While at Leipzig, Nietzsche met and became a devotee of composer Richard Wagner (1813–1883), although he eventually broke with Wagner, concluding that his music was overly decadent.

In 1879, Nietzsche resigned his university position because of a worsening of his probably psychosomatic illnesses, which produced symptoms such as migraine headaches, visual problems, and vomiting. He spent the next 10 years at resorts in France, Switzerland, Germany, and Italy trying to recover some semblance of health. Unfortunately, Nietzsche suffered a complete mental and physical breakdown early in 1889. His collapse has been attributed to a variety of causes, including tertiary syphilis, and for the remainder of his life, Nietzsche was cared for by his mother, and, following her death, by his sister. He never regained his sanity.

In the years between his resignation from Basel and his collapse, Nietzsche devoted himself to developing a philosophy "that would comprise both cool analysis and enthusiastic vision, a synthesis of a new religious creed and merciless criticism. Apollo, the god of lucid wisdom, and [Dionysus], the god of orgiastic mysticism, were taken for its symbols" (Runes, 1959, p. 299). For Nietzsche, Dionysus represented creative energy, whereas Apollo symbolized order and restraint, the forces that harness Dionysian energy. As he saw it, European culture since Socrates had been geared toward repressing the Dionysian creative force, with Christianity and Judaism being the chief agents in this repression.

According to Nietzsche, the one thing characterizing all humans is the "will to power," a need to dominate the environment. For Nietzsche, this natural will to power has been corrupted by Western religion, and, in response, Nietzsche called for a rejection of the dominant "morality of the weak." In its place he argued for a morality based on humankind's original nature, which is to strive for control and dominance. Nietzsche saw the next step in human evolution as the *Übermensch*, or superman—someone with the courage to reexamine all values and to respond freely to the internal will to power. Nietzsche did not envision this superman as a dictator or tyrant, however, but as a superior individual whose Dionysian nature was in harmony with his Apollonian intellect.

Philosophical Library, New York.

Friedrich Nietzsche (1844–1900) and his mother

Nietzsche's many literary works contain a variety of provocative themes, such as the repudiation of Christian and Judaic ethics, the death of God, the universal will to power, and the *Übermensch*. His reputation suffered greatly from the Nazis' embrace of his ideas, which were generally distorted. We will have more to say about Nietzsche's ideas and their similarity to components of psychoanalysis in Chapter 15 and will discuss his influence on 20th-century existentialists in Chapter 16.

In some respects, Nietzsche and Kierkegaard were poles apart in their thinking. For example, Kierkegaard was an earnest Christian theologian who felt that complacency and an uncritical acceptance of church doctrine represented a dangerous threat to an authentic Christian experience. Many of his works explore this theme subtly and indirectly, through the use of extended analogy and parables. Nietzsche, by contrast, was a self-proclaimed antichrist whose writing style was by no means subtle or indirect. Instead, Nietzsche appears to intentionally challenge the reader by presenting clever, but inflammatory, arguments that one cannot accept uncritically.

Despite their obvious differences, the goal of both philosophers was essentially the same and perhaps can be distilled into the statement, "Never let other people do your thinking for you." In Chapter 16, we will examine more contemporary existential thinkers, such as Heidegger, Sartre, and Camus, who incorporated this idea into their psychologies. There, we will also find that this simple principle is the centerpiece of humanistic approaches to clinical psychology.

CONCLUSIONS

Three points that define rationalism's legacy for psychology stand out: First, and most generally, we have the "rationalism versus empiricism" debate. Unlike the empiricists, who often conceived of mind as a passive receptacle of environmental sensations, the rationalists tended to view mind as an active, structuring agent and grounded "reality" in it, not in the world. Both an "active" mind and the study of mental representations are the hallmarks of many subsequent psychological theories.

Second, we have the nativist-nurturist conflict introduced in the first chapter. Rationalism is usually a philosophy supportive of nativist positions, and psychology and psychological theories have never entirely escaped this debate. As early as Lotze, it was clear that most psychological phenomena have both nativist (innate mental or biological structures) and nurturist (learning) components. Intelligence (Chapter 17) provides perhaps the best example of this conflict in modern psychology.

Third, we have the contrast between faculty psychology and associationism. Here, we find Kant aligned with the Scottish School on the side that saw various components of mind (e.g., language, memory, reasoning) as more or less discrete entities in opposition to the idea that one general principle—the association of ideas—characterizes the nature of mind. William James's *Principles of Psychology* is, to some extent, organized around this contrast, as are many contemporary theories in psychology.

Another important rationalist covered in this chapter was Hegel, whose evolutionary approach to phenomena (dialectical movement) sowed the seeds for many ideas in biology, psychology, and economics. In addition to Hegel, several others come close to earning the label of the first "true" psychologist, such as Herbart and Lotze.

Finally, with a focus on humans themselves, romanticism, as seen in the philosophies of Herder, Rousseau, and Goethe, and existentialism, as seen in the work of Kierkegaard and Nietzsche, represented reactions to the materialism and mechanism of the age. We will see their influence again in the more person-centered approaches to psychology, such as phenomenology and humanistic psychoanalysis (Chapter 16).

Although we have identified many influences on psychology from the romantic movement of the 19th century, Schneider (1998) has argued that present-day psychology has increasingly lost touch with romanticism's legacy. According to Schneider, the price of the movement away from romanticism "includes psychology's deepening neglect of its meaning and significance for the lifeworld [for persons' real lives]; its further dissociation from the arts and humanities; and its widening reductionism" (p. 286). From the romantic perspective, psychology should consider supporting approaches that stress wholeness of experience, the use of intuition and imagination, and qualitative/ descriptive accounts of behavior.

Last but not least, it can be argued that rationalism itself evolved directly into modern cognitive psychology through the transitional phase of Gestalt psychology. As we will see in Chapter 14, the Gestaltists were able to create a productive synthesis between rational philosophy and the growing body of psychologically relevant physiological phenomena, to which we turn next.

SUMMARY

The chapter's theme was the Continental reaction to and contrast with British empiricism and associationism.

Rationalism

Reading Hume stimulated Immanuel Kant to write *Critique of Pure Reason.* Reacting against Hume, Kant made causality part of the mind's inherent structure, along with such things as space and time forms, totality, and existence and nonexistence. After the mind coordinates sensations into perceptions, the perceptions are changed into knowledge by Kant's innate categories of thought. Our experience of the outside world (noumenal world) is filtered through the structure of our minds to give us the phenomenal world. Kant's work particularly influenced Gestalt psychology and the German physiologists Müller and Helmholtz.

Georg Wilhelm Friedrich Hegel accepted Kant's categories of thought and gave them objective status in the Absolute (God). In Hegel's philosophy, everything evolves toward the Absolute through dialectical movement in which a thesis leads to its opposite (antithesis), which begets an emerging whole (synthesis).

Johann Friedrich Herbart studied under a Kantian disciple and visited the educational reformer Johann Heinrich Pestalozzi. Herbart's application of psychology to education earns him the title of the founder of educational psychology. And by writing the first textbook on psychology, Herbart becomes a candidate for the honor of being the founder of psychology as a science. However, like Kant, Herbart saw psychology as a nonexperimental science. Herbart also considered psychology amenable to mathematical modeling, and his conception of the threshold of consciousness and the repression of incompatible ideas influenced Fechner and Freud, respectively.

Trained as a physician, Rudolf Hermann Lotze eventually filled Herbart's chair in philosophy at Göttingen. Lotze indirectly influenced psychology through his students and friends, including Ernst Weber and Gustav Fechner, G.E. Müller, Carl Stumpf, and Franz Brentano. His major direct contribution came through his theory of space perception in the empirical tradition.

Romanticism

In philosophy, romanticism was a reaction against both empiricism and rationalism and emphasized the whole person, particularly the person's feelings. An early romanticist, Johann Gottfried Herder was fascinated by unsophisticated human nature and stressed the importance of the historical method for understanding people. Herder influenced Wundt, whose *Völkerpsychologie* included the study of language, myths, and social customs through historical records.

Jean-Jacques Rousseau discussed the social contract between people and their legitimate government in *The Social Contract,* which became the bible of the French Revolution. Rousseau's *Émile* influenced the leading educationists and Kant, who saw in Rousseau's appeal to feelings the answer to the era's irreligion.

Johann Wolfgang von Goethe was a writer, critic, and scientist whose belief in the study of intact, meaningful phenomena led to phenomenology, which was an important antecedent of Gestalt psychology. Goethe's color vision observations stimulated the work of Jan Purkinje, of Purkinje shift fame.

In *The World as Will and Representation,* Arthur Schopenhauer presented his philosophy. For Schopenhauer, the world is idea and the world is will. The "will to live" is the driving impulse of nature, whose purpose is to enable us to live long enough to reproduce. Escape from the will's dictates can come through asceticism or aesthetics. Schopenhauer's pessimistic philosophy influenced Freud, Wundt, and the existential philosophers.

Existentialism

Sören Kierkegaard is considered the founder of existentialism, the philosophy stressing the individual's isolation in a hostile environment while emphasizing freedom of choice and accepting responsibility for one's actions. For Kierkegaard, an individual who lives life merely for sensory pleasure exists on the aesthetic level; achievement of the ethical level requires the individual to accept rules of conduct developed by reason. One achieves the ethical plane, on which the individual enters a relationship with God, through a leap of faith, not through reasoning.

Friedrich Nietzsche developed a philosophy combining creative energy with order and restraint. He saw the next step in human evolution as the *Übermensch,* or superman, who would have the courage to challenge all previous values and to respond to the internal will to power.

CONNECTIONS QUESTIONS

1. How does rationalism connect with, and contrast with, empiricism?
2. Of the individuals we have encountered so far, which seem most important for the rise of psychology as an independent discipline?
3. What is the nativist–empiricist debate, and why has it been so important for psychology?
4. In what ways was romanticism a part of psychology's beginning?
5. Describe as many examples of Hegel's dialectical process as you can from psychology and other sources.
6. Compare and contrast the central ideas of early existentialism with those of other "isms" we have considered (e.g., rationalism, romanticism, positivism).

KEY NAMES AND TERMS

apperceptive mass (p. 129)
categorical imperative (p. 125)
categories of thought (p. 124)
dialectical movement (p. 126)
existentialism (p. 137)
Johann Wolfgang von Goethe (p. 133)
Georg Wilhelm Friedrich Hegel (p. 125)
Johann Friedrich Herbart (p. 128)
Johann Gottfried Herder (p. 131)
Immanuel Kant (p. 122)
Sören Aabye Kierkegaard (p. 138)
local sign (p. 130)
Rudolf Hermann Lotze (p. 130)
Friedrich Wilhelm Nietzsche (p. 139)
noumenal world (p. 124)
phenomenal world (p. 124)
Jan Purkinje (p. 135)
rationalism (p. 122)
romanticism (p. 131)
Jean-Jacques Rousseau (p. 132)
Arthur Schopenhauer (p. 135)
threshold (limen of consciousness) (p. 129)
Giambattista Vico (p. 132)
will (p. 136)
Christian von Wolff (p. 123)

SUGGESTED READINGS

Archer, R. L. (Ed.) (1964). *Jean Jacques Rousseau: His educational theories selected from Émile, Julie and other writings.* Woodbury, NY: Barron's Educational Series, Inc. This is an excellent introduction to Rousseau's educational theories.

Durant, W. (1961). *The story of philosophy.* New York: Washington Square Press. Durant's chapters on Kant and Schopenhauer are entertaining and informative. The chapter on Schopenhauer is full of quotes from the philosopher, and Kant's chapter contains much *about* Kant but little *by* Kant. The reason for this, Durant noted, is that "Kant is the last person in the world whom we should read on Kant" (p. 253). The chapter on Kant ends with "A Note on Hegel."

Goethe, J.W.v. (1967). *Faust: A tragedy.* New York: Modern Library. (Original work published 1808, 1832) Perhaps Goethe's best-known work, it demonstrates not only the author's writing talents but his interest in such diverse topics as science and the occult. It is widely available in many formats and editions.

Kant, I. (1929). *Critique of pure reason* (N. K. Smith, Trans.). New York: St. Martin's Press. (Original work published 1787) Kant is an important thinker for both ethics and the philosophy of mind and perhaps the premier philosopher in this chapter. If you are interested in rationalism, it will be well worth your effort to read at least some of Kant's *Critique.*

Kaufmann, W. (1974). *Nietzsche: Philosopher, psychologist, antichrist* (4th ed.). Princeton, NJ: Princeton University Press. First published more than 50 years ago, this remains the definitive biography of Nietzsche. In addition, the book examines in detail Nietzsche's many (and often uncredited) contributions to psychology.

Nordentoft, K. (1972). *Kierkegaard's psychology* (B. Kirmmse, Trans.). Pittsburgh: Duquesne University Press. There are some who would argue that Kierkegaard should be considered a founder of modern psychology. Although we do not support that position, this book will help you understand why the argument is sometimes made.

Schopenhauer, A. (1969). *The world as will and representation* (E. F. J. Payne, Trans.). New York: Dover Publications, Inc. (Original work published 1844) Schopenhauer is more readable than Hegel and Kant, and this two-volume work is a good place to begin any investigation of his philosophy.

Physiological Influences on the Development of Psychology

CHAPTER 7

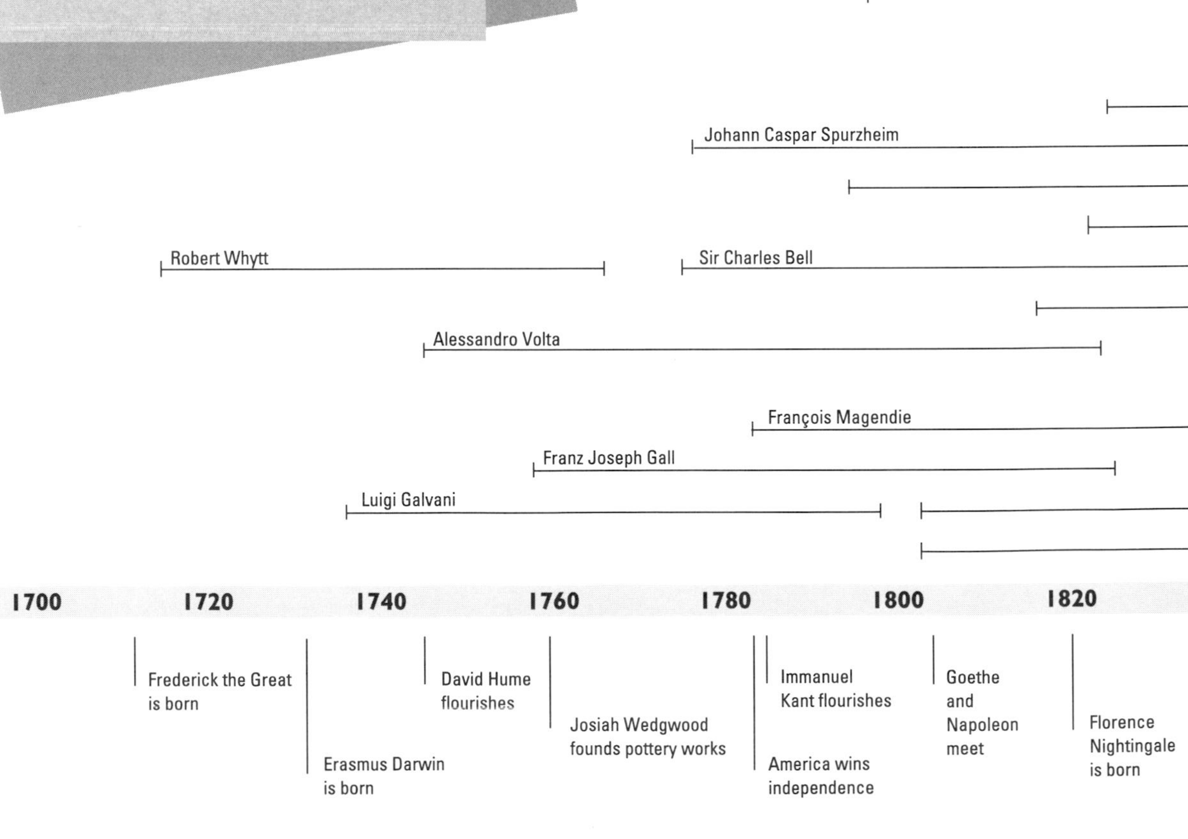

OUTLINE

Review of Early Speculation

Electricity and Nerve Function

- Hermann Ludwig von Helmholtz
- Ewald Hering and Opponent-Process Theory

Localization of Function

- The Bell-Magendie Law
- The Doctrine of Specific Nerve Energies
- Phrenology
- Pierre Flourens and the Ablation Method
- Phineas P. Gage—A Case of Accidental Ablation
- Localization of Language Areas
- Electrical Brain Stimulation and Localization of Function
- Neuron Doctrine or Nerve Network?

Psychophysics

- Ernst Weber
- Gustav Theodor Fechner

Conclusions

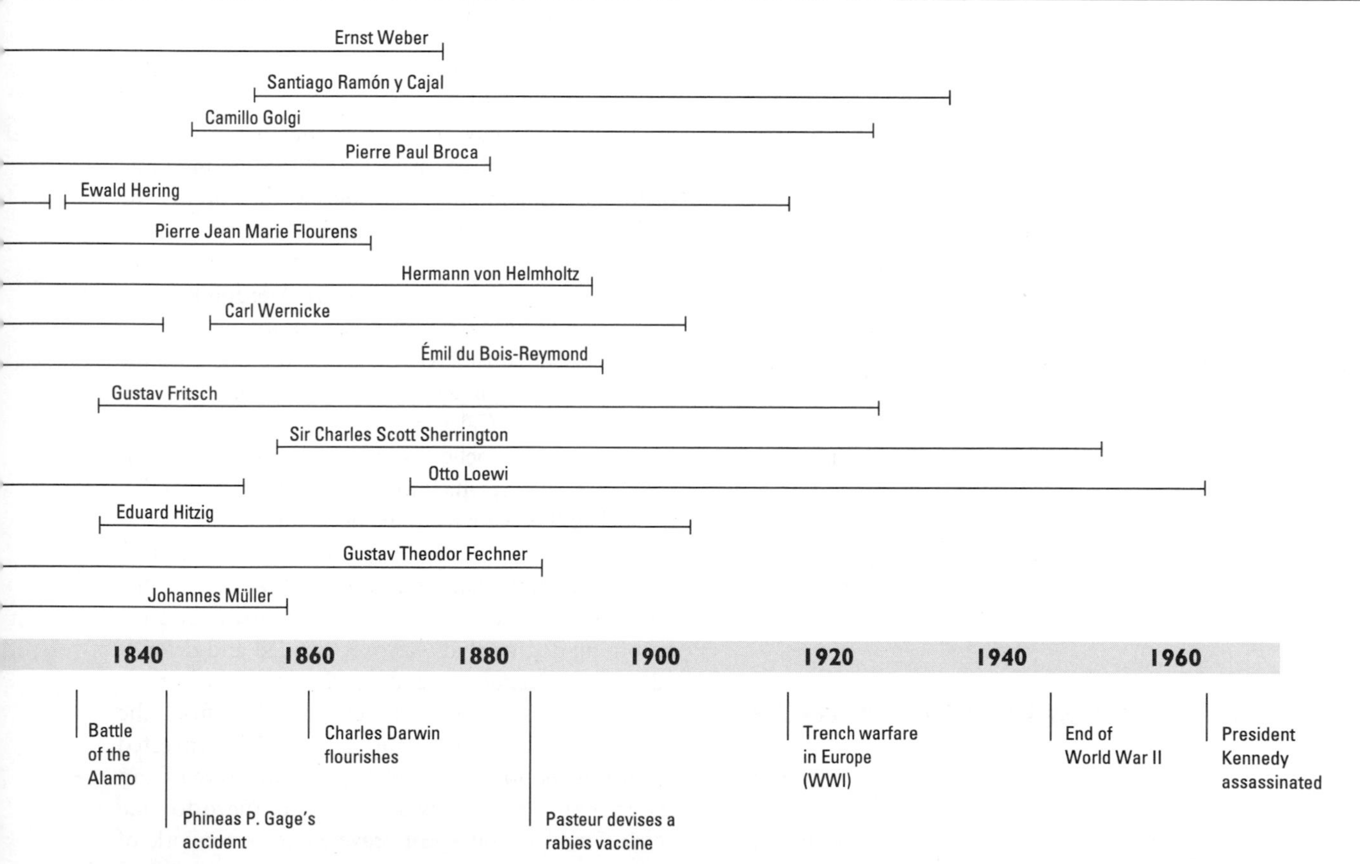

Realistically, all the early physiologists and philosophers could do was speculate about the nature and locus of "mind," because the technology necessary to achieve valid insights into the operations of the nervous system were often centuries in the future. Within their limitations, some of the ancients guessed correctly; but others had ideas that, from our 21st-century perspective, were amusing. Before we congratulate ourselves too quickly, we should note that our current theories may seem as outmoded to neuroscientists 100 years from now as many of the early theories of nervous system structure and function seem to us today. However, neuroscience has made great strides in the last 2 centuries, and in this chapter we will examine the people and the ideas that laid the foundation for our current knowledge.

One theme stands out in the early study of the physiological basis of mind: the demystification of the nervous system. This can be seen in the finally accepted conclusion that the brain is the organ of mind, emphasized by the phrenologists, supported by Flourens's animal research, and dramatically demonstrated by the personality changes in accident-victim P. P. Gage. This demystification will be revealed further with the recognition of the electrical nature of many nervous system activities and in the experimental recording by Helmholtz of the speed of the nerve impulse. Helmholtz's demonstrations of the susceptibility of the nervous system to investigation were amplified by the 19th-century development of such major investigative techniques as ablation, electrical stimulation, and the staining of neural tissue. We will see how the staining method enabled Ramón y Cajal to definitively support neuronal theory over the neural net idea. As a final example of the demystification, we will examine the controversy over localization or nonlocalization of function in the nervous system, which eventually produced evidence that many functions are localized in particular nervous system areas.

REVIEW OF EARLY SPECULATION

The first recorded reference to the brain is found in the Edwin Smith Surgical Papyrus, which was produced in Egypt in about 3000 B.C.E. and is known to us from a copy made in about 1600 B.C.E. (Marshall & Magoun, 1998). The reference appears in an account of a severe head injury that penetrated both the skull and underlying tissues to expose the brain itself. The next recorded account comes to us from the Greek physician Alcmaeon, discussed briefly in Chapter 2.

As certain as we are today that behavior is a function of brain activity, we have difficulty comprehending that in the past there was considerably less agreement. For example, Aristotle (Chapter 2) taught that the brain cooled the blood and that the mind was in the heart, even though 50 years earlier Hippocrates had said:

> Men ought to know that from the brain and from the brain only, arise our pleasures, joys, laughter and jests, as well as our sorrows, pains, griefs and tears. Through it, in particular, we think, see, hear, and distinguish the ugly from the beautiful, the bad from the good, the pleasant from the unpleasant. (Jones, 1923, p. 129)

As briefly mentioned in Chapter 2, **Herophilus** (ca. 335–280 B.C.E.), founder of the anatomy school at Alexandria, may have been the first to dissect the human body in order to study its anatomy. Although Herophilus considered the brain the main organ of the nervous system and the seat of intelligence, he located the mind in the brain's cavities or ventricles. In addition, Herophilus distinguished between sensory and motor nerves.

Galen also considered the brain the organ of the mind and was strongly opposed to Aristotle's placing it in the heart. Galen wrote extensively about the brain's ventricles, believing they were the reservoir for the animal spirits, which many ancient Greeks felt distinguished the living from the nonliving.

As we noted in Chapter 2, Galen's and Aristotle's views were important because they were accepted and systematized by the early Christian Church, becoming dogma that was propounded and defended until the Renaissance. According to the Church's model of mind, nutrients were absorbed from the intestines and passed to the liver, which converted them into *natural spirit.* Natural spirit flowed from the liver to the heart, where it was changed to *vital spirit.* Finally, vital spirit traveled to a network of blood vessels at the base of the brain, where it became *animal spirit* and was stored in the ventricles.

The Church's model of mind focused on the fluid-filled ventricles, which were incorrectly seen as three chambers, one behind the other. In 1490, **Leonardo da Vinci** (1452–1519) drew anatomical studies of the head incorporating the ventricular scheme. Note how the optic nerves converge on the first chamber in both the side view and the view from above. As you might guess, sensory analysis was believed to occur in the first ventricle. Images formed there were passed to the middle ventricle, which was considered to be the seat of reason, thought, and judgment. The last ventricle held memory.

Between 1504 and 1507, da Vinci dissected an ox brain. Instead of finding the nerves from the sense organs all ending in the first ventricle pair, da Vinci found that many terminated around the middle ventricle, in the brain area we call the thalamus. Accordingly, he decided that sensory analysis took place in the middle ventricle. Although still incorrect, da Vinci's conclusion cast doubt on the model the Church had so vigorously defended.

René Descartes (Chapter 4) broke completely with the prevailing model, conceptualizing the nervous system hydraulically, with hollow tubes (nerves) leading to empty bladders (muscles). For Descartes, the nerves contained threads connecting the sensory receptors to the brain. Sensory stimulation tightened the threads, which caused a "pore" to open in the brain, releasing animal spirits that flowed back to the appropriate muscle. Expanding from the animal spirits, the muscle caused movement. Descartes' model resembled the workings of the lifelike statues in the gardens of St. Germain (Chapter 4).

At least Descartes' hydraulic model was easy to test. Experiments by Jan Swammerdam (1637–1680) and Francis Glisson (ca. 1597–1677) did not support Descartes' nervous system model, and Luigi Galvani (discussed later) found that frog muscles could still contract after separation from the frog's body. Obviously, this is impossible if animal spirits from the brain produce muscle contraction.

Meanwhile, other investigators such as **Robert Whytt** (1714–1766) and George Prochaska (1749–1820) were overhauling Descartes' understanding of reflex action. Whytt studied frog spinal reflexes, demonstrating that automatic movements were possible with stimulation of only a portion of the spinal cord. He emphasized the difference between voluntary movements depending on an act of will and involuntary movements occurring too rapidly to involve reason. However, reflexes were not quite unconscious for Whytt, as he thought the nervous tissue contained a sentient (conscious) principle. In 1751, Whytt described the reflexive contraction of the pupil to light, which is sometimes called **Whytt's reflex.**

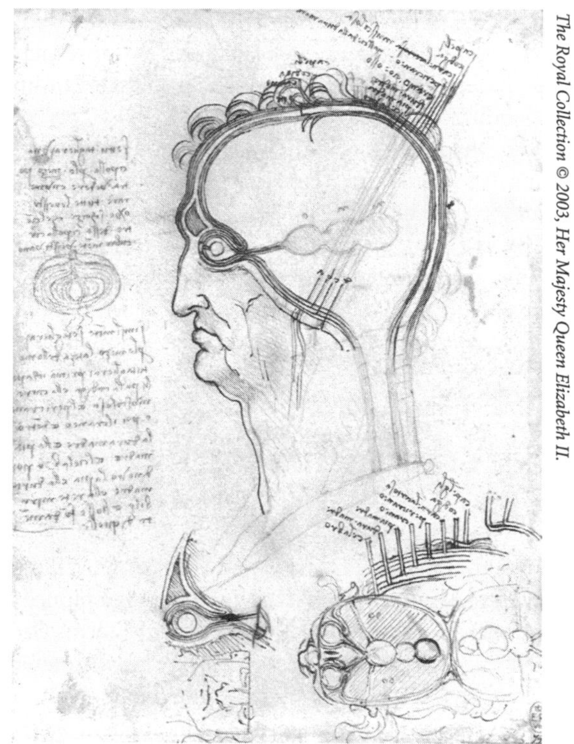

Leonardo da Vinci's drawing illustrating the Church's ventricular scheme

Scottish physician and physiologist **Marshall Hall** (1790–1857) worked to clarify reflex action in the first half of the 19th century. Hall distinguished voluntary movement (depending on consciousness and higher brain centers), respiratory movement (involuntary and depending on lower brain areas), involuntary movement (depending on muscular irritability when muscle is directly stimulated), and reflex movement. For Hall, reflex movement was independent of consciousness and the brain, depending only on the spinal cord. Hall's conception of the reflex paved the way for modern conceptions of the reflex arc (e.g., John Dewey, Chapter 11; Ivan Pavlov, Chapter 12).

By the end of the 18th century, the hydraulic model was completely overturned, and the ancient concept of animal spirits was replaced with something that seemed equally farfetched—electricity.

ELECTRICITY AND NERVE FUNCTION

In 1600, English physicist and physician William Gilbert (1540–1603) published *De Magnete,* a pioneering work on electricity that introduced the terms *electric force, electric attraction,* and *magnetic pole.* Interest in this mysterious force grew rapidly, and the 18th century has been called the "Age of Electricity." Scientists soon speculated that electricity might be responsible for nerve function, but testing this notion was a problem: Early investigators could neither reliably generate electricity nor measure it. Matters improved toward the end of the 18th century, however.

An Italian lecturer in anatomy and professor of obstetrics at the University of Bologna, **Luigi Galvani** (1737–1798) began experiments on electricity in about 1780. The results were published in 1791 in *De viribus electricitatis in motu muscularis commentarius* (*A Commentary on the Role of Electricity in Muscular Contractions*).

Galvani found that a frog's leg twitched when one of its nerves received an electrical charge, and he also found that twitching occurred when the leg muscles were hung between different metals. For example, iron and silver produced a vigorous reaction, and the leg would continue to twitch as long as it was suspended. Galvani had made an organic battery, because an electrical current is produced when a salt solution connects two dissimilar metals, and the frog's leg and motor nerve are essentially salt solutions.

Although Galvani's conclusion that his frogs had generated electricity was soon challenged, his belief that nervous energy has an electrical component was important. The **galvanic skin response** (GSR, a change in the skin's electrical conductivity) is named after him.

Italian physicist **Count Alessandro Volta** (1745–1827) concluded that Galvani's frogs had merely conducted electricity generated by the two metals and the attached frog leg. In 1800, Volta made the first battery without animal tissue. The Voltaic pile consisted of alternating layers of disks of silver, brine-moistened cardboard, and zinc. By constructing an inorganic battery, Volta believed he had disproved the notion that animals generated electricity, but other eminent scientists of the period (e.g., Johannes Müller, discussed later) did not abandon the idea.

Volta's reliable method for producing a "galvanic current" led physicists to make an instrument—called, appropriately enough, a galvanometer—to measure the current. As Galvani anticipated, an electrical current was observed when a galvanometer was applied to nervous tissue. This observation so captivated German-born Swiss physician **Émil du Bois-Reymond** (1818–1896) that he devoted his life to electrophysiology, the field he created.

While studying the electrical nature of nervous tissue, du Bois-Reymond formulated the idea that nervous and muscle tissue are charged with positive and negative particles. He demonstrated that when nerves are electrically stimulated, the charged particles reverse their positions. We call this reversal the **action potential,** and it is considered the nervous system's basic means of long-distance communication.

In keeping with this chapter's central theme, du Bois-Reymond's work demystified the nerve impulse, bringing it from the realm of animal spirits into the real world of science. This suggested to Hermann von Helmholtz that the speed of a nerve impulse might actually be measurable.

Hermann Ludwig von Helmholtz

Although Helmholtz is considered one of the greatest 19th-century scientists, this label may be doing him a disservice. In fact, Helmholtz was one of the greatest scientists of all time. Shortly after Helmholtz's death,

Wellcome Library, London.

Helmholtz (1821–1894) at about the time he first measured the speed of the nerve impulse

Carl Stumpf (Chapter 8) wrote: "Since the death of Darwin, the loss of no one in the scientific world has made such a deep impression as that of Helmholtz. . . . Whenever he smote the rock of nature, there gushed forth the living waters of knowledge" (1895, p. 1). "By inclination he was a physicist, but at various times he also was a physician, a psychologist, a physiologist, an anatomist, a meteorologist, a mathematician, and a chemist" (Adler, 2000, p. 15). Adler even suggested that Helmholtz's influence could be tied to the invention of the radio and television through his student Heinrich Hertz. Some have considered Helmholtz a physiological psychologist as well (e.g., Stumpf, 1895).

Hermann Ludwig Ferdinand von Helmholtz (1821–1894) was born in Potsdam, Germany. His father was a teacher of philology (the study of language and culture) and philosophy at a Potsdam *Gymnasium.* Helmholtz's mother was Caroline Penne, a descendant of William Penn, the English Quaker reformer who founded Pennsylvania.

A sickly child, Helmholtz was first tutored at home by his father. Often confined to his room for long periods of time, Helmholtz particularly liked playing with wooden blocks. At the age of 7, when he began school in Potsdam, he "astonished his masters in the Geometry Class, because (thanks to his toy blocks) he knew all the facts which they expected him to learn" (Koenigsberger, 1906/1965, p. 6).

At the *Gymnasium,* Helmholtz excelled in science but was less scholarly in languages and history. In fact, while his class studied Cicero or Virgil, Helmholtz could often be found under the table working out the passage of light rays through a telescope (Koenigsberger, 1906/1965). By the time Helmholtz graduated from the *Gymnasium,* he had decided to become a physicist.

Financially unable to pursue his interest in physics, Helmholtz entered a Berlin medical institute that charged no tuition to young men who promised to serve as Prussian Army surgeons. Although he was not a student at the University of Berlin, he was greatly influenced by a physiology professor there—Johannes Müller—and several of Müller's students, particularly du Bois-Reymond.

Müller's influence on Helmholtz did not extend to his mentor's belief in vitalism—the idea that life involves a vital principle distinct from physical and chemical forces. In fact, Helmholtz, along with du Bois-Reymond and others, eventually initiated a movement known as "Helmholtz's School of Medicine," whose chief purpose was to rid science of Müller's vitalism. As we will see in Chapter 15, Freud was importantly influenced by a member of this school in Austria, Ernst Brücke, who was another of Müller's students.

After graduating from the medical institute in 1842, Helmholtz began work in Potsdam as an army surgeon. However, he continued his studies in mathematics and physics. In 1847, the 26-year-old Helmholtz read his famous paper on the conservation of energy to the *Physikalische Gesellschaft* (Physical Society) in Berlin. Conservation of energy was important for psychology because it raised further doubts about the possibility of an immaterial mind affecting a material body. Accepting the principle leads to the conclusion that all physical changes have physical causes, which in turn suggests a materialistic, deterministic psychology. Helmholtz's mathematical formulation indicated to his fellow scientists that he belonged in academia, not in the military.

In 1849, Helmholtz went to the University of Königsberg as an untenured junior professor, but in 2 years he was promoted to a full professorship (Brauns, 1997). In just 7 years at Königsberg, Helmholtz measured the speed of the nerve impulse, invented the ophthalmoscope (a device to study the retina, which is the only part of the central nervous system that can be examined noninvasively without elaborate equipment), and revised an earlier color vision theory. Next, Helmholtz went to Bonn for 2 years as professor of physiology, which was followed by the same position at Heidelberg, where he stayed until 1871. Finally, Helmholtz was called to be professor of physics at the University of Berlin, the peak of German academia.

Helmholtz traveled to America in 1893 to see the Chicago World's Fair. On the return voyage, he fell down a stairway and never fully recovered. Helmholtz died in 1894.

Measuring the Speed of the Nerve Impulse

In his *Handbook of Human Physiology,* Müller (discussed later) listed three different estimates for the speed of the nerve impulse, which ranged from 9,000 feet per minute (at 150 feet per second, this was reasonable) to 57,600 million feet per second, which is nearly 60 times the speed of light! Although Müller disagreed with the fastest estimate, he thought that the speed was extremely rapid, perhaps approaching the speed of light, and would never be measured.

Helmholtz soon proved Müller wrong. Using frog motor nerves of different lengths and a pendulum myograph (an instrument for recording muscle contractions), which he had invented, Helmholtz measured the speed of nerve conduction and found it to be much slower than the speed of light. In fact, at about 90 feet per second, it was even slower than the speed of sound. Helmholtz closed a lecture with the following illustration of the slowness of the nerve impulse: A "whale probably feels a wound near its tail in about one second, and requires another second to send back orders to the tail to defend itself" (Koenigsberger, 1906/1965, p. 72).

Helmholtz next measured the speed of transmission in sensory nerves by stimulating a man on either the toe or the thigh and asking the man to respond by pushing a button. Helmholtz found that the man's reaction time was longer with the greater distance traveled. By subtracting the shorter reaction time from the longer, Helmholtz computed transmission speeds for impulses along sensory nerves ranging from approximately 50 to 100 meters per second (165 to 330 feet per second).

Although du Bois-Reymond later measured the speeds more precisely, the importance of the discovery that nervous transmission was not nearly instantaneous was incalculable. As Boring (1950) put it, "The most important effect of the experiment and all the research that followed upon it was . . . that it brought the soul to time, . . . [it] actually captured the essential agent of mind in the toils of natural science" (p. 42). On a more mundane level, Helmholtz's measurement of the speed of the impulse "paved the way for electrophysiological studies of somatic [bodily] sensation . . ." (Finger, 1994, p. 136).

Other Contributions of Helmholtz

Young-Helmholtz Theory. In 1798, John Dalton (1766–1844), the famed English chemist who developed atomic theory, wrote on color deficiencies shared by him and his brother. Dalton's work was followed in 1802 by English physician and physicist **Thomas Young**'s (1773–1829) proposal that color sensations come from patterns of stimulation of three different receptor types in the eye.

Almost universally recognized as a genius during his lifetime, Young was, among other things, the most important translator of the Rosetta Stone, the founder of the modern wave theory of light, the inventor of the diffraction grating, the first to attempt to measure the diameter of a molecule, and the developer of a theory of tides far superior to Newton's earlier one (Martin-

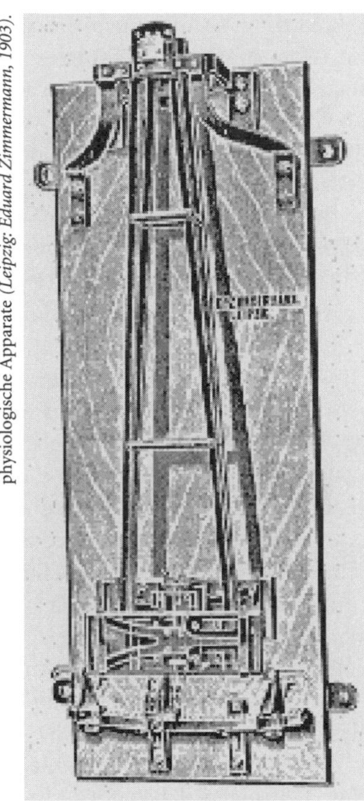

Helmholtz's pendulum myograph

dale, 2001). In the early 1850s, Helmholtz rediscovered Young's relatively ignored theory and modified it slightly; it became known as the **Young-Helmholtz theory,** or **trichromatic theory** (*trichromatic* means three colors). Helmholtz considered Young one of the brightest persons who ever lived but concluded it was Young's bad luck to live at a time in which he was so far ahead of his contemporaries. In fact, there may never have been a right time for a person with Young's remarkable talents and intelligence.

Helmholtz stated that there are three different sets of fibers in the eye, the stimulation of each producing a different color sensation (i.e., red, green, and violet). A color other than one of the primaries stimulates some combination of the three fibers, resulting in a perceived color different from the primaries. For example, looking at a ripe banana would activate some combination of red and green fibers, resulting in the perception of yellow. (If you think the combination of red and green results in brown, you are thinking of mixing pigments, which produces a subtractive color mixture. The eye's receptors perform an additive color mixture, which you obtain by combining colored lights.)

Critics of the Young-Helmholtz theory pointed out that the most common color defect is the inability to differentiate red and green. In trichromatic theory, yellow results from stimulation of red fibers and green fibers, which are assumed to be defective in red-green "blindness." Thus, the theory would predict incorrectly that a person with a red-green defect should also have trouble seeing yellow. Such incorrect predictions led to other color-vision theories, the most successful of which was proposed by Helmholtz-contemporary Ewald Hering (discussed later).

Place Theory of Pitch Perception. In studying the auditory system, Helmholtz was primarily concerned with accounting for the ability to discriminate between different pitched sounds. Helmholtz sought the mechanism we use to tell the difference between a high-pitched sound (e.g., a fingernail scraped across a blackboard) and a low-pitched sound (e.g., a foghorn).

The inner ear's cochlea contains a structure called the basilar membrane. Normally coiled, the basilar membrane looks like a harp when uncoiled—narrow at one end and wide at the other. Helmholtz assumed that fibers at the narrow end resonate to high-pitched sounds, whereas fibers at the wide end resonate to low-pitched sounds. Thus, Helmholtz's theory was an early version of place theory, which holds that the place of basilar stimulation determines a sound's pitch.

Georg von Békésy (1899–1972) won the Nobel Prize in physiology or medicine in 1961 for his modern **place theory of pitch perception.** To study the basilar membrane's movement in response to different sound frequencies, von Békésy drilled a tiny "observation window" in a cochlea from a recently deceased person. Then, he sprinkled silver particles on the normally transparent membrane to make it visible through a microscope. Using stroboscopic lighting timed to the stimulation frequency, von Békésy saw that the peak of the membrane's vibration depended on the frequency, with high-frequency stimulation causing peaks near the membrane's base and low-frequency stimulation producing less precise peaks closer to the apex. Von Békésy (1960) concluded that the place of maximal vibration determines a sound's perceived pitch.

Ewald Hering and Opponent-Process Theory

As a medical student at the University of Leipzig, **Ewald Hering** (1834–1918) was instructed by both Weber and Fechner (discussed later). Although Hering did not study with Johannes Müller, he was greatly influenced by Müller's work. Hering earned his M.D. but practiced for only 2 years before settling on physiology as a career. In 1870, Hering succeeded Jan Purkinje (Chapter 6) at Prague. In 1895, Hering accepted a professorship at Leipzig, where he became a colleague of Wundt (Chapter 8).

Hering proposed **opponent-process theory** in 1874. For Hering, there were four primaries, with the fourth being yellow. In his theory, three receptor complexes each respond in one of two opposing ways to signal either red or green, yellow or blue, or black or white. An example of a red-green system would be a retinal unit whose activity increased in response to red and decreased in response to green. Similarly, a yellow-blue complex might increase its activity when stimulated by blue and decrease its activity to yellow. The black-white process accounts for brightness perception.

Hering's opponent-process idea better explains color defect phenomena than does trichromatic theory. With Hering's theory, a person with a red-green weakness should have no trouble with blue and yellow. In addition, color weaknesses tend to be paired—there are red-green weaknesses and blue-yellow weaknesses—which is a feature of opponent-process theory.

Hering's theory also readily explains the **negative afterimage,** which is the perception of the complementary or opposite color after prolonged stimulation with a particular hue. For example, if you stare at a picture of a red dog for 2 minutes and then look at a white space, you will briefly see a green dog there. According to opponent-process theory, fatiguing the red response in a complex by staring at a red image causes the green system to account for more activity of the complex when you look at the white space. Hence, you see a green dog.

After Hering's theory was introduced, several color-vision theories appeared, of which **Christine Ladd-Franklin**'s became perhaps the best known (Boring, 1950). Christine Ladd (1847–1930) earned a Vassar degree in 1869 and began graduate studies at Johns Hopkins as a "special student," a status reflecting Hopkins's exclusion of women. Ladd was admitted because a prominent Hopkins mathematics professor, aware of her already-published work, interceded on her behalf. Although she completed the Ph.D. requirements in 1882, the degree was not actually granted until 1926, when Hopkins celebrated its 50th anniversary. Soon after finishing at Hopkins, Ladd married Fabian Franklin, a member of the mathematics department.

A trip to Europe in 1891–1892 introduced Ladd-Franklin to several outstanding German psychologists and physiologists. With G. E. Müller's (Chapter 8) support, she conducted experimental work in vision in his Göttingen laboratory. In addition, Ladd-Franklin worked in Helmholtz's Berlin laboratory and attended lectures by Arthur König (Chapter 8), who supported Helmholtz's trichromatic theory.

Ladd-Franklin's theory was based on the tetrachromatic (four-color) theory of Dutch ophthalmologist and physiologist Franciscus Cornelius Donders (Chapter 8). Donders had suggested that color discrimination could be explained in terms of the stimulation of optic nerve fibers by decomposing color-sensitive molecules. Ladd-Franklin's theory added a developmental focus to Donder's idea. She proposed that white receptors are basic to vision. Some white receptors developmentally split into either blue or yellow receptors, and some of the yellow receptors evolve into either red or green receptors. Hering's theory eventually supplanted Ladd-Franklin's attempted reconciliation of the Young-Helmholtz theory with Donders's theory.

Hering thought the opponent processes occurred at the level of the receptors (the rods and cones), an idea incompatible with trichromatic theory. Because of this incompatibility, Hering's theory did not

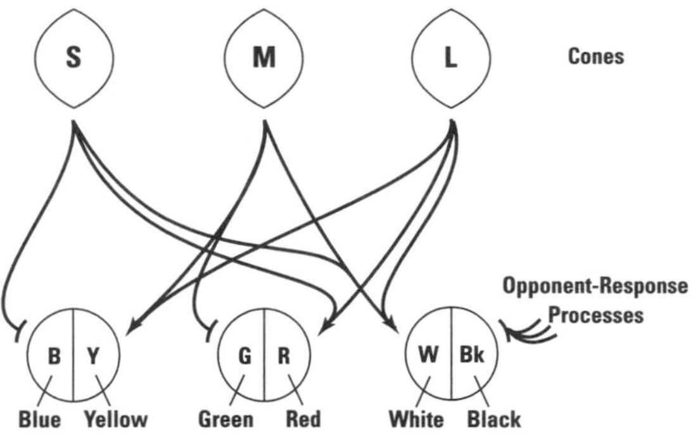

FIGURE 7.1 Wiring diagram

This diagram shows how it is possible to go from three receptors (trichromatic system) to an opponent-process system. "S," "M," and "L" refer to wavelengths of light; where "S" = short, "M" = medium, and "L" = long.

Source: From Hurvich, L. M. and Jameson, D. (1974). "Opponent Processes as a Model of Neural Organization," American Psychologist, 29, 88–102. Copyright © 1974 by the American Psychological Association. Adapted with permission.

catch on until L. M. Hurvich and Dorothea Jameson (1957) published "An Opponent-Process Theory of Color Vision." After physiological evidence supporting opponent-process theory appeared (e.g., Svaetichin & MacNichol, 1958), Hurvich and Jameson (1974) constructed a simple diagram (Figure 7.1) to show how three different cones might be "wired" to higher-level visual cells to produce opponent responses. Most authorities accept that both trichromatic theory and opponent-process theory are correct at different levels of the visual system—trichromatic theory at the receptor level and opponent-process theory at higher levels.

Helmholtz-Hering Debate

In addition to opposing Helmholtz's view of color vision, Hering was critical of Helmholtz's theory of visual space perception. Taking the nativist approach, Hering thought each retinal point innately has three local signs: one for height, one for lateral position, and one for depth. An empiricist, Helmholtz believed that space forms develop from experience and that the location of local signs is learned.

Hering's nativism was at least partly the result of Johannes Müller's influence; Müller was Kantian (Chapter 6) in his treatment of space as one of the innate intuitions. Hering, in turn, influenced Carl Stumpf, and through him, the Gestaltists (Chapter 14). On the other side, Helmholtz was following the lead of Lotze (Chapter 6) and the British empiricists (Chapter 5), and in this he influenced Wundt—briefly his assistant—who influenced Titchener and Külpe (both Chapter 8). We mention these connections because the **Helmholtz-Hering debate** became representative of the larger empiricist-nativist debate about the nature of perception, which remains with us today.

LOCALIZATION OF FUNCTION

In addition to the interest in the electrical nature of nervous activity, another thread running through 19th-century neuroscience was interest in localization of function. **Localizationists** believe specific functions reside in specific nervous system areas, whereas **nonlocalizationists** have been more impressed with the nervous system as a coordinated unit. The central question is, Are neural functions tied to one specific nervous system location?

The Bell-Magendie Law

A distinction between sensory nerves and motor nerves had been made by some (e.g., Herophilus, Galen) over the centuries, but by the beginning of the 19th century the distinction was not usually made. The spinal and cranial nerves were all assumed to have both sensory and motor functions, a nonlocalizationist position. Sir Charles Bell in England and François Magendie in France independently performed research that led to the distinction between sensory nerves and motor nerves known as the **Bell-Magendie law.** The law states that the dorsal roots of spinal nerves bring in sensory information and that the ventral roots of the spinal nerves carry motor fibers to the muscles (*dorsal* means "pertaining to the back of an organism," referring to the top of the spinal cord in a vertebrate; *ventral* refers to an animal's lower surface).

Sir Charles Bell (1774–1842)

Born in Edinburgh, Scotland, **Sir Charles Bell** (1774–1842) was a brilliant neurologist, surgeon, and physiologist whose fame extended to the Continent. One story tells of a French physiologist who, during a visit from Bell, dismissed his class without a lecture, telling the students, "*C'est assez, messieurs, vous avez vu* Charles Bell!" ("That's enough, gentlemen, you have seen Charles Bell!")

In 1811, Bell gave 100 copies of a privately published pamphlet to his friends. In it, he told of animal experiments in which he exposed the roots of the spinal nerves:

> I found that I could cut across the [dorsal root], which took its origin from the posterior portion of the spinal marrow without convulsing the muscles of the back; but that on touching the [ventral root] with the point of the knife, the muscles of the back were immediately convulsed. (Bell, 1811/1948, pp. 119–120)

Bell correctly surmised that the dorsal root was sensory and the ventral root was motor. Extending his research to cranial nerves (nerves entering the brain directly), Bell later demonstrated that some are entirely sensory, some entirely motor, and some are mixed.

In 1822, French physiologist **François Magendie** (1783–1855) published experiments on the spinal nerves of puppies. (Antivivisectionists—people opposed to surgical research on live animals—often cite Magendie's research as an example of science's cruelty to animals, because it was performed without anesthesia, like all the animal work of this period.) When Magendie cut the dorsal root, pinching the animal's affected limb produced no reaction, although the limb still moved spontaneously. Magendie concluded that the limb was anesthetized, not paralyzed, and the cut dorsal root had carried sensory information. Cutting a ventral root paralyzed the limb, indicating that the ventral root was motor.

Magendie's publication triggered a battle over priority. Although Magendie's research was more thorough and convincing than Bell's, the fact that most historians call the discovery the Bell-Magendie law suggests Bell and his supporters were victorious.

Magendie was also the teacher of **Claude Bernard** (1813–1878), whom some consider the "father" of experimental physiology (and psychology) in France. After an unsuccessful attempt at a literary career, Bernard studied medicine in Paris. In 1841, he became Magendie's assistant at the Collège de France and worked with Magendie until his own appointment to the chair of general physiology in 1854. The next year he succeeded Magendie as professor of experimental physiology. Bernard disliked philosophy, and his efforts in establishing experimentation in France greatly influenced William James's (Chapter 10) conception of psychology (Taylor, 1990).

The Bell-Magendie law supports localization of function, because it says that sensory and motor functions are separated in spinal nerve roots. Bell also speculated that the separation in the roots was maintained in the spinal cord and in the brain, which might therefore contain separate sensory and motor regions.

François Magendie (1783–1855)

In addition to differentiating the sensory and motor nerves, Bell anticipated Johannes Müller's later doctrine of specific nerve energies. Bell said each of the senses is mediated by its own kind of nerve. We don't see, hear, feel, taste, or smell anything directly. Instead, an object makes an impression upon a sense organ and then the sensory nerve acts as an intermediary between the object and the brain. This idea had been held by a number of Greek philosophers and had been familiar doctrine since Galen.

The Doctrine of Specific Nerve Energies

Born in Koblenz, Germany, **Johannes Müller** (1801–1858) became professor of physiology at the University of Berlin in 1833. He is best known for his *Handbuch der Physiologie des Menschen* (*Handbook of Human Physiology*), which appeared from 1833 to 1840. The *Handbuch* summarized the physiology of the day and included many original observations and speculations. In it, Müller formulated the **doctrine of specific nerve energies,** whose central principle is that we are directly aware only of the activity in our nerves, not of the external world itself. The nerves impose their own qualities on the mind (e.g., stimulation of the optic nerve always leads to a visual experience). Müller also considered and rejected the possibility that the specific sensory quality was imparted by the area of the brain to which the nerve travels.

According to Müller's doctrine, no matter how a particular sensory nerve is stimulated, the sensation will be appropriate to the stimulated nerve. For example, visual sensations result from stimulation of the optic nerve, even if the stimulation occurs mechanically, electrically, or in some other way. Close your eyes and *gently* press the right side of your right eye. The resulting visual sensation in your left visual field is a pressure phosphene, and it shows that mechanical stimulation of the optic nerve produces a visual sensation.

Note that Müller's doctrine is consistent with a primary element of German rationalism, which is that the mind (brain, in this context) actively structures, organizes, and interprets sensory information. Although you touched the side of your eye, your brain interpreted the sensation as visual, demonstrating that you are not just a passive receiver of information as it appears in the world.

Another corollary of the doctrine is that the same stimulus applied to different sensory nerves results in different sensations, with each nerve giving the sensation appropriate to itself. For example, a tactile stimulus on your arm produces the sensation of touch, whereas the same stimulus applied to your optic nerve gives a visual sensation.

Müller's doctrine of specific nerve energies also supports the concept of localization of function, because, as we have indicated, visual sensations result from optic nerve stimulation alone, auditory sensations result from auditory nerve stimulation alone, and so on. For Müller, the doctrine of specific nerve energies differentiated the various sensory modalities. Influenced by Müller, Helmholtz applied the doctrine *within* a sense modality, arriving at a doctrine of specific fiber energies (Boring, 1950).

As you will recall, the Young-Helmholtz theory maintains there are three different sets of fibers in the eye, each set giving rise to a different color sensation. Thus, not only does stimulation of the optic nerve produce visual sensations, but stimulation of particular fibers within the optic nerve should lead to specific color sensations. Because Young had the idea of different color qualities before Helmholtz, Young in a sense anticipated both Bell and Müller on the doctrine of specific nerve energies.

Bell, Magendie, Müller, and Helmholtz all supported the idea that nervous functions were localized, with the sensory theories of Helmholtz arguing for many specific nerve qualities. Localization of function in the nervous system received even greater support from the writings and lectures of Franz Joseph Gall and an associate, Johann Caspar Spurzheim.

National Library of Medicine, Washington, D.C.

Franz Joseph Gall (1758–1828)

Phrenology

Franz Joseph Gall (1758–1828) was born in Tiefenbrunn in Baden, a region in southwestern Germany. As a physician and anatomist, Gall made some excellent contributions to 19th-century science. For example, Gall examined the brains of many different animal species and of humans of different ages and mental status and concluded that the higher mental functions are associated with the size and integrity of the brain and particularly with its outer covering, or cortex. In fact, "Gall was the first to claim that mental activities were localized in the cortex alone; the white matter he relegated to the role of a system of conduction and projection" (Neuburger, 1897/1981, p. 268). Gall is most remembered, however, for founding the pseudoscience of **phrenology** (the "science of the mind").

As a youth, Gall was often irritated by the superior performance of some of his schoolmates whom he considered to be less intelligent than himself. His schoolmates compensated for whatever they lacked in intelligence by being better "memorizers." These better memorizers all seemed to have large and protuberant eyes. Perhaps their eyes protruded because the area of the brain behind the eyes was enlarged. Because these boys all had excellent memories, Gall reasoned that verbal memory resides in the part of the frontal lobes behind the eyes. And if one faculty of the mind can be assigned to a particular brain area, perhaps others can be similarly localized.

In his "research," Gall made three questionable assumptions. First, he assumed the skull's outer contours correspond to the contours of the underlying brain. Gall believed the brain's form is determined early in life, and the skull conforms to the brain's shape. Further, he thought enlargements in a particular brain area are reflected in a bump on the skull, whereas a smaller than normal brain area might cause an indentation. Gall's second assumption was that the mind can be divided into a limited number of faculties or functions. This assumption was neither novel nor necessarily wrong, and Gall selected his faculties from the lists of the Scottish philosophers Thomas Reid and Dugald Stewart (both Chapter 5). Third, Gall assumed the mind's functions are located in different places in the brain.

Armed with these assumptions, Gall specifically studied the heads of people with special qualities. To locate such people, he traveled to foundling homes, prisons, and mental asylums and gradually accumulated a catalog of "relations" between mental abilities and bumps on the skull. For example, Gall observed several people with strong sexual drives and concluded they all had well-developed necks and unusually thick skull bases. Because the cerebellum is at the base of the brain, Gall concluded that the faculty of "amativeness" (love, particularly sexual love) resides there.

Gall eventually settled on 27 highly specific faculties, including such abilities as acquisitiveness, benevolence, mirthfulness, and secretiveness, in addition to amativeness. Later phrenologists added to Gall's list, and the arbitrary choice of faculties was one of phrenology's great defects. Ironically, there is little more agreement today on the basic personality dimensions than there was in Gall's time (see Chapter 16).

Another methodological defect was the way Gall tested his hypotheses. Observations that did not fit the system—for example, a generous person with a bulge in the acquisitiveness area—were explained away rather than being allowed to cast doubt on the system's validity. With 27 or more potentially interacting faculties, Gall could easily dismiss discrepant findings, and the generous person might have an enlarged "benevolence" area, which would obviously counteract any acquisitive tendencies.

Gall was a model of experimental propriety compared to some of his followers, however. To illustrate this, Fancher (1996) wrote:

> When a cast of Napoleon's right skull predicted qualities markedly at variance with the emperor's known personality, one phrenologist replied that his dominant side had been the left—a cast of which was conveniently missing. When Descartes's skull was examined and found deficient in the regions for reason and reflection, phrenologists retorted that the philosopher's rationality had always been overrated. (p. 81)

It is perhaps poetic justice that a story widely circulated after Gall's death that his skull had been twice as thick as average.

Gall began lecturing about what he called either craniology (the study of skulls) or organology (the study of functional "organs" on the brain's surface; Clarke & Jacyna, 1987) in Vienna, where his teaching soon attracted a large following. The most important of his disciples was **Johann Caspar Spurzheim** (1776–1832). The first great work on phrenology was written by Gall, with Spurzheim's collaboration on the first two of four volumes. Appearing between 1810 and 1819, the publication was titled *The Anatomy and Physiology of the Nervous System in General, and of the Brain in Particular, With Observations on the Possibility of Discovering the Number of Intellectual and Moral Dispositions of Men and Animals Through the Configurations of Their Heads.*

Spurzheim was phrenology's great popularizer. In fact, it was he who adopted the term *phrenology* in 1815, 2 years after he and Gall separated in Paris because of their disagreements over the nature of phrenology. One of their major differences concerned the number of faculties into which the mind could be divided. Spurzheim wanted to add to Gall's list, but Gall believed if more faculties were added, the whole process would get out of control. On his own, Spurzheim adopted a list of 37, subdivided into affective and intellectual faculties. Examples of affective qualities included destructiveness and benevolence, whereas the intellectual faculties included calculation and language. A typical phrenological chart is shown in Figure 7.2.

Gall stayed in Paris, but Spurzheim took phrenology's message all over Europe, Great Britain, and even to the United States. Phrenology was popular in America, and Orson and Lorenzo Fowler, along with their brother-in-law, Samuel Wells, established the successful firm of Fowler and Wells in New York City. Fowler and Wells also published books on phrenology, including the widely used text by

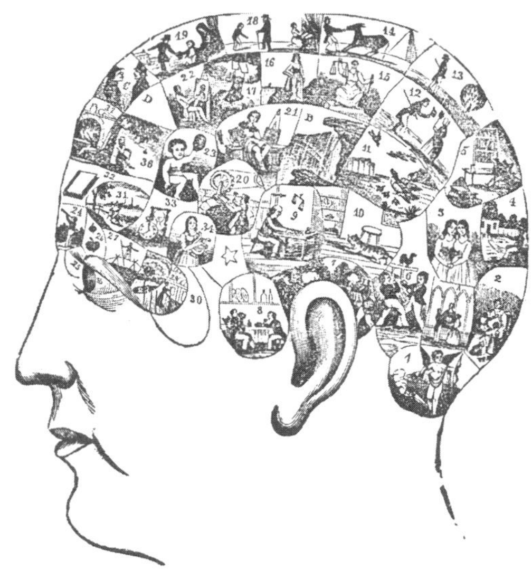

NUMBERING AND DEFINITION OF THE ORGANS.

1. AMATIVENESS, Sexual and connubial love.
2. PHILOPROGENITIVENESS. Parental love.
3. ADHESIVENESS, Friendship—sociability.
A. UNION FOR LIFE, Love of one only.
4. INHABITIVENESS, Love of home.
5. CONTINUITY, One thing at a time.
6. COMBATIVENESS, Resistance—defence.
7. DESTRUCTIVENESS, Executiveness-force.
8. ALIMENTIVENESS, Appetite, hunger.
9. ACQUISITIVENESS, Accumulation.
10. SECRETIVENESS, Policy—management.
11. CAUTIOUSNESS, Prudence, provision.
12. APPROBATIVENESS, Ambition—display.
13. SELF-ESTEEM, Self-respect—dignity.
14. FIRMNESS, Decision—perseverance.
15. CONSCIENTIOUSNESS, Justice—equity
16. HOPE, Expectation—enterprise.
17. SPIRITUALITY, Intuition--spiritual revery
18. VENERATION, Devotion—respect.
19. BENEVOLENCE, Kindness—goodness.
20. CONSTRUCTIVNESS. Mechanical ingenuity
21. IDEALITY, Refinement—taste—purity
B. SUBLIMITY, Love of grandeur.
22. IMITATION, Copying—patterning.
23. MIRTHFULNESS, Jocoseness—wit—fun
24. INDIVIDUALITY, Observation.
25. FORM, Recollection of shape.
26. SIZE, Measuring by the eye.
27. WEIGHT, Balancing—climbing.
28. COLOR, Judgment of colors.
29. ORDER, Method—system—arrangement
30. CALCULATION, Mental arithmetic.
31. LOCALITY. Recollection of places.
32. EVENTUALITY, Memory of facts
33. TIME, Cognizance of duration.
34. TUNE, Music—melody by ear.
35. LANGUAGE, Expression of ideas.
36. CAUSALITY. Applying causes to effects
37. COMPARISON, inductive reasoning.
C. HUMAN NATURE, perception of motives
D. AGREEABLENESS, Pleasantness—suavity

FIGURE 7.2 A typical phrenological chart

Drayton and McNeill (1879). The Institute of Phrenology was still in business in New York as late as 1912 (Boring, 1950), and Jesse Fowler gave phrenological examinations until her death in 1932 (Risse, 1976).

Phrenologists came to serve much the same function as some of today's applied psychologists. After performing an examination, the phrenologist could make predictions about a child's intellectual ability, about a couple's prospects for marital happiness, or about the honesty of a prospective employee. Phrenology was eventually replaced with a better method—psychological testing (Chapter 17)—early in the 20th century. In fact, the "firm of Fowler and Wells was the historical antecedent of The Psychology Corporation" (Bakan, 1966, p. 211), which publishes widely used intelligence tests and other psychological instruments.

Although widely accepted by the public, phrenology was not well received by scientists. However, phrenology did further the study of the brain. First and foremost, phrenology established the brain as the source of the mind. By doing this, it concentrated scientific efforts on understanding neural physiology and the psychophysics of sensation.

Phrenology also reinforced the idea that functions can be localized in the brain. Although the phrenologists were essentially incorrect about their choice of faculties and the faculties' locations, it remained for empirical studies to prove them wrong. Some of the most important of these studies were performed by Pierre Flourens, whose work is often viewed as supporting the nonlocalization position. In fact, Flourens handicapped the development of cortical localization theory by his successful attacks on Gall and phrenological localization of function (e.g., Clarke & Jacyna, 1987; Neuburger, 1897/1981).

Pierre Flourens and the Ablation Method

Born near Montpellier in southern France, **Pierre Jean Marie Flourens** (1794–1867) graduated from Montpellier's medical school at 19, having already published his first scientific article. Moving to Paris, he soon became the protégé of Georges Cuvier (1769–1832), a French anatomist known as the founder of comparative anatomy and paleontology. Flourens was elected to the *Académie des Sciences* in 1828, and at Cuvier's dying request, he was appointed its permanent secretary.

An ardent opponent of phrenology, Flourens performed experiments on animals to show that the functions the phrenologists had assigned to specific brain areas could not actually reside there. In his attack, Flourens used the ablation method, or, as it is sometimes called, the extirpation method. (**Ablation** is the surgical removal of part of the body.) Although Flourens did not invent the technique, he refined it greatly and has been called its father (e.g., Boring, 1950). The ablation method was widely used to study

Pierre Flourens (1794–1867)

the functions of the nervous system through at least the 1970s.

Flourens's method involved surgically damaging one of what he considered the nervous system's six basic anatomical units: the cerebral hemispheres or cerebrum, the cerebellum, the corpora quadrigemina, the medulla oblongata, the spinal cord, and the nerves themselves. Following surgery, Flourens nursed the animal back to health, if possible, and noted any changes in the animal's abilities. If a particular ability was permanently lost following the injury, Flourens inferred that the part of the nervous system removed normally controlled that ability.

Removal of the **cerebral lobes**—the outer part of the brain, lying immediately beneath the skull—abolished voluntary movements and perception. A pigeon without its cortex could be kept alive by force feeding, but it never moved voluntarily and appeared insensitive to visual or auditory stimulation. Flourens concluded the cerebrum was the site of perception, intelligence, and the will.

Without its **cerebellum** (a brain structure below and behind the cerebral lobes), a dog still possessed all its intellectual faculties and its perceptual abilities. What was destroyed was the animal's ability to coordinate its movements, which obviously had nothing to do with Gall's amativeness organ.

Without its **corpora quadrigemina** (an area in the center of the animal's brain), a bird was blind, even though the cerebral lobes were intact, and Flourens concluded the structures were necessary for vision. Damage to the **medulla oblongata**—the first brain structure after the spinal cord—resulted in an animal's death, and the medulla was called the "vital knot," even before Flourens's investigations.

Finally, Flourens concluded that the spinal cord's function was conduction, whereas the function of the nerves was excitation. Although Flourens had found that each of the six units has a specific function, he was more impressed by the nervous system's ability to function as a unitary system. In addition to a specific function, the units were subjected to a common action of the system working as a whole. Within each of the nervous system's major parts, Flourens thought there was no differentiation of function. For example, he believed perception and willing were properties of the whole cerebrum—a nonlocalizationist position—rather than of any specific areas within it.

Flourens found evidence for this communal action in animals subjected to ablation in which recovery of a lost function occurred over time. Knowing that brain tissue does not regenerate, Flourens reasoned that other brain areas must have assumed some of the ablated areas' lost functions. This phenomenon of **neural plasticity** is still investigated today (e.g., Finger, 1988).

Flourens's apparent evidence for a nonlocalizationist position resulted from the way he performed his ablations. By making slices across a region such as the cerebrum, Flourens in fact damaged several functional areas at once, producing a general deficit rather than more specific losses. "It is possible to

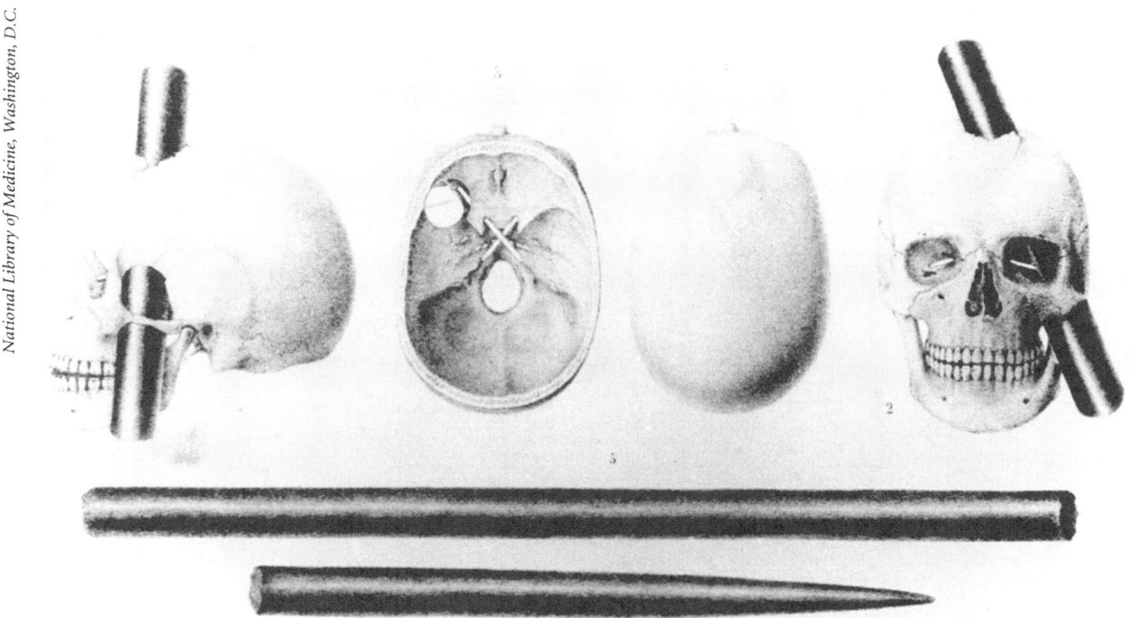

This photo illustrates the size of the tamping rod and Phineas Gage's skull

think of Gall as the visionary who had the right idea [functional localization] but the wrong method, and of Flourens as a laboratory scientist with the better method but the wrong theory [nonlocalization of function]" (Finger, 1994, p. 36).

Phineas P. Gage—A Case of Accidental Ablation

Although Flourens deliberately damaged the nervous system in animals in order to study its functions, a case of accidental brain damage provided clues to human prefrontal lobe function and helped establish the brain as the organ of mind once and for all. This was the celebrated case of railroad construction supervisor **Phineas P. Gage.**

On September 13, 1848, as Gage prepared a hole for blasting powder, a premature explosion blew an iron tamping rod through his head. The bar entered Gage's left cheek and exited above his right temple. To his crew's amazement, Gage almost immediately sat up and asked for the rod. The physician to whom Gage was taken, Dr. John Harlow, proved to himself the story of Gage's injury with the observation that his two index fingers touched when he inserted them into the entry and exit wounds.

Although Gage recovered physically, his personality was dramatically altered. According to Dr. Harlow (1868),

> His physical health is good, and I am inclined to say that he has recovered. . . . Applied for his situation as foreman, but is undecided whether to work or travel. His contractors, who regarded him as the most efficient and capable foreman in their employ previous to his injury, considered the change in his mind so marked that they could not give him his place again. . . . He is fitful, irreverent, indulging at times in the grossest profanity (which was not previously his custom), manifesting but little deference for his fellows, impatient of restraint or advice when it conflicts with his desires, at times

> pertinaciously obstinate, yet capricious and vacillating, devising many plans of future operation, which are no sooner arranged than they are abandoned in turn for others appearing more feasible. . . . [H]is mind was radically changed, so decidedly that his friends and acquaintances said he was "no longer Gage." (pp. 339–340)

Gage lived several years after his accident, flitting from one occupation to another and at one point exhibiting himself at Barnum's Museum in New York City. His lack of initiative and inability to carry through plans are characteristics of prefrontal lobe damage (e.g., Valenstein, 1973). Recent research on Gage's skull using modern neuroimaging techniques has confirmed the location of prefrontal damage that produces the defects described by Dr. Harlow (1868): an inability to make rational decisions and a defect in processing emotions (Damasio, 1994; Damasio, Grabowski, Frank, Galaburda, & Damasio, 1994).

In summary, Gage's accident definitively showed the importance of the brain for the mind. After his injury, Gage was "no longer Gage." Also, Gage's experience argued against Flourens's nonlocalizationist position by showing that specific human abilities depended on the integrity of the frontal lobes. Further support for localization of function soon appeared.

National Library of Medicine, Washington, D.C.

Pierre Paul Broca (1824–1880)

Localization of Language Areas

Although Flourens's nonlocalizationist beliefs held center stage through the mid-1850s because of the quality of his experiments and his opposition to phrenology, the tide of scientific opinion soon took a localizationist turn. The evidence for localization came from Paul Broca's study in 1861 of a patient sometimes called Tan. As is often the case, earlier work anticipated Broca's study.

Jean Baptiste Bouillaud (1796–1881) was a physician and an admirer of Gall and phrenology. In 1825, Bouillaud reported clinical evidence supporting Gall's claim for a language "organ" in the brain's frontal area. Because of the general acceptance of Flourens's antilocalizationist beliefs, Bouillaud's claim was discounted, and his offer of 500 francs for proof he was wrong went unchallenged.

His son-in-law Ernest Aubertin (1825–1893) supported Bouillaud. Aubertin was most convinced by a patient who had recovered from a gunshot wound to the left front of the head. Pressing the soft spot over the man's wound halted his ability to speak. Aubertin had another patient who had lost his speech, and he predicted that this patient would be found to have frontal lobe damage.

Before Aubertin could test his prediction, another speechless but otherwise intelligent patient came to the attention of **Pierre Paul Broca** (1824–1880), the chief of surgery at the Bicêtre hospital near Paris. Broca's patient was a 51-year-old man named Leborgne who had been at the hospital for 21 years. Although the man apparently understood everything said to him, all he could say was "*tan, tan*" or, when frustrated by his inability to communicate, he would utter the curse "*Sacré nom de Dieu*" (literally, Sacred name of God). His fellow patients considered him "an egoist, vindictive and objectionable, and his associates, who detested him, even accused him of stealing" (Broca, 1861; in Benjamin, 1988, p. 94).

Leborgne was transferred to Broca's ward after an infection in his paralyzed right leg became gangrenous. After satisfying himself there was nothing wrong with Leborne's larynx and tongue muscles, Broca asked Aubertin if the case was a suitable test of Aubertin's hypothesized frontal lobe language center. Aubertin agreed that it was, and Leborgne died 6 days after admission to Broca's ward. Broca's autopsy revealed a lesion about the size of a hen's egg to the third convolution of the left frontal lobe. He presented the brain to the *Société d'Anthropologie* a few hours after the autopsy.

If this were Broca's only contribution to the discovery of a left frontal lobe language area, we might conclude that Aubertin and Bouillaud deserve a kinder historical fate than to be almost completely overlooked. However, "while Broca may have been lucky to steal Aubertin's thunder in producing the first demonstration case, he proved his real mettle as a scientist by collecting more supportive evidence" (Fancher, 1996, p. 89).

Today we honor Broca by attaching his name to the left frontal lobe area, where damage produces an expressive aphasia (*aphasia* refers to a language defect). Damage to Broca's area produces labored, agrammatical speech—a difficulty in expressing oneself—in a person with relatively intact language comprehension.

Unfortunately, we also associate Broca's name with **craniometry**—the measurement of skulls—and a belief in a clear relationship between brain size and intelligence. In this, Broca was influenced by the *Zeitgeist*, which viewed certain racial groups and women as inferior to other racial groups and men, respectively. In 1861, Broca wrote,

> In general, the brain is larger in mature adults than in the elderly, in men than in women, in eminent men than in men of mediocre talent, in superior races than in inferior races. . . . Other things equal, there is a remarkable relationship between the development of intelligence and the volume of the brain. (cited in Gould, 1981, p. 83)

National Library of Medicine, Washington, D.C.

Carl Wernicke (1848–1904)

One of Broca's trainees drew quite different conclusions from his studies of brain size. Taking into account the differences in body size, Léonce Manouvrier concluded that women's brains "were proportionately heavier than were men's" (Hecht, 1997, p. 224) and, even more heretically for his era, that women were just as intelligent as men.

Slightly more than a decade after Broca's discovery, in 1874, German neurologist **Carl Wernicke** (1848–1904) reported an aphasia from damage to the superior (top) portion of the left temporal lobe. The symptoms include poor language comprehension and fluent, but meaningless, speech. Wernicke's aphasia is sometimes called

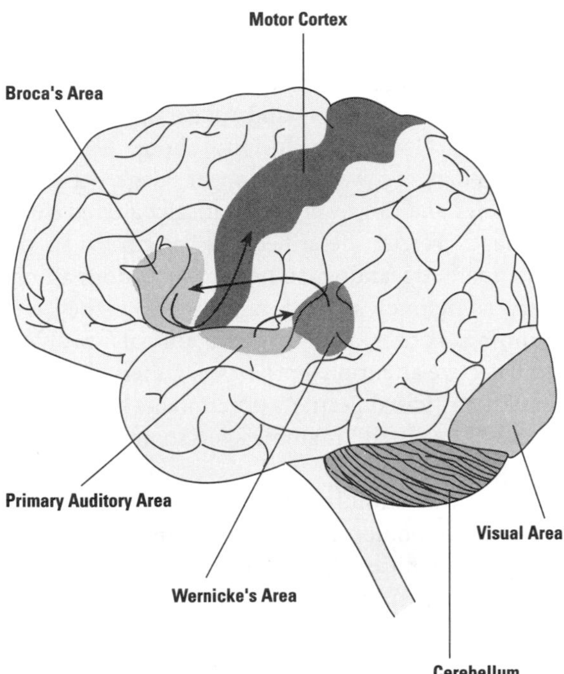

FIGURE 7.3 Lateral view of the left human neocortex, showing Wernicke's model as discussed in the text

receptive aphasia, because language meaning is poorly received. Figure 7.3 shows Broca's area and Wernicke's area in the context of Wernicke's model.

Wernicke's model forms the basis for current neural conceptions of language. Because Wernicke's area is adjacent to the primary auditory cortex, Wernicke concluded that it converts speech sounds into meaning. Broca's area, close to the motor cortex areas controlling the face and neck region, converts temporal lobe language representations from Wernicke's area into speech. Wernicke predicted that disconnection of the two areas would result in fluent, but nonsensical, speech in a person with intact language comprehension. His prediction was confirmed when people were discovered with damage to the arcuate fasciculus—fibers interconnecting Broca's area and Wernicke's area—which produces a language deficit called a conduction aphasia. Such people cannot "conduct" language information from Wernicke's area to Broca's area.

Electrical Brain Stimulation and Localization of Function

By the end of the 19th century, three major techniques had been developed for studying the nervous system: ablation, electrical stimulation, and tissue staining. In this section, we will see how electrical brain stimulation provided further evidence for functional localization.

Working with epileptic patients, including his wife, English neurologist **John Hughlings Jackson** (1835–1911) guessed there were discrete motor areas in the cerebral cortex before such areas were demonstrated experimentally. Among other things, Jackson is known for discovering a particular type of seizure, called Jacksonian epilepsy, in which the convulsion involves the musculature on only one side of the body and the patient remains conscious. Because all such seizures followed the same sequence of muscular involvement, Jackson surmised that the motor areas of the brain were divided into different sections that must be set. Perhaps electrical stimulation of these motor areas—which Jackson believed to be in the cortex—would result in motor movements. His speculation was verified by investigators applying electrical stimulation to the cortex of animals.

Electrical stimulation of the brain was initially hindered by the belief that the cortex, and perhaps the rest of the brain as well, was insensitive to stimulation. Several observations had contributed to this belief, held by Magendie, Flourens, and others. For example, operations on the brains of conscious people had produced no sensory phenomena; mechanical brain stimulation rarely caused motor movements; and cortical stimulation immediately after death was ineffective, even though the motor nerves briefly retained their excitability (recall Cabanis's conclusions in Chapter 5 about guillotine victims).

A major turning point occurred when German scientists **Gustav Fritsch** (1838–1927) and **Eduard**

Hitzig (1838–1907) reported in 1870 that they had found the motor cortex in the dog by using electrical brain stimulation. Both men had made earlier observations that foreshadowed their discovery. During the Prusso-Danish War, while dressing head wounds Fritsch had noticed that accidentally touching exposed brain tissue resulted in muscle twitches on the opposite side of the body. In the late 1860s Hitzig had discovered that electrical stimulation of the back of the head or the ears elicited eye movements in humans (Finger, 2000).

Working together in Hitzig's house, Fritsch and Hitzig exposed and electrically stimulated the cortex of several dogs. According to Finger (2000), in order to keep their electrical current from being too strong, the intrepid experimenters tested its strength by applying it to one or the other of their own tongues! After stimulating what they believed to be the motor cortex, Fritsch and Hitzig destroyed part of the area in two dogs to see if they would lose the appropriate function. As expected, both animals appeared to lose awareness of one of their forepaws.

Fritsch and Hitzig's results were soon replicated and extended by the Scottish neurologist **Sir David Ferrier** (1843–1928). Ferrier had studied with Alexander Bain for his M.A., and in Chapter 5 we noted that Bain may be considered an early physiological psychologist. Working with monkeys, Ferrier found vision in the occipital lobes, where stimulation produced scanning eye movements, and ablation caused blindness. Ferrier thought removal of one occipital lobe caused blindness in the eye opposite the side of the lesion. However, German physiologist **Hermann Munk** (1839–1912) demonstrated that the loss of one occipital lobe produces blindness in the opposite visual field. For example, destruction of the right occipital lobe causes blindness in the left visual field, not in the left eye.

Discovery of the temporal lobe auditory cortex is usually attributed to Ferrier, who used the ablation method to confirm his stimulation results in monkeys. Ferrier reported that monkeys with bilateral damage to the top part of the temporal lobes appeared unresponsive to sound (Finger, 1994). In other studies, Ferrier as well as Munk localized the skin senses (e.g., touch, temperature) in the parietal lobes.

Ferrier's experiments with anterior frontal lobe damage in monkeys and dogs supported Dr. Harlow's (1868) conclusions about Phineas P. Gage—that he was "no longer Gage." Ferrier's monkeys and dogs were dramatically altered by the damage; Ferrier described the monkeys as dull and apathetic, and when he threw the dogs a bone, they sometimes seemed to forget why they were running. Ferrier attributed the animals' problems to defective attentional processes. Others (including Munk) criticized Ferrier's experiments because they thought he tested his animals too soon after surgery (Finger, 1994).

Electrical stimulation results tended to refute Flourens's nonlocalization position, but without supporting phrenology. Functions were localized in the brain, but these functions and where they were found bore no resemblance to phrenology's teachings.

Electrical Stimulation of the Human Brain

In 1874, Cincinnati physician **Roberts Bartholow** (1831–1904) had the opportunity to electrically stimulate the exposed brain of one of his patients—a 30-year-old, somewhat feeble-minded woman named Mary Rafferty. Cancer had eaten a 2-inch hole in the top of her skull, which exposed the pulsations of her brain. Guided by the work of Fritsch and Hitzig and of Ferrier, Bartholow decided to stimulate Rafferty's brain with a needle insulated except for its tip, in order to prevent widespread distribution of the electrical current.

At first, the study went well and Bartholow was able to elicit some sensations and motor movements. Hoping to increase Rafferty's reaction, Bartholow then strengthened the current. As a result, Rafferty had a violent convulsion on her left side and lost consciousness. Two days later, Bartholow applied further stimulation with less current but decided to abandon the experiment, as Rafferty "was pale and depressed; her lips were blue; and she had evident difficulty in locomotion" (Bartholow, 1874, p. 311). Mary Rafferty died 2 days later.

Although Bartholow did not think his experiments caused Rafferty's death, his report of the investigation produced a scandal. Bartholow resigned from his staff position at a hospital in Cincinnati and was eventually forced to leave the city. He later developed a positive reputation for his books on practical medical therapeutics (Valenstein, 1973).

Lack of a therapeutic rationale clearly separates Bartholow's experiment and the later investigations of the American-born Canadian neurosurgeon **Wilder Graves Penfield** (1891–1976). In his operations on conscious epileptic patients, Penfield electrically stimulated their exposed brains to search for the locus of epileptic seizures (so that he could remove it) and for the locus of language areas (so that he could avoid damaging them as much as possible). Still, we must credit Bartholow with anticipating the later work of the "surgeon-experimenter."

To this point, we have discussed discoveries obtained through the use of ablation and electrical stimulation in the last half of the 19th century. In addition, the brain's anatomy had begun to be studied with chemical stains by the latter part of that century. This technique led to the resolution of a major question about nervous system anatomy: Is the nervous system a nerve net with all nerve cells interconnected, or is it made up of individual nerve cells (neurons)?

Neuron Doctrine or Nerve Network?

In 1891, German neurologist and anatomist **Wilhelm von Waldeyer** (1836–1921) introduced the term *neuron* to describe the independent nerve unit. This led to the development of the neuron doctrine in opposition to the idea that the nerves form an interconnected network. The network idea was consistent with Flourens's nonlocalizationist view of a nervous system in which each major part had a particular function but there was no differentiation of the function within the part. Thus, one major effect of the neuron doctrine's victory over the nerve network idea was to reinforce the concept of functional localization within the brain. In addition, the neuron doctrine appeared to provide an anatomical basis for ideas formed through associations (e.g., Boring, 1950).

One of the chief proponents of the nerve network theory was **Camillo Golgi** (1843–1926), an Italian histologist and physician whose work ironically led to the downfall of the nerve network notion. Golgi was born in Corteno, a village in northwest Italy. His father, a country doctor, sent him to study at the University of Pavia, where Golgi received his M.D. degree in 1865. He immediately went to work at a clinic for mental ailments directed by Cesare Lombroso (1836–1909), best known for his theory of a criminal type distinguishable from the normal man.

Golgi experimented with various methods for hardening and staining tissues originally invented by Joseph von Gerlach (1820–1896), Johannes Müller, and others. He found that osmic acid gave nerve cells and fibers a deep black color, which was well suited for microscopic work. Unfortunately, osmic acid was scarce, and Golgi was forced to seek a less costly substitute. In 1873, he announced his invention of a method of staining by immersing hardened brain tissue in a silver nitrate solution.

Golgi's method stains only a few cells at a time in a region, and the stained cells are shown in their entirety. Today, over 100 years later, no one knows exactly how Golgi's stain works to color completely only about 3% of neurons, while leaving the other cells unaffected (Finger, 2000).

Using his own modification of Golgi's stain, **Santiago Ramón y Cajal** (1852–1934), Spanish histologist and neurologist, demonstrated that nerve cells are independent cells, contiguous without being continuous. Like Golgi, the son of a physician, Cajal was a rebellious youth, often punished by his disciplinarian father for truancy, bad grades, and acts of vandalism. Finally, at his wit's end, Cajal's father decided to try to interest the boy in his own area of expertise, anatomy, and this proved to be the turning point in Cajal's life—he decided to become a physician. After a stint in the military during which he caught malaria and nearly died in Cuba, Cajal returned to Spain and an uncertain future.

Cajal's first experience with a microscope determined that future, and he embarked on the research career that led to his support for the neuron theory and undermined Golgi's neural net idea. In 1906, Golgi and Cajal shared the Nobel

Prize in physiology or medicine. In his acceptance speech, Golgi

> launched an attack on the theory championed by the man with whom he was sharing the honor. He stated that the neuron doctrine was a fad already going out of favor . . . and made it very clear that he did not see any hope for the reductionistic philosophy of cortical localization. (Finger, 2000, p. 215)

Cajal, on the other hand, took the high road in his address, at one point even referring to Golgi as his "illustrious colleague."

Thus, Cajal, the once rebellious youth with bad grades from a scientifically isolated country, went on to earn many honors and awards and even lived to see his image on stamps and currency. Golgi, unfortunately, never abandoned his belief in the nervous system's unitary nature, despite Cajal's overwhelming evidence refuting it.

Charles Sherrington and the Synapse

After Cajal's demonstration that neurons are separate units with tiny gaps between them, the key question became: What happens at the gaps? Is the information from one neuron to another transported the same way it travels the axon (a neuron's relatively long process)? Many properties of transmission across the gap were deduced by Charles Sherrington (1906) in his book, *The Integrative Action of the Nervous System.*

Born in London, **Sir Charles Scott Sherrington** (1857–1952) was a physician and physiologist. At Liverpool and then later at Oxford, Sherrington studied the reflex arc, a circuit consisting of at least three neurons: a sensory neuron, a motor neuron, and a neuron connecting the sensory and motor neurons called an "interneuron." In the basic reflex, a sensory neuron excites an interneuron, which excites a motor neuron, and the motor neuron stimulates a muscle to produce the reflex response.

Long before the electron microscope made it visible, Sherrington called the apparent gap between neurons the **synapse,** which means binding (*-apse*) together (*syn*). Studying the spinal reflex in dogs, Sherrington described several synaptic properties.

National Library of Medicine, Washington, D.C.

Sir Charles Sherrington (1857–1952)

For example, he found that reflexes were slower than conduction along an axon, suggesting that synaptic transmission introduces a slight delay. In addition, Sherrington found that summation of influences occurs at the synapse; for example, several weak stimuli presented at nearly the same time (temporal summation) or in nearly the same place (spatial summation) produce a greater response than does a single stimulus. Sherrington shared the 1932 Nobel Prize in physiology or medicine with another English physiologist, Edgar Douglas Adrian (1889–1977). Lord Adrian was also recognized for his work on the function of neurons.

Otto Loewi and Synaptic Transmission

Born in Frankfurt am Main, **Otto Loewi** (1873–1961) was a German pharmacologist and physician. Until 1921, the prevailing view was that synaptic transmission occurred from the spreading of an electrical wave from the end of the axon (nerve terminal) to an effector organ (e.g., a muscle). Loewi thought this could not be correct because he knew that the stimulation of certain nerves increases the function of one organ while decreasing the function of another, which is inexplicable if synaptic transmission is indeed electrical. As early as 1903, Loewi believed that the terminals of some nerves might contain chemicals that carry the nerve impulse to the effector organs.

On the night before Easter in 1920, Loewi awoke with the plan for an experimental test of the chemical theory of synaptic transmission. He jotted some notes on a slip of paper, only to discover the next morning that he could not decipher them. When the memory returned at 3 A.M. the following morning, Loewi went to his laboratory and did the experiment. In retrospect, Loewi (1960) wrote, "If carefully considered in the daytime, I would undoubtedly have rejected the kind of experiment I performed. . . . It was good fortune that at the moment of the hunch I did not think but acted immediately" (p. 18).

Loewi first placed two beating frog hearts, one with its vagus nerve attached and the other without the nerve, into a container with a little Ringer solution, which is physiological saline with chemicals added that are needed to preserve tissue function. Next, he stimulated the vagus nerve of the first heart, which caused its beating to slow. Loewi then transferred some of the Ringer solution from the first heart to the second heart, and the second heart slowed its beating as though its vagus nerve had been stimulated.

With this simple experiment, Loewi had shown that stimulation of the vagus nerve released a chemical onto the heart muscle that caused its beating to slow. Appropriately enough, he called the mysterious chemical *Vagusstoff*, meaning "stuff from the vagus nerve." *Vagusstoff* was soon found to be acetylcholine. For demonstrating that synaptic transmission was chemical and not electrical—that is, for acting on his nighttime hunch—Loewi was a cowinner of the 1936 Nobel Prize in physiology or medicine.

Loewi's discovery of chemical transmission at synapses eventually led to a wealth of information on neurotransmitters. Beginning in the 1950s, this development was in part fueled by the discovery in the brain of such chemical transmitters as norepinephrine, dopamine, and serotonin; a burgeoning interest in **psychopharmacology,** the field that uses psychological and pharmacological concepts to investigate the behavioral effects of drugs; and the discovery of the first major antipsychotic drugs (e.g., chlorpromazine). Exciting recent developments include the discovery of endogenous opioids (naturally occurring morphine-like neurotransmitters) and the synthesis of antidepressants that target a single transmitter substance such as serotonin.

New York University Archives, Photographic Collection.

Otto Loewi (1873–1961)

The Nerve Impulse

Meanwhile, additional research focused on how nerve cells transmit information axonally. That is, although Otto Loewi demonstrated that synaptic transmission was chemical and many subsequent studies sought to expand the list of transmitter substances, research was also aimed at discovering how the nerve cell delivers the information it receives to the synapse.

This research was enormously aided by a discovery in the 1930s by Oxford University scientist John

Z. Young: Young found that the squid has neurons large enough to be isolated and studied individually during transmission of the nerve impulse. Much of what we now know about axonal transmission came from experiments on the giant axon of the squid by the British neurophysiologists **Sir Alan Hodgkin** (1914–1998) and **Sir Andrew Huxley** (1917–). Hodgkin and Huxley, along with **Sir John Eccles** (1903–1997), received the Nobel Prize in physiology or medicine in 1963. Eccles, whose mentor was Charles Sherrington, performed research that furthered our understanding of synaptic transmission.

So far, we have examined research designed to uncover the mind-body connections by directly assaulting the brain, either by stimulating it or damaging it, or by studying the sequelae to naturally occurring damage. In addition, we have discussed late-19th-century/early-20th-century studies that answered fundamental questions about the construction of the nervous system and how it works. Another 19th-century physiological approach to the mind-body problem produced psychophysics, whose leading figure, Gustav Fechner, is considered a contender for the honor of having originated psychology as a science (e.g., Boring, 1950). We will begin our look at psychophysics, however, with an examination of the anticipatory work of Ernst Weber, Fechner's longtime Leipzig colleague and friend.

PSYCHOPHYSICS

Ernst Weber

Ernst Heinrich Weber (1795–1878) was born in the university community of Wittenberg, a German city on the Elbe River. Weber studied medicine at Wittenberg, receiving his M.D. in 1815 at the age of 20. Two years later he became a medical instructor at Leipzig University, where he taught for 50 years (1821–1871) as a professor of anatomy and physiology. Wilhelm Wundt (Chapter 8) "respected E. H. Weber as the 'honored senior professor' of Leipzig University and proudly lived for some time in Weber's former university apartment . . ." (Brauns, 1997, p. 98).

As an anatomist and physiologist, Weber's special interest lay in touch and kinesthesis (the sense of movement or the position of body parts). Weber was one of the first to demonstrate that touch is actually more than one sense. For him, the sense of touch provided sensations of pressure, temperature, and locality, with locality being secondary to, and its arousal dependent on, other sensations. Weber held that sensation varies only in quality and intensity. Localization in space depends on the mind's actions and the relations among sensations.

Although Weber attributed the sense of locality in part to the actions of the mind, this did not prevent him from attempting its investigation. This investigation led to the first of his major contributions to psychology, the measurement of the two-point threshold.

The Two-Point Threshold

Using a compass-like instrument with two points that can be separated greater or lesser distances, Weber mapped the body's sensitivity to dual, simultaneous touches. With the points slightly apart, a portion of the body is touched and the subject asked to report whether one or two touches has been felt. Weber found that sensitivity varied greatly for different body parts. For example, an observer could detect two touches on the tongue when the points were only about 1 mm apart, whereas separate touches on the back were not perceived until the points were separated by approximately 60 mm. Weber attributed this difference to receptor density; spatial discrimination is most accurate where the receptors are many and closely packed (e.g., on the tongue).

Although Weber was interested in measuring the sensitivity of spatial discrimination on the body, his "compass test" has become synonymous with the measurement of the **two-point threshold,** or limen. Incidentally, Weber did not use the word *threshold* in his discussion of what we call the two-point threshold; the term was introduced in this context by Fechner (Boudewijnse et al., 2001).

Ernst Weber (1795–1878)

Weber's research was important because it showed that for every change in stimulation (e.g., spreading apart the points) there is not always a corresponding change in sensation. On the back, only one touch is felt whether the points are 10 mm, 20 mm, or 30 mm apart. Apparently gross differences in stimulation result in no change in sensation. Do you remember Zeno's millet seed example in Chapter 2?

Weber's most important investigations of sensitivity dealt with judgments of lifted weights and gave rise to a mathematical relation Fechner called Weber's law. These were Weber's studies of the just noticeable difference (jnd) in weight judgments.

The Just Noticeable Difference

On each trial, Weber required a subject to lift an unvarying standard weight and a comparison weight, which varied in measured amounts from the standard. The subject then reported whether the comparison weight felt lighter, heavier, or the same as the standard. Weber found that the difference that could be reliably detected, the **just noticeable difference,** depended on the standard weight. With a light standard weight, small changes were detected. With a heavy standard, a relatively large change was needed for detection.

Although the absolute size of the jnd varied, Weber believed it varied by a constant ratio of the standard stimulus. For judgments of lifted weights, Weber found the ratio to be 1/40. For example, with a 40-g standard weight a change of at least 1 g was needed to detect a difference. A 39-g weight would be felt as lighter and a 41-g weight heavier, but a 39.5-g weight or a 40.5-g weight would appear to weigh the same as the standard. With an 80-g standard, a change of at least 2 g (2/80 = 1/40) would be needed for the difference to be detected.

Weber determined the jnds for other types of discriminations and found them also to be constant ratios of the standard stimulus, although the ratios varied for the different types of judgments. For example, the ratio was 1/40 for lifted weights, 1/30 for weights passively felt, and 1/100 for judgments of the length of two lines.

Following Fechner, we call the ratios **Weber fractions,** and they fit data reasonably well, deviating only at extreme intensities of the standard stimulus. However, Weber is important not for his fractions but for having a valid claim to being the first to measure the mind quantitatively. Although Weber did not recognize the importance of his research for psychology, a fellow scientist at Leipzig did.

Gustav Theodor Fechner

Gustav Theodor Fechner (1801–1887) was born in the village of Gross Särchen in southeastern Germany. His father was the local pastor, a man who shocked his congregation by installing a lightning rod on the church steeple, as the congregation considered this a lack of faith in the Lord's protection. The father's freethinking extended to preaching without a wig, which, he argued, Jesus must also have done. Pastor Fechner died when

Gustav was 5, and he and a brother went to live with an uncle who also was a minister.

Fechner enrolled at the University of Leipzig to study medicine in 1817, the same year Weber became a medical instructor there. Fechner's study was largely completed on his own, from books, although he did attend Weber's physiology course. Despite passing the required examinations for an undergraduate degree, Fechner did not obtain the doctorate that would have allowed him to practice medicine, confessing later that he had not learned any of the requisite skills for such practice (e.g., how to apply a bandage or how to deliver a baby).

However, Fechner had learned enough about the medicine of his day to satirize it. Under the pseudonym Dr. Mises, Fechner's first publication was *Beweiss, dass der Mond aus Iodine bestehe* (*Proof That the Moon Is Made of Iodine,* 1821), in which he lampooned the use of iodine to treat virtually every illness. Dr. Mises also commented on the *Vergleichende Anatomie der Engel* (*The Comparative Anatomy of Angels*), noting that the "basic angelic form is always the sphere, and we regard the sphere as no more than the basic form of Beauty" (Fechner, 1825/1969, p. 137). In this statement, Fechner revealed his interest in aesthetics, a topic he returned to late in life. Dr. Mises published 14 times between 1821 and 1876, revealing Fechner's lifelong tendency to follow his own mind rather than accepting the dogma of authority. For a commentary on *Comparative Anatomy*, see Marshall (1969).

With no academic appointment, Fechner stayed at Leipzig to study physics and mathematics, supplementing his meager income by translating a French physics textbook into German. The multitalented Fechner also translated several chemistry textbooks. In 1824, he began lecturing at the university, and he also started experiments on electricity. By 1834, Fechner's reputation was such that he became a full professor of physics at Leipzig, a position that commanded a good salary and a lifetime pension.

Fechner married in 1833, and his life settled into a frenetic pace of intellectual and social activity that soon took its toll. He began to have headaches and difficulty sleeping, and his worry about his health turned to depression. Fechner's eyesight began to deteriorate, undoubtedly aggravated by an experiment on afterimages in which he stared at the sun through colored glasses. Finally, his health almost gone, Fechner resigned his chair in physics and retired on his pension.

Philosophical Library, New York.

Gustav Theodor Fechner (1801–1887)

In the beginning of his illness, Fechner experienced a deep depression accompanied by a loss of interest in eating. Various remedies were tried, including laxatives, electricity, and violent counterirritants. Nothing worked, and Fechner was nearly dead from starvation and the remedies when an acquaintance offered him a dish of spiced raw ham soaked in Rhine wine and lemon juice whose recipe had appeared to her in a dream. Fechner accepted it, and his illness entered a new phase involving the wild flight of ideas, mutism, and a fear of light. During this period, Fechner sat in a darkened room, while his mother read to him through an opening in the door. His recovery came suddenly in October 1843, and the sight of flowers on his first venture outside without a blindfold led to another of Dr. Mises's books, *Nanna, oder über das Seelenleben der Pflanzen* (*Nanna, or Concerning the Mental Life of Plants,* 1848).

Nanna reveals a deepening of Fechner's religious convictions and argues against the scientific materialism of his day. "Miraculously" recovered, Fechner now considered he had a mission to reveal to all that consciousness pervaded the world of nature (panpsychism). *Nanna* was intended to be the wake-up call in Fechner's mission. His next call came in *Zend-Avesta, oder über die Dinge des Himmels und des Jenseits* (*Zend-Avesta, or Concerning Matters of Heaven and the Hereafter,* 1851). Although the public continued to sleep, *Zend-Avesta* was important because Fechner outlined psychophysics in it. Thus, *Zend-Avesta* anticipated Fechner's famous *Elemente der Psychophysik* (*Elements of Psychophysics,* 1860). Fechner's panpsychism is described in Woodward (1972).

Elements of Psychophysics

Fechner sought the relation between the spiritual and the material worlds, between the mind and the body. Although he had been thinking about this relation for many years (Adler, 1980, 1996), the insight for how to determine it came on the morning of October 22, 1850, while he was still in bed. (The importance of precise dates of discovery is a matter of conjecture [e.g., Rosenzweig, 1987].) He would develop a method to measure the relation between sensation (the mental) and the stimulus giving rise to it (the physical), and he would call the method and associated theory **psychophysics.** According to Fechner (1860/1966), "Psychophysics should be understood . . . as an exact theory of the functionally dependent relations of body and soul or, more generally, . . . of the physical and the psychological worlds" (p. 7).

Without Fechner's insight, a truly experimental psychology probably would have been only slightly delayed. The time was ripe for scientific psychology, and Fechner was in the right place at the right time with the right preparation. First, from Herbart (Chapter 6), Fechner had obtained the conception of psychology as an enterprise to which mathematics could be applied. More importantly, Herbart gave Fechner the idea that mind might be analyzed through exploration of the threshold of consciousness, an idea Herbart had gotten from Leibniz (Chapter 4).

Weber's measurement of the just noticeable difference also influenced Fechner. As we noted, Weber had found that the jnd for at least three sensory modalities was a constant ratio of the standard stimulus. Fechner gave Weber's relation mathematical form and called the result **Weber's law,** which may be written

$$\frac{\delta R}{R} = \text{a constant},$$

where R stands for the stimulus magnitude (the German word for stimulus is *Reiz*), and δR is the amount of stimulus change needed for detection (the jnd). Weber's law shows that "the magnitude of the stimulus increment must increase in precise proportion to the stimulus already present, in order to bring about an equal increase in sensation . . ." (Fechner, 1860/1966, p. 54).

According to Marshall (1990), Fechner also was substantially influenced by another Weber, the physicist Wilhelm Eduard Weber (1804–1891), one of Ernst's brothers. As Marshall sketched the events, Fechner had his famous insight in October 1850, wrote a description of it to Wilhelm Weber, received a recommendation from Weber to delay his "fancy quantitative analysis until he managed to find some facts to support his theory" (p. 52), outlined the idea in *Zend-Avesta,* and then devoted the better part of the next decade to securing the experimental evidence Wilhelm Weber had cautioned him to obtain.

Fechner did not claim that the function relating stimulus intensity and sensation magnitude originated either with him or with Weber. He noted that the relation had been recognized in other contexts by mathematicians such as Pierre Simon Laplace (1749–1827) and Siméon Denis Poisson (1781–1840), and particularly by Daniel Bernoulli (1700 –1782), who pointed out that the same monetary stimulus has dramatically different effects on people depending on their state of wealth. A dollar

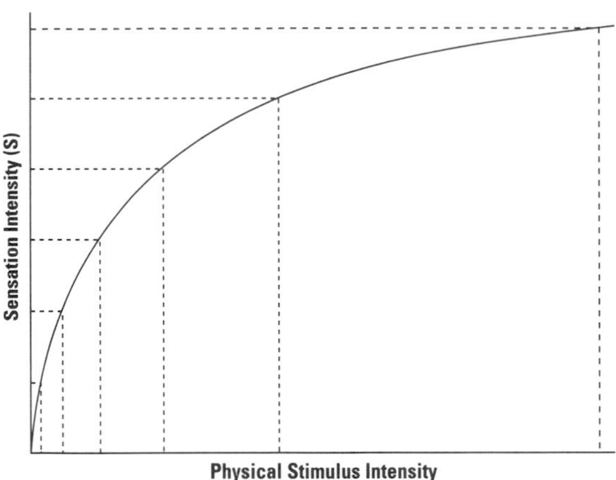

FIGURE 7.4 A graph of Fechner's law showing that with higher stimulus intensities, larger and larger increases are necessary for a change in sensation

is meaningless to a rich man but cause for celebration to a beggar.

Through a series of mathematical exercises, Fechner changed Weber's law into what we call **Fechner's law,** which is

$$S = k \log R,$$

where S is the psychological sensation, which is equal to a constant (k) times the logarithm of physical stimulus intensity (log R). As you can see from Figure 7.4, a graph of Fechner's law, with low levels of stimulus intensity even a small change produces a change in sensation. However, as the intensity of R increases, larger and larger changes are required for a change in sensation.

In recent years, Fechner's logarithmic relation between stimulus intensity and sensation has been modified into a power relation called **Stevens's law** (Stevens, 1956; Chapter 13). Still, Fechner had at least indirectly measured sensation. He had shown it is possible to measure the mind and had either developed or systematized psychophysics' major methods: the **method of limits,** the method of constant stimuli, and the method of average error.

To illustrate the methods, we will consider the method of limits, which can be used to determine detection thresholds. Suppose you want to know the least intense sound someone can hear. First, you gradually increase the volume of an undetectable sound until the person reports hearing it, noting the intensity at which the person's report changes from "I do not hear it" to "I hear it." Then, you start with a clearly detectable sound, decreasing it until the person says "I no longer hear it." After several such presentations, the average intensity at which the judgment changes is found and called the detection threshold. The name *method of limits* was coined in 1891 by Emil Kraepelin, one of Wundt's most famous students. The name refers to the fact that a stimulus series ends when the tested person reaches a limit or point of change in his or her judgments.

Other Contributions

After psychophysics, Fechner turned to art. His first publication in **experimental aesthetics** (the study of beauty) concerned the "golden section," the most aesthetically pleasing ratio of length to width in an object. To study their proportions, Fechner measured 20,000 paintings in 22 art museums. In 1876, he published *Vorschule der Aesthetik* (*Preparatory School of Aesthetics*), which became the foundation of experimental aesthetics. Arnheim (1985) argued that Fechner's view of aesthetics was derived from his psychophysics,

> with the consequence that the more strictly the investigators adhered to the criterion of preference, the more completely their results neglected everything that distinguishes the pleasure generated by a work of art from the pleasure generated by a dish of ice cream. Just as Fechner's study does not tell us why people prefer the ratio of the golden section to others, so most of the innumerable preference studies carried out since his time tell us deplorably little about what people see when they look at an aesthetic object, what they mean by saying that they like or dislike it, and why they prefer the objects they prefer. (p. 861)

One of Fechner's most interesting speculations dealt with the function of the brain's major interconnecting structure, the **corpus callosum.** Because

Fechner believed that consciousness is one of the brain's properties, he theorized that consciousness would become two streams if the corpus callosum were cut (Blakemore, 1977). Nearly 100 years later, the chance to test his speculation came in patients receiving split-brain operations as treatment for epilepsy. The study of these surgical patients by Roger Sperry and his associates will be discussed in Chapter 16.

Fechner's Influence

Response to Fechner's *Elements of Psychophysics* was immediate, and many of psychology's founders (e.g., Helmholtz and Wundt) conducted experiments similar to those of Weber and Fechner. As we will see, one of Wundt's major research areas was the study of sensation and perception using Fechner's psychophysical methods. Inspired by a used copy of *Elements,* Hermann Ebbinghaus (Chapter 8) applied Fechner's experimental methods in an elegant investigation of human memory.

Although Fechner's *Elements* stimulated the development of a scientific, experimental psychology, some scientists disagreed with various details of psychophysics (e.g., the use of the jnd as a unit of measurement or the validity of Weber's law and the mathematical transformations leading to Fechner's law). Although the work is not well known today, Fechner continued his psychophysical research the rest of his life, with most of his efforts aimed at answering his critics (Murray, 1990). According to Murray, Fechner's inner psychophysics—the relation of sensation to nervous system physiology—"foreshadowed modern notions such as signal detection theory [see also Link, 1994] and holographic memory" (p. 54). His outer psychophysics was the relation between sensation and stimulus, which he detailed in 1860.

One writer who saw little of value in Fechner's psychophysics (but much of value in his philosophy) was William James (Chapter 10). Three years after Fechner's death, James wrote:

> Fechner himself indeed was a German *Gelehrter* [scholar] of the ideal type, at once simple and shrewd, a mystic and an experimentalist, homely and daring, and as loyal to facts as to his theories. But it would be terrible if even such a dear old man as this could saddle our Science forever with his patient whimsies, and, in a world so full of more nutritious objects of attention, compel all future students to plough through the difficulties, not only of his own works, but of the still drier ones written in his refutation. . . . The only amusing part . . . is that Fechner's critics should always feel bound, after smiting his theories hip and thigh and leaving not a stick of them standing, to wind up by saying that nevertheless to him belongs the *imperishable glory* of first formulating them and thereby turning psychology into an *exact science*(!). (James, 1890, Vol. 1, p. 549, italics in the original)

Although James's opinion of Fechner's work was predominantly negative in 1890, his attitude changed over the years as he became better acquainted with Fechner's thoughts (Early, 1994).

Boring (1950) certainly did not agree with James's (1890) negative characterization of Fechner's work, concluding:

> Fechner, because of what he did and the time at which he did it, set experimental quantitative psychology off upon the course which it has followed. One may call him the "founder" of experimental psychology, or one may assign that title to Wundt. It does not matter. Fechner had a fertile idea which grew and brought forth fruit abundantly. (p. 295)

CONCLUSIONS

By the end of the 19th century, great strides had been made in demystifying the nervous system. The brain had been established unequivocally as the mind's substrate, in part thanks to phrenology and to Phineas Gage's accident, and the nerve impulse had been shown to have an electrical component through the studies of Galvani, Volta, and du Bois-Reymond. Helmholtz had measured the speed of the nerve impulse, demonstrating that at least one of the nervous system's functions was amenable to experimental study. In addition, three of the methods used so successfully for studying the brain and its functions in the 20th century were well established by the end of the 19th century (i.e., the ablation, electrical stimulation, and anatomical staining methods). The phrenologists' extreme localizationist position had given way to the nonlocalizationist beliefs of Flourens, which, in turn, were superseded by evidence for localization (but not the localization preached by the phrenologists) discovered by Broca, Wernicke, Fritsch and Hitzig, Ferrier, Munk, and others. A major motor area had been mapped in the cortex of the brain, along with sensory areas for all the senses except olfaction and taste. Using the clinical method, Broca and Wernicke had found language centers.

In addition, the anatomical staining methods developed by Camillo Golgi in the latter part of the 19th century had been used by Santiago Ramón y Cajal to demonstrate the validity of the neuron doctrine in contrast to the nerve network, which further supported functional localization in the nervous system. From studies of spinal reflexes in the dog, Sir Charles Sherrington deduced many synaptic properties before electron microscopy allowed visualization of a synapse, and Otto Loewi's elegant experiment with frog hearts proved that synaptic transmission from the vagus nerve to the heart muscle is chemical rather than electrical.

The 19th century also saw the development of another approach to the mind-body problem. Building on earlier experimental investigations of mind-body relations, particularly those of his Leipzig colleague Ernst Weber, Gustav Fechner developed the science of psychophysics. His 1860 publication, *Elements of Psychophysics*, written nearly 2 decades before Wundt organized his laboratory, is considered by some to mark the beginning of psychology as an experimental science.

The work we have examined in this chapter laid the foundation for the dramatic advances in knowledge of the nervous system that occurred in the 20th century. We will review some of this later work in Chapter 16.

SUMMARY

Review of Early Speculation

Except for Aristotle, most of the ancient philosophers guessed correctly that the brain was the biological substrate of thought and behavior. Early interest focused on the brain's ventricles as the reservoir for the animal spirits. In the Christian Church's three-chambered model of mind, sensory analysis occurred in the first chamber, reason and thought in the middle chamber, and memory in the third chamber. Leonardo da Vinci's anatomical studies cast serious doubt on the Church's model.

A century later, Descartes viewed the nervous system as a hydraulic affair. Descartes's model was quickly shown to be impossible by such investigators as Jan Swammerdam and Francis Glisson.

Electricity and Nerve Function

In the 18th century, electricity replaced animal spirits as the nervous system's activating substance. Electrical stimulation of a motor nerve caused contraction of a frog's leg muscle, and Luigi Galvani concluded the frogs had generated electricity. By contrast, inorganic battery inventor Alessandro Volta believed Galvani's frogs had conducted electricity instead of generating it. Studying nervous tissue's electrical nature, Émil du Bois-Reymond demonstrated that positively and negatively charged particles reverse positions with nerve stimulation. With this research, du Bois-Reymond brought the nerve impulse into the world of science and paved the way for Helmholtz to measure its speed.

As a student, Helmholtz was greatly influenced by Johannes Müller (famous for his *Handbook of Human Physiology*) and his students, particularly du Bois-Reymond. At Königsberg, Helmholtz measured the speed of the nerve impulse, invented the ophthalmoscope, and revised Thomas Young's trichromatic theory of color vision. Helmholtz also developed a place theory of auditory pitch perception.

Criticisms of trichromatic theory led Ewald Hering to propose opponent-process theory in which three receptor complexes signal either red or green, yellow or blue, or black or white. Helmholtz and Hering also disagreed on visual space perception: Hering took a nativist approach, whereas Helmholtz believed that space forms develop from experience.

Localization of Function

Localizationists believe that specific functions are located in specific nervous system areas, whereas nonlocalizationists are more impressed by the way the nervous system functions as a whole. The Bell-Magendie law—maintaining that the dorsal roots of spinal nerves are sensory and the ventral roots are motor—supported localization and suggested that discrete sensory and motor areas might be found in the brain.

Johannes Müller formulated the doctrine of specific nerve energies, whose central tenet is that we are aware only of the activity in our nerves, not of the external world itself. Helmholtz was greatly influenced by the doctrine, extending it to vision and audition.

Phrenology, the idea that bumps and indentations on the skull reflect functional areas underneath, was an extreme localizationist position. Founded by Franz Joseph Gall and supported by Johann Caspar Spurzheim, phrenology was important in emphasizing the brain as the organ of mind and in teaching that behavioral functions can be localized in the brain.

One of phrenology's chief opponents, Pierre Flourens used the ablation method to study brain function in animals. Although Flourens discovered the specific functions of individual nervous system parts, he was most impressed by the common action of the separate parts and of the whole system, a nonlocalizationist position.

In 1848, accidental damage to the prefrontal lobes of Phineas P. Gage demonstrated the importance of the brain for human behavior and gave clues to the functions of the brain's prefrontal area. Further evidence for functional localization came from Pierre Broca's and Carl Wernicke's discoveries of language areas in the brain. Broca's area in the frontal lobe is concerned with speech production, whereas damage to Wernicke's area in the temporal lobe results in fluent speech that is not meaningful. Wernicke's model connects Wernicke's area to Broca's area through the arcuate fasciculus.

Gustav Fritsch and Eduard Hitzig electrically stimulated a dog's brain and discovered the motor cortex. Their work was extended by scientists such as David Ferrier and Hermann Munk. Ferrier localized vision in the occipital lobes, and both Ferrier and Munk found a temporal lobe auditory center. Neural areas important for the skin senses were found in the parietal lobes. Cincinnati physician Roberts Bartholow electrically stimulated the exposed brain of a patient, marking the beginning of the clinical investigations of the surgeon-experimenter.

Neuron Doctrine or Nerve Network?

A major debate in the latter part of the 19th century was whether the neurons are separate or whether they form a nerve network. Using a stain developed by Camillo Golgi, Santiago Ramón y Cajal demonstrated that nerve cells are independent cells, thus supporting the neuron doctrine.

From his study of the spinal reflex arc in dogs, Sir Charles Sherrington hypothesized a functional gap or "synapse" between neurons and deduced many of its properties. Pharmacologist Otto Loewi demonstrated in 1920 that synaptic transmission was chemical rather than electrical.

Research on axonal transmission was aided by the discovery of the giant axons of the squid, which were used by British neurophysiologists Hodgkin and Huxley in their Nobel Prize–winning research.

Psychophysics

Leipzig physiologist Ernst Weber mapped the two-point threshold in studying the sense of touch. Of greater importance was his study of the just noticeable difference (jnd), which he found to vary by a constant ratio of a standard stimulus when a subject compared the standard with a comparison stimulus.

After recovering from a physical and mental breakdown, Leipzig physicist/philosopher Gustav Fechner set out to define an equation that would express the mind-body relation. Fechner gave Weber's relation between the jnd and the standard stimulus mathematical form, which he called Weber's law. Next, he mathematically derived Fechner's law, which states that there is a logarithmic relation between sensation and stimulus magnitude. Fechner also developed or systematized the major methods of psychophysics, and his *Elements of Psychophysics* stimulated the development of a scientific, experimental psychology.

CONNECTIONS QUESTIONS

1. What connections can you make between physics and physiology/psychology?
2. What connections exist between the study of color blindness and color vision?
3. In what ways was phrenology important for psychology?
4. In what sense does psychology emerge from the connection between physiology and philosophy?
5. Connect the signal physiological discoveries in the 19th century with the localization/nonlocalization of function controversy.

KEY NAMES AND TERMS

ablation (p. 158)
action potential (p. 148)
Roberts Bartholow (p. 164)
Sir Charles Bell (p. 154)
Bell-Magendie law (p. 153)
Claude Bernard (p. 154)
Pierre Paul Broca (p. 161)
Santiago Ramón y Cajal (p. 165)
cerebellum (p. 159)
cerebral lobes (p. 159)
corpora quadrigemina (p. 159)
corpus callosum (p. 172)
craniometry (p. 162)
Leonardo da Vinci (p. 147)
doctrine of specific nerve energies (p. 155)
Émil du Bois-Reymond (p. 148)
Sir John Eccles (p. 168)
experimental aesthetics (p. 172)
Gustav Theodor Fechner (p. 169)
Fechner's law (p. 172)
Sir David Ferrier (p. 164)
Pierre Jean Marie Flourens (p. 158)
Gustav Fritsch (p. 163)
Phineas P. Gage (p. 160)
Franz Joseph Gall (p. 156)
Luigi Galvani (p. 148)
galvanic skin response (p. 148)
Camillo Golgi (p. 165)
Marshall Hall (p. 147)
Hermann Ludwig Ferdinand von Helmholtz (p. 149)
Helmholtz-Hering debate (p. 153)
Ewald Hering (p. 152)
Herophilus (p. 146)
Eduard Hitzig (p. 164)
Sir Alan Hodgkin (p. 168)
Sir Andrew Huxley (p. 168)
John Hughlings Jackson (p. 163)
just noticeable difference (p. 169)
Christine Ladd-Franklin (p. 152)
localizationists (p. 153)
Otto Loewi (p. 166)
François Magendie (p. 154)
medulla oblongata (p. 159)
method of limits (p. 172)
Johannes Müller (p. 155)
Hermann Munk (p. 164)
negative afterimage (p. 152)
neural plasticity (p. 159)
nonlocalizationists (p. 153)
opponent-process theory (p. 152)
Wilder Graves Penfield (p. 165)
phrenology (p. 156)
place theory of pitch perception (p. 176)
psychopharmacology (p. 167)
psychophysics (p. 171)
Sir Charles Scott Sherrington (p. 166)
Johann Caspar Spurzheim (p. 157)
Stevens's law (p. 172)
synapse (p. 166)
trichromatic theory (p. 151)
two-point threshold (p. 168)
Count Alessandro Volta (p. 148)
Georg von Békésy (p. 151)
Wilhelm von Waldeyer (p. 165)
Ernst Heinrich Weber (p. 168)
Weber fractions (p. 169)
Weber's law (p. 171)
Carl Wernicke (p. 162)
Wernicke's model (p. 163)
Robert Whytt (p. 147)
Whytt's reflex (p. 147)
Thomas Young (p. 150)
Young-Helmholtz theory (p. 151)

SUGGESTED READINGS

Benjamin, L. T., Jr. (1988). *A history of psychology: Original sources and contemporary research.* New York: McGraw-Hill Book Company. Chapter 4 of this book of readings, "The Physiological Roots of Psychology," contains original works by Broca and Helmholtz. Broca's account of his discovery of the speech area that bears his name is entertaining. Benjamin's compilation is only one of several books of readings that provide convenient sources for original material.

Blakemore, C. (1977). *Mechanics of the mind.* Cambridge: Cambridge University Press. This is an excellent treatment of the development of scientific investigation of the brain. The illustrations are outstanding.

Clarke, E., & Jacyna, L. S. (1987). *Nineteenth-century origins of neuroscientific concepts.* Berkeley: University of California Press. Clarke and Jacyna have put together a magnificent account of the development of modern neuroscience from 19th-century discoveries and theoretical ideas. One of the book's reviewers called it "[a]n absolute must for anyone interested in history, neurology and neuroscience."

Fechner, G. (1966). *Elements of psychophysics* (Vol. 1; H. E. Adler, Trans.). New York: Holt, Rinehart and Winston. (Original work published 1860) Despite James's negative view of Fechner's work, it is always worthwhile to read the original writings of psychology's founders, at least in translation.

Finger, S. (1994). *Origins of neuroscience: A history of explorations into brain function.* Oxford: Oxford University Press. This is a monumental and well-illustrated volume devoted to the history of ideas about brain functioning from its beginnings in Egypt, Greece, and Rome to relatively modern times.

Loewi, O. (1960). An autobiographic sketch. *Perspectives in Biology and Medicine, 4,* 3–25. This is a highly readable account of Loewi's discovery that much synaptic transmission occurs chemically.

Stumpf, C. (1895). Hermann von Helmholtz and the new psychology. *Psychological Review, 2,* 1–12. Written by one of the key figures in the history of psychology, this is a good summary of Helmholtz's contributions to psychology.

The Origins of Modern Scientific Psychology in Germany

CHAPTER 8

Oswald Külpe

Georg Elias Müller

Hermann Ebbinghaus

Edmund Husserl

Carl Stumpf

Celestia Suzannah Parrish

Emil Kraepelin

Wilhelm Wundt

E. B. Titchener

Franz Brentano

1830 1840 1850 1860 1870 1880

Typewriter is patented

Goethe dies

U.S. Naval Academy opens

Work begins on the Suez Canal

Lee surrenders to Grant to end the Civil War

Gilbert and Sullivan publish *The Pirates of Penzance*

OUTLINE

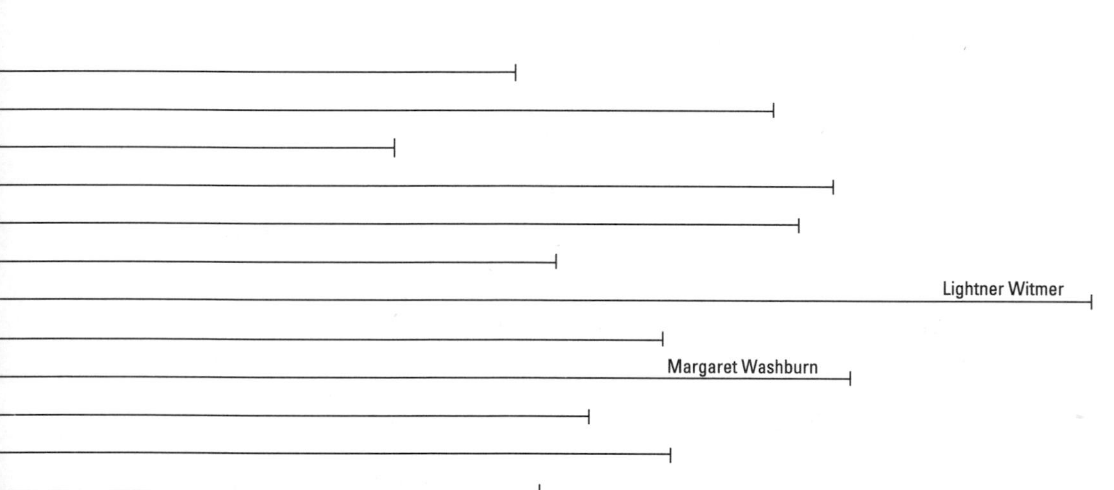

Lightner Witmer
Margaret Washburn
1890
1900
1910
1920
1930
1940
1950
1960
Babe Ruth is born
APA is founded
W.E.B. Du Bois founds NAACP
Armistice is signed by Germany; WWI ends
Orson Welles directs "War of the Worlds"
Japanese forces bomb Pearl Harbor

In the last six chapters, we have explored the events in philosophy and physiology (or medicine) that laid the foundation for psychology. In this chapter, we will see that scientific psychology arose when physiology's experimental methods were applied to certain philosophical problems. This combination of an interest in philosophy and a knowledge of physiology has often been seen in the same person. For example, in Chapter 5, Locke, Hartley, and Cabanis all had medical backgrounds. And in Chapter 6, we noted that Lotze earned a medical degree while retaining his interest in philosophy and the arts. In fact, of the men who have received some support as the "founders" of psychology, almost all had medical backgrounds plus strong interests in philosophy.

In Chapter 10, we will see that William James, trained as a physician, devoted his professional life to psychology and philosophy. Although James's 1875 demonstration laboratory at Harvard establishes his claim as psychology's founder, James was never really an experimentalist. Because this chapter's theme is the founding of psychology as an experimental science, as distinct from psychology as a philosophical enterprise, we will first review the work of Wilhelm Wundt at the University of Leipzig. Wundt is the man and Leipzig the location that most historians of psychology associate with the founding of a separate science of psychology. After Wundt, we will discuss Edward Bradford Titchener, who established a version of Wundt's psychology as America's first school—structuralism. We will end the chapter with an examination of several Germans whose approaches to psychology differed from Wundt's. Specifically, we will review the work of Franz Brentano, Carl Stumpf, Edmund Husserl, Hermann Ebbinghaus, Georg Elias Müller, and Oswald Külpe.

You might be curious about why psychology as an experimental science arose in Germany rather than in England or France or another country. Was there something about Germany's university system in the 19th century that fostered the development of psychology as a science? The answer is almost certainly yes.

For one thing, education, particularly higher education, was quite important in 19th-century Germany and was well supported by both the country's citizens and their rulers. According to Dobson and Bruce (1972), "The prevailing opinion seemed to be that education, not elegance or fine living, was the one thing every German must have" (p. 204).

German universities particularly encouraged scholarship through "freedom of teaching" and "freedom of learning." Freedom of teaching meant that instructors were free to choose their topics, to present them in their own styles, and to express their views without fear of interference from an outside party. Similarly, students were free to attend lectures on whatever topics interested them, taught by teachers they liked, and as frequently or infrequently as they wished. For example, freedom of learning allowed Carl Stumpf (discussed later), to take courses at the University of Würzburg on subjects as disparate as aesthetics and law and then to transfer to the University of Göttingen, where he was favorably impressed by the lectures of physiologist Wilhelm Weber. Examinations were held at the end of a course of study, which fostered freedom of learning by allowing individuals to study whatever interested them as long as they could pass a comprehensive examination.

Once psychology as a science began, the freedom of teaching and learning in German universities helped the movement spread throughout the country's universities (Dobson & Bruce, 1972). As we will see in our discussion of this chapter's central characters, ease of movement by professors and students was the norm in the German university system. For example, we have seen that Stumpf studied at Würzburg and Göttingen as a student; as a professor, he taught at Würzburg, Halle, Munich, and Berlin, with a digression between Würzburg and Halle to Prague, Czechoslovakia. Similarly, Oswald Külpe (discussed later) began his university career at Leipzig, transferred to Göttingen, and then returned to Leipzig for his Ph.D. As a professor, his career took him from Leipzig to Würzburg to Bonn and finally to Munich.

In addition, the German university system's research emphasis was probably largely responsible for giving psychology its scientific approach (Hilgard, 1987). In England and France, science meant physics and chemistry, but German academics considered any topic worthy of a scientific approach. Thus, they encouraged scientific investigations in subjects as diverse as chemistry, biology, literature, and music. "Given this atmosphere, the scientific study of the human mind by men such as Fechner and Wundt may be seen as an inevitable consequence" (Dobson & Bruce, 1972, p. 206). Wilhelm Wundt was trained in this German research tradition and took advantage of it to create a new synthesis of philosophy and physiology that has become modern scientific psychology.

We will see throughout our look at the beginnings of scientific psychology that the synthesis of physiology and philosophy is crucial for the development of the field. As we indicated in Chapter 6, Rudolph Hermann Lotze earned doctorates in both philosophy and medicine and was pivotal to the founding of psychology. Similarly, Gustav Fechner (Chapter 7) combined his training in medicine with philosophical interests to produce psychophysics, which some would argue began scientific psychology. In this chapter, we will introduce medically trained philosopher Wilhelm Wundt as the true founder of psychology as a science.

Archives of the History of American Psychology–The University of Akron.

Wilhelm Wundt (1832–1920) in about 1865

WILHELM MAXIMILIAN WUNDT AND VOLUNTARISM

Wilhelm Maximilian Wundt (1832–1920) was born in the village of Neckarau, part of Baden, which is a division of southwestern Germany. His parents' fourth child, Wundt had only one living brother, who was 8 years older. Wundt's father was a Lutheran minister, characterized by Wundt as a good-humored spendthrift. By contrast, his mother was a frugal shopper whose bargain hunting embarrassed her husband. Two of Wundt's ancestors on his father's side had been presidents of the University of Heidelberg, whereas others had scholarly interests in economics, geography, and history. On his mother's side were scientists, governmental administrators, and physicians.

Despite his accomplished ancestors, Wundt's daydreaming produced a mediocre academic record. Wundt's father once visited his class as the school inspector and became so angered at Wundt's inattentiveness "that he slapped him in the face" (Bringmann, Balance, & Evans, 1975, p. 288). In his autobiography, Wundt noted that this incident stood in marked contrast to the treatment he normally received from his father.

When he was 13, Wundt spent a year of academic torture at the Catholic *Gymnasium* at Bruchsal. This was followed by enrollment at the Lyceum in Heidelberg, where Wundt finally overcame his daydreaming tendency, experienced the death of his father during the school year, and developed friendships for the first time in his life. He also became an avid reader and found it reinforcing when a teacher read his essays to the class as examples of good writing.

When Wundt graduated in 1851, he and his mother were barely existing on her widow's pension. With his poor academic record, Wundt did not qualify for the scholarship normally available to ministers' sons. After a year studying medicine at Tübingen University, Wundt returned to Heidelberg and completed his medical training in just 3 years, ranking first in the medical state board examinations in 1855.

As a Heidelberg medical student, Wundt also developed an interest in research. Supervised by noted chemist Robert Bunsen (1811–1899), of Bunsen burner fame, Wundt deprived himself of salt in order to study the effect on the salt concentration of his urine. Wundt considered the resulting publication more enjoyable than any other because it was his first.

For 6 months after completing the state board examination, Wundt worked as the clinical assistant to one of his former teachers. He also continued his research on the touch sensitivity of hysterical patients, which he considered the first steps on his journey toward experimental psychology. This investigation became Wundt's medical dissertation, and on November 10, 1855, Wundt received his M.D., *summa cum laude.*

Next, Wundt spent a semester studying physiology in Berlin with Johannes Müller and Émil du Bois-Reymond (Chapter 7). Wundt returned to Heidelberg and applied for a second doctorate (*Habilitation*) to enable him to offer courses of his own. After initially rejecting him, the faculty relented and allowed Wundt to teach his first course in experimental physiology in the summer of 1857 as a *Privatdozent.*

From the stress of a class of four students held in his mother's apartment, Wundt nearly died of a lung hemorrhage. He went to the Swiss Alps to recover and, perhaps deciding that teaching was too demanding, applied for a position as assistant to Helmholtz (Chapter 7) in the newly established physiological institute at Heidelberg. As one of Helmholtz's assistants from 1858 until 1864, Wundt shared a room with Ivan Sechenov (Chapter 12), a Russian physiologist who greatly influenced Ivan Pavlov (Chapter 12). Sechenov later recalled that Wundt never spoke either to him or to the other three men who shared the room and that he had never even heard Wundt's voice!

According to G. Stanley Hall (Chapter 10), who visited Wundt in Leipzig and later wrote a biography of him, Helmholtz fired Wundt for mathematical incompetence. However, Wundt disputed Hall's claim, and Helmholtz wrote several recommendation letters for his former assistant "in which he praised Wundt for his teaching skills, his publication record and especially the integrity of his research methods" (Bringmann et al., 1975, p. 292).

In 1862, Wundt published *Beiträge zur Theorie der Sinneswahrnehmung* (*Contributions Toward a Theory of Sense Perception*). In *Contributions,* Wundt outlined his plans for psychology, which he envisioned as a science that would establish the facts of consciousness. Wundt planned to create an experimental psychology, a scientific metaphysics (i.e., "a philosophy which makes the results of all the other sciences the object of its own special investigations" [Titchener, 1921, p. 167]), and a social psychology. Two physiology textbooks followed, and Wundt's income from his writings allowed him to leave the physiological institute and start a small laboratory in his home, where he continued his experimentation.

After leaving Helmholtz, Wundt also had a brief political career. As president of the Heidelberg Workmen's Educational Association, he traveled and lectured on popular scientific topics. Appointed to serve in the Baden Parliament in 1866, Wundt was elected in 1867, but he resigned when he realized the position deserved his full attention, and he was still primarily interested in research.

In 1871, Wundt received a salaried appointment (*ausserordentlicher Professor* or *Professor extraordinarius*) at Heidelberg with an income nearly twice the amount he had received as Helmholtz's assistant. With his improved economic situation, Wundt married Sophie Mau, his fiancée of several years.

In 1873 and 1874, Wundt published in two volumes the first edition of his most influential book, *Grundzüge der physiologischen Psychologie* (*Principles of Physiological Psychology*). Note that *physiological psychology* did not mean the same thing to Wundt that it does to us. To Wundt, it meant experimental or laboratory psychology rather than psychological neuroscience. *Physiological* referred to the use of physiology's methods, not to what was studied.

From Heidelberg, Wundt went to the University of Zurich to assume a professorship in philosophy. Zurich was considered a stopover for young scholars ascending the academic ladder, and Wundt added to this reputation. In little more than a year, he was called to the chair of philosophy at the University of Leipzig, where he remained for the next 42 years. Note that Wundt accepted positions in philosophy at Zurich and Leipzig, despite having taken only one philosophy course as an undergraduate. He had established his philosophy credentials with a book on the philosophical analysis of the physical basis of causality.

At Leipzig, Wundt established psychology as an experimental science through his voluminous publications, his teaching and research, a journal, and the graduate students he trained. But all of this was in the future when he arrived in 1875. To store his equipment from Zurich, Wundt was assigned a small room in the dining hall, and it was here in 1879 that Wundt began some independent psychological research.

Although generally accepted as the date of scientific psychology's founding, the year 1879 is not etched in stone (Boring, 1965). In fact, a variety of other years have appeared in print, including 1874, 1875, and 1878. Sometimes more than one date has been given in the same article: for example, 1878 and 1879 in Baldwin (1894). However, Wundt himself spoke of the autumn of 1879 as the time when experimentation began in the Leipzig laboratory space, and there is a wealth of supporting documentation (e.g., Bringmann, Bringmann, & Ungerer, 1980; Bringmann & Ungerer, 1980; Bringmann, Voss, & Ungerer, 1997) for the 1879 date.

For 2 years, Wundt supported his "institute" with his own money, and his laboratory was not recognized in the university catalog until 1883. This belated official recognition was stimulated by an offer Wundt received from another university, which provided the leverage he needed to persuade the administration to give him more resources. Limited resources continued to be a problem as late as 1891, according to a recently translated article by a Belgian visitor to Wundt's laboratory, J. J. Van Biervliet (1859–1945). Van Biervliet noted that Wundt's annual allotment of 1,500 Deutschmarks was wholly inadequate for a laboratory with more than 20 persons a year in it. "Some Americans told us that laboratories of psychology in the United States are far better equipped" (Nicolas & Ferrand, 1999, p. 199).

Soon, Wundt was able to expand his laboratory into rooms vacated by the school of pharmacy. In 1892, the laboratory moved to 11 rooms in a building that had previously housed the department of gynecology. Finally, 5 years later, Wundt and his laboratory moved to a building constructed to his specifications. This building served as a model for many similar laboratories until its destruction during World War II.

During his career, Wundt taught more than 24,000 students. Wundt was a popular lecturer at Leipzig, and his lecture style has been described by one of his American students as follows:

> As soon as his familiar figure appeared, applause in the form of shuffling feet . . . would greet him. . . . Utterly unmoved, as if he had not heard us, Wundt would glide to his place on the dais, assume his accustomed position, fix his eyes on vacancy and begin his discourse. There could not be a better scientific lecturer. Without a scrap of writing, he would speak for three-quarters of an hour so clearly, concisely, and to the point, that, in listening to him, one would imagine one were reading a well-written book in which the paragraphs, the important text of the page, the small print, and the footnotes were plainly indicated. Wundt told no stories, gave few illustrations, scorned any attempt at popularity. His only thought was to deal with the topic of the day as thoroughly and exhaustively as the time permitted. . . . With all this, he was followed almost breathlessly, sometimes by eight hundred students, and, if the lecture had been unusually amazing, they would burst into spontaneous applause. (Worcester, 1932, p. 90)

Wundt supervised a large number of doctoral dissertations and apparently had close relationships with many of his graduate students. He also maintained friendly relations with former students who disagreed with his views, such as Hugo Münsterberg (Chapter 10). Wundt even recommended Münsterberg to the University of Zurich after a major disagreement.

Liked by his university colleagues, Wundt "regarded himself fortunate to have personally known the two psychophysicists [Ernst] Weber . . . and Gustav Theodor Fechner . . . and to have been a guest in their homes" (Bringmann et al., 1975, p. 295). Friedrich Sander (1889–1972), Wundt's last assistant, recalled a mellow Wundt, tired of controversy, who enjoyed their intimate conversations.

Wundt's home life was apparently pleasant and conventional. With his wife, he entertained faculty and students, and the Wundts went to the theater, to the opera, and to concerts. His wife also helped him professionally, and he kept her informed about his research and his classes (Hilgard, 1987). Wundt died in 1920 shortly after his 88th birthday and just 8 days after completing his autobiography, *Erlebtes und Erkanntes* (*What I Have Experienced and Discovered*).

Wundt's pendulum-clock experiment

From R. E. Fancher, Pioneers of Psychology *(2nd edition, New York: W. W. Norton, 1990).*

Wundt's Psychology

In 1861, Wundt rigged a pendulum clock into an apparatus (see illustration) that he used to perform an interesting experiment (Wundt, 1862). Below the pendulum (B), Wundt had placed a calibrated scale (M). As the pendulum swung, a knitting needle (S) struck a bell (g) when the pendulum reached either position b or d. However, Wundt found that when he tried to attend to both the bell's sound and the position of the pendulum, the pendulum was never precisely at b or d at the moment he heard the bell—it was always on its way back toward the center of the scale. In fact, he determined that it took him approximately 0.1 second to switch his attention from the bell's sound to the pendulum's location or vice versa. Although the sound of the bell and the pendulum's extreme position occurred simultaneously, Wundt had not consciously experienced the two sensations together. He had experienced the sensations successively, indicating that separate acts of attention were necessary.

Like Fechner, Wundt had experimentally measured a psychological process. As we noted earlier, in 1862 Wundt also published *Contributions Toward a Theory of Sense Perception* in which he proposed to create experimental psychology. Wundt's experimental psychology did not develop overnight, however, and 17 years passed before he began the Leipzig studies honored by the American Psychological Association in 1979. In the meantime, he published the two-volume first edition of *Principles of Physiological Psychology.* To keep up with the work pouring from his laboratory, Wundt revised the *Principles* five times, with the last two editions expanded to three volumes.

In the *Principles,* it is evident that Wundt was seeking to establish psychology as a "new domain of science," but not necessarily one completely independent of philosophy (Brock, 1993). In calling for a science of psychology, Wundt was refuting the claims of Comte (Chapter 5) and Kant (Chapter 6) that psychology could not be a science. And by arguing for an experimental psychology, Wundt was disagreeing with Herbart's (Chapter 6) belief that psychology could not be an experimental endeavor. In fact, Herbart "provided much of the background against which Wundt rebelled" (Blumenthal, 1979, p. 549).

Despite his regular revisions of the *Principles*, Wundt realized he needed a journal to provide more timely publication of his experimental results. In 1881, he began publishing *Philosophische Studien* (*Philosophical Studies*). Wundt initially planned to call the journal *Psychologische Studien* (*Psychological Studies*), but a journal with that title already existed, dealing with parapsychology and spiritism. According to Brock (1993), Wundt wrote in his autobiography that he deliberately chose the title *Philosophische Studien* to emphasize that psychology was part of philosophy. However, citing letters written in 1880 from Wundt to Emil Kraepelin (discussed later), Bringmann et al. (1980) reported conclusively that Wundt initially planned to call his journal *Psychologische Studien.* We use this slight discrepancy as a reminder of our Chapter 1 discussion of the difficulties of pinning down a completely accurate history. Whatever its intended title, this was the first journal devoted primarily to psychological experiments.

Wundt's Two Psychologies

For Wundt, the mind could be seen as a collection of conscious experiences produced by the interaction of external stimuli and higher mental processes. Psychology was the science of mind: that is, a science of conscious experiences. Wundt further assumed that consciousness could be experienced either directly or indirectly. For example, experienced directly, an apple produces sensations of redness and a rounded shape along with a feeling of mild pleasure. Wundt called this direct experience **immediate experience,** because it is based on an "immediate" reaction, uninfluenced by previous knowledge of the stimulus. Immediate experience gives the data for experimental psychology, which was one of Wundt's two psychologies.

By contrast, you may use a light meter to measure the amount of light the apple's surface reflects or a scale to determine its weight. This experience of the apple is indirect, mediated by the instruments used to collect the data. Wundt called this **mediate experience,** which produces data for physics and other natural sciences.

The part of Wundt's psychology with which most contemporary psychologists are familiar studied the lower mental processes—for example, sensing and feeling—using the methods of physiology. Wundt treated his physiological (experimental) psychology as a natural science (*Naturwissenschaft*).

Wundt did not believe that the higher mental processes—for example, language, memory, and thinking—could be studied experimentally, treating them instead as a cultural science (*Geisteswissenschaft*). Thus, he studied the *products* of the processes rather than the mental processes themselves, and the result grew into the 10 volumes of the *Völkerpsychologie*, which we will discuss briefly after we examine Wundt's experimental psychology.

Wundt's Use of Internal Perception

One of the most enduring misconceptions about Wundt's methodology concerns the use of introspection (*Selbstbeobachtung*, self-study or looking inward).

> Wundt was not an introspectionist as that term is popularly applied today [as looking into one's own mind to contemplate one's thoughts, sensations, and feelings]. The thrust behind his entire experimental program was the claim that progress in psychology had been slow because of reliance on casual, unsystematic introspection, which had led invariably to unresolvable debates. (Blumenthal, 1975, p. 1082)

That is, Wundt did not use the type of introspection (Chapter 3) implied by the term, although this use is often attributed to him.

Wundt distinguished between introspection and **internal perception** (*innere Wahrnehmung*). In principle, he thought internal perceptions could be as valid as external perceptions. Recognizing that conscious experiences are continually changing, Wundt developed specific rules for reporting them. First, the observer required proper training to ensure that he or she described immediate experience rather than mediate experience. Second, the observer needed to know when the stimulus would be presented so that he or she would not be caught by surprise. This was necessary because the report was supposed to occur as soon as the observations were made instead of being based on memory. Third, the observer had to be primed to experience the stimulus, in a state of strained attention. Fourth, the observations needed to be repeated many times, in order to reveal problems that might have occurred with early presentations. Finally, the experimental conditions had to be varied systematically to enhance the observations' generality. Given the lengthy training needed to become proficient at internal perception and the stringent rules for its use, it is easy to see why William James wrote that Wundt's experimental method "hardly could have arisen in a country whose natives could be *bored*" (1890, Vol. 1, p. 192, italics in the original).

Although it is sometimes implied that internal perception was the *only* technique Wundt and his students used, its use was limited to sensation and perception studies in which the rules could be applied. Wundt's disapproval of introspection (as opposed to internal perception) is clear from an analysis of nearly 180 studies from 20 years of *Philosophische Studien,* which revealed that only 4 had produced qualitative introspective data of the kind gathered in other laboratories in the first decade of the 20th century (Danziger, 1980). Danziger noted that 2 of the 4 were specifically criticized by Wundt, and a third concerned data not gathered in his laboratory.

Wundt's Research

Wundt's research was remarkable for its range of topics. Because Wundt assigned the research problems to his students, an analysis of *Philosophische Studien* (e.g., Boring, 1950) provides an indication of the scope and nature of the studies done in Wundt's laboratory.

Sensation and Perception. Approximately half of the Leipzig studies between 1881 and 1903 investigated sensation and perception topics, with most of the work being done in vision. For example, there were studies on the psychophysics of light and color, studies of negative afterimages, studies of color defects, and studies of optical illusions. There were also psychophysical studies of auditory sensations and studies of Weber's two-point threshold.

Reaction-Time Studies. With his 1861 clock experiment, Wundt had revealed an interest in how long it took to react to sensory stimulation. Probably this interest was fueled by Wundt's having been Helmholtz's assistant: As we noted in Chapter 7, Helmholtz used a reaction-time difference to measure the speed of the nerve impulse. However, interest in reaction-time measurement antedated Helmholtz's work by over half a century.

In 1796 at Greenwich Observatory, British astronomer-royal Nevil Maskelyne (1732–1811) fired his assistant, Kinnebrook, because of a significant difference in the two men's readings of the times of stellar transit—the time noted when an observed star crossed grid lines in the telescope. Stellar transit was measured by the "eye and ear" method, in which an observer watched a star move across a grid while counting the beats of a clock. This information was used to make a complex judgment, and, not surprisingly, the differences in judgments made by Maskelyne and his assistant were attributed to faults in Kinnebrook.

Twenty years later, German astronomer Friedrich Wilhelm Bessel (1784–1846) learned of the Kinnebrook-Maskelyne incident and decided to investigate any differences between himself and other astronomers. Following Bessel's work, the difference between any two astronomers became known as a "personal equation." Bessel's discovery forced astronomers to determine their personal equations and to correct for them. In addition, the Dutch physiologist Franciscus Cornelius Donders (1818–1889) took over the reaction experiment from the astronomers.

In measuring a "simple" reaction time, a subject reacts to a predetermined stimulus with a predetermined movement. In 1868, Donders complicated the task by adding other stimuli to which the subject either responded or did not respond. Complicating the task should lengthen the reaction time, presumably by the time it takes the subject to make additional judgments. Donders's **mental chronom-**

etry method was based on the following assumptions: It takes time to perform mental acts; complicated reaction times are the sum of the reaction times for each of the different mental acts involved; and the time required for a particular mental act can be found by subtraction. To illustrate, suppose a subject takes 0.2 seconds to release a telegraph key when a blue light appears. As a complication, the subject is given two telegraph keys and must now release the left key when a blue light appears and the right key when a yellow light appears. The result is a 0.3-second reaction time. Donders assumed the time needed to categorize the light's color (blue or yellow) and to make the appropriate response (release the left key or the right key) is 0.1 second (0.3 – 0.2 = 0.1).

At first, reaction-time experiments appeared to provide a true mental chronometry—a measure of the time each mental process took—and about 17% of the studies from Wundt's laboratory involved the reaction experiment. For example, James McKeen Cattell (Chapter 10), Wundt's first assistant, worked extensively with reaction times, using ingenious equipment he designed. Whereas in earlier studies the measurement of reaction times required a subject to either press or release a telegraph key, for later experiments Cattell invented keys activated by lip movements or by sound vibrations from a subject's voice. In one series of observations, Cattell presented letters or words and required subjects to name the stimuli by speaking. The finding that subjects took about the same time to name short words as they did individual letters led Cattell to the valid conclusion that people perceive words as wholes rather than perceiving each letter separately.

Wundt, and later his critics, were particularly interested in the 1888 reaction-time experiment by **Ludwig Lange** (1863–1936). Lange compared simple reaction times when the subject attended either to the expected stimulus or to the response to be made. Generally, reactions were about 0.1 second longer when the focus was on the stimulus. The personal equation problem appeared to have been solved: Astronomers who attend to the stimulus take longer to respond than astronomers who attend to making the response.

Archives of the History of American Psychology–The University of Akron.

Wundt and his collaborators in the reaction experiment, 1912

Wundt attributed the difference to Leibniz's distinction (Chapter 4) between simple perception and apperception. When concentrating on the response, the subject merely perceives the stimulus, leading to a quick response. When concentrating on the stimulus, the subject apperceives it, and apperception (or attention) requires 0.1-second longer. Thus, Lange's study led to a third major research area in Wundt's laboratory—attention.

Perhaps Wundt should have taken Helmholtz's experience with reaction times as instructive: Helmholtz abandoned them because of unreliability. Nevertheless, the recording of reaction times has proved useful in such areas as sensation and perception (e.g., Coren, Ward, & Enns, 1994), intelligence testing (e.g., Vernon, 1987), and cognitive psychology (e.g., Posner, 1978).

Attention. The study of attention accounted for about 10% of the articles in *Philosophische Studien.* To appreciate the importance of attention for Wundt, we must examine his system more closely.

For Wundt, simple reaction time involved three mental acts: First, the sensory stimulus enters consciousness (perception). Wundt assumed that perception occurs passively, determined by the actual stimulation and the individual's physiology and experiences. Next, attention is focused on the sensory impression (**apperception**). Finally, there is a voluntary release of the response (voluntary behavior). Wundt believed consciousness has two zones: The first, larger zone is the background of impressions that have entered consciousness, whereas the second zone consists of material on which attention is focused, resulting in clear perception or apperception. Think of a stage on which a spotlight is trained. At the center of the spotlight, characters and objects are apperceived, whereas the dimly illuminated objects and characters outside the spotlight are merely perceived.

Wundt considered apperception an act of will, an active desire to pay attention. You may recall the centrality of will in Schopenhauer's philosophy (Chapter 6). Rejecting Schopenhauer's metaphysics, Wundt made the voluntary nature of attention his "paradigm [model or pattern] psychological phenomenon." Because of this, Wundt called his system **voluntarism** and by the end of the century had placed it in opposition to Titchener's structuralism (discussed later), a term Wundt never applied to his own psychology (Blumenthal, 1979).

Wundt further held that different rules of organization and combination apply to perceived and apperceived ideas. Perceived ideas are organized automatically and mechanically, based on channels carved by experience, whereas apperceived ideas may be combined in novel ways. In other words, a **creative synthesis** of ideas may take place at the focus of attention, and Wundt speculated that this occurs in the brain's frontal lobes (Blumenthal, 1997). Although it has been suggested (see Chapter 5) that Wundt's creative synthesis is related to John Stuart Mill's mental chemistry, Blumenthal (1975) argued against making too much of the relationship.

> Wundt did in his early years make brief, passing references to J. S. Mill's use of a chemical analogy to describe certain perceptual processes. . . . Similarly, the qualities of a perception are not directly given in its underlying elements.
>
> But Wundt points out that this analogy does not go far enough, and by the end of the century he is describing it as a false analogy because the chemical synthesis is . . . wholly determined by its elements while the psychological synthesis is "truly a new formation, not merely the result of a chemical-like formation." . . . What the chemical analogy lacks is the independent, constructive, attentional process which in the psychological case is the source of the synthesis. (p. 1083)

Some of Wundt's students experimentally measured the apperception span to determine how many stimulus elements could be clearly fixed in consciousness with a single exposure. Random letters, numbers, or words were flashed briefly on a screen, and subjects tried to recall as many stimuli as possible. The number of recalled stimuli generally ranged from four to six, and this was true whether the stimuli were individual letters or familiar words. For example, if the stimulus was a four-by-four array of random letters, 4 to 6 letters were normally apperceived. However, with an array of 16 six-letter words, 4 to 6 words were recalled, supporting Cattell's finding that words are treated as wholes rather than as individual letters. (This works with *familiar* words; with unfamiliar words, apperception occurs at the level of individual letters.)

As Wundt's student, the German-born psychiatrist **Emil Kraepelin** (1856–1926) applied Wundt's attentional theory to schizophrenia, which he called *dementia praecox* (insanity of the young). He considered the abnormal behavior of schizophrenics the result of "flaws in the central control process that may take the form of either highly reduced attentional scanning, or highly erratic scanning, or extremes of attentional focusing" (Blumenthal, 1975, p. 1085). Reviving Kraepelin's analysis, Silverman (1964) discussed the importance of defective attention in schizophrenia.

Feelings. As we noted above, Wundt divided the contents of consciousness into sensations and feelings. In the 1890s, a great deal of Wundt's research focused on feelings, and such studies constituted about 10% of the experimental reports in *Philosophische Studien.*

Based on his own internal perceptions of the clicking of a metronome—an instrument for keeping time in music—Wundt concluded there are three different dimensions of feelings.

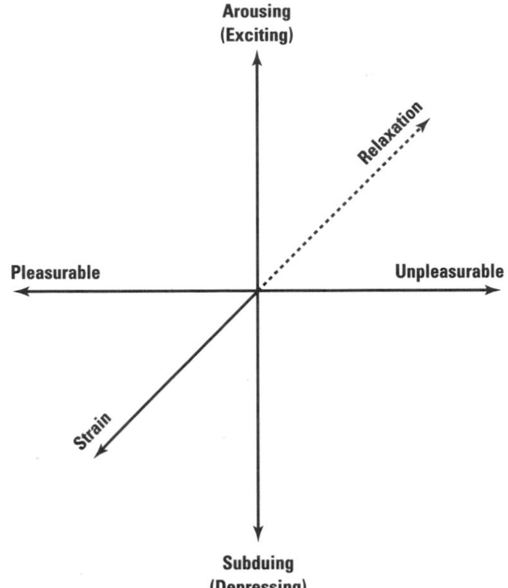

FIGURE 8.2 Wundt's three-dimensional theory of feeling

> *Three* such chief directions may be distinguished; we will call them the direction of *pleasurable* and *unpleasurable* feelings, that of *arousing* and *subduing* (exciting and depressing) feelings, and finally that of feelings of *strain* and *relaxation*. Any concrete feeling may belong to all of these directions or only two or even only one of them. (Wundt, 1897; cited in Sahakian, 1968, p. 127, italics in the original)

Figure 8.2 illustrates Wundt's three-dimensional theory of feelings.

Research at Leipzig tried to relate the three dimensions to unique bodily response patterns using the **method of expression.** According to Boring (1950),

> there were half a dozen researches on the method of expression, relating changes of pulse, breathing, muscular strength and so on, to correlated feelings. . . . Most of these papers sought to support Wundt's new theory and are now seen, with the theory, to have failed. (p. 343)

However, more recent research, using factor analytic statistical techniques (Chapter 17), has identified dimensions similar to Wundt's. For example, Schlosberg (1954) described three affective dimensions as "pleasantness-unpleasantness," "high-low activation," and "attention-rejection," whereas Osgood, Suci, and Tannenbaum's (1957) three dimensions were "good-bad," "active-passive," and "strong-weak."

The Völkerpsychologie

Beginning with the establishment of his laboratory in 1879, we can divide Wundt's career at Leipzig into two parts: the first part, in which he studied lower mental processes experimentally, and the second part, in which he studied the products of the higher mental processes from a comparative-historical point of view. As we noted, the latter part resulted in the publication, in 10 volumes, of the *Völkerpsychologie: Eine Untersuchung der Entwicklungsgesetz von Sprache, Mythus, und Sitte* (*Cultural Psychology: An Investigation of the Developmental Laws of Language, Myth, and Morality*). Consisting of two volumes on language, two on myth and religion, two on society, and one each on art, culture, law, and history, the ***Völkerpsychologie*** was published during the last 2 decades of Wundt's life and even today remains largely undiscovered by most American psychologists.

One reason for this lack of attention is that little of the *Völkerpsychologie* has been translated. In addition, except for one volume on language, the books contain "a massive collection of often outdated accounts of myths, rituals, religion, customs, and so on. It requires dogged persistence to plow through even a single volume, let alone the whole set" (Jahoda, 1997, p. 151). Another factor is that "Wundt's main English-speaking disciple . . . , Titchener, was totally unsympathetic to *völkerpsychologie,* misrepresenting Wundt's ideas on this topic even in the obituary he wrote" (p. 152).

On the other hand, the *Völkerpsychologie* has positively influenced other disciplines, such as anthropology (Blumenthal, 1997). For example, Wundt's belief that mental differences in human populations have a cultural basis was accepted by Franz Boas (1858–1942), who attended Wundt's lectures as a young student. As the founding figure in anthropology, Boas passed on this belief, indirectly shaping modern ideas about intelligence (Chapter 17) with Wundt's views.

Nerlich and Clarke (1998) have noted a similar influence of the *Völkerpsychologie* on the study of language. Despite Wundt's repudiation by linguists, in their criticisms of Wundt's approach to language, psychologist Karl Bühler (Chapter 14) and sociologist George Herbert Mead (Chapter 11) "both acknowledged that Wundt had been a true pioneer in the psychological study of language and that without his theories to test and criticize a more modern psychology of language would not have been possible" (p. 198).

Although there is a significant split between Wundt's earlier experimental work and the *Völkerpsychologie*, Greenwood (2003) has argued that the *Völkerpsychologie* is not necessarily an indication that Wundt believed it was impossible to study higher mental processes experimentally.

> Indeed, it may be reasonably argued that Wundt clearly recognized that "higher" cognitive processes, such as memory and cognition, can be experimentally manipulated. These were, after all, precisely the phenomena studied experimentally and introspectively by Wundt's American and German students in the Leipzig laboratory. (p. 80)

Greenwood (2003) argued that Wundt's efforts in the *Völkerpsychologie* can be seen as an early type of social psychology, continuing a tradition involving such people as Giambattista Vico and Johann Gottfried Herder (both Chapter 6). This tradition examines the evolution of a sort of group mentality in communities of people experiencing a common heritage and environment; we discussed a version of it in John Stuart Mill's ethology (Chapter 5) and in Hegel's concept of *Geist* (Chapter 6).

Wundt's Students

As we have seen, Wundt's Leipzig laboratory quickly became a busy place, and Wundt directed 186 dissertations, with 116 on psychological problems and the rest on philosophical topics. Although many of Wundt's Ph.D. recipients disappeared into the *Gymnasium* system without affecting psychology, there are still many important names in the roster of Wundt's students.

Americans who earned a Ph.D. with Wundt included James McKeen Cattell; **Edward W. Scripture** (1864–1945), an early director of the Yale Psychological Laboratory; **Lightner Witmer** (1867–1956), founder of the world's first psychological clinic in 1896 at the University of Pennsylvania (see the March 1996 issue of *American Psychologist* for more on Witmer and his contributions); **Charles H. Judd** (1873–1946), a pioneer educational and social psychologist at the University of Chicago; and Walter Dill Scott (1869–1955), who became perhaps the first industrial-organizational psychologist (Benjamin, 1997). Wundt's important Continental students included Oswald Külpe; Emil Kraepelin; Hugo Münsterberg; **Theodor Lipps** (1851–1914), best remembered for his empathy theory of aesthetic enjoyment; and Vladimir Bekhterev (Chapter 12). Edward Bradford Titchener was a famous British student.

As you can see, Wundt's influence on psychology's development was strong through his students. Although his experimentally trained American students quickly lost most vestiges of whatever version of Wundt's system they were taught, they brought from Leipzig an enthusiasm for laboratory psychology and a commitment to psychological research (Benjamin, Durkin, Link, Vestal, & Acord, 1992). Blumenthal (1980) suggested that Wundt's American students may have been quick to lose knowledge of Wundt's system because of their deficiencies in the German language. Perhaps their loss simply reflected their lack of understanding originally. According to Blumenthal, some of the American students survived their experience with Wundt only because Wundt knew enough English that he did not force them to answer his questions in German.

Despite their deficiencies in the German language, many young Americans traveled to Germany, and particularly to Leipzig, to earn their doctorates. Although some of the attraction was undoubtedly the opportunity to study with the founder of the new science of psychology, at least part of the appeal was related to the nature of the German doctorate, which was a 2-year degree approximately equivalent to our present-day master's degree (Blumenthal, 1998). An American student could spend a couple of years at

Leipzig and return to America with what was considered the equivalent of the American Ph.D. The German scholar at Leipzig, by contrast, first earned the doctorate and then was required to defend another dissertation to achieve *Habilitation*, which was essential for teaching at a German university.

Several of Wundt's American students founded psychology laboratories, including Cattell (University of Pennsylvania and Columbia University), Harry K. Wolfe (University of Nebraska; Chapter 13), Frank Angell (Cornell and Stanford University; Chapter 11), **George Stratton** (1865–1957; University of California-Berkeley), and Charles Judd (Wesleyan and New York Universities).

The Resurrection of Wundt

Over 3 decades have passed since Arthur Blumenthal began his pioneering reappraisal of Wundt (Blumenthal, 1970). Since 1970, Blumenthal (e.g., Blumenthal, 1975, 1979, 1980, 1997, 1998), Wolfgang Bringmann (e.g., Bringmann et al., 1975; Bringmann & Balk, 1992; Bringmann et al., 1980), Kurt Danziger (e.g., Danziger, 1979, 1980), and Thomas Leahey (e.g., Leahey, 1979, 1981) have been instrumental in revising our portrait of experimental psychology's founder.

As we indicated in Chapter 1, the traditional way to view Wundt was as Boring (1950), influenced by Titchener, portrayed him—as an introspectionist primarily concerned with unearthing the elements of consciousness. According to this view, Wundt's work led to structuralism, the school of psychology fleshed out by Titchener, who was responsible for bringing Wundt's psychology to America. Leahey (1981) and others (e.g., Koch, 1992) have written convincingly on the differences between the psychologies of Wundt and Titchener, and we will explore these differences in more detail shortly.

As we indicated, much of Wundt's research did not use introspection, and we have carefully referred to one of his methods as "internal perception" rather than introspection. In fact, according to Danziger (1980),

> Wundt would have been appalled to find himself categorized as an "introspective psychologist," not only because of his scorn for the introspectionist tradition, but also because of the implication that the reach of psychology was for him coextensive with the scope of introspection, an inference that was totally at variance with his whole approach to psychology. Quite apart from the ten volumes of his social psychology (*Völkerpsychologie*), his major text of experimental psychology, the *Grundzüge der physiologischen Psychologie,* contains a great deal of psychology that goes well beyond the data provided by experimental introspection. (p. 249)

Further, "Wundt [the introspectionist] became a convenient straw-man for behaviorists who wanted to demonstrate the superiority of their approach" (Brock, 1993, p. 236), and Wundt's reappraisal coincides with behaviorism's declining influence and the growing importance of cognitive psychology (e.g., Blumenthal, 1975; Danziger, 1979). As Blumenthal put it,

> Strange as it may seem, Wundt may be more easily understood today than he could have been just a few years ago. This is because of the current milieu of modern cognitive psychology and of the recent research on human information processing. (p. 1087)

By acknowledging that Wundt can be more easily interpreted in the era of cognitive psychology than he could have been in that of behaviorism, Blumenthal's statement may illustrate the "presentist bias," or the tendency to reinterpret people from the past in present-day terms, we discussed in Chapter 1.

According to Danziger (1979), at the beginning of psychology's development as a separate science, two models were proposed: First, there was Wundt's model, in which psychology kept at most one foot in the natural science camp. This observes Wundt's distinction between a *Naturwissenschaften* (experimental psychology) and a *Geisteswissenschaften* (social psychology or *Völkerpsychologie*). As we noted in Chapter 6, Herder earlier distinguished between *Naturwissenschaften* and *Geisteswissenschaften,* and his belief in the importance of the historical method influenced Wundt's *Völkerpsychologie.*

The main proponents of psychology wholly as a natural science (the second model) were Oswald Külpe, Hermann Ebbinghaus, and E. B. Titchener, men committed to the positivist philosophy associated with Mach and Avenarius. Külpe and his contemporaries aimed for psychology to have a scientific status equivalent to that of the physical sciences. In order to facilitate this process, Külpe rejected the "psychical individual" as an explanatory principle, opting instead for the "corporeal individual." Psychological explanations should be replaced as soon as possible with physiological explanations (reductionism).

Wundt adamantly opposed any positivistic or reductionistic approach that challenged his conception of psychology, arguing insightfully that psychology can be an independent science only if the psychical processes are interpreted in psychical terms, not in physical terms. If the psychical can be interpreted physiologically, then an independent science of psychology is unnecessary. Ironically, the same positivist *Zeitgeist* that aided Wundt's promotion of experimental psychology also set the stage for behaviorism and its repudiation of Wundt.

Wundt's Influence

Although first trained in physiology and often employed as a philosopher, Wundt is considered the first modern psychologist. His Leipzig laboratory qualifies as the first experimental psychology laboratory, and he trained many of the first generation of psychologists, several of whom established programs and/or laboratories that taught an experimental approach to psychology. Despite its title, Wundt's *Philosophische Studien* was the first experimental journal devoted primarily to psychology. Long overlooked, Wundt's surprisingly modern ideas in parts of the *Völkerpsychologie* have been rediscovered with the burgeoning interest in all things cognitive.

The scope of Wundt's influence has been tremendous, but the legacy of his work appears to be in transition. For example, a focus on his empirical science downplays his role as a German philosopher seeking to reconcile the new psychology with the rationalism of Kant and others. Some of the problem comes from the sheer volume of Wundt's output. With so much of his work published, it was not difficult for American and Russian (e.g., Bekhterev) objective psychologists to find elements in Wundt that seemed to anticipate their programs. Similarly, modern scholars such as Blumenthal have had little difficulty connecting Wundt to aspects of cognitive science.

Wundt's incredible publication record has been the subject of frequent commentaries, many based on Boring's (1950) analysis. Boring stated that "Wundt's penchant for writing can be statisticized, though one must not lose one's sense of humor in so doing" (p. 345). Boring then noted that "the adding-machine shows that Wundt . . . wrote about 53,375 pages in the sixty-eight years between 1853 and 1920 inclusive . . . which comes to about one word every two minutes, day and night, for the entire sixty-eight years" (p. 345).

Cattell suggested the secret to Wundt's productivity in a letter to his parents cited in Bringmann and Balk (1992): "[Wundt] works with great regularity, so in the course of a year accomplishes a great deal . . ." (p. 52). Cattell also contributed to Wundt's output by introducing him to the typewriter, a "new American invention." Although Cattell (1928) later claimed to have given Wundt his typewriter when he left Leipzig, "Wundt had already purchased his own machine in the summer of 1885 . . ." (Bringmann & Balk, p. 53).

Despite all of Wundt's well-documented accomplishments, there were detractors. Referring to the typewriter, Cattell wrote, "I am told that Avenarius said it was an evil gift, for with it Wundt wrote twice as many books as would otherwise have been possible" (Baldwin, 1921, p. 158). G. Stanley Hall characterized Wundt's writing style as solid and as lusterless as lead. And in a letter to Carl Stumpf, William James devoted four pages to Wundt, writing that he was trying to be

> a Napolean of the intellectual world. Unfortunately he will never have a Waterloo, for he is a Napoleon without genius and with no central idea which, if defeated, brings down the whole fabric in ruin.

Concerning Wundt and his critics, James wrote:

> Whilst they make mincemeat of some of his views by their criticisms, he is meanwhile writing a book on an entirely different subject. Cut him up like a worm, and each fragment crawls;

> there is no *noeud vital* in his mental medulla oblongata, so that you can't kill him all at once. (James, 1887; cited in Perry, 1935, Vol. II, p. 68)

Bringmann and Balk (1992) essentially agreed with Boring's (1950) assessment of the quantity of Wundt's writings. Their interpretation of Wundt's productivity was more flattering, however. In common with other particularly productive natural and social scientists, Bringmann and Balk noted that Wundt began publishing at an early age (not quite 21), which is comparable with Freud (21), Darwin (22), and Einstein (22). Like other eminent scientists, Wundt had a lengthy period of productivity (68 years), which is actually longer than Darwin (51+ years), Einstein (53 years), and Freud (55+ years). Albert (1975) defined a genius as someone who produces over a long period of time a large body of work, which has a significant influence on many people for many years. By this definition, Wundt was indeed a genius.

We will close our examination of Wundt's contributions to psychology with the words of one of his most famous students, Edward Bradford Titchener (1921), who brought a version of Wundt's experimental psychology to America:

> I take Wundt to be the first great figure in the history of thought whose temperament—disposition, attitude, habitual mode of approach to scientific problems—is that of the scientific psychologist. . . . I believe that when Wundt's special theories have utterly perished his fame will still endure; it will endure because . . . he established a new point of view and from it surveyed the whole scientific and philosophical domain. In this sense I am prepared to say that Wundt is the founder, not of experimental psychology alone, but of psychology. (pp. 176–177)

EDWARD BRADFORD TITCHENER AND STRUCTURALISM

Edward Bradford Titchener (1867–1927) was born in the Roman-established town of Chichester, which is in the south of England. Titchener was from an old English family steeped in tradition but not wealthy. Titchener's father went to America at the time of the American Civil War, fought with the Confederate army, returned to England, married, sired Titchener, and died while still in his 30s. Fortunately, Titchener's intellectual gifts earned him scholarships first to Malvern College and then to Oxford. At Malvern, he won so many academic prizes that the presenter remarked when Titchener appeared for yet another award, "I am tired of seeing you, Mr. Titchener."

During his first 4 years at Oxford, Titchener studied philosophy and the classics. As a temporary devotee of Herbert Spencer (Chapter 9), Titchener was attracted to Darwinian biology and developed an interest in comparative animal psychology. His publication of several articles on the topic is ironic, given his later indifference to animal psychology.

With a firm grounding in British philosophy, Titchener stayed an extra year to learn more science, working as a research student with noted experimental

From the collection of Rand B. Evans.

Edward Bradford Titchener (1867–1927)

physiologist Sir John Scott Burdon Sanderson (1828– 1905). Titchener was impressed with Burdon Sanderson's careful experimental technique and so respected the physiologist that he later dedicated two books to him.

At Oxford, Titchener learned of Wundt's new physiological psychology but received no encouragement from his friends for his idea to go to Leipzig. Undeterred, Titchener translated Wundt's third edition of *Grundzüge der physiologischen Psychologie* into English and took the translation to Leipzig in 1890, only 3 years after the book's publication. However, the fourth edition was nearly finished, so Titchener's translation was obsolete. The same thing happened with the fourth and nearly with the fifth editions. Persevering, Titchener translated the first volume of the fifth edition and published it immediately (Wundt, 1902/1904).

At Leipzig in the fall of 1890, Titchener roomed with **Ernst Meumann** (1862–1915), who became an outstanding educational psychologist before his untimely death from influenza. Oswald Külpe was Wundt's assistant, and the Americans there were Edward Pace, Edward W. Scripture, and Frank Angell, with whom Titchener formed a lifelong friendship. The next year the three Americans were replaced by Lightner Witmer and **Howard C. Warren** (1867–1934), the latter best known as the owner of the Psychological Review Company, which published such journals as *Psychological Review* and *Psychological Bulletin*, when it was sold to the American Psychological Association (APA).

At Leipzig, Külpe was developing his *Grundriss der Psychologie* (*Outlines of Psychology*), and Titchener was involved in its planning. The *Grundriss* was published in 1893, and Titchener translated it into English in 1895 and wrote his own *Outline of Psychology* in 1896. Both Külpe and Titchener were enormously influenced by the recently published works on positivism by the philosopher Avenarius and by the physicist Mach, and, according to Tweney (1987), Külpe had a stronger influence on Titchener than Wundt himself.

After receiving his Ph.D., Titchener returned briefly to Oxford as a lecturer in biology, having published 10 biology papers in *Nature* since 1889. Titchener would have liked to establish experimental psychology at Oxford, but the university was not interested in the new discipline. Besides, Titchener had already committed himself to a position at Cornell University in Ithaca, New York.

Titchener's Cornell offer came by way of Frank Angell, who had returned to America to found a laboratory at Cornell. When he departed for Stanford University, Angell suggested Titchener as his replacement. Initially, Titchener planned to stay a year or two, but he stayed instead for the rest of his life. In 1917, he rejected what he considered the best position in America, Münsterberg's Harvard professorship. Perhaps he would have gone to Oxford, but the call never came. In fact, it could be argued that German-style experimental psychology was slow to develop in England, although there were exceptions (e.g., James Ward; see Hilgard, 1987).

At Cornell, Titchener patterned his professorial style after that of his mentor. Although Titchener spent only 2 years at Leipzig, and his relationship with Wundt was not particularly close, Boring (1927)—one of Titchener's students—detailed several ways in which the pupil came to resemble the master. Like Wundt, Titchener ruled his laboratory autocratically. Also, both required their students to maintain a unified front, to work together with them in pursuing their goal of analyzing consciousness. Like Wundt, Titchener believed in formal psychological apparatus and the need to equip his laboratory with standardized pieces. Titchener adopted Wundt's practice of using experimental demonstrations in his elementary lectures and of dramatizing his lectures. One dramatic device was to speak in his Oxford master's gown, because it gave him "the right to be dogmatic." Like Wundt, Titchener required his staff to attend the elementary lectures, where they listened "with suppressed excitement to hear how, after some new discovery at Cornell, [Titchener] would alter the familiar treatment of the subject" (Boring, 1927, pp. 492–493).

Also like his mentor, Titchener needed a journal to express his views on what he considered true scientific psychology. But unlike Wundt, Titchener never achieved sole responsibility and ownership of a journal. For many years, however, he was one of the principal editors of *The American Journal of Psychology,* along with Edmund Clark Sanford (Chapter 10) and the journal's founder, G. Stanley Hall. When **Karl Dallenbach** (1887–1971), one of Titchener's students, bought the journal in 1921, Titchener became its sole editor. In 1925, Dallenbach suggested that the journal might begin to include some dignified advertising. Titchener resigned and was replaced by an editorial board consisting of four of his Ph.D. students.

In 1894, Titchener married Sophie K. Bedlow, and she provided invaluable assistance in his laboratory and with drawings for the books that poured from his prolific pen. As we noted, he translated Külpe's *Grundriss* in 1895, published his own *Outline* in 1896 and his *Primer of Psychology* in 1898, and started work on his monumental *Experimental Psychology,* published in four volumes in 1901 and 1905. Also, with assistance, Titchener translated some of Wundt's books (and subsequent editions) between 1894 and 1902. Meanwhile, he was developing his laboratory and publishing 62 articles between 1893 and 1900 (Boring, 1927). With this productivity record, Titchener became a full professor when he was only 28.

Titchener is sometimes considered a male chauvinist, which is curious given his training and encouragement of female students. Of the Titchener-directed Cornell Ph.D. students in psychology listed in Boring (1927), over a third are women, and Titchener's first Ph.D. student was Margaret Floy Washburn (discussed later).

Even before Washburn received her Ph.D., Titchener had shown his support for women in academia by helping **Celestia Suzannah Parrish** (1853–1918) learn about the new experimental psychology.

> Parrish persuaded Edward Bradford Titchener . . . to accept her as a student in the 1893 summer school. During this summer she also persuaded Titchener to provide her with a tailor-made correspondence course that she could take while teaching at R-MWC [Randolph-Macon Woman's College] that fall. (Rowe & Murray, 1979, p. 282)

Parrish established the first psychology laboratory in the South at R-MWC in Lynchburg, Virginia, using notes she had taken from Titchener as the textbook for her class until 1896, when he published his *Outline of Psychology.* Parrish's first publication in psychology was based on work she did at Cornell in the summers of 1894 and 1895. Parrish moved from R-MWC to the chair in psychology and pedagogy at the State Normal School, which later became part of the University of Georgia. In her honor, Randolph Macon's psychology laboratories became the Celestia S. Parrish Laboratories of Psychology in 1933 (Smith, 1995).

Paradoxically, Titchener has also been associated with misogyny, evidence for which comes mainly from his founding of **The Experimentalists,** an informal club of psychology laboratory directors. Titchener intended for the men he invited (or whose invitation he approved when the meeting was held away from Cornell) to meet annually to discuss their research with each other and with their most promising graduate students. Titchener "wanted oral reports that could be interrupted, dissented from and criticized, in a smoke-filled room with no women present—for in 1904, when The Experimentalists was founded, women were considered too pure to smoke" (Boring, 1967, p. 315). "Trapped by the social norms existing in his time, Titchener did exclude women from the meetings of the Experimentalists but this is something quite different from misogyny" (Evans, 1991, p. 90).

The Experimentalists resulted from Titchener's disaffection with the American Psychological Association, founded in 1892 (Chapter 10), and its failure to censure E. W. Scripture for what Titchener considered plagiarism. In 1895, Scripture published a popular introduction to the new experimental psychology in which he closely paraphrased J. E. Creighton and Titchener's translation of Wundt's *Vorlesungen über die Menschen- und Thierseele* (*Human and Animal Psychology*)—too closely, according to Titchener. When the APA failed to act, Titchener resigned. Beginning in 1904, The Experimentalists continued to meet throughout Titchener's lifetime. After Titchener's death, The Experimentalists reorganized as The Society of Experimental Psychologists, breaking two of the earlier association's taboos first by permitting the discussion of animal research and then by inviting women. Fittingly, Washburn was the first female member. More formally organized than when it began, Titchener's creation continues to this day.

Titchener was never fully integrated into American psychology, but this had more to do with Titchener himself than with American psychology. British by birth, Titchener's Leipzig years molded his character to the point where he was often considered a German, once even by a visiting British psychologist. After 35 years in America, "his work was generally spiced with German phrases and even German sentences. In fact, Titchener published a German-English dictionary of psychological terms that were essential to the understanding of his writings" (Hindeland, 1971, p. 23). Titchener never became a U.S. citizen, and during World War I, "his 'we' meant Great Britain and his 'you' America" (Boring, 1927, p. 490).

Boring (1927) speculated that Titchener's declining productivity (and perhaps interest) in psychology after 1910 stemmed from a loss of external drive. "It was becoming plain that Titchener would find no one who would carry on his torch as he had been carrying Wundt's, and he always wanted an able successor-disciple" (p. 502). Thus, Boring believed that Titchener simply allowed himself to be distracted by other interests.

Titchener and his wife were collectors of many things, including live reptiles. He and

> Mrs. Titchener early agreed that the house should be a museum. In it was a place for anything that represented the intimate habits of other times or other peoples; . . . devil's masks and idols, pewter galore and old American hardware, hair wreaths, chest handles, the ancestral furniture and silver—I mention only what occurs to me. (Boring, 1927, p. 495)

Titchener also developed an interest in Greek and Roman numismatics and in working out inscriptions on ancient coins. He enjoyed puzzles, and this pursuit allowed him to use his exceptional linguistic ability (Thorne, 1996).

Obviously, Titchener was a complex and fascinating individual. Boring (1967) characterized him as "brilliant, erudite, kindly, paternal, insultable, flexible yet intransigent, [someone] whose insistent contradictions were matched only by the ambivalences of his disciples, some of whom ultimately became his hesitant critics and detractors" (pp. 315–316). In Titchener's structuralism, psychologists of all types found something to criticize.

Titchener's Structural Psychology

Discussions of Titchener's system generally refer to Titchener's 1910 work, *A Text-Book of Psychology*. After 1910, followers and critics alike waited for Titchener's *magnum opus*, finding at his death

> only three chapters, and those dealt with general and introductory considerations. The important chapter on method, which was to be the final chapter of the first volume, the *Prolegomena*, was never written and no trace of notes on the other volumes has been found. (Evans, 1972, p. 168)

The three chapters were published as *Systematic Psychology: Prolegomena* in 1929. Before exploring how Titchener's system changed, we will consider its form in the first half of Titchener's career.

Science of the Mind

A reading of Ernst Mach (Chapter 5) laid the foundation for Titchener's conception of science as well as for his science of psychology. For Titchener, psychology was the science of the generalized, normal, human, adult mind. He was not interested in abnormal minds, animal minds, the minds of children, or individual minds—he was interested in mind in an idealized sense. Titchener saw his task as cataloging the elements (the structure) of consciousness, discovering how they are connected, and investigating the underlying physiological processes. Most of his career was devoted to the first chore, identifying and describing the components of conscious experience.

For Titchener, Wundt's distinction between immediate experience (direct experience uninfluenced by previous knowledge or instrumentation) and mediate experience (indirect experience that provides the data for the natural sciences) makes psychology's subject matter different from that of the natural sciences.

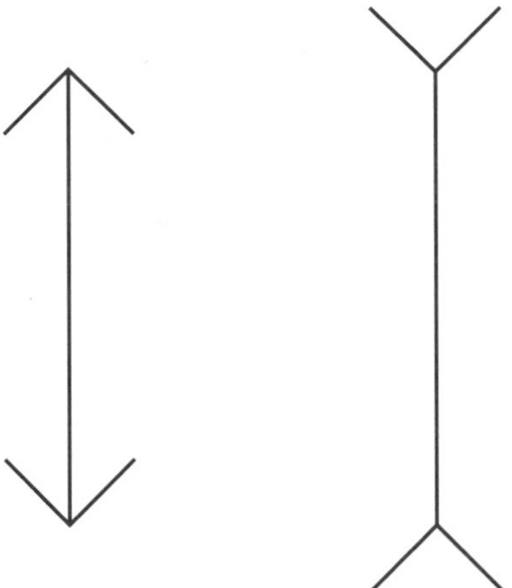

FIGURE 8.3 Müller-Lyer Illusion

This means psychology can never be a natural science. Thus, Titchener rejected Wundt's distinction for a position he felt allowed psychology to be on a par with the other natural sciences.

"All human knowledge is derived from human experience," Titchener (1910, p. 6) wrote. "But human experience . . . may be considered from different points of view." One point of view is that the experience is independent of any particular individual: It occurs whether or not anyone experiences it. For example, if no ear hears it, does a tree falling in the woods make a sound? From the viewpoint independent of an experiencing individual (e.g., of physics), the answer is clearly yes. Physics defines sound as transmitted vibrations, which can be detected and recorded even if no ear hears them.

A second viewpoint is that the experience is completely dependent upon an individual. Thus, without a conscious mind to perceive it, the claim that the falling tree makes a sound is meaningless. Therefore, the answer to the falling tree question depends on the point of view taken.

As another example, consider the Müller-Lyer Illusion in Figure 8.3. From the point of view independent of an individual, the vertical lines are equal, as shown by a ruler. However, from the perspective of an experiencing individual—your perspective—they appear to be different.

The psychological description in which Titchener was interested is that you see two visual extents, and one is longer than the other. Because you know the two lines are actually the same length, you might be tempted to describe the illusion as consisting of two equal lines, one of which *appears* longer. In this description, you have mixed the physical and psychological perspectives. You have committed Titchener's **stimulus error,** which is describing the stimulus itself rather than reporting the immediate sensations or feelings the stimulus produces.

To summarize, Wundt had said there were two different kinds of experience, one peculiar to the natural sciences and the other specific to psychology, which for Titchener meant psychology could never wholly be a natural science. Titchener believed that by insisting on only one kind of experience, viewed from different perspectives, he was ensuring that psychology was a natural science.

Introspection and the Elements of Consciousness

To investigate conscious experiences, Titchener used an "analytical or anatomical introspection. Unlike Wundt's, Titchener's subjects did not just briefly report an experimentally controlled experience, they had to dissect it, attempting to discover the sensation-elements given at that moment in consciousness" (Leahey, 1981, p. 275). Experience would thus be reduced to meaningless elements identical with the sensory elements forming the basis of physical science, the difference being in the point of view. Psychology studies the elements in their dependence on a mind, whereas physics studies them independently (Danziger, 1980).

The Basic Elements. Titchener identified three basic elements of consciousness: sensations, images, and affections or feelings. Sensations are the elements of perceptions and are the basis for everything else in the mind. Titchener concluded there were more than 44,000 different sensations (e.g., 32,000+ visual, nearly 12,000 auditory, but only 4 taste sensations—salty, sweet, sour, and bitter).

Images are the elements of ideas, which arise when a particular sensation has been experienced previously. We can form an image of an apple in the absence of the actual fruit, although the image is less distinct than its template. Similarly, feelings are the emotions' elements. Titchener's introspections produced only the pleasantness-unpleasantness dimension of Wundt's three dimensions of feelings: pleasantness-unpleasantness, arousing-subduing, and strain-relaxation.

Attributes. Sensations, images, and feelings all have certain attributes, and a mental element does not exist apart from its attributes. According to Titchener, the basic **attributes** are quality, intensity, duration, clearness, and extent. Quality allows us to differentiate sensations; examples include the "redness" of an apple and the "coldness" of ice. Intensity refers to the strength of an experience: for example, the loudness of a sound or the brightness of a light. Duration is the length of an experience, and clearness refers to how much an experience stands out from the background against which it appears. Finally, extent gives an experience a spatial dimension that tells how "spread out" the image or sensation is.

For sensations and images, all of the attributes apply, except that extent generally pertains only to sight and touch sensations. Feelings are accompanied by quality, intensity, and duration attributes but not by clearness or extent.

Attention. For Wundt, attention was related to apperception, which he saw as an active desire to pay attention. Whatever is at the point of apperception is clearly perceived. Titchener simplified **attention** by making it an attribute of sensations, equating it with clearness. "Where Wundt had explained sensory clarity by appealing to the process of attention, Titchener argued that 'attention' is just a descriptive label given to what we experience with clarity" (Leahey, 1981, p. 275). Because he considered it just a label attached to a clear sensation, Titchener believed attention could not be directly observed. In his system, he first called clearness *vividness* and then later *attensity*.

Meaning. Like attention, meaning cannot be directly observed. In fact, Titchener exhorted his observers to avoid confusing the meaning of a stimulus with the direct experience it produces, and, in this sense, giving the meaning of an observation rather than the immediate experience of it is analogous to committing the stimulus error. Both mistakes come from mixing the physical and psychological points of view.

According to Titchener (1910),

> [m]eaning, psychologically, is always context; one mental process is the meaning of another mental process if it is that other's context. And context, in this sense, is simply the mental process which accrues to the given process through the situation in which the organism finds itself. (p. 367)

Like attention, **meaning** is something we attribute to our conscious experiences based on the context in which we experience them. A shoulder tap has a different meaning to a person reading a horror novel than it does to the same person at a party.

Henle (1971) argued that Titchener himself may have committed the stimulus error in his conception of meaning. Using an example from Titchener's (1915) *A Beginner's Psychology*, Henle identified at least one type of experience as meaningful without the aid of Titchener's context theory, which suggests that other experiences may be similarly meaningful. Perhaps, she concluded, Boring's (1927) attribution of Titchener's declining productivity in later years to a lack of external incentives was incorrect. It is possible that "inconsistencies such as the ones I have mentioned were beginning to arise out of the inadequacies of his approach" (p. 282), were recognized by Titchener, and led to his choice not to start over.

Changes in Titchener's System

By 1915, Titchener's system had just two elements: sensations and feelings. Titchener's thinking on the mental elements continued to evolve, and in a 1923 letter to Boring, "Titchener announced . . . that he was ready to shelve the concept of elements [for] . . . attributive dimensions" (Evans, 1972, p. 172). Thus, images were the first of the mental elements to go, followed by sensations and affections. "So the first level of Titchener's old system reduced to the five dimensions of quality, intensity, protensity [duration], extensity, and attensity, with quality taking precedence over the others" (p. 174). Further, intensity as a dimension separate from quality was suspect.

Titchener's questioning even included his introspective method, and he apparently came to believe that a more flexible introspection might be fruitful for studying qualitative dimensions. Perhaps the arduous training of observers was unnecessary. In fact, Titchener (1912) may have been considering a phenomenological approach like that of Stumpf or Husserl (discussed later) for the study of consciousness when he wrote: "a roughly phenomenological account, a description of consciousness as it shows itself to common sense, may be useful or even necessary as the starting-point of a truly psychological description" (p. 490).

Actually, the last thesis Titchener edited for publication was a study using a phenomenological methodology (Evans, 1972). Although the method had changed, the topic was still the contents of consciousness, however. As we will see in Chapter 14, the phenomenological approach was an important antecedent to Gestalt psychology, but there is no hint before 1925 that Titchener was modifying his negative attitude toward Gestalt psychology. He called it a fad and said in a 1924 letter cited in Evans, "There is really no remedy for all these eccentric movements except time and the general logic involved in the progress of science all round" (p. 178). Still later, after one of Gestalt psychology's founders visited Cornell, Titchener's attitude softened considerably, and he acknowledged that the Gestaltists had done "much good work, and some brilliant work."

Archives of the History of American Psychology–The University of Akron.

Titchener's study

Titchener and Wundt Compared

In 1981, Leahey wrote: "It is widely believed by American psychologists that Edward Bradford Titchener was a loyal pupil of Wilhelm Wundt who acted as a kind of English-speaking double for the founder of psychology" (p. 273). The following statement from a recent introductory psychology textbook helps validate Leahey's statement: "The school of thought associated with Wundt and his student E. B. Titchener is called **structuralism,** or the science of the structure of the mind" (Pettijohn, 1998, p. 5). Pettijohn equates Wundt and Titchener and calls Wundt's school *structuralism* rather than voluntarism, which Wundt used to contrast his approach with Titchener's.

Although voluntarism and structuralism clearly differed in detail and in substance, it is also apparent that Titchener owed much to his former teacher. In the preface to *Experimental Psychology* (Vol. 1, *Qualitative Experiments:* Part II, *Instructor's Manual*), Titchener (1901) wrote: "My greatest debt, here as elsewhere, is to Wundt" (p. vii). Continuing, he acknowledged that his system was diverging from Wundt's: "If my recent writing has seemed rather to be directed against Wundtian doctrines, that is but the natural reaction of a pupil who cannot swear to the literal teaching of the Master" (pp. vii–viii). What are some of the major differences between the two systems?

As we noted, Wundt called for two psychologies, one to study lower mental processes experimentally (e.g., sensing, feeling) and another to study higher mental processes (e.g., language, thought). For Wundt, a "complete psychology thus had to include [experimental] psychology as a direct study of outer mental phenomena given in consciousness, and *Völkerpsychologie* as an indirect study of the inner phenomena of mind" (Leahey, 1981, p. 274). By rejecting Wundt's distinction, Titchener largely deleted the *Völkerpsychologie* from his system. Like Külpe, Titchener made a frontal assault on the higher mental processes, which he viewed as "completely analyzable complexes of conscious sensations to be reduced to their elemental constituents" (Leahey, p. 275).

Although Wundt distinguished between immediate experience and mediate experience, Titchener argued for one type of experience viewed from different perspectives. Whereas Titchener advocated a meaning-free depiction of the elements of consciousness, a structuralism, Wundt stressed the voluntary operation of the mind, a voluntarism. Wundt's voluntarism was particularly evident in his concept of apperception, attention through an act of will; Titchener viewed attention as merely one of the attributes of sensations and images. Instead of an act of will, he saw attention as just a label we apply to anything experienced with clarity.

As we have seen, Wundt's use of internal perception (*innere Wahrnehmung*) was different from Titchener's use of introspection (*Selbstbeobachtung*). Wundt's use of the internal perception method was quite circumscribed, and he would have bristled at the notion that he was an "introspective psychologist," a label that better fit Titchener.

From this description of several Wundt-Titchener contrasts, it is evident that the two systems differed significantly, and, given the difference in backgrounds of the two men, it is clear *why* they differed. "Although Titchener studied with Wundt, Titchener's earlier grounding in philosophy in England undoubtedly kept him from absorbing the Wundtian paradigm, and predisposed him to accept the Machian positivism espoused by some . . ." (Leahey, 1981, p. 276). After 2 years with Wundt, Titchener journeyed to America to establish himself, where, in a new environment, "he reverted to what he knew" (p. 276), which was traditional English psychology.

Titchener's Influence

Titchener's primary contribution was the strict, empirical, experimental approach he brought to American psychology. More specifically, he wrote *Experimental Psychology*, with the first two volumes, the *Student's* and *Instructor's Qualitative Manuals*, appearing in 1901. Publication of the *Student's* and *Instructor's Quantitative Manuals* was delayed until 1905 by the 1904 appearance of G. E. Müller's *Psychophysische Methodik*, which forced Titchener to revise his nearly completed manuscripts. Even with the hasty revision, they have been called "a monumental work that is perhaps the most thorough manual of experimental technique ever prepared in the English language" (Tweney, 1997, p. 157). According to Boring (1950), Külpe called them the most erudite such work. The books were widely used for decades, and many psychologists who would never have identified with Titchener's structuralism (e.g., John Watson) learned experimental psychology from them.

Titchener's influence was also significant through the large number of Ph.D. students he trained, 56 according to Boring's (1927) listing, including several Asiatic students. Some of Titchener's students later rose to prominence in American psychology, and over a third of his Ph.D. students were women, as we noted earlier. In 1950, Boring included Margaret Floy Washburn, Walter Pillsbury, Karl Dallenbach, and John Wallace Baird (Chapter 10) in his list of Titchener-trained Ph.D. students of importance. Note that Titchener trained Boring himself, the dean of historians of psychology, and that J. Paul Guilford (Chapter 17), the famous psychometrician, was one of Titchener's last students.

Titchener's first Ph.D. student, Vassar-trained **Margaret Floy Washburn** (1871–1939), worked briefly with James McKeen Cattell at Columbia before going to Cornell, noted for its liberal stance in admissions. Under Titchener, she became the first woman to earn a Ph.D. in psychology. Washburn remained an active "structuralist" researcher across a career that saw her teaching at several colleges and universities before returning to Vassar in 1903. Perhaps her most noted publication was *The Animal Mind*, which was the first book about animal psychology by an American. Washburn's honors included being elected APA president in 1921 and being elected to the National Academy of Sciences in 1931. In each case, Washburn was the second woman so honored; Mary Calkins (Chapter 10) was the first.

Archives of the History of American Psychology–The University of Akron.

Margaret Floy Washburn (1871–1939)

Titchener also was important for his willingness to argue against findings and theoretical matters he considered in error. Two controversies will illustrate Titchener's role as a gadfly.

To investigate thought, Oswald Külpe—one of Titchener's friends and teachers at Leipzig—and his Würzburg associates developed an experiment in which observers introspected on the thought processes that occurred when they solved complex problems. Most of the Würzburg subjects reported images and feelings while they performed higher mental activities, but for some, the solutions seemed to appear suddenly in consciousness without images or feelings. They had experienced **imageless thought,** which Wundt and Titchener considered impossible.

Wundt rejected Külpe's results in part because he did not believe that higher mental processes could be studied experimentally. Titchener accepted the experimental study of higher mental processes but rejected the findings because Cornell researchers always obtained images in their analysis of thought. In other words, he rejected "imageless thought" as an artifact of improper introspection. Ironically, by 1915, the year Külpe died, Titchener had abandoned images as a basic element of consciousness (Evans, 1972).

A second controversy was with James Mark Baldwin (Chapter 10). In discussing Wundt, we noted that when trained observers attended either to the presentation of a stimulus or to making a response, the sensorial reaction time was about 0.1-second longer than the muscular reaction time, and Titchener agreed with this result. Using untrained observers, Baldwin sometimes found that the muscular reaction time was longer than the sensorial reaction time. Further, he accused Titchener of being blind to a fact of nature—the Leipzig/Cornell reaction-time difference depended on trained observers. Titchener responded that his experimental psychology was concerned with the laws of the generalized mind, not with individual minds, and that Baldwin's individual differences led to no general law. The controversy further isolated Titchener in America, because one effect of it was that he avoided the *Psychological Review Publications,* begun by Baldwin and Cattell.

At a more general level, Titchener's development of structuralism was important because it gave competing approaches something to attack. Rebellion is always more effective with something to rebel against, and Titchener provided a convenient target until his death in 1927.

With Titchener's death, structuralism "suddenly collapsed, dwindling rapidly from the status of a vital faith in the importance of consciousness to the equally essential but wholly inglorious state of having been an unavoidable phase of historical development" (Boring, 1950, p. 420).

Tweney (1987) reached a more positive conclusion about Titchener's historical influence:

> We tend to regard his system as a failed one; there are no Titchnerian structuralists today. But there are, and have been, other experimentalists of a Titchnerian stripe—programmatic, data-driven, and open to the consequences of

disconfirmation. Historically, Titchener must then be credited with helping to collapse Wundt's distinction between the experimental study of basic mental processes and the comparative study of higher mental processes. . . . His view of the broad power of the experimental method is, in some quarters, received doctrine. For better or worse, Titchener helped to create the doctrine. (p. 52)

FRANZ BRENTANO AND ACT PSYCHOLOGY

At the beginning of this chapter, we examined the life and psychology of Wilhelm Wundt, who is credited with founding psychology as an experimental science. From the *Zeitgeist* view of history, Wundt's success in starting experimental psychology implies the time for it was right. Now we will turn our attention to further exploring the *Zeitgeist* that produced psychology by inspecting the efforts of Wundt's German contemporaries. What was the atmosphere that facilitated a productive synthesis of physiology and philosophy? If the time was right for the founding of experimental psychology, who would have filled the void if Wundt had not become a researcher? What would the first psychology have been like?

To answer these questions, we will consider the lives and work of several individuals, all of whom may have been more widely recognized as Germany's leading psychologists than was Wundt at the turn of the century. The most prominent name on this list is Franz Brentano, who published his system of psychology in 1874, the year Wundt completed publication of *Principles of Physiological Psychology*.

Franz Clemens Brentano (1838–1917) was born in Marienburg, Germany, into a family of renown and ability. An uncle was a poet/novelist and a leader in German romanticism, and an aunt was known as the "Sibyl of romanticism." Both Brentano's father and mother achieved some stature as writers of religious works (Rancurello, 1968), and a brother, Lujo Brentano (1844–1931), was a prominent pacifist and German political economist.

Brentano's early education came from a Catholic priest hired by his parents. He completed

Courtesy of Franz Brentano Forschung, Institute of Philosophy, University of Wuerzburg.

Franz Brentano (1838–1917) in Florence (ca. 1900)

his secondary education at the local *Gymnasium*, showing a talent for classical languages and mathematics. After a spiritual crisis, Brentano chose philosophy over mathematics, hoping philosophy could solve his religious quandary; he also decided to become a priest.

Following three semesters at the *Lyceum* in Aschaffenburg, Brentano studied successively at the Universities of Munich, Würzburg, and Berlin, as well as at the Academy of Münster, before receiving his doctorate in philosophy from the University of Tübingen in 1862, with a dissertation on Aristotle (Chapter 2). Frederick Trendelenburg (1802–1872), the leading German philologist and Aristotelian philosopher at the University of Berlin; Franz Clemens (1815–1862), another Aristotelian scholar and a modern scholastic at Münster; and Ignatius Döllinger (1799–1890), historian and theologian at the University of Munich, all significantly influenced Brentano.

Brentano became a priest in 1864 and was habilitated (accredited as a university lecturer) as a *Dozent* at Würzburg in 1866 based on his excellent studies of Aristotle's psychology. Brentano was also an outstanding teacher, and his ultimate influence on psychology was at least as great through his students as through his writings. Although popular with students, Brentano was less popular with some of the Würzburg faculty, who saw him as a mystic, a scholastic, and even as a disguised Jesuit and successfully blocked his promotion to professor on the grounds that he was a priest.

In the 1860s, the Catholic Church split over the doctrine of papal infallibility, which is the idea that the Pope is infallible when he defines doctrines of faith or morals from the throne of St. Peter. Asked to study the doctrine comprehensively, Brentano wrote a highly critical analysis that was published before the vote of the First Vatican Council in 1870. When the Council voted 533 to 2 for the doctrine, Bretano agonized for 3 years before resigning from the priesthood and from the University of Würzburg.

With no clerical or university commitments, in 1874 Brentano published the book that established his fame in psychology, *Psychologie vom empirischen Standpunkte* (*Psychology From an Empirical Standpoint*). Also, with Lotze's (Chapter 6) recommendation Brentano secured a professorship at the University of Vienna, which he lost in 1880 because of his marriage to a Catholic (former priests were forbidden to marry in Austria). Brentano returned to the university as a *Privatdozent,* hoping in vain to be reinstated to his former position.

In 1894, Brentano's wife died. He resigned from the University of Vienna, left Austria, and settled in Florence in 1896. In 1897, Brentano married Emilia Ruprecht, and he lived in Italy until 1915, when, as a pacifist, he moved to Zurich because of Italy's entry into World War I. Brentano died in 1917 at the age of 80.

Brentano's Psychology

The first half of Wundt's *Principles of Physiological Psychology* appeared in 1873, and Brentano addressed it in *Psychology From an Empirical Standpoint,* written in late 1873 and early 1874. However, Brentano was not simply motivated by opposition to Wundt. "The real reason behind his work was that he had something worth saying in its own right and he said it when the time was ripe for him" (Rancurello, 1968, p. 14).

Brentano's psychology was empirical primarily in the philosophical sense. He used the empirical method of comparing philosophic insights on a topic and then used his experience to try to resolve conflicts. Thus, it was empirical because it was based on experience, but it was not empirical in the sense in which the term is often used—as being experimental. Although Brentano's unsuccessful attempts to secure an institute and a laboratory in Vienna indicated his continuing interest in research, Titchener (1921) was probably correct in asserting that Brentano would not have performed Wundtian-type experiments even if he had had a laboratory.

Brentano intended for his completed *Psychology* to have six "books," the first two of which—"psychology as a science" and "psychic phenomena in general"—comprised the 1874 publication. The other books, which he never completed, "would have investigated 'the properties and laws' of representation . . . , of judgment . . . , and of 'affective and volitional states,' and 'the relationship between mind and body' . . ." (Rancurello, 1968, p. 15).

Act Psychology

For Brentano, psychic phenomena were characterized by their "intentional in-existence" or their "immanent objectivity." Psychic phenomena, or **acts,** are directed toward an object, which then exists within the act. The act has immanent objectivity, that is, it contains an object within itself. According to Brentano,

> Every mental phenomenon includes something as object within itself. . . . In presentation something is presented, in judgment something is affirmed or denied, in love loved, in hate hated, in desire desired and so on. . . . (Brentano, *Psychology From an Empirical Standpoint;* cited in Watson, 1979, p. 138)

As a further example, the act of seeing contains within it what is seen. If you see a red patch, seeing is the act, or psychic phenomenon, and the color red is the content. Brentano's psychology was an **act**

psychology, whereas Wundt's (and later Titchener's) was a psychology of content. Brentano's act psychology was also a holistic approach (e.g., act of seeing plus what is seen) compared to the elementism (e.g., only what is seen) of Wundt and Titchener.

According to Brentano, mental acts occur in three main categories: acts of *presentation* (or sometimes *ideating*), acts of *judging,* and acts of *desire* (sometimes *loving* and *hating*). Sensing and imagining are acts of presentation, and the acts of judging include rejecting, perceiving, and recalling. Acts of loving and hating include feeling, wishing, and intending. The object of an act may be either a real object, a fictional object (e.g., we can imagine a unicorn), or another act (e.g., we can imagine loving someone or we can reject our feelings).

Brentano's Method. According to Brentano, "Psychology, like the natural sciences, has its basis in perception and experience. Above all, however, its source is to be found in the *inner perception* of our own mental phenomena" (cited in Watson, 1979, p. 139, italics in the original). Like Wundt, Brentano distinguished between inner or internal perception (*innere Wahrnehmung*) and inner observation or introspection (*Selbstbeobachtung*), selecting internal perception as the "primary and essential source of psychology." In fact, Danziger (1980) suggested that Wundt may have adopted Brentano's terminology without giving him credit for it. Nevertheless, Brentano's inner perception method was decidedly different from Wundt's. Although we can direct our full attention to objects perceived externally, this is impossible for objects of inner perception. In the attempt, we change the object of study. Brentano wrote:

> If someone is in a state in which he wants to observe his own anger raging within him, the anger must already be somewhat diminished, and so his original object of observation would have disappeared. (cited in Watson, 1979, p. 140)

If we cannot use inner observation to study mental states such as anger directly, Brentano suggested, we can use our inner perception indirectly:

> It is only while our attention is turned toward a different object that we are able to perceive, incidentally, the mental processes which are directed toward that object. . . . Indeed, turning one's attention to physical phenomena in our imagination is, if not the only source of our knowledge of laws governing the mind, at least the immediate and principal source. . . . (cited in Watson, 1979, p. 140)

In addition to the indirect inner perception of our mental phenomena when they occur, we can observe past mental phenomena in memory. If our observation of anger as it occurs diminishes the anger, this is not a problem with anger remembered.

> Furthermore, we could say that it is even possible to undertake experimentation on our own mental phenomena in this manner. For we can, by various means, arouse certain mental phenomena in ourselves intentionally, in order to find out whether this or that other phenomenon occurs as a result. We can then contemplate the result of the experiment calmly and attentively in our memory. (cited in Watson, 1979, p. 141)

A third Brentano method can be called "objective observation." We can observe the "*externalization* of the psychic life of other persons" in their speech, autobiographies, achievements, and voluntary acts. Further, this observation can include the behavior of animals, children, people in primitive societies, the mentally ill, and "the physiological antecedents of our psychic states and outer behavior" (Rancurello, 1968, p. 32). However, lest these "objective observations" be seen as advocating a kind of behaviorism (Chapter 12), Brentano cautioned "that these techniques can never be more than supplemental" (Fancher, 1977, p. 219) to the use of inner perception in adult humans, which is consistent with act psychology's focus on understanding conscious mental events (Titchener, 1922).

Undoubtedly, Brentano's greatest contribution to philosophy and to psychology was his conception of intentionality. **Intentionality** is the defining feature of consciousness, as consciousness always intends something, and the act of being conscious of something manifests the property of intentionality. For Aristotelian expert Brentano, the recognition of intentionality as the central element of consciousness represented a restoration of Aristotle's concept of final cause, as it underscored the purposefulness of cognitive acts.

As an example, consider music. Hearing the music is a mental act (of presentation). The act of hearing "intends" the music; that is, it takes the music as its "immanent object." For Brentano, this simple scheme placed Aristotelian and scholastic concepts of intentionality within a modern empirical psychology.

Following Brentano, intentionality has been central to the philosophy of mind. Both his students Alexius Meinong and Edmund Husserl further developed the concept, and some modern philosophers of psychology have continued to argue for the centrality of intentionality in this era of cognitive science (e.g., Chisholm, 1981; Searle, 1983). One example can be found in John Searle's (1980) attack on artificial intelligence (Chapter 18). Searle argued that if consciousness is an intrinsic feature of truly intelligent systems, and if intentionality is an intrinsic feature of consciousness, then any truly intelligent system should manifest intrinsic intentionality. However, neither computers nor computer programs seem to exhibit such a quality. What they intend (are directed to) appears to be dictated by the way they are designed/programmed, which reflects the intentionality of a human builder. Because the machine itself has no intrinsic intentionality, it cannot be conscious, and for Searle, if it cannot be conscious, it cannot truly be intelligent. Although many writers (e.g., Henley, 1990) have contested Searle's analysis, this issue demonstrates the continued relevance of Brentano's ideas.

As psychology has matured, it has become clear that Brentano's general conception of a holistic psychology and his influence through his students were more important than the details of act psychology. Thus, we will review Brentano's influences on the development of psychology as a prelude to our consideration of some of his best-known students.

Brentano's Influence

First and foremost, Brentano developed a system different from Wundt's—but contemporaneous with it—to which non-Wundtians could turn. People who could not accept Wundt's content psychology had the alternative of Brentano's act psychology. By contrast with Wundt the researcher and educator, Brentano was a scholar and teacher. Some of his students of importance for psychology are Carl Stumpf and Edmund Husserl (discussed later); **Christian von Ehrenfels** (1859–1932); and **Alexius Meinong** (1853–1920, founder of the first psychological laboratory in Austria at Graz in 1894). Von Ehrenfels—devotee of Wagner, friend of Freud, and advocate of legalized polygamy (Heider, 1970)—developed the concept of *Gestaltqualität* as an extension of Ernst Mach's (Chapter 6) writings on perception. Meinong and others advanced this idea, which anticipated (or matured into) Gestalt theory (Chapter 14).

Others who found Brentano's system more appealing than Wundt's include Oswald Külpe (discussed later); the American pioneer William James (Chapter 10), a forerunner of functionalism and a friend of Stumpf; and the Gestalt psychologists. Husserl and Stumpf were greatly influenced by Brentano's descriptive psychology, which he subtitled "descriptive phenomenology" when he taught it in 1888–1889. With Goethe (Chapter 6), we defined phenomenology as the study of intact, meaningful experiences, which is precisely what Brentano advocated. Husserl is considered the founder of philosophical phenomenology, and both Husserl and Stumpf clearly influenced Gestalt psychology. As we suggested earlier, in his later years, even Titchener may have been drifting toward Brentano's phenomenological orientation.

Brentano's view of consciousness as an intentional, goal-directed activity was shared by the functionalists, whom we will consider in Chapters 10 and 11. Sigmund Freud (Chapter 15) also has been called a functionalist, and as Freud took all his nonmedical courses at Vienna from Brentano, it should not be surprising to find similarities between the two. Fancher (1977) detailed some important similarities between Brentano's system in 1874 and Freud's metapsychology as revealed in his 1895 *Project for a Scientific Psychology.* Brentano's influence on existential psychology (Chapter 16) will be apparent in our later discussion and has been noted by others (e.g., Gilbert, 1968).

As patriarch of the phenomenological alternatives to Wundt that foreshadowed cognitive psychology,

Brentano can be credited with at least an indirect influence on modern-day cognitive science. Baumgartner and Baumgartner (1997) have suggested that Brentano's core statement in 1874 about intentionality provided the foundation for several movements, including cognitive psychology. MacNamara (1993) has gone even further, suggesting that Brentano may have had a better understanding of the basic acts of cognition than some modern psychologists.

CARL STUMPF

Carl Stumpf (1848–1936) was born in Wiesenthied, a hamlet in the Bavarian province containing Würzburg. Like Brentano, Stumpf came from an accomplished family. His father was the County Court Physician, his paternal grandfather was a well-known Bavarian historian, and two paternal uncles were active scientists. His mother's family also included many physicians, and in his autobiography, Stumpf concluded, "It may be that the love of medicine and natural science was in my blood" (Stumpf, 1930, p. 389).

Stumpf and his family were also talented musicians. Stumpf learned to play the violin at 7 and five other instruments "with more or less success." He began composing at 10, and his first work was an oratorio for three male voices. After a normal elementary and secondary education, he entered the University of Würzburg with, as he reported, a greater love of music than of learning.

In Stumpf's second semester, Brentano joined the faculty, and Stumpf was captivated by his personality, his teaching, and his style of thinking. Under Brentano's tutelage, Stumpf learned to think like a philosopher.

Taking Brentano's advice, Stumpf went to Göttingen to study with Lotze, and he earned his Ph.D. in 1868 with a dissertation on "The Relationship Between Plato's God and His Idea of Goodness" (Sprung, 1997). Stumpf (1930) noted that Lotze's "mental attitude had greater influence on me than Brentano really wished" (p. 392). Following graduation, Stumpf returned to Würzburg for further study with Brentano and also to prepare for the priesthood. For Stumpf, just as for Brentano, the controversy over papal infallibility intervened, and Stumpf "took off the black robe."

Carl Stumpf (1848–1936)

In 1870, Stumpf continued his friendship with Lotze as an instructor at Göttingen. In addition, he met the two elderly Leipzig psychophysicists—Weber and Fechner (Chapter 7). At his brother Wilhelm Weber's house, Ernst demonstrated sensory fields on Stumpf's body, and during a field trip to Leipzig, Stumpf and a friend served as subjects for one of Fechner's experiments.

In 1872, Stumpf began work on the origin of space perception that led to his first psychological book, *Über den psychologischen Ursprung der Raumvorstellung* (*On the Psychological Origin of Space Perception*). Stumpf's theory was nativist, and he "argued that both color and extension are equally primitive part-contents of visual sensation" (Boring, 1950, p. 363). The book came at a good time, and with Lotze's and Brentano's recommendations, Stumpf secured a professorship in philosophy at Würzburg.

In 1875, Stumpf began work that combined his interests in music and psychology and resulted in the publication in two volumes in 1883 and 1890 of *Tonpsychologie* (*Tone Psychology*). Between 1873 and 1894, Stumpf went from Würzburg to Prague to Halle to Munich, and then finally to Berlin. At Prague, he was stimulated by contact with Ernst Mach and Ewald Hering (Chapter 7) and by a visit from William James, with whom he began a correspondence and friendship that lasted until James's death.

While at Munich in 1890, Stumpf began a quarrel with Wundt by criticizing the work on tonal distances of one of Wundt's students. Wundt quickly made the controversy personal, spicing his comments "with the most scathing invectives" (Stumpf, 1930, p. 401). Stumpf based his argument on his superior musical knowledge, whereas Wundt relied on laboratory results with apparatus and psychophysical methods. In the end, Stumpf concluded that he must have been correct because the offending experiments were never mentioned again, except in Wundt's textbook. "Wundt's methods . . . had been repellent to me since his Heidelberg days, . . . although I admire his extraordinary breadth of vision and his literary productivity, even in his extreme old age" (p. 401).

At Berlin, Stumpf was at the peak of German psychology, in a position that perhaps should have gone to Wundt as Germany's senior psychologist. Stumpf's productivity dramatically increased as his inherited laboratory grew into a large and important institute, and the demands on his energies drew him into many activities. For example, in 1900, he founded the Archive for Phonograms, which made primitive-music recordings, but much of the credit for this archive belongs to his student, **Erich von Hornbostel** (1877–1936). In the same year, Stumpf and a school principal began the Berlin *Gesellschaft für Kinderpsychologie* (Society for Child Psychology). Through the Society, Stumpf hoped to encourage the study and observation of the mental life of the child.

In 1904, Stumpf was involved in the celebrated case of Clever Hans (Chapter 1). Stumpf served as Rector of the University of Berlin in 1907–1908, and the position gave him access to "the leading personalities of all circles," including Kaiser Wilhelm II. In 1909, Stumpf represented the University at the centenary of Darwin's birth at Cambridge. "[T]he idea of evolution had been bred in my very bones—as was the case with all my contemporaries" (Stumpf, 1930, p. 409). In Chapter 9, we will examine Darwinian evolution and the *Zeitgeist* that favored its acceptance.

In 1913, Stumpf was asked to select someone to head an anthropoid (ape) research station on Tenerife, an island off the west coast of Africa. He suggested a former student, Wolfgang Köhler (Chapter 14), who eventually succeeded Stumpf as Director of the Berlin Psychological Institute.

Although Stumpf was heavily involved in organizing German psychologists for the war effort during World War I, he admitted that the German psychologists' cooperation was not as great as that of the Americans. However, in recording "the native dialects, songs, and other musical productions of the prisoners-of-war . . ." (Stumpf, 1930, p. 410) from all over the world, Stumpf felt Germany had surpassed other countries. Again, we see Stumpf's interest in music.

Stumpf retired in 1921 but continued lecturing until 1923. He also continued his research in tone psychology until he was well into his 80s, and a former student noted that it "was rather impressive to see the old gentleman well over eighty come from time to time to the institute . . . to make personal observations on the elaborate instrument he had built for the synthetic production of vowels" (Lewin, 1937, p. 190). Stumpf died on Christmas Day in 1936.

Stumpf's Psychology

As Brentano's student, Stumpf developed within an atmosphere of rigorous philosophy that culminated with Husserl's phenomenology. Stumpf's own focus concerned the classification of experience. His first class of experiences was that of phenomena such as tones, colors, and tastes, which comprise sensations and images. Appropriately, Stumpf called the study of such phenomena as sensations and images "phenomenology," which he considered preparatory to the study of the second class of experiences—the functions. Stumpf's functions were Brentano's acts, such things as perceiving, grouping, and willing. "Observation of the functions is the foundation of the mental sciences . . ." (Stumpf, 1930, p. 424). Stumpf devoted most of his career to his phenomenology, which, like Husserl, he considered antecedent to the real work of psychology.

Stumpf's Influence

As with Brentano, Stumpf's greatest legacy was his students. Unlike the authoritarian Wundt, Stumpf took a less directive approach in assigning research topics. This style is corroborated by one of his last students, Kurt Lewin (Chapter 14).

> Stumpf gave his students an unusual amount of freedom. For example, I selected my topic for a thesis and it was presented to Stumpf by the assistant while I waited in another room. The assistant came out to tell me that the topic was accepted and during the next three or four years I spent on this work, I do not remember having ever discussed the matter with Stumpf previous to my final presentation. . . . In respect to the guidance of students, as in most points, Stumpf's views were quite different from those of Wundt whose name was nearly taboo in the Berlin Institute. (Lewin, 1937, pp. 193–194)

Stumpf's influence was most evident on the men who made his rather than Husserl's phenomenology the basis for Gestalt psychology, and we can view Stumpf as an important link between Brentano and Gestalt psychology. Because of this link, Stumpf's psychology lived on through Gestalt psychology and phenomenology. By contrast, Wundt's voluntarism died with him.

Two of Gestalt psychology's three founders, Kurt Koffka and Wolfgang Köhler, took their Ph.D.s with Stumpf, and the man often listed as the fourth major Gestalt psychologist, Kurt Lewin, did also. As we noted, Köhler succeeded Stumpf at Berlin when the latter retired, and "the center for the new Gestalt school was seen to be where Stumpf's laboratory had been" (Boring, 1950, p. 370). Summarizing Stumpf's accomplishments, Sprung and Sprung (2000a) wrote,

> He was an ingenious experimenter, a pioneer in the psychology of hearing, a perceptive theoretician, the founder of a major institute of psychology in Berlin . . . , the individual behind the establishment of one of the most influential ethnomusicological collections in the world, and a significant forerunner, promoter, and critic of Gestalt theory. (p. 51)

Through it all, Stumpf remained a student of the psychology of music.

Never a large subfield, the psychology of music is still being studied (e.g., Handel, 1989). Stumpf is recognized as the area's pioneer, but another important early contributor was **Carl Emil Seashore** (1866–1949), the 1911 president of the American Psychological Association, who worked primarily at the University of Iowa.

EDMUND HUSSERL

Edmund Gustav Albrecht Husserl (1859–1938) was born in Prossnitz, Moravia, then part of the Austro-Hungarian Empire and today a part of the Czech Republic. At 17, Husserl began his higher education at the University of Leipzig, where he studied under Wundt. After 2 years, Wundt had failed "to make any special impression on him" (Misiak & Sexton, 1966, p. 406), and Husserl went to Berlin. At Berlin and then at Vienna, Husserl studied mathematics, completing his degree in 1883. He returned to Berlin, where he briefly taught mathematics before moving to Vienna to study logic with Brentano.

Husserl remained a lifelong friend of Brentano, and Brentano suggested he should work with Stumpf at Halle. Although Husserl considered Brentano his "one and only teacher," Husserl completed his philosophy degree as Stumpf's first graduate student.

Edmund Husserl (1859–1938)

Husserl's career as a philosopher of psychology began with his appointment at Halle in 1887. After 14 years, Husserl moved to Göttingen, where he taught until 1916. During his lifetime, phenomenology "was in the air, and so were Husserl's views" (Boring, 1950, p. 368). His Göttingen colleagues, David Katz and G. E. Müller (both discussed later), as well as Alexius Meinong and Carl Stumpf, all held similar phenomenological views about how to progress in psychology. In addition, through either Husserl or his friend Karl Bühler (Chapter 14), phenomenology's influence spread to Külpe's Würzburg laboratory. Although the various "phenomenologies" differed, Husserl's system was largely victorious, and it remains an active, although uncommon, approach to psychology (e.g., Buytendijk, 1959; Giorgi, 1970; Spiegelberg, 1960).

In 1916, Husserl moved to the University of Freiburg, where he retired in 1929. Although he was a Lutheran, Husserl had been born a Jew, and in 1933 the Nazis removed his titles and forbade him to lecture or to attend any academic conferences.

Husserl's Freiburg chair passed to Martin Heidegger (Chapter 16), his best-known pupil, and a man considered along with Ludwig Wittgenstein (Chapter 18) one of this century's most important philosophers. Husserl was clearly at the center of an important and far-reaching philosophical movement, and his impact on psychology should not be underestimated.

Edmund Husserl died in 1938, undoubtedly frustrated that large quantities of his work remained unpublished or untranslated. His personal library was considered such a fine collection that his wife Malvine went to great lengths to keep it from the Nazis as she fled. After failing to get nuns to transport the material across the Swiss border, Malvine convinced Belgium's prime minister to declare the material Belgian property. Fortunately, she and most of Husserl's books and papers escaped to Belgium, where much of the material can still be found at the Husserl Archives in Louvain.

Husserl's Phenomenology

The term *phenomenology* may be among the most misunderstood words in the history of psychology. Hegel's most important work, *The Phenomenology of Mind,* popularized the concept, and we first indicated that phenomenology is the study of intact, meaningful experiences in our discussion of Goethe. For Husserl and his contemporaries, however, the term had a more circumscribed and technical meaning. Heidegger, and many other philosophers and psychologists in the generation after Husserl (e.g., the Gestalt psychologists), shaped the term into the meaning that it carries for most modern-day philosophers and psychologists.

According to Husserl, **phenomenology** is the science of examining the data of conscious experience. As such, phenomenology seems neither overly complex nor unrelated to psychology, as critics have argued. In fact, Husserl's understanding of phenomenology closely resembles William James's conception of psychology, and several publications have explored the similarity between the two (e.g., Edie, 1987; Linschoten, 1968; Stevens, 1974; Wilshire, 1968).

Despite this similarity, Husserl saw phenomenology as a separate science that logically preceded psychology. Husserl's critics have stressed this "separateness" and have used Husserl's own words to argue that he should be of no interest to psychologists (e.g., Jennings, 1986; see Henley, 1988, for a reply).

Husserl's phenomenology first appeared in earnest with the publication of *Logical Investigations.* A popular variation appeared in 1913, with an English translation in 1931 known as the *Ideas* (Husserl, 1913/1931). Husserl also wrote the phenomenology entry for the *Encyclopedia Britannica,* an entry considered one of the finest presentations of phenomenology.

According to Husserl, beginning with Descartes, the history of philosophy and of psychology can be viewed as an attempt to find a suitably scientific system to structure further inquiry. Tracing this search through the works of Brentano and Stumpf, Husserl concluded that phenomenology was the appropriate system.

Husserl's phenomenology can be seen as a methodology for further inquiry into the structure and content of conscious experience. Husserl's system has several "steps," with the most essential being **description.** Description involves the intense concentration on, analysis of, and depiction of a given phenomenon. Central to Husserl's program, careful description remains the primary feature of modern-day phenomenological psychology (e.g., Pollio, Henley, & Thompson, 1997).

Wesensschau, or the cognition of essence, is another important step in Husserl's system. *Wesensschau*'s purpose is to apprehend something's essence through a consideration of phenomena. For example, looking at many green objects leads to the apprehension of greenness or color. Both *Wesensschau* and Husserl's notion of intentionality continue to be popular in philosophical theories of perception and other mental events (e.g., Føllesdal, 1974).

Although Husserl was a logician and a philosopher, the relation between phenomenology and psychology is central to most of his later writings. In fact, from his day until this, psychological philosophers have made the most use of Husserl's work. Husserl was critical of positivism (Chapter 5) and of the "mechanistic" psychology that endorsed it (e.g., associationism and behaviorism). Similarly, he was never impressed with Wundt's efforts or with Wundtian-style empirics.

For Husserl, phenomenology and psychology should be mutually beneficial. Phenomenology offered psychology a methodology for analyzing the data of consciousness and a structured program to guide the analysis. In turn, psychology was expected to provide new discoveries and factual data about the nature of conscious experience that could be used to refine phenomenology further. Examples of contemporary work linked to Husserl's approach include the study of topics such as learning and memory (e.g., Giorgi, 1989) and consumer behavior (e.g., Thompson, Locander, & Pollio, 1989).

More than a particular philosophical methodology, phenomenology represented a statement about how psychology should progress and what should count as its subject matter. Yet despite the efforts of various "phenomenological" contingents (e.g., the Gestaltists, James, the Würzburgers), no version of phenomenology ever became dominant. In fact, over Husserl's admonitions, Wundt's empiricism and positivistic forms of associationism and behaviorism gained center stage in the new science of psychology.

Husserl's Influence

The phenomenological tradition in psychology was, and is, influential. We have noted Husserl's impact on such contemporaries as Katz and Bühler, and through them on the Gestaltists and the Würzburgers, respectively. We have also mentioned the similarity between Husserl and James and have made connections to important philosophers, such as Heidegger. Through the French psychologist Maurice Merleau-Ponty, we can trace a direct connection between Husserl and much of modern-day phenomenological psychology (e.g., Pollio, 1982). In Chapter 16, in the context of "humanistic" psychology, we will examine further the connections between later phenomenologists such as Merleau-Ponty and existentialists such as Jean-Paul Sartre.

Despite significant differences between Husserl's phenomenology and cognitive psychology, Dreyfus (1982) suggested that without Husserl modern-day cognitive science might not exist. According to Dreyfus, Husserl anticipated concepts pivotal to cognitive psychology, particularly issues concerning the nature and structure of mental representations. As we noted, Husserl's views on perception and conception have remained popular among philosophical psychologists, many of whom helped start the "cognitive revolution" (Chapter 18).

Next, we consider a psychologist who did his most important work outside the university system, using himself as his only subject. Despite its limitations, the work of Hermann Ebbinghaus remains as relevant today as it was over a century ago.

Archives of the History of American Psychology–The University of Akron.

Hermann Ebbinghaus (1850–1909)

HERMANN EBBINGHAUS

Hermann Ebbinghaus (1850–1909) was born in Barmen, near Bonn, the son of a wealthy merchant. Ebbinghaus attended the Barmen *Gymnasium* and then went to the University of Bonn at 17. Planning to study history and philology, over the next 3 years he spent time at Halle and Berlin, where philosophy became his major interest.

In 1873, following a brief tour with the Prussian Army in the Franco-Prussian War, Ebbinghaus obtained the Ph.D. degree with a dissertation on Eduard von Hartmann's (1842–1906) recently published *Philosophie des Unbewussten* (*Philosophy of the Unconscious*). Ebbinghaus spent the next 7 years in independent study, first in Berlin, where he read science in keeping with the academic tradition of the time. From 1875 to 1878, Ebbinghaus traveled in France and England, studying and tutoring. In a used bookstore in London—not Paris as reported in E. R. Jaensch's obituary of Ebbinghaus (Traxel, 1985)—he purchased a copy of Fechner's *Elements of Psychophysics.* Its effect on him was so great that Ebbinghaus dedicated a 1902 book to Fechner, saying "*ich hab' es nur von Euch*" (I owe everything to you). Paradoxically, in his most famous work, *Über das Gedächtnis*, which was almost certainly inspired by *Elements of Psychophysics*, Fechner is nowhere mentioned, although Ebbinghaus even sent an autographed copy of his published monograph to the elderly psychophysicist (Hoffman, Bringmann, Bamberg, & Klein, 1987).

Ebbinghaus was impressed by Fechner's advances in studying sensation and perception with his psychophysical methods, and he was convinced that he could use similar methods to study higher mental processes that Wundt had said could not be studied experimentally. Thus, he began to study memory, a problem he may have gotten from the British associationists. In this, he treated psychology as *Naturwissenschaft* (natural science), something he did throughout his career (Shakow, 1930) and something that led to controversy with famed philosopher Wilhelm Dilthey (1833–1911), a former teacher.

Converted to psychology early, Ebbinghaus abandoned philosophy to make psychology a quantitative natural science. By contrast, Dilthey argued that the "new" psychology—apparently meaning Herbart's psychology—could never be more than descriptive, and the mind could not be analyzed. Ebbinghaus responded in part through his use of laboratory methods to study memory successfully. In this, Ebbinghaus also showed that higher mental functions could be investigated directly and that Wundt's *Völkerpsychologie* was not the only approach to their study.

In 1880, Ebbinghaus was habilitated as an instructor at Berlin, and in 1885, he published his studies of human memory in *Über das Gedächtnis: Untersuchungen zur experimentellen Psychologie* (*Concerning Memory: An Investigation in Experimental Psychology*). Shortly thereafter, Ebbinghaus was promoted, and, probably in the late 1880s, he founded the laboratory that Stumpf inherited in 1894. Shakow (1930) noted that Ebbinghaus's Berlin laboratory was perhaps the third in Germany, after Wundt's at Leipzig and G. E. Müller's at Göttingen.

One of Ebbinghaus's most significant contributions to psychology was the 1890 founding, with former Helmholtz student and physiologist **Arthur König** (1856–1901), of the *Zeitschrift für Psychologie und Physiologie der Sinnesorgane* (*Journal of Psychology and Physiology of the Sense Organs*). The cooperating editors included Helmholtz, Hering, Müller, and Stumpf, and the journal not only represented a German alternative to Wundt's *Philosophische Studien* but also helped advance psychology as a natural science (Lander, 1997). The journal is still published as *Zeitschrift für Psychologie*, and a 1985 volume celebrated the centennial of Ebbinghaus's *Über das Gedächtnis* with a variety of papers on Ebbinghaus and his legacy.

In 1894, Ebbinghaus was passed over for promotion to professor at Berlin, probably because he had too few publications, and Stumpf got the position. Ebbinghaus departed for a professorship at the University of Breslau. There, Ebbinghaus was on a commission charged with determining whether children's mental ability declined over their 5-hour school sessions. Although the central question got lost, the "Ebbinghaus Completion Test" proved useful for measuring general intellectual ability. For example, a child might be asked to complete the statement, "Children are ________ than their parents," with both the accuracy and speed of the answer important in scoring. Performance was highly correlated with the students' ranks in class, an indication of the test's potential for measuring intelligence. Partly because of the success of the Ebbinghaus Completion Test, Alfred Binet (Chapter 17) later used similar tasks in developing the first intelligence tests.

In 1902, Ebbinghaus published *Grundzüge der Psychologie* (*Principles of Psychology*), which was an immediate success, primarily because of its readability. Demands for revisions continued after Ebbinghaus's death; these were provided first by E. Dürr and then, after Dürr's death, by Karl Bühler.

Abriss der Psychologie (*Outline of Psychology*), a brief sketch of psychology that opens with Ebbinghaus's famous line, "Psychology has a long past, but only a short history," appeared in 1908. The book averaged a new edition every 2 years through its eighth edition in 1922.

By all accounts, Ebbinghaus was an exceptional lecturer. "His ever-youthful personality, his natural humor, and the unusual clarity and ease of his presentation assured him of an overflowing audience and of considerable influence on his auditors" (Shakow, 1930, pp. 507–508). According to Schwartz (1986), Ebbinghaus was also well liked as a person. Given his attractiveness, it is surprising that there were so few "Ebbinghausians." E. R. Jaensch (1909) accounted for the lack of disciples by writing that Ebbinghaus had no desire to create them.

William Stern and William Lowe Bryan were two of the better-known people who worked with Ebbinghaus. Stern made important contributions in cognition, developmental psychology, applied psychology, and individual differences. His suggestion for dividing mental age by chronological age as a measure of intelligence was adopted by Lewis Terman for the Stanford-Binet test (Chapter 17).

William Lowe Bryan (1860–1955) worked with Ebbinghaus in Berlin for a year, subsequently earned his Ph.D. with G. Stanley Hall (Chapter 10), and later worked with Külpe at Würzburg. An APA president, Bryan was also the long-time president of Indiana University, where he established the oldest continuing psychological laboratory in the United States.

In 1905, Ebbinghaus went from Breslau to Halle. In 1909, he developed pneumonia and died unexpectedly at 59. R. S. Woodworth (1909) expressed the feelings of many when he wrote:

> The sudden death, on February 26 . . . of Dr. Hermann Ebbinghaus . . . is felt as a severe loss throughout the psychological world, for few psychologists were more international in their reputation and sympathies. Nowhere, perhaps, will the loss be keener felt than on this side of the water, where his work has long been held in high esteem, and where his great book, the "Grundzüge der Psychologie," is by many regarded as the best general treatment of the subject. (p. 253)

Although the *Grundzüge* was an excellent general treatment of psychology, Ebbinghaus is most famous for his work on memory.

Ebbinghaus's Memory Research

As we indicated earlier, Fechner is not cited in *Über das Gedächtnis.* Frequently mentioned, however, is Herbart, who, as part of his mathematical approach to psychology, called for the search for lawful relations for mental events (Hoffman et al., 1987). Because Herbart had not conducted the research to determine these lawful relations, this is what Ebbinghaus aimed to do.

Following Fechner's lead, Ebbinghaus used objective research methods to study memory, believing that simplification was essential. His greatest simplification involved the **nonsense syllable,** or **CVC trigram** (two consonants with a vowel between), as it is often called. Actually, Ebbinghaus used the term "*sinlose Silben,*" which literally means "meaningless syllable," and even this may be inaccurate because in one passage Ebbinghaus (1885/1964) wrote: "The differences between sense and nonsense material were not nearly so great as one would be inclined a priori to imagine" (p. 23). Incidentally, Hoffman et al. (1987) indicated that it was the lists that were nonsense, not the syllables.

Although Ebbinghaus gave no examples, his "meaningless syllables" have been found in archival material (Hoffman et al., 1987). According to Hoffman et al.,

> [Ebbinghaus] first prepared a pool of 2300 syllables, but these were not consonant-vowel-consonant trigrams, as is reported in most history of psychology texts. . . . The stimuli were syllables, but quite a few were words or were at least very word-like. Here are some examples: *heim, beis, ship, dush, noir, noch, dach, wash, born, for, zuch, dauch, shok, hal, dauf, fich, theif, haum, shish,* and *rur.* In discussing the materials, Ebbinghaus referred to their simplicity or homogeneity and to the ease with which they could be systematically varied, but not to their "meaninglessness." (pp. 66–67, italics in the original)

Many texts report that Ebbinghaus invented the CVC trigram, because Ebbinghaus wrote that he constructed his syllables by placing a vowel sound between two consonants. His footnote specifying the vowels and consonants explains why some of Hoffman et al.'s (1987) unearthed syllables consisted of more than three letters.

> The vowel sounds employed were a, e, i, o, u, ä, ö, ü, au, ei, eu. For the beginning of the syllables the following consonants were employed: b, d, f, g, h, j, k, l, m, n, p, r, s, (= sz), t, w, and in addition ch, sch, soft s, and the French j (19 altogether); for the end of the syllables f, k, l, m, n, p, r, s, (= sz), t, ch, sch (11 altogether). For the final sound fewer consonants were employed than for the initial sound, because a German tongue even after several years practice in foreign languages does not quite accustom itself to the correct pronunciation of the mediae at the end. (Ebbinghaus, 1885/1964, p. 22)

G. E. Müller and F. Schumann later made the rules for constructing nonsense syllables even more explicit. In a review of their work, Bergström (1894) explained that the initial consonants were placed on separate cards in one box, the end consonants in another, with the vowels and diphthongs (complex vowel sounds involving two letters) in a third box between the other two. Syllables were then formed by drawing a card at random from each box in sequence. Thus, Müller and Schumann's method produced syllables consisting of an initial consonant and an end consonant with either a vowel or a combination of two vowel sounds—the German umlaut (e.g., ü)—between them. In short, the method resulted in CVC syllables, which were not necessarily trigrams.

For 2 years, Ebbinghaus learned and relearned syllable lists using a "complete mastery" procedure. Specifically, he read through a list at a set rate, timed with either a metronome or a watch, until he had mastered the list completely and could recite it from memory. Then he would measure his retention after varying time periods by relearning the list and computing a percentage savings score. Using this procedure and himself as the experimental subject, Ebbinghaus investigated such questions as the effect of practice (number of repetitions) on memory and the effect of time on memory.

Amount of Practice and Memory

You readily assume the time you spend studying some material translates into better retention later, but is this true? Ebbinghaus answered the question by learning and relearning lists of 16 syllables. He found that the number of repetitions in original learning was inversely related to the number of repetitions in relearning; the more times he rehearsed a list originally, the fewer the repetitions required to relearn the list to an errorless repetition 24 hours later.

This experiment also demonstrated the importance of **overlearning**—continued rehearsal beyond mastery—for retention. Once Ebbinghaus could say a 16-word list without error, continuing practice was overlearning, and overlearned lists were better retained than nonoverlearned lists. Further, the greater the overlearning, the greater the savings after 24 hours. Take it from Ebbinghaus: If you want to be sure you retain material for a test, overlearn it. Specifically, once you can recite it from memory, rehearse it some more.

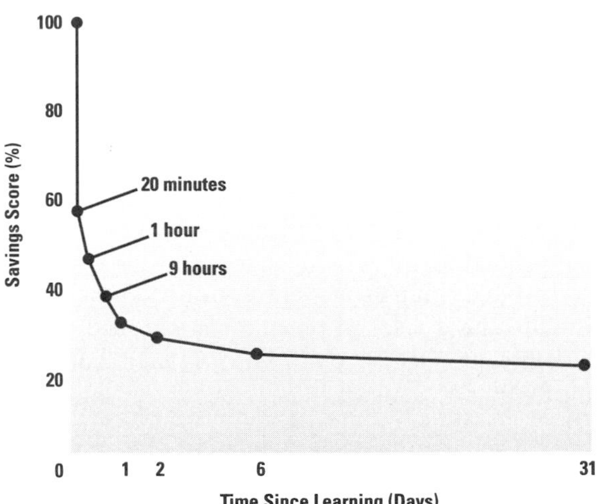

FIGURE 8.4 The classic Ebbinghaus forgetting curve

Memory and the Passage of Time

To determine the relation of forgetting to time since learning, Ebbinghaus learned 13-syllable lists to complete mastery and then tested his retention by relearning the lists after different time periods. Plotting Ebbinghaus's savings scores over time produces the classic forgetting curve (Figure 8.4), which reveals a large initial drop in retention followed by decreasing losses thereafter. As you can see, there was only 58% retention after 20 minutes, and by an hour after learning, less than half (44%) was retained. However, the curve also shows that most forgetting occurs within 24 hours, with relatively little beyond that.

Additional Observations

Some of Ebbinghaus's almost incidental observations are important and widely cited. For example, Ebbinghaus noted, "With any considerable number of repetitions a suitable distribution of them over a space of time is decidedly more advantageous than the massing of them at a single time" (Ebbinghaus,

1885/1964, p. 89). In other words, Ebbinghaus found that for learning syllable lists, **distributed practice** was better than **massed practice.** In addition, Ebbinghaus's work foreshadows various serial position effects (e.g., recency and primacy).

Discussing several experiments, Ebbinghaus concluded that "the number of syllables which I can repeat without error after a single reading is about seven. One can, with a certain justification, look upon this number as a measure of the ideas of this sort which I can grasp in a single unitary conscious act" (Ebbinghaus, 1885/1964, p. 109). This passage anticipates modern short-term memory discussions, one of which is in Miller's (1956) paper appropriately titled, "The magical number seven plus or minus two: Some limits on our capacity for processing information." Miller's paper is sometimes viewed as the start of the cognitive revolution (Chapter 18).

Ebbinghaus's Influence

Before Ebbinghaus, no experimental investigations of memory or anything else related to thinking had been done. Indeed, both Herbart and Kant had denied the possibility of measuring higher mental processes and thus developing a science of mental life (Boneau, 1998). Ebbinghaus's memory research showed that Herbart and Kant were wrong in their pessimism about psychology and refuted Wundt's claim that higher mental functions could not be studied experimentally. His experimental findings are still considered valid and are cited alongside much more recent work. In part, this continuing relevance stems from his careful experimental procedures, some of which we have described. Unlike some of his contemporaries (e.g., Wundt, Titchener, G. E. Müller), Ebbinghaus did not rush his findings into print. The following Ebbinghaus statement, quoted in Woodworth (1909), explains why:

> "the individual has to make innumerable studies for his own sake. He tests and rejects, tests once more and once more rejects. For certainly not every happy thought, bolstered up perhaps by a few rough-and-ready experiments, should be brought before the public. But sometimes the individual reaches a point where he is permanently clear and satisfied with his interpretation. Then the matter belongs to the scientific public for their further judgment." (p. 255)

Although Ebbinghaus completed his memory studies by 1880, he did not publish *Über das Gedächtnis* until 1885. He was replicating and extending his original findings in the meantime.

When considering the originality of Ebbinghaus's memory research, note that there were no others doing similar research. Ebbinghaus had no subject pool of undergraduate students; he had no colleagues to consult about a problem; his simplifying syllables were his own creation. This makes his accomplishment all the more remarkable.

Of course, not all the influences of Ebbinghaus's memory studies have been unequivocally positive. In 1985, the *Journal of Experimental Psychology: Learning, Memory, and Cognition* published commentaries on the article, "Ebbinghaus: Some Associations" (Slamecka, 1985). In one, Kintsch (1985) decried the invention of the nonsense syllable, writing: "What a terrible struggle our field has had just to overcome the nonsense syllable! Decades to discover the 'meaningfulness' of nonsense syllables, and decades more to finally turn away from the seductions of this chimera" (p. 461). Young (1985) criticized Ebbinghaus for doing research that was too good, with the consequence that he "put a stamp on this field which resulted in rigidifying, for nearly 80 years, the paradigms used to study human learning" (p. 491). According to Young, Ebbinghaus's simplifying methodology ruled out the study of mnemonics (memory aids) for almost 80 years.

By contrast, Endel Tulving (Chapter 18) argued that Ebbinghaus's memory research showed evidence of different components of memory (e.g., semantic and procedural), although Ebbinghaus himself held a unitary view of learning and memory. Tulving (1985) concluded that Ebbinghaus would probably have been open to the possibility of separate memory systems, as "he was an open-minded scientist, forever ready to reach beyond what is known" (p. 490).

Ebbinghaus's memory research alone would be enough to cement his place in the history of psychology. Yet, as we noted, he did two additional things of importance: The first was his cofounding of the *Zeitschrift,* which provided a place to publish psychological research outside Wundt's sphere. His second contribution was the discovery that complex tasks are useful for assessing mental ability.

In summary, Ebbinghaus did highly original work, which has stood the test of time. He was not a researcher who hits upon a useful method and problem and then mines it for all it is worth. Instead, he was content to show the way and leave the "mopping up" to others. One of those "others" was Georg Elias Müller, who spent a considerable portion of his career extending and refining Ebbinghaus's memory research.

Archives of the History of American Psychology–The University of Akron.

G. E. Müller (1850–1934)

GEORG ELIAS MÜLLER

In his obituary of Stumpf, Kurt Lewin (1937) wrote: "For a German graduate student of psychology around 1910, like myself, two men held the highest rank and dignity within the pyramid of psychologists actively participating in research . . . Stumpf and . . . G. E. Müller" (p. 189). Boring (1950) also held a high opinion of Müller, referring to him as the "last of the 'giants,' except for Stumpf . . ." (p. 379), and as one of the "pioneers in a very important undertaking, the bringing of the impalpable mind into the experimental laboratory" (Boring, 1935, p. 348). Despite the accolades, Müller is often slighted in histories of psychology, at least partly because his major works have not been translated into English (Behrens, 1997).

Georg Elias Müller (1850–1934) was born in Grimma, which is not far from Leipzig. After an early humanistic education that included little mathematics or science, Müller developed a philosophical bent by reading such works as Goethe's *Faust* and the poetry of Byron and Shelley. Reading Gotthold Ephraim Lessing (1729–1781)—a philosophically minded poet, playwright, essayist, and critic—taught Müller the value of careful, rigorous thought.

Müller's higher education included study at Leipzig, Berlin, and Göttingen, with a year off for the Franco-Prussian War. At Göttingen, Lotze completed Müller's training in precise thinking, and he also reinforced further the need to ground philosophy in science. Although the philosophers interested in psychology at this time believed psychology should be grounded in the scientific method, they rarely became experimentalists. Müller, Ebbinghaus, and Wundt were the exceptions.

At Leipzig, Müller had become acquainted with Fechner, and he maintained a scientific correspondence with the psychophysicist. Müller revised and extended the psychophysics methodology and used the work to secure an instructor's position at the University of Göttingen. Unlike Stumpf, who worked at five universities before settling in Berlin, Müller was professor of philosophy at Göttingen for

40 years, long enough to make him an institution there, much as Wundt was at Leipzig.

At Göttingen, Müller continued his psychophysical research, becoming the leader in the field with Fechner's death in 1887. As we noted earlier, the 1903 publication of Müller's handbook of psychophysics forced Titchener to delay publishing the second volumes of his *Experimental Psychology.*

In 1887, 2 years after Ebbinghaus's publication of *Über das Gedächtnis,* Müller and his assistant, **Friedrich Schumann** (1863–1940), began work on memory using Ebbinghaus's complete mastery method. To standardize nonsense syllable list presentation, Müller and Schumann invented the **memory drum,** which consists of a rotating piece of paper on which are printed verbal materials to be learned. Each verbal item appears for a set time in the "window" facing the subject.

An important behind-the-scenes psychologist, Schumann earned his degree at Göttingen with Müller and worked with him on memory. Schumann then went to Berlin, where he was Stumpf's right-hand man for 11 years, doing important work on visual space perception. With Ebbinghaus's death, Schumann assumed the editorship of *Zeitschrift für Psychologie.* In 1910, Schumann was at Frankfurt in time to give laboratory space and equipment to Max Wertheimer, so that Wertheimer, working with Kurt Koffka and Wolfgang Köhler, could do the experiments that led to Gestalt psychology.

Müller verified and extended Ebbinghaus's verbal learning research. His addition of introspective reports to Ebbinghaus's method convinced Müller that subjects had attempted to group items in the lists and to find meaning even in meaningless material, an observation usually associated with later researchers (e.g., Bousfield, 1953). In addition, a subject's preparatory set (*Anlage*) affected the memory processes, a finding we will see further investigated in Oswald Külpe's Würzburg laboratory. Külpe spent some time with Müller.

With Alfons Pilzecker, Müller developed the **interference theory of forgetting,** finding that new learning can interfere with the memory of material learned earlier. They called this interference **retroactive inhibition,** because it acts back upon (retro-active) an earlier memory. Interference theory continues to be an important explanation of forgetting.

Archives of the History of American Psychology—The University of Akron.

A memory drum

In addition, Müller was interested in visual perception, and particularly color perception. Ironically, Müller himself had defective color vision (Sprung & Sprung, 2000b). In a series of articles, he detailed and defended a theory of color vision that advanced Ewald Hering's opponent-process theory (Chapter 7). Hering's theory predicts that with equal stimulation of the black-white, blue-yellow, and red-green systems, the result should be that we see nothing, a visual "silence." Actually, we see gray, which Müller explained by proposing that there is a constant gray background caused by molecular activity in the cortex (cortical gray).

Several additional people who worked in Müller's laboratory figure prominently in the history of psychology. For example, **Erich R. Jaensch** (1883–1940), **David Katz** (1884–1957), and **Edgar Rubin** (1886–1951) all worked on or published phenomenological investigations at approximately the same time that Wertheimer, Koffka, and Köhler performed similar research that led to Gestalt psychology. This further demonstrates the persuasive power of the phenomenological *Zeitgeist* in non-Wundtian German psychology.

After earning her Ph.D. with Titchener in 1898, Eleanor Acheson McCulloch Gamble was Müller's student in 1906–1907. She subsequently published a classic work on the reconstruction method for measuring memory, which was based primarily on research performed at Wellesley before she went to Göttingen. In midlife, **Lillien Jane Martin** (1851–1943) discovered Wundt's work. Deciding to go to Germany to study, Martin arrived at Göttingen in 1894 and spent 4 years there, failing to earn a Ph.D. because the university was not granting them to women at the time. In 1898, Martin joined the faculty at Stanford University, where in 1915 she became the first woman to head a Stanford department. Finally, working with Müller, Adolph Jost published memory research that produced Jost's law, which states that "when two associations are of equal strength, a repetition strengthens the older more than the younger" (Boring, 1950, p. 375).

Müller's Influence

As you can see, Müller was a gifted researcher who made substantial contributions in the areas of psychophysics, memory, and vision. In addition, he provided a laboratory at Göttingen to rival Wundt's at Leipzig. As Boring (1950) put it,

> Within experimental psychology he exhibited a broad interest and a fertile mind. His students received from him more than their meed of inspiration and help, and through his own work and through theirs he exerted a great influence upon experimental psychology in its formative years. As a power and an institution he was second only to Wundt. (p. 379)

Similarly, Behrens (1997) called Müller the "Third Pillar of Experimental Psychology," after Wundt and Fechner.

Müller was particularly noted for his careful research methodology and served as a subject himself in each of his students' experiments, often over extended time periods (Sprung & Sprung, 2000b). The Gestalt psychologist David Katz referred to Müller as the "methodological conscience" of psychology.

We will conclude with an examination of the career and influence of a man who worked under both "institutions" in German psychology in the late 19th century, who found Brentano's psychology more appealing than that of the man whose assistant he had been, and who went on to found a research program with a lasting influence—Oswald Külpe.

OSWALD KÜLPE

Oswald Külpe (1862–1915) was born in Candau in Courland, Latvia, which at the time was part of Russia. However, both his family and his native tongue were German, and Külpe did not learn Russian until he entered the *Gymnasium* at Libau. Although the Külpes were probably not affluent, they were well educated.

In 1881, Külpe went to the University of Leipzig to study history. He attended Wundt's lectures, but Wundt's laboratory was just getting underway, so Külpe transferred to Berlin to again study history. From Berlin, Külpe went to Göttingen, where he studied under G. E. Müller, who supplied his dissertation topic. With a digression in Russia, Külpe returned to Leipzig and Wundt's seminar, and in 1887, he had his doctoral examination. In 1888, Külpe defended a second dissertation and became a *Privatdozent.* He also became Wundt's second assistant, James McKeen Cattell (Chapter 10) having returned to America.

In the early 1890s, Külpe planned to write a psychology textbook that would present the experimental work that had been done and be simpler than Wundt's *Principles.* Much of the planning involved discussions with Titchener, who translated Külpe's *Grundriss der Psychologie* into *Outlines of Psychology,* which was published only 2 years after *Grundriss* appeared (Külpe, 1895). Although Külpe dedicated his book to Wundt, Wundt did not approve of it and promptly wrote his own *Grundriss der Psychologie.*

Külpe was promoted at Leipzig shortly after the publication of the *Grundriss,* but in 1894 he went to the chair of philosophy at the University of Würzburg. There, Külpe developed a laboratory that soon rivaled Wundt's in quality. In 1909, Külpe moved to Bonn, and then in 1913, he moved to Munich, establishing laboratories at both universities. Before Christmas in 1915, Külpe had a bout with influenza, and he died on December 30, 1915, at only 53.

Oswald Külpe (1862–1915)

According to R. M. Ogden (1951; Chapter 14), one of his Ph.D. students, "Oswald Külpe was both an impressive and a lovable character. . . . Külpe's character is best described, I think, as that of an esthetic personality in a factual world" (pp. 6–7). Külpe never married and often said "with a twinkle in his eye: 'Science is my bride'" (p. 4).

Külpe's Psychology

At Leipzig, Külpe and Titchener were strongly influenced by the positivistic writings of Mach and Avenarius, which led them to accept the view that any mental state, no matter how complex, could be reduced to elementary states. This allowed them to study higher and lower mental processes with the same methodology, experimental introspection, rather than reserving experimental methodology only for the study of the lower processes, as Wundt taught.

By defining psychology as "a science of the facts of experience in their dependency upon experiencing individuals . . ." (p. 3), Külpe (1895) avoided Wundt's distinction between immediate experience as the province of psychology and mediate experience as the property of physics. Külpe could then define physics as a science of experience independent of an experiencing individual.

Külpe's *Outlines* attempted to cover everything known about experimental psychology at the time it was written. Thus, it omitted discussion of such unresearched topics as thought, which Wundt considered impossible to study experimentally. At Würzburg, Külpe and his students made thought a major topic of study, soon discovering that not all thought is accompanied by images. As we noted, this led to the imageless thought controversy with Wundt and Titchener.

The Würzburg School

Note that "none of the articles in the traditional Würzburg canon were written by the founder and father figure of the school, Oswald Külpe" (Lindenfeld, 1978, p. 132), which leads to the question: What was Külpe's relationship to the school associated with his name? Ogden (1951) considered Külpe the inspiration for work coming from his laboratory, writing:

> Unlike G. E. Müller, [Külpe] published no extensive experimental studies of his own. It should be noted, however, that he was intimately engaged in all that went on in his laboratory. It was a matter of principle with him to act as observer in the experimental work of his students. . . . His influence upon his students was never dominating. Instead, they were engaged together in a joint enterprise of scientific discovery. (p. 9)

The **Würzburg school** method was **systematic experimental introspection,** in which people performed a complex task involving such mental events as thinking, remembering, or judging and were then required to make a retrospective report of their mental experiences during the task. The mental events *during* the solution were what interested the Würzburgers, not the task solution itself.

Karl Marbe (1869–1953), who later became interested in such applied areas of psychology as advertising and developing aptitude tests (Marbe, 1936), reported one of the Würzburg school's first studies in 1901. Marbe asked subjects to judge which of two weights was heavier and then to report what happened in their consciousness during the judgment. Although the subjects usually made the correct judgment, they did not know how the judgment got into their minds. Marbe attributed such judgments to *Bewusstseinslagen,* or "conscious attitudes," which then became a new element of the mind, along with Wundt's sensations, images, and feelings.

Külpe's Scottish doctoral student, **Henry Jackson Watt** (1879–1925), performed the next key study. In 1904, Watt asked subjects to make partially restricted associations to stimulus words, for example, to the word *dog.* A subject might be required to make either a superordinate response (e.g., *animal*) or a subordinate response (e.g., *bulldog*). As before, Watt was interested in the thought processes preceding the response, and he found that subjects produced appropriate associations without conscious effort.

Watt's research introduced the technique of **fractionating** the introspections into four periods: (1) the preparatory period, (2) the period when the stimulus word was presented, (3) the period of search for the associated word, and (4) the response period. In addition, Watt's research placed the emphasis on the *Aufgabe,* or task. Once the subject was given and had accepted the task, Watt found the response followed the stimulus word automatically, without conscious content. That is, Watt found little conscious content in the period (3) when there should be the search for the response. The *Aufgabe* created an *Einstellung,* or "set" to respond.

Watt's work was followed in 1905 by the work of Külpe's junior colleague, **Narziss Ach** (1871–1946). Ach gave his subjects number pairs, after first giving them the instruction to either add, subtract, multiply, or divide the numbers. If 8 and 2 are printed on a piece of paper, with 8 above and 2 below, the typical associations are 10, 6, 16, and 4. However, the instruction to add strengthens one association so that the result is almost inevitably 10. The *Aufgabe,* or, as Ach called it, the **determining tendency,** effectively predetermines the result.

Külpe's interpretation of Ludwig Lange's reaction-time studies in Wundt's laboratory foreshadowed Ach's idea of determining tendency. Recall that Lange found that subjects concentrating on making a response showed shorter reaction times than subjects concentrating on the presentation of the stimulus. According to Wundt, concentrating on the stimulus added apperception to the perceptual-response sequence, which required an extra 0.1 second beyond simply perceiving it. By contrast, Külpe argued that changing the set did not merely add another element: It changed the whole process. Ach's research, and Watt's before it, showed that Külpe was right.

In addition to the "determining tendency," Ach's research uncovered an element of conscious content that was neither image nor sensation, which Ach called *Bewusstheit* (awareness). This "was the birth of an 'imageless thought content' . . ." (Ogden, 1951, p. 10).

Imageless Thought Controversy. Both Wundt and Titchener assumed that thinking depended on mental images, and thought without images, with *unanschaulische Bewusstheiten* (vague awareness), questioned this basic assumption. Neither man believed the Würzburg studies damaged his position. Wundt rejected imageless thought as being caused by faulty methodology—thought cannot be observed while one is thinking. The Würzburgers' retrospective introspection failed to observe the actual thought processes that occurred during the search-for-response period. After the response is made, the original thought processes cannot recur.

Although Titchener believed thought could be studied introspectively, he objected to imageless thought because at Cornell, introspectively analyzed thought always produced images. Titchener tried to reduce the Würzburgers' *unanschaulische Bewusstheiten* to kinesthetic sensations (sensations of position, movement, etc., of parts of the body).

> The introspective [reports] kept showing, for example, that the kinesthesis of an incipient smile or of a relaxed chest could mean familiarity. "The great god kinesthesis," exclaimed someone on reading a set of such [records], so pervasive were these somesthetic sensory processes in the stream of consciousness. (Boring, 1969, p. 28)

In addition to the Würzburgers, Robert S. Woodworth (Chapter 11) in America soon reported imageless thought, as did Alfred Binet in France. Binet even claimed that the "method of Würzburg" should be called the "method of Paris." Külpe responded by pointing to the early studies from his laboratory by Marbe and Ach, which antedated Binet's work.

Probably the most important effect of the imageless thought controversy was that it undermined confidence in introspection as a method. The data generated by introspection were unreliable, open to alternative interpretations, and, perhaps, too easily biased by the observer's viewpoint.

Külpe's Influence

Perhaps most important, Külpe's Würzburg program generated controversy, which tends to stimulate research. Controversy prevents the establishment of orthodoxy, which works to stifle dissent. Unfortunately for Külpe, there was a heavy personal price to pay: His unorthodox findings generated criticism, even attack, from the men he admired and liked the most.

> His break with Wundt over matters of principle, which occurred even in his Leipzig days, failed to weaken his reverent regard for his master teacher. He published three tributes to Wundt and was active in the preparation of the *Festschrift* that brought to a close the publication of Wundt's *Philosophische Studien.* Külpe retained a like regard for Müller, his second teacher, though he was deeply hurt when Müller saw fit to attack the methods and results of the Würzburg school. It was sadness rather than resentment that characterized his feelings when Titchener, his friend and companion of Leipzig days, turned the guns of his laboratory at Cornell against the Würzburg investigations of the thought-processes. "If I could only sit down with Titchener," he said to me, "I am sure I could make him see what we are driving at." (Ogden, 1951, p. 6)

Like Ebbinghaus's and Müller's memory experiments, Külpe's studies of thought showed that higher mental processes could be examined experimentally and that Wundt's "two psychologies" (experimental to study lower mental processes and cultural to study higher mental processes) were unnecessary. In addition, the Würzburgers' demonstration that mental operations frequently occur without definite images undermined the basic assumption of Wundt's and Titchener's approaches that the elements of consciousness are sensations, images, and feelings.

Throughout, Külpe's work showed the importance of mental set. Given the appropriate instructions, subjects extracted relevant information from a stimulus while failing to extract other, equally apparent information. Thus, the stimulus did not automatically produce sensations that became images, again showing a deficiency in Wundt's and Titchener's systems.

The Würzburgers' studies stressed the importance of motivation in terms like *Aufgabe* (task), *Einstellung* (set), and determining tendency. The subjects were not consciously aware of these directing tendencies, indicating they operated unconsciously. However, the Würzburgers viewed the tendencies as vague conscious elements, and it remained for Freud to make the unconscious control of behavior a vital concept.

Külpe's research sharpened the distinction between mental content and mental acts or functions, which brought him closer to Brentano than to Wundt. Because so many of Brentano's students were important for Gestalt psychology's development, it is not surprising that one of Külpe's doctoral students, Max Wertheimer, had the seminal insight that led to Gestalt psychology. The basic compatibility was there in the Würzburgers' tendency toward the holistic approach in contrast to Wundtian elementism. In addition, by studying such higher mental functions as thought and volition experimentally, the Würzburgers "contributed significantly to the development of modern cognitive . . . psychology" (Mack, 1997, p. 177).

Finally, the inconsistencies in the introspective reports that led to the imageless thought controversy hastened the demise of introspection as an experimental method of psychology.

CONCLUSIONS

Scientific psychology, whether it began in 1860 with Fechner's psychophysics or in 1879 with Wundt at Leipzig, arose from physiology and philosophy. Philosophy provided the issues—for example, the mind-body relation, the nature of perception, the structure of consciousness—and research in the tradition of physiology was used to seek the answers. Fechner and Wundt converted this from a possibility to an actuality, taking psychology from the philosopher's armchair to the laboratory. Psychology under Wundt became an empirical science, not just in the philosophical sense that Herbart had noted, but in the modern sense of that phrase.

Because of behaviorism's early dominance in America, we often assume that John Watson (Chapter 12) brought psychology in line with the other, more mature sciences (e.g., physics). In fact, it was Titchener who went beyond Wundt and first argued that the subject matter of psychology is no different in kind from that of physics. The subject matter of both physics and psychology is simply experience. Viewed from the individual's perspective, the experience is psychological, but viewed from a perspective independent of an individual, the experience is physical.

Despite the effects of several phenomenological alternatives we considered, psychology became a positivist enterprise just as Titchener desired. Wundt and Titchener, and whatever common elements of "structuralism" existed between them, formed the first schools of psychology and gave psychology its legacy. Today, psychology remains situated midway between philosophy and physiology, which a cursory glance at cognitive neuroscience will confirm. In addition, psychology continues to advance as an empirical science, adhering to the methods and conventions—although no longer positivistic—of the wider scientific community. As Koch (1992, p. 8) noted:

> What Wundt effectuated . . . was the stabilization of *a* meaning of a word that had been invited and worked toward over several prior centuries and an arrogation of that "new" meaning to sovereign status relative to all prior usages in the history of thought. Henceforward the core meaning of "psychology" would be dominated by the adjectives *scientific* and *experimental.*

Both Wundt and Titchener trained many of the next generation of psychologists. In Wundt's case, his students formed laboratories all across Europe and America, making him in a nontrivial sense the "father" of psychology.

In addition to Wundt and Titchener, we explored contemporary German alternatives to Wundtian psychology. Except for Ebbinghaus, all the major people we examined—Brentano, Stumpf, Husserl, Müller, and Külpe—can be considered "phenomenological" psychologists. As we indicated, phenomenological ideas were a major part of the era's *Zeitgeist.*

As presented in *Psychology From an Empirical Standpoint,* Brentano's system stands as the backdrop to the various phenomenologies (e.g., Stumpf's, Husserl's) and phenomenological approaches to psychology (e.g., the Würzburg school, Gestalt psychology) that came later. Like Brentano, Stumpf and Husserl were more important as philosophers of psychology than as experimental psychologists. By contrast, Müller and Külpe (and later the Gestaltists) made substantial laboratory contributions. We can only speculate about how the tension between Wundt's psychology and Brentano's psychology would have been resolved if World War II had not intervened. As we will see, the Gestaltists and other students of Stumpf seemed poised to control the field in German universities before the rise of the Nazis.

However, the Nazis did come to power, and individuals such as Husserl suffered as a result. Whether we blame it on the Nazis or not, Brentano's system and its descendants faded from mainstream psychology, which turned to America, first to Titchener's structuralism and then to behaviorism. Both structuralism and behaviorism were steeped in the positivist and empirical traditions attacked by subsequent phenomenologists (e.g., Husserl). Remnants of Brentano's alternate vision for psychology can be found in Freud and in functionalism (Chapter 11), mostly in the form of active conceptions of mind, which contrast with the empirical behaviorists' view.

The legacy of men Boring (1950) called giants (e.g., Stumpf and Müller) remained alive in Gestalt psychology and phenomenology for decades and has recently been "rediscovered" by cognitive psychologists. In fact, modern-day cognitive science, with its central interest in memory and thinking, owes much to the efforts of not only the various phenomenologists but to Ebbinghaus as well. Although the non-Wundtians in this chapter may not have strongly influenced American psychology's history, they may still shape its future.

Despite our having flagged Wundt as the "founder" of psychology, we are sensitive to the fact that during their day Brentano and Stumpf may have been seen as more "mature" psychologists. Both embodied a psychology built on the tradition of German rationalism, whereas Wundt's system was more "empirical." The phenomenologists in this chapter advocated an important point still lost on many contemporary psychologists—the primacy of perception. Consider the following: When a clinician gives a client a personality test, he or she is really measuring not personality but the perception of personality as reflected in the test used.

Kuhn (1970; Chapters 1 and 18) noted that history texts are usually written to justify current theories. With the rise of all things cognitive in modern psychology, you should not be surprised to see Wundt's legacy continue to be downplayed and his contemporaries continue to be "rediscovered." Does this change represent progress in our ability to capture the past accurately, or does it just demonstrate the phenomenological point that our judgments are always tempered by our pre-existing cognitions and current perceptions (i.e., the presentist bias we introduced in Chapter 1).

SUMMARY

Psychological topics have interested individuals trained in physiology and medicine throughout history. Of the potential "founders" of psychology, all were philosophers and almost all were trained in physiology. Wilhelm Wundt, credited with founding scientific psychology through the establishment of his laboratory at Leipzig in 1879, applied the methods of physiology to philosophical problems.

Wilhelm Maximilian Wundt and Voluntarism

In 1873 and 1874, Wundt published *Principles of Physiological Psychology,* in which it was evident he was seeking to create a new science. From the beginning of his Leipzig laboratory in 1879, Wundt eventually supervised 186 doctoral dissertations. So rapidly did his experimental psychology create new results that in 1881 Wundt started the journal *Philosophical Studies.*

Wundt distinguished between the immediate experience of a stimulus, which provides the data for psychology, and mediate experience, which provides data for physics and other natural sciences. Wundt saw the need for two psychologies: one to study the lower mental processes experimentally and another to study the products of the higher mental functions. Wundt treated his physiological (experimental) psychology as a natural science, whereas he conceived his indirect study of the higher mental processes as a cultural or mental science. Wundt's work in experimental psychology is better known than the *Völkerpsychologie,* his study of culture and language.

Wundt believed that the basic elements of consciousness were sensations and feelings and that subjects could be trained to report their internal perceptions. Other Wundt experimental techniques included the recording of reaction times and the method of expression, in which recording devices assessed the subject's physiological changes.

Most of the studies done in Wundt's laboratory concerned sensation and perception, reaction times, feelings, and attention. For Wundt, the focusing of attention in apperception involved an act of will, and he used the term *voluntarism* to describe his system of psychology.

Based on his own internal perceptions, Wundt developed a three-dimensional theory of feelings. Using the method of expression, Wundt tried to relate the dimensions to specific physiological responses.

Influenced by Titchener, E. G. Boring contributed, along with American behaviorism, to an overly narrow conception of Wundt. In recent years, we have discovered that much of the misinformation about Wundt came from confusing him with Titchener. In addition, Wundt was opposed to a reductionistic approach based on positivism. When behaviorism, by way of positivism, gained ascendancy in psychology, Wundt's contribution was seen as unimportant. With behaviorism's declining influence and the growing importance of cognitive psychology, Wundt has been favorably reappraised. For developing the first laboratory of experimental psychology and training many of the first generation of psychologists, Wundt is honored as the founder of psychology as a separate scientific discipline.

Edward Bradford Titchener and Structuralism

Edward Bradford Titchener was an Oxford-educated Englishman who studied with Wundt for 2 years at Leipzig. For Titchener, psychology was the science of the generalized, normal, human, adult mind, and he spent much of his career cataloging the elements (or structure) of consciousness. Unlike Wundt, Titchener did not distinguish between immediate and mediate experience, a distinction Titchener thought prevented psychology from being wholly a natural science. By insisting on only one kind of experience, viewed from different perspectives, Titchener made psychology a natural science. Describing an experience from the wrong perspective led to the stimulus error, which for Titchener involved describing the stimulus itself rather than reporting the sensations or feelings the stimulus produced.

Using an analytical introspection, Titchener sought to reduce experience to its most basic elements: sensations, images, and feelings. Titchener found more than 44,000 different sensations. For him, images were the elements of ideas, and feelings were the elements of the emotions. Titchener reduced Wundt's three-dimensional theory of feelings to pleasantness-unpleasantness.

The basic elements have the attributes of quality, intensity, duration, clearness, and extent. Quality allows us to differentiate sensations, and intensity describes the strength of an experience. Duration is how long an experience lasts, and clearness indicates how much an experience stands out from its background. Extent gives an experience spatial dimension. For Titchener, attention was equated with clearness, and meaning is something we attribute to our experiences based on context. By 1923, Titchener was ready to abandon the three basic elements of consciousness for attributive dimensions, and he initiated a phenomenological approach to the study of consciousness.

Titchener brought a strict, empirical, experimental approach to American psychology, and his structuralism gave other approaches a convenient target. Titchener's style invited controversy. One of his controversies was over imageless thought, and another controversy with James Mark Baldwin served to isolate Titchener further in America.

Titchener's influence was felt through the large number of Ph.D. students he trained. With Titchener's death, structuralism dwindled rapidly in importance.

Franz Brentano and Act Psychology

Franz Brentano's most important work for psychology was *Psychology From an Empirical Standpoint* (1874). Brentano's psychology was empirical in the sense of being based on experience.

Brentano's psychology was an act psychology, where acts are psychic phenomena falling into three broad categories: presentation (or ideating); judging; and desire, loving, and hating. Brentano's method included indirect inner perception, the observation of past mental phenomena in memory, and "objective observation," in which others are studied through their speech, autobiographies, and voluntary acts.

Brentano was important in establishing intentionality as a central issue for the philosophy of mind and through his influence on such students as Christian von Ehrenfels, Alexius Meinong, Carl Stumpf, Edmund Husserl, and Sigmund Freud. Stumpf, Husserl, Külpe, the Gestaltists, and such functionalists as Freud and James all found in Brentano's act psychology an attractive alternative to Wundt's experimental psychology.

Carl Stumpf

Carl Stumpf studied under Brentano and then Lotze. In 1875, he began work that combined his interests in psychology and music, which culminated in *Tone Psychology.*

Stumpf classified experience into phenomena and functions. Phenomena were such things as tones and colors, and Stumpf called their study "phenomenology." Stumpf's functions were Brentano's acts, and although he considered study of the functions to be the foundation of psychology, Stumpf devoted most of his career to investigating phenomena, which he considered preparatory to psychology. Stumpf's greatest influence came through the students who made his phenomenology the basis for Gestalt psychology: Koffka, Köhler, and Lewin.

Edmund Husserl

Edmund Husserl was a respected logician and philosopher whose phenomenology was the most detailed and eventually the most accepted of the "phenomenologies." Husserl's phenomenology was defined as the science of examining the data of conscious experience, and he considered phenomenology a science separate from psychology and preparatory to it. Husserl's approach examines the structure and content of conscious experience through a series of steps, which include description and *Wesensschau*—the cognition of essence.

Husserl criticized positivism and the mechanistic psychologies that endorsed it, and his influence extended to subsequent "phenomenological" approaches to psychology, including the Gestalt school and the Würzburg school. Similarly, he influenced existential-phenomenological philosophers and psychologists such as Martin Heidegger and Maurice Merleau-Ponty.

Hermann Ebbinghaus

Fechner's *Elements of Psychophysics* inspired Hermann Ebbinghaus to use Fechner's psychophysical methods to study the higher mental function of memory. In 1885, Ebbinghaus published his memory research in *Concerning Memory.*

To simplify the learning of verbal material, Ebbinghaus invented nonsense material, from which he constructed lists. Ebbinghaus found that the more time he spent practicing a list originally, the less time it took to relearn it later. He also found that overlearning was important for retention and that there is a large drop in retention soon after learning that is followed by a more gradual decline thereafter. In addition, Ebbinghaus found that distributed practice was superior to massed practice, and he anticipated modern discussions of short-term memory span by observing that he could remember a maximum of seven syllables after a single reading.

Ebbinghaus's memory research showed it was possible to study a higher mental function experimentally and produced many findings still considered valid. The *Zeitschrift für Psychologie* and the "Ebbinghaus completion method" were further significant contributions to psychology.

Georg Elias Müller

Georg Elias Müller's first experimental efforts gave him the leadership of psychophysics after Fechner's death. Following Ebbinghaus's lead, Müller began research on human memory. From these studies, Müller and Alfons Pilzecker developed the interference theory of forgetting, which says that new learning can interfere with the memory of material learned earlier. Müller also produced a theory of color vision that included Hering's theory. Müller was second only to Wundt as an institution in the early days of psychology.

Oswald Külpe

Oswald Külpe developed the Würzburg school, whose major method was systematic experimental introspection, in which subjects performed a task involving higher mental processes and were then asked to report their mental experiences during the task. Working at Würzburg, Karl Marbe attributed subjects' weight judgments to "conscious attitudes." Henry Watt found that partially restricted associations to stimulus words were made without conscious effort, because the task created a set to respond. Narziss Ach also showed the importance of the determining tendency and uncovered a conscious element that led to the imageless thought controversy with Wundt and Titchener. The controversy undermined confidence in introspection, and Külpe's research program showed it was possible to study higher mental processes experimentally.

CONNECTIONS QUESTIONS

1. What are the connections between Wundt and Titchener?
2. Given the differences in the systems of Wundt and Titchener, why was Titchener's structuralism considered to be just an Americanized version of voluntarism for half a century?
3. What evidence would you cite to support the claim that Wundt was the founder of scientific psychology?
4. Compare and contrast Brentano's psychology with Wundt's. List and discuss as many differences as you can.
5. In what ways did Külpe extend experimental psychology beyond the limits imposed on it by Wundt?
6. Compare and contrast the phenomenologies of Husserl and Stumpf.
7. Compare and contrast Wundt's and Brentano's *innere Wahrnehmung*. How would Brentano and Wundt have approached the study of the phenomenon of anger?

KEY NAMES AND TERMS

Narziss Ach (p. 220)
act psychology (p. 203)
acts (p. 203)
apperception (p. 188)
attention (p. 198)
attributes (p. 198)
Franz Clemens Brentano (p. 202)
William Lowe Bryan (p. 213)
creative synthesis (p. 188)
CVC trigram (p. 213)
Karl Dallenbach (p. 195)
description (p. 210)
determining tendency (p. 220)
distributed practice (p. 215)
Hermann Ebbinghaus (p. 211)
Christian von Ehrenfels (p. 205)
The Experimentalists (p. 195)
fractionating (p. 220)
Erich von Hornbostel (p. 207)
Edmund Gustav Albrecht Husserl (p. 208)
imageless thought (p. 201)
immediate experience (p. 185)
intentionality (p. 204)
interference theory of forgetting (p. 217)
internal perception (p. 185)
Erich R. Jaensch (p. 217)
Charles H. Judd (p. 190)
David Katz (p. 217)
Arthur König (p. 212)
Emil Kraepelin (p. 188)
Oswald Külpe (p. 218)
Ludwig Lange (p. 187)
Theodor Lipps (p. 190)
Karl Marbe (p. 220)
Lillien Jane Martin (p. 218)
massed practice (p. 215)
meaning (p. 198)
mediate experience (p. 185)
Alexius Meinong (p. 205)
memory drum (p. 217)
mental chronometry (p. 186)
method of expression (p. 189)
Ernst Meumann (p. 194)
Georg Elias Müller (p. 216)
nonsense syllable (p. 213)
overlearning (p. 214)
Celestia Suzannah Parrish (p. 195)
phenomenology (p. 209)
retroactive inhibition (p. 217)
Edgar Rubin (p. 217)
Friedrich Schumann (p. 217)
Edward W. Scripture (p. 190)
Carl Emil Seashore (p. 208)
stimulus error (p. 197)
George Stratton (p. 191)
structuralism (p. 199)
Carl Stumpf (p. 206)
systematic experimental introspection (p. 219)
Edward Bradford Titchener (p. 193)
Völkerpsychologie (p. 189)
voluntarism (p. 188)
Howard C. Warren (p. 194)
Margaret Floy Washburn (p. 200)
Henry Jackson Watt (p. 220)
Wesensschau (p. 210)
Lightner Witmer (p. 190)
Wilhelm Maximilian Wundt (p. 181)
Würzburg school (p. 219)

SUGGESTED READINGS

Blumenthal, A. L. (1975). A reappraisal of Wilhelm Wundt. *American Psychologist, 30,* 1081–1088.

Bringmann, W. G., Balance, W. D. G., & Evans, R. B. (1975). Wilhelm Wundt 1832–1920: A brief biographical sketch. *Journal of the History of the Behavioral Sciences, 11,* 287–297.

Leahey, T. H. (1981). The mistaken mirror: On Wundt and Titchener's psychologies. *Journal of the History of the Behavioral Sciences, 17,* 273–282. In recent years, there has been a "rediscovery" of Wilhelm Wundt and a reappraisal of his contributions. These articles will help you see psychology's "founding father" in this modern light. Leahey's article will help you understand the similarities and differences between Titchener and Wundt.

Baldwin, B. T. (Ed.) (1921). In memory of Wilhelm Wundt: By his American students. *Psychological Review, 28,* 153–188. This is a highly readable appreciation of Wundt written by several of his American students and visitors, including Titchener, Hall, Cattell, Frank Angell, and Bird T. Baldwin.

Boring, E. G. (1927). Edward Bradford Titchener: 1867–1927. *American Journal of Psychology, 38,* 488–506. Written by arguably his most famous student, this obituary of Titchener must be read by anyone interested in learning more about the man.

Danziger, K. (1980). The history of introspection reconsidered. *Journal of the History of the Behavioral Sciences, 16,* 241–262. Danziger's article traces the history of the use of introspection to explore the conscious mind. One particularly important focus is on the differences in the methods used by Wundt and Titchener, even though both are often uncritically called introspection.

Dreyfus, H. (1982). *Husserl, intentionality, and cognitive science.* Cambridge, MA: MIT Press. This is a fine collection of essays on Husserl and his connection to modern-day cognitive psychology and the philosophy of mind.

Ebbinghaus, H. (1964). *Memory: A contribution to experimental psychology.* New York: Dover. (Original work published 1885; translated 1913) Widely available, this slender book is must reading for anyone interested in the study of memory. Remembering that the research that led to this work was almost completely novel will help you appreciate Ebbinghaus's genius.

Lewin, K. (1937). Carl Stumpf. *Psychological Review, 44,* 188–194. Obituaries are often excellent sources of information about historical figures, and this is no exception. Lewin, as we will see, is an important historical figure in his own right.

Ogden, R. M. (1951). Oswald Külpe and the Würzburg school. *American Journal of Psychology, 64,* 4–19. Written by one of his doctoral students, this paper is an excellent overview of Külpe and the research of the Würzburg school.

Rancurello, A. C. (1968). *A study of Franz Brentano: His psychological standpoint and his significance in the history of psychology.* New York: Academic Press. This is an excellent monograph on a pivotal figure in the history of psychology.

Shakow, D. (1930). Hermann Ebbinghaus. *American Journal of Psychology, 17,* 504–518. Shakow's article is almost always cited in any treatment of Ebbinghaus—with good reason.

Stumpf, C. (1930). Carl Stumpf. In C. Murchison (Ed.), *A history of psychology in autobiography* (Vol. 1, pp. 389–441). Worcester, MA: Clark University Press. Any in-depth study of Stumpf should begin with his remarkably readable and candid autobiography.

Titchener, E. B. (1910). *A text-book of psychology.* New York: Macmillan. This book provides a readable overview of Titchener's psychological system.

Wundt, W. (1904). *Principles of physiological psychology* (5th ed.; Vol. 1; E. B. Titchener, Trans.). New York: Macmillan. (Original work published 1902). Translated by Titchener, this book provides an overview of the scientific psychology created by Wundt. Excerpts are often included in anthologies of readings in the history of psychology (e.g., Dennis, 1948).

Darwin's Influence

CHAPTER 9

Charles Darwin

Charles Lyell

Erasmus Darwin

Alphonse de Candolle

Thomas Malthus

Jean-Baptiste Lamarck

1700 1720 1740 1760 1780 1800 1820

Declaration of Independence is signed

Military steamships are built

University of Pennsylvania is founded

North and South Carolina become English Crown colonies

Count Allesandro Volta produces the battery

OUTLINE

Pre-Darwinian Evolution
- Herbert Spencer

Charles Robert Darwin
- *The Origin of Species*
- *The Descent of Man*
- *The Expression of the Emotions in Man and Animals*
- Darwin's Influence

Francis Galton
- *Hereditary Genius*
- Galton's "Intelligence" Tests
- Correlation and Regression
- Other Contributions to Psychology
- Galton's Influence

Conclusions

Francis Galton

Alfred Russel Wallace

Herbert Spencer

Thomas Henry Huxley

Karl Pearson

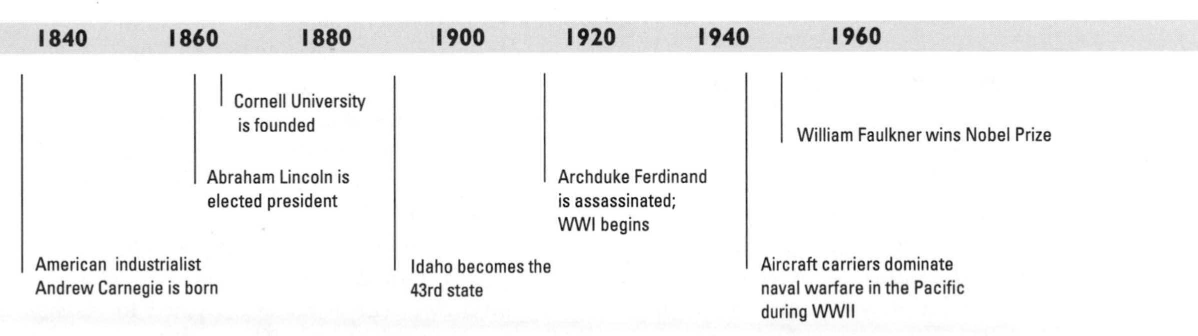

In Chapter 8, we examined Wundt's initiation of psychology as a separate science and reviewed Titchener's version of Wundt's system. Titchener's structuralism never achieved dominance in America, despite Titchener's efforts and the large number of psychologists he trained. More viable was the psychology of function to which Titchener compared his psychology of structure (Titchener, 1898). Instead of having Titchener's concern with identifying the mind's elements, many of America's first psychological theorists (e.g., William James, G. Stanley Hall, John Dewey) were more interested in the mind's functions. In large part, this interest in function had been stimulated by the concept of evolution, which gained scientific acceptance through Charles Darwin's efforts.

In Chapter 8, we saw that phenomenology was a major part of the 19th century's intellectual milieu. Evolution was another major part of that *Zeitgeist* and will be the primary theme of this chapter. Organic evolution, in which structures or systems change in response to external pressures, was important for psychology in many ways. For example, the evolution of consciousness as an aid to adaptation makes the study of the mind relevant. In addition, evolutionary theory requires variability within a species, suggesting the investigation of individual differences, which Darwin's cousin, Francis Galton (discussed later), pursued with vigor. Finally, evolution puts humans in the animal kingdom, thus legitimizing the study of animal behavior (comparative psychology and ethology) as a way to learn about human nature.

Although we tend to think of Charles Darwin as the discoverer of the concept of evolution, Darwin was definitely a product of his age. Other scientists, some of whom we have already mentioned, were important antecedents of Darwin.

PRE-DARWINIAN EVOLUTION

We suggested in Chapter 2 that a concept of evolution first appeared with the ancient Greeks (e.g., Aristotle, Heraclitus). In Chapters 5 and 6, we encountered three early contributors to the evolutionary *Zeitgeist* of the 19th century—Comte, Hegel, and Goethe. An idea of evolution was central to the philosophies of Comte and Hegel. For Goethe—author, philosopher, and scientist—there was a fascination with the metamorphosis of parts. From careful observation of plants, Goethe concluded that different plant forms can be established by the modification of one part into another, and he extended this principle to the animal kingdom.

Erasmus Darwin (1721–1802), Charles Darwin's grandfather by his first wife, and Francis Galton's grandfather by his second wife, reached similar conclusions independently of Goethe about the transmutation (change) of species. A popular physician known for his free-thinking opinions, his poetry, his botanical garden, and his mechanical inventions, Darwin saw evidence for the mutability of species in changes that occur during embryonic development, in changes following domestication and hybridization, and in the similar structural plan of vertebrates. Darwin speculated that change in species occurs through adaptations to the environment that result from the struggle for survival, and that many of these adaptations are transmitted to descendants. He set his ideas to verse, which weakened their power by making them seem less scientific than they might have seemed in prose.

The French naturalist **Jean-Baptiste Lamarck** (1744–1829) was another important pre-Darwinian evolutionist. The descendant of an impoverished noble family, Lamarck joined the French army at 17 and became interested in Mediterranean plants as a soldier, publishing in 1778 *Flore Français* (*French Flowers*). Lamarck resigned from the military after an injury and became a clerk in a Paris bank, using his income to study medicine and botany.

For a time, Lamarck tutored the sons of the **Comte de Buffon** (1707–1788), a famous French naturalist. Buffon theorized the earth was much older than the biblical account indicates, and his writings also foreshadowed a theory of evolution. At Buffon's death, Lamarck became keeper of the herbarium in the *Jardin du Roi* (the royal botanical gardens in Paris). With the French Revolution in 1789, the designation "*du Roi*" (of the King) fell from favor, and Lamarck's suggestion to rename the garden the *Jardin des Plantes* (Garden of Plants) was accepted.

Lamarck's interest moved from plants to animals and especially animals without backbones, which he called *invertébrés* (invertebrates). Asked to classify

Wellcome Library, London.

Jean-Baptiste Lamarck (1744–1829)

animal collections in the Paris Museum of Natural History, Lamarck was struck by the similarities in closely related species. Perhaps if enough closely related species were studied together, the differences between them would be undetectable. Although not exactly true, the idea led Lamarck to develop a theory of evolution in which there was the descent of species from other species over long time periods.

According to Lamarck, two factors accounted for evolution. The first was a supposed tendency in organisms toward perfection and increased complexity, a concept Lamarck considered so self-evident it required no proof. Because of this factor, Lamarck believed that simple organisms must have arisen recently by spontaneous generation; if they had arisen earlier, they would be more perfect and complex.

Lamarck's second factor was intended to account for the deviations in a perfect ordering of organisms from the lowliest at the bottom to humans at the top. The anomalies must reflect environmental interference. As he wrote in *Philosophie Zoologique* (*Zoological Philosophy*),

> Every considerable alteration in the local circumstances in which each race of animals exists causes a change in their wants, and these new wants excite them to new actions and habits. These actions require the more frequent [use] of some parts before but slightly exercised, and then greater development follows as a consequence of their more frequent use. Other organs no longer in use are impoverished and diminished in size, nay, are sometimes entirely annihilated, while in their place new parts are insensibly produced for the discharge of new functions. (Lamarck, 1809/1914, p. 234)

These acquired alterations are then passed on to offspring.

Lamarckism has been distilled into "the inheritance of acquired characteristics," as if an animal whose tail has been amputated should produce tailless progeny. But this phrase is a disservice to Lamarck, because it implies more than he intended. Lamarck stressed the transformation of body parts through the animal's efforts to adapt to its environment, with the subsequent inheritance of these changes. The heritable changes are wrought by an organism's internal need and effort, not by something imposed externally.

> It is, however, only fair to say that Lamarck has been treated with less than justice by history, for his name is associated with a hypothetic cause of evolution that he did not invent and that is unacceptable, whereas it was his genius in proposing a scheme of evolution that deserves commemoration in the term Lamarckism. (Sir Gavin de Beer; cited in Appleman, 1979, p. 5)

At the end of his life, Lamarck became blind and nearly destitute. "His life was a tribute to his courage, and his old age was a disgrace to his government" (Durant & Durant, 1975, p. 328).

French naturalist George Cuvier (mentioned in Chapter 7), a believer in the biblical account of creation, vigorously opposed Lamarck's view of the mutability of the species. The weight of Cuvier's opinion effectively prevented wide acceptance of Lamarck's ideas, much as Flourens's stature inhibited the search for and belief in the localization of function espoused by Gall and phrenology (Chapter 7).

However, at least one important evolutionist embraced Lamarckism—Herbert Spencer.

Herbert Spencer

Herbert Spencer (1820–1903) was born in Derby, an industrial town in central England. He was intermittently educated by an uncle and by his father, a schoolmaster, and this nontraditional education was perhaps responsible for Spencer's tendency to champion unorthodox beliefs and to form strong opinions without careful study.

After 10 years spent employed by small railway companies, in 1848 Spencer went to London to work as a journalist. There, he acquired friends that included writer George Henry Lewes, novelist Mary Ann Evans (better known as George Eliot), and **Thomas Henry Huxley** (1825–1895), a biologist who became one of Darwin's chief defenders. Huxley's relatives included Aldous Huxley (1894–1963), the author of *Brave New World* (1932), Sir Julian Huxley (1887–1975), biologist and humanist, and Sir Andrew Fielding Huxley (1917–), a co-winner of the 1963 Nobel Prize for physiology or medicine.

National Library of Medicine, Washington, D.C.

Herbert Spencer (1820–1903) at about the age at which he wrote *The Principles of Psychology*

Spencer's interest in evolution began in 1839 when a reading of **Sir Charles Lyell**'s (1797–1875) criticism of Lamarck in *Principles of Geology* paradoxically convinced Spencer of Lamarck's validity. In *The Principles of Psychology* (1855), Spencer detailed an evolutionary doctrine that anticipated Darwin's *The Origin of Species* (1859). Note that Spencer's *Principles* antedated by nearly 25 years the establishment of Wundt's laboratory at Leipzig. However, Spencer's views on evolution had little impact in the 1850s because they were based on Lamarckism, which was already familiar, and Spencer himself initially had little credibility with the scientific community because of his lack of training in science. Later acceptance of Darwin's work also resulted in greater acceptance of Spencer's more general ideas, as scientists and nonscientists alike became interested in reading about evolution.

Inspired by Darwin's publication of *The Origin of Species,* by the early 1860s Spencer had decided he would produce a comprehensive philosophy of science based on evolutionary concepts. Similar to Comte's ambitious enterprise, Spencer's **synthetic philosophy** aimed at examining the problems of sociology, psychology, biology, education, and ethics from the standpoint of evolution, in which an indefinite homogeneity becomes a differentiated heterogeneity.

Through funds generated from a syllabus sent to prospective subscribers and frugal living, Spencer produced 10 volumes of *The System of Synthetic Philosophy.* His work on psychology for the synthetic philosophy was actually the revision of his 1855 *Principles,* which encompassed two volumes published in 1870 and 1872. These works "were largely dictated on a boat, in between vigorous bouts of rowing on a lake in a London park" (Boakes, 1984, p. 12).

In Spencer's revised *Principles of Psychology,* the key concept for us is his **evolutionary associationism.** To Alexander Bain's (Chapter 5) development of voluntary behavior through the action of pleasurable or unpleasurable events, Spencer added a Lamarckian tendency for frequently made associations to be passed on to future generations. Thus, Bain's account of the development of voluntary behavior became known as the **Spencer-Bain principle.** Spencer saw his evolutionary associationism operating phylogenetically: Simple creatures respond in simple, undifferentiated ways to gross stimuli, their behavior analogous to reflex actions in higher organisms. On a higher level, instinct is "compound reflex action," capable of mediating an organism's response to more complex and differentiated conditions. Memory and cognition arise from instincts, and we see Spencer's evolutionary hierarchy of mental states.

Although there was little direct response to his 1855 *Principles,* by 1870 Spencer had a considerable reputation, particularly in America. His teleological approach to evolution—the idea that evolution has a final purpose toward which change is heading and that evolutionary change is always progressing—found favor with American functional psychology. American business particularly liked **social Darwinism,** which was the notion that societies and their institutions evolve like species and that the **survival of the fittest**—Spencer's phrase, not Darwin's—is morally justified. Because social Darwinism suggests progress will be maximized when free enterprise prevails, American capitalists applauded Spencer.

Reviews of Spencer's work were often mixed. About him, Darwin wrote in his autobiography, edited by his granddaughter, Nora Barlow:

> After reading any of his books, I generally feel enthusiastic admiration for his transcendent talents, and have often wondered whether in the distant future he would rank with such great men as Descartes, Leibnitz, etc., about whom, however, I know very little. Nevertheless I am not conscious of having profited in my own work by Spencer's writings. (Barlow, 1958, pp. 108–109)

William James (Chapter 10) used Spencer's *Principles of Psychology* as his text in 1876 in the first course in America on the new physiological (experimental) psychology and cited Spencer extensively in his own *Principles of Psychology* (James, 1890). However, James was also sometimes critical of Spencer's abilities (e.g., Boring, 1950).

Almost universally recognized as a brilliant thinker, Spencer was interested in discovering the relations between facts. By contrast, Darwin was a great observer, a man of dazzling insight, and one of functionalism's most important antecedents.

CHARLES ROBERT DARWIN

Charles Robert Darwin (1809–1882) was the son of Robert Darwin, a wealthy physician, and Susannah Wedgwood Darwin, the granddaughter of Josiah Wedgwood, the famous potter. As noted, Darwin's paternal grandfather was Erasmus Darwin, a distinguished thinker in his own right. Darwin was born in Shrewsbury, England, on February 12, 1809, the same day as Abraham Lincoln.

Darwin was an indifferent student who seemed fated not to fulfill the destiny of his heritage. After grammar school at Shrewsbury, Darwin went to medical school at the University of Edinburgh, where he found the lectures dull and the clinical experiences horrifying. Darwin wrote to a sister about one of the lecturers, "Dr. Duncan is so very learned that his wisdom has left no room for his sense, & he lectures . . . on the Materia Medica, which cannot be translated into any word expressive enough of its stupidity" (Burkhardt, 1996, p. 2).

After Darwin's failure to become a physician, his father decided a vocation in the church might prove more congenial. When Darwin acquiesced, he was dispatched to Cambridge, where he soon formed friendships with the Reverends Adam Sedgwick (1785–1873) and John Stevens Henslow (1796–1861). Darwin accompanied Cambridge professor of geology Sedgwick on a geological tour of north Wales after his graduation in 1831. As an indication of intellectual ability masked by his relatively average academic record, Darwin ranked 10th out of 168 on his examination for the B.A. degree (Burkhardt, 1996).

Botany professor Henslow encouraged Darwin's interest in zoology and geology, and the two men often walked the town together. At this point, Darwin saw his future in his friend: "More than anyone, Henslow was the kind of man he yearned to be—a clerical naturalist or professor—the sort that even [his father] might approve of" (Desmond & Moore, 1991, p. 89). Fate had other plans for Darwin, however: Henslow recommended that he accompany **Captain**

Drawing from Down House titled
HMS Beagle in the Strait of Magellan

Robert FitzRoy (1805–1865) on the HMS *Beagle*'s planned 2-year surveying voyage of South America. FitzRoy was looking for a "gentleman" to share his table and to give him someone other than the crew to talk to. If the gentleman happened to be a naturalist, there would be opportunity aplenty on the trip.

After an uncle convinced Darwin's father of the trip's benefits, it became a matter of convincing FitzRoy that Darwin was right for the position. However, FitzRoy believed in physiognomy, the notion that a person's character can be deduced from facial features, "and [FitzRoy] doubted whether anyone with [Darwin's] nose could possess sufficient energy and determination for the voyage. But I think he was afterwards well-satisfied that my nose had spoken falsely" (Barlow, 1958, p. 72). Darwin's amiability won over FitzRoy, who, ironically, saw the voyage as

> a grand opportunity to substantiate the Bible, especially the book of Genesis. As a naturalist, Darwin might easily find many evidences of the Flood and the first appearance of all created things upon the earth. He could perform a valuable service by interpreting his scientific discoveries in the light of the Bible. (Moorehead, 1969, p. 37)

Note that Darwin himself was earnestly religious at the beginning of the voyage, often "quoting the Bible as an unanswerable authority on some point of morality" (Barlow, p. 85).

For Darwin, the trip was the experience of a lifetime, although he suffered from seasickness throughout. Not long into the voyage, Darwin read the first volume of Lyell's *Principles of Geology*. Lyell advocated a controversial geological theory called uniformitarianism, which holds that the earth's major features are the result of observable processes that have operated in a uniform manner from the beginning of the earth until the present. In Chile, Darwin experienced an earthquake, which convinced him Lyell was correct: The earth is far older than the biblical account suggests, and its shaping processes are still occurring. Lyell and uniformitarianism encouraged Darwin to think in the lengthy time frames required by a gradual process of change.

In addition, the *Beagle*'s frequent landings gave Darwin opportunities to explore exotic animal and plant species. As a passionate collector from an early age, he "seemed . . . intent on putting the South American continent into specimen bottles" (Irvine, 1955, p. 47).

In the Galápagos Islands, Darwin found striking evidence for the changeability of species. Some 500 miles off the northwestern coast of South America, the Galápagos Islands lie on the equator and are home to species found nowhere else on earth. *Galápagos* is Spanish for "giant tortoise," one of the island chain's more well-known inhabitants, and Darwin discovered that each island contained its own tortoise variety. A local Englishman told him that he could tell at a glance which island a particular tortoise came from by the design of its shell.

Even more striking were the varieties of finches. Finches on one island had thick, strong beaks for cracking nuts, finches on another island had smaller beaks designed to catch insects, and so on. Apparently the finches on a particular island, separated by miles of ocean from other finches, had changed to fit the requirements of the island they inhabited. Although Darwin did not immediately recognize all the implications of what he had observed on the Galápagos Islands, his ideas about the immutability of species were undermined by his observations. Incidentally, as crucial as the finches may have been to Darwin's thinking about evolution, they are not mentioned explicitly in *The Origin of Species* (Hayes, 1993).

Arriving home in 1836, Darwin found he was already well regarded in scientific circles. The specimens he had shipped back had been well received, and Henslow had taken the liberty of publishing geological excerpts from Darwin's letters. In short order, Darwin became a fellow of the Royal Geological and Zoological Societies and began editing for publication the journal of his experiences on the voyage. He also found time in 1839 to marry his cousin, Emma Wedgwood (1808–1896). Finding London too exhausting, in 1842 the Darwins moved to Down House near the village of Downe.

Convinced of the mutability of species, in October 1838 Darwin read "for amusement" **Thomas Malthus**'s 1798 *Essay on the Principle of Population.* In it, Malthus (1766–1834), an economist and clergyman, discussed the tendency of the human population to increase faster than the means to support it. The result is a population suppressed by famine, disease, and war.

From his studies of the selective breeding of animal species, Darwin had already grasped the idea of selection. Obviously, humans select domestic animals for particular qualities. Malthus's essay suggested that nature selects by breeding an oversupply of a species and then killing off individuals whose characteristics fail to match the needs of their environments. Animals better adapted to the environment are more likely to survive to procreate and pass on their superior characteristics. Given the lengthy time frames Darwin had accepted from his reading of Lyell and his observations on the *Beagle,* extant species could have been drastically altered through a slow process of change.

Darwin did not rush to publish his theory of evolution, however. In fact, it was not until 1842 that he wrote a 35-page sketch. In 1844, Darwin expanded the sketch to 231 pages, which he gave to his wife with instructions on publishing it if he died. Considering Darwin's ill health, an early demise was distinctly possible.

Some historians wonder if Darwin's illness was a psychosomatic response to his theory's implications, or if it was the result of a then-undiagnosed malady he had caught on the *Beagle*'s voyage. The leading candidate for a "real" illness is Chagas disease, something Darwin might have contracted from handling the South American Benchuga bug. Darwin's symptoms included weakness, fatigue, headache, and insomnia, and as he grew older, any change from a set routine proved disastrous. His routine included 3 hours of scientific work (8 to 9:30 A.M. and 10:30 to noon), walking, resting, thinking, answering letters, and long hours of reading.

Although he had communicated his ideas to his closest friends, by the mid-1850s Darwin had still not published a paper on evolution. Lyell urged him to publish at least a brief account of his theory, which Lyell did not fully accept, to establish priority. Botanist **Joseph Hooker** (1817–1911) advised Darwin instead to publish an authoritative treatise, and Darwin was working on this project when he received the now-famous letter and essay in 1858 from **Alfred Russel Wallace** (1823–1913). As we saw in Chapter 1, Wallace's theory, developed in some 3 years, was similar to the one on which Darwin had been laboring for decades. Like Darwin, Wallace had read Malthus and had had the same insight about natural selection (Raby, 2001). Gruber and Wallace (2001) have argued, however, that Wallace's work was not completely independent of Darwin's, as the two had communicated, and also that Wallace differed fundamentally from Darwin on some matters, such as his failure to accept the human mind's evolution.

Darwin's immediate reaction was to have Wallace's paper published and to give him credit for the discovery, but Lyell and Hooker rejected this idea, believing Darwin should have priority. After an agonizing exchange of letters with Lyell and Hooker, Darwin, in despair at the death of one of his children, left the problem to his friends. Their solution was to have Wallace's paper read at the next meeting of the Linnean Society along with a paper by Darwin. To ensure that Darwin got the appropriate credit, his paper was accompanied by "a copy of Darwin's letter to Asa Gray [describing natural selection in some detail], written the previous year, and a statement certifying that Hooker had known of Darwin's work fifteen years earlier" (Rachels, 1986, p. 23). Although Rachels contends that Darwin and his friends acted badly, Wallace was pleased with the turn of events and apparently never considered that he should have received priority over Darwin. In fact, he called one of the many books he wrote *Darwinism.* Wallace made several contributions to our understanding of evolution, and some of his thoughts on matters such as the evolution of the human brain and the intelligence of native peoples were more enlightened than Darwin's (Eiseley, 1961).

Two of the suggested causes for Darwin's lengthy wait to publish his theory are work on other publications and fear of the theory's social consequences. As Masterton (1998) put it, between 1842 and 1854, Darwin worked on projects that "seem[ed] calculated to postpone the publication of the theory of evolution" (p. 19). As for fear of the social consequences, "Darwin was frightened by the prospect of excoriation for his unorthodox theory by the closely intertwined Christians and Tories. Even more distressing was the prospect of ostracism from the same Whig society that he and his family held dear" (p. 20).

Other suggested reasons are that Darwin needed time to accumulate supporting evidence and that he delayed because of what he considered a possibly fatal flaw in his theory (Richards, 1983). From Darwin's reading in the early 1840s, he knew that theologians were enthusiastic about one particular example from the animal kingdom that appeared to reveal God's hand—the instincts of worker bees and slave-making ants. If not for God's intervention, how else could the ants' ability to select the best servants be explained? What other explanation would apply to bees' ability to make perfectly hexagonal cells to house their larvae?

In the 1840s, Darwin's explanation for instinctive behavior was that—like anatomical structures—it evolved through natural selection. Unfortunately, this explanation appeared invalid for the neuter insects, who leave no offspring to inherit favorable variations. In fact, Darwin initially considered this an insurmountable problem, and he said as much in *The Origin of Species.* Thus, Darwin delayed until he felt he had resolved the issue. "Darwin came to recognize the solution to his difficulty [kin selection rather than selection at the individual level] and to flesh it out only in late December of 1857, as he wrote what would become the chapter on instinct in *The Origin of Species*" (Richards, 1983, p. 52). Darwin realized that evolution may have as its basic unit something bigger than the individual. That is, a kinship group such as a hive, a colony, or a family could be what was struggling to survive and propagate itself. As with earlier insights, Darwin's essentially correct understanding in the absence of a well-articulated genetic theory was remarkable.

Charles Darwin (1809–1882), at about the age at which he wrote *The Origin of Species*

Darwin and Wallace's joint papers to the Linnean Society in July 1858 attracted little attention. However, there was a decidedly different reaction to the publication in 1859 of *On the Origin of Species by Means of Natural Selection, or the Preservation of Favoured Races in the Struggle for Life.* The first edition's 1,250 printed copies sold out on the day of publication.

The reaction was predictably negative. Fortunately, Darwin had chosen his allies well. In addition to Lyell and Hooker, there was Thomas Huxley, Spencer's friend. Before the *Origin,* Huxley reacted to Darwin's ideas by giving up his belief in the biblical account of creation without fully accepting evolution. After reading *The Origin of Species,* his first reaction was to exclaim: "How extremely stupid not to have thought of that" (Irvine, 1955, p. 106). Huxley soon proved his mettle in the battle with the forces arrayed against Darwin.

In June 1860, the British Association for the Advancement of Science met at Oxford to debate

Darwin's evolutionary theory. The chief opponents were Bishop of Oxford Samuel Wilberforce (1805–1873), whose oratorical skills had earned him the nickname of "Soapy Sam," and Huxley and Hooker. As usual, Darwin was ill and did not attend. However, the attendance from Oxford undergraduates, clergy, and scientists and their wives was so great the meeting had to be moved from its usual venue.

After two days of meetings, Wilberforce began an oration against Darwinism that he unwisely punctuated with a jab at Huxley, demanding to know whether it was through his grandfather or his grandmother that he claimed to be descended from the apes. Huxley, speaking in an undertone, said, "The Lord hath delivered him into my hands." He then stood and

> announced that he would certainly prefer to be descended from an ape rather than from a cultivated man who prostituted the gifts of culture and eloquence to the service of prejudice and falsehood. The Bishop in short did not know what he was talking about. (Moorehead, 1969, p. 263)

Pandemonium ensued, and in its midst a slight, grey-haired man stood, waving a Bible. "Here was the truth, he cried, here and nowhere else. Long ago he had warned Darwin about his dangerous thoughts. Had he but known then that he was carrying in his ship such a . . ." (Moorehead, 1969, p. 266). It was Robert FitzRoy, the skipper of the *Beagle.* Less than 5 years later, financial and emotional problems drove him to suicide (Marks, 1991).

The Origin of Species

Although the book's main ideas came as a revelation to some and a threat to many, Darwin's most famous work is not exactly exciting. Instead, he marshals fact after fact to lead inevitably to the conclusion that species change over time in response to natural selection. Given the overabundance of life and the limited supply of essential ingredients to support it, any variation in a species that gives its possessor an advantage will increase the chances that the individual survives to breed and pass on the advantage.

Darwin's chapter on instinct—a term he used in several different ways (e.g., Beer, 1983)—is particularly important for psychology. In it, he treats behavior patterns the same way he treats bodily structure, as something inheritable. Behavior, even instinctual behavior, varies within a species. If an individual's behavior confers a reproductive advantage, then this too will be passed on to its offspring.

Given Darwin's evidence, it is difficult to imagine how a thoughtful person would not have reached the conclusion he expressed succinctly in the final chapter of *The Origin of Species:*

> That many and serious objections may be advanced against the theory of descent with modification through variation and natural selection, I do not deny. . . . Nothing at first can appear more difficult to believe than that the more complex organs and instincts have been perfected . . . by the accumulation of innumerable slight variations, each good for the individual possessor. Nevertheless, this difficulty, though appearing to our imagination insuperably great, cannot be considered real if we admit the following propositions, namely, that all parts of the organisation and instincts offer, at least, individual differences—that there is a struggle for existence leading to the preservation of profitable deviations of structure or instinct—and, lastly, that gradations in the state of perfection of each organ may have existed, each good of its kind. The truth of these propositions cannot, I think, be disputed. (Darwin, 1859/1958, p. 426)

But the truth of the propositions was, and sometimes still is, disputed, particularly by the nonscientific community. This illustrates that what is commonly accepted by scientists may be rejected or unknown to the majority of laypersons.

The Origin of Species did not mark the end of Darwin's career, and, in fact, two of his later books are of even more direct relevance for psychology. They are *The Descent of Man, and Selection in Relation to Sex* and *The Expression of the Emotions in Man and Animals.*

The Descent of Man

Near the end of *The Origin of Species,* Darwin wrote, "In the future . . . [m]uch light will be thrown on the origin of man and his history" (Darwin, 1859/1958, p. 449). In the first part of *The Descent of Man,* Darwin presented evidence that humans, like other species, had evolved from some "lower" form. He began by pointing to the similarity in structure between humans and the "higher" mammals:

> It is notorious that man is constructed on the same general type or model as other mammals. All the bones in his skeleton can be compared with corresponding bones in a monkey, bat, or seal. So it is with his muscles, nerves, blood-vessels, and internal viscera. The brain . . . follows the same law, as shown by Huxley and other anatomists. Bischoff, who is a hostile witness, admits that every chief fissure and fold in the brain of man has its analogy in that of the orang . . . (Darwin, 1874, p. 6)

The figure illustrates one of the many ways Darwin and his theory were lampooned in the contemporary press.

From March 22, 1871 issue of The Hornet.

Darwin as an orangutan, from the March 22, 1871, issue of the British publication *Hornet*

The structural similarity Darwin noted between the human brain and the orangutan brain points to a similarity in mental ability. He used innumerable examples of animal behavior to illustrate that animals exhibit the qualities typically attributed to humans: for example, jealousy, which illustrates that animals love and need to be loved; excitement and boredom; curiosity; imitation; memory; reason; sense of beauty; and so on. Darwin (1874) concluded, "the difference in mind between man and the higher animals, great as it is, certainly is one of degree and not of kind" (p. 143). For more on Darwin's views on human nature, see Alland's (1985) compilation drawn from Darwin's scattered writings.

Darwin's conclusion of continuity of mental ability in the animal kingdom sent his supporters, such as George Romanes (Chapter 12), to search for evidence of reasoning in animals. This was the context for the interest in animal geniuses like Clever Hans (Chapter 1). Another way to support the continuity was to search for animal origins of human behavior, and Darwin took this approach in his next work of importance for psychology.

The Expression of the Emotions in Man and Animals

In *The Descent of Man,* Darwin planned to include a chapter on emotions, but he set the chapter aside when it grew too large. The expanded chapter became *The Expression of the Emotions in Man and Animals* (1872). In the book, Darwin sought to demonstrate that human emotional expressions are inherited and have evolved because of their survival value.

Darwin used several methods for gathering information, including the observation of infants to see emotional expression at the earliest stage of life; the study of the expressions of the insane, because "they are liable to the strongest passions, and give uncontrolled vent to them" (Darwin, 1872/1979, p. 13); the study of cultural variations and similarities in emotional expression; and the examination of the emotional expressions in "some of the commoner animals." For information on the expressions of the insane, Darwin relied heavily on material he received from James Crichton Browne (1840–1938), a psychiatrist, amateur photographer, and the director of the West Riding Asylum (Gilman, 1979).

Darwin concluded that three principles account for most of the expressions used by humans and animals: the *principle of serviceable associated habits,* the *principle of antithesis,* and the *principle of the direct action of the nervous system.* According to the principle of serviceable associated habits, movements, facial expressions, and the like that have been long associated with some particular set of stimuli will tend to be performed when the associated stimuli are encountered, even though the movements are useless. Wrinkling the nose in a sneer in response to an offensive smell is an illustration.

The principle of antithesis is seen in the submissive posture of a dog who, moments before discovering that an intruder is its master, had bristled with hostility toward the approaching human. Instead of an upright posture with erected fur, bared fangs, and ears tight against the head, the dog now crouches with smooth fur, covered teeth, and formerly stiff tail wagging at its master's approach. The dog assumes postures that are the opposite (antithesis) of postures indicating hostility and aggressiveness.

Finally, there is the principle of the direct action of the nervous system. In highly aroused states, Darwin believed the "nerve-force" spills over to produce movements without functional benefit. For example, Darwin noted that either fear, anger, or joy might produce trembling. "I remember once seeing a boy who had just shot his first snipe on the wing, and his hands trembled to such a degree from delight, that he could not for some time reload his gun" (Darwin, 1872/1979, p. 67). In his autobiography, Darwin revealed he was the hunter (Barlow, 1958).

In *Expression of the Emotions,* Darwin devoted great effort to showing that human emotional expressions are similar in all humans, no matter what their culture or race. From this, he concluded that all races "descended from a single parent-stock, which must have been almost completely human in structure, and to a large extent in mind, before the period at which the races diverged from each other" (Darwin, 1872/1979, p. 361). In 1872, Darwin was still proselytizing, and in the book's last paragraph, he wrote:

> We have seen that the study of the theory of expression confirms to a certain limited extent the conclusion that man is derived from some lower animal form . . . but as far as my judgment serves, such confirmation was hardly needed. (p. 367)

Darwin's Influence

Although he has been called a genius,

> Darwin was the most unspectacular person of all time, a man known to his contemporaries as a quiet, methodical worker, devoted to his family, hard to prise out of his house in the country, averse to ostentation, utterly conventional in his behaviour, modest and unassuming about his results. (Browne, 1995, p. ix)

Yet, *The Origin of Species* changed forever our view of the world and the place of humans in it. No longer could we see a Cartesian split in the animal kingdom, with animals as automatons and humans as possessors of mind and reason. To an even greater degree, *The Descent of Man* made explicit the continuity between humans and animals, making the study of animals relevant for learning about humans. Darwin's encouragement of a young naturalist, George John Romanes, began comparative psychology, which was ably developed further by a committed Darwinian, C. Lloyd Morgan (Burghardt, 1985). The lives and work of Romanes and Morgan will be covered in Chapter 12.

Although behaviorism was not synonymous with animal psychology (Lyman-Henley & Henley, 2000), the study of animal behavior was a critical element in the development of the school, as we will also see in Chapter 12. In addition, behaviorism grew out of functionalism, and evolution was central to the psychology of function, the idea that abilities evolve because they play a part in their possessors' adaptation.

The "animal nature" of humans undoubtedly influenced Sigmund Freud (Chapter 15) and his conception of the id as a storehouse for biological drives. Interestingly, Darwin recognized his own tendency to use repression (motivated forgetting), a mechanism Freud saw as central to our attempts to keep ourselves from experiencing injurious self-revelations. In fact, Darwin attributed at least part of the success of *The Origin of Species* to his ability to *avoid* repression:

> I had . . . followed a golden rule, namely, that whenever a published fact, a new observation or thought came across me, which was opposed to my general results, to make a memorandum of it without fail and at once; for I had found by experience that such facts and thoughts were far

> more apt to escape from the memory than favourable ones. (Barlow, 1958, p. 123)

In 1877, Darwin published "Biographical sketch of an infant," which was based on his records of the early development of his first child. This important early paper in child development may have influenced Wilhelm Preyer (Chapter 11), whose 1882 book *Die Seele des Kindes* is sometimes considered the first work of modern child psychology (Fitzpatrick & Bringmann, 1997). Darwin suggested that the stages through which his son developed roughly approximated the stages through which humans may have proceeded in their evolution. For example, in language development the boy learned to connect names with important people or objects before inventing words for himself and stringing them together; Darwin wrote that this is what we might expect, because we know that some animals can learn to understand spoken words. And in developing locomotion, the boy first crawled (moved in a quadrupedal fashion) before learning to walk (moved bipedally), again illustrating the stages through which our ancestors may have evolved. The idea that an individual's development repeats in some fashion the development of the species ("ontogeny recapitulates phylogeny") was later popularized by the German naturalist and Darwinian **Ernst Haeckel** (1834–1919). The same idea was the key to G. Stanley Hall's developmental theories (Chapter 10).

Darwin's key contribution has to be his idea of evolution by natural selection, about which Dennett (1995) wrote:

> If I were to give an award for the single best idea anyone has ever had, I'd give it to Darwin, ahead of Newton and Einstein and everyone else. In a single stroke, the idea of evolution by natural selection unifies the realm of life, meaning, and purpose with the realm of space and time, cause and effect, mechanism and physical law. (p. 21)

According to Bowler (1990), Darwin's theory of natural selection was rejected in his own time even as the process of evolution was accepted. The Victorians preferred to believe in a progressionism, in which evolution had a purpose—the development of humans. Bowler noted that Darwin's open-ended selection theory has been revived in modern times, as the Dennett (1995) quote attests.

Darwin, for all his limitations, left behind an enormous amount of published work of high quality.

> The strongest proof of his greatness is that he—not Wallace, Huxley, nor anybody else—was the center of Darwinism. Despite his illnesses and his limitations, he had the largeness, sobriety, and concentration of mind to retain leadership within his own broad area of investigation. (Irvine, 1955, p. 73)

Darwin died at three o'clock on the morning of April 19, 1882. His family wanted him buried at Downe, but his friends and supporters had another idea: Because his country had not awarded him a knighthood (ironically, three of his sons were knighted), he would be canonized by burial in Westminster Abbey. With Huxley, Hooker, and Wallace among his pallbearers, Darwin was buried next to Sir Isaac Newton. Francis Galton "was sufficiently impressed [by Darwin's funeral] to urge in a letter to *The Pall Mall Gazette* that the old creation window [in Westminster Abbey] . . . be replaced by an evolutionary one in honor of his famous cousin" (Irvine, 1955, p. 229). Fittingly, long after Darwin died, one of his pallbearers was interred in the Abbey beside him—Alfred Russel Wallace (Marks, 1991).

FRANCIS GALTON

Of all the individuals affected by Darwin's theory of evolution, perhaps none was more influenced than Francis Galton. In response to a letter from Darwin giving his positive reaction to Galton's book, *Hereditary Genius* (1869), Galton penned the following:

> It would be idle to speak of the delight your letter has given me, as there is no one in the world whose approbation in these matters can have the same weight as yours. Neither is there any one whose approbation I prize more highly, . . . because I always think of you in the same way as converts from barbarism think of the teacher who first relieved them from the intollerable [*sic*] burden of their superstition. I used to be wretched under the weight of the old fashioned 'arguments [of Creation] from design', of which I felt though I was unable to

> prove it myself, the worthlessness. Consequently the appearance of your 'Origin of Species' formed a real crisis in my life; your book drove away the constraint of my old superstition as if it had been a nightmare and was the first to give me freedom of thought. (Galton, 1869; reproduced in Pearson, 1914–1930, Vol. 1, Plate II)

From his first reading of *The Origin of Species*, Galton's interest in the "natural history of human faculty" never diminished (McClearn, 1991). Galton, seeking to supply the evidence of human variability in mental and physical abilities required for human evolution, studied individual differences in contrast to the Continental studies of Fechner and Wundt, which aimed to discover the general principles of human nature. Studies of individual differences proved of paramount importance for American psychology. Galton's talents, experiences, and interests before 1859 prepared him admirably for his subsequent study of human abilities.

Francis Galton (1822–1911) was born in Birmingham, England, the ninth and youngest child in an upper-class British family that included the founders of the Quaker religion on his father's side and the Darwins on his mother's side. He was the grandson of Erasmus Darwin, and his mother was the half-sister of Charles Darwin's father. Galton's father was a wealthy banker, and when he died, Galton's inheritance freed him from the need to acquire a profession.

Galton's early education was directed by an invalid sister, Adèle. By all accounts, Galton was incredibly precocious. His letter to Adèle written shortly before his 5th birthday well illustrates his early abilities.

> My Dear Adèle,
>
> I am four years old and I can read any English book. I can say all the Latin Substantives and Adjectives and active verbs besides 52 lines of Latin poetry. I can cast up any sum in addition and can multiply by 2, 3, 4, 5, 6, 7, 8, [9], 10, [11]. I can also say the pence table. I read French a little and I know the Clock.
>
> Francis Galton.
> Feb[r]uary-15-1827
>
> (Pearson, 1914–1930, Vol. 1, p. 66)

Archives of the History of American Psychology–The University of Akron.

Francis Galton (1822–1911)

Pearson explained that Galton removed the numbers 9 and 11, the first with a penknife and the second with a piece of paper pasted over it. Galton knew he had claimed too much.

Although Galton was obviously a bright child, Fancher (1997, 1998) has argued convincingly that the idea of Galton's later genius contradicts his academic accomplishments. Indeed, "a sense of relative personal inferiority, rather than self-congratulatory superiority, provided one of the main dynamics for Galton's influential theory of innate and inherited intellectual differences" (1998, p. 103).

When he was 8, Galton began his education away from home. His experience at King Edward's School, Birmingham, which he entered at 13, began badly when he contracted scarlet fever. The illness was an educational setback from which his biographer said he probably never completely recovered. Finally, at 16, Galton was freed from the strictures of the private schools he had been attending and enrolled as a House Pupil at the General Hospital, Birmingham. His father had decided he would become a physician.

As unsuited to be a physician as his cousin, Galton was easily persuaded by Darwin to take time off from his medical studies to attend Cambridge (Gillham, 2001). There, he earned his bachelor's degree in mathematics in early 1844. His medical studies were interrupted for good when his father died later that year.

Following his father's death, Galton entered his "fallow years," during which he pursued "travel and sport for pure amusement's sake . . ." (Pearson, 1914–1930, Vol. 1, p. 209). By the summer of 1849, he had "sown his wild oats," and in 1850 he went to Africa, where for 2 years he explored uncharted territory in what today is Namibia. During this journey, he began to indulge in what became an obsession—measurement. To illustrate, at one point Galton wanted to measure the form of a particularly well-endowed Hottentot maiden. Unfortunately, he knew no Hottentot and did not want to ask his missionary host to translate.

> The object of my admiration stood under a tree, and was turning herself about . . . as ladies who wish to be admired usually do. Of a sudden my eye fell upon my sextant; . . . and I took a series of observations upon her figure in every direction, up and down, crossways, diagonally, and so forth, and I registered them carefully upon an outline drawing for fear of any mistake; this being done I . . . measured the distance from where I was to the place where she stood, and having thus obtained both base and angles, I worked out the results by trigonometry and logarithms. (Galton, 1853/1971, p. 88)

Galton returned to England as one of Great Britain's renowned 19th-century explorers (e.g., Sir Richard Burton, David Livingstone). Indeed, with his penchant for measurement and quantification, Galton's reports to the Royal Geographical Society of his travel in Africa were in some respects valued more highly than those of his "competitors," whose reports were often useless for accurate mapping (Gillham, 2001).

Galton's health and his marriage dimmed his wanderlust, however, and for the rest of his life he confined his travel to vacation rambles. He published *Art of Travel* (1855), which went through many editions, including a reprinting in 2001, and, according to Pearson (1914–1930, Vol. 2),

> remains still a treasury not only for the professed traveller, but for the leaders of the boy-scouts and girl-guides; nay, there are methods to be learnt in the *Art of Travel* which may bring profit to the ordinary household of to-day. (p. 2)

Along with Galton's geographical explorations, there was a parallel interest in meteorology, stemming first from a consideration of the effect of climate on the explorer. With his penchant for measuring, Galton prepared tables of climate, which led to meteorological maps. From his wind and pressure charts, he discovered the *anticyclone*, a weather system the opposite of the already recognized cyclone. Although the term caught on, few associate it with Francis Galton. Daily weather forecasts in England actually developed from storm warnings initiated by H.M.S *Beagle*'s Robert FitzRoy, who, unlike Galton, "had more enthusiasm than science" (Pearson, 1914–1930, Vol. 2, p. 43).

Hereditary Genius

Turning from the environment to humans themselves, Galton (1865) published a paper that anticipated the larger work to follow. In "Hereditary Talent and Character," he expressed his belief in the inheritance of both physical and mental characters and rejected the inheritance of acquired characteristics. Using biographical dictionaries and other sources, Galton demonstrated that distinguished fathers had many more distinguished sons than would be found in the general population. Anticipating by more than 50 years Lewis Terman's results from his longitudinal study of gifted children (Chapter 17), Galton concluded that high intelligence was not associated with physical weakness. In fact, the opposite was true.

Galton followed this essay with his most famous work, *Hereditary Genius: An Inquiry Into Its Laws and Consequences*, published in 1869. His purpose was clear from the outset: "I propose to show in this book that a man's natural abilities are derived by inheritance, under exactly the same limitations as are the form and physical features of the whole organic world" (Galton, 1892, p. 1).

Galton began by contradicting the notion that babies are born pretty much alike, contending that there is wide variability in human ability. In his argument, Galton made his first appeal to statistical method, using the "very curious theoretical law of 'deviation from an average'" (Galton, 1892, p. 22) proposed by Belgian astronomer and statistician **Jacques Quételet** (1796–1874). Quételet had shown that the distributions of such heritable physical characteristics as the heights of French conscripts conformed to a curve with a peak in the center and symmetrical tails on either side, which we call the **normal curve.** Galton found that the distribution of scores on a Cambridge mathematical examination fit Quételet's distribution, which suggested that mental characteristics, like physical ones, are inherited.

Next, Galton examined the family trees of people eminent in different areas, his subjects including judges, statesmen, military commanders, literary men, scientists, poets, and wrestlers. Galton found nearly 1,000 eminent men in the 300 families he studied. Because he had defined eminence as a position attained by only 1 out of 4,000, his discovery of so many men of eminence in a small number of families supported his belief in the inheritance of ability.

Further, Galton found that the incidence of eminence was greater the closer the kinship. He also found a tendency for relatives to exhibit their abilities in the same fields. For example, the relatives of eminent painters were often painters themselves, and the relatives of eminent writers were often writers.

Galton concluded that his results provided evidence for the inheritance of abilities, but the possibility of environmental influences was high and not addressed in *Hereditary Genius.* The offspring of eminent parents in the Victorian era received the best educational opportunities, the best medical treatment, and the best nutrition available, all of which might have contributed to their eventual success. Also, the model of a parent successful in science or music could easily encourage a child to develop skills similar to the parent's.

Swiss botanist **Alphonse de Candolle** (1806–1893) was more impressed with environmental influences on the development of eminence in families, and Galton's book stimulated him to publish *Histoire des Sciences et des Savants depuis deux Siècle* (*History of the Sciences and Scientists Over Two Centuries*) in 1872. Examining biographical information on over 300 eminent European scientists, de Candolle found that heredity played a role in their success, but he also found conclusive evidence for environmental influences such as the size and climate of a country, its type of government, and the degree of religious tolerance.

Galton's response to de Candolle's book began a correspondence that stimulated Galton to investigate further the heredity-environment question in scientists. For this, he developed an extensive questionnaire that he sent to nearly 200 distinguished Fellows of the Royal Society. This instrument, which marked the first use of the **questionnaire,** asked for information ranging from the respondent's political and social background to such physical information as hair color and hat size. Although some of Galton's biographers (e.g., Karl Pearson) have linked his interest in hat size (and head size) to the idea that Galton himself had a large head, Fancher (1997) indicated that Galton's head was actually rather small.

The scientists were also asked to describe their educational experiences, particularly experiences that might have interested them in science. In a question he considered crucial, Galton asked whether or not the respondents felt their interest in science was innate.

Although most responding Fellows considered their interest in science innate, there was also evidence for environmental influences. For example, Galton observed that a relatively large number of the scientists were Scottish, and many of the Scots noted the value of their educational experiences in fostering an interest in science. Acknowledging this influence, Galton called for a reform to make English schools more like schools in Scotland.

In the 1874 book that addressed his study of eminent British scientists, Galton used the phrase "**nature and nurture**" and clearly described the issues involved.

> The phrase "nature and nurture" is a convenient jingle of words, for it separates under two distinct heads the innumerable elements of which personality is composed. Nature is all that a man brings with himself into the world; nurture is every influence that affects him after his birth. (Galton, 1874, p. 12)

The phrase was even part of the book's title: *English Men of Science: Their Nature and Nurture.* Although the phrase may have been stimulated by Galton's awareness of de Candolle's work (Fancher, 1979), and its origin may be much earlier—for example, Shakespeare (Conley, 1984) or Richard Mulcaster, an early writer of educational treatises (Teigen, 1984)—there is no question that Galton deserves credit for popularizing it (Fancher, 1984).

Galton also introduced the **study of twins** in his attempt to measure the relative effects of nature and nurture. Twins are important because monozygotic (identical) twins share both their genes and their environments (if raised together), whereas dizygotic (fraternal) twins share their environments but only half their genes. Cases of identical twins separated soon after birth are particularly important. If the twins turn out to be very similar, the similarity may be attributed to heredity. As we will see in Chapter 17, twin studies continue to be a powerful methodology for psychologists.

Galton gathered detailed case histories from nearly 100 twin pairs, finding that the pairs separated into two broad categories: pairs of twins with evidence for close similarity and pairs of twins in which there were marked dissimilarities. He concluded: "The impression that all this evidence leaves on the mind is one of some wonder whether nurture can do anything at all beyond giving instruction and professional training" (Galton, 1876, p. 404).

Galton's "Intelligence" Tests

Galton's hereditarian position led to his interest in **eugenics,** a term he coined, which is the improvement of humankind by selectively breeding the "best" people. Buss (1976) argued that Galton was deeply committed to individual freedom and equal opportunity, but equally convinced of the inheritance of abilities. This latter belief led him to adopt an ideology—eugenics—that would abridge personal freedom.

But how would the most "fit" people be determined? If we waited until a person became eminent, the person might be too old to use as breeding stock. Galton needed a test to identify the brightest and best people while they were still in their reproductive prime. This led him to establish the first **anthropometric laboratory** at the International Health Exhibition in London in 1884. For a small fee, a person could have a variety of measurements performed. The measurements were primarily physiological, as Galton assumed the ablest individuals would have the best sensory acuity and the quickest reaction times. During the Exhibition, 9,337 people were measured, and when the Exhibition closed, the laboratory was moved to the Science Museum in South Kensington. Galton's monumental data set is still considered worth analyzing (e.g., Johnson et al., 1985).

To analyze his data, Galton developed the statistical method of correlation.

Correlation and Regression

Faced with mountains of numbers relating such variables as height and weight and the height of parents to the height of their offspring, Galton eventually began trying to visualize the relationship with graphs. Specifically, he plotted his data as **scatter plots,** graphs with one variable on the *X* axis and the other variable on the *Y* axis. Here, you will note the connection to Descartes and Cartesian coordinates.

From the graphs, Galton concluded there was *reversion,* the term he first used, or, as it came to be known, **regression toward the mean.** For example, although children of tall parents tend to be tall themselves, they tend to be closer to the average height than their parents. Similarly, short parents tend to have short offspring, but their children tend to be closer to the average—that is, taller—than their parents. Earlier, Galton had seen the same relationship in his study of the size and weight of sweet pea seeds over generations. For example, the mean weights of offspring seeds tend not to be as extreme as the mean weights of the parental seeds (Cowles, 2001). Although Galton interpreted the decreased variability in the offspring as a trend toward a decrease in the population with succeeding generations, Cowles noted that it is actually a mathematical artifact caused by an imperfect correlation between the two generations.

Galton's final work on heredity and regression was published in his 1889 book, *Natural Inheritance,* which highly stimulated Walter Weldon (1860–1906), a University Lecturer at Cambridge in invertebrate morphology. Weldon was intrigued by the possibility of mathematical solutions to problems of variability in the animals he studied. In 1890, Weldon became a professor at University College, London, and a paper he submitted to the Royal Society went to Galton for review. Galton's subsequent help with the

Galton's anthropometric laboratory at the International Health Exhibition in London in 1884

statistical analyses began Weldon's friendship with Galton. Through Weldon, Galton and **Karl Pearson** (1857–1936) also developed a relationship (Cowles, 2001). Pearson, an able mathematician, soon derived the now-familiar deviation score equation to compute a coefficient of correlation, which is called *r*, for regression. Pearson's index is known as the **Pearson product-moment correlation coefficient,** or **Pearson *r*.** Karl Pearson and his contemporary rival Sir Ronald Fisher (Chapter 17) are usually considered the founders of modern statistics.

Other Contributions to Psychology

Galton is also recognized for his study of word associations, mental imagery, and comparative sensory abilities. His first attempt to study associations came on a leisurely walk down London's Pall Mall. During his stroll, he was struck by the large number of associations stimulated by the objects he saw. A second walk a few days later also stimulated a variety of associations, but many were repetitions from the previous outing. Fascinated, Galton developed a method for studying his associations more scientifically.

Galton made a list of 75 different words, each written on a separate piece of paper. Next, he exposed the words one at a time, recording the associations and, with a stopwatch, the length of time it took to produce two associations. He repeated this procedure four times at intervals of a month.

Again, he found many repetitions. Of greater importance, Galton was able to identify in 124 cases when the association had occurred in his life. He found that 39% had occurred in his boyhood and youth, 46% in adulthood, and only 15% in the recent past—an early demonstration of the importance of childhood experiences for adult behavior.

Galton's **word-association experiment** was appropriated and developed extensively by Wundt and his students as well as by Carl Jung (Chapter 15). In addition, Freud's development of free association may have been influenced by Galton's experiment. Finally, association-based studies of language and memory can be found in both the behaviorist and cognitive traditions (e.g., Crovitz, 1970).

In studying word associations, Galton found that imagery—picturing something in his mind—was more likely to be the second association than the first. This observation stimulated his interest in mental imagery, which he studied with a questionnaire that asked his respondents to visualize the morning's breakfast table and then to answer questions about their images. He then asked whether the respondents could visualize such concrete objects as furniture, people, and scenery.

Galton was amazed to find that many scientists claimed to have no imagery at all. In fact, he found wide individual differences and concluded there is a continuum of imaging ability, from people who form clear and distinct mental images to people with no ability. In the middle, the majority of people have some, but not much, imaging ability.

Because of his interest in measuring human sensory abilities, Galton invented a whistle that produced sounds of different frequencies. In addition to testing human auditory acuity with his whistle, Galton performed animal experiments with it. Attaching a whistle to the end of a walking stick, Galton would produce a sound near an animal and observe whether the animal responded. In this way, Galton found that little dogs were more likely to respond than big dogs and that cats were superior to all other animals he tested. He attributed the cats' better ability to natural selection, reasoning that cats who heard the high-pitched sounds of small animals fared better in the search for food and were more likely to breed and pass on this acuity to future generations.

Galton's Influence

Blessed with a long life, independent means, and unending curiosity, Sir Francis Galton—he was knighted in 1909—achieved an enviable record of innovations. As we have seen, he was an explorer who wrote a popular book of practical suggestions for travellers. He was the inventor of weather maps and the discoverer of the anticyclone. And later in his life, Galton developed fingerprinting as a means of identification (Pearson, 1914–1930, Vol. 3) and the technique of **composite portraiture,** in which several images are combined onto one photograph. Galton was interested in producing a picture of the "average" criminal of a particular type—for example, a murderer.

In the spirit of Galton, modern psychological researchers have adapted Galton's method to study physical attractiveness. For example, Langlois and Roggman (1990) found that composite faces, produced by averaging samples of faces, were considered more attractive than almost all of the individual faces comprising the composites. The researchers concluded this is consistent with evolutionary forces favoring characteristics close to the population mean. Galton would have endorsed the conclusion.

As noted, Galton was an avid user of statistics, and his development of the idea of correlation and regression has immensely benefited psychology and other sciences as well. Indeed, no "rival claims of priority, no record of independent discovery by others, dims the brilliance of this discovery" (Diamond, 1980, p. 51). Additionally, Galton originated the questionnaire, which we will see extensively used by G. Stanley Hall, one of functionalism's forerunners. Galton also invented the word-association test, which became an important research tool in Wundt's laboratory and beyond. Further, the use of twins to investigate the effects of inheritance on physiology and/or behavior was first employed by Galton to study the relative contributions of "nature and nurture," a phrase he popularized. Strongly influenced by Galton, Sir Cyril Burt (Chapter 17) later used (and possibly misused) twin studies to argue for the inheritance of intelligence.

It is interesting to compare Galton with some of his more famous contemporaries. For example, Darwin employed a more "Baconian" method (Chapter 4), collecting facts without having a theory in mind. Then, with the facts in hand, he searched for a law to explain them. By contrast, Galton first formed a problem and then devised experiments to answer it. Obviously, in capable hands, both methods can be successful.

Comparing Galton to Wundt, Pearson (1914–1930, Vol. 2) observed that Wundt progressed from psychology to anthropology (folk or cultural psychology), whereas Galton went from anthropology to psychology. Their work was independent; Wundt pioneered experimental psychology in Germany, Galton in England. Wundt's interest was in the generalized human mind, whereas Galton's interest was in the mental ability of individuals, which illustrates the nomothetic (Wundt)/idiographic (Galton) distinction we described in Chapter 1. Galton's creative methods to study human capabilities became part of American functional psychology (Diamond, 1980), earning him an important place as a forerunner of functionalism.

Although Galton never had an academic position, he was influential in establishing the Psychological Laboratory at University College London (Valentine, 1999), and he did have disciples, as we have noted. One was Karl Pearson, his biographer, and another was James McKeen Cattell (Chapter 10), sometimes called a "Galtonian" in America.

CONCLUSIONS

In this chapter, we have described how evolution was a major part of the *Zeitgeist* of the late 18th century and the 19th century. Although evolutionary ideas have a long history, the modern concept of evolution presented in different versions by Lamarck, Spencer, Wallace, and Darwin was particularly important for psychology and all the life sciences. In the absence of an understanding of genetics, the details of evolutionary theory were subject to debate—as evidenced by the "Neo-Darwinians" and other movements favoring one mechanism over another—but evolution's broad outline and its implications for psychology were readily embraced by the scientific community. The population at large has not universally accepted evolutionary theory, and even today the teaching of evolution sometimes evokes passionate debate and in some areas legislative initiatives.

With its interest in comparative animal studies, American functionalism was the foremost beneficiary of evolutionary theory in psychology. The acceptance of evolution led to a concern with the function of consciousness and behavior. As we will see in the next two chapters, the focus on function and on the application of psychological knowledge was part of what made a psychology of function more popular in America than Titchener's structuralism. In addition, the theory of evolution bridged the Cartesian split between humans and animals, making the study of animals—such as in ethology (Chapter 12) and in the comparative study of animals and people—a respectable enterprise for psychology (see Armstrong, 1993, for an examination of Darwin as an ethologist).

This chapter also examined the work of Darwin's cousin, Sir Francis Galton. Galton was remarkable for the scope and nature of his accomplishments, many of which—for example, the formalization of the nature versus nurture debate, the use of questionnaires, twin studies, the study of individual differences, the development of important statistical techniques—remain defining features of modern-day psychology. Together with Alexander Bain and Herbert Spencer, Galton represents an important landmark in the development of a true science of psychology in Great Britain. Although England has produced many other noted psychologists—for example, James Ward (1843–1925), W. H. R. Rivers (1864–1922), and Sir Frederic Bartlett (Chapter 18)—Galton's contributions stand out.

SUMMARY

Just as phenomenology was part of the *Zeitgeist* that produced scientific psychology, so too was the concept of evolution.

Pre-Darwinian Evolution

Although it first appeared in the writing of the ancient Greeks, in more recent times, the concept of evolution can be found in the work of Hegel, Comte, Goethe, and Charles Darwin's grandfather, Erasmus Darwin. Among the first of several important precursors to Charles Darwin and modern evolutionary theory, French naturalist Jean-Baptiste Lamarck saw a striving for perfection and environmental influences as factors accounting for evolution. Lamarck's ideas are often distilled into the phrase "the inheritance of acquired characteristics."

Evolution formed the centerpiece for Herbert Spencer's comprehensive philosophy of science. Spencer's synthetic philosophy included a revision of his 1855 *Principles of*

Psychology in which he introduced an evolutionary associationism by adding an evolutionary principle to Bain's account of voluntary behavior. Spencer is also famous for social Darwinism, the idea that society and its institutions evolve like animal species.

Charles Robert Darwin

Charles Darwin accompanied Captain Robert FitzRoy on the H.M.S *Beagle*'s surveying voyage of South America. On the trip, Darwin became convinced the earth was far older than the biblical account of creation suggested. In the Galápagos Islands, Darwin found compelling evidence for the mutability of species. Malthus's *Essay on the Principle of Population* gave Darwin the insight that nature selects by breeding an excess of a species and then killing members that are not well adapted to their environment.

Botanist Joseph Hooker advised Darwin to publish an authoritative treatise on evolution, and Darwin was working on this when he received a letter and essay from Alfred Russel Wallace, which expressed a theory virtually identical to Darwin's. At the urging of his friends, Darwin allowed Wallace's paper along with one of his own to be read to the Linnean Society in July 1858.

After little reaction to the first public exposure of Darwin's ideas, there was an enormous reaction to the later publication of *On the Origin of Species by Means of Natural Selection, or the Preservation of Favoured Races in the Struggle for Life*. In *The Origin of Species,* Darwin presented facts that led almost inevitably to the conclusion that species change over time in response to natural selection.

In *Descent of Man,* Darwin argued that humans, like other species, have evolved through natural selection. In *The Expression of the Emotions in Man and Animals,* Darwin demonstrated that human emotional expressions have evolved because of their survival value.

The Origin of Species changed forever our view of the world and our place in it. The *Origin* and to a greater extent *The Descent of Man* abolished the Cartesian split in the animal kingdom, making explicit the continuity between humans and animals. Following Darwin, mind too could be seen as something that evolved because it facilitated adaptation.

Francis Galton

Influenced by Darwin's *The Origin of Species,* his cousin, Francis Galton, collected data to substantiate his belief in eugenics—the improvement of mankind through selective breeding. In *Hereditary Genius,* Galton tried to show that the natural abilities of humans are subject to inheritance just as are the form and physical features of the organic world.

Galton's interest in human ability made him a pioneer in studying individual differences and facilitated his development of methodological and statistical techniques. Galton purportedly found evidence for a relationship between kinship and eminence. In order to study further the nature and nurture issue, Galton distributed a questionnaire to the Fellows of the Royal Society. He also introduced the study of twins as a method to assess the relative contributions of nature and nurture.

In an effort to identify the most "fit" people for eugenics, Galton developed measures of human ability that he administered to people visiting his Anthropometric Laboratory in London. Galton's physiological measurements stimulated him to develop correlation. Karl Pearson, Galton's disciple and biographer, invented the Pearson product-moment correlation coefficient.

Galton's other contributions to psychology include the word-association experiment, the study of visual imagery, and a whistle that produced sounds of different frequencies, which Galton used to test human and animal auditory acuity. As the pioneer of experimental psychology in England, Galton can be compared with Wundt, who was a similar developer in Germany.

CONNECTIONS QUESTIONS

1. Trace the connections between Alfred Russel Wallace and Charles Darwin. Should Wallace have been given credit for the theory of evolution, as Rachels (1986) implies, or do you think Darwin deserved the credit he received?
2. Connect all the elements you can that contributed to Darwin's development of the concept of organic evolution.
3. Compare and contrast Wundt and Galton.
4. What are the connections between Galton and Darwin?
5. How many connections can you make between Galton's work and contemporary methods/issues in the social sciences?

KEY NAMES AND TERMS

anthropometric laboratory (p. 244)
Comte de Buffon (p. 230)
Alphonse de Candolle (p. 243)
composite portraiture (p. 246)
Charles Robert Darwin (p. 233)
Erasmus Darwin (p. 230)
eugenics (p. 244)
evolutionary associationism (p. 232)
Captain Robert FitzRoy (p. 234)
Francis Galton (p. 241)
Ernst Haeckel (p. 240)
Joseph Hooker (p. 235)
Thomas Henry Huxley (p. 232)
Jean-Baptiste Lamarck (p. 230)
Sir Charles Lyell (p. 232)
Thomas Malthus (p. 235)
nature and nurture (p. 243)
normal curve (p. 243)
Karl Pearson (p. 245)
Pearson product-moment correlation coefficient (Pearson *r*) (p. 245)
questionnaire (p. 243)
Jacques Quételet (p. 243)
regression toward the mean (p. 244)
scatter plots (p. 244)
social Darwinism (p. 233)
Herbert Spencer (p. 232)
Spencer-Bain principle (p. 233)
study of twins (p. 244)
survival of the fittest (p. 233)
synthetic philosophy (p. 232)
Alfred Russel Wallace (p. 235)
word-association experiment (p. 245)

SUGGESTED READINGS

Barlow, N. (Ed.) (1958). *The autobiography of Charles Darwin, 1809–1882.* New York: W. W. Norton. (Original work published as part of *Life and letters of Charles Darwin* in 1887) Edited by his granddaughter, Nora Barlow, Darwin's autobiography was written for his family and for himself and reveals an intelligent, witty, and ultimately very human individual. The picture is of a singularly unconceited man who was comforted by the thought that "I have worked as hard and as well as I could, and no man can do more than this" (p. 126).

Burkhardt, F. (Ed.) (1996). *Charles Darwin's letters: A selection 1825–1859.* Cambridge: Cambridge University Press. Darwin's intelligence, wide range of interests, and friendships shine through in this selection of letters extending from his Edinburgh years through the publication of *The Origin of Species.*

Darwin, C. (1958). *The origin of species, by means of natural selection or the preservation of favoured races in the struggle for life.* New York: New American Library. (Original work published 1859)

Darwin, C. (1874). *The descent of man, and selection in relation to sex* (2nd ed.). New York: A. L. Burt, Publisher.

Darwin, C. (1979). *The expression of emotions in man and animals.* London: Julian Friedmann Publishers. (Original work published 1872) There are many different modern reprints of Darwin's major works. You will find that his writing is remarkably clear and understandable and just as relevant today as it was over a century ago.

Desmond, A., & Moore, J. (1991). *Darwin.* New York: Warner Books. Stephen Jay Gould, an acclaimed science writer himself, called this "the finest [biography] ever written about Darwin." In it, the callow youth becomes a famous naturalist and then the tortured purveyor of a theory that changed his world and ours. The book's 90 pictures alone are worth its price.

Galton, F. (1892). *Hereditary genius: An inquiry into its laws and consequences* (2nd ed.). London: Watts & Co. Galton's most famous book, this is a good introduction to the man's thoughts and interests.

Gillham, N. W. (2001). *A life of Sir Francis Galton: From African exploration to the birth of eugenics.* New York: Oxford University Press. As the title indicates, this is a new biography of Darwin's cousin, Francis Galton. The book includes good descriptions of Galton's contributions to African exploration, meteorology, statistics, and psychology, and personalizes one of the giants of Victorian England.

Irvine, W. (1955). *Apes, angels, and Victorians.* Cleveland, OH: World Publishing Co. This is the well-researched and eminently readable story of the lives and time of two famous men of the Victorian era, Charles Darwin and Thomas Henry Huxley. In many ways, Huxley was the more brilliant of the two, but it was Darwin who had the ultimate insight and the perseverance to ensure the near-total scientific acceptance of the idea of evolution.

Marks, R. L. (1991). *Three men of the* Beagle. New York: Alfred A. Knopf, Inc. This is an account of the interesting relationship between Darwin and FitzRoy and of how Darwin's successes and beliefs affected the latter.

Pearson, K. (1914–1930). *The life, letters and labours of Francis Galton* (Vols. 1–3). Cambridge, England: Cambridge University Press. Pearson's three volumes constitute the definitive biography of an extraordinary Victorian, Sir Francis Galton.

Early American Psychology

CHAPTER 10

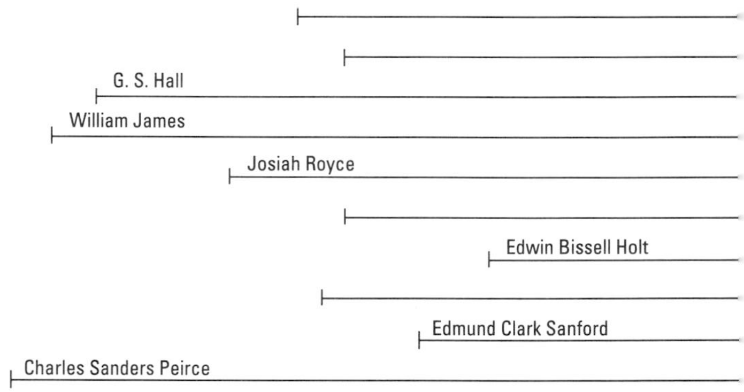

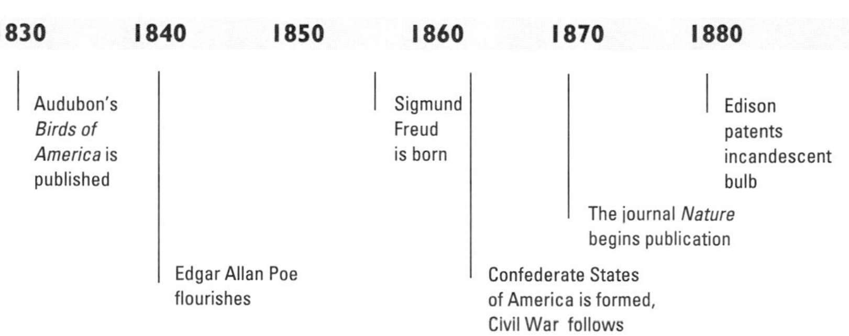

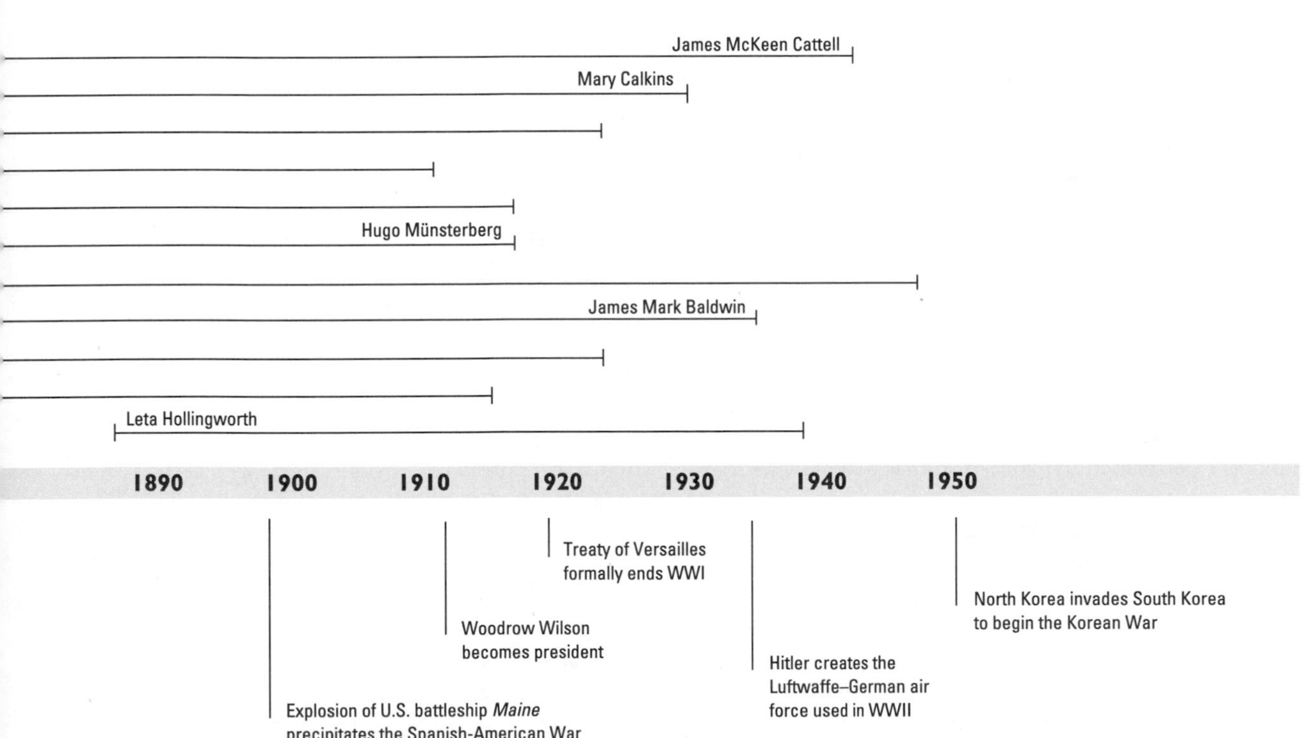
James McKeen Cattell
Mary Calkins
Hugo Münsterberg
James Mark Baldwin
Leta Hollingworth
1890
1900
1910
1920
1930
1940
1950
Treaty of Versailles formally ends WWI
North Korea invades South Korea to begin the Korean War
Woodrow Wilson becomes president
Hitler creates the Luftwaffe–German air force used in WWII
Explosion of U.S. battleship *Maine* precipitates the Spanish-American War

As we noted in Chapter 9, evolution was a major theme during the 19th century. In England as well as in the United States, Herbert Spencer's social Darwinism—the idea that institutions and societies evolve—met with great favor. When Spencer came to America in 1882, he was enthusiastically received. His principle of survival of the fittest captured our developing nation's mood by stressing the importance of individual initiative, independence from regulation, and the ability of the more successful among us to adapt to a demanding environment.

By 1882, few were more influenced by the evolutionary *Zeitgeist* than two American psychologists—William James and G. Stanley Hall. Both believed that consciousness has a function, which is to aid its possessor in the struggle for survival. Although psychologists of function, neither was quite a functionalist in the formal sense of the term.

The American psychologists we will survey in this chapter established the foundation for functionalism by taking psychology into areas avoided by "pure" psychologists (i.e., psychologists interested in understanding the generalized mind, not in applying psychological knowledge to practical problems) such as Titchener (Chapter 8). Again, the mood in America in the 19th century favored a more practical psychology. As noted in Chapter 9, Galton pioneered the study and testing of individual differences, and we will see this interest continued in America by James McKeen Cattell (discussed later) and others. After Darwinian evolution legitimized the study of animal behavior, Romanes and Lloyd Morgan (both Chapter 12) established comparative psychology, which was further developed by the research of functionalists such as Harvey A. Carr (Chapter 11). Following Morgan's lead, Edward Lee Thorndike (Chapters 11 and 12) performed the animal studies that cemented his fame for psychology.

This chapter's central theme is the origin of American psychology. Our main characters will be William James and G. Stanley Hall. Although neither had the personality to become a laboratory scientist, James and Hall were instrumental in moving American psychology away from mere philosophy and toward science. Both had backgrounds in the disciplines from which psychology arose—philosophy and physiology. Of the two, Hall became the more thoroughgoing psychologist, as James returned to philosophy after establishing American scientific psychology almost singlehandedly. However, before discussing William James, we need to describe briefly psychology in America before he arrived on the scene.

EARLY PHILOSOPHY AND PSYCHOLOGY IN AMERICA

Published statements often reinforce the view that American psychology leapt full-blown from William James's pen, with the 1890 publication of *The Principles of Psychology*. For example, Boring (1950) wrote that "James began psychology in America with his recognition of the significance of the new physiological [experimental] psychology of Germany" (p. 505). And without specifically mentioning James, Cattell told the Ninth International Congress of Psychology in 1929 that a history of American psychology before the 1880s "would be as short as a book on snakes in Ireland since the time of St. Patrick" (Cattell, 1929, p. 336; according to legend, St. Patrick rid Ireland of snakes in the 5th century).

Although James taught the first courses in the new scientific psychology in America and his *Principles* effectively communicated this psychology to a waiting and willing audience, there was some "psychology" in America before James. It was primarily moral, or mental, philosophy, however. According to Fuchs (2000a), this mental philosophy helped pave the way for the development of the system of functionalism in America.

Jonathan Edwards (1703–1758) is perhaps America's first noteworthy home-grown philosopher. Educated at Yale, where he read Locke's *An Essay Concerning Human Understanding* (Chapter 5), Edwards preached hard-line Calvinism as minister of the Congregationalist Church at Northampton, Massachusetts. Edwards urged people to return to God's absolute rule, as humanity, born with nothing (Locke's mind as "white paper, void of all characters"), has received everything from God. Tweney (1997) noted that Edwards's deterministic psychology was grounded in Newtonian determinism (Chapter 4).

Locke's *Essay* also influenced **Samuel Johnson** (1696–1772), Columbia University's first president. Johnson wrote a book that popularized many of empiricism's ideas and also discussed a number of relevant topics such as child psychology, the use of introspection, consciousness, and perception.

Although Edwards and Johnson are frequently mentioned as early American psychologists, neither actually "attempted to present a real psychological point of view . . ." (Harms, 1972, p. 120). The distinction between moral philosophers with some relevance to psychology and ones who were "doing psychology" emerged less clearly in America than in Europe, but we can see it in the comparison of Edwards and Johnson with **Laurens Perseus Hickok** (1798–1888). Hickok's work differed from many of his contemporaries in that he attempted to provide a system of scientific psychology based on his analysis of philosophical positions from Aristotle through Kant. In *Empirical Psychology,* Hickok stressed "observation, investigation, and experiment," by which he meant studying consciousness through introspection. Harms concluded, "Hickok's whole psychology and this book are . . . unique in the psychology of the 19th century, claiming to be an exact and fully worthy psychology based totally upon self observation" (p. 122).

Bare (1998) concluded that Hickok accepted the challenge implicit in Kant's negative prognosis for a science of psychology and surmounted it "in ways that foreshadowed the thinking of psychologists in generations yet to come" (p. 14). According to Bare, Hickok clearly anticipated elements of structuralism, such Freudian concepts as the pleasure principle, various cognitive processes, and modern ideas of emotion. "All of these contributions identify Hickok as an important pioneer in the history of general psychology" (p. 15).

One of Hickok's contemporaries, **Thomas C. Upham** (1799–1872) could also be considered "one of the principal founders of a truly indigenous American system of Psychology" (Rieber, 1980, p. 104). A professor of mental and moral philosophy at Maine's Bowdoin College, Upham wrote the first textbook in intellectual philosophy, later mental philosophy, with the undergraduate student in mind (Fuchs, 2000a). Upham also developed a doctrine emphasizing "the teaching of proper moral action and the 'cure of the soul.' . . . [T]hese can be seen as earlier versions of the twentieth-century concept of mental hygiene and psychotherapy" (Rieber, p. 105).

After the American Revolution, psychology in America fell largely under the influence of Scottish common-sense philosophy (Chapter 5). Textbooks written by the Scottish philosophers included such topics as sensation, perception, association, memory, and thinking. Written by Dugald Stewart (Chapter 5), one such textbook was used at Yale in the early part of the 19th century. As we will see, the textbooks that provided competition to James's *Principles* included one by Princeton's President James McCosh, who was a leader in America of Scottish philosophical psychology. There were also textbooks based on German rational psychology, and the ideas of Hegel and Herbart (both Chapter 6) form some of the background for functionalism in America. In part, James's genius lay in his ability to synthesize such diverse elements.

WILLIAM JAMES

With the publication of *The Principles of Psychology,* William James almost overnight became America's foremost psychologist. In addition to its literary quality, the *Principles* is noted for its scope and its tolerant tone. The origin of that tolerance can perhaps be found in James's unusual childhood in a family that also produced one of America's most brilliant novelists—Henry James (1843–1916).

William James (1842–1910) was the oldest of five children born to Henry James, often called Henry James Senior to distinguish him from his novelist son. Henry Senior was the son of an Irish immigrant, the original William James, who had amassed a fortune through land speculation. Among his purchases was the village of Syracuse, New York, for $30,000. As a result of his inheritance, Henry Senior never had to work for a living.

After initially planning to be a Methodist minister, in his zeal Henry Senior managed to become permanently alienated from organized religion. At 35, he was introduced by a friend to the writings of Emanuel Swedenborg (1688–1772), a Swedish scientist/mystic/theologian. Enamored with the Swedish theologian, Henry Senior devoted himself to the study of Swedenborg and to the spread of his doctrines by lecturing and writing. Henry Senior's writing was not always enlightening; after the publication of *The Secret of Swedenborg*, a friend joked that Henry had not only found the secret, he had kept it.

Although affectionate and loving, Henry Senior was an erratic parent, given his depression and his nearly constant search for the meaning of his life. Further, William, with an exuberant and willful nature, appears to have borne the brunt of parental discipline, administered as spankings by his father with a "paper cutter" (Simon, 1998).

Transatlantic travel was a frequent occurrence in the James's household, as Henry Senior searched for himself. William James took his first trip to Europe when he was 2, and later in life any crisis calling for a decision or any refractory ailment sent him across the Atlantic. As a result, James "became adept in French and passable in German and Italian, languages that would aid him in his scholarly life. He also spoke a little Portuguese and read Latin and Greek" (Evans, 1990, p. 12).

James's nomadic childhood produced a markedly abnormal education, as his father sought "to protect his offspring from the corrupting influence of anyone else's ideas" (Simon, 1998, p. 47). James emerged well-read and intellectually curious, with a dislike of mathematics and logic, ready to become an artist. Perhaps realizing his son's interest in art would be brief, James's father surreptitiously ordered a dissecting microscope, saying, "Willy needs it and will be much obliged" (Lewis, 1991, p. 108).

After a brief interest in chemistry that included a course taught by a neighbor of the Jameses, Charles W. Eliot (1834–1926), James shifted toward biology. Fearing a biologist's income would not allow him to support a family, he then opted for medicine, entering Harvard Medical School in 1864. His interest in medicine was never wholehearted, however, and James accompanied Harvard's brilliant Swiss-born naturalist Louis Agassiz (1807–1873) on an expedition to Brazil in 1865. The experience taught James he was not cut out to be a field naturalist.

James withdrew again from his medical studies in the spring of 1867, beset by ailments that included "insomnia, digestive disorders, eye-troubles, weakness of the back, and sometimes deep depression . . ." (James, 1920, Vol. I, p. 84). These may have been psychosomatic, as James was 25 years old, without a vocation, and not sure he was suited for medicine. At some point during all his misery, James had himself committed to McLean's Asylum in Somerville, Massachusetts (Townsend, 1996). Finally, to partake of the medicinal baths and to perfect his German while studying the physiology of the nervous system, James went to Europe.

James spent the next 2 years mainly in Germany, often suffering from depression so deep he considered suicide. In this season of melancholy, two events stand out: James had his first literary effort published, and he revealed a burgeoning interest in psychology. In a letter to a friend, he wrote:

> I have blocked out some reading in physiology and psychology which I hope to execute this winter. . . . It seems to me that perhaps the time has come for psychology to begin to be a science. . . . I am going on to study what is already known, and perhaps may be able to do some work at it. Helmholtz and a man named Wundt at Heidelberg are working at it, and I hope I live through this winter to go to them in the summer. (James, 1920, Vol. I, pp. 118–119)

James heard physiology lectures by du Bois-Reymond in Berlin and Helmholtz in Heidelberg (both Chapter 7) before returning to his Harvard medical studies in November 1868. During this period, he also became something of a disciple of French physiologist Claude Bernard (Chapter 7) and may have considered psychiatry as a profession (Howard, 1992; Taylor, 1990). In June 1869, James finally received his Harvard medical degree.

For the next 3 years, James lived at home, reading voraciously, writing an occasional article or review, and spending "most of the time in a state of hypochondriacal misery" (Knight, 1950, p. 29). He was finally rescued from his morbid preoccupations by reading the French philosopher **Charles Bernard Renouvier** (1815–1903). In one of his notebooks, James wrote:

> I think that yesterday was a crisis in my life. I finished the first part of Renouvier's second "Essais" and see no reason why his definition of Free Will—"the sustaining of a thought *because I choose to* when I might have other thoughts"—need be the definition of an illusion. At any rate, I will assume for the present—until next year—that it is no illusion. My first act of free will shall be to believe in free will. (James, 1920, Vol. I, p. 147)

Before this "crisis," James had believed in the physical basis of his mental states, which led him to seek physiological remedies. When these failed, he had come to view his depression as something to be endured. Renouvier had shown him that perhaps he had the ability (free will) to sustain a thought of his own choosing. Croce (1999) documented how his thinking and public statements during this period ultimately shaped James's approach to psychology.

Two years after the worst of his depression, Charles W. Eliot, now Harvard's president, asked James to teach the physiology portion of an undergraduate course in anatomy and physiology. James taught the course and thereby found the vocation he had sought.

According to Ross (1991), James was an excellent teacher because of his unusual education, his personal philosophy, and his age and experience.

> Having been included in intellectual discussions from an early age in his liberal household, James was at ease with students and they with him. His varied background and his attempts to relate class material to life situations were appealing to students. The breadth of his experiences and reading, his ability to communicate, and his engaging style added to his popularity. (p. 18)

In 1875, James added to his teaching repertoire a course in physiological psychology, teaching it first to graduate students and then the next year to undergraduates. Along with the new course, James obtained two rooms to house psychological apparatus, which became the first experimental psychology "laboratory" in America. However, although James did produce a few carefully designed studies (see Taylor, 1992), experimental research was not his true love.

James married Alice Howe Gibbens in 1878, and he began to draft the opening chapters of the *Principles* on his honeymoon. Although he told Henry Holt, the publisher, that he did not think he would be able to complete the book in under 2 years, it actually took him nearly 12.

The *Principles* was finally finished in May 1890, and in a letter to Holt, James, perhaps disingenuously, expressed his feelings about the manuscript:

> No one could be more disgusted than I at the sight of the book. *No* subject is worth being treated of in 1000 pages! Had I ten years more, I could rewrite it in 500; but as it stands it is this or nothing—a loathsome, distended, tumefied, bloated, dropsical mass, testifying to nothing but two facts: *1st,* that there is no such thing as a *science* of psychology, and *2nd,* that W.J. is an incapable. (James, 1920, Vol. I, p. 294, italics in the original)

The "James," as it was known, was an immediate success, and it took James only another 2 years to complete his 500-page abridgement, *Psychology: The Briefer Course.* An excellent introductory textbook, the "Jimmy" remained for years the most widely used psychology textbook in the English language.

The Principles of Psychology

Competition and Criticism

The Principles of Psychology entered a textbook market containing several competitors. As Holt waited for James's manuscript, three major books appeared in 1886 alone: James McCosh's *Psychology: The Cognitive Powers,* John Dewey's *Psychology,* and Bordon P.

By permission of the Houghton Library, Harvard University.

William James (1842–1910) and daughter in 1892, the year the "Jimmy" was published

Bowne's *Introduction to Psychological Theory.* In 1887, Yale philosophy professor **George Trumbull Ladd** (1842–1920) published the well-received *Elements of Physiological Psychology.* Like James's, Ladd's psychology was largely self-taught. His 1887 book was based on Wundt's *Principles of Physiological Psychology* (Chapter 8). Although Ladd's *Elements* was a work about experimental psychology by someone who had never done a psychological experiment, it was widely used as a textbook in the United States and in England. For further details about Ladd and his textbook writing, see Mills (1974).

Praise for the *Principles* was swift, but not universal. For example, **James Sully** (1842–1923), a British textbook writer and a friend of Alexander Bain (Chapter 5), found James's style too brilliant, contending that a textbook should be duller. Perhaps Sully feared the competition his own *Outlines of Psychology* (1884) would receive from the *Principles.*

More recently, B. F. Skinner (Chapter 13), writing from William James Hall at Harvard, praised the writer but not his message in a 1986 letter to one of this book's authors:

> William James is generally accepted as the last important figure in the history of mentalistic psychology. He was a careful thinker and a *charming writer* but my own feeling is that *those traits are to be regretted.* He made altogether too good a case for what could be said at the time about the human mind. (italics added)

Reviewers also criticized the *Principles'* unsystematic arrangement. For example, James's chapter on sensation does not appear until Chapter 17. The discussion of perception, which often follows the discussion of sensation, occurs in Chapters 15 ("The Perception of Time"), 19 ("The Perception of 'Things'"), 20 ("The Perception of Space"), and 21 ("The Perception of Reality"). The instinct material, which might logically precede Chapter 4's discussion of habit, is in Chapter 24.

Some of the apparently random arrangement of chapters may simply reflect James's personal interests and priorities; that is, topics of greater interest were covered earlier. More importantly, the arrangement may have stemmed from James's attempts to be inclusive and systematic of both a phenomenological account of psychology and a physiological account.

Some reviewers criticized James's physiological approach, objecting that the *Principles* was "materialistic to the core." Although the book carefully balances phenomenology and physiology, in his materialistic moments James was merely incorporating the view that psychology could not be taught as a living science by anyone without a knowledge of nervous physiology.

Selected Topics from the Principles

Instead of attempting an overview of the *Principles'* nearly 1,400 pages, we will discuss briefly three of James's most influential concepts—the stream of consciousness, habit, and his theory of emotions—citing the *Principles* liberally to give the flavor of his writing. For further information on James and his many important contributions to psychology through the *Principles,* we recommend Blanshard and Schneider (1942), Donnelly (1992), Johnson and Henley (1990), Kimble (1990), and McLeod (1969). Each work examines topics in which James's views were pioneering, such as the mind-body problem, association, will and free will, and the self, which we will not treat in detail here. Indeed, the scope of James's work as well as the contemporary scholarship it continues to generate cannot be overstated. Recent examples of such scholarship include Bordogna's (2001) article about James's "temperament thesis" and Coon's (2000) work on James's conception of self.

Stream of Consciousness. As we noted in Chapter 8, Wundt and Titchener approached consciousness by seeking to identify its elements, beginning with sensations. According to James, this is the wrong place to start.

> It is astonishing what havoc is wrought in psychology by admitting at the outset apparently innocent suppositions, that nevertheless contain a flaw. . . . The notion that sensations, being the simplest things, are the first things to take up in psychology is one of these suppositions. The only thing which psychology has a right to postulate at the outset is the fact of thinking itself, and that must first be taken up and analyzed. If sensations then prove to be amongst the elements of the thinking, we shall be no worse off as respects them than if we had taken them for granted at the start. (James, 1890, Vol. 1, p. 224)

If we begin with thinking, we find that thought is a continuous stream rather than a collection of pieces susceptible to the analysis to which Wundt and Titchener and others had subjected it. James concluded that thought has five characteristics:

1. Our thoughts are part of a personal consciousness. My thoughts are mine; your thoughts are yours.
2. Thought is always changing. As Heraclitus (Chapter 2) believed, you cannot step into the same stream twice, or, as James expressed it, ". . . *no state once gone can recur and be identical with what it was before*" (James, 1890, Vol. 1, p. 230, italics in the original).
3. Our thoughts are sensibly continuous. As long as we are not unconscious, we are unaware of gaps in our consciousness.
4. Our consciousness appears to deal with objects outside of itself. That is, we believe our thoughts deal with objects having an external reality. The reason for this belief "is that there are *many* human thoughts, each with the *same* objects. . . . The judgment that *my* thought has the same object as *his* thought is what makes the psychologist call my thought cognitive of an outer reality" (Vol. 1, pp. 271–272, italics in the original).
5. Consciousness is selective; attention is focused more on some elements of our experiences than on others.

James believed consciousness evolved because it has a function, which is to aid in its possessor's adaptation. He wrote:

> It is very generally admitted . . . that consciousness grows the more complex and intense the higher we rise in the animal kingdom. That of a man must exceed that of an oyster. From this point of view it seems an organ, superadded to the other organs which maintain the animal in the struggle for existence; and the presumption . . . is that it helps him in some way in the struggle, just as they do. But it cannot help him without being in some way efficacious and influencing the course of his bodily history. If now it could be shown in what consciousness might help him, and if . . . the defects of his other organs . . . are such as to make them need just the kind of help that consciousness would bring provided it were efficacious; why, then the plausible inference would be that it came just because of its efficacy . . . (James, 1890, Vol. 1, pp. 138–139)

In summary, consciousness is a continuous, ever-changing, yet selective stream unique to its possessor. Consciousness also has a purpose or function, which is to aid in its possessor's adaptation to the environment. The image of consciousness James offered remains the view of modern psychology.

For a discussion of the stream of consciousness concept since James, see Pollio (1990).

Habit. For James, habit was a well-learned pattern of behavior resulting from the malleability of our nervous systems, which he described as follows:

> It is to the infinitely attenuated currents that pour in through [the sensory nerve-roots] that the hemispherical cortex shows itself to be so peculiarly susceptible. The currents, once in, must find a way out. In getting out they leave their traces in the paths which they take. The only thing they *can* do, in short, is to deepen old paths or to make new ones. . . . The most complex habits . . . are . . . nothing but *concatenated* discharges in the nerve-centres, due to the presence there of systems of reflex paths, so organized as to wake each other up successively—the impression produced by one muscular contraction serving as a stimulus to provoke the next, until a final impression inhibits the process and closes the chain. (James, 1890, Vol. 1, pp. 107–108, italics in the original)

For James, the anatomical substrate of habit was a pathway in the brain, so altered that it could be traversed more easily in the future.

Habits are essential for maintaining society's integrity, according to James, and in a frequently cited passage, he wrote:

> Habit is thus the enormous fly-wheel of society, its most precious conservative agent. It alone is what keeps us all within the bounds of ordinance, and saves the children of fortune from the envious uprisings of the poor. It alone prevents the hardest and most repulsive walks of life from being deserted by those brought up to tread therein. It keeps the fisherman and the deck-hand at sea through the winter; it holds the miner in his darkness, and nails the countryman to his log-cabin and his lonely farm through all the months of snow. . . . It dooms us all to fight out the battle of life upon the lines of our nurture or our early choice. . . . (James, 1890, Vol. 1, p. 121)

James offered some practical suggestions on how to acquire new habits or to remove old ones, following Bain's advice. For example, "we must take care to *launch ourselves with as strong and decided an initiative as possible*" (James, 1890, Vol. 1, p. 123, italics in the original). Thus, if you want to quit smoking, you might make a public pledge that you are going to stop, or you might spend as much time as possible in a nonsmoking environment. These actions

> will give your new beginning such a momentum that the temptation to break down will not occur as soon as it otherwise might; and every day during which a breakdown is postponed adds to the chances of its not occurring at all. (p. 123)

In addition, "*Never suffer an exception to occur till the new habit is securely rooted in your life*" (James, 1890, Vol. 1, p. 123, italics in the original). Practice your new habit (or the absence of an old one) until it becomes second nature, for each "lapse is like the letting fall of a ball of string which one is carefully winding up; a single slip undoes more than a great many turns will wind again" (p. 123). How many times has your latest diet been undone by eating a single snack or dessert?

Although today James is more often associated with cognitive psychology than with behaviorism, his discussion of habit proved to be central to functionalism (behaviorism's parent) and to learning theory. At the same time that behaviorists (Chapters 12 and 13) distanced themselves from James's mentalism, his analysis of habit was fundamental to all subsequent American psychology.

Emotion. In 1884, James described a novel theory of emotion, and in 1885, Danish physiologist **Carl Lange** (1834–1900) independently published a similar theory, which we call the **James-Lange theory of emotion.** Normally, we believe that a stimulus (e.g., a phone call saying you have won a sweepstakes) produces an emotion (e.g., joy), and the emotion triggers your response (e.g., increased heart rate, shouting, hugging family members). Instead, James said, the stimulus first triggers the response, and awareness of the response constitutes the emotion.

> Common-sense says, we lose our fortune, are sorry and weep; we meet a bear, are frightened and run; we are insulted by a rival, are angry and

> strike. The hypothesis here to be defended says that this order of sequence is incorrect, that the one mental state is not immediately induced by the other, that the bodily manifestations must first be interposed between, and that the more rational statement is that we feel sorry because we cry, angry because we strike, afraid because we tremble, and not that we cry, strike, or tremble, because we are sorry, angry, or fearful, as the case may be. (James, 1890, Vol. 2, pp. 449–450)

One criterion of a good theory is that it can be tested, and by this criterion the James-Lange theory succeeded. In 1927, Harvard physiologist and former student of James **Walter B. Cannon** (1871–1945) attacked the theory on several fronts, with apparent success. Among his other contributions, Cannon argued that stimulation of the sympathetic nervous system prepares an organism for "fight or flight," and he coined the term *homeostasis* to describe the body's relatively constant internal conditions. Let us consider two of Cannon's objections to the James-Lange theory and how they might be reinterpreted today. Although Cannon (1927) had additional criticisms, none was any more telling than the ones discussed here.

James had argued that an emotion-producing stimulus triggers a bodily response and response awareness is the emotional feeling. In addition to the external manifestations of the response (e.g., laughing, crying, running), there are less visible, but no less important, "internal" bodily changes, such as heart rate changes and inhibition of digestive processes. If feedback from bodily changes produces an emotional feeling, then blocking the feedback should prevent the emotional feeling.

Thus, Cannon's (1927) first criticism was that "*Total separation of the viscera* [internal organs] *from the central nervous system does not alter emotional behavior*" (p. 108, italics in the original). In support, Cannon reviewed research showing that emotional responses continued in animals after the sensory nerves between the viscera and the central nervous system had been cut. Cannon concluded that "operations which largely or completely destroy emotional feeling, nevertheless leave the animals behaving as angrily, as joyfully, as fearfully as ever" (p. 109).

However, the fact that cats with no visceral feedback still manifest external signs of rage does not mean they still *feel* rage. Obviously, cats cannot tell us what they feel, and they might *appear* angry without any corresponding *feeling*. More importantly, James did not say *all* emotional feelings depend on visceral feedback. He also thought muscular feedback was important, and Cannon's operations did not abolish feedback from the muscles.

But what about emotional feelings in humans with altered bodily feedback? Hohman (1966) asked people with spinal cord injuries about the intensity of their feelings, and, supporting the James-Lange theory, he found a clear correlation between level of injury and intensity of feelings. People with high spinal injuries (less bodily feedback) reported less intense feelings than people with lower spinal damage (greater bodily feedback). James (1894) himself cited similar data in a reply to critics of the James-Lange theory.

Another Cannon objection was that the "*Artificial induction of the visceral changes typical of strong emotions does not produce them*" (Cannon, 1927, p. 113, italics in the original). In support, Cannon reported studies in which people injected with adrenalin—which produces the bodily changes that normally accompany strong emotions—generally did not experience any emotions. In other words, artificially inducing the physiological changes that accompany an emotion usually failed to cause a true emotional feeling.

More recently, Stanley Schachter and Jerome Singer (1962) studied subjects who received either a placebo or adrenalin, were either informed or misinformed about what to expect physiologically, and were exposed either to a euphoric or to an angry confederate while they responded to a questionnaire. Schachter and Singer concluded their results supported a two-factor theory of emotion: A stimulus causes arousal, and our emotional feeling depends on how we label the stimulus. Presumably, subjects in the studies Cannon reviewed did not feel any particular emotion because they experienced their physiological changes in a neutral environment to which they could not attach a label (see also Zillmann, Katcher, & Milavsky, 1972).

One corollary to the James-Lange theory is that simulating the emotion (e.g., smiling when you are unhappy) should produce the appropriate feeling. James had actually used this technique to combat his grief following his parents' deaths, and he was speaking from personal experience when he wrote:

> Whistling to keep up courage is no mere figure of speech. On the other hand, sit all day in a moping posture, sigh, and reply to everything with a dismal voice, and your melancholy lingers. . . . [I]f we wish to conquer undesirable emotional tendencies in ourselves, we must assiduously . . . go through the *outward movements* of those contrary dispositions which we prefer to cultivate. The reward of persistency will infallibly come, in the fading out of the sullenness or depression, and the advent of real cheerfulness and kindliness in their stead. Smooth the brow, brighten the eye, . . . and speak in a major key, pass the genial compliment, and your heart must be frigid indeed if it do not gradually thaw! (James, 1890, Vol. 2, p. 463)

Carlson (1994) reported that "several experiments suggest that feedback from the contraction of facial muscles can affect people's moods and even alter the activity of the autonomic nervous system" (p. 351). A physiological mechanism for the effect has been proposed: By influencing blood flow to the brain, facial expressions may alter the release of neurotransmitters that affect our moods (Zajonc, Murphy, & Ingelhart, 1989). As you can see, the James-Lange theory of emotion is still generating research and commentary (e.g., Ellsworth, 1994; Lang, 1994) long after it was first proposed.

After the *Principles*

Having virtually created American scientific psychology with his book, James, never a laboratory scientist, wanted to be freed from it. To gain his freedom, James chose Hugo Münsterberg (discussed later), a young German who had received his Ph.D. from Leipzig, to head his Harvard laboratory.

James also became increasingly interested in being freed from psychology, calling it "a nasty little subject" and turning instead toward philosophy. Nevertheless, in his last 2 decades, James continued to engage in psychological activities and to write books with a strong psychological flavor. For example, he served twice as APA president (1894, 1904). In 1899, he published *Talks to Teachers,* which applied his psychological ideas to pedagogy. Three years later, *The Varieties of Religious Experience* examined, among other things, the relations between religious experience and abnormal psychology. And in 1909, although gravely ill, he traveled to Clark University to hear and meet Sigmund Freud during Freud's only visit to America. According to Freud's colleague and biographer Ernest Jones (Chapter 15), James responded to Freud and his associates on the occasion of their meeting by saying, "The future of psychology belongs to your work" (Jones, 1955, p. 57). About the man himself, James wrote, "I confess that [Freud] made on me personally the impression of a man obsessed with fixed ideas" (James, 1920, Vol. 2, p. 328).

Unfortunately, James's future was nearly over by the time of the Clark Conference (discussed later). For the last decade of his life, James suffered increasingly from heart disease, searching valiantly in both America and Europe for a definitive diagnosis and treatment regimen to restore his health. After a final European trip in the summer of 1910, James returned to his summer home in Chocorua, New Hampshire, where, at "2:30 in the afternoon of August 26, William James died in Alice's arms" (Bjork, 1988, p. 261).

James's Pragmatism

Although James first detailed his philosophy of pragmatism in *The Will to Believe and Other Essays in Popular Philosophy* (1897), his thinking about it preceded this publication by at least 2 decades. When he was in his 20s, James had been part of an informal group that included Chauncey Wright, Oliver Wendell Holmes, and **Charles Sanders Peirce** (1839–1914). Peirce later called the group the "Metaphysical Club." Only a few years older than James, Peirce became one of his lifelong friends. Philosopher, logician, and mathematician, Peirce never obtained an academic position beyond a half-time appointment as a lecturer in logic at Johns Hopkins from 1879 until 1884. "Despite his universally acknowledged genius, he was considered too difficult to deal with and too abstract to be a good teacher" (Cadwallader, 1974, p. 291). His ideas aided in the establishment of semiotics (a theory of meaning), a concept now central to linguistics and the philosophy of language. Peirce actually introduced the term **pragmatism** into philosophy in an article in *Popular Science Monthly* (Peirce, 1878).

At Metaphysical Club meetings, Peirce promoted his theory of pragmatism, which, among other things, stressed the uses for science and knowledge. In order to find the meaning of an idea, we must understand the consequences to which the idea leads. In other words, the pragmatist asks what is the function of an idea? Does the idea work? Further, an idea that works in one context may not work in another, with the result that ideas, like organisms and societies, evolve. Here, you can see the relation between pragmatism and the relatively new Darwinian evolution.

Pragmatism's central test—Does it work?—led James to reconsider the nature of truth. For James, truth became, not an objective entity (Truth with a capital "T"), but something that works—that is functional. His decision in the early 1870s to believe in free will was true in the sense that it brought him out of his depression. Truth, according to James, was the value of an idea within a context. If it works in that context, it is true.

In *The Will to Believe,* James defended empirical methods against rationalistic or absolutist methods in philosophy. He was particularly opposed to systems developed by deductive reasoning, such as that of Hegel. Instead, James believed that philosophy could advance only by using the inductive, empirical method of the natural sciences, which means advancing from one working hypothesis to another and abandoning the search for absolute truths.

The main point of *The Will to Believe* is that we often may be justified in embracing a belief as a working hypothesis whose validity cannot be proved. Although few would argue with this idea, James carried it a step further in *Pragmatism,* when he defined truth in terms of whether or not an idea works. That is, he now believed that an idea that works is true *by definition.* Critics pointed to his definition's circularity; logically, a true belief becomes a belief that it is to our advantage to regard as true.

Although some critics consider *Pragmatism* James's least satisfactory work, James himself liked it, and it remains widely read and enormously influential. As one illustration of its influence, Thomas Kuhn's philosophy of science that we introduced in Chapter 1 reflects many of the tenets of James's pragmatism. Nevertheless, Peirce tried in vain to relabel his philosophy "pragmaticism" to distinguish it from James's pragmatism.

James's Students

Although James attracted a variety of people who became important psychologists, there were never "Jamesians" as there were "Wundtians," "Freudians," "Skinnerians," and so on (Robinson, 1993). Some of the most well known of James's students included philosopher, historian, poet, and novelist **George Santayana** (1863–1952), American writer Gertrude Stein (1874–1946), and W. E. B. Du Bois (1868–1963). Du Bois, a cofounder of the National Association for the Advancement of Colored People in 1909, entered Harvard in 1888 and later wrote movingly of his relationship with James, whom he considered a friend and his guide to clarity of thought (Myers, 1986).

Some of the psychologists who studied with James were Morton Prince (Chapter 16), James Rowland Angell, Edward Lee Thorndike, Robert S. Woodworth (all in Chapter 11), and **Edwin Bissell Holt** (1873–1946), as well as Mary Calkins and G. Stanley Hall (discussed later). Often viewed as an early behaviorist, Holt was one of James's favorite students. First at Harvard, then at Princeton, Holt continued the Jamesian tradition of combining sophisticated philosophical analysis with his psychological inquiries.

James's Influence

James's specific contributions to psychology include, with Lange, his theory of emotion; the importance of habit as an organizing principle of mind; and his stream of consciousness idea, which diverted attention from the atomism of structuralism and anticipated Gestalt psychology's emphasis on wholes (Chapter 14).

Debate continues over the degree to which James directly influenced the eventual rise of American behaviorism (Robinson, 1993). Clearly, by suggesting that "feelings" do not cause emotions, as well as by grounding psychological inquiry within a pragmatic philosophy, James at the least provided a foundation for both functionalism and behaviorism.

In fact, the ideas James expressed in both the *Principles* and his pragmatic philosophical writings led rather directly to functionalism. For example, James saw consciousness as useful and adaptive—functional, in a word. John Dewey (Chapter 11) and James Rowland Angell, considered founders of functionalism, acknowledged their debt to James. James was also influential through the people he attracted to psychology, foremost among whom were Edward Lee Thorndike and Robert S. Woodworth.

The open-mindedness and wide interests that made James popular sometimes divided opinion of him as a scientist. One example is his interest in psychical research. In America,

> James for years stood almost alone among men of high intellectual repute, and although he was eminently conservative in his estimate of the results of the work of the [psychical research] society, he nevertheless committed himself to belief in certain mediumistic phenomena in a way which seriously offended many of his professional colleagues. At best, they regarded him as a man whose judgment could not be trusted, at worst as an unwitting backer of quackery and fraud.
>
> His position on the issue was all of a piece with his insistent and never failing protestantism, his passion for fair play, and a just hearing for all sides of every question. . . . (Angell, 1911, p. 81)

James, along with Münsterberg and Josiah Royce (discussed later), helped establish Harvard as one of the principal sites for psychology in America. As we will see, R. M. Yerkes (Chapter 12), **Herbert S. Langfeld** (1879–1958), E. B. Holt, and E. G. Boring (Chapter 1)—psychology's best-known historian—all served as part of Harvard's early psychology faculty. Langfeld received his Ph.D. under Stumpf (Chapter 8) in Berlin, and then spent most of his professional life at Princeton, where he directed the psychological laboratory.

James's kindness and creativity are revealed in a visit he paid to Helen Keller (1880–1968), who, blind and deaf from the age of 19 months, achieved distinction as a lecturer, writer, and scholar.

> Helen Keller wrote that James visited her and Anne Sullivan [her teacher] when Keller was a young girl at the Perkins Institution for the Blind in South Boston. Comparing him to Plato and to Francis Bacon, she recalled in 1929 that he had brought her an ostrich feather. "'I thought,' he said, 'you would like the feather, it is soft and light and caressing.'" . . . The creative touch in this gesture was another of James's trademarks. (Myers, 1986, p. 42)

In summary,

> William James was that rarest of human beings—a great man who was also simple, kindly, brave and true. His memory will always be with us as an inspiration and a benediction. (Angell, 1911, p. 82)

We will now examine the life and career of an early psychologist who was significantly influenced by James. Her difficulties well illustrate the problems faced by women who wanted to earn the Ph.D. in psychology. Although early American psychology was more accepting of women in academia than other sciences, it was still a male-dominated field and projected masculine values (Minton, 2000). To be accepted by this androgenic society, many early women psychologists adopted the approach to psychology of their male counterparts. Mary Calkins, by contrast, chose an approach more sensitive to the female experience.

MARY WHITON CALKINS

Mary Whiton Calkins (1863–1930) was the oldest child of Wolcott and Charlotte Calkins. Her father was a strong-willed evangelical minister, described by his wife as "unconventional." Both of Mary Calkins's parents "were intimately involved in directing the education of their children, sons and daughters alike" (Scarborough & Furumoto, 1987, p. 30).

After earning a B.A. degree with a concentration in the classics from Smith College in western Massachusetts, Calkins was offered an appointment in the Greek Department at Wellesley College, a prestigious women's school near Boston. In 1888, Wellesley decided to introduce the new scientific psychology, and Calkins was offered the teaching position, provided she first study psychology for a year. Initially, Calkins thought of going to Germany, but she was deterred by a letter giving her a firsthand look at the difficulties—for example, inability to gain access to lectures—she would encounter.

In 1890, there were few American schools with graduate psychology programs, and the graduate schools admitting women were even fewer. Calkins eventually sought to take courses at Harvard's "Annex." Not officially part of Harvard, the Annex was a Harvard faculty method for offering private courses to women. At first, Calkins was encouraged to take regular advanced courses taught by James and Royce, but this plan ran into President Eliot's opposition. Finally, through the intercession of James and her father, Calkins was allowed to attend the courses taught by Royce and James without registering as a Harvard student. Two days later, James welcomed Calkins into his seminar.

According to Calkins (1930):

> I began the serious study of psychology with William James. Most unhappily for them and most fortunately for me the other members of his seminary in psychology dropped away in the early weeks of the fall of 1890; and James and I were left . . . quite literally at either side of a library fire. The *Principles of Psychology* was warm from the press; and my absorbed study of those brilliant, erudite, and provocative volumes, as interpreted by their writer was my introduction to psychology. (p. 31)

Courtesy of Wellesley College Archives.

Mary Calkins (1863–1930) as a young Wellesley faculty member

In essence, Calkins had a private tutorial with James, using as a textbook the just-published *Principles.* But there was more:

> I was equally fortunate . . . in entering on laboratory work under the guidance of Edmund Sanford [at Clark University in Worcester, MA], a teacher unrivalled for the richness and precision of his knowledge of experimental procedure and for the prodigality with which he lavished time and interest upon his students. (p. 32)

Edmund Clark Sanford (1869–1924) was an innovator of early psychological apparatus and published the first laboratory manual for experimental psychology. Just 3 years older than Calkins, Sanford had earned a Ph.D. at Johns Hopkins.

When Sanford recommended that Calkins look to Germany for a Ph.D. and noted he had seen a picture of Münsterberg and his seminar that contained at least one woman, Calkins considered working with Münsterberg in Freiburg. However, James urged her to postpone her decision about where to study. The reason for the delay was that Münsterberg was coming to Harvard.

Calkins worked with Münsterberg from 1893 to 1895, and he sent a letter to the Harvard Corporation describing her as the strongest student working in the laboratory during his tenure and asking if she could be admitted as a Ph.D. candidate. He concluded that a Harvard Ph.D. associated with her name would honor both her and the university. Unfortunately, women did not become eligible for the Harvard Ph.D. until 1963.

Calkins was granted an unofficial examination for the Ph.D. by the philosophy department. Although her performance was outstanding, the report of it had no effect on the Harvard authorities.

Radcliffe College replaced the Harvard Annex in 1894, and in 1902 Radcliffe's governing board offered Calkins a Ph.D. for her Harvard work. Viewing the offer as a way for Harvard to continue to deny degree recognition to women, Calkins reluctantly rejected it.

Calkins taught at Wellesley for the rest of her career, retiring in 1929. Her list of publications includes four books and over 100 papers, divided equally between psychology and philosophy. According to Furumoto (1979), Calkins's main contributions were the establishment of an early psychology laboratory at Wellesley, the invention of a paired-associates method for studying memory, and the development of a system of self-psychology. Calkins's (1894) report of the **paired-associates method** first appeared in a publication in which she stated that she had shown subjects colors paired with numbers. G. E. Müller (Chapter 8) further refined the method, which Calkins did not pursue (Strunk, 1972). In a recent examination of Calkins's immediate-memory research, Madigan and O'Hara (1992) concluded that Calkins actually identified several phenomena (e.g., primacy and recency effects) rediscovered long after her unacknowledged work.

Calkins viewed her **self-psychology** system as having much greater importance. Building on many of James's conceptions of psychology and the self (Coon, 2000), Calkins's own view of psychology was that it "should be conceived as the science of the self, or person, as related to its environment, physical and social" (Calkins, 1930, p. 42). Self-psychology, or personalistic psychology, is an introspectionist psychology, with three basic concepts: "that of the self, that of the object, and that of the self's relation or attitude toward its object" (p. 45). Although undefinable, the self has describable characteristics, which include that it is a unique being (I am I and you are you), an identical but changing being (my adult self is the same being as my 10-year-old self, but at the same time the two differ), and "a being related in a distinctive fashion both to itself and its experiences and to environing objects, personal and impersonal." The self's relation to the objects "is called its consciousness of them" (p. 45).

Calkins (1906) proposed self-theory as a way to reconcile structural and functional psychology. By 1930, Calkins confidently noted the compatibility of her system with the other systems of psychology proposed to that point—structuralism, functionalism, behaviorism, and Gestalt psychology—and with "every one of the psychoanalytic systems" (p. 53). Heidbreder (1972) suggested that Calkins was trying to develop a conceptual scheme that would allow psychology to deal "with its empirical subject-matter, not only as that subject-matter appears when observed under laboratory conditions and by certain approved methods, but as it presents itself in ordinary experience and in common-sense knowledge" (p. 66). Heidbreder concluded that Calkins did not succeed in her conceptual efforts, but her way of perceiving the problem and her approach to it are instructive.

Wentworth (1999) addressed the question of why Calkins continued to stress her self-psychology in the face of widespread opposition from the psychological community. As the daughter of a Protestant minister, Calkins remained deeply religious herself, and her self-psychology had strongly moral and religious overtones. Hence, Wentworth concluded, "[i]t is conceivable that Calkins's unwavering commitment to self-psychology was a consequence of the theory's very interconnectedness to her own many-sided self" (p. 128).

Furumoto (1989) has suggested another explanation for Calkins's continuing commitment to a psychology of the self, and particularly to a psychology of interacting social selves, at a time when behaviorism reigned supreme in American psychology. Calkins developed her self psychology in the context of the close-knit Wellesley academic community. Given this context, it is little wonder that Calkins eventually rejected the atomistic, impersonal approach to laboratory psychology in which she had been trained for "the reality and importance of selves in everyday experience" (p. 29).

Calkins was elected president of the APA in 1905 and of the American Philosophical Association in 1918, in each case being the first woman to hold the post. In a 1903 ranking of the 50 leading American psychologists, Calkins ranked 12th. Calkins received honorary degrees from Columbia in 1909 and from Smith College in 1910, and she received an honorary membership in the British Psychological Association in 1928 (Furumoto, 1991). For a further look at the experiences of the first generation of women psychologists, see Milar (2000).

We will now examine the contributions of the third of Calkins's major teachers—Hugo Münsterberg.

Courtesy of Harvard University Archives.

Hugo Münsterberg (1863–1916)

HUGO MÜNSTERBERG

Hugo Münsterberg (1863–1916) was born in Danzig, East Prussia, which is now Gdansk, Poland. His father was a prominent Jewish lumber merchant, and his mother was an avid painter and musician. Both of his parents died before Münsterberg was 20, and Münsterberg converted to Protestantism following their deaths (Spillmann & Spillmann, 1993).

Münsterberg attended Wundt's lectures and earned his Ph.D. from Leipzig in 1885, then studied medicine and received his M.D. at Heidelberg in 1887. That same year, Münsterberg was appointed a *Dozent* at the University of Freiburg, establishing a laboratory there with equipment purchased with his own money.

In 1888, Münsterberg published the work he had intended as his dissertation but had not used at Wundt's request, *Die Willenshandlung* (*Voluntary Action*), a book James called "a little masterpiece" in the *Principles.* In it, Münsterberg criticized Wundt's position on will while he "railed at statistics-gathering empiricism as well. Hence from James's view young Münsterberg had attacked the humbug of an artificial idealism as well as the excesses of a dry positivism" (Bjork, 1983, p. 43). When G. E. Müller brutally reviewed Münsterberg's book, James wrote Münsterberg a letter of "consolation." At the time of Münsterberg's first meeting with James at the First International Congress of Psychology in Paris in 1889, Münsterberg had broken with Wundt, established a laboratory at Freiburg, and was beginning to publish a series of four volumes entitled *Beiträge zur experimentelle Psychologie* (*Contributions to Experimental Psychology*). In Münsterberg, James believed he had found his director for the Harvard laboratory.

However, Münsterberg spoke no English and was nationalistically German. "He seems to have always seen himself as a missionary of enlightenment amidst naive hosts" (Watkins, 1989, p. 3) and appears never to have considered becoming a United States citizen. Still, he was interested enough in the Harvard position to come to America in 1892 for a 3-year trial.

During Münsterberg's test period, James went to Europe on sabbatical, leaving **Josiah Royce** (1855–1916) in charge of the department. Although Royce and James were close personally, Royce was thoroughly a rationalist, a Hegelian, believing in an Absolute Mind. By contrast, James considered Hegel his "philosophic *bête noire* [literally black beast, or "pet peeve"]" (Knight, 1950, p. 39).

Through correspondence with Royce, James learned that his new laboratory director was an "immense success." For example, taking full advantage of Harvard's enormous financial resources and the equipment James had already gathered, Münsterberg quickly built a first-class experimental psychology laboratory (Benjamin, 2000). He also trained students, worked on a German textbook, and learned English (Moskowitz, 1977).

In 1895, Münsterberg returned to Germany but was unable to find a chair at a major university. Thus, Münsterberg formally joined the Harvard faculty in 1897 and stayed until his death in 1916 from a cerebral hemorrhage during a lecture to an introductory psychology class at Radcliffe College. "At the time of his death he was widely despised and ridiculed, and essentially friendless. Harvard refused to pay any pension to his widow. By provision of his will, his remains were returned to Germany" (Watkins, 1989, p. 3). According to Benjamin (2000), "His papers, housed today in the Rare Books and Manuscripts Collection of the Boston Public Library, include four folders of hate mail" (p. 113). Indeed, some of the letters even contain death threats. From a promising beginning—Münsterberg was elected the seventh APA president in 1898—what led to such an ignominious ending?

The problem was that Münsterberg developed and pursued interests outside academia. Although many of these interests led to important contributions, they also gave Münsterberg a visibility that became a liability because of his pro-German activities at a time when American sentiment was decidedly anti-German.

> Although Münsterberg actively fomented experimentalism among his students in the laboratory, he . . . had heard the siren voice of philosophy and was rapidly becoming more interested in the "principles" of psychology than in the discovery of new facts. He became famous in America for his personal brilliancy, his participation in public affairs, his voluminous popular writings, and his innovating applications of psychology to industry, jurisprudence, and medicine. (Perry, 1935, p. 201)

A listing of just a few of Münsterberg's book titles shows his versatility: *On the Witness Stand* (1909), *Psychology and the Teacher* (1909), *Psychotherapy* (1909), and *Psychology and Industrial Efficiency* (1913). A best seller, *On the Witness Stand* was concerned with what we would call forensic or legal psychology. *Psychology and Industrial Efficiency* was important in the development of industrial psychology in America. *On the Witness Stand* and *Psychology and Industrial Efficiency* established Münsterberg as a pioneer in applied psychology (Chapter 17).

It is historically interesting to compare the contributions and long-term influence of Münsterberg and Titchener, two of Wundt's students who came to America to take charge of experimental laboratories at major universities. As we have noted, Titchener's psychology studied the adult, human, generalized mind to determine its basic elements and structure; Münsterberg's psychology was considerably broader and less easily characterized. In particular, Münsterberg sought to apply psychology to the betterment of life, and as part of this effort, invented a new science called psychotechnics. Psychotechnics was a forerunner of what is known today as **ergonomics** (designing equipment that can be more efficiently used by humans; also called human factors engineering) and industrial psychology. The term *psychotechnics* was coined by William Stern (Chapter 8) but popularized by Münsterberg (Lück & Bringmann, 1997).

Although Kuna (1978) noted a number of applied studies before Münsterberg began his work, Spillmann and Spillmann (1993) concluded, "Hugo Münsterberg is regarded as the founder of applied psychology in the United States, as well as in Europe" (p. 332). We can see Münsterberg's influence in such applied areas as business and industry, the legal profession, and the psychological clinic. By contrast, Titchener's structuralism did not long survive him. Thus, of the two, Münsterberg has had by far the greater impact on contemporary psychology, although he rarely receives the recognition his contributions merit.

Münsterberg's publications, many aimed at and read by the general public, made him perhaps the best-known psychologist in America in the early part of the 20th century and "helped sell the American public on the worth of psychology" (Benjamin, 2000, p. 127). This was a time of steadily worsening relations between Germany and its Western European neighbors, culminating in World War I. As a German in America, Münsterberg worked actively to keep America neutral.

The Harvard administration was frequently embarrassed by Münsterberg's pro-German activities, and President Eliot rebuked Münsterberg on a number of occasions. Unfortunately, Münsterberg continued such activities after war began in Europe. In 1914, a former Harvard student, Major Clarence Wiener of London, sent an open letter to the Dean of Harvard College and several newspapers threatening to withdraw his promise of a sizable bequest unless Münsterberg was removed from the faculty. Although the Harvard administration intended to ignore the threat, Münsterberg made matters worse by declaring publicly that he would resign if Wiener would give half the gift immediately. Wiener refused, but the administration found itself having to defend Münsterberg's unpopular antics—such as writing articles and books defending Germany's position. "Consequently, he was vilified as 'Professor Hugo Monsterbug' . . . by the same newspapers which had praised and popularized his accomplishments as an applied psychologist" (Lück & Bringmann, 1997, p. 473). Stemming from Münsterberg's belief system, his activities continued after the 1915 German sinking of the *Lusitania*, with the loss of over 100 Americans. Despite the accomplishments of his campaign of applied psychology, in the end Münsterberg was so despised that no eulogy was published when he died.

Although Münsterberg contributed significantly to the shift of psychology from an exclusively academic discipline to one with professional and applied interests (Moskowitz, 1977), the person universally recognized as second only to William James in shaping the course of American psychology was G. Stanley Hall.

GRANVILLE STANLEY HALL

William James's influence on psychology continues primarily because of his writing of the *Principles.* G. Stanley Hall's influence continues because of his organizational talents, exemplified by the founding of the American Psychological Association, by journals such as *The American Journal of Psychology,* and by the department of psychology at Clark University that Hall, as Clark's first president, developed. In short, despite his personal faults, Hall was a pioneering founder of psychology in America. Like James, but for different reasons, Hall's development as a psychologist was circuitous.

Granville Stanley Hall (1844–1924) was born near Ashfield, Massachusetts, the first child of descendants of colonists who arrived on the *Mayflower.* Although both of Hall's parents had been schoolteachers, his father was a farmer when Hall was born and remained so for the rest of his life.

Hall's father was harshly puritanical, stern, and quick-tempered, whereas his mother was gently pious. Hall's feelings toward his father combined love and admiration with hostility. Perhaps stemming from "these ambivalent feelings, Stanley developed a character at once aggressive and constrained" (Ross, 1972, p. 11).

In a letter to a student cited in Pruette (1926), Hall described his life as a series of intense interests. Infatuated with Wundt's psychology, Hall rushed to Leipzig and then came back to establish the first psychological laboratory in the country. Next came his child-study craze, with the use of questionnaires, followed by an obsession with psychoanalysis. Hall indicated this was his last obsession, "unless I except war psychology, on which I have a book coming out" (p. 4). With this overview, we will examine how Hall became one of American psychology's great founders.

Hall's Early Years

At 23, Hall graduated with Phi Beta Kappa honors from Williams College in Massachusetts. Upon graduation, he wanted to further the philosophical interests gained from reading John Stuart Mill (Chapter 5) with study in Germany, but he could not afford to go. Selecting the only advanced educational avenue open to someone of limited means with an interest in philosophy—theology—Hall enrolled at New York City's Union Theological Seminary.

Hall found New York exhilarating. In his spare time,

> [h]e attended all kinds of church services, from Catholic to Seventh-Day Adventist to Spiritist. He tested the city's famous phrenologists and mediums, repeatedly visited the police courts and the morgue, and dabbled in a few of the reform movements of the day. . . . Twice he went to see "The Black Crook," a popular and scandalous ballet spectacle which featured . . . one hundred female dancers very scantily attired. After the second visit, Hall wrote his parents that he "sat very near and this time was disgusted." (Ross, 1972, pp. 32–33).

Still, Hall dreamed of becoming a professor of philosophy. With a loan, he sailed for Europe in June 1869. In Germany, Hall's main studies were as a member of the seminar of Frederick Trendelenburg, the Berlin philosopher who influenced Brentano (Chapter 8). Trendelenburg's emphasis on development encouraged Hall to investigate Hegel, and both Hegel and Trendelenburg confirmed Hall's belief in the value of historical process. When Hall's money ran out, he reluctantly returned to America in the fall of 1870.

Back at Union, Hall's trial sermon revealed his rapidly waning religious orthodoxy: Instead of the usual critique by the president, the latter instead "knelt and prayed that I might be shown the true light and saved from mortal errors of doctrine, and then excused me without a word" (Hall, 1923, p. 178). Thus, Hall decided to use his divinity degree to gain a position teaching philosophy rather than to become a minister. Unfortunately, he found it difficult to obtain such a position because philosophy was usually taught by a more traditional cleric.

Hall finally received an offer to teach rhetoric and English literature at Ohio's Antioch College. Because of Antioch's financial straits, Hall also taught French, German, and Anglo-Saxon. In his "spare time," he was also the college librarian, debate coach, and drillmaster. During Hall's 4 years at the school, he earned a reputation as one of Antioch's best teachers. However, even with the authorities' liberal Unitarian beliefs, Hall found his attitudes incompatible with those in Ohio. Above all, his ambitions were unfulfilled.

Hall's philosophy continued to evolve. The second edition of Spencer's *Principles of Psychology* (1872) is probably where Hall found the principle (psychology) to unify his diverse philosophical interests, and he introduced lectures on psychology into his philosophy course. Soon thereafter, Hall was greatly excited by the first volume of Wundt's *Principles of Physiological Psychology,* as his studies in Germany and his independent readings had prepared him to appreciate Wundt's effort to found a science of psychology from physiological and philosophical bases. Hall took a leave of absence from Antioch in order to attend lectures at Harvard.

According to Hall, he stayed at Harvard to earn his Ph.D. after he was offered a teaching post in English by President Eliot. "This story is not supported by contemporary evidence. . . . The story appears to reflect Hall's desire to minimize the importance of his debt to William James" (Ross, 1972, p. 61), which was considerable, as Hall took most of his work with James. This illustrates our Chapter 1 discussion of both the reconstructive nature of some autobiographical material and the need to consult multiple sources when attempting to verify historical events.

Hall's largely theoretical dissertation was on the muscular perception of space, supported by experiments he performed in Henry P. Bowditch's (1840–1911) laboratory at Harvard Medical School. In addition to his 1878 Ph.D.—the first doctorate awarded by Harvard's philosophy department and the first psychology doctorate in America—Hall took from his experience with James a functional and pragmatic approach to the mind. With no immediate employment prospects, Hall left for a second visit to the German universities and the laboratories of several physiologists we introduced in Chapter 7.

Hall traveled first to du Bois-Reymond's Berlin laboratory. In addition, Helmholtz's efforts to explain the processes of life physically and chemically caught Hall's imagination. Hall began increasingly to feel that philosophy rested upon psychology and psychology upon physiology, a reductionistic view. Hall also heard and was impressed by Hermann Munk (Chapter 7). Finally, Hall's Berlin experience exposed him to the study of psychopathology.

In the fall of 1879, Hall moved to Leipzig, where he spent most of his time working in Karl Ludwig's (1816–1895) physiology laboratory. Hall also worked in Wundt's newly established laboratory, but nothing publishable resulted, and Hall's opinion of Wundt decreased with greater contact. In a letter to James, he described Wundt "as a man who has done more speculation and less valuable observing than any man I know who has had his career" (cited in Ross, 1972, p. 85).

Ernst Haeckel's theories formed a major part of the scientific backdrop during Hall's stay in Germany. Haeckel (Chapter 9) believed that an individual repeats the evolutionary history of the species in its development, and this recapitulation idea became central to Hall's theory of child development (discussed later).

After being rejected initially for employment at Johns Hopkins University, Hall hit upon the idea of applying psychology to education. He assembled pedagogical materials and quickly toured schools in Germany, France, and England. This tour and his interest in psychology applied to education proved important for his later career.

Hall and Psychology in America

Employed as a teacher of the history of philosophy at Williams College, Hall gave a series of lectures on pedagogy on Saturday mornings at the request of Harvard's president. The lectures' success led to an offer for Hall to do a similar series at Johns Hopkins.

Hall gave 10 lectures on the "new" psychology in January 1882, and in March, Hopkins' President Daniel Gilman offered him a 3-year appointment in the philosophy department as a lecturer in psychology and pedagogy. Hall found himself competing for a professorial slot with a Union mentor, George Morris, and with James's friend, Charles S. Peirce. After Peirce was dismissed in early 1884, Hall was chosen over Morris, at least partly because Hall was forceful and dynamic whereas Morris was quiet and retiring.

Because Hall considered the principal division of the "new" psychology to be experimental psychology, in 1883 he developed a small psychological laboratory that some consider America's first formally established psychological laboratory (e.g., Cattell, 1929). By 1887, Hall's laboratory had expanded to four rooms. When he left in 1888, Hall took with him the laboratory apparatus, and Johns Hopkins did not re-establish a psychological laboratory until 1903. Hall's Hopkins laboratory forced other universities in America to create laboratories in order to stay current.

In addition to James McKeen Cattell (discussed later) and John Dewey, a number of Hall's Hopkins students had significant careers. **Joseph Jastrow** (1863–1944) and Henry Donaldson (Chapter 12) were among the earliest contingent. The founder of the laboratory at the University of Wisconsin and APA president in 1900, Jastrow is perhaps best known for his books popularizing psychology, including *The House That Freud Built,* as well as for his duck-rabbit reversible figure (see Chapter 14). Jastrow and Donaldson were soon joined by Edmund Sanford, and Sanford and Donaldson accompanied Hall to Clark University.

The most famous of Hall's students at Hopkins was T. W. Wilson, "who spent a long Sunday afternoon walking and debating with Hall whether he should leave the study of politics and history and come definitely into psychology . . ." (Pruette, 1926, p. 91). As history records it, Thomas Woodrow Wilson (1856–1924) became a lawyer, then president of Princeton, governor of New Jersey, and finally, America's 28th president.

Hall's efforts at Hopkins included psychical research. In Germany, Hall had established contact with some of the spiritualists in the Leipzig academic community, which included his neighbor, Gustav Fechner (Chapter 7). The Society for Psychical Research was formed in England in 1882, and William James was a member. In 1885, at James's initiative, an American version was founded, with Hall as one of the vice-presidents (Bauer, 1997). Hall believed many "psychic phenomena" were created by deception, and to help him detect the deception, he studied magic, becoming an expert performer. He used this expertise to expose mediums and became one of the first of the scientific leaders to resign from the Society. In fact, Hall used his attacks on the "pseudoscience" of spiritualism to enhance psychology's scientific image (Coon, 1992).

Perhaps Hall's foremost accomplishment at Hopkins was the 1887 founding of America's first psychological journal, *The American Journal of Psychology.* Ironically, some of the funds for the *Journal* came from a gift from a member of the American Society for Psychical Research, who undoubtedly assumed Hall's *Journal* would treat psychical research favorably. When this proved not to be the case, there were no more contributions. Also, in his enthusiasm, Hall ordered far more copies of the first volume than he actually sold, a financial setback from which he apparently never recovered psychologically. As testimony to his obsession with fiscal economy, when he died, Hall had more than $172,000 in small amounts in 78 different Massachusetts banks.

At about the time Hall founded his journal, Jonas Clark and eight other citizens of Worcester, Massachusetts, were petitioning the state legislature to incorporate an institution of higher learning. After earning a fortune as a merchant in the California gold rush in the mid-19th century, Clark (1815–1900) returned to his birthplace to establish a monument to himself in the form of a university bearing his name. Clark apparently wanted a school in the mold of Johns Hopkins, and to head his institution, Clark and his board of trustees chose Hall.

At Clark's expense, Hall toured European universities to gather the latest thinking on higher education, using the opportunity to create a positive image of Clark University in the minds of all he met. Before and after this trip, Hall assembled a talented faculty, with many recruited from Hopkins. In addition, Hall hired many professors for low wages by promising them reduced teaching loads, maximum research time, and ample equipment support. For example, Franz Boas (Chapter 8), who became the country's premier anthropologist, was lured to Clark for half the $2,000 he made at *Science* magazine by the promise of free summers to pursue fieldwork.

When Clark University opened in 1889, the 18 faculty members indeed had light teaching duties, devoting most of their time to directing the research of 34 students. Unfortunately, this idyllic situation was short-lived, its ending presaged in 1890 by a personal disaster for Hall. While recuperating from diphtheria in Ashfield, Hall learned his wife and daughter had been asphyxiated by a faulty heater, with only his 9-year-old son surviving. Hall sought solace in a renewed faith in God and a passion for work, neither of which were enough to save his dream for Clark.

Initially, the problem was Jonas Clark's unrealistic expectations of a university's cost. Forced to pay operating expenses out of his own pocket, Clark's ardor cooled rapidly. Hall did think of one way to generate public approval and needed funds for the University, however. In 1891, he opened a summer school for area educators. That same year Hall founded the journal *Pedagogical Seminary,* which later became the *Journal of Genetic Psychology.*

But summer school for educators did not bring in enough money, and Clark became stingier with his funds. In response, Hall became increasingly autocratic and devious. His alienation of the faculty proved disastrous, as it came when President William Harper was trying to attract high-quality personnel to his newly organized University of Chicago. "In the end, two-thirds of all those of faculty rank and 70 percent of the student body left Clark in the spring of 1892" (Ross, 1972, p. 227). With the loss of most of the students and faculty, Clark was left with only one strong department: psychology, with its pedagogy subdivision (Hogan, 2003). Further, after word spread about the university's problems, Hall found it nearly impossible to hire well-qualified replacements for the lost faculty.

However, 1892 was not all bad for Hall's ambitions. In that year, he was instrumental in founding the American Psychological Association and was elected its first president. It is worth noting that Clark University survived its early hardships and remains a prestigious center for psychological research.

Hall and the Founding of the APA

Hall invited over 25 people interested in scientific psychology to an organizational meeting of the **American Psychological Association** (APA) at Clark University on July 8, 1892. The charter members included Hall and Sanford at Clark; James, Royce, and Münsterberg at Harvard; Cattell at Columbia; Witmer (Chapter 8) at Pennsylvania; James Mark Baldwin (discussed later) at Toronto; Titchener at Cornell; Dewey at Michigan; and Jastrow at Wisconsin. As president, Hall presided over the APA's first annual meeting, which was held at the University of Pennsylvania on December 27, 1892. With his election again in 1924, Hall became only the second person to be elected twice; James was the other.

From the 31 charter members, the membership of the APA has increased rapidly, with the organization claiming more than 150,000 members in 2003. Table 10.1 lists the APA presidents, and you will see that most of this chapter's people are on the list. For an examination of the APA's origins and early development, see Sokal (1992).

Since the APA's founding, a number of rival organizations have formed, generally with the goal of being more accommodating to scientific and academic psychology. Titchener's The Experimentalists (later The Society of Experimental Psychologists) is one example. Another is the **Psychonomic Society,** founded in 1959–1960 by Clifford T. Morgan (1915–1976), William Verplanck (1916–2002), and other well-respected experimentalists. A physiological psychologist, Morgan served as chairman of the organizing committee. Like The Society of Experimental Psychologists, the Psychonomic Society was organized to serve the needs of basic scientists in psychology.

The APA's apparent applied-clinical focus triggered a mass defection in 1988. The resulting **American Psychological Society** (APS) has an explicit focus on scientific psychology. By 2003, the APS had more than 15,000 members. More than anything, the various professional organizations for psychologists highlight the field's diversity, which is well illustrated by the more than 50 different APA divisions to which a member can belong.

Hall's Fall From Glory

By the end of the 19th century, Hall had passed his peak of influence in American psychology. Although his Ph.D. output had been prodigious—by 1898, 30 of the 54 American psychology Ph.D.s had gone to Hall's students—this would not continue. With Clark impoverished, its psychology department could not compete against departments at wealthier schools.

In addition, Hall's editorship of *The American Journal of Psychology* damaged his relations with other psychologists. In part, the difficulty lay in his continuing attacks—often through brutal book reviews—on some of his "friends." For example, Hall criticized the haphazard chapter arrangement in James's *Principles* by implying "that the book sounded as though it were written with a shotgun or water hose. . . . So much did James's personality intrude on his work, that it sometimes reminded one of Rousseau or a cheap popular diarist" (cited in Ross, 1972, p. 233).

The idiosyncrasy and exclusiveness of Hall's *Journal* led other psychologists to start rival journals. Baldwin and Cattell were the leaders in this effort, founding the *Psychological Review.* When the *Review* appeared in 1894, Hall reluctantly took steps to meet the challenge to his *Journal:* He named Sanford and Titchener as co-editors and a cooperative board

TABLE 10.1

Presidents of the American Psychological Association

1892 G. Stanley Hall	1930 Herbert S. Langfeld	1968 Abraham Maslow
1893 G. T. Ladd	1931 Walter S. Hunter	1969 George A. Miller
1894 William James	1932 Walter R. Miles	1970 George W. Albee
1895 J. McKeen Cattell	1933 L. L. Thurstone	1971 Kenneth B. Clark
1896 G. S. Fullerton	1934 Joseph Peterson	1972 Anne Anastasi
1897 J. M. Baldwin	1935 A. T. Poffenberger	1973 Leona E. Tyler
1898 Hugo Münsterberg	1936 Clark L. Hull	1974 Albert Bandura
1899 John Dewey	1937 Edward C. Tolman	1975 Donald T. Campbell
1900 Joseph Jastrow	1938 J. F. Dashiell	1976 Wilbert McKeachie
1901 Josiah Royce	1939 Gordon Allport	1977 Theodore H. Blau
1902 E. C. Sanford	1940 Leonard Carmichael	1978 M. Brewster Smith
1903 William L. Bryan	1941 Herbert Woodrow	1979 Nicholas A. Cummings
1904 William James	1942 Calvin P. Stone	1980 Florence L. Denmark
1905 Mary W. Calkins	1943 John E. Anderson	1981 John J. Conger
1906 James R. Angell	1944 Gardner Murphy	1982 William Bevan
1907 Henry R. Marshall	1945 Edwin R. Guthrie	1983 Max Siegel
1908 George M. Stratton	1946 Henry E. Garrett	1984 Janet T. Spence
1909 Charles H. Judd	1947 Carl R. Rogers	1985 Robert Perloff
1910 Walter B. Pillsbury	1948 Donald G. Marquis	1986 Logan Wright
1911 Carl E. Seashore	1949 Ernest R. Hilgard	1987 Bonnie R. Strickland
1912 Edward L. Thorndike	1950 J. P. Guilford	1988 Raymond D. Fowler
1913 Howard C. Warren	1951 Robert R. Sears	1989 Joseph D. Matarazzo
1914 R. S. Woodworth	1952 J. McVickers Hunt	1990 Stanley R. Graham
1915 John B. Watson	1953 Laurance F. Shaffer	1991 Charles Spielberger
1916 Raymond Dodge	1954 O. Hobart Mowrer	1992 Jack G. Wiggins
1917 Robert M. Yerkes	1955 E. Lowell Kelly	1993 Frank Farley
1918 J. W. Baird	1956 T. M. Newcomb	1994 Ronald E. Fox
1919 Walter D. Scott	1957 Lee J. Cronbach	1995 Robert J. Resnick
1920 Shepherd I. Franz	1958 Harry F. Harlow	1996 Dorothy Cantor
1921 Margaret Washburn	1959 Wolfgang Köhler	1997 Norman Ables
1922 Knight Dunlap	1960 D. O. Hebb	1998 Martin E. P. Seligman
1923 Lewis M. Terman	1961 Neal Miller	1999 Richard M. Suinn
1924 G. Stanley Hall	1962 Paul Meehl	2000 Patrick H. DeLeon
1925 Madison Bentley	1963 Charles Osgood	2001 Norine G. Johnson
1926 Harvey A. Carr	1964 Quinn McNemar	2002 Philip Zimbardo
1927 H.H. Hollingworth	1965 Jerome S. Bruner	2003 Robert Sternberg
1928 E. G. Boring	1966 Nicholas Hobbs	2004 Diane Halpern
1929 Karl S. Lashley	1967 Gardner Lindzey	2005 Ronald Levant

consisting of his and Titchener's friends and supporters. Unfortunately, Hall's editorial opening the "new" *Journal* included the claim that his influence had been responsible "for the founding of departments of experimental psychology and laboratories at Harvard, Yale, Pennsylvania, Columbia, Toronto, Wisconsin, and many other universities" (Ross, 1972, p. 243). Letters to *Science* from James, Ladd, Baldwin, and Cattell refuted Hall's claims. Hall's subsequent conciliatory letter to *Science* failed to heal the rift that developed between him and James—and, perhaps, between Hall and the rest of American psychology.

Hall's Research Interests

Hall is best known for research that combined his interests in psychology, pedagogy, and evolution in the study of child development. Hall's data were collected with questionnaires, which he used so extensively that he is often credited with developing the technique, although the originator was actually Galton (Chapter 9).

Before leaving Boston for Baltimore and Johns Hopkins, Hall gathered questionnaire data on schoolchildren, which was published as "The Contents of Children's Minds" (Hall, 1883). This was followed by his 1904 two-volume *Adolescence: Its Psychology and Its Relations to Physiology, Anthropology, Sociology, Sex, Crime, Religion, and Education.* Much of *Adolescence* is filled with comments about sexuality, and Hall frequently coined new terms without adequately defining them. Yet despite its faults, the book is important as perhaps the first systematic recognition in modern times of the period from puberty to young adulthood as a distinct stage in the life cycle.

Adolescence was remarkably successful given its size and topic, selling more than 25,000 copies in America. Although popular reviewers often approved of it, psychologists were less enthusiastic. For example, Thorndike reviewed Hall's book negatively and privately wrote Cattell that it was "'chock full of errors, masturbation and Jesus. He is a mad man'" (Ross, 1972, p. 385).

In *Adolescence,* Hall described his **recapitulation theory** of child development, which maintains that every human being passes "through all the stages of the race's evolution in his personal development (thus Hall's nickname as the 'Darwin of the mind')" (Schlossman, 1973, p. 143). Accordingly, the child is reliving the period when humans were little more than savages; in this stage, what is needed is drilling in the correct habits—indoctrination, in other words. Adolescence thus becomes "the time for training the will and shaping ideals" (p. 143), and Hall's supporters touted boys' clubs as ideal venues for such tuition. For psychology, recapitulation theory died at the hands of Thorndike, who criticized it from a biological standpoint (its parallels are more apparent than real) and concluded that the theory's influence was due primarily to its rhetorical attractiveness.

Although Hall's study of childhood and adolescence amply qualify him as an early child psychologist (Nance, 1970; White, 1990), his interest in development continued with *Senescence: The Last Half of Life* (1922). *Senescence* looks at the problems of old age and the psychological states they engender. Mirroring earlier works, *Senescence* is a personal record of what it was like for Hall himself to grow old. In keeping with the methodology he had used to develop data for *Adolescence,* Hall used interviews and questionnaires to gain information on aging from a large group of aging persons. His rationale was that the older persons themselves were the authorities on aging (Hirshbein, 2002). Currently, gerontology—the study of aging and the aged—is a "hot" topic in psychology, and Hall deserves recognition as an early investigator.

Despite his contributions to religious psychology, Hall's role in its founding is often unrecognized. "In most recent psychology of religion texts, Hall is either conspicuously absent or overwhelmingly dwarfed by James" (Vande Kemp, 1992, p. 296). Hall, who first offered courses in religious psychology at Hopkins and taught at least one course on the topic nearly every year after 1900, clearly played a role in founding the psychology of religion. In 1904, "Hall founded a library department of religious psychology and education to concentrate on acquiring a special book collection and publishing a journal" (Vande Kemp, p. 292). Hall's *The American Journal of Religious Psychology and Education* was published for a decade beginning in 1904, its impetus perhaps partly caused by James's 1902 book, *The Varieties of Religious Experience* (Ross, 1972).

Hall initially edited the journal with two former students—**James H. Leuba** (1868–1946) and **Edwin D. Starbuck** (1866–1947). Leuba was an 1895 Clark graduate who stayed on as a fellow before moving to Bryn Mawr College to head the psychology department. He published the first empirical study of religious conversion and the first book with the title

The Psychology of Religion (Beit-Hallahmi, 1974). Starbuck was James's student at Harvard before transferring to Clark. Like Leuba, Starbuck stayed at Clark as a fellow after receiving his Ph.D.

In 1917, Hall published *Jesus, the Christ, in the Light of Psychology,* which is primarily "a historical study of Jesus' life and its humane meaning . . ." (Ross, 1972, p. 418). Hall delayed publication because of the possible reaction of fundamentalists and the fear of damaging the rest of his career. "The book was indeed criticized severely in the conservative religious press but taken in stride in other quarters" (p. 418), as "Hall's psychological colleagues were accustomed to his eccentricities" (Vande Kemp, 1992, p. 294).

Hall and Psychoanalysis

Because of his interest in physiology, Hall invited "Father of the Neuron Theory" Santiago Ramón y Cajal (Chapter 7) to the celebration of Clark's 10th anniversary (Rosenzweig, 1997). A further interest in psychopathology led Hall to invite Swiss medical researcher and psychiatrist **Auguste-Henri Forel** (1848–1931) as well. Also known for his studies of ants, Forel spoke in 1899 about hypnotism and cerebral activity and about the work of Breuer and Freud (both Chapter 15). In that same year, Hall's *Journal* favorably reviewed Freud's and Breuer's work on hysteria.

As Clark's 20th anniversary (1909) approached, Hall decided to invite Wundt and Freud to the psychology conference. Wundt refused Hall's offer of 3,000 marks ($750) and an honorary degree, pleading advanced age and the 500th Jubilee of Leipzig University as his excuse. Freud also rejected Hall's offer of 1,600 marks ($400), his main objection being the scheduled date of the conference (Evans & Koelsch, 1985). Hall's invitation was rejected by Alfred Binet (Chapter 17) as well, but Wundt's slot was filled by Hermann Ebbinghaus (Chapter 8). Unfortunately, Ebbinghaus died unexpectedly in 1909 before the conference took place.

When Hall changed the conference date and offered Wundt's honorarium, Freud accepted the invitation. Psychoanalysts Carl Jung, Sandor Ferenczi, Ernest Jones, and A. A. Brill (all Chapter 15) also attended, with only Jung and Freud scheduled to speak.

Freud's five lectures in German were well received both by the attendees and by the local press, and a positive article about the meeting subsequently appeared in *The Nation* and several other periodicals (Cromer & Anderson, 1970). Apparently, Hall himself wrote *The Nation* article (Evans & Koelsch, 1985), possibly fearing a repeat of the lack of coverage his 10th anniversary meeting had received.

For Freud, the opportunity to present his work to interested psychologists in the United States was a dream come true. The subsequent publication of his lectures in Hall's *Journal* (Freud, 1910) completed his successful introduction of psychoanalytic ideas to the New World.

Although Hall remained an advocate of psychoanalysis, his public support of Freud ended in 1911. The problem apparently lay in Freud's attribution of sexual symbolism to many different objects and to a highly critical review of Hall's *Educational Problems* in 1911. Upbraided for his apparent preoccupation with sexuality, Hall was probably reluctant to continue to support publicly psychoanalysis's sexual emphasis (Ross, 1972).

As a postscript to Hall's interest in psychoanalysis, he began corresponding with Alfred Adler (Chapter 15) in 1914 and at one point considered inviting Adler to the United States (Ansbacher, 1971). Finally, Hall's influence on Carl Jung has been suggested (Hinkelman & Aderman, 1968). When they met at the Clark Conference, Jung was a relatively unknown psychologist and Hall was a well-known university president.

Hall and Subordinates

Hall's interpersonal relationships were often less than satisfactory and were frequently characterized by dissembling when he felt his intellectual superiority threatened. For example, Cattell probably lost his Hopkins fellowship because he was highly intelligent and brashly confident. Feeling threatened, Hall worked behind the scenes to deny Cattell his fellowship and then repeated his performance with John Dewey, another able graduate student.

Archives of the History of American Psychology–The University of Akron.

Attendees at the Clark Conference in 1909

Beginning with first row, left to right: Franz Boas, E. B. Titchener, William James, William Stern, Leo Burgerstein, G. Stanley Hall, Sigmund Freud, Carl G. Jung, Adolf Meyer, H. S. Jennings. *Second row:* C. E. Seashore, Joseph Jastrow, J. McK. Cattell, E. F. Buchner, E. Katzenellenbogen, Ernest Jones, A. A. Brill, Wm. H. Burnham, A. F. Chamberlain. *Third row:* Albert Schinz, J. A. Magni, B. T. Baldwin, F. Lyman Wells, G. M. Forbes, E. A. Kirkpatrick, Sandor Ferenczi, E. C. Sanford, J. P. Porter, Sakyo Kanda, Kikoso Kakise. *Fourth row:* G. E. Dawson, S. P. Hayes, E. B. Holt, C. S. Berry, G. M. Whipple, Frank Drew, J. W. A. Young, L. N. Wilson, K. J. Karlson, H. H. Goddard, H. I. Klopp, S. C. Fuller.

Hall did not alienate all of his competent associates, however. Edmund Sanford was both capable and steadfastly loyal. In addition, Sanford was always willing to be subordinate to Hall, and this was perhaps the key to their relationship. Hall "recognized ability and nurtured it effectively so long as it remained in a subordinate role" (Sokal, 1990, p. 116). Recognizing the quality of his relationship with Hall, Sanford "wrote late in his life that 'the relation of pupil and teacher was never wholly lost'" (p. 118). Apparently, one reason for Sanford's loyalty was that Hall stood by him during Sanford's frequent illnesses. At a time when a disability such as a loss of hearing could cause dismissal, Sanford's loyalty becomes more understandable. According to Goodwin (1987), Sanford's attachment to Hall cost him recognition he might have had if he had gone his own way.

Another illustration of Hall's support for people in ill health was his hiring of Titchener-trained **John Wallace Baird** (1873–1919) to head Clark's psychological laboratory. Influenced by the Würzburg school (Chapter 8), Baird shared Sanford's unstable health, as did Lewis Terman (Chapter 17). Terman studied at Clark perhaps because Hall was the only psychologist of note willing to offer a graduate fellowship to "a midwesterner with active tuberculosis" (Sokal, 1990, p. 119).

Hall's need for a dominant/subordinate relationship with students and colleagues may also explain the apparent contradiction between his stated objection to the coeducation of the sexes and the fact that Clark was one of the leading institutions for the graduate education of women in the early 20th century. Hall believed that women needed to be educated apart from men in adolescence to avoid damage to their reproductive organs and to prepare them for their appointed role in life—motherhood. Further, Hall opposed women teachers in high school, "for it was during adolescence that boys needed the firm hand of a man and a model to emulate" (Diehl, 1986, p. 872).

Although Hall's coeducation position never changed, he was a shrewd administrator of a perennially underfunded institution. In 1909, in response to a request for information about what Clark was doing for the common good that would enable it to keep its tax-exempt status, Hall created an Educational Department that would grant higher degrees to women. Privately, Hall noted the political desirability of continuing to award the occasional Ph.D. to a woman in order to prevent trouble from feminists (Diehl, 1986).

Theodate Louise Smith's (1859–1914) career well illustrates Hall's relationships with women junior colleagues. Born in Hallowell, Maine, Smith earned a Yale Ph.D. in 1896. After unsuccessfully seeking university employment until 1902, Smith became Hall's research assistant. Apparently, Smith shared Hall's views on the role of women and fulfilled her subordinate role so well that, after her sudden death, "Hall wrote a glowing tribute to her deference to him . . ." (Sokal, 1990, p. 121).

Howard University.

Francis Sumner (1895–1954)

Hall's last graduate student, **Francis Cecil Sumner** (1895–1954), further illustrates Hall's tendency to attract to Clark students and faculty who would have found it difficult or impossible to enter academia elsewhere. Sumner was the first African American student to earn a Ph.D. in psychology in the United States, with a dissertation comparing the psychoanalytic theories of Freud and Adler (Guthrie, 2000).

Although Sumner published two articles in the 1920s calling for unequal and segregated education for African Americans and Caucasians, Sawyer (2000) argued that Sumner was just responding to the prevailing paradigm of the Caucasian establishment in order to further his "hidden agenda" of obtaining support from the white community for higher education for African Americans. A few years later, as head of the psychology department at Howard University, Sumner served as teacher and mentor to Kenneth B. Clark (Chapter 17). Clark's research on discrimination and segregation was cited in the 1954 Supreme Court decision abolishing segregated education in the United States. Unfortunately, the final ruling came 4 months after Sumner's fatal heart attack.

Sumner was also a major producer of entries for *Psychological Abstracts*, composing nearly 2,000 abstracts of articles written in English, Spanish, French, German, and Russian. *Psychological Abstracts* is a principal library tool for psychology students and psychological researchers.

Hall's Influence

As we have noted, Hall had more "firsts" than perhaps any psychologist before or since. For example, Hall received the first Ph.D. from Harvard's philosophy department; he was the first American student at the world's first psychology laboratory (Wundt's at Leipzig); his *American Journal of Psychology* was the first exclusively psychological journal in English; his Hopkins laboratory is considered the first psychological laboratory in America (James's earlier Harvard laboratory was primarily for teaching); he was the first president of Clark University; he was the main organizer of the APA and its first president; he was instrumental in giving American psychology its first look at Freud and psychoanalysis; he was among the first to write about adolescence and senescence; and he directed the program of Francis Sumner, the first African American to earn a Ph.D. in psychology.

Through his many students, Hall's influence extended beyond the journals, laboratories, and institutions he founded. Some of Hall's students developed unswerving loyalty, and Sanford's comment in his obituary to Hall well illustrates Hall's effect on this group: "To those who were his pupils, the inspiration, the illumination, the friendliness are unforgettable" (Sanford, 1924, pp. 320–321). Others saw Hall differently and "were baffled by his inconsistent anger or approval, his evidences of harshness, meanness, and selfishness. His most perceptive student sensed that he was a very accomplished actor" (Ross, 1972, p. 426).

Hall's influence on his students was perhaps most effective through his Monday night seminars, held in Hall's home. Usually, two doctoral candidates would present papers, with a discussion session following. When questioning slowed, Hall, hitherto silent, "opened his deceitfully half-closed eyes to express his interest in the student's research" (Averill, 1982, p. 342). Hall used Socratic questioning with conceited or ill-prepared students, at first complimenting the student on the presentation and then asking for some minor clarification. "Locating the essential weakness of the paper he blandly followed up his lead question by question until the man either threw up his hands or became furiously angry, usually the former" (Sheldon, 1946, p. 234). According to Averill, none "of the hundreds of pursuers of the graduate gleam who ever experienced the intellectual ravishment of these soul-stirring seminars of Stanley Hall ever forgot them" (p. 342).

Hall also contributed importantly to the history of psychology (Bringmann, Bringmann, & Early, 1992), in the form of biographies. Hall's historical interests directly influenced a number of colleagues, including the dean of psychological historians, E. G. Boring, whose first academic position was at Clark University under Hall. In addition, Boring began writing his monumental *A History of Experimental Psychology* shortly after he left Clark, and the book contains many stories first mentioned in Hall's writings (Bringmann et al.).

Like the other major figures we have surveyed in this chapter (James and Münsterberg), Hall was a forerunner of functionalism and not a "true" functionalist. Although in part chronological, this distinction occurs primarily because each man (and Cattell, as well) was an eclectic thinker. Temperamentally, these pioneers were ill-suited to adherence to a formal system—even one as nondoctrinaire as functionalism.

It is difficult to summarize the accomplishments and character of a person as complex as G. Stanley Hall. As Clark's president, he created an environment conducive to research, and his broad range of interests gave a variety of students an opportunity to express themselves. As builder, organizer, administrator, and propagandist for the "new" psychology, Hall succeeded.

As a person, he was less successful. A man of immense personal magnetism, Hall possessed a character that was all too flawed. "Loyalty to persons is something which Hall probably never had," wrote Lorine Pruette (1926, p. 180), a sympathetic biographer and former student. Noting his inconsistency with people, Pruette concluded that it "made him appear a greater liar than he really was . . ." (p. 180).

EARLY STUDIES OF GENDER DIFFERENCES: THE WORK OF LETA STETTER HOLLINGWORTH

Hall's view of women as best suited for subordinate positions was shared by many of his contemporaries. Pioneering American psychologist Leta Hollingworth challenged experimentally one of the tenets upon which the idea of male intellectual superiority rested and found little supporting evidence.

Her work provides a brief case study of the contributions made by women to the rise of American psychology.

In the Victorian era, the dominant political and social positions held by men were considered confirmation that men were more capable intellectually than women. When the mental testing movement failed to find a difference in the average abilities of men and women, believers in the innate inequality of the sexes turned to Darwin. In *Descent of Man,* Darwin had noted that in many species there was more differentiation of secondary sex characteristics in the male, suggesting that the male was the more variable sex. "Because variation from the average had already been proposed as a primary evolutionary mechanism, the alleged greater variation among males was seen as . . . a sign of the superiority of their sex" (Shields, 1975, p. 853).

Because of the social implications of the variability hypothesis—for example, if women were less likely to possess high abilities, their graduate education was probably a waste of resources—**Leta Stetter Hollingworth** (1886–1939) investigated its validity. Born in a dugout canoe along the White River in northwestern Nebraska (Ware, 1993), Hollingworth received her psychology Ph.D. from Columbia in 1916, with Thorndike as her major professor. Hollingworth's graduate school expenses were ensured by a contract her husband received from the Coca-Cola Company to study the behavioral effects of Coke's caffeine (Benjamin, Rogers, & Rosenbaum, 1991).

Because Thorndike advocated the variability hypothesis, Hollingworth's motive for her studies may have been to prove him wrong. It is a testimony to Thorndike's willingness to face facts, however, that he accepted Hollingworth's experimental results (Shields, 1991). Shortly after earning her Ph.D., Hollingworth joined the Columbia faculty.

Examining the variability hypothesis, Hollingworth (1913) looked at gender differences in the numbers of mentally retarded women and men, finding there were more institutionalized men than women, which might be taken as evidence for greater male variability. However, Hollingworth argued that women "belong to a non-competitive and dependent class and are not so readily recognized as defective since they do not have to compete mentally to maintain themselves in the social milieu" (p. 753). From this, she reasoned that women would be more likely to be institutionalized at older ages, when they were too old to be "useful," and she found statistical support for this.

Later, Hollingworth and Helen Montague (Montague & Hollingworth, 1914) examined hospital records of 2,000 neonates (1,000 of each gender), searching for greater physical variability in males. If anything, they found greater female variability. For this study and the earlier one, Hollingworth was recognized by feminists as the scientific cornerstone of their cause (Shields, 1975).

Much of Hollingworth's later career was devoted to the study of children at the extremes of ability: For example, two of her books were *The Psychology of Subnormal Children* and *Gifted Children.* Like Hall, she wrote on adolescence, and her textbook, *The Psychology of the Adolescent,* was widely adopted. At Columbia, Hollingworth influenced several graduate students, including Carl Rogers (Chapter 16). Cattell included her in his 1921 *American Men of Science.*

Hollingworth's husband, **Harry L. Hollingworth** (1880–1956), earned a Ph.D. under Cattell at Columbia and served as head of the psychology department at Barnard College for many years. The author of some 25 books on such diverse psychological topics as abnormal, applied (the area for which he is primarily known [Benjamin, 1996]), and educational, Harry Hollingworth was the APA president in 1927. The work of both Hollingworths and their connections to Columbia serve to introduce the next of our early American psychologists—James McKeen Cattell.

JAMES MCKEEN CATTELL

James McKeen Cattell (1860–1944) was born the year after Darwin's publication of *The Origin of Species,* and the theory of evolution was central to his thinking. As Boring (1950) wrote:

Columbia University Archives–Columbiana Library.

James McKeen Cattell (1860–1944)

> Evolution had taken hold of American thought, and evolution . . . meant in psychology an emphasis upon individual differences. Cattell was convinced of the importance of the psychology of individual differences even before he went to Wundt. . . . He did not get this idea from Galton, but presumably got it out of the same atmosphere that gave it to Galton. (p. 533)

Like Galton, Cattell believed he had inherited ability, but he also realized the importance of his environment. He wrote: "It was my fortune to find a birthplace in the sun. A germplasm fairly well compounded [good genes] met circumstances to which it was unusually fit to react" (Sokal, 1971, p. 629).

Cattell was born in Easton, Pennsylvania, into a family that combined ambition, education, wealth, and social connections. His father was a Presbyterian minister and professor of Latin and Greek at Lafayette College and, from 1863 to 1883, president of the College. Many years later, Cattell noted, "In my statistical studies I found that one who wanted to become a scientific man had the best chance if he chose a professor or a clergyman for his father. . . . My father was both a professor and a clergyman" (Sokal, 1971, p. 633). An advocate of eugenics, Cattell offered each of *his* children $1,000 if he or she would marry the child of a college professor.

Cattell was admitted to Lafayette College before his 16th birthday, and his genetic and environmental promise was amply fulfilled: "I stood first in my class without much effort" (cited in Sokal, 1971, p. 634). In addition, Cattell maintained a lifelong interest in sports and games, learning to play tennis (at Leipzig with James Mark Baldwin) when there were no courts in America and golf "when there were only three courses in the world" (p. 634).

When Cattell left for Europe in 1880, his knowledge of psychology had come mainly from a moral philosophy book he had used in a course at Lafayette College. His main purpose in the journey was ostensibly to learn to speak French and German. Cattell heard Lotze (Chapter 6) lecture at Göttingen and Wundt at Leipzig and was impressed with both men.

In Leipzig, Cattell wrote an essay on the philosophy of Lotze that earned him a fellowship at Johns Hopkins. On his own, Cattell began measuring simple mental processes, but his fellowship was withdrawn and given to his fellow student and lifelong friend, John Dewey. At the end of Dewey's fellowship year, he too had the fellowship taken away. As Cattell wrote to his parents,

> Dr. Hall has not acted honorably towards me. When I was at [Johns Hopkins] he praised me highly, said there was no one he would so gladly see holding the fellowship, but unfortunately, he had nothing to say in the matter, and Dewey was a great favorite of . . . Pres. Gilman's. He added he hoped the university authorities would grant him an assistant, and if so he knew no one so well fitted for the post as me. Pres. Gilman showed me Dr. Hall's recommendation for the fellowship. Dewey stood first and I fourth. (Cattell to his parents, Oct. 27, 1884; cited in Ross, 1972, p. 146)

Sokal (1980) suggested another possible reason for Cattell's loss of the fellowship: "[Cattell's] continual bickering with Daniel Coit Gilman, the university's president" (p. 43).

At any rate, Cattell's year at Hopkins was not wasted. In addition to measuring individual differences, he undertook to "make psychological experiments on stimulant and intoxicating drugs. I have full notes on these, but they have never been published, for on reaching years of somewhat greater discretion I was not altogether proud of my enterprise" (cited in Sokal, 1971, p. 632). Cattell had drunk beer in Germany, but he had never tried other alcoholic beverages, coffee, or tobacco. The substances Cattell ingested at Hopkins included hashish, "morphine, opium, and other psychedelic and narcotic drugs, in part for the sensation and in part out of interest in what they do to the mind" (Sokal, 1987, p. 25). Cattell admitted that the dose of hashish he ingested was "perhaps the largest . . . ever taken without suicidal intent (cited in Sokal, 1971, p. 632).

From Hopkins, Cattell returned to Leipzig in 1883, earning his Ph.D. from Wundt in 1886, having spent part of the time as Wundt's first laboratory assistant. Cattell's Leipzig research was unusual in that he studied problems of his own choice using instruments of his own construction. In addition, he was interested in individual differences, a pursuit Wundt characterized as *ganz amerikanisch* (wholly American) but was flexible enough to permit, although not in his laboratory. Cattell received permission to perform his experiments in his room. Perhaps it was just as Cattell wrote to his parents: "Prof. Wundt seems to like me and to appreciate my phenomenal genius" (Letter dated February 13, 1885; cited in Benjamin, 1993, p. 50).

Cattell did not idolize Wundt, despite Wundt's reputation and standing in the scientific community. Disparaging comments were frequent in his letters home:

> Prof. Wundt lectured yesterday and today on my subject—I suppose you won't consider it egotistical when I say that I know a great deal more about it than he does, but you will be surprised when I say that half of the statements he made were wrong. (Letter dated January 16, 1885; cited in Benjamin, 1993, p. 49)

From 1883 to 1886, Cattell published nine papers, all on either reaction time or individual differences or some combination of the two topics.

For the next 2 years, Cattell divided his time between Cambridge, England, where he met Galton, and America at Bryn Mawr College and the University of Pennsylvania. Galton confirmed Cattell's long-standing interest in measuring individual differences, and Cattell subsequently called him "the greatest man whom I have known" (Woodworth, 1944, p. 203).

Cattell and Psychology in America

From 1888 to 1891, Cattell was Professor of Psychology at the University of Pennsylvania, a position his father had had created for him (Sokal, 1994). There, Cattell founded a laboratory and began to administer 10 tests to student volunteers, introducing the term **mental tests** to describe the battery (Cattell, 1890). The series included tests of sensation by means of the two-point threshold, just noticeable differences in weight judgments, reaction time for noises, memory span for letters, and rate of movement. Cattell left Lightner Witmer in charge when he departed for Columbia.

For his first decade at Columbia, Cattell continued administering his "mental tests" to entering freshmen. Using Pearson's correlation coefficient, in 1901 Cattell's graduate student **Clark Wissler** (1870–1947) tested Cattell's (and Galton's) assumption that measures of physical and sensory ability were assessing intelligence. The resulting correlations between Cattell's tests and college standing were low, suggesting that Cattell had not developed a valid measure of intelligence. However, reevaluation of Wissler's study has revealed deficiencies that make its conclusions questionable at best. Deary (1994) concluded that both early and more recent studies consistently find a positive relation between pitch discrimination and psychometric measures of intelligence, indicating that Galton and Cattell may have been on the right track.

Cattell's "mental tests" were soon superseded by Alfred Binet's intelligence tests (Chapter 17), and Cattell devoted himself to administration, science editing and publishing, and the development of a method for ranking according to merit. Wissler switched to anthropology and made a name for himself as an ardent environmentalist.

Cattell initially applied his order-of-merit ranking method to the psychophysical problem of arranging various shades of gray, which differed by almost imperceptible steps from black to white. The method was soon extended to value judgments, and Cattell applied it to the ranking of American men of science. For psychologists, he first made a list of 200 men and women, which he gave to 10 competent psychologists with instructions to rank the names by order of scientific merit.

The 1903 ranking did not become public until Cattell's 1929 address as President of the Ninth International Congress of Psychology. In order, the top 10 psychologists were James, Cattell, Münsterberg, Hall, Baldwin, Titchener, Royce, Ladd, Dewey, and Jastrow. Mary Calkins ranked 12th, ahead of Thorndike in 16th place, and Christine Ladd-Franklin (Chapter 7) ranked 19th. Cattell used his ranking method to compile the *Biographical Directory of American Men of Science* (plus some women), which he edited through the first six editions. *American Men of Science* continues to be published as a basic reference work, a veritable Who's Who of science.

Cattell's academic career ended with his 1917 dismissal from Columbia. In the midst of American involvement in World War I, Cattell used university stationery to write a letter to Congress protesting the use of conscientious objectors in combat. Cattell had long been an irritant to Columbia President Nicholas Murray Butler, and Butler used the letter as a pretext to rid himself of Cattell. (Ironically, Butler received the Nobel Peace Prize in 1931.) Cattell sued the University for libel and won.

Out of academia, Cattell pursued his publishing and editing ventures. These had begun over 20 years before his dismissal, when, with James Mark Baldwin, he founded first *Psychological Review* and then *Psychological Index* and *Psychological Monographs* as alternatives to Hall's *American Journal of Psychology*. Baldwin bought Cattell out in 1903, and in 1925, the journals they had founded became the nucleus of the APA's stable of successful journals (Johnson, 2000). Note the irony: The organization founded by Hall ultimately acquired the journals founded in opposition to Hall's first journal.

In 1895, Cattell purchased the floundering journal *Science* from Alexander Graham Bell. Under Cattell, *Science* overcame its financial difficulties and became one of the foremost general scientific publications in the world. In 1900, it became the official publication of the American Association for the Advancement of Science (AAAS).

At one time or another, Cattell edited *Psychological Review, Science, Scientific Monthly* (originally known as *Popular Science Monthly*), *American Naturalist, School and Society,* and *American Men of Science.* In addition, in 1921 Cattell organized the Psychological Corporation to promote applied psychology. In keeping with Cattell's original idea, the Corporation has returned much of its profits to psychologists for further research. The Psychological Corporation publishes the popular Wechsler intelligence tests (e.g., the Wechsler Adult Intelligence Scale or WAIS, Chapter 17), among many other psychological instruments.

Cattell's Influence

Cattell was one of the APA's founding members and its fourth president. Shortly after arriving at Columbia, Cattell joined the New York Academy of Sciences (NYAS), and soon persuaded the Academy to establish a Section of Anthropology and Psychology. He was elected NYAS president in 1902.

In 1924, Cattell was elected president of the AAAS, the first psychologist so honored. He was also the first psychologist to be admitted to the National Academy of Sciences (1901). Cattell's crowning glory came in 1929 when he was chosen by American psychologists to serve as president of the Ninth International Congress of Psychology, the first such meeting held in the United States.

Like Hall, Cattell is a study in contrasts. His letters from Leipzig reveal a self-confidence some might view as arrogance or conceit. Always the diplomat, Woodworth accounted for Cattell's lack of a published autobiography by accepting Cattell's excuse that any

> autobiography such as he would write would land him in the position of defendant in a number of libel suits. He felt sure he could not bring himself to delete all the pungent comments that would occur to him, and he had found by long experience that such comments were not always accepted in the spirit of raillery [good-natured teasing] that motivated them. . . . (Woodworth, 1944, pp. 207–208)

By contrast, Sokal (1971) noted that "Cattell's conversation and correspondence were full of sarcasm and 'pungent comments' that were usually taken seriously, for it was never clear whether the 'spirit of raillery' to which Woodworth refers actually existed" (p. 627).

In fact, Cattell engendered controversy throughout his career. As we noted, Cattell's dismissal from academia ultimately stemmed from his antagonism of Columbia's president. There was also controversy between Cattell and Baldwin over control of *Psychological Review* and conflict between Cattell and William McDougall (Chapter 12). Of the five-person committee that selected nominees for Carl Murchison's (1930) *A History of Psychology in Autobiography,* three voted for Cattell and two voted against. Cattell's decision not to write an autobiography for Murchison's project was largely the result of controversies he had had with Murchison, who actually voted for Cattell's inclusion.

Cattell had more influence on his students through his ability to inspire than through his teaching. His approach to his graduate students was as nondirective as Wundt's and Titchener's approaches were directive:

> In research it is doubtful if a department has existed in this country where students were thrown more upon their own resources. . . . Cattell pointed clearly the way and said "Go," but the greatest teacher must be able to say "Come." (Wells, 1944, p. 271)

In addition to F. L. Wells, students inspired by Cattell included Thorndike, Woodworth, S. I. Franz (Chapter 16), and E. K. Strong, an industrial and vocational psychologist. Margaret Washburn (Chapter 8), America's first major female experimental psychologist, had studied with Cattell before going to Cornell and earning a Ph.D. with Titchener. She wrote, "I feel an affectionate gratitude to [Cattell], as my first teacher, which in these later years I have courage to express; in earlier times I stood too much in awe of him" (Washburn, 1932, p. 339). Although Lightner Witmer (Chapter 8) received his Ph.D. from study with Wundt, he wrote to E. G. Boring that he considered his main debt to Cattell, under whom he had been an assistant at Pennsylvania (McReynolds, 1996).

Cattell is important to the stream of ideas in American psychology because he provided a bridge between the British psychology of the individual (idiographic) and the German (including Titchener's) psychology of the generalized mind (nomothetic). Cattell understood and communicated the value of both approaches for a mature psychological system.

With his interest in measuring mental ability, Cattell's psychology was a psychology of human capacity and thus a psychology of function. As we will see, Columbia and Chicago were the centers of functionalism, and during Cattell's tenure, Columbia became the foremost producer of psychology Ph.D.s. When the first international psychology congress was held in the United States, 704 APA members had doctorates. Of these, 155 had degrees from Columbia; Chicago was a distant second with 91 (Cattell, 1929).

However, Cattell's influence was perhaps greatest through his scientific editing. Serving as editor of *Science* for half a century enabled Cattell to promote psychology's image as a science. "[T]here is no denying that [Cattell's editorship] significantly enhanced psychology's visibility and status among the older sciences" (Benjamin, 1993, p. 39).

Before concluding our examination of early American psychology, we will consider briefly the life and career of a man mentioned frequently in this chapter and elsewhere: James Mark Baldwin. APA president in 1897 and fifth on Cattell's list of prominent psychologists in 1903, Baldwin's enthusiasm for evolution and functional view of mind make him well suited for placement as another American forerunner of functionalism.

James Mark Baldwin (1861–1934)

JAMES MARK BALDWIN

Born in Columbia, South Carolina, **James Mark Baldwin** (1861–1934) spent a year with Wundt in Leipzig and Friedrich Paulsen in Berlin before earning his Ph.D. in philosophy from Princeton in 1889, supervised by Scottish philosopher James McCosh. Following an appointment at Lake Forest College in Illinois, Baldwin went to Toronto, where he founded the first psychology laboratory in Canada. From Toronto, Baldwin returned to Princeton, where he established his second laboratory. A decade later, Baldwin moved to Johns Hopkins, reopening the laboratory Hall had closed when he went to Clark. Baldwin was forced to resign from Hopkins in 1909 in a scandal over his presence in a Boston house of prostitution.

Like many of his contemporaries, Baldwin was an ardent evolutionist. In his autobiographical essay (Baldwin, 1930), one of the contributions he valued most was his theory of organic selection, which combined Darwinian and Lamarckian concepts to account for the directedness of evolution, and another was his study of children. Baldwin and Hall are often jointly considered the founders of developmental psychology.

Although Baldwin was younger than Hall, his initial book on genetic psychology, *Mental Development in the Child and the Race,* first appeared in 1895. Despite several publications related to developmental psychology, however (see Kahlbaugh, 1993), as well as pioneering work in experimental social psychology and an early text on the history of psychology, Baldwin's greatest contribution may have been through his influence on Jean Piaget, whose efforts in cognitive development we will examine in Chapter 18.

After resigning from Hopkins, Baldwin took up residence in England, not in Mexico City as reported by Boring (1950). He did make several trips to Mexico City, where he consulted with officials from the National University of Mexico and presented a lecture series (Horley, 2001).

Baldwin also made frequent visits to the Continent, and eventually moved to France after World War I. For a time, Baldwin had an appointment at the *École des Hautes Études Sociales* in Paris (Horley, 2001). He died at the American Hospital in Paris following a brief bout with pneumonia and was buried in Princeton, with none of his American contemporary psychologists in attendance. Perhaps their absence is a reflection of his personality: "Not only was Baldwin an ambitious individual who alienated many on his way to the top, but also he appears to have been arrogant and dismissive of colleagues at times. . . . Overall, he appears to have been a difficult person to work with in any capacity" (Horley, p. 26).

CONCLUSIONS

When we think of America's founding, we think of its early leaders and their accomplishments, and of certain themes that capture our country's spirit. The same framework can be used in our consideration of the founding of psychology in America.

Thus, William James, G. Stanley Hall, and James McKeen Cattell were early leaders of psychology in America. James produced a classic text, brought experimental psychology to Harvard, and established an important psychology department there. Hall's importance lay chiefly in his organizational skills, which are well illustrated by his "foundings": for example, the departments of psychology at Johns Hopkins and at Clark, the first American journal of psychology, and the American Psychological Association. In addition, Hall brought Freud and psychoanalysis to America for the Clark Conference. Like Hall, Cattell was a master publicist of psychology in America. Through his publishing ventures and his association with the American Association for the Advancement of Science, Cattell helped make psychology a respected scientific discipline.

America is often seen thematically as the home of pioneers, who were rugged individualists fighting for the freedom of their beliefs. That same characterization may well apply to James, Hall, and Cattell. Although some limited psychological speculation predated James, he was the first pioneer of American psychology, charting a new intellectual territory. Hall's many "firsts" and "foundings" echo that same pioneer theme, as do the efforts of Mary Calkins and Leta Hollingworth.

Clearly, the people we covered in this chapter were willing to "do their own thing," in today's jargon. This is well illustrated by the brash young Cattell performing his own experiments in his room while studying with the normally autocratic Wundt, by James's sense of fair play in treating both Wundt and his phenomenological contemporaries equally within his *Principles,* and by Hall's eclectic interests from development to psychoanalysis. James, Hall, and Cattell represented no established system, such as structuralism, nor did they found one directly. However, their efforts were all directed toward a psychology of function and laid the foundation for functionalism, America's first native school of psychology.

SUMMARY

Evolution was a major 19th-century theme, and Herbert Spencer's social Darwinism fit American society's mood. Few were more influenced by Darwinism than William James and G. Stanley Hall, who believed that consciousness has a function. The first true American psychologists took psychology into areas avoided by "pure" psychologists such as Titchener.

Early Philosophy and Psychology in America

There was little psychology in America before the publication of William James's *Principles.* Although Jonathan Edwards and Samuel Johnson made contributions in the tradition of Locke and British empiricism, mainly the ideas of the Scottish school and to a lesser degree the German rationalists formed the basis of American psychology before James.

William James

After an unusual childhood and education, James's first academic position was as a Harvard physiology instructor. James soon added a physiological psychology course and contracted to write *The Principles of Psychology,* published in 1890.

In the *Principles,* James argued that psychology should arise not from the study of individual sensations but from the study of complete conscious experiences. James's analysis suggested that consciousness is personal, always changing, continuous, always directed at some object, and selective. Further, James believed consciousness has evolved because it functions to aid its possessor in adapting to an environment.

For James, habits result from changes in the brain, and he offered practical suggestions for acquiring new habits and for getting rid of old ones. He and Carl Lange independently produced the James-Lange theory of emotion, which holds that a stimulus triggers a response and awareness of the response constitutes the emotion. Despite criticisms, the theory's core idea remains a part of the modern psychology of emotion.

After publishing the *Principles,* James wrote on a variety of philosophical topics including pragmatism. Pragmatism replaced the rationalist notion of truth as an objective entity with a functionally defined understanding of truth. According to James, truth is the value of an idea. If an idea works, it is true.

Through his students and his writings, James shaped psychology in America. Both Gestalt psychology and functionalism acknowledged a debt to James, and he was influential in founding the important Harvard psychology department.

Mary Whiton Calkins

One of James's brightest students, Calkins took courses at Harvard but never received a Harvard Ph.D., despite her superior performance. Calkins spent her career at Wellesley and was the first woman elected president of the APA and of the American Philosophical Association. Her main contributions to psychology include an early psychology laboratory, the paired-associates method for studying memory, and a self-psychology system.

Hugo Münsterberg

Hugo Münsterberg earned his Ph.D. under Wundt, received a Heidelberg M.D., and then founded a laboratory at Freiburg. James secured a position for him in charge of the Harvard psychological laboratory.

Many of Münsterberg's works were major contributions to applied psychology, and he published volumes on forensics, pedagogy, psychotherapy, and industrial psychology. Despite his productivity, Münsterberg is not remembered more favorably because he continued to promote German-American ties when relations between Germany and its neighbors were worsening and World War I was underway.

Granville Stanley Hall

A man of many "firsts," G. Stanley Hall helped shape the course of American psychology. At Johns Hopkins, Hall founded an important early psychological laboratory, attracted several noteworthy students, and founded *The American Journal of Psychology* (the first psychology journal in America).

In 1889, Hall became the first president of Clark University. Although most of Hall's outstanding faculty and students left Clark in 1892, in that year Hall was instrumental in founding the American Psychological Association and was elected its first president.

Hall is perhaps best known for his work in developmental psychology. Using questionnaires, Hall gathered data that led to *Adolescence,* which included his recapitulation theory of child development. Hall also published *Senescence,* which is about the last part of life.

Like James, Hall was an early contributor to the study of the psychology of religion. He founded a journal in the area, and two of his students were instrumental in developing what some call the Clark School of Religious Psychology.

At Clark's 20th anniversary, Freud's lectures gave America its first look at psychoanalysis. Hall later initiated a dialogue with Alfred Adler and may have influenced Carl Jung.

Hall's relations were perhaps best with subordinates, and this is apparent in his relations with several junior colleagues at Clark. Although Hall and Clark University trained several female psychologists, this fact can also be viewed as supporting Hall's need to have relationships in which he was dominant. Hall's last graduate student was Francis Sumner, the first African American to receive a Ph.D. in psychology.

Early Studies of Gender Differences: The Work of Leta Stetter Hollingworth

True to the *Zeitgeist,* Hall viewed women as intellectually inferior to men. Leta Stetter Hollingworth obtained early empirical evidence refuting this view.

James McKeen Cattell

James McKeen Cattell completed his Ph.D. under Wundt in 1886. After meeting Galton in Cambridge, England, Cattell became Professor of Psychology at the University of Pennsylvania. There, Cattell founded a laboratory and developed his battery of mental tests before leaving for Columbia, where he continued his research on mental testing. When Cattell-student Clark Wissler found low correlations between physiological measures and intelligence, Cattell went into administration and Wissler became an anthropologist.

After being fired from Columbia, Cattell continued his publishing and editing ventures. In 1921, he founded the Psychological Corporation, which remains the publisher of several important psychological tests, including the WAIS.

A founding APA member and its fourth president, in 1929 Cattell served as president of the Ninth International Congress of Psychology, which was the first such meeting held in America. Cattell's influence was perhaps greatest through his editing of the journal *Science,* in which he was able to promote psychology's image as a science.

James Mark Baldwin

Considered one of the creators of developmental psychology along with Hall, Baldwin founded the first laboratory of psychology in Canada and a second laboratory at Princeton; he also reopened the laboratory at Johns Hopkins. An ardent evolutionist, he valued as a scientific contribution his theory of organic selection that combined Darwinian and Lamarckian features to account for evolution's directedness.

CONNECTIONS QUESTIONS

1. Compare and contrast the psychologies and the personalities of Hall and James.
2. How would you connect Cattell's contributions to psychology's present status as an experimental science?
3. Compare and contrast Titchener and Münsterberg. Why is Titchener so celebrated in the history of psychology, whereas Münsterberg is all but forgotten?
4. How did Mary Calkins's and Leta Hollingworth's research contribute to the place of women in American psychology?
5. How does William James connect to the scientific psychology that preceded him in Europe? To the scientific psychology that followed him in America?
6. Hall is remembered for his many "firsts." How many connections can you make between Hall and something he initiated for American psychology?

KEY NAMES AND TERMS

American Psychological Association (p. 271)
American Psychological Society (p. 271)
John Wallace Baird (p. 275)
James Mark Baldwin (p. 283)
Mary Whiton Calkins (p. 263)
Walter B. Cannon (p. 259)
James McKeen Cattell (p. 278)
Jonathan Edwards (p. 252)
ergonomics (p. 267)
Auguste-Henri Forel (p. 274)
Granville Stanley Hall (p. 267)
Laurens Perseus Hickok (p. 253)
Harry L. Hollingworth (p. 278)
Leta Stetter Hollingworth (p. 278)
Edwin Bissell Holt (p. 261)
William James (p. 253)
James-Lange theory of emotion (p. 258)
Joseph Jastrow (p. 269)
Samuel Johnson (p. 253)
George Trumbull Ladd (p. 256)
Carl Lange (p. 258)
Herbert S. Langfeld (p. 262)
James H. Leuba (p. 273)
mental tests (p. 280)
Hugo Münsterberg (p. 265)
paired-associates method (p. 264)
Charles Sanders Peirce (p. 260)
pragmatism (p. 261)
Psychonomic Society (p. 271)
recapitulation theory (p. 273)
Charles Bernard Renouvier (p. 255)
Josiah Royce (p. 266)
Edmund Clark Sanford (p. 263)
George Santayana (p. 261)
self-psychology (p. 264)
Theodate Louise Smith (p. 276)
Edwin D. Starbuck (p. 273)
James Sully (p. 256)
Francis Cecil Sumner (p. 276)
Thomas C. Upham (p. 253)
Clark Wissler (p. 280)

SUGGESTED READINGS

Cattell, J. M. (1929). Psychology in America. *Science, 70,* 335–347. This is the published version of Cattell's presidential address to the Ninth International Congress of Psychology, and it is an interesting overview of early American psychology from the perspective of one of the pioneers.

Donnelly, M. (Ed.) (1992). *Reinterpreting the legacy of William James.* Washington, DC: American Psychological Association. This anthology was born from symposia held at the 1990 meeting of the APA to honor the 100th anniversary of the publication of the *Principles.* In contributions by well-known psychologists, this work makes connections between James and many other persons and topics (e.g., James and Darwin, James and psychic research).

James, W. (1890). *The principles of psychology* (Vols. 1–2). New York: Henry Holt. Any serious consideration of William James's place in the history of American psychology should begin with his magnum opus, the *Principles.* Open these volumes anywhere and read a paragraph or two, and you may agree with Thorndike who found the work more stimulating than any he had read before or since.

Johnson, M. G., & Henley, T. B. (Eds.) (1990). *Reflections on* The Principles of Psychology. Hillsdale, NJ: Lawrence Erlbaum Associates, Publishers. Johnson and Henley's edited book is a compilation of essays on James's *Principles* written on the 100th anniversary of its publication.

Ross, D. (1972). *G. Stanley Hall: The psychologist as prophet.* Chicago: The University of Chicago Press. Ross's biography of Hall should be the starting point for anyone who desires a better understanding of a complicated and talented, but ultimately flawed, individual.

Simon, L. (1998). *Genuine reality: A life of William James.* New York: Harcourt Brace & Company. Linda Simon's book is the first full biography of William James in nearly a generation. Although James has been the subject of many biographical books and articles, the scope and recency of this work make it one we highly recommend.

Sokal, M. (1971). The unpublished autobiography of James McKeen Cattell. *American Psychologist, 26,* 626–635. Cattell's preliminary draft of an autobiographical essay and Sokal's introduction to it provide a fascinating look at a pioneering American psychologist who "was not a modest man . . ." (p. 629).

Spillmann, J., & Spillmann, L. (1993). The rise and fall of Hugo Münsterberg. *Journal of the History of the Behavioral Sciences, 29,* 322–338. The Spillmanns' paper presents an objective but sympathetic look at a man whose contributions to applied psychology are often overlooked in histories of psychology.

Functionalism

CHAPTER 11

Milicent Shinn

Harvey Carr

George H. Mead

Walter Hunter

Edward L. Thorndike

Robert Woodworth

James R. Angell

Ethel Puffer Howes

Edna Heidbreder

John Dewey

1850 1860 1870 1880 1890 1900 1910

Auguste Comte dies

The Gatling gun invented and used in Civil War

The first milk chocolate for eating is invented

First tetanus antitoxin

Britain's Edward VII dies and is succeeded by his son, who becomes George V

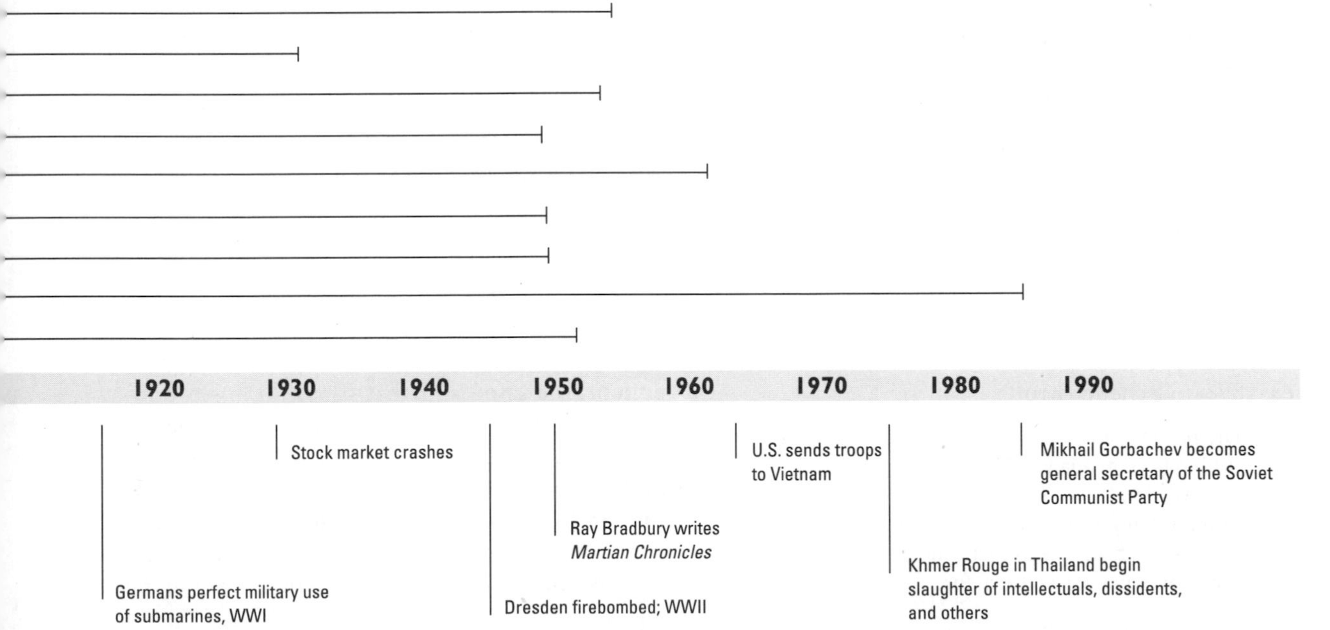

1920
1930
1940
1950
1960
1970
1980
1990
Stock market crashes
U.S. sends troops to Vietnam
Mikhail Gorbachev becomes general secretary of the Soviet Communist Party
Ray Bradbury writes *Martian Chronicles*
Khmer Rouge in Thailand begin slaughter of intellectuals, dissidents, and others
Germans perfect military use of submarines, WWI
Dresden firebombed; WWII

Functionalism was a psychological system that studied the functions of mind and behavior in the context of the organism's adaptation to the environment. As a formal system of psychology, functionalism was remarkably informal. Unlike structuralism, founded and dominated in America by Titchener, functionalism had no central individual. Nevertheless, functionalism was the first truly American system of psychology and was important both in its own right and as a forerunner of behaviorism.

As this chapter will document, functionalism was a diverse school. Using the analogy of America as an ethnic melting pot, American functionalism served as an intellectual smelter. Given functionalism's eclectic nature, historians of psychology typically list several individuals as important influences on functionalism rather than focusing on a founder. As we saw in Chapter 10, James, Hall, and Cattell were all interested in the mind's functions and were psychologists of function without really being functionalists. For example, although James supported functionalism's strongly empirical, experimental approach, he lacked the temperament to sustain such a research effort. Instead, he imported Wundt-trained Münsterberg to lead the laboratory he had established. Münsterberg's forays into applied psychology were also compatible with the pragmatic psychology of function. Hall, too, abandoned laboratory science early in his career. Both James and Hall had such diverse interests that they could never become members of even such a loosely knit school as functionalism.

With his single-minded approach to psychology, Titchener (Chapter 8) was better suited to become the founder and leader of a school. Ironically, Titchener is often credited with establishing functionalism as a "formal" school, by objectifying the differences between his structural approach and the functional psychology of others (Titchener, 1898). Titchener wrote:

> The primary aim of the experimental psychologist has been to analyze the structure of mind.... His task is . . . a vivisection which shall yield structural, not functional results. He tries to discover, first of all, what is there and in what quantity, not what it is there for. . . . There is, however, a functional psychology, over and above this psychology of structure. . . . Just as experimental psychology is to a large extent concerned with problems of structure, so is 'descriptive' psychology . . . chiefly occupied with problems of function. (pp. 450–452)

As you can see, Titchener was interested in the "what" of consciousness rather than the "why," or, alternatively, he was interested in the "is" rather than the "is for."

Titchener clearly saw his structuralism as preferable to the functional approach in the work of William James, John Dewey, and, later, that of James Rowland Angell and Harvey A. Carr. As he expressed it,

> The burden of the argument has been that there is reasonable agreement, within the experimental camp, as to the postulates of a purely structural psychology, whereas there is pretty radical disagreement among the psychologists of function.... I believe ... that the best hope for psychology lies to day in a continuance of structural analysis, and that the study of function will not yield final fruit until it can be controlled by the genetic, and, still more, by the experimental method.... (Titchener, 1898, pp. 464–465)

As we revealed in Chapter 10 and will show in this chapter, functionalism bore abundant fruit, whereas Titchener's structuralism essentially died with him.

Titchener's 1898 paper was a response to John Dewey's (1896) paper, "The Reflex Arc Concept in Psychology," which is usually honored as functionalism's seminal article.

JOHN DEWEY

John Dewey (1859–1952) was born in Burlington, Vermont, the same year that Charles Darwin published *The Origin of Species.* A shy youth, Dewey attended the University of Vermont in his hometown, turning to philosophy in his senior year. After graduation in 1879, the year Wundt established his laboratory, Dewey taught all subjects in high school for a few years, where he first developed the interest in the

University of Chicago Library, Department of Special Collections.

John Dewey (1859–1952)

problems and purpose of education that shaped much of his career. Famous for his contributions to the American educational system and to teaching, by some accounts Dewey was himself a poor teacher.

> It remains indeed one of the sociological paradoxes of American culture . . . why a man, by the usual outward, visible signs not a good—and indeed by all conventional criteria a poor—teacher, should have so deeply inspired and remade the thinking of crucial individuals in all the professions, teaching above all. (Edman, 1955, p. 24)

While teaching high school, Dewey had two philosophical papers accepted by the *Journal of Speculative Philosophy*, and the editor encouraged Dewey to become a philosopher. With this in mind, Dewey enrolled at Johns Hopkins in 1882.

At Hopkins, Dewey took courses from the three men on trial for the professor of philosophy position: Peirce, Hall, and Morris (as noted in Chapter 10). Of the three, Dewey was most influenced by the Hegelian idealism of Morris. When Morris became chairman of the University of Michigan philosophy department, one of his first actions was to offer Dewey—who earned his Ph.D. from Hopkins in 1884—an instructorship at Michigan, which Dewey accepted.

Except for a year at the University of Minnesota, Dewey spent the next 10 years at Michigan, becoming philosophy department chairman upon Morris's untimely death. In his first term at Michigan, Dewey taught a course in empirical psychology for which he wrote a textbook published in 1886 as *Psychology*. *Psychology* was a synthesis of the new empirical, experimental psychology with the older, primarily Hegelian, idealistic philosophy. Along with other psychology books of the period immediately preceding James's *Principles of Psychology* (Chapter 10), it was a psychology text written from a philosopher's perspective.

After reading James's *Principles,* Dewey felt encouraged to move toward a more empirical and objective functionalism (Raphelson, 1973). There were other influences, however, including Wundt (Shook, 1995) and the neo-Hegelian philosophies of Thomas Hill Green and George S. Morris (Backe, 2001). Morris had been Dewey's mentor at Hopkins. Because of Dewey's Hegelian influence, Backe stresses the difference between Dewey's philosophy and the later functionalism systematized by James Rowland Angell (discussed later). Dewey (1896) expressed his new approach to psychology most clearly in "The Reflex Arc Concept in Psychology."

The Reflex Arc Concept

Dewey began by accepting the reflex arc—a stimulus produces a sensation that triggers a response—as a unifying principle in psychology, but he was critical of the arc as "a patchwork of disjointed parts, a mechanical conjunction of unallied processes" (Dewey, 1896, p. 358). Instead, "what is wanted is that sensory stimulus, central connections and motor responses shall be viewed, not as separate and complete entities in themselves, but as divisions of labor, functioning factors, within the single concrete *whole,* now designated the reflex arc" (p. 358, italics added).

To illustrate what he considered wrong with dividing the reflex arc into three components (sensory stimulus, central activity, and motor discharge), Dewey used the child-candle reflex from James's *Principles.* As usually interpreted, the candle's light is a stimulus leading to the child's grasping response, which produces a burning stimulus causing hand withdrawal, and so on, the reflex being broken neatly—but perhaps artificially—into its stimulus-response components. According to Dewey, the candle's light does not begin the reflex: "the real beginning is with the act of seeing; it is looking, and not a sensation of light" (pp. 358–359). And the act of seeing is really part of the whole act of seeing and reaching, "because seeing and grasping have been so often bound together to reinforce each other . . . that each may be considered practically a subordinate member of a bigger coördination" (p. 359). Add the burning sensation, and the original seeing and reaching coordination becomes a "seeing-of-a-light-that-means-pain-when-contact-occurs" (p. 360) coordination.

Dewey's point was that the traditionally interpreted reflex arc led to a disjointed psychology because it assumed that sensory stimulus and motor response were separate psychical entities. Actually, the sensory stimulus and motor response "are always inside a coördination and have their significance purely from the part played in maintaining or reconstituting the coördination . . ." (Dewey, 1896, p. 360). In other words, Dewey was arguing against Wundt and Titchener's elementism (their tendency to divide consciousness into its elements, which they believed to be sensations, images, and feelings). Dewey believed the reflex arc should be viewed as a coordinated whole with a purpose or function, not as a series of individual components. In his stress on behavior as a total coordination, Dewey was anticipating one of Gestalt psychology's (Chapter 14) central tenets and also agreeing with the holistic emphasis of Brentano's act psychology (Chapter 8). Note also the similarity of Dewey's holistic approach to the reflex arc and James's description of consciousness as a stream (Chapter 10).

Boring (1953) called Dewey's paper "a declaration of independence for American functional psychology" (p. 146) and viewed it as an anticipation of Gestalt psychology's complaints about the Wundtians' elementism. As evidence of the importance of Dewey's article for American psychology, it ranked first in a preferential vote on the articles appearing in *Psychological Review*'s initial 50 volumes (Langfeld, 1943).

Dewey's Influence

Although he was no longer interested in teaching psychology courses, as head of the philosophy department at Michigan, Dewey did not abandon the psychological program he had initiated. Instead, he hired **James H. Tufts** (1862–1942) to teach the psychology courses. Tufts established a laboratory course that enrolled Michigan's president's son, James Rowland Angell (discussed later). When Tufts left for Chicago in 1891, student interest forced Dewey to hire two instructors to replace him, one of whom was **George Herbert Mead** (1863–1931). Born in South Hadley, Massachusetts, Mead studied at Oberlin College, Harvard (where he met James), and at the Universities of Leipzig and Berlin. A Hegelian like Dewey, Mead is best known for his concept of the self, and his ideas anticipated movements in both social and clinical psychology, including elements of contemporary humanistic psychology (Chapter 16). One of Mead's best-known works is *Mind, Self and Society* (Mead, 1934), which purports to be a social psychology from a behaviorist viewpoint. However, as Cook (1977, 1994) emphasized, Mead's social behaviorism was rooted in Dewey's functionalism, not in Watsonian behaviorism (Chapter 12). Mead also influenced sociology's rise as a formal discipline in America.

At Tufts's urging, University of Chicago President William Harper offered Dewey the chairmanship of the philosophy department, which also included psychology and pedagogy. Dewey accepted, in part because the position offered possibilities in his three major interests. Mead came with Dewey, and in 1895

Dewey attracted a former Michigan student, James R. Angell, to direct the department's psychological laboratory. With a young and vigorous staff, Chicago's department flourished.

In 1896, Dewey developed a working laboratory to study the learning processes of children and put his "progressive education" theories into practice. Dewey emphasized learning by doing, the importance of a student's interest in a task, and intelligent problem solving rather than rote memorization. The progressive education movement spawned by Dewey's approach declined and eventually died in the 1950s (Hilgard, 1987). Gestalt psychologist Max Wertheimer's *Productive Thinking* (Chapter 14) presented a similar approach to education, and, in fact, Dewey and Wertheimer had their own radio program in 1935 devoted to such topics as education and anarchy.

Dewey's laboratory/school was never intended to be a teacher-training school, and this irritated some of the education faculty, who persuaded Chicago's president to merge Dewey's school with the Teacher Training Institute. Dewey was so offended that he took a post in 1904 at Columbia University secured for him by Hopkins classmate and friend, James McKeen Cattell (Chapter 10). Dewey stayed at Columbia for the rest of his life.

One of the charter members of the American Psychological Association, Dewey remained an APA member until 1927, even though his career as a psychologist is often said to have ended when he left Chicago. Elected APA president in 1899, in 1910 Dewey became the fourth psychologist elected to the National Academy of Sciences, his three predecessors having been Cattell (1901), James (1903), and Royce (1906). After Dewey, the psychologists elected were Hall, Thorndike, and James Rowland Angell (Boring, 1953). Dewey was also involved in liberal causes, such as the American Civil Liberties Union, the founding of the American Association of University Professors, and the women's suffrage movement in America.

As noted, Dewey's formal contact with psychology effectively ended with his departure from Chicago. His position as nominal leader of functionalism was filled by a former student who became head of the psychology department at Chicago—James Rowland Angell.

JAMES ROWLAND ANGELL

Like Dewey, **James Rowland Angell** (1869–1949) was born in Burlington, Vermont. His father was president of the University of Vermont from 1866 to 1871 and of the University of Michigan from 1871 to 1909, and his maternal grandfather had been president of Brown University. As a child in an environment frequented by distinguished political and academic leaders, Angell undoubtedly developed interpersonal skills that made him well suited for administration, and he eventually became a university president himself.

Angell entered the University of Michigan in 1886, pursuing classical studies—Latin, Greek, and mathematics—along with history, English, modern languages, and science as fillers. His first psychology course "instantly opened up a new world, which it seemed to me I had been waiting for, and for the first time I felt a deep and pervasive sense of the intellectual importance of the material I was facing" (Angell, 1936, p. 5). This material was the newly published *Psychology* by his teacher, John Dewey.

In his last year at Michigan, Angell took a seminar with Dewey to study James's just-published *Principles.* With master's degree in hand and Dewey's encouragement, Angell next went to Harvard, where he studied under William James and Josiah Royce (Chapter 10). With James, Angell "enjoyed a peculiarly intimate contact" (Angell, 1936, p. 7), because James turned over to him a mass of material from the American Society for Psychical Research. Although ultimately unimportant for psychical research, the work put Angell "in direct contact with one of the most inspiring and spiritually beautiful human beings I have ever known" (p. 7).

After earning a second master's degree at Harvard, Angell went to Leipzig, taking with him a letter of introduction from his cousin **Frank Angell** (1857–1939), founder of psychological laboratories at Cornell and at Stanford. Unfortunately, Wundt's laboratory was full, so Angell moved on to Berlin, where he heard lectures by Ebbinghaus (Chapter 8) and Helmholtz (Chapter 7), who "especially impressed" him.

James Rowland Angell (1869–1949)

Angell next went to Halle, where he wrote a doctoral thesis on Kant (Chapter 6) while working with Hans Vaihinger (1852–1933). Angell's dissertation was accepted pending its revision into more acceptable German. Faced with the decision of whether to finish his degree or to accept a job offer at either Minnesota or at Harvard (for considerably less money), Angell chose the Minnesota position and marriage. He never returned to Germany to complete his degree.

A year later, Angell joined Dewey, Tufts, and Mead at the University of Chicago, where his neighbors and friends included the famous physiologist Jacques Loeb and the neurologist Henry Donaldson (both Chapter 12). Angell quickly established a research program, and his first paper (Angell & Moore, 1896) showed the importance of research from the functionalist position by successfully addressing the Titchener-Baldwin reaction-time controversy (Chapter 8).

Specifically, Titchener found that attention to the motor reaction produced reliably shorter reaction times than attention to the sensory stimulus; using naive subjects rather than Titchener's (and Wundt's) highly trained ones, Baldwin (Chapter 10) often obtained the opposite result. Angell and A. W. Moore discovered that without training, subjects produced Baldwin's variable results, whereas with further experience, subjects produced the kind of reaction times that Titchener observed. Obviously, both men were right—Baldwin with untrained observers and Titchener with highly trained ones. For the functionalist, however, the study's importance lay in the adaptive change that occurred in subjects during exposure to the task. Also important was the demonstration of the relevance of individual differences for task performance. Structuralists, in their desire to illuminate the generalized mind, considered individual differences a nuisance to be overcome through long training.

Note that the Titchener-Baldwin controversy and its resolution by Angell shows the importance of the *nomothetic* (study of the generalized mind)/ *idiographic* (psychology of the individual) distinction we mentioned at the end of Chapter 10. Titchener's nomothetic approach led to different results than Baldwin's idiographic work, as Angell and Moore (1896) demonstrated.

Perhaps because of his lack of the Ph.D. degree, during his first 7 years at Chicago, Angell received neither raise nor promotion. Beginning to listen seriously to other job offers, Angell was finally promoted to associate professor in 1901 and then to professor in 1904, with the promise that he would be made department head when psychology separated from philosophy. The promise was fulfilled the next year.

Elected APA president in 1906, at the annual convention Angell spoke on "The Province of Functional Psychology." To begin, he noted that functional psychology was nothing new. "In certain of its phases it is plainly discernible in the psychology of Aristotle and in its more modern garb it has been increasingly in evidence since Spencer wrote his *Psychology* and Darwin his *Origin of Species*" (Angell, 1907, p. 62).

Angell advanced three main conceptions of functionalism:

> (1) functionalism conceived as the psychology of mental operations in contrast to the psychology of mental elements; or . . . the psychology of the *how* and *why* of consciousness as distinguished from the psychology of the *what* of consciousness.
> (2) the functionalism which deals with the problem of mind conceived as primarily engaged in mediating between the environment and the needs of the organism. This is the psychology of the fundamental utilities of consciousness. . . .
> (3) functionalism described as psychophysical psychology, that is the psychology which constantly recognizes and insists upon the essential significance of the mind-body relationship for any just and comprehensive appreciation of mental life itself. (Angell, 1907, pp. 85–86, italics added)

First, Angell contrasted functionalism's interest in the how and why of consciousness with structuralism's concern over the what—mental activity versus mental content, in other words. Second, Angell saw a functional psychology whose task was to understand the mind's mediation between the environment and the organism's needs. For the functionalist, consciousness is concerned with "accommodation to the novel"; actions frequently repeated become habit, and "the mental direction tends to subside and give way to a condition approximating physiological automatism . . ." (Angell, 1907, p. 72). Finally, Angell conceived of functionalism as "a form of psychophysics," a psychology of the total mind-body organism. Functionalism "finds its major interest in determining the relations to one another of the physical and mental portions of the organism" (p. 80). Functionalism's biological orientation encouraged further development of animal psychology, which Angell supported at Chicago.

Over the years, administrative duties took increasingly more time away from Angell's efforts in psychology. From a variety of posts at Chicago, including having been acting president on a number of occasions (Angell could not have become president at the time because of a rule that the officeholder had to be a Baptist), Angell left in 1920 to become the Carnegie Corporation's president. The Corporation had been created in the United States to promote human welfare, principally along educational lines. After only a year as its head, Angell accepted the presidency of Yale University, at exactly half his Carnegie salary. Angell served with distinction from 1921 until his retirement in 1937.

Angell's Influence

Although Angell essentially retired from psychology in 1911, his position as president of Yale enabled him to promote psychology and its interests. As we have seen, Angell was instrumental in articulating the functionalist position, most importantly in his 1907 paper. Angell's influence was also felt through *Psychology: An Introductory Study of the Structure and Functions of Human Consciousness* (Angell, 1904). Angell's textbook—popular enough to go through four editions by 1908—was in part a response to the lack of an integrating system in James's *Briefer Course.* Thus, although James had many of the basic ideas of functionalism, Angell and others integrated them into a system.

Like James and Hall, Angell attracted loyal followers, and several of the 50 psychology doctorates awarded during his Chicago tenure went to people who had significant careers in psychology. As we noted in our Münsterberg discussion in Chapter 10, applied psychology was particularly compatible with functionalism, given the system's focus on pragmatic rather than philosophical solutions. We can see this applied focus in many of Angell's students. For example, **Helen Thompson Woolley** (1874–1947) received a Ph.D. in 1900 and became the director in Cincinnati of the Bureau for the Investigation of Working Children. Her research made her an ardent proponent of child welfare reform. In Detroit, she organized one of America's first nursery schools, where she studied child development and the mental abilities of young children and applied what she had learned to benefit her charges.

Another of Angell's stars was **June Etta Downey** (1875–1932), who founded the psychology laboratory at the University of Wyoming and in 1915 became head of the university's department of psychology and philosophy, a position she held until her death (Hogan & Broudy, 2000). Downey's applied approach produced many personality tests, and she became an expert on handwriting analysis (graphology), which was the subject of her doctoral research. Both Angell and John Watson served as subjects for her dissertation.

Walter S. Hunter (1889–1953), converted to psychology at 17 by reading James's *Principles* (Hunter, 1952), earned a Chicago Ph.D. in 1912 and then gravitated from functionalism toward the behaviorist movement begun by another Angell student—John Watson. The 1931 APA president, Hunter eventually became psychology department head at Brown University, after stints at Texas, Kansas, and Clark University. For his doctoral dissertation, Hunter developed the **delayed-response problem** to study memory in animals, a problem suggested to him by Harvey A. Carr. An animal is first shown the problem's solution (e.g., the door hiding a reward) and is then restrained for varying times before being released. To solve the problem, the animal must "remember" the reward's position during the delay. Hunter was a pioneer in comparative psychology, including the comparison of animals and humans (e.g., Hunter, 1913). Comparative psychology was neglected by the structuralists but embraced by American functionalists.

Further important comparative work came from Robert Yerkes (Chapter 12) and his pupil—later his teacher—**Gilbert Van Tassell Hamilton** (1877–1948). Considered a major figure in the history of psychiatry (Sears, 1992), Hamilton was another pioneer in American comparative psychology (e.g., Hamilton, 1911, 1916), with interests in contrasting animals and humans on the same behavioral phenomena.

Angell himself was an important figure in the growing interest in "behavior" that came to dominate American psychology (Leahey, 1993). Two years before Watson's "behaviorist manifesto," Angell (1911) wrote,

> But there is unquestionably a movement on foot in which interest is centered in the *results* of conscious process, rather than in the *processes* themselves. This is peculiarly true in animal psychology; it is only less true in human psychology. In these cases interest is in what may for lack of a better term be called 'behavior'; and the analysis of consciousness is primarily justified by the light it throws on behavior, rather than *vice-versa.*
>
> If this movement should go forward, we should probably have a general science of behavior. . . . (p. 47, italics in the original)

One of Angell's best-known students was Harvey A. Carr, who received his Ph.D. in 1905. Carr eventually succeeded Angell as functionalism's primary spokesperson.

HARVEY A. CARR

Harvey A. Carr (1873–1954) was born on an Indiana farm. He began his college career at DePauw University, where he majored in mathematics. Although he liked physics and was curious about the biological sciences, there was little taught in the latter at DePauw—rumor had it that school authorities disliked "biology because of its evolutionary implications" (Carr, 1936, p. 69). Illness at the beginning of his third year interrupted Carr's education at DePauw. His recovery was followed by a period of teaching, which Carr felt was partly responsible for his later specialization in psychology.

Carr next entered the University of Colorado, planning to resume his studies in mathematics. However, Carr found he liked the professor of psychology and education and disliked the mathematics instructor, so he opted for psychology.

After earning bachelor's and master's degrees from Colorado, Carr pursued a Ph.D. in experimental psychology at the University of Chicago. When he arrived, Dewey was the department head, and Angell was in charge of the experimental psychology course. At the end of Carr's first year, Dewey left, Angell became head of a separate department of psychology, and John Watson was hired as an instructor.

Carr's first reaction to Watson was "of slight reserve and suspicion," but this soon changed to a spirit of comradeship. After Carr received his Ph.D. in 1905, his first university employment was at Chicago in 1908 when he took the opening left by Watson's departure. Carr remained at Chicago, becoming department head in 1925. During Carr's 30-year association with the department, 130 doctorates were conferred. According to Fred McKinney (1978), a Chicago student from 1929 to 1931, Carr was

> held in special regard by most of the graduate students. . . . To me he was like a favorite uncle: warm, friendly, teasing at times, oblivious to everyone when he was preoccupied. He was a quiet, apparently happy family man who came to the office regularly and did his work unostentatiously. He was no academic prima donna, but was quite comfortable in the background; he seemed emotionally mature and unpretentious. . . . [N]o one doubted the keenness of his intellect or the depth of his concern for students. (pp. 143–144)

Under Carr, functionalism at Chicago reached its zenith, and his approach is representative of functionalism's most mature position. Our discussion will center on the system described in Carr's (1925) influential textbook, *Psychology: A Study of Mental Activity.*

University of Chicago Library, Department of Special Collections.

Harvey A. Carr (1873–1954)

Carr's Functionalism

For Carr, psychology was the study of mental activity, whose aim is to manipulate experience to achieve a better adjustment between the organism and its environment. Mental activity is a generic term for specific activities such as perception, memory, feelings, and reasoning. For Carr, as for William James and other psychologists of function, we see the importance of evolutionary theory. Mental activity, or consciousness, has evolved because it has the function of helping the organism adapt to its environment. Mental activity produces adaptive behavior, and the essence of adaptive behavior is the adaptive act.

For Carr, the **adaptive act** was a key concept consisting of three essential elements: (1) a motivating stimulus, (2) a sensory situation, and (3) a response that changes the situation to satisfy the motivating conditions. Carr saw a motive as a stimulus that dominates and directs behavior until the organism responds so that the motivating stimulus is no longer effective. Resolution of the motive may come in any of three ways: The adaptive act may remove the stimulus or disrupt it by substituting a more powerful stimulus, or the organism may adapt to the motivating stimulus.

To illustrate, consider the last time you were hungry. There was a motivating stimulus—for example, hunger pangs, time on the clock; a sensory situation—for example, nothing desirable in your refrigerator or cupboard; and a response that changed the sensory situation—for example, you drove to a fast-food restaurant, ordered, and then ate a hamburger to remove the motivating stimulus. Although our example is oversimplified, each adaptive act consists of a coordinated series of stimuli and responses, with each response altering the stimulus situation. Like Dewey's reflex arc concept, in Carr's adaptive act, behavior is a continuous and integrated process.

The adaptive act ends when a response removes the motivating stimulus, and this is the basis for learning.

> The usual explanation of the adaptive character of our acquired reactions is that of the law of effect, which accounts for the selection and elimination of acts on the basis of their consequents. . . . The law merely accounts for the fixation of the adaptive acts and the elimination of the nonadaptive ones. . . . (Carr; cited in Hilgard, 1991, p. 128)

The law of effect, mentioned first in our discussion of Bain (Chapter 5), was formulated by Thorndike (discussed later).

Like most of the psychologists before him—for example, Wundt, Brentano, Titchener, James—Angell saw introspection as a fundamental method of psychology, although their approaches to introspection differed. Carr's mature functionalist position accepted that mental acts could be either subjectively (through introspective self-report) or objectively observed, without implying one method was preferable. He considered self-reports necessary to learn about human mental events, but the subjective method could be used only with "subjects of training and ability." Psychologists must use the objective method (observation of behavior) in studying animals, children, primitive peoples, and the insane.

The Chicago functionalists preferred experimentation to naturalistic observation, and learning became a key area of study. In fact, psychologists working in the functionalist tradition obtained a large amount of objective data by studying learning in animals, and Carr himself worked with rats early in his career.

Carr's Influence

Carr's and functionalism's eclecticism permitted a variety of disparate areas to develop. Because of their concern for the adaptive nature of mental acts—the uses to which the acts could be put—functionalists supported applied fields such as educational psychology, industrial psychology, abnormal psychology, and mental hygiene. Put another way, applied psychology, by stressing the application of psychological knowledge for enhancing the human condition, is by definition functional (i.e., adaptive).

In addition, because of their nondoctrinaire positions, functionalists tended to be skeptical of the more extreme, although sometimes related, systems such as behaviorism and psychoanalysis. By advocating the study of overt behavior, behaviorists were merely embracing a position included under the functionalist umbrella; the objective, scientific study of animals clearly interested functionalists. When psychoanalysts stressed motivation's importance for behavior, functionalists could say that motivation had always been important in their conception of adaptive behavior. Because of its inclusiveness, functionalism saw little need for these "new" schools.

Basically, Carr's view was that functional psychology was American psychology, "and he might have included France and Britain too, as well as animal psychology and all applied psychology . . ." (Boring, 1950, p. 559). Unfortunately, by being so catholic in what it accepted, functionalism lost the dynamic that comes in opposing and being opposed.

Still, there were functionalists at places other than Chicago. As we saw in Chapter 10, Cattell, a psychologist of function, if not formally a functionalist, had a Columbia career spanning more than 25 years (1891–1917). In 1904, Cattell brought John Dewey from Chicago, but by this time Dewey was more concerned with philosophy and education than with psychology. Two of Cattell's students were particularly instrumental in imparting a functionalist flavor to psychology at Columbia and for making Columbia an important center for American psychology. Both studied under James at Harvard before taking their Ph.D.s with Cattell. They were Robert Sessions Woodworth and Edward Lee Thorndike.

ROBERT SESSIONS WOODWORTH

Robert Sessions Woodworth (1869–1962) was born in Massachusetts, the oldest son of his father's third wife. His father was a sternly religious Congregational minister, and his mother was an early gradu-

Robert Sessions Woodworth (1869–1962)

ate of Mount Holyoke Seminary (now College). In 1859, she was instrumental in founding a women's seminary in Ohio.

For the most part, Woodworth grew up in New England, and he considered his environment the neighborhood more than his immediate family. As he put it, "from the age of six or seven, I had a chum, I had 'a girl,' I had a group of friends, whose doings loom larger in my memory than what went on within the four walls of home" (Woodworth, 1932, p. 360).

Woodworth earned his Amherst College bachelor's degree in 1891, with exposure to psychology in his senior philosophy course, taught by Amherst's exceptional instructor, **Charles E. Garman** (1850–1907). Garman, with a Yale master's degree, also founded the psychology laboratory at Amherst. James H. Tufts, mentioned earlier in the chapter, was another psychologist importantly influenced by Garman.

For the next 4 years, Woodworth taught mathematics, first at a secondary school, then at Washburn College. During this period, he found James's *Principles* stimulating and heard an inspiring lecture by G. Stanley Hall. Hall's lecture motivated Woodworth to inscribe the word *INVESTIGATION* on a card he hung over his desk, and a year later he abandoned mathematics to study psychology and philosophy at Harvard.

At Harvard, James and Royce were Woodworth's main teachers, and his experimental training came from **E. B. Delabarre** (1863–1945). In charge of the Harvard laboratory in Münsterberg's absence, Delabarre had earned an M.A. under James and a Ph.D. from Freiburg and was on leave from Brown University, where he had established a psychology laboratory. Delabarre's main contributions to psychology were in visual perception.

James had Woodworth work on the study of dreams, and he thought he saw a pattern of dreaming about matters begun but not completed during the day, which anticipates the Zeigarnik effect (Chapter 14) by more than 2 decades. Motivation also interested Woodworth during his Harvard days and afterward, and at one point he told Thorndike he was going to try to develop a "motivology," or science of motives.

In 1897, both Woodworth and Thorndike earned master's degrees from Harvard. Woodworth spent a year in physiology at the Harvard Medical School before going to Columbia, where he got his Ph.D. in 1899.

Woodworth spent 5 of the 6 years following his master's degree studying or teaching physiology, and as Charles Sherrington's (Chapter 7) assistant at Liverpool in 1903, he was "much minded to make [his] psychology contribute to a career in brain physiology, rather than vice versa" (Woodworth, 1932, p. 368). Sherrington's physiological work on the reflex provided the neurological basis for Dewey's reflex arc concept.

However, at this point, Cattell asked Woodworth to return to Columbia to "work at experimental and physiological psychology," and Woodworth decided this was the work for which he was best prepared. Except for the year 1912 in Külpe's (Chapter 8) laboratory, Woodworth stayed at Columbia until he retired in 1942, having succeeded Cattell as department head when Cattell was fired in 1917.

Perhaps reflecting his lengthy and varied training before becoming fully committed to psychology—he was 34 when he returned to Columbia—Woodworth was remarkably broad in his concerns. In addition to his interests in experimental and physiological psychology, Woodworth lectured on abnormal psychology, tests and statistics, and social psychology and offered seminars on such diverse topics as movement, vision, thinking, and motivation. He was also interested in the history of psychology as it established itself as a science. His "bogey men"—psychologists who most irritated him—were individuals who tried to dictate method and results, whose aim was to restrict.

Woodworth's Contribution to Functionalism

Woodworth's most systematic contribution to functionalism can be found in his 1918 *Dynamic Psychology*, revised 40 years later as *Dynamics of Behavior*. The eclectic Woodworth saw psychology encompassing both the introspectionist tradition and the newer interest in the study of behavior. For him, psychology's subject matter was both consciousness *and* behavior. Thus, he sought a healing of the schism between traditional introspectionism and revolutionary behaviorism, or between the psychologies of his two biggest bogey men—Titchener and Watson.

In his psychology, Woodworth stressed the importance of the state of the organism itself, changing the classic stimulus-response (S-R) formula to S-O-R. It is not enough just to describe the stimuli; in order to know what the organism will do, we must know its internal state, its motivation. Here we see Woodworth working to develop his **motivology,** or science of motivation, that he had mentioned to Thorndike 2 decades earlier. To illustrate the importance of the "O" for behavior, consider your actions when grocery shopping. If you go to the store *before* you have eaten, you will probably buy more food than if you shop *after* a meal. The difference is in the O—the organism.

Two of Woodworth's most important concepts were mechanism and drive. **Mechanism** refers to *how* something is accomplished, whereas **drive** indicates *why*. For example, take a hungry rat in a maze. The rat's behavior leading to the goal box and food—its running and exploring the maze's alleys—is the mechanism that leads to success; its hunger is the drive.

Mechanism itself might become a drive, according to Woodworth. For example, consider a woman who works to earn money to satisfy her needs for food, clothing, and shelter. Initially, her work is the mechanism that satisfies her basic drives. At some point, the work may not be necessary to satisfy basic drives; she may have earned enough money to provide for her basic needs with money left over. However, the woman continues to work because the mechanism itself has become a drive.

Woodworth is often credited with coining the term *drive*, but the term actually appeared at least several months before *Dynamic Psychology* was published, in an article by Watson and Morgan (1917). Although he did not introduce the word, Woodworth certainly popularized it.

Woodworth's Other Contributions

In a career spanning nearly 60 years, Woodworth wrote several major books, almost any one of which would have capped a lesser psychologist's career. For example, in 1911 he revised G. T. Ladd's (Chapter 10) *Elements of Physiological Psychology*, "which became the standard handbook for this field until 1934" (Boring, 1950, p. 564). We have already mentioned *Dynamic Psychology* and its revision. And in 1921, Woodworth published *Psychology: A Study of Mental Life*, an introductory textbook whose several editions outsold its competition for 25 years.

Woodworth revealed his interest in psychology's history with the 1931 publication of *Contemporary Schools of Psychology*. His general eclecticism is evident in his even-handed treatment of the various systematic positions; Woodworth denied that any approach to psychology was the *only* approach, even his own. *Contemporary Schools* went through three revisions, the last published with a co-author 2 years after Woodworth's death.

One of Woodworth's students, **Edna Heidbreder** (1890–1985), is best known for *Seven Psychologies,* a book on the same topic as *Contemporary Schools.* Heidbreder received her Ph.D. from Columbia in 1924, spent a decade at the University of Minnesota, and then went to Wellesley College, where she worked until her retirement. Like many other functional psychologists, Heidbreder made significant contributions to applied psychology, particularly to the psychological testing movement and personality testing (see Henle, 1991).

Perhaps the publication for which Woodworth is best known is *Experimental Psychology,* which first appeared in 1938, although a mimeographed version had been used for nearly 20 years by then. The 1938 version and its revision with Harold Schlosberg in 1954 taught experimental psychology to literally thousands of students, becoming for its generation what Titchener's *Experimental Psychology* had been for an earlier one. One of Woodworth's many contributions to experimental psychology was his popularization of the terms *independent* and *dependent variable* (Winston, 1990).

In 1914, Woodworth was elected APA president, and his presidential speech presented his contribution to the imageless thought controversy we first mentioned in Chapter 8. Of perhaps greater interest, Woodworth called for psychology to develop its own technical vocabulary. The problem is that many of psychology's technical terms are part of everyday language, with all the imprecision that implies. Terms such as *thoughts, mind, memory, behavior,* and even *psychology* itself have both common and technical definitions, with the former frequently interfering with the latter (for a critique of the term *behavior,* see Hibbard & Henley, 1994). Woodworth called for psychology to develop a technical vocabulary, following the lead of physics and chemistry in naming something after its discoverer. For example, you may recall that in Chapter 8, we said that Külpe and his students made thought a major research topic at Würzburg.

> [S]ince . . . the "thoughts" were gradually brought to light by the school of which Külpe was the guiding spirit, I would suggest calling them "kulps," defining this term similarly by reference to the original works. These terms [Woodworth suggested others] are certainly beautifully compact and euphonious, and those who can bring themselves to use them will find them very convenient. (Woodworth, 1915/1978, p. 126)

Although the problem Woodworth highlighted is real, his technical terms never caught on. That is unfortunate, because drives might have become "woods."

For his many contributions to psychology, Woodworth received numerous honors. In addition to being APA president, in 1921 he was elected to the first board of directors of the Psychological Corporation, Cattell's organization to promote applied psychology. In 1956, he received the first American Psychological Foundation Gold Medal Award for his contributions to the growth of psychology.

As we indicated, Cattell's two most important students at Columbia were Woodworth and Thorndike. They had very different dispositions: Woodworth was patient and thoughtful, whereas Thorndike was anxious to get on with whatever he was doing. Despite their differences, there were similarities in their systematic positions, and the two remained lifelong friends.

EDWARD LEE THORNDIKE

Edward Lee Thorndike (1874–1949) was the son of a Methodist minister, who, in the custom of the Methodist church at the time, moved his family every 2 or 3 years to another little New England town. Thorndike's mother was the perfect minister's wife, regarding as wicked such pleasures as dancing

From Boakes, From Darwin to Behaviourism (1984), by courtesy of Cambridge University Press.

Edward Lee Thorndike (1874–1949) at Harvard

and Sunday newspapers. Seriousness and diligence were the order of the day.

Thorndike was a serious and diligent student, and his record at Wesleyan University in Middletown, Connecticut, testified to his brilliance. At Wesleyan, Thorndike's religious faith yielded to a trust in science. This background and commitment are reflected in Thorndike's scientific productivity, which was prodigious even by the standards of the people we have so far considered.

During his junior year, Thorndike heard the word *psychology* for the first time, when he took a required course in the subject, using James Sully's *Outlines of Psychology* as the text. Thorndike considered Sully's book unremarkable, but he had a different reaction to the chapters of James's *Principles of Psychology* he read for a competition, which he won. He found the *Principles* stimulating, "more so than any book that I had read before, and possibly more so than any read since" (Thorndike, 1936, p. 263). As a consequence, Thorndike purchased the two volumes, the only books outside his English major that he bought voluntarily during his Wesleyan years, and chided the psychology professor for not using the *Principles* as a text.

From Wesleyan, Thorndike went to Harvard, initially planning to major in English and also taking psychology and philosophy courses. However, work in English was abandoned for psychology in his first graduate year. As with Woodworth, Thorndike's research training in psychology was primarily directed by E. B. Delabarre.

Thorndike's first research was an attempted study of "mind-reading ability" in children. The study's rationale came from James's belief that "mind reading," if it occurred, resulted from the detection of slight (and unconscious) changes in facial expression or movements. As close observers of their parents and other adults, children might be particularly adept at detecting such signals.

In his experiment, Thorndike would think of one of a set of numbers, letters, or objects, and a child, seated facing him, would try to guess the correct item. Thorndike found little evidence for "mind reading," despite rewarding correct guesses with a piece of candy.

You may recognize similarities between Thorndike's "mind-reading" experiments and Oskar Pfungst's work with Clever Hans (Chapter 1). Through careful observation, Pfungst found the horse was using barely discernible changes in the body posture and/or facial expressions of his questioners to answer their questions correctly. When Pfungst used Hans's method with human subjects, many of them thought he was reading their minds. Specifically, Pfungst asked a subject to think of a number, which Pfungst then tried to guess by tapping it out with his hand. Pfungst would stop tapping when he saw the kind of signal Hans had responded to.

Although the study of Clever Hans occurred nearly a decade after Thorndike's experiment with children, the rationale for the "mind-reading" experiments was the same. Thorndike's lack of results appears to contradict the study by Pfungst, but there is a key methodological difference: In Pfungst's demonstration, the correct answer invariably occurred during his tapping, and Pfungst had only to stop tapping when he detected the signal for the correct number. By contrast, the children in Thorndike's experiment were allowed to make only one guess of the item Thorndike had selected. If Thorndike had allowed a child to name each of the possible items on each trial, stopping with the correct one, then Clever Hans–type "mind reading" might have been revealed.

Although the children enjoyed the experiments, the authorities decided they should not be continued. "I then suggested experiments with the instinctive and intelligent behavior of chickens as a topic, and this was accepted" (Thorndike, 1936, p. 264). Although never explicitly acknowledged by Thorndike, the reason for his choice seems to be an influence from Lloyd Morgan (Chapter 12), as we noted in Chapter 5. Morgan lectured at Harvard in 1896 on his learning studies with chickens, which illustrated the Spencer-Bain principle that behavior is modified by its consequences.

At first, Thorndike kept his subjects in his room, but his landlady's protests forced him to move them to new quarters. James,

> with his habitual kindness and devotion to underdogs and eccentric aspects of science, harbored my chickens in the cellar of his own home for the rest of the year. The nuisance to Mrs. James was, I hope, somewhat mitigated by the entertainment to the two youngest children. (Thorndike, 1936, p. 264)

In the fall of 1897, Thorndike accepted a fellowship from Cattell at Columbia and moved to New York with two educated chickens he planned to breed as part of a test of the inheritance of acquired mental traits (Lamarckism; Chapter 9). Thorndike scrapped the project when he realized how long it would take to train and breed several generations of chickens.

At Columbia, Thorndike began training animals, chiefly young cats, to escape from puzzle or problem boxes he had constructed. Because of their importance for behaviorism, we will discuss Thorndike's animal experiments in detail in Chapter 12. Here, we will just note that within 16 months of his arrival at Columbia, Thorndike had written and successfully defended his dissertation, published it as a monograph supplement to *Psychological Review*, and presented his results to both the American Psychological Association and the New York Academy of Sciences.

After a year at the College for Women at Western Reserve University in Cleveland, Thorndike returned to New York to accept a position at Teachers College, Columbia. With the exception of one more brief foray into animal research—he studied monkeys from 1899 to 1901—Thorndike devoted himself to research with humans. The reason for this was his employment at Teachers College—a school with a focus on pedagogy. As he wrote in 1936, "it has been my custom to fulfill my contractual obligations as a professor before doing anything else" (p. 270).

Thorndike's Psychology

For Thorndike, psychology was the study of stimulus-response (S-R) connections, and he assumed that behavior can be analyzed into such associations or connections, as he called them. However, Thorndike's idea of S-R bonds was broader than his critics often assumed. Instead of just simple associations between discrete phenomena, Thorndike's conception included the type of associations we saw in Dewey's reflex arc.

> [Connections] often occur in long series wherein the response to one situation becomes the situation producing the next response and so on. They may be from parts or elements or features of a situation as well as from the situation as a whole. . . . The things connected may be subtle relations or elusive attitudes and intentions. (Thorndike, 1949, p. 81)

Of course, specific S-R connections were certainly possible in Thorndike's learning theory, and this is what he found in his dissertation research. Highly specific S-R bonds were also found in a famous study in which Thorndike and Woodworth tested the **doctrine of formal discipline.** This doctrine was the widely held belief that exercising the mind by learning disciplinary subjects such as Latin, Greek, and mathematics would improve the mind's ability to learn other unrelated subjects. In this "mind-as-a-muscle" idea, exercise would strengthen the mind's "fibers" and make them more capable of profiting from future training.

William James had informally tested the doctrine by memorizing passages from Victor Hugo and John Milton. Reporting his results in the *Principles,* James (1890) concluded, "*No amount of culture would seem capable of modifying a man's* GENERAL *retentiveness*" (Vol. 1, pp. 663–664, emphasis in the original).

Thorndike and Woodworth (1901) examined the doctrine by training subjects on various tasks such as estimating geometrical areas and then testing the subjects to see if their ability to perform tasks more or less similar to the original had improved. **Transfer of training**—improvement in one task following training on another—was slight and, when it occurred, seemed to require "identical elements" between the tasks, not the learning of something unrelated. Thorndike and Woodworth's results helped shift educational practices toward specifically task-oriented teaching and away from nonspecifically disciplinary training—that is, away from the doctrine of formal discipline.

For Thorndike, the S-R connections were formed through so-called trial-and-error learning, although it is more accurate to call it trial-and-success. As we will see in Chapter 12, Thorndike's animals demonstrated that the strengthening of S-R bonds occurred through the action of the Spencer-Bain principle, which he dubbed the *law of effect*—success strengthens the bond between a stimulus situation and a particular response. Thorndike's learning theory was so influential that even a psychologist who disagreed with it could say, "The psychology of animal learning—not to mention that of child learning—has been and still is primarily a matter of agreeing or disagreeing with Thorndike, or trying in minor ways to improve upon him" (Tolman, 1938, p. 11). B. F. Skinner's learning theory (Chapter 13) is primarily an extension of Thorndike's, and Skinner acknowledged that his most important contribution to psychology was to take Thorndike's law of effect seriously. In his monumental work, *The Behavior of Organisms,* however, Skinner (1938) provided little mention of Thorndike's research. He was criticized for this omission in a book review by Hilgard (1939). In response to Hilgard's criticism, Skinner sent Thorndike a letter in which he wrote:

> I seem to have identified your point of view with the modern psychological view as a whole. It has always been obvious that I was merely carrying on your puzzle box experiments, but it never occurred to me to remind my readers of that fact. (Skinner, cited in Hearst, 1999, p. 445)

Thorndike's Applied Contributions

Thorndike's influence on pedagogy and psychology was felt in several ways beyond his learning theory. For example, Thorndike wrote a number of practical educational works that literally changed how children were taught in America. With an interest in how best to teach children to read and spell, he measured the frequency with which different words occur in print, determining the 10,000, 20,000, and finally, 30,000 most common words. Thorndike thought teachers should teach children to read and spell the most common rather than the most obscure words.

Thorndike also revolutionized children's dictionaries. At the time, school dictionaries were abbreviated adult dictionaries, with definitions often incomprehensible to a child. By contrast, Thorndike defined each word with words simpler than itself, and the simplest words were merely used in sentences rather than being defined. Additionally, pictures were widely used to illustrate objects being defined. Thorndike's dictionaries were quite successful, and later producers of dictionaries for children generally adopted his principles.

After children have been taught to read and to spell, some progress measure is desirable, and Thorndike developed scales to measure reading ability, just as he created ability scales for spelling, drawing, handwriting, and arithmetic. Like Galton and Cattell, Thorndike loved to measure things, particularly things objectively difficult to measure. "Whatever exists, exists in some amount. To measure it is simply to know its varying amounts" (Thorndike, 1921, p. 379). Paradoxically for one who so loved to measure, Thorndike recognized his deficient mathematical training, which he "tried to remedy . . . by private study, but something else always seemed more important" (Thorndike, 1936, p. 267). However, he encouraged his children to get a strong mathematical grounding, with the result that two of his sons earned doctorates in physics and his daughter received a Ph.D. in mathematics. The "only intellectually disreputable member of the family" (R. L. Thorndike, 1991, p. 141) was the other son—respected psychometric psychologist Robert L. Thorndike.

Consistent with his love of measurement, Thorndike developed tests to measure intelligence, culminating in his *Intelligence Scale CAVD.* From his belief that intelligence was a combination of many different skills, the *CAVD* measured sentence completion (*C*), arithmetic ability (*A*), vocabulary (*V*), and the ability to follow directions (*D*). Robert L. Thorndike (1991) cited the example of his father to illustrate the multidimensionality of intelligence: "In abstract intelligence, he was unquestionably in the top fraction of a percent of the population, while in mechanical intelligence he was a slow learner. He never learned to drive a car; I never saw him fix any device" (p. 145). Although this comment may strike you as odd given Thorndike's methodological innovation of the puzzle boxes for studying animal learning, when you see examples of the actual apparatus in Chapter 12, the statement will become more meaningful.

Like so many of his contemporaries, Thorndike was an avowed hereditarian. Like Galton (Chapter 9), Thorndike advocated eugenics. Although much of his research and writing benefited the education of all, Thorndike himself was opposed to universal equal educational opportunities. Different intellectual abilities called for different instruction.

Thorndike's Influence

Thorndike was incredibly prolific, averaging one publication per *month* throughout his career, and many of them were textbooks based on his lectures. As he explained, "It has always seemed to me better for an instructor to present his contributions in black and white than to require the labor and risk the errors of note-taking" (Thorndike, 1936, p. 266). In addition to taking Thorndike swiftly to the top in psychology—a 1921 poll of psychologists for Cattell's *American Men of Science* found Thorndike ranked first—his books earned him a good income. In 1924 alone, his annual royalty income was five times his salary as a professor.

As you would expect, Thorndike received many honors during his lifetime. He was elected APA president in 1912, elected to membership in the National Academy of Sciences in 1917, and received the Butler Medal from Columbia in 1925 in recognition of his contributions to education. Thorndike was the president of the American Association for the Advancement of Science in 1933.

As R. L. Thorndike (1991) put it, his father was "in some ways the original workaholic, reading the *Encyclopaedia Britannica* in bed to locate good passages for reading comprehension tests, . . . because he would rather be getting or analyzing data than most anything else" (p. 151). Although he was not a social person, according to his son, Thorndike could inspire great loyalty. To illustrate, his student Herbert Toops named his first son Edward L. Toops and his second son Thorndike Toops.

Thorndike was particularly influential in educational psychology because of his learning theory, his studies on the learning of specific skills, his many published instructional materials, and his investigations of intelligence and the tools to measure it. Much of his learning theory came from his dissertation experiment, a study that began systematic laboratory research in animal learning. His further investigation of human learning led to a revision of his learning theory, as we will see in Chapter 12. Thorndike's approach to education became known as the "scientific movement" in contrast to Dewey's "progressive movement."

Thorndike is a transitional figure between functionalism and behaviorism. His animal research fits well into the behaviorist tradition, whereas the bulk of his research had functionalism's applied, utilitarian flavor. There is little contradiction in our placing Thorndike astraddle the functionalism-behaviorism fence, however, because the behaviorist movement grew out of functionalism.

In Chapter 10, we discussed the research of one of Thorndike's female students, Leta Stetter Hollingworth, who joined the Columbia faculty after receiving her Ph.D. To close this chapter, we will examine two additional women who were part of the functionalist school—Milicent W. Shinn and Ethel Puffer Howes.

Courtesy of The Bancroft Library, University of California, Berkeley.

Milicent W. Shinn (1858–1940)

WOMEN IN AMERICA'S FIRST SCHOOL

From its beginnings, women have been disproportionately represented in American psychology relative to their presence in the more "mature" sciences such as physics and chemistry (Scarborough & Furumoto, 1987). However, despite their numbers, women's accomplishments largely have been overlooked in most reconstructions of the discipline's past. In part, their absence simply reflects "the problematic absence or invisibility of women in historical accounts in general" (p. 8), and Bohan (1990, 1992) has developed a framework for "re-placing" women in psychology's history. Their relative invisibility may also reflect a corresponding lack of accomplishments, which was caused by the difficulties many women faced in establishing their careers.

Milicent W. Shinn

California native and cousin of Edmund Sanford (Chapter 10), **Milicent Shinn** (1858–1940) entered the University of California in 1874, only a year after it opened its doors to women and just 2 years after it moved to Berkeley. There, she met President Daniel Gilman, the man we mentioned as the president of Johns Hopkins University in the last chapter. Gilman went to Baltimore in 1875, and in 1879, after a chance meeting with Shinn at a social science convention in the East, began a correspondence with her that lasted many years. Although Gilman wrote her about opportunities at the Harvard Annex, Shinn could not escape her family ties. Instead, she assumed the nonpaying editorship of a San Francisco literary magazine, *Overland Monthly,* continuing to live on the rural family farm near Niles, California, and commuting to the city.

In 1890, Shinn began a project that eventually led her back to Berkeley as a psychology graduate student. One of her brothers had brought his wife to the family homestead, and when their daughter was born, Shinn kept a detailed record of the infant's growth and development for more than 2 years. This systematic description of a child's physical and mental development established Shinn's place in psychology.

In 1893, Shinn was invited to present her findings at the World's Columbian Exposition in Chicago. Sandwiched among experimental papers in a conference on education, Shinn's "The First Two Years of the Child" was hailed as an outstanding early American contribution to the topic of child development. Convinced by others of the importance of her efforts, Shinn resigned her editorship and entered graduate school at Berkeley in 1894. In 1898, she received the 11th Ph.D. awarded by the University of California and the first given to a woman. Shinn's studies of her niece were published in 1900 as *The Biography of a Baby.*

Shinn's work was not the first systematic description of child development, however. Darwin (Chapter 9) kept a record of his infant son's development, which he published in 1877 as "Biographical sketch of an infant." Similarly, the German philosopher Dietrich Tiedemann (1748–1803) kept a diary record of the first 3 years of his son's life, which he published in 1787 (Bringmann, Hewett, & Ungerer, 1997), nearly a century before Darwin's article.

After Darwin, but before Shinn, **Wilhelm Preyer** (1842–1897) published *Die Seele des Kindes* in 1882, which was translated and published in 1888–89 as *The Mind of the Child.* Strongly based on Herbart's (Chapter 6) theory of education (Boudewijnse et al., 2001), Preyer's observational study of his own son is sometimes credited with being the first work of modern child psychology (Scarborough & Furumoto, 1987). A physiologist, Preyer was a friend of Fechner (Chapter 7) and one of the original editors of Ebbinghaus and König's *Zeitschrift für Psychologie* (Chapter 8). After 1882, Preyer devoted most of his time to child psychology.

Shinn acknowledged being guided by Preyer's book at the beginning of her observations, but she later diverged more and more from Preyer's method. After reading portions of Shinn's dissertation, Preyer acknowledged its value, suggesting in a letter to an American colleague that it should be translated into German so that German mothers could read it.

Unfortunately for psychology, after graduating Shinn returned to the family home. Scarborough and Furumoto (1987) wrote, "her sense of responsibility to her family emerges as the overriding factor deterring her from forging a professional identity" (p. 61).

Of course, Shinn was not the only woman of her era to face the dilemma posed by family obligations and career. Although Mary Calkins (Chapter 10) enjoyed a successful psychology career, she did not consider the scholarly life an easy one for a woman. Particularly problematic, in her view, were the conflicting demands of work and social responsibilities.

> In an observation that reflected her own personal experience as well as the existing social norms, [Calkins] remarked [in a 1913 address] that it was an unmarried daughter rather than a son who was likely to become responsible for the care of aging parents. For the woman who chose to marry, the balancing act between career and family demands was even more difficult. (Scarborough & Furumoto, 1987, p. 51)

This was especially true for Ethel Puffer Howes.

Ethel Puffer Howes

Born in Framingham, Massachusetts, **Ethel Puffer Howes** (1872–1950) was the oldest of four daughters of George and Ella Puffer. Ella had been a high school teacher before her marriage, and George had gone to business school in Boston before working as a stationmaster for the Albany railroad.

Ethel Puffer graduated from Smith College in western Massachusetts in 1891. As you may recall from Chapter 10, both Mary Calkins and Theodate Smith also earned degrees from Smith. In 1895, Puffer went to Germany to study psychology, eventually working with Münsterberg in Freiberg, where she was essentially adopted by the Münsterberg family. Back in New England on a fellowship received with Münsterberg's support, Puffer completed the Radcliffe Ph.D. requirements, among which was an examination by a committee that included James, Santayana, and Münsterberg.

Ethel Puffer Howes (1872–1950)

For the next decade, Puffer held academic positions in the Boston area and served as Münsterberg's laboratory assistant. In 1908, she married Benjamin Howes, a young man she apparently met as one of her students during a year of high school teaching (Scarborough, 1991). For much of the rest of her life, Ethel Puffer Howes was a homemaker.

Unlike Shinn, however, Ethel Howes did not completely relinquish the scholarly life. At various times, she wrote articles for the popular press, worked for the war effort and for women's suffrage, and had a brief (but exhausting) second career in the 1920s as the director of an institute at Smith College devoted to studying the status of women.

In her last word on the marriage-versus-career dilemma, it is evident Howes (1929) no longer believed it was possible for a woman to have a satisfactory career by making personal adjustments either in her family life or in her attitudes. What was needed instead was a redefinition of the traditional role of the woman, a changing of the inner attitudes of both men and women toward accepting the need of educated women for both familial and intellectual satisfaction. Society must change to eliminate "the intolerable choice" of the woman.

CONCLUSIONS

In this chapter, we have sketched the maturation of a peculiarly American school of psychology, functionalism. Functionalism declined as a recognized school primarily because of the success of its offspring, behaviorism, which we will examine in the next two chapters. As we have noted more than once, behaviorism's founder, John Watson, received his training in the functionalist tradition at the University of Chicago.

In a very real sense, Chicago's functionalism, exemplified by the work of James Rowland Angell and Harvey Carr, gave scientific substance to many of William James's pronouncements in the *Principles.* Watson's behaviorism can be seen as a logical outgrowth of the functional psychology he had learned, stripped of its mentalistic flavor. Although he accepted many of functionalism's principles—the strongly empirical, scientific approach to psychology, the importance of applied research, the study of animals—Watson rejected functionalism's continued interest in studying consciousness.

Despite behaviorism's early success, the case can be made that behaviorism did not murder functionalism, which lives on in its quiet, nonrestrictive way. For example, in our examination of cognitive psychology (Chapter 18), we will see that studies of human consciousness using both subjective and objective data in a manner consistent with functionalism are once again popular. As Fred McKinney (1978), one of Harvey Carr's students, expressed it,

> As I look back to the late twenties and then turn to observe psychology today, I conclude that *the functional tradition quietly persists.*

> Among all the systems of psychology that have emerged, it produced the greatest number of residuals. American psychology (which started with the functionalist William James, was institutionalized by John Dewey and James Angell as functionalism, and was regarded as the mainstream of psychology by Carr) generally continues in that tradition. American psychology serves as the model for psychologists and laboratories arising in the many new departments around the world; as a result, the functional tradition is worldwide. . . . Functionalism, present in the time of Ancient Greece, had its heyday as a school in the twenties and thirties of this century and lives on without the trappings of a school to this very day. (p. 147, italics in the original)

SUMMARY

As a school, functionalism had no dominant individual, and its formal founding is often credited to Titchener's 1898 criticism of John Dewey's earlier paper. Contrary to Titchener's predictions, the study of function proved fruitful.

John Dewey

In 1896, John Dewey wrote an article that Titchener criticized, "The reflex arc concept in psychology." Dewey's analysis of the reflex arc was intended to show that strong distinctions between stimulus and response are artificial and that an event such as seeing a candle, touching the flame, and drawing back in pain are part of one coherent whole. At the University of Chicago, Dewey built a strong functionalist philosophy department, while pursuing his interests in education. He went to Columbia in 1904, directing his efforts thereafter toward philosophy and education.

James Rowland Angell

James Rowland Angell became head of the psychology department at Chicago in 1905. In his APA presidential address, Angell characterized functionalism as (1) the study of mental operations in contrast to the study of mental elements, (2) the study of the mind engaged in mediating between the environment and the organism, and (3) the study of the relationship between the mind and the body.

Harvey A. Carr

With a Chicago Ph.D., Harvey A. Carr eventually became department head, and under him functionalism at Chicago reached its peak. For Carr, psychology was the study of mental activity, which produces adaptive behavior. A key concept was the adaptive act, which consists of (1) a motivating stimulus, (2) a sensory situation, and (3) a change in the situation that satisfies the motivating conditions. The adaptive act ends when a response removes the motivating stimulus, providing the basis for learning. Under Carr's direction, functionalism supported a variety of methods and applications, although it stood in opposition to the increasingly extreme positions of behaviorism and psychoanalysis.

Robert Sessions Woodworth

Harvard- and Columbia-trained Robert S. Woodworth's dynamic psychology stressed the state of the organism, changing the classic (and Thorndike's) S-R formulation to S-O-R. To know what an organism will do in a situation, we must know its motivation, and Woodworth is perhaps best known for his motivology, or science of motivation. Motivology was the study of the mechanisms (how something is accomplished) and drives (why something is accomplished) that form our motivations.

Woodworth's important textbooks included *Contemporary Schools of Psychology,* on the history of psychology, and the work for which he is best known, *Experimental Psychology.* Woodworth also called in vain for psychology to develop a technical vocabulary.

Edward Lee Thorndike

Probably Edward Lee Thorndike's most important research for psychology was the animal research for his dissertation. Soon after receiving his Ph.D., Thorndike permanently joined the faculty of Teacher's College at Columbia.

Although Thorndike's psychology can be understood as a psychology of S-R connections, his conception of stimulus and response was influenced by Dewey. In a test of the doctrine of formal discipline (with Woodworth), Thorndike found little evidence for the doctrine, and transfer of training seemed to require "identical elements" between the tasks. In his study of animal learning, Thorndike found that success strengthened a bond between a stimulus situation and a particular response, and he dubbed this updating of the Spencer-Bain principle the law of effect.

Much of Thorndike's work dealt with practical matters of education such as reading, spelling, children's dictionaries, and the measurement of children's abilities. In many ways, Thorndike represents the transition in American psychology from functionalism to behaviorism.

Women in America's First School

Milicent Shinn's career illustrates the struggles and accomplishments of women in America's first psychological school. Shinn received the first Ph.D. given to a woman by the University of California at Berkeley. Her primary work concerned her observations of an infant's development across a 2-year span. In Germany, Wilhelm Preyer had done similar work and suggested Shinn's work should be translated into German. After receiving her Ph.D., Shinn returned to the family home.

Also trained in the functional school, Ethel Puffer Howes struggled to combine marriage and a career. Howes eventually concluded it was impossible for a woman to have a satisfactory career by making personal adjustments in her family life or in her attitudes. Instead, society needed to redefine the woman's role.

CONNECTIONS QUESTIONS

1. What connections can you make between William James and the major functionalists reviewed in this chapter?
2. What is the connection between Dewey's reflex arc concept and James's stream of consciousness? Between Carr's adaptive act and Dewey's reflex arc concept?
3. What connections can you draw between Thorndike's "mind-reading" experiments and Pfungst's work with Clever Hans?
4. What connection can you make between the "founding" of functionalism as a school of psychology and Titchener?
5. What connections can you make between the women pioneers of American psychology? What sorts of common obstacles did they face?
6. What connections can you draw between Thorndike and Woodworth?

KEY NAMES AND TERMS

adaptive act (p. 297)
Frank Angell (p. 294)
James Rowland Angell (p. 293)
Harvey A. Carr (p. 296)
E. B. Delabarre (p. 299)
delayed-response problem (p. 296)
John Dewey (p. 290)
doctrine of formal discipline (p. 304)
June Etta Downey (p. 295)
drive (p. 300)
functionalism (p. 290)
Charles E. Garman (p. 299)
Gilbert Van Tassell Hamilton (p. 296)
Edna Heidbreder (p. 301)
Ethel Puffer Howes (p. 307)
Walter S. Hunter (p. 296)
George Herbert Mead (p. 292)
mechanism (p. 300)
motivology (p. 300)
Wilhelm Preyer (p. 307)
Milicent Shinn (p. 306)
Edward Lee Thorndike (p. 301)
transfer of training (p. 304)
James H. Tufts (p. 292)
Robert Sessions Woodworth (p. 298)
Helen Thompson Woolley (p. 295)

SUGGESTED READINGS

Angell, J. R. (1936). James Rowland Angell. In C. Murchison (Ed.), *A history of psychology in autobiography* (Vol. 3, pp. 1–38). Worcester, MA: Clark University Press.

Carr, H. A. (1936). Harvey A. Carr. In C. Murchison (Ed.), *A history of psychology in autobiography* (Vol. 3, pp. 69–82). Worcester, MA: Clark University Press.

Thorndike, E. L. (1936). Edward Lee Thorndike. In C. Murchison (Ed.), *A history of psychology in autobiography* (Vol. 3, pp. 263–270). Worcester, MA: Clark University Press.

Woodworth, R. S. (1932). Robert S. Woodworth. In C. Murchison (Ed.), *A history of psychology in autobiography* (Vol. 2, pp. 359–380). Worcester, MA: Clark University Press. These autobiographical essays in Murchison's *History of Psychology in Autobiography* are excellent starting points in the search for information on their authors. In reading Woodworth's autobiographical account, keep in mind that he lived and worked for another 3 decades after writing it.

Angell, J. R. (1907). The province of functional psychology. *Psychological Review, 14,* 61–91. This published version of Angell's 1906 APA presidential address provides both an excellent overview of a mature conception of functionalism and a glimpse of Angell's tendency toward verbosity.

Dewey, J. (1896). The reflex arc concept in psychology. *Psychological Review, 3,* 357–370. As we noted, this is the paper usually credited with initiating functionalism as a separate school of psychology. As a companion piece, it is worthwhile to read Titchener's critique: Titchener, E. B. (1898). The postulates of a structural psychology. *Philosophical Review, 7,* 449–465.

Scarborough, E., & Furumoto, L. (1987). *Untold lives: The first generation of American women psychologists.* New York: Columbia University Press. This is an excellent source for information on early women psychologists. In addition to chapters on Milicent Shinn and Ethel Puffer, Scarborough and Furumoto examine the travails and successes of Mary Calkins, Margaret Washburn, and Christine Ladd-Franklin. Cameo portraits are presented of such early women psychologists as Lillien Martin, Naomi Norsworthy, Theodate Smith, and Helen Woolley.

Animal Psychology and Early Behaviorism

CHAPTER 12

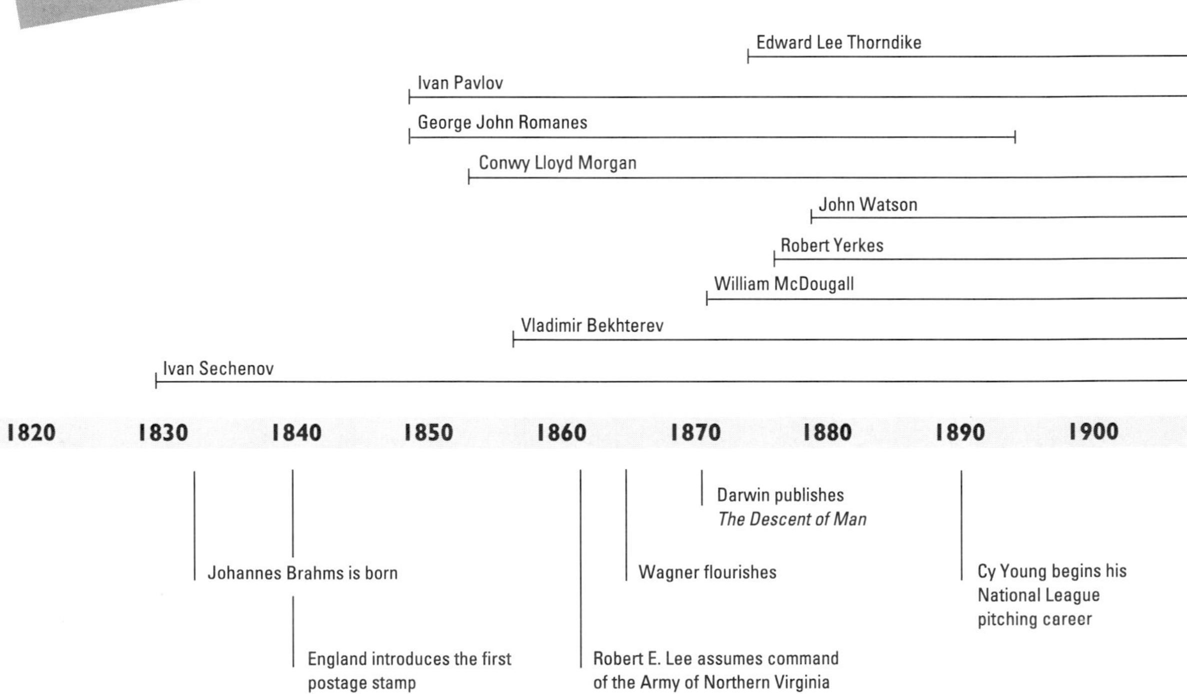

OUTLINE

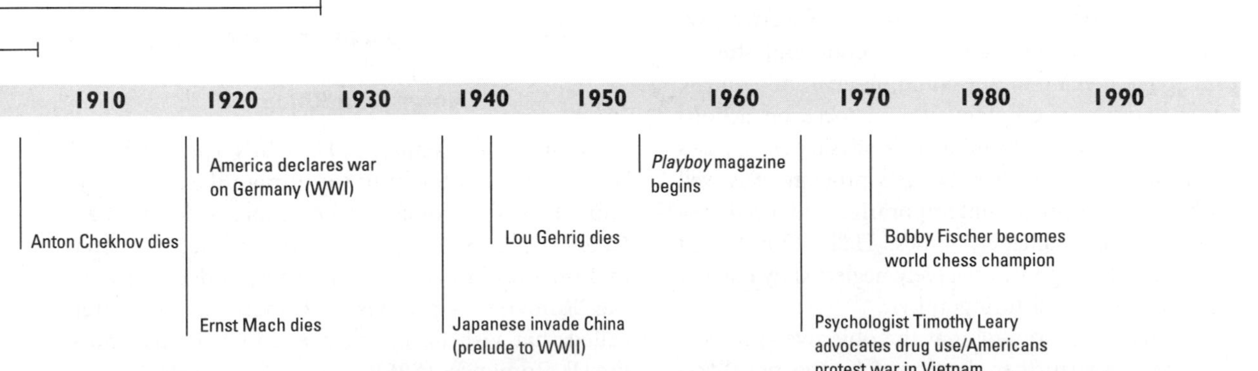
1910
1920
1930
1940
1950
1960
1970
1980
1990
America declares war on Germany (WWI)
Playboy magazine begins
Anton Chekhov dies
Lou Gehrig dies
Bobby Fischer becomes world chess champion
Ernst Mach dies
Japanese invade China (prelude to WWII)
Psychologist Timothy Leary advocates drug use/Americans protest war in Vietnam

Defined as the system that stresses the use of objective methods to study the overt behavior of organisms, **behaviorism**'s formal beginning is generally attributed to John Watson's (1913) article, "Psychology as the behaviorist views it." As we have seen, however, no system arises in isolation, and behaviorism, like structuralism and functionalism, had many antecedents. One element of behaviorism was the associative psychology of the early British and French empiricists (Chapter 5; see also Walsh, 1971). From its beginning, behaviorism had a strong French influence, which we saw first in Descartes' (Chapter 4) and in La Mettrie's (Chapter 4) objective, mechanistic explanations of body and mind. Some authorities (e.g., Fraisse, 1970) have even suggested that a French pioneer such as Henri Piéron (1881–1964) should be credited with behaviorism's founding as a system of psychology.

A few generations after La Mettrie, Comte developed the philosophy of positivism (Chapter 5), which became a major part of the European *Zeitgeist.* Comte's early 19th-century philosophy had at its core his Law of Three Stages, with the highest being the positivistic or scientific stage. At this stage, a field relies on experimentation and observation and tries to explain its phenomena objectively, by the laws of natural cause and effect. Comte did not think a science of the mind relying chiefly on introspection was possible. Watson also rejected introspection and substituted a science of behavior for a science of the mind. As the wags put it: With Darwin, psychology lost its soul; with Watson, it lost its mind.

Before Watson, German philosopher Friedrich Albert Lange (1828–1875) advocated Darwinism for a soulless psychology. According to Teo (2002), in an 1866 publication Lange called for an objective psychology that did not use introspection and studied only phenomena that one could observe and control. Lange thought psychology should focus on actions and speech, and determine the physiological bases for such events. Further, Lange's program was well known to Watson's contemporaries and predecessors, such as Titchener, James, Hall, Wundt, and Brentano, although it is relatvely neglected by current English-speaking historiography.

In Chapter 5, we saw that the objective approach to science was further developed by the positivists Mach and Avenarius. Carnap and Schlick (both Chapter 5) and other Vienna Circle members continued to refine positivism, and positivism's objective approach to science facilitated psychology's takeover by behaviorism—a singularly objective approach.

Evolution—a major part of the 19th-century *Zeitgeist*—was another important antecedent of behaviorism. As we saw in Chapters 9 through 11, evolution was central to the psychology of function, the idea that abilities evolved because they play a part in their possessors' adaptation. A direct descendant of functionalism, behaviorism accepted many of its principles—for example, a strongly empirical, scientific approach; the importance of applied research; the study of animals—while rejecting the study of consciousness.

Darwinian evolution placed humans squarely in the animal kingdom, and George Romanes's efforts to find intellectual continuity among animals began comparative psychology, which was further developed by Romanes's protégé—C. Lloyd Morgan. We will begin our look at animal behavior research with Romanes and Morgan.

Although animal psychology was not synonymous with behaviorism, it was critical for behaviorism's development, and Watson's early animal studies contributed significantly to his formulation of behaviorism. After we examine animal psychology's influences on behaviorism, we will describe developments in Russia that importantly anticipated and affected American behaviorism's course.

ANIMAL PSYCHOLOGY

British Comparative Psychology

George John Romanes

As we noted in Chapter 9, Darwin's *The Descent of Man* stimulated the hunt for humanlike abilities in animals, and no one searched more ardently than George John Romanes. Darwin had seen a letter by Romanes in *Nature,* and he responded by inviting Romanes for a visit. Romanes's wife later called that visit an epoch event in her husband's life (E. Romanes, 1896).

George John Romanes (1848–1894)

Born in Canada, **George John Romanes** (1848–1894) was the son of a minister who received a major inheritance the year Romanes was born and moved the family back to England. After a spotty education at home, where he was considered a "shocking dunce," in 1867 Romanes entered Cambridge, and he earned a Second Class degree in 1870, without having read Darwin. In fact, he did not read Darwin until about 1873 and paid his first visit in about 1874, the same year he began to work in the physiology laboratory of Dr. Burdon Sanderson, Titchener's first mentor (Chapter 8). By this time, Romanes had decided to devote himself to scientific research.

Although Romanes was a prolific researcher, with varied publications, he is most remembered for *Animal Intelligence* (1881). This and his later book, *Mental Evolution in Animals,* were "designed to prove that the law of evolution is universal, and applies to the mind of man as well as to his bodily organisation" (E. Romanes, 1896, p. 170). *Animal Intelligence* quite literally began comparative psychology: "I have thought it desirable that there should be something resembling a text-book of the facts of Comparative Psychology . . ." (Romanes, 1881/1895, p. v).

Despite his many positive contributions to animal psychology (Burghardt, 1985), Romanes feared *Animal Intelligence* might be judged badly, and he was right. Today, Romanes is generally considered "the archetypal purveyor of anecdotes about animals" (Boakes, 1984, p. 25). In reality, Romanes was more critical of the anecdotes he collected than many of his contemporaries, including Darwin. Romanes used only stories reported by observers he knew to be competent (anything Darwin reported was automatically incorporated), reports based on careful observation, and anecdotes that described an animal ability noted by independent observers. Despite these stringent criteria, *Animal Intelligence* contains much we would reject today. As Boakes put it, "In many cases the observed behaviour was interesting and believable; it was the observer's rich interpretation in terms of current ideas from human psychology that was wide open to objection" (p. 26).

To illustrate, after carefully describing a cat that had learned to open a door with a half-hoop handle and a thumb-latch, Romanes interpreted the cat's behavior as follows:

> Hence we can only conclude that the cats in such cases have a very definite idea as to the mechanical properties of a door; they know that to make it open, even when unlatched, it requires to be *pushed*. . . . The whole psychological process, therefore, implied by the fact of a cat opening a door in this way is really most complex. First the animal must have observed that the door is opened by the hand grasping the handle and moving the latch. Next she must reason . . . If a hand can do it, why not a paw? Then, strongly moved by this idea, she makes the first trial. The steps which follow have not been observed, so we cannot certainly say whether she learns by a succession of trials that depression of the thumb-piece constitutes the essential part of the process, or, perhaps more probably, that her initial observations supplied her with the idea of clicking the thumb-piece. (Romanes, 1881/1895, pp. 421–422)

As we will see, Edward Lee Thorndike made the observations Romanes had not made and concluded the animals did not use reasoning.

The fact that Romanes is remembered mainly for *Animal Intelligence* was in part caused by his loyalty to Darwin and to his acceptance of Darwin's addition of a Lamarckian principle to natural selection to explain the development of instincts. By the 1880s, Alfred Russel Wallace's position that evolution could be explained by natural selection, without resort to Lamarckism, was called "Neo-Darwinism" by Romanes. Neo-Darwinism was strongly supported by German biologist August Weismann's (1834–1914) "germ-plasm" theory of heredity, which contributed to the modern theory of genetics (see Johnston, 1995).

Note that Darwin had no real understanding of genetics as the vehicle of inheritance, which explains his attachment to some Lamarckian concepts and underscores the remarkable insights he had into the evolutionary process. Austrian monk and botanist **Gregor Johann Mendel** (1822–1884) had published work on the genetics of pea plants that would have solved problems of inheritance that Darwin agonized over both before and after *The Origin of Species.* Unfortunately, Mendel's research appeared in an obscure journal and was not "discovered" until 1900, long after both he and Darwin had died.

Like Romanes, C. Lloyd Morgan supported the "unadulterated" Darwinism (i.e., with some Lamarckism), at least during his friendship with Romanes. In his last year, Romanes summoned Morgan and gave him instructions about unfinished work that Morgan carried out diligently (E. Romanes, 1896). Romanes was still devising plans for experiments concerning Weismann's theory at the end, which occurred just 3 days after his 46th birthday.

From Boakes, From Darwin to Behaviourism (1984), by courtesy of Cambridge University Press.

Conwy Lloyd Morgan (1852–1936) and family

Conwy Lloyd Morgan

Like Romanes's experience with Darwin, Morgan's relationship with Romanes began with a letter Morgan sent to *Nature.* In it, Morgan criticized a passage in *Animal Intelligence* suggesting that scorpions under stress commit suicide. Morgan's experiments indicated instead that the animals' tail movements were reflexive attempts to rid themselves of sources of irritation, which incidentally resulted in their being stung.

Darwin's friend and supporter Thomas Huxley played a major role in **Conwy Lloyd Morgan**'s (1852–1936) intellectual development. Too poor for Oxford, the school of his forebears, Morgan went to London's Royal School of Mines to be trained as a mining engineer. After a conversation at one of the school's annual dinners, Huxley, professor of natural history, suggested that Morgan "put in a year under him" (Morgan, 1932, p. 241), which Morgan did following a 3-month trip to America.

After a series of jobs, Morgan obtained a teaching post in South Africa, where he made the scorpion observations. In addition, he continued the self-education that had begun in his teens when he had read Berkeley (Chapter 5). Eventually Morgan read *Origin of Species,* "browsed in Romanes' *Animal Intelligence;* and resolutely tackled Herbert Spencer" (Morgan, 1932, p. 247). Concerning Romanes's anecdotes, Morgan

> felt . . . that not on such anecdotal foundations could a science of comparative psychology be built. . . . I then entertained doubts whether

> one could extract from the minds of animals (wholly inferential from their observable behavior) the data requisite for a science. . . . Did one get out of the animal mind aught else than that which one put into it? (pp. 247–248)

In 1884, Morgan returned to England to teach at University College, Bristol. Approximately 10 years later, he began research designed to enable him to "get into the animal mind." Reasoning that instinctive behavior is characterized by "*like* performance on the first and on all subsequent occasions" (Morgan, 1932, p. 249), Morgan made sure he was studying behavior on its first occasion. In one study, Morgan allowed chicks to peck and consume edible caterpillars before exposing them to bad-tasting and brilliantly decorated caterpillars. After a few pecks, the chicks avoided these caterpillars. Morgan considered the chicks' behavior an example of the Spencer-Bain principle, in which behavior is modified by its consequences. As we noted in Chapter 5, Morgan's lectures at Harvard in 1896 undoubtedly influenced Thorndike.

By 1900, Morgan's support for "unadulterated Darwinism" had waned, and he now rejected any appeal to Lamarckism because of the success of Weismann's germ-plasm doctrine, which precluded any effect on heritable material of an individual's bodily or psychological changes. Although he rejected Lamarckism, Morgan could not accept a second assumption that was part of Neo-Darwinism: the Cartesian perception of the organism as an automaton. In Chapter 4, we noted that Descartes believed animals were totally mechanical, without mind or soul. Huxley, the modern pioneer of the notion of animals as automatons, treated animals like machines while accepting animal consciousness as a side effect (epiphenomenon) of a certain amount of brain tissue.

Supported by the more Lamarckian James Mark Baldwin (Chapter 10), Morgan developed a theory of organic selection as "an attempt to repair evolutionary theory by treating evolution not as a random, mechanical process, but as reflecting the organism's *intentional* relation to its environment" (Costall, 1993, p. 115, italics added). Morgan and Baldwin saw their theory as an extension of Darwin that Darwin would have approved.

However, Lloyd Morgan also created **Morgan's Canon,** which was supposedly an effort to avoid the dangers of Romanes's anecdotal method by invoking the Law of Parsimony, or Ockham's razor, named for William of Ockham (Chapter 3). In this context, the Law of Parsimony says we should explain behavior by the simplest mental processes that will account for the facts. As Morgan (1894) put it, "In no case may we interpret an action as the outcome of the exercise of a higher psychical faculty, if it can be interpreted as the outcome of one which stands lower in the psychological scale" (p. 53). How can we reconcile Morgan's Canon, generally interpreted as an attempt to eliminate mind or consciousness in animals, with Morgan's theory of organic selection, which stresses the importance of mind (intentionality) in the evolutionary process?

According to Costall (1993), Morgan did not intend for the Canon to be a rigid prohibition against *any* explanation of animal behavior in terms of higher mental processes. Morgan's main concern was that Darwin's supporters had read too much into their accounts of animal behavior in order to find mental continuity. "The real aim of Morgan's Canon was to alert the Darwinians to the need to establish the existence of modes of relations between organisms and environments other than that of reflective, rational thought . . ." (p. 117). Rather than being a revolt against Romanes, as it is usually portrayed, Costall contends Morgan's Canon was

> an acceptance of Romanes's conception of a true comparative psychology, as opposed to a mere study of animal conduct. . . . Contrary to Morgan's original intentions, [Morgan's Canon] has been used with great rhetorical effect to perpetuate exactly the kind of psychology and biology Morgan sought to displace, the essentially Cartesian notion of the animal as "a mere puppet in the hand of circumstances." . . . (pp. 120–121)

We can conclude our look at Romanes and Morgan by noting that Romanes began comparative psychology to support Darwin, and Morgan developed it experimentally. As we indicated, Romanes was more than an uncritical anecdotalist, and interpreting Morgan's Canon as a refutation of Romanes's interpretations needs to be examined more closely.

Animal Psychology in America

Animal psychology was a relatively small part of American psychology's rapid expansion at the turn of the century (Boakes, 1984), and some of the most important early contributors to animal psychology were biologists. For example, mentioned in Chapter 11 as Angell's neighbor at the University of Chicago, **Jacques Loeb** (1859–1924) was a major influence on Watson. With an assistantship to study medicine in Berlin, Loeb's first experimental work dealt with brain lesions and the behavior of dogs, which he abandoned when inflicting injuries on the animals became too distasteful. Later, in Würzburg, Loeb became interested in the reactions of simple animals to light and also in plant movement, which physiologists explained by elementary chemical and physical forces acting on the plant's structure. Loeb extended the idea of tropistic reactions to simple animals such as cockroaches and caterpillars and believed that **tropisms**—directed, mechanical movements—could account for much behavior in higher animals as well (e.g., Pauly, 1981).

For the mechanistic and materialistic Loeb, science was merely a tool to use to alter and ultimately control the behavior of existing creatures (Buckley, 1989). Further, he was committed to the idea of biological engineering as a means of achieving control over biological phenomena. An emphasis on control permeates the psychology of his student, John Watson.

With limited employment prospects because of his Jewish background, Loeb emigrated to the United States in 1891. In 1892, he obtained a position at the newly founded University of Chicago, which is where he was when Watson arrived. Loeb eventually became head of the general physiology division at the Rockefeller Institute for Medical Research, a post he held from 1910 until his death in 1924.

American biologist **Herbert Spencer Jennings** (1868–1947) strongly opposed Loeb's mechanistic approach to animal behavior. Jennings was born in Tonica, Illinois, the son of a physician. Reading Herbert Spencer (Chapter 9) stimulated Jennings's father to abandon religious belief and so influenced him that he named one son Herbert Spencer and another Darwin.

Entering in 1890, Jennings worked his way through the University of Michigan and then went to Harvard, where he earned his doctorate in just 2 years. A travel fellowship to Europe in 1896 enabled Jennings to work with zoologist Max Verworn, who had been with Ernst Haeckel (Chapter 9) at Jena. In Verworn's laboratory, Jennings became fascinated with the behavior of the unicellular paramecia. This behavior's complexity convinced Jennings that Loeb's theory of tropisms was invalid for the behavior of even simple creatures.

Although they disagreed on the basis for animal behavior, both Loeb and Jennings believed in and popularized the idea that the study of simple creatures would tell much about the behavior of complex organisms. In addition, they agreed on the importance of experimental work and on the necessity for the objective description of behavior. Finally, both were important for the training of early behaviorists, Loeb for Watson and Jennings for Karl Lashley (Chapter 16).

Jennings's last behavioral work occurred in 1906, the year he published *The Behavior of Lower Organisms*, a review of 20 years of research on protozoa (a group of unicellular, usually microscopic organisms) and other simple multicellular creatures. In his book, Jennings discussed his microscopic animals' learning ability, although there was little evidence for it. Herrnstein (1969) called Jennings "the most modern of the early behaviorists . . . for his objective use of psychological terms is most like what goes on among today's behaviorists . . ." (p. 60).

Thorndike's Animal Research

Poorly supported in biology departments, animal research was even less encouraged in philosophy and psychology departments. For example, Edward Lee Thorndike's initial animal study was conducted in William James's (Chapter 10) basement when Thorndike found no space for it at Harvard. And at Columbia, Cattell (Chapter 10) initially supported Thorndike's animal work, but "Cattell's commitment was not long-lasting. After a few short years of animal work, Thorndike followed the professional path of least resistance by turning to educational psychology" (O'Donnell, 1985, p. 192). Thorndike's "few short years of animal work" was the effort for which he is

Courtesy of Wiley Publishers.

Four puzzle boxes actually used by Thorndike

usually remembered outside of education and provided the data that laid the foundation for his learning theory and for behaviorism's ascendance.

As we noted in Chapter 11, Thorndike is a transitional figure between functionalism and behaviorism. Thorndike's animal research ties in well with behaviorism, and passages from *Animal Intelligence* (1911)—a compilation of his animal research performed around the turn of the century—sound remarkably like Watson's later writings. For example, here is what Thorndike wrote about introspection as psychology's primary method:

> So long as introspection was lauded as the chief method of psychology, a psychologist would tend to expect too little from mere studies, from the outside, of creatures who could not report their inner experiences to him in the manner to which he was accustomed. In the literature of the time will be found many comments on the extreme difficulty of studying the psychology of animals and children. But difficulty exists only in the case of their *consciousness*. Their *behavior*, by its simpler nature and causation, is often far easier to study than that of adults. . . . The studies reprinted in this volume produced in their author an increased respect for psychology as the science of behavior. . . . (pp. 3–5, italics in the original)

Thorndike's study of animal behavior included testing cats in several homemade **puzzle boxes.** The neatly constructed box shown in Thorndike's dissertation is an idealized picture. Recall that Thorndike's son, Robert L. Thorndike, wrote that his father had little mechanical aptitude. This is apparent in photos of the boxes actually used in Thorndike's experiments.

Thorndike tested 13 kittens and young cats in 15 puzzle boxes, with each solution requiring a different response or sequence of responses. For example, a cat was required to turn a button to open the door in Box C, whereas in Box G, operating a thumb latch freed the cat.

Thorndike's inspiration for the puzzle boxes came from Romanes's claims about the mechanical abilities of cats, which Romanes (1881/1895) published as part of *Animal Intelligence*. It is no coincidence that Thorndike titled the version of his dissertation published in *Psychological Review* "Animal intelligence: An experimental study of the associative processes in animals" and the 1911 book simply *Animal Intelligence.* Despite the similarity in titles, Thorndike's approach to the subject was decidedly different from that of his predecessors, as he quickly pointed out:

> Although no work done in this field is enough like the present investigation to require an account of its results, the *method* hitherto in use invites comparison by its contrast, and . . . by its faults. In the first place, most of the books do not give us a psychology, but rather a *eulogy*, of animals. They have all been about animal *intelligence*, never about animal *stupidity*. . . . (Thorndike, 1911, p. 22, italics in the original)

Thorndike charged previous researchers with being biased observers, ruled by "the well-nigh universal tendency in human nature to find the marvelous wherever it can" (p. 23). By contrast, Thorndike aimed for an objective appraisal of animal ability. First, he studied in a systematic, quantitative fashion an animal's ability to escape confinement. Next, he examined animal memory by training animals on the puzzle box task and then testing their retention later. Finally, he assessed the possibly beneficial effects of imitation and of passive tuition—guiding an animal through the appropriate response.

On each trial, Thorndike placed a hungry cat into a box with food in view outside and then timed the latency of the animal's escape. Thorndike's use of the motive of "practically utter hunger" was widely criticized, with detractors accusing him of starving animals and of experimenting on animals panic-stricken from hunger (e.g., Mills, 1899). In response, Thorndike (1899) admitted that many of his animals exhibited "great violence and fury of activity" on early trials, but animals that did not display "mental panic" performed no better than ones that did. Thorndike explained in 1911 that by "utter hunger" he had meant the animal was hungry enough to eat a hearty meal after the experiments were completed for the day. At that time, "the cats received abundant food to maintain health, growth and spirits . . ." (p. 27).

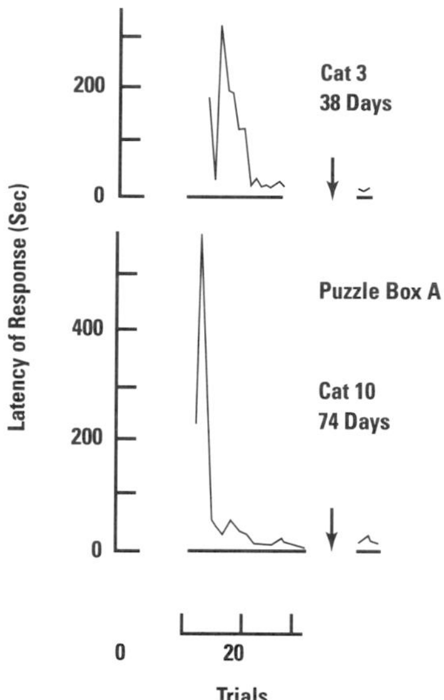

FIGURE 12.1 Examples of the first learning curves; retention is also shown.

Thorndike plotted the first animal learning curves, with redrawn examples shown in Figure 12.1. As you can see, freedom on the early trials in Box A occurred after long latencies, with the cats exhibiting many unsuccessful responses before accidentally making the correct response. On succeeding trials, the successful movement was performed more and more efficiently until by the end a cat would perform the appropriate response rapidly and smoothly. Cats 3 and 10 both showed excellent memory for the correct response after lengthy intervals without training (38 and 74 days, respectively).

Thorndike concluded that his dissertation illustrated **stimulus-response** (**S-R**) **learning,** the association of "the sense-impression of the interior of the box" with a successful movement. For Thorndike, the animal did not learn to associate ideas—for example, the idea of confinement with the idea of a movement to produce freedom. Instead, his cats learned "the association of idea or sense impression [S] with *impulse* [R]" (Thorndike, 1911, p. 106). On the issue of animal consciousness, Thorndike was not optimistic:

> The possibility is that animals may have *no images or memories at all, no ideas to associate.* Perhaps the entire fact of association in animals is the presence of sense-impressions with which are associated, by resultant pleasure, certain impulses, and that, therefore, and therefore only, a certain situation brings forth a certain act. (pp. 108–109, italics in the original)

Thorndike's Laws. Thorndike saw association learning in animals as the bonding of sense-impressions (stimuli) with impulses (acts, responses) by "resultant pleasure." Correspondingly, Thorndike believed initially that "discomfort" weakened the bond. He called this principle of association the law of effect, although not for several years after his dissertation experiment (Hearst, 1999). Thorndike's law of effect is a restatement of the Spencer-Bain principle (Chapter 9). In 1911, Thorndike defined the **law of effect** as follows:

> *Of several responses made to the same situation, those which are accompanied or closely followed by satisfaction to the animal will, other things being equal, be more firmly connected with the situation, so that, when it recurs, they will be more likely to recur; those which are accompanied or closely followed by discomfort to the animal will, other things being equal, have their connections with that situation weakened, so that, when it recurs, they will be less likely to recur.* (Thorndike, 1911, p. 244, italics in the original)

In addition, Thorndike called a second law to account for the learning phenomena he had observed the **law of exercise:**

> *Any response to a situation will, other things being equal, be more strongly connected with the situation in proportion to the number of times it has been connected with that situation and to the average vigor and duration of the connections.* (Thorndike, 1911, p. 244, italics in the original)

We have encountered the law of exercise in different guises in earlier chapters: for example, in Aristotle's (Chapter 2) statement, "we remember easily what we often ponder," and in much of Ebbinghaus's memory research (Chapter 8). Many human learning studies later, Thorndike modified his laws of effect and exercise (e.g., Thorndike, 1932), concluding that repetition (exercise) without consequences produced little effect and that reinforcement outweighed punishment.

Thorndike realized his phrases *satisfaction to the animal* and *discomfort to the animal* lacked precision, and he struggled with general definitions for reward and punishment before adopting a behavioral one:

> [b]y a satisfying state of affairs is meant one which the animal does nothing to avoid, often doing such things as attain and preserve it. By a discomforting or annoying state of affairs is meant one which the animal commonly avoids and abandons. (Thorndike, 1911, p. 245)

Thorndike's behavioral definition dodges the issue of whether a particular event is inherently satisfying or annoying. If the organism works to obtain the event, then it is reinforcing, no matter how negative the event might be in an absolute sense.

Observations Important for Later Animal Research. Based on his dissertation research, Thorndike's conclusions about cats' reasoning ability were dramatically different from Romanes's. For example, he pointed to the gradual acquisition of associations shown in his learning curves, arguing that reasoning ability should lead to sudden mastery, which his animals never exhibited. Instead, everything indicated the gradual strengthening of a bond between an accidental act leading to pleasure and the stimulus situation of confinement in a particular box.

Can animals learn by imitation or by passive tuition? In experiments with both cats and dogs, Thorndike saw no evidence for imitation, and passive tuition was similarly ineffective, despite widespread belief in its efficacy. Thorndike's (1911) results with passive tuition demonstrated "that no animal who fails to perform an act in the course of his own impulsive activity will learn it by being put through it" (p. 103).

Thorndike made a number of additional observations explored further by later animal researchers. For example, data from cats placed into Box Z raised the question of whether all types of behavior are equally sensitive to reinforcement. All cats had to do to escape from Box Z was to lick or scratch themselves. Because cats ordinarily spend much time in self-grooming, you might expect the association to be easily formed. However, Thorndike found it was remarkably difficult to train cats to groom themselves in order to escape from the box. Thorndike's observation of the difficulty of such training and others like it have led to the concept of **learning predispositions,** the idea that evolution has shaped an organism's "associative apparatus" as well as its sensory and motor abilities (e.g., Breland & Breland, 1966; Seligman, 1970). Presumably, hungry cats that groomed themselves instead of seeking food did not survive to pass on this tendency.

Aristotle anticipated Thorndike's observations in *Parva Naturalia,* noting that some experiences are better remembered after only a few repetitions than others often encountered. One example of a human biological predisposition is conditioned taste aversion, associated with John Locke in Chapter 5. Most of us have developed an aversion to a particular food, when eating it was followed by illness (e.g., Logue, 1985). Such conditioning requires only one pairing of the food with stomach upset, and there may be a relatively long interval between the meal and illness. Important research on conditioned taste aversion has been performed by **John Garcia** (1917–), one of the first Hispanic Americans to earn a Ph.D. in psychology. Garcia received APA's Distinguished Scientific Contribution Award in 1979.

Another observation Thorndike made with his animals that he explored further with humans was transfer of training (Chapter 11). Thorndike found his cats became progressively better at solving new puzzle boxes. This positive transfer may be seen as an example of **stimulus generalization,** a learning phenomenon extensively investigated by Ivan Pavlov (discussed later). In stimulus generalization, a response associated with a particular stimulus is made to other, similar stimuli. Learning predispositions and transfer of training are only two of Thorndike's many observations about human and animal learning that remain a part of contemporary learning theory.

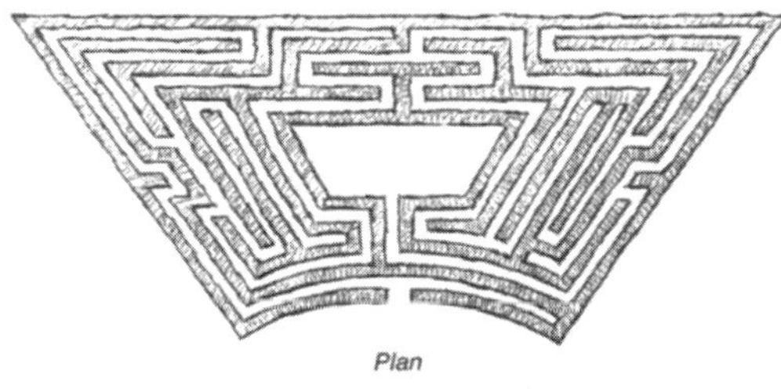

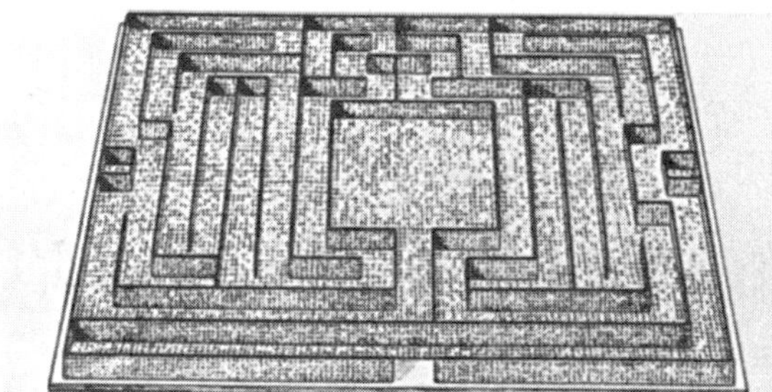

Overhead view and plan of the Hampton Court Palace maze on which Small's rat maze was based

Thorndike and Behaviorism. Although we have noted the importance of Thorndike's animal work for behaviorism, the early behaviorists did not consider Thorndike solidly in their camp. Unlike Watson, Thorndike did not reject the study of subjective experience as a part of psychology: He just preferred to study behavior. If animal research had been more supported when Thorndike completed his animal studies, perhaps we would honor him instead of Watson as behaviorism's founder, but Thorndike's employment at Teachers College made him an educational psychologist for most of his career.

Thorndike's dissertation research almost completely overshadowed animal studies performed at about the same time by **Willard Stanton Small** (1870–1943) at Clark University. Small's studies are important for two things they introduced to psychology: the laboratory rat (Small, 1900) and the maze task (Small, 1901). The introduction of the white rat to biological research had occurred slightly earlier, also at Clark, through the individual most responsible for the "institutionalization" of the rat for research—Henry Donaldson (Logan, 1999).

Unlike Thorndike, Small wanted to study his animals as naturally as possible, which led him to the maze as an analog of the burrows of wild rats. For the pattern of his maze, Small constructed a miniature replica of the famous Hampton Court Palace maze. Near London, Hampton Court Palace was built by Cardinal Thomas Wolsey, who occupied it until 1529. Afterward, it became a favorite residence of British monarchs, including Henry VIII. Its gardens and maze are popular tourist attractions. One of your authors remembers his wife displaying ratlike behavior when frustrated by the Hampton Court maze.

Small's studies were primarily observational, and his hesitant conclusions were more in Romanes's style than in Thorndike's objective mold. For example, in describing the difference between cats and rats, he wrote:

> The cat, primarily a hunter, is bold, independent, and aggressively open; the rat, . . . primarily the hunted, and only secondarily a hunter, is timid and furtive. . . . His boldness when displayed is impudent and half apologetic, never self-contained and unconscious like that of the cat. (Small, 1901, p. 208)

In addition, Small's comments on the rat's olfactory sensitivity and on its ability to traverse a maze without vision led to the question of the sensory mechanisms the rat uses in solving a maze, which Watson investigated extensively.

In his 1898 monograph, Thorndike offered photographs of his apparatus to anyone who requested them, and Harvard graduate student Robert Yerkes sent such a request. Thorndike found Yerkes's interest flattering and eventually sent several puzzle box pictures, which are preserved today in the Robert M. Yerkes Papers at Yale University Medical Library (Burnham, 1972).

Robert Mearns Yerkes

Robert Mearns Yerkes (1876–1956) was the first-born child in a family of farmers who lived near Philadelphia. He described his mother as "a woman of rare sweetness of disposition and unusual ability, beloved of all who knew her . . ." (Yerkes, 1932, p. 382). Yerkes's negative feelings for his father turned him away from the family's agricultural tradition, and the care he received from the family physician, his cousin, during a childhood illness initially inclined him toward medicine.

In 1892 Yerkes entered Ursinus College in Pennsylvania, and in 1897 he received his A.B. degree. Offered a $1,000 loan for graduate work in biology at Harvard, he took it, assuming he could begin his medical studies in Philadelphia after a year. At the end of his first year, Yerkes received another A.B. degree and was given graduate status. With his teachers' encouragement, he became a candidate for the Ph.D. rather than for the M.D.

Interested in both zoology and psychology, Yerkes took Josiah Royce's (Chapter 10) advice and combined his interests by devoting himself to comparative psychology. After transferring from the laboratories of zoology to the laboratory of psychology, for the next 18 years Yerkes was associated with Harvard as student, assistant, instructor, and assistant professor. His research was in psychobiology, and he taught courses in comparative and genetic psychology.

Throughout, Münsterberg's (Chapter 10) support was crucial, and Yerkes (1932) wrote, "I seriously doubt whether I should have remained in Harvard more than one or two years except for his influence and encouragement" (p. 389). When Münsterberg asked him if he could afford to accept an instructorship paying only $1,000, Yerkes said, "No, . . . but I shall, nevertheless" (p. 389).

In fact, Yerkes remained woefully underpaid at Harvard because of his interest in comparative psychology. To supplement his meager salary, he taught at Radcliffe, at Harvard's summer school, and in the University Extension Department in Boston. Instead

Archives of the History of American Psychology–The University of Akron.

Robert Mearns Yerkes (1876–1956) and friends

of switching to educational psychology to gain a promotion, as Thorndike did at Columbia, Yerkes continued his animal research. As a result, he was still an assistant professor when he was elected APA president in 1917, 15 years after he had received his Harvard Ph.D.

Nevertheless, Yerkes enjoyed his Harvard animal research and especially his associations with his colleagues, who, in addition to Royce and Münsterberg, included William James, George Santayana, Edwin B. Holt, and Ralph Barton Perry. In his research, Yerkes may be said to have worked his way up from primitive creatures to primates, investigating sensory ability, adaptive behavior, and instinct in various invertebrates, amphibians and reptiles, mice, rats, crows and doves, pigs, monkeys and apes, and finally humans. Yerkes's interests at Harvard later broadened to include human psychopathology and mental testing (see Reed, 1987).

Much of Yerkes's animal research was included in the first animal psychology book written by an American, *The Animal Mind* by Margaret Washburn (Chapter 8). After receiving her Titchener-directed Ph.D. from Cornell in 1894, Washburn taught at Wells College in Aurora, New York, before becoming warden of Sage College, which was the women's dormitory at Cornell. In addition to her administrative duties, Washburn taught a course in animal psychology; she later cited this as the beginning of her interest in the topic (Washburn, 1932), which culminated in *The Animal Mind,* first published in 1908. The book was an unbiased, readable review of experimental studies of animal behavior. Washburn adopted Morgan's view that the reason for studying an animal's behavior was to infer its conscious states in order to provide a basis for analyzing subjective experience in humans.

Many of the studies Washburn reviewed reflected the influence of Thorndike's dissertation. In some cases, Thorndike's methods for studying trial-and-error learning were extended to different species, whereas other studies examined his negative conclusions about imitation learning and learning by passive tuition. Nearly all of the reviewed experiments were conducted at either Clark, Chicago, Johns Hopkins, or Harvard.

In 1917, Yerkes received an offer to reorganize psychology at the University of Minnesota. He accepted it, and without moving to Minneapolis, he made staffing recommendations, planned the department, and arranged to move the laboratory. In addition, as APA president, he led psychologists mobilized to support the American war effort in World War I. His group developed the first group intelligence tests, the Army Alpha and Army Beta (Chapter 17).

After the war, Yerkes resigned from Minnesota and stayed in Washington to supervise the completion of the final report on the psychological work during the war and to continue his search for support for psychobiological research on anthropoid apes. This search ended successfully when Yerkes accepted a professorship at Yale, where James Rowland Angell (Chapter 11) was the new president.

Supported by a Laura Spellman Rockefeller memorial grant to Yale to establish an Institute of Psychology and by a Rockefeller Foundation grant to Yerkes himself for anthropoid research (Reed, 1987), Yerkes established a laboratory in New Haven to study apes, which was followed by a larger facility at Orange Park, Florida. Yerkes headed the Orange Park laboratory from 1930 until 1942, when Karl Lashley (Chapter 16) took over as director. Finally, the primate center moved to Atlanta, Georgia, where it is now the Yerkes Regional Primate Center of Emory University.

Based on his primate work, Yerkes and his colleagues and students published many papers and monographs and a few semipopular books (e.g., Yerkes & Learned, 1925). One of his greatest works (Yerkes & Yerkes, 1929) was a compilation of all that was known about apes (in English; German, Russian, and Japanese researchers were also pioneers in primatology) before the Orange Park facility opened. *The Great Apes: A Study of Anthropoid Life* was co-authored with his wife, Ada Watterson Yerkes, a Ph.D. biologist.

Yerkes had extensive contact with many people we have considered. For example, correspondence with Titchener (Chapter 8) grew out of his teaching the introductory course in psychology, and Yerkes considered Titchener the most learned psychologist he had ever known. He also corresponded extensively with Watson when the two were working to improve the methodology for studying vision comparatively in animals.

Although Yerkes and Watson were comfortable collaborators, Yerkes was not a behaviorist. Like Woodworth (Chapter 11), Yerkes objected to people who tried to dictate the "appropriate" method and results. He rejected both the extreme objectivism of Loeb and Watson's behaviorism because of their restrictiveness. Despite his interest in organic structure and function, Yerkes was not opposed to the study of consciousness and mind, and he credited Titchener with "[w]hatever interest I have in introspection, competence in its use, and appreciation of its results, and whatever I know of the psychology of the self . . ." (p. 392).

Yerkes is also remembered for the **Yerkes-Dodson law,** which holds that the optimal arousal level depends on task difficulty: For a simple task, high arousal aids performance, whereas for more complex tasks, the optimal level declines. This relation was based on the work of one of the many Harvard doctoral students Yerkes supervised (Yerkes & Dodson, 1908).

E. G. Boring (Chapter 1) considered Yerkes the leader in American comparative psychology, both because of his belief in comparative study, and "also because of the volume of his work, his persistence, and the way . . . he threw his influence toward the organization of investigation" (Boring, 1950, p. 628). *Determined* and *persistent* are frequently used in describing Yerkes's temperament (e.g., Dewsbury, 1996). As we have noted, Yerkes contributed significantly to mental testing and to the study of primates, particularly the apes.

In 1909, Yerkes co-authored a paper introducing Pavlov's animal work to an American audience (Yerkes & Morgulis, 1909). The paper carefully discussed Pavlov's method of salivary conditioning in dogs, although the authors failed to see the technique's generality. "It seems . . . as if Pawlow's method were especially important in animal psychology as a means to the intensive study of the mental life of a limited number of mammals. The dog evidently is especially well suited to the experiments" (p. 262). (The use of *w*'s rather than *v*'s in spelling *Pavlov* suggests Yerkes and Morgulis [and American psychologists in general] first discovered Pavlov through German publications [Skinner, 1981].) Pavlov's reflex conditioning became a major part of the psychology of Watson—who recognized its generality—and Russian objective psychology is another important antecedent of modern behaviorism.

OBJECTIVE PSYCHOLOGY IN RUSSIA

Russian objective psychology began not with Pavlov, but with Ivan Sechenov, who is also considered modern Russian physiology's founder.

Ivan Mikhailovich Sechenov

Ivan Mikhailovich Sechenov (1829–1905) was born in a village now called Sechenovo. As a youth, he had a governess who taught him French and German, which he later used on trips to study in Europe. When he was 14, Sechenov entered a St. Petersburg college of military engineering. Trouble with the college authorities in Sechenov's 4th year led to an unattractive posting near Kiev, illustrating the difficulty Sechenov often experienced when dealing with authority figures (Kimble, 1996). After a disappointing infatuation in Kiev, Sechenov set out for Moscow to study medicine.

At this point in Russian history, the teaching of medicine was in a sorry state. Lectures on any topic were usually out of date because of efforts to exclude foreign ideas. Sechenov's exposure to stimulating lectures from a professor of physiology convinced him to become a researcher in physiology instead of a physician.

Following the death of his parents, Sechenov sold his claim to the family inheritance and left for Germany to study with Johannes Müller (Chapter 7). Müller's lectures on vertebrate genitals disappointed Sechenov, and he was more impressed with Émil du Bois-Reymond (Chapter 7), although the latter treated the young Russian with coolness. With little guidance, Sechenov learned all he could about electrophysiological research before departing for Leipzig and Vienna.

From Vienna, Sechenov went to Heidelberg to study chemistry with Bunsen and physiology with Helmholtz (Chapter 7). In 1859, Sechenov returned to St. Petersburg to find that during his travels, there had been momentous changes in Russia. Now there was great interest in learning about the new discoveries in physiology, and Sechenov was in demand as the first Russian in years to return after extensive training abroad. He became an assistant professor at the Military-Medical Academy, which was part of the University of St. Petersburg.

In 1862, Sechenov left Russia for Paris to study voluntary control over normally involuntary actions (e.g., the ability to avoid scratching an itch) with Claude Bernard (Chapter 7). Earlier, Eduard Weber (1804–1891), Ernst Weber's (Chapter 7) brother, had made an important discovery related to Sechenov's interest: Electrical stimulation of a frog's vagus nerve decreased the animal's heart rate, showing that nerve excitation could produce physiological inhibition. Weber also noticed that spinal reflexes were sometimes more reduced in normal animals than in animals without their cerebrums, which led him to theorize that the cerebrum might have inhibitory influences on reflex activity.

From Selected Psychological and Physiological Works by I. M. Sechenov (Bonset, 1968).

Ivan Sechenov (1829–1905) in his laboratory at the Military-Medical Academy

Using the reflexive withdrawal of a frog's leg dipped in a mild acid solution, Sechenov extended Weber's finding. He found that stimulation of certain parts of the frog's brain with a salt crystal depressed the withdrawal reflex, an experimental illustration supporting Weber's suggestion that brain stimulation might inhibit reflex activity. Sechenov believed his demonstration of inhibitory actions in the central nervous system paved the way for a physiological analysis of mental processes.

Back in St. Petersburg, Sechenov wrote a paper expressing his view that the brain is simply a center for organizing reflexes. Sechenov planned to call his work *An Attempt to Bring Physiological Bases Into Mental Processes,* but the St. Petersburg censor made him change it to *Reflexes of the Brain* (1863). This change was supposed to make the article seem technical and uninteresting (Boakes, 1984), so that its mechanistic approach to the brain would be little read by people who might have their religious faith undermined.

In fact, La Mettrie's materialistic philosophy (Chapter 4) became in Sechenov's hands a physiological theory in which all forms of behavior are reflexes of the brain. For example, Sechenov considered emotional behavior merely reflexes whose intensity is heightened by brain activity, and he saw voluntary behavior as reflex chains assembled during development as the result of involuntary learning. We will see Sechenov's view of thought as reflexes with inhibited motor expression (Gray, 1979) echoed in Watson's notion of thought as subvocal activity.

Sechenov learned psychology from the French philosophers after La Mettrie, and La Mettrie's belief that appropriate tuition would transform an ape into "a little gentleman" is reflected in Sechenov's suggestion that with a European upbringing, various ethnic minorities (e.g., Lapps and Bashkirs) would develop skills and interests little different from those of an educated European. Watson's (1924/1970) pronouncement, "Give me a dozen healthy infants, well-formed, and my own specified world to bring them up in and I'll guarantee to take any one at random and train him to become any type of specialist I might select" (p. 104), makes the same point. Contrast these attitudes with the ones Francis Galton (Chapter 9), Sechenov's British contemporary, expressed in *Hereditary Genius.*

Sechenov resigned his St. Petersburg position in 1870 and found employment at Odessa, where he wrote another article on physiology and psychology. In *Who Must Investigate the Problems of Psychology and How,* Sechenov asked psychologists to abandon the introspective analysis of subjective experience and concentrate on studying reflexive behavior in animals. He believed that if physiologists studied psychology, the result might be slow, but real, progress rather than the illusory rapid progress he felt characterized psychology. To his question of who must investigate, the answer was the physiologist. To the question of how, the answer was by studying reflexes.

Sechenov's most important contributions for psychology were the idea of inhibitory action in the nervous system, the extension of physiology into psychology's domain, and his influence on the next generation of Russian neurophysiologists. Although Sechenov's own neurophysiological speculations were dazzling, there was little evidence to sustain them. Ivan Pavlov's research supplied the needed empirical observations (Windholz & Lamal, 1986).

Ivan Petrovich Pavlov

Ivan Petrovich Pavlov (1849–1936) was born in Ryazan, a small Russian town southeast of Moscow. His father was the town's priest; his mother, a priest's daughter. From his father, Pavlov developed a love of gardening and of physical exercise. As the oldest of 11 children, Pavlov developed responsibility and learned the value of hard work.

A severe fall as a youth delayed his entrance to the local school, and Pavlov recuperated with his godfather, the abbot of a nearby monastery. His godfather devoted his life to his duties and studies; as an adult, Pavlov did likewise.

Pavlov's formal education began at the Ryazan Ecclesiastical High School, where he obtained a more progressive education than if he had attended the secular state schools. A rigid educational program at the state high schools excluded the teaching of science. By contrast, Pavlov was exposed to the "literature of the '60s," which included such topics as Darwin's theory of evolution.

In 1870, Pavlov left Ryazan for St. Petersburg University, planning to study science. By his third year, he had chosen to be a physiologist. Because Sechenov left St. Petersburg in 1870, Pavlov's introduction to physiology came from Sechenov's successor, Ilya Cyon (Boakes, 1984). Cyon was an excellent researcher and an inspirational lecturer whose unpleasant personality led to his eventual expulsion from the university and departure from Russia. Under Cyon's supervision, Pavlov studied pancreatic nerves, earning a gold medal and graduating in 1875.

Next, Pavlov studied at the Medico-Surgical Academy in St. Petersburg, where he received his second degree in 1879 and earned a second gold medal for his research on innervation of the heart. Because of his exceptional research ability, in 1878 Pavlov was put in charge of the small-animal laboratory of the academy's

Ivan (1849–1936) and Sara Pavlov at about the time of their marriage

medical clinic director, Sergei Botkin. Botkin had attended du Bois-Reymond's lectures in Berlin with Sechenov and had become one of Russian medicine's most influential men. Botkin's belief in nervism, the pervasive importance of the nervous system for disease, undoubtedly influenced Pavlov's later commitment to the same view.

In 1883, Pavlov received his Doctorate of Medicine, but his financial situation remained precarious. He had married in 1881, and he and his wife Sara suffered extreme poverty for the first several years of their marriage. Their poverty was caused by the scarcity of decent research jobs, by Pavlov's refusal to allow Sara to work, and by his lack of concern over worldly matters.

The story of Sara's visit to Pavlov in St. Petersburg during their engagement illustrates Pavlov's impracticality. Aware of her tendency to spend money too freely, Sara gave her funds to Pavlov at the beginning of the visit, and he paid for everything except a pair of shoes she bought for herself. Unfortunately, Pavlov spent all of Sara's money and all of his own, and Sara returned home in nearly penniless misery. Upon arriving, she found only one shoe in her luggage, Pavlov having kept the other shoe to remember her by (Babkin, 1949).

Pavlov's carelessness with money even extended to a 1923 trip to America, when he lost nearly all of the money he had brought for the trip. According to one account, Pavlov had placed a handbag with most of his money on the seat next to him in Manhattan's Grand Central Station. When he rose to leave, the handbag had disappeared. "Ah, well," sighed Pavlov gently, "one must not put temptation in the way of the needy" (Gerow, 1988, p. 12). Thomas (1997) has argued convincingly that this account, which appeared in *Time* magazine in 1928, is almost completely fabricated. Apparently, Pavlov was accosted by three men soon after entering an empty train car with his son. His wallet containing funds for the trip was snatched from a coat pocket, and there is no indication Pavlov actually made the comment attributed to him in the *Time* article.

Pavlov's negligence in his personal life was offset by his practicality, ingenuity, and dedication to science. "Pavlov said of himself: 'I am an experimenter from head to foot. My whole life has been given to experiment'" (Babkin, 1949, p. 110). As an example of his dedication, one day during the Russian Revolution, Pavlov arrived at his laboratory at his usual 9 A.M. An assistant came in 10 minutes late, explaining he had been delayed by the Revolution and shooting in the streets. Unsympathetically, Pavlov scolded the assistant, admonishing him to get up 10 minutes earlier the next time there was a revolution.

Even Pavlov's final illness illustrates his dedication to his work. After an apparently mild attack of the grippe (influenza), against his family's advice Pavlov went to his laboratory on February 21, 1936, worked all day, and returned home at dinnertime. The next day he awoke with a fever, and his condition worsened rapidly. Pavlov died on February 27.

Pavlov's Research on the Digestive System

In his research, Pavlov almost always avoided *acute* experiments, in which an animal is anesthetized, an organ isolated and studied quickly, and then the animal is sacrificed. Instead, he used *chronic* preparations, in which his animal subjects were conscious, healthy, and capable of being repeatedly observed. Like many animal researchers of the period, Pavlov agonized over vivisection experiments. Pavlov felt his work was justified because the only way humans can learn many of the organic world's laws is through animal experimentation and observation. Although he was often criticized by antivivisectionists, there is ample evidence of Pavlov's kindness toward and dedication to his experimental animals.

> On a monument at the Institute of Experimental Medicine to the dogs used in his experiments Pavlov had carved, "The dog, man's helper and friend from pre-historic times, may justly be offered as a sacrifice to science; but let this always be done without unnecessary suffering" . . . (Dewsbury, 1990, pp. 322–323)

Pavlov's research on the mechanisms for the secretion of different digestive juices began in earnest in 1890, when he became both a professor of pharmacology at the Military-Medical Academy in St. Petersburg and director of the Physiology Department at the Institute of Experimental Medicine. These appointments gave Pavlov the space and facilities to pursue his interests.

In an early study, Pavlov's chronic preparation involved an operation to create an isolated portion of the stomach, a "gastric pouch," open to the outside of the dog's body so that he could study its contents at will. The German physiologist Heidenhain had nearly accomplished such a preparation, and Pavlov had studied the method in Heidenhain's Breslau laboratory. However, Heidenhain's pouch required cutting nearly all the nerves to the externalized stomach tissue. Because Pavlov believed in nervism, he sought to preserve the nerves to the isolated stomach tissue. Pavlov—called by Sechenov the best surgeon in Europe (Gray, 1979)—eventually succeeded with the extremely difficult surgical procedure.

Pavlov pioneered "sham feeding" experiments, in which a dog was allowed to eat but the food fell out through a hole cut in the esophagus. Feeding actually occurred through a second opening—or fistula—in the dog's stomach, through which Pavlov could study the animal's gastric secretions.

Pavlov found that the taste of food triggered the release of gastric juices in the stomach even though the food never reached that organ. These "psychical secretions" prepare the stomach to digest the food that normally reaches it. Pavlov demonstrated that psychic secretion release is under nervous system control and, in particular, controlled by the vagus nerve. In the days before over-the-counter antacids, Pavlov bottled and sold his dogs' gastric juices to treat human stomach ailments, nearly doubling his laboratory's income (Babkin, 1949).

In 1897, Pavlov published *Work of the Principal Digestive Glands,* which dealt with his digestive system research and only incidentally mentioned psychical secretions. This book is considered so important for psychology that the centennial of its publication was the rationale for a special section of the September 1997 *American Psychologist* devoted to excerpts and articles about Pavlov's contributions (see Dewsbury, 1997). From the book, Pavlov gained an international reputation and the Nobel Prize in medicine in 1904. However, by 1904, Pavlov had already begun the research for which he is most famous, and his address at Stockholm was about conditioned reflexes.

The Conditioned Reflex

Pavlov's serious study of psychical secretions or psychic reflexes started in the late 1890s, at about the same time Thorndike was doing his animal learning experiments. Pavlov later credited Thorndike's research with providing the experimental groundwork for studies of animal conditioning:

> [T]he American School of Psychologists—already interested in the comparative study of psychology—evinced a disposition to subject the highest nervous activities of animals to experimental analysis under various specially devised conditions. We may fairly regard the treatise by

> Thorndyke [*sic*], *The Animal Intelligence* (1898), as the starting point for systematic investigations of this kind. (Pavlov, 1927/1960, pp. 5–6)

Although Pavlov's psychical secretions had been observed in both the gastric glands and the salivary glands, Pavlov concentrated on the latter, using a method one of his colleagues had developed for their long-term study (Koshtoyants, 1957). The first experiments on psychical secretions were conducted by Stefan Wolfson (or Vul'fson; Windholz, 1990), working under Pavlov's direction. (Like many other names in translations of Russian literature [see Bagg, 1972, for a listing of different spellings of Pavlov and others], various spellings of Wolfson can be found. Our spelling is that used in Pavlov [1928].) Wolfson found the sight of food was enough to elicit salivary secretion. Further, the saliva's quantity and quality depended on what was actually shown—whether it was edible or inedible, for example.

Another student, Anton Snarsky, conducted similar experiments, interpreting his results introspectively in terms of the dog's inner world of thoughts, desires, and emotions. For Snarsky, the dog's salivation resulted from its psychical reaction, and this inner state was unavailable to physiological investigation.

By this time, however, Pavlov had decided to replace the psychical secretion notion with physiological concepts. As a result, he and Snarsky differed bitterly, and Snarsky was finally forced to leave Pavlov's laboratory. As Pavlov expressed the controversy,

> Snarsky clung to his subjective explanation of the phenomena, but I . . . decided finally . . . to remain in the role of a pure physiologist, i.e., of *an objective external observer and experimenter, having to do exclusively with external phenomena and their relations.* I attacked this problem with a new co-worker, . . . and from this beginning there followed a series of investigations . . . , which has lasted for more than twenty years. (Pavlov, 1928, Vol. 1, pp. 38–39, italics added)

As an "objective external observer [of] . . . external phenomena and their relations," Pavlov was clearly in the behaviorist mold.

Having rejected an explanation of conditioning by appeal to the dog's mental life, Pavlov dropped *psychical reflex* for *conditional reflex.* Note the word is *conditional,* not *conditioned.* Yerkes and Morgulis (1909) decided to use the *-ed* versions, because they considered it likely Pavlov himself had sanctioned *conditioned* and *unconditioned* in lectures given in London in 1906. Following Yerkes and Morgulis and many others, we will use the *-ed* forms (e.g., conditioned reflex).

Conditioning was still a side issue for Pavlov until a 1902 report about a momentous finding by two British physiologists, Sir William Maddock Bayliss (1860–1924) and Ernest Henry Starling (1866–1927). Bayliss and Starling found that some digestive system information is conveyed by chemical signals, or hormones (their word), and they discovered the first hormone (secretin).

With his nervism bias, Pavlov had assumed signals from one digestive system part (e.g., the mouth) to another (e.g., secretory glands in the stomach) were conveyed by the nervous system. Perhaps some of this information was carried via chemical messages. When full details of Bayliss and Starling's experiment became available, Pavlov asked an assistant to replicate it, and it was soon obvious that secretin stimulated secretion from a digestive system organ Pavlov had assumed was under nervous control. As a result, Pavlov's study of digestive system physiology decreased, and his research on conditioned reflexes increased.

As we indicated, Pavlov's Nobel Prize address concerned reflexive conditioning, and the reaction of physiologists to his new work was quite negative. For example, Sir Charles Sherrington (Chapter 7) advised Pavlov to return to "real physiology." However, Pavlov's Nobel Prize insulated him from such criticism, and his work on conditioning continued.

In contrast to Pavlov, University of Pennsylvania doctoral student **Edwin Burket Twitmyer** (1873–1943) had no established position when he observed patellar (knee-jerk) reflex conditioning to the sound of a bell. Although he reported his observations at the 1904 APA convention, his discovery drew only an uncomfortable silence from the gathered American psychologists. It is likely that Twitmyer's contemporaries, chiefly interested in identifying the contents of consciousness, were poorly prepared to realize the conditioned reflex's significance (e.g., Coon, 1982; Irwin, 1943). Although Dallenbach (1959) suggested

Pavlov's dog prepared for conditioning

Archives of the History of American Psychology—The University of Akron.

Twitmyer's study of the knee-jerk reflex had priority over Pavlov's work, Windholz (1986) argued that Pavlov's research on conditioned reflexes actually began 3 or 4 years before Twitmyer's dissertation.

As a physiologist, Pavlov had no qualms about studying a "primitive" reflex as a window on the central nervous system's operations, and Pavlov, not Twitmyer, is recognized as the discoverer of the conditioned reflex. Actually, it is more precise to say that Pavlov was the first person to investigate the conditioned reflex systematically, as several individuals (e.g., Robert Whytt, Johannes Müller, Erasmus Darwin, Claude Bernard) recognized and commented about salivary conditioning before Pavlov began his studies (Rosenzweig, 1959).

As for priority, Logan (2002) has reported that Austrian physiologist Alois Kreidl (1864–1928) demonstrated the development of conditioned reflexes in 1896 in his study of fish called to food. Further, Kreidl stated that his observation of such conditioning had been known to science since the 1830s. Logan contends that Kreidl's work was overlooked for a variety of reasons, such as his focus on sensory abilities rather than conditioning, his testing in a monastery rather than in a laboratory, and his use of imprecise methods of measurement.

Research on Conditioning

Pavlov assumed all behavior consists of reflexes, some depending on inborn anatomical connections between the central nervous system and effectors (muscles and glands), and some acquired through experience with the environment. Pavlov systematically studied acquired reflexes for the last 3 decades of his life.

To study reflex conditioning, Pavlov and his colleagues typically used the preparation illustrated in the photo above, which shows a dog that has had a minor surgical procedure so that its salivation can be precisely recorded. The dog has been trained to stand quietly in the harness.

Note that Pavlov's choice of animal and of the salivary response was essentially arbitrary. He believed he was studying the general laws of higher nervous activity, which were applicable to any higher animal and to any reflex. Subsequent reflexive conditioning research has tended to support this belief, and the principles Pavlov established have been validated over a broad array of different behaviors, in a variety of species.

In a typical Pavlovian study, a reflex was conditioned by presenting a neutral stimulus (**conditioned stimulus** or **CS**—a stimulus that does not initially trigger salivation) with an **unconditioned stimulus** (**UCS**—a stimulus that innately triggers salivation). Salivation to the UCS is the **unconditioned response (UCR).** After several CS-UCS pairings, the CS alone begins to elicit salivation, which is called the **conditioned response (CR).**

Pavlov found two conditions necessary for developing a CR: temporal contiguity and repeatedly pairing the CS and UCS. Contiguity and repetition were first mentioned by Aristotle and developed further by Hume (Chapter 5) and his successors. Further, Pavlov found it important for the CS to precede the UCS; neither strict simultaneity (**simultaneous conditioning**) nor presenting the UCS before the CS (**backward conditioning**) results in significant conditioning. A slight delay between the CS and UCS (**delayed conditioning**) is often optimal for conditioning, as long as the CS is still present when the UCS begins. If the CS has ended and some time passes before the UCS begins, the conditioning is called **trace conditioning,** which Pavlov found difficult to achieve.

Using the basic procedure, perhaps pairing a tuning fork tone (CS) with meat powder (UCS), Pavlov and his associates elucidated virtually all of the basic conditioning phenomena. For example, they found that once a conditioned reflex has been acquired, repeatedly presenting the CS without the UCS eventually causes the animal to stop salivating to the CS (**extinction**).

In further studies, another colleague, B. P. Babkin, found the extinguished CR reappears under certain conditions. For example, a dog conditioned to salivate at the sight of a dish of food by being allowed to eat from it had its salivary response extinguished. Once the CR had disappeared, the animal rested for a few hours, and then the dish was again presented. The CR reappeared at almost full strength. This reappearance of the CR after a rest interval following extinction is called **spontaneous recovery.**

Spontaneous recovery also occurred if Babkin presented another strong, but irrelevant, stimulus. For example, a dog whose salivary response had been extinguished began to salivate again to the dish after Babkin placed a little dilute acid into its mouth. Later study indicated that the irrelevant stimulus did not have to produce the UCR in order for **disinhibition** to occur. A loud sound was sufficient to restore the CR, if it happened during the CS presentation to an animal whose response had been extinguished.

Pavlov and his colleagues also studied **higher-order conditioning,** the use of a CS as a UCS in further conditioning. For example, once a dog has been conditioned to salivate to a tone (CS) paired with meat powder (UCS), another neutral stimulus (e.g., a light) can be paired with the tone to eventually produce the conditioned response. The demonstration of higher-order conditioning was considered essential for the claim that all behavior represents chains of conditioned reflexes. Although Pavlov did not actually make this claim (see Windholz, 1996, for a discussion of how Pavlov accounted for the formation of complex behavior patterns), others did, including Clark Hull (Chapter 13) and John Watson (Malone, 1991).

Pavlov also called the stimuli that come to signal biologically important events (CSs) the **first-signal system**—that is, the first signals of reality. But humans have a **second-signal system,** language, or symbols of symbols, which are presumably learned by higher-order conditioning. Pavlov used the distinction between the two systems to categorize people into artistic types, dependent on the first-signal system, and intellectual types who depend primarily on the second-signal system.

Pavlov and his co-workers also studied stimulus generalization—responding to a stimulus similar, but not identical, to the original CS. For example, a dog trained to salivate to one tone also salivates (less copiously) to a slightly higher or lower tone. If two tones are presented alternately, with one always followed by the UCS and the other never followed by it, the dog learns to discriminate between them (**conditioned discrimination**). Specifically, the generalized response extinguishes, leaving only the conditioned response.

However, when the discrimination became too difficult, Pavlov observed a phenomenon important both for his brain function theory and for generalizing his findings to humans: **experimental neurosis.** Experimental neurosis was first observed in 1921 in visual discrimination experiments performed by one of Pavlov's female students, N. R. Shenger-Krestovnikova, in which a dog learned to distinguish a circle from an ellipse. As the ellipse became more circular, discrimination slowed until the animal reached its discrimination limit. At this point, the animal's behavior changed dramatically: Learned discriminations easily made previously broke down; a previously docile animal became hard to handle; a previously silent dog barked violently; and so on.

Pavlov believed experimental neurosis developed when his animals experienced a conflict between incompatible conditioned-response tendencies—in this case, between the tendency to salivate at the sight of the nearly circular ellipse or to not salivate to it. As a physiologist, Pavlov incorporated this idea into a theory of brain functioning, for which he failed to develop any evidence. Pavlov's theory involved hypothetical mechanisms of brain function that were not all that farfetched at the time he proposed them; however, discoveries by Ramón y Cajal, Sherrington, and others soon rendered Pavlov's explanatory ideas impossible. Pavlov failed to alter his theory accordingly. As Gray (1979) put it, "it is as though, in 1900 or thereabouts, he stopped listening to what was going on elsewhere" (p. 102). Fortunately, Pavlov's importance for psychology does not rest on his theory of brain function.

Personality Types and Psychopathology

In order to appreciate Pavlov's theory of personality types, recall that he and his colleagues observed the same dogs over long periods, often for years, becoming quite familiar with their dogs' temperaments. Also, each dog's behavior was studied in many different experimental situations, and behavioral consistencies were easy to see.

Pavlov categorized his animals into four temperament types based on the strengths of their excitatory and inhibitory processes, the balance or equilibrium between the processes, and the mobility or lability of the processes. He took his four temperament types from Galen's (Chapter 2) temperaments based on the Hippocratic humors: sanguine (excessive blood), melancholic (excessive black bile), choleric (too much yellow bile), and phlegmatic (excessive phlegm). Before concluding Pavlov's categories were archaic, note that some modern personality theorists (e.g., Eysenck; Chapter 16) have also used these labels and temperaments.

For Pavlov, strong but balanced excitatory and inhibitory processes lead to different types of dogs depending on how easily the processes can be set in motion. Easily triggered processes produce a sanguine dog (lively, readily conditioned); relatively inactive processes, a phlegmatic personality (inert, slow to condition). The excitatory processes dominate the inhibitory to produce a choleric temperament (impetuous, difficulty with discriminations). Finally, weak excitatory and inhibitory processes lead to a melancholic personality (depressed, slow to condition), irrespective of the ease with which the processes can be activated. For Pavlov, environmental conditioning was mediated by an animal's temperament, which differentiates Pavlov from most later behaviorists.

While developing his theory of personality differences, Pavlov also studied psychopathology. As we indicated, too fine a discrimination caused experimental neurosis in the dogs. The question was, How do stress and personality combine to produce a particular mental disorder?

At 80, Pavlov began to visit psychiatric wards, where he observed and discussed cases with psychiatrists. Soon he began to talk of psychotics and neurotics as though they were dogs whose conditioning had gone awry; his explanations and treatments for the human disorders were based on his theories of brain function. For example, the sedative bromide was assumed to strengthen the inhibitory process, and it became Pavlov's main remedy, along with sleep. Because of Pavlov's recommendation, sleep therapy became popular in the Soviet Union, but it has not caught on elsewhere. In general, Pavlov's importance for psychopathology stems more from his method than from his actual findings and theorizing: He was among the first to bring abnormal behavior under experimental investigation (Gray, 1979). Dews (1981) concluded Pavlov's direct impact on psychiatry was slight, and it was too early to assess his indirect effect.

Pavlov and His Laboratory Coworkers

From 1897 to 1936, Pavlov was assisted by at least 146 different students and colleagues, most of whom were from the Soviet Union (Windholz, 1990). Pavlov excluded women in the early 1900s because of an early conflict with a woman in the laboratory, admitted only 3 women from 1905 until 1910, but after 1910 included them readily among his laboratory personnel. Ultimately, his coworkers in the study of higher nervous activity included at least 20 women, among them his daughter.

New workers in Pavlov's laboratory were required to read previous dissertations, because before the 1920s there was no systematic exposition of the work on conditioned reflexes. They were also assigned to a project and required to attend Pavlov's seminars. Finally, the new worker was given a dog with a fistula in one parotic gland to allow measurement of its salivary response.

According to Jasper Ten-Cate, a Dutch citizen, the atmosphere in Pavlov's laboratories was congenial, and a new worker was quickly made to feel "at home" (Windholz, 1990). Pavlov was not a distant figure, as he spent most of his workday in the laboratory. "Every morning Pavlov would sit in a large room, where any co-worker could approach him. The co-workers would report new experimental findings, listen to his comments and explanations, and occasionally dare to disagree with him" (p. 67).

The reminiscences of former Pavlovians give the impression that having worked with the master was a signal event in their lives. Although Pavlov was often approachable and pleasant, many Pavlovians experienced "Pavlov's loud verbal abuse and threatening gestures" (Windholz, 1990, p. 68). Most of these attacks occurred because of a coworker's failure to follow established procedures precisely. Easily angered, Pavlov was also quick to apologize if he was wrong. Student and long-time friend Boris Babkin (1949) attributed Pavlov's yelling at his associates to the style among Russian officials of the period, who "considered it necessary to instill fear into their subordinates by raising their voices" (p. 120). Despite his fiery temperament, Babkin concluded that Pavlov's closest associates were not afraid of him.

In the 40 years Pavlov studied higher nervous activity, he and his coworkers published at least 532 papers (Windholz, 1990). Given the turmoil in Russia during much of Pavlov's research (e.g., World War I, the Bolshevik Revolution), his research output was remarkable and surely a credit to the inspiration of Pavlov himself.

Pavlov's Influence

Pavlov was a great Soviet hero, both because of his international reputation and because his materialistic approach to the problems of mind and behavior fit nicely with the Soviet rejection of spiritualism. As evidence of Soviet support, a 1921 decree over Lenin's signature established a committee to see that the conditions were optimal for the work of Pavlov and his colleagues. By the same decree, Pavlov and his wife received double food rations.

In 1950, Pavlov was in effect canonized by the Soviet Academy of Sciences (Windholz, 1997). As a result, in the ensuing decades there has been a great accumulation of experimental psychological data in Russia but little critical examination of Pavlovian theory.

Outside Russia, Pavlov's influence has had several phases. First, behaviorism adopted Pavlov's objective language of conditioned reflexes, without adding his actual methods and theories to its repertoire. In part, this was caused by the early lack of American access to English translations of his major papers. The scarcity of translated material had an even greater effect on the international influence of Pavlov's contemporaries and rivals, such as Vladimir Bekhterev (discussed later) and Lev Vygotsky (Chapter 18).

Pavlov reciprocated behaviorism's interest in him. He particularly approved of the behaviorist belief that the behavior of people is more important than speculation about their conscious states, and Pavlov almost certainly knew of the similarity between his methods and assumptions and those of behaviorism (Windholz, 1983). Pavlov's approval of Watsonian behaviorism is probably at least partly responsible for Pavlov's extreme reaction to criticisms by Lashley in his 1929 APA presidential address and Edwin Guthrie (Chapter 13) in 1930. Pavlov (1932) responded to both in a *Psychological Review* article, "The reply of a physiologist to psychologists." Lashley's and Guthrie's criticisms aside, Pavlov fully expected American behaviorism to continue his work on the conditioned reflex.

Although Pavlov approved of the school of behaviorism, he held widely differing opinions of its various members. "Pavlov greatly admired the work of E. L. Thorndike . . . , was contemptuous of C. L. Hull . . . and E. R. Guthrie . . . , [and] hostile toward Lashley . . ." (Windholz, 1987, p. 105). Windholz further argued that Pavlov was always attracted to psychology, and a chronological summary of Pavlov's work after 1901 shows it to be devoted almost completely to traditional psychological topics.

The second phase of Pavlov's American influence came with Clark Hull's attempt to develop a comprehensive, mathematically formulated learning theory in the 1930s and 1940s. Hull borrowed freely from Pavlov's data, adopted many of his concepts, but discarded any Pavlovian references to brain physiology. As in the earlier influence, Pavlov's methodology was not used to study animal behavior; Thorndike's technique continued to dominate American comparative psychology.

The third phase of Pavlov's influence came in the 1950s and 1960s, when the distinction between Pavlovian (or classical) conditioning and Thorndikian (or instrumental) conditioning had been clearly drawn (Gray, 1979). The distinction led psychologists such as O. H. Mowrer (Chapter 13) to construct "two-factor" theories, which assume that classical conditioning teaches an animal the significance of environmental events, whereas instrumental conditioning enables the animal to learn to do something about such events. This type of theorizing eventually led to the use of Pavlovian conditioning to explore questions Pavlov posed over half a century ago, and Gray concluded: "The influence of Pavlov on the study of animal learning is stronger and more direct now than at any time in the past; and it appears still to be growing" (p. 127).

Note that Pavlov, at least toward the end of his life, did not consider that all learning was of the conditioned reflex variety (Windholz, 1987). In fact, he specifically credited Thorndike with "the systematic investigation of a natural phenomenon . . . of immense importance to humankind and science in particular—trial and error learning" (p. 109). Pavlov considered conditioned reflexes important for the organism's adaptation to a changing environment, whereas trial-and-error learning led to the accumulation of knowledge.

Although we will explore classical conditioning in the context of early American behaviorism in the rest of this chapter and parts of the next, Pavlovian conditioning is by no means extinct. For example, **Robert A. Rescorla** (1940–) won the APA's Distinguished Scientific Contribution Award in 1986 for "[h]is use of Pavlovian conditioning as a representative associative process [that] has enabled him to question and expand the laws of association put forth by Aristotle and the British Associationists" (*American Psychologist,* 1987, p. 285). Rescorla's Pavlovian interest began at the University of Pennsylvania, where he received his Ph.D. in 1966. At Yale, Rescorla's research focused on animal learning, conditioned inhibition, and Pavlovian higher-order conditioning. His more recent efforts have examined contextual effects on learning.

To conclude our look at Ivan Pavlov, we will let Pavlov speak for himself:

> I must say that looking back on my life I would describe it as being happy and successful. I have received all that can be demanded of life: the complete realization of the principles with which I began life. I dreamed of finding happiness in intellectual work, in science—and I found it. I wanted to have a kind person as a companion in life and I found this companion in my wife . . . , who patiently endured all the hardships of our existence before my professorship, always encouraged my scientific aspirations and who devoted herself to our family just as I devoted myself to the laboratory. (Pavlov, 1957, p. 62)

Vladimir Mikhailovich Bekhterev

Vladimir Bekhterev (1857–1927)

Although **Vladimir Mikhailovich Bekhterev** (1857–1927) was nearly 8 years younger than Pavlov, he climbed the educational ladder rapidly and received his first degree in medicine in 1878, a year before Pavlov. In 1881, Bekhterev received his M.D. from St. Petersburg and for the next several years, he studied abroad with such notables as du Bois-Reymond, Wundt (Chapter 8), and Charcot (Chapter 15). Bekhterev returned to found the first two experimental psychology laboratories in Russia—in 1886 at Kazan and in 1895 at St. Petersburg. Most of his career was spent as a colleague of Pavlov's in St. Petersburg.

Throughout his career, Bekhterev was more of a psychiatrist than a physiologist. In Kazan, he became convinced that more could be gained from objectively studying a neurotic patient's life than from trying to analyze the neurotic's subjective experience. Bekhterev was also interested in neural localization of conditioning experiences, and his animal research often involved conditioning a dog and then damaging its brain to see which areas controlled the conditioning.

Like Pavlov, Bekhterev believed that study of conditioned reflexes, which he called "associated reflexes," was the key to the scientific study of the mind. Also like Pavlov, Bekhterev was committed to an objective science. The two were completely unlike in virtually every other area, however.

In many respects, Bekhterev's career mirrored G. Stanley Hall's (Chapter 10). Like Hall, Bekhterev was a great organizer and innovator, with little interest in the repetition and tedium often characterizing laboratory work. Like Hall, Bekhterev founded clinics, laboratories, institutes, and journals. In fact, his *Review of Psychiatry, Neuropathology, and Experimental Psychology,* established in 1896, was the first journal with *experimental psychology* in its title. In addition to editing the journal, Bekhterev was for a time its most prolific author, contributing a third of the first volume's reports.

As a result of Bekhterev's dizzying pace, students and colleagues saw little of him and his family even less. For years he worked 18 hours a day, requiring no more than 5 hours sleep, often writing in bed while his wife slept beside him. The result was an amazing number of papers and books.

In a 1904 article, Bekhterev argued against introspection in psychology and, like Sechenov, proposed the reflex as a key concept for an objective psychology. Bekhterev expanded the paper into a book that clearly presented his work on conditioning and animal behavior and should have enhanced his reputation. Its failure to do so can be attributed to controversies between Bekhterev and Pavlov, which Pavlov won.

The most important controversy involved whether destruction of a cortical salivary "center" would prevent a dog from re-establishing a conditioned reflex. In Bekhterev's laboratory, this appeared to be the case, whereas Pavlov's results convinced him such dogs could reacquire a conditioned response. The matter came to a head at a meeting at which Bekhterev arranged for a public demonstration to prove he was right. One of Bekhterev's students tested two animals with cortical ablations, and neither showed any signs of salivating to a stimulus that had produced a CR before surgery. Testing the dogs himself, Pavlov demonstrated that with the appropriate technique, conditioned reflexes were easily re-established. Bekhterev's interest in animal research subsequently declined dramatically (Boakes, 1984).

In 1917, Bekhterev published a series of lectures in *General Principles of Human Reflexology,* in which he again argued for an objective approach to psychology's problems and expressed his opposition to mentalistic terms. **Reflexology** was Bekhterev's word for an objective psychology that would study the relationship between behavior and physiological and environmental conditions. However, despite his approximately 600 publications, when Bekhterev died in 1927 his influence rapidly waned.

As you can see, the study of animal behavior and Russian objective psychology were quite compatible with behaviorism. However, as we noted above, American behaviorism's founding is usually marked by Watson's 1913 publication. We will now examine the colorful life and controversial career of behaviorism's founder.

JOHN BROADUS WATSON

By heredity and upbringing, **John Broadus Watson** (1878–1958) was different from most of the other American psychologists of his generation. For example, he was from the small Southern village of Travelers Rest, near Greenville, South Carolina. Unlike most of his contemporaries, Watson was not the son of a minister or professional—his father was by most accounts a disreputable character who spent much of his time away from the family.

Watson's mother was the family's strength, moving her six children (Watson was the fourth-born) to Greenville when Watson was 12, because of better schools in town than in the country. Emma Watson was devoutly religious, and Watson was named for John Broadus, a fire-and-brimstone Baptist minister. At some point, Emma made Watson promise to become a Baptist minister himself, probably hoping he would follow in his namesake's footsteps (Brewer, 1991). It was a forlorn hope: According to his son, James B. Watson,

> Dad was not just without religion; he was an atheist. He had been required to go to church regularly as a child and was steeped in the Baptist religion as he grew up. As he turned to science he rejected religion. . . . (Hannush, 1987, p. 148)

Given his circumstances, it is not surprising Watson was a wild youth. In his autobiographical essay, he described himself as "lazy, somewhat insubordinate . . ." (Watson, 1936, p. 271) and a poor student. He was arrested twice, "once for . . . fighting, and the second time for shooting off firearms inside the city limits" (p. 271).

Although we will cite frequently Watson's autobiographical essay, its tone is generally negative, and it is difficult to know how much stock to place in it. Positive comments are quickly negated. For example, Watson noted he was the youngest person to receive his Ph.D. from Chicago at the time he finished, and then added,

> I got my first deep-seated inferiority at the same time. I received my degree Magna Cum Laude and was told . . . by Dewey and Angell that my exam was much inferior to that of Miss Helen Thompson who had graduated two years before with a Summa Cum Laude. (p. 274)

In 1894, Watson enrolled at Greenville's Furman University as a subfreshman, a status reflecting his lack of college preparation. He was introduced to philosophy and psychology by Gordon B. Moore, who was up on the latest in psychology after a sabbatical year at the University of Chicago. Although Watson felt Moore "gave us his best," he still managed to challenge Moore in his senior year, as Moore had promised to fail any student who "handed in a paper backwards." Watson, "by some strange streak of luck . . ." (Watson, 1936, p. 272), committed that very crime, perhaps as a way to delay his Furman graduation and scheduled enrollment in Princeton Theological Seminary (Creelan, 1974). As a result, Watson stayed an extra year, graduating from Furman with an A.M. rather than an A.B. in 1899, with a resolve to become a Ph.D. psychologist so he could get even with Moore.

> Imagine my surprise and real sorrow during the second year of my stay at Hopkins, when I received a letter from [Moore] asking to come to me as a research student. Before we could arrange it, his eyesight failed, and he died a few years later. (p. 272)

For a year, Watson taught in a one-room country school, where he impressed the children with his trained rats. In July 1900, Watson's mother died, and Watson promptly applied to the University of Chicago to do graduate work.

Watson in Chicago

In 1900, the distinguished instructors at Chicago included Jacques Loeb, John Dewey, George Herbert Mead, James Rowland Angell (all from Chapter 11), and **Henry H. Donaldson** (1857–1938). Donaldson had been one of Hall's students at Hopkins and was among the first American scientists to work with laboratory rats. As a neurologist, his interest was mainly in their nervous systems.

Arriving in Chicago with only $50, Watson worked at a variety of jobs to pay his way. One of his jobs was as an assistant janitor, which included taking care of Donaldson's rats. At first, Watson leaned toward Loeb as his dissertation director because he found mechanical explanations of behavior through tropisms appealing. However, Angell convinced Watson that Loeb was not a "safe" supervisor, and Angell and Donaldson became his dissertation advisers.

In a project combining animal learning and neurology, Watson first established a baseline of what infant rats of different ages could learn. He then sacrificed different-aged animals and microscopically examined their nervous systems, finding that increasing behavioral complexity was strongly correlated with increasing maturation of nerve fibers. This was an important result, and Watson borrowed $350 from Donaldson to have his dissertation published in 1903 as *Animal Education: The Psychical Development of the White Rat.* Watson's work was generally well received (see Dewsbury, 1990).

After graduating, Watson stayed at Chicago, first as an assistant to Angell and then as an instructor. In his animal laboratory, Watson investigated the cues rats use in learning their way through the maze, a problem suggested by Small. Assisted by Carr (Chapter 11), Watson (1907) suggested that kinesthetic sensations might provide the necessary cues for maze learning; that is, the rats learn a series of muscular movements. To test this, he built a maze in which the "straightaways [could] be shortened or lengthened without disturbing any of the *turning* relations" (p. 96). Watson reasoned that if a rat learns to run a particular distance and then turn, the rat should turn into a side wall if the arm has been lengthened or run into the end wall in a shortened pathway. In fact, this is what he and Carr found (Carr & Watson, 1908).

Watson's (1907) paper was viciously attacked by antivivisectionists, many of whom probably had not read the actual report (Dewsbury, 1990). Watson was ably defended by Baldwin (Chapter 10) and by his department head, Angell. Accused of cruelty to his rats, Watson was actually "loving to animals and very sensitive to their needs," according to his son (Hannush, 1987, p. 141). Watson's animal work during his Chicago years also included the study, with Yerkes, of sensory processes in animals and investigations of the behavior of terns (a sea bird). Watson's successful animal work helped establish him as a rising star in psychology.

In 1904, Watson publicly married Mary Amelia Ickes, a former student. Earlier, he had married her secretly, primarily because of opposition to him by her brother, Harold Ickes, who later became Secretary of the Interior in Franklin D. Roosevelt's cabinet. Watson and Mary had two children, Mary (or Polly) and John. Polly's daughter, John B. Watson's granddaughter, is the television and stage actress Mariette Hartley (see Hartley & Commire, 1990).

Although Watson enjoyed his work at Chicago, he was less satisfied with his salary and his academic position—he was still an instructor in 1908. Thus, when Baldwin offered Watson a position at Johns Hopkins as professor and director of the psychological laboratory at a salary nearly twice what he was making at Chicago, his decision was easy.

John Watson (1878–1958) in 1912, voted the most handsome professor by Johns Hopkins students

Watson at Johns Hopkins

As we noted in Chapter 10, scandal over a brothel visit forced Baldwin's resignation from Hopkins in 1909, soon after Watson's arrival. With Baldwin's departure, responsibility for leading the psychology department and for editing *The Psychological Review* fell to Watson, who was only 31 when he moved to Baltimore. From his new position of power, Watson began pressuring the administration to separate psychology from philosophy and to develop more ties between psychology and biology. In May 1912, Watson established a separate department of psychology with himself as head (O'Donnell, 1985).

Meanwhile, Watson still taught a Jamesian general psychology course and used Titchener's experimental manuals in his experimental courses, but his animal research was steering him toward behaviorism. In fact, he had broached the idea of the nonintrospective study of behavior to his Chicago colleagues as early as 1904, but their response had not been encouraging.

Watson's dislike of introspection was at least partly caused by his lack of facility at it (e.g., Creelan, 1974). In his autobiographical essay, Watson (1936) admitted he did not like to use human subjects and hated serving as a subject himself. More and more he began to think that from watching the behavior of rats he could learn everything other psychologists were discovering by using human observers.

Watson now had the freedom and power to pursue his ideas aggressively, or as Angell (1936) wrote, to develop his behaviorism "in such an extravagant manner" (p. 26). In addition, Watson had the influence of **Knight Dunlap** (1875–1949), one of the psychologists Baldwin recruited to bolster the department at Hopkins. Dunlap had earned his Ph.D. from Harvard, working primarily under Münsterberg, and then came to Hopkins in 1906, where he spent much of his professional life. Dunlap's dissatisfaction with psychology's focus on introspection and consciousness encouraged Watson to make the final break with the traditional, introspective approach to psychology. Watson made his break with a vengeance in "Psychology as the Behaviorist Views It" (Watson, 1913), which was based on lectures he had given at Columbia in early 1913.

Psychology as the Behaviorist Views It

Watson revealed his hand in the opening paragraph:

> Psychology as the behaviorist views it is a purely objective experimental branch of natural science. Its theoretical goal is the prediction and control of behavior. Introspection forms no essential part of its methods, nor is the scientific value of its data dependent upon the readiness with which they lend themselves to interpretation in terms of consciousness. (Watson, 1913, p. 158)

Watson described his uncertainty about how to respond when other psychologists asked him about his animal work's relevance for human psychology. The prevailing attitude was that it was essential to fabricate the conscious content of the animal whose behavior had been studied in order to relate the results to human consciousness. Recall this was what Snarsky wanted to do in Pavlov's laboratory, and Pavlov had found the approach absurd. For Watson, there were two solutions to the problem of how to handle the gulf between the study of animal behavior and the study of human consciousness: Either animal behavior could be studied independently of psychology or psychology could be changed to the study of behavior. Watson chose to change psychology.

"I do not wish unduly to criticize psychology," Watson (1913) wrote, before noting "It has failed signally . . . during the fifty-odd years of its existence as an experimental discipline to make its place in the world as an undisputed natural science" (p. 163). In Watson's opinion, introspection was the problem, and if psychology continued using it, future psychologists would still disagree over the conscious mind's elements. Thus, psychology should "discard all reference to consciousness . . ." (p. 163).

Watson's criticism was not reserved solely for the structuralists, however. He considered functionalism little different from structural psychology and attacked it on the same grounds—for using introspection to study conscious processes. Without consciousness and introspection, psychology would become the objective, positivistic study of behavior.

Although Watson was confident beneficial changes would come once consciousness was discarded, he made few specific predictions about what these changes would be. Instead, he was more interested in showing the need for uniformity in experimental procedures and in reporting the results from both animal and human research.

It would be difficult to overstate the impact of Watson's "manifesto." As an illustration of its lasting significance, Skinner (1964) used Watson's article as a point of departure in one of his most famous essays, "Behaviorism at fifty." More recently, Kimble (1994) began an 80-year report on behaviorism's status using Watson (1913) as his starting point. However, it would not be fair to say Watson's manifesto immediately converted most psychologists to behaviorism, as Samelson's (1981) search of the psychological literature from 1913 to 1920 revealed only limited support at best.

Watson worked diligently for the next few years to fill in the gaps in his behaviorist agenda. With Karl Lashley (Chapter 16), he worked unsuccessfully to study thought as faint contractions in the speech musculature (i.e., as subvocal speech).

Watson's next major behaviorist statement appeared in *Behavior: An Introduction to Comparative Psychology* (1914). After essentially repeating his 1913 manifesto, Watson presented a review of animal behavior work that, except for its theoretical stance, was similar to Washburn's *The Animal Mind.* In addition to claiming thought was subvocal speech, Watson gave a behavioristic view of feelings, arguing they were based on sensations arising from the reproductive organs and erogenous zones. To illustrate, Watson gave an example of how the pleasing effect to the male of the sight of a female animal could be explained physiologically. Watson's explicit discussion of sex was ahead of its time.

Behavior was well received as a comprehensive look at contemporary animal behavior and added to Watson's stature at a time when he was campaigning for the APA presidency. In his presidential speech in late 1915, Watson (1916) appealed again for behaviorism. In place of introspection, he proposed using the conditioned reflex method. After listing difficulties with Pavlov's conditioned salivary reflex, he noted that his work with Lashley had focused on Bekhterev's conditioned motor reflex. The rest of his talk detailed human and animal conditioning work he and Lashley had done.

Watson at Phipps Psychiatric Clinic

Soon after Watson's APA address, he found himself with reduced laboratory space, because of a move by arts and sciences to a new campus. **Adolf Meyer** (1866–1950), a Swiss psychiatrist and the director of Hopkins' Phipps Psychiatric Clinic, offered and Watson eagerly accepted space at the Clinic for his laboratory. A leading figure in American psychiatry, Meyer believed in close contact with academic psychology and invented the term *psychobiology* to describe the union of psychological and biological approaches he thought was necessary to solve psychiatric problems.

In a 1916 paper, Watson advocated the application of his ideas on conditioning to clinical problems, and he sent Meyer a prepublication copy. Meyer was disturbed by Watson's apparent ridicule of treatment methods other than conditioning, by his ignorance of mental illness, and by his lack of understanding of Meyer's views. Although Watson's response did little to satisfy Meyer's objections, Meyer continued to encourage Watson's presence at Phipps Clinic (Leys, 1984). With easy access to newborn infants at the hospital, Watson began a program to extend behavioral research to humans.

Watson had been engaged in this work for about a year when World War I intervened, and he was called to active duty in 1917. Poor eyesight kept him from service as a line officer, and he was assigned at first to organize and oversee the aviation examining boards. With his typically negative attitude toward people in authority, during his military service Watson was nearly court-martialed and then ordered to the front line. "[I]n other words," Watson (1936, p. 278) wrote, "the wish was implied that I be killed speedily." Fortunately, the war ended, and Watson summarized his experiences with the military by writing, "The whole army experience is a nightmare to me" (p. 278).

By December 1918, Watson was back at Phipps. Before his involvement in the war, Watson had published an article in which he talked about three basic emotions in infants—fear, rage, and love—from which all others are derived by conditioning (Watson & Morgan, 1917). Before training, Watson found the emotions were triggered by only a limited range of stimuli. For example, fear was elicited reliably by loud sounds and sudden loss of support (infants were dropped by the experimenter and caught by an assistant). Although many have attributed instinctive fears of darkness and animals to newborns, Watson (like John Locke in Chapter 5) concluded such fears were conditioned. Afraid of the dark most of his life, Watson revealed what he believed to be his fear's origin: "From time immemorial children have been 'scared' in the dark, either unintentionally or as a means of controlling them (this is especially true of children reared in the South)" (p. 166). Rage was elicited reliably by hampering an infant's movements, and love responses—for example, smiling, gurgling, and cooing—followed "the stroking or manipulation of some erogenous zone, tickling, shaking, gentle rocking, patting, turning upon the stomach across the attendant's knee, etc." (Watson & Morgan, 1917, p. 167).

In 1919, Watson published *Psychology From the Standpoint of a Behaviorist* (Watson, 1919a), in which he presented a clear outline of his behaviorist program. Devoted to solving practical problems, the program would include the study of the development of emotional reactions, the clarification of habit formation's basic laws, and the effect of such factors as alcohol, climate, sex, and age on human performance. Again, Watson repeated his proposal to study thinking by recording movements of the larynx. Psychopathology, perhaps because Watson was still smarting over Meyer's reaction, was treated only in the book's final two pages.

Although a central theme of *Psychology* was the development of "conditioned emotional reactions" in the child, Watson had little hard data. He soon remedied this deficit with what is surely his most widely quoted (and misquoted) experiment.

Fear Conditioning in Little Albert

In an experiment that would almost certainly not pass institutional review today, Watson and Rosalie Rayner (1920) deliberately attempted to create a conditioned emotional response in an infant. Their efforts to condition an infant were certainly not the first; Wesley (1968) cited the work of German ophthalmologist E. Raehlmann, "who . . . reported an infant conditioning experiment in 1903" (p. 161). Published in an ophthalmological journal, Raehlmann's excellently designed study remains obscure.

For his study, Watson selected a son of a wet nurse (a woman paid to nurse another woman's child). At the age of about 9 months, Albert B., or **Little Albert,** was afraid only of a suddenly produced loud noise.

Attempts to condition Little Albert began approximately 2 months later. Albert received two training trials at the first session. On each trial, a white rat was placed in front of the child, he reached for it, and as soon as he touched the animal, a loud

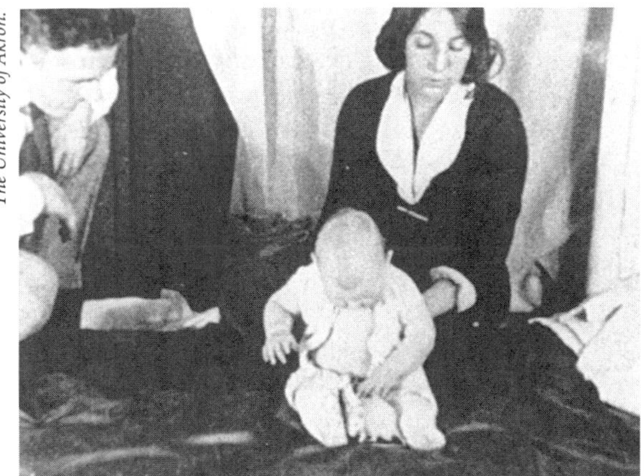

Archives of the History of American Psychology—The University of Akron.

Watson, Rayner, Little Albert and a white rat

sound was made behind his head by striking a steel bar with a hammer. To the second presentation, Albert jumped violently, fell forward, and began to whimper.

A week later, Albert received five joint rat/loud noise presentations. After this, when the rat was presented alone, Albert began to cry and crawled away so swiftly "that he was caught with difficulty before reaching the edge of the table" (Watson & Rayner, 1920, p. 5).

Five days later, Albert was tested to see if he was still afraid of the rat (he was) and then to see if his fear response generalized to other similar objects. Albert reacted fearfully to a rabbit, a dog, and a seal fur coat but had little reaction to cotton wool. Albert also reacted negatively to Watson's hair and to a Santa Claus mask.

After another 5 days, Albert was again given generalization tests and tests of his reaction to the rat. In addition, Watson decided to strengthen Albert's reaction to various stimuli by making the loud noise in their presence. At the end of the session, the dog was presented to Albert without the loud noise, and the child initially had little reaction. When the animal barked unexpectedly, Albert fell over and began wailing until the dog was removed.

A month later, Albert was given his final test, and the authors concluded that their "experiments would seem to show conclusively that directly conditioned emotional responses as well as those conditioned by transfer persist, although with a certain loss in the intensity of the reaction, for a longer period than one month" (Watson & Rayner, 1920, p. 12). Because Albert left the hospital after these final tests, Watson and Rayner did not try to remove the conditioned emotional response.

In conclusion, Watson and Rayner (1920) suggested that many phobias are either conditioned emotional reactions or their generalizations and ridiculed the possible Freudian (Chapter 15) interpretation of the cause of Albert's fear of seal skin coats:

> The Freudians twenty years from now, . . . when they come to analyze Albert's fear of a seal skin coat . . . analysis at that age—will probably tease from him the recital of a dream which upon their analysis will show that Albert at three years of age attempted to play with the pubic hair of the mother and was scolded violently for it. . . . If the analyst has sufficiently prepared Albert to accept such a dream . . . as an explanation of his avoiding tendencies, and if the analyst has the authority and personality to put it over, Albert may be fully convinced that the dream was a true revealer of the factors which brought about the fear. (Watson & Rayner, 1920, p. 14)

Despite Watson and Rayner's (1920) ridicule of a possible Freudian interpretation of Little Albert's conditioned emotional response, Rilling (2000) concluded that the Little Albert study was, in fact, an effort "to validate in the laboratory Freud's ideas that emotions can be displaced or transferred from one object to another" (p. 311). Thus, when Albert responded fearfully to a rabbit after being conditioned to fear a rat, Watson reported that the fear had transferred from one stimulus to the other. According to Rilling, "Watson repeatedly used the Freudian inspired word *transfer*, and he never used the Pavlovian concept of generalization in describing the stimulus generalization that was the most dramatic finding of his most famous experiment" (p. 309).

Although the Little Albert study appears in most introductory psychology textbooks and in most learning textbooks as a paradigmatic example of human Pavlovian conditioning, careful examination of the various reports would lead most objective observers to conclude that "this study with a sample of one [is] an interesting but not very compelling pilot study" (Samelson, 1980, p. 621). In addition, as reported, the study's details are not always accurate. Harris (1979) indicated that some of the inaccuracies involve minor details such as the child's age and the initial object Albert was taught to fear (i.e., a rabbit instead of a rat). More significant distortions involve the generalized fear items and the story's ending.

Harris (1979) reported that some of the distortion resulted from Watson's own varied recountings. In addition, discrepancies about the animal Albert was taught to fear and the study's outcome may have come from confusing the Little Albert report with a later project involving Watson, the study of a child named Peter by Mary Cover Jones (Jones, 1924a, 1924b, 1974).

During her last semester at Vassar, **Mary Cover Jones** (1896–1987) attended a lecture by Watson on Little Albert's conditioning. Watson was working in New York City by the time Jones became a graduate student at Columbia, where she earned her Ph.D. Because Jones had been a classmate and friend of Rosalie Rayner, by this time Watson's wife, Watson was willing to advise Jones on most Saturday afternoons during the project to cure Peter. As Peter was successfully treated by someone associated with Watson, and Peter was initially afraid of rabbits (and rats), you can see how confusion might occur.

To eliminate the 3-year-old Peter's fear of a rabbit, Jones first used social imitation (modeling therapy) by placing Peter in a room with three other children playing fearlessly with a rabbit. Although this reduced Peter's fear, an accidental encounter with a frightening dog brought it back. Jones next used a "direct conditioning" method in which Peter sat in a highchair eating a preferred food while the rabbit was moved successively closer to him over a period of several days. By the end, Peter showed "a genuine fondness for the rabbit. . . . The fear of the cotton, the fur coat, feathers, was entirely absent" (Jones, 1924a, p. 314).

Elsewhere, Jones (1924b) discussed different procedures she had tried for removing fear responses, concluding that only direct conditioning and social imitation worked consistently. The sometimes-successful methods included talking about the feared object, elimination through disuse, negative adaptation (stimulation with the feared object until the child grows used to it), repression (punishment by social ridicule), and distraction (using a substitute activity to divert the child's attention from the feared object).

Jones spent most of her career at the Institute of Human Development of the University of California, Berkeley, where she collaborated with her husband, Harold E. Jones, on longitudinal studies of development. However, she is best known for having been the first researcher in modern times—recall Locke's method for removing "vain Terrors"—to use counterconditioning to remove a child's fear. In fact, Joseph Wolpe (Chapter 5), the person usually credited with inventing systematic desensitization and behavior therapy, called Mary Cover Jones "the mother of behavior therapy" for the work we have described (Rutherford, 2000).

From Behaviorism to Advertising

In his autobiographical essay, Watson (1936) treated his divorce and dismissal from Hopkins in three sentences: "I was divorced in 1920 and was married immediately to Rosalie Rayner, of Baltimore" (p. 271) and "All of this work abruptly came to a close with my divorce in 1920. I was asked to resign" (p. 279). Of course, there is more to the story than that.

By 1920, Watson's career was soaring, but his home life was in shambles. Perhaps describing his own situation, at the end of an article Watson (1919b) wrote about a man with a low level of adjustment who seemed to have a wall around him in terms of his emotional attitudes. Watson suggested that emotionally exciting stimuli might be able to break through the wall, and he soon encountered such stimuli in his laboratory assistant, Rosalie Rayner.

Although it is true that Watson and Rayner's passionate affair led to his divorce and their marriage, it is probably not the case that the romance stemmed from a sexual research study in which he and his laboratory assistant were the subjects (e.g., Magoun, 1981; McConnell & Philipchalk, 1992). After examining records that included Watson's divorce trial transcripts and the private correspondence of university officials and involved faculty, biographer Kerry Buckley (1989) dismissed the sex research allegations as speculation. Watson's involvement with a Hopkins student, particularly one whose prominent family had given significant amounts of money to the university, offended the administration. The affair, combined with his very public divorce, resulted in his dismissal. In addition, "after the newspaper publicity, no university could afford to risk the inevitable public outcry by hiring Watson" (p. 129), who became an outcast from academic psychology. Paradoxically, the psychologist who was perhaps most supportive of Watson in his time of trouble was the person whose psychological school was most negatively impacted by behaviorism—Titchener (Larson & Sullivan, 1965). Watson and Rayner were married on New Year's Eve in 1920, and he began a new career in advertising.

Out of academia, Watson was confident he would be able to find employment in the business community. A friend introduced him to Stanley Resor, head of the J. Walter Thompson advertising agency, which at the time was possibly the world's largest such agency (Kreshel, 1990). Watson, who had said psychology's "goal is the prediction and control of behavior" (Watson, 1913, p. 158), now had the opportunity to apply that goal.

Initially, Watson was assigned to study the rubber boot market along the Mississippi River. Offered a permanent position with the agency, Watson entered J. Walter Thompson's rigorous training program, which was sometimes called a "University of Advertising" (Kreshel, 1990). During his training, Watson spent some time "Yubanning" (selling Yuban coffee to retailers and wholesalers) and clerking at Macy's department store in New York City.

Watson (1936) reported that after a little over a year in the agency, he "began to learn that it can be just as thrilling to watch the growth of a sales curve of a new product as to watch the learning curve of animals or men" (p. 280). He was promoted to a vice presidency in 1924 and worked at J. Walter Thompson until resigning in 1936 to become a vice president at another advertising agency, William Esty and Company. He retired from Esty in 1947.

At J. Walter Thompson, Watson became a company ambassador, standing in for Resor as a speaker at conventions and conferences (Kreshel, 1990). Watson excelled in this role: He was handsome, well educated, practiced in public speaking, and he loved the limelight (Larson, 1979). Furthermore, Watson's hiring showed the business community the Thompson agency was committed to seeking scientific solutions for marketing problems. Watson's task "was to develop campaigns of mass appeal that would create reliable markets for goods created by mass production" (Buckley, 1982, p. 211).

Watson proved adept at creating markets by applying behaviorist principles. Instead of just giving consumers product information, Watson told the advertising community that advertising's purpose was to create a society of consumers whose buying activities could be controlled, and this control could be achieved by conditioning emotional responses. Recall that Watson had concluded that the three basic emotional responses were fear, rage, and love.

Using fear, Watson created Johnson and Johnson Baby Powder ads in which pediatricians stressed the dangers of infection to infants, the "cleanliness" of baby powder and its infection-fighting properties, and the need to use the powder frequently to keep the baby well. To illustrate Watson's use of love (or sex), an ad for Pebeco toothpaste showed an enticingly dressed young woman smoking a cigarette. Although the ad implied smoking enhanced a woman's sex appeal, it also suggested her appeal would be diminished if she did not brush with Pebeco toothpaste to freshen her breath and brighten her smile.

Other techniques Watson employed effectively included using demographic information and celebrity testimonials. For example, Watson used demographic information to target young, upwardly mobile middle-class mothers as consumers of baby powder, and he employed Queen Marie of Romania to endorse Pond's cold cream. Note that celebrity testimonials take advantage of Pavlovian conditioning by pairing a product, initially a neutral stimulus, with the image of a famous person as an unconditioned stimulus. After several repetitions of the ad, the consumer presumably begins to respond to the advertised product the way he or she responds to the celebrity.

In one of Watson's few experiments after leaving academia, he studied Thompson employees and found that despite specific brand preferences, smokers could not discriminate between cigarette brands.

This reinforced Watson's belief that successful product marketing depended not on appeals to reason but on the creation of desire. Watson himself was a smoker who, according to his son, smoked about half a pack a day without inhaling. Watson smoked Lucky Strikes until he went to the William Esty Company; because Esty handled the Camel account, he dutifully switched to Camels.

Although Kreshel (1990) cited authors who concluded Watson's influence on advertising was "nothing short of phenomenal" (p. 54), Kreshel interpreted Watson's advertising career differently. According to her, many of the advertising techniques Watson supposedly originated had entered the industry long before he was employed by J. Walter Thompson. For example, testimonial advertising was first popular in the late 19th century. Kreshel concluded that "Watson was quite simply an advertising man who became very good at what he did" (p. 54).

As an advertising executive, Watson had the time and the skills needed to present his thoughts on psychology in general and on behaviorism in particular to a new, larger audience. He thereby became one of the first psychologists to package psychology in a digestible form to the general public—that is, to popularize it. From 1922 on, Watson wrote articles for such magazines as *Harper's, McCall's, Collier's,* and *Cosmopolitan.* He was well paid for the articles, which averaged about one per month, and was never rejected until he submitted what he considered a "good" article under the unappealing title, "Why I Don't Commit Suicide" (Brewer, 1991).

Behaviorism and Childrearing

Another opportunity for Watson to put his behaviorism to the test came with his and Rosalie Rayner's children. The Watsons' behavioristic childrearing approach was published as *Psychological Care of Infant and Child* in 1928 and quickly became a controversial bestseller.

Watson's work was controversial not only because of its specific recommendations, which we will explore later, but also because of developmental psychology's changing nature. As Elkind (1985) noted, the important distinction between children and adults—that is, children are not just little adults—was not fully realized until relatively modern times. Maria Montessori was one of the first to argue for this distinction.

Born into a wealthy home in Rome, **Maria Montessori** (1870–1952) was the first woman in Italy to receive a medical degree (1894). Later study in philosophy and psychology helped her better understand intellectually challenged children, and she helped found a school for retarded children in 1899. Learning from the children and pioneering many educational techniques—often credited to better-known American psychologists—Montessori developed a legacy that remains today in schools employing the Montessori Method.

Two psychologists who focused primarily on the physiological phenomena of maturation—Arnold Gesell and Leonard Carmichael—were closer rivals to Watson in child development than Montessori, however. Nearly Watson's age and with a chronologically overlapping career, Gesell was more interested in children's maturational growth processes than Watson, who, as an extreme environmentalist, was more concerned with changes occurring through learning. **Arnold Gesell** (1880–1961) received his undergraduate degree at the University of Wisconsin. There, he was influenced by Joseph Jastrow (Chapter 10) to pursue his Ph.D. under Jastrow's mentor, G. Stanley Hall, whom Gesell considered "the acknowledged genius of the group at Clark" (Gesell, 1952, p. 123). After earning his Ph.D. in 1906, Gesell had brief stints with some of American psychology's best-known researchers—Lewis Terman, Henry Goddard (both Chapter 17), and Lightner Witmer (Chapter 8)—before settling at Yale.

At Yale, Gesell founded a psychology clinic in 1911, completed his M.D. in 1915, and conducted research that established maturational standards for children. Gesell is most remembered for his contributions to the methodology used by developmental psychologists, particularly for the use of photography and one-way mirror observation.

Like Gesell, **Leonard Carmichael** (1898–1973) worked to establish the physiology of maturation. With a Harvard Ph.D., Carmichael's disparate accomplishments include the first recording of the electroencephalogram in America, being president of Yale, and work at the Smithsonian Institution and the National Geographic Society. He is probably best known in developmental psychology for his editorial work and for his writing in the *Manual of Child Psychology,* subsequently known as *Carmichael's Manual of Child Psychology.*

Watson's approach to childrearing was a harsh regimen that avoided, as much as possible, any expressions of tenderness and affection to the child. As he put it,

> A certain amount of affectionate response is socially necessary but few parents realize how easily they can overtrain the child in this direction. . . . Mothers just don't know, when they kiss their children and pick them up and rock them, caress them and jiggle them upon their knee, that they are slowly building up a human being totally unable to cope with the world it must later live in. (Watson, 1928/1972, pp. 43–44)

Watson acknowledged how parents would react to his prescription: "Once at the close of a lecture before parents, a dear old lady got up and said, 'Thank God, my children are grown—and that I had a chance to enjoy them before I met you'" (Watson, 1928/1972, p. 69). But, according to Watson, this was the attitude responsible for the unhappiness of children in general—they were too coddled, which made them whiners.

Watson and Rayner apparently practiced what they preached on their two sons, Bill and James, although Rayner may not have wholeheartedly supported strict behaviorist childrearing practices (Duke, Fried, Pliley, & Walker, 1989). However, her untimely death in 1935 (Thorne, 1998) at the age of 35 (Thorne & Watson, 1999) and the effect this had on Watson make it difficult to attribute Bill's and James's subsequent problems solely to their unemotional upbringing. Still, it is interesting to read James Watson's thoughts about the effect of his father's behavioristic principles on him.

> I have some unhappy thoughts about my upbringing, . . . about the effects of behavioristic principles on my being raised into an adult. It is difficult not to let these thoughts affect my feelings about my father. In many ways I adored him as an individual and as a character. He had a nice sense of humor. He was bright; he was charming; he was masculine, witty, and reflective. But he was also conversely unresponsive, . . . unable to express and cope with any feelings of emotion of his own, and determined unwittingly to deprive, I think, my brother and me of any kind of emotional foundation. . . . We were never kissed or held as children; we were never shown any kind of emotional closeness. (Hannush, 1987, pp. 137–138)

Bill became a psychiatrist, whereas James finished college in industrial psychology and became a successful executive with Hunt-Wesson Foods. Both brothers experienced bouts of depression; an attempted suicide sent James into psychoanalytic therapy, which he continued for several years after Bill killed himself. According to James,

> I believe [depression] happens to a lot of people who are not raised by behaviorists, but I strongly believe that strict adherence to the principles established in behaviorism, particularly as advocated in some of Dad's earlier books, tends to . . . cause a great deal of difficulty in later life. (Hannush, 1987, p. 139)

Watson's Learning Theory and the Decline of the Instinct Concept in Psychology

As illustrated in *Psychological Care of Infant and Child,* Watson was an extreme environmentalist by 1928. In fact, his ideas about learning and instinct changed during his academic career and beyond. For example, he did not incorporate Pavlovian conditioning into his view of learning until 1915, when he endorsed it wholeheartedly.

Conditioning allowed a stimulus and response to occur together so they could be associated together. Thus, Watson's central learning principle was contiguity. Watson considered Thorndike's law of effect too mentalistic, emphasizing instead repetition and recency. That is, because each learning trial ends with the animal making the correct response, it is this response that occurs most frequently. Also, because the trial ends with the successful act, the act's recency makes it likely to occur the next time the animal encounters the learning situation.

In *Behaviorism* (Watson, 1924/1970)—based on a series of lectures Watson gave at the New School for Social Research—Watson argued for a radical environmentalism in which learning rather than heredity determines behavior. *Behaviorism* contains two chapters entitled "Are there any human instincts?" Watson's answer was "There are then for us no instincts—we no longer need the term in psychology" (p. 94). As we find so often in our review of history, Watson's anti-instinct position was anticipated many years earlier. In a paper entitled "Animal Psychology" presented in 1857, Lewis Henry Morgan (1818–1881) rejected the idea of instinct as a "stupendous blunder" and a "fraud upon the animal races" (Johnston, 2002). Morgan is better known as a founder of evolutionary anthropology and a pioneering student of Native American ethnography than he is as a comparative psychologist.

Watson's (1924/1970) response to the question of human instincts implies the term was once needed by psychologists. In fact, Darwin's theory of evolution encouraged the search for inherited behavior patterns (instincts) in animal species including man, and the concept has an even earlier history (Diamond, 1971). William James (1890) defined instinct "*as the faculty of acting in such a way as to produce certain ends, without foresight of the ends, and without previous education in the performance*" (Vol. 2, p. 383, italics in the original). After listing many "special human instincts," such as hunting instinct and acquisitiveness, James concluded that humans have the greatest repertoire of instincts in the animal kingdom.

Another avid proponent of human instincts was a man who considered himself James's successor—**William McDougall** (1871–1938). After becoming a leading British psychologist, McDougall came to America in 1920 to fill the Harvard professorship created by Münsterberg's 1916 death. Unfortunately, McDougall left his experimental work behind him, except for a lengthy rat study to find evidence for or against Lamarckism (McDougall, 1930), and never became fully accepted by American psychologists. Jones (1987) concluded that one significant reason for McDougall's isolation in America may have been the negative way he was treated by the mass media of his day. Another was his inability to modify his positions to be more in tune with the behavioristic *Zeitgeist.* McDougall developed hormic psychology, a system of striving or purpose, which he contrasted vehemently with behaviorism's mechanistic approach (Krantz, Hall, & Allen, 1969).

Psychology Department, University College, London.

William McDougall (1871–1938)

McDougall accepted the chairmanship of the newly created psychology department at Duke University in 1927, where his support of **Joseph Banks Rhine**'s (1895–1980) controversial extrasensory perception research did little to enhance McDougall's image in American psychology. Unlike many other American psychologists, Rhine held McDougall in the highest esteem, telling his daughter "in serious tones that [McDougall] was the greatest man [she] would ever meet" (Feather, 1996, p. 188).

In *An Introduction to Social Psychology,* McDougall (1908) presented his theory of instincts to explain human behavior. Although his definition of psychology as the science of behavior antedated Watson's manifesto, McDougall was not a behaviorist. Instead, his outspoken opposition to mechanistic behaviorism led to a 1924 debate with Watson, which was won by Watson, according to McDougall, because the women in the audience voted overwhelmingly for his handsome opponent (Boakes, 1984).

Debate about the relative contributions to behavior of nature and nurture (e.g., instinct vs. learning, heredity vs. environment) began in earnest around 1920. One problem identified by Knight Dunlap (1919), Watson's Hopkins colleague, was a tendency to perceive the instinct labels as something more than they really were. "Having posited a 'pugnacious instinct,' for example, one writer proceeds gravely to infer that war is forever a necessity, as the expression of this 'instinct'" (p. 309). This type of inference would be justified only if the underlying psychological processes were understood, which they were not, leading Dunlap to write "for psychology there are no 'instincts'" (p. 311).

Dunlap was not opposed to the instinct concept in principle, just to the way it was then defined. **Zing Yang Kuo** (1898–1970) opposed the concept in principle, arguing that "the term *instinct* was a cloak for ignorance of the subtle behavioral changes that accompany maturation" (Blowers, 2001, p. 368). A Chinese psychologist, Kuo studied in the United States, with Edward Tolman (Chapter 13) as his dissertation advisor. Kuo (1921) wrote an influential anti-instinct paper stating that the "so-called instincts are in the last analysis acquired trends rather than inherited tendencies" (p. 648).

Kuo's environmentalism was even more extreme than Watson's, based in part on studies in which Kuo demonstrated environmental effects on purportedly inherited behaviors. For example, Kuo (1930) raised kittens under a variety of conditions to assess environmental effects on rat or mouse killing. In one study, he found most kittens raised with mothers allowed to kill rats subsequently killed rats before they were 4 months old. By contrast, kittens raised in the same cages with rats never killed their cagemates. Kuo concluded, "kittens can be made to kill a rat, to love it, to hate it, to fear it or to play with it: it depends on the life history of the kitten" (p. 34). For a look at Kuo's career in China as a politically connected university administrator, see Blowers (2001).

Archives of the History of American Psychology—The University of Akron.

Zing Yang Kuo (1898–1970)

In the final analysis, three major criticisms were leveled against the instinct concept (Krantz & Allen, 1967). First, there was a tendency for the proliferation of instincts. Whereas McDougall (1908) listed 11 basic human instincts, Angell (1908) listed 17, Warren (1919) listed 26, Woodworth (1921) listed 110, and Bernard (1921) wrote that he had collected several thousand examples before listing 14,000 different instincts that had been identified since 1900 (Bernard, 1924).

A second criticism was the use of the instinct concept to "explain" behavior, which is the **nominal fallacy.** Instinct proponents tended to attach the label to any poorly understood behavior pattern, which largely accounts for the proliferation of instincts. Often the explanation of a particular instinct became an exercise in tautology or circular reasoning. An example of circular reasoning would be the following: The reason there are so many wars is that humans are instinctively aggressive. How do we know humans are instinctively aggressive? Because there are so many wars.

The third criticism was that, with proper analysis, instincts turn out to be merely learned responses. Kuo initially advocated this view, but later his radical environmentalism led him to conclude that both instinct (heredity) *and* habit (learning) should be eliminated from psychology. The cat studies leading to his 1930 paper resulted in his earlier comment that

> [a] psychology without heredity is a psychology which proposes to do away with not only the concepts of heredity and instinct but also all their related concepts such as habit, trial and error, imitation, insight and purpose. . . . Its view is essentially passivistic in that it considers every action as a 'forced' response to be described solely in terms of the functioning of the environmental stimulation. (Kuo, 1929, p. 199)

Despite the cogency of Kuo's arguments, few were willing to go as far as he did.

By the middle of the 1930s, instinct theory had been driven out of American psychology. As McDougall (1921) realized, the instinct controversy was a disagreement between his purposive view of behavior and Watson's mechanistic paradigm. In this, as in so many areas, behaviorism carried the day but not necessarily the future. The instinct concept was successfully revived by such biologists as the 1973 Nobel Prize winners **Karl von Frisch** (1886–1982), **Niko Tinbergen** (1907–1988), and **Konrad Lorenz** (1903–1989). Von Frisch is best known for his studies of communication by "dances" in honeybees. Considered the founders of the study of animal behavior known as **ethology,** Lorenz and Tinbergen were honored for their biological explanations of behavior. Tinbergen is perhaps best known for his analysis of the reproductive behavior of the three-spined stickleback fish and other studies of instinct (e.g., Tinbergen, 1951/1969). And as many psychology texts note, Lorenz described the social attachment (learning) called imprinting and also studied such phenomena as aggression (e.g., Lorenz, 1963/1966). Actually, Lorenz's view of instinct as behavior having an innate basis but showing the effects of environmental modification was originally developed by Lloyd Morgan (Richards, 1977).

Unlike behaviorism, which often used animal models to explore general principles of learning, or comparative psychology, in which different species are contrasted on a particular phenomenon, ethologists study animal behavior for its own sake (Lyman-Henley & Henley, 2000). Typically, the focus has been instinctive, species-specific action patterns rather than learned behaviors. Also, ethologists favor naturalistic observations over controlled laboratory studies, with some major exceptions (see Dewsbury, 1992). Although it never achieved the status of behaviorism within American psychology, ethology remains a respected alternative to the study of behavior.

Watson's Influence

As one writer put it, "Second only to Freud, . . . John B. Watson is, in my judgment, the most important figure in the history of psychological thought during the first half of the century" (Bergmann, 1956, p. 265). Bergmann saw Watson as a tarnished idol, however, writing, "His social philosophy is, in my opinion, deplorable. His metaphysics is silly" (p. 266).

According to Bergmann (1956), Watson's greatest contribution was his methodological behaviorism—that is, his advocacy of psychology as an experimental, objective science free from mentalistic concepts and introspection's subjectivity. With Watson, the definition of psychology became "the scientific study of behavior." According to at least one recent psychology textbook, this "definition lasted until the 1960s, when interest in studying the mind returned and led to the current, broader definition of *psychology* as 'the science of behavior and mental processes'" (Sdorow, 1990, p. 4; see also Henley, Johnson, Herzog, & Jones, 1989).

In 1974, Mary Cover Jones captured the impact Watson had on her generation of psychologists:

> As graduate students at Columbia University, my husband, . . . myself, and other members of our student group were among those to whom Watson "sold" behaviorism. I can still remember the excitement with which we greeted Watson's (1919) *Psychology From the Standpoint of a Behaviorist.* It shook the foundations of traditional

> European-bred psychology, and we welcomed it. This was in 1919; it pointed the way from armchair psychology to action and reform and was therefore hailed as a panacea. (p. 582)

Watson's advertising career provided him a position from which he could advocate his version of psychology without academia's limitations. His popularization of psychology enhanced the public's view of the usefulness of science and particularly of the science of psychology. At the same time, his popularization of psychology brought him into disrepute within the academic community.

By 1957, the year before he died, a new generation of psychologists had forgotten (or forgiven) Watson's earlier transgressions, and his contributions were recognized by the APA's Gold Medal Award. In New York to receive the award, at the last minute Watson dispatched his eldest son to the APA convention to accept it. In gratitude for the recognition, Watson dedicated a 1958 reprint of *Behaviorism* to the members of the APA. Bergmann (1956), who saw in Watson both the good and the ill, concluded:

> Yet I have not the slightest doubt that, with all the light and all the shadow, he is a very major figure. Psychology owes him much. His place in the history of our civilization is not inconsiderable and it is secure. Such men are exceedingly rare. We ought to accept them and appreciate them for what they are. (p. 276)

CONCLUSIONS

Without exception, the major anticipators of behaviorism and the first behaviorists began their careers studying animals, which is incompatible with introspection. Because animals cannot give subjective, phenomenological reports, studying them requires an objective methodology similar to that used by physicists. Watson recognized that an objective psychology of behavior would make psychology like physics in other ways as well. Psychology would become a science in the positivistic sense of being grounded in public observations. We will have more to say about behaviorism's connections with positivism in the next chapter, but for now note that, armed with the positivist agenda, Watson took behaviorism to the leading position in American psychology that it enjoyed for over half a century.

Strongly anticipated by such elements of functionalism as Thorndike's animal research, behaviorism began with the work of Pavlov and Watson. It was grounded in a truly scientific methodology (Thorndike's trial-and-error learning, Pavlovian conditioning), and, as Thorndike's work in education and Watson's career in advertising illustrated, behaviorism could be applied outside the laboratory to affect people's lives. In the next chapter, we will continue our story of behaviorism by looking at the important behaviorists after Watson—the neobehaviorists.

SUMMARY

Behaviorism's antecedents include the mechanistic explanations of body and mind of Descartes, La Mettrie, and Cabanis, as well as Comte's philosophy of positivism. Further positivist anticipations of behaviorism came from Mach, Avenarius, and the Vienna Circle. Darwinian evolution set the stage for the animal research of George Romanes and Lloyd Morgan.

Animal Psychology

George Romanes was the pioneer of comparative psychology. He is most remembered for *Animal Intelligence,* often criticized as a collection of animal anecdotes. Actually, Romanes's problem was his tendency to interpret animal behavior in human terms.

When he was over 40, C. Lloyd Morgan began research to "get him into the animal mind." Morgan concluded from his study of newly hatched chickens that the birds learned to avoid a bad-tasting caterpillar through the Spencer-Bain principle. Supported by James Mark Baldwin, Morgan developed a theory of organic selection, which treated evolution as a process reflecting the organism's intentional relation to its environment, thus stressing the importance of mind. Morgan's Canon—do not attribute to the animal mind higher mental abilities than necessary to explain its behavior—seems to contradict his theory of organic selection. However, the interpretation of Morgan's Canon as a prohibition against Romanes's excesses needs closer examination.

Although animal psychology was a relatively small part of American psychology at the turn of the century, all of the early behaviorists began as animal researchers. Both Jacques Loeb, with his tropism concept, and H. S. Jennings were important influences on the early behaviorists, particularly Watson.

Although Edward Lee Thorndike is usually viewed as a transitional figure between functionalism and behaviorism, his animal research particularly influenced behaviorism. Thorndike tested the ability of cats to escape from puzzle boxes, finding evidence for the law of effect and the law of exercise. Although Thorndike found no evidence for reasoning in animals or for animal learning by imitation or passive tuition, he did see evidence for stimulus generalization and for learning predispositions. Thorndike's animal research overshadowed the contributions of Willard Small, who introduced the maze problem to psychology.

Comparative psychologist Robert Yerkes studied sensory ability, adaptive behavior, and instinct in invertebrates, reptiles, birds, and mammals such as rats, monkeys, and apes. After World War I, Yerkes established a Yale laboratory to study apes. This was followed by a larger facility in Orange Park, Florida, which was directed by Karl Lashley after Yerkes's retirement. Yerkes is also remembered for the Yerkes-Dodson law.

Objective Psychology in Russia

Ivan Sechenov studied with such outstanding European physiologists as Müller, du Bois-Reymond, Helmholtz, and Bernard. In his research, Sechenov found support for Eduard Weber's suggestion that brain stimulation might inhibit reflex activity, and in *Reflexes of the Brain,* Sechenov asserted that the brain is a center for organizing reflexes.

Physiologist Ivan Pavlov won a 1904 Nobel Prize for his research on the digestive processes in the dog. Along the way, he became interested in salivary responses to novel stimuli. For the rest of his career, Pavlov studied the conditioned reflex.

Pavlov and his coworkers studied such learning phenomena as extinction, higher-order conditioning, stimulus generalization, discrimination, and experimental neurosis. Pavlov believed his dogs had different personality types, which were important for ease of conditioning and for mental illness. Pavlov's conditioned reflex became an important part of behaviorism's methodology.

Throughout his career, Vladimir Bekhterev was more of a psychiatrist than a physiologist. Like Pavlov, Bekhterev thought a study of conditioned reflexes was the key to the scientific study of the mind. The advocate of an objective psychology he called reflexology, Bekhterev was also a founder of clinics, laboratories, institutes, and journals.

John Broadus Watson

Staying at Chicago after he earned his Ph.D., Watson established an animal laboratory, where his studies included the cues rats use in learning a maze. In 1908, he went to Johns Hopkins as professor and director of the psychological laboratory.

From his position as leader of the Hopkins psychology department and editor of *Psychological Review,* Watson began behaviorism with the article "Psychology as the Behaviorist Views It." The article called for discarding the introspective method and the study of human consciousness and advocated the objective study of behavior.

After World War I, Watson continued studying human infants at Phipps Psychiatric Clinic. With Rosalie Rayner, he demonstrated the conditioning of a fear response in Little Albert. Later, Mary Cover Jones, with Watson's advice, developed techniques for removing an abnormal fear response from a child named Peter. Peter was most successfully treated with a counterconditioning method similar to one suggested by John Locke.

In 1920, Watson's affair with Rosalie Rayner resulted in his divorce and forced resignation from Johns Hopkins. After marrying Rayner, Watson worked in advertising, where he demonstrated that behaviorism could be applied to real-world situations. Another application of behaviorism's principles that Watson presented in *Psychological Care of Infant and Child* was less successful.

Watson's central learning principle was contiguity, and in *Behaviorism,* he argued for a radical environmentalism, denying the existence of human instincts. Watson's instinct position was consistent with that of most psychologists by the 1930s, due in part to the work of Zing Yang Kuo. Ethologists such as Lorenz, Tinbergen, and von Frisch developed an alternative approach to the study of instincts in animal behavior.

Watson's most important contribution was probably his advocacy of psychology as an experimental, objective science free from mentalism and the introspective method. For the next 40 years after Watson, the definition of psychology became "the study of behavior."

CONNECTIONS QUESTIONS

1. How is behaviorism connected to the 19th-century *Zeitgeist*? Specifically, what connections can you make between behaviorism and Darwin's theory of evolution? Between behaviorism and logical positivism?
2. How would you connect the following to behaviorism: Aristotle, La Mettrie, Locke, Darwin, Romanes, Morgan, Loeb, and Yerkes?
3. How is the disagreement between Pavlov and Snarsky connected with Pavlov's importance for behaviorism?
4. What are the connections between American functionalism and American behaviorism?
5. Connect Watson's mechanistic behaviorism with the decline of the instinct concept in American psychology. How is Kuo's research connected to this decline?
6. Sechenov and Watson held extreme environmentalist views. Contrast their views with Galton's ideas on heredity.
7. Describe the context in which Romanes collected his animal anecdotes and critique his interpretations. Have you been guilty of similar interpretations of the behavior of your own pets? How was Morgan's Canon designed to prevent extravagant interpretations of animal rationality?

KEY NAMES AND TERMS

backward conditioning (p. 332)
behaviorism (p. 314)
Vladimir Mikhailovich Bekhterev (p. 336)
Leonard Carmichael (p. 345)
conditioned discrimination (p. 333)
conditioned response (CR) (p. 332)
conditioned stimulus (CS) (p. 332)
delayed conditioning (p. 332)
disinhibition (p. 332)
Henry H. Donaldson (p. 338)
Knight Dunlap (p. 339)
ethology (p. 349)
experimental neurosis (p. 333)
extinction (p. 332)
first-signal system (p. 332)
John Garcia (p. 322)
Arnold Gesell (p. 345)
higher-order conditioning (p. 332)
Herbert Spencer Jennings (p. 318)
Mary Cover Jones (p. 343)
Zing Yang Kuo (p. 348)
law of effect (p. 321)
law of exercise (p. 321)
learning predispositions (p. 322)
Little Albert (p. 341)
Jacques Loeb (p. 318)
Konrad Lorenz (p. 349)
William McDougall (p. 347)
Gregor Johann Mendel (p. 316)
Adolf Meyer (p. 340)
Maria Montessori (p. 345)
Conwy Lloyd Morgan (p. 316)
Morgan's Canon (p. 317)
nominal fallacy (p. 348)
Ivan Petrovich Pavlov (p. 327)
puzzle boxes (p. 319)
reflexology (p. 337)
Robert A. Rescorla (p. 335)
Joseph Banks Rhine (p. 347)
George John Romanes (p. 315)
Ivan Mikhailovich Sechenov (p. 325)
second-signal system (p. 332)
simultaneous conditioning (p. 332)
Willard Stanton Small (p. 323)
spontaneous recovery (p. 332)
stimulus generalization (p. 322)
stimulus-response (S-R) learning (p. 320)
Niko Tinbergen (p. 349)
trace conditioning (p. 332)
tropisms (p. 318)
Edwin Burket Twitmyer (p. 330)
unconditioned response (UCR) (p. 332)
unconditioned stimulus (UCS) (p. 332)
Karl von Frisch (p. 349)
John Broadus Watson (p. 337)
Robert Mearns Yerkes (p. 323)
Yerkes-Dodson law (p. 325)

SUGGESTED READINGS

Babkin, B. P. (1949). *Pavlov: A biography.* Chicago: The University of Chicago Press. Boris Babkin was a student and long-time friend and associate of Pavlov. Although obviously sympathetic to his subject, Babkin's book provides a balanced consideration of Pavlov's personality, temperament, and work.

Brewer, C. L. (1991). Perspectives on John B. Watson. In G. A. Kimble, M. Wertheimer, & C. White (Eds.), *Portraits of pioneers in psychology* (pp. 170–186). Hillsdale, NJ: Lawrence Erlbaum Associates, Publishers. Charles Brewer, a professor at Watson's alma mater, Furman University, is an expert on Watson. His chapter contains background material on Watson not found in other sources.

Buckley, K. W. (1989). *Mechanical man: John Broadus Watson and the beginnings of behaviorism.* New York: The Guilford Press. Buckley's definitive biography is an interesting account of the life, times, and contributions to psychology of a man who was ultimately more successful in his careers than in his personal life.

Gray, J. A. (1979). *Ivan Pavlov.* New York: Viking Press. Gray's biography is a brief, highly readable account of the context and contributions of one of the world's foremost scientists.

Morgan, C. L. (1932). C. Lloyd Morgan. In C. Murchison (Ed.), *A history of psychology in autobiography* (Vol. 2, pp. 237–264). Worcester, MA: Clark University Press. Morgan's autobiographical account is readable and entertaining, whereas his psychology is worthwhile but will require careful reading in order to be fully grasped.

Pavlov, I. P. (1960). *Conditioned reflexes: An investigation of the physiological activity of the cerebral cortex.* New York: Dover Publications, Inc. (Original work published 1927)

Pavlov, I. P. (1928). *Lectures on conditioned reflexes.* New York: International Publishers. These are the two classical collections of Pavlov's work. The writing (or the translation) is straightforward and easily understandable. The detail and care with which Pavlov and his associates made their observations is evident.

Romanes, E. (1896). *The life and letters of George John Romanes.* London: Longmans, Green, and Co.

Romanes, G. J. (1895). *Animal intelligence.* New York: D. Appleton and Company. (Original work published 1881) *The life and letters of George John Romanes* is a readable and very sympathetic account of the brief life of Romanes, edited and written by his wife. Before condemning Romanes as the quintessential anecdotalist, be sure to read this book and *Animal Intelligence,* Romanes's most famous work.

Thorndike, E. L. (1911). *Animal intelligence.* New York: The Macmillan Co. Any career devoted to the study of animal learning should begin with a careful reading of this book. The brashness and self-confidence of the young Thorndike is obvious, and it is also apparent why so many animal researchers of the period were offended. Thorndike's dissertation, included in this work, can still provide insight into the animal "mind" more than a century after its publication.

Watson, J. B. (1913). Psychology as the behaviorist views it. *Psychological Review, 20,* 158–177. Watson's "behaviorist manifesto" is still must reading for the student of the schools of psychology.

Watson, J. B. (1919). *Psychology from the standpoint of a behaviorist.* Philadelphia: Lippincott.

Watson, J. B. (1970). *Behaviorism.* New York: Norton. (Original work published 1924) These are two of Watson's best-known books. The first was written while Watson was still in academia, and, as Mary Cover Jones wrote, it "shook the foundations of European-bred psychology." *Behaviorism* was written after Watson had become a successful advertising executive, and it is pitched at a wider audience than its predecessor. Reprinted editions are readily available.

Watson, J. B. (1936). John Broadus Watson. In C. Murchison (Ed.), *A history of psychology in autobiography* (Vol. 3, pp. 271–281). Worcester, MA: Clark University Press.

Yerkes, R. M. (1932). Robert Mearns Yerkes: Psychobiologist. In C. Murchison (Ed.), *A history of psychology in autobiography* (Vol. 2, pp. 381–407). Worcester, MA: Clark University Press. The autobiographical essays in *A History of Psychology in Autobiography* are often fascinating. Watson's essay is particularly intriguing because of its terseness and its generally negative tone.

Neobehaviorism

CHAPTER 13

Edward Chace Tolman
Eleanor Gibson
J. R. Kantor
Roger Barker
B. F. Skinner
J. J. Gibson
Kenneth Spence
O. H. Mowrer
Neal Miller
Edwin Guthrie
Clark Hull

1875 1885 1895 1905 1915 1925 1935

The world's first birth control clinic opens in Amsterdam

Montana becomes a state

Ford Motor Company is founded

Bertrand Russell publishes *Introduction to Mathematical Philosophy*

Woodrow Wilson's "14 points for world peace" (close of WWI)

Robert Frost flourishes

OUTLINE

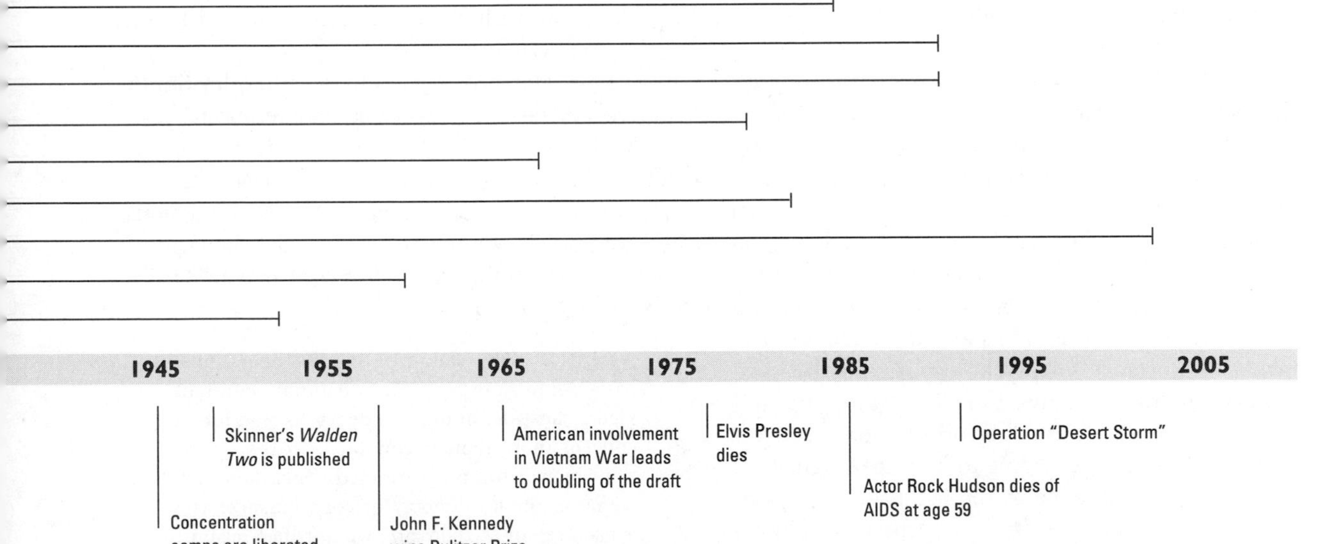
1945
1955
1965
1975
1985
1995
2005
Concentration camps are liberated (close of WWII)
Skinner's *Walden Two* is published
John F. Kennedy wins Pulitzer Prize
American involvement in Vietnam War leads to doubling of the draft
Elvis Presley dies
Actor Rock Hudson dies of AIDS at age 59
Operation "Desert Storm"

"For a while in the 1920s it seemed as if all America had gone behaviorist. Everyone . . . was a behaviorist and no behaviorist agreed with any other" (Boring, 1950, p. 645). Although behaviorism became American psychology's predominant and relatively unchallenged paradigm for more than 50 years, there were many versions of it (see O'Neil, 1995). Our interest in this introduction will be in what made behaviorism so dominant, and in the body of the chapter, we will examine its most important versions.

In general, behaviorism was the culmination of a line of influences that led to an emphasis on a strongly objective, rigorously experimental psychology. Accordingly, the empirical tradition of Locke and Hume (Chapter 5) represents one early influence, with later influences coming from Darwinian evolutionary theory (Chapter 9) and American functionalism (Chapters 10 and 11).

Additional influences came from the positivism of people like Avenarius and Mach (Chapter 5) and from the later positivism of the Vienna Circle, whose chief members were Carnap, Schlick (both Chapter 5), and Feigl. Herbert Feigl, with a 1927 Ph.D. in philosophy from the University of Vienna, used the term *logical positivism* to describe the Vienna Circle's position and to differentiate it from earlier positivism. Logical positivism held that all of science's assertions should be analyzed, and only assertions that can be verified empirically, or are connected logically to verifiable assertions, are meaningful.

Mentioned in Chapter 5, German-born **Rudolph Carnap** (1891–1970) taught in Vienna and Prague before coming to the United States in 1936, where he worked first at the University of Chicago and then at UCLA from 1954 until his death. Carnap proposed that philosophy's proper task is logical analysis, which would be applied to all scientific assertions to clarify the sense of each statement and to illuminate how the claims are connected. Of particular importance for psychology, Carnap believed that psychological propositions belong to empirical science just as surely as do the propositions of chemistry and biology. According to him, the language of psychology is reducible to the language of physics; psychology would become an aspect of physics because all science would ultimately reduce to physics. This concept of the reduction of all science to physics is an aspect of the logical positivist's plan for the *unity of science*—the idea that the sciences are all fundamentally similar in that they use the same methods and have the same goals.

Simultaneously with the formation of the Vienna Circle, a general approach to science with its roots in positivism was introduced to physics, always psychology's model science, by **Percy Williams Bridgman** (1882–1961). Bridgman was born in Cambridge, Massachusetts, and educated at Harvard, where he became professor of mathematics and physics in 1919. Bridgman won the Nobel Prize in physics in 1946. In *The Logic of Modern Physics,* Bridgman (1927) argued for **operationism,** which states that scientific concepts should be defined by the operations used to measure them. To illustrate an **operational definition** in psychology, hunger can be defined as the length of time since the last meal or as the number of calories consumed in a meal—that is, by the operations used to measure hunger.

With operationism, concepts that cannot be tested by observation are pointless, and operational definitions should permit psychology to discard questions that are unanswerable by any available observational tests. Thus, the notion of private conscious experience is operationally meaningless. A number of psychologists had taken this view of the study of consciousness by the time Bridgman's book appeared, which meant that Bridgman's call for operationism in science fell on fertile grounds in psychology.

In 1935, Harvard psychophysicist **Stanley Smith Stevens** (1906–1973) advocated an operational basis for psychology, and by the end of the decade, operationism had swept the field. According to Stevens, "[operationism] insures us against hazy, ambiguous and contradictory notions and provides the rigor of definition which silences useless controversy" (1935, p. 323). He concluded,

> with psychology stabilized on the operational basis, we must expect still to maintain constant vigil against the human tendency to read into a concept more than is contained in the operations by which it is determined. Only then shall we never think of energy or consciousness as a substance; only then are we fortified against meaningless concepts. (p. 330)

For Stevens, operationism would make psychology an undisputed natural science, and thus it would fit into the plan of the logical positivists for the unity of science.

Consistent with behaviorism's aims, operationism's acceptance by psychology aided behaviorism's domination. As were most psychologists of the period, this chapter's major psychologists were philosophically attuned to logical positivism and operationism. Because their main contributions came after Watson's, they are, by definition, neobehaviorists. In reviewing the neobehaviorists' psychologies, we will see that neobehaviorism is nearly synonymous with learning theory. The reason is that behaviorists studied behavior, which they assumed, following Watson and the abandonment of the instinct concept (Chapter 12), to be learned. If behavior is learned, then a theory of behavior will also be a theory of learning. We will first consider Edwin Guthrie's learning theory, as it is more similar to Watson's (and Pavlovian conditioning) than the others.

Archives of the History of American Psychology – The University of Akron.

Edwin Ray Guthrie (1886–1959)

EDWIN RAY GUTHRIE

Edwin Ray Guthrie (1886–1959) was born in Lincoln, Nebraska, the oldest of five children. Guthrie's father was a minister's son who operated a Lincoln piano store; his mother had taught school before her marriage, and Guthrie acquired "the efficient work habits that he exhibited all his life" (Prenzel-Guthrie, 1996, p. 138) from her.

Guthrie demonstrated exceptional scholastic ability early, and he read Darwin's *Origin of Species* and *Expression of the Emotions* while just in the eighth grade. In fact, his high school senior thesis was so insightful the principal interviewed him to be sure it was not plagiarized.

Guthrie entered the University of Nebraska in 1903, majoring in mathematics with an interest in philosophy. In 1907, he received the bachelor's degree in mathematics and philosophy with Phi Beta Kappa honors, having taken only a general course in psychology during his 4-year program.

Guthrie continued his education as a graduate student at the University of Nebraska, changing his major to philosophy, and he earned his master's degree in 1910. Guthrie's master's program included psychology courses from **Harry Kirke Wolfe** (1858–1918), one of Wundt's early Ph.D. students. Wolfe was also the high school principal who interviewed Guthrie about his senior thesis, having served at several high schools during a period when he had been terminated from the University of Nebraska in a "debate over his orthodoxy." As the only student in one of his courses with Wolfe, Guthrie (1959) later recalled that Wolfe's "views on the philosophy of science were of great interest" (p. 160).

Guthrie's readings at Nebraska were all philosophical, and he wrote, "Mach and Avenarius were later read with that same conviction that had accompanied reading Darwin's *Origin of Species* and his *Expression of the Emotions* . . ." (Guthrie, 1959, p. 160). Thus, Guthrie, like many others, was strongly influenced by twin aspects of the era's *Zeitgeist*—evolution and positivism.

Guthrie went to the University of Pennsylvania in 1910 to work on his Ph.D. Still a philosopher, his dissertation dealt with symbolic logic and Nobel Prize–winning philosopher **Bertrand Russell**'s (1872–1970) paradoxes—propositions whose truth implies their falsity, and vice versa. An example is the statement "This proposition is false."

Earning his Ph.D. in 1912, Guthrie taught high school mathematics until he was appointed as an instructor in the philosophy department at the University of Washington in 1914. In 1919, Guthrie changed to the department of psychology, where he remained until he became dean of the graduate school in 1943. After attaining emeritus status in 1951, Guthrie continued to teach and participate in university affairs until he retired in 1956 (Sheffield, 1959).

At the end of his life, Guthrie wrote that his "chief interest lay in undergraduate teaching, a fact that probably accounts for a strong bent toward simplification which, with some justification, has been described as oversimplification" (Guthrie, 1959, p. 161). In fact, simplicity is the hallmark of Guthrie's learning theory.

One-Trial, Nonreinforcement, Contiguity Learning

Like Watson, Guthrie adopted one main principle for his learning theory—contiguity. As Guthrie noted (Guthrie, 1952), the law of association by contiguity has been a key feature of the learning theories of Berkeley, Hume, James Mill, Hartley, Bain (all Chapter 5), and James (Chapter 10), to list only a few. Guthrie's formal statement of the contiguity principle was: "*A combination of stimuli which has accompanied a movement will on its recurrence tend to be followed by that movement*" (p. 23, italics in the original). Note there is nothing about association requiring "satisfiers," or reward, or pleasant effects. Guthrie explicitly rejected Thorndike's law of effect as a necessary condition for learning.

Guthrie's point was that an organism will tend to do in a situation whatever it did when it was last in the situation. However, a problem quickly arises: Which of the many things an organism actually does will it tend to repeat? Guthrie's answer is simple: The response that will tend to be repeated is the very last one made previously. For example, suppose you are trying to solve a mechanical puzzle. After many erroneous responses, you finally select one that works. The next time you attempt the puzzle, Guthrie's theory predicts, you will perform the response that solved it previously—that is, the last thing you did earlier.

Again, this sounds like one of Watson's ideas, the recency principle. Guthrie disagreed with Watson's frequency principle, however. Although Watson considered learning as the formation of stimulus-response connections that strengthen with practice (frequency), Guthrie saw the bonds as all-or-none. A movement becomes attached to a stimulus situation on the first occasion of its pairing either completely or not at all, and the bond's strength does not change with practice.

But this idea seemingly violates common sense. If practice does not produce gradual improvement, why else would you spend so much time on the putting green or solving a particular type of math problem? How can all-or-none learning be involved in learning to ride a bicycle or drive a car?

We need to reconsider Guthrie's definition of contiguity: "A combination of stimuli which has accompanied a *movement* will on its recurrence tend to be followed by that *movement*." Guthrie differentiated movements from acts, a movement being a small unit of behavior such as the contraction of particular muscles, whereas an act is a larger unit consisting of many movements. We tend to think of learning occurring on the level of acts—for example, the act of successfully making a 15-foot putt—when what is learned on each practice putt is to make a specific set of muscle movements in response to the specific set of stimuli in effect on that particular stroke. Guthrie's differentiation of an act from the movements comprising it accounts for how performance improves with practice (repetition, frequency) at the same time it allows one-trial learning. Learning a particular movement to a specific set of stimuli occurs in one trial, but the act—for example, making a 15-foot putt—requires many trials for mastery because it consists of many movements.

Like Watson, Guthrie often wrote of human behavior as a mechanical affair. For him, behavior was tightly controlled by stimuli, and the changes in the S-R connections occurred through simple mechanical laws. However, unlike Watson, Guthrie admitted to concepts like desire and purpose, recognizing that much behavior is goal directed. Guthrie interpreted such concepts in terms of actual movements that may be too minute to be readily detected. He particularly emphasized **movement-produced stimuli**—sensations produced by the movements themselves—in maintaining sequential responding. For example, each movement of a rat running a maze produces a stimulus for the animal's next movement, which produces another stimulus, and so on. These movement-produced stimuli are also important in thought (remember Watson's subvocal speech), and in producing trains of responding leading to stimuli that are not present.

As we indicated, Guthrie did not consider reinforcement necessary for the S-R bond. For Guthrie, reinforcement changed the stimulus situation, thereby protecting the S-R bond between a stimulus situation and the last movement before the reinforcement.

Consider a hungry rat in a T-maze. The rat ambles down the long part of the T, comes to the crossing alley, turns right, and discovers food at the end of the alley. The reinforcement stops the rat's movement and changes the situation so that the last behavior before the food was located (turning right on the T) is the last thing done and thus is the movement learned. "*What encountering the food does is not to intensify a previous item of behavior but to protect that item from being unlearned*" (Guthrie, 1940, p. 144, italics in the original).

Guthrie's definition of reinforcement leads to testable predictions. For example, consider a hungry rat that presses a bar to receive tiny food pellets. Guthrie would say that receiving a food pellet changes the situation in the box, and the rat becomes increasingly likely to press the bar because this is the last thing it does before receiving the food. However, simply removing the rat after each bar press changes the stimulus conditions even more dramatically than giving the rat a food pellet. If reinforcement is simply a matter of changing the stimulus conditions, then removing the rat should also increase the probability of the rat's pressing the bar.

Seward (1942) found that rats that received food were much more likely to press the bar than rats taken from the box. Although this and similar results appear to cast doubt on Guthrie's definition of reinforcement, there are other possible explanations for this study that may save Guthrie. Remember that the animals were hungry. In this case, hunger produces and maintains movement. Thus, removing the rat from the box each time it presses the bar does not change the rat's internal state, because the animal is at least as hungry as it was before being removed. Therefore, pressing the bar is never connected with a change in the stimulus situation that matters to the animal—its internal state of hunger.

Note that the rat's hunger drive also has not been removed by eating the tiny food pellet. As Guthrie (1939) put it,

> The rat at the end of the maze may be given only a small pellet of food, not enough to put an end to the state of hunger which made him restless, but enough to cause the rat to stop and eat. (p. 482)

Another interpretation of Seward's (1942) experiment compatible with Guthrie's theory is that removing the rat was punishment rather than reinforcement. For Guthrie, a punisher was a stimulus that triggers new behaviors incompatible with what was last done in the stimulus situation. "It is what the punishment makes the [animal] *do* that counts or what it makes a man do, not what it makes him feel" (Guthrie, 1934a, p. 458, italics in the original).

Because Guthrie did not believe reinforcement strengthens S-R bonds, he explained the extinction of the conditioned response that occurs with reinforcement removal by arguing that the organism has learned to do something else. Similarly, Guthrie's interpretation of forgetting was that habits do not fade away with disuse or lack of practice—they are replaced by other habits. In this interference theory (Chapter 8), forgetting occurs because new learning interferes with previous learning, or vice versa.

Although it is one thing to confound your critics with reason, it is quite another to provide experimental evidence for your theory, and this is why the 50-year-old Guthrie embarked on a lengthy study with a colleague, George P. Horton. The result was published in 1946 as *Cats in a Puzzle Box.*

Cats in a Puzzle Box

Like Thorndike, Guthrie and Horton (1946) put cats individually into puzzle boxes and watched them escape. Unlike Thorndike, they were interested in the cats' escape movements, not just in whether escape occurred and how long it took. Thorndike believed his cat experiments revealed a learning curve showing a gradual decline in escape latencies, which is accompanied by a slow increase in the strength of the association between the stimulus situation and the successful response.

By contrast, Guthrie sought evidence for one-trial learning, which he believed would be shown by a stereotyping of behavior. Assuming the cat learns the last thing it did in the puzzle box, then it should precisely repeat on subsequent trials the movements that freed it. Guthrie and Horton constructed a puzzle box that enabled them to observe all the animal's movements, as well as allowing them to photograph the successful movement and to record all behavior with a movie camera.

In the puzzle box, there was either a post on the floor or a tube hanging from the ceiling. Contact with this post or tube released the front door and simultaneously triggered a camera, which photographed the cat's last response before being freed. Guthrie and Horton found striking evidence for stereotyped behavior, and Guthrie (1952) reported that what happens on each trial/escape from the box—one association—differs from what Thorndike thought happened. Instead, in its wanderings on each trial, the animal establishes many associations that are subsequently replaced by others. The "escape routine, the essential movements of escape, are repeated because they remove the cat from the puzzle box and, being removed, *no new associations with the puzzle-box situation are possible*" (p. 270, italics in the original).

However, rather than observing learning in the cat, what Guthrie and Horton (1946) may have watched was the cats' species-typical "greeting" reaction of rubbing. Using a similar apparatus and procedure, Moore and Stuttard (1979) reported, "When we watched unobtrusively, the reaction did not occur; but when we were visible [as Guthrie and Horton were], the animals rubbed heads, flanks, or tails against the (convenient) vertical rod" (p. 1032). Further, Moore and Stuttard found the food reward was irrelevant, as naive, unrewarded animals performed the same rubbing motions in response to a human observer entering the room.

Guthrie was interested in demonstrating his theory through real problems of real people, not just in how well the model predicted the behavior of cats in boxes. One illustration of this application can be seen in Guthrie's methods for changing habits.

Guthrie's Methods for Breaking Habits

The key to Guthrie's methods for breaking habits is that they are designed to produce a new behavior in the old situation. For example, if the old stimulus situation (e.g., the end of a meal) results in smoking a cigarette, the person trying to "kick the habit" should do something else instead (e.g., eat a piece of fruit). Unfortunately, this does not always work.

> I once had a caller to whom I was explaining that the apple I had just finished was a splendid device for avoiding a smoke. The caller pointed out that I was smoking at that moment. The habit of lighting a cigarette was so attached to the finish of eating that smoking had been started automatically. (Guthrie, 1952, p. 116)

The success of Guthrie's methods in breaking habits has resulted in their being adopted by behavior therapists, who usually do not acknowledge their source. One example is the fatigue or exhaustion method.

The **fatigue** or **exhaustion method** is the typical technique used for breaking horses in which an experienced "horsebreaker" saddles, bridles, and mounts the horse, staying aboard while the horse bucks until it is too exhausted to struggle any more. At this point, the horse has learned a new habit to replace the old habit of bucking to the weight of a rider on its back.

Using the exhaustion method, a person who wants to quit smoking enters a small room and chain smokes until he or she exhausts the urge for another cigarette. Of course, nausea may occur, which leads to behavior incompatible with further smoking.

In Chapter 12, we discussed the case of Peter, who had a fear of white rabbits and rats. Mary Cover Jones cured Peter of his fear by exposing the child gradually to the rabbit. In the **toleration** or **threshold method,** cues that trigger the behavior are presented at such a low level that the response does not occur. Then the stimuli are gradually increased, and the threshold for triggering the response is raised.

In the method of **incompatible stimuli,** the stimulus for the behavior we want to remove is presented when other aspects of the situation will prevent the response. Guthrie illustrated the method with a college student who is unable to read in the bustle of the library. If the student starts by reading a book so interesting it absorbs her full attention, she will quickly become used to the ambient noise and later will be able to read study material without being distracted. The response of looking up from her reading has been inhibited by the engrossing nature of what she is reading, which results in the cues of the library sounds becoming associated with the response of not looking up.

Guthrie and Pavlov: The Reply of a Psychologist to a Physiologist

Guthrie took a simple idea with a basis in antiquity—that learning occurs through stimulus-response contiguity—and derived from it an important learning theory. Retaining the practical, useful flavor of Thorndike, Guthrie's theory used Pavlov's terminology but not the conditioned reflex itself. Guthrie (1930) reinterpreted 10 "established facts of learning" in light of his contiguity conditioning theory. In the paper, he carefully distinguished his conditioning theory of learning and Pavlov's theory of learning through conditioned reflexes. Not surprisingly, Guthrie concluded that all the main characteristics of learning could be understood as examples of conditioning by contiguity.

Pavlov (Chapter 12) was so disturbed at what he perceived as attacks from American behaviorists (Guthrie and Lashley) that he wrote his only article for an American psychological journal (Pavlov, 1932). He began by attacking Guthrie, primarily for not recognizing the need to analyze conditioning and conditioned reflexes further. The physiologist and the psychologist differ in their approaches, with the psychologist using deduction from logic without verifying by experiment and the physiologist analyzing through investigation every step of the way.

Guthrie (1934b) acknowledged that Pavlov's characterization of the difference between the physiologist and the psychologist was "substantially correct." Guthrie *was* interested in "painting with a broad brush." He discussed each of Pavlov's objections, concluding,

> It is evident that the differences between us do not concern Pavlov's laboratory findings. . . . Our differences concern a strong tendency found throughout Pavlov's reports to interpret the facts in terms of [counterfeit] events and states in the cortex. These events and states are not the characteristics of nerve conduction . . . directly demonstrable in the laboratory. (p. 205)

As we noted, Pavlov's theory of nervous activity in conditioning did include mechanisms that were problematic in light of then-current knowledge of cortical function. Guthrie's reply ended the exchange.

Guthrie's Influence

The simplicity of Guthrie's learning theory elicited both criticism and praise. The praise has come from psychologists who prefer parsimonious theories; with its one main principle, Guthrie's theory is elegant in its simplicity. Praise has also come from psychologists who dislike jargon. As many have noted (e.g., Bower & Hilgard, 1981; Sheffield, 1959), Guthrie masterfully used anecdote and simple terms to illustrate complex theoretical ideas.

But the theory's simplicity has also led to complaints of incompleteness and vagueness. Another valid criticism is that Guthrie often relied on his anecdotes to demonstrate his ideas rather than performing controlled experiments. Recall that Guthrie's sole research test of his theory came in his study of stereotypy in cats learning to escape a puzzle box (Guthrie & Horton, 1946). The quality of Guthrie's anecdotes was such that he often succeeded in convincing his readers of the validity of the point he was making. For example, Skinner-trained **William K. Estes** (1919–) found Guthrie's theory so compelling he developed a statistical learning theory based on contiguity (Chapter 17). For his efforts, Estes received the National Medal of Science in 1997.

Guthrie's influence extended beyond learning theory with the publication of *The Psychology of Human Conflict* (Guthrie, 1938). Guthrie acknowledged his debt to Pierre Janet's writings (Chapter 15), and, in fact, he and his wife (Helen Macdonald Guthrie) had earlier translated Janet's *Principles of Psychotherapy. Human Conflict* "was not too well received in some quarters, perhaps because it favored Janet over Freud and took a generally critical attitude toward psychoanalysis" (Sheffield, 1959, p. 646). In addition, Guthrie's influence in abnormal psychology can be seen in the adoption by behavior therapists of many of his suggestions for breaking bad habits.

Guthrie's honors included being elected APA president in 1945 and receiving an honorary doctorate from the University of Nebraska the same year. In 1958, Guthrie was given the American Psychological Foundation's Gold Medal Award for his contributions to the science of learning. The University of Washington honored Guthrie in 1956 by naming a building after him.

Archives of the History of American Psychology – The University of Akron.

Edward Tolman (1886–1959) in about 1911, the year he graduated from MIT

EDWARD CHACE TOLMAN

Edward Chace Tolman (1886–1959) was born in Newton, Massachusetts, the son of the president of a manufacturing company and "a warm, loving, but in some areas Puritanical mother . . ." (Tolman, 1952, p. 324). Bowing to family pressure, Tolman followed his older brother to the Massachusetts Institute of Technology, where he received a B.S. in electrochemistry in 1911. After reading some William James (Chapter 10) in his senior year, Tolman decided to be a philosopher, and he enrolled in summer school at Harvard planning to become one.

That summer, Tolman took a course in philosophy taught by **Ralph Barton Perry** (1876–1957) and a course in psychology taught by Robert Yerkes (Chapter 12). Perry's course convinced him he was not bright enough to become a philosopher, and psychology seemed a good compromise between philosophy and science. Tolman also acknowledged that Perry's course "laid the basis for my later interest in motivation and . . . gave me the main concepts . . . which I have retained ever since . . ." (Tolman, 1952, p. 325). Perry's attitudes toward Watsonian behaviorism were also influential, as he welcomed Watson's methodological objectivity but rejected Watson's reductionism. Anticipating the importance of purpose in Tolman's behaviorism, Perry (1918) suggested a learning process in which purpose was "significantly applicable."

With only the two summer courses as background, Tolman enrolled at Harvard in 1911 in the joint department of philosophy and psychology. Tolman's graduate research experience held a dilemma: On the one hand, Münsterberg (Chapter 8), who nominally directed the laboratory, often made opening speeches to the students in which he claimed introspection was *the* method of psychology. On the other hand, most of the laboratory's research—supervised by Langfeld (Chapter 10)—was quite objective. "If introspection were 'the' method of psychology and we weren't doing it, shouldn't I really go to Cornell where Titchener taught one to do it properly?" (Tolman, 1952, p. 326).

Tolman's conflict was resolved by Yerkes's comparative psychology course, which introduced Tolman to Watson's behaviorism. Watson's idea that psychology's true method was the objective measurement of behavior and not introspection came as a great relief to Tolman.

After his first Harvard year, Tolman went to Germany for the summer to practice the language in preparation for the required Ph.D. examination. Tolman spent part of the summer in Giessen with Kurt Koffka, the Gestalt psychologist (Chapter 14), and this made him receptive to Gestalt concepts when they became widely available to American psychology after World War I. In 1923, Tolman returned to Giessen to learn more from Koffka.

Tolman received his Harvard Ph.D. in 1915 and took an instructorship at Northwestern University in Illinois. There, he was "self-conscious and inarticulate, and was afraid of my classes" (Tolman, 1952, p. 327), and he was dismissed in 1918 because of "war retrenchment and my not too successful teaching" (p. 327). Tolman's avowed pacifism—his mother had grown up in the Quaker tradition—may also have been involved in his dismissal. With Langfeld's aid, Tolman obtained an instructorship at the University of California at Berkeley, where he spent the rest of his career.

Arriving at Berkeley, Tolman learned it was up to him to suggest a new course. "Remembering Yerkes' course and Watson's textbook I proposed 'comparative psychology.' And it was this that finally launched me down the behavioristic slope" (Tolman, 1952, p. 329).

Purposive Behaviorism

Unlike Guthrie, Tolman relished laboratory research, particularly with rats and mazes. In fact, it can be argued that Tolman thought of the world as a giant maze (Smith, 1990), and he built mazes and used them and his rats to test key elements of the learning theories of Watson and Thorndike and later, Hull.

As a behaviorist, Tolman was concerned with objective behavior—not with conscious experience—and with the effect of external stimuli on behavior. However, unlike Watson and Guthrie, Tolman was little interested in molecular behavior, behavior analyzed into single movements of individual muscles. Instead, he studied molar behavior, or behavior considered in large units—for example, Guthrie's acts. Examples included

> A rat running a maze; . . . a man driving home to dinner; . . . my friend and I telling one another our thoughts and feelings—*these are behaviors* (qua [as] *molar*). And it must be noted that in mentioning no one of them have we referred to, or . . . even known what were the exact muscles and glands, sensory nerves, and motor nerves involved. (Tolman, 1932/1967, p. 8, italics in the original)

In addition, Tolman stressed the relation of behavior toward goals, recognizing that much behavior is concerned with a search for a goal. In other words, behavior has a purpose, and Tolman's brand of behaviorism has been called "**purposive behaviorism.**" In fact, Tolman (1932/1967) titled his most important statement of his system *Purposive Behavior in Animals and Men* and dedicated it to M.N.A.—*Mus norvegicus albinus* (literally "white Norway mouse," but Tolman meant the white rat). Tolman's self-deprecating humor is immediately apparent: "First, I would ask forgiveness in that, as a presentation of a system, this book is not shorter and more to the point. No mere system is worth so many pages nor deserves so laborious and minute a treatment" (p. xvii). Later, he apologized for all the "neologisms I have introduced" (p. xviii). Many of Tolman's neologisms—newly created words or expressions—have been incorporated into psychology's language. One example is Tolman's *cognitive map.*

Purposive Behavior in Animals and Men

Initially, Tolman was attracted to Watson's and Guthrie's denial of the law of effect and to Watson's emphasis on frequency and recency. However, he did not like Watson's atomistic notions of stimulus and response.

> I was already becoming influenced by Gestalt psychology and conceived that a rat in running a maze must be learning a lay-out or pattern and not just having connections between atom-like stimuli and atom-like responses 'stamped in' or 'stamped out,' whether by exercise *or* by effect. (Tolman, 1952, p. 329, italics in the original)

Tolman soon saw experimental evidence that argued against the primacy of Watson's ideas of frequency and recency.

With advice from Tolman, Zing Yang Kuo (Chapter 12) gave rats a choice of four different routes leading to food (Kuo, 1922). Kuo's study showed Tolman "that the successive droppings out of the bad routes were in no case due to a preceding greater frequency or recency on the other routes" (Tolman, 1932/1967, p. 349).

Like Watson, Tolman did not believe that the consequence of a response, its reinforcement, is important for learning. However, unlike Watson, Tolman recognized the importance of reinforcement for motivating learning. Thus, he distinguished learning from **performance,** holding that learning occurs in the absence of reward but reward is important for an animal's performance—that is, its actual behavior. In other words, learning may have occurred without appearing in the organism's behavior; a reward motivates performance and reveals the learning that has occurred. The key early study that reinforced the learning-performance distinction was contained in H. C. Blodgett's 1925 dissertation, which provided evidence for **latent learning.**

Blodgett ran three groups of hungry rats in a maze: Group I was fed in the food box at the end of the maze after each day's run; Group II received no reward for the first 6 days and then was rewarded on subsequent days; Group III received no reward for the first 2 days, with reward thereafter. Before receiving reward, rats in Groups II and III showed no evidence for learning. However, errors were halved on the day after the reward was introduced, and by the day after that, animals in Groups II and III were performing as well as the rats rewarded throughout. Tolman concluded that learning had been occurring in the absence of reward —was latent—but an incentive was necessary for the learning to appear in the rats' performance (Tolman, 1932/1967).

Tolman found further evidence against Thorndike's mechanical view of reinforcement's effect on learning. "According to Thorndike, an animal learned . . . merely because a quite irrelevant 'pleasantness' or 'unpleasantness' was . . . shot at it, as from a squirt gun, after it had reached the given goal-box or gone into the given *cul de sac*" (Tolman, 1952, p. 330). According to Tolman, an animal's experience with a particular reward in a particular situation leads to the expectation that in future occurrences of the situation, the particular reward will be encountered.

Otto Tinklepaugh (1928) observed perhaps the most dramatic evidence for reward expectancies in monkeys. In a delayed-response task—an animal is shown the reward location but prevented from responding for different lengths of time—Tinklepaugh surreptitiously substituted a piece of lettuce for the piece of banana he had shown the animal. Here is Tinklepaugh's description of a typical test:

> After the delay, the monkey is told to 'come get the food.' She . . . rushes to the proper container and picks it up. She extends her hand to seize the food. But her hand drops to the floor without touching it. She looks at the lettuce but (unless very hungry) does not touch it. She looks around the cup and behind the board. She stands up and looks under and around her. She picks the cup up and examines it thoroughly inside and out. She has on occasion turned toward the observers . . . and shrieked at them in apparent anger. (p. 224)

It is difficult not to conclude, as Tinklepaugh did, that the monkey's memory included a representation of the banana piece under the container.

Tolman's program also included studies challenging Carr and Watson's (1908) conclusion that rats learn a sequence of motor responses in a maze. For example, D. A. Macfarlane trained one group of rats to swim through a maze initially, whereas the other group waded through the maze at first. Then, the required responses were reversed, with the "swimming" rats wading and the "wading" rats swimming.

> [T]he results of this experiment were . . . such as to prove surprising to anyone convinced of the old kinesthetic doctrine of maze learning. . . . The kinesthetic impulses received as a result of wading must have been quite different in quality, and very different in quantity, from those received from swimming and *vice versa,* and yet the change from the one condition to the other, although it caused evident disruption, surprise, etc., did not cause any considerable increase in the error scores, per se. The rats still "*knew*" *where to go,* although at first their behavior was obviously upset . . . at finding free water instead of submerged bottom, or *vice versa.* (Tolman, 1932/1967, pp. 80–81, italics in the original)

A study by Tolman and Honzik illustrated even more dramatically that rats typically learn *where* to go in a maze for reward rather than learning a sequence of specific motor responses. Tolman and Honzik used the maze shown in Figure 13.1, which had three pathways to the food box: Path 1 was the shortest and most direct; Path 2 was intermediate in length; and Path 3 was the longest.

When Path 1 was blocked at A, the rats backed out of Path 1 and chose Path 2 more than 90% of the time; because Path 2 was the second most direct path, this was not surprising. But what would the rats do if they found Path 1 blocked at B, which would also prevent them from reaching the goal by Path 2? Would they try Path 2, the S-R prediction, or would their awareness of the maze layout cause them to select Path 3? This problem is similar to Wolfgang Köhler's (Chapter 14) *Umweg* (detour) problem. Köhler visited Tolman's laboratory in the mid-1920s, and the English translation of Köhler's classic, *The Mentality of Apes*, was published in 1925, well before Tolman and Honzik's experiment.

On the first "test" run, 14 out of 15 rats (93%) selected Path 3. The S-R prediction failed, as the rats had gotten the "big picture" of the maze. Using Köhler's terminology, they had developed "insight." Although later studies showed that Tolman and Honzik's results were reproducible, they also found that one could alter the results by manipulating such experimental conditions as the width of the alleys, which should not have an effect on a rat's "reasoning ability." Thus, Tolman and Honzik's "insight" explanation became only one of the various possible interpretations of the study (Bower & Hilgard, 1981).

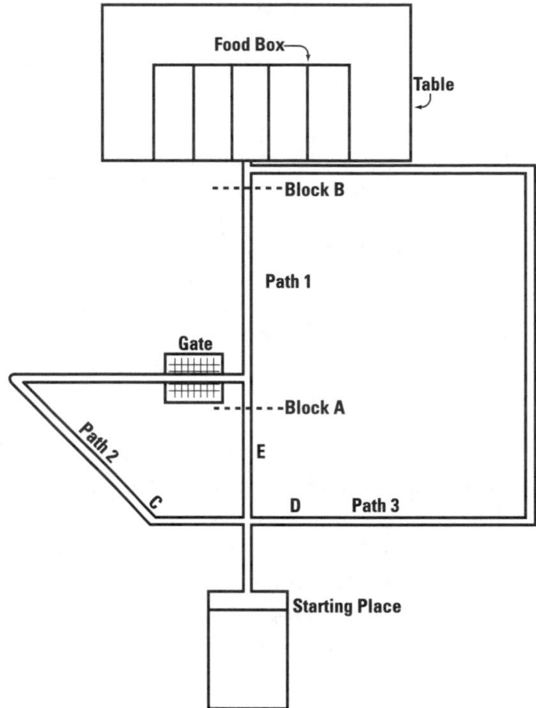

FIGURE 13.1 Tolman and Honzik's maze on which rats demonstrated "insight"

Source: Tolman's (1967), Purposive Behavior in Animals and Men. *New York: Irvington Publishers, Inc. (original work published 1932 by Appleton Century Crofts). Reprinted by permission of Irvington Publishers, Inc.*

Intervening Variables

As noted, Tolman believed that behavior is goal oriented. A particular goal can be obtained through many different acts, and Tolman's theory was designed to explain the complexity of behavior used to obtain goals. Thus, he considered it essential to incorporate the organism's cognitions—its knowledge of the world. This knowledge constitutes behavior space, which is closely related to Kurt Lewin's "life space" (Chapter 14), and Tolman frequently acknowledged his debt to Lewin's ideas (e.g., Tolman, 1939/1951, 1952).

In accounting for behavioral complexity, Tolman extensively used **intervening variables,** which are constructs that come between the stimulus and the response and are completely defined by the S-R conditions. Innis (1997) suggested that Tolman's intervening variables were perhaps his most important contribution to psychology. Yet the intervening variable is a purely abstract behavioral concept, without any presumed underlying physiological mechanism. Although the exact list of intervening variables changed throughout Tolman's career, we can illustrate the concept with a well-known example: the cognitive map.

In 1959, Tolman wrote, "Learning . . . is conceived by me as the acquisition of . . . connections I have called means-end readinesses or beliefs" (p. 124). The combination of these beliefs becomes the organism's **cognitive map,** or an organism's understanding of the layout of its environment. In the case of a rat learning a maze,

> the incoming impulses [sensory stimuli from the maze and its surroundings] are usually worked over and elaborated in the central control room into a tentative, cognitive-like map of the environment. And it is this tentative map, indicating routes and paths and environmental relationships, which finally determines what responses, if any, the animal will finally release. (Tolman, 1948, p. 192)

Note that the cognitive map, which we have called an intervening variable, appears to have a physiological basis. In the quotation, Tolman referred to the "map" as being "elaborated in the central control room," meaning the brain. MacCorquodale and Meehl (1948) differentiated between intervening variables and constructs with more surplus meaning and at least an implied physiological basis, which they called **hypothetical constructs** (Chapter 17). According to this differentiation, Tolman's cognitive map is a hypothetical construct, not an intervening variable. Tolman acknowledged MacCorquodale and Meehl's distinction but disagreed with it.

Tolman's evidence for the rat's development of cognitive maps came from several different types of study. For example, during the nonreward period in latent learning studies, rats were learning the location of the blind alleys. "They had been building up a 'map,' and could utilize the latter as soon as they were motivated to do so" (Tolman, 1948, p. 195).

Studies of vicarious trial and error (VTE) also support the cognitive map idea. VTE refers to a rat's looking-back-and-forth behavior at a maze choice point, or to similar behavior when an animal has to choose between two stimuli in a discrimination test. Tolman (1939/1951) found the VTEing began at the time the animals started to learn and that it decreased when the learning was established. He concluded, "VTEing . . . is evidence that in the critical stages [of learning] . . . the animal's activity is not just one of responding passively to discrete stimuli, but rather one of the active selecting and comparing of stimuli" (Tolman, 1948, p. 200)—that is, of developing a cognitive map.

Further evidence for cognitive maps came from Ira Krechevsky's so-called **hypothesis experiments** (Tolman, 1948). Krechevsky—later known as David Krech—observed that rats often exhibit systematic responses on discrimination problems that appear to result from the rats' testing a particular hypothesis. For example, in a two-choice situation in which the stimuli are separated laterally, rats often go to one particular side initially, apparently testing a spatial position hypothesis. If this hypothesis fails to maximize success, rats select another hypothesis, which might be discarded for a third, and so on. Tolman wrote that Krech used the term *hypothesis* to refer to what Tolman had "been calling cognitive maps which, it appears from his experiments, get set up in a tentative fashion to be tried out first one and then another until, if possible, one is found which works" (p. 202).

Finally, the cognitive map idea is supported by experiments in **place learning,** in which an animal learns to go to a specific place rather than learning a specific sequence of motor responses. Macfarlane's study of swimming and/or wading rats and Tolman and Honzik's blocked-pathway experiment indicated that rats learn about the maze, if they are permitted to do so.

Another type of place-learning experiment directly pitted place learning against response learning to see which rats learned more readily. For example, Tolman, Ritchie, and Kalish (1946) used the apparatus shown in Figure 13.2. Half of the animals were reinforced for always going to a particular place on the elevated maze, whereas the other animals were reinforced for always making the same response. That is, if a place-learning rat was being taught to find food at F_1, then it should turn right when started from S_1 but left when started from S_2. A response-learning rat reinforced for always turning right at point C would find food at F_1 when it started from S_1 and at F_2 when it started from S_2. In this experiment, all place-learning rats learned within 8 trials, whereas none of the response learners learned as quickly and several still had not learned after 72 trials.

Subsequent place-learning studies gave conflicting results. In resolving the controversy, Restle (1957) noted there is nothing that makes rats inherently "place" learners or "response" learners. Rats use the cues available to them, and if such cues favor

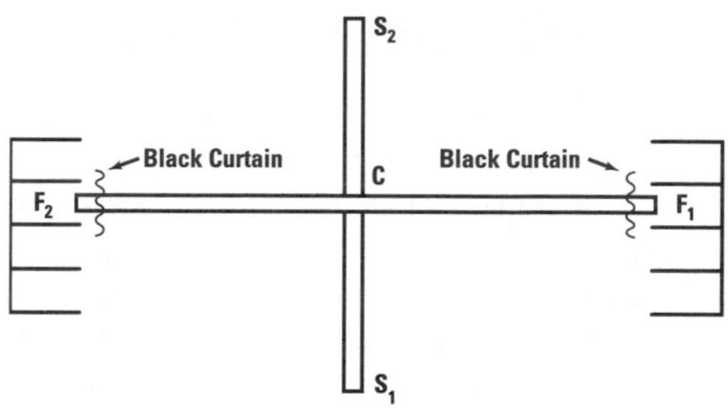

FIGURE 13.2 Elevated maze used to compare place-learning and response-learning rats

Source: Tolman, Ritchie, & Kalish (1946), p. 223. Studies in spatial learning. II. Place learning versus response learning. Journal of Experimental Psychology, *36, 221–229.*

place learning, then place learners perform better than response learners. Restle concluded that further "definitive" studies would prove fruitless.

Tolman's Influence

As you can see, Tolman introduced apparently subjective, mentalistic concepts into his accounts of the learned behavior of rats. Although the notion that rats form cognitive maps and behave purposefully seems foreign to Watson's aims for behaviorism, Tolman considered himself a behaviorist. In 1932, Tolman explained how he could use mentalistic terms such as *purpose* and *cognition* while remaining true to behaviorism:

> Finally . . . it must . . . be emphasized that purposes and cognitions which are thus immediately, immanently [directly], in behavior are wholly objective as to definition. They are defined by characters and the relationships which we observe out there in the behavior. We, the observers, watch the behavior of the rat, the cat, or the man, and note its character as a getting to such and such by means of such and such a selected pattern of commerces-with. It is we . . . who note these perfectly objective characters as immanent in the behavior and have happened to choose the terms *purpose* and *cognition* as generic names for such characters. (pp. 12–13)

Thus, Tolman believed it was possible to introduce apparently mentalistic, but common-sense, ideas such as insight, purpose, and expectancy into an objective psychology. In addition, his provocative experimental results challenged contemporary learning theorists—particularly Hull (discussed later)—and forced them to modify their theories in order to deal with his findings.

As we noted in Chapter 12, it was said that with Watson, psychology lost its mind. But Krech (1967) wrote "that it was actually Tolman and his rats who sought to give back to psychology its mind—its insights, its cognitions, its purposes" (p. xv). By including such apparently relevant concepts as insight, cognition, and purpose, Tolman's behaviorism was less easily dismissed by "people psychologists"—for example, clinical, child, and social psychologists—than Watsonian behaviorism or Pavlovian conditioning. In this sense, Tolman's work "helped to preserve animal experimentation, learning theory, and Behaviorism as viable forces in the development of American psychology" (p. xv). Also, Tolman's "cognitive behaviorism" was clearly an important influence on modern cognitive psychology (Chapter 18).

In addition and related to his research on learning, Tolman played an important role in developing the field of behavior genetics (Innis, 1992). Specifically, Tolman (1924) performed the first study examining the genetic basis for rat maze learning with a selective breeding program: He paired and bred "maze bright" and "maze dull" rats and then tested their offspring. This initial study was expanded by Tolman's student Robert C. Tryon, who eventually reported on work with more than 20 rat generations (e.g., Tryon, 1940). By the 8th generation, Tryon found virtually no overlap in performance by the "brights" and "dulls" on a type of maze task.

Unlike such professional rivals as Hull and Skinner, Tolman did not seek converts or disciples. According to former pupil Henry Gleitman (1991), students "mattered much more to Tolman than his own beliefs, or, rather more than instilling his own beliefs in students" (p. 240). When Tolman learned of Gleitman's brief defection to Hullian theory, his reaction was characteristically straightforward:

> "Gleitman, you son of a bitch, I hear you are becoming a Hullian! So okay. Just be a good Hullian!" (p. 240)

As a result of "the loose, exploratory style of [Tolman's] research and theorizing . . ." (Smith, 1990, p. 248) and Tolman's unwillingness to proselytize, there were no Tolmanians, as there were Hullians and Skinnerians. As Hill (1971) expressed it,

> [Tolman] wanted not so much to build a truly adequate theory as to explore the whole activity of theory building, both playing with it himself and puncturing the excessive claims of others. As a result, he has been widely respected and widely loved, but not widely followed. (p. 129)

Despite his lack of followers, Tolman's professional accomplishments resulted in the 1937 APA presidency, an invitation to membership in the Society of Experimental Psychologists, and an APA Distinguished Scientific Contribution Award in 1957.

Tolman was also widely respected at Berkeley. Toward the end of the McCarthy era, the university attempted to force its faculty to sign loyalty oaths. In 1949–1950, Tolman led the faculty in opposition to signing. Acknowledging that his refusal to sign would cause him little economic hardship, he advised his younger colleagues to sign the oath and leave the battle to those who could afford to pursue it. For his courageous stand, Tolman received wide acclaim and honorary degrees from several major universities.

Of his career in psychology, Tolman wrote in 1959,

> I have liked to think about psychology in ways that have proved congenial to me. Since all the sciences, and especially psychology, are still immersed in such tremendous realms of the uncertain and the unknown, the best that any individual scientist, especially any psychologist, can do seems to be to follow his own gleam and his own bent, however inadequate they may be. In fact, I suppose that actually this is what we all do. In the end, the only sure criterion is to have fun. And I have had fun. (p. 152)

During the 1940s, Tolman offered a major alternative to Hull's neobehaviorism, which was arguably the dominant view at the time. Hull's "gleam and bent" lay in developing the most systematic learning theory ever attempted.

CLARK LEONARD HULL

Born in a log house on a farm near Akron, New York, **Clark Leonard Hull** (1884–1952) grew up on a farm in Michigan, where the family moved when he was very young. Hull attended a one-room rural school until he was 16; he was an able student with a lifelong interest in building machines. At 17, he passed a teachers' examination and taught for a year in the same school, an experience that motivated him to continue his education.

After a year of high school, Hull attended the academy of Alma College in Michigan, where the study of geometry "proved to be the most important event of [his] intellectual life . . ." (Hull, 1952a, p. 144). At the academy graduation dinner, he contracted typhoid fever, which nearly killed him and left him with a generalized bad memory for names.

Hull studied at Alma College to become a mining engineer and took a job at a company that owned iron mines in Hibbing, Minnesota. He contracted polio 2 months later, which made a mining career impossible, as it left him with a permanently paralyzed left leg supported by a steel brace he designed himself. Hull briefly considered becoming a Unitarian minister before turning to psychology. As a preliminary survey of the subject, he read both volumes of James's *Principles of Psychology*. After another brief stint as a teacher, Hull married Bertha Iutzi, and the newlyweds pooled their resources and entered the University of Michigan. There, Hull's most memorable course was a year in experimental psychology, with W. B. Pillsbury's lectures and J. F. Shepard's laboratory. APA president in 1910, Walter Bowers Pillsbury (1872–1960) was also known as an early historian of psychology.

Hull received his bachelor's degree in 1913, at the age of 30. After graduation, he took a teaching position in Richmond, Kentucky. Despite a heavy teaching load, Hull found time to build an exposure apparatus he later used for his dissertation.

Through Pillsbury's assistance, Hull became a part-time teaching assistant in psychology at the University of Wisconsin, working under Joseph Jastrow (Chapter 10). In his spare time, Hull worked on problems concerning concept formation, using his exposure apparatus. He received his Ph.D. in 1918, continuing as a staff member at Wisconsin.

Hull's Three Interests

Although the sequential discussion of Hull's disparate areas of interest—aptitude testing, hypnosis, and learning theory—makes it appear that each was developed serendipitously, Triplet (1982) argued that they all fit within a major theme "that ties Hull's life work together as a unified whole" (p. 24). The theme is Hull's ambition to achieve personal recognition. At the time Hull began work on them, aptitude testing, hypnosis, and learning theory had not been investigated systematically in a manner that met Hull's stringent criteria. By employing his talents in these areas, Hull believed he would attain the recognition he sought.

Archives of the History of American Psychology – The University of Akron.

Clark Leonard Hull (1884–1952)

Aptitude Testing

Hull's interest in aptitude testing began when he was asked to teach a course in psychological tests and measurements. Calling the course "Aptitude Testing," Hull found that much of the work in the area was methodologically weak and little concerned with test validation. "With characteristic energy he set about the task of organizing the field systematically"(Hovland, 1952, pp. 347–348), which he accomplished by publishing *Aptitude Testing* in 1928.

Hull also developed an aptitude test and invented a machine to compute correlation coefficients. As he later explained, "It happens that I am very prone to make small errors in such computations, . . . [and] I conceived the idea of building a machine which would do nearly all of the correlation work automatically" (Hull, 1952a, p. 151). Hull built two such machines, one of which is in the Smithsonian Institution, but he abandoned aptitude testing when his survey of the field made him pessimistic about the future of such work.

Hypnosis

In addition to the aptitude testing course, Hull was asked to teach Jastrow's introductory course in psychology for premedical students. One of Hull's innovations was the topic of suggestion, which he believed was used extensively in contemporary medicine. Hull began to study hypnotic suggestion, using the quantitative methodology of experimental psychology to make his work more robust than most earlier research (see Chapter 15).

Hull's hypnosis research (performed mostly at Wisconsin) yielded 32 published papers and a major book, *Hypnosis and Suggestibility: An Experimental Approach* (1933). Hull concluded that hypnosis was merely a hypersuggestibility state differing quantitatively, but not qualitatively, from the normal state. Further, he believed there were no hypnotic phenomena that could not occur in the normal state, given appropriate suggestion.

Hull's hypnosis research was attacked almost immediately at Yale, where he went in 1929. The opposition came first from medical authorities and then from one of Hull's female subjects, who sued the university. Despite the bizarre nature of the charges, Yale bought the woman's silence, and Hull was forced to pursue a new research interest (Kimble, 1991).

Hypothetico-Deductive Learning Theory

Although Hull was sympathetic with Watson's rejection of introspection and with his desire for objectivity in psychology, he was uncertain about Watson's more dogmatic claims and repelled by the fanaticism on both sides of the behaviorism debate. Briefly, he was attracted to the Gestalt movement that began at about the same time as behaviorism. In fact, Mills (1988) suggested the primary motive driving Hull's development of a learning theory was his need to respond to the Gestaltists' challenge. While listening to Koffka's lectures, Hull agreed with most of Koffka's criticisms of behaviorism. However, exposure to Koffka—Hull had him brought to Wisconsin in 1926–1927—had the opposite effect on Hull that it had on Tolman: "Instead of converting me to *Gestalttheorie,* the result was a belated conversion to a . . . behaviorism mainly concerned with the determination of the quantitative laws of behavior and their deductive systematization" (Hull, 1952a, p. 154). At the same time, Hull was positively influenced by Pavlov's *Conditioned Reflexes* and by the empiricist approach to animal behavior exemplified by Morgan's and Thorndike's work (Triplet, 1982). Rather than concluding that Gestalt theory was sound, Hull decided "that Watson had not made out as clear a case for behaviorism as the facts warranted" (Hull, 1952a, p. 154). He would remedy Watson's failure with a system immune from "the damaging criticisms of Koffka and the other [Gestaltists]" (Mills, 1988, p. 397). In other words, he would develop a **hypothetico-deductive learning theory.**

In 1929, President Angell (Chapter 11) invited Hull to the Institute of Psychology at Yale, which soon became part of the Institute of Human Relations. Beyond a weekly 2-hour seminar, Hull's lack of formal teaching duties gave him freedom to pursue his goal of a systematic learning theory. In addition, his work was aided by the many capable psychologists his seminar attracted, including such subsequent luminaries as Kenneth Spence, Neal Miller, John Dollard, O. H. Mowrer (all discussed later), and Carl I. Hovland (Chapter 17).

In Hull's (1929) first learning theory essay he described the conditioned reflex "as an automatic trial-and-error mechanism which mediates, blindly but beautifully, the adjustment of the organism to a complex environment" (p. 498), and the same theme reappears in Hull's later work (e.g., Hull, 1937, 1952b). Around 1930, Hull concluded that psychology is a true natural science and that he could describe its primary laws with equations. As he began to develop his system, Hull realized it would take at least three books to detail it adequately: one volume introducing the system and stating its primary principles; one in which he would deduce the more common forms of individual behavior from the primary principles; and a third providing similar deductions for social or group behavior. Hull's *Principles of Behavior* appeared in 1943, and *A Behavior System* was published shortly after his death. To some degree, the third volume's aims were accomplished by his students (e.g., Neal Miller).

Fifty years before he died, Hull began a journal of his thoughts on his work, on his life's progress, and on things in general. He called these his "idea books," and he filled 73 of them, with his last entry coming just 18 days before he died (Hays, 1962). In Hull's June 16, 1930, entry, he gave the rationale for and a clear statement of his novel approach to system building:

> Every time I start reading writers of the classic theories of knowledge I am at once struck with the extreme subjectivity of their point of departure. . . . [A]ll have started from introspective experience as the more primary and more basic, and attempted to derive a system with which to explain action and human nature as well. . . . I propose to develop a system which starts from exactly the opposite end. . . . I shall start with action—habit—and proceed to deduce all the rest, including conscious experience, from action, i.e., habit. (Hull, 1962, pp. 836–837)

In his APA presidential address, Hull (1937) listed three requirements for a sound theoretical system: First, there should be a set of postulates with all important terms defined operationally. Next, using logic, a series of interlocking theorems about the field's most important phenomena should be deduced from the postulates. Finally, the theorems should agree with the discipline's known facts. If they agree, the system is probably true; if they do not agree, the system is demonstrably false. If it is impossible to tell whether the theorems agree or disagree, the system is scientifically meaningless. Note the similarity between Hull's conception of a sound theoretical system and logical positivism's tenets presented early in the chapter.

For Hull, a valid theory was one containing a logical system of postulates from which theorems could be derived. Hull's postulates would not be proven but would be the starting points for subsequent proofs. From them, theorems—as laws of behavior—could be deduced logically. Then, experiments would test the theorems; a positive outcome would support the whole theory, whereas a negative outcome would weaken the overall theory, forcing revision.

Hull's (1952b) final learning system contained 17 postulates, several with corollaries, from which he had derived more than 130 theorems, many with multiple parts. Obviously, this was a grand attempt to systematize a particular area of psychology. Because of the complexity of Hull's unfinished system, we will present only a simplified version to give you some of the system's flavor.

For Hull, as for others before him, all learned behavior involved stimulus-response connections. Like the functionalist Woodworth (Chapter 11), Hull realized the importance of internal factors that can affect an organism's response to a stimulus, and one of Hull's students wrote: "Hull's S-R diagrams . . . may be thought of as being essentially an elaboration of the S-O-R formula of Woodworth" (Spence, 1952, pp. 645–646). Hull followed Tolman's lead in filling the organism with intervening variables mediating between stimulus and response.

Hull's predictive scheme contained four stages: Stages 1 and 4 detailed independent variables and dependent variables, respectively. Stages 2 and 3 consisted of intervening variables assumed to connect the stimuli and responses. Figure 13.3 shows a schematic representation of the stages, along with some representative intervening variables.

Note that independent variables—experimenter-manipulated variables—can refer to stimulation the organism is receiving at the moment (e.g., electric shock), stimulation from preceding events (e.g., time since the last meal), or previous experience in the particular learning situation (e.g., number of times the response to be learned has been made). The independent variables affect intervening variables in the second stage. For example, food or water

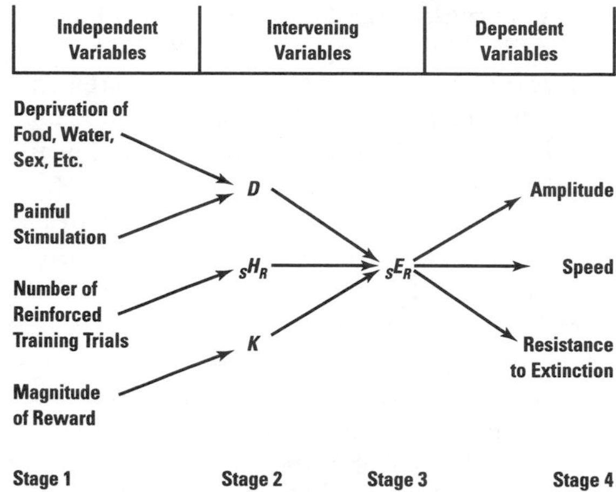

FIGURE 13.3 Simplified schematic representation of the four stages in Hull's system

Source: Adapted from Figure 5 from Learning: a survey of psychological interpretations, *4th ed. by Winfred Hill. Published by Allyn and Bacon, Boston, MA. Copyright © 1985 by Pearson Education. Adapted by permission of the publisher.*

deprivation and painful stimulation affect the intervening variable labelled "*D*" for **drive,** an activated state of the organism; reward is drive reduction.

The number of reinforced training trials affects **habit strength** ($_SH_R$)—the strength of the S-R connection—one of Hull's most important intervening variables. "*H*" stands for habit, which is a permanent connection between the particular stimulus (S) and the response (R). Each time a response occurs in the presence of a stimulus and is quickly followed by reinforcement, the bond between S and R is strengthened. A simplified version of Hull's equation to express the relationship between habit strength and the number of reinforced trials is

$$_SH_R = 1 - 10^{-.0305N},$$

where *N* is the number of reinforced trials. Exact values like the exponent –.0305 generally came from the results of a single experiment. As *N* grows, the fraction subtracted from 1 becomes smaller so that the limit of habit strength is 1, which is approached more slowly with each additional reinforced trial. Herbart (Chapter 6) considered psychology mathematical, and his equation to express the rise of a concept in consciousness is similar to Hull's function for the rise of habit strength (Bakan, 1952).

Reward magnitude on the previous response affects the intervening variable labelled "*K*," Hull's symbol for **incentive motivation.** *K*'s inclusion as a separate intervening variable was a change in Hull's system from 1943 to 1952. In 1943, Hull treated reward quality or quantity as just another aspect of reinforcement—the larger (or more preferred) the reward, the greater the drive reduction and the larger the increase in habit strength. However, experiments showed that increasing the reward resulted in more rapid performance improvements than would be possible given the slow growth of habit strength. Even more problematic, a decrease in reward actually produced a performance decrement, suggesting decreased habit strength. Such a decrease is impossible assuming a permanent S-R bond whose strength is increased with successive reinforcements, no matter what their size.

Thus, Hull adopted Kenneth Spence's idea of incentive motivation ("*K*" for Kenneth; Malone, 1991), which is affected independently of habit strength. Finding a large reward on a trial after receiving small rewards previously increases the organism's motivation for the incentive, even though each rewarded trial adds only a little to habit strength. Making *K* separate from ${}_SH_R$ provided a way to account for dramatic increases or decreases in performance with changes in reward magnitude. Here, note the importance of Tolman's learning-performance distinction: Habit strength is a learning variable; incentive motivation, a performance variable. Also, recall Tolman's expectancy effect—animals learn to expect a particular quantity (or quality) of reward, and there are dramatic behavior changes when this expectation is not fulfilled (e.g., Tinklepaugh's monkey discovering lettuce instead of banana).

Now we come to Stage 3 and ${}_SE_R$, which Hull called **excitatory potential** and **reaction potential** in 1952. Reaction potential is the total tendency to make a particular response to a particular stimulus and is the product of the Stage 2 intervening variables, or

$${}_SE_R = {}_SH_R \times D \times K.$$

Specifically, an organism's tendency to make a given response to a given stimulus is the product of habit strength developed through reinforced practice (${}_SH_R$), an internal state of the organism (*D*), and the incentive magnitude found on the immediately preceding trial (*K*).

Hull's fourth stage contains the dependent variables, which are measurements of behavior. In Figure 13.3, reaction potential (${}_SE_R$) determines the amplitude or size of the response, response speed, and resistance to extinction. As reaction potential increases, so does the size of the response, its speed, and how many responses are made before the organism stops responding. Hull's system included a variety of additional variables, such as R_G (goal response) and r_G (anticipatory goal response).

Believe it or not, we have barely scratched the surface of Hull's learning theory. In the final analysis, Hull conceded that a given subject's reaction potential on a given learning trial was not a precise value, as it would appear to be from the ${}_SE_R$ equation. Instead, there is a random variation in reaction potential, which means that "[v]ariability, inconsistency, and specific unpredictability of reaction under seemingly constant conditions are universal characteristics of the molar behavior of organisms . . . " (Hull, 1943, p. 317). Hull's system—for all its complexity and apparent scientific precision—never achieved perfect prediction or control of behavior.

Hull's Influence

Both Hull's mathematical/logical analysis of learning and his propensity to build machines reinforce the idea that for Hull the metaphor of mechanism was central to understanding behavior and advancing psychology (Smith, 1990). Hull was an anticipator of modern cognitive psychology's efforts in artificial intelligence and machine learning (Chapter 18), as you can see from the following comment: "It should be a matter of no great difficulty to construct parallel inanimate mechanisms, even from inorganic materials, which will genuinely manifest the qualities of intelligence, insight, and purpose, and which, in so far, will be truly psychic" (Hull, 1930, p. 256).

Thus, Hull held that the brain functioned like a machine and that machines would ultimately be built that displayed genuine intelligence. For Karl Lashley (Chapter 16), one problem with Hull's view was it assumed the Watsonian S-R switchboard connectionism Lashley believed his brain research had disproved (e.g., Lashley, 1929). Lashley's disagreement with Hull's use of a mind-machine metaphor led to a lengthy, and ultimately unresolved, correspondence debate between the two men (Weidman, 1994).

Like his contemporary learning theorists, Hull was interested in general learning principles, and whether the study object was a rat, a person, or a machine was of secondary importance. In Hull's day, the focus on the general principles of learning per se was used to validate generalizations from animal studies—for example, of rats in mazes—to human behavior. At the present time, the same sort of focus is used to explain how analyzing computer programs can produce important insights into human learning and cognition.

Hull's dominance during the 1930s and 1940s is shown in Ruja's (1956) examination of reference citations in three major journals during the years from 1949 to 1952. For example, in 183 articles in the *Journal of Experimental Psychology*, Hull received more than twice as many citations as his nearest rival. Perhaps more importantly, the four psychologists below Hull were all Hull's students or associates. Ruja also found that the work most frequently cited was Hull's (1943) *Principles of Behavior*.

Coan and Zagona's (1962) obtained ratings of psychological theorists provides another illustration of Hull's stature. Coan and Zagona received ratings both for the period from 1880 to 1960 and by decades within the period. Overall, Hull ranked second only to Freud. In the 2 decades from 1930 to 1949, Hull had the highest ranking, with Tolman second. However, Hull's name was not among the top 10 in the decade from 1950 to 1959—Skinner topped the list—and Tolman slipped to ninth. Still, three of Hull's students and associates were included among the decade's top 10 theorists.

Hull's honors included election to the APA presidency in 1936, election to the American Academy of Arts and Sciences in 1935, and acceptance into the National Academy of Sciences in 1936. Hull particularly enjoyed the meetings of the Society of Experimental Psychologists, and he received the society's coveted Warren Medal in 1945. According to the citation for the medal:

> [Hull's] theory has stimulated much research and it has been developed in a precise and quantitative form so as to permit predictions which can be tested empirically. The theory thus contains within itself the seeds of its own ultimate verification and of its possible final disproof. A truly unique achievement in the history of psychology to date. (Hovland, 1952, p. 349)

The line about Hull's theory possibly containing the seeds of its final disproof was prophetic. In an evaluation of Hull's system shortly after his death, Seward (1954) concluded,

> If a building is no more solid than its foundations, neither is a system more stable than its postulates. That Hull's postulates are far from "finished" is obvious from their rate of revision during the past few years. He is said to have remarked, "I reserve the right to change my postulates every morning before breakfast." There is no reason why we should regard them with greater awe. (pp. 155–156)

Although critical of the foundation of Hull's grand system of behavior, Seward acknowledged probably the most important effect of Hull's attempt in his last sentence: "High on any list of his contributions to psychology should go the many challenging targets he gave us to shoot at" (pp. 156–157). By making his theory explicit and testable, Hull stimulated an enormous amount of research in laboratories all over the country.

As we have indicated, Hull's direct influence on psychology did not long survive his death, which came a few weeks before his planned retirement from Yale in 1952. Overly ambitious and mathematically tedious, Hull's learning theory has been considered a failure by some. "Moreover, his failure has probably discouraged others from attempting such a task. Many observers have noted a trend in learning theory away from . . . all-encompassing theories . . . toward theories of smaller scope designed to explain only certain kinds of learning" (Hill, 1971, p. 157). Although this trend was undoubtedly true for at least a couple of decades following Hull's death, recent advances in machine learning, of which Hull would have approved, can be seen as a return to a general theory of behavior with similarities to Hull's system (e.g., Rumelhart, McClelland, & the PDP Research Group, 1986).

Nevertheless, Hull set the stage for the inductive approach to learning adopted by the man who supplanted him in theoretical importance in the 1950s: B. F. Skinner. Before examining Skinner's life and accomplishments, we will briefly look at the careers of a number of Hull's most important students and associates.

Hull's disciples continued his line of research after they had gone to other universities. In turn, they motivated their own students to continue similar work, with the result that there were soon "a large number of enthusiastic fourth and fifth generation students [of Hull] throughout the country" (Hovland, 1952, p. 349). The reasons why Hull inspired such loyalty may be found in the introduction by Ruth Hays (1962), Hull's long-time assistant, to excerpts from Hull's idea books.

> Those who worked with him were deeply conscious of his intellect and ability, his integrity and courage; they respected his sincerity and singleness of purpose; . . . they stood almost in awe of his constant achievements and hard work, often in the face of physical weakness and suffering; and they loved him for his humanness—his forthright likes and dislikes, his keen sense of humor, . . . his quick contempt of sham or affectation or pomposity. Above all they appreciated his unstinting generosity in giving an assistant all or even more than his due or credit in recognition of work done and in the matter of publication. (p. 805)

HULL'S STUDENTS AND ASSOCIATES

Kenneth Spence

Kenneth W. Spence (1907–1967) was raised in Montreal, Canada, where he attended McGill University, earning B.A. and M.A. degrees. Spence went to Yale to work on his Ph.D., which he received in 1933, with a dissertation directed by Robert Yerkes. Although he moved to the University of Texas in 1964, most of his career was spent at the State University of Iowa. There, he built a human eyeblink-conditioning laboratory to study how motivation contributed to human learning. Wiseman (2000) assessed Spence's human learning research program in terms of several disputes and controversies in learning theory at the time, which often hinged on subtle interpretations of events by Spence and his contemporaries. Although Spence's conditioning research outwardly appeared to be objective, Wiseman contends there were elements of subjectivity that prevented him from developing "a body of reliable knowledge with predictive accuracy" (p. 277). Kendler (2001) subsequently challenged Wiseman's claim that Spence's science was subjective, but Wiseman's (2001) basic belief remains intact.

Spence's eminence as a theorist, experimentalist, and methodologist resulted in his election to the National Academy of Sciences. Despite this achievement, Spence is little remembered by today's psychologists, perhaps because of his ability to alienate his contemporaries (Kimble, 1998). However, Kimble predicted that future psychologists will come to honor Spence's memory.

Throughout his career, Spence's name was closely associated with Hull's, and when Hull died, Spence continued his mentor's theoretical efforts. Although their approaches and views differed in significant ways—for example, Spence opposed Hull's tendency to interpret his intervening variables physiologically (O'Neil, 1995; Smith, 1990)—both Spence and Hull were dedicated to developing an objective theory of behavior based on conditioning. Spence's major contributions were his theory of discrimination learning and his invention and elaboration of incentive motivation.

Discrimination Learning and Relational Responding

Spence's theory of discrimination learning was proposed as an S-R theorist's response to learning experiments by Wolfgang Köhler. In what became known as the transposition problem, discussed in Chapter 14, Köhler (e.g., 1925) trained chickens to peck at a dark gray card and to avoid pecking at a lighter gray card. To see what an animal had learned, Köhler tested it with the dark gray card and a still darker card, reasoning that if a chicken had learned a specific response to a specific stimulus, it would peck at the same card as in the original learning. However, if the animal originally had learned the relationship between the stimuli, it would peck at the darker stimulus in the test, which is what most animals did.

Spence (1937) developed an explanation for Köhler's results based on the S-R concepts of habit strength, conditioned inhibition, and stimulus generalization that did not require innate tendencies to "get the big picture," as the Gestaltists suggested. Spence's solution to the relational versus absolute responding controversy stimulated much research, and the "decline in [relational responding] with distance [between the stimuli] has indeed been found many times and it provides a difficulty for the relational view" (Bower & Hilgard, 1981, p. 115). When tests with children showed relational responding based on verbalization, two of Spence's students, Howard and Tracy Kendler, further modified and extended Spence's solution (Kimble, 1998).

Incentive Motivation

As we noted, Spence suggested to Hull that motivation based on a reward's quantity or quality should be separated from habit strength, thus giving Hull the idea of incentive motivation (K). When Hull died, K was not completely assimilated into his system, and Spence worked to clarify K's status, eventually changing Hull's theory in ways that took it closer to the theories of Hull's competitors.

Hull believed habit strength ($_{S}H_{R}$) was a function of the number of reinforced S-R pairings. By about 1950, Spence had decided that habit strength development did not depend on reward as drive reduction. He believed "if the response occurs there will be an increment in [habit strength] regardless of whether a reinforcer does or does not result" (Spence, 1960, p. 96). From this, habit formation became strictly a matter of S-R contiguity, a basic tenet of Guthrie and Watson.

Further, Spence continued modifying K, eventually suggesting a physiological basis for it consisting of movement-produced stimuli. Such stimuli help maintain an animal's movement toward a goal, which is a thoroughly Guthrian concept. But Spence also drifted toward cognitive behaviorism. Incentive motivation can be seen as reward anticipation with a physiological basis. Reward anticipation is a completely Tolmanian idea.

Neal E. Miller

Neal Elgar Miller (1909–2002) earned his B.S. from the University of Washington, his M.A. from Stanford, and his Ph.D. from Yale in 1935, with Hull as his advisor. Miller then went to the Vienna Psychoanalytic Institute to learn about Freudian therapy, which was incorporated into *Personality and Psychotherapy* (Dollard & Miller, 1950), published with his long-time collaborator, the sociologist **John Dollard** (1900–1980).

Returning to Yale, Miller was a member of the Institute of Human Relations—as was Dollard—from 1936 to 1950, a professor of psychology from 1950 to 1952, and the James Rowland Angell Professor of Psychology from 1952 to 1966. He then went to New York's Rockefeller University, where he served as a professor and head of a physiological psychology laboratory from 1966 to 1980, when he acquired emeritus status.

Miller's contributions occurred in several different areas: First, with Dollard, he presented a simplified version of Hullian theory and began social learning theory. Second, starting with Kurt Lewin's ideas on conflict (Chapter 14), Miller elaborated and developed a precise account of conflict theory. Third, Miller collaborated with Dollard to apply learning theory to such phenomena as psychopathology and aggression. Fourth, in his physiological research, Miller demonstrated that learning can be motivated by electrical brain stimulation (Miller, 1958) and investigated autonomic response (visceral) conditioning (Miller, 1969), which was important for the field of biofeedback. Once Miller had demonstrated instrumental conditioning of the viscera in animals, it was a small step to try biofeedback conditioning for treating such human pathologies as hypertension, epilepsy, and insomnia (see reviews by Miller, 1978; Yates, 1980). Unfortunately, later attempts to replicate some of his earlier autonomic conditioning work in rats were unsuccessful (e.g., Miller & Dworkin, 1974). We will briefly consider Miller's version of Hull and its application to psychopathology.

Social Learning and Imitation

In 1941, Miller and Dollard published *Social Learning and Imitation,* which contains Miller's adaptation of Hull and provides the impetus for Albert Bandura's social learning theory (Chapter 17). Miller's central concept is drive, which causes an organism to act. Further, a drive always involves a strong stimulus, and any stimulus, if strong enough, can function as a drive. Drive is the basis of motivation.

Drive stimulates activity, and one of the organism's responses may reduce the drive's strength. This reduction reinforces whatever response produced it, which means the response tends to be learned—that is, repeated in a similar stimulus situation. Thus, we have presented the four elements Miller and Dollard used to anticipate Hull's elaborate postulates and theorems: drive, cue, response, and reward. That is, *drive* causes a *response* in the presence of certain *cues* (the stimulus situation). If the result reduces the drive, this is *rewarding*, and the response is connected to the cues.

Miller and Dollard used their theory to account for imitation, which they believed is a learned behavior. To illustrate, consider the behavior of two young boys. On one occasion, the older brother heard his father's footsteps entering the house and ran to greet him. His brother happened to be running in the same direction at the same time. The father gave both boys candy. Thus, this was a learning situation for the younger boy, with his desire for candy the drive, his brother's running the cue, his own running the response, and eating the candy the reward. From this event and other similar ones, the younger boy learned to imitate his brother.

In *Social Learning and Imitation,* Miller and Dollard (1941) presented a wealth of data from animal and human experiments on imitation. From their studies with people, the authors concluded that good human models tend to be similar demographically, older and of higher social status, technically skilled, and more knowledgeable.

Secondary Drives and Neurosis

In addition to such primary drives as hunger, pain, and fatigue, Miller and Dollard were particularly interested in **secondary drives.** A secondary—learned or acquired—drive gains its motivating status from initially being paired with a primary drive and its reduction. For example, money, a secondary reinforcer, and the urge to acquire it, a secondary drive, earn their status from being paired with hunger and its alleviation.

In *Personality and Psychotherapy,* Dollard and Miller (1950) were interested in the learning and unlearning of neuroses. According to them, neurotics have three characteristics: They are unhappy because of their conflicts, at least some of their behavior is irrational because they are acting on unresolved conflicts, and they present a variety of symptoms. At the root of the neurotic's conflicts is the learned drive of fear.

In a classic experiment, Miller (1948) demonstrated that stimuli paired with an aversive reinforcer become capable themselves of motivating and reinforcing behavior—in other words, the stimuli become secondary aversive reinforcers. In the study, rats were placed individually into a box with one white compartment with a grid floor and one black compartment with a wooden floor. Strong grid shock caused the rats to learn quickly to escape to the black box. After several shock presentations, the rats were placed into the white compartment without shock—all ran to the black chamber. Because pain did not motivate this escape behavior, Miller concluded the rats had learned a secondary drive of fear, which motivated the escape.

Further, Miller showed the learned fear could motivate new learning. To do this, he closed the door between the two compartments and made it possible for a rat to open the door by turning a wheel. Over half the animals learned the response, and the successful learners then acquired a lever-pressing response in order to enter the black compartment. Miller's experiment showed that cues occurring with an aversive stimulus acquire the power to produce fear, and new responses permitting escape from the cues will be reinforced and thus learned.

What does this animal work have to do with neurotics? According to Dollard and Miller (1950), through maladaptive learning the neurotic has acquired a fear drive triggered by stimuli not normally associated with fear. Behavior that reduces the fear is rewarding and is likely to increase. For example, suppose a boy is consistently punished for displaying assertive behavior. The punishment triggers emotional responses, which produce the secondary drive of fear. As a consequence, the child's assertive behavior comes to trigger fear, and submissiveness reduces the fear.

As an adult, the man encounters situations in which assertiveness might bring him the goals he wants, but he has learned to fear his assertiveness. This fear produces a conflict between his desire for certain goals and his fear of the assertive behavior that would possibly bring goals. His conflict—with learned fear at its heart—makes him unhappy, causes apparently irrational behavior in some situations, and may produce the symptoms of a disorder.

Because the fear is learned, extinguishing it is the key to curing the man through psychotherapy. If he can be convinced to make assertive responses under nonpunitive conditions, his fear will eventually extinguish. Because the cues for the fear come from his own emotional responses, the responses should be induced weakly at first, gradually building in intensity.

In addition to all the other contributions we have outlined, "Miller's practice of reaching across the disciplines of psychology, physiology, pharmacology, immunology, and public health, led to the development of behavioral medicine and health psychology, in which he played pioneering and pivotal roles" (Brandon, 2002, p. 13). His honors included being elected president of the APA and of the Society for Neuroscience. In addition, he was elected to the National Academy of Sciences and to the American Philosophical Society, and he received the National Medal of Science, the APA Gold Medal Award, and several honorary degrees.

O. H. Mowrer

The last of Hull's talented students and associates we will consider here is **Orval Hobart Mowrer** (1907–1982), born and raised on a farm near Unionville, Missouri. Mowrer suffered bouts of depression throughout his life, the first coming at 14. This experience motivated him to study psychology in college (Mowrer, 1974).

As a University of Missouri undergraduate, Mowrer studied with Max Frederick Meyer (1873–1967), a staunch behaviorist who had taken his Ph.D. under Carl Stumpf (Chapter 8) at Berlin. For a sociology course, Mowrer constructed a questionnaire that asked, among other things, about attitudes toward premarital sex and divorce. Mowrer was nearly dismissed as a result of the outcry, and Meyer was suspended for a year without pay and fired the next year for giving his interpretation of the incident at a professional meeting. Mowrer's undergraduate transgressions were ultimately forgiven, and Missouri honored him with a Certificate of Merit in 1956 (Hunt, 1984).

Mowrer received his Ph.D. from Johns Hopkins in 1932 and had an appointment from 1934 to 1940 at Yale's Institute of Human Relations. Mowrer's motivation for becoming a psychologist attracted him to the Institute's program geared toward integrating psychoanalysis with learning theory in the hope of achieving a mental health breakthrough. At the Institute, he participated in Hull's psychoanalytic seminar with a number of psychologists who included Dollard and Miller. At Yale, Mowrer made his major contributions to learning theory (discussed later).

From 1940 until 1948, Mowrer was an assistant and then an associate professor in the Harvard Graduate School of Education, with a courtesy appointment in the psychology department. At Harvard, Mowrer began counseling students on their personal problems, and this eventually led to a type of treatment he called *integrity therapy*. From Harvard, Mowrer went to the University of Illinois as a research professor of psychology, a position he held until he retired in 1975. Mowrer was APA president in 1954.

At the end of his life, Mowrer concluded that his frequently distressing depression had spurred him to a usefulness he would not otherwise have had. Three years after his wife died, Mowrer decided to end his own life in order not to deprive his children of whatever financial assistance he might leave them.

Mowrer's Two-Factor Theory

During the era of Watson and Guthrie, little distinction was drawn between Thorndikian and Pavlovian conditioning. Despite obvious procedural differences, the learning was assumed to be the same in each. In 1938 (and earlier), Skinner (discussed later) suggested there was a fundamental difference between Pavlovian conditioning and the type of conditioning he was studying, and Mowrer (1947) further elaborated this distinction with sign learning and solution learning.

Sign learning refers to Pavlovian or classical conditioning of involuntary responses controlled by the autonomic nervous system. It requires only temporal contiguity of a neutral stimulus (e.g., a white box) and an unconditioned stimulus (e.g., pain from shock). Mowrer called this sign learning because the CS becomes a sign of danger that triggers an emotional response of fear. This was Pavlov's first-signal system (Chapter 12).

Solution learning involves instrumental conditioning of voluntary responses of the striped, skeletal muscles controlled by the central nervous system, with reinforcement occurring through drive reduction. Mowrer called it solution learning because the instrumental response solves the problem created by the drive. Hilgard and Marquis (1940) advanced the more familiar terms *classical conditioning* and *instrumental conditioning.*

Later, Mowrer (1960) reduced his two-factor theory to only one factor—conditioning or sign learning—with solution learning seen as just a special kind of sign learning. Unlike Mowrer, two-factor theorist B. F. Skinner did not change his thinking.

B. F. SKINNER

Burrhus Frederick Skinner (1904–1990) was born and spent his first 18 years in the small railroad town of Susquehanna, Pennsylvania. Skinner was the first-born son of attorney William A. Skinner and Grace Burrhus Skinner. Grace had rigid standards of right and wrong, and the only physical punishment Skinner received from either of his parents came at her hands: She washed his mouth out with soap for using a dirty word.

Skinner described his home environment as "warm and stable," and he and his parents graduated, as salutatorians, from the same high school. Skinner was fond of his younger brother, Ebbie, who was more athletic and more popular than Skinner. In Skinner's presence, Ebbie died suddenly at 16, probably of a cerebral aneurism (Skinner, 1976).

As a youth, Skinner was a gadgeteer, an amateur inventor who delighted in building things. He also enjoyed school and was fortunate to have a teacher named Mary Graves, who taught him art in grammar school and English in high school. She was probably responsible for Skinner's early decision to major in English literature in college and to become a writer.

In high school, Skinner discovered Francis Bacon (Chapter 4) by challenging Shakespeare's authorship of a play his 8th-grade class was reading (some have suggested that Bacon really wrote the works we attribute to Shakespeare). Miss Graves responded that Skinner did not know what he was talking about, which stimulated him to acquire the knowledge to defend his contention. Many years later Skinner described his attitude toward science as Baconian:

> I reject verbal authority. I have "studied nature not books," asking questions of the organism rather than of those who have studied the organism. I think it can be said, as it was said of Bacon, that I get my books out of life, not out of other books. (Skinner, 1967, p. 409)

Skinner's first year at Hamilton College in New York was a period of major adjustment. He pledged the "wrong" fraternity, made few friends, and suffered humiliation over his mispronunciations (e.g., "crick" for "creek"; Bjork, 1993). Then, at Easter break, Ebbie died.

After his freshman year, Skinner became acquainted with the Saunders family through tutoring their youngest son in mathematics. The Saunders were sophisticated and well connected, and Percy Saunders remained a vital confidant to Skinner long after he graduated from Hamilton.

In his junior year, Skinner's anatomy and embryology professor recommended he read work by Jacques Loeb (Chapter 12), and Skinner was impressed by Loeb's tropism concept, much as Watson had been earlier. However, his literary inclinations were reinforced by attending the Bread Loaf School of English in Vermont during the summer following his junior year. There he met Robert Frost, who suggested that Skinner send him some of his work. Skinner sent three short stories, and Frost responded positively: "*You are worth twice anyone else I have seen in prose this year*" (Letter from Frost, 1926; cited in Skinner, 1976, p. 249, italics in the original).

After graduation, Skinner entered his "Dark Year," living at home in part because his brother's recent death still weighed heavily on the family (Bjork, 1998). Skinner did essentially nothing productive as a writer and decided to go to graduate school. He spent the 6 months before graduate school living in New York City's Greenwich Village, where he worked in a bookstore. Much of his reading pointed him toward a psychology career and particularly toward behaviorism. For example, Bertrand Russell's (1925) *Philosophy* directed him to Watson's *Behaviorism.* Many years later, Skinner sat across the table from Russell at a luncheon in the philosopher's honor. According to Skinner (1979), "I told him that his *Philosophy* had converted me to behaviorism. 'Good heavens,' he said, "I thought it had demolished behaviorism'" (p. 224). After a summer in Europe, Skinner applied to Harvard and was accepted for graduate school in psychology.

Skinner at Harvard

At Harvard, Skinner was apparently less influenced in his interests by the psychology faculty than he was by fellow graduate student Fred S. Keller (1899–1996), with whom he corresponded throughout his life, and the physiologist William Crozier. A student of Loeb, Crozier studied tropisms in intact lower organisms and also worked with rats. Crozier encouraged Skinner throughout his graduate and postgraduate Harvard tenure, and Skinner worked independently for several years in a laboratory offered by Crozier in the biology building. However, despite his proximity to biology and physiology, Skinner became increasingly convinced the study of behavior should concentrate on behavior and not on its physiological substrate. Thus, "Skinner would become a 'descriptive' or 'radical' behaviorist precisely because he denied that behavior is determined by processes within the physiology of the organism" (Bjork, 1993, p. 80).

Skinner's Harvard research combined his belief in the orderliness of individual animal behavior with his love of building gadgets. Beginning with a silent-release box designed to prevent a rat introduced into an apparatus from being disturbed, Skinner tinkered until he had invented what Hull later called the **Skinner box.** In it, a rat could be conditioned to press a lever to receive a food pellet, and a cumulative record of the animal's responding could be obtained. In his effort to develop experimental control over an individual animal's behavior, Skinner had constructed an apparatus that recorded behavior with relatively little variability and produced apparently lawful results. Skinner wrote his parents that it was the best birthday present he had gotten—he was 26.

An accomplished student, at his doctoral oral examination Skinner suffered only one moment of chagrin: Gordon Allport (Chapter 17) asked him to name some objections to behaviorism, and Skinner could not think of any. After receiving his Ph.D., Skinner stayed at Harvard on a fellowship that lasted the rest of the academic year. With Crozier's assistance, Skinner spent the next 2 years on a National Research Council Fellowship. On his 29th birthday in 1933, Skinner was interviewed by the Harvard Society of Fellows for the prestigious Junior Fellowship, which enabled him to stay at Harvard until 1936.

Skinner at Minnesota

Despite Skinner's research accomplishments, the Depression made finding a university position difficult. Finally, with a strong recommendation to a Harvard Ph.D., Richard Elliott, psychology department chairman at Minnesota, Skinner found himself in a teaching position for the first time. Staying one step ahead of his students, Skinner began to learn college psychology, and later he wrote, "I have never again been so richly reinforced as a teacher" (Skinner, 1967, p. 400).

Before leaving Harvard, Skinner had met Yvonne Blue, later known as Eve, the daughter of a wealthy ophthalmologist. She had majored in literature at the University of Chicago, had mixed with a bohemian crowd, and had horrified her parents by smoking in public. She and Skinner were married in late 1937, and their first child, Julie, was born in 1938.

The Behavior of Organisms

In 1938, Skinner published *The Behavior of Organisms,* which represented the culmination of his research efforts since 1930. Through *The Behavior of Organisms* and earlier papers, Skinner demonstrated that the rat's lever-pressing response was a behavioral unit that could be studied as scientifically as Pavlov's conditioned reflex. In fact, it illustrated a second type of conditioning, which he had identified earlier (Skinner, 1935). Describing the difference, Skinner noted that Pavlovian conditioning prepared the organism for food, whereas his version—which he dubbed "Type I"—obtained the food for which the organism was prepared.

Polish physiologists Konorski and Miller (1937) criticized Skinner's two conditioning types, renaming them Type I for Pavlovian conditioning and Type II for Skinner's "new type of reflex." Replying to Konorski and Miller, Skinner (1937) introduced another pair of names: Type R for his type of conditioning and Type S for Pavlov's. Further, he wrote, "All conditioned reflexes of Type R are by definition operants and all of Type S, respondents . . ." (p. 274). This was Skinner's first use of the term **operant,** which he defined as "a kind of response which occurs spontaneously in the absence of any stimulation with which it may be specifically correlated" (p. 274). Operant behaviors operate on the environment to produce consequences, which determine whether the behavior will be repeated in the given situation. A **respondent** was a reflex in the more traditional sense, involving the correlation between a stimulus and the response to it. Skinner did not claim to have discovered Type R or operant conditioning, noting that "The behavior characteristic of Type *R* was studied as early as 1898 (Thorndike)" (Skinner, 1937, p. 278).

Konorski and Miller (1937) had implied that a conditioning procedure relying on a response to occur spontaneously could not be universally valid because many responses never occur spontaneously. In response, Skinner (1937) described **shaping,** in which "elaborate and peculiar forms of response may be generated from undifferentiated operant behavior *through successive approximation to a final form*" (p. 277, italics added).

Most reviewers of *The Behavior of Organisms* thought it contained serious flaws. For example, some reviewers considered the title pretentious, arguing against the leap from rat conditioning experiments to "the behavior of organisms." Skinner's rebuttal was that he was just following the lead of Pavlov, who had not added "in the dog" to the title *Conditioned Reflexes.* Further, several reviewers criticized Skinner for neglecting previous work on learning and motivation. Skinner's justification was that he had had little success in finding completely relevant material elsewhere because his paradigm was so novel. Other criticisms included the book's lack of coverage of such important psychological fields as perception and thinking, and its lack of statistical fortification. Despite the book's unprofitability—as of 1946 there were still 250 copies unsold from the original 800-copy printing—Keller (1991) considered it Skinner's "most important book, . . . assuring him of an honored place in the history of science" (p. 4).

Project Pigeon

With World War II underway, Skinner knew about the Nazis' use of the airplane as a potent offensive weapon, and he began to wonder about a missile that would zero in on a bomber. On a 1939 train ride, Skinner noticed a flock of birds flying alongside the train. "Suddenly I saw them as 'devices' with excellent vision and extraordinary maneuverability. Could they not guide a missile?" (Skinner, 1979, p. 241).

Skinner bought some pigeons and began to train them to guide missiles. Following a successful demonstration of the pigeons' ability to guide missiles, the dean of the Minnesota faculty wrote to Richard Tolman, Edward Tolman's brother, who was affiliated with the National Defense Research Committee (NDRC). Tolman decided not to support the experimentation needed to see if Skinner's pigeons could function under combat conditions.

After the December 1941 Pearl Harbor attack, Skinner resurrected the pigeon project. With graduate students Keller and Marian Breland, Norman Guttman, and later William Estes, Skinner began working on a steerable bomb rather than a surface-to-air missile as before. Although Tolman again denied funding, Skinner's efforts came to the attention of Chairman Bell of General Mills, who appropriated $5,000 to fund the project until it could be supported by a governmental agency.

A successful 1943 demonstration led the newly formed Office of Scientific Research and Development (OSRD) to award General Mills a contract to "develop a homing device" under the name **Project Pigeon.** Of course, some of the pigeon studies Skinner and his group performed had nothing to do with the project. In a letter to Fred Keller, Skinner wrote they had replicated almost all of the work reported "in [*The Behavior* *of Organisms*] (with a different species) plus oodles of new stuff" (Skinner, 1979, p. 267). Key pecking in pigeons proved a more satisfying model than rat lever pressing, and Skinner never returned to rats.

After another successful feasibility demonstration to OSRD officials, Skinner was told that further project support would delay other developments promising more immediate military application. Although the pigeons had performed beautifully, "all our efforts with the scientists came to nothing. My verbal behavior with respect to Washington underwent extinction, and the effect generalized" (Skinner, 1979, p. 274).

In the early 1950s, Skinner acted as consultant on a Navy project to use pigeons for missile guidance, which was called Project ORCON (ORganic CONtrol). With the discovery of alternative electronic guidance systems, ORCON was discontinued in 1953.

Skinner at Indiana

In 1940, **Jacob Robert Kantor** (1888–1984) asked Skinner if he would be willing to come to Indiana. A Chicago Ph.D., Kantor called his approach **interbehaviorism** and stressed the interactions of an organism with stimulus objects. Both the responding organism and the stimulus objects were considered of equal importance (e.g., Mountjoy & Hansor, 1986).

Skinner rejected the Indiana position in 1940, but he was interested in 1945 when the offer included the department's chairmanship. Feeling out of the mainstream of psychology in Minneapolis, Skinner accepted Indiana's offer.

The Baby in a Box

Because Yvonne had disliked caring for their first child, Skinner suggested they simplify the care of the new baby that arrived in 1943. He started work on

> a crib-sized living space that we began to call the "baby-tender." It had sound-absorbing walls and a large picture window. Air entered through filters at the bottom and, after being warmed and moistened, moved upward through and around the edges of a tightly stretched canvas, which served as a mattress. A strip of sheeting ten yards long passed over the canvas, a clean section of which could be cranked into place in a few seconds. (Skinner, 1979, p. 275)

Home from the hospital, Deborah was immediately placed into Skinner's **baby-tender.**

Deborah thrived in the box for the first 2 1/2 years of her life. Despite rumors of insanity and suicide, she was a healthy, happy infant who grew into an accomplished adult. According to her father, "she's actually a happily married woman, living in London at the moment, [and] cooperating in writing a book on the best hotels in England and Scotland" (Trudeau, 1990, p. 10). The only long-term effects Deborah recalls from her life in the box "are unusually prehensile toes and the habit of sleeping with only a sheet" (Bjork, 1998, p. 269). Although Julie Skinner had not been raised in the baby-tender, she elected to raise her children in one.

After failing to interest General Mills in developing the baby-tender, Skinner wrote an article describing the device's advantages, which was published in *Ladies' Home Journal* as "Baby in a Box" in the fall of 1945. Although there were negative letters from people who assumed Skinner was experimenting on his daughter as he had done on rats and pigeons, there were far more positive letters. "Within a month after the article's appearance, seventy-five to one hundred baby tenders were being built by *Journal* readers" (Bjork, 1993, p. 132).

After further publicity, Skinner turned the project of building and marketing "heir conditioners" over to Cleveland businessman J. J. Weste. Unfortunately, Skinner soon learned that Weste had disappeared, taking with him money from lending agencies, from Skinner himself, and from several potential customers. For years afterward, Skinner felt the embarrassing effects of Weste's dishonesty.

In the 1950s, Skinner finally became involved in a successful effort to produce baby-tenders (now called aircribs) commercially. In 1957, John Gray's Aircrib Corporation began to manufacture and sell Skinner's invention. Approximately a thousand aircribs were sold by the time Gray died a decade later, and several surveys of users indicated that "overall . . . parents were quite satisfied with their aircribs" (Benjamin & Nielsen-Gammon, 1999, p. 163). Although Skinner always believed his first social invention failed to find greater acceptance because of the difficulties of getting aircribs mass-produced by a large manufacturer, Benjamin and Nielsen-Gammon suggested the problem was instead one of image—the aircrib

Skinner (1904–1990) demonstrating the operant conditioning of a pigeon

was erroneously seen as reducing parent-infant contact. Skinner's next social invention effort came in novel form.

Walden Two

At a party in 1945, Skinner talked to a dinner companion about what young people would do after the war and how it was a shame for them to lose their crusading zeal. Perhaps they should explore new ways of living, as people had done in 19th-century utopian communities. Skinner's dinner companion asked for details and later suggested that he write it all down.

In June 1945, Skinner began to write what he planned to call *The Sun Is But a Morning Star.* In the book, Skinner (1948) adopted a standard utopian strategy by having people visit a community whose concept is described and defended by its founder. The book's narrator is Burris (as in Burrhus), a college professor who has unhappily returned to the classroom after an exciting wartime experience. The community's founder is Frazier, "a self-proclaimed genius who has deserted academic psychology for behavioral engineering, the new discipline upon which the community is based" (Skinner, 1979, p. 296). Skinner speculated that "Frazier" was a combination of "Fred" (either himself or his friend, Fred Keller) and "Crozier," his Harvard mentor.

Skinner's utopian community operates by the operant conditioning principles its author had discovered. The environment is arranged so that each person can engage in work, hobbies, the arts—all inherently reinforcing activities. Not surprisingly, babies are raised in aircribs. Also not surprisingly, Frazier contends that behavioral science is superior to other ways of improving the human condition. All that is necessary for the good life is to apply operant techniques to society.

Skinner found writing the book to be cathartic, as Frazier was able to "say things that I myself was not yet ready to say to anyone" (Skinner, 1979, p. 298). However, Skinner's catharsis did not ensure the book's publication, and four large publishing firms rejected it before Macmillan accepted it if Skinner would write an introductory psychology textbook for them. *Walden Two* was published in 1948.

Several early reviews were quite favorable: For example, "the *New Yorker* called it 'an extremely interesting discourse on the possibilities of social organization'" (Skinner, 1979, pp. 346–347). Unfortunately, *Life,* a magazine with broad national circulation, published a particularly damning critique. Possibly because of such reviews, *Walden Two* sold poorly for many years. However, with the growing interest in alternative lifestyles in the 1960s, sales blossomed, and by Skinner's death in 1990, sales recorded on a cumulative response curve in his study had reached nearly 2,500,000 copies.

Skinner (1971) made another attempt to advocate social change from the behaviorist perspective in

Beyond Freedom and Dignity. In it, he argued that only operant science is capable of properly modifying human culture. Skinner concluded, "We have not yet seen what man can make of man" (p. 215).

Negative reactions to *Beyond Freedom and Dignity* were legion, coming from sources ranging from scholarly journals to television and radio talk shows. Most critics objected to Skinner's apparent disparagement of individual freedom and dignity, and more than one suggested Skinner's approach to individual freedom was compatible with Germany and Italy in the late 1930s. Certainly the most colorfully negative critique came from philosopher/novelist Ayn Rand, whose novels *The Fountainhead* and *Atlas Shrugged* stress the importance for society of the autonomous individual. Rand compared *Beyond Freedom and Dignity* to "'Boris Karloff's embodiment of Frankenstein's monster: a corpse patched with nuts, bolts and screws from the junkyard of philosophy, Darwinism, Positivism, Linguistic Analysis, with some nails by Hume, threads by Russell and glue by the *New York Post*" (Rand, as cited in Bjork, 1993, p. 205).

Obviously, *Beyond Freedom and Dignity* struck a sensitive chord. Skinner was not, as his critics contended, advocating the loss of individual freedom, because he already believed such freedom was an illusion. As products of our environments, he argued, we should strive to structure our environments to produce behavior that maximizes the benefits to society. Perhaps the novelty of Skinner's argument *shaped* his critics' reactions.

Beyond Freedom and Dignity was certainly not Skinner's last word on the ills of modern—and particularly Western—society from the behaviorist perspective. With an audience confined to psychologists, Skinner (1986) specified cultural practices he believed have violated the reinforcement contingencies in effect throughout human evolution. Among other things, he pointed to the separation of workers from the products of their efforts and the tendency to do things because we have been told to do them rather than because we have been reinforced for doing them as practices that have weakened human behavior in the West. As you would expect, Skinner argued that an experimental analysis of behavior holds the key to strengthening behavior.

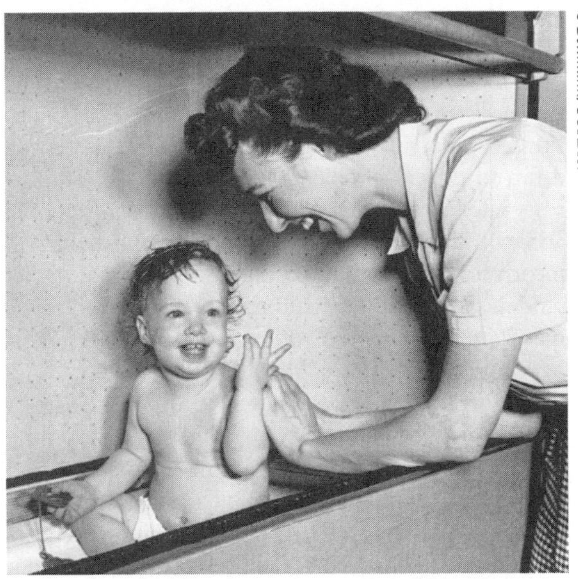

A happy Debbie Skinner playing in the baby-tender

Skinner at Harvard Again

In 1947, Boring (Chapter 1) invited Skinner to give the William James Lectures at Harvard, and Skinner spoke on "Verbal Behavior: A Psychological Analysis." On the strength of the lectures and his many accomplishments, Skinner was invited to return to Harvard, and he remained there until his retirement in 1974. On retiring, fittingly enough, Skinner was presented a first edition of Thoreau's *Walden*.

Teaching Machines

During a visit to his daughter Debbie's 4th-grade arithmetic class, Skinner observed some students finishing their task early and sitting idly while other students strained with their problems. Afterward, the teacher collected the papers to grade and return the next day. The situation violated two fundamental learning principles: Knowledge of consequences was delayed and individual differences in ability were ignored. Skinner responded by building a **teaching machine** that presented arithmetic problems singly, in a fixed order, that the student had to solve before proceeding. A student could work at his or her own pace, and reinforcement—getting the problem right—was immediate.

Skinner's teaching machine was anticipated by the work of Ohio State University professor Sidney Pressey, who, in 1926, built a box with a revolving drum to present problems to a student. The student responded by pressing one of four buttons. A correct answer triggered a new problem to appear, whereas an incorrect response blocked the drum's rotation. After sending Skinner information about his work, Pressey met Skinner at the next APA convention, where Skinner convinced him a brighter future lay ahead.

Unfortunately, it was not to be. Although Skinner had some limited success in building a teaching machine that delivered programmed instruction and even used the machine in teaching one of his courses at Harvard, his attempts to get his teaching machines mass-marketed proved as fruitless as his baby-tender efforts. Rutherford (2003) attributed both failures to bad timing in terms of the cultural milieu in which the new technologies were introduced. Skinner's baby-tender came at a time of more permissive parenting and was rejected by many who thought it would interfere with essential parent-child interactions. Similarly, Skinner's teaching machines appeared when the humanistic movement was on the rise because of a growing public fear of the dehumanizing effects of technology. The teaching machines were seen as contributing to this dehumanization.

Although Skinner's revolution in American education failed, "The seeds he sowed are still alive and, to a limited extent, have been integrated in some computer-learning software" (Bjork, 1993, p. 186). Still, at the end of his life, Skinner was discouraged about American education's future, calling his efforts to change education his life's greatest disappointment.

Schedules of Reinforcement

Soon after he arrived at Harvard, Skinner established a pigeon laboratory in which he and Charles Ferster worked happily for several years, studying the effects of different schedules of reinforcement on behavior. In *The Behavior of Organisms,* Skinner (1938) had discussed the effect on behavior of intermittent or partial reinforcement—which he at first called "periodic reconditioning" (Skinner, 1980)—and had indicated that intermittent reinforcement could be scheduled in many ways. *Schedules of Reinforcement* (Ferster & Skinner, 1957) was an "exhaustive extension" of that theme. As an indication of the book's thoroughness, it contains 921 figures, which mostly depict cumulative response curves.

The basic intermittent schedules are based on either time between reinforcements (interval schedules) or number of responses between reinforcements (ratio schedules). Further, the time between reinforcements can be either fixed or variable, resulting in **fixed-interval (FI)** and **variable-interval (VI)** schedules. Similarly, the number of responses between reinforcements can be fixed or variable, giving **fixed-ratio (FR)** and **variable-ratio (VR)** schedules.

Schedules of Reinforcement was an enormous achievement, and a decade later, Skinner (1967) described his collaborative work with Ferster as "the high point in my research history" (p. 405). Figure 13.4 shows cumulative response curves illustrating the basic schedules.

Verbal Behavior

In the same year that *Schedules of Reinforcement* appeared, Skinner (1957) finally saw the publication of *Verbal Behavior,* a book he had begun in 1934 following a friendly challenge from Alfred North Whitehead (mentioned in Chapter 2). Whitehead was willing to agree that science might successfully account for all human behavior except verbal behavior. Naturally, Skinner began work on a behavioristic account of human language.

For the behaviorist, human speech is just another behavior, which, like any operant behavior, is controlled by its consequences. We learn to speak by being reinforced for our verbal behavior, and we learn what to say (and what not to say) through reinforcement and punishment. Speech becomes a way to obtain reinforcement from others around us and a way for us to reinforce others. Literature, poetry, and other forms of creative writing are variations of verbal behavior acquired and retained through operant conditioning.

Along with favorable reviews of *Verbal Behavior,* which Skinner predicted in 1980 would "prove to be [his] most important work" (p. 198), Skinner received a strongly negative critique from Noam Chomsky. Skinner put the critique aside when the "first pages were not reassuring," but Chomsky's criticisms were published in the journal *Language,* and they soon began to receive more attention than *Verbal Behavior.* According to Skinner (1983), one of his former students was said to have begun a speech with, "Behaviorism is dead and it was a linguist [Chomsky] who killed it" (p. 155). We will have more to say about Chomsky's views of language and their impact on behaviorism's decline in Chapter 18.

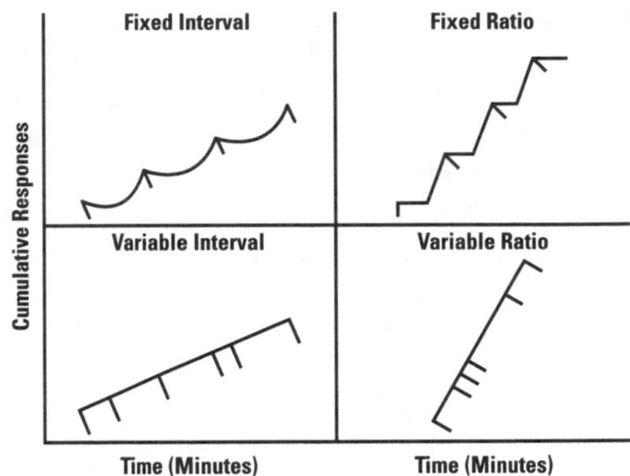

FIGURE 13.4 Cumulative response curves
The curves illustrate performance on each of the basic reinforcement schedules. Each downward mark indicates delivery of a reward.

Skinner's Influence

In our examination of Skinner's contributions, we have avoided discussing a learning theory. This omission is consistent with the conclusion of Skinner's (1950) article, "Are theories of learning necessary?" Skinner noted that although "[t]heories are fun . . . it is possible that the most rapid progress toward an understanding of learning may be made by research that is not designed to test theories" (p. 215). Following Francis Bacon's precept to experiment, Skinner made lasting contributions to many areas of psychology.

In addition to such contributions as the identification and study of operant conditioning, the invention of the Skinner box, the elucidation of schedules of reinforcement, the scientific beginnings of programmed instruction, and the illustration of the power of shaping (e.g., in Project Pigeon), operant conditioning has been used in myriad ways. One example has been its use in testing the psychoactive effects of different drugs and/or the effects on behavior of different types of brain damage (e.g., Aaron & Thorne, 1975; Thorne, Rager, & Topping, 1976). As another example, Skinner's students Ogden Lindsley, Nathan Azrin, and others have used operant conditioning to treat psychopathology. In one of the best-known studies, Teodoro Ayllon and Azrin (1968) used a **token economy** to treat schizophrenic females in a state hospital. The women received plastic tokens for cooperative behaviors such as making their beds and eating properly. The tokens could be exchanged for privileges (e.g., being allowed to go for a walk on the grounds) or for desired items (e.g., candy). Under the token economy, desirable behaviors increased dramatically, and removing the tokens produced swift extinction of the desirable behaviors.

Skinner's influence can also be seen in the journals and associations his work spawned. The *Journal of the Experimental Analysis of Behavior* came first (1958), followed by the *Journal of Applied Behavior Analysis* (1968). In 1974, the Midwestern Association for Behavior Analysis was organized, and it was followed 4 years later by the Association for Behavior Analysis.

Despite his acclaim, Skinner was never elected APA president, primarily because he did not want the job. The office then and now involves "political" work for which Skinner considered himself unsuited. The APA recognized Skinner's research efforts with the Distinguished Scientific Contribution Award in 1958, and shortly before his death, the organization presented Skinner with a Lifetime Contribution to Psychology Award.

Skinner was less successful in changing such society's institutions as education and early childrearing practices, and Prilleltensky (1994) has argued that Skinner and other radical behaviorists were more concerned with changing people to fit society than in modifying society's institutions. Perhaps Skinner's failure came from embracing the Baconian technological ideal, which seeks to control and remake the world (Smith, 1992). In this, Skinner followed Watson's lead by declaring that the aim of behavioral science is the prediction and control of behavior. According to Smith, some historians of science have identified another approach, the Aristotle-originated contemplative ideal, which seeks to understand the natural world and its causes.

Skinner's adoption of the Baconian approach and defense of behavioral technology came at a time in America when technological advances were viewed as a mixed blessing at best. *Walden Two* was finished shortly before the destruction of two Japanese cities with atomic bombs, an event that raised the specter of humanity's destruction through the unwise application of technology. Rachel Carson's (1962) *Silent Spring* was an early harbinger of the negative environmental effects of modern industrial technology, just as earlier novels such as George Orwell's *1984* and Aldous Huxley's *Brave New World* had cautioned against behaviorism's social engineering.

In a National Public Radio interview shortly before his death, Skinner summarized his successes and failures in this way: "I've had a very good life. It would be very foolish of me to complain in any way about it" (Trudeau, 1990, p. 12). We will let the final comment on this outstanding figure of the 20th century come from a psychologist who probably knew him best, his friend from graduate school—Fred Keller.

> B. F. Skinner, as he signed himself professionally, was a many-sided genius, a product of small-town America, with a liberal education at the hands of a few good teachers, an exposure to some of the finest thinkers of our past, and a natural endowment that permitted him to take advantage of these benefits to the full. He was an independent worker, an expert in self-management, and was undistracted by personal attacks or by high honors (of which there were very many). He was never an office-seeker or a hail-fellow-well-met, but he played an active part in every group of which he was a member. He was not a do-gooder, but all of his attempts to apply the principles of behavior to practical affairs were aimed at the improvement of the lot of human beings everywhere. (Keller, 1991, p. 5)

It would be impossible to overemphasize behaviorism's importance, or Skinner's importance as its leading contributor (although see O'Neil, 1995, for a less sanguine view of Skinner's contributions). Boring's 1950 comment about all America having gone behaviorist was valid, and later it was not just behaviorism, but Skinnerian behaviorism (e.g., Skinner, 1974), that dominated modern scientific psychology. "[O]ne can confidently assert that B. F. Skinner was the most visible and influential American psychologist in the second half of the 20th century" (Coleman, 1997, p. 213).

Behavioral analysis focuses on the environment as the source of stimulus information, and a psychology whose goal is the prediction and control of behavior typically involves the study and manipulation of the environment. Instead of unseen mental or biological events, the radical behaviorists provided explanations of psychological phenomena in terms of observable environmental conditions. Not surprisingly, one of the camps of behaviorism focused on analyzing the environment itself, and we will call this ecological psychology. Because the ecological behaviorists have been more readily embraced by contemporary cognitive psychology than most other behaviorists, it seems appropriate to close our consideration of behaviorism with them.

ECOLOGICAL PSYCHOLOGY

We are using the term **ecological psychology** to signify a behaviorist movement that stressed examining the environmental conditions and fully understanding the nature of the stimulus in any behavioral event. This attention to the stimulus, and thus to the organism's perception of the information it contains, paradoxically gives the ideas of the ecological behaviorists a somewhat "cognitive" feel. By expanding the consideration of the stimulus to matters of perception and information, these behaviorists represent a connection to both the underlying physiology of behavior and to phenomena often considered mentalistic (Chapter 18). However, as behaviorists, the ecological psychologists provided alternative explanations for many "cognitive" phenomena.

J. R. Kantor and his interbehaviorism, mentioned earlier, can be viewed as the forerunner to the ecological movement, which we will examine in the work of Roger Barker and James J. Gibson.

Roger Barker

Roger Barker (1903–1990) was born in Iowa and raised in California and Canada. Barker was sickly as a child, an invalid from the ages of 14 to 21, and suffered health problems intermittently throughout his adult life. After starting college at the University of Redlands in California, he earned a Ph.D. in psychology from Stanford.

From Stanford, Barker returned to Iowa as a research assistant to the Gestalt psychologists Kurt Lewin and Tamara Dembo (Chapter 14). Barker (1989) acknowledged his debt to Lewin for introducing him to the "stream of behavior" metaphor that Barker made central to his own research (e.g., Barker, 1963). Also, Barker adapted Lewin's "life space" concept into a more behavioral analysis of the environment and the invitations and constraints it places on our actions.

Leaving Iowa, Barker held positions at Harvard, Illinois, Stanford, and Clark before becoming chairman of the psychology department at the University of Kansas in Lawrence. His best-known work, *One Boy's Day* (Barker & Wright, 1951), is a microanalysis of just that—one boy's day—and is a methodological masterpiece of environmental analysis. The book also illustrates the main work at the Midwest Psychological Field Station of the University of Kansas, which was established in 1947 by Barker and his colleague H. F. Wright in nearby Oskaloosa, Kansas, where Barker and his wife Louise lived for more than 40 years (Kaminski, 1997). The field station's mission included the discovery and description of the environments in Oskaloosa for the town's children, the recording of the children's behavior in the environments, and the study of the relations in the town between behavior and environment.

James Jerome Gibson

Like Barker, **James Jerome Gibson**'s (1904–1979) career was shaped by contact with Gestalt psychology. Gibson was a Princeton Ph.D. who studied under Herbert Langfeld (Chapter 10) and was also influenced by E. B. Holt (Chapter 10) and Leonard Carmichael (Chapter 12). Carmichael visited Germany after Köhler assumed leadership of the Berlin Institute from Stumpf (Chapter 8) and brought back news of Gestalt psychology (Reed, 1996). Gibson's dissertation on form perception offered a behaviorist alternative to phenomena reported by Gestalt pyschologist Kurt Koffka.

Gibson (1966a) credited his interest in behaviorism to H. C. Warren's (Chapter 8) zeal over Watson's ideas and to E. B. Holt's motor theory of consciousness, which Gibson thought allowed a place for studying consciousness within a behavioral, scientific psychology. Moving to Smith College, Gibson found that one of his new colleagues was Kurt Koffka, a psychologist he came to admire greatly. Professionally, Gibson wrote, "Koffka, along with Holt, was a main influence on my psychological thinking"(p. 131), and the Gestalt tempering of Gibson's behaviorism is clear in his classic works (e.g., Gibson, 1966b, 1979).

J. J. Gibson's primary interests were in the relations between the perceived properties of a stimulus and behavior. Gibson studied several tasks to demonstrate the importance of the stimulus, of which the best known was his work for the military on the ability to land aircraft successfully (e.g., Gibson, 1947). After the war—a boon for Gibson because his research was useful in training pilots—Gibson moved to Cornell, where he concluded his academic career. He was a recipient of the APA's Distinguished Scientific Contribution Award.

Gibson's major work, *The Ecological Approach to Visual Perception,* appeared the year he died. Many believe that Gibson succeeded in presenting a grand, unifying behavior theory that provides both a behaviorist account of mentalistic concepts and the appropriate conception of the relations between behavior and physiological processes. In so doing, Gibson may have reduced psychology's three rival modes of explanation—the mentalistic, the physiologically reductive, and the behavioral focus on the environment—into a holistic way of understanding the action of organisms.

Although not everyone is convinced that Gibson succeeded (e.g., Fodor & Pylyshyn, 1981), Gibson's ideas have had an impact both on behaviorism and on cognitive psychology. The core idea of Gibson's final book is **affordance,** which is the information contained in a stimulus that we perceive and respond to directly because of our evolutionary history. For the behaviorist, affordance is attractive because of this **direct perception;** that is, the information is not processed by an unseen mental structure but is interpreted directly by the biological equipment evolved for survival in an ecological niche.

Gibson's views have been most criticized for their explicit disinterest in discovering physiological mechanisms mediating direct perception. In an "appreciation" of Gibson, Nakayama (1994) indicated he had "turned a blind eye" to Gibson's unwavering stance "because, early on, I decided that Gibson's ideas were just too good to pass up" (p. 334). Nakayama's article was one of three papers in a 1994 issue of *Pyschological Review,* which presented comments following a reprinting of Gibson's 1954 article, "The Visual Perception of Objective Motion and Subjective Movement."

At Smith, Gibson married Eleanor Jack, a former student of his and later one of Hull's Ph.D.s at Yale after being rejected by Yerkes, who allowed no women in his laboratory (Gibson, 1980). Gibson's relationship to his wife kept him in touch with important changes in learning theory (Reed, 1996). A member of the National Academy of Sciences, a fellow of the American Association for the Advancement of Science, and a winner of the APA's Distinguished Scientific Contribution Award, **Eleanor Jack Gibson** (1910–2002) is best known for her visual cliff work.

One illustration of an affordance is infant (human and animal) **visual cliff** performance. Studies by Eleanor J. Gibson and others have shown that infant organisms avoid an apparent "cliff" despite a lack of experience with falling, which suggests an evolutionary advantage for an innate association between edges and danger. Falling is dangerous for organisms because it brings the head and the rest of the body to the ground with great force. Thus, we have evolved a visual system vigilant for signals, such as edges, warning of environmental contexts that can lead to falling. In Gibson's view, the affordance of falling is not a consciously mediated event but a direct perception that influences our behavior in a particular situation.

CONCLUSIONS

It would be misleading to suggest there were no important behaviorists after Skinner or Gibson, or that behaviorism's impact faded from psychology with the deaths of the major figures we have examined in Chapters 12 and 13. Still, it is true that although behaviorism was American psychology's pre-eminent school from the 1920s until the 1970s, in the last 2 decades psychology's center has shifted away from the behaviorist focus on learning theory.

For example, social psychology (Chapter 17) increased dramatically in popularity following World War II, and, as we suggested earlier, the Chomsky-Skinner debate over language was fundamental to the rise of cognitive psychology and perhaps to behaviorism's fall. Cognitive psychology was not the only critic of behaviorism's dominance over psychological research, however. The ethologists (Chapter 12) mounted an attack on the proper analysis of animal behavior, and humanistic (often clinical) psychologists (Chapter 16) saw behaviorism as too narrow to explain adequately the vagaries of human existence.

Broader changes in science and philosophy also contributed to behaviorism's decline. Logical positivism lost respectability as new problems in physics and further analysis by philosophers of science challenged its core assumptions. In fact, it can be argued that positivism's embrace by such behaviorists as Watson, Hull, and Skinner was too tight, and behavioral psychologists represent some of the final holdouts to the increasingly discredited positivist view of science.

Still, behaviorists have made so many contributions that seem permanently entrenched in the body of psychological fact that, in at least this sense, behaviorism has achieved immortality. Although the ideas of Guthrie and Tolman seem to garner less coverage in each new introductory psychology textbook, we can point to a return of Hullian concepts with modern interest in machine learning. Additionally, such principles as those Skinner derived from his reinforcement schedules research seem etched in stone.

Although one of Skinner's students is supposed to have said, "Behaviorism is dead and it was a linguist who killed it" (Skinner, 1983, p. 155), behaviorism's demise may be more apparent than real. Kendler (2002) pointed out that "[b]ehaviorism was not a monolithic system" (p. 70), and the behaviorism that cognitive psychology "killed" was a very restrictive form of the system. Kendler notes that an early cognitivist, George Mandler, "clearly acknowledged that the cognitive revolution did not reject methodological behaviorism" (p. 71). Kendler's article also provides an interesting retrospective on his more than 60 years in psychology.

Perhaps the proper conclusion to our review of behaviorism can be found in Gregory Kimble's (2000) article, "Behaviorism and Unity in Psychology." As the title indicates, Kimble's thesis is that behaviorism, which he defines as "any psychology that sees its mission as the explanation of behavior and accepts stimuli . . . and responses as its basic data" (p. 208), is capable of unifying the disparate strains in psychology. He concludes by writing,

> The materials I have used to paint a portrait of behaviorism with S-R and R-R faces show that this orientation provides an environment in which the psychology of tests and measures can live in harmony with biological, cognitive, and humanistic psychology. . . . It softens the antagonism between the academic psychologists and practitioners. It gives subjective concepts scientific legitimacy and may even promote peace between psychology's scientific and humanistic cultures. . . . (p. 211)

SUMMARY

Behaviorism was the culmination of a line of influences toward a strongly objective, rigorously experimental psychology. These influences included British empiricism, Darwinian evolutionary theory, American functionalism, logical positivism, and operationism. After S. S. Stevens called for operationism in psychology, its principles swept the field, as did behaviorism.

Edwin Ray Guthrie

Guthrie's learning theory is one-trial, nonreinforcement, contiguity learning, because he believed that a connection between a stimulus and a response occurs at full strength on each trial, without reinforcement, by stimulus-response contiguity. Practice improves performance because the learning of a particular movement occurs in one trial, but an act consists of many movements, each of which must be acquired before the act is performed skillfully.

Guthrie developed several ways to break bad habits: for example, by fatiguing the response. He also recognized that much behavior is goal directed and emphasized the role of movement-produced stimuli in sequential responding. William K. Estes applied a mathematical model to Guthrie's learning theory.

Edward Chace Tolman

Tolman was interested in behavior considered in large units, and he, too, believed that behavior is goal oriented. Tolman differentiated learning from performance, holding that although learning may occur in the absence of reinforcement, reward is necessary for performance. Evidence for the distinction came from latent learning studies.

From studies of rats in mazes, Tolman concluded that animals developed cognitive maps they could use to achieve alternative solutions when a particular pathway was blocked. Support for the cognitive map idea included studies of vicarious trial and error behavior, hypothesis-testing experiments, and studies comparing place-learning and response-learning rats.

Clark Leonard Hull

After research on aptitude testing and hypnosis, at Yale, Hull began work on hypothetico-deductive learning theory. Hull's final system contained 17 postulates and over 130 theorems. Like Tolman, Hull used intervening variables in his theorizing, including such variables as drive, habit strength, excitatory potential, and incentive motivation.

Hull's Students and Associates

After Hull's death, Spence continued his mentor's experimental efforts. One of Spence's main contributions was an S-R explanation for Köhler's demonstration of relational responding in chickens. Over time, Spence's theorizing edged closer to Tolman's and Guthrie's.

With John Dollard, Neal Miller presented a simplified version of Hull's theory, reducing Hull's postulates and theorems to the elements of drive, cue, response, and reward. Miller and Dollard provided data for the importance of imitation, and they were also interested in secondary drives—learned drives that gain their motivating status from pairing with primary drives.

O. H. Mowrer proposed a two-factor theory of reinforcement and, correspondingly, two types of learning.

Skinner had earlier distinguished between Pavlovian conditioning and Skinner's Thorndike-based type of conditioning. Mowrer elaborated Skinner's distinction into sign learning (Pavlovian conditioning) and solution learning (instrumental conditioning).

B. F. Skinner

Through a process of development, Skinner invented the Skinner box, in which an organism is conditioned to make a response for reinforcement. Skinner called his conditioning "operant conditioning," because the organism operates on the environment to produce consequences, which determine whether the behavior will be repeated. By reinforcing successive approximations of the desired behavior, an organism's operant behavior can be shaped.

Skinner and his associates demonstrated operant conditioning's power by training pigeons to be missile guidance systems. A more practical demonstration came in Skinner's development of teaching machines. Skinner's inventiveness also led to the baby-tender, a protected environment for early childrearing. Neither invention achieved commercial success.

At Harvard, Skinner worked with Charles Ferster to study the effects of different reinforcement schedules on behavior. Skinner also developed a behavioristic analysis of language, and its attack by linguist Noam Chomsky may have led to behaviorism's death.

Often controversial, Skinner penned such social commentaries as *Walden Two* and *Beyond Freedom and Dignity.* Skinner's radical behaviorism forms the foundation of modern scientific psychology.

Ecological Psychology

Ecological psychology was a behaviorist movement stressing the importance of fully understanding the environmental conditions and the nature of the stimulus in any behavioral event. Roger Barker and James J. Gibson were leading ecological psychologists who were influenced by Gestalt psychologists. Gibson was married to Eleanor Jack Gibson, perhaps best known for visual cliff experiments with young animals.

Some psychologists think J. J. Gibson's *The Ecological Approach to Visual Perception* achieved a holistic understanding of the behavior of organisms that combines the mentalistic, the physiologically reductive, and the behavioral focus on the environment. The core idea is the affordance, which is stimulus information we respond to directly because of our evolutionary history.

CONNECTIONS QUESTIONS

1. What were some of the connections Skinner foresaw between behaviorism and how we live in the everyday world?
2. How is Guthrie's brand of behaviorism connected to our everyday lives?
3. What connections can you make between the functionalists and the neobehaviorists?
4. What events in the lives of Hull and Skinner seem to connect with their psychological positions and research interests?
5. What connections can you make to support the claim that Skinner's most important contribution to psychology was to take Thorndike's law of effect seriously?
6. What enduring connections can you make between learning theory (behaviorism) and other areas of psychology such as clinical, social, developmental, and cognitive?

KEY NAMES AND TERMS

habit strength (p. 371)
Clark Leonard Hull (p. 368)
hypothesis experiments (p. 366)
hypothetical constructs (p. 366)
hypothetico-deductive learning theory (p. 370)
incentive motivation (p. 372)
incompatible stimuli (p. 361)
interbehaviorism (p. 381)
intervening variable (p. 365)
Jacob Robert Kantor (p. 381)
latent learning (p. 364)
Neal Elgar Miller (p. 375)
movement-produced stimuli (p. 359)
Orval Hobart Mowrer (p. 377)
operant (p. 380)
operational definition (p. 356)
operationism (p. 356)
performance (p. 364)
Ralph Barton Perry (p. 362)
place learning (p. 366)
Project Pigeon (p. 380)
purposive behaviorism (p. 363)
reaction potential (p. 372)
respondent (p. 380)
Bertrand Russell (p. 358)
secondary drive (p. 376)
shaping (p. 380)
sign learning (p. 378)
Burrhus Frederick Skinner (p. 378)
Skinner box (p. 379)
solution learning (p. 378)
Kenneth W. Spence (p. 374)
Stanley Smith Stevens (p. 356)
teaching machine (p. 383)
token economy (p. 385)
toleration or threshold method (p. 360)
Edward Chace Tolman (p. 362)
variable-interval (VI) schedule (p. 384)
variable-ratio (VR) schedule (p. 384)
visual cliff (p. 388)
Harry Kirke Wolfe (p. 357)

SUGGESTED READINGS

Bjork, D. W. (1993). *B. F. Skinner: A life.* New York: BasicBooks. Bjork was aided in producing this highly readable biography by interviews with Skinner, his family, and Fred Keller, Skinner's long-time friend. Access to the Harvard Archives and to the "Basement Archives" at Skinner's home were invaluable.

Gibson, J. J. (1979). *The ecological approach to visual perception.* Boston: Houghton Mifflin. As Gibson's most well-known work, this is foundational reading in ecological psychology.

Guthrie, E. R. (1952). *The psychology of learning* (Rev. ed.). New York: Harper & Brothers, Publishers. This book will show you why Guthrie is considered a peerless user of anecdote and simple terms to illustrate complex theoretical ideas.

Hull, C. L. (1943). *Principles of behavior: An introduction to behavior theory.* New York: Appleton-Century-Crofts, Inc. If you want to learn more about Hull's learning theory by reading him in the original, this book is less technical and formulaic than his later *Behavior System.*

Hull, C. L. (1952a). Clark L. Hull. In E. G. Boring, H. S. Langfeld, H. Werner, & R. M. Yerkes (Eds.), *A history of psychology in autobiography* (Vol. 4, pp. 143–162). Worcester, MA: Clark University Press. Written shortly before he died, Hull's autobiographical essay is an excellent introduction to the man, providing details about his preprofessional life, his different "careers" in psychology, and his behavior system.

Skinner, B. F. (1967). B. F. Skinner. In E. G. Boring & G. Lindzey, *A history of psychology in autobiography* (Vol. 5, pp. 385–413). New York: Appleton-Century-Crofts.

Skinner, B. F. (1976). *Particulars of my life.* New York: Alfred A. Knopf.

Skinner, B. F. (1979). *The shaping of a behaviorist.* New York: Alfred A. Knopf.

Skinner, B. F. (1983). *A matter of consequences.* New York: Alfred A. Knopf. Here you have a choice: Skinner's autobiographical essay or his three-volume autobiography. The essay is a remarkably detailed, amusing summary of the contents of his autobiography.

Skinner, B. F. (1974). *About behaviorism.* New York: Vintage Books. *About Behaviorism* is an outstanding collection of Skinner's ideas about most of the topics (e.g., learning, language development, social engineering) explored in this chapter.

Tolman, E. C. (1967). *Purposive behavior in animals and men.* New York: Meredith Publishing Co. (Original work published 1932) Despite Tolman's penchant for creating neologisms, this is an entertaining and informative account of much of his early animal research.

Tolman, E. C. (1952). Edward Chace Tolman. In E. G. Boring, H. S. Langfeld, H. Werner, & R. M. Yerkes (Eds.), *A history of psychology in autobiography* (Vol. 4, pp. 323–339). Worcester, MA: Clark University Press. Tolman's essay gives a summary of changes in Tolman's thinking 2 decades after *Purposive Behavior.*

Gestalt Psychology

CHAPTER 14

Kurt Lewin
Kurt Koffka
Wolfgang Köhler
Max Wertheimer
Bliuma Zeigarnik
Rudolph Arnheim
Mary Henle
Leon Festinger

1870 1880 1890 1900 1910 1920 1930

The first milk bottles appear in Brooklyn, NY

Although electric lights are installed in the White House, neither Pres. Harrison nor his wife will touch the switches

H. G. Wells flourishes

Hindenberg leads German troops (WWI)

Einstein flourishes

OUTLINE

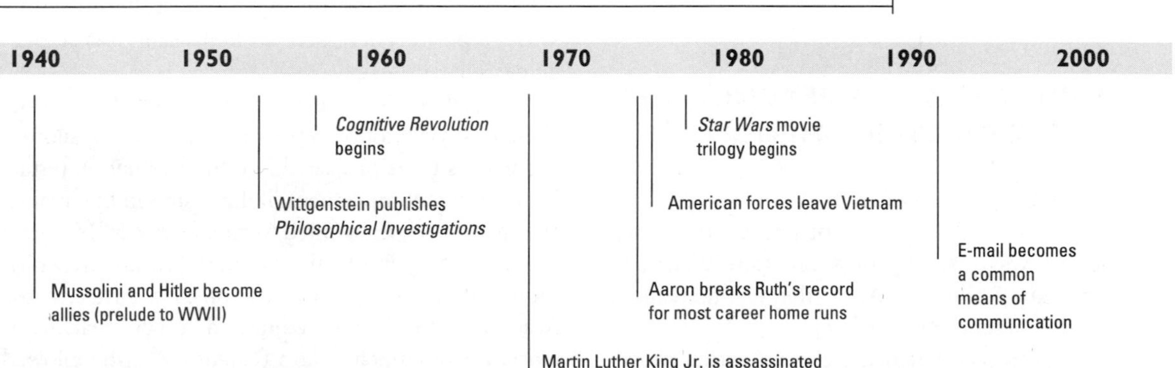

1940
1950
1960
1970
1980
1990
2000
Cognitive Revolution begins
Star Wars movie trilogy begins
Wittgenstein publishes Philosophical Investigations
American forces leave Vietnam
E-mail becomes a common means of communication
Mussolini and Hitler become allies (prelude to WWII)
Aaron breaks Ruth's record for most career home runs
Martin Luther King Jr. is assassinated

Max Wertheimer (1880–1943) standing next to a type of tachistoscope he used in his apparent-movement experiments

Synonyms for the German word *Gestalt* include shape, form, and configuration, and Titchener (Chapter 8) even suggested configurationism as the name for this psychological school. "Total structure" is sometimes included as a dictionary definition, and Boring (1950) indicated that *Strukturpsychologie* (structural psychology) might have been an appropriate name, "since a structure is a whole in which the total organization is altered by the change of any part . . ." (p. 588). Although Boring's suggestion was consistent with a major Gestalt theme, the problem with structural psychology was that James (Chapter 10) had already applied the label to contrast Titchener's approach with functionalism. In fact, Titchener's structuralism, with its focus on identifying the elements of consciousness (a molecular approach), is in a sense the exact opposite of Gestalt psychology's molar approach.

Thus, following the lead of many historians of psychology, we will leave the German word untranslated. Indeed, *Gestalt* has become part of our English vocabulary and is usually taken to mean "a structured whole." That is, Gestalt psychology dealt with organized wholes that could not be explained by breaking them into their component parts. As a system that held psychologists should study and discover useful and meaningful laws about the relations between parts and wholes, **Gestalt psychology** was particularly opposed to the reductive elementism characterizing structuralism and behaviorism. But Gestalt psychology was much more than a group of Germans opposed to structuralism and behaviorism: It was a new way of looking at experimental psychology from the perspective of rational philosophy, the phenomenology of experience, and early neuroscience.

FOUNDING GESTALT PSYCHOLOGY: THE PHI PHENOMENON

In 1910, Max Wertheimer had an insight that began Gestalt psychology. According to the story, Wertheimer was traveling by train from Vienna to vacation in the Rhineland. Along the way, he realized that the phenomenon in which a perception of movement is experienced when there is no actual movement has great significance for psychology. It must mean that perception does not necessarily correspond on a one-to-one basis with sensory stimulation. Perceptions may have properties that cannot be predicted from the sensations comprising them. The whole percept is not necessarily equal to just the sum of its sensory parts. Therefore, structuralism was a misguided enterprise.

Wertheimer left the train at Frankfurt and purchased a stroboscope—a then-popular toy that allowed still images to be projected in a time sequence, resulting in apparent movement of the figures in the images. Wertheimer experimented with the toy in his hotel room before going to the Frankfurt Academy, which soon became the University of Frankfurt. At the Academy, Wertheimer contacted a Berlin acquaintance, Friedrich Schumann (Chapter 8), who allowed

Wertheimer to use his new **tachistoscope**—a device used to display visual stimuli for brief time intervals. Wertheimer used the tachistoscope to flash lights on and off for very short periods of time.

Wertheimer conducted several experiments of apparent motion, which he called the **phi phenomenon.** Illustrations of the phi phenomenon in everyday life include the movement you see in motion pictures, or movies. When you watch the action in a movie, the movement is apparent rather than real—the phi phenomenon, in other words. The phi phenomenon also creates the illusion of movement with neon lights outside nightclubs and restaurants in major cities.

In his experiments, Wertheimer used as subjects two younger psychologists at Frankfurt, Wolfgang Köhler and Kurt Koffka (both discussed later), as well as Koffka's wife. Typically, two lights were briefly shone successively, one through a vertical slit and the other through a horizontal slit, in that order. With too-short intervals between their presentations, both lights appeared to be on simultaneously; with too-long intervals, the lights appeared stationary—vertical light followed by horizontal light. However, with the correct time interval, the vertical line appeared to rotate to the horizontal position. Wertheimer's description of his apparent-movement experiments in the 1912 publication, "Experimental Studies on the Seeing of Motion," is often said to mark Gestalt psychology's formal beginning. Wertheimer, Köhler, and Koffka became Gestalt psychology's triumvirate.

What was the significance of Wertheimer's studies of apparent motion? After all, Wertheimer did not discover the phenomenon, and Wundt (Chapter 8) had an explanation for it based on learned eye movements. Wertheimer had nevertheless demonstrated that perceptions were not reducible to sensory stimulation alone and had rendered Wundt's eye-movement explanation untenable with his critical experiment (Figure 14.1). When line "a" was followed by line "b," "the phenomenon of rotation clearly appeared, both to the left and to the right at the same time . . ." (Max Wertheimer, 1912/1968, p. 421). Because the eyes cannot move in two directions simultaneously, apparent movement cannot be explained by sensations from the eye muscles. Thus, the phi phenomenon could not be understood by breaking the phenomenon into its component elements.

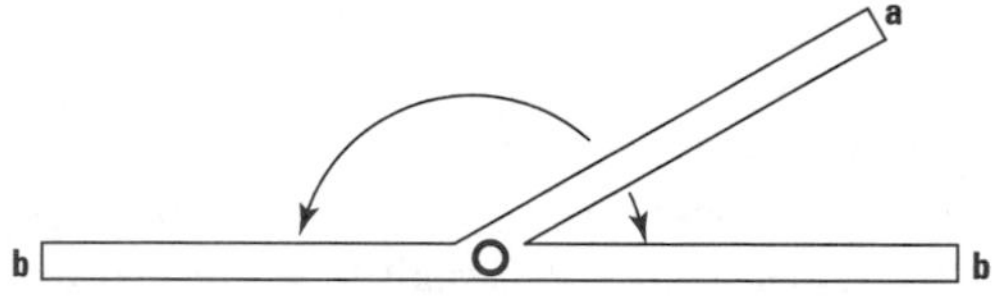

FIGURE 14.1 Experimental figure that resulted in a perception of movement from "a" to "b" in both directions simultaneously

Was Wertheimer's initial study a turning point in psychology or merely "a rallying point"? Arguing from the *Zeitgeist* perspective, O'Neil and Landauer (1966) stated that Wertheimer's experiment was no more than a rallying point for like-minded psychologists. However, Seaman (1984), in concluding his rebuttal of O'Neil and Landauer, observed that all the major Gestalt ideas can be found in Wertheimer's 1912 article. Because of this, Seaman saw no reason for not regarding Wertheimer's article as a turning point for Gestalt thinkers rather than simply a rallying point.

Michael Wertheimer (1927–), Max Wertheimer's son and a historian of psychology at the University of Colorado at Boulder, has presented an entirely different view of the 1912 article (Michael Wertheimer, 1980, 1991). According to him, two earlier Wertheimer publications, one on musicology and one on thinking, are considerably more relevant for Gestalt theory than the more-famous later publication. Michael Wertheimer (1980) further noted that the first published version of Gestalt theory can be found in a 1914 monograph by Gabriele Wartensleben, whose information on Gestalt theory came from a Wertheimer lecture she had attended at the Frankfurt Academy in 1913.

GESTALT PSYCHOLOGY'S ANTECEDENTS

Wertheimer's 1912 article can be seen as fundamental to modern perceptual theory and to cognitive psychology. The article demonstrates the role of previous knowledge and ongoing perception, revealing the power of expectation on cognition. Specifically, if your previous knowledge and current sensations suggest movement is occurring, then you experience either the phi phenomenon (apparent movement) or real movement; for the Gestaltist, there is no difference in the experiences. Still, if Wertheimer had gone into another field or had not ridden the train along the Rhine, would someone else have had the insight leading to Gestalt psychology? The answer is probably yes. Like the other schools we have considered, Gestalt psychology had many antecedents.

Sprung and Sprung (1997) observed that the sort of holistic thinking we associate with Gestalt psychology can be seen in the Chinese theory of yin and yang, first recorded by Confucius (552–479 B.C.E.) in the *I Ching*. One can find similar views in Aristotle's philosophy (Chapter 2) and in Leibniz's theory of monads (Chapter 4). Clearly, the Gestaltists were influenced by Leibniz, one of the cornerstones of German rationalism. In fact, the Gestalt movement can be seen as the pinnacle of evolution of the German rationalistic philosophy of mind, which led to a true science of psychology.

More recently, Wertheimer's insight was anticipated in part by both Ernst Mach (Chapter 5) and Christian von Ehrenfels (Chapter 8), the latter a scientist with whom Wertheimer studied. A physicist who developed a version of positivism, Mach studied the nature of sensations and introduced two "new" types—space form and time form—which he considered independent of their elements. For example, a space form such as a triangle could be large or small, or drawn in red ink or green ink, without losing its triangularity. Similarly, a time form, such as a melody, could be played with different instruments or in another key without losing its essential quality (Mach, 1886/1914).

In 1890, Christian von Ehrenfels criticized Wundt's failure to include another element—***Gestaltqualitäten*** or form qualities—with sensations, images, and feelings (Heider, 1970). To illustrate form qualities, von Ehrenfels, like Mach, pointed to a musical melody. The melody is more than simply a collection of individual notes, because it can be transposed to different keys or played by different instruments without loss of recognition.

Wertheimer's insight was that the qualities of the whole, the Gestalt or form qualities, determine the characteristics of the parts, rather than the other way around. Form quality was not just another of Wundt's basic elements, as von Ehrenfels thought, but a new concept altogether. This was a rationalistic, Kantian (Chapter 6), "top down" analysis rather than the empirical, sensation-based, "bottom up" approach of the structuralists.

Actually, Wundt himself could be considered a forerunner to Gestalt psychology. His idea of the creative synthesis of elements—similar to John Stuart Mill's (Chapter 5) mental chemistry—acknowledged the difference between wholes and the sum of their parts. Both Mill and Wundt realized something new might arise from the combining of elements into a whole, although neither developed the idea as fully as the Gestaltists.

Franz Brentano (Chapter 8) is another of Gestalt psychology's forerunners. In addition to Brentano's profound influence on von Ehrenfels, his use of introspection was quite different from the technique Wundt and his students practiced. Brentano's introspection tended to be phenomenological, meaning the study of intact experiences without further analysis into smaller, artificial, discrete units. Brentano directly anticipated the analysis of whole and psychologically meaningful experiences practiced by later phenomenologists (Chapter 16), William James, and the Gestaltists.

Oswald Külpe (Chapter 8) directed Wertheimer's dissertation and "Külpe may . . . have had something to do with Wertheimer's progress away from sensationism toward phenomenology" (Boring, 1950, p. 594). All the major Gestaltists also studied with Carl Stumpf (Chapter 8), with Koffka, Köhler, and Kurt Lewin (below) earning Ph.D.s at the University of Berlin under his supervision. Despite this obvious connection, the Gestalt psychologists never admitted Stumpf had directly shaped their thinking, and Stumpf himself denied influencing the Gestalt school.

Edmund Husserl (Chapter 8) has been called modern phenomenological psychology's "father." The many similarities between Gestalt psychology and phenomenological psychology suggest at least an indirect influence of Husserl and Stumpf on Gestalt theory.

Alternatively, phenomenology may have borrowed heavily from Gestalt psychology (see Henley, 1988; Schmidt, 1985).

Both William James and John Dewey (Chapter 11), can be considered Gestalt psychology's precursors. In his dislike of elementism and his conception of the stream of consciousness, James was far from structuralism, and the Gestaltists undoubtedly found support in the phenomenological flair of James's (1890) *Principles.* In fact, Woody (1999) has detailed "striking similarities" in Gestalt theory and James's work. Like James, Dewey argued against the artificial elementism that dominated psychology under the structuralists.

One of James's best-known biographers, Ralph Barton Perry (1935; Chapter 13), contended that James, even more than Stumpf, was the major influence upon the Gestaltists. However, Mary Henle (1990) suggested Perry's connection between Gestalt psychology and William James was overblown. Although Henle found similarities between James and Gestalt theory, she also noted important differences, particularly on such issues as mechanism, atomism, and organization. For example, James's mechanistic view of the nervous system prevented him from seeing the more dynamic processes (and organization) the Gestaltists considered necessary to "permit the interactions needed to make understandable many corresponding psychological phenomena" (Henle, p. 79). Although James generally rejected the sort of atomism the Gestaltists opposed, he often lapsed into it.

Beyond the German phenomenologists and American philosophical psychologists, theorists from Jean Piaget (Chapter 18) and Jean-Paul Sartre (Chapter 16) to J. J. Gibson and Edward Tolman (both Chapter 13) have been linked to the Gestaltists because of similarities of some of their ideas to Gestalt positions. We can see from this brief survey of antecedents and "relatives" that Wertheimer's insight fell on fertile soil.

These various connections also suggest the thematic elements of Gestalt psychology. First and foremost, it was a rationalistic approach consistent with the tradition of Kant, Herbart (Chapter 6), Brentano, Stumpf, and Külpe. Second, Gestalt psychology involved the search for what sort of a priori (innate) structures organize and direct our mental experiences, not just our perceptual experiences, but our learning and thinking as well. Finally, perhaps more than any other school, Gestalt psychology attempted to synthesize sophisticated philosophical analysis, physiological data from neuroscience, and our everyday, phenomenological experiences. More than a school about "wholes and parts," Gestalt psychology prospered because of its important advances on long-standing issues such as the mind-body problem and the relationship between perception and consciousness.

GESTALT PSYCHOLOGY'S TRIUMVIRATE

Max Wertheimer

Max Wertheimer (1880–1943) was born into an intellectual and artistic family in Prague. Wertheimer's father was a financially successful educator, whose success triggered in his son a lifelong interest in education and gave him the financial independence to pursue his own intellectual interests, at least in the first half of his life.

As a child, Wertheimer was gifted in mathematics, philosophy, literature, and especially music. He played the piano and the violin and composed symphonies and chamber music. As a psychologist, Wertheimer often used musical examples to illustrate his ideas and typically had a piano at his lectures for demonstrations such as how a melody's early notes constrain how it can be completed (Michael Wertheimer, 1992; Michael Wertheimer & King, 1994).

In adolescence, Wertheimer's interest centered on literature, and he became fascinated with Spinoza (Chapter 4). With so many talents and interests, Wertheimer had difficulty deciding on a career, and he considered law before turning to philosophy and then to psychology.

Wertheimer took classes from Stumpf at the University of Berlin before moving to the University of Würzburg, where he got his Ph.D. summa cum laude in 1904, with Külpe as his advisor. With a dissertation on lie detection, he developed a word association test he used to evaluate the truth of legal testimony.

Between 1904 and 1910, Wertheimer was at the Universities of Prague, Vienna, and Berlin. In 1910, his phi phenomenon insight took him to Frankfurt, where he stayed until 1916, with time out for World War I. As a German army captain, he studied sound localization with Erich von Hornbostel (Chapter 8), which ultimately led to the invention of a type of sonar that Wertheimer and his family called the "Wertbostel" (Michael Wertheimer, 1980). From 1916 to 1929, Wertheimer was a *Privatdozent* (nonsalaried university lecturer) at the University of Berlin, where, along with Koffka, Köhler, and neurologist Kurt Goldstein (discussed later), he established the journal *Psychologische Forschung* (*Psychological Research*). He served as editor for the first 20 volumes.

Despite his undisputed contributions, Wertheimer was not given a professorship until 1929, when he replaced the retiring Friedrich Schumann at the University of Frankfurt. At Frankfurt, he was also the department chair (Sarris, 1997). This delayed promotion was caused partly by his Jewish heritage and partly by his lack of systematic publications of his Gestalt theoretical position. In fact, his first such publication came in 1921, more than a decade following his original insight. Although this "provocatively fragmentary, open-ended mode of presentation was characteristic of Wertheimer, . . . it was not standard procedure for scholars in Germany who wished to become full professors . . ." (Ash, 1989, p. 53). In 1933, Wertheimer immigrated to the United States to escape the growing Nazi threat that led to World War II and the Jewish Holocaust.

In America, Wertheimer took a position in New York City at the New School for Social Research, an institution established to employ refugee scholars from Europe. Along with Köhler, Wertheimer was invited in 1936 to join the prestigious Society of Experimental Psychologists (Chapter 8); Koffka had been invited in 1929. Beyond his continued academic affiliations, Wertheimer remained broadly interested in education throughout his life, as indicated by his participation with John Dewey and others in a radio panel discussion on education in 1935 (Michael Wertheimer & King, 1994).

Wertheimer became a U.S. citizen the day before his 59th birthday and died 4 years later of a coronary embolism at his home in New Rochelle, New York. In 1945, one of his best-known works, *Productive Thinking*, was published. *Productive Thinking* was based in part on interviews with people known for their problem-solving abilities. For example, Wertheimer spent many pleasant and productive hours with one of his friends in America, another Jewish refugee, the Nobel Prize–winning physicist Albert Einstein. (See Michael Wertheimer, 1965, for more on Max Wertheimer's relationship with Einstein.) Like Einstein, Wertheimer was one of the people Abraham Maslow (Chapter 16) considered self-actualized (with a fully realized personality). In fact, Maslow began his investigations of self-actualization as an effort to understand two of his most revered teachers—anthropologist Ruth Benedict and Max Wertheimer (Michael Wertheimer & King, 1994).

Kurt Koffka

Recalled by his biographers as a charismatic and charming man whom women found attractive, Berlin-born **Kurt Koffka** (1886–1941) earned a Ph.D. from the University of Berlin in 1908, under Stumpf's supervision. His Berlin studies were interrupted by a year at the University of Edinburgh, during which he became fluent in English. This language proficiency enabled Koffka to spread the Gestalt message to America in a 1922 *Psychological Bulletin* article, "Perception: An Introduction to *Gestalt-Theorie*."

Unfortunately, Koffka's article led most American psychologists to assume the Gestalt psychologists were interested *only* in perceptual phenomena, when, in fact, they were interested in philosophical issues, learning, thinking, and many other topics. Their interests were so broad that Sprung and Sprung (1997) have characterized the perspective of the leaders of the Gestalt movement in Germany as "monopolistic," in that they "were convinced that their theories and methods were applicable to all psychological problems" (p. 272). This led them to challenge any alternative positions, no matter how reasonable they might have been.

It is true that the Gestaltists' early publications focused on perception. According to Michael Wertheimer (2000), they were rebelling against Wundt's system, and much of Wundt's work had been in sensation and perception. That is, the Gestaltists stud-

Smith College Archives.

Kurt Koffka (1886–1941) in 1928

ied perceptual phenomena "in order to attack Wundt in his own stronghold . . ." (p. 126).

As we noted, Koffka was at Frankfurt when Wertheimer arrived in 1910. In 1911, Koffka took a position at the University of Giessen, 40 miles from Frankfurt, and stayed there until 1924. He was a visiting professor at Cornell University from 1924 to 1925 and at the University of Wisconsin 2 years later. In 1927, Koffka accepted a position at Smith College, where he remained until his death in 1941.

At Smith College, Koffka befriended J. J. Gibson (Chapter 13), an important, and increasingly influential, perceptual theorist. Gibson's approach to perception was both strongly nativist and "behavioristic." However, Gibson's theory can also be seen as an extension of Koffka's thoughts on perception, an idea supported by Gibson's (1979) discussions of Koffka in his classic work, *The Ecological Approach to Visual Perception.*

A prolific writer, Koffka was Gestalt psychology's major spokesperson. One of his most important works was a book on child psychology from the Gestalt perspective, which was translated as *The Growth of the Mind* (Koffka, 1924). Another major work, *Principles of Gestalt Psychology* (Koffka, 1935), which Koffka dedicated to Wertheimer and Köhler, was intended to be a systematic application of Gestalt theory to such diverse areas of psychology as perception, learning and memory, social psychology, and personality. Although *Principles* was intended for a lay audience and was actually written "for 19 year old girls" (Gibson, 1971, p. 3), it "was probably read only by professional psychologists . . ." (Henle, 1987, p. 14). Henle recommended that "we pay our respects to Koffka's *Principles* . . . not as an illustrious antique, but as a 'fount of questions' and a continuing aid in clarification of contemporary thinking" (p. 20).

Wolfgang Köhler

Born in Reval, Estonia, **Wolfgang Köhler** (1887–1967) grew up in northern Germany. Like Koffka, he attended the University of Berlin, receiving his Ph.D. in 1909 under Stumpf. At Berlin, Köhler also studied with Max Planck, the famous physicist, and "was always a physicist in his thinking, indebted for stimulus in his student days at Berlin to Max Planck rather than to Stumpf" (Boring, 1950, p. 597). From Berlin, Köhler went to Frankfurt, where he participated in Wertheimer's phi phenomenon experiments.

In 1913, the Prussian Academy of Science sent Köhler to study a group of apes on Tenerife, one of the Canary Islands in the Atlantic, off the west coast of Africa. Apes are not endemic to the island, and the Anthropoid Research Station Köhler supervised was stocked with animals imported from a German colony in west central Africa. Although he expected to stay only a short time, Köhler was marooned for the duration of World War I.

During the war, British intelligence suspected Köhler of being a German spy. In the mid-1970s, Ronald Ley, an American psychology professor, visited Tenerife and subsequently published *A Whisper of Espionage: Wolfgang Köhler and the Apes of Tenerife* (Ley, 1990). Ley concluded Köhler had "served the cause of the German military through his part in building, maintaining, and operating a concealed radio for the purpose of communicating information that would contribute to the German war effort" (p. 253).

Wolfgang Köhler (1887–1967) in about 1947

However, the likelihood Köhler actually engaged in espionage was highly discounted by Marianne Teuber (1994), in an article about the founding of the primate research facility.

Köhler summarized his work with the apes and other animals on Tenerife in *Intelligenzprufungen an Menschenaffen* (*Intelligence Tests With Anthropoid Apes*), published in 1917. It was translated into English in 1925 and published as *The Mentality of Apes.* We will discuss Köhler's contributions to learning theory later.

In a brief mention of his stay on Tenerife, Köhler (in Henle, 1971) acknowledged he did not always work on animal psychology. Instead, his thoughts turned to the possibility of a connection between what he had learned from the physicist Planck and Wertheimer's Gestalt ideas. Referring to the anti-elementism of Gestalt psychology, the desire to study wholes rather than elements, Köhler indicated he was relieved to find a similar approach in physics. Further, Köhler noted that in studying many specific physical situations, physicists handled the situations as wholes rather than as collections of independent facts.

Köhler returned to Germany in 1920, succeeding first G. E. Müller (Chapter 8) at the University of Göttingen in 1921 and then Stumpf at the University of Berlin in 1922. With his replacement of Stumpf, Köhler attained the academic pinnacle of psychology in that era.

Ley's (1990) investigations included an interview with one of Köhler's students and later his University of Berlin assistant—Professor Wolfgang Metzger (1899–1979). Metzger gave Ley "the impression that Köhler did not talk very much about anything, except, perhaps, psychology" (p. 76). In addition, Köhler apparently suffered from stage fright whenever he had to give a lecture, and he later developed a hand tremor that his students and assistants used to gauge his mood—the worse the mood, the greater the tremor. Metzger's wife told Ley that Köhler did not like small children, and during the early years of his second marriage, his daughter by his second wife was placed in a foundling home.

According to Metzger, Wertheimer was Köhler's exact opposite. Whereas Köhler was cold and aloof, Wertheimer was warm and friendly, which is at least part of the reason Metzger worked to be transferred from Berlin to Frankfurt so that he could become Wertheimer's assistant (Götzl, 2003). Metzger also suggested that Wertheimer's slow promotion stemmed from German anti-Semitic attitudes even before the Nazis came to power. Köhler's influence as director of the Psychological Institute at the University of Berlin probably helped Wertheimer achieve his Frankfurt professorship.

During his University of Berlin tenure, Köhler made two trips to America. In the 1925–1926 academic year, he was a visiting professor at Clark University, and he was the William James lecturer at Harvard from 1934 to 1935. Later in 1935, he was a visiting professor at the University of Chicago. Köhler also lectured at Yale in 1929; in France, Spain, and Uruguay in 1930; and in Brazil and Argentina in 1932 (Jaeger, 1997).

Unlike some non-Jewish German academics, Köhler staunchly opposed the rise of Nazism and the dismissal of Jews and anti-Nazis from their university positions (e.g., Crannell, 1970). In fact, in 1933, Köhler wrote the last anti-Nazi article published in a German newspaper. In it, he referred to the great patriotism of the valuable people who had *not* joined the Nazi party and criticized the wholesale dismissal of Jews from universities and other positions by citing examples of outstanding contributions made by such Jews as Spinoza and the experimental physicist James Franck (Henle, 1978a). Although his renown prevented his arrest, Köhler's position in Germany became increasingly precarious, and he immigrated to the United States in 1935. With the departure of the founders of Gestalt psychology from Germany, Metzger became the leader of the movement, aided undoubtedly by his collaboration with the Nazi regime (Götzl, 2003; Mandler, 2002). After visiting professorships at Harvard and Chicago, Köhler taught at Swarthmore College in Pennsylvania until his retirement in 1958. His research and writing continued at Dartmouth College in New Hampshire, where he moved after retiring.

In a revealing footnote, Michael Wertheimer (2000) described Köhler as follows:

> A fastidious, meticulous man with the highest personal standards, Köhler loved to be immaculate in everything he did. The present writer remembers seeing Köhler, bent on recreation, spending a Sunday afternoon during the mid-1940s chopping firewood in his back yard—using a razor-sharp, well-polished axe, and dressed in a spotless white suit, with white shirt and tie. (p. 128)

Soon after coming to America, Köhler became a favorite reader of works in progress by his colleagues because of his superior command of English. Although we have tried to give you some impressions of Köhler's scientific work and his personality, note that we have merely scratched the surface of this complex man. Köhler's scope was phenomenal, encompassing not only the topics we mention in this chapter but also the mind-body problem (e.g., Köhler, 1966), intelligence, physiology, and philosophy (notably ethics and aesthetics).

Köhler, who survived in the United States much longer than the other major Gestalt psychologists, received several awards for his scientific contributions. In 1947, he received the Warren Medal for "his studies on figural after-effects and an approach to a more general theory of perceptual responses" (Wilkening, 1973, p. 94). He received one of the first three Distinguished Scientific Contribution Awards from the APA in 1956 and was elected APA president in 1959. Köhler was selected to receive the APA's Gold Medal Award in 1967 but died before he could accept it, and the award is not given posthumously.

PRINCIPLES OF GESTALT PSYCHOLOGY

The Gestalt psychology literature is voluminous, and Harry Helson (1933)—an American supporter of Gestalt psychology and a 1962 recipient of the APA's Distinguished Contribution Award—identified 114 different laws of *Gestalten* assumed to structure perceptions and thinking. Here, we will cover briefly a few of the most important points, beginning with the so-called principles of perceptual grouping, which Wertheimer developed to better understand motion perception (Sarris, 1989).

In 1923, Wertheimer published a paper on visual perceptual grouping in which he tried to show we perceive objects in a way analogous to the way we see perceived movement in the phi phenomenon: We see objects as unified wholes rather than as elemental sensations. Wertheimer used simple stimuli (e.g., lines, dots, and simple line figures) to avoid the criticism that the meaningfulness of real objects might force their organization in particular ways. That is, meaningless stimuli should not suggest any form of organization. In a sense, this is analogous to Ebbinghaus's invention of the nonsense syllable (Chapter 8); Ebbinghaus wanted to study verbal learning and memory uncontaminated by the meaning of words. Similarly, Titchener emphasized the use of meaningless stimuli to prevent his students from committing the "stimulus error." Following Wertheimer's lead, we will use simple visual stimuli to illustrate the Gestalt perceptual principles of organization.

Gestalt Principles of Perceptual Grouping

Figure-Ground

The **figure-ground relationship** was borrowed from the work of Danish psychologist Edgar Rubin (Chapter 8), although it can be traced to a political art form in which faces of the unpopular could be hidden. According to Rubin, the perceptual field is divided into figure and ground; figure is the part we are attending to, and ground is the remainder of the field we are not attending to. Factors that distinguish figure from ground include the following: The figure's shape is fully defined, whereas the ground appears shapeless; the ground seems to continue behind the figure; and the figure looks both closer and brighter than the ground. What is figure and what is ground are both dynamic and context-dependent, which is clearly illustrated through reversible figures like the ones shown in Figure 14.2.

FIGURE 14.2 The figure-ground relationship Switching of the figure-ground relationship makes each of these figures ambiguous. The figures are called vase/face and duck/rabbit, respectively.

Continuity

In **continuity,** there is a perceptual tendency to follow elements that appear to be proceeding in the same direction, to "continue" in the direction they appear to be heading. For example, in Figure 14.3a, we tend to see the figure at the top as a semicircle with a line through it rather than as a combination of the two figures below it.

Proximity

In **proximity**, elements close to each other in time or space are seen as belonging together. You see Figure 14.3b as three pairs of lines rather than as six individual lines or a collection of six lines, because of the principle of proximity.

Similarity

The old saying, "birds of a feather flock together," is one way to think of **similarity.** Similar elements are seen as belonging together, and in Figure 14.3c, there is a tendency to see alternating rows of circles and squares rather than columns of mixed circles and squares.

Closure

The principle of **closure** accounts for why we tend to see incomplete figures as complete; we tend to fill in the gaps. You will probably see Figure 14.3d as complete geometric figures (circle, square, and triangle) rather than as collections of unconnected dashes. Closure makes it difficult for many people to to proofread material—they tend to see the material the way it should be rather than the way it really is. Did you catch the error in the previous sentence? If not, closure may have prevented you from seeing it.

Other Gestalt Principles and Phenomena

The Law of Prägnanz

The Gestalt principles of perceptual grouping we have considered may be seen as illustrations of a general Gestalt principle, the **law of *Prägnanz.*** The law asserts that innate psychological organization tends toward the perception of a "good Gestalt," or that we

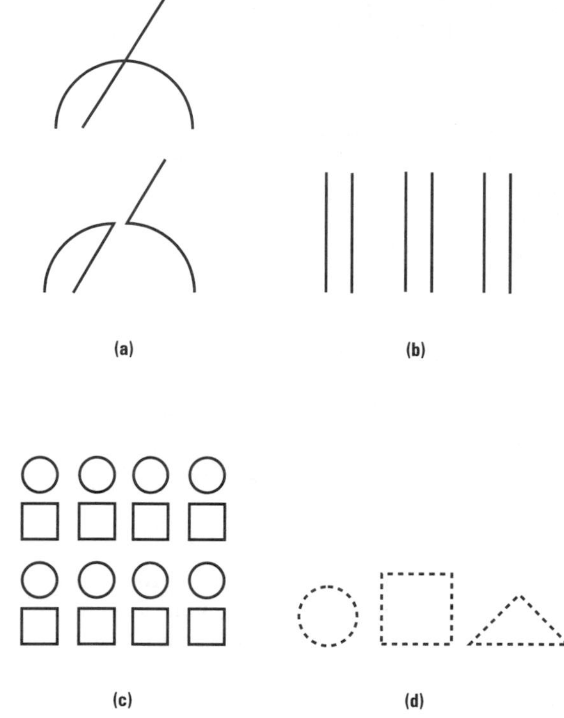

FIGURE 14.3 Gestalt principles of perception
Illustration of the Gestalt perceptual principles of (a) continuity, (b) proximity, (c) similarity, and (d) closure.

will perceive a stimulus to be as good and meaningful as prevailing conditions allow. For example, closure works because a completed circle is more meaningful than a circle with a gap in it. Similarly, we see the semicircle with a line through it in Figure 14.3a because it forms a better Gestalt than the two figures below it.

Note that the law of *Prägnanz* has important implications beyond perceptual organization. Memory changes over time may also reveal the law's influence, with possible consequences for eyewitness testimony's validity (Chapter 18). You may recall our Chapter 1 discussion of a study in which subjects viewed a film of an automobile accident and were later asked questions about it. Subjects asked if they saw broken glass in accidents involving cars that *smashed* were more likely to "recall" broken glass than subjects asked the same question about cars that *hit*. In reality, there was no broken glass in the film. *Smashed* establishes a context in which broken glass is more likely to be present, and the subjects' responses were consistent with the created context.

The Zeigarnik Effect

The **Zeigarnik effect**—the tendency to remember incomplete tasks longer than finished tasks—is another illustration of the law of *Prägnanz* generally and of the principle of closure specifically. The effect was investigated by and named for the Russian-born psychologist **Bliuma Vul'Fovna Zeigarnik** (1890–1990), who did her doctoral work under Kurt Lewin (discussed later). In Russia, where psychotherapy tended to be the province of psychiatrists, Zeigarnik became one of a small number of what we would call clinical psychologists. Her research focused on the psychoses, and she also published papers on the history of abnormal psychology.

Zeigarnik's dissertation research was stimulated by an occurrence at a Berlin cafe. During one of their regular meetings at the cafe, someone in Lewin's group called for the bill, and their waiter knew exactly what everyone had ordered even though he had no written record. A short time later, Lewin asked the waiter to write the check again. This time, the waiter indignantly explained he no longer knew what they had ordered because they had already paid the bill. Thus, the unpaid bill (incomplete task) created tension that was relieved with payment (task completion).

To test Lewin's theory that attaining a goal relieves tension, Zeigarnik (1927) gave various tasks to a large number of subjects, allowing them to finish some of the tasks but not others. In a later recall test, many more of the uncompleted tasks were remembered than the completed ones.

Examples of the Zeigarnik effect are legion. Assuming you studied and learned the material, you are more likely to remember test questions you missed—did not complete—than ones you got right. Have you ever noticed how many TV series end a season with a cliffhanger episode, hoping the lack of completion will force you to tune in next season? Some people tend to finish the sentences of the person speaking to them, which may be another example of the Zeigarnik effect.

Isomorphism

Another important Gestalt principle is called isomorphism, which literally means identical (*iso*) form (*morphism*), and it provides part of the Gestalt answer to the mind-body problem. According to Köhler (1947), "*Experienced order in space is always structurally identical with a functional order in the distribution of underlying brain processes*" (p. 61, italics in the original). **Isomorphism** assumes there is a direct correspondence between brain processes and mental experiences. The direct correspondence does not mean brain processes and perception have identical form, however. For example, it does not mean that when you see a cube, a neural pattern shaped like a cube exists in the brain.

One analogy frequently used to illustrate the relationship between neural processes and corresponding perceptions is that of a map and the country it represents. Although the map and the country are obviously not the same, an identity exists in the sense that we can discern much about the country's characteristics from studying the map. The map tells us about the location of cities, about the country's topography, about the presence of rivers, and so forth, without being in any sense a literal copy of what it depicts.

All three founding Gestaltists accepted isomorphism, beginning with Wertheimer's 1912 discussion of experiments on the phi phenomenon. Wertheimer noted that the brain processes for apparent motion and for true motion must be essentially the same, because real and apparent motion are experienced as identical. To account for phi, there must be a correspondence between the conscious experience of motion and the underlying neural experience (i.e., there must be a psychophysical isomorphism).

Furthermore, the Gestaltists believed the fact that we experience perceptions as coordinated wholes instead of a simple sum of interconnected sensations argues against a telephone switchboard analogy of the brain's structure and function. In other words, the phi phenomenon shows that the successive stimulation of neural units that would occur in the perception of the real movement of a line is unnecessary for perceiving apparent movement. Recent advances in machine learning, called neural networks (see Chapter 18), have further strengthened the idea that the nervous system does not have to be organized into interlocking elements. In fact, several authors have discussed the similarity between Gestalt psychology and this new artificial intelligence technology (e.g., van Leeuwen, 1989).

Gestalt Learning Principles

As we noted, Köhler spent at least some of his time on Tenerife studying the behavior of an ape colony. In his studies, Köhler developed the problems and learning principles that challenged the prevailing learning theory of the time, Thorndike's (Chapter 12) trial-and-error learning.

***Umweg* or Detour Problem.** For Thorndike, learning occurred when an animal made a response and was either rewarded or not rewarded for it. Reward (a satisfier) strengthened the stimulus-response bond, whereas lack of reward (an annoyer) weakened the S-R bond. Learning developed gradually through trials and errors and trials and successes.

Köhler believed Thorndike's task, the problem boxes, made it difficult for Thorndike's animals to see the whole situation. The boxes forced the animals into random activity to solve the problem, rather than allowing them to get an overview of it. Thorndike's cats used trial-and-error learning because that was all the task permitted them to use.

Köhler's tasks enabled his animals to see all the problem elements, although not necessarily in the sequence or format that would permit solution. Solution required a restructuring of the field (i.e., seeing it in a different perspective). Köhler used the term **insight** to refer to the sudden behavior change that often appeared when the animal (or human) accomplished the restructuring. Insight occurred when the subject recognized the relationships among the problem's relevant stimuli.

One task used both by Köhler and by later Gestalt psychologists (e.g., Lewin) was the ***Umweg*** or **detour problem**, which allowed an animal to see the entire problem at one time. In the simple *Umweg* task shown in Figure 14.4, the goal is clearly visible to the

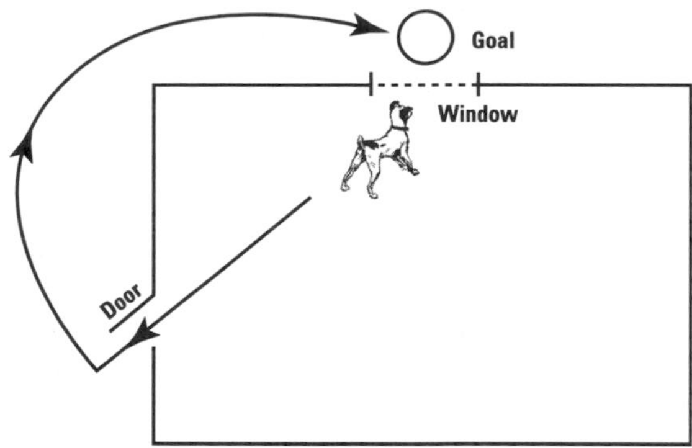

FIGURE 14.4 A typical *Umweg* or detour problem

subject, although it cannot be reached directly. The organism must take a detour by initially going away from the goal in order ultimately to obtain it. In one version of the problem, Köhler tested a dog, a child, and some chickens. The dog and the child solved the problem readily, but the chickens were less successful (Köhler, 1917/1925).

Apes, Boxes, Sticks, and Bananas. Köhler's ape research provided further evidence for insight learning. In a typical task, a banana hung from the ceiling of an ape's enclosure. Boxes and/or sticks were available for use as tools in obtaining the fruit. The boxes could be stacked by an animal and then ascended like a ladder.

One of the most widely quoted passages from *The Mentality of Apes* involves the insightful behavior of an ape named **Sultan.** Sultan's task required him to rake in a banana placed outside his cage, but neither stick available to the ape was long enough to reach the fruit. The problem's solution required Sultan to join the two sticks together into a longer tool. After an initial period of failure, Köhler left the ape alone with the keeper. Animal caretaker Manuel González y García described Sultan's development of insight as follows:

> Sultan first of all squats indifferently on the box, which has been left standing a little back from the railings; then he gets up, picks up the two sticks, sits down again on the box and plays carelessly with them. While doing this, it happens that he finds himself holding one rod in either hand in such a way that they lie in a straight line; he pushes the thinner one a little way into the opening of the thicker, jumps up and is already on the run toward the railings, to which he has up to now half turned his back, and begins to draw a banana towards him with the double stick. (Köhler, 1917/1925, p. 127)

Köhler concluded that insight learning had several important characteristics differentiating it from Thorndike's trial-and-error learning. Because the task solution is based on a perceptual restructuring of the field, it often occurs suddenly and completely, without a gradual accumulation of associations. The learning is all or none, the "aha" phenomenon drawn as a light coming on over a cartoon character's head.

In addition, insight learning does not depend on reinforcement. Sultan had already solved the problem before he ran to rake in the banana. The banana provided the incentive for his response without being necessary for the learning. Tolman's studies of latent learning and insight learning in rats also showed that learning could occur without reinforcement, at least reinforcement as traditionally defined. We noted that Tolman always credited the Gestaltists for influencing his thinking.

Insight solutions are long remembered and easily generalized to similar problems. Once Köhler's apes learned to stack boxes to reach a banana or learned to use a pole to rake in a banana from outside the compound, they could apply this knowledge to solve other, similar problems. There was a large amount of positive transfer.

Despite the importance that Köhler and the other Gestaltists attached to the distinction between insight and trial-and-error learning, the difference may be less clear-cut than the Gestaltists believed. For example, in one "insight" learning study, Birch (1945) tested young chimpanzees on a problem like one often used by Köhler: Food was placed outside the animals' cages, with a hoe available to rake it in. An ape with extensive experience using sticks as tools readily solved the problem. Four animals that could not solve the problem initially were given sticks to play with for 3 days. Although they were never observed using the sticks as rakes, when they were retested with food and a hoe, they soon solved the task. Apparently, in order for insight to occur, the animals must have earlier

Grande stacks boxes to retrieve a banana, while Sultan watches with interest

acquired at least one component skill of the eventual solution (i.e., using sticks as extensions of their arms).

Born Harry Frederick Israel, **Harry F. Harlow** (1905–1981) was an experimental psychologist who did extensive research with monkeys at the University of Wisconsin. Harlow noted that the typical insight learning problem was one in which the previous experience of the animals with problem components was unknown. In his studies of monkeys, Harlow (1951) found that insight sometimes did not occur in animals without some relevant prior experience, just as Birch's (1945) study had showed. Harlow's alternative to insight learning involved the formation of a **learning set,** or the gradual elimination of error-producing tendencies in a long series of similar problems until an animal could solve a problem swiftly, and apparently insightfully (LeRoy & Kimble, 2003). In other words, the animals developed what looked like insight because of their experience (Rumbaugh, 1997). Harlow is also known for studying affectional systems ("love") in infant monkeys and maternal behavior in so-called motherless mothers—female monkeys who gave birth after being raised by surrogate (wire or wire-and-cloth) mothers (e.g., Harlow, 1962; Harlow & Harlow, 1965). Arguing against Watson and Rayner's behaviorist prescription for childrearing (Watson, 1928/1972), Harlow's research showed the necessity of affection for the physical, emotional, and intellectual development of primates (Blum, 2002; LeRoy & Kimble).

Köhler's insight learning studies stimulated replication by Pavlov (Chapter 12) in the 1930s. Although Pavlov confirmed Köhler's results, his explanations for the learning he observed stressed, not surprisingly, Pavlovian and Thorndikian conditioning. Pavlov saw insight learning as the progressive development of associations, more in the manner of Harlow's learning set formation (Windholz, 1984).

As with so many historical milestones, the idea of insight learning did not originate with the person whose name is so closely associated with it. Instead, the first recorded example may well be the experience of the famous Greek mathematician **Archimedes** (ca. 287–212 B.C.E.). According to the story, King Hieron gave an artisan some gold to fashion into a crown. The resulting crown weighed as much as the gold the king had supplied, but Hieron suspected that silver had been substituted for some of the gold. The king told Archimedes his suspicions and gave him the crown to test—without damaging it.

Weeks later, Archimedes noticed that as he stepped into the water at the public baths, it overflowed according to how deep he was. This observation led Archimedes to infer that

> a floating body loses in weight an amount equal to the weight of the water it displaces. Surmising that a *submerged* body would displace water according to its volume, and perceiving that this principle offered a test for the crown, Archimedes . . . dashed out naked into the street . . . crying out "Eureka! eureka!" (Durant, 1939, pp. 630–631)

which means "I have found it." Archimedes exhibited the sudden behavior change that accompanies the insightful restructuring of a field, when he discovered a test for the specific gravity of an object. Because gold and silver have different specific gravities, Archimedes demonstrated both that the crown's gold had been alloyed with silver and also exactly how much gold had been stolen.

The Transposition Problem. One of the most interesting tasks Köhler developed was supposed to contrast directly the Gestalt approach with Thorndike's trial-and-error learning. As noted in Chapter 13, Köhler first trained chickens to peck corn on the darker of two shades of gray paper. If they pecked it on the lighter gray, they were chased away. After hundreds of trials, the chickens pecked corn only on the darker gray paper. To see what they had learned, Köhler next gave the birds a choice between corn on the dark gray paper from their training trials and corn on a still darker gray paper. S-R theory predicts the chickens will peck the corn on the reinforced gray paper from the original task, but the Gestalt view is they have learned the pattern or Gestalt. Hence, Köhler predicted the chickens would choose the new, darker gray paper, demonstrating they had learned the relations between the original training stimuli.

Köhler's chickens generally showed relational responding by choosing the darker of the test stimuli. He called the phenomenon **transposition,** the analogy being that notes from musical melodies do not change their relationship to each other when the melodies are *transposed* to different instruments or to different keys on the musical scale. The darker gray card in the test had the same relation to the dark gray card as the dark gray card had to the light gray card during training.

Dozens of ingenious experiments examined the transposition effect's generality, and the results did not uniformly favor the Gestalt position. However, one outcome of the transposition phenomenon was to force the S-R theorists to develop alternative explanations for it. As we noted in Chapter 13, Kenneth Spence developed one elaborate interpretation that enabled him to predict when transposition would and would not occur (Spence, 1937). Further studies sometimes supported the Gestalt relational-responding view and sometimes supported the Hull-Spence absolute stimulus view. Modern learning theorists (e.g., Klein, 2002) conclude that both positions may be valid, with Gestalt relational responding occurring in tasks allowing simultaneous stimulus comparison and Hull-Spence absolute responding in tasks permitting the subject to see only one stimulus at a time.

Wertheimer and Thinking

Productive Thinking, published 2 years after Wertheimer's death, represents the culmination of his study of thinking. His interest in the topic began much earlier; in fact, Wertheimer published his first article on thinking the same year (1912) his famous article on the phi phenomenon appeared.

The case material in *Productive Thinking* ranges from schoolchildren solving simple geometric problems to Albert Einstein's thought processes resulting in his theory of relativity. Applying Gestalt principles, Wertheimer believed problem solving should proceed from the whole problem down to its parts rather than vice versa. Again, this is a "top down" or holistic approach in which students should get the "big picture," which, in turn, should help organize the particular details into a "good" or meaningful form. By contrast, learning by rote memorization and repetition leads to a "bottom up," elemental, mechanical performance rather than to creative or productive thinking. "Wertheimer felt keenly that the concentration of schools on drill, memory, [and] habit forming is inimical to productive thinking, and even damages the strong trend in children to deal with problems in a direct way" (Asch, 1946, p. 97).

Furthermore, holistic learning should result in comprehension of the principles behind a problem's solution, and these principles can be applied readily to future problems. Given his emphasis on holistic learning, Wertheimer believed a teacher should present the whole problem to students from the beginning. This approach contrasted with Thorndike's trial-and-error learning in which the problem's solution is hidden, and the learner is forced to make errors before "accidentally" selecting the correct solution.

Thus, according to Gestalt principles, learning is based on understanding the nature of the problem. The problem itself creates a cognitive disequilibrium that lasts until it is solved. Note that this is the essence of the Zeigarnik effect—an unfinished or unsolved task creates tension that motivates solution.

If you have had a social psychology course, you may notice the similarity between cognitive disequilibrium and its resolution and **cognitive dissonance** theory. According to the latter, people cannot tolerate cognitions (beliefs, thoughts, perceptions, etc.) that conflict. Something has to give, and the person resolves the inner conflict by revaluing one or more of the conflicting beliefs. Cognitive dissonance theory is attributed to **Leon Festinger** (1919–1989), a prominent social psychologist who earned his Ph.D. at the State University of Iowa in 1942—under the direction of the fourth major Gestalt psychologist, Kurt Lewin.

In addition, Gestalt principles suggest that restoring cognitive equilibrium is reinforcing. For example, the banana Sultan raked in with the joined sticks was not the reinforcement that led the ape to solve the problem; reinforcement came from problem solving itself.

As an illustration of insight learning's benefits, Michael Wertheimer (1980) described an experiment in which subjects studied 15 digits for 15 seconds, the object being to try to remember as many as possible. The digits were 1 4 9 1 6 2 5 3 6 4 9 6 4 8 1. Given only the instruction to try to remember as many as possible, most subjects could remember only a few, and even these were lost after a week.

Instructed to look for a pattern, some subjects in another group realized the 15 numbers are just the squares of the numbers from 1 to 9. With this insight, the subjects then reproduced all the digits correctly and probably would *always* be able to recall the 15 numbers, further illustrating the advantage of the insightful approach compared to rote memorization.

In summary, Gestalt psychology contributed significantly to problem solving and learning. In fact, present-day cognitive psychology (Chapter 18), which includes studies of problem solving, can be viewed as a direct descendant of Gestalt psychology (e.g., Gardner, 1985).

KURT LEWIN

Kurt Lewin (1890–1947) was born on September 9, 1890, in the town of Mogilno, Prussia (a former German state). He grew up on a farm, and his family moved to Berlin in 1905. After studies at the Universities of Freiburg and Munich, Lewin began his formal training in psychology at the University of Berlin in 1910. He had completed all the Ph.D. requirements under Stumpf by 1914, but because of World War I, he did not receive his degree until 1916. During the war, Lewin rose from private to officer and won the Iron Cross.

After the war, Lewin returned to the Psychological Institute in Berlin. He became a *Privatdozent* in 1921 and an *Ausserordentlicher Professor* (associate professor) in 1927, an advance over his previous rank, but a position without tenure. He was a Visiting Professor of Psychology at Stanford University in 1932 and left Germany in 1933 to escape the growing Nazi threat to Jews.

For the next 2 years, Lewin was an Acting Professor of Psychology at Cornell, with an appointment in the home economics department because of the department's responsibility for training nursery school teachers (Lück, 1997). Lewin's research with children involved filmmaking, which probably began through home movies of his own children. According to Lück, Lewin's talent as a filmmaker was widely recognized both in Germany and abroad.

After Cornell, Lewin spent 10 years as Professor of Child Psychology at the Child Welfare Research Station, University of Iowa. Shortly before his death, he accepted the position of Professor of Psychology and Director of the Research Center for Group Dynamics, Massachusetts Institute of Technology. Lewin died at Newtonville, Massachusetts, of a massive heart attack on February 12, 1947.

Lewin's programs in both Germany and the United States interested women students. Perhaps this was because of his subject matter—the more social elements of cognition and perception, children, applied topics—and the *Zeitgeist* that constrained the place of women and the topics in which they were interested. Four female graduate students began to work with Lewin in 1924: Gita Birenbaum, Tamara Dembo (who came with him to America), Maria Ovsiankina, and Bliuma Zeigarnik. Lewin continued to work with women in the United States, but they were not in the majority as they had been in Germany (Ash, 1992).

Almost without exception, people who knew Lewin described him in glowing terms. For example,

Archives of the History of American Psychology – The University of Akron.

Kurt Lewin (1890–1947)

Rensis Likert (1903–1981), a Lewin associate and the developer of the Likert Scale, said, "all who knew him had a singular unanimity of feeling about him. Here was an individual who was a great scientist, a great teacher and a great man" (Likert, 1947, p. 132). According to Lewin-student Jerome Frank (1978), the word best summarizing Lewin's personality is *zest:* "He was a little man with an apparently inexhaustible supply of energy. . . . Although he must often have been seated in my presence, in my memories he is almost always in motion" (p. 223).

Lewin also had a keen intellect and a high degree of mental flexibility; he was always willing to listen receptively to new ideas from any source (Cartwright, 1947). Lewin had a talent for attracting capable students, and his group discussions with them were conducted in an open manner. Lippitt (1947) wrote, "Over and over he made clear that the atmosphere of the discussion must be such that no one had any fears of 'sticking out his neck' in expressing any idea, no matter how unformulated it might seem" (p. 88).

By all accounts, Lewin fit easily into the American way of life. For example, Tolman (1948) referred to an essay Lewin had written about social psychological differences between Americans and Germans. Lewin described Americans as more open and communicative than Germans, resulting in "greater ease and friendliness in ordinary social relations, and greater contact with immediate practical problems in the American, and a more private and idea-centered life in the German" (p. 2). Tolman cited Lewin's distinction because according to his own analysis, Lewin himself was "very American."

To end his obituary of Lewin, Tolman (1948) predicted:

> In the future history of our psychological era there are two names which, I believe, will stand out above all others: those of Freud and of Lewin. . . . Freud, the clinician, and Lewin, the experimentalist, these are the two men who will always be remembered because of the fact that their contrasting but complementary insights first made of psychology a science which was applicable both to real individuals and to real society. (p. 4)

To the general public, Freud's name is much better known than Lewin's, but to many psychologists, Lewin's contributions are of considerably more than historical interest.

Lewin's Topological Psychology

Lewin is known for applying Gestalt principles to the study of motivation, personality, and social processes. To do this, Lewin developed **field theory,** in which a person interacts continually within a field of psychological forces. For Lewin, the behavior (B) of a person (P) is a function of the person's interaction with his or her environment (E); that is, $B = f(PE)$. By environment, Lewin meant the psychological (or psychobiological) environment.

A person's psychological activities occur within the **life space,** which consists of all the influences on the person at a given time. Lewin referred to the influences themselves as "psychological facts." These influences can include motivational states (e.g., hunger), memories (how good food tastes at a particular restaurant), and sensations (the smells

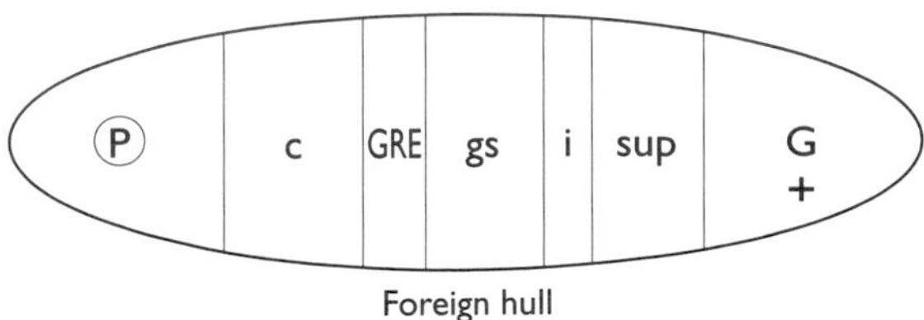

FIGURE 14.5 Life space of a person who wants to become a practicing clinical psychologist

from a restaurant's kitchen). The only restriction on what is in the person's life space is that it must be something the person is aware of.

To illustrate the person's life space with its psychological facts, Lewin borrowed symbols from *topology*—a form of mathematics that deals with the unvarying properties of a geometric figure when the figure is changed in certain ways. For example, the relative positions of regions within a bounded form are maintained despite changes in size or distortions of the form. In addition, Lewin invented **hodology,** which he used to show paths of energy within the life space. Lewin used Jordan curves (elliptical shapes) to enclose a person's life space. Psychological facts are contained within the curve; events and objects that are not part of the person's life space lie outside the curve and constitute the foreign hull.

For Lewin, the life space of an individual is divided into regions with boundaries, or barriers. The boundaries vary in their permeability, with some easier to cross than others. As an illustration, consider the life space of a psychology undergraduate student who decides she wants to go to graduate school, earn a Ph.D., and become a practicing clinical psychologist. Her life space at the time of her decision might look like the illustration in Figure 14.5.

As you can see, the student (P, for person) has several boundaries and regions to traverse before attaining her ultimate goal (G) of being a clinical psychologist with a private practice. She must first finish college (c), take the Graduate Record Examination (GRE) and score well, go to graduate school (gs), complete an internship (i), and set up a practice (sup) before she can achieve her goal. Some of the boundaries might prove more difficult to penetrate than others. For example, if the student does not do well on standardized aptitude tests such as the GRE, then for her, the barrier to entrance into graduate school may be impenetrable.

The psychological facts have value (or valence in Lewin's terminology), which is represented with either a plus (+) or minus (–) sign; a fact with no value to the individual receives no sign. Lewin used vectors to show either impelling or repelling psychological forces acting on a person. As a further illustration of Lewin's topological psychology, we will examine some of the concepts Lewin (1931) explored in his invited chapter for *A Handbook of Child Psychology.*

One basic concept was that the life space becomes larger and more differentiated with age. This differentiation occurs temporally as well as physically. That is, the older child's life space contains not only *present* psychological facts but both past and future psychological facts. The older child begins to plan for the future and also begins to use imagery and fantasy. This means the child lives to some extent on an irreality level (Lewin, 1936). Lewin used the term *irreality* to describe an unrealistic aspect of a person's life space.

In his *Handbook* chapter, Lewin (1931) described three types of conflict experienced by the child (and the adult as well). These are the approach-approach conflict, approach-avoidance conflict, and avoidance-avoidance conflict. Lewin defined *conflict* "as the opposition of approximately equally strong field forces" (p. 109).

In **approach-approach conflict,** the child must decide between two goals, both with positive valence. In Figure 14.6a, the child (C) must choose between going on a picnic (P) and playing with friends (Pl.). Approach-approach conflict is usually easy to resolve because both choices are positively valued, but Lewin noted that once the choice is made, the child often sees the chosen goal as inferior to the rejected goal.

Approach-avoidance conflict occurs when a goal simultaneously has both positive *and* negative valence. Shown in Figure 14.6b, Lewin's example is of a child who wants to climb a tree (Tr) but is fearful of doing

(a) Approach – approach conflict

(b) Approach – avoidance conflict

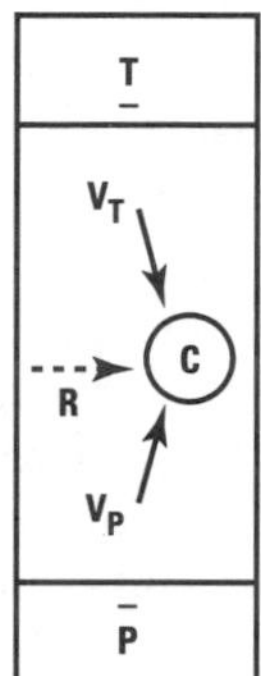

(c) Avoidance – avoidance conflict

FIGURE 14.6 Lewin's three types of conflict

Source: from Lewin, K. (1931) "Environmental Forces in Child Behavior and Development." In C. Murchison (Ed.), Handbook of child psychology *(pp. 94–127). Worcester, MA: Clark University Press. Reprinted by permission.*

so. The length of the vectors can be drawn to indicate which of the impelling and repelling forces is stronger. Thus, if the enjoyment from climbing the tree is likely to be greater than the child's fear of heights, then he or she will climb the tree.

In **avoidance-avoidance conflict,** the child must choose between two goals with negative valence. Shown in Figure 14.6c, in Lewin's example the child is told to perform an unpleasant task (T) or she will be punished (P). V_T is the vector pushing the child away from the unpleasant task, and V_P pushes the child away from punishment. The result is often attempted escape from the field, shown in the figure by R, the "sideways resultant." One of the authors remembers telling his son to do his homework or he would be punished; invariably the son chose the sideways resultant, escaping from the field by falling asleep.

Lewin at the Iowa Child Welfare Research Station (ICWRS)

In Iowa, as in Germany, Lewin was open to the ideas of his group, and daily discussions involved a constantly changing set of participants. This aspect of Lewin's approach to research had a special name, *die Quasselstrippe* (the chatter line), a term that appears repeatedly in the reminiscences of Lewin's American students (e.g., Ash, 1992).

From these discussions came two ideas that led to especially significant and widely cited studies. According to Dorwin Cartwright, one of Lewin's students, the idea to study the effect of different types of group leadership on children's behavior probably originated with conversations Lewin had with Ronald Lippitt in 1936 (Ash, 1992). In the most extensive study, Lewin, Lippitt, and White (1939) organized groups of 10-year-old boys to perform various activities under different adult-leadership types: authoritarian, democratic, and *laissez-faire* (not interfering in the boys' pursuits). Authoritarian leadership led to increased aggression within the group and "scapegoating," selecting a target for the aggression. The social atmosphere was friendlier in the democratically led group, and more assigned tasks were accomplished. Little was accomplished in the *laissez-faire* group.

As noted, Lewin believed the individual's life space becomes more differentiated with development. Thus, going backward developmentally (regressing) should result in less personality differentiation, or, as Lewin put it, "dedifferentiation." To study the dedifferentiation hypothesis, Barker, Dembo, and Lewin (1943) first allowed children to play with such ordinary toys as blocks, a teapot, a cup, crayons, and writing paper. During this period, the experimenters rated the constructiveness or destructiveness of the children's play, assigning a developmental age to each child's play. Next, the children were allowed to play with vastly superior toys on the other side of a screen from their original playthings. These toys included a dollhouse large enough to admit a child and "a toy lake . . . filled with real water. It contained an island with a lighthouse, a wharf, a ferryboat, small boats, fishes, ducks, and frogs. The lake had sand beaches" (p. 445). Finally, the children were forced to return to the original toys, but they could see what they were missing through the screen.

The resulting frustration led to dedifferentiation, which was evidenced by a dramatic decline in the children's quality of play. The average rated play age was over 17 months less than originally. Children threw blocks at each other, used crayons to scribble on paper rather than to draw or color pictures, had tantrums, and so on. This study provided dramatic evidence for the frustration-aggression hypothesis (Dollard, Doob, Miller, Mowrer, & Sears, 1939).

Lewin After Iowa

After leaving Iowa, Lewin began his "action research" (applied research) which was intended to solve actual problems. John, Eckardt, and Hiebsch (1989) have suggested that the roots of Lewin's action research can be seen in an essay Lewin wrote in 1920, long before he came to America. Eng (1978) suggested that Lewin's action research, although valuable from the standpoint of positively affecting the human condition, may have been compensation for the "sterility in the long run [of Lewin's field theory] as a paradigm for a new psychology" (p. 232). By contrast, Henle (1978b) did not consider Lewin's field theory approach a failure. She characterized Lewin's work as metatheory rather than theory—Lewin "was writing a *theory of personality theory*" (p. 234, italics in the original)—and concluded that personality theory would be more advanced if its formulators had appreciated Lewin's contribution.

One example of action research examined the most effective way to change opinions about various food items during World War II. In one study, women either heard a dynamic lecture praising some unpalatable, but abundant, food item or participated in group discussions on the desirability of buying and eating the disliked item. Group discussions and public commitment to changing behavior were clearly more effective than either discussions with individuals or dynamic lectures.

With Lewin's formation of the Research Center for Group Dynamics at MIT, the study of group dynamics became more focused. Some concepts that Lewin and his followers studied included group cohesiveness, identification with the group, within-group communication, and group decision processes. Lewin also thought a great deal about social change, especially about the problem of changing the entire culture. Specifically, "he looked to the methods of group dynamics to provide effective tools for reform, which, although exerting some pressures on people, would on the whole respect the freedom and dignity of individuals" (Heims, 1978, p. 239). After Lewin died, the Research Center for Group Dynamics moved to the University of Michigan. In addition, a National Training Laboratory was begun at Bethel, Maine, to conduct summer workshops to train leaders using the principles of group dynamics. These training groups were called "T groups" and became popular in the 1970s.

We see in Lewin a diverse thinker who contributed to a variety of areas in psychology. Even today, Lewin's field theory has adherents in both industrial psychology and personality theory.

LESSER-KNOWN GESTALT PSYCHOLOGISTS

In Germany and, later, America, many other theorists and researchers were associated with Gestalt psychology. For example, David Katz (Chapter 8) was a well-known perceptual theorist in Europe in the 1920s and was always counted as an ally of Gestalt psychology and a contributor to its store of facts. Earlier we mentioned **Kurt Goldstein** (1878–1965) as one of the editors of *Psychologische Forschung.* Goldstein studied under Carl Wernicke (Chapter 7), whose interest in aphasia (language deficits) became a lifelong obsession of Goldstein (Simmel, 1966). A pioneer in clinical neuroscience, Goldstein's work with brain-damaged World War I soldiers enabled him to make many substantive contributions to our understanding of the relationship between neurology and behavior within a Gestalt framework (Goldstein, 1967).

Karl Bühler (1879–1963) can be associated with several phenomenological movements in Germany, Gestalt psychology among them. What little of Bühler's work has been translated into English has been well received by contemporary cognitive psychologists (e.g., Bransford, 1979).

A student of both Wertheimer and Köhler, **Karl Duncker** (1903–1940) was one of the most notable of the Gestalt psychologists with interests in thinking. Duncker committed suicide while staying with the Köhlers (Harrower, 1983). Duncker's (1945) posthumously published work on problem solving provides much of the basis for our current understanding of how linguistic relations constrain human reasoning and for **functional fixedness.** Functional fixedness is defined most simply as the inability to use objects to attain a goal in a manner different from their previously established use.

To illustrate how linguistic relations constrain our thinking, consider the following problem adapted from Duncker (1945): You have a cancer that cannot be surgically or chemically treated because it is located deep inside the body surrounded by vital tissue. The only option is to destroy it with a laser. However, because the tumor is surrounded by essential organs, a laser beam that would destroy the tumor would also destroy the vital tissue it had to pass through to reach the tumor. A hint from Crovitz (1970) may help you find the solution. Try thinking through the phrase "Take a ray _______ a ray," inserting different prepositions in the blank. Modern work on psycholinguistics has continued to build on Duncker's insights into the importance of relations in human problem solving (e.g., Johnson & Henley, 1992).

Mary Henle (1913–) and **Rudolph Arnheim** (1904–) are two noteworthy modern-day Gestalt psychologists. Henle is perhaps best known as the "chronicler of Gestalt psychology." She has compiled several essay collections (e.g., *Documents of Gestalt Psychology* [Henle, 1961]; *The Selected Papers of Wolfgang Köhler* [Henle, 1971]) and has written articles comparing Gestalt psychology and such things (or people) as phenomenology (Henle, 1979), William James (Henle, 1990), and gestalt therapy. Concerning Gestalt psychology and gestalt therapy, Henle (1986) wrote, "The difference is so crucial that I could conclude at this point that there is no substantive relation between Gestalt psychology and gestalt therapy" (p. 26). Henle is currently Professor Emeritus at the New School for Social Research.

Rudolph Arnheim has continued to write articles on classical Gestalt topics (e.g., 1986a), to be a critic of misconceptions of Gestalt psychology (e.g., 1986b), and to take Gestalt psychology in new directions, such as into art and architecture. *Visual Thinking* (Arnheim, 1969), *Art and Visual Perception* (Arnheim, 1974), and many related articles have pioneered the fields of the psychology of art and of architecture.

GESTALT PSYCHOLOGY'S INFLUENCE

As we indicated, Wertheimer, Köhler, and Lewin all came to America to escape the Nazis. Other, lesser-known Gestaltists left Germany as well, going to Scandinavia, Russia, and other countries (Henle, 1986). The Gestalt psychologists left behind them in Germany their well-established careers, large laboratories, many students, and a major journal (*Psychologische Forschung*). As Henle (1980) noted, "the first generation of young Gestalt psychologists was essentially wiped out" (p. 178). And it was not just the Gestalt school that was destroyed with the advent of the Nazi regime. According to Mandler (2002), psychology as a viable field in Germany was ruined when the Nazis came to power in 1933.

The story of how the Gestaltists came to America and found academic positions is interesting. Mary Henle (1984) argued that their immigration and subsequent employment may be attributed primarily to **R. M. Ogden**'s (1877–1959) efforts. Ogden was Titchener's student at Cornell before taking his degree in 1903 with Külpe at Würzburg. While in Germany, Ogden met Koffka, Külpe's assistant at the time (ca. 1909). Returning to America, Ogden taught at Missouri, Tennessee, and Kansas before settling at Cornell. During this time, Ogden kept in contact with Koffka and was instrumental in the publication of Koffka's article introducing Gestalt psychology to America in the *Psychological Bulletin* (1922).

By the mid-1920s, it was clear that the major Gestaltists were interested in coming to America, and Ogden acted as a facilitator (Freeman, 1977). After considering an offer at Wisconsin, where he had taught in the 1926–1927 academic year (Chapter 13), Koffka settled at Smith College in 1927. In 1929, Ogden arranged for Köhler to give visiting lectures at

Cornell after failing to get Wertheimer for them. In 1933, Lewin came to Cornell at Ogden's bidding.

Although all the major Gestaltists except Wertheimer spent brief periods as visiting professors at several major American schools both before and after immigrating to America, the places they eventually chose all had drawbacks. For example, although Koffka's interactions at Smith College with J. J. Gibson proved important for perceptual theory, Smith was an undergraduate institution that could not train a new generation of Ph.D.s. Actually, Koffka did have one Ph.D. student in America—Molly Harrower. Despite Smith's lack of a Ph.D. program, **Molly Harrower** (1906–1999) earned her degree in 1934 with a committee that included Arnold Gesell, E. G. Boring, and Koffka (Dewsbury, 1999). Harrower's postdoctoral training included work with Kurt Goldstein and neurosurgeon Wilder Penfield (Chapter 7), which enabled her to "become one of the first experimental psychologists to move into a field now known as neuropsychology" (Popplestone, 1983, p. viii). Important for Gestalt psychology, Harrower (1983) published an edited version of her voluminous correspondence with Koffka between 1928 and 1941. In his obituary of Harrower, Dewsbury (2000b) described her as a "modern-day Renaissance woman." Among other things, Harrower was "a gifted clinician and serious researcher, a fine university teacher and one of the first psychologists in full-time private practice, a Gestalt psychologist and devotee of psychoanalysis, a psychologist and poet" (p. 1058).

Köhler stayed at Swarthmore, also an undergraduate institution, but he influenced some students (e.g., Mary Henle and Hans Wallach). In fact, **Hans Wallach** (1904–1998) joined Köhler at Swarthmore in 1936 and lived in the small town of Swarthmore, Pennsylvania, for the rest of his long life. Wallach is particularly known for his studies in perception, and he received the APA's Award for Distinguished Scientific Contributions in 1983 and the Howard Cosby Warren Medal from the Society of Experimental Psychologists in 1987 (Harris, 2001). Finally, when Wertheimer started at the New School for Social Research, it offered no degrees. Wertheimer did not have Ph.D. students in America until near the end of his life (Henle, 1980).

Not only did the Gestaltists leave behind their "establishment," their arrival in America coincided with behaviorism's heyday. In addition, although seldom stated, the fact that the major Gestaltists were Germans at a time of escalating international tensions with Germany could not have helped their careers. Thus, it is easy to see why Gestalt psychology did not prosper in America.

World War II's events played a major role in fragmenting Gestalt psychology as a school, leading one social psychologist to comment: "If I were required to name the one person who has had the greatest impact on the field, it would have to be Adolph Hitler" (Cartwright, 1979, p. 84). The major Gestaltists' move to America cost them their place in the sun and relocated them in well-respected, but not powerful, academic settings. Also, because American psychology at the time was deeply rooted in behaviorism, the Gestaltists did not find fertile soil for their ideas.

However, Köhler never gave up the fight for the recognition that Gestalt psychology deserved. He continued to publish and to grow in stature as a psychological theorist and philosopher throughout his long career. Indeed, Gestalt theory as a philosophy of psychology flourished. First exposed to Gestalt psychology by Karl Bühler, Ludwig Wittgenstein (Chapter 18) became the major figure in modern philosophy largely through his later writings in the philosophy of psychology. Wittgenstein frequently used Gestalt principles as his point of departure, and Gestalt figures often appeared in his books, as he grappled with difficult questions about perception, language, and the structure of knowledge. For more details on Wittgenstein's analysis of Gestalt psychology, see Pastore (1991).

Köhler (1959) began his presidential address to the American Psychological Association by tracing Gestalt psychology from Wertheimer through its then-current works in social psychology by Solomon Asch and Fritz Heider (both Chapter 17). Next, he proposed that the age of such competing schools as Gestalt psychology and behaviorism was waning. Köhler closed by suggesting that the time had come to combine the wisdom of all the schools into one psychology.

In part, what Köhler suggested in 1959 has occurred. Modern cognitive-behavioral therapies and new "cognitive science" advances in learning theory exemplify the combining of disparate areas of psychology. Within 10 years of Köhler's APA address, the last two great schools—behaviorism and Gestalt psychology—were gone. In their place was a loose confederation known as cognitive psychology, which can be viewed as a marriage of both the behaviorist and the Gestalt traditions (e.g., Simon, 1992).

Howard Gardner (1985) traced the origins of the "Cognitive Revolution" in *The Mind's New Science,* in which he referred to Gestalt psychology as "the most direct link" between older works on thinking and modern cognitive psychology (see also Michael Wertheimer, 1991). Throughout their careers, many Gestalt psychologists were interested in conception and thinking, in addition to perception.

Obviously, Gestalt psychology has continued to influence modern psychology long after its decline as a formal school. It lives on as a viable perceptual theory and underpins many modern insights in cognitive psychology and social psychology, as we will see in subsequent chapters.

CONCLUSIONS

Gestalt psychology emerged in Germany as the fullest expression of the phenomenological alternative to Wundt's system (see Chapter 8). At its peak just before World War II, it represented perhaps the most complete and sophisticated system of psychology extant. Unfortunately, the rise of the Nazis led to the dismantling of the German academic community, and with it Gestalt psychology. With its principals scattered across Europe and America, Gestalt psychology never regained its former status.

Although introductory textbooks cover the contributions that Gestalt psychologists made to our understanding of perceptual phenomena, often without giving appropriate credit, equally important contributions to learning, child development, cognition, biological psychology, and social and applied areas are largely ignored. Still, Gestalt psychology did not fade away completely. In America, many of the original Gestalt theorists found a niche, and new students (e.g., Asch, Festinger, Heider), in social cognition. In addition, Gestalt psychology can be seen as an important forerunner of modern cognitive psychology.

Because of the negative effect of world events on Gestalt psychology before it reached maturity, we cannot conclude that Gestalt psychology fully succeeded as a psychological school. However, the impact of Gestalt psychology on the future of psychology should not be underestimated. We are left with the perennial "what if" question: What would the landscape of psychology look like today if the Gestaltists had not been among World War II's casualties?

SUMMARY

The German word *Gestalt* has become part of the English language and is usually taken to mean "whole." Gestalt psychology dealt with wholes unexplained by knowledge of their components.

Max Wertheimer's 1910 insight about apparent movement (the phi phenomenon) was that perceptions may have properties that are different and cannot be predicted from the sensations that comprise them. He studied the phi phenomenon at Frankfurt with Wolfgang Köhler and Kurt Koffka.

The most immediate forerunners of Gestalt psychology were Ernst Mach and Christian von Ehrenfels, who recognized that whole perceptions may have qualities independent of the individual sensations comprising them (*Gestalt-qualitäten*). Others often mentioned as anticipators include John Stuart Mill, Wundt, Brentano, Külpe, Stumpf, Husserl, James, and Dewey.

Gestalt Psychology's Triumvirate

After studying the phi phenomenon at Frankfurt, Max Wertheimer taught at the University of Berlin before becoming a professor at the University of Frankfurt. Coming to the United States in 1933, he was employed by the New School for Social Research in New York City until his death in 1943. His well-known *Productive Thinking* was published in 1945.

Both Kurt Koffka and Wolfgang Köhler earned Ph.D.s from the University of Berlin under Stumpf's supervision. Koffka's "Perception: An Introduction to *Gestalt-Theorie*" introduced Gestalt psychology to America. In 1913,

Köhler went to Tenerife to study an ape colony, publishing his results in English as *The Mentality of Apes.* Köhler immigrated to America in 1935 and held visiting professorships at Harvard and the University of Chicago before settling at Swarthmore College.

Principles of Gestalt Psychology

The Gestalt principles of perceptual grouping include the figure-ground relationship, continuity, proximity, similarity, and closure.

Other Gestalt Principles and Phenomena

The Gestalt perceptual principles may be viewed as special cases of the law of *Prägnanz.* Studied by Bliuma Zeigarnik, the Zeigarnik effect—the tendency to remember incomplete tasks longer than finished tasks—illustrates the law of *Prägnanz.* Isomorphism is the Gestalt principle that assumes a direct correspondence between brain processes and what is being experienced.

Köhler developed the Gestalt learning principles from his studies of animals solving *Umweg* (detour) problems, learning to stack boxes or use sticks to get bananas, and being trained and tested on the transposition problem. Animals sometimes showed sudden awareness or "insight" of a problem's solution.

In *Productive Thinking,* Wertheimer applied Gestalt principles to problem solving and learning. Wertheimer favored a holistic approach to problem solving rather than rote memorization.

Kurt Lewin

Kurt Lewin received his Ph.D. under Stumpf and was at the Berlin Psychological Institute until he immigrated to the United States in the early 1930s. After stints at Cornell and in Iowa, Lewin became Director of the Research Center for Group Dynamics at MIT.

Lewin applied Gestalt principles to the study of motivation, personality, and social processes, developing field theory in which a person is seen to interact in a field of psychological forces. To illustrate his theory, Lewin borrowed symbols from topology. He invented hodology to show the paths of energy in the life space.

In an article for *A Handbook of Child Psychology,* Lewin described approach-approach conflict, approach-avoidance conflict, and avoidance-avoidance conflict. In Iowa, Lewin and his colleagues studied groups of boys performing activities under either authoritarian, democratic, or *laissez-faire* adult leadership. Authoritarian leadership led to increased within-group aggression and scapegoating. Also in Iowa, Lewin and his colleagues found that when children were first allowed to play with desirable toys and were then prevented from such play, the resulting frustration caused behavioral regression. In a study during World War II, Lewin found that housewives who participated in group discussions of the benefits of unpopular food items were more likely to use the items than housewives given a dynamic lecture.

Lesser-Known Gestalt Psychologists

Lesser-known contributors to Gestalt psychology include Karl Duncker, David Katz, Kurt Goldstein, Karl Bühler, Mary Henle, and Rudolph Arnheim.

Gestalt Psychology's Influence

All the major German figures in Gestalt psychology immigrated to the United States in the 1920s and 1930s, leaving behind their laboratories, careers, and many students. The institutions where these psychologists eventually settled did not have Ph.D. programs, which, along with behaviorism's popularity, contributed to Gestalt psychology's failure to prosper in the United States. However, Gestalt psychology lives on in perceptual theory, social psychology, and cognitive psychology.

CONNECTIONS QUESTIONS

1. Name and discuss as many connections as you can between World War II and Gestalt psychology.
2. Who were some of the forerunners of Gestalt psychology, and what are some of the connections between them?
3. What connections can you trace between Gestalt psychology and learning theory?
4. Draw as many connections as you can between Gestalt psychology and social psychology.
5. What are some of the connections between Gestalt psychology and cognitive psychology?
6. Defend the thesis that Gestalt psychology is the culmination of a rational approach to psychology.

KEY NAMES AND TERMS

approach-approach conflict (p. 410)
approach-avoidance conflict (p. 410)
Archimedes (p. 406)
Rudolph Arnheim (p. 413)
avoidance-avoidance conflict (p. 411)
Karl Bühler (p. 412)
closure (p. 402)
cognitive dissonance (p. 408)
continuity (p. 402)
Karl Duncker (p. 413)
Leon Festinger (p. 408)
field theory (p. 409)
figure-ground relationship (p. 402)
functional fixedness (p. 413)
Gestalt psychology (p. 394)
Gestaltqualitäten (p. 396)
Kurt Goldstein (p. 412)
Harry F. Harlow (p. 406)
Molly Harrower (p. 414)
Mary Henle (p. 413)
hodology (p. 410)
insight (p. 404)
isomorphism (p. 404)
Kurt Koffka (p. 398)
Wolfgang Köhler (p. 399)
law of *Prägnanz* (p. 402)
learning set (p. 406)
Kurt Lewin (p. 408)
life space (p. 409)
Rensis Likert (p. 409)
R. M. Ogden (p. 413)
phi phenomenon (p. 395)
proximity (p. 402)
similarity (p. 402)
Sultan (p. 405)
tachistoscope (p. 395)
transposition (p. 407)
Umweg or detour problem (p. 404)
Hans Wallach (p. 414)
Max Wertheimer (p. 397)
Michael Wertheimer (p. 395)
Bliuma Vul'Fovna Zeigarnik (p. 403)
Zeigarnik effect (p. 403)

SUGGESTED READINGS

Harrower, M. (1983). *Kurt Koffka: An unwitting self-portrait.* Gainesville, FL: University Presses of Florida. Harrower's book is composed of the exchange of correspondence between her and one of Gestalt psychology's founders. The time period covered is from 1928 (not long after Koffka's arrival in America) to 1941, the year Koffka died. Koffka emerges from his "unwitting self-portrait" as a genuinely sympathetic figure in the history of Gestalt psychology.

Henle, M. (1961). *Documents of Gestalt psychology.* Berkeley, CA: University of California Press. This volume contains classic papers in Gestalt psychology. Several famous articles are translated and reprinted, and the book includes several essays by the "lesser-known" Gestalt psychologists.

Henle, M. (1986). *1879 and all that: Essays in the theory and history of psychology.* New York: Columbia University Press. Mary Henle has become the chronicler of Gestalt psychology, as well as its leading spokesperson in modern times, and you can also find essays by her on Gestalt psychology in several history anthologies. This volume explores selected elements of the history and theory of Gestalt psychology.

Köhler, W. (1925). *The mentality of apes.* London: Routledge and Kegan Paul. (Original work published 1917) This is the work for which Köhler first became known to American psychologists. In it, he introduced the *Umweg* problem and made other contributions to the study of learning in animals.

Köhler, W. (1947). *Gestalt psychology: An introduction to new concepts in modern psychology.* New York: Liveright. (Original work published 1929) This book provides an excellent overview of Gestalt psychology's key concepts, its stance on several major issues—mind-body, reductionism, molar-molecular analysis—and its relationship to other schools, such as structuralism and behaviorism.

Köhler, W. (1966). *The place of value in a world of fact.* New York: Liveright. (Original work published 1938) This book is listed for those of you interested in the more philosophical aspects of Gestalt psychology. The essays it includes were first given by Köhler as a series of lectures at Harvard in 1934–1935.

Ley, R. (1990). *A whisper of espionage.* Garden City Park, NY: Avery Publishing Group, Inc. Ley's book is recommended as "fun" reading and as a further introduction to Köhler and some of the other Gestalt psychologists. We will allow you to draw your own conclusions about Köhler's possible role as a German spy in World War I.

Wertheimer, Max (1945). *Productive thinking.* New York: Harper. As we discussed in the chapter, this work explores cognition in a variety of ways, some theoretical and some applied.

Psychoanalysis

CHAPTER 15

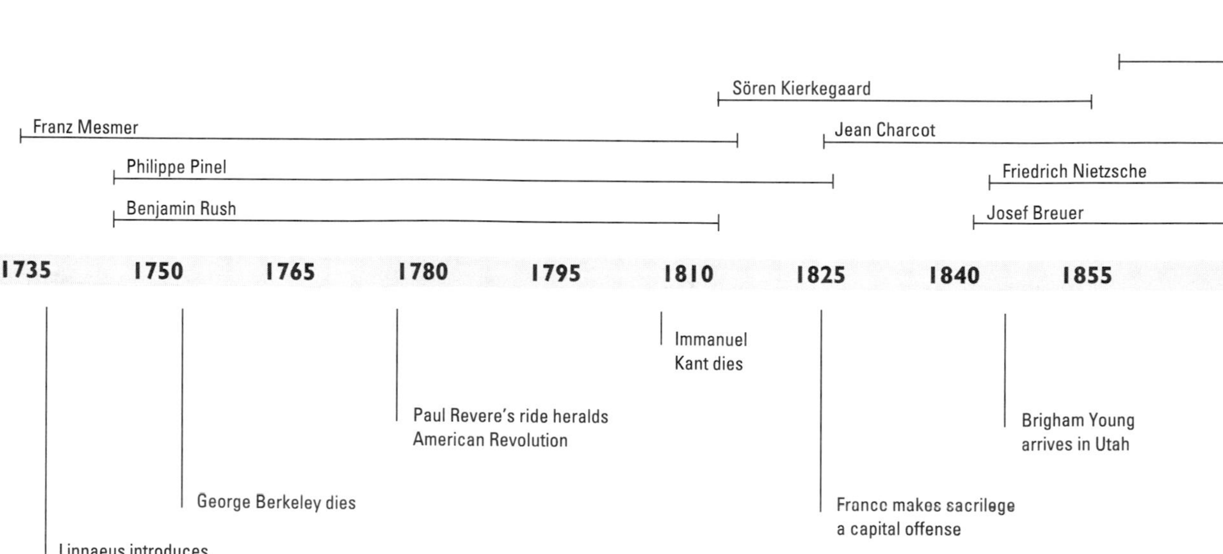

OUTLINE

Early Treatment of the Mentally Ill

Hypnosis

- Mesmerism
- Hypnotism
- Nancy Versus Salpêtrière
- Pierre Janet

Existential Precursors to Freud

Sigmund Freud

- *The Interpretation of Dreams*
- Freud Gains Recognition
- Freud's Theory of Personality
- Freud's Influence

Neo-Freudians

- Anna Freud
- Karen Horney
- The Formation of Attachments
- Erik Erikson: Life-Span Development
- Alfred Adler
- Carl Gustav Jung

Conclusions

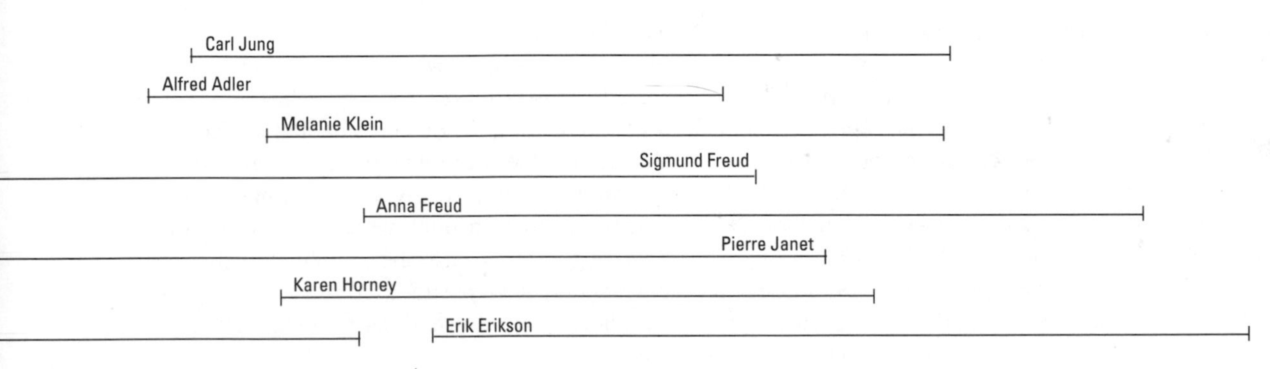

1870 | 1885 | 1900 | 1915 | 1930 | 1945 | 1960 | 1975 | 1990

Jefferson Davis, Confederate president, is captured

Stanford University is founded by Leland Stanford to honor his son who died the previous year

Ty Cobb enters major league baseball

League of Nations created in Paris after WWI

Jewish Holocaust is part of WWII

Hitler commits suicide

Kurt Vonnegut flourishes

Soviet Union collapses

We can define **psychoanalysis** as the system developed by Sigmund Freud to study human motivation, personality, and psychopathology, using such techniques as free association and the analysis of dreams and everyday errors. Chronologically, the development of psychoanalysis precedes two of the systems we have discussed—behaviorism and Gestalt psychology—but we have saved the discussion of psychoanalysis for last because its origin was quite different from those of the other psychological systems. Specifically, unlike structuralism, functionalism, behaviorism, and Gestalt psychology, which all developed within academic settings, psychoanalysis focused on human abnormal behavior and how to treat it, acquiring its theoretical concepts primarily from the clinical setting. Quantification of phenomena, experimentation, and the laboratory were key ingredients in the development of the previously examined systems, whereas they were much less important for psychoanalysis.

Psychoanalysis grew initially from Sigmund Freud's clinical experiences, but Freud, like the founders of the other systems, did not develop his ideas in isolation. Five traditions in late-19th-century academia importantly influenced Freud's thinking: hypnotism (discussed later); the Helmholtz School and Brücke's dynamic physiology (discussed later); Darwin's theory of evolution (Chapter 9); German rationalism, especially the works of Hegel and Schopenhauer (both Chapter 6); and contemporary conceptions of the unconscious. Of course, other influences have been proposed as well. For example, Fine (1979) suggested association psychology (Chapter 5), with Freud's free association technique coming directly from this school.

Born 3 years before publication of the *Origin of Species*, Freud credited Darwinian theory with paving the way for his optimism about the possibility of major advances in understanding the world. More specific connections from Darwin to Freud have also been suggested—for example, from Darwin's *The Expression of Emotions* on Freud's thinking about human emotions (Shakow, 1969).

The idea of unconscious processes was a major part of 19th-century rationalistic, German academia, as we have noted in earlier chapters. In Chapter 6, we discussed Herbart's conception of the apperceptive mass in consciousness, with incompatible unconscious ideas being prevented from entering the mass. Similarly, Schopenhauer wrote about repressing unwanted thoughts into the unconscious, with resistance hindering retrieval of such thoughts. Although Freud credited Schopenhauer with originating this notion, he claimed to have discovered it independently. In Chapter 8, we noted Ebbinghaus's dissertation on Eduard von Hartmann's influential *Philosophy of the Unconscious*, with which Freud was probably familiar.

Other influences on Freud (Pierre Janet, the existential philosophers Sören Kierkegaard and Friedrich Nietzsche) will be examined after we have surveyed briefly pre-Freudian concepts of, and treatments for, mental illness. To fully understand Freud's significance, we must first explore the conceptions of mental illness before his revolutionary ideas.

EARLY TREATMENT OF THE MENTALLY ILL

Treatment for mental illness is generally consistent with the contemporary concept of the cause of a disorder. For example, when demonic possession was considered the root of abnormal behavior, treatment involved making the demon's habitat as uncomfortable as possible. In prehistoric times, exorcising the demon may have involved trephining—cutting a hole in the skull through which the evil spirit could leave (e.g., Maher & Maher, 1985). At other times, the mentally ill were subjected to such treatments as loud noises, vile concoctions, flogging, starving, and burning.

Alongside such barbaric practices, there have been pockets of "enlightened" individuals whose conceptions of mental illness suggested more humane approaches. For example, Hippocrates (Chapter 2) attributed illness, including insanity, to natural causes, which led to natural remedies such as rest, moderation in food and drink, and sexual abstinence. The Greeks and Romans, at least through Galen (Chapter 2), generally accepted the Hippocratic approach.

Treatment of the mentally ill during the Middle Ages (ca. 500 to 1500) was mostly handled by the clergy. Consisting mainly of prayer, the application of holy water and sanctified relics, and mild exorcism, treatment was relatively benign at the beginning of this era. The more well-developed exorcistic rituals emphasized insulting the devil in the hope that the demons afflicting the patient would depart.

By the middle of the 13th century, the Inquisition sought to root out heresy, including witchcraft. For the next several centuries, a populace suffering from famines, plagues, and social unrest became obsessed with the devil as the upheaval's chief cause. Some historians of psychiatry (e.g., Alexander & Selesnick, 1966) have assumed that most of the witches were, in fact, mentally ill, as evidenced by their confessions of having performed impossible acts such as flying. Another possibility is that grain contaminated by ergot (an LSD-like fungus) may have been a common cause for the medieval witch craze. No matter what the cause, although the afflicted were often believed to be demonically possessed, the "demoniac was frequently construed as an individual smitten by witchcraft (i.e., bewitched) and was encouraged to accuse the witch who had caused him or her to become possessed . . ." (Spanos, 1978, p. 419). That is, the demented person was often considered a witch's victim, rather than a witch. Spanos noted, "There is some evidence that individuals then defined as insane were *less likely* than others to be accused of witchcraft" (p. 425, italics added). Also, confessions of having performed incredible feats probably resulted from torture, not from mental illness (e.g., Clark, 1997). Fortunately, witch hunting began to abate in the early 1600s.

Although histories of psychiatry (e.g., Zilboorg, 1941) have often depicted medieval treatment of the mentally ill as barbaric, the truth may be considerably different (Neugebauer, 1978). Reviewing manuscripts rather than just published documents from medieval and early modern England, Neugebauer found the mental status of disturbed individuals was measured with common-sense criteria, and in cases of disability, the Crown appointed supervised guardians.

Mental asylums were almost unknown before the 15th century, with many of the institutions that eventually housed the insane being used for lepers. As leprosy (Hansen's disease) gradually disappeared from Europe, leprosariums often became insane asylums. Some of the asylums were notorious for their deplorable conditions—for example, filthy surroundings, horrible food, brutality. One of the worst was London's priory of St. Mary of Bethlehem, which officially became a mental hospital in 1547 when Henry VIII gave it for this purpose to the city. Bethlehem, or Bedlam as it became known, "was a favorite Sunday excursion spot for Londoners, who came to stare at the madmen through the iron gates" (Alexander & Selesnick, 1966, p. 154). Tickets to see the violent patients continued to be sold into the 19th century.

Across Europe, the mentally ill began to receive more humane treatment toward the end of the 18th century, with the signal event being **Philippe Pinel**'s action (1745–1826). Put in charge at La Bicêtre asylum in Paris, in 1793, Pinel freed the insane men from their shackles and bonds. He improved the lot of the insane women at Salpêtrière the next year.

In Italy, Pinel contemporary **Vicenzio Chiarugi** (1759–1826) was another humanitarian reformer in his position as director of a large public hospital in Florence (Gerard, 1997). Chiarugi's work was anticipated by a 1774 ordinance in Tuscany, an Italian region, concerning hospitalization of the mentally ill (Mora, 1975). Mora called this ordinance "the first decree in any country attempting to provide adequate care to the mentally ill . . ." (p. 247).

Another of Pinel's contemporaries, English Quaker philanthropist **William Tuke** (1732–1822) established the York Retreat, which housed the mentally ill in a quiet, religious atmosphere. Samuel Tuke (1784–1857), William Tuke's grandson, was a leading psychiatric reformer, and his son, Daniel Hack Tuke (1827–1895), became an outstanding British psychiatrist. Samuel's published description of the retreat set forth the principles of the "moral therapy" practiced there.

In America, **Benjamin Rush** (1745–1813), who had studied in France and Great Britain, encouraged more humane treatment of the mentally ill while he was associated with the Pennsylvania Hospital. In lectures to the medical students at the University of Pennsylvania, Rush expounded a psychology combining Hartley's associationism and the Scottish school's faculty psychology (both Chapter 5; Noel & Carlson, 1973). Considered the founder of American psychiatry, Rush also advocated "public schools, free dispensaries for the indigent, higher educational facilities for

Rush's tranquilizing chair (1811)

women, and hospitals for alcoholics" (Alexander & Selesnick, 1966, p. 162). Rush was against the intemperate use of "spirituous liquors," and his most successful publication was a pamphlet discussing, among other things, alcohol's devastating effect on the mind (Carlson, 1977).

Enlightened in many respects, Rush nevertheless was an ardent proponent of bloodletting, the use of fear to change a mental patient's thinking, and a "tranquilizing chair," on which leather straps around the patient's arms and legs restrained movement. Still, Rush was genuinely concerned with his patients' welfare and represented an important positive force in American psychiatry.

Dorothea Dix (1802–1887) was another tireless American worker for humane treatment of the insane. Forced by recurring bouts of tuberculosis or possibly pneumonia to abandon classroom teaching, Dix offered to teach a Sunday school class for women in jail (Viney, 1996). This exposed her to the shocking conditions in jails and asylums, and for 40 years Dix effectively advocated reform. Through her efforts, hospital conditions improved in the United States, Canada, Scotland, and several other countries. Dix was personally responsible for establishing more than 30 mental hospitals, and she served during the Civil War as the superintendent of women nurses in the Union Army.

More humane treatment also followed a change in the suspected basis of mental disorders. Reviving Hippocrates' hypothesis of the bodily origin of illness, in the mid-19th century German physician Wilhelm Griesinger suggested the diagnosis of a mental disorder should indicate a physiological cause. One of Griesinger's followers, Emil Kraepelin (Chapter 8), divided mental illness into two major categories—dementia praecox (schizophrenia) and manic-depressive psychosis—attributing the former to a chemical imbalance and the latter to a metabolic defect.

In other parts of western Europe in the 19th century, particularly in France and Austria, mental disorders were thought to be caused by psychic malfunction rather than by physiological disturbance. For reasons not entirely clear to us today—although women's constrictive clothing has been blamed—hysteria was one of the period's most common disorders. Major symptoms are sensory or motor problems (e.g., hand anesthesia) without a known anatomical basis. Initially attributing hysteria to a physiological cause, the famous Parisian neurologist **Jean Martin Charcot** (1825–1893) came to view its origin as psychogenic instead. His change in thinking involves hypnosis.

HYPNOSIS

The story of hypnosis begins with another once-mysterious force—magnetism. Swiss alchemist, physician, and mystic **Paracelsus** (1493–1541)—an early opponent of witch hunts and the authority of such ancient physicians as Galen—believed magnets, like stars, influenced humans by means of a celestial fluid. The Flemish chemist **Jan Baptista van Helmont** (1577–1644) initiated the notion of **animal magnetism,** which was the idea that people emit a magnetic fluid that can be used to influence and even cure others. Animal magnetism's most important proponent was a Viennese physician whose name became synonymous with a disreputable methodology.

Mesmerism

Franz Anton Mesmer (1734–1815) graduated in 1766 from the University of Vienna Medical School, with a dissertation on the influence of the planets on human physiology. At least some of Mesmer's dissertation was apparently plagiarized, however (Gallo & Finger, 2000). As a physician, Mesmer developed a method of treating diseases using a magnet. Soon he discarded the magnet, believing that transmission of a magnetic force from his own body was sufficient to effect cures. When his treatment procedures were not accepted by the medical community, Mesmer left Vienna in 1778.

Franz Anton Mesmer (1734–1815)

Settling in Paris, Mesmer was spectacularly successful with hysterical patients, whereas the medical community was nearly unanimous in its disapproval. For his treatment performance, Mesmer charged the poor nothing and the wealthy exorbitant fees; "cures" were often obtained.

Treated in groups in a dimly lit, carpeted room suffused with soft music and the odor of orange blossoms, patients joined hands around a covered *baquet* (tub) filled with "magnetized" water. The music came from an instrument called either an armonica or glass harmonica, which had been invented by Benjamin Franklin to facilitate the playing of musical glasses (Gallo & Finger, 2000). Iron rods protruded from the *baquet*, and Mesmer, clad in a lilac robe, would extract a rod and touch a patient in an afflicted place in an effort to induce a "crisis," in which the patient would scream and go into convulsions. Generally, other patients followed suit, presumably affected by group suggestion (see Chapter 17).

Although Mesmer tried diligently to convince the medical community of animal magnetism's reality, he succeeded only with Charles d'Eslon, the physician to Louis XVI's brother. Despite d'Eslon's continuing loyalty, eventually Mesmer came to regard his most influential follower as a rival.

Mesmer left Paris in 1781 (Alexander & Selesnick, 1966), returning in 1784 to a professional defeat from which he never recovered. Because of pressure from d'Eslon and a society founded to promote animal magnetism, Louis XVI appointed a commission to study Mesmer's claims. Headed by Benjamin Franklin (other members included famed chemist Antoine Lavoisier and Joseph Guillotin, inventor of the guillotine), the Franklin Commission "concluded that Mesmer's animal magnetism was unrelated to physical magnetism and that any beneficial effects were due to pressure of the hands and feet, imagination, or the imitation of other patients" (Hoffeld, 1980, p. 383). After the commission's report, Mesmer fled to Switzerland, where he died in obscurity.

After Mesmer's death, **mesmerism**—the name given to his treatment method—continued in different parts of the world. One of its practitioners was Mesmer's former student—the **Marquis de Puységur** (1751–1825). In experiments on the family estate, Puységur and his brother discovered most of the hypnotic phenomena known today, such as the subjects' extreme suggestibility, their power to forget trance events, and their responsiveness to posthypnotic suggestion. Puységur also found that the crisis state and convulsive fit Mesmer considered essential for mesmerism were unnecessary. Puységur is important for demonstrating that mesmerism occurred and could be studied outside the sensationalistic environment of Mesmer's *baquet*.

Portuguese priest **José Custodio di Faria** (1756–1819) examined why some people are less responsive to "animal magnetism" than others, a problem even Mesmer had noticed. Faria showed he could induce deep trance states in about 20% of his subjects just by commanding them to "sleep." Anyone, even a child, could induce such "lucid sleep" in appropriate subjects, which suggested that the power to achieve the state lay in the hypnotized person, not in the hypnotizer. Unfortunately, Faria's ideas faded away after his death (Fancher, 1996).

Mesmerism remained in the hands of traveling showmen, who connected it with either magnetism or the occult. A standard demonstration involved the production of anesthesia in a subject, and this intrigued a few physicians and surgeons in the time before chemical anesthetics. One physician whose curiosity was piqued by such a demonstration was **John Elliotson** (1791–1868), a physician at London's University College Hospital.

No stranger to controversy, Elliotson was among the first to use the newly invented stethoscope to listen to heart sounds. In fact, Elliotson profoundly distrusted "old" medicine and was always eager to examine the "new." However, when the hospital administrators learned he planned to study mesmerism's anesthetic properties, they passed a resolution to prevent mesmerism's use at the institution. Elliotson resigned and never again entered the hospital he had been instrumental in founding (Boring, 1950).

Elliotson continued to use mesmerism to treat certain conditions, although not for surgical anesthesia, leaving that study to other physicians. For example, a Scottish physician practicing in India, **James Esdaile** (1808–1859), reported a mortality rate of less than 6% in 261 operations on mesmerized patients (Magner, 1992). Unfortunately, Esdaile found mesmerism less effective for anesthesia in Scotland than it had been in India. However, by this time, chemical anesthesia had come to dominate the medical community.

Hypnotism

After losing out to the reliable and universally applicable anesthetic actions of nitrous oxide, ether, and chloroform, mesmerism gained something close to scientific respectability and a new name through Scottish surgeon **James Braid**'s (1795–1860) efforts. In 1841, Braid attended public demonstrations of mesmerism, becoming convinced at the second demonstration that the mesmerized state was real, and he decided to investigate the phenomenon to bring it into line with scientific physiology.

Braid confirmed the findings of Puységur and Faria. Also like Faria and Puységur, Braid thought the trance state resembled sleep, so he called it *neurypnology*, which is a contraction of the Greek *neuro* for "nerve" and *hypnos* for "sleep." Braid later settled on "**hypnotism.**" Because Braid presented his work as an attack on mesmerism, the scientific community accepted it, and hypnotism became a scientific phenomenon that could be studied in the laboratory (Boring, 1950). For a detailed examination of hypnotism's history, see the appropriately titled *A History of Hypnotism* (Gauld, 1992).

Nancy Versus Salpêtrière

Nancy is a town in northeastern France where **Auguste Ambroise Liébeault** (1823–1904) began to practice medicine in 1864. At first, Liébeault charged nothing for hypnotic treatments and a standard fee for orthodox treatment, but he soon found that many of his patients wanted to be hypnotized, and he was forced to "allow" them to pay whatever they thought was fair. Liébeault's success attracted the attention of **Hippolyte Bernheim** (1840–1919), a younger physician from Nancy.

Bernheim visited Liébeault's hypnotic clinic in 1882, and he was so impressed with Liébeault's achievements he abandoned internal medicine for hypnotherapy. Bernheim's subsequent experience with hypnotically treated patients led him to conclude that people vary on a general trait of suggestibility and that their hypnotic susceptibility varies accordingly. Bernheim's many books and articles effectively presented the Nancy school of hypnotism's principles.

Jean Martin Charcot (1825–1893) and hypnotic subject

Meanwhile, Charcot was developing another school of hypnotism at Paris's Salpêtrière Hospital. As we noted, Charcot initially considered hysteria a physiological disorder, but he became convinced of its psychological basis when some of his students hypnotized a normal woman, suggested to her the display of hysterical symptoms, and Charcot believed she was really suffering from hysteria. He then began to concentrate on his hysterical patients, noting their various symptoms and treating them with hypnosis. He came to regard hypnotizability as a characteristic of hysteria, not part of the normal range of human behavior as Bernheim believed. Charcot was wrong in this, and the "verdict of time has favored the Nancy school . . ." (Boring, 1950, p. 130). However, Charcot's studies of hysteria changed medical thinking about the disorder.

Contemporary medical opinion held that hysterics were probably pretending to be ill, because their symptoms usually did not conform to known neuroanatomy. Physicians who believed in the disorder's reality considered it exclusively a disease of women and attributed it to a defect in their reproductive systems. Charcot's observations convinced him the symptoms were not simulated, and he had examined men outside Salpêtrière with similar conditions, which meant hysteria could not be caused by a defective female reproductive system. Charcot's opinions greatly influenced two of his pupils: Sigmund Freud and Pierre Janet.

Pierre Janet

Mentioned in Chapter 13, Paris-born **Pierre Janet** (1859–1947) was interested in psychology from an early age. At 22, Janet began teaching philosophy at a lycée (a secondary school that prepares students for university study) in Le Havre. Because he wanted to write a thesis on hallucination, Janet asked a physician if he knew of anyone with hallucinations whom Janet might study. The doctor put Janet in contact with a woman named Léonie who had been hypnotized in her youth and "had been observed to perform some curious things with clairvoyance, mental suggestion, and hypnotism from a distance, etc." (Janet, 1930, p. 125).

Janet studied Léonie for years, apparently demonstrating hypnotic somnambulism (sleepwalking) induced from a distance. For example, on one occasion, Janet found that "16 times out of 20 somnambulism has exactly coincided with a mental suggestion made at a distance of one kilometer" (Janet, 1930, p. 125). Repeating Janet's experiments, **Charles Richet** (1850–1935) also succeeded in inducing a somnambulistic state in Léonie from afar. A Nobel Prize–winning physiologist, Richet had concluded hypnosis was a genuine phenomenon in 1875, and his support helped Charcot decide to investigate hypnosis. Janet's discussion of his work with Léonie, whose interpretation he eventually came to doubt, put him in contact with Charcot and led to his return to Paris (Kopell, 1968).

In 1889, Janet received his doctorate at the University of Paris, and in 1890, he accepted Charcot's offer of the directorship of the psychological laboratory at the Salpêtrière. Janet immediately began to systematize the work on hysteria and to bring it into line with academic psychology, which shows his long-term interest in integrating clinical and academic psychology. The resulting publication earned Janet the M.D. degree in 1893.

Janet went to the Sorbonne in 1895 and then succeeded Ribot (Chapter 5) in 1902 at the Collège de France, from which he retired in 1936. As dean of French psychology, Janet served as honorary president of the XIth International Congress of Psychology, which met in Paris in 1937.

Janet believed a psychologically healthy person has a stable psychic energy level, whereas fluctuations of psychic energy and lowered mental tension cause an inability to deal with life's problems and neurosis. The psychic weakness in his hysteric patients produced exaggerated suggestibility (increased hypnotic susceptibility), faulty memory, and fixed ideas. Further, the lack of integration in their personalities meant there could be a dissociation into conscious and unconscious processes; hence, they could develop multiple personalities. The hysteric's fixed ideas narrowed the focus of consciousness, forcing unacceptable ideas into the unconscious mind. In the unconscious, the unacceptable ideas would be converted into symbolic symptoms.

Janet believed the neurotic's psychic weakness might result from negative events in the past.

Archives of The History of American Psychology – The University of Akron.

Pierre Janet (1859–1947)

> These events, which had established a violent emotion and a destruction of the psychological system, had left traces. The remembrance of these events, the mental work involved in their recall and settlement, persisted in the form of lower and more or less conscious psychological processes, absorbed a great deal of strength, and played a part in the persistent weakening. (Janet, 1930, p. 128)

Other potential sources of the psychic weakness included faulty heredity, disease, fatigue, and deficient education.

Janet's psychopathological system and Freudian psychoanalysis have many similarities, and Janet believed psychoanalysis originated in his and Charcot's work. In addition, Freud and Janet disagreed over priority of the unconscious-mind concept. Janet's 1889 dissertation on "automatic" activities formed the basis for his later claim of priority. Apparently with good cause, Freud argued that Janet's use of the term *unconscious mind* in 1889 was more or less coincidental and not a serious attempt to establish the concept (Boring, 1950).

Like Freud, Janet thought the key to treating the hysteric successfully was to make the forgotten, negative experiences conscious, and he used hypnosis to uncover the dissociated memories. Making the patient consciously aware of the memories often caused the hysterical symptoms to abate.

Regardless of whether Janet's work significantly influenced Freud's development of psychoanalysis, Freud has received the primary credit for developing the system. Before we consider Freud's life and work, we will look at existentialism's influence on him. Our discussion of the historical context of the psychoanalytic view of human nature and mental illness would be incomplete without mention of Sören Kierkegaard and Friedrich Nietzsche (both introduced in Chapter 6).

EXISTENTIAL PRECURSORS TO FREUD

As we noted earlier, Sören Aabye Kierkegaard (1813–1855) was educated at the peak of Hegel's (Chapter 6) popularity in Germany and Denmark, and many of Kierkegaard's ideas stemmed from his disagreement with Hegel's system. For Kierkegaard, Hegel had missed one important element in his system—personal existence—and this led Kierkegaard to found existentialism, which stresses individual freedom of choice and personal responsibility for one's actions, among other things.

In our examination of influences on Freud, Kierkegaard's work on anxiety and despair is important. Kierkegaard's *The Concept of Anxiety* (alternatively, *The Concept of Dread*) and *The Sickness Unto Death* carefully analyze disorders we might today characterize as anxiety disorders and depression, respectively. Kierkegaard was a devout, if unorthodox, Christian, and his theology permeated his analysis of psychological conditions. Although his association of pathology with sin may seem misplaced, if one views "sin" metaphorically as difficulties caused by repressed conflicts or problems of conscience, then the association resembles explanatory mechanisms we will see in Freudian psychoanalytic theory. Given his interest in psychopathology and his position as one of existentialism's founders, Kierkegaard represents another important element of the European *Zeitgeist* surrounding Freud.

The connection between Freud and German philosopher Friedrich Wilhelm Nietzsche (1844–1900) is even more explicit than that between Freud and Kierkegaard. Although considered the next great existential philosopher after Kierkegaard, Nietzsche did not share Kierkegaard's appreciation of theology. Kierkegaard was an earnest Christian who feared that organized religion could hamper a personal, meaningful relationship with God. Nietzsche, by contrast, saw religion as central to humankind's problems.

Although *id* and *superego* are Freudian terms, Nietzsche first recognized these opposing psychic forces. The superego (the internalization of external standards of behavior) and the id (our animalistic passions) were examined in Nietzsche's best-known works—for example, *Beyond Good and Evil* (Nietzsche, 1886/1966) and *On the Genealogy of Morals* (Nietzsche, 1887/ 1967). The superego is the essence of civilization, whereas the id represents baser instincts. Their relationship is that societal rules and religious dictates become our conscience, which keeps us from acting on our immediate impulses. Unlike Freud, Nietzsche viewed this relationship as something humans need to transcend; the superego must be restrained in order for our more fundamental nature to emerge. Nietzsche saw pathology as the submission of our will and nature to the rules of society and religion.

Nietzsche predated Freud only slightly—his classic works were published mainly in the 1880s—and was well known and controversial enough that Freud undoubtedly was aware of his ideas. Greer (2002) argued that, more than simply being aware of Nietzsche's ideas as part of the intellectual *Zeitgeist*, Freud was directly influenced by him. In fact, the recent publication of much of Freud's early correspondence makes it possible to determine the order in which Freud read Nietzsche's works. Although Freud denied an early interest in Nietzsche on multiple occasions, Greer noted that at least on one such occasion, "we may even interpret Freud's own odd denial as an admission [of interest]" (p. 307). Greer concluded, "In the end, it seems fair to say that in spite of (or, more so, because of) Freud's denial, Nietzsche had a far greater effect on him than he wanted to admit, or perhaps even realized" (p. 314). What Freud did admit was that Nietzsche was second only to Schopenhauer as a philosopher who anticipated elements of psychoanalytic theory (Kaufmann, 1974).

Several of the existential and humanistic theorists we will examine in Chapter 16 acknowledged Kierkegaard's (e.g., Rollo May) or Nietzsche's influence (e.g., Viktor Frankl) on their systems of psychotherapy. In addition, psychologists and philosophers from diverse areas (e.g., social, cognitive) still explore the works of these two influential pioneers of existentialism.

SIGMUND FREUD

Sigmund Freud, or Sigismund Schlomo Freud, according to the family Bible, was born on May 6, 1856, in Freiburg, Moravia (now part of the Czech Republic). Freud's father was Jakob Freud, a gentle wool merchant loved by all in the family; Freud considered himself a duplicate of his father, both physically and mentally. Freud's mother, Amalia Nathansohn Freud, was Jakob's second wife (or perhaps his third; Federn, 1997; Gay, 1988), and Freud had two half-brothers from his father's previous marriage. Amalia's firstborn child (of eight), Freud was clearly the family favorite—as an illustration, he was the only one to have his own room.

Because of anti-Semitism, a failing business, and limited small-town educational opportunities, the Freuds moved to Leipzig in 1859 and then to Vienna. Freud lived in Vienna from 1860 until 1938, when he emigrated to London to escape Nazi persecution. Although Freud was not religious, he identified with Jewish cultural values and ideals throughout his life (e.g., Levin, 1975).

After Freud's early lessons with his mother, Jakob took over his education until Freud qualified by examination for admission to the Sperl Gymnasium, where he usually ranked first in his class and graduated summa cum laude at 17. His reward was a trip to England 2 years later.

Freud was gifted in languages. According to Jones (1953), he had learned Latin and Greek in his early education, had a thorough knowledge of English and French, taught himself Spanish and Italian, and had been taught Hebrew. Freud was also a "recognized master of German prose" and was nominated more than once for the Nobel Prize in literature. In 1930, he won the prestigious Goethe Prize.

Entering the University of Vienna at 17, Freud studied medicine. As we noted, Freud took several philosophy courses under Brentano (Chapter 8), perhaps reinforcing Freud's long-standing interest in the ancient Greeks, as Brentano was an Aristotelian expert (Tourney, 1965). In 1876, Freud began the first of several original studies with a grant from his zoology professor, Carl Claus. At Trieste, a northeastern Italian city on the Adriatic Sea, Freud sought the testes of eels. As Jones (1953) dryly stated: "One is tempted to . . . remark that the future discoverer of the castration complex was disappointed at not being able to find the testes of the eel" (p. 38).

Freud was more impressed by his physiology professor, **Ernst Brücke** (1819–1892), than by Claus. Brücke's institute was part of the movement known as Helmholtz's School of Medicine. The School began with the friendship of Émil du Bois-Reymond and Hermann von Helmholtz (Chapter 7), Karl Ludwig (mentioned in Chapter 10), and Brücke. Its chief purpose was to rid science of Johannes Müller's vitalism—the idea that life involves a vital principle distinct from physical and chemical forces—and most of the School's members had studied under Müller. By the time Freud was a student, Helmholtz's School dominated German physiology and medicine and had made impressive discoveries in physiology. Brücke's dynamic physiology, in which organisms were seen as part of a system of forces, became assimilated into Freud's dynamic psychology, and "it can be shown that the principles on which [Freud] constructed his theories were those he had acquired as a medical student under Brücke's influence" (Jones, 1953, p. 45).

In 1876, Freud was accepted into Brücke's institute as a research scholar. Freud's first published effort contributed to the work leading to the neuron doctrine (Chapter 7), although Freud is not credited with being part of the discovery.

Freud also developed a new staining technique and, while studying cocaine's uses, anticipated its value as an anesthetic in eye surgery. Unfortunately,

Sigmund Freud (1856–1939) and his fiancée, Martha Bernays, in 1885

Freud's enthusiasm for cocaine in 1884 became a major embarrassment when its potential for addiction became generally known soon thereafter (Julien, 1995). Rumors of Freud's own cocaine addiction seem to be baseless, as Gay (1988) reported there is no evidence suggesting Freud ever acquired the habit, although "he continued to use [cocaine] in modest quantities at least until the mid-1890s" (p. 45).

Freud received his M.D. in 1881 and continued at Brücke's institute. In May, he was promoted to Demonstrator, a post with teaching duties. At this point, he probably planned to work his way through the ranks, eventually becoming Professor of Physiology. However, in June of the next year, Freud decided to become a physician. Brücke's warning that Freud's poverty could hamper his scientific career (Freud, 1925/1963) and the fact that the normal path to promotion may have contained racial obstacles undoubtedly influenced his decision.

Accordingly, Freud entered the General Hospital of Vienna to prepare for private practice. In 3 years at the Hospital, Freud worked in surgery, dermatology, and ophthalmology and spent 5 months in Meynert's Psychiatric Clinic. A German like Brücke, **Theodor Meynert** (1833–1893) was a pioneer in cytoarchitectonics—the study of cellular architecture—and made the first detailed description of the cerebral cortex. Although Freud considered Meynert an outstanding neuroanatomist (e.g., James, 1890), he was less impressed with Meynert's psychiatric ability. However, in later writings he spoke of following in Meynert's footsteps, and "he always recalled him as the most brilliant genius he had ever encountered" (Jones, 1953, p. 65).

In 1885, Freud was appointed a *Privatdozent* in neuropathology, a highly prized position affording occasional lectures but no salary. To Freud, the position demonstrated a professional competence that would enable him to secure a medical practice, which in turn would allow him to marry his fiancée, Martha Bernays.

In late 1885 and early 1886, Freud studied under Jean Martin Charcot in Paris, and the experience turned him from neurology to psychopathology. Freud probably would have made little impression on Charcot if he had not overheard Charcot complain about a lack of response from the German translator of his lectures (Freud, 1925/1963). Freud offered to tackle the translation, and his offer was promptly accepted.

From Charcot, Freud received two major "gifts," which ultimately led to psychoanalysis (Wollheim, 1971). The first was a therapeutic method that aimed to remove a mental disorder's symptoms through the use of words, whereas the second "was a diagnosis, according to which the symptoms of the disorder were traceable to the influence of ideas" (p. xi). Freud was so impressed with Charcot that he named his firstborn son Jean Martin after him.

Although he continued to publish and present physiological work for the next several years, Freud returned to Vienna as a clinician. In 1891, he published *Aphasia,* attacking Carl Wernicke's (Chapter 7) model of language deficits and challenging Meynert's cortical localization of ideas and memories. *Aphasia* apparently was little noticed. A monograph that same year on paralysis in children was more successful and is the work for which Freud is best known in neurology. Freud dedicated *Aphasia* to his friend Josef Breuer.

Josef Breuer (1842–1925) was a Viennese physician Freud met in the late 1870s. Breuer's scientific research had earned him an excellent reputation, and like Brücke, Breuer was a follower of the Helmholtz School.

In late 1882, Breuer told Freud about a patient whose story was later published under the name of **Anna O.** Anna O was **Bertha Pappenheim** (1859–1936), an intelligent, attractive young woman from a distinguished Jewish family. Before seeing Breuer, Anna O had developed several physical symptoms—including a nervous cough—while caring for her gravely ill father. Breuer decided the nervous character of her cough and the calming effect of his listening to her stories suggested a functional illness, not something organic. Breuer also found that some of Anna's whims disappeared when traced back to their origins.

Because of the cough, Anna was not allowed to tend her father, and the additional symptoms she developed included paralyses from muscle contractions, vivid hallucinations, and language disturbances. For example, at one point Anna spoke only English, although she could understand what people told her in German.

Her father's death triggered a new set of symptoms, and at one point an expert on forensic psychiatry and sexual pathology, **Richard Krafft-Ebing** (1840–1902), was summoned (Ellenberger, 1972). Anna behaved as if Krafft-Ebing were not there, even when he blew smoke toward her face. Throughout his treatment of her, Breuer found that getting Anna to talk out her vivid hallucinations under hypnosis brought some relief. Anna called this procedure a "talking cure" or "chimney-sweeping" (Freud & Breuer, 1895/1966).

Finally, Anna developed two personalities, one "normal" and the other "sick," with the "sick" personality existing in time exactly 1 year earlier than the "normal" one. In this condition, Anna told Breuer in reverse order about the appearance of each symptom; when she reached the initial triggering event, the symptom disappeared.

Although Jones (1953) presented Anna O's story as an illustration of hysteria cured by the **cathartic method,** or talking cure, in which symptomatic relief is achieved by bringing forgotten memories and feelings to consciousness, the story is more complicated. Referring to an unpublished report by Breuer, Ellenberger (1972) noted several discrepancies. For example, Anna O was not a hysteric, and "the word catharsis appears nowhere in the 1882 report" (p. 277). Further, Bertha Pappenheim was not cured, and she spent several weeks in the fall of 1882 in a Swiss sanitarium. She eventually recovered and became "the respectable figure of a pioneer of social work, fighter for the rights of women and the welfare of her people . . ." (p. 279). Recently, Kimball (2000) has provided a contextualized study of Pappenheim's life both before and after her Breuer-treated illness.

Fascinated by Anna O's case, Freud related it to Charcot, who was not interested. As we noted, Charcot had come to realize hysteria's symptoms had a psychogenic origin, and he also recognized the disorder was not found exclusively in women. Impressed with these new ideas, on his return to Vienna, Freud read a paper on male hysteria to the Medical Society. He felt the report was badly received, and his old mentor Meynert challenged Freud to produce a case of male hysteria with the appropriate symptoms. Ironically, on his deathbed, Meynert confessed to Freud that he had been a classic case of male hysteria, a fact he had always concealed (Jones, 1953). Shortly after his "bad report," Freud found a male hysteric who had developed visual defects after a quarrel with a brother. Along with an ophthalmologist, Freud demonstrated the case to the Medical Society before 1886 ended. For more on Charcot's influence on Freud's thinking about hysteria, see Libbrecht and Quackelbeen (1995).

At this point, Freud was just beginning to develop a private neurological practice. Unlike the patients a neurologist typically encounters today, Freud's patients were primarily neurotics. At first, Freud used electricity to treat them, along with such auxiliary remedies as ice baths and massages. Although he was still using these methods into the 1890s, in late 1887 he began to try hypnotic suggestion, which he employed for 18 months.

Freud soon found he could not induce a trance in some of his patients, and with others the suggestible state was too shallow for therapeutic purposes. In order to improve his technique, Freud traveled to Nancy in 1889, where he observed the work of Liébeault and Bernheim. While watching Bernheim, Freud was struck by the possibility there might be interesting mental processes unavailable to consciousness. He also learned Bernheim's success with hypnotic suggestion occurred only with his hospital patients, and Bernheim had no more success than Freud with one of Freud's private patients who, at Freud's request, had followed him to Nancy. Obviously, something more was needed than hypnotic suggestion for treating hysterics.

Initially, Freud used hypnotism to give therapeutic suggestions and to try to uncover the traumatic incident(s) responsible for the patient's illness. In his search for trauma, he was guided by Charcot's teachings. Working with Breuer's cathartic method, Freud would direct the patient's attention to the traumatic scene, looking for the psychic conflict that would give the desired beneficial effect when brought to consciousness. Freud discovered something even more interesting, however: His efforts to follow his patients' associations to the traumatic incident led back to their earliest childhood memories.

Freud's **free association** method gradually evolved between 1892 and 1895, and he dispensed with hypnosis for the first time in a case in 1892. This was also the first case in which Freud felt satisfied with the patient's "psychical analysis" and the first case in which he began to realize the importance of urging the patient to say whatever came into her or his mind without trying to make it more socially desirable.

Freud's abandonment of hypnosis has been attributed to difficulties in hypnotizing some patients and to the fact that hypnotic suggestions were not always effective, particularly with private patients. Schneck (1965) suggested another possibility: "[T]he key to Freud's abandonment of hypnosis may be found in his great ambition and drive for prestige, in his striving for originality and his desire to make a name for himself" (p. 194). Hypnosis had a long past, with many names associated with it; Freud's name would be the first linked with free association.

Although he was not using hypnosis, Freud was active in the treatment, questioning, probing, urging the patient to divulge the information needed for a successful outcome. Finally, one of his patients reproved him for interrupting her train of thought, and Freud got the message. Careful listening, without frequent queries, became part of free association.

In fact, Freud may not have completely abandoned hypnosis for treating mental illness. Gravitz and Gerton (1981) cited a little-known autobiography of Hungarian-born hypnotist Franz Polgar as an indication of Freud's continuing interest in the method long after he had supposedly rejected it. Polgar reported that in 1924 he watched Freud's method for inducing hypnosis and afterward became the psychoanalyst's medical hypnotist. Freud's negative expressions about hypnosis eventually so undermined Polgar's self-confidence that he returned to Budapest to study psychology.

In 1895, Freud and Breuer (1895/1966) jointly published *Studies on Hysteria*, which is usually considered the seminal event in the development of psychoanalysis. Freud's break with Breuer—whom Freud called the true founder of psychoanalysis at his Clark University lectures in 1909 (Green & Rieber, 1980)—came within the next 2 years, precipitated by Freud's growing belief in the importance of sex in the origin of neuroses. Freud also decided the therapeutic relationship between himself and his patients had an erotic basis when a female patient suddenly embraced him. Freud called this **transference,** because he thought the patient had transferred her feelings for a childhood object onto him. Instead of being frightened by transference, as Breuer had been with Anna O's similar behavior, Freud saw it as an important part of the therapeutic relationship and as proof of the neuroses' sexual origin.

For the next several years, Freud developed his technique and theory of psychoanalysis—a term he first used in a paper published in French in 1896—in relative isolation, although it was apparently more self-isolation than isolation imposed from without (Esterson, 2002b). After losing Breuer's advice, encouragement, and financial support, Freud turned to Berlin ear, nose, and throat specialist **Wilhelm Fliess** (1858–1928).

From our perspective, Fliess, whom Freud initially idealized (Blum, 1990), appears to have been a crackpot. For example, as a numerologist, he believed it was possible to ground biology in symbolic mathematics.

Also, Fliess considered the nose the body's dominant organ, and "Freud even allowed Fliess to operate on his own nose several times in an attempt to dispel 'neurotic disturbances'" (Grosskurth, 1991, p. 8).

Despite his strange ideas, Fliess was an intelligent reader of Freud's manuscripts, supported Freud's ideas of infantile sexuality in publications of his own, and introduced the notion of human bisexuality, which Freud subsequently elaborated. In addition, Fliess served as Freud's informal analyst during a period when Freud's relationship with his wife was changing because of her repeated pregnancies and the birth of their children (Blum, 1990). Freud's sister-in-law, Minna Bernays, was another important confidante. Bernays, whose fiancé had died young, eventually came to live in the Freud household. At times, she accompanied Freud—without her sister—on summer vacations. Carl Jung's (discussed later) rumor that Freud and Minna had an affair lacks persuasive evidence (Gay, 1988).

Freud's isolation primarily resulted from his ideas about the sexual origin of neurosis, which he later claimed to have gotten from three people he greatly respected: Breuer, Charcot, and Chrobak, a University of Vienna gynecologist. For example, when Freud was a young hospital doctor, Breuer said about a female patient's neurotic behavior, "Those are always secrets of the alcove" (Freud, 1938a, p. 937), meaning such disorders always resulted from a couple's sexual problems. Later, Freud overheard Charcot talking to an assistant about a young married couple in which the husband was impotent and the wife was "a great sufferer." When the assistant appeared astonished, Charcot said emphatically: "*Mais, dans des cas pareils, c'est toujours la chose génital, toujours—toujours—toujours*" (p. 938). (But, in such cases, it is always a genital thing, always—always—always.)

The third incident came when Chrobak asked Freud to take a case in which the patient suffered from debilitating anxiety attacks. Chrobak "disclosed to [Freud] that the patient's anxiety was due to the fact that although she had been married eighteen years, she was still a [virgin], that her husband was utterly impotent." Chrobak added, "The only prescription for such troubles is the one well-known to us, but which we cannot prescribe. It is: Penis normalis dosim Repetatur!" (Freud, 1938a, p. 938), which means "repeated doses of a normal penis."

In his work with hysterics, Freud reached the startling conclusion, which he presented in an 1896 address, that in every case the disorder was precipitated by a sexual experience before puberty. This is Freud's **seduction theory,** the idea that neuroses result from childhood sexual abuse.

Not surprisingly, Freud's talk received an "icy reception," although this may have had more to do with skepticism about the methodology he used in uncovering supporting evidence for his theory than with distaste over the theory's sexual nature (Esterson, 2002b). What Freud actually said about his seduction theory, both in public and in private, continues to be debated (e.g., Esterson, 2002a; Gleaves & Hernandez, 1999, 2002).

Although Freud wrote Fliess in the fall of 1897 that he was now convinced the traumatic seductions had never occurred, he did not publicly abandon the theory for another 9 years (Schusdek, 1966). Masson (1984) has argued that Freud abandoned his seduction theory because his colleagues rejected him after he announced it. After a careful examination of Masson's evidence for this assertion, Esterson (2002b) concluded, "There is abundant documentary evidence that demonstrates that Masson's account of Freud's being shunned by his colleagues is contradicted by the historical facts" (p. 130). In fact, Freud's move away from the seduction theory revealed something new about his understanding of the mind: Patients might have fantasized the sexual episodes they thought had really occurred, which, for Freud, was further proof of hysteria's sexual origin.

The Interpretation of Dreams

Freud's followers became psychoanalysts after an analysis of their personalities conducted with someone else. As the first psychoanalyst, Freud underwent a self-analysis, which he began in 1897, relying primarily on an examination of his dreams. This purportedly led to *The Interpretation of Dreams,* completed in the summer of 1899 but published with a 1900 date. It took 8 years to sell 600 copies of what many consider Freud's most important book, and Freud received little money for his effort. Although

Freud and Ernest Jones—Freud's friend, disciple, and biographer—thought the book had been treated negatively, in fact it was extensively and favorably reviewed in Germany and was well known to the educated German public (Decker, 1975). The book was not reviewed at all in the United States, and Freud himself remained virtually unknown (Fancher, 2000).

Although the impression is typically conveyed that Freud's dream theory developed out of his efforts to interpret his own and his patients' dreams, Fancher (1971) argued for a different origin. Specifically, he suggested Freud's dream theory—and much of the rest of psychoanalytic theory—could be deduced from Freud's neurological model of the mind set forth in a paper Freud sent to Fliess in 1895, fully 4 years before *The Interpretation of Dreams.* The paper was never revised, published, or even mentioned in Freud's later publications, yet its neurological speculations readily explain some of the more inexplicable elements of dream interpretation, such as wish-fulfillment (see below).

In *The Interpretation of Dreams,* Freud stressed the importance of dream analysis for understanding psychic life: "*[T]he interpretation of dreams is the [royal road] to a knowledge of the unconscious element in our psychic life*" (Freud, 1938b, p. 540, italics in the original). Further, Freud believed that dreams have meaning and that he held the key to understanding them: free association to the various dream elements.

Freud believed it was crucial to distinguish the dream's **manifest content**—the details we remember—from its **latent content**—the dream's true meaning. Dream analysis is aimed at deciphering the latent content from the manifest content.

Freud believed all dreams represent **wish-fulfillment,** even ones with troubling manifest content (Freud, 1938b). The reason the manifest content may not appear to represent the dreamer's wish is that two psychic forces are the primary cause of a dream's formation: The first system forms the wish expressed, whereas the second system censors the first system's work, distorting the dream-wish.

"Dream work," which protects sleep by altering troubling impulses and memories to make them relatively innocuous, distorts the dream-wish. Some of the methods used to disguise the latent content include condensation, displacement, and symbolization. *Condensation* is the tendency for a dream to be abbreviated relative to its expressed ideas. In *displacement,* "the emotional charge is separated from its real object . . . and attached to an entirely different one" (Stafford-Clark, 1965, p. 77). Thus, an innocuous manifest content may conceal great emotion, or vice versa. *Symbolization* is the dream work's use of certain universal elements to stand for something else.

Freud did not consider symbolism important at first, but in later editions of *The Interpretation of Dreams* he added a sizable section on symbols because of prodding by **Wilhelm Stekel** (1868–1940) and other early followers. Educated at the University of Vienna, Stekel had a brief analysis with Freud in 1902 and became one of the original group of psychoanalysts to gather around him. Stekel's break with Freud around 1912 was undoubtedly responsible for Freud's comment in later editions of *The Interpretation of Dreams* that "[Stekel]. . . has perhaps injured psychoanalysis as much as he has benefited it . . ." (Freud, 1938b, p. 368). Freud warned against overusing the symbols, noting that precedence should be given to the dreamer's associations. For more on Stekel and his relationship with Freud, see Bos (2003).

Many of the dream symbols have sexual connotations. For example, weapons, tools, and elongated objects (e.g., cigars and neckties) are phallic symbols; small boxes and vessels represent female genitalia. Castration is indicated by baldness, haircutting, and the loss of teeth. Steep inclines, ladders, stairs, and going up or down them symbolize the sex act. Freud also noted nonsexual symbols, such as "to depart" means death and a traveler's luggage refers to "the burden of sin." In addition, he carefully noted that the "assertion that *all dreams call for a sexual interpretation* . . . is quite foreign to my *Interpretation of Dreams*" (Freud, 1938b, p. 392, italics in the original).

The Interpretation of Dreams was Freud's first comprehensive, albeit incomplete, statement of his psychology. Throughout the book, Freud's belief in psychological determinism is apparent. Therefore, it is fitting that at the same time he was working on his dream book, Freud was also collecting material for *The Psychopathology of Everyday Life* (1901).

In *The Psychopathology of Everyday Life,* Freud amassed examples of slips of the tongue or pen, the forgetting of common names, and other behaviors previously considered accidental and not worth analyzing. Freud believed such (Freudian) slips reveal repressed psychic material, and their analysis became another way, with free association and dream analysis, to understand the patient. As one example of a Freudian slip, Freud wrote,

> Two women stopped in front of a drugstore, and one said to her companion, "If you will wait a few *moments*, I'll soon be back," but she said *movements* instead. She was on her way to buy [a laxative] for her child. (Freud, 1938c, p. 77, italics in the original)

Publication of *The Interpretation of Dreams* and *The Psychopathology of Everyday Life* signaled Freud's emergence from the relative isolation that had followed his emphasis on the sexual basis of the neuroses and heralded an important series of new contributions for psychology.

Freud Gains Recognition

Following these publications, Freud's reputation began to grow (e.g., Jones, 1955). In 1902, "a number of young doctors gathered around [him] with the expressed intention of learning, practising, and spreading psychoanalysis. The impetus for this came from a colleague who had himself experienced the beneficial effects of the analytic therapy" (Freud, 1938a, p. 946).

Freud's Inner Circle

Wilhelm Stekel was Freud's unnamed colleague, and the rest of the group consisted of Alfred Adler (discussed later), Max Kahane, and Rudolf Reitler. Meeting on Wednesday nights, the group called itself the Wednesday Psychological Society; by 1908, it had formed the nucleus of the Vienna Psychoanalytic Society.

Freud's circle of disciples incorporated Otto Rank in 1906, Carl Jung, Karl Abraham, Sandor Ferenczi, and Max Eitingon in 1907, and Ernest Jones in 1908. Some of Freud's inner circle eventually broke away, usually over matters of theory. For example, Adler resigned in 1911, taking 9 of 35 members with him; Stekel followed in 1912. Jung, once Freud's heir apparent, resigned in 1914 from the International Psychoanalytic Association, which had been founded in 1910. **Otto Rank** (1884–1939) was removed from Freud's inner circle after publishing *The Trauma of Birth* in 1924. Rank's emphasis on anxiety from birth trauma instead of sexual conflict was the theoretical issue on which he and Freud parted company. Rank's place was filled by Anna Freud (discussed later), Freud's daughter.

Introduced by Jung to Freud's work, **Karl Abraham** (1877–1925) moved from Zurich to Berlin in 1907 and became the first German psychoanalyst as well as the founder of the Berlin Psychoanalytic Society. A close collaborator with Freud, Abraham contributed significantly to Freud's theory of psychosexual development.

Hungarian-born **Sandor Ferenczi** (1873–1933) received his M.D. at the University of Vienna, met and became a follower of Freud in 1908, and was one of the group accompanying Freud to Clark University in 1909 (Chapter 10); the others were Jung, Jones, and A. A. Brill. Ferenczi founded the Hungarian Psychoanalytic Society in 1913 and collaborated with Rank in writing *The Development of Psychoanalysis* (1924). Austrian **A. A. Brill** (1874–1948) was America's first practicing psychoanalyst and a translator of many of Freud's works into English. He was instrumental in founding the American Psychoanalytic Association.

Ernest Jones (1879–1958) was born in Wales, obtaining his medical degree from University College Hospital in London. Jones encountered Freud through neurological research, learned German in order to study Freud's work more closely, and, starting in 1908, became a lifelong friend of Freud. Jones introduced psychoanalysis to Great Britain and founded the British Psycho-Analytical Society (1913). He was a professor of psychiatry at the University of Toronto from 1909 to 1912, establishing important psychoanalytic connections in North America. Jones's three-volume biography is considered the definitive work on Freud, and Jones himself arguably became Freud's heir.

Freud's Journey to America

As we indicated in Chapter 10, Clark University's president G. Stanley Hall invited Freud to America to lecture on psychoanalysis during Clark's 20th anniversary celebration and, after his arrival, "worked hard to promote Freud as a star" (Fancher, 2000, p. 1026). The journey marked a turning point in both Freud's life and the psychoanalytic movement. It not only introduced psychoanalysis to America but "constituted the first public recognition of [Freud's] professional contribution to psychology, psychiatry and the other behavioral sciences—a recognition that in Europe had been meager and largely negative" (Rosenzweig, 1992, p. 13). For more on Freud's visit, see Saul Rosenzweig's *Freud, Jung, and Hall the King-Maker: The Historic Expedition to America (1909).*

Freud's Last Years

Despite the growing acceptance of psychoanalysis as an important force in psychology (see Green and Rieber, 1980, for a discussion of its assimilation in America), Freud's last 2 decades contained much personal suffering. World War I was particularly stressful because of worry about the safety of his two sons in the army, a shortage of food, and a lack of heating during two severe winters. Runaway inflation after the war took Freud's life savings, and it was not until late 1920 that he again began to earn a reasonable income.

In 1920, Freud's daughter Sophie died in the influenza pandemic. Unfortunately, Sophie's death was the first of many that occurred among Freud's family and friends during his lifetime. Perhaps the hardest loss came in 1923 with the death of Sophie's 4-year-old son Heinele. Freud, who was not one for tears, broke down. "I find this loss very hard to bear," he wrote to friends shortly before the boy died. "I don't think I have ever experienced such grief," he continued, insightfully concluding that "perhaps my own sickness contributes to the shock" (Freud, 1923; cited in E. L. Freud, 1992, p. 344). Diagnosed the same year Heinele died, Freud's illness was cancer of the mouth and jaw. Freud eventually underwent 33 operations for his malignancy, which was attributed to his cigar smoking. Although he tried several times, Freud was never able to give up his addiction to tobacco.

Lifelong friend and colleague Karl Abraham died in late 1925, and Freud's mother died in 1930. In 1933, the Nazis burned Freud's books in Berlin, and the German Society for Psychotherapy fell under Nazi control. In March 1938, Germany invaded Austria, and Freud's apartment was visited first by the SA (*Sturmabteilung,* storm troops) and then a week later by the Gestapo (*Geheime Staatspolizei,* German state police). With the aid of friends and admirers, who included Ernest Jones and President Roosevelt, Freud and his immediate family left Austria, arriving in England in June. Freud's four sisters were detained, and all perished in Nazi gas chambers, a fact that, mercifully, Freud never learned.

Freud received an enthusiastic welcome in England, but his cancer was far advanced. His health declined steadily and further surgery was not an option. Freud died on September 23, 1939.

Freud's Theory of Personality

As we noted, Freud's conception of human personality was strongly influenced by Brücke's dynamic physiology, which viewed the living organism as a dynamic system. Freud took the same view, considering personality a system in which energy changes and exchanges are important. From his clinical practice, Freud grew more and more convinced that much of the operation of the dynamic forces within an individual personality occurs unconsciously, and he came to see himself as an explorer of the unconscious. Thus, even in his early work (e.g., *The Interpretation of Dreams*), the unconscious was central to his theory, and Freud conceptualized personality in terms of the **unconscious** (the site of relatively irretrievable material, some of which may be repressed), the **preconscious** (antechamber to consciousness, containing relatively accessible material), and the **conscious** (what we are aware of). Later, Freud shifted emphasis from the three levels of consciousness to the three systems of the id, ego, and superego.

In the mentally healthy individual, the three systems work harmoniously, enabling the person to interact in a satisfying way with the environment to fulfill his or her needs and desires. Disharmony among the systems leads to the maladjustment that psychoanalysis was developed to treat.

Silverstein (1989) has argued convincingly that Freud's view of the mind-body relation was an interactive dualism. Further, this position was needed for Freud's development of psychoanalysis: "It facilitated the development of a psychology which stressed the importance of unconscious wishes which, although rooted in somatic processes, had to be considered a unique form of reality" (p. 1095).

The Id

The only system present at birth, the **id** (literally, "it") functions to discharge energy released in the organism by external or internal stimulation. This function satisfies the first principle of life, Freud's **pleasure principle,** which strives to eliminate or at least to reduce tension to an acceptably low and stable level. One experiences tension as discomfort, whereas relief from tension is satisfying; the pleasure principle's aim is to seek pleasure while avoiding pain (e.g., Freud, 1920). We saw a form of hedonism in the philosophy of Epicurus (Chapter 2), who sought pleasure in serenity and freedom from fear.

The id is a primitive reservoir of undifferentiated energy, which is derived from the instincts. Freud thought of an instinct as an innate condition imparting direction to psychological processes, and he eventually divided the instincts into the life instincts (*Eros*) and death instincts (*Thanatos*). Freud used the term **libido** to refer to the form of energy used by the life instincts, and originally identified it with sexual energy. Later, he broadened the definition of libido to include all the life instincts. Perhaps *sensual drive* better expresses Freud's intended meaning.

At first, Freud used the terms *death instinct* and *destructive instinct* interchangeably, "but in his discussion with [Albert] Einstein about war he made the distinction that the former is directed against the self and the latter, derived from it, is directed outward" (Jones, 1957, p. 273). The death instincts strive for the individual's disintegration, whereas the life instincts function to maintain the organism's integration. Of all the components of Freudian personality theory, the notion of death instincts was among the least accepted by other psychoanalysts, and Freud himself was not completely committed to it.

The id is initially a reflex apparatus, and if an infant's reflex responses could discharge all the tensions aroused by sensory stimulation, no further development would be necessary. However, the organism soon experiences tensions that cannot be reduced by reflexes. For example, hunger pangs bring tension that produces crying and restlessness. Because the baby's reflexive responses do not produce food, the pangs increase until either the baby is fed or it becomes exhausted from its unsuccessful efforts.

No matter how diligent the parents, the infant experiences some frustration in discharging tensions, which leads the id to develop the **primary process.** This is the production of a memory image of the object needed to reduce tension. For the hungry baby, the primary process produces the image of food or the mother's breast, and the id treats the memory image and the real thing as identical. Freud called the image formation of a tension-reducing object "wish-fulfillment," suggesting he considered dreaming an example of the primary process.

Of course, dreaming or imagining something ultimately fails to reduce tension: The hungry infant imagining its mother's breast remains hungry. This failure of the primary process leads to the development of the secondary process, which is an ego function.

The Ego

Because of the id's ineffectiveness in dealing with the external environment, the **ego** (Latin for "I"; the self) develops. The ego functions according to the **reality principle,** whose aim is to prevent energy discharge until the actual tension-reducing object is produced. The hungry child, as opposed to the hungry infant, has learned to postpone eating until food is located. In order to postpone behavior, the ego must be able to tolerate a certain level of tension. The id's pleasure principle still dictates the ultimate aim of gratification. To attain this aim, the reality principle deals with the environment and tolerates discomfort.

The ego's **secondary process** supersedes the id's primary process. Instead of fantasizing or dreaming, the ego develops an action plan through thought and reason—through cognition, in other words. The secondary process corresponds to thinking or problem solving.

To deal effectively with the environment, the ego must be able to function on all three levels of consciousness. Like the id, the ego can use the primary process; however, the ego recognizes that its fantasy images are not real. Also like the id, the ego ultimately strives for pleasure, which is not necessarily the case for the superego.

The Superego

The **superego** is the personality's moral component, striving for perfection rather than for sensual pleasure. It develops from the ego by incorporating the parental and societal standards of appropriate behavior. A child not only learns to obey the reality principle, he or she also learns to obey the moral dictates of parents and society.

The superego has two subsystems: the ego-ideal and the conscience. The **ego-ideal** contains the rules the child perceives that his parents consider right and proper—the "thou shalts," in other words. Donating your time and money to charity is a rule that might be in your ego-ideal. Acting according to this rule brings you pleasure from a sense of pride.

The **conscience** punishes inappropriate behaviors through guilt. In it are found the parental (and societal) "thou shalt nots"—the Ten Commandments, for example. If you cheat on a test, you will feel guilty if your conscience is well developed.

As with the id, the superego's operation is primarily unconscious, and it, too, operates mainly through the primary process. The superego exerts control over the ego by rewarding or punishing it. In reality, the ego may be punished or rewarded for just *thinking* of doing something "bad" or "good." Like the id, the superego fails to differentiate between subjective and objective reality.

Although we have discussed the personality systems under separate headings, their boundaries are not sharply drawn. The ego develops from the id, and the superego comes from the ego, and the systems continue to be closely associated and interactive throughout life.

Psychosexual Development

As we indicated, Freud believed the animal instincts provide the energy for the life processes. Although an instinct's aim does not change, its source—bodily excitation—may change during development. This sort of change is evident in the development of the sexual instinct, which Freud considered a central example for understanding psychic life.

For Freud, the sexual instinct included stimulation of more than just the genitals. In fact, Freud considered any part of the body where sensations become focalized and create tension—which can then be relieved by such actions as stroking and sucking—to be an erogenous zone.

Freud was convinced childhood sexuality begins long before puberty. The reproductive function awakens at puberty, and people who deny infantile sexuality are "making the mistake of confounding sexuality and reproduction with each other . . ." (Freud, 1920, p. 320). Thus, children have a sexual life divorced from reproduction, which includes receiving enjoyment from the body's erogenous zones. The mouth is the first of these zones.

The Oral Stage. Initially, all the infant's efforts revolve around obtaining satisfaction through the oral zone, which produces the **oral stage.** Eventually, the mouth develops at least five modes of functioning—taking in, holding on, biting, spitting out, and closing—which are prototypes for different personality traits. Frustration or overindulgence of any of the functions may cause fixation on a prototype. For example, anxiety over "taking in" may lead to the adult desire to incorporate such things as love, knowledge, power, money, and material possessions. Biting is the prototype for such adult "biting" as sarcasm and cynicism, and the person may become a movie critic or acerbic essayist (e.g., Hall, 1954).

The adult manifestation may also appear as the opposite of what the prototype seems to dictate. Thus, an extremely gullible person ("She'll swallow anything") may have received frustration over either "spitting out" or "taking in." Other typical adult manifestations of oral fixation include excessive eating, smoking, and drinking. The oral stage typically lasts until some time within the infant's second year.

The Anal Stage. At about age 2, libidinal satisfaction switches from the mouth and lips to the anal sphincter. Toilet training becomes a key event in the child's life, as it often represents the child's first major experience with external authority. Toilet training that is either too harsh or too lax can have permanent effects on the child's adult personality concerning rules and cleanliness.

Punitive toilet training may cause **anal stage** fixation leading to adult messiness, irresponsibility, and wastefulness—or to their exact opposite: The harshly trained child may become a fastidious, compulsive, and overcontrolled adult. Lavish praise for a child's bowel movements may also cause fixation, and the resulting adult may be motivated to create things or to give them away. Alternatively, the excessively praised child may become a thrifty adult or one with an interest in collecting objects. The anal stage ordinarily lasts until late in the third or early in the fourth year.

The Phallic Stage. Interest centers on the genitals in the third stage, or **phallic stage,** the name reflecting Freud's emphasis on the male's anatomy and development. In focusing on the male, Freud was merely mirroring the prevailing attitudes of the late Victorian era in which he worked, and present-day critics of this emphasis illustrate the dangers of presentism (Chapter 1). To differentiate the events for the sexes, Freud called the two stages the "male phallic stage" and the "female phallic stage."

In the male phallic stage, the boy's love for his mother develops, and he becomes jealous of the control of his father over his mother. Freud called the stage in which the little boy would like to possess his mother exclusively and remove his father as a rival the **Oedipus complex,** after the Greek mythological character who unwittingly killed his father and married his mother. Recall that Freud had a lifelong enthusiasm for the ancient Greeks and their work (Tourney, 1965).

One problem the little boy faces is that his father is too powerful to be displaced. In addition, there is the fear that the father will remove the child's genitalia—the little boy may have seen a little girl naked and discovered she has no penis. Perhaps the father cut it off! Called **castration anxiety,** the child's fear motivates him to resolve the Oedipus complex by repressing his desire for his mother and identifying with his father.

At the beginning of the female phallic stage, the little girl, like the little boy, loves her mother, but she does not relate to the father the way a brother might. When she discovers her "missing" penis, the little girl feels cheated, and her cathexis (attachment) to the mother is weakened. At the same time, the little girl begins to prefer the father, who possesses the organ she lacks. Because her love for her father is mixed with envy—he has what she does not have—the little girl experiences **penis envy.** Whereas castration anxiety causes the boy to resolve his Oedipus complex, the girl's penis envy introduces her Oedipus complex; now she loves the father and is jealous of the mother. Eventually, **identification** with the mother (unconsciously trying to think, feel, and act like her) enables the little girl to experience the father vicariously while partly compensating for her lost love relation with the mother. The complex we have called the Oedipus complex in both sexes is sometimes called the **Electra complex** in females, after the character in Greek mythology who avenges her father's death by joining forces with her brother to kill their mother and her lover.

The various identifications that end the phallic stage result in the formation of the superego, which is sometimes called the "heir of the Oedipus complex," because it replaces it. At the end of the phallic stage, at about age 6, "a standstill or retrogression is observed in the sexual development, which . . . deserves to be called a *latency period*" (Freud, 1920, p. 335, italics in the original). The so-called **latency stage** is followed at puberty by the genital stage.

The Genital Stage. The oral, anal, and phallic stages are collectively known as the pregenital period. During this period, sexual gratification is self-directed, or autoerotic, because of the child's primary narcissism, or self-love. Secondary narcissism is a feeling of pride when the ego identifies with the superego's ideals. As we noted, the pregenital child's sexual instinct is not directed toward others, and reproduction, until puberty.

After the latency period, the adolescent begins to direct the libido outward, toward the opposite sex and reproduction. The resulting **genital stage** is a period of socialization, marriage, and rearing a family. Like the earlier stages, the genital stage does not completely replace its predecessors, and activities that satisfy pregenital urges become part of the mating experience. For example, kissing clearly involves the erogenous zone that was the oral stage's focus.

Note that we have spent more time discussing the pregenital stages, which occur in the first 5 or 6 years of life, than we have in discussing the two stages that occupy a much longer period of a person's life. The reason is that the Freudian theory of psychosexual development emphasizes the importance of the first few years of life for later development.

Freud's Influence

With his central interests in sexuality and the darkly aggressive id, Freud was easily and often caricatured. Discussion of sex was a two-edged sword: Although it attracted attention to his ideas, it also alienated many potential allies. Often Freud used sex as a sensational metaphor, when he could have couched his ideas in less provocative terms.

Although there was much in the intellectual European *Zeitgeist* compatible with Freudian thinking (e.g., evolution, conceptions of the unconscious), Freud made an important break with prevailing opinion in developing a psychological approach to mental illness rather than a physiological one. According to Gay (1988), Freud's "most eminent colleagues in the field of psychiatry were neurologists at heart" (p. 119). For example, Krafft-Ebing published an 1895 monograph that concluded essentially that psychological suffering was a matter of physiology. Nearly 20 years earlier, American neurologist William Hammond wrote, "The modern science of psychology is neither more nor less than *the science of the mind considered as a physical function*" (cited in Gay, p. 121, italics in the original). Freud was thoroughly exposed to this physiological view through his neurological training, and it is a measure of his thinking's independence that he was able to break with it.

Psychoanalysis suffered from Freud's rationalistic, nonexperimental approach, and the system as a whole has experienced devastating critiques in recent years. For example, in reviewing a book he considers "the most comprehensive, coherent, and unimpeachable assessment of Freud's concepts and tenets that has yet been mounted" (Crews, 1996, p. 64), Crews listed several "marks of pseudoscience" and discussed their applicability to psychoanalysis. To illustrate, although "[a] theory should not create its own facts" (p. 66), psychoanalysis is filled with such creations. As we indicated, Freud considered a dream's manifest content to be a disguised version of its latent content—the dream-thoughts—which can be determined only by Freudian dream analysis. That is, Freud first theorized a dream's hidden meaning and then relied on psychoanalytic dream analysis to produce "supporting evidence."

Further, a theory should be testable and potentially refutable, and Crews (1996) noted that Freudian theory is notorious for remaining unscathed by outcomes at variance with theory. "The vagueness of the theory is such that it can withstand almost any number of surprises and be endlessly revised according to the theorist's whim, without reference to data" (p. 67).

Nevertheless, it is virtually impossible to overestimate Freud's impact on Western civilization. Psychoanalysis has contributed abundantly to our everyday language, in which such terms as *id, ego, superego, the unconscious,* and *Freudian slip* are immediately recognized. Books on Freud, including major biographies, continue to be published and read. And despite an array of alternatives, psychoanalysis as a treatment method is still widely used.

Freud also contributed importantly to such areas as social psychology and cognitive psychology. For example, he had a continuing interest in the relationship between an individual's intrapsychic events and social and cultural concerns. Across a variety of books and essays (e.g., *Character and Culture, Civilization and Its Discontents, Moses to Monotheism,* and *Totem and Taboo*), Freud explored art, humor, political change, religion, and war. Although Freud's writings on psychoanalysis, personality, and psychopathology remain our first association between him and psychology, the scope of Freud's "social psychology" should be underscored. In addition, it is largely through these "nonpsychological" works that Freud's ideas and theories influenced disciplines such as anthropology, literary criticism, and sociology.

As an illustration of Freud's "nonpsychological" writing, *Civilization and Its Discontents* is particularly intriguing. Written toward the end of his life, it is "Freud's most somber book" (Gay, 1988, p. 543), with good reason. By this time, Freud had experienced war, famine, economic turmoil, and the deaths of people close to him, and he was dying of cancer; it is little wonder he would write an essentially pessimistic essay. The work's theme is that civilization has been created to hold our aggressive and erotic instincts in check, but the cost of this creation is unhappiness, neuroticism. "Freud's theory of civilization . . . views life in society as an imposed compromise and hence as an essentially insoluble predicament. The very institutions that work to protect mankind's survival also produce its discontents" (Gay, p. 547). *Civilization*'s message seems as relevant today as it was when Freud wrote it.

Matthew Erdelyi (1985) considered Freud a "grand" theorist—that is, as providing a comprehensive theory of psychology rather than simply making contributions to such selected areas as personality theory and psychopathology. He concluded that Freud aimed to provide a complete consideration of human existence and, in so doing, anticipated important advances in both social and cognitive psychology.

In addition to Freud's contributions to psychology, Beier (1991) characterized the contributions of psychoanalysis to humankind as (1) bringing people closer together, (2) focusing attention on the importance of childhood experience for later life, and (3) stressing the idea that people gain pleasure from their symptoms. By the first contribution Beier meant that Freud showed us that people are pretty much alike—"We all have significant sexual goals, trouble with controls, and internal conflicts and anxieties" (p. 47). Freud used the idea of a pleasurable aspect of a neurotic's symptoms to explain the so-called neurotic paradox, which is the resistance patients exhibit in discarding their abnormal behavior. As in so much of psychoanalytic theory, the source of the pleasure is rooted in childhood experiences.

An ambitious person, Freud was fabulously successful in his quest for personal recognition, as evidenced by his *third* appearance on the cover of *Time* magazine—for the March 29, 1999 issue. The picture of Freud psychoanalyzing Albert Einstein shows 2 of the 20th century's 100 "greatest minds." Freud's fame is also illustrated by a memorial poem penned by W. H. Auden shortly after Freud's death. Auden mourned Freud's death as he mourned the death of others "who were doing us some good, who knew it was never enough but hoped to improve a little by living" (Auden; cited in Mendelson, 1976, p. 215). As for Freud's method, Auden wrote,

> He wasn't clever at all: he merely told
> The unhappy Present to recite the Past
>   Like a poetry lesson till sooner
>   Or later it faltered at the line where
>
> Long ago the accusations had begun, . . . (p. 216)

Freud as one of the 20th century's greatest minds

Auden acknowledged Freud's widespread influence in the passage

> If often he was wrong and at times, absurd,
>   To us he is no more a person
>   Now but a whole climate of opinion
>
> Under whom we conduct our differing lives: . . .
> (p. 217)

NEO-FREUDIANS

Of the many psychoanalysts who followed Freud, some adhered more closely than others to his original teachings. In this section, we will briefly consider some neo-Freudians who, although they diverged from Freud on certain matters, still remained relatively close to his core theory. Each also sought to embellish Freud's understanding of the developmental process. We will begin with Freud's daughter, Anna Freud.

Anna Freud

The last of Freud's six children, **Anna Freud** (1895–1982) became indispensable to her father and was eventually his successor in the continued advancement of psychoanalytic theory. As Freud's illness deprived him of his speaking abilities, Anna Freud was dispatched to read his papers at international psychoanalytic meetings. This both publicized Freud's ideas and exposed her to the psychoanalytic community. Anna Freud also assumed Minna Bernays's role as sympathetic listener and functioned as her father's private nurse toward the end of his life.

When Anna Freud was 17, her father advised her to become more easygoing. Despite her tendency toward seriousness, she did not finish the *Gymnasium* and received no formal scientific training. Initially, she worked as an elementary school teacher, while also attending Freud's lectures at the University of Vienna and meetings of the Vienna Psychoanalytic Society without being a member. Undergoing analysis with her father—a violation of the rules of analytic technique and something that would never happen today (e.g., Coles, 1992)—Anna Freud became a member of the Vienna Society in 1922 and a practicing child analyst the next year. If she ever felt deprived of a life outside psychoanalysis, she sublimated it well.

Anna Freud (1895–1982) in the early 1920s

Anna Freud's Contributions to Psychoanalysis

"During Freud's lifetime Anna Freud was never in her own right a leader in psychoanalysis, but . . . [eventually] she has inherited Freud's throne" (Roazen, 1975, p. 453). After her father's death, Anna Freud became one of the psychoanalytic school's major developers, making several important contributions, including the popularization of child analysis. For Anna Freud, the main distinction between child analysis and adult analysis was that children are incapable of establishing an adult form of transference. Thus, she did not attempt to treat children in exactly the same way as adults.

Additionally, Anna Freud was one of the earliest of the orthodox psychoanalysts to stress ego psychology and particularly the ego's defensive mechanisms. Freud had introduced the term *defense mechanism* in 1894 but did not use it for the next 30 years (Wolman, 1968). In her best-known work, *The Ego and the Mechanisms of Defence,* which she handed a copy of to her father on his 80th birthday (Coles, 1992), Anna Freud (1937) detailed the mechanisms.

Defense mechanisms are methods the ego uses when threatened by conflicting demands of the id and superego. The most basic mechanism is **repression,** defined as an unconscious removal from consciousness of unacceptable ideas, memories, and impulses. The ego forces such material into the unconscious mind and expends energy to keep it there. Freud believed repression accounted for his inability to remember nonpaying patients' names.

Regression is a retreat to an earlier stage of development as an attempt to escape frustration and anxiety. For example, a child may respond to the stresses of the first day of school by thumbsucking and crying. **Rationalization** is the ego's attempt to account for mistakes and failures by providing a reasonable, but untrue, explanation for behavior. For example, a student may attribute a poor grade in a course to a biased teacher rather than to his or her own lack of motivation.

Projection is attibuting our unpleasant or disturbing desires to others while rejecting them in ourselves. For instance, a woman who no longer loves her husband may project her feelings and accuse him of no longer loving her. In **reaction formation,** a person professes the desire for the opposite of what he or she really wants; a person with a phobia of homosexuals may in fact have latent homosexual tendencies.

In **displacement,** emotion is shifted from its real object to a safer one, as when a punished child acts aggressively against a younger sibling or the family pet. **Sublimation** is displacement in which the substituted object of the displacement is socially approved. For example, a person may channel disturbing tendencies into art, becoming a famous painter.

Anna Freud was not the only neo-Freudian interested in child analysis. In London, Melanie Klein became Anna Freud's rival in a conflict leading to alternative approaches to child analysis that endure today (Viner, 1996).

Melanie Klein Trust.

Melanie Klein (1882–1960)

Melanie Klein

Initially trained as a nursery school teacher, **Melanie Klein** (1882–1960) was first analyzed by Ferenczi in Budapest and then later by Abraham in Berlin. Through another woman undergoing analysis with Abraham, Klein's name became known to Ernest Jones. With an interest in improving the intellectual quality of the London psychoanalytic group and in securing the services of a good child analyst for his children, Jones invited Klein to London, and she settled there in 1926.

Although Klein's personal relationship with Freud was slight, he saw her ideas as a challenge to his daughter's, and the arrival of Freud and his immediate family in England in 1938 caused a rift within the British psychoanalytic movement. Klein's suffering from the schism was intensified by attacks from her own daughter, also a physician and an analyst. Because of Klein's outspokenness, "until she died in 1960 the situation in the British Psychoanalytic Society was tense and difficult. But the fact that psychoanalysis in England is not intellectually complacent is due in part to her energy and absorption in life" (Roazen, 1975, p. 488).

Despite the Freud family's opposition, Klein's ideas actually conformed rather closely to an orthodox Freudian framework. One difference was Klein's emphasis on the pre-oedipal layers of personality development and her stress on the importance of the mother's early nurturing of the child. Although Klein agreed with Freud's concepts of the id, ego, and superego, she thought each system was relatively distinct almost from the beginning of life.

Because she emphasized the importance of the mother's nurturing function, the female breast assumed almost mythic proportions for Klein. In her view, men experienced both castration anxiety and "breast envy." Ironically, Klein reportedly did not nurse her own children (Roazen, 1975).

Unlike Anna Freud, Klein applied the same psychoanalytic technique to both children and adults. In addition, she at one point advocated universal child psychoanalysis, differing in this respect from Anna Freud and many others. Interestingly, many analysts sent their children to Klein for treatment.

Klein differed from Freud in her approach to adult psychoanalysis as well. For example, although Freud was willing to bypass certain patient defenses, Klein believed in leaving nothing unanalyzed. As a result, her English followers have spoken of 10-year (or longer) analyses (Roazen, 1975).

Both Anna Freud and Melanie Klein were also important as pioneering women therapists. As women became increasingly involved with psychoanalysis, some of the more male chauvinistic elements of Freud's system were challenged, particularly by Karen Horney.

Karen Horney

Born near Hamburg, Germany, **Karen Horney** (1885–1952), née Danielson, was the daughter of a stern, authoritative sea captain. Horney's mother protected her daughter against the father's rigidity and encouraged her to pursue a career. Entering medical school in 1906, she met and married Oskar Horney in 1909 and subsequently received her M.D. from the University of Berlin in 1915. Horney was psychoanalyzed by Karl Abraham and was associated with the Berlin Psychoanalytic Institute from 1918 until 1932.

In 1932, Franz Alexander (1891–1964)—formerly a student at the Berlin Institute—invited Horney to join him at the Chicago Psychoanalytic Institute, where she became Associate Director. Alexander's and Horney's incompatibility soon resulted in Horney's move to New York, where she initially practiced psychoanalysis and taught at the New York Psychoanalytic Institute. Dissatisfaction with a wholly orthodox psychoanalysis led Horney to found, along with others of like mind, the Association for the Advancement of Psychoanalysis and the American Institute for Psychoanalysis, where she served as dean until her death in 1952.

Throughout her life, Horney's relationships with men were problematic, at best. According to Paris (2000), "[t]he typical pattern of her relationships was first idealization of the man, followed by disappointment, depression, and efforts to comprehend why the relationship failed" (p. 165). This pattern led Horney from man to man and sometimes to several simultaneously. Horney's troubled relationships and her nearly continuous struggle to gain relief from emotional problems stimulated recurring self-analysis and led to a creative burst of activity in the last 15 years of her life. Among other things, during this period Horney published five major books, founded and edited *The American Journal of Psychoanalysis,* took up painting, maintained a busy social life, and read and traveled widely. Paris concluded, "Her belief both in the human potential for growth and in the difficulty of achieving it was based on her own experience" (p. 179).

Horney's Version of Psychoanalysis

Although Horney accepted much of Freudian theory, she strongly objected to some of its tenets, such as Freud's notion of penis envy as a determining factor in feminine psychology. It is not the penis itself that young girls envy; it is the "accessibility and acceptability of the male genitalia" (Murphy, 1992, p. 12). Horney's problem was that psychoanalysis was the product of a male genius, and most of its later developers were also men. Hence, it is little wonder that Freudian psychoanalysis was a masculine psychology in which the development of men was more completely portrayed than that of women. Horney concluded that feminine psychology owed more to a lack of confidence and an overemphasis on the love relationship than it did to a feeling of genital inferiority and jealousy of men.

Like many neo-Freudians, Horney disagreed with Freud's emphasis on the sexual instinct and on the controlling effects of instincts in general, preferring to focus on the effects of cultural and social conditions on the individual. For Horney, Freud's basic theoretical contributions were psychic determinism, unconscious motivation, and the notion of nonrational motives (Horney, 1939).

One of Horney's most fundamental concepts was **basic anxiety,** which is a child's feeling of helplessness and isolation within a potentially hostile world. In general, anything that disturbs the relationship between the child and its parents produces basic anxiety. Examples of potential causes include unpredictable parental behavior, lack of consistent warmth, and lack of respect for the child's feelings.

Karen Horney (1885–1952)

To counteract basic anxiety, the child develops various strategies or defenses, any of which may become permanent personality patterns. Horney identified 10 needs she considered neurotic because they represent irrational problem solutions. Of the neurotic needs, Horney found women particularly susceptible to the need for affection and approval, the need for a "partner" to take over one's life, and the need to restrict one's life within narrow borders. Other neurotic needs include the need for power, the need to exploit others, the need for personal admiration, and the need for perfection and unassailability.

In later work, Horney classified the 10 neurotic needs into three groups: needs that involve moving toward people (e.g., the need for affection and approval); needs that involve moving away from people (e.g., the need for self-sufficiency and independence); and the need for moving against people (e.g., the need for power). Whereas a normal person can effectively integrate the three orientations and reduce his or her conflicts, because of greater basic anxiety the neurotic cannot achieve a similar integration. Prevention is the best answer to the conflicts; in a home and society providing warmth, security, love, tolerance, and respect, children grow into adults who can either avoid or resolve the conflicts.

Rather than try to replace Freudian psychoanalysis, Horney aimed to correct the errors in Freud's thinking she felt were caused by his mechanistic, biological, male-oriented approach. For example, as an alternative to Freud's penis envy notion for women, it might be just as appropriate to say men suffer "womb envy," as they envy a woman's ability to give birth (Hale, 1995). In particular, she sought to replace Freud's portrayal of women dominated by penis envy with concepts that had little to do with a woman's sexual anatomy, that resulted from experience in a male-dominated culture rather than from unchangeable biology. Changes to psychoanalysis such as Horney's soon led to new concerns, such as the problem of the formation of attachments.

The Formation of Attachments

With the close relation between development and personality assumed by Freud and his followers, the interactions between a child and significant others (e.g., parents, siblings) became a particularly important topic for psychoanalytic theorists, who referred to the general class of relations as **attachments.** For example, **John Bowlby** (1907–1990) and **Mary Salter Ainsworth** (1913–1999) shared the 1990 APA Award for Distinguished Scientific Contribution for their work on attachment. Bowlby and Ainsworth's theory of a human attachment behavioral system forms the core of our current view of attachment and the basis for a new connection between child development and personality formation (e.g., Ainsworth & Bowlby, 1991).

Born in Ohio, Mary Salter was raised from the age of 4 in Canada. She received her Ph.D. in 1939 from the University of Toronto, with a dissertation that "contained the first published mention of the *secure base* concept, which John Bowlby later incorporated into attachment theory" (Bretherton, 2000, p. 1148, italics in the original). Following her marriage in 1950, Mary Salter Ainsworth moved to England and secured a position at London's Tavistock Clinic. Under Bowlby's direction, Ainsworth investigated the effects of infant-mother separation on the infant's behavior. In the laboratory, Ainsworth pioneered the "strange situation" methodology for studying mother-infant attachment. By placing a mother-infant pair in a strange room and then having the mother leave the infant and return, Ainsworth could examine the type of bond exhibited by a particular pair (i.e., secure attachment, insecure attachment) and the effect of this bond on the infant's exploration and learning.

John Bowlby was born in London, completed his initial studies at Cambridge, taught at a coeducational school modeled on Montessori's (Chapter 12) principles, and earned his medical degree in 1933, specializing in psychiatry and psychoanalysis. After 5 years as an Army psychiatrist, Bowlby resumed work as a child psychiatrist and accepted a position at the Tavistock Clinic. His views on childhood deviancy were importantly influenced by his Cambridge years, by his time as a teacher, and by his work at a child guidance clinic (Van Dijken, Van der Veer, Van Ijzendoorn, & Kuipers, 1998).

Bowlby became an important innovator of modern psychoanalytic theory by turning toward biologically based explanations that better corresponded to the growing data about children and mental health. Bowlby was particularly interested in ethology (Chapter 12), and, working with Cambridge ethologist Robert A. Hinde (1923–), he produced the first outline of his theory of attachment behavior in 1957.

Primate studies of mother-infant attachment, such as Harry Harlow's (Chapter 14), provided part of the empirical basis for Bowlby's ideas and helped sensitize the psychological community to the importance of proper attachments for developing a healthy personality. With Bowlby the theorist, Ainsworth was primarily responsible for collecting the empirical data to advance the theories. Bowlby and Ainsworth's 40-year collaboration produced a new field of scientific study. In addition to sharing the Distinguished Scientific Contribution Award, Ainsworth received the award for Distinguished Professional Contributions to Knowledge (1987) and was elected a fellow of the American Academy of Arts and Sciences in 1992.

Although interest in developmental issues such as attachment has usually meant work with children, Erik Erikson realized that that did not have to be the case.

Archives of the History of American Psychology – The University of Akron.

Erik Erikson (1902–1994)

Erik Erikson: Life-Span Development

As an artist hitchhiking around Europe in 1927, **Erik Erikson** (1902–1994) got a job painting children in analysis with Anna Freud. This led to Erikson's own analysis with her, and he completed training at the Vienna Psychoanalytic Institute in 1933. Erikson emigrated with his American wife to the United States, where his rise was meteoric (Roazen, 1975). With no earned degrees after his high school diploma, Erikson became Professor of Human Development at Harvard in 1960, and he stayed there until his 1970 retirement (Hopkins, 1995).

Trained as a child psychoanalyst, Erikson is best known for his work in developmental psychology (e.g., Erikson, 1963, 1982). Erikson's additions to Freud's psychosexual stages brought the total to eight: oral-sensory, muscular-anal, locomotor-genital, latency, puberty or adolescence, young adulthood, adulthood, maturity and old age. Erikson believed each stage has an accompanying identity crisis, with a desired developmental outcome. For example, the crisis in the oral-sensory

STAGE	IDENTITY CRISIS
Maturity and Old Age	Ego Integrity vs. Despair
Adulthood	Generativity vs. Stagnation
Young Adulthood	Intimacy vs. Isolation
Puberty or Adolescence	Identity vs. Identity Confusion
Latency (Elementary School Age)	Industry vs. Inferiority
Locomotor-Genital (Early Childhood)	Initiative vs. Guilt
Muscular-Anal (Toddler)	Autonomy vs. Shame and Doubt
Oral-Sensory (Infancy)	Trust vs. Mistrust

FIGURE 15.1 Erikson's eight stages of development

stage is one of trust versus mistrust, for which the desired outcome is hope. At the other end of development—maturity and old age—the crisis is over integrity versus despair. If a person considers his or her life has had meaning, then he or she will gain a sense of integrity. Despair can result if the person feels his or her life has not been meaningful. Erikson's eight stages are illustrated in Figure 15.1.

Erikson's additional developmental stages can be linked to a growing modern interest in **gerontology,** the study of aging and the exploration of issues that emerge as we age. Erikson's additions also anticipate the current interest in a life-span approach to personality development. According to a life-span approach, development is a process that does not stop at puberty or at any other developmental milestone but continues throughout life—that is, across the life span. Psychologists are now taking life-span approaches to many topics in psychology, such as creativity and sexuality.

In addition to his developmental theorizing, Erikson popularized "psycho-history"—the psychoanalytic analysis of a historical figure. His first such effort produced *Young Man Luther* (Erikson, 1962), an excellent study of Martin Luther (Chapter 3). His second psychohistory, *Gandhi's Truth,* won a Pulitzer Prize.

So far, we have discussed one group of neo-Freudians—Anna Freud, Melanie Klein, and Karen Horney—but it is important to realize this is only one group among many. In fact, several forms of psychotherapy appeared after Freud, and those with some connection to Freud's system are now often called either "psychoanalytic" or "psychodynamic." Within this tradition, further distinctions are possible. For example, although Freud emphasized intrapsychic conflicts related to the satisfaction of basic desires or needs, one later approach highlights conflicts based on object relations, which are interpersonal relationships as represented in the individual's mind. This approach is called **object-relations theory** (e.g., Kernberg, 1976). Two other variations on the Freudian system were developed by one-time members of Freud's inner circle: Alfred Adler and Carl Jung.

Alfred Adler

Alfred Adler (1870–1937) was born in a suburb of Vienna, the second child in a family of six. His father was a prosperous grain merchant, and Adler was his father's favorite. Young Adler suffered from rickets, which prevented him from competing successfully with his older brother and perhaps set the stage for his later conception of organ inferiority and compensation.

At 5, Adler nearly died from pneumonia, an experience that determined his choice of a medical career. Adler enrolled at the University of Vienna, receiving his M.D. degree in 1895. Initially specializing in ophthalmology, he became a general practitioner and then abandoned general practice for psychiatry because of his distress when young patients died. Two years after he graduated, Adler married Raissa Timofejewna, a Russian, and they had three girls and a boy, two of whom became Adlerian psychiatrists.

According to Bottome (1939), Adler gained Freud's attention by defending Freud's dream analysis book against a highly critical review, although after a "thorough search," Jones (1955) was unable to confirm this account. At any rate, in the autumn of 1902, Freud sent postcards to Adler, Kahane, Reitler, and Stekel, who became the nucleus of the Vienna Psychoanalytic Society. Adler succeeded Freud as the Society's president in 1910, and, at the same time, he and Stekel became co-editors of the newly founded *Zentralblatt für Psychoanalyse.* However, by this time Adler's views on psychoanalysis had evolved, and his separation from Freud was inevitable.

Early in 1911, Adler presented his views at two Society meetings, with two additional meetings devoted to discussing Adler's theories. Freud was unstinting in his criticisms. When Stekel suggested there was no contradiction between the two theories, Freud indicated that both he and Adler thought there was (Jones, 1955). Adler immediately resigned as president and soon resigned from both the Society and his editorship of the *Zentralblatt.* Despite Adler's resignations, there was some merit to Stekel's observation. Here, we will focus on Adler and Freud's differences, not on their many similarities.

Adler formed his own group, which became known as the Society of Individual Psychology. After World War I, he became interested in preventing neurosis by establishing child-guidance centers in Vienna's public schools. Through the 1920s and early 1930s, Individual Psychology attracted many adherents, reaching a peak in Europe just before Hitler came to power.

National Library of Medicine, Washington, D.C.

Alfred Adler (1870–1937)

A prolific author and almost compulsive lecturer, Adler began making regular trips to America in 1925, lecturing to audiences of all types and sizes. In 1932, Adler became Professor of Medical Psychology at the Long Island College of Medicine, and in 1934, he settled permanently in New York City. While on a 1937 lecture tour, he died of a heart attack in Aberdeen, Scotland.

Adler's Individual Psychology

Individual Psychology, Adler's personality theory, differs from Freud's in several fundamental ways: First, he downplayed sexuality and particularly infantile sexuality. Second, Adler developed an ego-oriented psychology that made consciousness, not the unconscious, the center of personality. In contrast to Freud's view of behavior ruled by instincts, Adler stressed human social urges, and social interest molds the Adlerian personality. Although Freud "assumed an innate evil component of human nature . . . which must be suppressed . . . to make life in society possible, Adler . . . postulated an innate readiness for social living, which through encouragement can be . . . developed into a full-fledged social interest" (Ansbacher, 1959, p. 380).

Adler's desire to be in touch with the masses extended to his psychiatric practice: Freud tended to treat the upper classes, whereas Adler focused on the middle class and the working poor (Wassermann, 1958). This difference undoubtedly influenced Freud's and Adler's theories, with Freud's patients exhibiting a "comparatively high degree of sexual misery alongside the freedom from financial cares" (p. 624). By contrast, Adler's patients were more concerned with basic problems of existence. "Where Freud sees nothing but a distressed Eros, Adler finds the drive for success to be the motivating force of the human psyche" (Wassermann, p. 625).

Inferiority and Striving for Superiority. In 1907, as a physician, Adler considered why one person develops an illness involving one organ (e.g., the heart), whereas in another person a different organ (e.g., the liver) is at fault. Organ inferiority was Adler's answer: The heart patient has a basically inferior heart, whereas the liver is inherently defective in the other. Adler also noted that a person with an organ weakness often tries to compensate through training. For example, after stuttering as a child, with practice Demosthenes (384–322 B.C.E.) became Greece's greatest orator.

Soon, Adler broadened his organ-inferiority concept to include any feelings of inferiority, whether physically or psychologically based. Initially, Adler equated inferiority with femininity and called the resulting compensation the "masculine protest." The masculine protest became a **striving for superiority** when Adler replaced his male chauvinistic view with the idea that inferiority feelings result from incompleteness or imperfection in any realm of life. The feeling of inferiority and the effort to compensate become humanity's great driving forces—people are pushed by the need to overcome inferiority and drawn by the need for superiority. Feelings of inferiority can be traced to such things as a cold upbringing, actual organ inferiority, and negative cultural ideas—for example, toward women or minorities (Bruder-Bezzel & Schiferer, 1997).

Adopting a less intense version of Nietzsche's "will to power," Adler believed the striving for superiority is innate, carrying us from one developmental stage to the next throughout life. In addition, what Adler meant by a striving for superiority was that the healthy person works for a sense of completeness or self-actualization and is not necessarily trying to achieve leadership or eminence. By contrast, the neurotic strives for personal recognition and power—for egotistical or selfish goals.

After breaking with psychoanalysis, Adler was greatly influenced by German philosopher Hans Vaihinger's *The Psychology of "As If,"* which suggests people live according to many ideas—for example, "the ends justify the means"—that have no counterparts in reality. We treat these fictional goals as if they were real and strive toward them. For Adler, this was the answer to Freud's rigid determinism resulting from constitutional factors and early experiences: We are motivated more by our expectations of the future than by our past experiences.

In striving toward fictional goals, we develop our own unique styles of life. Adler tied his idea of the **style of life** to the concepts we have discussed in the following way:

> We have seen how human beings with weak organs . . . suffer from a feeling or complex of inferiority. But as human beings cannot endure this for long, the inferiority feeling stimulates them . . . to movement and action. This results in a person having a goal. Individual Psychology has long called the consistent movement toward the goal a plan of life. But because this name has sometimes led to mistakes among students, it is now called a style of life. (Adler, 1929; cited in Ansbacher & Ansbacher, 1956, p. 173)

Each of us has the goal to achieve superiority (completeness or mastery), but there are many ways to attain this goal, which constitute the different possible lifestyles. Once an individual's lifestyle has been formed, usually by 4 or 5, all subsequent experiences are interpreted and incorporated according to it.

Adler believed in a coherence of the personality and the unity of the individual, concepts with a Gestalt flavor. In fact, he acknowledged that "Gestalt psychology shows a better understanding of this coherence [than psychoanalysis]" (Adler, 1929; cited in Ansbacher & Ansbacher, 1956, p. 175), and Max Wertheimer (Chapter 14) proposed a concept similar to Adler's "style of life."

Adlerian Therapy. According to Adler, psychopathology results from a lifestyle inadequate for solving problems in the person's current life situation. Therapy's task is to reorganize the patient's style of life, but the first step is to give the patient an understanding of the current lifestyle by investigating the person's earliest memories, birth-order position, and dreams.

Adler was interested in a person's earliest memory because it shows "some dominant interest of the individual, since the creative tendency of the imagination always produces fragments of the life ideal . . ." (Adler, 1930, p. 404). Adler found the early-memory method an economical way to assess an individual's personality.

Adler considered birth order important for personality, because each child encounters an environment different from that of its siblings (Orgler, 1963). For example, the first-born child initially receives a lot of attention but is dethroned with the next child's birth. Oldest children usually show an interest in the past—when they were the center of attention—and often develop into responsible, protective adults. However, Adler noted that criminals, drunkards, and neurotics are frequently first-born children.

The second-born or middle child may grow up to be ambitious, because he or she is always trying to compete with the older sibling. Later, the middle child may become a revolutionary, believing because of his or her earlier striving that there is no power that cannot be overcome.

Spoiled, the youngest child is most likely to have problems in adulthood. One reason for later difficulties is that the youngest child may develop severe inferiority feelings, because the older children are bigger, stronger, and more experienced.

Adler viewed dreams as just another expression of a person's style of life and considered a person's fabricated dream as meaningful as a real one, because "the person's imagination cannot create anything but that which his style of life commands" (Adler, 1929; cited in Ansbacher & Ansbacher, 1956, p. 359). For Adler, dreams have a problem-solving function, connecting the dreamer's problem with its goal of attainment.

Like Freud, Adler believed dreams contain common elements—symbols—that can be interpreted. However, the hallmark of Individual Psychology is that the individual is unique, and we should not look for universal symbols. The same element in two individuals' dreams may have different meanings and must be interpreted in terms of each person's total personality. For example, if two people dream of having an examination, the meaning for one might be that the person is unprepared to face some current problem, whereas the interpretation for the other is that the person enjoys challenges.

Adler's Influence

Adler's contributions to personality theory included an emphasis on social determinants of behavior and on the uniqueness of personality (i.e., Individual Psychology), a de-emphasis on sexuality's contributions to personality, and a focus on consciousness and the ego. Adler also strongly influenced the founders of humanistic psychology such as Abraham Maslow and Carl Rogers (Chapter 16; Ansbacher, 1990). Paradoxically, although Adler's concepts have been incorporated into many modern personality theories, including psychoanalytic theories in particular, his contribution has not always been recognized (Ansbacher, 1994).

Adler's approach to theory and therapy is sustained through a number of organizations, including the North American Society of Adlerian Psychology, which publishes a newsletter and the quarterly journal *Individual Psychology*. In Europe, the largest Adlerian society is in Germany, and its journal is the *Zeitschrift für Individualpsychologie*, published quarterly.

Carl Gustav Jung

Carl Gustav Jung (1875–1961) was born in Kesswil, which is on Lake Constance in Switzerland, the son of a Swiss Reformed Church minister. Jung's father was also an Oriental and classical scholar whom Jung described as kind, tolerant, somewhat conventional, and weak, at least compared to Jung's mother. Jung characterized his mother, a minister's daughter, as having two dispositions: one unstable and mystical

Archives of the History of American Psychology – The University of Akron.

Carl Jung (1875–1961)

and the other more traditional and practical. Jung identified with his mother's mystical side.

For his first 9 years, Jung was an only child in a family plagued by marital discord. Perhaps because of this, Jung "developed a deep distrust of women in general, and an ambivalent attitude toward his mother in particular" (Storr, 1973, p. 2). Another possible residue of his childhood was Jung's ability to leave completely contradictory impressions in the minds of people who knew him. For example, Gay (1988) noted that people found Jung "sociable but difficult, amusing at times and taciturn at others, outwardly self-confident yet vulnerable to criticism" (p. 198). Similarly, Alexander (1991) found Jung described as "arrogant, vain, ambitious, status seeking, competitive, and even untrustworthy . . . ," these negative characteristics occurring alongside such positive traits as "humble, caring, undefensive, even saintly . . ." (p. 157).

Jung completed his medical degree at the University of Basel in 1900 and had nearly decided to become a surgeon when he encountered a psychiatry textbook by Krafft-Ebing. Krafft-Ebing considered the field to be in such a primitive state that textbooks about it were inevitably marked by the authors' subjective assumptions and personality. This description appealed to Jung because of his dual need for association with an objective natural science and for freedom to pursue his lifelong interests in religious speculation, the search for meaning, and mysticism. Perhaps amorphous psychiatry would afford what he needed (Storr, 1973).

With his medical degree, Jung became an assistant to **Eugen Bleuler** (1857–1939) at Zurich's Burghölzli Mental Hospital. Bleuler had studied briefly with Charcot and is known particularly as an early expert on schizophrenia, a term he coined. Bleuler had succeeded Auguste-Henri Forel in 1898 as director of the Burghölzli. As you may recall, Forel spoke in America on hysteria at Hall's invitation (Chapter 10).

Bleuler had made the Burghölzli an outstanding psychiatric research center by the early 1900s, and physicians from other countries often came to observe the latest in the diagnosis and treatment of mental illness. In addition, Bleuler encouraged the staff physicians to travel, and this allowed Jung to spend a semester in 1902 at the Salpêtrière psychiatric center that earlier influenced Freud. There, he heard Janet lecture on psychopathology.

Shortly after joining Bleuler, Jung reviewed Freud's *The Interpretation of Dreams* for the staff. From Freud's book, Jung became familiar with repression of material into the unconscious, which dovetailed nicely with work on word associations he undertook for Bleuler. Using Galton's method (Chapter 9), Jung asked individuals to respond to singly presented words with the first word that came to mind, recording both the response and its latency. Jung believed that words a person responded to relatively slowly had special personal meaning, which could be found in a unified core of ideas in the unconscious accompanied by excessive or inappropriate affect. Jung called this core of ideas a "complex." Repression had forced the complex into the unconscious.

A conflict between Jung and Max Wertheimer (Chapter 14) over priority of the use of word associations to diagnose complexes (or criminal guilt) has been resolved in Jung's favor, although investigation of the published literature suggests the two developed the usage independently and Wertheimer's publication of it (with Julius Klein) preceded Jung's by a couple of weeks (Michael Wertheimer, King, Peckler, Raney, & Schaef, 1992).

Jung's discovery of the agreement between his word association studies and Freudian concepts created a dilemma: Should he become a Freudian and risk damaging his contemplated academic career (Freud had a negative standing in academic circles at this point), or should he publish his results without mentioning Freud? Jung heeded the inner voice that told him to become a "partisan of Freud's."

In 1906, Jung sent Freud a copy of his word association paper, and then the following year a copy of his monograph *On the Psychology of Dementia Praecox,* in which he had singled out Freud's "brilliant conceptions." However, Jung was unwilling to attribute as much significance to youthful sexual trauma as Freud, and this became the rock on which their relationship eventually foundered. In 1906, Freud and Jung began a correspondence lasting until 1913 and involving over 300 letters. The following year they had their first meeting, with Jung (1961) later reporting they had "met at one o'clock in the afternoon and talked virtually without a pause for thirteen hours" (p. 149).

Although Freud apparently truly liked Jung (Gay, 1988), he was also elated over what Jung brought to the psychoanalytic movement. Jung was young, dynamic, handsome, brilliant, associated with a famous mental hospital, and, above all, not Jewish. Heretofore the movement had involved primarily Viennese Jewish physicians, and Freud saw Jung as a propagandist who would significantly expand psychoanalysis beyond its provincial boundaries. He also saw Jung as inheriting the throne of psychoanalysis.

Jung saw Freud as a father-figure and also "seems to have believed that Freud could serve as his personal guide to the dark and mysterious regions of the soul" (Graf-Nold, 1997, p. 425). Despite their frequent expressions of affection, there were hints of future difficulties throughout their association. One came in 1909, when Freud, Jung, and Ferenczi were waiting to board ship for the voyage to America to attend Hall's Clark Conference (Chapter 10). With a longstanding interest in archeology, Jung began talking about prehistoric remains being unearthed in Germany, and Freud, interpreting this as a veiled death wish against him, fainted.

In 1909, Jung resigned from the Burghölzli because of a growing private practice, and in 1913 he resigned his University of Zurich instructorship to devote himself to his practice, his writing, his training and research, and his travel. The final separation from Freud and psychoanalysis also came that year. Although it is likely that Jung was never able to accept Freud's emphasis on sexuality, other factors ranging from Jung's interest in mystical experiences to jealousy over Freud's writing skills may have contributed to the breakup. Freud's advantage in writing is nowhere more evident than in their correspondence, in which "it is everywhere apparent that Freud is the superior literary stylist" (McLynn, 1996, p. 103).

In an exploration of the two men's eventual rift, Stepansky (1976) argued that Jung was never totally committed to Freudian concepts and that Freud was aware of this and even approved of it, at least for a time. Stepansky concluded that "Jung never 'broke' with Freud" (p. 239), although he remained loyal to his own "limited conception of psychoanalysis." The whole affair was an "ominous testimony to Freud's emotional investment in the institutionalized movement his work had created" (p. 239).

Throughout their relationship, Jung had sought to expand the meaning of Freudian libido to encompass a general mental energy instead of focusing on sensual drives. On a 1912 lecture tour in America, Jung divested himself of what he considered psychoanalytic baggage—such concepts as childhood sexuality and the Oedipus complex—and redefined libido. Adding insult to injury, Jung then told Freud that his revised psychoanalysis had converted many people offended by Freud's pansexuality. Despite some brief reconciliations, Freud was exultant when Jung finally resigned as president of the International Psychoanalytic Association.

Freud considered Jung's departure "a great loss," but Jung was even more disturbed by it. "After the parting of the ways with Freud, a period of inner uncertainty began for me," he wrote in his autobiography. "It would be no exaggeration to call it a state of disorientation" (Jung, 1961, p. 170). Jung's disoriented state included a feeling of inner pressure that seemed to be from "something in the air," which was revealed to him on August 1, 1914, when World War I began. In response, Jung began a self-analysis that led to his own personality theory, which became known as **Analytical Psychology.** "The rest of his life was devoted to the elaboration of the insights which he attained during his self-analysis . . ." (Storr, 1973, p. 18). The end of Jung's mental turmoil was signalled by the publication of *Psychological Types or the Psychology of Individuation* (Jung, 1921/1923).

Psychological Types

As Jung saw it, libido is directed either inward by the person or outward. Jung called the inward-directed attitude **introversion** and the outward-directed one **extraversion.** Introverts are oriented toward the inner, subjective world of ideas, extraverts toward the external, objective world of objects and people. Introverts tend toward self-sufficiency; extraverts need people around. Although both attitudes are present in everyone, usually one is dominant.

In addition, Jung identified four psychological functions: thinking, feeling, sensation, and intuition. Thinking and feeling are ways of making decisions. The thinking person decides through logical and objective considerations, whereas the feeling person uses personal, subjective values.

Sensation and intuition are called the perceiving functions because they are two different ways of taking in information. A person using sensation acquires information through the primary senses, whereas the intuitive individual acquires and processes information unconsciously—through a hunch, for example.

Summarizing the four functions, Jung (1933) wrote, "Sensation establishes what is actually given, thinking enables us to recognize its meaning, feeling tells us its value, and finally intuition points to the possibilities of the whence and whither that lie within the immediate facts" (p. 93). The **Myers-Briggs Type Indicator** or **MBTI** (Myers, McCaulley, Quenk, & Hammer, 1998) is a personality assessment device developed to implement Jung's type theory. In addition to Jung's attitudes and functions, the MBTI includes the judging-perceiving scale.

Personality Structure

For Jung, the personality, or psyche, consisted of several different, interacting systems. The major systems are the ego, the personal unconscious and its complexes, and the collective unconscious and its archetypes (persona, anima and animus, shadow, and self).

The Ego. The ego is the conscious mind, which comprises our perceptions, thoughts, memories, and feelings. It is the mechanism through which we interact with the environment. Before work indicating the importance of the unconscious, the ego was considered to express the psychic totality. Now, the "ego, once the monarch of this totality, is dethroned. It remains merely the centre of consciousness" (Jung, 1939, p. 4).

The Personal Unconscious. The **personal unconscious** contains relatively accessible experiences that were once conscious but have been repressed, suppressed, or simply forgotten, as well as experiences too weak to affect the ego. It also contains an unknown number of **complexes,** which are organized groups of memories, thoughts, perceptions, and feelings. "Complexes are autonomous groups of associations that have a tendency to move by themselves, to live their own life apart from our intentions" (Jung, 1968, p. 81).

The Collective Unconscious. Jung chose the term *collective* to illustrate that the deepest layer of the unconscious, the **collective unconscious,** is universal. It contains behavioral contents and modes that are more or less the same in everyone and thus constitutes a "psychic foundation" in us all (Jung, 1939).

The collective unconscious contains the **archetypes,** a concept from St. Augustine (Chapter 3) meaning universal thought-forms (ideas) that transcend the individual's experience. The traces of humanity's collective experience, archetypes are unconscious, inherited predispositions to perceive or respond in particular ways. Myths, fables, dreams, visions, and works of art reveal such archetypes as birth, death, power, magic, and God.

Although all archetypes can be considered autonomous, some are so developed they may be treated as separate personality systems. These evolved archetypes include the persona, the shadow, and the anima and animus.

The **persona** is the role a person assumes in society, the side of personality for public consumption, which may or may not reveal a person's true nature. If a person becomes too identified with the persona—the judge who can never take off the judicial robes, for example—this is detrimental to the personality because other personality parts are being neglected. An example of such a neglected part is the archetype often paired with the persona—the shadow.

The **shadow** is the residue of the human being's animal nature, what we have inherited from more "primitive" forms of life. It is our nature's dark side and is considered responsible for our socially unwanted thoughts, feelings, and actions. The shadow is also a potent source of creative energy.

Jung's recognition of the importance of human sexual duality is evident in the anima and the animus. Simply put, the **anima** is "the woman in a man . . . ," and the **animus** is "the man in a woman" (Jung, 1939, p. 19). By living together through the ages, women have acquired some of the characteristics of men and vice versa. Men and women have the potential to understand each other because of the anima and animus, respectively.

The interactions between the ego and the archetypal realm involve the persona, the shadow, and the anima and animus. In addition, there is an overall integrating archetype Jung called the "self."

The self arises through **individuation,** which is the process that makes someone a unique, whole entity. Through individuation, the self becomes the totality of the psyche. "The self is not only the centre, but also the circumference that encloses consciousness and the unconscious; it is the centre of this totality, as the ego is the centre of consciousness" (Jung, 1939, p. 96). The self archetype is revealed in symbols such as the mandala, or magic circle, which is any of a variety of geometric designs representing the universe.

Life's ultimate goal is the realization of the self, which, often sought, is seldom achieved. Because complete development of the different personality components is needed before the self can emerge, self-realization does not appear, if at all, before middle age. Childhood, adolescence, and early adulthood are periods when personality's conflicting components are being reconciled. But during middle age, a person seriously begins trying to reorient the personality's center from the conscious ego to a region midway between the consciousness and the unconscious, which is the self's domain.

Personality Development

The importance of opposites for personality development has been implicit in much of our discussion. Jung held that conflict between personality systems creates tension that is the essence of life. Without such tension, personality does not exist. Both Freud and Hegel before him (Chapter 6) were also conflict theorists.

Opposition is seen in Jung's attitudes and functions —between introversion and extraversion, for example. There is further opposition between the ego and the collective unconscious, between the anima and the animus, and so on. Jung saw conflict everywhere in the personality.

Nevertheless, Jung believed that the union of opposites is possible and that the different systems can be integrated into perfect wholeness. This is the ultimate goal of self-realization, revealed in symbols found in such venues as dreams, myths, art, and religion.

Unlike Freud, Jung did not detail the stages through which personality develops. Taking an optimistic viewpoint, Jung believed we are continually trying to progress from a less perfect to a more perfect developmental stage. In practice, perfection will not be achieved, but the ultimate goal is the realization of the self, which represents a harmonious blending of the various personality systems.

Jung saw the transition from a youthful, passionate person into a wise, spiritual one as the most important event in life, but one fraught with pitfalls. For example, if the spiritual values of middle age fail to use all the energy formerly invested in early adulthood's aims (e.g., acquiring a family, marriage, rearing a family), then there will be excess energy that will act against the psyche's integration. Jung was perhaps most successful treating middle-aged persons whose core problem was a need to find satisfactory outlets for this excessive, undirected energy.

Jung's Influence

Jung's influence on academic psychology has been limited, as revealed by even a cursory look at histories of psychology. For example, Boring's (1950) *A History of Experimental Psychology* contains six pages devoted to Freud and only six *lines* to Jung; Fancher's (1990) *Pioneers of Psychology* contains a lengthy chapter on Freud but just two sentences mentioning Jung.

One reason for traditional psychology's lack of acceptance of Jungian concepts is that Jung's writing is difficult, at best. Jung often wrote feverishly, flinging material together hastily to form a difficult hodgepodge of ideas. In addition, the source of many of Jung's concepts—for example, religion, astrology, alchemy—militates against their unbiased appraisal from most psychologists. For the same reason, Jung's thinking has had a much greater influence on disciplines outside psychology, including such diverse areas as literature, filmmaking, and art education (e.g., McWhinnie, 1985). Jung's ideas have also resonated with nonscientific groups interested in such phenomena as occultism, mysticism, meditation, and self-fulfillment.

Jung's characterization of personality types is perhaps the work for which he is best known in psychology. Using the statistical technique of factor analysis, Hans Eysenck (Chapter 17), a vocal opponent of psychoanalysis, found support for Jung's introvert-extravert distinction (Eysenck & Rachman, 1965). Tests to identify personality type based on Jung's work have been developed, and the Myers-Briggs Type Indicator is particularly popular with the public, if not with mainstream psychology. From his interests in such mysterious phenomena as "synchronicity" to his personality theory, a brief survey of Jung's life and analytical psychology cannot do justice to the breadth of canvas on which he worked.

CONCLUSIONS

Compared to the systems that developed out of the academic tradition, psychoanalysis largely arose from a different culture—clinical medicine. In addition, many of Freud's followers, coming from nonacademic backgrounds, were openly disdainful of "scholarship," with all its apparently stultifying dictates (Shakow, 1969). Thus, including psychoanalysis as one of psychology's major historical systems is problematic.

Nevertheless, the impact of Freud and psychoanalysis has been profound on both psychology and Western society. Academic psychology has added to its repertoire such psychoanalytic concepts as the goal-directed unconscious, the importance of early experience, and ego psychology, including the defense mechanisms. These additions illustrate one of the tactics employed by mainstream psychology when faced with the public popularity of psychoanalysis: co-opting psychoanalytic concepts into the corpus of psychological knowledge (Hornstein, 1992).

Psychoanalysis has clearly made inroads into traditional psychology. Early evidence of this can be seen in *Personality and Psychotherapy,* the 1950 book by Neal Miller, who had studied psychoanalysis at the Vienna Psychoanalytic Institute, and John Dollard (both Chapter 13). More recently, Matthew Erdelyi (1985) has shown that psychoanalysis can be transposed into a cognitive framework, bringing the final integration of psychoanalysis with experimental psychology perhaps a step closer.

We briefly examined some of the first important women psychoanalysts—Anna Freud, Melanie Klein, and Karen Horney. Following these pioneers, women have continued to be attracted to clinical psychology and related areas in large numbers. For example, over the decade from 1981 to 1991, "the pool of new entrants into the clinical, counseling, and school psychology workforce was primarily comprised of women (64% of the 1991 new doctorate recipients in these subfields)" (American Psychological Association, 1995, p. 10).

Although Freud pioneered psychoanalysis, as we have seen in this chapter, others had much to contribute. As Freud knew, our world is remarkably dynamic. The development of psychoanalysis did not end with Freud, or even with Anna Freud, Melanie Klein, Karen Horney, or Erik Erikson. The work of Alfred Adler and Carl Jung, two of Freud's one-time disciples who separated from him to establish successful variations of psychoanalysis, demonstrates further substantive changes to Freud's system.

SUMMARY

Unlike the other psychological systems we have considered, psychoanalysis arose from Sigmund Freud's clinical experiences, not from academia.

Early Treatment of the Mentally Ill

The early treatment of the mentally ill was at times barbaric and at other times (and places) relatively enlightened. In the late Middle Ages, the mentally ill were generally seen as bewitched rather than as witches. By the end of the 18th century, the *Zeitgeist* produced more humane treatment than earlier, with the actions of Philippe Pinel in Paris considered the signal events in this era of improved treatment. In the United States, Benjamin Rush and Dorothea Dix represented important positive forces in American psychiatry.

In the 19th century, Wilhelm Griesinger and his followers, especially Emil Kraepelin, attributed mental illness to organic causes. At the same time, particularly in France and Austria, an approach grew that considered mental disorders caused instead by psychic malfunction.

Hypnosis

Franz Mesmer was an early practitioner of a treatment method for hysteria variously called animal magnetism, mesmerism, and later, hypnosis. The method was used and studied by such individuals as the Marquis de Puységur, José di Faria, John Elliotson, and James Esdaile, before James Braid gave it a name and scientific respectability.

In the 19th century, competing schools of hypnosis developed in France, with Liébeault and Bernheim at Nancy and Charcot at Salpêtrière Hospital. Pierre Janet used hypnosis to treat hysteric patients and developed a system of psychology with similarities to Freud's psychoanalysis.

Existential Precursors to Freud

Sören Kierkegaard is considered one of the founders of existentialism, the philosophy stressing the individual's isolation in a hostile environment while emphasizing freedom of choice and responsibility for actions. Like Freud, Friedrich Nietzsche recognized the opposing psychic forces of the superego and the id; unlike Freud, Nietzsche viewed the relationship between the opposing forces as something that humans need to transcend. Freud considered Nietzsche second only to Schopenhauer as an anticipator of elements of psychoanalysis.

Sigmund Freud

Trained as a neurophysiologist, Freud eventually opened a private practice in psychiatry. Using ideas from various sources, he developed a treatment method that became known as psychoanalysis in the latter part of the 19th century. To analyze the unconscious mind of his patients, Freud first used hypnosis, eventually abandoning it for free association and dream interpretation. His analysis of his patients convinced him sex was at the root of most neurotic disorders.

The Interpretation of Dreams is often considered Freud's most important book. Freud considered dream analysis essential for understanding psychic life, and believed that dreams represent wish-fulfillment and that many dream elements are symbolic.

Freud's reputation and circle of devotees began to expand after his books were published at the turn of the century. Early disciples included Alfred Adler, Otto Rank, Carl Jung, Sandor Ferenczi, Karl Abraham, and Ernest Jones. Adler, Jung, and Rank became the most conspicuous defectors from Freud's inner circle.

In Freudian theory, three personality systems—the id, the ego, and the superego—operate on different levels of consciousness. As the storehouse of innate drives, the id seeks pleasure through the primary process, or fantasizing about the desired object. The ego contends with the environment by means of the reality principle, whereas the superego is the personality's moral component.

For Freud, the instincts, and particularly the sexual instinct, provide the energy for life's processes. Personality development passes through five stages: oral, anal, phallic, latency, and genital. Fixation at any of the first three stages has consequences for adult behavior. The phallic stage is crucial, because during it the little boy experiences the Oedipus complex and the little girl the Electra complex. Castration anxiety is the impetus for termination of the former, whereas the latter ends because of penis envy.

Freud's influence can be seen in our language, in psychoanalysis as a treatment method for mental illness, and in the many disciples he created.

Neo-Freudians

Anna Freud, Freud's daughter, became his successor in psychoanalysis. In her best-known work, Anna Freud described the ego defense mechanisms her father had earlier identified. Some of the major mechanisms are repression, regression, rationalization, projection, reaction formation, displacement, and sublimation.

Like Anna Freud, Melanie Klein was a child analyst. She became a rival of Anna Freud, and the Freuds' arrival in England produced a rift within the British psychoanalytic movement.

Karen Horney's version of psychoanalysis disagreed with Freud's approach to feminine psychology and with

Freud's emphasis on the sexual instinct. Horney identified 10 neurotic needs, which include the need for affection and approval, the need for power, the ambition for personal achievement, and the need for perfection.

John Bowlby and Mary Ainsworth studied attachment behavior in children and developed a theory of human attachment. Part of the empirical basis for Bowlby's theory came from primate mother-infant attachment studies, such as those of Harry Harlow.

Analyzed by Anna Freud, Erik Erikson is best known for his work in developmental psychology. To Freud's psychosexual stages of development, Erikson added adolescence, young adulthood, adulthood, and maturity and old age.

Alfred Adler's Individual Psychology de-emphasized the sexual instinct and made consciousness the center of personality. For Adler, humanity's great driving forces were feelings of inferiority and efforts to compensate, with birth order another important determinant of personality.

Carl Jung's self-analysis led to Analytical Psychology. Jung's conception of psychological types divided people according to introversion and extraversion and the functions of thinking, feeling, sensation, and intuition. For Jung, the personality consisted of several different, interacting systems, the major ones being the ego, the personal unconscious and its complexes, and the collective unconscious and its archetypes.

CONNECTIONS QUESTIONS

1. Describe as many connections as you can between conceptions of mental illness and treatments for it.
2. How might the late 19th century's social *Zeitgeist* and the various wars involving Germany be connected to Freud's theory?
3. How are mesmerism and hypnosis connected to psychoanalytic theory and treatment?
4. What effects on Freud's theory might we expect to see from Freud's association with Brentano? With Meynert? With Brücke and the "Helmholtz School"?
5. What sort of connections can you draw between Freud's work and subfields of psychology such as developmental, social, and cognitive?
6. What connections can you make between the various neo-Freudians and changes in the psychoanalytic conceptions of development?
7. In what ways did Adler and Jung "disconnect" themselves from Freud?

KEY NAMES AND TERMS

Karl Abraham (p. 434)
Alfred Adler (p. 446)
Mary Salter Ainsworth (p. 444)
anal stage (p. 438)
Analytical Psychology (p. 452)
anima (p. 453)
animal magnetism (p. 422)
animus (p. 453)
Anna O (Bertha Pappenheim) (p. 430)
archetype (p. 452)
attachments (p. 444)
basic anxiety (p. 443)
Hippolyte Bernheim (p. 424)
Eugen Bleuler (p. 450)
John Bowlby (p. 444)
James Braid (p. 424)
Josef Breuer (p. 430)
A. A. Brill (p. 434)
Ernst Brücke (p. 428)
castration anxiety (p. 438)
cathartic method (p. 430)
Jean Martin Charcot (p. 422)
Vicenzio Chiarugi (p. 421)
collective unconscious (p. 452)
complexes (p. 452)
conscience (p. 437)
conscious (p. 435)
defense mechanisms (p. 444)
displacement (p. 442)
Dorothea Dix (p. 422)
ego (p. 436)
ego-ideal (p. 437)
Electra complex (p. 438)
John Elliotson (p. 424)
Erik Erikson (p. 445)
James Esdaile (p. 424)
extraversion (p. 452)
José Custodio di Faria (p. 424)
Sandor Ferenczi (p. 434)
Wilhelm Fliess (p. 431)
free association (p. 431)
Anna Freud (p. 441)
Sigmund Freud (p. 428)
genital stage (p. 438)
gerontology (p. 446)
Jan Baptista van Helmont (p. 422)
Karen Horney (p. 443)
hypnotism (p. 424)
id (p. 436)
identification (p. 438)
Individual Psychology (p. 447)
individuation (p. 453)
introversion (p. 452)

Pierre Janet (p. 425)
Ernest Jones (p. 434)
Carl Gustav Jung (p. 449)
Melanie Klein (p. 442)
Richard Krafft-Ebing (p. 430)
latency stage (p. 438)
latent content (p. 433)
libido (p. 436)
Auguste Ambroise Liébeault (p. 424)
manifest content (p. 433)
Franz Anton Mesmer (p. 423)
mesmerism (p. 423)
Theodor Meynert (p. 429)
Myers-Briggs Type Indicator (MBTI) (p. 452)
object-relations theory (p. 446)
Oedipus complex (p. 438)
oral stage (p. 437)
Paracelsus (p. 422)
penis envy (p. 438)
persona (p. 453)
personal unconscious (p. 452)
phallic stage (p. 438)
Philippe Pinel (p. 421)
pleasure principle (p. 436)
preconscious (p. 435)
primary process (p. 436)
projection (p. 442)
psychoanalysis (p. 420)
Marquis de Puységur (p. 423)
Otto Rank (p. 434)
rationalization (p. 441)
reaction formation (p. 442)
reality principle (p. 436)
regression (p. 441)
repression (p. 441)
Charles Richet (p. 426)
Benjamin Rush (p. 421)
secondary process (p. 436)
seduction theory (p. 432)
shadow (p. 453)
Wilhelm Stekel (p. 433)
striving for superiority (p. 448)
style of life (p. 448)
sublimation (p. 442)
superego (p. 437)
transference (p. 431)
William Tuke (p. 421)
unconscious (p. 435)
wish-fulfillment (p. 433)

SUGGESTED READINGS

Ansbacher, H. L., & Ansbacher, R. R. (Eds.) (1956). *The Individual Psychology of Alfred Adler: A systematic presentation in selections from his writings.* New York: Basic Books, Inc. This volume includes both interpretations and voluminous citations from primary works and is a good place to begin the study of Adler's psychology.

Brill, A. A. (Ed. and Trans.) (1938). *The basic writings of Sigmund Freud.* New York: The Modern Library. This collection of Freud's works consists of such classic writings as *Psychopathology of Everyday Life, The Interpretation of Dreams, Totem and Taboo,* and *The History of the Psychoanalytic Movement.* Many similar volumes can be found.

Erdelyi, M. H. (1985). *Psychoanalysis: Freud's cognitive psychology.* New York: W. H. Freeman and Company. This is a scholarly work that advances the thesis that Freud was much more than just a psychotherapist. In addition, it has high intrinsic interest, because many of its examples are drawn from sources such as dreams, religion, and art.

Freud, A. (1937). *The ego and the mechanisms of defence.* London: The Hogarth Press Ltd. This is Anna Freud's most important work, which details the various ways in which the ego seeks to protect itself when threatened by conflicting demands of the id and superego.

Freud, E. L. (Ed.) (1992). *Letters of Sigmund Freud.* New York: Dover Publications. The letters of famous people are good sources of information about them and their times, and this collection of Freud's is no exception.

Gay, P. (1988). *Freud: A life for our time.* New York: W. W. Norton & Company. This is a readable and scholarly biography of Freud. Gay's qualifications for writing the work include the fact that he is a graduate of the Western New England Institute for Psychoanalysis.

Jones, E. (1953–1957). *The life and work of Sigmund Freud* (Vols. 1–3). New York: Basic Books, Inc. One of Freud's most loyal disciples, Jones produced what is considered the definitive biography of his mentor and friend.

McLynn, F. (1996). *Carl Gustav Jung.* New York: St. Martin's Press. According to the dust jacket, this is the first full-length biography of Jung, who was an intriguing character. Controversial because of his alleged anti-Semitism and his sexual promiscuity, Jung was nevertheless a more acceptable icon than Freud, at least partly because of his opposition to Freud's atheism.

Roazen, P. (1975). *Freud and his followers.* New York: Alfred A. Knopf. Roazen's book contains excellent pictures and interesting biographies of all the major, and most of the minor, characters in the history of the psychoanalytic movement.

Shakow, D. (1969). Psychoanalysis. In D. L. Krantz (Ed.), *Schools of psychology: A symposium* (pp. 87–122). New York: Appleton-Century-Crofts. Shakow's essay is an excellent overview of the psychoanalytic movement.

Storr, A. (1973). *C. G. Jung.* New York: The Viking Press. In slightly more than 100 pages, Storr has written a worthwhile overview of the life and theories of one of the psychoanalytic movement's most complex figures.

Mind and Brain: Clinical Psychology Meets Neuroscience

CHAPTER 16

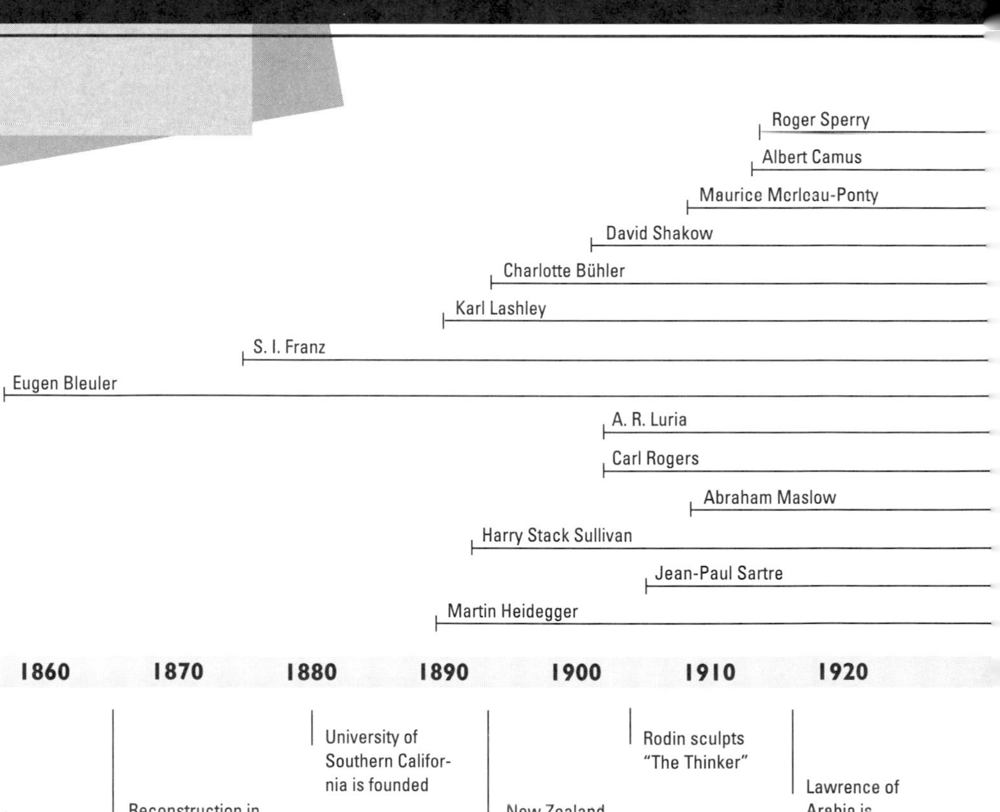

OUTLINE

Existential and Humanistic Approaches to Clinical Psychology

The Backdrop of Existential Philosophy

The Third Force

Recent Advances in Psychotherapy

Psychiatric Influences

The Growth of Clinical Psychology

Neuropsychology

Shepherd Ivory Franz

Karl Spencer Lashley

Alexander Romanovich Luria

Conclusions

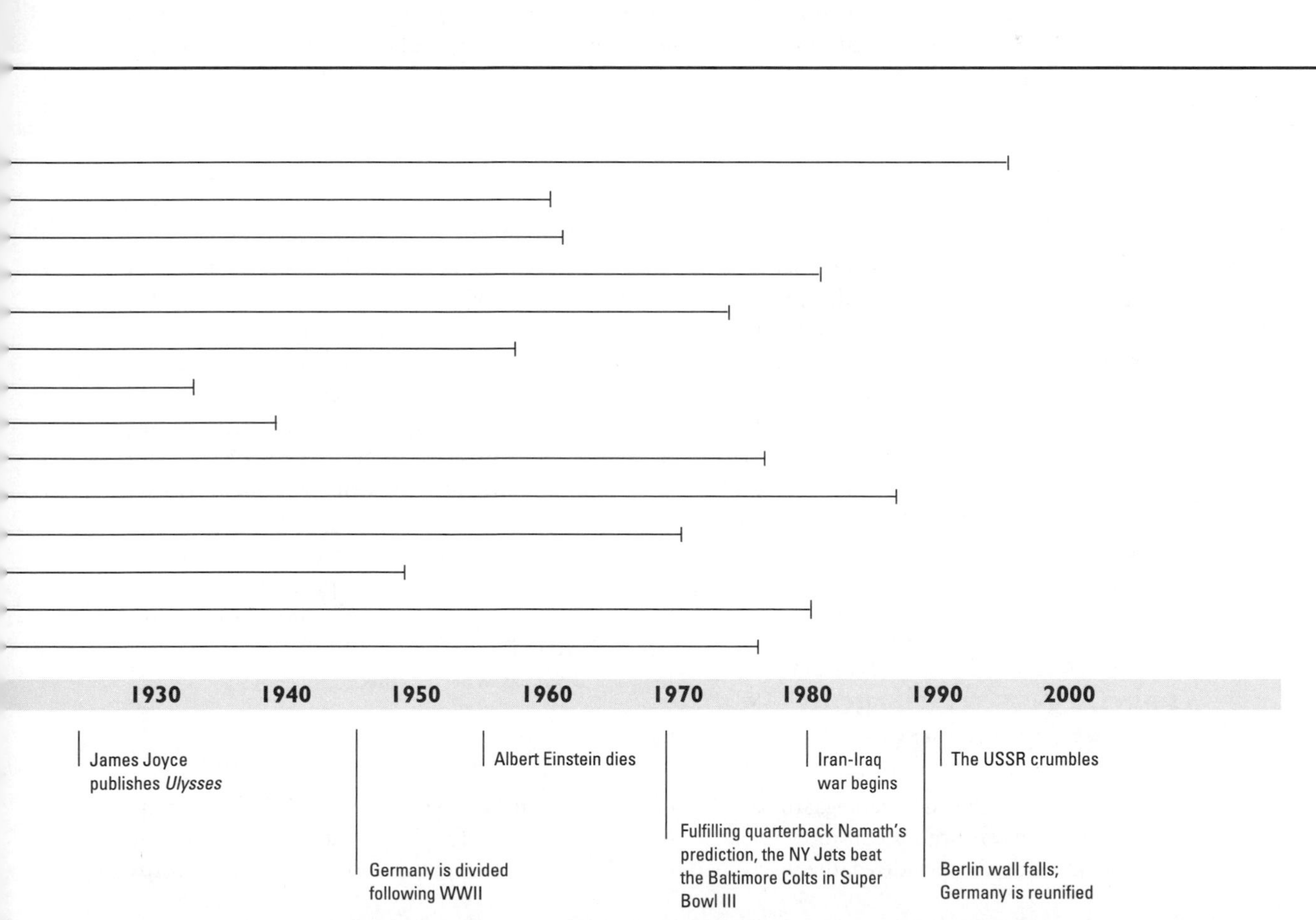

In Chapter 15, we examined the work and influence of Sigmund Freud, the patriarch of psychoanalysis, and also that of neo-Freudians Anna Freud, Melanie Klein, Karen Horney, Erik Erikson, Alfred Adler, and Carl Jung. In this chapter, we will consider clinical psychology's existential and humanistic approaches, as well as important developments in clinical practice, including connections between American clinical psychology and the psychiatric community. For example, David Shakow's career (discussed later) began when there were virtually no clinical training programs and ended recently, when there were more than 150 APA-approved clinical programs. Throughout Shakow's lifetime, clinical psychology greatly expanded on its Freudian foundation, with many elements of clinical theory and practice becoming part of academic psychology (e.g., a required course in abnormal psychology).

We will also look at the beginnings of neuropsychology and how neuroscience has enhanced our ability to treat mental illness and other clinical disorders. For example, the finding that people with Parkinson's disease—a major motor disorder characterized by tremors at rest and decreased voluntary movement—display a massive depletion of the brain's neurotransmitter, dopamine, resulted in at least temporarily successful treatment of many patients with L-dopa, which increases dopamine in the patient's brain. Similarly, increasingly successful pharmacological treatments for such disorders as depression and schizophrenia have stimulated and been stimulated by enhanced knowledge of the nervous system and its operations. Experimental neuropsychology has helped develop that knowledge, whereas clinical neuropsychology has fostered the successful diagnosis and treatment of neurological disorders.

EXISTENTIAL AND HUMANISTIC APPROACHES TO CLINICAL PSYCHOLOGY

In Chapter 6, we introduced Kierkegaard and Nietzsche, two of the 19th century's better-known existential philosophers, and we considered them again briefly in Chapter 15. Existentialism in general, and Kierkegaard and Nietzsche in particular, have had a significant impact on the evolution of psychology—especially clinical psychology. A humanistic "Third Force" (discussed later) emerged in post–World War II American psychology, which incorporated many ideas from existential philosophy.

The Backdrop of Existential Philosophy

Beyond being existential philosophy's founders, Kierkegaard and Nietzsche represent the beginnings of something new within psychology. From Kierkegaard's interest in anxiety and depression through Nietzsche's analysis of man relative to society, both philosophers placed questions about personal freedom and life's meaning at the forefront.

Two themes perhaps best capture existential philosophy's appeal for psychology. The first is that subjective meaning, rather than a third-person account of brain or behavior, should be psychology's central focus. This theme is not peculiar to existentialism, as the same idea can be found clearly in James (Chapter 10), Freud (Chapter 15), and others.

Existential philosophy's second major theme is that humans have the freedom to make choices and thus must take responsibility for their choices. For Kierkegaard and Nietzsche, this meant resisting the tendency to consider God or society responsible for failures and successes instead of accepting them as the result of freely chosen actions. In contemporary psychology, this theme means resisting reductionistic and deterministic accounts of human behavior that attribute human actions either to biology or to the environment.

In addition to Kierkegaard and Nietzsche, several existential philosophers have important connections to psychology. Two of the best known also won the Nobel Prize in literature: Albert Camus in 1957, and Jean-Paul Sartre, who declined it in 1964.

Jean-Paul Sartre and Albert Camus

Paris-born **Jean-Paul Sartre** (1905–1980) had a military officer father and a mother who was the first cousin of famed theologian/physician Albert Schweitzer. Sartre completed his doctorate in philosophy at the École Normale Supérieure in the late 1920s, with a focus on French philosopher **Henri Bergson** (1859–1941), winner of the 1927 Nobel Prize in literature. Bergson is sometimes called the French William James because of the similarity of their work. Before World War II, Sartre taught philosophy at several prestigious French universities and studied phenomenology under both Husserl (Chapter 8) and Heidegger (discussed later) in Germany. Captured early in the war, Sartre spent 9 months as a prisoner before being released and joining the French Resistance as an essayist and reporter.

Several of Sartre's major works first appeared during the tumultuous years before and during World War II, including his psychological novel, *Nausea* (Sartre, 1938), which tells the story of a French writer who uses a diary format to relentlessly catalog his every feeling and sensation about the world and the people around him. As a result, he experiences an overwhelming feeling of nausea, hence the title. The central character's philosophical and psychological struggles to come to terms with life enable Sartre to dramatically portray his existentialist philosophy.

Sartre's most substantive contribution to theoretical psychology and the philosophy of mind—*Being and Nothingness* (Sartre, 1943)—provides an existential analysis of the structure and function of consciousness. His best-known play, *No Exit* (Sartre, 1947), looks harshly at the relationship between one's self and others, exploring how we carefully try to manage the public aspects of our self. After the war, Sartre never returned to a full-time academic position, working instead as a writer in different forms (e.g., plays, novels) and on an array of topics including philosophy, psychology, and social criticism.

Even without a university position's advantages, Sartre exerted an enormous influence on French intellectuals and existential philosophy and psychology internationally. For example, Sartre's long-time associate, **Simone de Beauvoir** (1908–1986), produced pioneering writings in existentialism and feminism. In *The Second Sex,* de Beauvoir combined information from interviews with women of all ages and from all walks of life with research about women's bodies, minds, and historic and economic roles to produce an encyclopedic work on the forced inequality of the sexes. *The Second Sex* well illustrates existential thought's impact on psychology beyond clinical theory and practice. Sartre's own psychological works are perhaps best classified as social psychological—an example is his analysis of the dreadful power of the human gaze (How do you feel when someone stares at you?)—or as existential clinical theory.

The son of a farm laborer, **Albert Camus** (1913–1960) was born in Mondovi, Algeria. After his father's death in World War I, his mother moved to a suburb of Algiers to better support the family. An able student and soccer player, Camus nevertheless struggled with tuberculosis.

Before World War II, Camus studied philosophy, completing a thesis on Plotinus (Chapter 3) in 1936. Like Sartre, during the war Camus served as a writer for the French underground and also produced many of his own classic works. These include *The Myth of Sisyphus,* Camus's existential treatise exploring the meaning of life, the nature of absurdity, and the possibility of suicide, and his gripping novel *The Stranger.* In *The Stranger,* Camus considers a range of psychological phenomena including the causes of aggression, the nature of guilt and grief, and the social aspects of emotional display.

After the war, Camus worked as a writer until his death in an automobile accident. Later works that contributed to Camus's winning the Nobel Prize include *The Plague,* which explores the social psychology of quarantine, and *The Fall,* perhaps his most classic statement of such basic existential issues as personal choice and subjective meaning. Although Camus was never closely associated with academia, his short and engaging novels are often required reading for university courses in existential philosophy and existential psychology, and Camus may be the most commonly read postwar existentialist.

Sartre and Camus were writers who found Cold War anxieties fertile ground in which to sow the seeds of existentialism for the general public through works of fiction. At the other extreme, the academician Martin Heidegger felt that everyday language inadequately conveyed the ideas of his rich existential, phenomenological, philosophical system.

Martin Heidegger

A student of Edmund Husserl, **Martin Heidegger** (1889–1976) has become an increasingly controversial figure. On the one hand, his contributions to philosophy are considered among the most significant of the 20th century. On the other hand, questions about his character and about his relations with the Nazis continue to cast a shadow over his legacy.

The son of a Catholic sexton, Heidegger was born in Germany's Black Forest region. When he was just 17, reading Brentano (Chapter 8) stimulated his interest in philosophy and psychology. Struck by the basic questions of metaphysics, Heidegger began a lifelong quest to understand such fundamental issues as "What is the meaning of being?"

Heidegger began at the University of Freiburg as a theology major, but the influence of Kierkegaard, Nietzsche, and particularly Husserl pulled him toward philosophy. After completing a dissertation on Duns Scotus (Chapter 3), Heidegger was Husserl's assistant until he accepted his own position at the University of Marburg in 1923. For the next several years, Heidegger undertook a synthesis of classic existential philosophy and contemporary Husserlian phenomenology, creating his own existential-phenomenology with the publication of *Being and Time* (Heidegger, 1927/1962).

Succeeding Husserl at Freiburg, Heidegger became the world's leading phenomenologist. On May 3, 1933, Heidegger joined Hitler's National Socialist German Workers' Party (NSDAP), which was the second largest party in Germany. A month earlier, he had been elected rector of the university, and on May 27, Heidegger gave his inaugural rector's address. The ambiguous text of that address is often cited as evidence of Heidegger's support for the Nazis, and it is certainly true that during his tenure as rector, Heidegger helped bring the university into alignment with the National Socialist policies. Heidegger resigned as rector less than a year after the inaugural speech, however, which was subsequently found to be incompatible with the party line, its text banned by the Nazis.

For the duration of the war, Heidegger's freedom to publish and travel to conferences was restricted, and at one point, he was under Gestapo surveillance. His lectures often subtly criticized Nazi ideology. Still, because of his alleged Nazi sympathies, Heidegger was forbidden to teach at the end of the war in 1945 and the following year was dismissed from his chair of philosophy. The ban was lifted in 1949, and Heidegger remained an influential writer and lecturer.

Philosophical Library, New York.

Martin Heidegger (1889–1976)

Heidegger's Philosophy. Heidegger aimed to transform questions about being and existence from abstract concerns into a discussion of the nature and place of humans in the world that would be of interest to almost everyone. By deliberately manipulating ordinary language, he sought to illustrate that humans alone question "Being" and that only people are aware of their Being.

In an effort to clarify his ideas, Heidegger not only distorted the standard uses of many terms but also created new ones, the most important of which was *Dasein*. In German, ***Dasein*** means "being there," and Heidegger used the word to represent humanity. *Dasein* was intended to capture the idea that people are always aware, always thinking, and are not like the world's other objects. Humans, *Dasein*, do not exist as things in the world like other things in the world; rather, *Dasein* has a **being-in-the-world** (another of Heidegger's linguistic constructions) that differs from all other objects. People exist by being-in-the-world; conversely, the world as a meaningful reality exists because humans are in it.

Because of their awareness of Being, humans are also aware of their impermanence. This realization creates the fundamental mood of people, which is anxiety. Humans are "thrown into the world" not of their making or choosing and must constantly strive to realize their fullest potentials by making appropriate decisions. In trying to create a worthwhile existence, to live toward death, the person lives an "authentic" life.

Failure to accept death's inevitability leads to an "inauthentic" life, in which the person experiences no sense of urgency to become all that he or she can become. An inauthentic person is always giving away his or her ability to choose. For example, the person may become involved in a social organization in which the rules of behavior are manifestly clear. By doing this, the individual surrenders his or her choices in living life. The person has elected to live an inauthentic life by accepting the decisions of others about how life should be lived.

As you can see, Heidegger's ideas are both intriguing and difficult. Nevertheless, no existential philosopher has had a more direct connection to clinical psychology than Heidegger. The reason for this influence is that several German psychotherapists fashioned therapeutic techniques based on Heidegger's *Dasein* concept.

Daseinanalysis. Two of Europe's leading psychiatrists, **Medard Boss** (1903–1990) and **Ludwig Binswanger** (1881–1966) founded a system of psychotherapy after World War II based partly on Heidegger's existential phenomenology. As is true for Boss and Binswanger, people trained in the Freudian psychoanalytic school developed the humanistic psychotherapies, in most cases.

Boss was born in Switzerland and started his medical studies in Vienna, where he worked briefly with Freud. Returning to Switzerland, Boss trained with Eugen Bleuler (Chapter 15) and then studied in London and Berlin with such notables as Karen Horney, Ernest Jones (both Chapter 15), and Kurt Goldstein (Chapter 14). Again returning to Switzerland, Boss became closely associated with Carl Jung and was an "orthodox psychoanalyst" (Craig, 1988).

An encounter with fellow Swiss psychiatrist Ludwig Binswanger led Boss to read Heidegger, whom he met in 1947 at Heidegger's Black Forest residence. Binswanger had completed his medical degree from the University of Zurich in 1907, before studying with Bleuler and Jung. Although he was considered one of Switzerland's premier Freudian therapists, Binswanger was moving toward a more phenomenological approach based on the ideas of Husserl and Heidegger when he met Boss.

Because of its foundation in existential philosophy, ***Daseinanalysis*** (existential psychoanalysis) differs from traditional psychoanalysis in placing a greater emphasis on present choices, minimizing the past as a cause of current problems. People are responsible for their lives and are free to make choices about what to do or what not to do. The central fact of existence is being-in-the-world; people cannot live apart from the world or in a world apart from themselves. *Daseinanalysis* aims to help the person live an authentic life.

Other Existential Psychotherapies. Existentialism was increasingly a part of the postwar European *Zeitgeist*, and many psychotherapists began to connect existential philosophy and clinical practice. Such a connection is evident in the work of German-born Swiss philosopher, psychologist, and psychiatrist **Karl Jaspers** (1883–1969). With a 1909 M.D. degree from Heidelberg, Jaspers was Professor of Philosophy at the university from 1921 until 1937, when the Nazis dismissed him. Jaspers stayed in Germany throughout the war, received the Goethe Prize in 1947 for his uncompromising stand, and then a year later became a Swiss citizen.

Jaspers indirectly popularized Heidegger by advocating an existential psychology, although he did not like being called an existentialist and preferred the label of philosopher (Stierlin, 1974). Nevertheless, Kierkegaard was Jaspers's primary point of departure in developing his approach. In his three-volume *Philosophy*, Jaspers distinguished three modes of being: being-there, being-oneself, and being-in-itself. Being-there refers to the world we know through our observations; being-oneself is the subjective awareness of our own difficulties, wishes, and expectancies; and being-in-itself is the ability to surmount the world and to know other worlds.

Jaspers found such existential, philosophical considerations a useful framework for structuring psychotherapy and for understanding psychopathology. For Jaspers (e.g., 1932/1969), psychotherapy was a form of *Existenzphilosophie* (analysis of existence), which focused on understanding a person's existence through an active analysis of consciousness as it relates to the self and to objects in the world. In turn, Jaspers's thought strongly impacted psychiatry and psychology in America, whereas his many comprehensive volumes in the history of philosophy were popular with academicians interested in an existential perspective.

Viktor Frankl (1905–1997) was another contributor to existential psychotherapy. A Viennese psychiatrist and holocaust survivor, Frankl emerged from 3 years in Nazi concentration camps—including the notorious Auschwitz—with a renewed appreciation of Nietzsche and other existential philosophers. *Man's Search for Meaning* (Frankl, 1946/1959) chronicles Frankl's experiences during the war and the creation of **logotherapy,** his brand of existential psychotherapy.

Logotherapy involves the search for meaning, focusing on what Frankl calls "the will to meaning" as opposed to Nietzsche's "will to power" or "the will to pleasure" (i.e., hedonism). Frankl believed many of our era's ills can be traced to a frustrated search for personal meaning, resulting in depression, aggression, and addiction. But the logotherapist cannot prescribe meaning for the individual. Instead, it "is the objective of logotherapy to *describe* the process of meaning perception by way of a phenomenological analysis, so as to find out how normal people arrive at meaning and consequently at a sense of fulfillment" (Frankl, 1994, p. 350).

Not all of the influential European existentialists were therapists or philosophers, however. In fact, the most influential theorist for an existential-phenomenological psychology, Maurice Merleau-Ponty, was primarily a child psychologist, with strong interests in cognition and consciousness.

Maurice Merleau-Ponty

Like Camus, **Maurice Merleau-Ponty** (1908–1961) lost his father in World War I, and like Sartre, he was educated in Paris, graduating from the École Normale Supérieure in 1930. Until he joined the war effort in 1939, Merleau-Ponty was affiliated with various movements, including the structural movement in sociology championed by social anthropologist Claude Levi-Strauss (1908–1990). Merleau-Ponty's most relevant works for theoretical psychology are *The Structure of Behavior* and *The Phenomenology of Perception,* both first published during the war.

In *The Structure of Behavior* and *The Phenomenology of Perception,* Merleau-Ponty revealed his interest in the relation between consciousness and human nature. For Merleau-Ponty, the appropriate method for studying consciousness was the phenomenology of perception, and he rejected extreme methodological approaches such as that found in Watson's behaviorism (Chapter 12).

Merleau-Ponty taught courses in Gestalt psychology, sociology, psychoanalysis, and the philosophy of language at the University of Lyon and at the École Normale before being named Professor of Child Psychology and Pedagogy at the Sorbonne in 1949. For the next several years, Merleau-Ponty conducted research in cognitive development. In 1952, he accepted what had been Bergson's prestigious chair at the Collège de France, from which he continued to write about language, consciousness, and existential-phenomenological psychology until his death in 1961.

Although Merleau-Ponty was knowledgeable about both psychoanalysis and philosophy, he left his mark on psychology primarily through advocating an existential-phenomenological approach to experimental psychology. Using less of traditional existential and Husserlian philosophy than most of his contemporaries, Merleau-Ponty built on such starting points as William James and Gestalt theory (Schmidt, 1985). Methodologically, Merleau-Ponty focused on analyzing perceptual processes and what that revealed about the structure and function of consciousness. His findings suggested that the experience of time, our own bodies, and of other people were primary elements in organizing our conscious processes.

AP/Wide World Photos.

Maurice Merleau-Ponty (1908–1961)

Merleau-Ponty marks an important transition in phenomenology from its status as a psychologically sophisticated philosophical system (e.g., Brentano and others in Chapter 8) to a school of psychology. Because of his more experimental nature and his connection to established psychological systems, Merleau-Ponty's existential-phenomenology approach became the most popular among academic psychologists (e.g., Ihde, 1979; Pollio, 1982; Pollio, Henley, & Thompson, 1997; Valle & King, 1978).

Other Existential Contributors

Our survey of the philosophical backdrop to a more humanistic psychology has been highly selective. Many people have made important contributions, some far removed from psychology. For example, some historians view Russian novelist Fyodor Dostoevsky (1821–1881) as one of the principal contributors to modern existential philosophy (e.g., Kaufmann, 1956), and college existentialism courses often list his *Notes From Underground* as required reading. Additionally, the Austrian Jewish theologian/philosopher **Martin Buber** (1878–1965) wrote both clinically relevant articles (e.g., Buber, 1957) and what has become the classic existential analysis of language use—*I and Thou* (Buber, 1923/1970). Buber's work remains a key volume for clinicians, social psychologists, and cognitive psychologists interested in language.

In America, **Rollo May** (1909–1994) was an early advocate for an existential psychology and has been called the "Father of American Existential Psychology" (Bugental, 1996). Born in Ada, Ohio, May obtained his B.A. from Oberlin College in 1930, a divinity degree from Union Theological Seminary in 1938, and a clinical psychology Ph.D. *summa cum laude* from Columbia in 1949. Battles with tuberculosis partly account for how long May took to earn his Ph.D. Study with Alfred Adler in Vienna and May's experiences as a tuberculosis patient profoundly influenced his outlook on life.

May's dissertation on the meaning of anxiety drew heavily from Kierkegaard's analysis of dread. May's subsequent publications (e.g., May, 1950) marked the first exposure most American psychologists had to Kierkegaard's ideas. Further books included several that focused on Heidegger (e.g., May, 1961), and May became perhaps the most celebrated American existential psychotherapist of his era.

One of May's contemporaries, George Kelly, further illustrates the increasingly humanistic nature of American psychology during and after World War II. Born in Kansas, **George A. Kelly** (1905–1967) completed his Ph.D. in physiological psychology from the University of Iowa in 1931. Kelly spent most of his career at The Ohio State University, where he worked with Julian Rotter to build the clinical program. **Julian Rotter** (1916–) is known for his construct "locus of control" (Rotter, 1966), which distinguishes individuals who see themselves as the source of what happens to them (internal locus) and people who believe their fate largely rests with forces beyond their control (external locus).

Kelly began his academic career in the depths of the Depression. Because he was unable to see how behavioristic S-R psychology or Freudian psychoanalytic theory could help most Americans during this era, Kelly began searching for a more relevant system, which he detailed in *The Psychology of Personal Constructs* (Kelly, 1955). Like the scientist who develops a theory to help predict and control the environment, individuals develop **personal constructs** from their experiences with the world, which they then use to organize and make sense of experience. Personal constructs lead to predictions about the world, and when the predictions prove to be accurate, the construct system is strengthened. Inaccurate predictions, by contrast, may force the person to reconstrue, or look for alternative ways to make sense of, his or her experiences. Although originally more "clinical" in nature, Kelly's personal construct theory is similar to the contemporary schema theory used by cognitive psychologists (Chapter 18) to explore such things as our perception and understanding of the world.

From a therapeutic perspective, to understand a person's world, it is necessary to understand his or her personal constructs. It is not enough just to examine the person's background (e.g., heredity, environment), because identical backgrounds may produce different personal constructs. Kelly believed people are free to choose how they interpret the events that affect them and how the events will impact their lives.

In more contemporary American psychology, several well-respected theorists, such as Amedeo Giorgi (e.g., Giorgi, 1970) and Joseph Rychlak (e.g., Rychlak, 1991), have lobbied for a more "humanistic" approach to all psychology, not just to clinical psychology. Articles representing an existential and/or phenomenological orientation can be found in almost every area of psychology, including artificial intelligence, social psychology, and consumer psychology. We will now examine the area of American psychology on which existentialism has had perhaps the greatest impact—humanistic clinical psychology, which some have called the Third Force.

The Third Force

Charlotte B. Bühler (1893–1974), Karl Bühler's (Chapter 14) wife, came to America in 1923 on a fellowship to work with Thorndike (Chapters 11 and 12) and did studies of age-specific cognitive abilities (e.g., Bühler, 1930) that were similar to research often associated with Piaget's stage model (Chapter 18). Bühler's later works anticipated Erik Erikson's (Chapter 15) modern life-span developmental approach. Additionally, her child psychology work is thought to have strongly influenced American child psychologist Arnold Gesell (Chapter 12).

After 1940, Charlotte Bühler's interests increasingly focused on the new humanistic psychology movement, which Abraham Maslow called American psychology's **Third Force,** the first force being behaviorism and the second force psychoanalysis. With Maslow, Carl Rogers (both discussed later), and Viktor Frankl, Bühler founded the Association for Humanistic Psychology in 1964, serving as its president in 1965–1966. Bühler is also known for producing one of the first widely read position papers outlining and popularizing this new humanistic approach to psychology (Bühler, 1971).

Humanistic psychology can be defined as a focus on the positive rather than the negative aspects of the self—an orientation more concerned with present choices than with past events. Such a definition encompasses people who may or may not have considered themselves humanists. For example, by this definition, Alfred Adler was a humanist and could be considered modern humanistic psychology's founder. Although some historians and Adlerians would welcome this designation, others would not.

From another perspective, existentialists frequently focused on the self, and existential approaches to clinical psychology are often considered a subset of humanistic orientations. Nevertheless, existentialism, with its roots in European philosophy, is not synonymous with a humanistic approach to clinical psychology in America. To convey what Charlotte Bühler and her colleagues intended, we will concentrate on some of the individuals involved in a movement in America in the late 1950s that led to the founding of the APA's Division of Humanistic Psychology in the early 1970s.

Several individuals mentioned in other contexts were part of the humanistic movement in psychology, including social psychologist Hadley Cantril (Chapter 1), Gestalt neuroscientist Kurt Goldstein (Chapter 14), and the novelist Aldous Huxley (Chapters 9 and 13). The movement also included America's leading existential psychologist, Rollo May, and a clinician known for client-centered therapy, Carl Rogers. We will start with the person most associated with the movement's position as the Third Force in modern psychology—Abraham Maslow.

Abraham Maslow

Abraham Maslow (1908–1970) was born in Brooklyn, the eldest child in a large immigrant household of Russian Jews. After brief college tries in New York, Maslow settled at the University of Wisconsin to earn his B.A. (1930), M.A. (1931), Ph.D. (1934), and first job. At Wisconsin, Maslow worked with Harry Harlow (Chapter 14) and contributed importantly to the study of primate social behavior (e.g., Maslow, 1936). Maslow returned to New York from Wisconsin, first on a fellowship to work with Thorndike at Columbia and later as part of the Brooklyn College faculty.

During his tenure under Thorndike, Maslow's interests shifted to human behavior and eventually into motivation, personality, and clinical psychology. This shift coincides with Maslow's association with such German refugee psychologists as Wertheimer and Koffka (both Chapter 14) and Horney and Adler. In 1951, Maslow accepted a position at Brandeis University in Waltham, Massachusetts, where he soon became closely associated with Kurt Goldstein.

Maslow is best remembered for his hierarchy of human needs and his theories of personality and motivation. Maslow's **need hierarchy** (Figure 16.1) is often depicted as a pyramid at whose base are the physiological needs, such as the need for food and water. Next are the safety needs, followed by the needs for belongingness and love. Once the needs to love and be loved are satisfied, the person can begin to satisfy the needs for esteem (e.g., self-esteem, achievement, independence). Finally, after meeting the deficiency needs, the need for self-actualization can be addressed.

Maslow believed subjective experience is central to psychology's subject matter, which implies that animal models are worth little for understanding human psychology, as are studies of group tendencies. Maslow felt psychology should be a future-oriented and applied enterprise, and research efforts

Abraham Maslow (1908–1970)

should focus on solving real human problems and expanding human potential.

Maslow's conception was clearly opposed to many aspects of behavioral and biological psychology seen as fundamental for establishing psychology as a true science. For example, Maslow and most other humanists would reject reductionistic attempts to study units smaller than a complete human being, or efforts to reduce human existence to elements such as the stimulus and response. Also anathema is the idea that a psychological science's goal involves prediction and *control* of human nature (e.g., Maslow, 1966). Indeed, Maslow's work to develop a "Third Force" in American psychology grew out of his dissatisfaction with behaviorism's dominance and its effect on psychology. For more background on the rise of the Third Force, see deCarvalho (1990).

Maslow's death in 1970 came on the eve of the APA's recognition of humanism, and it is unfortunate he did not live to see the fruits of his labor.

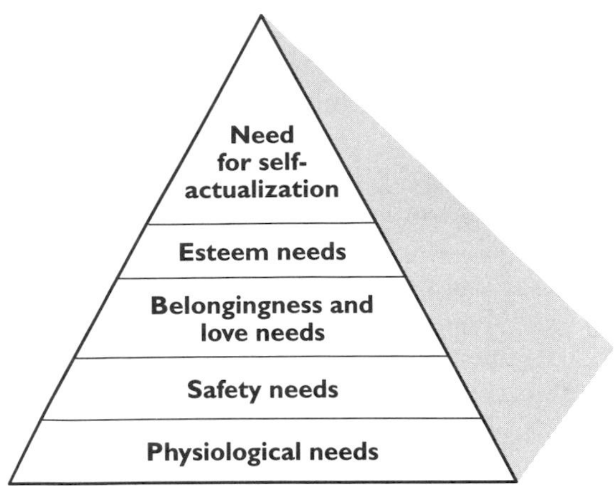

FIGURE 16.1 Maslow's need hierarchy

Source: Adapted from Maslow, 1943.

Maslow's demise was a serious blow to the humanistic movement, as neither of the leading candidates to fill his leadership role, Rollo May and Carl Rogers, had Maslow's impressive academic pedigree. Despite objections to Maslow's specific claims for a humanistic psychology, Maslow's early work in animal behavior and his connections to such scientific stalwarts as Thorndike, Wertheimer, and Harlow ensured that his opponents took him seriously.

Carl Rogers

Born in a Chicago suburb, in his teens **Carl Ransom Rogers** (1902–1987) moved with his family to a rural farming area. This background led to his first major in "scientific agriculture" (Rogers, 1967) at the University of Wisconsin, but Rogers's interests soon shifted to theology and history.

Rogers traveled to China as part of a student missionary group, and this trip combined with a hospitalization for an ulcer delayed his graduation until 1924. Next, he went to New York's Union Theological Seminary. Rogers (1967) later recalled that Leta Hollingworth's (Chapter 10) clinical psychology course at Columbia facilitated his shift from theology to clinical psychology.

In 1926, Rogers started work at the Institute of Child Guidance and began his education in psychology in earnest at the eclectic but psychodynamically oriented program at Columbia. After completing his Ed.D. from Teachers College, Rogers accepted a position at a guidance clinic in Rochester, New York. During the next several years, he developed an approach to psychotherapy based in part on variations of Otto Rank's (Chapter 15) techniques (deCarvalho, 1999).

In his first academic appointment, Rogers spent 5 years at The Ohio State University before moving to the University of Chicago. During the 1940s, Rogers's reputation grew quickly, and the psychoanalytic community began to view him as the most serious challenge to their control over American therapeutic practice (Gendlin, 1988). Rogers achieved this status mainly through conflicts with the medical community at Chicago, including disputes with the head of the psychology department, **James Grier Miller** (1916–2002). With both a psychology Ph.D. and an M.D. from Harvard, Miller was particularly noted for his contributions to systems theory—the idea that all things (e.g., cells, people, groups) can be viewed as systems of essential functions.

In 1951, Rogers published *Client-Centered Therapy,* which described his therapeutic approach. By the end of the 1950s, the client-centered (now called person-centered) treatment was being widely reviewed and discussed by both academics and practitioners. Rogers assumed each person has the capacity to become psychologically healthy and self-actualized, and people become maladjusted when they deny important parts of their personalities. Borrowing from Kierkegaard, he held that the goal of life is "to be the self which one truly is." He was also inspired by Kurt Goldstein, who coined the term *self-actualization* (deCarvalho, 1989). The emphasis on trusting the client led to a number of applications at the University of Chicago, which included student-centered educational approaches and providing therapy to children even when their parents did not participate. Virginia Axline (1947) discussed this latter application in *Play Therapy: The Inner Dynamics of Childhood.*

Client-centered therapy provides an accepting environment to which the therapist contributes congruence, unconditional positive regard, and empathic understanding. Congruence refers to genuineness by the therapist, who is willing to be

Carl Rogers (1902–1987)

transparent in the relationship—to express his or her feelings. Unconditional positive regard means the therapist respects the client as a unique individual and is willing to accept whatever the client says. Finally, the therapist displays empathic understanding by listening to what the client is attempting to communicate, particularly on the feeling level, and then sharing his or her understanding with the client. The therapist's acceptance of the client's feelings as worthwhile helps restore the client's self-confidence and self-image.

Rogers and his associates were instrumental in promoting the attitude that psychotherapy could be studied objectively. By taping therapy sessions and publishing complete transcriptions of the recordings, Rogers opened the doors of psychotherapeutic interventions and stimulated an enormous amount of research.

In 1956, Rogers was selected along with Wolfgang Köhler (Chapter 14) and Kenneth Spence (Chapter 13) to receive the first APA Distinguished Scientific Contribution Award. Rogers found this award profoundly moving, and he "was astonished that psychologists deeply and significantly regarded me as 'one of them'" (Rogers, 1967, p. 375). In 1957, Rogers returned to the University of Wisconsin, which proved as turbulent an environment as Chicago had been, because psychology's Third Force was still not well received by either of the first two. Rogers soon left academic psychology for California's greater tolerance. From 1964 on, his primary affiliation was with what is now La Jolla's Center for the Study of the Person.

Given Rogers's focus on inner feelings and experiences, his theories were particularly at odds with the emphasis on external behavior and the effects of the environment of B. F. Skinner (Chapter 13). In fact, the two men held friendly debates at different universities (e.g., Rice University; see Wann, 1964). Audiences generally perceived that Rogers and Skinner were not communicating in any fashion that could serve to reconcile their positions.

Rogers remained an active contributor to humanistic conceptions of therapy and to the Center until his death. Because of his lack of interest in renewing his ties with academic psychology, Rogers was a relatively ineffective leader of the humanistic movement following Maslow's death. With the 1961 publication of *On Becoming a Person,* Rogers secured his place as a spokesperson for the humanistic movement.

Although the humanistic movement never fully became a Third Force commensurate with behaviorism and psychoanalysis, it did enjoy a decade in the spotlight from the mid-1960s through the mid-1970s and continues to be an important voice in modern psychology. We will next consider some elements other than humanism that have shaped contemporary clinical psychology.

RECENT ADVANCES IN PSYCHOTHERAPY

Because of clinical psychology's connection to both academic psychology and the real-world problem of psychopathology, the influences on it have been diverse. We will conclude our overview by looking at connections with psychiatry and by surveying some signal events in the field's development.

Psychiatric Influences

Any history of clinical psychology's development in America should at least mention Lightner Witmer (Chapter 8) and **Morton Prince** (1854–1929). Witmer started the first psychological clinic, named the field (e.g., Witmer, 1907), and began an early journal—*The Psychological Clinic*—in 1907. Additionally, it was through Morris Viteles (Chapter 17), one of Witmer's students, that Prince also influenced industrial psychology and vocational guidance (McWhirter & McWhirter, 1997). Despite all these achievements, Witmer's interests diverged from the direction taken by clinical treatment "into the comparatively low-status school psychology and remedial education" (O'Donnell, 1979, p. 4). Although some historians of psychology have proclaimed Witmer the "father of clinical psychology" (e.g., McReynolds, 1996, 1997), Taylor (2000) has argued persuasively against such a designation: "Psychotherapy or, as it was originally called around the turn of the past century, *psychotherapeutics,* was an endeavor that Witmer clearly detested and actually knew very little about" (p. 1029, italics in the original). Taylor further argues that clinical psychology and related areas had roots in a psychotherapeutic alliance originating in French neurophysiology, which preceded psychoanalysis by several decades.

Prince founded the Harvard clinic in 1927 (which he deemed his "most meaningful accomplishment"; Marx, 1970), is considered modern psychotherapy's creator in America (Hilgard, 1987), and started the *Journal of Abnormal Psychology* in 1906. With connections to James, Pavlov (Chapter 12), Charcot, and Münsterberg (Chapter 10), Prince was an eclectic theorist with ideas on complexes, conflicts, repression, and symbols that predated Freud (Murray, 1956). His relative decline in importance following these early accomplishments resulted from his independence from Freudian psychoanalysis at a time when "libido theory" conquered psychiatry. Although both Witmer and Prince demonstrate the contributions of American "psychologists," many important developments occurred in psychiatry.

As we have suggested, the psychodynamic approach to clinical psychology was internationally the most influential technique until after World War II. Then as now, a psychodynamic procedure and the ability to prescribe drugs and such medical interventions as electroconvulsive shock and psychosurgery have been favored by the medical mental health community. As we noted in discussing Carl Rogers, the relationship between psychiatrists and clinical psychologists has not always been harmonious. However, psychiatrists and other physicians (e.g., neurosurgeons) have contributed substantially to psychology. In addition, psychiatry continues to be intimately connected to clinical psychology practice through such venues as its guide to diagnosis (discussed later) and drug therapy.

In Chapter 15, we noted that Benjamin Rush is considered the father of American psychiatry. Subsequently, **Harry Stack Sullivan** (1892–1949) was one of the important neo-Freudian psychiatrists responsible for shaping much of American clinical psychology's theory and practice. Sullivan never earned an undergraduate degree, received his M.D. from a school he described as a "diploma mill," and, except for a few months in 1939, did not hold an academic appointment. Unfortunately, Sullivan died from a cerebral hemorrhage before most of his major works were published. Among his posthumous publications, *The Psychiatric Interview* (Sullivan, 1954/1970) remains a primer in client-therapist interaction.

For Sullivan, therapy was an interpersonal process in which the clinical interview was crucial. In talking with clients, therapists needed a structured framework for their questions to ensure that they discovered the clients' patterns, living conditions, and salient experiences. Sullivan's approach established this framework, which many still consider essential for successful therapy.

Today, the psychiatric community tremendously influences all mental health professionals through its publication of the *Diagnostic and Statistical Manual (DSM),* currently in its 4th edition (American Psychiatric Association, 1994). The *DSM* is a catalog of identifiable mental disorders, and it provides a consistent language that mental health professionals use to communicate with each other and with the public about psychopathology. The *DSM* is also a guide to the diagnosis of, information about, and possible treatments for each of its recognized conditions.

All *DSM* editions have been organized around contemporary conceptions of the cause of mental illness. Early editions assumed more of a psychodynamic basis, whereas the current publication is slanted toward biological explanations. This schism over etiology has produced continuing tensions between many psychiatrists and psychologists.

Belief in biological explanations has led to a wide panoply of psychiatric medications, which are generally among the most commonly prescribed drugs in the United States. Currently popular are the tranquilizer Xanax and the antidepressant Prozac; a generation ago, the tranquilizers Valium and Librium topped the list of most frequently prescribed medications. Although we will not trace drug therapy's history, because of psychiatric influences new medications will continue to play an important role in treating a wide range of mental disorders.

Some of the most controversial statements about the nature of mental disorders have come from psychiatrists. For example, **Ronald D. Laing** (1927– 1989) described psychopathology as something occurring in a relationship, not in a person. From studying schizophrenics, Laing (1979) concluded schizophrenia is a method invented by the person to deal with an impossible situation. The schizophrenic is no longer able to maintain the false persona society requires, and his or her schizophrenic behavior is viewed as abnormal.

Hungarian-born **Thomas S. Szasz** (1920–) has also been controversial in his discussions of mental illness. Szasz came to America when he was 18 and earned his M.D. from the University of Cincinnati in 1944. He received training in psychiatry at the University of Chicago and in psychoanalysis at the Chicago Institute for Psychoanalysis.

Szasz's (1961/1974) thesis is contained in the title of his most famous work—*The Myth of Mental Illness.* Seen by many humanists as their most important statement, Szasz asserted that true illness is by definition biological and that the so-called mental illnesses either result from bodily illnesses with mental symptoms (e.g., the organic psychoses) or are not illnesses at all. Most of what psychologists and psychiatrists call mental illness Szasz labels "problems in living" with no connections to underlying physiological disturbance. Although most practitioners in both the medical and the psychological communities disagree with his exact thesis, Szasz's work continues to generate discussion and to stimulate research into psychotherapy's nature and practice.

The Growth of Clinical Psychology

By contrast, clinical psychologist David Shakow's work was less controversial but perhaps equally influential. Shakow is particularly known for his interest in schizophrenia. Our focus on David Shakow as a case study in American clinical psychology will permit us to examine changes that occurred in the 20th century, as well as recent advances. Shakow was both a clinician and a researcher, and he was active in the American Psychological Association from a time when clinicians were a small subset of psychologists into the period when clinicians came to dominate the APA.

David Shakow (1901–1981) was born on the Lower East Side of New York City. An early fascination with William James took him to Harvard, where he completed undergraduate courses with such figures as Floyd Allport (Chapter 17), Herbert Langfeld (Chapter 10), and William McDougall (Chapter 12). Following his undergraduate degree, Shakow took a job at the Worcester State Hospital with **Grace Kent** (1875–1973), who is best known for her collaborations with psychiatrist Aran Rosanoff in the early development of clinical diagnostic scales (e.g., Kent & Rosanoff, 1910).

In 1925, Shakow returned to Harvard for graduate training, which he took in the standard experimental psychology program, because the Harvard Psychological Clinic was not yet underway. Shakow's dissertation on subliminal perception under E. G. Boring (Chapter 1) proved so inconclusive Shakow was forced to take a job back at Worcester without completing his degree. Fourteen years later, after World War II, Shakow's dissertation on schizophrenia was accepted, and he finally received his Harvard Ph.D.

In 1946, Shakow accepted a faculty position at the University of Illinois Medical School, and in 1948, he added a psychology appointment at the University of Chicago. In the postwar years, Shakow was involved in clinical education matters, including work for the APA on the nature of clinical training and internship

Archives of the History of American Psychology – The University of Akron.

David Shakow (1901–1981)

programs. Specific activities included being an original member of APA's Board of Examiners in Professional Psychology, chairman of the APA's Committee on Training in Clinical Psychology, APA's representative to the World Federation of Mental Health, and president of APA's Division of Clinical Psychology.

After a suggestion in 1947 by Shakow's Committee on Training in Clinical Psychology, a formal recommendation was made in 1949, at a conference in Boulder, Colorado, that clinical psychologists should be trained first as psychologists—that is, scientists—and second as practicing clinicians. Thus, the **Boulder model** of clinical training views the modern clinical psychologist as both scientist and practitioner and serves as a guide in universities where this approach is adopted. Subsequent conferences have been held to explore clinical training issues further, including the 1973 meeting in Vail, Colorado. The Vail conference recognized professional clinical training (as distinct from training as a scientist-clinician) as an acceptable model. In programs devoted to training clinical practitioners, the terminal degree is the Psy.D., whereas the Ph.D. is preferred by programs that focus on developing new knowledge in psychology.

In the last 3 decades, programs awarding the Psy.D. degree and the number of degree recipients have grown dramatically, as indicated by statistics in the APA's *Monitor on Psychology* (Murray, 2000). Nearly 9,000 Psy.D.s had been awarded as of 2000, with approximately two-thirds of them given after 1992. "In fact, the number of Psy.D.s—whose programs stress practice more than research—has been increasing at the same time that Ph.D.s in clinical psychology have leveled off . . ." (p. 52). In response to the criticism that the Psy.D. is unscientific, Psy.D. pioneer Donald Peterson contends the degree is based in science, and degree recipients are trained to be "'local scientists' who apply the scientific method to problems in the field" (p. 54).

From 1954 until 1966, Shakow served as the National Institute of Mental Health's (NIMH) psychology laboratory director. As such, he was able to return to his research interest in schizophrenia. In 1966, Shakow retired from his administrative position to become an NIMH Senior Research Scientist. Among his many honors, he received the APA's 1975 Distinguished Scientific Contribution Award and the Distinguished Professional Contribution Award the next year.

Shakow's professional biography offers a snapshot of clinical psychology's evolution. His initial Harvard training was ill-suited to the practice of clinical psychology, despite his tuition by several major figures in the history of psychology (e.g., William McDougall, Floyd Allport, Morton Prince). When Shakow entered Harvard, an education into the symptoms, causes, and treatment of psychopathology was not available outside a medical school. In the years after World War II, Shakow played a vital role in creating standards for clinical training programs and for clinical research.

At the time of Shakow's entry and before his work within it, the APA was dominated by experimental psychologists (Chapter 10), who had little conception of how to oversee clinical practitioners. By the time of his death, the APA had changed dramatically, and clinical practitioners had become much more numerous than experimental researchers.

Shakow himself embodied what many graduate programs today try to encourage—the dual role of scientist and practitioner.

NEUROPSYCHOLOGY

Defined as "the study of the relation between brain function and behavior" (Kolb & Whishaw, 1996, p. 3), neuropsychology encompasses all behavioral neuroscience. Histories of the discipline often begin with the observations and speculations of the ancient Greeks, such as Alcmaeon, Hippocrates, Aristotle, and Galen. In other words, everything we have had to say about the brain and behavior in this book could be included under this broad definition of the term.

Because the term *neuropsychology* is actually a recent invention (Kolb & Whishaw, 1996), however, and Luria (1973, p. 16) calls neuropsychology "a new branch of science," we will adopt a definition and approach that limit our historical overview to approximately the last century. At the beginning of the 21st century, no one questions the brain as the organ of mind and consciousness. In order to understand fully the nature of mental events, many psychologists have considered it essential to understand the biological substrate. Because all behavior has a biological basis, clinical psychologists must be aware that a "mental" illness, or disorder, ultimately has its roots in the brain.

This undeniable connection between clinical psychology and **neuropsychology**—defined here as "the clinical and experimental field devoted to the study, understanding, assessment, and treatment of behaviors directly related to the function of the brain" (Golden, 1994, p. 478)—can be seen in the establishment of the first psychological laboratory in a mental hospital. According to Thomas (2003), the plan for such a laboratory originated with Edward Cowles, superintendent of McLean Hospital (a teaching facility associated with Harvard Medical School), and G. Stanley Hall (Chapter 10). S. I. Franz implemented the plan, and for this, as well as other reasons, he deserves to be considered the first modern experimental neuropsychologist, although sometimes this honor is accorded to his more famous student, Karl Lashley.

From Finger, Origins of Neuroscience (Oxford University Press, 1994).

Shepherd Ivory Franz (1874–1933)

Shepherd Ivory Franz

Born in Jersey City, New Jersey, **Shepherd Ivory Franz** (1874–1933) earned a B.A. in 1894 and a Ph.D. in psychology in 1899 from Columbia University. Franz's introduction to psychology came through reading William James's (Chapter 10) *Briefer Course* (Franz, 1932). While still an undergraduate, Franz began working with James McKeen Cattell (Chapter 10), who directed his doctoral dissertation. Although Franz spent a semester in 1896 in Wundt's (Chapter 8) laboratory, he considered that the training that led to his physiological study of brain function came from his first two postdoctoral positions, the first as assistant in physiology at Harvard Medical School (1899–1901) and the second as instructor in physiology at Dartmouth Medical School (1901–1904). At Harvard, Franz worked in Henry P. Bowditch's (Chapter 10) laboratory, the same laboratory in which G. Stanley Hall performed his dissertation experiments.

At Dartmouth, Franz published the research that led to his claim of being the first investigator to combine the physiologist's ablation method with the training methods—based on Thorndike's dissertation research—of the psychologist. Franz used the combination of these methods to investigate the frontal lobes in cats (Franz, 1902).

In 1904, Cowles employed Franz to establish a research laboratory at McLean Hospital, as we noted. At the beginning of 1907, Franz was hired for a similar purpose by Superintendent William A. White at the Government Hospital for the Insane in Washington, D.C., also known as St. Elizabeth's Hospital. Franz's tenure at St. Elizabeth's came to an abrupt end in 1924, with his resignation following a rancorous dispute with White (Thomas, 2003).

From St. Elizabeth's, Franz went to the University of California, Los Angeles (UCLA), where he soon became a professor and head of the psychology department. He held this position until his death from amyotrophic lateral sclerosis in 1933 (Thomas, 2003).

For much of his career, Franz used the training/ablation method to study brain function. Like Flourens (Chapter 7), Franz believed the recovery of functions initially lost after cerebral destruction argued against a fixed localization of function in the cortex. Ablation work with Karl Lashley in 1916 and Lashley's subsequent brain-ablation research further reinforced Franz's position.

Karl Spencer Lashley

Born in Davis, West Virginia, **Karl Spencer Lashley** (1890–1958) went to the University of West Virginia, planning to major in either English or Latin. As a freshman, Lashley discovered zoology through neurologist John Black Johnston. An encounter with a set of frog brain slides led to Lashley's decision to study behavior. Taking the slides to his instructor, Lashley naively proposed to work out all the connections, so "we should know how the frog worked" (Hebb, 1963, p. viii).

Lashley received his M.S. in bacteriology at the University of Pittsburgh and his introduction to psychology there through an experimental psychology course with Karl Dallenbach (Chapter 8), one of Edward Bradford Titchener's Ph.D.s. Lashley subsequently earned his Ph.D. in genetics with H. S. Jennings (Chapter 12) at Johns Hopkins University in 1914. At Hopkins, Lashley was influenced greatly by John Broadus Watson (Chapter 12), with whom he pursued a psychology minor. Lashley continued to work with Watson after he received his Ph.D., and their collaboration produced 14 articles (Bruce, 1986). During this period, Lashley also joined S. I. Franz on two studies of cortical ablations and learning in the rat, setting the stage for Lashley's research career.

From 1917 until 1926, Lashley worked at the University of Minnesota. He might have gone from there to Stanford, as Lewis Terman (Chapter 17) had asked for Lashley to be brought to California. Stanford's President Wilbur traveled to Minnesota to offer Lashley a position. Unfortunately, Lashley's nonconformist appearance—"long hair and pince-nez glasses, with a ribbon flowing in the breeze" (Hilgard, 1987, p. 429)—offended Wilbur, and Lashley was not invited to Stanford. Instead, Wilbur hired one of Lashley's Ph.D.s, **Calvin P. Stone** (1892–1954), who was the 1942 APA president. Harry Harlow (Chapter 14) was perhaps Stone's best-known student.

In 1926, Lashley went to the Institute for Juvenile Research in Chicago, where he began the experiments reported in *Brain Mechanisms and Intelligence* (Lashley, 1929/1963). From 1929 until 1935, Lashley was a professor at the University of Chicago.

From Chicago, Lashley went to Harvard, where he quickly became dissatisfied with what he perceived as excessive administrative work and insufficient research funds. He demanded and received a "roving" professorship, which allowed him to become the director of the Yerkes Laboratory of Primate Biology in Orange Park, Florida, the position from which he retired in 1955. Lashley died unexpectedly in 1958—the same year Watson died—while vacationing in France.

Lashley is often viewed as the quintessentially objective scientist, who sought truth in a disinterested manner and often found evidence that overturned others' theories as well as his own. In recent years, however, this picture has been disputed by historian Nadine Weidman (1994, 1999), who has characterized Lashley as a racist whose staunch belief in genetic determinism informed his science. Both Bruce (1998a, 1998b) and Dewsbury (2002b, 2002c) have taken issue with Weidman's portrayal, presenting

Karl Lashley (1890–1958) in the 1930s

alternative interpretations of the historical record, to which Weidman (1998, 2002) has responded. If for no other reason, the debate has been valuable for its focus on the historical record surrounding a leading figure in experimental neuropsychology.

Lashley's Search for the Engram

Lashley's search for the **engram** (memory trace; the location of specific memories) began with the "simple aim of demonstrating the soundness of Watson's ideas of . . . the formation of stimulus-response connections through the cortex" (Hebb, 1963, p. viii). Faced with conflicting evidence from studies in which he tested brain-damaged rats on a variety of problems, Lashley abandoned Watson's simplistic idea of stimulus-response connections across the cortex (Lashley, 1950). Note that this illustrates the importance of neuropsychological research for testing and constraining theories in psychology. Watson's telephone-switchboard S-R approach to memory formation in the brain seemed reasonable until Lashley's research revealed its implausibility. Lashley's search for the engram also led to his best-known concepts: mass action and equipotentiality.

By **mass action,** Lashley meant that the amount of cortical tissue destroyed is more important for complex learning than the tissue's location. The greater the area destroyed, the greater the negative effect on learning. "Complex learning" is the key phrase—mass action is true for learning involving many different cues and motor responses (as in a maze) and correspondingly many different cortical areas.

By **equipotentiality,** Lashley meant that any part of a functional area could carry out a particular function. Within an area, the parts are equal in their potential to mediate the function. Loss of the function requires ablation of the entire area; sparing of any part allows the function to be displayed. Lashley (1929/1963) suggested that equipotentiality held only for the so-called cortical association areas (cortical areas neither primarily sensory nor primarily motor) and for relatively complex functions such as maze learning.

Lashley did not deny the possibility of cortical localization of simple functions such as brightness discrimination. In the rat, lesions of the posterior cortex disrupt brightness discrimination, whereas anterior cortical lesions have no effect. Lashley's equipotentiality and mass action held for complex learning involving many sensory cues.

Toward the end of his famous paper "In Search of the Engram," Lashley (1950) wrote, somewhat facetiously, "I sometimes feel, in reviewing the evidence on the localization of the memory trace, that the necessary conclusion is that learning is just not possible" (pp. 477–478). He reluctantly assigned the memory trace to cortical sensory areas, concluding that "the memory trace is located in all parts of the functional area; that various parts are equipotential for its maintenance and activation" (p. 469).

Lashley's inability to locate the memory trace definitively stimulated the career of **Robert Thompson** (1927–1989), a research assistant at the Yerkes Laboratory for a year during Lashley's tenure. Thompson thought that by concentrating on the cortex Lashley may have been looking in the wrong place for the engram; perhaps Lashley (1950) had dismissed subcortical areas prematurely.

Thompson received his Ph.D. in 1955 from the University of Texas, where he and fellow graduate student **James V. McConnell** (1925–1990) became the first modern researchers to classically condition the planarian, or flatworm (Thompson & McConnell, 1955). McConnell's career included controversial memory transfer research, the APA's Distinguished Teaching Award, and a lighthearted journal called the *Worm Runner's Digest* (Sommer, 1991).

Thompson began his search for the engram by adopting Wilder Penfield's (Chapter 7) idea of a collection of subcortical structures that coordinates and integrates the activities of the cerebral hemispheres—the **centrencephalic system** (e.g., Penfield, 1958). Penfield attributed to the system many of the qualities Descartes (Chapter 4) claimed for the pineal gland. For example, Penfield (1952) believed that if a person wants to perform a particular action, the centrencephalic system directs impulses to the cortical area that stores the action's instructions.

Using carefully placed lesions, Thompson and his associates amassed evidence for a set of rat brain structures involved either in the retention of preoperatively acquired tasks or in the postoperative learning of such tasks. Thompson's memory studies culminated in *A Behavioral Atlas of the Rat Brain* (Thompson, 1978); his learning work led to the posthumously published *Brain Mechanisms in Problem Solving and Intelligence: A Lesion Survey of the Rat Brain* (Thompson, Crinella, & Yu, 1990). Thompson (1993) gives a final summary of his centrencephalic system.

Thus, Thompson essentially succeeded where Lashley failed, as indicated by Jan Bures of the Czechoslovak Academy of Sciences. In a 1986 letter, Bures wrote, "[Robert Thompson] is a true heir of Karl Lashley" (cited in Thorne, 1995, p. 129).

Lashley's Influence

Several of Lashley's students characterized him as a poor classroom teacher (e.g., Beach, 1974; Hebb, 1980). For example, Beach wrote, "By any usual standard Lashley was a poor if not an atrocious classroom lecturer" (p. 39). Beach (1961) thought Lashley's failure as a teacher probably stemmed from his attitude toward teaching: "It was Lashley's professed philosophy that trying to teach people is useless, 'Those who need to be taught can't learn, and those who can learn don't need to be taught' " (p. 182). Compare this philosophy with Kant's similar thoughts on pedagogy (Chapter 6).

According to Hebb (1959), Lashley was much more effective in the laboratory and interacting with small groups. His influence in psychology came mainly through his publications and his many graduate students. This influence was not always positive, however. By appearing to characterize the brain as a relatively homogeneous structure in whose parts the principle of equipotentiality reigned, Lashley's (1929/1963) *Brain Mechanisms and Intelligence* dampened interest in "physiologizing"—giving neurophysiological explanations of behavioral events (e.g., Hebb). Despite this negative impact, Orbach (1982) dated modern experimental physiological psychology from the book's publication. From about 1930 until 1950, theoretical psychology concerned itself with the behavioral aspects of learning (i.e., the work of the neobehaviorists we presented in Chapter 13), avoiding speculation on the neural basis of learning. Ironically, such speculation was rekindled by one of Lashley's students, D. O. Hebb.

Born in Chester, Nova Scotia, **Donald Olding Hebb** (1904–1985) received a B.A. from Dalhousie University, planning to be a novelist. Because a novelist needs to know something about psychology, Hebb went to McGill University as a part-time graduate student in psychology, where he worked with two Pavlov-trained scientists, Boris P. Babkin and Leonid Andreyev. When Hebb became disenchanted with Pavlov, Babkin urged him to study with Lashley at Harvard in 1936. From 1937 to 1939, Hebb worked with neurosurgeon Wilder Penfield. At Lashley's invitation, Hebb spent 5 years (1942–1947) at the Yerkes laboratory, and in 1949 he published his most famous book, *The Organization of Behavior.*

In *The Organization of Behavior,* Hebb developed hypothetical neural mechanisms such as the *cell assembly*—a circuit of neurons activated by a particular stimulus. Hebb used these mechanisms to account for a wide array of behavior, including perceptual phenomena such as reversible images, inverted images, and closure; learning phenomena such as all-or-none learning and insight; motivation; attention; forgetting;

sleep; and emotional disturbance. Because of this inclusiveness, Hebb's book was still being cited 30 years later to support the work of various authors writing on diverse topics (e.g., sensation and perception, emotion, motivation, cognitive science, physiological psychology) in Hearst's (1979) book, *The First Century of Experimental Psychology*. In fact, present-day theorists interested in machine learning (see Chapter 18) consider Hebb's contributions so important that one element of machine learning is called the "Hebbian Rule" (Rumelhart, McClelland, & the PDP Research Group, 1986). This rule is an equation that predicts the learning rate given the number and strength of neural connections.

Lashley's opinion of Hebb's book was ambivalent at best. In a letter to Hebb, Lashley admitted he was unconvinced by Hebb's arguments but ended by writing, "Hearty congratulations on an outstanding achievement" (cited in Glickman, 1996, p. 237). On the other hand, Mark Rosenzweig, a student in Hebb's Harvard seminar in the summer of 1947, remembered "Lashley saying that the ideas in the book were garbled versions of his (Lashley's) that Hebb had misunderstood" (Glickman, p. 237).

Hebb returned to McGill in 1947 and became head of the psychology department the following year. He spent the rest of his career at McGill, serving as the university chancellor from 1970 through 1974. Among his many honors, Hebb was one of the few non-American APA presidents (1960), and he received the gold medal of the American Psychological Foundation for his contributions to psychology.

One of Lashley's Chicago Ph.D.s, **Frank A. Beach** (1911–1988) was another experimental neuropsychologist influenced by Lashley, whom he described as "one of the great psychologists of our time," as an "*eminent psychologist with no earned degree in psychology*," a "*famous theorist who specialized in disproving theories, including his own*," and an "*inspiring teacher who described all teaching as useless*" (Beach, 1961, p. 163, italics in the original). In contrast to his mentor, Beach has been described as a "master teacher," and in 1986, he received the American Psychological Foundation's Award for Distinguished Teaching in Biopsychology (Dewsbury, 2000a). In a classic paper, Beach (1950) chided comparative psychology for its overemphasis on the behavior of only a few species, particularly the white rat. For the most part, his target audience has ignored the message. Beach is best known for his work in human and animal sexual behavior (see Beach, 1985).

Lashley also influenced people other than Robert Thompson who did not take degrees with him. For example, Lashley was one of two men to whom Clifford T. Morgan (mentioned in Chapter 10), a Harvard instructor during Lashley's tenure there, dedicated his 1943 book, *Physiological Psychology*. Also, at Orange Park, Florida, Lashley had such an influence on the practicing neurosurgeon **Karl Pribram** (1919–) that Pribram abandoned his medical practice for an academic career in experimental neuropsychology. Pribram (1985) wrote, "Lashley taught me the techniques of experimental psychology, a field of inquiry I did not know existed" (p. 67). In addition to contributing many studies to the experimental neuropsychology literature, Pribram has been a theorist of brain function in the Hebbian mold. Pribram's theories have been expounded in major reviews (e.g., Pribram, 1960) and books (e.g., Miller, Galanter, & Pribram, 1960; Pribram, 1971), and he remains a leader in the field.

Of all the persons influenced by Karl Lashley, perhaps the most important was Roger Sperry, cowinner of the 1981 Nobel Prize for medicine or physiology. Born in Hartford, Connecticut, **Roger Wolcott Sperry** (1913–1994) received his A.B. in English and an M.A. in psychology from Oberlin College, followed by a Ph.D. in zoology from the University of Chicago in 1941. From Chicago, Sperry went to Harvard to work with Lashley as a postdoctoral student and then followed Lashley to the Yerkes Laboratory in Florida, where he interacted with Lashley students including Hebb, Beach, and Pribram. The research methodologies and surgical techniques Sperry acquired at Orange Park greatly benefited his later research program (Puente, 2000).

From 1946 to 1952, Sperry was an assistant professor in the department of anatomy at the University of Chicago. When denied tenure in that department, Sperry served for a year as a section chief of the Institute of Neurological Diseases and Blindness at the National Institutes of Health. At the same time, he also accepted a position as an associate professor of psychology at the University of Chicago. In 1954,

AP/Wide World Photos.

Roger Sperry (1913–1994) receiving the Nobel Prize from King Gustaf XVI (right) in Stockholm

Sperry moved to the California Institute of Technology, where he was Hixon professor of psychology until his retirement in 1984. Sperry's many awards included the Karl Lashley Award of the American Philosophical Society in 1976.

In Chapter 7, we noted Gustav Fechner's prediction of dual consciousness if the brain's major interconnecting structure, the corpus callosum, were cut. The work for which Sperry received the Nobel Prize essentially tested Fechner's prediction.

Working with cats whose corpus callosum and optic chiasm (a structure beneath the brain where the two optic nerves come together and some fiber crossing occurs) had been cut, Myers and Sperry (1953) found the animals functioned as though they had two independent brains. For example, the left hemisphere could learn a problem requiring a solution diametrically opposed to a problem learned by the right hemisphere. After studies of the **split-brain operation** in animals revealed little mental impairment, surgeons P. J. Vogel and J. E. Bogen of the California College of Medicine tried the operation on humans with uncontrollable epilepsy, hoping the surgery would reduce the intensity of the patients' seizures by limiting them to one hemisphere. The operation proved quite beneficial, and many patients never had another seizure. Beginning with the first patient in 1961, Sperry and various associates, particularly Michael S. Gazzaniga, studied the patients postoperatively to see if the animal findings generalized to humans.

Under ordinary circumstances, the surgical patients appeared normal, but sophisticated testing procedures revealed striking differences in the abilities of the two hemispheres. According to Sperry (1982), the left hemisphere's specialties tend to be verbal, mathematical, and sequential, and because of its language capacity, the left hemisphere is sometimes called the "dominant" hemisphere. The mute right hemisphere typically specializes in spatial and imagistic ability, the kind in which "a picture is worth a thousand words." Block design and map reading are tasks at which the right hemisphere excels.

Concerning Fechner's prediction of separate consciousness from splitting the brain, Gazzaniga (1967) wrote, "All the evidence indicates that separation of the hemispheres creates two independent spheres of consciousness within a single cranium. . . . This conclusion is disturbing to some people who view consciousness as an indivisible property of the human brain" (p. 374).

The work of Sperry and his associates has brought us to the present time, where we find that experimental neuropsychology has particularly benefited from advances in technology. For example, the combination of nuclear physics, computer technology, and medicine has given us new methods for studying the anatomy and function of the living brain. First came computerized axial tomography (CT or CAT), which has been replaced almost completely by magnetic resonance imaging (MRI; Barnes, 1988). MRI has higher powers of resolution than CT, and neuropsychological researchers are using MRI to try to develop an index that will allow them to detect brain abnormalities with better than 90% accuracy. If accomplished, this will undoubtedly revolutionize the diagnosis of at least some types of mental illness.

Although CT and MRI are excellent for detecting structural abnormalities in the brain, positron emission tomography (PET) is used to study the metabolic activity of the living brain. For example, with PET, researchers can actually visualize the brain areas most active during panic attacks, when a person is performing mental arithmetic, or when someone diagnosed with schizophrenia is hallucinating.

MRI technology can be modified to provide a picture of metabolic activity in the brain and thus to reveal which brain areas are most active when a person is performing a particular function. The resulting procedure is called functional MRI (fMRI), and one advantage of fMRI scans over PET scans is that they have greater resolution, so they present more detailed information. The new technology we have outlined is making it possible for experimental neuropsychologists to solve the problems of functional localization that first intrigued scientists from Gall and Flourens in the 19th century to Lashley and his students and associates in the 20th century.

Building on this foundation in experimental neuropsychology, we will now examine the history of clinical neuropsychology. This is the branch of neuropsychology concerned with the assessment and treatment of neurological disorders typically caused by such disease processes as tumors or strokes or by accidental damage to the brain. Early contributors to the knowledge base of clinical neuropsychology include many of the people discussed in Chapter 7, such as Franz Joseph Gall with the creation of phrenology, Pierre Paul Broca with the discovery of Broca's area, Carl Wernicke with the study of Wernicke's area, John Hughlings Jackson with his work with epileptic patients, and Roberts Bartholow with his electrical stimulation of Mary Rafferty's brain. Dr. John Harlow's study of accident victim Phineas P. Gage is another important early contribution to clinical neuropsychology. In modern times, A. R. Luria is considered one of the discipline's founders (e.g., Cole, 1997; Zinchenko, 1997).

Alexander Romanovich Luria

Alexander Romanovich Luria (1902–1977) was a physician's son, born in Kazan, a Russian university town east of Moscow. Luria attended the town's university, earning a degree in the humanities in 1921, at which time he began working in psychology. Recognizing the importance of preparation in the natural sciences for his career in psychology, Luria began studying medicine at Kazan University, eventually completing his medical training at the First Moscow Medical School in 1936.

In 1923, Luria began to work at the Institute of Psychology of Moscow University. A year later, he met Lev Vygotsky (Chapter 18), "who was to become a decisive influence in all of [his] later life" (Luria, 1974, p. 254). Luria and Vygotsky, along with A. N. Leont'ev (sometimes Leontiev), set out to develop an approach to psychology emphasizing maturational processes and cultural-historical influences on adult psychological functions. Their approach also strongly emphasized the role of language. In 1931, the three men founded the Center of Psychology of the Ukrainian Psychoneurological Academy.

According to an autobiographical essay, Luria (1974) moved into clinical neuropsychology in 1936, creating the Laboratory of Neuropsychology in the Institute of Neurosurgery. There, he developed methods for studying the effects of localized brain damage, which proved essential for his work with people who had suffered traumatic brain injury during World War II. Luria continued this work for the rest of his life, except for a period in the 1950s when he was removed from the Institute of Neurosurgery as a result of anti-Semitic pressure.

Luria's honors included election as a foreign member to the American Academy of Arts and Sciences (1966), to the American Pedagogical Academy (1967), and to the National Academy of Sciences (1968). His empirical and theoretical contributions to neuropsychology particularly involved understanding the effects of frontal lobe damage and of damage to the left hemisphere language areas of the brain.

Luria's Model of Cortical Function

Luria (1970) conceptualized the brain as divided into three blocks, the first of which determines the state of alertness of the cortex. The reticular formation is particularly involved in this function. The second block consists of the posterior parts of the cortex (the parietal, occipital, and temporal lobes) and can be thought of as the sensory unit, as specific areas in it are responsible for receiving and analyzing visual, auditory, kinesthetic, and cutaneous stimuli. The third block, comprising the anterior cortex (the frontal lobes), is the motor unit. The motor unit formulates intentions to act and carries out these intentions through programs of behavior.

Courtesy Michael Cole.

A. R. Luria (1902–1977) with Karl Pribram (right)

Each of the cortical blocks is further divided into three zones arranged hierarchically. In the posterior cortical sensory unit, sensory information first enters the primary zone, is further developed in the secondary zone, and then is integrated in the tertiary zone. For a response to the sensory input, activation travels from the tertiary sensory zone to the tertiary motor zone in the frontal cortex, then to the secondary motor zone, and from there to the primary motor zone for the beginning of the response.

In developing his theory, Luria made three basic assumptions: serial processing of information by the brain, hierarchical processing, and unity of perception. As Kolb and Whishaw (1996) indicated, Luria's theory used known cortical organization to simply and elegantly explain his clinical observations. More recent findings, however, have questioned Luria's basic assumptions. For example, all cortical areas do not appear to be linked serially, which is required by hierarchical serial processing. Further, because no single area receives input from all other areas, it is difficult to see exactly where unity of perception would occur as Luria envisioned it.

As more has been learned about the organization and functioning of the cortex, Luria's simple model of cortical processing has given way to more complicated models (e.g., Felleman & van Essen, 1991). Luria's neurological assessment method has suffered a kinder fate, however, in its extended life as the Luria-Nebraska Neuropsychological Battery.

Neuropsychological Assessment

Before the advent of modern neuroimaging methods, such as CT and MRI, neuropsychological evaluation methods were developed to aid in localizing brain damage, as well as in assessing cognitive abilities. Now that it is easy to establish the anatomical locus of damage definitively with neuroimaging, the focus of neuropsychological assessment is on establishing current functioning ability, along with residual capacities, which can then be used to plan and tailor rehabilitation.

Developed in the context of his work with brain-injured patients, Luria's assessment procedures relied heavily on clinical judgments by the examiner and stressed qualitative factors rather than standardized and quantified ones. Because of this focus, American practitioners did not initially accept his testing procedures. Charles J. Golden (1978) organized Luria's approach into a standardized test, however, which subsequently became known as the Luria-Nebraska Neuropsychological Battery (Golden, Hammeke, & Purisch, 1980).

The Luria-Nebraska test consists of 269 items, which comprise 14 scales. The neuropsychological functions it measures include motor functions, visual functions, receptive and expressive speech, reading skills, arithmetical skills, and memory. The testing time averages more than 2 hours.

The Luria-Nebraska test illustrates the fixed-battery approach to neuropsychological assessment, because the test items are administered in a set order. Currently, there are two major fixed-battery tests, the Luria-Nebraska and the Halstead-Reitan Neuropsychological Test Battery (Reitan & Wolfson, 1985), although recently a fixed-battery instrument has been developed for use with elderly patients (Mayo Cognitive Factor Scales; Ivnik, Smith, Malec, Kokmen, & Tangalos, 1994). Of the two major tests, the Halstead-Reitan is the most widely used (Tsushima, 1994). Advantages of fixed-battery tests include their comprehensiveness and standardization; disadvantages include the length of administration time and their inflexibility (Vanderploeg, 1994).

Both of these disadvantages are overcome with the flexible-battery approaches to neuropsychological assessment. As a consequence, there are many flexible-battery tests (e.g., see Spreen & Strauss, 1998), and their use is increasing relative to fixed-battery tests (Sweet, Moberg, & Westergaard, 1996). Unfortunately, flexible battery procedures have disadvantages of their own. For example, such tests are not standardized across patients or facilities, and they may fail to identify specific deficits if the particular battery administered does not specifically target them.

CONCLUSIONS

Modern clinical psychology has often tried to dissociate itself from Freud. For example, one currently popular approach to therapy, Albert Ellis's and Aaron Beck's cognitive-behavioral paradigm, has more salient connections to neobehaviorism (Chapter 13) and to cognitive psychology than it does to Freud's system.

Although historians may attribute the shape of modern psychology to Wundt, James, or perhaps Watson, the aura and impact of Freud remain with us. Ask any introductory psychology student to name a psychologist, and the response is likely to be "Freud." Perhaps too often these days Freud's seminal role in such areas as development, personality, and abnormal psychology is minimized. Clinical psychology—Freud's legacy—continues to be the most popular and attractive subdiscipline for undergraduate and graduate students alike.

Because of the dynamic nature of our world, the development of psychoanalysis did not end with Freud, as the work of such neo-Freudians as Adler and Jung demonstrates. Further developments came in World War II, which provided a fertile ground for existentialism, and subsequently a more humanistic approach to psychotherapy grew in popularity. In America, during the last 75 years or so, clinical psychology has gone from nonexistence to its place of eminence among psychology's subdisciplines.

Considered a subdivision of clinical psychology, neuropsychology is a relatively new discipline. Defined broadly as the study of the brain and behavior, neuropsychology encompasses virtually all that neuroscientists have learned from many disciplines in the past centuries. In our narrow view of the field, we traced the development of experimental neuropsychology through the career of its founder, S. I. Franz, and particularly through the activities and influence of Franz's most famous student, Karl Lashley. Lashley's endeavors first stimulated and then depressed behavioral neuroscience until its renaissance through the writings of one of his students, D. O. Hebb.

The beginning of clinical neuropsychology and some of the accomplishments in the field were traced through the career of the famous Russian psychologist, A. R. Luria. Recent advances in imaging technology, such as CT, PET, and fMRI will facilitate both the clinical neuropsychology and the experimental neuropsychology of tomorrow. These techniques have set the stage for the definitive localization of functions in the human brain, which has been the goal of most of the brain's investigators for the last 2 centuries.

SUMMARY

This chapter surveyed developments in personality theory and psychotherapy that originated in, but went beyond, Freud's system. Important connections between clinical psychology and the psychiatric community were also explored, along with the beginnings of neuropsychology.

Existential and Humanistic Approaches to Clinical Psychology

Two existential philosophy themes important to psychology are that subjective meaning should be psychology's central focus and that humans have the freedom to make choices for which they should be prepared to take responsibility. The idea of choice represents a resistance to reductionistic and deterministic accounts of human behavior.

Jean-Paul Sartre and Albert Camus were two existentialists whose writings influenced philosophy, psychology, and the general public. Martin Heidegger's philosophy included the idea of humanity as *Dasein*, German for "being there." For Heidegger, the human effort to create a worthwhile existence leads to an authentic life, whereas giving up the ability to make decisions leads to an inauthentic life. Medard Boss and

Ludwig Binswanger developed *Daseinanalysis*, a psychotherapy based on Heidegger's philosophy. Karl Jaspers and Viktor Frankl developed additional existential psychotherapies.

Maurice Merleau-Ponty's primary influence on psychology came through his development of a scientifically respectable approach to a phenomenological experimental psychology. Martin Buber wrote the classic existential analysis of language, and Rollo May provided the first exposure of most American psychologists to Kierkegaard's existential ideas. May's contemporaries, George Kelly and Julian Rotter, further illustrate the increasingly humanistic nature of American clinical and social psychology during and after World War II.

Charlotte Bühler's work anticipated Erik Erikson's lifespan developmental approach and focused on the humanistic psychology movement that Abraham Maslow called the Third Force. Maslow is perhaps best remembered for his human need hierarchy.

Carl Rogers developed a client-centered psychotherapy in which the therapist provides an accepting environment to which he or she contributes congruence, unconditional positive regard, and empathic understanding.

Recent Advances in Psychotherapy

Psychiatric influences on clinical psychology include the work of Harry Stack Sullivan, the American Psychiatric Association's *Diagnostic and Statistical Manual*, and the controversial statements of Ronald D. Laing and Thomas Szasz.

David Shakow's career traces clinical psychology's evolution in America. Shakow was instrumental in creating standards for clinical training programs (e.g., the Boulder model) and for clinical research. As such, he exemplified the dual role of scientist and practitioner.

Neuropsychology

Depending on how it is defined, one can view neuropsychology as either all neuroscience throughout history, or as a relatively recent invention, encompassing perhaps the last century. Modern experimental neuropsychology can be said to have begun with the work of S. I. Franz, who combined the physiologist's ablation method with the training methods of the psychologist. Franz's student, Karl Lashley, further developed experimental neuropsychology through his research and his influence on people such as D. O. Hebb, Frank Beach, Karl Pribram, and Nobel Prize–winner Roger Sperry. Sperry's work included the study of humans who had had a split-brain operation to treat epilepsy. Both experimental and clinical neuropsychology have benefitted and will continue to benefit from recently invented brain-imaging techniques such as CT, PET, and fMRI.

A. R. Luria was one of the foremost founders of modern clinical neuropsychology. A Russian psychologist, Luria studied clinical patients with brain damage resulting from a variety of causes. Based on his clinical work, Luria developed a simple model of cortical function that has been superseded by more complex models. His neurological assessment methods are still widely used.

CONNECTIONS QUESTIONS

1. What connections can you make between the rise of existential approaches to philosophy and psychology and World War II?
2. How is Freud connected to the various existential and humanistic approaches to psychology?
3. What is the connection between Heidegger and *Daseinanalysis*?
4. Connect David Shakow's career in psychology with the evolution of clinical psychology in America.
5. Connect A. R. Luria with as many 19th-century neuroscientists as you can in terms of methodology and findings.
6. How is Karl Lashley connected to French brain researcher Pierre Flourens in terms of methodology and findings?

KEY NAMES AND TERMS

Frank A. Beach (p. 477)
being-in-the-world (p. 463)
Henri Bergson (p. 461)
Ludwig Binswanger (p. 463)
Medard Boss (p. 463)
Boulder model (p. 472)
Martin Buber (p. 465)
Charlotte B. Bühler (p. 466)
Albert Camus (p. 461)
centrencephalic system (p. 476)
client-centered therapy (p. 468)
***Dasein* (p. 462)**

Daseinanalysis (p. 463)
Simone de Beauvoir (p. 461)
engram (p. 475)
equipotentiality (p. 475)
Viktor Frankl (p. 464)
Shepherd Ivory Franz (p. 473)
Donald Olding Hebb (p. 476)
Martin Heidegger (p. 462)
Karl Jaspers (p. 463)
George A. Kelly (p. 465)
Grace Kent (p. 471)
Ronald D. Laing (p. 471)
Karl Spencer Lashley (p. 474)
logotherapy (p. 464)
Alexander Romanovich Luria (p. 479)
Abraham Maslow (p. 467)
mass action (p. 475)
Rollo May (p. 465)
James V. McConnell (p. 476)
Maurice Merleau-Ponty (p. 464)
James Grier Miller (p. 468)
need hierarchy (p. 467)
neuropsychology (p. 473)
personal construct (p. 466)
Karl Pribram (p. 477)
Morton Prince (p. 470)
Carl Ransom Rogers (p. 468)
Julian Rotter (p. 465)
Jean-Paul Sartre (p. 460)
David Shakow (p. 471)
Roger Wolcott Sperry (p. 477)
split-brain operation (p. 478)
Calvin P. Stone (p. 474)
Harry Stack Sullivan (p. 470)
Thomas S. Szasz (p. 471)
Third Force (p. 466)
Robert Thompson (p. 475)

SUGGESTED READINGS

Frankl, V. E. (1959). *Man's search for meaning.* Boston: Beacon Press. (Original work published in 1946) The original German edition was published in 1946 as *Ein Psycholog erlebt das Konzentrationslager.* In English translation, *Man's Search for Meaning* is available as a paperback and has been a long-standing international best seller. Short and readable, this volume is actually two different books. The first is a vivid account of Frankl's personal experiences in the Nazi death camps, and the second is an outline of the existential therapy (logotherapy) Frankl derived from his survival of the Holocaust. This is a book everyone should read.

Ihde, D. (1979). *Experimental phenomenology.* New York: Paragon Books. This is a delightful little book filled with several simple experiments designed to illustrate basic concepts in phenomenology. These thought-provoking exercises nicely demonstrate some of the methodology used by modern-day phenomenological psychologists.

Luria, A. R. (1973). *The working brain: An introduction to neuropsychology.* New York: BasicBooks. This is an excellent introduction to neuropsychology and to the work of one of its founders, A. R. Luria.

Rogers, C. R. (1961). *On becoming a person.* Boston: Houghton Mifflin. With this book, Rogers became one of the major voices in the humanistic movement. *On Becoming a Person* presented a perspective of psychology's Third Force that proved both popular and influential.

Sartre, J.-P. (1947). *Huis Clos [No exit].* Paris: Gallimard. Published in French as *Huis Clos, No Exit* is a short, intensely psychological play that appears in almost any anthology of Sartre's work or any collection of modern drama. Without divulging the plot, we can say that the key line is "Hell is—other people"; in other words, the story is an eye-opener.

Schmidt, J. (1985). *Maurice Merleau-Ponty: Between phenomenology and structuralism.* New York: St. Martin's Press. With only a small amount of biographical information on Merleau-Ponty, this book is rich in its consideration of his thought and work. It is an important work for anyone interested in the origins of existential-phenomenology as a methodology for psychology.

Szasz, T. (1974). *The myth of mental illness* (Rev. ed.). New York: Harper & Row. (Original work published 1961) Szasz's book challenges many of our basic conceptions about psychopathology and the practice of "mental health" professionals. *The Myth* remains standard reading for first-year graduate students in many clinical psychology programs.

Weidman, N. M. (1999). *Constructing scientific psychology: Karl Lashley's mind-brain debates.* Cambridge: Cambridge University Press. Based on Weidman's dissertation research, this is a good overview of the life and work of Karl Lashley. Note that Weidman's theme for Lashley's research may or may not be a valid interpretation. Before drawing your own conclusions, it would be worthwhile to read the rebuttals of Bruce and Dewsbury, as cited in the chapter.

Applied Psychology

CHAPTER 17

Solomon Asch
David Wechsler
Cyril Burt
Muzafer Sherif
Lewis Terman
William Stern
Gordon Allport
Charles Spearman
Gardner Murphy
Herbert Goddard
Alfred Binet
Anne Anastasi
Floyd Allport

1850 1860 1870 1880 1890 1900 1910 1920

Melville's *Moby Dick* is published

U. S. Grant, subsequently president, is a hero of the Civil War

Dostoevsky's *Brothers Karamazov* is published

Basketball is invented by James Naismith

Hawaii becomes a United States Territory

Mark Twain dies

Wundt dies

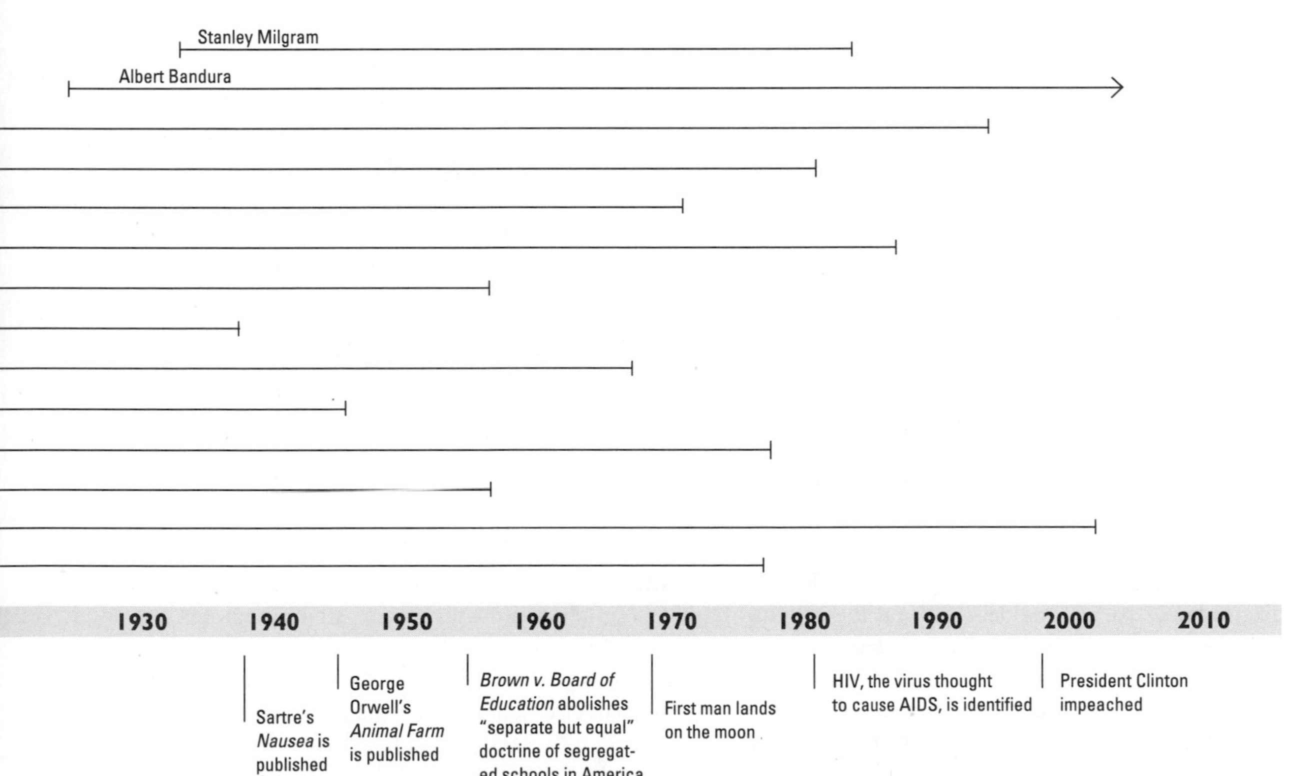

Stanley Milgram
Albert Bandura
1930
1940
1950
1960
1970
1980
1990
2000
2010
Sartre's *Nausea* is published
George Orwell's *Animal Farm* is published
Brown v. Board of Education abolishes "separate but equal" doctrine of segregated schools in America
First man lands on the moon
HIV, the virus thought to cause AIDS, is identified
President Clinton impeached

In this chapter, we continue our overview of psychological topics that either are outside the scope of or followed the decline of the major systems of psychology. In Chapter 16, we examined 20th-century advances in one domain of applied psychology–clinical practice. This chapter's theme is psychometrics and some of psychology's more socially relevant applications. Although we have focused on areas of applied psychology such as intelligence testing, psychometrics, social psychology, and industrial psychology, we do not mean to imply that these areas represent all the topics in applied psychology. Some of the other topics we might have chosen include forensic psychology, educational psychology, health psychology, and environmental psychology. Thus, the areas we have selected and the people we have highlighted should be viewed as representative of applied psychology rather than as an exhaustive catalog.

In modern psychology, the term **psychometrics**—literally, measuring the mind—is sometimes used synonymously with *statistics* and *methodology*, although it is perhaps better defined as the measurement of mental processes through psychological tests. The most celebrated example of psychometrics and the application of psychological ideas to the "real world" is undoubtedly intelligence testing.

INTELLIGENCE TESTING

A number of historians (e.g., Doyle, 1974) have argued that psychological testing began over 4,000 years ago in China, where civil service candidates were given batteries of exams. However, as Yang and Sternberg (1997) noted, ancient Chinese conceptions of intelligence differed markedly from our currently held ideas. In the West, reflections on why one person seems more intelligent than another can be traced back as far as the Greeks (Chapter 2). For example, Socrates was concerned with issues we would recognize today as part of the debate about the origins of intelligence (Chapter 9). Plato's *Republic* touches on such practical matters as how a society should handle the intellectual variation of its citizens. Subsequently, Aristotle's thoughts about the nature, origin, and organization of intelligence were explored by both Christian and Islamic scholars throughout the Middle Ages (Chapter 3). Although Bondy (1974) identified several forerunners of psychological testing during the Renaissance and early Modern period, scientific (or pseudoscientific) advances in measurement laid the foundation for contemporary ideas.

For example, although Gall's phrenological work (Chapter 7) was scientifically bankrupt, it did involve an initial attempt to measure various mental faculties, including intelligence. From that point on, such "scientific" measurements were assumed to be potentially applicable to business and industry.

In Chapter 9, we examined Sir Francis Galton's contributions, many of which are important for the history of intelligence testing, psychometrics, and applying psychology to everyday problems. Additionally, Galton first framed the still ongoing nature-nurture debate over the origins of intellectual ability, favoring the nature explanation.

In America, no one was more influenced by Galton than James McKeen Cattell (Chapter 10), who coined the term *mental tests* to describe the psychometric measurements (including intelligence tests) that he conducted and popularized in the late 19th century. Additional American pioneers included Joseph Jastrow (Chapter 10), Franz Boas (Chapter 10), and one of Titchener's (Chapter 8) students, Stella Sharp. At Harvard, Hugo Münsterberg (Chapter 10) in some ways represented the continuation of work initiated by German researchers such as Hermann Ebbinghaus and William Stern (both Chapter 8). As we indicated, Münsterberg was also an important early advocate in America of applied psychology. Any serious discussion of intelligence testing, however, best begins with the work of Alfred Binet.

Alfred Binet and the First Intelligence Tests

Alfred Binet (1857–1911) was born in Nice, France, the son of a wealthy physician. After his parents separated, Binet was raised by his mother. He maintained a lifelong fear of his father after an incident in which the man attempted to cure his son's timidity by forcing him to encounter a cadaver (Fancher, 1985).

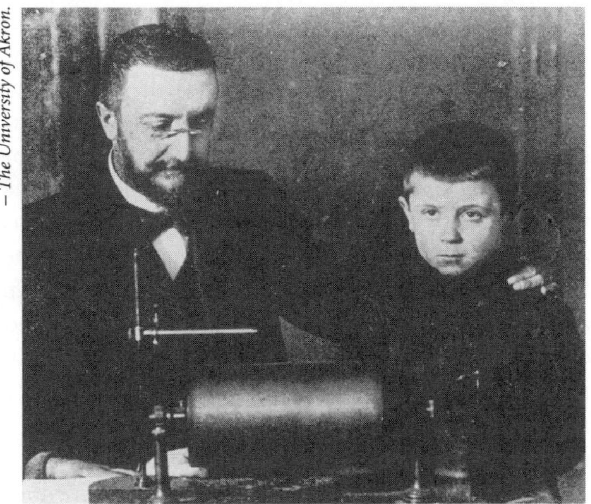
Archives of the History of American Psychology – The University of Akron.

Alfred Binet (1857–1911) testing an unknown boy

Binet was educated at schools in Nice and Paris, where he won awards for his compositions. After completing a law degree, Binet turned to medicine, but his medical school career was cut short by his psychological conflicts concerning his father and cadavers.

From 1879 through 1883, Binet undertook a course of self-directed study at the prestigious *Bibliothèque Nationale* (National Library) in Paris, focusing on the available works in psychology. Discovering an interest in John Stuart Mill's (Chapter 5) writings, Binet sought someone who could further advance his understanding of an empirical, associationistic psychology. The person he found was Charcot (Chapter 15) at the Salpêtrière.

Under Charcot's influence, Binet's interests expanded to include hypnotism and psychopathology. In conjunction with the psychiatrist Charles Féré (1852–1907), these new interests culminated in *Animal Magnetism* (1888), which offered some empirical support for Charcot's model of hypnotism.

At the Salpêtrière, Binet worked on such diverse topics as child development, sexual fetishes, and illusions. In addition, he continued to hone his experimental skills and to publish his findings, producing two additional books and more than 20 articles, most of which appeared in Ribot's (Chapter 5) *Revue Philosophique.* During this period, Binet's interest in individual differences and mental tests began as a result of observing his two young daughters.

With a growing interest in testing and individual differences, in 1891 the independently wealthy Binet became an unpaid assistant to Henri Beaunis (1830–1921), director of the newly formed Laboratory of Physiological Psychology in the Sorbonne's School of Advanced Studies. In 1894, Binet replaced Beaunis as laboratory director, establishing himself as one of the foremost experimental psychologists in France. That same year, with Beaunis's support, Binet created the journal *L'Année Psychologique* to further develop the laboratory's research reputation (Nicolas, Segui, & Ferrand, 2000).

Although he completed an advanced degree in natural science in order to become a professor, Binet continued as the unpaid laboratory director for the rest of his career. In part, this was caused by low enrollment at a facility that offered no degree. During his Sorbonne tenure, Binet saw the chairs held by Ribot and Janet (Chapter 15) go to other candidates, despite his excellent qualities as an experimental psychologist (Nicolas & Ferrand, 2002). According to Nicolas and Ferrand, the orientation of French psychology to psychopathology prevented Binet's (and French psychology's) advancement.

Individual Measurement

In 1895, Binet and his assistant Victor Henri (1872–1940) began a research program they called "Individual Psychology" to create a mental test battery that would allow them to examine the individual differences between people in detail. Some tests existed—mostly the work of Galton and Cattell—but whole intellectual faculties remained unexplored.

Beginning in about 1899, Binet's research program gradually evolved into a more specialized consideration of children and intelligence. In the French public school system, a new universal education law required that all children be given a certain amount of instruction. Problems soon emerged. In some cases, there was the practical question of what to do with children who could not keep up, whereas in other cases the problem concerned children with such low intelligence they could not benefit from a standard education.

In 1899, Binet was fortuitously approached by **Théodore Simon** (1873–1961), a young physician with access to retarded subjects. Binet immediately recognized the value of working with subjects of below-average intelligence.

In 1904, a government-appointed commission began to investigate the problems of educating "weak ones," or students who were retarded, and Binet was named a member. For the French government, the problem was to objectively and impartially identify children who could not benefit from a standard education.

The Tests of Binet and Simon

Based on 30 tasks of varied difficulty, Binet and Simon's first test appeared in 1905. The easiest task required the child to follow a light with his or her eyes, something very young normal children could do but some retarded children could not do. The tasks' difficulty increased through sentence completions that could be solved only by clever 11-year-olds.

Although the test successfully identified retarded children in an objective, empirical manner, Binet saw it as merely the starting point. Important test revisions occurred in 1908 and then in 1911, the year Binet died. The revisions increased the test's length, reflected research with an ever-increasing subject pool of both normals and subnormals, extended the age range of children who could be tested, and, most importantly, allowed for more subtle distinctions than simply whether or not the child was retarded. Having developed a test to meet the commission's needs, Binet was moving toward a test that would allow him to state with empirical precision if a particular child was performing at the level of an average child of that age.

For example, suppose André is 8 years old and performing poorly in school. Binet's test might demonstrate that André's intellectual abilities are equal to the skills of the average 6-year-old, accounting for his poor performance. Alternatively, imagine Marie, a bright 7-year-old. Marie's test results might indicate she scores as well as the average 10-year-old on an array of tasks.

By using experimental research techniques, Binet had demonstrated the utility of psychometrics for solving real-world problems. Always the empiricist, he resisted philosophical speculations about intelligence—such as what the construct actually was or how to define it—and even felt that it mattered little what the tests were as long as they were numerous and well designed. In 1911, Binet was 54 and at the height of his public prestige, but his personal life appears to have been in ruin. Fancher (1985) noted evidence that Binet's wife was struggling with mental illness, that Binet himself was growing increasingly more macabre, and that his exact cause of death is unknown.

In a discussion of intelligence testing in France after Binet's death, Schneider (1992) contrasted the French understanding of intelligence as multifaceted with the prevailing English notion that intelligence was best understood as a single factor. Charles Spearman is most associated with this idea.

Spearman and Factor Analysis

In 1890, **Charles Spearman** (1863–1945) was a decorated British army officer who liked reading philosophy texts, when, like Binet, his encounter with J. S. Mill's works steered him toward a career in psychology. At 34, Spearman started work at Leipzig under Wundt (Chapter 8). Seven years and another stint of active duty later, Spearman completed his Ph.D. Following a brief tour of the major European psychology laboratories (e.g., Oswald Külpe's, Karl Bühler's, G. E. Müller's [all Chapter 8]), Spearman began work in psychometrics at University College in London (Spearman, 1930).

Spearman represents the continuation of ideas about intelligence and psychometrics conceived by Galton, developed by Pearson (Chapter 9), and systematized by Burt (below). Spearman was an early theorist concerning the nature of intelligence (e.g., Spearman, 1904), and his initially rejected ideas (e.g., Binet, 1905; Thorndike, Lay, & Dean, 1909) were eventually accepted by many hereditarians who played an important role in developing intelligence tests.

Although Spearman's intelligence tests were unsophisticated, leading to their initial rejection, his

Charles Spearman (1863–1945)

data analysis method was not. Statistically accomplished, Spearman invented a way to analyze and interpret a series of correlations, which was an early form of **factor analysis,** and he applied it to data obtained from tasks he assumed were related to intelligence.

Spearman observed that people who excel on one intelligence measure—for example, solving mathematics problems—also tend to do well on other tests such as measures of vocabulary and block assembly. This high intercorrelation of test scores indicates the work of an underlying general factor, which he abbreviated "**g.**" Spearman also believed that each of the particular tests reflects a specific ability, an "**s**" factor, and his theory can be called a *two-factor theory of intelligence,* although this may be misleading given the importance Spearman and others placed on g.

From Spearman came the idea that the most important thing to know about a person's intelligence is the level of g, or general intelligence. Spearman's g continues to anchor one side of the debate over the nature of intelligence (e.g., Jensen, 1985). As Gould (1981) also noted, the widely held belief that the construct of intelligence as measured through intelligence tests actually corresponds to something real—something biological—originated with Spearman. The "Intelligence: One or many debate?" remains active today (and is covered later), and it also interested Ebbinghaus's student, William Stern.

Stern and the Intelligence Quotient

Although the 1908 version of the Binet-Simon test can be seen as the starting point for all subsequent intelligence tests we will consider, **William Stern** (1871–1938) introduced both the term **intelligence quotient** (or **IQ**) and the modern concept of an IQ score in *The Psychological Methods of Intelligence Testing* (1912). Stern undoubtedly will always be remembered for developing the intelligence quotient concept, but by his death in 1938, he may well have wished that he had never suggested using a single number to represent intelligence (Allport, 1968). As we will see, the IQ idea quickly became controversial.

In addition to his book on intelligence, Stern advanced applied psychology in Germany by founding an early journal. Many of his efforts are perhaps best categorized as either cognitive or developmental psychology (e.g., see also Chapter 18). In keeping with his interest in developmental psychology, Stern and his wife kept detailed diaries on the growth and development of their three children, amassing more than 4,800 pages of observations (Lamiell, 1996). After establishing himself as one of Germany's leading psychologists, Stern completed his career at Duke University.

The Psychological Methods of Intelligence Testing provided a detailed and critical review of early theory and research in intelligence testing—that is, of the work of Binet and Simon, as well as that of Spearman. Stern also presented his own ideas, including the concept of an intelligence quotient. The actual formula for the intelligence quotient is simple—mental age divided by chronological age—and follows directly from Binet's work. To illustrate, André has a chronological age of 8 (he is 8 years old) and a mental age of 6 (the age of most children at his skill level); 6/8 = 0.75. By contrast, Marie's chronological

Archives of the History of American Psychology – The University of Akron.

William Stern (1871–1938) riding on top of an open-air bus in Hamburg in 1932

age is only 7, but her mental age is 10, which gives her an IQ of 10/7 = 1.43. As you can see, Stern's approach results in a fractional term not quite in the form with which you are probably familiar. Lewis Terman removed the fraction.

Terman and the Stanford-Binet

Born in rural Indiana, **Lewis Madison Terman** (1877–1956) completed all the formal education available to a farmboy by the time he was 12. As the 12th of 14 children, Terman was probably not slated for higher education. However, after a phrenological examination predicted great things for him (Terman, 1932), at 15 he began taking classes at the unaccredited Central Normal College in Danville, Indiana (Minton, 1987). At Central, Terman completed degrees in arts, sciences, and pedagogy while he continued to farm part-time and, starting at 17, became a full-time schoolteacher.

In 1901, married, with one child, having been the principal of a high school without ever attending one, Terman borrowed money to attend Indiana University. There, he earned both an A.B. and an A.M. degree in just 2 years. Faced with the prospect of a teaching position that would not allow him to pay his debts or save for further education, Terman accepted a fellowship offer from Clark University.

At Clark, Terman flourished in the atmosphere of freedom of teaching and learning. Drawn to Clark by the inspiration of Hall's writings, Terman soon tired of the questionnaire method then in vogue with Hall and began to work with Edmund Clark Sanford (Chapter 10), who allowed Terman to pursue his interest in a study of mental tests. With a few suggestions from Sanford, Terman completed his doctoral work in 1905 and saw it published in 1906, despite suffering from tuberculosis in the interim. As we noted, 1905 was the date of the first Binet and Simon test. Although Terman was not seeking to identify the retarded, the conceptual similarity between his initial test and Binet and Simon's first test is striking.

Because of his health problems, Terman sought employment either in the South or the Southwest, eventually accepting a post as principal of a high school in San Bernardino, California. After a year, he moved to the Los Angeles State Normal School, where he remained for 4 years. In 1910, he joined the faculty of Stanford University as a professor of education, moving over to the psychology department in 1922 to succeed Frank Angell (Chapter 11) as head of the department.

At Stanford, Terman modified the efforts of Binet and Stern (Terman, 1916). Terman had the 1908 Binet and Simon test translated into English and its content revised to reflect the experiences of American children, creating the **Stanford-Binet.** Applying Terman's slight modification of multiplying Stern's intelligence quotient by 100, André has an IQ of 75 (.75 × 100) and Marie an IQ of 143 (1.43 × 100).

In addition to his publication that created the widely used Stanford-Binet and popularized IQ scores, Terman was part of the Robert Yerkes (Chapter 12) team that developed the Army Alpha and Beta tests (discussed later) used during and after World War I. Terman also initiated a famous longitudinal study of the gifted, the results of which were released from 1925 through 1959.

Longitudinal studies—research on a group over an extended time period—represent a powerful but difficult methodology. Like Terman, **Nancy Bayley** (1899–1994) distinguished herself in part through longitudinal studies of intelligence. Born in The Dalles, Oregon, Bayley completed the B.S. and M.S. at the University of Washington before earning her

Archives of the History of American Psychology – The University of Akron.

Lewis Terman (1877–1956)

Ph.D. from the University of Iowa in 1926. In 1966, Bayley became the first woman to win the APA's Distinguished Scientific Contribution Award for her work, which includes the internationally used Bayley Scales of Infant Development.

Terman initially tested over 250,000 schoolchildren and from this group selected a sample of 1,500 subjects with average IQs of 150. Periodic followups have continued through the present time (see Cravens, 1992; Friedman et al., 1995). In general, this sample has been healthier, happier, and more successful than the population from which it came. Terman's study and other similar research (e.g., Janos & Robinson, 1985) contradict the stereotype of the gifted as weak, sickly, and socially inept "bookworms."

Terman's Stanford-Binet has been through 5 major revisions and remains a widely used intelligence test. Following Binet's original model, the Stanford-Binet has a variety of items scaled to various ages. Sample items include questions like "An inch is short, a mile is ______" (for age 6). The current version is designed for both children and adults and includes an array of tasks designed to be administered by a psychologist to one individual at a time.

Although we have focused on Terman's work with intelligence, he also made substantive contributions to other areas of psychology. For example, his study of marital satisfaction was both epic in scope and groundbreaking in its consideration of women (Terman, 1938). In addition, Terman was an excellent administrator. Hilgard (1987) suggested that Terman's administrative skills as department head were largely responsible for Stanford's development of one of America's foremost psychology programs. Terman served as APA president in 1923.

The Wechsler Tests

In 1939, David Wechsler first released the Wechsler-Bellevue test, which evolved into a series of widely used intelligence tests that challenged the Stanford-Binet's position as the optimal measure of intelligence. Born in Romania, **David Wechsler** (1896–1981) came to America at age 6. He completed his A.B. at the City College of New York and his master's and doctorate at Columbia. At Columbia, Wechsler encountered psychological luminaries involved in mental testing, including Thorndike (Chapters 11 and 12) and Cattell (Chapter 10).

When World War I began, Wechsler was studying memory loss for his master's degree. He initially served as a volunteer with the psychologists working on IQ testing for the military, work that he continued after he enlisted. Before completing his tour of duty, Wechsler was sent to England, where he worked with both Pearson and Spearman. Before returning to America in 1922, Wechsler also spent some time studying psychology in Paris. In 1925, he completed his dissertation at Columbia on the psychological measurement of emotional reactions, reflecting his training as an experimental psychologist (Edwards, 1982).

By 1932, Wechsler was the Chief Psychologist at the famed Bellevue Psychiatric Hospital in New York. Wechsler's first mental test—The Wechsler-Bellevue—had the advantage of being better suited

David Wechsler (1896–1981)

to, and normed for, use with adults than the contemporary version of the Stanford-Binet.

During World War II, Wechsler modified his test for use with a younger population—military volunteers were often around 16—and after the war further revisions produced first the **Wechsler Intelligence Scale for Children (WISC)** and later the **Wechsler Adult Intelligence Scale (WAIS).** The WAIS was particularly well received because the Stanford-Binet was better suited for children than for adults. The WAIS introduced a more precisely standardized scoring system establishing 100 as the mean IQ score and linking other IQ values to percentiles along a normal distribution. This change in calculating the IQ has been incorporated into the Stanford-Binet's scoring as well.

The WAIS has 11 subscales divided into two general groups. The verbal group includes measures of general information, vocabulary, and comprehension, whereas the performance subscales include such tasks as picture completion and block and puzzle assembly. Both the WISC and the WAIS continue to be revised and today join the Stanford-Binet as the most widely used intelligence tests (Matarazzo, 1979).

The Mismeasure of Mental Ability

Our survey of intelligence testing to this point has been quite selective, in part because we have focused on advances, omitting several false starts and bad ideas that are part of a complete history of intelligence testing. Some of these false starts and bad ideas deserve mention.

Craniometry

Although modern science has proven otherwise, and modern sensibilities find the discussion offensive, in Darwin's era (Chapter 9) it was widely believed that different races represented different levels of evolution. Evidence for this view often came from wildly exaggerated caricatures of facial features illustrating the "obvious" evolution from ape to the Nordic ideal. The efforts in **craniometry**—the measurement of skulls—were ostensibly more scientific, and Gould (1981) reviewed the skull-related evidence marking the initial attempts at measuring intelligence. Few of the otherwise respectable scientists with an interest in intelligence emerge unblemished. For example, Darwin and Galton, Agassiz (Chapter 10), Broca (Chapter 7), and Binet (among others) all at some point endorsed a racial elitism based on craniometric data.

The basic argument was simple: Bigger heads mean bigger brains, and bigger brains mean greater intelligence. In the absence of real understanding of how brains work, it is possible to sympathize with the assumption that bigger brains equal better brains. Gould's (1981) point was not so much to vilify over-zealous craniometrists as it was to show how the initial pseudoscientific mistakes established the groundwork for hereditarian assumptions that followed. Actually, recent work (e.g., Rushton & Ankney, 1996) has called Gould's own efforts into question and has confirmed many of the earlier observations.

Goddard and the Kallikaks

One of the most infamous examples of "the mismeasure of man" involved **Henry Herbert Goddard** (1866–1957), who earned a Ph.D. under G. Stanley Hall at Clark University. In 1906, Goddard became the director of the Training School for the Feebleminded at Vineland, New Jersey, where he began to collect information on his charges. The information he collected led him to champion Binet's mental testing approach, and Goddard's efforts to translate Binet's material anticipated by several years Terman's development of the Stanford-Binet.

Like many of his generation of American psychologists, Goddard believed in the inheritance of intelligence. In his 1912 publication, *The Kallikak Family: A Study in the Heredity of Feeble-Mindedness,* Goddard felt he had proved the hereditary nature of mental retardation by showing its much higher occurrence in the "bad" side of a New Jersey family than in the family's "good" side. Even **Kallikak,** the pseudonym Goddard coined for the family, expresses the relationship he thought he had seen, as *kalos* and *kakos* are Greek for "good" and "bad," respectively.

The moral of Goddard's book was simple: If the feebleminded are allowed to interbreed with normal people, their feeblemindedness will spread like a cancer through future generations. Note that terms considered offensive today (e.g., *feebleminded, moron, imbecile, idiot*) once had fairly precise technical meanings for intelligence testers. At the time it appeared, the book's hereditarian-eugenic message (that intelligence is hereditary and breeding should be prohibited among the feebleminded) was well received.

By the 1920s, however, the study's scientific weaknesses were coming to light—for example, "Goddard's impressionistic methods of assessing intelligence . . . and his failure to acknowledge that environmental factors could have created many of the effects that he attributed solely to heredity" (Fancher, 1987, p. 585)—and by the 1950s, few took the work seriously. Goddard's account of the Kallikaks is generally perceived today as an example of bad science with unfortunate consequences because of the policies and attitudes it influenced.

Archives of the History of American Psychology – The University of Akron.

Henry Herbert Goddard (1866–1957) surveying Egypt from the Great Pyramid at El Gîza

In 1981, Harvard paleontologist Stephen Jay Gould added a new wrinkle to the criticism of Goddard's book. In *The Mismeasure of Man,* Gould wrote that he had "discovered a bit of more conscious skulduggery. . . . It is now clear that all the photos of the noninstitutionalized kakos were phonied by inserting heavy dark lines to give eyes and mouths their diabolical appearance" (Gould, 1981, p. 171). In other words, Gould charged that Goddard (or someone) had intentionally altered the pictures of Kallikaks from the family's "bad" side to make them appear more retarded and menacing. Goddard himself had admitted in the book's preface that, for the benefit of educating the public, "we have made rather dogmatic statements and drawn conclusions that do not seem scientifically warranted" (Goddard, 1912, p. x).

In fact, the Kallikak photographs do appear to have been crudely retouched. After seeing the pictures in a copy of Goddard's book, the director of

Some of the Kallikaks in front of their rural home. From Goddard's *The Kallikak Family.*

Photographic Services at the Smithsonian Institution wrote,

> There can be no doubt that the photographs of the Kallikak family members have been retouched. Further, it appears that this retouching was limited to the . . . eyes, eyebrows, mouths, nose and hair. . . . The harshness clearly gives the appearance of dark, staring features, sometimes evilness, and sometimes mental retardation. It would be difficult to understand why any of this retouching was done were it not to give the viewer a false impression of the characteristics of those depicted. (James H. Wallace, Jr., letter cited in Gould, 1981, p. 171)

Is it possible that the retouching of some of the photographs in Goddard's book could have a less sinister explanation? Raymond Fancher (1987) suggested two possibilities in his article. The first is that the pictures could have been retouched to enhance their reproducibility in the book, and the second is that Goddard himself might have altered the photographs "to protect the innocent" by disguising their appearance. Fancher concluded "that any 'evil,' 'sinister,' or 'retarded' qualities added to the Kallikak photos by retouching may lie more in the eye of the beholder than in the ulterior or dishonest motives of the retoucher" (p. 588).

What conclusions can we draw from the story of Goddard and the Kallikaks? By today's standards, Goddard's methodology was unscientific and his conclusions were unfortunate in their consequences. However, the evidence of "skulduggery" uncovered by Gould (1981) seems unfounded. For a scathing critique of many of Gould's other examples of "mismeasure," see Jensen (1982). We agree with Fancher (1987) that "when trying to understand Goddard and our other predecessors as *people*, it seems appropriate to try to view them with the same openness and fairness that we hope will be applied to us by *our* successors" (p. 589, italics in the original).

Subsequent work by Goddard targeted Eastern European immigrants—as Fancher (1985) ironically observed—such as David Wechsler. Goddard's questionable findings about Eastern Europeans have often been linked to the dark eugenic aspects of the U.S. Immigration Act of 1924, although Snyderman and Herrnstein (1983) found little factual basis for the connection.

Army Alpha and Army Beta

The United States entered World War I in 1917, and psychologists became involved in the war effort in diverse ways (see Mayrhauser, 1989; Popplestone & McPherson, 1994; Samelson, 1977). For example, Robert Yerkes, although primarily an animal psychologist, had experience and interest in intelligence testing. Thus, he was selected to head the committee to create a test for the American military that would serve two functions: (1) to identify mentally deficient individuals who could not be counted on to serve; and (2) to assign individuals to the military service they could be trained to perform given their intellectual potential.

Yerkes recruited five other psychologists to assist, including Terman and Goddard; Wechsler was part of the project, but he was not involved in the initial test development. Yerkes's group produced the Army Alpha and Beta tests.

The **Army Alpha** was similar to Terman's Stanford-Binet test with one important difference: a design simplified for group administration. Essentially the same test as the Army Alpha, the **Army Beta** had a pictorial format so that illiterate subjects could be tested. Almost 2 million people were examined before the end of 1918, and in some ways the program was a huge success.

First, like Binet's work for the French government, the Army Alpha and Beta demonstrated that psychology could be applied to real-world problems. Second, with group-administered tests, over 200,000 men a month had been tested. The time constraints produced by individual testing had been solved, and the viability of now-familiar pencil-and-paper measures had been established. The idea of intelligence testing and its use in applied settings were here to stay.

There were problems, however. With little previous experience, test administrators may have encountered technical difficulties that could have affected some scores adversely (e.g., people in the back of the room may have been unable to hear the instructions or see the examiners). Worse, published reports of the results (e.g., Yerkes, 1921) were often misinterpreted by the public as suggesting that many test takers had below-average intelligence, because the mental age averaged around 13. In reality, this figure, based on a test sample of nearly 100,000 recruits, was a better estimate of average mental age than the average with which it was compared—a value of 16, based on a sample of fewer than 100 subjects (Pastore, 1978).

Another problem was more troubling. All the major American mental testers at the time believed heredity was the source of intelligence. With this bias, published results were presented as evidence for the intellectual inferiority of some ethnic groups. Although subsequent research softened the views of some hereditarians such as Terman (Hilgard, 1957), the disparate racial results stimulated a great deal of tension. Questions such as "Should we really have a democracy in which every person has one vote, if some races in America are clearly inferior to others?" remained in the public arena for years (e.g., Block & Dworkin, 1976).

Gould (1981) found that some claims made by hereditarians based on the Army Alpha and Army Beta data were ludicrous. For example,

> How could Yerkes and company attribute the low scores of recent immigrants to innate stupidity when their multiple-choice test consisted entirely of questions like:
>
> > Crisco is a: patent medicine, disinfectant, toothpaste, food product
> > The number of a Kaffir's legs is: 2, 4, 6, 8
> > Christy Mathewson is famous as a: writer, artist, baseball player, comedian
>
> I got the last one, but my intelligent brother, who, to my distress, grew up in New York utterly oblivious to the heroics of three great baseball teams then resident, did not.
>
> Yerkes might have responded that recent immigrants generally took Beta rather than Alpha, but Beta contains a pictorial version of the same theme. In this complete-a-picture test, early items might be defended as sufficiently universal: adding a mouth to a face or an ear to

> a rabbit. But later items required a rivet in a pocket knife, a filament in a light bulb, a horn on a phonograph, a net on a tennis court, and a ball in a bowler's hand (marked wrong, Yerkes explained, if an examinee drew the ball in the alley, for you can tell from the bowler's posture that he has not yet released the ball). (pp. 199–200)

Gould's (1981) point was that most of the observed racial differences were artifacts of the tests' cultural biases. Still, in the 1920s, few people recognized such test-item bias, and the results made sense in light of the hereditarian views of the leading psychologists interested in intelligence at the time, such as Sir Cyril Burt.

Although they represent the best-known examples, it is important to note that the Army Alpha and Beta tests were not the only group intelligence tests developed at this time. For example, psychologists Luella Cole and Sidney Pressey (mentioned in Chapter 13 as the inventor of the teaching machine) developed their "Group Point Scale" of intelligence, which they administered to literally thousands of Indiana school children in the period from 1917 to 1921 (Petrina, 2001). Cole and Pressey also successfully marketed their various group tests.

Sir Cyril Burt

The son of the Galtons' family physician, **Cyril Lodowic Burt** (1883–1971) was born in London. He entered Oxford in 1902 on a scholarship in the classics, although his interests lay more in science and medicine, and school authorities insisted he pursue a curriculum appropriate to his scholarship (Burt, 1952). Fortunately, as a subcategory of philosophy, the subject of psychology was open to him.

In 1904, William McDougall (Chapter 12) took the chair in psychology and became Burt's first mentor. Burt had already had contact with Galton, Pearson, and Spearman, and his interest in psychometrics was developing while he continued studying the classics.

For his Oxford efforts, Burt was awarded the John Locke Scholarship in Moral Philosophy, which allowed him to continue his psychology studies more directly. Following McDougall's advice, Burt worked with Külpe in Würzburg and then returned to England, where in 1908 he began teaching psychology to medical students at Liverpool under Sherrington's (Chapter 7) direction.

Around 1910, Burt started revising the Binet and Simon test for British use. His initial efforts included collaborations with Charles Spearman, England's foremost contributor to intelligence testing at that time. World War I—during which Burt worked as a statistician—created in England as in America a greater appreciation for the usefulness of psychometrics and applied psychology. Following the war, Burt resumed his governmental work on intelligence tests for children.

In 1932, Burt succeeded Spearman in the Chair of Psychology at the University College of London, a prestigious position created by Galton and first occupied by Karl Pearson. From it, Burt became one of England's foremost psychological researchers. His widespread interests included studies of personality, vocational selection, the psychology of aesthetics, and mental telepathy. Burt's outstanding students included Raymond Cattell and Hans Eysenck, both of whom will be considered later.

In 1946, Burt became the first psychologist to receive knighthood (Osborne, 1994). However, at 63, he suffered from poor health, a failed marriage, and the stresses of war. In addition, his hereditarian views had fallen out of favor. Unwilling or perhaps unable (e.g., Kuhn, 1970) to discard his beliefs about the origins of intelligence, Burt found his contemporaries forcing him out of his department and also away from the editorship of his own journal—the *British Journal of Statistical Psychology.* Worse, the war had destroyed much of his data. Perhaps some of it was human error, but several sources (e.g., Dorfman, 1978; Gould, 1981; Hearnshaw, 1979) argue that at least part of Burt's postwar research was fabricated, resulting in one of the 20th century's largest scientific scandals.

As early as the late 1930s, exaggerations, minor inconsistencies, and dubious editorial practices became associated with Burt. More serious questions began to arise in the mid-1970s about Burt's empirical work (e.g., Jensen, 1974; Kamin, 1974).

Because Burt was no longer alive to answer the accusations, Leslie Hearnshaw, a psychologist and Burt supporter, was asked to investigate. Hearnshaw reluctantly concluded that some of Burt's most famous work on twins appeared to have been fraudulent. Even more disturbing, Burt possibly published concocted supporting articles under false names in his own journal. Finally, it appeared that as Burt grew older he began to take personal credit for more and more of the early factor analysis work actually pioneered by Spearman (e.g., Lovie & Lovie, 1993).

Although Hearnshaw's (1979) biography of Burt was damning, more recent books (e.g., Fletcher, 1991; Joynson, 1989) make a strong "case that Burt was innocent of outright fraud, and that some of his detractors were guilty of character assassination" (Green, 1992, p. 328). Green concluded that Burt's primary mistake was in not recognizing that data collection standards had changed and that his data were substandard and should not have been published. However, adding to the ongoing Burt saga, Tucker (1997) concluded there is "little doubt that he committed fraud" (p. 145).

With Burt's data suspect and his reputation compromised, you might think the hereditarian position was weakened. However, the nature-nurture debate remains one of the most heated contemporary issues in intelligence testing.

Contemporary Issues in Intelligence Testing

Intelligence testing remains a vital area of modern psychology and continues to be associated with social and political policy. Recently, some psychologists have damned and some have praised Herrnstein and Murray's (1994) *The Bell Curve,* a book that reconsiders issues we have discussed, such as the nature-nurture controversy and single-factor versus multiple-factor theories of intelligence. Although Sternberg (1995) scathingly reviewed *The Bell Curve* (for other commentaries on the book and the firestorm it created, see Samelson [1997], Weidman [1997], and Zenderland [1997]), we will look at these major issues as part of the ongoing debate about both intelligence and intelligence testing.

Heredity Revisited

In this chapter, we have noted many who have taken a hereditarian position on the nature-nurture controversy. On the nurture side, we have cited the views of environmentalists such as Watson (Chapter 12) and Skinner (Chapter 13). Additional nurturists include George Stoddard (1897–1981) and Beth Wellman (1895–1952)—affiliated with the Iowa Research Station—who in 1940 summarized several research projects and concluded that environmental changes can dramatically alter an individual's IQ on a standard measure of intelligence.

Florence Goodenough (1886–1959), best known for the Draw-a-Person Test, challenged Stoddard and Wellman's findings through a more sophisticated psychometric analysis. Terman and the Stanford IQ testing community tended to side with Goodenough, although many developmental psychologists continued to endorse Stoddard and Wellman. In many respects, the debate degenerated into a "turf war" over intellectual development. Although Anne Anastasi (1958, discussed later) offered an attractive compromise position, the nature-nurture debate remains a contentious topic.

As we indicated, **Arthur Jensen** (1923–) and **Leon Kamin** (1927–) released the initial reports of errors in Burt's work in 1974 (for an analysis of Kamin's contribution to and credit for the controversy, see Tucker, 1994). Since then, Jensen and Kamin have come to represent the extreme positions in the continuing debate.

In 1969, Jensen published a controversial and critical review of postwar programs such as Head Start, which were designed to improve intelligence and scholastic achievement in America. Jensen suggested the programs had failed because intelligence was mainly inherited. As evidence, he relied heavily on Burt's research, which had suggested that as much as 80% of the variance in the British public's intelligence could be linked to heredity. Criticism of Jensen's scholarly work became acrimonious when he raised the topic of race.

Jensen (1969) observed that blacks have produced distributions with means about 15 points lower than the means of distributions of whites on almost all intelligence measures since World War I. Jensen explained that these were group means and should not be used to predict individual cases. Additionally, Jensen suggested that environmental factors undoubtedly play a major role in the differences. Still, Jensen asked, if the tests are culturally balanced and populations are controlled for economic factors, does not any remaining variance suggest some biological difference? Even some of the hereditarian position's supporters feel that Jensen needlessly linked biology and race, observing that any underlying biological determinants for intelligence do not have to be linked to ethnicity (e.g., Jensen, 1980).

In contrast to Jensen, Kamin believed that if Burt's data were fraudulent, the hereditarian position should be virtually destroyed, as Burt was that camp's central figure. The son of Eastern European immigrants, Leon Kamin was so publicly vilified by Senator Joseph McCarthy's hunt for communists in academia during the 1950s that he continued his career in Canada. Kamin's accomplishments and changes in the political climate allowed him to move to Princeton in 1968.

Kamin (1974) advanced several bold claims that often seemed based more on conviction and moral principle than on data. His claims typically asserted that the *actual* research with twins suggested little or no contribution to IQ from heredity.

However, even without Burt's studies, the hereditarians still have abundant data that many find persuasive (e.g., Eysenck & Kamin, 1981; Jensen, 1985). For example, work with twins and nontwins suggests a correlation of about .74 for twins raised apart but only about .16 for unrelated children raised together (Jensen, 1981), strong evidence for a large genetic component in IQ.

Most psychologists today endorse some intermediate position that includes the effects of both nature and nurture. Psychologists such as Sandra Scarr (a winner of the American Psychological Society's James McKeen Cattell Award for applied psychology) have advocated a balance of evidence from such diverse areas as behavioral genetics and environmental influences on child development (e.g., Scarr & Weinberg, 1978). Scarr has emerged as a respected critic of extremes in psychological theory (e.g., Scarr, 1985), and she contends that nature *or* nurture is a false dichotomy, recognizing that for intelligence and many other phenomena, both nature *and* nurture play a role.

Another debate issue is that some see IQ tests themselves as culturally biased (e.g., Gould, 1981). One way to eliminate this factor might be to develop a physiological measure of intelligence. Eysenck (1982) found the most promising approach to be a measure of brain wave activity called the average evoked potential, which is determined by examining the subject's EEG pattern in response to a brief stimulus such as a sound. Correlations between the average evoked potential and the WAIS have been high, suggesting that average evoked potential may be a useful measure of intelligence. Former APA president and IQ test expert Joseph Matarazzo (1992) noted that it is possible that future psychological testing may employ advanced physiological measures instead of traditional IQ tests.

Intelligence: One or Many?

Joy Paul Guilford (1897–1987) was perhaps the first to provide a reasoned, multifactor alternative to Spearman's g. Presumably Spearman's g is summarized by the intelligence quotient, the single-number concept first proposed by Stern. Although g is one idea of the nature of intelligence, other psychologists believe that intelligence is composed of many factors. Titchener's student at Cornell, Guilford completed his 1927 Ph.D. under Karl Dallenbach (Chapter 8), whose course in psychophysics "impressed [Guilford] with the . . . precision with which psychological data could be obtained and treated and with the fact that numerical values and mathematical functions could be employed" (Guilford, 1967, p. 178). Winner of the APA's Distinguished Scientific Contribution Award in 1964, Guilford argued that his research suggested more than 100 components of intelligence (e.g., Guilford, 1967, 1985). Guilford's research was indebted to another pioneer in factor analysis, L. L. Thurstone.

Chicago-born **Louis L. Thurstone** (1887–1955) was the son of Swedish immigrants who Americanized the family name (Thurstone, 1952). Thurstone's route to success in psychology was circuitous—before going to college, he was educated in places as diverse as Stockholm, Sweden, and Centerville, Mississippi.

Archives of the History of American Psychology – The University of Akron.

Louis L. Thurstone (1887–1955)

Thurstone's initial college education was in engineering at Cornell, and on the basis of early work, he was invited to join the laboratory of famed inventor Thomas Edison, which he did briefly before starting to teach geometry at the University of Minnesota.

Exposure to psychology lectures at Minnesota stimulated Thurstone's interest, and he enrolled for graduate study in psychology with James Rowland Angell (Chapter 11) at the University of Chicago. Thurstone completed his Ph.D. in 1917, having already accepted a position at the Carnegie Institute of Technology, where Walter Bingham (discussed later) was building the first applied psychology department.

In 1924, Thurstone returned to the University of Chicago. There, his psychometrics laboratory flourished, and eventually Thurstone became the head of the department. In 1952, Thurstone moved to the University of North Carolina, and after his death, his wife Thelma Thurstone (1897–1993) succeeded him as director of the newly established psychometrics laboratory.

Thurstone's major contributions came from his advances in factor analysis. As we indicated, Spearman observed that several independent measures of intelligence (e.g., verbal tests, mathematical tests) were highly correlated with each other. This intercorrelation suggested an underlying factor (g) measured through the various tests. Factor analysis attempted to quantify the effect produced by this underlying factor. A series of variations of the basic procedure Spearman and Burt developed led Thurstone (1938) to suggest that seven factors underlay the observed correlations: verbal comprehension, word fluency, use of numbers, spatial visualization, associative memory, perceptual speed, and reasoning skills. Thurstone's work was fundamental to later advances in scholastic aptitude or achievement testing and to the debate over one or many factors in intelligence.

Robert Sternberg and Howard Gardner have each suggested a more manageable number of components than Guilford. Gardner (1983) identified six—linguistic, logical-mathematical, spatial, musical, bodily-kinesthetic, and personal—whereas Sternberg (1986) proposed only three: componential, experiential, and contextual. Sternberg's componential intelligence is our usual conception of intelligence as the ability to think abstractly and to solve word problems and mathematics problems. Experiential intelligence is the ability to formulate new ideas and to find novel relationships by drawing on past experiences. Contextual intelligence—the ability to adapt to changing environmental conditions—has been the most difficult type to measure reliably.

Just as with the nature-nurture debate, many psychologists have sought a middle ground on the number of different types of intelligence. For example, Burt's student **Raymond Bernard Cattell** (1905–1998) introduced the terms *fluid* and *crystallized*, by which he meant there is a single, biological factor (called fluid or g) that establishes the broad outlines of our intellectual potential. Within this outline, environmental conditions, life experiences, and other factors determine the specifics (crystallization) of our intellect (e.g., Cattell, 1963). Although Cattell was the announced 1997 winner of the American Psychological

Foundation's Gold Medal for Lifetime Achievement, some critics objected to the award, accusing Cattell of racism in some of his writings. In one of his books in the 1930s, for example, Cattell reported that parents of lower intelligence had more offspring than parents of higher intelligence. Because this trend would ultimately lower our national intelligence, Cattell argued for incentives to encourage higher birth rates in parents with higher intelligence and lower rates in their less able counterparts (Horn, 2001). When the APF decided to delay the award until a committee could investigate the accusations, Cattell declined the award and died soon thereafter. Cattell's open letter to the APA in response to the allegations of racism could be found online at the time of this writing (*http://www.cattell.net/devon/openletter.htm*).

PSYCHOMETRICS

If psychometrics is the construction of psychological tests and measures, then all psychologists who ever designed, conducted, or analyzed research were psychometricians in some sense. Although that probably overstates the issue, to the degree that psychology is an empirical, experimental science, some mathematical and statistical knowledge is essential. Thus, it is not surprising that several individuals we covered earlier were also pioneers in mathematics and statistics. Examples from Chapter 4 include Descartes, the inventor of analytical geometry; Leibniz, an inventor of calculus; and Pascal, often considered the "father" of statistics. In Chapter 7, we saw important psychometric advances in Fechner's measurement of sensory experiences and in Helmholtz's measurement of the speed of the nerve impulse. We have also noted Galton's, Pearson's, and Spearman's impact on psychometric methods.

More contemporary psychologists have also made key contributions to data analysis. Some have invented new statistical techniques, whereas others have applied existing statistical techniques and standards to psychological phenomena—for example, to intelligence testing. We have already noted one such method—factor analysis—invented by Spearman and refined by Burt. L. L. Thurstone's student, Quinn McNemar, made further developments.

Advances in Methods of Analysis

Quinn McNemar (1900–1986) was one of the first to ask if a single factor of intellectual ability, or a set of multiple factors (such as Thurstone's primary mental abilities), would better predict some "real-world" intellectual event, such as college grades. Apparently, there is little difference (McNemar, 1964), another reason why the more parsimonious idea of generalized intelligence (g) remains viable.

Born in West Virginia, McNemar completed his Ph.D. under Terman at Stanford and did postdoctoral work with Thurstone at Chicago. Such geographical diversity seems appropriate for a man who hitchhiked from Stanford to Yale in 1929 to attend the International Congress of Psychology. In remembering the Congress, McNemar (1980) reported he had never heard anyone so "cocksure" as Spearman. Terman (1932) used the same term to describe his initial reaction to Spearman's prose. McNemar's contributions to psychometrics included further refinements of factor analysis, work on a revision of the Stanford-Binet, and one of the classic texts in psychology, *Psychological Statistics* (1949).

In 1964, McNemar served as president of the APA. Like Spearman, McNemar achieved a certain degree of immortality by having a variation of the chi-square statistical test named after him. Spearman's name is attached to the Spearman rank-order correlation coefficient.

Factor analysis is more than just a tool for intelligence testing. Raymond Cattell's 16 PF (discussed later) is one example of factor analysis used in measuring personality. A Yale Ph.D., **Charles Osgood** (1916–1991) extended factor analysis to understanding semantics (word meanings), developing the **semantic differential** (Osgood, Suci, & Tannenbaum, 1957) as a technique to assess word meanings. Osgood received the 1960 Distinguished Scientific Contribution Award from the APA and was elected APA president in 1963.

In recent years, newer statistical techniques have tended to overshadow traditional factor analysis. In 1988, Frederic Lord (1912–2000), a researcher at the Educational Testing Service from 1949 to 1985, received the APA's Distinguished Scientific Contribution Award. Lord's major contribution was Item Response Theory, a mathematical advance in test analysis that has been used to determine racially biased items on a psychological test such as an IQ test.

Hilgard (1993) recognized the importance of not only statistical but also mathematical contributions to the analysis of behavior. For example, as we noted in Chapter 13, William Estes introduced a mathematically formalized version of Guthrie's learning theory. In addition, for recognizing some of the ways mathematics can be applied to analyze psychological problems, **Wendell Richard "Tex" Garner** (1921–) won the APA's Distinguished Scientific Contribution Award in 1964. Garner's analysis of information and communication (e.g., Garner, 1962) and his applied work in radar jamming illustrate his interests.

E. G. Boring's student S. S. Stevens (Chapter 13) received the APA's Distinguished Scientific Contribution Award in 1960, along with Osgood. Stevens is primarily known for his mathematical refinements of many of Fechner's original psychophysical principles (e.g., Stevens, 1961). John Swets won the same APA award in 1990 for his extension of **signal detection theory**—a mathematically based theory that assumes a perceptual experiment observer is an active decision maker who makes perceptual judgments under conditions of uncertainty (e.g., Swets, 1961)—as an alternative to the magnitude estimations of Fechner and Stevens. Swets also extended signal detection theory to such applied areas as aptitude testing and decision making.

Reliability, Validity, and Generalizability

If you have taken a research methodology course, you are almost certainly familiar with **reliability** (measurement consistency over time), **validity** (the extent to which a test measures what it is supposed to measure), and **generalizability** (the extent to which sample results apply to different populations). Several psychologists have made important contributions to these and related concepts; we will primarily discuss two of the most important contributors: Anne Anastasi and Lee Cronbach.

Anne Anastasi

Anne Anastasi (1908–2001) was born, raised, and educated in New York City. She earned a B.A. from Barnard College, the women's college of Columbia, and a Ph.D. from Columbia at 21. Although her initial interests were in mathematics, a course with Harry Hollingworth (Chapter 10) and an article by Spearman convinced her psychology and mathematics could be combined.

Anastasi started at Columbia in 1928, a time when Columbia was active in psychometrics. Thorndike was there, and some of his students—for example, **E. E. "Ted" Cureton** (1902–1992)—were working on methodological dissertations. Like Anastasi, Cureton contributed substantially to psychometric issues such as reliability and validity (e.g., Cureton, 1950). Working under Henry Garrett, a psychologist who developed a casebook of classic experiments (Garrett, 1951), Anastasi's doctoral thesis was a factor analytic consideration of memory.

Archives of the History of American Psychology – The University of Akron.

Anne Anastasi (1908–2001)

After receiving her Ph.D., Anastasi worked at Barnard until she founded the psychology department at New York's Queens College in 1939. In 1933, Anastasi married another Columbia student, John Foley. Anastasi (1980) noted that being married to a psychologist was almost like having a second degree, and through her husband she was exposed to the ideas of Kantor (Chapter 13). In 1947, Anastasi moved to New York's Fordham University, where she remained until her 1979 retirement.

Anastasi's contributions included work on test construction and validation (e.g., Anastasi & Foley, 1952), reliability (e.g., Anastasi, 1934), and psychological testing in general (e.g., Anastasi, 1954). In an autobiographical essay, Anastasi (1980) noted that one theme underlying much of her efforts concerned the effect of environmental and experiential factors on psychological development. As an illustration, Anastasi and her colleagues conducted a long-term project to examine the role of such factors in the development of creativity in children and adolescents (e.g., Anastasi & Schaefer, 1969; Schaefer & Anastasi, 1968). Anastasi (1964) also wrote a widely used text surveying applied psychology. She was elected APA president in 1972.

Lee Cronbach

Lee J. Cronbach (1916–2001) was born and initially educated in Fresno, California, completing his A.B. at Fresno State College in 1934. Master's and doctoral degrees in education followed from Berkeley and Chicago, respectively, and Cronbach joined the psychology faculty at the State College of Washington.

After World War II, Cronbach was employed first at the University of Chicago and then at the University of Illinois before returning to California and Stanford. Like Anastasi, Cronbach distinguished himself in psychometrics through both classic papers (e.g., Cronbach & Meehl, 1955) and textbooks (e.g., Cronbach, 1949). In addition, the most common statistical measure of the relation between a given scale item and the overall score of a scale bears his name (Cronbach's alpha).

Cronbach's (1957) APA presidential address has also become a classic. In it, he asserted that scientific psychology has produced two very different cultures: one consisting of researchers from areas well suited for experimentation and the discovery of general principles (e.g., psychophysics, physiological psychology) and the other of researchers from areas in which experimental designs are not always practical and individual differences are of interest (e.g., clinical psychology, developmental psychology). Cronbach contrasted and compared the experimental-design approach with the correlational procedure to illustrate the "two cultures," concluding that neither approach in isolation is the path to a complete, and psychometrically sophisticated, psychology. In 1974, Cronbach received the APA's Distinguished Scientific Contribution Award.

In addition to reliability, validity, and generalizability, there are many other philosophical and practical matters relating to psychometrics. Perhaps the most important of these concerns hypothesis testing and how we apply statistics to psychological data.

Hypothesis Testing and Its Critics

Much of psychology's basic understanding about designing an experiment and the statistical analyses to perform on the data comes from Cambridge mathematician **Sir Ronald A. Fisher**'s (1890–1962) work. Fisher was an innovator in the analysis of variance and a variety of nonparametric statistics (techniques that do not require estimating measurable characteristics of populations). The second holder of Galton's eugenics chair at University College, London (Pearson was the first), Fisher was an outspoken opponent of Pearson's correlational paradigm.

Despite his reliance on agricultural examples, Fisher's 1925 text, *Statistical Methods for Research Workers,* was arguably the first classic book for psychometricians. Fisher's greatest contribution was undoubtedly his conceptualization of testing the null hypothesis. As typically explained, the null hypothesis is the opposite of the thesis being tested, so that rejecting it supports the thesis.

Jacob Cohen (1923–1998) was one of the most relentless watchdogs of the misapplication of statistics in psychology. Although he won many awards, such as the Distinguished Lifetime Contribution Award from a division of the APA, his life and career were not without difficulties. The worst of these were several episodes of debilitating major clinical depression, from which he recovered only after electroshock treatment (Shrout, 2001).

Cohen's most recent admonition against what he considered psychology's misuse of statistics involved hypothesis testing. Cohen (1994) noted, "What we want to know is 'Given these data, what is the probability that [the null hypothesis] is true?' But . . . what [hypothesis testing] tells us is 'Given that [the null hypothesis] is true, what is the probability of these (or more extreme) data?' These are not the same" (p. 997), although psychologists often proceed as if they were. For additional discussion of the pros and cons of hypothesis testing, see the special section in the January 1997 issue of *Psychological Science* introduced by Shrout (1997).

Cohen (1962) initially achieved notoriety with his critical review of research and data analysis from selected areas of psychology. He reported that as a result of insufficient power, which is a statistical concept involving sample size and effect size, the findings of perhaps half the studies reviewed were dubious. A more recent followup reported no improvement (Sedlmeier & Gigerenzer, 1989).

Paul E. Meehl (1920–2003) was perhaps the foremost critic of psychological methodology (e.g., Meehl, 1967, 1978, 1992). Meehl's concern stemmed largely from the recognition that psychology's subject matter is often quite different from the subject matter in such natural sciences as chemistry, although psychology's hypothesis-testing procedures are the same. For example, four gold samples are more homogeneous, more readily controlled, and more easily measured than are four behavior samples, but we frequently analyze the data using the same sorts of statistics and assumptions.

Meehl began college at the University of Minnesota in 1938—when Skinner was on the faculty—and entered Minnesota's graduate program in 1941 under the direction of Starke Hathaway (Meehl, 1989). Meehl's initial publications, often with Hathaway, led to the popularity of the MMPI (discussed later). Additionally, his interest in the growing tension between practicing clinicians and academically based experimentalists produced *Clinical Versus Statistical Prediction* (1954), a volume still often selected as required reading. With other notables, Meehl edited *Modern Learning Theory* (1954), a book some have said proved the untenability of a grand theory of psychology and is responsible for the absence of any meaningful attempts at a unifying theory in the last 4 decades.

Perhaps more than any other individual, Meehl explored the significance of psychology's dependence on hypothetical constructs (Chapter 13). With Lee Cronbach, Meehl virtually created the modern understanding of psychological constructs and the concept of validity (Cronbach & Meehl, 1955). In association with Vienna Circle (Chapter 5) philosopher Herbert Feigl, Meehl co-founded the prestigious Minnesota Center for Philosophy in Science in 1953. In addition, Meehl saw patients as a clinician and developed a theory of schizophrenia, taught courses in law school and published in law reviews, and produced work on parapsychology. Meehl's honors included the 1962 APA presidency, the APA's Distinguished Scientific Contribution Award (1958), and being elected a fellow of the American Academy of Arts and Sciences.

Cohen and Meehl represent two contemporary advocates for psychometric sophistication. Perhaps the most important point from their admonitions is that psychologists need to always seek the most appropriate ways to conceptualize their data. Change in psychometric methodology is often resisted: For example, social scientists have only recently begun implementing Bayesian probability, developed by the Reverend Thomas Bayes (1702–1761). Bayes's theorem recognizes that previous empirical findings can be applied to estimations of probability for current events, thus making predictions based on conditional probabilities more accurate. As we noted, nowhere is the need for accuracy in prediction more urgent than in applied psychology.

Psychological Testing in Applied Contexts

In modern times, personality theories have been judged primarily by the psychometric sophistication of the instruments they employ to assess personality. The lack of demonstrably reliable and valid personality tests associated with Freudian and neo-Freudian theory (Chapter 15) has been problematic.

If you can think of a personality characteristic (e.g., Machiavellianism, narcissism, optimism), chances are good that one or more tests have been developed to appraise it. Because of the large number of personality tests, we will confine our coverage to some of the more general and widely used ones.

Introduced earlier, Raymond Cattell created the **16 Personality Factors Test (16 PF)** by using Gordon Allport's (discussed later) insight that our everyday language about personality traits might be a useful starting point in their study (e.g., Allport & Odbert, 1936). Cattell and his associates used such techniques as factor analysis and personality questionnaires to reduce some 4,000 trait descriptions to 16 binary personality factors (e.g., Cattell, 1957, 1973). Although the 16 PF is still used, subsequent personality scales derived from newer factor analytic techniques have suggested fewer than 16 primary traits. For example, the **NEO Personality Inventory-Revised (NEO PI-R**; e.g., Costa & McCrae, 1992) contends that only neuroticism, extraversion, openness (to experience), agreeableness/antagonism, and conscientiousness are needed to characterize personality.

Hans J. Eysenck (1916–1997) left Germany in 1934 in opposition to the Nazis to study in France and England, earning his Ph.D. in 1940 from the University of London. Far from helping Eysenck obtain a position, his mentor, Cyril Burt, "was a somewhat unstable person who distrusted any of his students whom he suspected of possibly criticizing or supplanting him in any way" (Eysenck, 1980, p. 159). By the time Eysenck became a postgraduate, Burt's feelings toward him had gone from favorable to ambivalent to hostile.

Eysenck's diverse research interests included personality theory and measurement, intelligence, behavioral genetics, and behavior therapy and led to an astounding publication output: 79 books and more than 1,000 journal articles (Farley, 2000). Not surprisingly, before his death, Eysenck was one of the world's most often cited psychologists, and Jensen (2000) called him "probably the world's most famous psychologist of his period" (p. 339). Or infamous: Eysenck achieved a high degree of notoriety in the early 1950s with his contention, based on a review of evidence for the therapeutic effectiveness of psychotherapy, that such treatment was no more effective than none at all. As a result, Eysenck was an early advocate and practitioner of what became known as behavior therapy (Jensen).

Eysenck suggested personality can be understood through perhaps as few as two factors (e.g., Eysenck & Rachman, 1965). One component, **neuroticism,** is based on an individual's emotional stability or instability. The other factor is more social and is usually called introversion/extraversion (see Chapter 15). Combining stability/instability with introversion/extraversion produces four personality types that can be mapped readily onto Galen's four temperaments (Chapter 2). Specifically, an unstable, introverted type corresponds to Galen's melancholic; unstable, extraverted to choleric; stable, introverted to phlegmatic; and stable, extraverted to sanguine.

Although tests such as the NEO PI-R have many uses, much personality appraisal work has been aimed at developing tests to assist clinical psychologists. The best-known such test is the **Minnesota Multiphasic Personality Inventory (MMPI).** Created by **Starke Hathaway** (1903–1984) and J. Charnley McKinley (see Buchanan, 1994), the MMPI has become a vital tool in both the clinical and the research communities. According to Butcher (2000), Hathaway was a strongly pragmatic individual who earned a Ph.D. in physiological psychology at the University of Minnesota, where he was influenced by psychologists such as Karl Lashley (Chapter 16) and B. F. Skinner (Chapter 13). Hathaway and McKinley developed the MMPI in a strictly empirical manner, without resorting to theory or any preconceived notion of what they were trying to assess. Although the test has been revised recently and a special version for adolescents has been introduced, the inventory's core structure remains intact.

On the MMPI, subjects agree or disagree with 550 simple statements (504 on the original test), which range from innocuous items such as "I like to read newspaper editorials" to more obvious clinical probes like "Several people are following me everywhere." Each item is linked to one or more of the test's 10 clinical scales, examples of which are depression, psychopathic-deviate, schizophrenia, and social introversion. Another MMPI feature is the inclusion of three "validity" scales designed to detect intentional faking.

A profile of scores on the scales graphically illustrates the relations between the various scales, and clinicians are often trained to evaluate the profile according to the two most elevated scales. The MMPI has spawned over 500 additional personality scales from its question pool (Murphy & Davidshofer, 1988) and has stimulated the publication of more than 13,000 books and articles (Butcher, 2000).

Whereas most clinical psychologists greatly respect the "theory-free" MMPI, several well-known measures are more closely linked to a given personality theory and are thus more controversial. For example, the **Rorschach Inkblot Test** and the **Thematic Apperception Test (TAT)** are based on the psychodynamic approach to personality.

Although inkblots had been suggested earlier to assess both personality (e.g., Binet and Henri suggested measuring imagination with them in 1896) and medical problems, the use of standardized inkblots as a clinical measure is linked with Swiss psychiatrist **Hermann Rorschach** (1884–1922). Rorschach earned his Ph.D. in Zurich in 1912, with a dissertation supervised by Eugen Bleuler (Chapter 15). Rorschach published the first version of his inkblot test in 1921, and it became immensely popular when the psychoanalytic movement was dominant. As an index of this popularity, during "the Twenties, there appeared 38 titles having to do with the Rorschach Test. This rose to about 230 during the Thirties and after that there were thousands" (Klopfer, 1973, p. 60).

Courtesy Rorschach Archives and Museum.

Hermann Rorschach (1884–1922)

Later, in an era increasingly interested in psychometric precision, the initially attractive free-form nature of the test began to be seen as its biggest problem. Test respondents describe what they see when they look at the randomly generated, symmetrical images. In scoring, attention is given to how commonplace or unusual the responses are, to their amount of detail, to whole versus part responses, and so forth. Although a reliable and valid approach to Rorschach interpretation appeared to have been developed by Exner (e.g., Exner, 1974, 1993), a recent critical examination has called the Exner scoring system into question (Wood, Nezworski, & Stejskal, 1996). Still, the Rorschach test is widely used, particularly by practitioners with a psychodynamic orientation.

The TAT's development followed a pattern similar to that of the Rorschach, with initial enthusiasm for the test's ambiguity yielding to a desire for psychometric precision in scoring. Christiana Morgan and Henry Murray introduced the TAT in 1935. **Christiana Drummond Morgan** (1897–1967) was a striking individual who was both muse and longtime lover to Murray. Both were analyzed by Jung, with Morgan's analysis leading to "visions" that Jung encouraged her to draw; these eventually set the stage for the TAT. When Murray became obsessed with a younger woman in the 1960s, Morgan apparently drowned herself in shallow water during a trip with Murray to the Virgin Islands (Milite, 2001). For a fascinating glimpse of both Morgan and Murray, see Schneidman (2001).

Henry A. Murray (1893–1988) earned a B.A. in history from Harvard and then an M.D. from Columbia in 1919. After studying embryology at the Rockefeller Institute for 4 years, he next earned a Cambridge Ph.D. in biochemistry. Murray's interest in Jung sparked his move toward psychology, and he returned to America to become Morton Prince's

(Chapter 16) assistant at Harvard's newly established psychological clinic. During World War II, Murray served as an officer in the Office of Strategic Services (OSS), where he was involved in the selection of secret agents (Schneidman, 2001).

Murray's (1967) autobiographical essay is written as a third-person analysis of "Murr," whose passion for the novelist Herman Melville's works is central to his career as a psychologist. Indeed, Murray, a 1961 recipient of the APA's Distinguished Contribution Award and a winner of the 1969 Gold Medal Award of the American Psychological Foundation, planned to analyze Melville's writings, but failing health prevented him from completing the task. Perhaps Murray's idiosyncrasies contributed to his reputation as a great teacher of psychology (Triplet, 1992).

Initially known as the Morgan-Murray Thematic Apperception Test, the TAT consists of 30 pictures depicting ambiguous social situations. A respondent typically views a subset of cards and is asked to create a story about each. The stories are then examined for common themes. Although various scoring systems exist, problems in developing reliable and valid methods to interpret the TAT's results have contributed to its decline in popularity.

Murray's best-known work, *Explorations in Personality,* first appeared in 1938, and it remains a classic analysis of human needs and motives. In it, Murray identified 20 psychological needs, of which the most thoroughly studied is "need achievement." This need for achievement represents a desire to excel, "to overcome obstacles, to exercise power, to strive to do something difficult as well and as quickly as possible" (Murray, 1938, pp. 80–81). In many studies, need achievement was assessed by analyzing TAT stories (e.g., McClelland, Atkinson, Clark, & Lowell, 1953).

We will conclude our survey by briefly examining an approach to personality appraisal that once held great interest for the psychology community but is all but forgotten today because of psychometric criticisms of it. The approach was developed by **William Herbert Sheldon** (1899–1977), William James's (Chapter 10) godson. Sheldon's interest in psychology can be traced to his memory of sitting on James's knee (Hilgard, 1987). Sheldon earned both a Ph.D. and an M.D. from the University of Chicago. Next, Sheldon spent 2 years in Europe, mostly studying with Jung, but Sheldon also visited Freud and German psychiatrist **Ernst Kretschmer** (1888–1964).

Kretschmer divided body type into three categories, and, following Kretschmer's lead, Sheldon's personality theory was based on three body types: endomorph, mesomorph, and ectomorph. Endomorphs are characterized by soft roundness of the body and a large belly compared to other body parts; mesomorphs are hard and rectangular, with a body heavier than it looks; ectomorphs are thin and lightly muscled, flat chested, and have a large brain relative to body size.

Sheldon found high correlations between his body types and temperament (i.e., between endomorphy and a love of comfort, social contact, food, people, and affection; between mesomorphy and a love of physical activity, risk-taking, and adventure; between ectomorphy and a tendency to be secretive and to love small, enclosed places). In fact, Sheldon's critics found the correlations so high they assumed his results must have been in error. Additional research produced more modest correlations, but Sheldon's results continued to support his hypothesis of a relation between body type and temperament. As criticism continued, Sheldon, like Titchener, turned to numismatics (see Thorne, 1995), developing a scale for grading coins that has been adopted by collectors of U.S. coins.

SOCIAL PSYCHOLOGY

Modern social science cuts across many academic fields. Political scientists and social philosophers pose theories about society and the individual's relation to it. Sociologists provide empirical studies of social trends and phenomena within a given society, whereas social psychologists focus on the individuals affected by the social trends and phenomena. In this section, we will first examine social psychology's origins, concentrating particularly on early American contributors, then focus on some classic works that have made social psychology popular and valuable.

For additional information about the history of social psychology, see the Fall 2000 issue of the *Journal of the History of the Behavioral Sciences.*

As we will see, the period immediately following World War II brought an enormous increase in topics of interest to psychologists, as well as an influx of European psychologists to America. Still, the idea of using an understanding of human nature to improve the world did not arise *de novo* after the war, and neither did interest in social behavior. Plato's *Republic* and Marcus Aurelius's *Meditations* (Chapter 2) contain advice about how the individual should behave relative to the state and what sort of society would be optimal for humankind. Machiavelli's *The Prince* (Chapter 4), Hobbes's *Leviathan* (Chapter 5), and Locke's and Hume's political philosophies (Chapter 5) are enduring classics of social psychology, although they anticipate by centuries the field's formal beginning. Rousseau's (Chapter 6) social contract idea, as well as Comte's (Chapter 5) original conception of a science of sociology, are further anticipations of social psychology.

French jurist **Gabriel Tarde** (1843–1904) was a more recent anticipator of social psychology. Long before Tolman, Miller (both Chapter 13), or Bandura (discussed later), Tarde (1890/1903) was struck by the importance of imitation in human social behavior. In a related development, another Frenchman, **Gustave LeBon** (1841–1931), saw group suggestion as central to social behavior (Faber, 1996).

Although his book *The Crowd* (LeBon, 1895/1960) was possibly the point of departure for a true social psychology, LeBon was medically trained. Analysis of groups and group behavior led LeBon to assert that people in groups exhibit characteristics different from the individuals comprising the group. Social contagion—the spread of behaviors through a crowd—may occur through unconscious suggestion. A current example might be the movement of the "wave" through sports' spectators. Although few people would be willing to stand and sway individually, the behavior, and the spreading suggestion to engage in it, often turns the crowd into a single waving entity.

LeBon's views represented tangible ideas about a "group mind," or *Volksgeist* (group mind or spirit), a concept Hegel (Chapter 6) originally popularized. Through his analysis of the crowd, LeBon's impact on later psychologists was substantial. For example, Freud's conception of and great interest in social psychology has been linked to LeBon (e.g., Freud, 1921), and LeBon also inspired the first American to write a textbook concerning social psychology, Edward Ross (1866–1951). However, **Emile Durkheim** (1858–1917), LeBon's contemporary, is credited with founding modern social science as an accepted academic discipline in France.

Durkheim was the pioneer in empirical sociology, although many of his works (e.g., *Rules of Sociological Method* and *Suicide: A Study in Sociology*) are fundamental to social psychology. Durkheim was also one of the many foreign visitors to Wundt's laboratory, and later the two corresponded. Perhaps Wundt's career-long interest in the *Völkerpsychologie,* 10 volumes devoted to various aspects of social psychology, influenced Durkheim's later interest in social science and sociology.

Although Wundt was important, **Max Weber** (1864–1920) was the leading German social scientist. Often considered a sociologist, Weber is best known in psychology for his writings on the protestant work ethic and on charisma (a word he coined) in leaders. Both topics illustrate the correspondence between applied and social psychology.

Thus, we can view the turn of the 20th century (plus or minus a decade) as the time when social psychology began. In addition to the French and German contributors, the sociological *Zeitgeist* extended to England and America. For example, Herbert Spencer (Chapter 9) published a textbook in sociology in 1876 and popularized the notion of "social Darwinism" to explain the success and failure of social institutions. We noted George Herbert Mead's connection to sociology's rise in America in Chapter 11, and his Chicago contemporary John Dewey (also Chapter 11) advocated a recognized subdiscipline of social psychology (Dewey, 1917), and contributed to the field's growing literature (e.g., Dewey, 1922).

James Mark Baldwin (Chapter 10) was perhaps the first to use the phrase *social psychology* in an English title (Baldwin, 1897). Like Wundt, Baldwin probably intended *social* to indicate an area he did not think could be studied experimentally. One of Hall's (Chapter 10) Ph.D. students, **Norman Triplett** (1861–1934) is frequently credited with conducting social psychology's first empirical study (Triplett, 1898). Among other things, Triplett investigated the effects of competition on the turning of a fishing reel by children. He found that half of the children were positively stimulated by competition and tended to reduce their times on competition trials relative to trials alone. Triplett also found a clear gender difference in that a higher percentage of girls than boys were stimulated positively by the competition. Triplett's study has been suggested as the first sports psychology experiment.

As we noted, Edward Ross was the first American to write a text about social psychology (Ross, 1908). Arguably more of a sociology work, Ross's text appeared the same year that William McDougall at Oxford produced perhaps the first true social psychology textbook (McDougall, 1908). Other texts followed, such as Dewey's 1922 volume and Kantor's (1929) classic, and social psychology had begun.

An Overview of Early Advances in Social Psychology

Triplett's 1898 experiment and McDougall's 1908 textbook are commonly cited signals for social psychology's formal beginning. The initial topic of interest remained the group, broadly defined, with little agreement in the field over theory and method. However, following Triplett, other researchers (e.g., Moede, 1920) experimentally investigated how the presence of others affects an individual's behavior. In general, this research demonstrated that people tend to perform tasks better with other people around. Floyd Allport, one of social psychology's first pioneers, called the effect **social facilitation.**

Floyd Allport and Gordon Allport

Although both **Floyd H. Allport** (1890–1978) and his younger brother **Gordon W. Allport** (1897–1968) had diverse interests and contributed to several areas of psychology, each made a lasting impact on social psychology. Floyd Allport's 1924 textbook, *Social Psychology,* helped solidify the field as an empirical discipline and explicitly associated social psychology with the behaviorist school. The association is not surprising, because, as we noted in Chapter 13, "in the 1920s it seemed as if all America had gone behaviorist" (Boring, 1950, p. 645).

Floyd Allport was born in Milwaukee, Wisconsin; his brother Gordon in Montezuma, Indiana. Floyd Allport completed his A.B. at Harvard in 1914, served as a balloon-based observer in World War I, and returned to Harvard to complete his psychology Ph.D. in 1919, the year Gordon finished his Harvard undergraduate career. Both Floyd (1974) and Gordon Allport (1967) recalled fondly several of the Harvard faculty, which, with the philosophy and psychology departments still combined, included Langfeld, Holt, Perry, Santayana, Münsterberg (all Chapter 10), and McDougall.

Münsterberg's applied interests first turned Floyd Allport toward social psychology. After receiving his Ph.D., he stayed at Harvard before moving to the University of North Carolina at Chapel Hill, where his career overlapped John F. Dashiell's (1888–1975). APA president in 1938, Dashiell is known for his many methodological contributions to experimental social psychology.

From 1924 until his 1957 retirement, Floyd Allport was at Syracuse University, where his major contributions occurred. In addition to his 1924 textbook anchoring experimental social psychology within the behaviorist framework, his best-known efforts in social psychology include *Institutional Behavior* (Allport, 1933) and his social facilitation work.

In examining social facilitation, Floyd Allport (1924) reported that in most cases subjects tested on cognitive tasks (e.g., math problems) and psychomotor problems (e.g., working a fishing reel) perform better when tested with others than when tested alone. Subsequent research has shown that social facilitation is a robust phenomenon across species from cockroaches (e.g., Allee, 1938) to humans (e.g., Zajonc, 1965).

Floyd Allport (1955) is also remembered for his comprehensive integrative review of theories of

Archives of the History of American Psychology – The University of Akron.

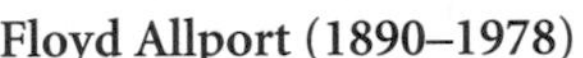

Floyd Allport (1890–1978)

Archives of the History of American Psychology – The University of Akron.

Gordon Allport (1897–1968)

perception, *Theories of Perception and the Concept of Structure.* Although *Theories* is usually seen as unconnected with social psychology, it actually was intended as an introduction to a complete theory of psychology. Some historians (e.g., Post, 1980) credit Allport with creating modern experimental social psychology by synthesizing and deleting the disparate elements—for example, interest in groups, evolution, sociology—of the *Zeitgeist* that preceded him.

After earning his A.B. degree from Harvard, Gordon Allport spent a year teaching English and sociology in Constantinople, Turkey (now Istanbul). On his way back to Cambridge, Allport visited Freud in Vienna. Unprepared for Freud's expectant silence, Allport described an episode he had just witnessed on a tram car, in which a small boy with an obvious dirt phobia kept saying to his mother, "I don't want to sit there . . . don't let that dirty man sit beside me" (Allport, 1967, p. 8). When he finished, Freud asked, "And was that little boy you?" assuming Allport was revealing something from his own past. Feeling slightly guilty, Allport changed the subject.

Gordon Allport completed his Ph.D. at Harvard (1922) and then received a 2-year travel fellowship enabling him to tour European universities. In Germany, Allport studied with Stumpf (Chapter 8), Wertheimer and Köhler (both Chapter 14), and Stern. In England, Allport worked with Frederic Bartlett (Chapter 18) and noted linguist I. A. Richards. Allport returned from his trip to a Harvard position.

Gordon Allport's primary interest is perhaps best described as a social psychological and humanistic (or spiritualistic) approach to personality (Rosenzweig & Fisher, 1997). His dissertation was on personality, and his Harvard teaching load usually included personality and social psychology courses. "By 1937 Allport was widely acknowledged as personality's leading spokesman in American psychology" (Nicholson, 1998, p. 53). According to Nicholson, Allport's version of personality psychology replaced the earlier idea of *character*, or the internal qualities of an individual, with something more scientific and quantifiable. Allport's concept of the "mature personality," however, included many of the ideals of character with which his upbringing had infused him.

Briefly at Dartmouth, Allport returned to Harvard in 1928 as the social psychologist, following McDougall's departure to Duke. In 1946, a departmental faction that included Allport broke off and cofounded the Department of Social Relations. The two departments remained almost totally distinct until 1964, the year Allport retired.

Despite important differences, the two Allports had much in common. For example, each began his career at Harvard, and each for a time edited Morton Prince's (Chapter 16) *Journal of Abnormal and Social Psychology*—an early outlet for social psychology articles. Each Allport also won the APA's Distinguished Scientific Contribution Award. The two brothers even collaborated on some works, including an early personality scale.

Despite his many contributions to social psychology, Gordon Allport's interests remained varied. His key social psychology publications include a pioneering chapter on the nature of attitudes (Allport, 1935), possibly the first history of social psychology (Allport, 1954a), and the groundbreaking *The Nature of Prejudice* (Allport, 1954b). Additional interests led to publications on Gestalt psychology, imagery, and issues of war and peace. As is true of many social psychologists, Gordon Allport's work at times drifted into applied topics. The book he cowrote with his student Hadley Cantril (Chapter 1) on *The Psychology of Radio* is just one example. In addition, Gordon Allport was an important "pillar" of the humanistic side of American psychology (deCarvalho, 1990).

As Gordon Allport (1967) recalled, many important psychologists passed through the Harvard program. Those he highlighted included contributors to cognitive psychology Jerome Bruner and Roger Brown (Chapter 18), social psychologist Stanley Milgram (discussed later), and Gardner Lindzey and Elliot Aronson, who independently have been prolific and respected researchers and jointly the editors of *The Handbook of Social Psychology* (e.g., Lindzey & Aronson, 1985). The *Handbook* was started by **Carl Murchison** (1887–1961), remembered as the editor of several early and long-standing journals friendly to social psychology and the first three volumes of *A History of Psychology in Autobiography*. (For more on Murchison at Clark University, see Koelsch, 1990.) Finally, Allport particularly recognized **David McClelland** (1917–1998), best known for his many studies of achievement and motivation (e.g., McClelland, 1961), which earned him the APA's Distinguished Scientific Contribution Award in 1987.

Gordon Allport's work first introduced the association of a humanistic interest in personality with social behavior. This connection proved fruitful, and Gardner and Lois Murphy continued a similar line of work.

Gardner Murphy and Lois Murphy

Gardner Murphy (1895–1979) married **Lois Barclay Murphy** (1902–2003) in 1926, when he was on the faculty at Columbia, and she was doing postgraduate work at Union Theological Seminary. Gardner earned his A.B. from Yale in 1916, entered graduate school at Columbia after World War I, completed his Ph.D. in 1923, and remained affiliated with Columbia until 1940. Between 1922 and 1925, Gardner also held a fellowship in psychical research at Harvard; you may recall McDougall's interest in this area from Chapter 12.

Gardner moved from Columbia to the City College of New York, where he remained through 1950. An outstanding teacher, graduating seniors at CCNY routinely voted him "best-liked teacher." After an extended trip to India, Gardner became Director of Research at the Menninger Foundation in Topeka, Kansas, a position he held from 1952 until 1972.

Lois Barclay completed her undergraduate work at Vassar in 1923, earned a B.D. at Union in 1928, and completed her Ph.D. in 1937 from Columbia. From 1937 until the Kansas move in 1952, Lois held academic positions in the New York area. At the Menninger Foundation, she served as a research psychologist and completed psychoanalytic training (Hilgard, 1987).

Lois Murphy (1902–2003) and Gardner Murphy (1895–1979)

At Columbia, Gardner distinguished himself as an emerging leader in social psychology. His social psychology program produced such important students as Rensis Likert (Chapter 14), Theodore Newcomb, and Muzafer Sherif (both discussed later). Gardner's publications at Columbia included a book with Lois on experimental social psychology (Murphy & Murphy, 1931), which became the defining text for the next generation of social psychologists.

Experimental Social Psychology blended biological, social, and personality factors into what the Murphys saw as the proper recipe for social psychology. Like Gordon Allport, they believed personality development should be the centerpiece of social psychology. Combining personality and social psychology was also evident in the works of the individual Murphys. For example, the theme of Lois Murphy's dissertation, published as *Social Behavior and Child Personality* (Murphy, 1937), was the interplay between personality and social influences within the developing child.

Gardner Murphy advocated a holistic study of psychological phenomena, seeking to integrate data from such seemingly disparate areas as evolutionary biology and cross-cultural anthropology. His own research was equally aimed at unifying, combining behavioral concepts like needs with Gestalt principles such as fields and more "clinical" elements such as personality. An emphasis on factors such as personality represented just one of the emerging content areas for the new discipline of social psychology. The consideration and analysis of attitudes was another prominent area.

The Study of Attitudes

To collect data for a widely cited attitude study, Richard LaPiere (1934) traveled across the United States with a young Chinese couple, staying at over 50 hotels and eating at nearly 200 restaurants. After the trip, LaPiere wrote the hotels and restaurants to ask if Chinese patrons were allowed. Although only one business had refused them service, over 90% of the respondents reported that the Chinese were not welcome in their establishments.

Although LaPiere's work is methodologically flawed (e.g., the people who served them may not have been the ones who answered LaPiere's letter), his study illustrates the early work with attitudes and the growing interest in the relation between attitudes and behavior. By the time of Gordon Allport's 1935 chapter on attitudes in the first *Handbook of Social Psychology*, it was clear that research on attitudes had become ". . . the most distinctive and indispensable concept in American social psychology" (p. 798). Early psychometric measures of attitudes were developed by Thurstone (Thurstone, 1928; Thurstone & Chave, 1929) and Likert (1932).

Because psychologists were employed in various ways during World War II, it is not surprising that some social psychologists focused on measuring soldiers' attitudes. Just as World War I provided subjects for intelligence testing, World War II allowed psychologists to study attitudes in thousands of young recruits. In fact, World War II gave social psychology the same sort of lift World War I had given psychometrics. Carl Hovland was one of the leaders in measuring soldiers' attitudes during the war (e.g., Hovland, Janis, & Kelley, 1953; Hovland, Lumsdaine, & Sheffield, 1949).

A Hull Ph.D. from Yale, **Carl Iver Hovland** (1912–1961) had been an experimental psychologist with industrial research experience before the war. After the war, he became the leader of Yale's social psychology program and winner of the APA's Distinguished Scientific Contribution Award (1957). He died from cancer at 49 and is remembered as a "gifted researcher, statesman of science, and incomparable human being" (Shepard, 2000, p. 299).

According to Shepard (2000), Hovland made significant research contributions in experimental (human learning), social (attitude change), and cognitive psychology (concept acquisition). In social psychology, Hovland revolutionized the study of attitudes by exploring attitude change in detail. For example, Hovland and Weiss (1951) examined the effects of a communicator's credibility on persuasion. Although being perceived as knowledgeable and trustworthy are beneficial for changing attitudes, there also can be a **sleeper effect.** With time, the association between the message and its source may fade so that the message is remembered after the source has been forgotten. Thus, even if the source is not credible, after a month or so the effects of the message exposure may appear as a change in attitude.

Like Hovland, Theodore Newcomb and Muzafer Sherif were winners of the APA's Distinguished Scientific Contribution Award who conducted important early studies on attitudes. **Theodore M. Newcomb** (1903–1984) began his college career at Ohio's Oberlin College, attended Union Theological Seminary, and then "crossed the street" to complete his Ph.D. at Columbia (Newcomb, 1974). Although Thorndike and Woodworth (Chapter 11) were also members of the faculty, Gardner Murphy became Newcomb's primary mentor.

After completing his dissertation, Newcomb was affiliated most notably with Vermont's Bennington College and the University of Michigan. At Bennington, Newcomb studied attitude change longitudinally, and at Michigan, he helped create a doctoral program that established the school as one of the centers for social psychological research.

Newcomb's Bennington research began in the 1930s and originally involved measuring student attitudes at the small women's college. The parents of Bennington students tended to be traditional and conservative, and Newcomb reported the process through which the students became more liberal. In his initial study, Newcomb (1943) found that attitudes were influenced importantly by an interaction between individual characteristics and group memberships. The results from his 25-year followup study were even more interesting and important, however.

Newcomb had expected the liberal attitudes to regress as the young women left college and eventually adopted societal roles similar to their parents' earlier roles. However, he found that the liberal attitudes persisted, which he explained by suggesting that the women had selected a lifestyle consistent with their college-developed attitudes. Newcomb's explanation led to a "balance theory" of attitude formation and change similar to Fritz Heider's theory of cognitive balance (discussed later).

Born in Odemis, Turkey, **Muzafer Sherif** (originally Muzaffer Serif Basoglu; 1906–1988) came to America in 1929 with a master's degree. After earning a second master's degree at Harvard in 1932, he traveled to Berlin to study with Köhler. The growing Nazi influence chased him from Germany, and he settled at Columbia to study with Gardner Murphy.

The Psychology of Social Norms (Sherif, 1936), Sherif's dissertation, soon became one of social psychology's key works. Returning to Turkey, Sherif was arrested for his outspoken opposition to the Nazis and spent time in prison, an experience that may have influenced his later interest in intergroup conflict. Several social psychologists, including Hadley Cantril and Gardner Murphy, helped facilitate his release and return to America.

By the end of his career, Sherif had written more than 24 books and 60 articles, many with his wife (and fellow social psychologist) Carolyn Wood Sherif (1922–1982). Several of Sherif's works advanced the understanding of attitude formation and attitude change (e.g., Sherif & Cantril, 1947; Sherif & Hovland, 1961). However, Sherif is perhaps best known for his intergroup conflict research (e.g., Sherif, Harvey, White, Hood, & Sherif, 1961), in which he first created, and then alleviated, hostile attitudes between two groups of boys at a summer camp.

The two groups had been put into direct competition for desirable prizes (medals, pocket knives), and relations between them quickly deteriorated until the researchers intervened to prevent serious consequences. The study showed how easily group biases could arise even when group membership was arbitrary and further demonstrated competition's role in arousing hostility between groups. Sherif et al. (1961) also found that intergroup hostility could be removed by forcing the groups to cooperate in completing a goal (e.g., restoring a water supply that the experimenters had "sabotaged").

Sherif's return to America is another illustration of the many ways social psychology benefited indirectly from World War II. Further examples include an increased interest in and appreciation of attitude research and innovations in the measurement of attitude change. As we noted in Chapter 14, Hitler's rise led to an outflow of Gestalt psychologists, some of whom (e.g., Kurt Lewin) came to America and found their niche in the new field of social psychology (Cartwright, 1979).

Gestalt Influences and Related Studies

After Lewin's arrival in America in 1932, his field theory quickly became the most attractive and complete alternative to a strictly behavioral explanation of social phenomena. As we noted, Lewin also pioneered applied social research and the study of group dynamics, and many of his ideas are still being applied in industrial psychology. In fact, leaders in the social psychological community came to view Lewin as "the giant of social psychology" (Hilgard, 1987, p. 604).

In Chapter 14, we also mentioned Solomon Asch, Leon Festinger, and Fritz Heider as three researchers closely affiliated with the Gestalt tradition. Each became a distinguished social psychologist in America; both Asch and Heider were early recipients of the APA's Distinguished Scientific Contribution Award.

Perhaps even more than Lewin, **Solomon Asch** (1907–1996) represented the clearest extension of the primary Gestalt ideals into social psychology, and in his obituary, Gleitman, Rozin, and Sabini (1997) called him "Solomon E. Asch, Gestalt psychologist" (p. 984). According to McCauley and Rozin (2003), "Asch aimed . . . to represent the scope and depth of Homo sapiens in a Gestalt psychology that focused on context and relationships" (p. 249).

A 1932 Columbia Ph.D., Asch first recognized the potential in exploring the social factors related to everyday perception, thus building directly upon one of the Gestalt program's major strengths—perceptual theory. In fact, Asch's best-known studies can be linked to Wertheimer's (Chapter 14) influence (Leyens & Corneille, 1999). Asch also understood that with the behaviorists' control of experimental psychology, the study of attitudes provided a point of attack for Gestalt psychology's more phenomenological and cognitive orientation. In many respects, Asch can be seen as the founder of such contemporary topics as social perception and social cognition, and his work illustrates why Gestalt theory provided such a fertile breeding ground for social psychology's development.

Friends Historical Library of Swarthmore College.

Solomon Asch (1907–1996)

The works for which Asch is best known are probably his demonstration of our willingness to conform our perceptions to group expectations (e.g., Asch, 1956) and his pioneering studies of impression formation (e.g., Asch, 1946). These were the first studies in person perception, an increasingly important topic for social psychologists today. In his research, Asch demonstrated that an individual's impression of another person represents a dynamic, creative integration of information about the person rather than a simple addition of separate facts (McCauley & Rozin, 2003).

To study conformity, Asch (1956) had a subject come to the laboratory to participate in an apparent study of visual perception, conducted with groups of subjects. Unknown to the real subject, the other 9 or 10 people were actually the researcher's confederates, who had been told how to respond to the stimulus material, which consisted of pairs of large cards. One card in each pair displayed a single line about 6 to 8 inches long. The other card had three lines of different lengths, and the task was to say which of the three matched the line on the first card. Although the discrimination was easy, after the first few trials the confederates unanimously began selecting one of the wrong answers. Asch found that fewer than 25% of the subjects resisted conforming on at least some of the trials.

Asch's research on conformity to group pressure had a significant impact on the field of group dynamics (Levine, 1999). Stanley Milgram's research on obedience was a conscious continuation of the study of conformity Asch pioneered (Sabini, 1986).

Born in New York City, **Stanley Milgram** (1933–1984) completed his bachelor's degree at Queens College and his Ph.D. at Harvard in 1960, with Gordon Allport as his advisor. Milgram was at Yale from 1960 until 1963, during which time he conducted his famed studies of obedience. In 1963, Milgram returned to Harvard, moving in 1967 to the Graduate Center of the City University of New York to lead the social psychology program.

At CUNY, Milgram's research focused on urban living, and he wrote and produced an award-winning film—*The City and the Self*—on the topic of life in cities. At the time of his death, Milgram was working with "cyranoids," subjects who speak thoughts that are a confederate's during a conversation with another person. Typically, the confederate tells the cyranoid what to say via a small radio transmitter. The cyranoid paradigm was developed to help explore the basic processes of communication and person perception. (The name *cyranoid* comes from a famous play about Cyrano de Bergerac, who put words in the mouth of a suitor to a woman Cyrano himself loved. The real Cyrano de Bergerac [1619–1655] was a French writer and dramatist who is said to have fought more than 1,000 duels because of his enormous nose.)

Although the urban living research was widely celebrated, Milgram's work on obedience brought greater fame. As a followup to Asch's conformity studies and in response to Nazi war criminals who claimed innocence because "they were just following orders," Milgram explored the boundaries of obedience in normal people. Milgram's (1974) book, *Obedience to Authority: An Experimental View,* provides a complete account of his research and theory on human obedience.

Photograph by Eric Kroll. Permission granted by Alexandra Milgram.

Stanley Milgram (1933–1984)

Milgram first asked many people, including 40 psychiatrists, to predict how normal subjects would respond in the following experiment: An experimental subject is seated before a large machine designed to administer a shock to another person as part of a study of the effects of punishment on learning. The machine has 30 switches, each delivering a more intense shock than the last (Figure 17.1 illustrates what the subject might see). An experimenter tells the subject when to increase the shock and when to administer it. Although the person receiv-

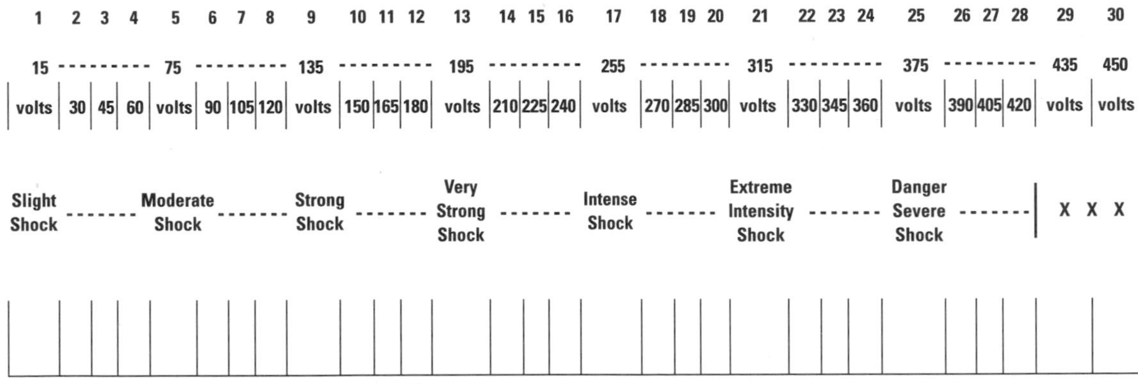

FIGURE 17.1 Adaptation of control panel from Milgram's famous obedience study

ing the shock is not visible, the subject receives auditory feedback, such as grunts in response to Switch 6, shouts in response to Switch 8, and groans by Switch 10. At Switch 12, the person cries, "I can't stand the pain!" After that, the screams become more agonized, and after Switch 20, the person stops responding to the learning task and insists on being freed. The experimenter tells the subject to treat each failure to respond as an error and to continue increasing the shock intensity through the switch marked "XXX," which is beyond the label "Danger Severe Shock."

At what point will experimental subjects disobey the experimenter and stop administering the shock? Psychiatrists predicted most subjects would not go beyond the 10th switch, and fewer than 4% would reach the 20th switch. Further, they estimated only 1 person in 1,000 would flip Switch 30 (Milgram, 1992). Actually, in a laboratory test, Milgram found that 62% of the subjects completely obeyed the experimenter, including throwing Switch 30.

Milgram conducted many studies of obedience using the situation we have described. In the studies, subjects were tricked into believing another person was being shocked as part of a learning experiment. In fact, the only person shocked in Milgram's studies was the subject, who got a mild shock at the beginning to show the equipment worked. The "victim" was actually the researcher's confederate, who gave programmed feedback on both the learning task and the "shocks."

Milgram systematically manipulated variables across the studies, and his results changed substantially with the different manipulations. However, even when factors were set to give minimal obedience—for example, having to touch the person being shocked, or the shocked person reporting a history of heart trouble—usually about 25% of the subjects still administered the highest shock level.

Milgram's purpose was to give people a clear conflict in order to explore the boundaries of obedience. Of course, the subjects had been paid a modest fee to participate in a "scientific study" and were told what to do by a "real scientist" wearing a white lab coat. However, it was obvious the other person was in pain, and the subject was the source of the pain. Except in situations employing disobedient models, Milgram found people generally obeyed the authority figure, even when it seemed the person being shocked was in danger. As the psychiatrists responding to a hypothetical case like Milgram's study demonstrated, the findings were not what most people would predict.

Although many people showed high levels of obedience, you should not assume they were unaffected by what they apparently had done. Many subjects remained upset even after learning what had really happened. Milgram's deception quickly led to a heated debate about the ethical guidelines for using subjects in psychological experiments (e.g., Baumrind, 1964).

Note that a prediction of the study's results by trained experts varied significantly from what really happened. Thus, a realistic analysis of the issue of obedience to an authority figure required a behavioral measurement, which leads to the question, "Are the results important enough to justify the deception necessary to obtain them?" Unfortunately, there is no simple answer. Milgram's research suggests that under the appropriate conditions, most people will follow orders, no matter how repugnant the orders' results might be. In addition, Milgram's obedience studies stimulated discussion and led to updated ethical standards concerning research on human and animal subjects. There is little doubt that a present-day researcher following the APA's ethical guidelines would not be allowed to repeat Milgram's research.

Milgram (1967) was also responsible for the so-called small-world study, which led to the frequently expressed idea that people are connected through an average of no more than "six degrees of separation." This idea, based on flimsy empirical evidence, according to a careful investigation of original sources by Judith Kleinfeld (2001), spawned a hit Broadway play and a 1993 movie with the title *Six Degrees of Separation.*

In Chapter 14's survey of Gestalt psychology, we briefly summarized Leon Festinger's concept of cognitive dissonance (e.g., Festinger, 1957; Festinger & Carlsmith, 1959). Festinger theorized that people resolve conflicting cognitions by revaluing one or more of them, citing a study in which subjects judged a poorly compensated, unpleasant task more favorably than expected given the nature of the work. Cognitive dissonance is closely associated with Fritz Heider's theory of cognitive balance.

Although generally considered an early contributor to social psychology, **Fritz Heider** (1896–1988) spent much of his career as a perceptual researcher in the Gestalt tradition. Heider began his work in psychology with Karl and Charlotte Bühler (Chapters 14 and 16, respectively) in Munich, focusing on methodology and child development. Next, he completed his dissertation in perception under Alexius Meinong (Chapter 8) at his hometown university in Graz, Austria (Heider, 1989). After receiving his degree, Heider attended the lectures of Köhler, Wertheimer, and Lewin at Berlin, before accepting a position at Hamburg with Stern in 1927.

On Stern's advice, Heider traveled to Smith College, where he worked with Kurt Koffka (Chapter 14) on projects involving deaf children. After World War II, Heider was invited to the University of Kansas by Roger Barker (Chapter 13), who you may recall as an associate of Lewin. At Kansas, Heider met the Murphys (then at Menninger), and about a decade later his classic work in social psychology—*The Psychology of Interpersonal Relations* (Heider, 1958)—appeared. After the book appeared, Heider finally gained recognition in the academic community, receiving, for example, the Lewin Memorial Award in 1959 and the APA Distinguished Scientific Contribution Award in 1965 (Malle & Ickes, 2000).

Despite its title, Heider's book contains a great deal of perceptual theory. Heider offered a phenomenological account of our everyday perceptions of other people based on the Gestalt assumption that some underlying cognitive structure organizes the perceptions. The organizing principle involves **cognitive balance,** which refers to a tendency to perceive information in ways consistent with pre-existing beliefs and attitudes.

Heider's balance construct provided a framework within which counterintuitive phenomena from such areas as impression formation (e.g., Asch) and cognitive dissonance (e.g., Festinger) could be explained. Heider's ideas were also fundamental in creating a new research area in social psychology, **attribution,** which refers to how we perceive, interpret, and account for people's actions. Four basic attribution modes can be illustrated by the common explanations for behavior we use daily. For example, we may attribute "John's" success on a test to *effort* (John did well because he studied), to *ability* (John did well because he was born with an excellent memory), to the *task* (John did well because the test was easy), or to *luck* (John must have gotten lucky to have done so well).

Edward Jones (1926–1993) and **Harold Kelley** (1921–2003) both earned the APA's Distinguished

Stanley Schachter (1922–1997)

Scientific Contribution Award for work on attribution. Jones (e.g., Jones & Davis, 1965) is perhaps best known for his research on how we modify our attributions as a function of how events directly affect us. This general tendency predisposes us to evaluate ourselves differently than we evaluate other people. In fact, we may blame the situation or bad luck for most of our failures, whereas we may attribute our accomplishments to either our own effort or to natural abilities (e.g., Jones & Nisbett, 1972). For others, we may attribute negative situations to the individual, not to the environment or to luck. This inconsistency between how we evaluate ourselves and others is sometimes called the **fundamental attribution error.**

Kelley (1972) recognized that we frequently incorporate aspects of both the environmental situation and the individual we are evaluating when we make attributions. This led him to suggest a system with three key concepts: distinctiveness, consensus, and consistency. For example, if we know John is doing poorly in other classes, then his excellent performance on a psychology test is *distinctive* and may prevent us from making attributions that would apply to some general or pervasive trait John might have (e.g., high intelligence). *Consensus* refers to our consideration of how other people behaved in the same circumstance—that is, if everybody did well on the test, then it must have been easy. However, if only John did well, then we may appeal to the *consistency* of his past behavior in similar situations. If it turns out John always does well in psychology courses but poorly in other subjects, we might conclude John exerts himself only in classes he enjoys.

We can further illustrate the fertility of attribution theory by briefly considering Stanley Schachter's studies of the attributions of emotions. Schachter, like Milgram, was involved in a controversy over research ethics when he and his colleagues reported data gathered from the infiltration of a doomsday cult (Festinger, Riecken, & Schachter, 1956). The authors and several other observers joined a group around a suburban housewife who believed she was receiving messages from the planet Clarion predicting a catastrophic flood. In *When Prophecy Fails,* Festinger et al. reported their observations of the conviction, commitment, and proselyting activity of the people associated with the cult.

The son of eastern European immigrant parents, **Stanley Schachter** (1922–1997) was born in New York City. He began college at Yale at 17 with some interest in psychology, and a class with Hull sealed the matter. Schachter was drafted about the time he started graduate school and decided not to return to Yale after leaving the army. Instead, he went to study with Lewin and Festinger at MIT.

After Lewin's death in 1947, interest in group dynamics faded at MIT, and many of the faculty and students, including Schachter and Festinger, moved to the University of Michigan (Schachter, 1989), which quickly became the leading center for social psychology in the postwar period. After earning his Ph.D., Schachter spent 12 years at the University of Minnesota before moving to Columbia University, where he remained for the rest of his career (Singer, 1998).

Schachter is perhaps best known for his research on the social factors related to the attribution of emotions. His classic study (Schachter & Singer, 1962) was a response to Walter B. Cannon's (1927) criticism of the James-Lange theory of emotion as discussed in Chapter 10.

In the study, subjects received either a placebo or adrenalin, were either told what to expect physiologically or misinformed about what to expect, and were exposed either to a euphoric confederate or to an angry confederate while they responded to a questionnaire. The findings supported a two-factor theory of emotion: A stimulus causes arousal, and the emotion experienced depends on how the stimulus is labeled.

Subsequent research on the attribution of emotions (e.g., Zillmann, 1983) has generally supported Schachter's two-factor theory, even demonstrating it is possible to mislabel emotions. For example, a teenaged couple watches the final seconds of an exciting high school football game. After the game, the couple's high arousal persists but now the most salient environmental feature is the other person, not the game. In this situation, the teens may experience "excitation transfer," mislabeling their continued excitement as sexual tension or love.

Schachter also studied obesity and eating disorders, as well as the addictive properties of nicotine. According to Nisbett (2000), it can be argued that such research led to the founding of health psychology, with many of the early studies in the field specifically referencing Schachter's work.

Selected Topics in Contemporary Social Psychology

Schachter's and Zillman's research exemplifies the interesting and relevant work that has characterized social psychology in the last few decades. Sex and aggression have emerged as popular research areas, and the study of attitudes, attribution, and groups continues to be central to the field. Several APA awards for distinguished scientific contributions have been made in recent years to psychologists with interests in social phenomena. These awards include the 1978 recognition of Robert Zajonc for his work in social cognition, of Paul Eckman in 1991 for his research on the communication of emotion, and of Paul Slovic in 1993 for his studies of applied decision making. Although it is possible to mention only a smattering of the work that has shaped social psychology, a few classic studies and contemporary issues should be noted.

Social Learning Theory

Born in Mundare, Alberta, Canada, **Albert Bandura** (1925–) completed his B.A. from the University of British Columbia in 1949. Because of an interest in Kenneth Spence (Chapter 13), Bandura went to the University of Iowa for his M.A. and Ph.D. degrees. Since 1953, Bandura has been affiliated with Stanford University in various capacities. He was elected APA president in 1974 and received the APA's Distinguished Scientific Contribution Award in 1980.

Bandura's work has often dealt with aggression (e.g., Bandura, 1973), and he has always advocated a social learning theory explanation of phenomena. **Social learning theory** focuses on the role of *modeling* or *imitation* in acquiring social behavior. Although much of social learning theory's empirical basis was developed earlier by behavioral learning theorists such as Edward Tolman and Neal Miller, Bandura's classic research with "BoBo" popularized the ideas behind the theory.

Bandura, Ross, and Ross (1961) studied children's behavior toward BoBo—a large inflatable toy doll (see photo)—after the children had observed models aggressing against the doll. As you can see, the children closely modeled some of the aggressive behavior (e.g., Bandura, Ross, & Ross, 1963a).

Bandura and his associates demonstrated that children acted more aggressively toward BoBo after exposure to an aggressive model. Similar results were obtained for films of human aggression and when the aggressive display was a cartoon featuring a cat (Bandura et al., 1963a). Bandura and his colleagues also found that imitative aggression increased when it was rewarded or ignored, but decreased if the model was punished (e.g., Bandura, Ross, & Ross, 1963b).

The implications of Bandura's work were twofold: First, the studies demonstrated imitative modeling as a source of human learning. Second, and perhaps more importantly, the research addressed the social

Modeling aggression

The top row of stills show an adult model aggressing against a BoBo doll. The bottom rows show imitative aggressive behavior in two children.

problem of aggression. Many researchers and social activists have used Bandura's work as a point of departure in further considerations of violence.

One of the ongoing debates connected to Bandura's research concerns media violence. Following Bandura's logic, violent films, TV shows, and even cartoons ought to facilitate aggression in children who watch them. In fact, laboratory studies (e.g., Liebert & Baron, 1972) have demonstrated such facilitation. Popular press coverage has led some to assume that if violence were no longer televised, the problem of aggression would be solved. However, aggression is far older than TV, and across different cultures (e.g., American, Japanese, South African) little relationship has been found between levels of media violence and aggressive crimes.

Although it is not the whole story, there is little doubt that children (and adults) learn by imitation and can learn to behave aggressively by observing aggressive models. With the connection of Bandura's work to TV violence, we again see the association between social psychology and applied psychology. Philip Zimbardo's exploration of social roles reveals another element in the learning and aggression story.

Social Roles

Philip Zimbardo (1933–) obtained his B.A. from Brooklyn College of the City University of New York and his M.S. and Ph.D. degrees from Yale. After graduation, Zimbardo moved to New York University and then in 1968 to Stanford University, where he is today.

Zimbardo (1992) provided a vivid narrative of the arrest and processing of nine college students 20 years earlier. Arrested by the police, the students were handcuffed, booked, fingerprinted, strip-searched, sprayed with disinfectant, given degrading uniforms, and locked up in the "Stanford County Prison." The students were identified only by number and were instructed to address the guards, who wore matching khaki uniforms, reflective glasses, and carried clubs, as "Mr. Correctional Officer, Sir." Failure to obey any rule meant loss of privileges or worse—as the inmates, locked in closets or forced to clean toilets with their hands, soon learned.

Conditions deteriorated following an aborted prisoner rebellion. When officials found the prisoners suffering from depression, psychosomatic rashes, and disorganized thinking, they decided the guards at Stanford County Prison had become too punitive, and the facility was closed only 6 days after it opened.

In fact, the Stanford County Prison was a real facility, but it was housed in the basement of the Stanford University Psychology Department. Although the police were real, the guards and the prisoners were drawn from college student volunteers who had been carefully screened to try to prevent the sort of thing that happened. Thus, Zimbardo's account was of events at a simulated prison, and the official who decided to close the prison was Philip Zimbardo.

Because assignment to the position of "prisoner" or "guard" was random, Zimbardo and his colleagues concluded the social role and not personal traits produced the increasingly sadistic guard behavior and the increasingly pathetic prisoner behavior (e.g., Zimbardo, Haney, Banks, & Jaffe, 1973). Zimbardo's demonstration dramatically revealed the power of environmental conditions to shape behavior.

An attempted replication of Zimbardo's experiment by the BBC for broadcast television apparently met a similar fate to the original experiment—early termination—despite the network's cautious approach (Wells, 2002). Zimbardo was skeptical of the BBC's project from the beginning, stating, "That kind of research is now considered to be unethical and should not be redone just for sensational TV and *Survivor*-type glamour. I am amazed a British university psychology department [Exeter University] would be involved" (p. 2).

The study of social roles has continued to be central to social psychology from a general, theoretical standpoint and as a vehicle for exploring special situations. One particular situation receiving a great deal of experimental attention in recent years examines the social role of the bystander.

Bystander "Apathy"

At 3:20 A.M. on March 13th, 1964, New York resident Kitty Genovese was attacked on her way home from work. Although she fought off her attacker several times, she was finally stabbed to death. At least 38 of Genovese's neighbors later reported hearing her screams, and some even stood at their windows watching her ordeal below them on the street. None came to her aid, and not one neighbor called the police until the attacker was gone. The research area this incident led to became known as the study of **bystander apathy.**

This case and others like it garnered much attention in the late 1960s. Newspaper and magazine articles, TV specials, Broadway plays, and Hollywood movies explored how such an event could occur. Although noted writer Harlan Ellison (1983) offered a science fictional explanation, John Darley and Bibb Latané's work led to a better understanding of the unresponsive bystander.

Born in Minneapolis, Minnesota, **John Darley** (1938–) received his B.A. from Swarthmore College, where he worked with Solomon Asch. In 1965, he earned a Ph.D. from Harvard, working with Jerome Bruner (Chapter 18). At New York University from 1964 to 1972, Darley has been at Princeton ever since.

Bibb Latané (1937–) was born in New York but raised in Chapel Hill, North Carolina, where his father was a member of the university faculty. Latané earned an undergraduate degree from Yale in 1958, and he began work on a Ph.D. in psychology at the University of Minnesota, where his primary mentor was Stanley Schachter. In 1961, both Latané and Schachter accepted positions at Columbia, although Latané did not complete his Minnesota Ph.D. until 1963. Since leaving Columbia in 1968, Latané has held positions at The Ohio State University and the University of North Carolina, and is currently at Florida Atlantic University.

Beginning in the late 1960s, Darley and Latané conducted several studies of bystander apathy (see

Latané & Darley, 1970, for an early summary). The researchers theorized that bystander unresponsiveness results from a **diffusion of responsibility,** which refers to a situation in which several individuals have the possibility of acting, but no individual has a clear responsibility to act.

To test their hypothesis, Darley and Latané created experiments in which they could stage an apparent emergency, control for the number of bystanders and other variables, and observe the responses of their experimental subjects. For example, in Darley and Latané (1968), the subject was told he or she was part of a group discussion held via intercom to avoid embarrassment. At some point, the primary confederate appeared to be having a seizure. With five other students present, the average delay in seeking aid was 166 seconds, and help was attempted in less than a third of the trials. With two other students, help was sought 62% of the time, with an average latency of 93 seconds. With only one bystander—the actual subject—help was obtained in less than 60 seconds on 85% of the trials and eventually on 100% of them.

Although subsequent studies found that factors such as time pressure inhibited helping (e.g., Darley & Batson, 1973), Latané and Darley's results showed that if an individual recognized a problem and perceived it as his or her responsibility, help would probably be sought. The more people witnessing the emergency event, the less likely that any one person will perceive the incident as his or her responsibility. Hence, diffusion of responsibility delays assistance and suggests how Genovese could be murdered in full view of many of her neighbors. Because they could see others viewing the incident, each probably assumed that someone else would act or had already acted.

Advances in the Study of Race and Gender

Throughout this book, we have tried to highlight the contributions of women and people of color, which, unfortunately, have often been marginalized. With this in mind, we will consider briefly the study of race and gender by social psychologists—areas in which contributions by a diverse group of researchers have been recognized.

Although we cannot attribute all of the interest in the study of ethnicity to World War II, there is little doubt that the persecution of the Jews in Europe stimulated social psychologists to study racial issues. Gordon Allport's *The Nature of Prejudice* (1954b) is one of the first major works in this area.

Born in Canada, **Otto Klineberg** (1899–1992) received his B.A. from McGill and earned his Ph.D. in psychology from Columbia, where in 1961 he became the first head of the university's social psychology department. At Columbia from 1925 to 1962, Klineberg developed an interest in anthropology, and in *Race Differences,* he concluded that the racial differences he observed were primarily culturally determined. For example, better educational opportunities in the North accounted for intelligence differences between African Americans in the northern United States and African Americans in the South.

Although the number of minorities in the American academic system historically has been small (Guthrie, 1998), as more people of color have entered psychology in America, they have broadened and stimulated interest in the study of race and cultural differences. From 1920 through 1966, an estimated 8 Blacks received Ph.D.s in psychology out of 3,700 degrees awarded. Of the 8, Francis Sumner (Chapter 10), Hall's student at Clark, was the first. Earning a 1933 Ph.D. from the University of Cincinnati, Beverly Prossor became the first Black female psychologist. **Kenneth B. Clark** (1914–2000), a social psychologist, became the first African American president of the APA in 1971. Clark received his B.A. and M.S. from Howard University and his Ph.D. from Columbia in 1940. In a famous study of self-concept and racial identification in the late 1930s, Clark and his wife, Mamie Phipps Clark, found that Black preschool children preferred white dolls to black ones. In 1987, Clark received the APA's Gold Medal Award for his contributions to the public interest.

In recent years, there has been great interest in topics related to race and racial identity (e.g., Parham & Helms, 1985). Additionally, the study of cultural differences has become a popular subdiscipline of social psychology, and journals devoted to

Kenneth B. Clark (1914–2000)

special populations (e.g., Asian Americans, Hispanics) encourage research in the area.

Erving Goffman's (1963) *Stigma* is one of the most important works on the general topic of difference and identity. A sociologist, Goffman argued that we all have some stigma that we manage carefully when we present ourselves to others. A stigma can be as obvious as race, gender, or being bound to a wheelchair, or it can be more subtle, such as speaking with an accent, having cancer, or being homosexual.

Although gender can be a stigma, Goffman also considered other issues concerning gender differences and the social presentation of gender. In publications such as *Gender Advertisements*—which explores the portrayal of women in the popular press—Goffman (1976) addressed gender difference issues. He contended that print and television advertisements reinforce many stereotypes of women (e.g., that they are typically passive, that they function best in the home).

As we have seen in previous chapters, some early women in psychology have made significant contributions. For example, Mary Calkins (Chapter 10) and Christine Ladd-Franklin (Chapter 7) were early members of the APA; Calkins became the first woman president of the organization in 1905. Margaret Floy Washburn (Chapter 8) was the first woman to receive a Ph.D. in psychology in America and became the second woman elected president of the APA. Following Washburn's election in 1921, more than half a century passed before the APA elected another woman president. Since the early 1970s, however, women have become much more visible in APA leadership roles (Etaugh & Bridges, 2004).

As we have noted, several of the first generation of women psychologists performed research that assessed the idea of female inferiority so prevalent at the time. For example, Leta Stetter Hollingworth (Chapter 10) examined the notion of greater variability (and thus greater ability) in men relative to women and found no support for the idea. Hollingworth's research was inspired by an earlier study by Helen Thompson Woolley (Chapter 11), who found little difference in the intellectual abilities of men and women (Crawford & Unger, 2000; Etaugh & Bridges, 2004).

Interest in the psychology of women and gender died out in the 1920s (Crawford & Unger, 2000), however, probably killed, paradoxically, by the success of the suffrage movement in the United States. When women gained the right to vote in 1920 with the ratification of the 19th Amendment to the Constitution, it appeared their struggle for equality had ended. With the vote, women would be able to elect people who were truly representative of their interests. Unfortunately, women's suffrage did not lead to a feminization of politics as the suffragists had hoped (Hoffert, 2003). In fact, passage of the amendment led to a fracturing of the women's suffrage movement and thus to a loss of momentum in pursuing the goal of equality of the sexes.

Taking another tack, one group of former suffragists, led by Alice Paul (1885–1977), began to promote the passage of an equal rights amendment. The Equal Rights Amendment (ERA) was first introduced in Congress in 1923 and was reintroduced in each session from 1923 to 1970. Although it was eventually approved by both houses of Congress, the ERA was stopped in 1982 just three states short of ratification. Since that time, it has continued to be reintroduced annually in Congress.

After the bombing of Pearl Harbor brought America into World War II, women moved into all areas of the workplace, filling jobs and leadership roles formerly considered the exclusive province of men. The gender-altering effects of World War II were only temporary, however, as women quickly resumed their roles in the home, as wives and mothers, after the war ended.

Several events in the 1960s resurrected the women's movement and consequently the study of gender issues: the publication of Betty Friedan's *The Feminine Mystique,* the passage of the Equal Pay Act, and the founding of the National Organization for Women by Friedan, who served as its first president. *The Feminine Mystique* was "arguably one of the most socially influential books written in twentieth-century America" (Hoffert, 2003, p. 360). In it, Friedan, who has an undergraduate degree in psychology from Smith College, argued that by accepting the housewife/mother role, women gained economic security at the cost of their sense of self. A controversial bestseller, *The Feminine Mystique* encouraged women to seek sources other than home and family for personal fulfillment.

As a new women's movement gained strength in the 1970s, psychologists developed a renewed interest in studying gender issues. One of the major contributors to modern social psychology's interest in women and gender differences is **Janet Taylor Spence** (1923–), who received her undergraduate degree from Oberlin College, entered the clinical psychology program at Yale, and completed her doctorate at the University of Iowa in 1949. Among her achievements is the Manifest Anxiety Scale, developed to test a theory she held with her husband, Kenneth Spence, about the interaction of task difficulty with arousal level in determining task performance. Janet Spence has the distinction of being the only person elected president of both the American Psychological Association and the American Psychological Society.

After she moved to the University of Texas, Spence turned to the examination of differences in men and women, for which she and Robert Helmreich developed the **Personal Attributes Questionnaire** (**PAQ;** Spence, Helmreich, & Stapp, 1974). Reported in *Masculinity & Femininity* (Spence & Helmreich, 1978), their work with the PAQ convinced Spence that looking at the sexes as bipolar opposites is incorrect. Instead, she and Helmreich found that in high school students, college students, and many other groups, masculinity and femininity are essentially independent constructs.

Sandra Bem (1944–) is another explorer of the concepts of masculinity, femininity, and how gender-based social roles are acquired. A 1968 University of Michigan Ph.D., Bem is perhaps best known for the **Bem Sex Role Inventory (BSRI),** a widely used scale that describes how much a person conforms to traditional sex-role stereotypes. Spence and Bem have been at the forefront of the study of sex roles, and their results have challenged many of society's preconceptions about gender by showing that "male" and "female" traits are not always in opposition.

One of the most interesting and controversial issues in the study of gender is over what differences—beyond the obvious ones in reproductive physiology—actually exist between the sexes. Eleanor Maccoby has been involved in some of the most important attempts to determine such differences.

Eleanor Emmons Maccoby (1917–) was born and raised in Tacoma, Washington. As evidence of her early interest in experimental psychology, Maccoby (1989) recalled that in her youth she wrote to J. B. Rhine (Chapter 12) at Duke, who responded by sending her materials with which to conduct ESP experiments.

Maccoby began her collegiate work at Reed College in Portland, Oregon, where she took her first psychology class from a former student of Edwin Guthrie (Chapter 13). Following a transfer to the University of Washington, Maccoby was able to work directly with Guthrie in her further study of psychology.

At Washington, she married fellow psychology student Nathan Maccoby (1912–1992), and his acceptance of a position at Oregon State College in 1939 complicated her pursuit of the graduate degree. The couple moved to Washington, D.C., during the war, and Maccoby assisted in survey work psychologists were doing for the government. This experience gave her professional connections that allowed her to complete her graduate work at the University of Michigan in 1950. After her husband accepted a position at Boston University, Maccoby was associated with Harvard for several years before going to Stanford, with her husband, as a professor of psychology.

At Harvard and at Stanford, **Robert "Bob" Sears** (1908–1989) was important for Maccoby's developmental interests. Sears and Maccoby co-authored *Patterns of Child Rearing* (Sears, Maccoby, & Levin, 1957), and Maccoby's subsequent works in sex differences and socialization reflect her continuing interests in developmental psychology. In fact, Maccoby's 1988 APA Distinguished Scientific Contribution Award noted her efforts in both developmental psychology and social psychology. In 1996, she received the American Psychological Foundation Gold Medal Award for Life Achievement.

Bob Sears and **Pauline "Pat" S. Sears** (1908–1993) met as undergraduates at Stanford, and both completed their Ph.D.s from Yale. At Yale, Bob Sears was associated with John Dollard and Neal Miller and the growing Neo-Hullian interest in connecting learning theory with other areas of psychology (e.g., social, clinical). Bob Sears's dissertation was on conditionability in decorticate goldfish (Sears, 1980).

From Yale, Bob and Pat Sears moved to Iowa, where Bob Sears directed the Child Welfare Research Station from 1942 until 1949. Becoming involved with the station's research efforts, Pat Sears collaborated with such notables as Lewin, Dembo, and Festinger (e.g., Lewin, Dembo, Festinger, & Sears, 1944). After a brief period at Harvard, during which Bob Sears served as APA president, Bob and Pat Sears returned to Stanford in 1953. Following their 1973 retirement, they both remained active, continuing Terman's longitudinal research on gifted children. In addition, Bob Sears became interested in the psychobiographical analysis of Mark Twain (e.g., Sears, Lapidus, & Cozzens, 1978). For his many contributions to developmental psychology, Bob Sears received the APA's Distinguished Scientific Contribution Award in 1975, and in 1980 Bob and Pat Sears were jointly awarded the American Psychological Foundation's Gold Medal Award.

Maccoby's interest in gender issues grew during the 1960s and early 1970s (Maccoby, 1989), culminating in *The Psychology of Sex Differences,* published in 1974 with Carol N. Jacklin (Maccoby & Jacklin, 1974). In *Sex Differences,* Maccoby and Jacklin conducted a comparative review of almost 1,600 studies. Their review produced evidence for just four unambiguous gender differences: (1) females have better verbal abilities; (2) males have better visual-spatial abilities; (3) males do better on tests of mathematical ability; and (4) females are less aggressive.

Research in gender difference and gender identity continues to be popular in social psychology. Rhoda Unger and Mary Crawford have independently, and jointly (e.g., Unger & Crawford, 1992), emerged as influential authors on these topics in recent years. In addition, **social constructionism** emerged in the mid-1960s as a theory in sociology (e.g., Berger & Luckmann, 1966), was quickly generalized to all of the social sciences (e.g., Harré & Secord, 1973), and has been popularized in psychology by Sandra Scarr and Kenneth Gergen (e.g., Gergen, 1994). Gergen's work has been well received, particularly by psychologists with interests in race and gender.

INDUSTRIAL PSYCHOLOGY

In some sense, almost everything psychologists do can be applied to the "real world." However, endeavors such as personnel selection, treating mental illness, or designing control panels for machines to better fit human perceptual capabilities have a more salient connection to everyday life than analyzing the functions of the olfactory bulbs in rats, for example. In addition to applying psychological knowledge to the treatment of mental illness (Chapters 15 and 16), psychologists have long been interested in applying their skills to the occupational world.

Hilgard (1987) suggested 1910 as a convenient starting point for applied/industrial psychology in America, noting that William Stern founded the first journal of applied psychology in Germany in 1907. Before World War I, interest in phrenological, intelligence, and other kinds of testing was already widespread in America. Some of the first books by psychologists on applied topics had appeared—for example, Münsterberg's *On the Witness Stand* (1909) and Walter Dill Scott's (below) *Human Efficiency in Business* (1910)—and specifically applied programs, such as the one directed by **Walter Van Dyke Bingham** (1880–1952) at the Carnegie Institute of Technology, were being developed.

Bingham was educated at the University of Chicago in its heyday (1905–1908), with James Rowland Angell and George Herbert Mead on the faculty, and John Watson running the animal and experimental labs (Bingham, 1952). In 1907, Bingham traveled to Harvard and to Europe before completing his dissertation on the nature of melody. In Germany, he visited psychology's leading musicology experts, Stumpf and von Hornbostel (Chapter 8); in England, he encountered Spearman and Burt; and at Harvard, he spent time with Münsterberg and Holt.

Bingham was an instructor in educational psychology under Thorndike at Columbia, was briefly at Dartmouth, and then went to Carnegie Tech as head of the Division of Applied Psychology. In conjunction with several businesses, the program soon focused on the psychology of marketing and sales.

During World War I, Bingham was part of Yerkes's committee that produced the Army Alpha and Beta tests and may have been responsible for the details of group intelligence test administration. After the war, Bingham continued at Carnegie Tech until 1924, when the Division of Applied Psychology was dismantled.

From 1924 until 1940, Bingham promoted the relevance of psychology in fields ranging from economics to engineering. In 1940, Bingham returned to work for the military on matters of personnel selection. His committee was asked to develop a test to sort recruits into roles for which they were best qualified. The result was the Army General Classification Test, which was eventually administered to 10 million men and women recruits.

The committee's duties were expanded to include consultation on applied psychology issues (e.g., training and efficiency), and Bingham continued to work with the military until 1947, with the title of Chief Psychologist. Bingham's World War II efforts gave applied psychology an enormous boost.

Walter Dill Scott (1869–1955) was one of Bingham's Carnegie group before World War I. A Wundt-trained Ph.D., Scott developed a small psychology laboratory at Northwestern University upon advice from Titchener at Cornell (Benjamin, 1997). Scott was at Northwestern when Bingham asked for his assistance. At Carnegie, Scott became one of the first professors of applied psychology. Through several books, he introduced psychology into the world of work, thereby helping to create industrial psychology.

During World War I, Scott was responsible for the military's initial interest in personnel psychology as distinct from intelligence testing. Although more has been written about Yerkes's committee, Scott's ideas endured in the military and shaped the tests given to modern recruits. For his efforts, Scott was awarded the Distinguished Service Medal in 1919.

In 1919, Scott formed his own corporation to do personnel selection and to consult on management issues. Applied psychology was advancing in both academics and the business world—Cattell's Psychological Corporation was founded in 1921, and both Hall and Bingham started applied psychology journals during the period. Despite Scott's importance, Morris Viteles pioneered the connection between academic psychology and the world of work.

Morris S. Viteles (1898–1996) was born in Russia just before his family resettled in England (Viteles, 1974). At 5, Viteles came to America and was educated in Philadelphia, eventually attending the University of Pennsylvania, where the psychology program was directed by Lightner Witmer (Chapter 8), an applied, clinical psychologist. After completing his Ph.D. under Witmer, Viteles balanced a successful academic career at Pennsylvania with work for various industries: for example, The Philadelphia Electric Company, The Yellow Cab Company, and The Bell Telephone Company of Pennsylvania. With a foot in both academics and industry, Viteles was well positioned to write some of the early industrial psychology classics such as *Industrial Psychology* (1932) and *Motivation and Morale in Industry* (1953).

The Hawthorne Effect

The **Hawthorne Effect**—named for a place near Chicago—is still used today to suggest that any workplace change that makes people feel important is likely to improve their work performance. Although they are over 50 years old, the studies leading to the Effect stand as perhaps the best examples of applied psychology's importance. The studies began as a series of experiments conducted between 1924 and 1927 at the Hawthorne Works of the Western Electric Company, a division of American Telephone and Telegraph.

The initial projects explored the relationships among workplace lighting, changes in rest breaks, and productivity. At the completion of the second project, the researchers realized that more was involved in worker productivity than just the physical conditions in the workplace; that is, the social impact of the research was far larger than the effect of lighting changes or breaks.

Actually, psychologists were minimally involved in the Hawthorne studies. Engineers, public health experts, and people from business schools did most of the work. An Australian, Elton Mayo (1880–1949), did have some psychology background, and it was largely through his participation that the results became popular material (Mayo, 1933). It was also through Mayo and the Hawthorne studies that Jean Piaget's (Chapter 18) clinical interview method was introduced to American industrial psychology as a technique for questioning Western Electric workers (Hsueh, 2002). Developed for use in studying child development, Piaget's interview approach grew out of Pierre Janet's clinical work.

Applied/Industrial Psychology Since World War II

Following World War II, several issues within both applied and social psychology became topics of public interest, as the American war experience motivated questions about war and peace, race, and aggression. Centers for applied psychology began to emerge, and existing institutes hummed with new activity. As noted in Chapter 14, Kurt Lewin founded the Research Center for Group Dynamics at MIT in 1944. Lewin-associate Rensis Likert directed perhaps the most prestigious of the centers for applied psychology at the University of Michigan. In addition, many industries have developed a tradition of hiring their own psychologists. Bell Laboratories is perhaps best known for its use of research psychologists, but other firms, such as Honeywell and IBM, have also become centers of applied psychological research.

Without diminishing perennial concerns like marketing and advertising, as well as personnel selection and worker productivity, applied psychology continues to evolve in new directions. Health psychology—for example, the use of psychological techniques to control chronic pain—is one such area. Social psychologists work on problems like AIDS awareness and drunk driving. Cognitive psychologists now frequently consult on product warning label design, computer interfaces, and, as a concluding example, recall the research of Elizabeth Loftus, whose work on memory in applied settings was introduced in Chapter 1. Loftus's contributions have focused on eyewitness memory (e.g., Loftus, 1979; Wells & Loftus, 1984). Psychology and law have enjoyed a long relationship that in recent years has included such new areas as jury selection and the image management of clients.

CONCLUSIONS

In this chapter, we have covered such seemingly disparate topics as intelligence testing, statistics, social psychology, and industrial psychology, which actually are closely associated. Psychometrics understood as mental tests is closely linked with psychometrics understood as advances in statistics and methodology. Mental testing has been just as important for applied psychology and industrial psychology as have interests in personnel selection and workplace efficiency. In addition, from its beginnings with Binet and the French government, the effort to measure intelligence has been coupled with the need to do so accurately. As the mental tests have become more complex and our understanding of mental phenomena more complete, advances in data analysis and reporting have also become more sophisticated.

Making recommendations that will influence people's lives is essential, but difficult, work. Psychologists shaping public policy, consulting in the courtroom, or administering personality and intelligence tests are participating in tasks society considers vitally important. The importance to individual lives of many of the tasks in which applied psychologists are involved has undoubtedly fueled debates such as the degree to which nature (heredity) or nurture (environment) affect intelligence.

Perhaps the most important conclusion that can be drawn from our overview of social psychology is that the field's scope and relevance are incredibly broad. Humans are social animals, and it is clear that a meaningful connection can be found between almost any aspect of human existence and social psychology. In particular, it is possible to connect modern social psychology to real-world applied psychology in innumerable ways (e.g., in the study of aggression, consumer behavior, attitudes). Research on race and gender are further examples that have been especially prominent in modern times.

As social psychology has evolved, its original focus on the group has receded, especially with the establishment of connections to other subfields of psychology. Gordon Allport's and Gardner and Lois Murphy's interest in personality represent one example of this linkage; the pioneering work of Solomon Asch and Fritz Heider in such areas as social cognition and social perception provides further illustrations.

Amid the diversity, social psychology has been frequently colorful, often controversial, and almost always socially relevant. Here we particularly note Darley and Latané's work on bystander apathy, Milgram's obedience studies, and Bandura's social learning theory research, although many other studies (e.g., Schachter and Singer's study of emotional attributions, Zimbardo's research on a simulated prison experience) also deserve highlighting.

SUMMARY

The term *psychometrics*—measuring the mind—is often used synonymously with *statistics.* Intelligence testing illustrates psychometrics applied to the "real world."

Intelligence Testing

Sir Francis Galton and his American disciple, James McKeen Cattell, made pioneering efforts in psychometrics. Ebbinghaus and Stern were also early contributors to intelligence testing.

In 1895, Binet and Victor Henri began research to create a battery of mental tests to identify individual differences between people. After 1900, Binet's work evolved into a consideration of the intelligence of children because of applied problems in the French public school system. Working with Théodore Simon, Binet produced his first test to measure intelligence in children in 1905.

William Stern introduced the term *intelligence quotient* and the modern idea of an IQ score. Stern's intelligence quotient was defined as mental age divided by chronological age. Translating the Binet-Simon test into English to produce the Stanford-Binet, Terman eliminated Stern's fractional intelligence quotient by multiplying it by 100. Terman also was part of the team that developed the Army Alpha and Beta tests during World War I, and he initiated a longitudinal study of gifted individuals in California, which found that the gifted were often more successful relative to the average population.

David Wechsler's initial intelligence test evolved into the Wechsler Adult Intelligence Scale (WAIS) and the Wechsler Intelligence Scale for Children (WISC). The WAIS and the WISC are now among the most widely used IQ tests.

Craniometry, the measurement of skulls, was often used to verify the measurers' biases, and hereditarians sometimes misused such measures to show the inferiority of one group to another. Additionally, results from the administration of group intelligence tests, the Army Alpha and Beta, were used to support the inferiority of certain groups. Sir Cyril Burt was so convinced of hereditary inferiority he may have falsified data to reinforce his belief in the inheritance of intelligence.

Believing IQ has a large hereditary component, Arthur Jensen published a controversial review in 1969. On the other hand, Leon Kamin felt that removing Burt's suspect data would destroy the hereditarian position, but this has not happened. Eysenck's successful work on measuring biological intelligence suggests that traditional IQ tests may not be culturally biased.

In the question of one component of intelligence or several, Spearman's work revealed a general intelligence factor, which he called "g." Other theorists favor a multifactor alternative. For example, J. P. Guilford argued for over 100 different components, whereas Thurstone chose 7, Gardner identified 6, and Sternberg just 3. In a middle-ground approach, Raymond Cattell introduced the terms *fluid* and *crystallized,* with fluid referring to Spearman's g factor and crystallized to specific aspects of intellect.

Psychometrics

Virtually all psychologists can be considered psychometricians, although the label is more properly applied to those who have attempted to measure mental processes or made important contributions to data analysis. Factor analysis was invented by Spearman, refined by Burt, and further developed by L. L. Thurstone and his student, Quinn McNemar. McNemar was one of the first to ask which would do better at predicting a "real-world" intellectual event—a single intelligence factor or multiple factors. The answer—that there is little difference between the positions—supports the idea of a g factor. Factor analysis also has been extended to an understanding of semantics by Charles Osgood, who developed the semantic differential.

Anne Anastasi's major contributions were on test construction and validation. Lee Cronbach was another well-known contributor to psychometrics; the Cronbach-Meehl model of the construct of validity and the validation of psychological constructs is a cornerstone of many psychometrics courses.

Much of psychology's basic knowledge on experimental design and statistical analyses comes from Sir Ronald A. Fisher's work. Fisher's greatest contribution was probably his conceptualization of testing the null hypothesis. Critics of the traditional hypothesis testing procedures include Jacob Cohen and Paul Meehl.

Using factor analysis and other methods, Raymond Cattell reduced numerous trait descriptions to develop the 16 Personality Factors Test. Further work suggests that even fewer factors are needed to characterize personality, leading to such personality tests as the NEO Personality Inventory.

Created by Starke Hathaway and J. C. McKinley, the Minnesota Multiphasic Personality Inventory is the most widely used personality appraisal instrument for assessing clinical populations. Over 500 personality scales have been developed from the MMPI's question pool.

The most popular tests based on the psychodynamic approach to personality have been Hermann Rorschach's Inkblot Test and the Thematic Apperception Test developed by Henry Murray and Christiana Morgan. Murray is also known for his list of psychological needs, of which the most thoroughly studied is called "need achievement."

William Sheldon created a personality theory based on Ernst Kretschmer's body type theory. Sheldon presented evidence that body type is related to temperament.

Social Psychology

Interest in social psychology began before World War II, although the war produced a dramatic increase in relevant social topics. Early people interested in social behavior include Plato, Machiavelli, Hobbes, Locke, Hume, and Comte. More recent forerunners include the Europeans Gabriel Tarde, Gustave LeBon, Emile Durkheim, and Max Weber and the Americans George Mead, James Mark Baldwin, and Edward Ross.

Floyd and Gordon Allport were two of social psychology's pioneers. Floyd studied social facilitation, in which people perform better when tested with others than when tested alone. Gordon's primary interest can be described as a humanistic and social psychological approach to personality.

Gardner and Lois Murphy continued the association of a humanistic interest in personality with social behavior. Gardner's social psychology program at Columbia produced such important psychologists as Rensis Likert, Theodore Newcomb, and Muzafer Sherif. Much of Lois's work concerned the interaction of personality and social influences on the developing child.

Richard LaPiere performed an early formal study on attitudes by touring the country with a Chinese couple. Although only one business refused service, over 90% of the people who responded to LaPiere's inquiry said that Chinese were not welcome in their establishments. Continuing the study of attitudes, Carl Hovland explored attitude change, finding evidence for a sleeper effect. Theodore Newcomb examined change and stability in attitudes.

Muzafer Sherif is known for his intergroup conflict research. Sherif created and then alleviated hostile attitudes between groups of boys at a summer camp.

Gestalt contributors to social psychology include Kurt Lewin, Solomon Asch, Leon Festinger, and Fritz Heider. Asch became famous for his work in conformity to group pressure, which was continued as the study of obedience by his student, Stanley Milgram. Fritz Heider's cognitive balance theory is closely related to Festinger's cognitive dissonance idea. Heider's theory was instrumental in creating the study of attribution—how we perceive, interpret, and account for people's actions. Attribution theory stimulated Stanley Schachter's study, which found that social factors are linked to how we attribute our emotions.

Albert Bandura developed social learning theory, which focuses on modeling or imitation in the acquisition of social behavior. Bandura found that imitative aggression increased when the modeled behavior was reinforced and decreased when the modeled behavior was punished.

Philip Zimbardo simulated a prison environment with normal adults and found that subjects quickly learned social roles appropriate to their status as either guards or prisoners. Zimbardo's work illustrates the power of environmental conditions to shape behavior.

Following Kitty Genovese's murder, witnessed by many of her neighbors, social psychologists began to study bystander apathy. John Darley and Bibb Latané conducted experiments showing that bystander unresponsiveness stems from a diffusion of responsibility rather than from a lack of concern for the victim.

The study of race and ethnicity became major psychological topics after World War II. Kenneth Clark, the APA's first African American president, was one of a handful of African Americans to earn Ph.D.s in psychology in the period from 1920 through 1966.

One of the issues addressed by sociologist Erving Goffman in *Stigma* was that of gender differences. Janet Spence and Sandra Bem are also leaders in studying gender differences, Spence for her work reported in *Masculinity and Femininity* and Bem for the Bem Sex Role Inventory scale. Eleanor Maccoby concluded from a review of many studies that only four gender differences had been demonstrated unambiguously: less aggression and better verbal abilities in females and better mathematical and visual-spatial abilities in males.

Industrial Psychology

Walter Van Dyke Bingham developed one of psychology's first applied programs at the Carnegie Institute of Technology. Bingham's work with the military during World War II gave applied/industrial psychology an enormous boost. Walter Dill Scott and Morris Viteles were two other early contributors to applied psychology's advancement.

The Hawthorne Effect suggests that any workplace change that makes people feel more important is likely to enhance their work performance. The popularity of the Hawthorne Effect was aided by Australian Elton Mayo.

After World War II, centers for applied psychology began to emerge, including Kurt Lewin's at MIT. Rensis Likert, a Lewin associate, directed one of the most prestigious centers. Applied psychology continues to expand in new directions, because psychology's applications to the real world seem limitless.

CONNECTIONS QUESTIONS

1. How is intelligence testing connected to World War I?
2. What different connections can you make among Francis Galton, James McKeen Cattell, and later intelligence testing?
3. How are advances in psychometrics as statistics connected to advances in psychometrics as mental testing?
4. How are the social changes in America that began during and following World War II connected to social psychology?
5. What are the connections among the European events leading to World War II, Gestalt psychology, and American social psychology?
6. Describe as many connections as you can between Gestalt psychology and social psychology. For example, what connections can you make between Asch and Milgram in terms of their most well-known research?

KEY NAMES AND TERMS

Floyd H. Allport (p. 508)
Gordon W. Allport (p. 508)
Anne Anastasi (p. 501)
Army Alpha (p. 495)
Army Beta (p. 495)
Solomon Asch (p. 513)
attribution (p. 516)
Albert Bandura (p. 518)
Nancy Bayley (p. 490)
Sandra Bem (p. 523)
Bem Sex Role Inventory (BSRI) (p. 523)
Alfred Binet (p. 486)
Walter Van Dyke Bingham (p. 525)
Cyril Lodowic Burt (p. 496)
bystander apathy (p. 520)
Raymond Bernard Cattell (p. 499)
Kenneth B. Clark (p. 521)
cognitive balance (p. 516)
Jacob Cohen (p. 502)
craniometry (p. 492)
Lee J. Cronbach (p. 502)
E. E. "Ted" Cureton (p. 501)
John Darley (p. 520)
diffusion of responsibility (p. 521)
Emile Durkheim (p. 507)
Hans J. Eysenck (p. 504)
factor analysis (p. 489)
Sir Ronald A. Fisher (p. 502)
fundamental attribution error (p. 517)
"g" factor (p. 489)
Wendell Richard "Tex" Garner (p. 501)
generalizability (p. 501)
Henry Herbert Goddard (p. 493)
Florence Goodenough (p. 497)
Joy Paul Guilford (p. 498)
Starke Hathaway (p. 504)
Hawthorne Effect (p. 526)
Fritz Heider (p. 516)
Carl Iver Hovland (p. 511)
intelligence quotient (IQ) (p. 489)
Arthur Jensen (p. 497)
Edward Jones (p. 516)
Kallikak (p. 493)
Leon Kamin (p. 497)
Harold Kelley (p. 516)
Otto Klineberg (p. 521)
Ernst Kretschmer (p. 506)
Bibb Latané (p. 520)
Gustave LeBon (p. 507)
longitudinal studies (p. 490)
Eleanor Emmons Maccoby (p. 523)
David McClelland (p. 510)
Quinn McNemar (p. 500)
Paul E. Meehl (p. 503)
Stanley Milgram (p. 514)
Minnesota Multiphasic Personality Inventory (MMPI) (p. 504)
Christiana Drummond Morgan (p. 505)
Carl Murchison (p. 510)
Gardner Murphy (p. 510)
Lois Barclay Murphy (p. 510)
Henry A. Murray (p. 505)
NEO Personality Inventory-Revised (NEO PI-R) (p. 504)
neuroticism (p. 504)
Theodore M. Newcomb (p. 512)
Charles Osgood (p. 500)
Personal Attributes Questionnaire (PAQ) (p. 523)
psychometrics (p. 486)
reliability (p. 501)
Hermann Rorschach (p. 505)
Rorschach Inkblot Test (p. 505)
"s" factor (p. 489)
Stanley Schachter (p. 517)
Walter Dill Scott (p. 525)
Pauline "Pat" S. Sears (p. 524)
Robert "Bob" Sears (p. 524)
semantic differential (p. 500)
William Herbert Sheldon (p. 506)
Muzafer Sherif (p. 512)
signal detection theory (p. 501)
Théodore Simon (p. 488)
16 Personality Factors Test (16 PF) (p. 504)
sleeper effect (p. 512)
social constructionism (p. 524)
social facilitation (p. 508)
social learning theory (p. 518)
Charles Spearman (p. 488)
Janet Taylor Spence (p. 523)
Stanford-Binet (p. 490)
William Stern (p. 489)
Gabriel Tarde (p. 507)
Lewis Madison Terman (p. 490)
Thematic Apperception Test (TAT) (p. 505)
Louis L. Thurstone (p. 498)
Norman Triplett (p. 508)
validity (p. 501)
Morris S. Viteles (p. 525)
Max Weber (p. 507)
David Wechsler (p. 491)
Wechsler Adult Intelligence Scale (WAIS) (p. 492)
Wechsler Intelligence Scale for Children (WISC) (p. 492)
Philip Zimbardo (p. 519)

SUGGESTED READINGS

Allport, G. W. (1954). *The nature of prejudice.* Cambridge, MA: Addison-Wesley. This is perhaps the first detailed consideration of racial prejudice by a psychologist. *The Nature of Prejudice* continues to be a relevant source book for researchers interested in race or prejudice.

Fancher, R. E. (1985). *The intelligence men.* New York: W. W. Norton & Company. Fancher's work traces the history of intelligence testing from before Binet through the early 1980s. Fancher is a well-known and respected historian, and his book stands out for its objective review of the sensitive topic of intelligence.

Latané, B., & Darley, J. M. (1970). *The unresponsive bystander: Why doesn't he help?* New York: Appleton-Century-Crofts. This book is an early summary of the work done on bystander apathy. Many studies are discussed, in addition to the one on which we focused.

Lindzey, G., & Aronson, E. (Eds.) (1985). *The handbook of social psychology* (3rd ed., Vols. 1–2). New York: Random House. Considered the definitive source book for social psychologists, *The Handbook* contains a comprehensive review of every major topic within the field. Although it may prove too expensive for your budget, the library's copy should be your first stop when you are exploring any topic in social psychology.

Matarazzo, J. D. (1979). *Wechsler's measurement and appraisal of adult intelligence* (5th ed.). New York: Oxford University Press. This book's title implies a narrower scope than is actually addressed. In addition to Wechsler, the book covers all the details of modern IQ testing and has several chapters on the history of both the concept of intelligence and intelligence tests.

Milgram, S. (1992). *The individual in a social world* (2nd ed.). New York: McGraw-Hill. This book surveys the work of Stanley Milgram, with considerable coverage given to his studies of obedience. Other topics include research ethics, urban living, and social cognition.

Popplestone, J. A., & McPherson, M. W. (1994). *An illustrated history of American psychology.* Madison, WI: Brown & Benchmark. This is a wonderful "picture book" that is great fun to flip through. Several chapters examine the impact of the two world wars on American applied psychology, and the format allows you to actually "see" some of the innovations.

Spence, J., & Helmreich, R. (1978). *Masculinity & femininity: Their psychological dimensions, correlates, & antecedents.* Austin, TX: University of Texas Press. Spence and Helmreich's book is one of the pioneering works in the social psychology of gender, and it remains an excellent source of information for anyone with interests in the area of gender.

The Cognitive "Revolution"

CHAPTER 18

Herbert Simon
Jerome Bruner
Lev Vygotsky
Jean Piaget
Ludwig Wittgenstein
Frederic Bartlett

1880 1890 1900 1910 1920 1930

Franz Kafka is born

Adolf Hitler is born

Paul Gauguin paints *Two Tahitian Women*

The *Titanic* sinks, over 1,500 drown

German torpedoes sink the *Lusitania,* killing 1,198 during WWI

The last Allied troops leave the Rhineland

OUTLINE

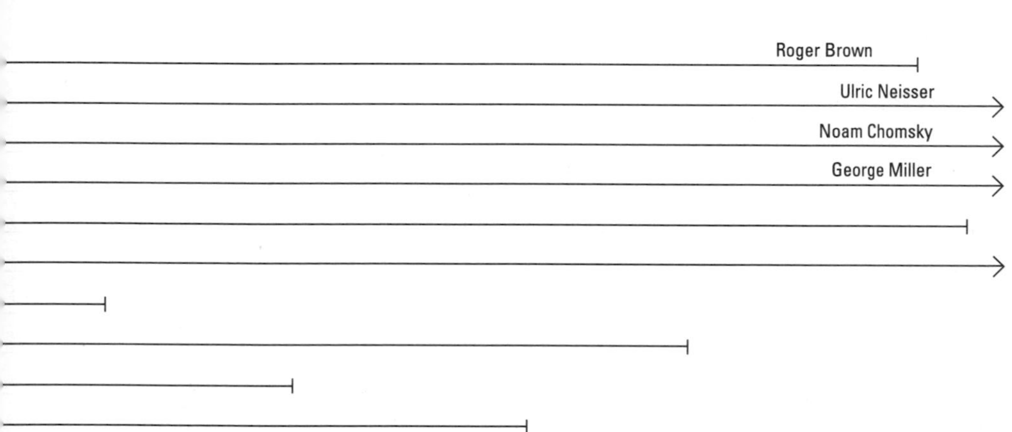

1940 1950 1960 1970 1980 1990 2000 2010

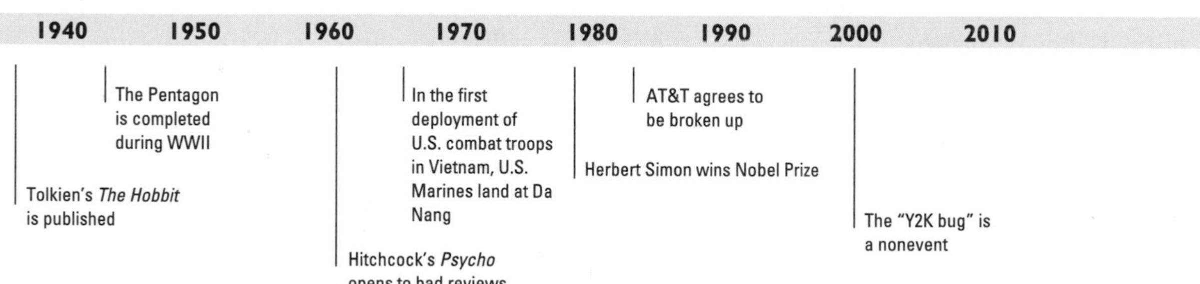

In the first chapter, we mentioned the philosopher of science Thomas Kuhn and his conception of scientific revolutions (Kuhn, 1970). Although Kuhn's thesis was developed to explain the evolution of theories and paradigms in the physical sciences (e.g., physics, chemistry, geology), many writers have applied Kuhn's work to psychology, especially to the waning of behaviorism and the rise of cognitive psychology (Gholson & Barker, 1985; Henley, 1989; Koch, 1975; Palermo, 1971). Kuhn's ideas have even been used to structure history of psychology texts (e.g., Bolles, 1993), although some historians have argued against using Kuhn in this way (e.g., Leahey, 1992).

For Kuhn (1970), theoretical revolution in science was a matter of evolving paradigms. A science begins with a period of agreement about what a given discipline is, about its subject matter, and about its appropriate methodology. At this point, there is only one paradigm (model or world view). Kuhn called this "normal" science, because the period tends to be long, calm, and concerned with working out the details of a grand theory that everyone in the science endorses. During this time, what needs to be done and how to do it are clear. Staying focused on the task is enforced socially and economically via such rewards as promotion, tenure, publications, and grants.

This "normal" science period *inevitably* ends when the discipline encounters a phenomenon anomalous to the theory. An anomaly is an event that does not fit within the standard pattern, and as Kuhn (1970) observed, an anomaly in science often requires substantive theoretical change. Discovery of the anomalous phenomenon causes the discipline's veteran researchers to begin patching the holes the phenomenon has created within their theoretical framework. Concurrently, younger researchers are likely to suggest radically different and competing theories to explain the new phenomenon. The young must provide such new theories, as more seasoned researchers have the old explanatory system at the core of their understanding of their science.

During the unstable period, competition exists between the old theory and a number of new alternatives. Eventually one of the new competitors emerges "victorious." Once all the old guard have been deposed at granting agencies and editorial boards, and as department heads, a new paradigm and a new era of normal science begins. The new theory in turn will rise, flourish, and prosper, but it too will eventually encounter the anomaly that will be its undoing.

There are certainly aspects of Kuhn's (1970) theory that should seem familiar to you. As the systems of psychology matured, they acquired some paradigmatic elements: for example, a grand theory, a shared methodology, and a system of rewards. We can view Darwin's theory of evolution, or positivistic conceptions of science, as the anomaly, and the new systems can be seen as the young competitors arising to replace long-standing folk theories of human behavior. From the Kuhnian perspective, we might argue that behaviorism emerged as the new paradigm for scientific psychology. Language can be viewed as the anomaly that undermined behaviorism and, in turn, provided the foundation for a new, cognitive paradigm. Note, however, that it is also possible to argue that the shift from behaviorism to cognitive psychology may not be best characterized as a "paradigm shift" (e.g., Greenwood, 1999).

FORERUNNERS TO THE COGNITIVE REVOLUTION

Although the widely used phrase *cognitive revolution* seems to affirm the value of using Kuhn's (1970) theory as a tool for understanding the history of psychology, there are inconsistencies between Kuhn's model and the historical record. One important inconsistency is that the study of cognition did not emerge as a new theory in the latter half of this century but, rather, has a long history of its own. The ideas of Plato (Chapter 2) provide much of the foundation of modern cognitive science, including what could perhaps be seen as its central question—the nature and structure of knowledge.

Descartes, Locke, and Kant (Chapters 4, 5, and 6, respectively) are important—and in Kant's case perhaps essential—stepping stones to modern cognitive science. Descartes's concern with the mind-body relationship, Locke's analysis of thought and thinking, and Kant's a priori categories each, in turn, advanced our interest and understanding of mental events. Following Kant, German rationalism in all its guises—phenomenology and act psychology (Chapter 8), Gestalt psychology (Chapter 14)—had as its central interest ideas that broadly defined were cognitive. In fact, we suggested several connections between Gestalt psychology and the modern interest in cognition at the conclusion of the Gestalt chapter. Good examples include works on thinking by Bühler, Duncker, Wertheimer, and Zeigarnik, as well as several important contributions to social psychology (Chapter 17), such as Asch's work on conformity and Festinger's studies of *cognitive* dissonance.

Also in Germany, we must recall the contributions of Ebbinghaus (Chapter 8) for his study of memory, and his student Stern, who helped introduce the term *cognition* into academic psychology. In Chapter 10, we reviewed James's interest in the mind, and both Dewey (Chapter 11) and Münsterberg (Chapter 10) provided arguably cognitive works (e.g., Dewey's *How We Think* [1910] and Münsterberg's *On the Witness Stand* [1908]). Schönpflug (1994) has argued that Münsterberg's presidential address to the APA in 1898 presented a plan for psychology as a cognitive science; it was a "road not taken" for the better part of a century.

Mandler (2002a) has argued that the cognitive themes and attitudes were in fact alive in Europe during the heyday of behaviorism in the United States, and you will see that the early contributors to cognitive psychology we will discuss are almost all European psychologists. Consistent with our use of quotation marks around the word *revolution* in this chapter's title, Mandler suggests that the change from behaviorism to the cognitive approach in American psychology evolved over a decade or more. "The term 'revolution' is probably inappropriate—there were no cataclysmic events . . ." (p. 339).

In America, Tolman's purposive behaviorism (Chapter 13) is the clearest, but not the only, example of an interest in cognition by someone we more commonly associate with behaviorism. Clark Hull's (Chapter 13) dissertation was on concept formation, and Jacob Kantor (1936; Chapter 13) produced an early work on psychology and language (*Objective Psychology of Grammar*). From physiological psychology, D. O. Hebb (Chapter 16) "may justly be regarded as a forerunner of contemporary cognitive neuroscience" (Dewsbury, 2002a, p. 20). In Chapter 15, we noted that even Freud can be considered an antecedent to the contemporary study of cognition. A few additional important antecedents remain to be examined, some from within psychology and some from outside the discipline.

Early Contributors in Psychology

Sir Frederic Bartlett

Even in some of his early works (e.g., Bartlett, 1923), Cambridge psychologist **Sir Frederic Charles Bartlett** (1886–1969) was critical of American behaviorism's limited focus. Thus, it is not surprising that *Remembering: A Study in Experimental and Social Psychology* (Bartlett, 1932), his magnum opus, was initially ignored in America. Despite its subtitle, *Remembering* is one of the most important contributions to cognitive psychology ever written. The book marks a departure from thinking about knowledge as occurring in static, atomic bits and focuses instead on larger, meaningful units of information, as well as on the dynamic nature of these units. The new unit is called the **schema,** which can be understood as a mental structure that organizes and summarizes a large number of related experiences. The schemata (*schema* is singular) allow us to combine many particular experiences—for example, our interactions with dogs—into one composite representation, our dog schema.

Bartlett adapted the term *schema* from earlier physiological work by Sir Henry Head (1861–1940), a friend and contemporary of Sir Charles Sherrington (Chapter 7). Although Bartlett was not the first to use the term, both his work and Jean Piaget's (discussed later) demonstrated the concept's utility. Bartlett's methodology included the use of long paragraphs that formed a cohesive, meaningful, whole story. The most famous example is the Kwakiutl Indian tale, the "War of the Ghosts," translated by Franz Boas (Chapter 10).

Bartlett (1932) asked subjects to read the material twice, and then at different time intervals ranging

Courtesy of Harvard College Library.

Frederic Charles Bartlett (1886–1969)

from minutes to weeks, he had subjects reproduce the story as completely as possible. Although subjects tended to omit details, they seemed to recall that the story was a coherent and meaningful narrative and worked to preserve that more "schematic" structure. As they forgot or misremembered actual story details, they reconstructed plausible new elements and connections to maintain a coherent narrative in the story they retold; hence the term **reconstructive memory.**

For example, an important element near the end of the story read: "When the sun rose he fell down. Something black came out of his mouth. His face became contorted." In one study of serial reproductions, the element became over time:

> When the sun rose he fell down. And he gave a cry, and as he opened his mouth a black thing rushed from it.

> He felt no pain until sunrise the next day, when, on trying to rise, a great black thing flew out of his mouth.

> He lived that night, and the next day, but at sunset his soul fled black from his mouth.

> He lived through the night and the next day, but died at sunset, and his soul passed out from his mouth.

> His spirit left the world. (Selections from Bartlett, 1932, p. 127)

The changes suggested to Bartlett (1932) that memory was schematic, with subjects tending to capture the meaningful "big picture" and reconstructing the details based on a combination of what they actually recalled and what, based on other knowledge and similar events, seemed likely to have occurred. Bartlett's research suggests that our reported knowledge of an event can be contaminated by factors such as our own interests and prior experiences, an observation similar to that of Francis Bacon (Chapter 4) in his discussion of idols.

In Chapter 1, we mentioned the empirical works of both Ulric Neisser and Elizabeth Loftus (also Chapter 17) and first raised the issue of reconstructive memory in the context of the goodness of source material in writing a history text. In Neisser's and Loftus's work, we see modern research directly connected to Bartlett's ideas. Because Bartlett concluded that memories are almost certain to contain multiple errors, his work is likely to be cited in any discussion of such phenomena as false memory retrieval, inaccurate eyewitness testimony, and memory errors in general (Roediger, 2000).

After examining the effect of Bartlett's *Remembering* on psychology, Johnston (2001) has identified three historical peaks of interest in the work. The first occurred at the time the book was published and consisted of attempts to replicate and extend Bartlett's study. The second occurred during the 1960s and 1970s, when cognitive psychology supplanted behaviorism. At that time, Bartlett's schema idea superseded behaviorism's S-R, trace concept of memory. The third peak is a current interest in the second part of Bartlett's book, which focuses on social factors affecting memory recall.

Lev Vygotsky

Lev Vygotsky is another forerunner of modern cognitive psychology who deserves mention. Although Vygotsky is not as intimately connected to the modern research agenda as Bartlett, he is a person whose ideas have recently come of age.

Lev S. Vygotsky (1896–1934) was born into a middle-class Jewish banking family that lived near Minsk in Byelorussia. By age 18, although Vygotsky's primary interests were art and Hegel (Chapter 6), his family insisted that he attend the medical school at the Moscow State University. Vygotsky soon transferred to the law school and enrolled concurrently at another university to continue his studies in the humanities. Whereas his goal seems to have been to become a literary critic, Vygotsky clearly absorbed a broad and quality education during his university years.

After finishing college in 1917, Vygotsky moved to Gomel, where his parents were living. The postrevolutionary period was difficult for many, and Vygotsky found humble employment teaching literature first in a high school and then at a teachers' college, which also allowed him to offer lectures in psychology. During this period, Vygotsky educated himself in both psychology and linguistics by reading classic works, including books by James and Freud (Kozulin, 1986). Vygotsky also stayed active in the arts, working in the theater, publishing several articles, and founding the literary journal *Verask.*

In 1924, Vygotsky delivered his first paper in psychology, a work on the limits of studying the reflex, at the second Psychoneurological Congress in Leningrad. Based on this work, A. R. Luria (Chapter 16) invited him to join the Moscow Institute of Psychology. Like Vygotsky, Luria was an eclectic psychologist. His research on human conflict (Luria, 1932) earned him early acclaim in America. Later studies with a man with a spectacular "photographic memory" (Luria, 1968) and a variety of works in psychoneurology combined to make Luria perhaps the most important Russian psychologist in the post-Pavlov period. Despite his acclaim, in an autobiographical essay, much of which was devoted to Vygotsky, Luria (1974) repeatedly stressed the importance of Vygotsky's influence both on himself and on the development of Soviet psychology.

Archives of the History of American Psychology – The University of Akron.

Lev Vygotsky (1896–1934)

In 1925, Vygotsky submitted what became *The Psychology of Art* as his doctoral thesis. Beyond art, Vygotsky worked with children and animals and investigated such diverse phenomena as intelligence, memory, and cultural influences on cognition. An excellent sample of Vygotsky's writings has been collected and published in English as *Mind and Society* (Vygotsky, 1978). Vygotsky's most famous work, *Thought and Language* (Vygotsky, 1934/1986), was written, like most of his publications, to compare divergent opinions from different psychological systems. In the process, Vygotsky attempted to explain the systems' differences and also to offer a new and unifying solution. Thus, William Stern (Chapter 8),

Karl Bühler and Wolfgang Köhler (Chapter 14), Jean Piaget (below), and Robert Yerkes and John Watson (both Chapter 12) all played a central role in Vygotsky's attempt to account for the relationship between thought and language.

In many ways, Vygotsky anticipated the "Cognitive Revolution" itself, as his central thesis was that mainstream empirical psychology—the Wundtian program and behaviorism—was not well suited to explain higher cognitive processes. In content, his preference most resembled Gestalt psychology and the works of Stern and the Würzburgers (Chapter 8). Vygotsky's goal was a unified psychology that would provide an account of mind within the context of the other natural sciences and accepted scientific methodology. Unfortunately, although Vygotsky developed an ambitious plan for psychology's unification, he actually had the opposite effect (Joravsky, 1988).

Dead of tuberculosis at 38, much of Vygotsky's work was published posthumously and was not translated from Russian until decades later. Probably because of anti-Semitism, *Thought and Language* was banned in the Soviet Union from 1936 until 1956 and was not translated into English for many years after that.

Until recently, Bartlett's work on schema theory and Vygotsky's contributions to cognitive development have been overshadowed by another European psychologist's interest in the same topics.

Jean Piaget

Jean Piaget (1896–1980) was born in Neuchâtel, Switzerland. In an autobiographical essay, Piaget (1952) recalled his father as an academic who worked primarily in medieval literature, and he described his mother as having a "rather neurotic temperament." Perhaps because of his mother, Piaget's first interests in psychology were in psychoanalysis and psychopathology.

Like some others we have encountered—for example, Leibniz (Chapter 4) and John Stuart Mill (Chapter 5)—Piaget was incredibly precocious, producing his first scientific paper at age 10. Recognizing the boy's abilities and interests, the director of Neuchâtel's natural history museum, an authority on molluscs, took Piaget under his wing. After the director's death, Piaget continued his mentor's research, producing over 20 publications on molluscs when he was between the ages of 15 and 19. Piaget's international reputation led one of his readers to offer him a curator's position in Geneva, which Piaget declined because he had not finished high school.

A vacation with his godfather, who aimed to "teach [him] the 'creative evolution' of Bergson" (Piaget, 1952, p. 240), resulted in a profound revelation: "The identification of God with life . . . enabled me to see in biology the explanation of all things and of the mind itself" (p. 240). Piaget dedicated his life to the search for biological explanations of knowledge. Somewhat later, he found that Bergson (Chapter 16) had not presented science's last word, as his godfather had led him to believe. "Between biology and the analysis of knowledge I needed something other than a philosophy. I believe it was at that moment that I discovered a need that could be satisfied only by psychology" (p. 240).

To fulfill this need, Piaget began reading everything that came his way, including the work of such philosophers as Kant, Spencer (Chapter 9), Comte (Chapter 5), and Tarde (Chapter 17), and that of such psychologists as James, Ribot (Chapter 5), and Janet (Chapter 15). This reading led to Piaget's "system," whose core principle was the idea that in all areas of life there are "totalities" different from their parts and that these "wholes" impose organization on the parts. Not surprisingly, Piaget (1952) wrote, "If I had known at that time (1913–1915) the work of Wertheimer and of Köhler, I would have become a Gestaltist . . ." (p. 242). James Mark Baldwin (Chapter 10) was another major influence on Piaget (Inhelder, 1977).

Piaget earned his bachelor's degree at 18 and his Ph.D. in biology (with a thesis on molluscs) at 22. In 1918, he spent a year in Zurich, where he worked in Bleuler's (Chapter 16) clinic, studied briefly with Jung (Chapter 15), and continued to study molluscs. In Paris in 1919, Piaget was recommended to Binet's associate, Théodore Simon (Chapter 17), who gave Piaget the task of adapting some of Cyril Burt's (Chapter 17) British work for use with French children. Piaget developed a different approach to children's intelligence than that taken by Binet and Simon, carefully questioning the children to tease out their thought processes. In this way, Piaget discovered that intelligence grows qualitatively with age as well as quantitatively, as Binet had assumed. That is, older children may use cognitive abilities to solve a particular problem that a younger child, without the particular abilities, cannot grasp. In the study of children's cognitive abilities, Piaget had found his niche: He would investigate the biological development of knowledge through the psychogenetic development of the child. Piaget called his program **genetic epistemology,** genetic in the sense of developmental rather than hereditary, and epistemology by reference to the branch of philosophy that studies the nature and foundations of knowledge.

Based on his initial studies of cognitive development in children, Piaget published two articles in the *Journal de Psychologie,* and a third was accepted by the Swiss psychologist **Edouard Claparède** (1873–1940) for the journal he had founded, *Archives de Psychologie.* Claparède, professor at Geneva and the founder of the Rousseau Institute for the study of educational science, offered Piaget the position of "director of studies" at the Institute (Brainerd, 1996). At the Institute, Piaget had the freedom to perform research in which he was interested and had excellent collaborators, including Valentine Châtenay, whom Piaget subsequently married.

Piaget was professor of psychology at the University of Geneva from 1929 to 1954, and in 1956 he founded the Institute for Genetic Epistemology at the University, where scholars from all over the world can come to discuss issues in cognitive development. The results of these discussions are published annually in the monograph *Studies in Genetic Epistemology.* Always a man of broad interests, Piaget was affiliated with other area universities in contexts ranging from sociology to molluscs.

Although Piaget received some early acclaim in America (e.g., an honorary Harvard doctorate in 1936), from 1933 until 1950 none of his works were translated into English. After World War II, this neglect was mainly caused by American psychology's behaviorist *Zeitgeist.* However, with behaviorism's relative decline and the 1960s growth of interest in cognitive psychology, Piaget was rediscovered. The translation of Piaget's *Psychology of Intelligence* in 1950 was the first of a wave of publications that resulted in his becoming perhaps the world's leading child development theorist. In 1969, Piaget received the APA's Distinguished Scientific Contribution Award.

Piaget (1896–1980) and unidentified child

Piaget's Psychology. Two important components of Piaget's psychology warrant discussion here: his stage model of cognitive development and his contribution to modern schema theory. Piaget's work was not the first of its kind in either case. Several similar stage theories of development predated Piaget's theory, and some alternatives (e.g., Vygotsky's) were perhaps better articulated. Key elements of Piaget's schema theory can be traced both to Baldwin (1898) and to certain Gestalt psychology principles. Still, Piaget's contributions to both areas were substantial, primarily because it was *his* presentation of cognitive developmental stages and schema theory that mainstream psychology eventually incorporated.

From observations of his own and many other children, Piaget concluded that the child is born with certain simple reflex actions, such as the grasping reflex and the suckling reflex, that it uses to interact with its world. He called these independent reflexes schemata, because they organize the infant's responses to experience. The child also has an inherent predisposition to organize the simple schemata into higher-order ones, such as when the infant combines its grasping schema with its suckling schema and holds the bottle while sucking from it.

Additionally, an infant inherits the processes of **assimilation** and **accommodation.** If an experience fits the individual's schemata, then the experience is assimilated into the mind. On the other hand, if there is not a match between the experience and existing schemata, then the schemata will be altered to accommodate reality. To illustrate, a young child initially may have a broad schema for the concept of *dog,* calling all four-legged animals *doggies.* The child soon encounters a quadruped that meows and purrs rather than barks and wags its tail, and this mismatch between the existing schema and reality produces disequilibrium, which is the incentive for the child to refine his or her dog schema (assimilation) and to develop a cat schema (accommodation).

Piaget divided the cognitive development of a child into four stages, which he believed all children go through, although not necessarily at exactly the same ages. Each stage is organized around a dominant theme, and each contains qualitatively different behaviors.

Piaget's first stage is the **sensorimotor stage,** which lasts from birth until approximately age 2. During this stage, the infant is learning the relations between its sensory apparatus and its motor responses. One of the period's defining features is a lack of the **object permanence** concept. That is, the infant responds as though he or she does not realize an object continues to exist if it is no longer being sensed (i.e., out of sight, out of mind).

From 2 until approximately 7, the child is in Piaget's **preoperational stage,** during which he or she discovers the operations (e.g., plans, strategies, rules) that will be used for solving problems and classifying information. During this stage, the child's thinking is likely to exhibit animism—the tendency to attribute life to inanimate objects—and egocentrism—the view that the self is the center of everything. The preoperational stage's hallmark is a lack of the concept of **conservation of quantity:** that is, the child does not realize that something's quantity remains the same with changes in appearance.

Between about 7 and 11, the child has developed the concept of conservation when dealing with concrete objects and is in what Piaget called the **concrete operational stage.** As long as a problem concerns tangible things the child can deal with directly, then the child can probably solve it. Problems involving abstract concepts, imagined realities, and symbols require cognitive skills not fully developed until Piaget's final stage.

The **formal operational stage** extends from about 12 or 13 through adulthood. Now the young person can think abstractly and has the cognitive ability to test problem solutions hypothetically and systematically.

Piaget's Influence. Piaget's theory of cognitive development has fostered a wealth of research, some of which has disagreed with specific aspects of the theory (see Halford, 1989, for a review of research testing Piagetian concepts). For example, it is now considered less certain that the child goes through distinct stages and that children at higher stages have abilities younger children completely lack. That is, development is apparently more continuous than Piaget thought. Also, questions have been raised about the degree to which Piaget's hypothesized stages are tied to Western civilization and may not generalize to other cultures.

Although the theory may be wrong in certain details, Piaget's general concepts are still considered valid (e.g., see the July 1996 issue of *Psychological Science* for an appraisal of his work). The cognitive abilities of the child are not the same as those of the adult. Through a combination of biological maturation and increasing experience with the world, the child's schemata are altered to better represent reality and cognitive development occurs.

We will conclude our discussion of Piaget and his contributions with a brief review of the life and work of perhaps his most important student at the University of Geneva and his long-time collaborator, Bärbel Inhelder.

Bärbel Inhelder

Bärbel Inhelder (1913–1997) was born in St. Gallen, Switzerland. From her zoologist father, Inhelder learned pre-Socratic philosophy and Darwin (Chapter 9), whereas her mother, a writer, exposed her to Shakespeare and the German classics (Inhelder, 1989). In 1932, Inhelder began work at the Rousseau Institute in Geneva, where she came into contact with Claparède and Piaget.

Inhelder began a lengthy collaboration with Piaget at the Institute, quickly producing several major publications (e.g., *The Child's Construction of Quantities;* Piaget & Inhelder, 1941) before she completed her doctoral thesis. After receiving her degree in 1943, Inhelder continued to work with Piaget, once again producing several important efforts (e.g., *The Origin of the Idea of Chance in Children;* Piaget & Inhelder, 1951). In 1948, the Institute began offering graduate degrees, and Inhelder was named part of the psychology faculty.

The rise of interest in cognitive psychology in America in the late 1960s led to interactions between Inhelder and cognitive pioneers such as Jerome Bruner (discussed later) at Harvard. These interactions facilitated the rediscovery of Piaget's ideas and the discovery of Inhelder's many contributions. Indeed, Inhelder deserves recognition as one of the first and most important female contributors to cognitive psychology.

Moral Development

When Inhelder first met Piaget in 1932, he had just completed *The Moral Judgment of the Child.* Although Piaget was an important contributor to the study of moral reasoning in children, his book was not the first work by a psychologist on morality, as Wendorf (2001) has documented an extensive history of the topic in the period from 1894 to 1932. Following Piaget, the central figure became Lawrence Kohlberg.

Lawrence Kohlberg (1927–1987)

Born in Bronxville, New York, **Lawrence Kohlberg** (1927–1987) was the son of a wealthy businessman and the product of the finest college preparatory schools. Kohlberg joined the Merchant Marines following high school graduation, and the experience of smuggling Jews from Europe to Palestine may have been the spark leading to his later interest in differences in moral reasoning.

Returning to America after his Merchant Marine service, Kohlberg completed his B.A. at the University of Chicago in only a year. Based primarily on Piaget's earlier efforts, Kohlberg's 1958 Ph.D. thesis at Chicago signaled the beginning of his lifelong devotion to studying moral development. Following several interim positions, Kohlberg settled at Harvard in 1967. On a Central American trip in 1973, Kohlberg contracted a disease that ruined his health and led to his suicide in 1987.

Kohlberg theorized three major stages of moral reasoning, each containing two levels. In the **preconventional stage,** moral behavior is motivated by the avoidance of punishment in the first level and by the desire to be rewarded in the second level.

In the **conventional stage,** moral decisions are motivated by social rules. At the third level, good behavior is behavior that earns the praise of other people, whereas behaving correctly at the fourth level means obeying the laws established by people in power.

In the **postconventional stage,** the individual is guided by internalized moral principles. At the fifth level, these are the principles established by society for its members' benefit. Finally, at the sixth level, the individual has incorporated and is influenced by universally ethical principles of right and wrong (e.g., by rules such as "Do unto others as you would have them do unto you").

Although Kohlberg's stage theory is still widely taught and respected, it has not escaped criticism. As we noted earlier, stage theories can always be challenged for de-emphasizing continuous changes in development and for depending on the cultural context from which they are derived.

One of Kohlberg's best-known critics, Carol Gilligan has largely focused on gender differences in moral development. Gilligan (1982) noted that theorists such as Freud, Piaget, and Kohlberg (with whom Gilligan taught a course on moral development at Harvard-Radcliffe) concluded that women are morally inferior to men because of how they reason about hypothetical moral dilemmas. Instead, Gilligan has found that women are more likely to consider the interpersonal context of the problem, probably because they are socialized to be caring rather than judgmental. Gilligan's speculations highlight the importance of experience for moral development and the relevance of gender-based issues outside of personality and social psychology.

Early Contributions Outside of Psychology

Although human development is one element of contemporary cognitive psychology, it is not the only one. For example, Claude Shannon (1938) observed that basic logic could be contained in an electronic relay, an insight that gave birth to the modern computer era. From the outset, computing machines and psychology have been related. In 1948, the term **cybernetics** was coined by applied mathematician Norbert Wiener (1894–1964) to cover the study of the fundamental control processes of behavior in both animals and machines. You may recall that in Chapter 13 we mentioned Hull's thoughts on machines and general principles of learning. By 1950, theorists such as **Alan Turing** (1912–1954), the "father" of artificial intelligence, had already observed both how much of human cognitive activity the computer could be programmed to display and the implications this would have for modeling and studying higher cognitive processes such as language and thought (Turing, 1950).

In an area related to cybernetics, McCulloch and Pitts (1943) showed that the operations of nerve cells could be modeled with symbolic logic. Their paper is considered "a landmark event in the history of cybernetics, and fundamental to the development of cognitive science and artificial intelligence" (Abraham, 2002, p. 3). Abraham has presented a fascinating look at the context within which the collaboration between Warren McCulloch (1898–1969), a philosophically minded neuropsychiatrist, and Walter Pitts (1923–1969), a mathematical genius, occurred. McCulloch and Pitts's efforts further reinforced the idea that one could use computers as models of such basic psychological processes as learning and perception.

Thus, several events outside cognitive psychology, or even psychology per se, have relevance for the rise of cognitive science. Gardner (1985) stressed the importance of a 1948 meeting at the California Institute of Technology concerning "Cerebral Mechanisms in Behavior." In the opening address, the eminent quantum theory mathematician John von Neumann reviewed evidence that the brain is analogous to a computer. Gardner credited the third speaker, Karl Lashley (Chapter 16), with outlining a program that became the interdisciplinary new cognitive science.

Computer science is not the only area outside psychology relevant to the modern interest in cognition. Gardner (1985) listed key changes in linguistics, the philosophy of language (and psychology) as pioneered by Gilbert Ryle (1949) and Ludwig Wittgenstein (1953), the rise of cultural anthropology, and many advances in neurology as being important to cognitive science's development. We will next examine one of the changes in linguistics that was most salient for psychology.

NOAM CHOMSKY

Avram Noam Chomsky (1928–) was born in Philadelphia and completed his undergraduate and graduate work in linguistics at the University of Pennsylvania before joining the Massachusetts Institute of Technology (MIT) faculty in 1955. Chomsky is considered the historically most important contributor to linguistics. In addition, his contributions to political theory are held in almost as much esteem.

The interplay between psychology and linguistics before Chomsky was limited. **Charles Kay Ogden** (1889–1957) represents perhaps the most notable bridge (e.g., Ogden & Richards, 1923). An English linguistic reformer, Ogden was an insightful investigator of the relationship between language and thought. However, if there has been a cognitive revolution, no person is more responsible for it than Noam Chomsky, whose review of Skinner's *Verbal Behavior* (Chomsky, 1959; Chapter 13) came as a rallying cry to foes of radical behaviorism.

Donna Coveney/MIT.

Noam Chomsky (1928–)

Chomsky (1959) began his response to Skinner's analysis of language by attacking behaviorism's fundamental concepts—reinforcement, stimulus, and so on—as being ineffectual when directed to the topic of human language. Although Lashley had already observed that there seemed to be more to language than the behaviorist analysis revealed, Chomsky popularized a rationalistic, and in his own terms Cartesian (Chomsky, 1966), alternative to language and language acquisition. By *Cartesian* Chomsky meant Descartes's innate characteristics of the mind, which Chomsky believes include a language acquisition device (**LAD**). For Chomsky, the story of language development has less to do with learning than it does with inherent structures in the mind (or brain) preprogrammed for language acquisition.

Chomsky argued that what a child must learn in order to speak correctly and understand a language is too complicated to be acquired through behaviorist learning principles and accounted for through stimulus and reinforcement. Chomsky insisted the language spoken to children was too poor a stimulus (his **poverty-of-stimulus argument**) and that reinforcement of correct grammar was too haphazard to provide a satisfactory behavioral account of language acquisition. What psychology needed was a revolutionary way of thinking about language. Chomsky's nativist alternative revitalized ideas first expressed by Wilhelm von Humboldt (1767–1835). For Chomsky (1957), various biological, **syntactic structures** exist that contain the basic grammar rules of human language.

Chomsky's poverty-of-stimulus argument has matured into a widely accepted criticism of Skinner in particular, and behaviorism in general, as a unified theory of all aspects of (human) behavior (e.g., Chomsky, 1980). For many, language was the Kuhnian anomaly that led to behaviorism's downfall.

Thus, the task of psycholinguistics was to discover and analyze the inherent mental structures that provide for language, and much of the important research has been conducted by psychologists such as George Miller and Roger Brown (both discussed later). Following Chomsky, American psychology's focus has shifted from an almost exclusive analysis of behavior back to the study of mental events. Also, the interaction between psychology and linguistics has strengthened with psychology's new cognitive focus. Currently, the study of figurative language (e.g., metaphor, analogy, irony), as pioneered by George Lakoff (1941–), is an increasingly important area of collaboration between psychology and linguistics (e.g., Lakoff & Johnson, 1980).

Courtesy of the Harvard University Archives.

Jerome Seymour Bruner (1915–)

JEROME BRUNER AND GEORGE MILLER

Jerome Bruner and George Miller are considered foundational figures in the renewed study of cognition. Bruner and Miller together were founders in 1962 of the Center for Cognitive Studies at Harvard, an event Hilgard (1987) called a "genuine milestone" in the history of cognitive psychology.

Jerome Seymour Bruner

New York–born **Jerome Seymour Bruner** (1915–) was trained initially by William McDougall (Chapter 12) at Duke and by Gordon Allport (Chapter 17) at Harvard, where he completed his Ph.D. in 1941. In a biographical sketch, Anglin (1973) also listed Lashley, Piaget, and Tolman (Chapter 13) as Bruner's intellectual mentors. During World War II, Bruner studied public morale with the Rensis Likert group (Chapter 17) and later surveyed public opinion with Hadley Cantril (mentioned in Chapter 1) at Princeton's Office of Public Opinion Research.

Bruner returned to Harvard and teaching in 1945 and conducted studies in both social psychology and perception. In the early 1950s, Bruner became interested in thinking and concept formation and assisted Sir Frederic Bartlett in holding one of the first conferences on cognition at Cambridge in 1955 (Bruner, 1980).

Bruner's classic *A Study of Thinking* (Bruner, Goodnow, & Austin, 1956) appeared the next year. The interdisciplinary nature of cognitive science and some of its historical connections are evident from the acknowledgments in the book's preface, which include nuclear physicist J. Robert Oppenheimer; perceptual researcher Egon Brunswick (1903–1955), who worked under Karl Bühler before coming to America at Tolman's invitation; and Herbert Langfeld (Chapter 10).

In another historical connection, Bruner (1986) told about how he first heard of Lev Vygotsky at a 1954 party at Wilder Penfield's home (Chapter 7). Bruner's independently formed ideas about language and memory were similar to Vygotsky's, and Bruner was instrumental in introducing Vygotsky to an increasingly receptive American audience.

Bruner eventually settled at the New School for Social Research in New York. Several recurrent themes in Bruner's writings that illustrate both his personal interests and cognitive psychology's broader aims include (1) the relationship between perception and conception, (2) the developmental aspects of cognition, and (3) applications—such as educational applications—of the study of cognition. For example, after first calling attention to the more intuitive and creative aspects of knowing decades ago (Bruner, 1962), Bruner's more recent works (e.g., Bruner, 1986) have criticized cognitive psychology trends that continue to focus on the logical and systematic aspects of thinking while neglecting other, more flexible and imaginative, aspects of knowing. The recognition of diverse cognitive styles holds promise for how children may be optimally educated.

George Armitage Miller

George Armitage Miller (1920–) wrote that his first experience with psychology came via a chance conversation with a textbook salesman. About the conversation's subject matter, Miller (1989) recalled that "I could recognize the devil when I saw him" (p. 391).

At the University of Alabama, Miller attended his first psychology seminar, which focused on Kurt Goldstein (Chapter 14), although Miller himself focused more on Katherine James, who soon became his wife (Miller, 1989). After earning a master's degree in speech, Miller stayed at Alabama as a psychology instructor. In 1942, his psychology mentor persuaded him to go to Harvard to work with E. G. Boring (Chapters 1 and 8) and S. S. Stevens (Chapters 13 and 17).

At Harvard, Miller became close friends with Wendell Garner (Chapter 17), and his work for the military on jamming signals was accepted for his dissertation. Miller stayed at Harvard until 1951, and his initial contributions were in pioneering "mathematical psychology" in the tradition of Claude Shannon and Norbert Wiener. After establishing a laboratory and a speech-perception research program during 2 years at MIT, Miller returned to Harvard to replace the retiring Boring. Miller's (1951) *Language and Communication* summarized much of his research to that point and is considered one of the seminal publications in psycholinguistics (e.g., Crowther-Heyck, 1999).

John T. Miller, courtesy Princeton University Communications Office.

George Armitage Miller (1920–)

The Magical Number Seven

Miller's (1956) famous paper, "The Magical Number Seven, Plus or Minus Two: Some Limits on Our Capacity for Processing Information," involves the intersection of mathematical information theory and human communication. The paper's central point was that **short-term memory**—consciousness—has an average capacity of 7 ± 2 **chunks** (items of information) independent of the size of the chunks (recall J. M. Cattell's similar findings from Chapter 8). Although the idea of chunking stimulated various related memory studies, the paper is also important because of its nativist implications about the fixed capacity of our ability to process information. In addition, it was a paper about *consciousness* published during the hegemony of behaviorism. As testimony to the paper's continuing relevance, it was partially reprinted in 1994 in *Psychological Review* as a prelude to two commentaries (Baddeley, 1994; Shiffrin & Nosofsky, 1994).

In 1955, Miller attended Bruner and Bartlett's conference at Cambridge, and in 1956 Miller and Chomsky met at a symposium on information theory at MIT. In 1957, the two began to collaborate on several works (e.g., Chomsky & Miller, 1958). In 1958–1959, Miller was a fellow at the Center for the Advanced Study of the Behavioral Sciences at Stanford, where he was exposed to the growing interest in and research on language by anthropologists. He also came into contact with Karl Pribram (Chapter 16) and learned of related advances in neuroscience.

Plans and the Structure of Behavior

Cambridge engineering psychologist **Donald Broadbent** (1926–1993) was an early popularizer of the information-processing metaphor with his book *Perception and Communication* (Broadbent, 1958). **Information processing** describes the application of cybernetic information and control theories to human behavior and mental events, and the first generation of cognitive psychologists accepted this term as a shorthand for their interests. Miller's "The Magical Number Seven" and *Perception and Communication* by Broadbent—who was educated by, worked with, and then replaced Bartlett at Cambridge—are often heralded as the publications that marked the beginning of the cognitive revolution.

However, Miller, Galanter, and Pribram's (1960) *Plans and the Structure of Behavior* may be a better candidate for the signal publication. This book introduced the **TOTE** (Test-Operate-Test-Exit) unit as the structure of behavior. A TOTE unit is a hypothetical, hierarchical, feedback loop that includes cognitive as well as behavioral components and is assumed to occupy the same theoretical space as the reflex arc. The TOTE was intended to be a general unit of analysis to explain behavioral processes—*Test* the environment for stimulus information, then *Operate*, or respond, to that information. The TOTE also includes further *Testing* of feedback for the congruence between the organism's planned state and its current state that could continue until the *Exit* conditions are met. If you have ever done any computer programming, you may be struck by how similar the TOTE is to any computational routine that analyzes a variable and then responds differently given the variable's state.

Miller (1989) conceded that the TOTE suffered from the same key problem as the S-R concept: It was too vague. However, the whole information-processing approach to the study of cognitive phenomena emerged from this new analysis of human behavior that included a role for the cognitive processing of information.

Back at Harvard in 1960, Miller approached Bruner about establishing a center for cognitive work, and the two established the Center for Cognitive Studies in 1962. Initial work there focused on empirical, psychological support for Chomsky's linguistic theories (Chomsky became a Center fellow in 1962). Miller (1989) recalled this as the period during which his presentations began to include an opening attack on the narrowness of behaviorism for understanding human cognition. Vygotsky would have been pleased.

By 1965, Chomsky's influence on Miller was clear, as Miller (1965) blasted behavioral approaches to human communication, including his own 1955 text. Other changes were also in the air. Just a few years after being named head of a department at Harvard that then included B. F. Skinner, Miller left and went to Rockefeller University.

Miller remained at Rockefeller for over a decade, during which time his attention shifted from a Chomskyian interest in syntax to broader issues of language and thought. Miller's *Language and Perception* (Miller & Johnson-Laird, 1976) presented the still-prevailing theory of how information about language is stored in the mind. Miller moved to Princeton in 1979 and founded the Princeton Cognitive Science Laboratory in 1986. Still active, he is currently engaged in a computer-based project known as WordNet, which represents a continuation of his interest in the structure and representation of language.

CLASSICAL CONTRIBUTIONS

It would be impossible for us to survey all of modern cognitive psychology in the remainder of this chapter. Instead, we will briefly explore some areas and individuals that are representative of modern cognitive research and illustrate some changes and trends in the area over the last 3 decades.

Words and Things

We have suggested that the study of language is central to modern cognitive psychology, which is not to say that behaviorists had neglected it. Interest in "verbal behavior" existed before Chomsky and certainly before empirical support for his position. In a Kuhnian fashion, several of the younger researchers during the 1960s shifted from the study of word associations in the behaviorist paradigm to the new psycholinguistics. For example, James Deese (1965) wrote the swan song on word associations before writing an important early psycholinguistics textbook (Deese, 1970). Irvin Rock (e.g., Rock, 1957) migrated from associative-learning work to other areas, such as perception. William Estes (Chapter 13) is also an important figure in the change from positivism and behaviorism, through statistical learning, into cognitive psychology. Another important language researcher, James Jenkins (1993) has written reflectively about this transition from behaviorism to cognitive psychology.

We have already noted nonpsychologist Noam Chomsky's foundational impact on psycholinguistics, as did the APA when it honored him with the Distinguished Scientific Contribution Award in 1984. Likewise, George Miller is a candidate for the "dean" of psycholinguistics, as is Roger Brown.

Born of Canadian émigrés, **Roger Brown** (1925–1997) grew up in America. He credited his reading of "thousands" of comic books as one positive factor in his early education. As a member of the Navy aboard the USS *Wichita* in the Pacific Theater following the Battle of Okinawa, Brown read Watson's *Behaviorism,* an event that he felt led him to study psychology after the war (Brown, 1989).

Brown completed his Ph.D. at Michigan and took a position at Harvard in 1952. Although his own teaching and research interests involved social psychology, he was attracted to Bruner's work in cognition, and so Brown, along with Bruner and Miller, attended the conference at Cambridge in 1955. With *Words and Things,* Brown (1958) made his initial mark in psychology and language.

In 1957, Brown moved to MIT, where he came into contact with Noam Chomsky. In 1962, Brown returned to Harvard and began work on two of his best-known publications: *Social Psychology* (Brown, 1965), a classic text that also pioneered social cognition; and *A First Language* (Brown, 1973), which is a careful, empirical analysis of language acquisition in children.

Although Brown did important work in other areas of cognitive psychology—such as research on **flashbulb memories** (Brown & Kulik, 1977), which are memories of first learning about a surprising or emotional experience—he was at the center of the psychological study of language. His work on language acquisition with young children was the first empirical work of its kind and provided much of the data that fueled the lingering Chomsky-Skinner debate.

Although his original analysis and stage model of the language development process has been modified over the last 25 years, the changes often have come from his students' further exploration of phenomena that Brown first recognized (e.g., Maratsos, 1983). For example, Dan Slobin (1985) performed a cross-cultural study of language acquisition. In addition, Jill de Villiers (de Villiers & de Villiers, 1978) analyzed telegraphic speech (e.g., a child saying "hungry" to mean "I am hungry"), and Steven Pinker (1984) examined underextensions of words (using a term too narrowly, such as resisting calling a mosquito an animal). Through his continued interest in social psychology, Brown pioneered the expansion of psycholinguistics from the mere study of words and things into a host of applied settings.

Cognition and Reality

Born in Germany but educated at Harvard, **Ulric Neisser** (1928–) received his undergraduate degree in 1950 and his Ph.D. in 1956. Neisser has taught at

Ulric Neisser (1928–)

several locations, including Cornell, where he was a colleague of James J. Gibson (Chapter 13).

Although he was already a well-established perceptual researcher (e.g., Selfridge & Neisser, 1960), his *Cognitive Psychology* (Neisser, 1967) was the first widely used textbook devoted to the new study of cognition. *Cognitive Psychology* owes a great deal to Bartlett's work on the schema, and Neisser clearly acknowledged his debt to the British psychologist (Roediger, 2000). The book's success catapulted Neisser to center stage, a position from which he published *Cognition and Reality* (Neisser, 1976).

Cognition and Reality advanced the schema as the basis of cognitive psychology and used schema theory to provide a general account of human behavior and development through what Neisser called the **perceptual cycle.** The perceptual cycle suggests that our mental structures (schema) direct our behavior, and our experiences modify our mental representations in an unending cycle.

The book also had three more implicit themes that reflected both Neisser's interests and changes that occurred in the field during the late 1960s and early 1970s. The first theme involved critical appraisal. Neisser offered a critical appraisal of many of the ideas he presented in *Cognitive Psychology* and of the initial information-processing approach to cognition that followed Miller's *Plans and the Structure of Behavior.* Neisser advised future cognitive psychologists to ensure that their laboratory experiments have **ecological validity**—that is, that their results will also generalize to the world outside the laboratory. In fact, Neisser considered the study of real-world problems necessary for a mature cognitive psychology (see Neisser, 1991).

Ecological validity dovetails nicely with a second theme of *Cognition and Reality,* which is a focus on applications of cognitive theories. Neisser acknowledged behaviorism's success as a psychological theory that proved itself useful in everyday life and admonished cognitive theorists to follow that lead. For Neisser, cognitive psychology's ultimate success will rest as much on what it can accomplish outside of academia as with the quality and veracity of its research within academia. Donald Norman's (1988) *The Psychology of Everyday Things* is an excellent example of such a focus on real-world applications. By exploring the cognitive elements in product design, Norman's book has become widely used both in human factors engineering courses and in environmental psychology courses. His examples range from automobiles to kitchen appliances, and throughout the book he shows the relevance of cognitive theory and data (e.g., in areas such as memory, perception, and reasoning) to the design of optimally functional mechanisms.

Cognition and Reality's third theme also has elements of a reconciliation with behaviorism. Neisser advocated a holistic, ecological approach to understanding human nature, and his perceptual cycle includes perception, development, and behavior, as well as cognition. Neisser extensively used the work of self-proclaimed behaviorist James J. Gibson to accomplish the reconciliation. Because Gibson is associated with an ecological approach to perception, Neisser's work is often viewed similarly.

Memory, Categorization, and Reasoning

Since the publication of *Cognition and Reality,* Neisser has also made substantive contributions to two of cognitive psychology's major subfields, memory (e.g., Neisser, 1981; Neisser & Harsch, 1993) and categorization (e.g., Neisser, 1987). We will briefly examine these subfields, along with reasoning.

Memory

Within the cognitive framework, two important discoveries have been made about memory. First, Bartlett found that memory is often schematic and reconstructive, and memory's reconstructive nature continues to be an active research area. For example, Neisser (1981) explored the memory of Watergate principal John Dean and also the flashbulb memory college students had of the space shuttle *Challenger* disaster (Neisser & Harsch, 1993). Both studies further supported memory's schematic nature and provided new information about the factors and conditions that facilitate misleading reconstructions.

The second memory research development began with Atkinson and Shiffrin's (1968) work. As we noted, Miller (1956) distinguished short-term memory—information we can keep in mind for about 1 minute or less (e.g., the start of this sentence, so that you know what the whole sentence means when you get to its end)—from long-term memory, events that may have happened to you years ago that you still remember. But Atkinson and Shiffrin provided the first model of memory from the information-processing point of view. Their work attempted to trace a concept from its initial conscious perception, through a short-term memory storage stage, on into long-term memory. This attempt was important for the recognition that memory was not a unitary phenomenon.

Subsequently, **Endel Tulving** (1927–) has advocated various memory types. Born in Estonia, Tulving listed among his "occupations" (in order) poacher, soldier, prisoner of war, interpreter for the U.S. Army, medical student at Heidelberg, undergraduate psychology major at the University of Toronto, psychology graduate student at Harvard, and, for 35 years, psychology faculty member at the University of Toronto (*American Psychologist,* 1994).

Tulving (e.g., 1972) distinguished between **episodic memory** and **semantic memory.** He observed that some memories are of isolated, emotionless, atemporal facts; these semantic memories include such things as your student identification number and the capital of Texas. Semantic memories resist forgetting and are probably less subject to reconstruction. In contrast, there are also episodic memories that tend to have lots of associations, often include an emotional sense, and have a temporal, narrative structure. Examples include your memory of your first day of school, your last romantic encounter, or breakfast this morning. Episodic memories seem more likely to be both misremembered and forgotten. Tulving's later research (e.g., Tulving, 1985) suggested that the semantic-episodic dichotomy may be too simple and that further distinctions may be required.

Categorization

In *Principles of Psychology,* William James (1890) asserted that **categorization** is the fundamental act of cognition. However, Wittgenstein (1953)—like James, a psychological philosopher—introduced the ideas that brought categorization to the forefront of cognitive psychology. **Ludwig Wittgenstein** (1889–1951) was born into a Viennese family of wealth and connection. His brother Paul was an acclaimed pianist who lost his right arm in World War I. Undeterred, Paul developed a left-handed repertoire, including pieces written for him by such famous composers as Richard Strauss and Maurice Ravel. Ludwig and Paul's sister facilitated Freud's exodus from Austria.

Wittgenstein was formally educated in mathematics and mechanical engineering, and his initial philosophical work was viewed as an important contribution to both logical positivism and applied mathematics. After his release as a World War I military prisoner, Wittgenstein returned to Austria, where he became friends with Karl Bühler. During this period, he taught elementary school, worked at a Catholic monastery he considered joining, and stayed in contact with the leading

European intelligentsia in mathematics and logic (e.g., Bertrand Russell and Rudolph Carnap).

In 1930, Wittgenstein joined the Cambridge faculty, an affiliation he retained for the rest of his academic life. The remainder of Wittgenstein's career was mostly occupied with the philosophy of language and the philosophy of psychology—two subdisciplines of philosophy that Wittgenstein and Gilbert Ryle (below), his Oxford contemporary, largely founded.

Wittgenstein's magnum opus was *Philosophical Investigations* (Wittgenstein, 1953), whose title is probably a play on the title of Husserl's *Logical Investigations* (Chapter 8). *Philosophical Investigations* contains Wittgenstein's discussion of **family resemblance,** which is the point of departure for modern cognitive psychology's interest in categorization. Before Wittgenstein's analysis, it was assumed that to be a member of a category required sharing in some defining attribute. Without reflection, we might say that flight is the defining feature of birds. But observation reveals that not all birds fly (e.g., penguins). If we are not attending to defining features, how can we recognize the penguin as a bird?

The family resemblance concept asserts that a category does not have to have a defining feature that all members share. Instead, there can be a set of features distributed across the category members, with no single feature essential for category inclusion. According to this view, we recognize a member more in terms of its schematic similarity to other members than by perceiving a key trait. Although the idea of family resemblance helped Wittgenstein solve problems he recognized in perception and semantics, he died before seeing the impact of his ideas on psychology, which he spent the latter part of his career criticizing.

More than 20 years after the publication of *Philosophical Investigations,* Eleanor Rosch and Carolyn Mervis (1975) brought Wittgenstein's family resemblance idea into cognitive psychology. Rosch found empirical support for Wittgenstein's suggestion that family resemblances, not defining features, are the core of human categorization. She (e.g., Rosch, 1978) continued to explore empirically the structure and function of our categories and discovered, for example, that categories exist at three levels: superordinate (such as animal or pet); basic (such as dog or cat), which is the level at which we most often speak and think; and subordinate (such as poodle or pomeranian).

Following Rosch's work, categorization came to be understood (as James had suggested) as the fundamental act of cognition, the process by which we organize and access all of our perceptions, knowledge, and memory. The basic-level category's structure remains the focus of much research. For example, Neisser (1987) explored how different contexts affect the formation and use of categories, and Lakoff (1987) examined several possible theories for the structure and internal organization of our mental categories, finding support in anthropology and linguistics as well as in cognitive psychology.

Reasoning

Both Wittgenstein and **Gilbert Ryle** (1900–1976) are sometimes called philosophical behaviorists, although that term may be misleading. Neither supported behaviorism per se, and both considered the psychology of their day terribly confused in its conception of mental events. Both Wittgenstein and Ryle advocated a more phenomenological analysis of language—an analysis of what we say and the behavioral and environmental contexts in which we say it—as part of the corrective they offered to psychology.

A long-time editor of Bain's (Chapter 5) journal *Mind,* Ryle (1949) published *The Concept of Mind,* a book about the mind-body problem, which he called "the ghost in the machine." In an attempt to provide a fresh perspective on the nature of mind, Ryle suggested that we reflect on how we talk and think about it—indeed, about how we talk and think in general. In this vein, Ryle's discussion of the **category mistake** became the book's centerpiece. To illustrate a category mistake, Ryle related the following story, which, by analogy, also illustrates how the mind-body problem had been misconceived.

> A foreigner visiting Oxford or Cambridge for the first time is shown a number of colleges, libraries, playing fields, museums, scientific departments and administrative offices. He then asks "But where is the University? I have seen where the members of the Colleges live, where the Registrar works, where the scientists experiment and the

> rest. But I have not yet seen the University in which reside and work the members of your University." It has then to be explained to him that the University is not another collateral institution, some ulterior counterpart to the colleges, laboratories and offices which he has seen. The University is just the way in which all that he has already seen is organized. (p. 16)

In other words, Ryle (1949) was suggesting that the mind and body are not at the same "level" of analysis, just as the University and the physical buildings at Oxford are not at the same level, even though philosophers and psychologists have long spoken and theorized about the mind and the body as if they exist on the same plane.

Ryle (1949) made another observation about how we think, and it has had a more direct impact on research in cognitive psychology than his discussion of the category mistake. His observation concerns two types of things we might claim to know: "Knowing that" is an intellectual knowing that includes knowing that a bow is used to play the violin, for example. "Knowing how" refers to procedural knowledge, such as how to use a bow to play the violin. Ryle's point is that much of our knowledge is known only intellectually and not through direct experience. Likewise, there are other things we know—such as how to play the violin—that are difficult to express intellectually; instead, our knowledge is demonstrated through motor skills. With this distinction between "knowing that" and "knowing how," Ryle can be seen as a forerunner to modern cognitive psychology's critical study of human knowledge and reasoning. The work of Daniel Kahneman and Amos Tversky provides a more contemporary illustration of research on reasoning.

Daniel Kahneman (1934–) was born in Tel Aviv and raised in France and Israel. He was educated first at Israel's The Hebrew University and later at the University of California at Berkeley. **Amos Tversky** (1937–1996) was born in Haifa, Israel, and attended first The Hebrew University and later the University of Michigan. Kahneman and Tversky's collaboration on research in human reasoning began in 1969.

Kahneman and Tversky's work showed that people do not follow the rules of logic and statistics when they reason about problems in the everyday world. Instead, they use a series of heuristics, or rules of thumb, to process information. This occurs even when subjects actually know the underlying logical and statistical concepts. Unfortunately, the heuristics often produce errors in reasoning and risk assessment.

One example is the **representative heuristic,** which concerns the misunderstanding of randomness and such related concepts as base rates and sample sizes (Kahneman & Tversky, 1972, 1973). For example, research subjects are given information about a character: for example, that the person is bright and interested in helping others. Then the subjects are asked to select the job the character might hold. Although subjects usually select options like physician or psychologist, they typically fail to choose occupations such as sales, at which many more people are employed. By ignoring the base rates of the various occupations, the subjects may be making mistakes in their choices.

Another case is the **availability heuristic,** which is the tendency to base estimates of frequency or probability on information that is easy to remember (because it is familiar, vivid, or recent) instead of on the most relevant information (Tversky & Kahneman, 1973). Try the following quiz on your friends: First, prepare a list of 40 names that includes 18 or 19 well-known women (e.g., Agatha Christie, Hillary Clinton) and 21 or 22 ordinary men's names (e.g., Randy Denton, Sam Burns). With no special instructions, read the list to your friends and then ask them if there were more women or men. If your results are like Tversky and Kahneman's (1973), about 80% of your friends will say there were more women. The familiarity of the names presumably makes them more available, which misleads us as we reason.

Because of the importance of their work on reasoning, Tversky and Kahneman won the APA's Distinguished Scientific Contribution Award in 1982. We have noted that Chomsky also won this award, as did Bruner, Miller, Brown, Broadbent, Tulving, and three others among the researchers we will consider next: Herbert Simon, Alan Newell, and Robert Abelson. Daniel Kahneman was also the cowinner of the 2002 Nobel Prize in Economics, becoming the first person with a Ph.D. in *psychology* to win a Nobel Prize (MacCoun, 2002).

Artificial Intelligence

Herbert Alexander Simon (1916–2001) was born in Milwaukee, Wisconsin. In 1943, Simon completed his Ph.D. in political science at the University of Chicago. His primary interests were in organizational behavior and decision making, areas that led to his 1978 Nobel Prize in economics. Simon also won the 1993 APA Award for Outstanding Lifetime Contributions to Psychology, which perhaps illustrates the breadth of his interests. In addition to economics and psychology, he was claimed by computer science and political science (Anderson, 2001).

Postwar advances in cybernetics attracted Simon's interest, and for the remainder of his career he blended psychology and computer models with his original focus areas of economics and management. In 1952, Simon met **Allen Newell** (1927–1992) while both were working at the RAND Corporation (*APS Observer*, 1992). A San Francisco native, Newell completed a degree in physics from Stanford and a Ph.D. in industrial administration at the Carnegie Institute of Technology (now Carnegie-Mellon University).

As Simon (1980) noted, psychology was not eager to adopt "the new information-processing paradigm. . . . There was too big a leap from Hullian S-R psychology (not to mention Skinnerian behaviorism) to computer simulation" (p. 465). Because both Simon and Newell had little standing in the psychological community, they were fortunate that their approach attracted the interest of two prominent psychologists—George A. Miller and Carl Hovland (Chapter 17). Simon and Newell collaborated with Miller and Hovland to organize a workshop at RAND at which several other psychologists were introduced to simulation and additional computer techniques. Simon noted, "Some of them were infected in the process" (p. 465).

Together, Simon and Newell empirically explored human problem solving, produced computer simulations of their findings, and worked to advance artificial intelligence computing.

Artificial intelligence (AI) has two slightly different meanings in the psychological community, and at different times, Simon and Newell's research program was associated with both of them. On the one hand, AI involves the construction of machines that model how humans think, learn, or perceive; on the other hand, AI refers to developing machines that perform some activity as well as a person, or even as well as an expert at that activity. In the first sense of the term, Newell and Simon (1972) developed the **General Problem Solver,** a computer program designed to mimic how humans solve diverse problems and logic puzzles. Earlier, Simon and Newell produced probably the first general problem-solving computer program (Logic Theorist) designed to be in some way analogous to human cognition.

Other programs derived from the General Problem Solver were adapted to specific problems and illustrate the second sense of artificial intelligence, which is perhaps best understood by considering Alan Turing's (1950) original definition of AI. This can be seen in the **Turing test,** a test for "artificial," computer intelligence. In the cited passage, "the problem" is the question of how we would establish the existence of such intelligence in a computer.

> The new form of the problem can be described in terms of a game which we will call the "imitation game". It is played with three people, a man (A), a woman (B), and an interrogator (C) who may be of either sex. The interrogator stays in a room apart from the other two. The object of the game for the interrogator is to determine which of the other two is the man and which is the woman. . . . The interrogator is allowed to put questions to A and B thus:
>
> C: Will X please tell me the length of his or her hair?
>
> Now suppose X is actually A, then A must answer. It is A's object in the game to try and cause C to make the wrong identification. His answer might therefore be
>
> "My hair is shingled, and the longest strands are about nine inches long."
>
> In order that tones of voice may not help the interrogator . . . [an] . . . ideal arrangement is to have a teleprinter communicating between the two rooms. . . .
>
> We now ask the question, "What will happen when a machine takes the part of A in this game?" Will the interrogator decide wrongly as often when the game is played like this as he does when

> the game is played between a man and a woman? These questions replace our original, "Can machines think"? (Turing, 1950, pp. 433–434)

In its general form, the Turing test can be seen as an empirical, behavioral, pragmatic test. If a computer's performance in a given situation is indistinguishable from human performance, then we must conclude that, in the context, the machine is intelligent. For his work in computer science, Herbert Simon received the A. M. Turing Award in 1975 (Anderson, 2001).

Interest in artificial intelligence was widespread in psychology (and other fields) from the mid-1950s through the early 1970s. Carnegie-Mellon University, Simon and Newell's academic home, was then and remains a center of AI activity. At MIT, Marvin Minsky (e.g., Minsky, 1985) was a founder of the artificial intelligence laboratory and oversaw a variety of important demonstration projects. MIT and Minsky continue to be at the forefront of AI research, as is Roger Schank.

In 1974, **Roger Schank** (1946–), along with social psychologist **Robert Abelson** (1928–), set out to make Yale another center of AI research. Schank and Abelson's (1977) *Scripts, Plans, Goals, and Understanding* demonstrated clearly how the interplay between computer models and cognitive psychology could advance our understanding of human knowledge structures. Abelson (1981) defined a **script** as a special type of schema involving a structured sequence of behavioral events. For example, consider the sequence we follow when we dine at a restaurant. We go in, wait to be seated, study the menu, place our order, wait for the food, eat it, perhaps order dessert, finish our meal, get the check, pay the bill, and exit.

If we ordered dessert, did we eat it? And if we left a tip, when was that done? These questions do not present problems, because the script has more slots than we illustrated, and as members of this culture, we all know the location of the slots and their default values. For example, if someone tells you about eating at a new restaurant and does not comment on the quality of the food or service, you will probably assume it was acceptable but not outstanding—the default value. Because people share that default assumption, they would need to mention the quality of the food or the service only if it was above or below the shared expectation. Moreover, there is a set place in the sequence of telling about the restaurant at which the information is presented.

Schank (1972, 1982) showed that computers can be programmed with scripts and that computers programmed in this way answer questions and reason through the data available to them in much the same way as people. Schank's research represented a true breakthrough in AI and also in our conception of the structure of human reasoning.

The 1970s saw other advances in AI, especially in machine understanding and natural language interactions with computers (e.g., Winograd, 1972). There was a widespread sense that truly spectacular computer programs capable of thinking and speaking exactly like people were just around the corner. Alternatively, others saw problems with AI and were not optimistic about its future (e.g., Dreyfus, 1972). Whereas it is easy to imagine how to program a computer to make a certain judgment if a particular condition is met (if X, then Y), how can we get a computer to see a family resemblance? As Wittgenstein and Rosch observed, if there are no rules or defining attributes that we use to categorize information, then the computers of the day, rule-based systems, had serious problems.

The truth apparently lies somewhere between the two extremes. Advances in AI programs written as rule-based systems have continued, and probably you have enjoyed such progress as you interact with your automated bank teller and play sophisticated computer games. On the other hand, we do not yet communicate with our personal computers in ordinary language, nor do we see computer systems that reason like people outside the narrow domain in which the computers are programmed to be expert.

Rule-based systems have limits, and one of AI's remaining problems is that humans gain new knowledge by learning, something most computers do not do, and something neglected by most cognitive psychologists. Instead, rule-based systems come programmed with all the information that they know and with a program composed of rules governing how to analyze new information. In 1986, **David Rumelhart** (1942–) and his colleagues first published their efforts to resurrect an older computer architecture that had been neglected in recent years (Rumelhart, McClelland, & the PDP Research Group, 1986). This architecture, variously called connectionism, parallel processing, or **neural networks,** represents a non-rule-based alternative to computing.

Parallel processing also represents a return to learning theory and a strengthening of cognitive psychology's ties with neuroscience. Computers are being programmed as models of the underlying neurology, not as models of higher cognitive processes. Indeed, parallel processing brings us back to the initial observations of McCulloch and Pitts (1943) that a computer could be made to simulate neural activity.

Although still in its infancy, connectionism has shown promise in circumventing the limits of rule-based systems, while at the same time allowing us to retain most of the advances discovered under that architecture. For example, machines can learn a family resemblance (Rumelhart et al., 1986). In addition, there are systems that truly (nonmetaphorically) learn on their own by making adjustments to their own neural connections as a function of new experience. Many such systems are now used in industry and in the military.

CONCLUSIONS

What does the future hold for psychology? Bartlett (1936) concluded his autobiographical essay with these thoughts:

> I will finish with the sort of remark that ought to be perfectly obvious. A psychologist who thinks that his work is done, that all that is now needed is the application of a final scheme to new instances is dead. Psychology will go on and leave him lamenting. Like the reactions it studies, psychology is living and oriented forward: there can be no end to its achievements. (pp. 51–52)

Perhaps some clues can be found by examining the themes that structure our current interest in cognition.

At times in this chapter we have talked about cognitive psychology, and at other times about cognitive science. Whether this usage reflects two synonymous terms, or two different fields, is largely a matter of opinion. The term *cognitive science* is often applied to cognitive psychology, although some have defined cognitive science more broadly, viewing cognitive psychology along with cultural anthropology, computer science, linguistics, neuroscience, and the philosophy of mind as components (e.g., Gardner, 1985).

Is this collaboration among disciplines the new trend? Will psychology vanish into fields such as cognitive science and neuroscience, or will the study of behavior always remain? Either way, the modern study of cognition is an interdisciplinary affair, and psychology has come a long way since Wundt (Chapter 8).

Or has it? Horgan (1999) has argued that "there has been little progress in understanding the mind, replicating its properties, or treating its disorders—especially compared with the extravagant claims made by proponents of certain approaches" (p. 470). In fact, he concludes pessimistically that the human mind may, in certain respects, ultimately be unknowable. Horgan's point of view may be reinforced by historian of psychology Michael Wertheimer's conclusion about the history of psychology: "If there's one lesson in history, it's that yesterday's theory and yesterday's problem is today something to laugh at" (Sharps & Wertheimer, 2000, p. 330).

We tend to be more sanguine than Horgan (1999) while at the same time recognizing the truth in Wertheimer's comment. As we complete the third edition of this book, topics such as language, human factors engineering, memory, categorization, reasoning, and artificial intelligence are among the "hottest" in psychology, but how long will it be before another change—a Kuhnian paradigm shift perhaps—sends the focus elsewhere? Does the machine learning of the parallel processing advocates and the ecological approach of Neisser represent a reunification in psychology? Will machine learning bring a final synthesis of cognition, physiology, and behavior? Are there trends in areas such as social or clinical psychology that reflect this union?

We began this book with a series of questions, and we close the same way. The answers to the questions in the first chapter were found in the past. The answers to our closing questions lie in the future.

SUMMARY

According to Kuhn, theories inevitably encounter an anomaly they cannot explain, and the encounter leads to a theoretical revolution. Language may have been such an anomaly for behaviorism, resulting in the cognitive revolution.

Forerunners to the Cognitive Revolution

Important antecedents of cognitive psychology include Plato, Kant, and Gestalt psychology. Sir Charles Bartlett and Lev Vygotsky were also major early contributors. Bartlett popularized the "schema" as the basic unit of thought and illustrated it through studies of reconstructive memory. Best known for analyzing the relationship between language and thought, Vygotsky imagined and argued for a scientific study of the mind that resembles modern cognitive science.

Piaget called his program genetic epistemology, because it dealt with knowledge development in children. From his research, Piaget believed children pass through developmental stages he called the sensorimotor stage, the preoperational stage, the concrete operational stage, and the formal operational stage.

Although Piaget contributed to the topic of moral development, the central figure was Lawrence Kohlberg. In Kohlberg's theory, the stages of moral reasoning are the preconventional stage, the conventional stage, and the postconventional stage.

Gardner observed that important advances outside psychology have also been important for the cognitive revolution. Specifically, Gardner noted cybernetics—the study of control processes in machines or animals—that became artificial intelligence, the philosophy of mind, and linguistics.

Noam Chomsky

The interplay between psychology and linguistics was limited before Noam Chomsky. Chomsky felt that behavioral explanations for the language acquisition process were inadequate. His poverty-of-stimulus argument suggested that behaviorist principles such as "stimulus" and "reinforcement" could not explain language learning. This argument can be expanded to question the completeness of a behavioral explanation of human behavior. As an alternative, Chomsky suggested that we have innate syntactic structures that allow us to acquire language, and the empirical study of language has remained central to cognitive psychology.

Jerome Bruner and George Miller

Jerome Bruner and George Miller's creation of the Center for Cognitive Studies at Harvard in 1962 was a signal event in cognitive psychology. Bruner's early work was in perception and social psychology, but his interests shifted to thinking after a Cambridge conference on cognition hosted by Sir Charles Bartlett. In his research on thinking, Bruner has stressed the relations between thinking and perception, the developmental aspects of cognition, the applications of cognitive research, and the creative aspects of thought.

George Miller entered psychology via his interest in communication and was interested in cybernetics from the outset. Miller is famous for "The Magical Number Seven," which is an analysis of short-term memory; *Plans and the Structure of Behavior,* which introduced the TOTE concept and popularized, along with Donald Broadbent's work, the information-processing metaphor; and *Language and Perception,* which explores various mental events.

Classical Contributions

Language remains central to cognitive psychology, and Roger Brown is arguably the "dean" of psycholinguistics. Associated with Chomsky, Bruner, and Miller, Brown was the first to provide empirical data for some of Chomsky's claims about language acquisition. Brown is known also for his flashbulb-memory studies and for his contributions to social psychology.

Ulric Neisser's *Cognitive Psychology* was widely used until he published *Cognition and Reality,* which represents a shift away from the information-processing approach toward a more applied, ecological perspective. *Cognition and Reality* further advances the schema as the fundamental unit of thought by making it central to the "perceptual cycle." Also, the book advocates the need for research with real-world applications. Neisser has advanced our understanding of the reconstructive nature of memory, which was first noted by Bartlett.

Memory researcher Endel Tulving distinguished between semantic and episodic long-term memories. Episodic memories are eventlike and seem to be the kind of memories on which work on reconstructive memory has focused. Semantic memories are memories of discrete facts, such as your telephone number.

Modern interest in categorization can be traced to philosopher Ludwig Wittgenstein and his analysis of family resemblance. Eleanor Rosch showed that categorizing the information we constantly acquire is the most fundamental act of cognition.

Current reasoning research also has its roots in philosophy. Like Wittgenstein, Gilbert Ryle was interested in pointing out problems that psychology seemed to have either neglected or misunderstood. Ryle's most famous work concerned the "category mistake," which involves confusing the ontological level of two objects: for example, confusing the buildings that comprise a university with the abstract notion of university. For Ryle, the mind-body problem was the most important category mistake.

In contemporary research in reasoning, Daniel Kahneman and Amos Tversky focused on the use of heuristics that lead to erroneous judgments. For example, the representative heuristic often causes us to ignore such important information as base rates.

Artificial intelligence (AI) is a component of cognitive science in which Herbert Simon and Allen Newell were pioneers. In psychology, AI may refer to using computers as tools to model cognitive operations, or it can refer to building machines that perform some task as well as an expert.

One way to determine whether intelligence exists in an entity is to apply the Turing Test. If performance by the entity is indistinguishable from intelligent human behavior in the same situation, then the entity has intelligence. AI pioneers Roger Schank and Robert Abelson programmed machines with scripts—modified versions of schema—and achieved success both in getting machines to perform interesting tasks in ways analogous to people and in using computers to advance our understanding of human cognition.

The most recent innovation in computing technology is often called the neural network because what is being modeled is a basic physiological process rather than a more abstract cognition. Neural networks have overcome some of the limits of the older, rule-based technology.

CONNECTIONS QUESTIONS

1. What connections can you make between advances in other academic disciplines and the rise of cognitive science?
2. What connections can you make between cognitive psychology and technological advances?
3. What are the connections between cognitive psychology and Gestalt psychology? Between behaviorism and the modern study of cognition?
4. What events in this chapter and in the two chapters preceding it do you feel will be most connected to the shape of psychology in the 21st century?
5. What connections can you trace to support the idea that psychology had a "cognitive revolution" of the Kuhnian variety?

KEY NAMES AND TERMS

Robert Abelson (p. 553)
accommodation (p. 540)
artificial intelligence (AI) (p. 552)
assimilation (p. 540)
availability heuristic (p. 551)
Sir Frederic Charles Bartlett (p. 535)
Donald Broadbent (p. 546)
Roger Brown (p. 547)
Jerome Seymour Bruner (p. 544)
categorization (p. 549)
category mistake (p. 550)
Avram Noam Chomsky (p. 543)
chunks (p. 545)
Edouard Claparède (p. 539)
concrete operational stage (p. 540)
conservation of quantity (p. 540)
conventional stage (p. 542)
cybernetics (p. 542)
ecological validity (p. 548)
episodic memory (p. 549)
family resemblance (p. 550)
flashbulb memories (p. 547)
formal operational stage (p. 540)
General Problem Solver (p. 552)
genetic epistemology (p. 539)
information processing (p. 546)
Bärbel Inhelder (p. 541)
Daniel Kahneman (p. 551)
Lawrence Kohlberg (p. 541)
LAD (p. 543)
George Armitage Miller (p. 545)
Ulric Neisser (p. 547)
neural networks (p. 554)
Allen Newell (p. 552)
object permanence (p. 540)
Charles Kay Ogden (p. 543)
perceptual cycle (p. 548)
Jean Piaget (p. 538)
postconventional stage (p. 542)

poverty-of-stimulus argument (p. 543)
preconventional stage (p. 541)
preoperational stage (p. 540)
reconstructive memory (p. 536)
representative heuristic (p. 551)
David Rumelhart (p. 553)
Gilbert Ryle (p. 550)
Roger Schank (p. 553)
schema (p. 535)
script (p. 553)
semantic memory (p. 549)
sensorimotor stage (p. 540)
short-term memory (p. 545)
Herbert Alexander Simon (p. 552)
syntactic structures (p. 543)
TOTE (p. 546)
Endel Tulving (p. 549)
Alan Turing (p. 542)
Turing test (p. 552)
Amos Tversky (p. 551)
Lev Vygotsky (p. 537)
Ludwig Wittgenstein (p. 549)

SUGGESTED READINGS

Gardner, H. (1985). *The mind's new science: A history of the cognitive revolution.* New York: Basic Books. Gardner's book contains a nice sketch of the early events in psychology and other fields (e.g., anthropology, computer science, linguistics, neuroscience, philosophy) related to cognitive science. This work is not highly technical and would be of interest to anyone who enjoys the history of ideas.

Miller, G., Galanter, E., & Pribram, K. (1960). *Plans and the structure of behavior.* New York: Adams-Bannister-Cox. This is perhaps the "signal" work in the cognitive revolution. Although the details are dated, *Plans and the Structure of Behavior* remains a classic look at early cognitive science.

Minsky, M. (1985). *The society of mind.* New York: Simon & Schuster. A cognitive science classic, this book provides a complete theory of human behavior and mental events from the perspective of the cognitive paradigm. Lighthearted, yet informative, the more recent paperback edition should be easy to find.

Neisser, U. (1987). *Concepts and conceptual development.* New York: Cambridge University Press. *Concepts and Conceptual Development* was the first in a series edited by Neisser. This volume focuses on categorization, and the theory and research it contains represents the most current ideas in cognitive psychology about categories and concepts.

Piaget, J. (1952). Jean Piaget. In E. G. Boring, H. S. Langfeld, H. Werner, & R. M. Yerkes (Eds.), *A history of psychology in autobiography* (Vol. 4, pp. 237–256). Worcester, MA: Clark University Press. Like many of the essays in this series, Piaget's makes interesting reading and reveals many of the influences on him that led to his seminal research on child development.

Vygotsky, L. S. (1978). *Mind in society: The development of higher psychological processes.* Cambridge, MA: Harvard University Press. *Mind in Society* is a nice sampler of Vygotsky's work, and it includes a short biographical sketch by Vygotsky's associate, A. R. Luria.

Glossary of Terms and Names

Abélard, Peter (1079–1142) A key figure in the nominalism-realism debate; one of the first in the West to emphasize Aristotle's works.

Abelson, Robert (1928–) A social psychologist who worked with Roger Schank on the concept of scripts—an area of AI research.

ablation The surgical removal of part of the brain to study its function.

Abraham, Karl (1877–1925) One of Freud's inner circle who became the first German psychoanalyst and founded the Berlin Psychoanalytic Society; Abraham contributed significantly to Freud's theory of the psychosexual stages of development.

Academy Plato's school, founded around 387 B.C.E. and closed in 529 C.E.

accommodation In Piaget's psychology, the changing of existing schemata to make them conform to reality.

Ach, Narziss (1871–1946) An associate of Külpe at Würzburg who discovered the importance of the *Aufgabe* or determining tendency.

action potential A reversal of polarity across a cell membrane that is the basic means of long-distance communication in the nervous system.

act psychology The name of Franz Brentano's system of psychology that studied psychological acts or functions rather than the contents of consciousness.

acts Also known as the functions of consciousness; according to Brentano, mental acts fell into three broad categories: presentation (or ideating), judging, and the acts of desire (or loving and hating).

adaptive act For Carr, the adaptive act had three elements: (1) a motivating stimulus, (2) a sensory situation, and (3) a response that changes the situation to satisfy the motivating conditions.

Adelard of Bath First of a series of British scholars; went to Syria in the 12th century in search of science.

Adler, Alfred (1870–1937) A one-time disciple of Freud who developed his own system of psychotherapy that focused more on social interests than on sexuality.

affordance J. J. Gibson's term for a stimulus whose information we perceive and respond to directly because of our evolutionary history.

Ainsworth, Mary Salter (1913–1999) A co-developer of a theory of human attachment behavior; particularly known for her "strange situation" methodology for studying infant attachments.

Alcmaeon (ca. 500 B.C.E.) One of the first recorded anatomists and an early proponent of rational medicine.

Alcuin (ca. 735–804) The court philosopher to Charlemagne; founded the Palatine school, which may have been the conceptual model for the University of Paris.

al-Kindi (ca. 800–870) Sometimes called "the philosopher of the Arabs"; was particularly interested in vision.

Allport, Floyd H. (1890–1978) A pioneer of social psychology whose 1924 textbook, *Social Psychology,* helped solidify the field as an empirical discipline and who is known for his studies of social facilitation.

Allport, Gordon W. (1897–1968) A pioneer of social psychology whose primary interest was a humanistic and social psychological approach to personality.

American Psychological Association Founded in 1892 by G. Stanley Hall and others, one of the primary organizations of psychologists in America.

American Psychological Society Founded in 1988 and organized primarily for experimental and academic psychologists.

anal stage The second of Freud's psychosexual stages in which pressure on the anal sphincter and its release with defecation provide for libidinal satisfaction that becomes central for the child at about the age of 2.

Analytical Psychology The system of psychology developed by Carl Jung after his break with Freud.

anamnesis The recollection of knowledge we already possess.

Anastasi, Anne (1908–2001) A psychologist whose main contributions include work on test construction and validation as well as on psychological testing in general.

Anaxagoras (ca. 500–428 B.C.E.) Greek philosopher with whom Pericles studied; prosecuted for arguing that the sun was a red-hot mass of rock at a time when the sun was a god to many.

Angell, Frank (1857–1939) James Rowland Angell's cousin who received his Ph.D. from Wundt and founded laboratories at Cornell and Stanford.

Angell, James Rowland (1869–1949) Developed a mature functionalist position at the University of Chicago before moving into administration.

anima The feminine aspect of an individual's personality, according to Jung.

animal magnetism The notion that people emit a magnetic fluid that can influence others.

animal spirits The substance many Greeks believed distinguished the living from the dead.

animus The masculine aspect of an individual's personality, according to Jung.

Anna O The name given to Bertha Pappenheim (1859–1936) by Breuer and Freud to conceal the woman's true identity. The case of Anna O's hysteria significantly influenced Freud's thinking about the disorder and its treatment. Pappenheim subsequently became an important social reformer.

anthropometric laboratory A laboratory Galton first established for the measurement of man (anthropometric) at the International Health Exhibition in London in 1884.

Antisthenes (ca. 455–360 B.C.E.) One of the founders of the school of Cynicism.

apperception Wundt's term for the focus of attention on a particular region of consciousness, resulting in clear perception of that region's contents.

apperceptive mass For Herbart, a formation of a group of compatible ideas in consciousness.

approach-approach conflict Conflict in which the person must decide on one of two goals, both with positive valence.

approach-avoidance conflict Conflict in which the person is forced to choose whether to pursue a goal with both positive and negative valence.

archetype For Jung, a universal, unconscious idea transcending individual experience that resides in the collective unconscious.

Archimedes A famous Greek mathematician who ran naked from his bath when he had the insight for how to test the specific gravity of an object.

Aristotle (384–322 B.C.E.) Plato's pupil and the teacher of Alexander the Great; founded a school called the Lyceum and invented the syllogism.

Army Alpha One of the first IQ tests designed for group administration, the Army Alpha was appropriate for literate takers.

Army Beta One of the first IQ tests designed for group administration, the Army Beta was made for illiterate test takers.

Arnheim, Rudolph (1904–) A Gestalt psychologist who has taken the field in new directions, such as art and architecture.

artificial intelligence (AI) The construction of machines that model how humans think, learn, or perceive, and the development of machines that can perform some activities as well as a person.

Asch, Solomon (1907–1996) A Gestalt-oriented social psychologist best known for his studies of conformity to group social pressure and person perception.

assimilation In Piaget's psychology, the incorporation of experiences that fit the infant's schemata.

association of ideas Hume's associative principles were originally resemblance, contiguity, and cause and effect.

associationism Derived from empiricism; includes formal rules for the association of ideas in the mind.

atomism The theory of Leucippus and Democritus that holds that everything is made of tiny, indivisible particles (atoms).

attachments The general class of interactions between a child and significant others.

attention For Titchener, an attribute of a sensation, its clearness (vividness, attensity).

attributes For Titchener, the basic attributes of sensations, images, and feelings were quality, intensity, duration, clearness, and extent.

attribution Refers to how we perceive, interpret, and account for people's actions.

availability heuristic The tendency for people to base estimates of frequency or probability on information that is easy to remember instead of on the most relevant information.

Avenarius, Richard (1843–1896) A University of Zurich philosophy professor who developed positivistic ideas independently of Mach.

Averroës (1126–1198) An Islamic Aristotelian scholar quoted frequently by Aquinas.

Avicenna (980–1037) An Arabic physician whose philosophy centered around Aristotle.

avoidance-avoidance conflict Conflict in which the person must choose between two goals, both with negative valence.

baby-tender A self-contained box that Skinner built to facilitate the early rearing of children.

backward conditioning In Pavlovian conditioning, the presentation of the UCS before the CS.

Bacon, Roger (ca. 1214–1292) An Englishman whose struggles for science and his reputation for knowledge earned him the contemporary nickname of *Doctor mirabilis* (wonderful doctor).

Bacon, Sir Francis (1561–1626) An Englishman who rejected the deductive logic of his predecessors and championed experimentation as the means for understanding nature; known for his discussion of idols.

Bain, Alexander (1818–1903) A British associationist, Bain represents the end of philosophical associationism. His journal, *Mind,* and his books, *The Senses and the Intellect* and *The Emotions and the Will,* were important contributions to the development of psychology.

Baird, John Wallace (1873–1919) Succeeded E. C. Sanford as director of the psychology laboratory at Clark University.

Baldwin, James Mark (1861–1934) Founded psychology laboratories in Canada and at Princeton, and reopened a laboratory at Johns Hopkins; considered a founder of developmental psychology.

Bandura, Albert (1925–) The developer of social learning theory; his work often dealt with aggression.

Barker, Roger G. (1903–1990) An ecological psychologist best known for *One Boy's Day,* a microanalysis of "one boy's day."

Bartholow, Roberts (1831–1904) Cincinnati physician who electrically stimulated the brain of a human patient.

Bartlett, Sir Frederic Charles (1886–1969) An early contributor to the

study of cognition who popularized the schema as the basic unit of thought.

basic anxiety In Horney's theory, a child's feeling of helplessness and isolation within a potentially hostile world.

Bayley, Nancy (1899–1994) A psychologist best known for her Bayley Scales of Infant Development and for her longitudinal studies of intelligence and its stability across a changing environment.

Beach, Frank A. (1911–1988) A student of Lashley who was known for his work on the physiology of human and animal sexual behavior.

behaviorism A psychological system that stresses the use of objective methods to study the overt behavior of organisms.

being-in-the-world In Heidegger's existential-phenomenology, being-in-the-world addresses an entity's mode of existence. Heidegger was especially interested in humanity's being-in-the-world.

Bekhterev, Vladimir Mikhailovich (1857–1927) Pavlov's contemporary and competitor who studied reflexive conditioning and developed a program he called reflexology.

Bell, Sir Charles (1774–1842) British physician whose research suggested that the dorsal roots of spinal nerves were sensory and the ventral roots motor.

Bell-Magendie law Independently proposed by Bell and Magendie, the law states that the dorsal root of spinal nerves brings in sensory information, and the ventral root takes out motor impulses.

Bem, Sandra (1944–) A pioneer in the study of gender differences who is perhaps best known for developing the Bem Sex Role Inventory.

Bem Sex Role Inventory (BSRI) Developed by Sandra Bem, the widely used scale that describes the degree to which a person conforms to traditional sex-role stereotypes.

Bentham, Jeremy (1748–1832) A pioneer of the social philosophy called Utilitarianism.

Bergson, Henri (1859–1924) Winner of the 1924 Nobel Prize for literature who has been called the "French William James" because of the scope and tenor of his philosophy.

Berkeley, George (1685–1753) An Irish philosopher who developed an empirical theory of depth perception and argued that objects exist in being perceived.

Bernard, Claude (1813–1878) Magendie's student; considered the father of experimental physiology in France.

Bernheim, Hippolyte (1840–1919) An internist who was attracted to hypnotherapy by Liébeault's success with it. His many books and articles presented the principles of the Nancy school of hypnotism.

Binet, Alfred (1857–1911) A French psychologist usually credited with inventing the intelligence test; he worked to create a battery of mental tests to identify individual differences and produced the first test to measure intelligence in children in 1905.

Bingham, Walter Van Dyke (1880–1952) A psychologist who was one of the original developers of the Army Alpha and Beta tests; chaired a committee that developed the Army General Classification Test, which was used to sort recruits in World War II.

Binswanger, Ludwig (1881–1966) A developer of *Daseinanalysis,* which is a system of psychotherapy based on Heidegger's existential-phenomenology.

Bleuler, Eugen (1857–1939) An expert on schizophrenia who coined the term and who influenced many important psychotherapists in his capacity as director of the Burghölzi Mental Hospital in Zurich.

Boethius, Anicius Manlius Severinus (ca. 480–525) Boethius's most famous work was *The Consolation of Philosophy;* his writings were mostly Aristotelian.

Bonnet, Charles Étienne (1720–1793) A Swiss empiricist who added physiology to Condillac's sentient statue.

Boring, Edwin Garrigues (1886–1968) Best known as an historian of psychology; a student of Titchener.

Boss, Medard (1903–1990) A developer of *Daseinanalysis,* a system of psychotherapy based on Heidegger's existential phenomenology.

Boulder model Named for a 1949 conference at Boulder, Colorado, the model holds that graduate education should train clinical psychologists to be both scientists and practitioners.

Bowlby, John (1907–1990) A British child psychiatrist who was a co-developer of a theory of a human attachment behavioral system.

Brahe, Tycho (1564–1601) Considered the greatest of the pretelescope astronomers.

Braid, James (1795–1860) A Scottish surgeon who developed an interest in studying mesmerism, verified many of its properties, and changed its name to hypnotism.

Brentano, Franz Clemens (1838–1917) The founder of act psychology, an early alternative to Wundt's voluntarism; also the "father" of several phenomenological alternatives to Wundt's psychology.

Breuer, Josef (1842–1925) A Viennese physician who became Freud's friend and early collaborator but later broke with Freud over the issue of sexuality.

Bridgman, Percy Williams (1882–1961) A Nobel Prize–winning physicist who argued for operationism in science.

Brill, A. A. (1874–1948) An Austrian who was the first practicing psychoanalyst in America and a translator of many of Freud's works into English.

Broadbent, Donald (1926–1993) An engineering psychologist who was one of the first to popularize the information processing metaphor.

Broca, Pierre Paul (1824–1880) Credited with establishing the importance of a frontal lobe area for speech production.

Brown, Roger (1925–1997) A social and cognitive psychologist particularly known for his work in psycholinguistics.

Brown, Thomas (1778–1820) Dugald Stewart's successor who compromised common-sense psychology with associationism.

Brücke, Ernst (1819–1892) Freud's physiology professor at the University of Vienna whose dynamic physiology was an important influence on Freud's dynamic psychology.

Bruner, Jerome Seymour (1915–) The themes in Bruner's work as a cognitive psychologist include the relationship between perception and conception, developmental aspects of cognitions, and applications of the study of cognition.

Bruno, Giordano (1548–1600) Italian philosopher who extended the Copernican system and was burned at the stake by the Inquisition.

Bryan, William Lowe (1860–1955) Worked with Ebbinghaus and Külpe before founding a psychological laboratory at Indiana University.

Buber, Martin (1878–1965) A Jewish theologian and philosopher known for his existentially oriented works of relevance for psychology.

Buffon, Comte de (1707–1788) A famous French naturalist whose evolutionary ideas influenced Lamarck.

Bühler, Charlotte B. (1893–1974) Known for her contributions to developmental psychology, Bühler later became an activist for humanistic psychology, publishing a key position paper on the topic in 1971.

Bühler, Karl (1879–1963) A forerunner of modern cognitive psychology who was associated with several phenomenological movements in Germany, including Gestalt psychology.

Burt, Cyril Lodowic (1883–1971) An important early worker in the study of intelligence and intelligence tests and the first psychologist to be knighted. His ardent hereditarian views of intelligence may have led to fraudulent results from some of his twin studies.

bystander apathy An area of research in which emergency situations are simulated to observe their effects on people exposed to them.

Cabanis, Pierre Jean Georges (1757–1808) A French empiricist/physician who held that the brain was the organ of thought; considered by some the first physiological psychologist.

Cajal, Santiago Ramón y (1852–1934) Spanish histologist and neurologist who, using the Golgi stain, demonstrated that nerve cells are independent cells.

Calkins, Mary Whiton (1863–1930) A student of James who was the first woman elected president of the APA and of the American Philosophical Association and who developed a system of self-psychology.

Camus, Albert (1913–1960) Born in Algeria, a French existentialist known for such powerful psychological works of fiction as *The Stranger.*

Candolle, Alphonse de (1806–1893) A Swiss botanist who produced an "environmentalist" (or nurturist) response to Galton's *Hereditary Genius.*

Cannon, Walter B. (1871–1945) A Harvard physiologist who coined the word *homeostasis* and criticized the James-Lange theory of emotion.

Carmichael, Leonard (1898–1973) The first person in the US to record electroencephalograms; probably best known in developmental psychology for his editorial work and for his writing in the *Manual of Child Psychology.*

Carnap, Rudolph (1891–1970) A member of the Vienna Circle—advocates of positivism; according to him, the language of psychology was reducible to the language of physics.

Carr, Harvey A. (1873–1954) Replaced Angell as chairman of the University of Chicago psychology department; under his tenure, functionalism reached its zenith.

castration anxiety The fear the little boy develops during the Oedipus complex that his father will remove his penis. Castration anxiety is the motive for resolving the Oedipus complex.

categorical imperative The central a priori principle in Kant's conception of morality. According to it, a person should act in such a way that the rule behind his or her actions could serve as a universal law for all to follow.

categories of thought According to Kant, the mind's 12 categories of thought that shape but are independent of experience.

categorization Refers to how we assign objects and concepts to particular groups; William James called categorization the fundamental act of cognition.

category mistake Introduced by Ryle, this is the idea that errors sometimes occur when concepts are considered together although they actually require different levels of analysis.

catharsis The purging of negative thoughts or emotions.

cathartic method A method for treating mental illness in which symptomatic relief is achieved by bringing forgotten memories and feelings to consciousness.

Cattell, James McKeen (1860–1944) A pioneer in the area of measurement as well as being important through his establishment and control over several scientific journals.

Cattell, Raymond Bernard (1905–1998) A psychologist influenced by Spearman and Burt who used factor analysis and questionnaires to create the 16 Personality Factors Test, among his many other contributions.

causality Belief of Hume that causality was a habit of mind in which we infer that one thing causes another when we have seen them constantly together in the past.

causes Aristotle's belief that to understand anything completely, we must know its four basic causes: material, formal, efficient, and final.

centrencephalic system Penfield's name for a collection of subcortical structures that coordinates and integrates the activities of the cerebral hemispheres.

cerebellum The nervous system unit that Flourens thought enabled an animal to coordinate its movements.

cerebral lobes The nervous system unit Flourens concluded was responsible for voluntary movements and perception.

chaos theory A modern-day theory that contends that systems may be more complex and variable than we realize. Heraclitus can be seen as a forerunner of this theory.

Charcot, Jean Martin (1825–1893) A famous Parisian neurologist whose views on hysteria greatly influenced Freud.

Chiarugi, Vicenzio (1759–1826) Pinel contemporary who was another humanitarian reformer in his position as director of a large public hospital in Florence.

Chomsky, Avram Noam (1928–) Considered historically the most important contributor to the science of linguistics, he may have started the "cognitive revolution" with his critique of Skinner's book on language acquisition.

chunks A term referring to collected items of information in memory.

Claparède, Edouard (1873–1940) The Swiss psychologist and the founder of the Rousseau Institute for the study of educational science who offered Piaget a position there.

Clark, Kenneth B. (1914–2000) The first Black president of the APA who, in a famous study of self-concept and racial identification, found that African American preschool children preferred white dolls to black ones.

Clever Hans A horse that had apparently been taught to solve math problems. Oskar Pfungst found that Hans was responding to involuntary cues given by the questioner.

client-centered therapy The name Carl Rogers gave to his humanistic approach to psychotherapy.

closure The Gestalt perceptual principle that says that people tend to see incomplete figures as complete.

cognitive balance Refers to a tendency to perceive information in ways consistent with pre-existing beliefs and attitudes.

cognitive dissonance According to Leon Festinger's theory, people cannot tolerate conflicting cognitions, and one or more of the conflicting beliefs is rejected or devalued.

cognitive map Tolman's term for an organism's complete understanding of the layout of its environment.

Cohen, Jacob (1923–1998) Critic of the misapplication of statistics in psychology; particularly opposed the misuse of hypothesis testing.

Coleridge, Samuel Taylor (1772–1834) English poet and philosopher whose self-examination anticipated modern research in psychopathology.

collective unconscious For Jung, the part of the unconscious reflecting aspects of behavior that are common to all individuals.

complexes For Jung, the organized groups of memories, thoughts, perceptions, and feelings contained in the personal unconscious.

complex ideas Ideas formed by combining simple ideas of both sensation and reflection.

composite portraiture A method developed by Galton for creating a picture of the "average" individual by combining several photographic images onto one picture.

Comte, Auguste Marie François Xavier (1798–1857) Considered the originator of positivism, a philosophy of science.

concrete operational stage The third stage in Piaget's theory of child development, lasting between the ages of about 7 and 11. During this stage the child displays conservation when dealing with concrete objects but not with abstract concepts.

Condillac, Étienne Bonnot de (1715–1780) A French empiricist famous for his discussion of a "sentient statue."

conditioned discrimination In Pavlovian conditioning, learning to respond to only one of a pair of similar stimuli.

conditioned response (CR) In Pavlovian conditioning, the response made to the conditioned stimulus.

conditioned stimulus (CS) In Pavlovian conditioning, the initially neutral stimulus that is paired with a stimulus that reliably elicits a reflex.

conditioned taste aversion A negative reaction to a taste following an illness associated with the taste.

conscience One of the two subsystems of the superego that contains the parental and societal prohibitions.

conscious In Freudian theory, the part of the mind that we are aware of at any moment in time.

conservation of quantity In Piaget's developmental theory, the realization that the quantity of something remains the same even with changes in appearance. Conservation of quantity is lacking in children in the preoperational stage.

continuity The Gestalt perceptual principle that says people tend to follow elements that appear to be heading in the same direction.

conventional stage The second of Kohlberg's stages of moral reasoning in which moral decisions are motivated by social rules.

convergence The eyes' inward rotation to keep an object in focus as it nears the observer; as recognized by Berkeley.

Copernicus, Nicolas (1473–1543) The Polish founder of modern astronomy who argued for a heliocentric or sun-centered view of the universe.

corpora quadrigemina The nervous system unit Flourens thought was necessary for vision.

corpus callosum The brain's major interconnecting structure.

Coster, Laurens Janszoon (ca. 1370–1440) One of the possible inventors of printing in the West.

craniometry Literally, the measurement of skulls.

creative synthesis Wundt's term for the possibility that apperceived ideas may be combined in novel ways.

Cronbach, Lee J. (1916–2001) A psychologist whose contributions to psychometrics include the Cronbach-Meehl model of the construct of valid-ity and Cronbach alpha, which is the most common statistical measure of the relation between a given scale item and the overall score on a scale.

Crusades A series of wars sanctioned by the pope that, among other things, exposed western Europeans to classical knowledge and to Islamic and Judaic scholarship. The various Crusades began in the late 11th century and lasted through most of the 13th century.

Cureton, E. E. "Ted" (1902–1992) A psychologist and student of E. L. Thorndike who made substantial contributions to psychometric issues such as reliability and validity.

CVC trigram Consisting of two consonants with a vowel between, the wordlike unit Ebbinghaus created in order to study memory; also called a nonsense syllable.

cybernetics The term coined by Norbert Wiener to refer to the study of the fundamental control processes of behavior in both animals and machines.

Cynicism School of thought advocating a back-to-nature life free from society's conventions.

Dallenbach, Karl (1887–1971) One of Titchener's well-known Ph.D. students who bought *The American Journal of Psychology* in 1921 and made Titchener its sole editor.

Darley, John (1938–) The researcher who, with Bibb Latané, has conducted important studies of bystander apathy.

Darwin, Charles Robert (1809–1882) Best known for his theory of evolution, detailed in *The Origin of Species;* additional works of importance for psychology include *The Descent of Man* and *The Expression of the Emotions in Man and Animals.*

Darwin, Erasmus (1721–1802) An early evolutionist, the grandfather of both Charles Darwin and Francis Galton.

Dasein Literally "being there"; Heidegger's term representing humanity.

Daseinanalysis A system of psychotherapy based on the existential-phenomenology of Heidegger and popularized by Boss and Binswanger.

da Vinci, Leonardo (1452–1519) Renaissance genius whose dissection of the brain of an ox cast doubt on the model of mind taught by the Church.

de Beauvoir, Simone (1908–1986) Sartre's long-time associate who was a pioneer in both existentialism and feminism. One of her most important works for psychology is *The Second Sex.*

deductive reasoning Reasoning from a known principle to an unknown one; Plato relied on deductive reasoning.

defense mechanisms Methods the ego uses when it is threatened by conflicting demands of the id and superego.

Delabarre, E. B. (1863–1945) Founded the psychology laboratory at Brown and served briefly as Münsterberg's replacement at Harvard, which made him the mentor to several important Harvard graduates.

delayed conditioning In delayed Pavlovian conditioning, the CS begins before the UCS and continues at least until the UCS begins.

delayed-response problem Problem developed by Hunter to study memory in animals. An snimal is shown the problem's solution while being prevented from responding; to solve the problem, the animal must remember the solution during the delay.

Democritus (ca. 460–370 B.C.E.) Further developed Leucippus's theory of atomism, which holds there are only atoms and the void.

derived ideas For Descartes, ideas that come from experience.

Descartes, René (1596–1650) A French mathematician and philosopher who wrenched philosophy away from its concern with the ancient Greeks, hypothesizing a mind-body interactive dualism.

description The most essential step in Husserl's phenomenological method, description involves intense concentration on, analysis of, and careful depiction of a phenomenon.

determining tendency For Ach, the tendency that predisposes a subject to have a particular association to stimulus material; also known as *Aufgabe* or *Einstellung.*

determinist Someone who believes all events are determined by prior causes.

Dewey, John (1859–1952) Primarily a philosopher whose 1896 paper, "The Reflex Arc Concept in Psychology," is often cited as the publication that initiated the school of functionalism.

dialectic The use of logical argument to arrive at the truth of an issue.

dialectical movement Hegel's evolutionary concept in which every condition leads to its opposite, and the conflict of opposites produces a new, higher whole.

diffusion of responsibility Refers to a situation in which several people have the possibility of acting, but no individual has the clear responsibility to act.

Diogenes (ca. 410–320 B.C.E.) One of the cofounders of Cynicism.

direct perception Stimulus information that is interpreted directly by biological equipment evolved for survival in an ecological niche.

disinhibition In Pavlovian conditioning, the recovery of a previously extinguished CR caused by the presentation of a strong, but irrelevant stimulus.

displacement The ego defense mechanism in which emotion is shifted from its real object to a safer object.

distributed practice Training with rest periods between repetitions, which Ebbinghaus found to be superior to massed practice.

Dix, Dorothea (1802–1887) An American who advocated reform in jails, hospitals, and asylums.

doctrine of formal discipline The idea that the study of disciplinary subjects strengthens the mind for future learning.

doctrine of specific nerve energies Formulated by Johannes Müller, the doctrine's central principle is that the nerves impose their own specific qualities on the sensory information they convey.

Dollard, John (1900–1980) A sociologist and long-time collaborator of Neal Miller.

Donaldson, Henry H. (1857–1938) A neurologist who was one of the first scientists to work with rats and one of Watson's dissertation advisers.

double aspectism The mind-body solution that contends that mind and body are two aspects of the same thing.

Downey, June Etta (1875–1932) One of James Rowland Angell's students who worked in the area of personality.

drive As defined by Woodworth, the "why" of motivation as opposed to mechanism, which concerns the "how"; for Hull, an activated state of the organism whose reduction results in reinforcement.

dualism The mind-body position that holds that both mind and body exist.

du Bois-Reymond, Émil (1818–1896) Devoted his life to the study of the electrical nature of nervous tissue.

Duncker, Karl (1903–1940) A Gestalt psychologist with interests in thinking who worked on problem solving; this work provides the basis for understanding how linguistic relationships constrain reasoning.

Dunlap, Knight (1875–1949) Watson's Hopkins colleague who, dissatisfied with introspection, encouraged Watson to break with the traditional, introspective approach to psychology.

duplex idea James Mill's duplex idea results from the uniting of two complex ideas.

Durkheim, Emile (1858–1917) A pioneer in empirical sociology who is credited with founding modern social science as an accepted academic discipline in France. Many of his works are fundamental to social psychology.

Ebbinghaus, Hermann (1850–1909) Pioneered the study of memory and made important contributions to methodology, intelligence testing, and other areas.

Eccles, Sir John (1903–1997) Winner of the Nobel Prize in physiology or medicine in 1963 for his work that increased our understanding of synaptic transmission.

ecological psychology A movement in behaviorism that stressed the importance of examining environmental conditions and fully understanding the nature of the stimuli in any environmental event.

ecological validity Popularized by Neisser, the idea that laboratory experiments should be generalizable to the world outside the laboratory.

Edwards, Jonathan (1703–1758) Considered by some to be America's first substantive philosopher; his thoughts on psychology were a mixture of Locke and theology.

ego "The self," the personality pro-cess introduced to deal more effectively with the environment than the id can.

ego-ideal One of the subsystems of the superego that contains the rules the child perceives that his or her parents think are right.

Ehrenfels, Christian von (1859–1932) A student of Brentano who developed the concept of *Gestaltqualität,* which anticipated Gestalt theory.

Electra complex The name sometimes given to the Oedipus complex in girls.

Elliotson, John (1791–1868) A British physician who expressed interest in mesmerism's anesthetic properties and used mesmerism to treat certain conditions.

empiricism The search for knowledge through experience rather than through reasoning.

engram Another name for the memory trace—the location of specific memories in the brain.

entelechy The built-in purpose of things, which is complete actuality rather than potentiality.

Epicureanism Founded by Epicurus, a school in which true pleasure was to be found in simplicity and moderation.

Epicurus (ca. 341–270 B.C.E.) The founder of Epicureanism.

epiphenomenalism The mind-body position that says that the brain's activity produces mind as a byproduct.

episodic memory A type of long-term memory introduced by Tulving that refers to memories for events, such as your first day at school or breakfast this morning.

equipotentiality Lashley's term for the idea that all parts of a given brain structure are equal in their potential to mediate a particular function.

Erasmus, Desiderius (1466–1536) A humanist and a "debunker" who was influential in saving Martin Luther's life at the beginning of the Protestant Reformation.

ergonomics Also called human factors engineering, the designing of equipment that can be efficiently used by humans; Münsterberg called it psychotechnics.

Erigena, John Scotus (ca. 810–877) Master of the Palatine school under Charles the Bald; tried to fuse Neoplatonism with Christian doctrines and to reconcile faith and reason.

Erikson, Erik (1902–1994) Trained as a child psychoanalyst, but is best known for his work in developmental psychology, which expanded Freud's psychosexual stages of development.

Esdaile, James (1808–1859) A Scottish physician who used mesmerism to induce anesthesia in surgical patients in India.

Estes, William K. (1919–) Developed a statistical theory of learning based on the central idea of Guthrie's learning theory, which was association by contiguity.

ethology The name for the biological approach to the study of animal behavior.

eugenics The idea that the human race can be improved through selectively breeding people for desirable traits.

evolutionary associationism Herbert Spencer's idea that frequently made associations can be passed on to future generations.

excitatory potential In Hull's system, the total tendency to make a particular response to a particular stimulus; it is the product of habit strength, drive, and incentive motivation. Also called reaction potential.

existentialism A philosophy that stresses the isolation of the individual in a hostile universe and emphasizes freedom of choice and responsibility for the consequences of actions.

experimental aesthetics The data-based study of beauty, a field founded by Gustav Fechner.

Experimentalists, The Titchener's informal club of laboratory directors who met annually to give reports in a "smoke-filled room with no women present"; after Titchener's death, was reorganized as the Society of Experimental Psychologists.

experimental neurosis The name for abnormal behavior often observed in Pavlov's dogs when discrimination training became too difficult for them.

extinction In Pavlovian conditioning, the presentation of the CS without the UCS.

extraversion An outward-directed attitude that Jung made a central component of his theory of psychological types.

Eysenck, Hans J. (1916–1997) An eclectic psychologist who was a developer of biological measures of intelligence and who suggested that personality can be understood through the use of as few as two factors—neuroticism and introversion/extraversion.

factor analysis A statistical procedure to analyze and interpret a series of correlations within a data set.

faculty psychology A position first associated with the Scottish School of common-sense psychology whose adherents believed that the mind can be divided into a number of different powers, or faculties.

family Subdivision of a school consisting of psychologists sharing a common developmental influence.

family resemblance A key concept of categorization proposed by Wittgenstein, the idea of family resemblance asserts that a category does not have to have a defining feature shared by all of the category's members. Instead, there can be a set of features distributed across the category members, with no one feature essential for inclusion in the category.

Faria, José Custodio di (1756–1819) Portuguese priest who investigated why some people are easier to hypnotize than others and suggested that the power to achieve a state of "lucid sleep" lay in the hypnotized person, not in the hypnotist.

fatigue or exhaustion method One of Guthrie's methods for breaking a habit by forcing its performance until the person could no longer do it.

Fechner, Gustav Theodor (1801–1887) The physicist, physiologist, and philosopher who created psychophysics.

Fechner's law S = k log R, where S is the sensation, which is equal to a constant (k) times the logarithm of stimulus intensity.

Ferenczi, Sandor (1873–1933) One of Freud's inner circle who accompanied Freud to Clark University in 1909, founded the Hungarian Psychoanalytic Society, and collaborated with Rank in writing *The Development of Psychoanalysis.*

Ferrier, Sir David (1843–1928) A Scottish neurologist knighted for his electrical stimulation studies of localization of function in the monkey brain.

Festinger, Leon (1919–1989) One of Kurt Lewin's Ph.D. students who was a prominent social psychologist credited with introducing and developing the theory of cognitive dissonance.

field theory Lewin's social-psychological theory in which a person is assumed to be continually interacting within a field of psychological forces.

figure-ground relationship Borrowed from the work of Edgar Rubin, the Gestalt perceptual principle in which the perceptual field is divided into two parts: The figure is the part of the field attended to, whereas the ground is the remainder of the field.

first-signal system Another name Pavlov gave to CSs, because he considered them the first signals of reality.

Fisher, Sir Ronald A. (1890–1962) A British statistician and innovator in the analysis of variance and several nonparametric statistical procedures whose greatest contribution was his conceptualization of testing the null hypothesis.

FitzRoy, Captain Robert (1805–1865) The captain of the HMS *Beagle,* the ship on which Darwin was an unpaid naturalist during a 5-year voyage.

fixed-interval (FI) schedule An operant conditioning schedule in which reinforcements are given after set periods of time.

fixed-ratio (FR) schedule An operant conditioning schedule in which rewards occur after fixed numbers of responses.

flashbulb memories Memories of first learning about a surprising or emotional experience.

Fliess, Wilhelm (1858–1928) An ear, nose, and throat specialist from Berlin who was a friend and confidant to Freud.

Flourens, Pierre Jean Marie (1794–1867) Developed the ablation method and used it to study the function of different parts of the nervous system.

Forel, Auguste-Henri (1848–1931) An expert on ants, the Swiss medical researcher and psychiatrist who was invited by Hall to speak at the 10th anniversary of Clark University's founding.

formal operational stage The fourth stage of Piaget's theory, which extends from about 12 or 13 through adulthood. The person in this stage can think abstractly and has the cognitive ability to test problem solutions hypothetically and systematically.

Forms Plato's universals known fully only through reasoning; also called Ideas.

fractionating A technique developed by Watt at Würzburg that involved dividing introspections into four distinct periods.

Frankl, Viktor (1905–1997) A Holocaust survivor and Viennese psychiatrist who was best known for his approach to existential psychotherapy called logotherapy.

Franz, Shepherd Ivory (1874–1933) The first person to combine the ablation method of the physiologist with the training methods of the psychologist, using the combination to study the functions of the frontal lobes in cats.

free association The name given to Freud's "talking cure," in which the patient is told to say anything that comes into the conscious mind, without trying to censor it.

Freud, Anna (1895–1982) The last born of Freud's children who became her father's successor in the advancement of psychoanalytic theory and is best known for her elaboration of Freudian ego defense mechanisms.

Freud, Sigmund (1856–1939) An Austrian psychiatrist who is considered the founder of psychoanalysis. *The Interpretation of Dreams* is considered his most important early work, and many of Freud's concepts are now a part of Western civilization.

Fritsch, Gustav (1838–1927) German scientist credited (with Eduard Hitzig) with introducing the electrical stimulation method to brain research.

functional fixedness The inability to see novel uses or possibilities for something.

functionalism A psychological system that studied the functions of mind and behavior in the context of the organism's adaptation to the environment.

fundamental attribution error The inconsistency between how we evaluate ourselves and how we evaluate others.

"g" factor A general intelligence factor that purportedly accounts for the high intercorrelation of scores on various tests comprising an IQ test.

Gage, Phineas P. Construction supervisor who had an iron bar blown through his head, the injury producing dramatic personality changes.

Galen (ca. 130–200 C.E.) Greek physician who incorporated Hippocrates' humors into a primitive personality theory.

Galilei, Galileo (1564–1642) Used a refracting telescope to make many astronomical discoveries; was forced by the Inquisition to recant his ideas.

Gall, Franz Joseph (1758–1828) A German physician and anatomist most remembered for the introduction of phrenology.

Galton, Francis (1822–1911) Darwin's cousin who wrote *Hereditary Genius* and was a pioneer in the study of individual differences, the use of statistics, and in the development of methods used by later psychologists; the person most associated with the nature-nurture debate.

Galvani, Luigi (1737–1798) An Italian lecturer in anatomy and professor of obstetrics who studied frogs and electricity and concluded that frogs generated electricity.

galvanic skin response (GSR) Named after Galvani; a change in the skin's ability to conduct electricity.

Garcia, John (1917–) Particularly known for his studies of conditioned taste aversion; one of the first Hispanic Americans to earn a Ph.D. in psychology.

Garman, Charles E. (1850–1907) Exceptional teacher at Amherst who also founded the psychology laboratory there; influenced Woodworth and other important psychologists.

Garner, Wendell Richard "Tex" (1921–) A psychologist who, by applying mathematics to the analysis of psychological problems, has analyzed information and communication and has done applied work in radar jamming.

Gassendi, Pierre (1592–1655) A critic of Descartes who supported Copernican astronomical ideas, Democritus's atomism, and Epicurus's moral philosophy.

generalizability The extent to which sample results apply to different populations.

General Problem Solver A computer program developed by Newell and Simon designed to mimic how humans solve a number of diverse problems and logic puzzles.

genetic epistemology The name Piaget gave to his program of study, which was genetic in the sense of developmental and epistemological because it studied the foundations of human knowledge.

genital stage The final psychosexual stage in Freudian psychoanalysis during which the person begins to direct the libido outward, toward the opposite sex, and to the goal of reproduction.

gerontology The study of aging and the exploration of issues that emerge as we age.

Gesell, Arnold (1880–1961) Founder of a psychology clinic at Yale; conducted research establishing maturational standards for children and is particularly known for his methodological contributions to developmental psychology, such as photography and observation through a one-way mirror.

Gestalt psychology A system that held that psychologists should study and discover useful and meaningful laws about the relations between parts and wholes.

Gestaltqualitäten von Ehrenfels's term, which means "a quality of the forms" or "form quality."

Gibson, Eleanor Jack (1910–2002) One of Hull's Yale Ph.D. students best known for her work on the visual cliff; she was married to J. J. Gibson.

Gibson, James Jerome (1904–1979) Considered an ecological psychologist whose primary interests were in the relationships between the perceived properties of a stimulus and behavior.

Goddard, Henry Herbert (1866–1957) A psychologist who was an ardent supporter of the hereditarian position concerning intelligence; best known for his book on the inheritance of "feeblemindedness" in the Kallikak family.

Goethe, Johann Wolfgang von (1749–1832) Literary masterpieces include *Faust* and *The Sorrows of Young Werther;* in science, Goethe believed in the study of intact, meaningful experiences, which became the essence of phenomenology.

Golden Age of Greece The time period between the birth of Pericles (ca. 490 B.C.E.) and the death of Aristotle (322 B.C.E.).

Goldstein, Kurt (1878–1965) A neurologist affiliated with Gestalt psychology who also served as one of the initial editors of the Gestaltist journal, *Psychologische Forschung.*

Golgi, Camillo (1843–1926) The Italian histologist and physician who won a Nobel Prize for his discovery of a type of stain that selectively colors only a few cells in a region.

Goodenough, Florence (1886–1959) A psychologist best known for the Draw-a-Person Test, Goodenough rebutted Stoddard and Wellman's work on the effects of environment on IQ scores.

Grosseteste, Robert (ca. 1175–1253) The first Chancellor of Oxford University and a writer of treatises of interest to psychology.

Guilford, Joy Paul (1897–1987) A psychologist who was one of the first to provide a multifactor alternative to Spearman's g, arguing for more than 100 components of intelligence.

Gutenberg, Johannes (1400–1468) One of the inventors of printing in the West.

Guthrie, Edwin Ray (1886–1959) An American psychologist who developed a one-trial, contiguity, nonreinforcement theory of learning.

habit strength In Hull's system, the strength of the bond between the stimulus and the response.

Haeckel, Ernst (1834–1919) A German naturalist who popularized the idea that the development of the individual repeats the development of the species (ontogeny recapitulates phylogeny).

Hall, Granville Stanley (1844–1924) Primarily a developmental psychologist whose "foundings" include the APA, the first American journal of psychology, and the psychology departments at Johns Hopkins and Clark. Hall is also known for his pioneering work in the psychology of religion and for his interest in psychoanalysis.

Hall, Marshall (1790–1857) A Scottish physician and physiologist who helped clarify knowledge of reflex action.

Hamilton, Gilbert Van Tassell (1877–1948) Considered a major figure in the history of psychiatry; also a pioneer in comparative psychology in America.

Harlow, Harry F. (1905–1981) An experimental psychologist who studied monkeys at the University of Wisconsin; he pointed to the importance of prior experience for the development of insight.

Harrower, Molly (1906–1999) Kurt Koffka's Ph.D. student who became one of the first experimental psychologists in neuropsychology.

Hartley, David (1705–1757) A physician who founded associationism and tried to give its ideas a physiological basis.

Harvey, William (1578–1657) Used the experimental method to show that the heart is a pump used to circulate blood.

Hathaway, Starke (1903–1984) A psychologist who, along with J. C. McKinley, developed the MMPI.

Hawthorne Effect Derived from a series of studies of workplace conditions and job performance, the Hawthorne Effect suggests that any workplace change that makes people feel important is likely to improve their work performance.

Hebb, Donald Olding (1904–1985) A student of Lashley who is probably most remembered for *The Organization of Behavior,* which reawakened interest in psychologists for neurological explanations of behavior.

hedonism The search for pleasure and the avoidance of pain.

Hegel, Georg Wilhelm Friedrich (1770–1831) A German philosopher who saw the universe as an interconnected unity that he called the Absolute. Everything was evolving toward the Absolute by dialectical movement.

Heidbreder, Edna (1890–1985) A student of Woodworth's whose best-known contribution to psychology was her book on the psychological schools entitled *Seven Psychologies.*

Heidegger, Martin (1889–1976) Heidegger is considered among the most significant philosophers in the 20th century. His existential-phenomenology underpins a form of therapy called *Daseinanalysis.*

Heider, Fritz (1896–1988) A perceptual researcher in the Gestalt tradition whose cognitive balance theory was instrumental in creating the study of attribution.

Helmholtz, Hermann Ludwig Ferdinand von (1821–1894) One of the greatest physiologists of all time, Helmholtz measured the speed of the nerve impulse, invented the ophthalmoscope, revised a theory of color vision, and proposed a place theory of auditory pitch perception, among other things.

Helmholtz–Hering debate A debate over the development of visual space perception, in which Helm-holtz took an empiricist approach (it is learned) and Hering argued for the nativist position (it is there from the beginning).

Helmont, Jan Baptista van (1577–1644) A Flemish chemist who introduced the idea of animal magnetism.

Henle, Mary (1913–) A Gestalt psychologist who is probably best known as a chronicler of Gestalt psychology.

Heraclitus (ca. 540–480 B.C.E.) Known as "the riddler"; focused on the changing nature of things.

Herbart, Johann Friedrich (1776–1841) A German rationalist who founded educational psychology and whose concept of a threshold of consciousness influenced Fechner.

Herder, Johann Gottfried (1744–1803) A German critic and poet who stressed the importance of the historical method for an understanding of humankind.

Hering, Ewald (1834–1918) Physiologist best known for his opponent-process theory of color vision.

Herophilus (ca. 335–280 B.C.E.) An anatomist and the founder of the school of anatomy at Alexandria who thought mind was located in the brain's ventricles.

Hickok, Laurens Perseus (1798–1888) A minister and theologian who may have been the first to develop a science of psychology in America.

higher-order conditioning In Pavlovian conditioning, the use of a previous CS as a UCS in further conditioning.

Hilgard, Ernest R. (1904–2001) An honored psychologist whose perhaps greatest contribution to the history of psychology is his monumental work, *Psychology in America: A Historical Survey.*

Hippocrates (ca. 460–377 B.C.E.) Called the father of medicine; remembered for, among other things, his humoral theory of illness.

historiography The field devoted to the study of how historical events are reported in writing.

Hitzig, Eduard (1838–1907) German scientist credited (with Gustav Fritsch) with introducing the electrical stimulation method to brain research.

Hobbes, Thomas (1588–1679) An English political philosopher whose empiricism and materialism influenced the later British empiricists; *Leviathan* was his most famous work.

Hodgkin, Sir Alan (1914–1998) A neurophysiologist who shared a Nobel Prize for his study of axonal transmission in the giant axon of the squid.

hodology Term invented by Lewin to show paths of energy within a person's life space.

Hollingworth, Harry L. (1880–1956) 1927 APA president and Leta Hollingworth's husband who was head of the psychology department at Bernard college for many years.

Hollingworth, Leta Stetter (1886–1939) An early female contributor to American psychology who provided scientific underpinnings for the feminist movement.

Holt, Edwin Bissell (1873–1946) An early behaviorist and an early member of the Harvard psychology faculty.

Hooker, Joseph (1817–1911) A botanist who was a friend and champion of Charles Darwin.

Hornbostel, Erich von (1877–1936) Stumpf's student, who, with Stumpf, founded the Archive for Phonograms in 1900.

Horney, Karen (1885–1952) A German psychoanalyst who came to America and helped found the American Institute of Psychoanalysis. One of Horney's most fundamental theoretical concepts was basic anxiety, and she identified 10 irrational problem solutions that she called neurotic needs.

Hovland, Carl Iver (1912–1961) A Hull Ph.D. from Yale who, after World War II, became the leader of Yale's social psychology program. In his research, he explored attitude change, finding evidence for a "sleeper effect," among other contributions.

Howes, Ethel Puffer (1872–1950) Primarily a student of Münsterberg who made contributions not only to psychology but also to a variety of women's issues.

Hull, Clark Leonard (1884–1952) An American psychologist who attempted to develop a complete learning system from postulates giving rise to testable theorems.

humanism A concern with the individual person as part of the world of nature; a primary factor contributing to the Renaissance.

Hume, David (1711–1776) The last of the British empiricists; closely anticipated British associationism.

humors The bodily fluids Hippocrates thought were distilled from the universe's basic elements. The humors were blood, black bile, yellow bile, and phlegm.

Hunter, Walter S. (1889–1953) A comparative psychologist from the functionalist/behaviorist tradition who developed the delayed-response problem.

Husserl, Edmund Gustav Albrecht (1859–1938) Husserl is best known in psychology for the formalization of the phenomenological method.

Huxley, Sir Andrew (1917–) A neurophysiologist who shared a Nobel Prize for his study of axonal transmission in the giant axon of the squid.

Huxley, Thomas Henry (1825–1895) A friend of both Spencer and Darwin and an ardent defender of evolutionary ideas.

hypnotism Named by James Braid, a state of heightened suggestibility in humans.

hypothesis experiments Experiments by David Krech in which rats appeared to test hypotheses about response strategies in order to maximize their success on the task.

hypothetical constructs Intervening variables with surplus meaning and at least the implication of a physiological basis.

hypothetico-deductive learning theory The name given to Hull's learning system in which general statements (postulates) gave rise to testable theorems.

id Literally "it," the totally unconscious, biological storehouse for drives, derived from instincts.

idealism The point of view stating that the objects of perception are ideas of the perceiving mind and that it is impossible to know whether reality exists apart from the mind; also called immaterialism or mentalism.

identification Unconsciously trying to think, feel, and act like another, identification ends the Oedipus complex.

Idols The term Francis Bacon used for preconceived notions that contaminate reasoning.

imageless thought Found by Külpe and others, referred to introspections during problem solving that yielded either no or vague images and feelings. Wundt and Titchener did not believe it was possible, and this led to controversy.

immaterialism See **mentalism.**

immediate experience Wundt's term for the direct experience of a stimulus, uninfluenced by any previous knowledge of it. Immediate experience provides the data for experimental psychology.

impressions The mind's active perceptions, according to Hume.

incentive motivation Kenneth Spence's idea, adopted by Hull, that the quantity and quality of a reward affects performance.

incompatible stimuli Guthrie's method for breaking a habit by presenting the stimulus that would normally trigger the undesirable behavior when other aspects of the situation will prevent the behavior's occurrence.

Individual Psychology The name for Adler's form of psychology.

individuation For Jung, the process through which the self became the whole psyche.

inductive reasoning Reasoning from the particular to the general; Aristotle used inductive reasoning.

information processing The term used to describe the application of cybernetic information and control theories to human behavior and mental events.

Inhelder, Bärbel (1913–1997) A longtime colleague and collaborator of Piaget and one of the first important female contributors to cognitive psychology.

innate ideas The ideas that Descartes believed come to mind with certainty and inevitability; they do not come from experience.

insight Köhler's term referring to a sudden behavior change that often appears when a human or animal restructures a field and solves a problem.

intelligence quotient (IQ) Mental age divided by chronological age—a term introduced by William Stern; the abbreviation "IQ" was coined by Lewis Terman.

intentionality A concept central to Brentano's act psychology, to be conscious is to be conscious of something (i.e., consciousness always intends something).

interactionism The mind-body position that says the mind and body are separate but interacting.

interbehaviorism The name Kantor gave to his psychology stressing the interactions of the organism with stimulus objects.

interference theory of forgetting The observation by Müller and Pilzecker that new learning can interfere with the memory of previously learned material.

internal perception Used by Wundt rather than introspection as one method to aid in the study of the lower mental processes; the German term is *innere Wahrnehmung.*

interposition One of three depth perception cues in which near objects hide, or partially hide, more distant objects; as recognized by George Berkeley.

intervening variable A construct coming between the stimulus and the response that is completely defined by the S-R conditions.

introspection Meaning "to look within"; a method for studying inner experience first suggested by St. Augustine.

introversion An inward-directed attitude that Jung made a central component of his theory of psychological types.

isomorphism A Gestalt principle that assumes a direct correspondence between brain processes and what is being experienced.

Jackson, John Hughlings (1835–1911) An English neurologist who guessed that there were motor areas in the cerebral cortex whose stimulation resulted in the motor convulsions of epilepsy.

Jaensch, Erich R. (1883–1940) Worked in G. E. Müller's laboratory and performed phenomenological investigations at the same time that the founders of Gestalt psychology were doing their seminal research.

James, William (1842–1910) The father of American psychology; best remembered for *The Principles of Psychology,* for his contributions to research areas in psychology such as consciousness and emotion, for his many important students, and for his role in founding Harvard's department of psychology.

James-Lange theory of emotion Theory of emotion, which put the physiological expression of emotion before the emotional feeling; proposed independently by William James and Carl Lange.

Janet, Pierre (1859–1947) Considered the dean of French psychology by the end of his career; developed a system of psychopathology that was in some respects similar to Freud's psychoanalysis.

Jaspers, Karl (1883–1969) An existential philosopher, historian, and psychotherapist whose approach to therapy was based on the analysis of existence.

Jastrow, Joseph (1863–1944) One of Hall's students at Hopkins who became well-known as a popularizer of psychology.

Jennings, Herbert Spencer (1868–1947) An American biologist who believed that simple animals exhibit complex behavior and opposed Loeb's use of tropisms to explain behavior.

Jensen, Arthur (1923–) A psychologist who published a controversial paper contending that programs designed to improve intelligence and scholastic achievement have failed because intelligence is mainly inherited; one of the first to report errors in Burt's work.

Jesus Lived from approximately 4 B.C.E. until his crucifixion in about 30 C.E. and is known mostly through the Gospels of Matthew, Mark, Luke, and John; he became the central figure in the religion of Christianity.

Johnson, Samuel (1696–1772) Columbia University's first president and the author of an early work that explored psychological topics from the perspective of British empiricism.

Jones, Edward (1926–1993) A social psychologist who is best known for his research on how we modify our attributions as a function of how events directly affect us.

Jones, Ernest (1879–1958) A lifelong friend of Freud and his biographer; introduced psychoanalysis to Great Britain and founded the British Psycho-Analytical Society.

Jones, Mary Cover (1896–1987) Psychologist who is probably best known for her study (with Watson's advice) of the removal of a fear of animals in a child named Peter.

Judd, Charles H. (1873–1946) A student of Wundt who was a pioneer educational and social psychologist at the University of Chicago and who founded laboratories at Wesleyan and New York Universities.

Jung, Carl Gustav (1875–1961) Once Freud's heir-apparent who broke away to develop Analytical Psychology, which contained more mystical elements but fewer sexual elements than Freud's system.

just noticeable difference The amount that a comparison stimulus must differ from a standard stimulus in order to be reliably detected as different.

Kahneman, Daniel (1934–) Known for his collaboration with Tversky on studies of human reasoning.

Kallikak Pseudonym for the family Goddard studied that he believed proved the hereditary nature of mental retardation.

Kamin, Leon (1927–) A psychologist who was one of the first to report errors in Burt's work; Kamin has claimed that research with twins suggests little contribution to IQ from heredity.

Kant, Immanuel (1724–1804) A German philosopher whose *Critique of Pure Reason* was written in reaction to David Hume's skeptical philosophy. In contrast to the empiricists, Kant believed the mind contains categories of understanding that exist before experience.

Kantor, Jacob Robert (1888–1984) A Chicago Ph.D. who developed an approach to behaviorism called interbehaviorism; a forerunner of later ecological approaches.

Katz, David (1884–1957) Performed phenomenological investigations in G. E. Müller's laboratory at the same time that Gestalt psychology's founders did their seminal research.

Kelley, Harold (1921–2003) A social psychologist whose attribution research indicated that we frequently incorporate aspects of both the environmental situation and the individual we are evaluating when we make attributions.

Kelly, George A. (1905–1967) Best known for his personal construct theory, Kelly sought a more humanistic alternative than he found in either Freud or behaviorism.

Kent, Grace (1875–1973) A psychologist best known for her work on clinical diagnostic scales.

Kepler, Johann (1571–1630) Proposed three fundamental laws of planetary motion that formed the basis for Isaac Newton's later discoveries.

Kierkegaard, Sören Aabye (1813–1855) Poet, philosopher, theologian, and psychological theorist who is considered the founder of existentialism.

Klein, Melanie (1882–1960) Seen as a rival to Anna Freud in England who differed from Freud in her stress on the importance of the mother's early nurturing of the child.

Klineberg, Otto (1899–1992) The first head of Columbia University's social psychology department and the author of *Race Differences,* in which he described differences between races on a variety of psychological characteristics.

Koffka, Kurt (1886–1941) One of the founders of Gestalt psychology; his 1922 *Psychological Bulletin* article introduced Gestalt psychology to American psychologists.

Kohlberg, Lawrence (1927–1987) Particularly known for his study of moral development.

Köhler, Wolfgang (1887–1967) One of the founders of Gestalt psychology, who, during World War I, did studies that provided the Gestalt answer to learning—insight learning.

König, Arthur (1856–1901) With Ebbinghaus, one of the founders of *Zeitschrift für Psychologie und Physiologie der Sinnesorgane (Journal of Psychology and Physiology of Sense Organs).*

Kraepelin, Emil (1856–1926) A student of Wundt who was a psychiatrist; applied attentional theory to schizophrenia.

Krafft-Ebing, Richard (1840–1902) An expert on forensic psychiatry and sexual pathology who was called to consult with Breuer on the case of Anna O.

Kretschmer, Ernst (1888–1964) A German psychiatrist who developed a body type theory that influenced William Sheldon.

Kuhn, Thomas (1922–1996) A philosopher of science who developed a model for scientific revolution.

Külpe, Oswald (1862–1915) Founder of the Würzburg school, which frequently challenged Wundt and Titchener.

Kuo, Zing Yang (1898–1970) A Chinese psychologist famous for his anti-instinct studies.

LAD The acronym for "language acquisition device," Chomsky's term for an innate characteristic of the human mind that enables children to acquire language easily.

Ladd, George Trumbull (1842–1920) Associated with the development of the psychology department at Yale; the author of an important early textbook based on Wundt's experimental psychology.

Ladd-Franklin, Christine (1847–1930) Researcher who is most remembered for her theory of color vision that was an attempted reconciliation of the Young-Helmholtz trichromatic theory with Donders's tetrachromatic theory.

Laing, Ronald D. (1927–1989) A psychiatrist who is best known for his description of psychopathology as something that occurs in a relationship, not in an individual.

Lamarck, Jean-Baptiste (1744–1829) An important pre-Darwinian evolutionary theorist whose central idea is often summarized by the phrase "the inheritance of acquired characteristics."

La Mettrie, Julien Offray de (1709–1751) Author of *Man a Machine,* the French empiricist who went a step beyond Descartes to argue against a mind-body dichotomy. Human mind and behavior are as mechanically controlled as they are in animals.

Lange, Carl (1834–1900) A Danish physiologist who independently developed a theory of emotion similar to the one developed by William James.

Lange, Ludwig (1863–1936) Working under Wundt, Lange did a reaction-time study in which a focus on the stimulus rather than on the response resulted in slightly longer reaction times than when the subjects focused on the response.

Langfeld, Herbert S. (1879–1958) One of Stumpf's Berlin Ph.D. students who spent most of his career at Princeton, where he directed the laboratory.

Lashley, Karl Spencer (1890–1958) Often considered the "father of neuropsychology," Lashley used the ablation method to study the neural basis of complex learning and memory in animals. He is considered to have provided evidence for a nonlocalizationist position.

Latané, Bibb (1937–) The researcher who, with John Darley, has conducted important studies of bystander apathy.

latency stage The relatively uneventful period in psychosexual development that occurs between the phallic stage and the genital stage.

latent content The dream's true meaning, which may differ from its manifest content.

latent learning Learning that is assumed to have occurred but is not evident in the organism's performance.

law of effect Thorndike's statement that responses in a situation followed closely by satisfaction will be more firmly attached to the situation and more likely to recur when the situation is repeated, whereas responses followed by discomfort will have their connections to the situation weakened and be less likely to recur when the situation is repeated.

law of exercise Thorndike's statement of the long-held belief that repetition of an association strengthens the bond between a situation and the reponse to it.

law of *Prägnanz* A general Gestalt principle asserting that any psychological organization will tend toward a "good Gestalt" or good form; the organization will tend to be as good as prevailing conditions allow.

Law of Three Stages According to Comte, the stages each field of thought passes through: theological, metaphysical, and positivistic, or scientific.

learning predispositions The idea that evolution has shaped an organism's associative system so that some associations are more easily made than others.

learning set The extraction of one key to the solution of a series of similar problems.

LeBon, Gustave (1841–1931) Trained as a physician, LeBon's book *The Crowd*—containing an analysis of groups and group behavior—may be considered the major point of departure for an actual social psychology.

Leibniz, Gottfried Wilhelm von (1646–1716) German mathematician/philosopher whose solution to the mind-body problem is called psychophysical parallelism: Mind and body appear to interact because they are perfectly constructed and set into motion simultaneously.

Leuba, James H. (1868–1946) A student of Hall's who was a pioneer in the psychology of religion.

Lewin, Kurt (1890–1947) A major Gestalt theorist who developed field theory and experimental social psychology.

libido Freud's term for the form of energy used by the life instincts.

Liébeault, Auguste Ambroise (1823–1904) A physician in Nancy who treated many of his patients with hypnotism.

life space Lewin's term for a field within which a person's psychological activities occur; it consists of all the influences on the person at a given moment in time.

Likert, Rensis (1903–1981) An associate of Kurt Lewin who is best known for the scaling procedure bearing his name.

Lipps, Theodor (1851–1914) A student of Wundt best known for his empathy theory of aesthetic enjoyment.

Little Albert The child Watson and Rayner used in their study of a conditioned fear reaction in humans.

localizationists Neuroscientists who hold that specific functions are located in specific brain areas.

local sign For Lotze, a particular pattern of stimulation somewhere on the body that carried with it a sense of location.

Locke, John (1632–1704) British philosopher considered to have begun British empiricism with *An Essay Concerning Human Understanding.*

Loeb, Jacques (1859–1924) A major influence on Watson; Loeb is best known for his idea that tropisms account for much of the behavior of animals.

Loewi, Otto (1873–1961) A German pharmacologist who proved that synaptic transmission may occur by chemical means.

logical positivism Another name for operationism; a movement started by the members of the Vienna Circle that continued the refinement of positivism through a systematic investigation of the logic of science.

logotherapy The existential psychotherapy developed by Frankl that involves the search for meaning.

longitudinal studies Studies performed on a group over an extended time period.

Lorenz, Konrad (1903–1989) Considered one of the founders of ethology; described the phenomenon of imprinting.

Lotze, Rudolf Hermann (1817–1881) The German physician and philosopher whose major contribution to psychology included an empirical theory of space perception in which local signs convey a sense of location.

Lucretius (ca. 99–55 B.C.E.) An advocate and popularizer of Epicureanism.

Lull, Raymond (ca. 1232–1315) Conceived of a machine programmed with elementary concepts that would generate all knowledge; an adversary of Averroës.

Luria, Alexander Romanovich (1902–1977) Arguably the most important Russian psychologist in the post-Pavlov period, considered one of the founders of modern clinical neuropsychology.

Luther, Martin (1483–1546) The German founder of the Protestant Reformation.

Lyceum Aristotle's school that came to rival Plato's Academy.

Lyell, Sir Charles (1797–1875) Author of *Principles of Geology,* which started both Darwin and Spencer on the road to evolutionary theories. Lyell became a constant friend and supporter of Darwin.

Mach, Ernst (1838–1916) A physicist who established Machian positivism, the main idea of which is that sensations are the basic data of all science.

Machiavelli, Noccolò (1469–1527) His book, *The Prince,* resulted in his name becoming synonymous with the use of any means to achieve one's goals.

Maccoby, Eleanor Emmons (1917–) A social and developmental psychologist who is particularly known for her study of gender issues, which culminated in 1974 with the publication of *Sex Differences,* with Carol Jacklin.

Magendie, François (1783–1855) French physiologist whose animal research established his claim as the codiscoverer of the Bell-Magendie law.

Maimonides (1135–1204) A Jewish scholar who tried to harmonize the teachings of Judaism with Aristotle.

Maine de Biran, François-Pierre (1766–1824) Part vitalist philosopher and part physiologist who advocated a type of introspection he called "experimental psychology."

Malebranche, Nicolas (1638–1715) A French philosopher whose solution to the mind-body problem is called occasionalism: Mind-body interaction is caused by the intervention of God.

Malthus, Thomas (1766–1834) Author of *Essay on the Principle of Population,* which discussed the tendency of the human population to increase faster than the means to support it, which results in suppression of the population by natural disasters. The essay gave Darwin the insight of natural selection for his theory of evolution.

manifest content The literal details of a dream that a person remembers upon awakening.

Marbe, Karl (1869–1953) A member of the Würzburg school who found that weight judgments often just appeared in the subjects' minds, which Marbe attributed to "conscious attitudes."

Marcus Aurelius (121–180 C.E.) One of the great Roman emperors whose *Meditations* is a classic work in Stoic philosophy.

Martin, Lillien Jane (1851–1943) A student of G. E. Müller at Göttingen who subsequently secured a position at Stanford.

Maslow, Abraham (1908–1970) Maslow became the major spokesperson for humanistic psychology and was largely responsible for humanistic psychology's viability as a "Third Force." Maslow is perhaps best known for his work on motivation in which he posited a hierarchy of needs.

mass action Lashley's term that meant that the amount of loss of function following brain damage was proportional to the amount of damage to the brain, not to its locus.

massed practice Practice without rest periods that Ebbinghaus found is inferior to distributed practice.

materialism The mind-body position that holds there is only body; the underlying reality is physical; form of monism.

May, Rollo (1909–1994) An early advocate for existential psychology in America, where his works largely introduced the topic.

McClelland, David (1917–1998) A social psychologist best known for his many studies of achievement and motivation.

McConnell, James V. (1925–1990) A researcher whose career in psychology included controversial work on memory transfer in the flatworm.

McDougall, William (1871–1938) A British social psychologist who came to America; an ardent opponent of Watson's behaviorism and a supporter of the instinct concept.

McNemar, Quinn (1900–1986) A psychologist whose contributions to psychometrics include refinements in factor analysis, a test bearing his name, and the idea that there may be little difference in predicting from a single intelligence factor or from several.

Mead, George Herbert (1863–1931) Part of the early faculty at Chicago, his work on the self is important to both clinical and social psychology as well as to sociology.

meaning For Titchener, the context in which something was experienced.

mechanism As defined by Woodworth, the "how" of motivation, as opposed to drive, which concerns the "why" of motivation.

mediate experience Wundt's term for the indirect experience that produces the data for physics and the other natural sciences.

medulla oblongata The first brain structure after the spinal cord; it is essential for life.

Meehl, Paul E. (1920–2003) Contributor to many diverse areas of psychology, perhaps the foremost critic of psychological methodology and an advocate for psychometric sophistication.

Meinong, Alexius (1853–1920) A student of Brentano who founded the first psychological laboratory in Austria.

memory drum A mechanical device invented by G. E. Müller and Schumann to systematize presentation of syllables in memory experiments.

Mendel, Gregor Johann (1822–1884) An Austrian biologist and botanist who studied inheritance in pea plants and published work that became the basis for modern genetics.

mental chemistry In John Stuart Mill's mental chemistry, an idea is generated by its components rather than consisting of them.

mental chronometry A method developed by Donders to study the time taken by the mind to perform different mental acts.

mentalism Also called **immaterialism** or **subjective idealism,** the mind-body solution that holds that reality ultimately exists in the mind; form of monism.

mental tests A term coined by Cattell for his measurements of such things as sensation, reaction time, and memory.

Merleau-Ponty, Maurice (1908–1961) An existential-phenomenological philosopher and psychologist whose books and methods remain popular today among psychologists interested in existentialism or phenomenology.

Mesmer, Franz Anton (1734–1815) A Viennese physician who went to Paris and developed a method of treatment—called mesmerism—that treated people by suggestion.

mesmerism In psychology, an early name for hypnosis.

method of expression The recording of physiological changes used by Wundt to study feelings.

method of limits One of Fechner's psychophysical techniques. In using it to determine the threshold of detection, the subject is presented with an undetectable stimulus that is gradually increased until the person reports it; then, a clearly detectable stimulus is gradually decreased until it is no longer sensed. The average intensity at which judgment changes is called the detection threshold.

Meumann, Ernst (1862–1915) A student of Wundt who roomed with Titchener at Leipzig and became an outstanding educational psychologist.

Meyer, Adolf (1866–1950) A leader in American psychiatry and director of Phipps Psychiatric Clinic who had close contact with Watson until he disagreed with Watson's paper on the application of conditioning to clinical problems.

Meynert, Theodor (1833–1893) A pioneer in the study of cellular architecture and one of Freud's professors.

Middle Ages The period extending from roughly 500 to 1500—from the fall of the Roman Empire until the beginning of the Renaissance.

Milgram, Stanley (1933–1984) A social psychologist known particularly for his studies of obedience. In his most famous experiment, Milgram found that most people would subject other people to apparently harmful electric shock if told to do so by someone in authority.

Mill, James (1773–1836) John Stuart Mill's father; took the passive association of ideas to its peak in his mental compounding model.

Mill, John Stuart (1806–1873) James Mill's son; added the idea of mental chemistry to his father's mental compounding.

Miller, George Armitage (1920–) Psychologist who is particularly known for his famous "The Magical Number Seven Plus or Minus Two" paper, which established limits (7 ± 2) on the human capacity for processing information.

Miller, James Grier (1916–2002) A contributor to systems theory—the idea that all things can be viewed as systems of essential functions.

Miller, Neal Elgar (1909–2002) One of Hull's Ph.D. students who, among other contributions, presented (with John Dollard) a simplified version of Hullian theory and began social learning theory, developed a precise account of conflict theory, applied learning theory to psychopathology and aggression, and demonstrated instrumental conditioning of autonomic responses.

Mind A journal of philosophy and psychology founded by Alexander Bain.

mind-body dualism Descartes' idea that the mind and the body are separate, with the mind unextended and without substance and the body extended and having substance.

mind-body problem One of the basic issues in the history of psychology that asks whether organisms have both mind and body, and, if so, how the two are related.

Minnesota Multiphasic Personality Inventory (MMPI) Created by Hathaway and McKinley, a personality assessment device consisting of 550 statements with which the person either agrees or disagrees. Each statement is linked to one or more of the test's 10 clinical scales. The MMPI also has three "validity" scales designed to detect faking.

Mirandola, Giovanni Pico della (1463–1494) An Italian humanist whose work emphasized individualism.

Mohammed (ca. 570–632) Born in Mecca, the founder of the Islamic religion.

Molyneux, William (1656–1696) An Irish scientist who argued that a person born blind and then made to see as an adult would not initially be able to identify objects visually but would first have to acquire visual ideas through sensations.

monads Leibniz term for the unextended, uncreatable, indestructible, and immutable particles he thought comprised everything.

monism The mind-body solution that holds there is only one underlying reality, either mind or body.

Montessori, Maria (1870–1952) The first woman in Italy to receive a medical degree and the pioneer of educational techniques that are still used in schools employing the Montessori Method.

Morgan, Christiana Drummond (1897–1967) Co-inventor of the TAT with Henry Murray.

Morgan, Conwy Lloyd (1852–1936) A protégé of Romanes and a leading contributor to the field of comparative psychology; perhaps best known for Morgan's Canon.

Morgan's Canon The suggestion that higher mental abilities should not be attributed to the animal mind than are necessary to explain the animal's behavior.

motivology Woodworth's term for the study of the drives and mechanisms related to motivation.

movement-produced stimuli Used to explain sequential responding, sensations produced by movements that lead to further movements.

Mowrer, Orval Hobart (1907–1982) One of Hull's associates who argued for a two-factor theory of conditioning in which he distinguished Thorndikian and Pavlovian conditioning.

Müller, Georg Elias (1850–1934) One of the early giants of experimental psychology who worked on psychophysics, memory, and vision.

Müller, Johannes (1801–1858) A German physiologist who taught Helmholtz and du Bois-Reymond and is perhaps best known for his doctrine of specific nerve energies.

Munk, Hermann (1839–1912) An investigator of brain function, German physiologist Munk concluded that loss of the occipital lobe on one side produced blindness in the opposite visual field rather than in the opposite eye.

Münsterberg, Hugo (1863–1916) Brought to America by William James to take over the psychology laboratory at Harvard; Münsterberg made several substantive contributions to psychology, especially to applied psychology.

Murchison, Carl (1887–1961) The initiator of *The Handbook of Social Psychology,* and most remembered as the editor of several early journals friendly to social psychology and the first three volumes of *A History of Psychology in Autobiography.*

Murphy, Gardner (1895–1979) An early leader in social psychology who created the program at Columbia that produced such important students as Rensis Likert, Theodore Newcomb, and Muzafer Sherif.

Murphy, Lois Barclay (1902–2003) A research psychologist, much of whose work concerned the interaction of personality and social influences on the developing child.

Murray, Henry A. (1893–1988) The psychologist and co-developer of the TAT test who wrote *Explorations in Personality,* in which he identified 20 psychological needs, such as a need for achievement.

Myers-Briggs Type Indicator (MBTI) A contemporary personality test based on Jung's theory of personality type.

nativists People adopting a nature position on the nature-nurture controversy.

nature and nurture A phrase popularized by Galton used to describe the longstanding debate about the relative importance of inherited or environmental influences on human behavior.

nature-nurture controversy Controversy over how much of behavior is inherited or instinctive (nature) and how much is acquired or learned (nurture).

need hierarchy The part of Maslow's theory of motivation often shown as a pyramid with basic physiological needs at its base and self-actualization at its apex.

negative afterimage The perception of the opposite color after prolonged stimulation with a particular color.

Neisser, Ulric (1928–) The cognitive scientist who has advanced the schema concept as the basis of cognitive psychology and used schema theory to provide a general account of human behavior and development.

NEO Personality Inventory-Revised (NEO PI-R) A personality assessment device suggesting that only five factors are needed to characterize personality—neuroticism, extraversion, openness, agreeableness/antagonism, and conscientiousness.

Neoplatonism A school that tried to combine Plato's views with various theologies.

neural networks A nonrule-based alternative to AI computing; also called parallel processing and connectionism.

neural plasticity A phenomenon in which remaining brain areas are believed to assume a lost function when a brain area is ablated.

neuropsychology The clinical and experimental field concerned with the study, understanding, evaluation, and treatment of behaviors rooted in brain function.

neuroticism One of Eysenck's personality components that is a measure of an individual's emotional stability or instability.

Newcomb, Theodore M. (1903–1984) A social psychologist whose most remembered research involved the longitudinal assessment of attitude changes in students at a small women's college.

Newell, Allen (1927–1992) With a Ph.D. in industrial administration, Newell worked with Simon on such things as human problem solving and artificial intelligence computing.

Newton, Sir Isaac (1642–1727) An inventor of integral calculus and the discoverer of the law of gravity.

Nietzsche, Friedrich Wilhelm (1844–1900) One of existentialism's founders, Nietzsche thought humans are characterized by a "will to power," or a need to dominate the environment. He saw the *Übermensch*, or superman, as the next step in human evolution.

nominalist One who believed that universals, concepts like truth and beauty, existed in name only, not in reality.

nominal fallacy The mistaken idea that naming something explains it.

nonlocalizationists Neuroscientists who are impressed with the way the nervous system works as a coordinated unit.

nonreductionism The position that psychological phenomena can stand on their own, without the need for biological or biochemical explanations.

nonsense syllable Consisting of two consonants with a vowel between, the wordlike unit Ebbinghaus created to study memory; also called a CVC trigram.

normal curve The bell-shaped curve that is often approximated when the distribution of scores from some physiological or behavioral measurement is plotted.

noumenal world Kant's term for the world outside our minds, which consists of "things-in-themselves."

nurturists People adopting a nurture position on the nature-nurture controversy.

object permanence In Piaget's theory, a child displays object permanence when it responds as though it realizes an object continues to exist even when it is no longer being sensed.

object-relations theory A psychoanalytic variation stressing conflicts based on object relations, which are interpersonal relationships as they are represented in an individual's mind.

occasionalism The mind-body position of Malebranche in which the need to act becomes the "occasion" for God's intervention.

Ockham's razor Belief of William of Ockham that the simplest explanation for a phenomenon is preferred over an explanation with more assumptions; sometimes called the Law of Parsimony.

Oedipus complex Part of the phallic stage during which the little boy would like to possess his mother and remove his father as a rival for her affections.

Ogden, Charles Kay (1889–1957) An English linguistic reformer; the most important bridge between psychology and linguistics before Chomsky.

Ogden, R. M. (1877–1959) Facilitator of the immigration to and employment in America of the founders of Gestalt psychology.

ontological argument St. Anselm's argument that says that God is the greatest thing that can be thought, and if God did not exist, then something greater could be thought. Hence, God must exist.

operant Skinner's term for a spontaneously occurring response.

operational definition A definition of something in terms of the way it is measured.

operationism Also called **logical positivism;** the philosophical approach to science that states that concepts should be defined operationally.

opponent-process theory Ewald Hering's theory of color vision in which three receptor systems each respond in one of two opposing ways: red-green, blue-yellow, and black-white.

oral stage The first of Freud's psychosexual stages during which the infant's efforts to achieve satisfaction are centered around the oral zone—the mouth.

Osgood, Charles (1916–1991) A psychologist who extended the idea of factor analysis to develop a measurement technique to assess word meanings—the semantic differential.

overlearning Continued practice beyond mastery; Ebbinghaus observed that overlearning facilitates retention.

paired-associates method An experimental technique for studying the nature of association that was introduced by Mary Calkins and further developed by G. E. Müller and others.

panpsychism The idea that mind or soul pervades the world of nature.

pantheism The belief that God and the universe are the same.

Paracelsus (1493–1541) A Swiss alchemist, physician, and mystic who was an early opponent of witch hunts and who believed that magnets influenced humans.

parallelism The view that mind and body are separate and noninteracting entities; also called psychophysical parallelism.

Parmenides (ca. 504–456 B.C.E.) Believed that change does not exist; distinguished between appearances (evidence from senses) and reality (known through reason).

Parrish, Celestia Suzannah (1853–1918) Studied briefly under Titchener and established the first psychology laboratory in the South at Randolph-Macon Woman's College.

Pascal, Blaise (1623–1662) The mathematician, physicist, and psychological philosopher who invented an early mathematical calculator.

Pavlov, Ivan Petrovich (1849–1936) An outstanding Russian physiologist who is known particularly for his detailed examination of a type of learning now called Pavlovian conditioning or classical conditioning.

Pearson, Karl (1857–1936) A friend, disciple, and biographer of Galton and the developer of statistical techniques such as the Pearson *r*.

Pearson product-moment correlation coefficient (Pearson *r*) The standard statistic computed to reveal the degree of relationship (correlation) between two variables.

Peirce, Charles Sanders (1839–1914) James's friend who is best known as a pragmatic philosopher and for the development of semiotics.

Penfield, Wilder Graves (1891–1976) A Canadian neurosurgeon who used electrical stimulation to study the human neocortex during brain surgery on patients.

penis envy The desire by females to possess the organ that they lack; penis envy introduces the Oedipus complex.

perceptual cycle Introduced by Neisser, the perceptual cycle suggests that our mental structures direct our behavior, and our experiences modify our mental representations in an unending cycle.

performance Refers to a distinction first made by Tolman between learning and performance; performance—the organism's actual behavior—may or may not reveal learning that has occurred.

Pericles (ca. 490–429 B.C.E.) Ruler under whom Athens enjoyed the privileges of democracy and benign dictatorship.

Perry, Ralph Barton (1876–1957) A Harvard philosopher from whom Tolman took a course that turned him toward psychology and gave him several of his main concepts.

persona In Jung's system, the part of the self that reflects a person's role in society.

Personal Attributes Questionnaire (PAQ) The questionnaire developed by Janet Spence and Robert Helmreich for use in studying gender differences.

personal construct From George Kelly's psychology, a theory an individual develops to help organize and make sense of his or her world.

personal unconscious In Jungian theory, the layer of the unconscious containing material that was once conscious but has now been repressed, suppressed, or simply forgotten.

petite perceptions The term Leibniz called perceptions that never reach consciousness.

Petrarch (1304–1374) An Italian poet and scholar strongly opposed to Averroës and Aristotle; his opposition to scholasticism and to religious authority aided later challenges to scientific dogma.

Pfungst, Oskar (1874–1932) A student of Carl Stumpf who is best known for resolving the Clever Hans mystery.

phallic stage The third of Freud's psychosexual stages of development during which interest in the child centers on the genitals.

phenomenal world Kant's term for the inner world created by the intuitions and categories of the mind.

phenomenology Often defined as the study of intact, meaningful experiences; Husserl defined it as the examination of the data of conscious experience.

phi phenomenon Wertheimer's name for apparent movement caused by the flashing of lights in the correct temporal sequence.

phrenology The pseudoscience that held that the mind's "faculties" were related to the bumps on the skull.

Piaget, Jean (1896–1980) A Swiss psychologist who made pioneering contributions in the study of child cognitive development.

pineal gland The gland in the brain Descartes chose for the point of interaction between the mind and the body.

Pinel, Philippe (1745–1826) Put in charge of asylums in Paris, Pinel freed the insane from their shackles.

place learning Contrasted with response learning, in Tolman's experiments rats were taught either to go to a specific place or to make a particular response; place learning proved to be superior to response learning, at least in Tolman's studies.

place theory of pitch perception The theory that the place of stimulation on the basilar membrane determines pitch perception.

Plato (427–347 B.C.E.) The founder of the Academy, famous for his theory of Forms and his Socratic dialogues.

pleasure principle The principle by which the id operates to try to eliminate or reduce tension to an acceptably low level.

Plotinus (ca. 205–270) A Neoplatonist philosopher who greatly influenced Christian thought.

Popper, Karl (1902–1994) Austrian philosopher of science who said that a truly scientific theory is one that can be refuted by a false instance.

positive afterimage A brief image of an object that remains after the object has been withdrawn; which Hartley attributed to continuing vibrations of tiny particles in the brain.

positivism A philosophical approach advocating a science based on observable facts and their logical relations to each other; scientific facts are to be gathered through empirical, objective observations.

postconventional stage Kohlberg's third stage of moral reasoning in which the individual is guided by internalized moral principles.

poverty-of-stimulus argument Chomsky's idea that the language spoken to children is too poor a stimulus and reinforcement of correct grammar is too haphazard to support a satisfactory behavioral account of language acquisition.

pragmatism A philosophical theory usually associated with William James or with its originator, C. S. Peirce. According to pragmatism, the meaning of an idea or proposition lies in its observable consequences; if an idea works in a context, it is true.

preconscious In Freudian theory, the part of the mind that is the antechamber to consciousness, containing relatively accessible material.

preconventional stage The first stage in Kohlberg's theory of moral reasoning in which moral behavior is motivated by the avoidance of punishment and the desire to be rewarded.

preoperational stage The second stage in Piaget's developmental theory, lasting from about age 2 to age 7. During this stage, the child discovers the operations that will be used for solving problems later.

presentist bias The tendency for historians to discuss and analyze past ideas, people, and events in terms of present issues and contexts.

Preyer, Wilhelm (1842–1897) A physiologist and friend of Fechner who was among the first to make detailed observations of child development.

Pribram, Karl (1919–) A practicing neurosurgeon who was influenced by Lashley to become a neuropsychologist in academia, where he has become a leading theorist of brain function.

primary process The production of a memory image of the object needed to reduce tension.

primary qualities Qualities inherent in matter (e.g., shape, quantity, and motion).

Prince, Morton (1854–1929) Sometimes considered the father of modern psychotherapy in America, Prince founded the clinic at Harvard in 1927.

principle of falsifiability Popper's principle that states that a scientific theory has the capability of being falsified or refuted.

principles of association Three principles—similarity, contrast, and contiguity—Aristotle used in describing recall.

projection The attribution of our unpleasant or disturbing desires to others while rejecting them in ourselves.

Project Pigeon A project devised by Skinner to train pigeons to guide missiles to their targets.

Protagoras (ca. 490–420 B.C.E.) A famous Sophist who refused to speculate beyond what we can know through our senses, and who taught that knowledge is relative.

proximity The Gestalt principle of perceptual grouping stating that elements that are close together are seen as belonging together.

psyche Term Aristotle used to refer to a vital principle that differentiated the living from the nonliving. For him, there were three different *psyches:* vegetative, sensitive, and rational.

psychic determinism The idea that all psychological events are determined.

psychoanalysis The system developed by Sigmund Freud to study human motivation, personality, and psychopathology, using such techniques as free association and the analysis of dreams and everyday errors.

psychometrics The measurement of mental processes through psychological tests; the term is sometimes used interchangeably with advances in statistics and data analysis.

Psychonomic Society Founded by Clifford Morgan and others in 1959–1960 in response to a growing perception that the APA was spending an increasing amount of time on concerns affecting primarily clinical psychologists.

psychopharmacology The field that uses psychological and pharmacological concepts to investigate the behavioral effects of drugs.

psychophysical parallelism The view that mind and body are separate and noninteracting entities.

psychophysics Fechner's term for the method he developed to measure the relation between sensation and the stimulus that produces it.

Purkinje, Jan (1787–1869) A Czechoslovakian physiologist who described the shift from cone vision to rod vision at twilight, which we call the Purkinje shift.

purposive behaviorism The name given to Tolman's version of behaviorism, which stressed the relation of behavior toward goals.

Puységur, Marquis de (1751–1825) Puységur and his brother investigated animal magnetism and discovered many of the phenomena of hypnosis known today.

puzzle boxes The pieces of apparatus Thorndike built to study learning in animals.

Pyrrho (ca. 365–270 B.C.E.) The founder of the school of Skepticism.

Pythagoras (ca. 580–500 B.C.E.) The founder of a mystical cult associated with important mathematical discoveries.

questionnaire This method to obtain data relevant to psychology was first introduced by Galton and is still popular today.

Quételet, Jacques (1796–1874) The Belgian astronomer and statistician who developed the idea of the normal curve.

Rank, Otto (1884–1939) One of Freud's inner circle who was removed after his publication of *The Trauma of Birth.* Rank differed from Freud in his emphasis on anxiety from birth trauma rather than sexual conflict.

rationalism Philosophical approach based on the use of reason to develop knowledge.

rationalization The ego's attempt to account for mistakes and failures by providing a reasonable, but untrue, explanation for behavior.

reaction formation The defense mechanism in which a person professes the desire for the opposite of what he or she really wants.

reaction potential See **excitatory potential.**

realist In medieval philosophy, one who believed that universals had a "real" existence apart from specific examples.

reality principle The principle by which the ego operates; its aim is to prevent energy discharge until the actual object needed for tension-reduction is produced.

recapitulation theory Ernst Haeckel's idea that the development of the individual reprises the development of the species; Hall applied the theory to child development.

reconstructive memory Refers to a tendency to construct plausible, but not necessarily accurate, memory elements when the actual memory details have been lost.

reductionism In psychology, the search for increasingly elemental explanations of psychological phenomena.

reflection The perception of the operations of the mind, according to Locke, which included perception, thinking, doubting, and reasoning.

reflexology The name Bekhterev gave to his objective psychology that would study the relationships between behavior and physiological and environmental conditions.

regression A retreat to an earlier stage of development as a result of a difficult experience.

regression toward the mean The tendency over time for the measurements of a variable to come closer to the mean or average for that variable.

Reid, Thomas (1710–1796) First member of the Scottish School whose common-sense psychology replaced the empiricist's view of the mind with a faculty-based, action-oriented psychology.

relative size One of three cues to distance perception. When two objects the same size are at different distances from the observer, the near object appears larger than the more distant object; as recognized by Berkeley.

relativism The theory that truth and moral values are not absolute but relative to the context.

reliability A test's consistency of measurement over time.

Renouvier, Charles Bernard (1815–1903) A French philosopher of free will whose writings are often seen as the "cure" to James's depression.

representative heuristic Refers to a tendency for people to use the wrong sort of heuristic in solving problems because of a misunderstanding of such concepts as randomness, base rates, and sample sizes.

repression The unconscious removal from consciousness of unacceptable ideas, memories, and impulses.

Rescorla, Robert A. (1940–) The winner of an APA Distinguished Scientific Contribution Award who is best known for modern studies of Pavlovian conditioning.

respondent Skinner's term for a reflex in the traditional sense; he called Pavlovian conditioning respondent conditioning.

retroactive inhibition Interference that acts back upon an earlier memory.

Rhine, Joseph Banks (1895–1980) His work on extrasensory perception at Duke University was supported by William McDougall.

Ribot, Théodule Armand (1839–1916) Founded a journal central to the establishment of French psychology as a scientific discipline.

Richet, Charles (1850–1935) A Nobel Prize–winning physiologist whose support for hypnosis influenced Charcot to investigate the phenomenon.

risky predictions Predictions made by scientific theories that may result in the theories being overturned.

Robertson, George Croom (1842–1892) First editor of Bain's journal *Mind.*

Rogers, Carl Ransom (1902–1987) A distinguished clinical theorist who advocated a humanistic approach to therapy; his system is called either client-centered or person-centered therapy.

Romanes, George John (1848–1894) A disciple of Darwin and a pioneer of comparative psychology; most remembered for his collection of animal anecdotes in *Animal Intelligence.*

romanticism A philosophical approach emphasizing the whole person and particularly the person's feelings; romanticism was a reaction against empiricism and rationalism.

Rorschach, Hermann (1884–1922) A Swiss psychiatrist who developed the popular inkblot test that bears his name.

Rorschach Inkblot Test Based on the psychodynamic approach to personality, the test assesses a person's responses to a series of inkblots.

Rotter, Julian (1916–) Rotter is best known for his scale that measures "locus of control," which distinguishes between people who see themselves as responsible for their actions and people who see outside agencies as responsible.

Rousseau, Jean-Jacques (1712–1778) Considered the founder of romanticism, Rousseau wrote *The Social Contract,* which became the bible of the French Revolution, and *Émile,* an essay on education.

Royce, Josiah (1855–1916) A longtime friend and colleague of James at Harvard whose philosophical positions were very different from James's.

Rubin, Edgar (1886–1951) Worked in G. E. Müller's laboratory and performed phenomenological investigations at the same time that the founders of Gestalt psychology did their seminal research; known for the vase/face reversible figure.

Rumelhart, David (1942–) Rumelhart has worked with his colleagues to resurrect a neglected computer architecture called variously connectionism, parallel processing, or neural networks.

Rush, Benjamin (1745–1813) Considered the founder of American psychiatry; basically a force for good in the treatment of mental illness in the late 18th to early 19th century.

Russell, Bertrand (1872–1970) A Nobel Prize–winning philosopher/mathematician with many interests related to psychology.

Ryle, Gilbert (1900–1976) A philosophical behaviorist whose discussion of the category mistake was the centerpiece of *The Concept of Mind.*

"s" factor Spearman's term for the specific ability reflected in a subtest of an intelligence test.

Sanford, Edmund Clark (1869–1924) Hall's student at Hopkins who was the director of the psychological laboratory during Hall's tenure as Clark's president.

Santayana, George (1863–1952) A Harvard student and contemporary of James who is best known for his contributions to poetry, history, and philosophy.

Sartre, Jean-Paul (1905–1980) A French existentialist who is known for his many essays and fictional works of relevance for psychology.

scatter plots Graphic representations of two variables, with one variable plotted on the *X* axis and the other variable plotted on the *Y* axis.

Schachter, Stanley (1922–1997) A social psychologist of wide scope who, in one of his best-known studies, found that social factors are linked to the way we attribute our emotions.

Schank, Roger (1946–) Schank worked with Robert Abelson to make Yale a center of AI research, through a consideration of scripts.

schema The schema (plural, schemata) is a mental structure that organizes and summarizes related experiences. Schema theory is central to modern cognitive psychology.

Schlick, Moritz (1882–1936) A member of the Vienna Circle and one of the founders of logical positivism.

scholasticism During the Middle Ages, a system of thought and method designed to join faith to reason through the use of logical deduction; adherents were called schoolmen.

school A psychological school consists of all the people who more or less agree with a particular system of psychology.

Schopenhauer, Arthur (1788–1860) Known as the philosopher of pessimism; best-known work is *The World as Will and Representation.*

Schumann, Friedrich (1863–1940) Coinventor with Müller of the memory drum; also worked with Stumpf and the first Gestalt psychologists.

Scott, Walter Dill (1869–1955) Wundt's student who became perhaps the first industrial/organizational psychologist. One of the first professors of applied psychology; he formed a corporation after World War I to do personnel selection and consultation on management issues.

Scottish School A philosophical school whose members were all Scottish; founded by Thomas Reid in opposition to Hume's skepticism.

Scotus, John Duns (ca. 1265–1308) Philosopher opposed to Aristotle and Aquinas who argued for the supremacy of the will, a view that became known as *voluntarism.*

script According to Abelson, a special type of schema involving a structured sequence of behavioral events.

Scripture, Edward W. (1864–1945) A student of Wundt who was an early director of the Yale Psychological Laboratory.

Sears, Pauline "Pat" S. (1908–1993) Collaborated with such researchers as Kurt Lewin and Leon Festinger at Iowa's Child Welfare Research Station. With Bob Sears, she continued Terman's longitudinal research on gifted children after she and her husband retired.

Sears, Robert "Bob" (1908–1989) A social and developmental psychologist who was APA president in 1951 and directed the Child Welfare Research Station at Iowa from 1942–1949.

Seashore, Carl Emil (1866–1949) A pioneer in the study of the psychology of music who worked primarily at the University of Iowa.

Sechenov, Ivan Mikhailovich (1829–1905) A Russian physiologist who is considered both the founder of Russian objective psychology and of modern Russian physiology; his most famous work was entitled *Reflexes of the Brain.*

secondary drive A learned drive that has acquired its motivating status from being paired with a primary drive and its reduction.

secondary process The process the ego uses to handle reality by developing an action plan through thought and reason; it corresponds to what we call thinking or problem solving.

secondary qualities Qualities (e.g., color, smell, and taste) that require the presence of a sensing observer.

second-signal system What Pavlov called human language to contrast it with what he considered the first-signal system, basic conditioned stimuli.

seduction theory The idea that neuroses are the result of childhood sexual abuse.

self-psychology The psychological system developed by Mary Calkins; also known as personalistic psychology.

semantic differential A measurement technique developed by Charles Osgood used to assess word meanings.

semantic memory A type of long-term memory introduced by Tulving that is a memory of an isolated, emotionless, atemporal fact, such as your memory or the name of the capital of Louisiana.

sensation Locke's term for impressions received by sense organs that are transmitted to our minds.

sensorimotor stage In Piaget's stage theory of development, the first stage, lasting from birth until about age 2. During the stage, the infant learns the relations between its sensory apparatus and its motor responses.

shadow For Jung, the residue of the animal nature in humans, which provides a potential source of creative energy.

Shakow, David (1901–1981) An important figure in the rise of clinical psychology as an academic discipline in America who, in addition to his research on schizophrenia, is known for his contributions to clinical education.

shaping An operant conditioning technique in which successive approximations to the desired behavior are rewarded.

Sheldon, William Herbert (1899–1977) A psychologist most remembered for his body type theory and a personality theory based on the body types.

Sherif, Muzafer (1906–1988) The social psychologist who is best known for his research on intergroup conflict, in which he created and then alleviated hostile attitudes between two groups of boys at a summer camp.

Sherrington, Sir Charles Scott (1857–1952) A British physician and physiologist who hypothesized the synapse and deduced most of its properties while studying the spinal reflex arc.

Shinn, Milicent (1858–1940) The first woman to receive a Ph.D. from the University of California at Berkeley and a pioneer in the observation of child development.

short-term memory Another name for consciousness; refers to a brief memory stage having a capacity of 7 ± 2 chunks.

signal detection theory A mathematically based theory that assumes the observer in a perceptual experiment is an active decision-maker who makes perceptual judgments under conditions of uncertainty.

sign learning Mowrer's term referring to Pavlovian conditioning in which the conditioned stimulus becomes a signal for an environmentally meaningful event.

similarity The Gestalt perceptual principle that says that similar elements are seen as belonging together.

Simon, Herbert Alexander (1916–2001) Winner of a Nobel Prize in economics, Simon blended psychology and computer models with his original focus areas of economics and management.

Simon, Théodore (1873–1961) A physician who worked with Binet to produce the first intelligence test.

simple ideas Ideas that have their origin in sensations and reflection; they cannot be divided further.

simultaneous conditioning In Pavlovian conditioning, the presentation of the CS and the UCS at the same time.

16 Personality Factors Test (16PF) The test created by Raymond B. Cattell, who constructed it by reducing some 4,000 trait descriptions to 16 binary personality factors.

Skepticism The philosophical position holding that we can never know anything with certainty, so the way to avoid believing something false is to not believe in anything.

Skinner, Burrhus Frederick (1904–1990) A radical behaviorist who, among other things, invented the Skinner box, developed operant conditioning, studied schedules of reinforcement, and wrote controversial social commentaries.

Skinner box Named by Hull, the apparatus Skinner developed to study operant conditioning in rats and pigeons.

sleeper effect Refers to attitude changes over time in which the association between the message and its source may fade, with the result that one remembers the content of the message after the source has been forgotten.

Small, Willard Stanton (1870–1943) A contemporary of Thorndike who is remembered for having introduced the maze problem to psychology and for having been one of the first psychologists to study behavior in the rat.

Smith, Theodate Louise (1859–1914) After earning a Ph.D. from Yale in 1896, she became one of Hall's research assistants.

social constructionism A theory in sociology that emerged in the mid-1960s and quickly generalized to all the social sciences.

social Darwinism The idea that society and its institutions evolve, facilitating the survival of the fittest.

social facilitation Floyd Allport's term for the improved performance on tasks when others are present.

social learning theory The theory developed by Bandura that focuses on the role of modeling or imitation in the acquisition of social behavior.

Socrates (469–399 B.C.E.) The teacher of Plato who used logical argumentation to help people understand general concepts like truth, beauty, and justice.

solution learning Mowrer's term for instrumental conditioning of voluntary responses.

Sophists Traveling teachers who taught young Greek men logic, science, philosophy, and especially rhetoric.

Spearman, Charles (1863–1945) A psychologist who invented an early form of the statistical technique of factor analysis and introduced the idea that there is a general factor of intelligence, as well as specific factors.

Spence, Janet Taylor (1923–) The APA president in 1984 who, among other things, is known for her studies of gender differences.

Spence, Kenneth W. (1907–1967) A long-time associate of Hull who continued to work on Hull's system after Hull's death. Among other things, Spence developed the idea of incentive motivation and presented an explanation of the Gestaltists' transposition problem based on S-R learning theory.

Spencer, Herbert (1820–1903) A brilliant thinker in the 19th century who wrote a comprehensive philosophy of science, which included a revision of his 1855 textbook, *Principles of Psychology,* and the concept of social Darwinism, with its notion of the "survival of the fittest."

Spencer-Bain principle Spencer's revision of Bain's explanation of voluntary behavior to include evolutionary ideas.

Sperry, Roger Wolcott (1913–1994) Winner of a Nobel Prize in 1981 for his investigations of split-brain preparations in animals and humans.

Spinoza, Baruch (Benedictus) (1632–1677) A Jewish philosopher who equated God with Nature; his mind-body solution is called double aspectism because the mind and the body are held to be like two sides of the same coin.

split-brain operation An operation in which some or all of the major connections between the brain's hemispheres are severed.

spontaneous recovery In Pavlovian conditioning, the reappearance of a conditioned response following a rest interval after extinction.

Spurzheim, Johann Caspar (1776–1832) A disciple of Gall who helped popularize phrenology.

St. Anselm (1033–1109) Known for the ontological argument for the existence of God, St. Anselm valued rationalism; often considered the founder of scholasticism.

St. Thomas Aquinas (1225–1274) Probably the person most responsible for the synthesis of Aristotle and Christianity. He believed that faith and reason were compatible.

St. Augustine (354–430) A major church figure who was skeptical of science divorced from theology; the first to suggest introspection as a method for studying inner experience; also known as Augustine of Hippo.

St. Albertus Magnus (ca. 1193–1280) A major Aristotelian scholar whose pupil was St. Thomas Aquinas.

St. Paul (ca. 10–64) Originally Saul of Tarsus; authored much of Christian thought, as revealed in the Bible's New Testament.

Stanford-Binet An intelligence test devised by Terman from the original test introduced by Binet and Simon.

Starbuck, Edwin D. (1866–1947) Initially a student of James at Harvard who went to Clark to study under Hall and became a pioneer in the psychology of religion.

Stekel, Wilhelm (1868–1940) One of the original followers of Freud whose prodding made Freud add a sizable section on symbols in dreams to *The Interpretation of Dreams.*

Stern, William (1871–1938) A pioneer in the study of cognitive development, applied psychology, and intelligence testing; one of Ebbinghaus's best-known students.

Stevens, Stanley Smith (1906–1973) A Harvard psychophysicist who advocated operationism in psychology.

Stevens's law Law holding that there is a power relation between sensory intensity and stimulus magnitude.

Stewart, Dugald (1753–1828) Longtime Professor of Moral Philosophy at Edinburgh; Thomas Reid's chief interpreter and popularizer.

stimulus error For Titchener, describing the stimulus itself rather than the immediate sensations and feelings produced by the stimulus.

stimulus generalization A learning phenomenon in which a response made to a particular stimulus is made to other, similar stimuli.

stimulus-response (S-R) learning The association of a particular stimulus with a particular response with the result that future encounters of the stimulus will lead to the response.

Stoicism A school of thought that taught acceptance of whatever comes.

Stone, Calvin P. (1892–1954) A student of Lashley who was hired by Stanford in Lashley's stead; Stone's best-known student was Harry Harlow.

Stratton, George (1865–1957) A student of Wundt who founded a psychological laboratory at the University of California-Berkeley.

striving for superiority For Adler, the idea that people are pushed by the need to overcome inferiority and pulled by the need for superiority over their environments.

structuralism The name often given to Titchener's psychology; the system in which psychologists used introspection to try to find the basic elements of adult, human consciousness.

study of twins A technique Galton introduced for examining the relative importance of heredity and the environment.

Stumpf, Carl (1848–1936) A student of Brentano who taught a number of important figures in psychology and phenomenology; his most famous work was *Tone Psychology,* a phenomenology of tones.

style of life For Adler, each person's unique response to the goal of achieving superiority.

subjective idealism See **mentalism.**

sublimation A form of displacement in which the substituted object of the emotional shift is socially approved.

Sullivan, Harry Stack (1892–1949) An important neo-Freudian in the psychiatric community who was responsible for shaping much of the theory and practice of American clinical psychology.

Sully, James (1842–1923) A British writer of textbooks and a friend of Alexander Bain who criticized William James's *Principles.*

Sultan Köhler's ape that insightfully solved a two-stick problem by joining the two sticks to make one pole long enough to reach a banana outside its cage.

Sumner, Francis Cecil (1895–1954) Hall's last graduate student and the first African American to receive a Ph.D. in psychology. He developed the undergraduate psychology program at Howard University and was a major contributor to *Psychological Abstracts.*

superego In psychoanalysis, the moral component of personality, which strives for perfection rather than for sensual pleasure.

survival of the fittest Spencer's term to indicate that only the best adapted organisms or entities survive.

syllogism Aristotle's invention of reasoning that begins with a fundamental general statement from which additional statements necessarily follow.

synapse A gap between neurons, which was hypothesized by Sir Charles Sherrington.

syntactic structures Chomsky's idea of innate, biological structures that contain the basic grammar rules of human language.

synthetic philosophy The name Herbert Spencer gave to his comprehensive program for a unified philosophy of science.

system A collection of ideas defining what is psychological and the methods that will be used to study it.

systematic desensitization A technique developed by Joseph Wolpe for removing an irrational fear.

systematic experimental introspection A method used at Würzburg in which subjects performed complex mental tasks and then introspected on their mental experiences during the solution of the task.

Szasz, Thomas S. (1920–) A Hungarian-born American psychiatrist who has taken the controversial position that mental illness as portrayed in contemporary psychology is largely a myth.

tachistoscope A piece of apparatus used to present visual stimuli for short time periods.

Taine, Hippolyte Adolphe (1828–1893) Sometimes called the French Bain, Taine's similarities to Bain include a psychophysical parallelism, the belief in associationism, and an interest in the physiology of mental events.

Tarde, Gabriel (1843–1904) A French jurist and an important early anticipator of social psychology who was particularly struck by the importance of imitation in human behavior.

teaching machine An educational device that Skinner worked on that would present problems to students at their own pace and would provide immediate reinforcement of their responses.

teleology The idea that everything has a definite end or final purpose.

Terman, Louis Madison (1877–1956) Psychologist who, while at Stanford, translated Binet and Simon's intelligence test into English and revised its content to create the Stanford-Binet; also known for initiating a longitudinal study of gifted California school children.

Thales (ca. 624–545 B.C.E.) Considered the first of the philosophers of ancient Greece.

Thematic Apperception Test (TAT) The test, originally developed by Henry Murray and Christiana Morgan, that consists of 30 pictures depicting ambiguous social situations to which a person responds by creating a story about the situation shown in each scene.

Theophrastus (ca. 372–286 B.C.E.) The head of the Lyceum after Aristotle's death; his special interest was botany.

theory of Forms The belief that there are universal Ideas, or "Forms," that underlie what we know through our senses.

Third Force With behaviorism and psychoanalysis as the first two forces, Maslow argued for a humanistic approach as the Third Force in psychology.

Thompson, Robert (1927–1989) A physiological psychologist who spent the bulk of his career searching for the locus of the engram in animals subjected to surgical ablations either before or after training.

Thorndike, Edward Lee (1874–1949) Trained at Harvard and Columbia, the principles Thorndike developed from his dissertation research became the foundation for modern learning theory. Thorndike represents the transition between functionalism and behaviorism, as well as the early American interest in having a useful, applied psychology.

threshold (limen of consciousness) Herbart's term for a limit that an idea had to surpass in order to become conscious.

Thurstone, Louis L. (1887–1955) A psychologist whose major contributions to psychology came from his advances in factor analysis, which he used to argue for seven primary mental abilities.

Tinbergen, Niko (1907–1988) Considered one of the founders of ethology; best known for his analysis of instinctive behavior in the three-spined stickleback fish.

Titchener, Edward Bradford (1867–1927) Perhaps Wundt's most famous Ph.D. student; his variation of Wundt's psychology came to be known as structuralism; he was responsible for bringing a refined, experimental approach to psychology to America.

token economy Derived from operant conditioning, a situation in which patients are given tokens that can be exchanged for privileges, in an effort to shape their behavior.

toleration or threshold method In this method Guthrie introduced for breaking habits, cues that normally trigger the behavior are presented at such a low level that the response does not occur, and then the cues are gradually increased.

Tolman, Edward Chace (1886–1959) American psychologist whose ingenious studies of rats in mazes led to his development of purposive behaviorism, advances in learning theory, and the idea of cognitive maps.

TOTE The acronym for Test-Operate-Test-Exit unit, which is a hypothetical, hierarchical, feedback loop that has both cognitive and behavioral components and is assumed to occupy the same theoretical space as the reflex arc.

trace conditioning In Pavlovian conditioning, the conditioning that occurs when the CS is presented and ends before the UCS occurs.

Tracy, Antoine Destutt de (1754–1836) A French mechanist who believed that mental phenomena are caused by biological phenomena.

transference An important part of the therapeutic relationship in which the patient unconsciously shifts her or his feelings for something or somebody onto the therapist.

transfer of training The improvement in one task following training on another.

transposition Köhler's term for the relational responding seen in certain learning problems.

trichromatic theory Theory of color vision proposed initially by Thomas Young and revised by Helmholtz; basic statement is that all colors arise from some pattern of stimulation of three different receptor types in the eye. Same as Young-Helmholtz theory.

tripartite soul Plato's idea that the soul has three parts: reason, spirit, and appetite.

Triplett, Norman (1861–1934) Investigated the effects of competition on performance in what is often considered social psychology's first empirical study.

tropisms Directed, mechanical movements of a plant or animal in response to a stimulus.

Tufts, James H. (1862–1942) An early psychologist associated with functionalism first at the University of Michigan, and then at the University of Chicago.

Tuke, William (1732–1822) An English philanthropist who established the York Retreat, where the insane were housed in a quiet, religious atmosphere.

Tulving, Endel (1927–) A memory researcher who has distinguished between episodic and semantic long-term memory.

Turing, Alan (1912–1954) Considered the "father" of artificial intelligence.

Turing test A test for computer intelligence that asks whether the computer output is indistinguishable from what would be expected from a human under the same circumstances. If it is indistinguishable, then the conclusion is that the machine is intelligent within that context.

Tversky, Amos (1937–1996) A cognitive psychologist who was known for his collaborative studies with Kahneman on human reasoning.

Twitmyer, Edwin Burket (1873–1943) American psychologist who observed the development of a conditioned reflex at about the same time as Pavlov but failed to follow through on the study of the conditioned reflex.

two-point threshold The minimum distance two simultaneously applied points must be separated before they are experienced as separate touches.

***Umweg* or detour problem** The problem in which a goal is clearly visible to the subject, but it can't be reached directly; the subject must make a "detour" in order to get the goal.

unconditioned response (UCR) In Pavlovian conditioning, the reflex response made to the unconditioned stimulus.

unconditioned stimulus (UCS) In Pavlovian conditioning, the stimulus that always elicits the reflex response.

unconscious For Freud, the part of the mind that was the site of relatively irretrievable material.

Upham, Thomas C. (1799–1872) Professor of mental and moral philosophy at Maine's Bowdoin College who can be considered one of the founders of a truly American system of psychology.

Utilitarianism A social and ethical philosophy that holds that the goal of all behavior should be to achieve the "greatest good for the greatest number."

validity The extent to which a test measures what it is supposed to measure.

variable-interval (VI) schedule An operant schedule in which rewards occur after varying periods of time.

variable-ratio (VR) schedule An operant schedule in which reinforcements occur after varying numbers of responses.

vibratiuncles For Hartley, tiny vibrations in the brain that represented sensory vibrations in the nerves.

Vico, Giambattista (1668–1744) An Italian philosopher and historian who, like Herder, sought to understand historical developments by studying the changes in human nature shown through language, myth, and culture.

Vienna Circle A group of scientists who refined positivism into the movement known as logical positivism.

visual cliff An apparent "cliff" used by Eleanor Gibson and others to determine if depth perception is innate.

vitalism The idea that life is caused by a principle different from chemical and physical forces.

Viteles, Morris (1898–1996) A psychologist who combined a successful academic career at the University of Pennsylvania with work for a variety of industries. He wrote some of the early classic books in industrial psychology.

Vives, Juan Luls (1492–1540) An early humanist important for his writings on psychology and the scientific method.

Völkerpsychologie A 10-volume work on language, culture, religion, etc., that resulted from Wundt's efforts to study the products of human-kind's higher mental processes, as he did not believe that higher mental processes could be investigated experimentally.

Volta, Count Alessandro (1745–1827) An Italian physicist who invented an electric battery (a Voltaic pile) and questioned Galvani's conclusion that frogs generate electricity.

voluntarism Wundt's name for his system of psychology, in which there is a voluntary focusing of attention.

von Békésy, Georg (1899–1972) The Hungarian-born physiologist who developed a modern place theory of pitch perception and won a Nobel Prize in 1961.

von Frisch, Karl (1886–1982) A 1973 Nobel Prize winner best known for his studies of communication in honeybees by means of a kind of "dance."

von Waldeyer, Wilhelm (1836–1921) The German neurologist and anatomist who introduced the term "neuron" to describe the independent nerve unit.

Vygotsky, Lev (1896–1934) An anticipator of the cognitive revolution who held that mainstream empirical psychology was not well suited to explain higher cognitive processes.

Wallace, Alfred Russel (1823–1913) A British naturalist who independently arrived at a theory of evolution very similar to Darwin's and made several other important contributions to science.

Wallach, Hans (1904–1998) Gestalt psychologist particularly known for his studies in perception.

Warren, Howard C. (1867–1934) Briefly a student of Wundt who spent his career in psychology at Princeton.

Washburn, Margaret Floy (1871–1939) Receiver of the first Ph.D. awarded under Titchener's supervision and the first woman to earn a Ph.D. in psychology.

Watson, John Broadus (1878–1958) Considered the founder of the psychological school of behaviorism in America; after being forced to leave academia in 1920, he had a successful career as an advertising executive.

Watson, Robert I. (1909–1980) A historian of psychology whose contributions included developing the first doctoral degree program in the history of psychology and helping to launch the *Journal of the History of the Behavioral Sciences.*

Watt, Henry Jackson (1879–1925) Külpe's Scottish student who introduced the technique of fractionating introspections.

Weber, Ernst Heinrich (1795–1878) The Leipzig physiologist who studied the two-point threshold and just noticeable differences.

Weber fractions Weber found jnds to be constant ratios of a standard stimulus, and his colleague Fechner called the ratios Weber fractions.

Weber, Max (1864–1920) Often classified as a sociologist, he is best known in psychology for his writings on the protestant work ethic and on charisma in leaders.

Weber's law Fechner gave the relation Weber found for jnds mathematical form and called it Weber's law, which is

$$\frac{\delta R}{R} = \text{a constant,}$$

where R (*Reiz*) stands for the magnitude of the stimulus, and δR is the jnd.

Wechsler, David (1896–1981) A psychologist who invented a mental test called The Wechsler-Bellevue, which evolved into the WISC and the WAIS.

Wechsler Adult Intelligence Scale (WAIS) A popular intelligence test invented by David Wechsler for determining adult IQ.

Wechsler Intelligence Scale for Children (WISC) Invented by David Wechsler, an important alternative to the Stanford-Binet test for assessing IQ in children.

Wernicke, Carl (1848–1905) A German neurologist who is credited with discovering the brain area whose damage results in the poor reception of language meaning.

Wernicke's model Wernicke's proposal that an area of the temporal lobe converts speech sounds into comprehended language, and this information travels through the arcuate fasciculus to Broca's area for speech production.

Wertheimer, Max (1880–1943) His 1910 insight about the importance of apparent movement (the phi phenomenon) for psychology led to the founding of the school of Gestalt psychology.

Wertheimer, Michael (1927–) Max Wertheimer's son and a historian of psychology at the University of Colorado.

Wesensschau The step in Husserl's system that is the cognition of essence; that is, the apprehension of the nature of a thing through a consideration of phenomena.

Whytt, Robert (1714–1766) Studied spinal reflexes in the frog and emphasized the difference between voluntary and involuntary movements.

Whytt's reflex Named for its discoverer, another name for the pupillary reflex to light.

will The central theme of Schopenhauer's philosophy, will is in everything and is the driving force of all nature.

William of Ockham (ca. 1285–1349) Successfully defended nominalism against realism and advocated using what we call Ockham's razor.

wish-fulfillment Freud's idea that all dreams represent events the dreamer really wants to happen, no matter how troubling the events seem to be.

Wissler, Clark (1870–1947) Cattell's graduate student who found little correlation between physical and sensory abilities and intelligence and became an anthropologist.

Witmer, Lightner (1867–1956) A student of Wundt who founded the first psychological clinic at the University of Pennsylvania.

Wittgenstein, Ludwig (1889–1951) Trained in mathematics and mechanical engineering, Wittgenstein's discussion of "family resemblance" is considered the point of departure for modern cognitive psychology's interest in categorization.

Wolfe, Harry Kirke (1858–1918) An early student of Wundt, he taught Guthrie at the University of Nebraska, where he established a psychological laboratory.

Wolff, Christian von (1679–1754) An early German proponent of faculty psychology; he distinguished between empirical and rational psychology.

Wolpe, Joseph (1915–1997) Considered the originator of systematic desensitization.

Woodworth, Robert Sessions (1869–1962) A functionalist at Columbia with lifelong interests in the study of motivation who made substantive contributions to many fields of psychology.

Woolley, Helen Thompson (1874–1947) Angell's student whose child development interests led to one of America's first nursery schools.

word-association experiment An experiment in which Galton looked at each of 75 different words and recorded his associations; the use of word associations was developed further by others, including Wundt and Jung.

Wundt, Wilhelm Maximilian (1832–1920) The German philosopher/psychologist who is credited with founding psychology as a separate science in 1879 at the University of Leipzig.

Würzburg school A collection of psychologists under Külpe's direction at the University of Würzburg. Much of their research was concerned with thought.

Yerkes, Robert Mearns (1876–1956) An early American comparative psychologist who is particularly known for his studies of primates and his involvement with IQ testing in World War I.

Yerkes-Dodson law The law stating that the optimal level of arousal for performance of a task depends on the difficulty of the task—for example, for easy tasks, a high level of arousal results in superior performance, whereas for difficult tasks, a high level of arousal is detrimental.

Young, Thomas (1773–1829) An English physician and physicist who proposed a three-color theory of color vision.

Young-Helmholtz theory First proposed by Thomas Young and revised by Helmholtz, this theory of color vision proposes that color sensations come from some pattern of stimulation of three different types of receptors in the eye. Same as trichromatic theory.

Zeigarnik, Bliuma Vul'Fovna (1900–1990) One of Lewin's doctoral students, the Russian-born psychologist who investigated the hypothesis that the tension created by an incomplete task is dissipated when the task is completed.

Zeigarnik effect An illustration of the principle that shows there is a tendency to remember incomplete tasks longer than finished tasks.

Zeitgeist "The spirit of the times"; view of history saying that the historical context plays a major role in determining which ideas are accepted and which are rejected.

Zeno of Citium (ca. 333–262 B.C.E.) The originator of Stoicism.

Zeno of Elea (ca. 490–430 B.C.E.) A follower of Parmenides who invented several paradoxes to show change was illusory.

Zimbardo, Philip (1933–) A psychologist and researcher who conducted an important study on the nature of social roles. He simulated a prison environment with normal adults and found that subjects quickly learned social roles appropriate to their status as either guards or prisoners.

References

Aaron, M., & Thorne, B. M. (1975). Omission training and extinction in rats with septal damage. *Physiology and Behavior, 15,* 149–154.

Abelson, R. P. (1981). Psychological status of the script concept. *American Psychologist, 36,* 715–729.

Abraham, T. H. (2002). (Physio)logical circuits: The intellectual origins of the McCulloch-Pitts neural networks. *Journal of the History of the Behavioral Sciences, 38,* 3–25.

Adler, A. (1930). Individual psychology. In C. Murchison (Ed.), *Psychologies of 1930* (pp. 395–405). Worcester, MA: Clark University Press.

Adler, H. E. (1980). Vicissitudes of Fechnerian psychophysics in America. In R. W. Rieber & K. Salzinger (Eds.), *Psychology: Theoretical-historical perspectives* (pp. 11–23). New York: Academic Press.

Adler, H. E. (1996). Gustav Theodor Fechner: A German *Gelehrter.* In G. A. Kimble, C. A. Bonneau, & M. Wertheimer (Eds.), *Portraits of pioneers in psychology* (Vol. II, pp. 1–13). Mahwah, NJ: Lawrence Erlbaum Associates, Publishers.

Adler, H. E. (2000). Hermann Ludwig Ferdinand von Helmholtz: Physicist as psychologist. In G. A. Kimble & M. Wertheimer (Eds.), *Portraits of pioneers in psychology* (Vol. IV, pp. 15–31). Mahwah, NJ: Lawrence Erlbaum Associates, Publishers.

Ainsworth, M. D. S., & Bowlby, J. (1991). An ethological approach to personality development. *American Psychologist, 46,* 333–341.

Albert, R. (1975). Toward a behavioral definition of genius. *American Psychologist, 30,* 140–151.

Alexander, F. G., & Selesnick, S. T. (1966). *The history of psychiatry: An evaluation of psychiatric thought and practice from prehistoric times to the present.* New York: Mentor.

Alexander, I. E. (1991). C. G. Jung: The man and his work, then and now. In G. A. Kimble, M. Wertheimer, & C. L. White (Eds.), *Portraits of pioneers in psychology* (pp. 153–169). Hillsdale, NJ: Lawrence Erlbaum Associates, Inc.

Alland, A., Jr. (1985). *Human nature: Darwin's view.* New York: Columbia University Press.

Allee, W. (1938). *The social life of animals.* Boston: Beacon Press.

Allen, R. E. (Ed.) (1966). *Greek philosophy: Thales to Aristotle.* New York: Macmillan.

Allport, F. H. (1924). *Social psychology.* Boston: Houghton Mifflin.

Allport, F. H. (1933). *Institutional behavior.* Chapel Hill, NC: University of North Carolina Press.

Allport, F. H. (1955). *Theories of perception and the concept of structure.* New York: Wiley.

Allport, F. H. (1974). Floyd H. Allport. In G. Lindzey (Ed.), *A history of psychology in autobiography* (Vol. 6, pp. 1–29). Englewood Cliffs, NJ: Prentice-Hall.

Allport, G. W. (1935). Attitudes. In C. Murchison (Ed.), *A handbook of social psychology* (pp. 798–844). Worchester, MA: Clark University Press.

Allport, G. W. (1954a). The historical background of modern social psychology. In G. Lindzey (Ed.), *A handbook of social psychology* (Vol. 1, pp. 3–56). Reading, MA: Addison-Wesley.

Allport, G. W. (1954b). *The nature of prejudice.* Cambridge, MA: Addison-Wesley.

Allport, G. W. (1967). G. W. Allport. In E. G. Boring & G. Lindzey (Eds.), *A history of psychology in autobiography* (Vol. 5, pp. 3–25). New York: Appleton-Century-Crofts.

Allport, G. W. (1968). *The person in psychology: Selected essays.* Boston: Beacon Press.

Allport, G. W., & Odbert, H. S. (1936). Trait names: A psycholexical study. *Psychological Monographs, 47,* (1, Whole No. 211).

American Psychiatric Association (1994). *Diagnostic and statistical manual of mental disorders* (4th ed.). Washington, DC: Author.

American Psychological Association. (1995, October). *Report of the task force on the changing gender composition of psychology.* Washington, DC: Author.

American Psychologist. (1987). Robert A. Rescorla. *American Psychologist, 42,* 285–288.

American Psychologist. (1994). Endel Tulving. *American Psychologist, 49,* 551–553.

Anastasi, A. (1934). The influence of practice upon test reliability. *Journal of Educational Psychology, 25,* 321–335.

Anastasi, A. (1954). *Psychological testing.* New York: Macmillan.

Anastasi, A. (1958). Heredity, environment, and the question "How?" *Psychological Review, 65,* 197–208.

Anastasi, A. (1964). *Fields of applied psychology.* New York: McGraw-Hill.

Anastasi, A. (1980). Anne Anastasi. In G. Lindzey (Ed.), *A history of psychology in autobiography* (Vol. 7, pp. 1–37). San Francisco: W. H. Freeman and Company.

Anastasi, A., & Foley, J. P., Jr. (1952). *The Human-Figure Drawing Test as an objective psychiatric screening aid for student pilots.* USAF School of Aviation Medicine, Project No. 21-37-002, Report No. 5.

Anastasi, A., & Schaefer, C. E. (1969). Biographical correlates of artistic and literary creativity in adolescent girls. *Journal of Applied Psychology, 53,* 267–273.

Anderson, J. R. (2001). Herbert A. Simon (1916–2001). *American Psychologist, 56,* 516–518.

Angell, J. R. (1904). *Psychology: An introductory study of the structure and functions of human consciousness.* New York: Holt.

Angell, J. R. (1907). The province of functional psychology. *Psychological Review, 14,* 61–91.

Angell, J. R. (1908). *Psychology* (4th ed.). New York: Henry Holt & Co.

Angell, J. R. (1911). Editorial: William James. *Psychological Review, 18,* 78–82.

Angell, J. R. (1911). Topic: Philosophical and psychological usages of the terms mind, consciousness, and soul. *Psychological Bulletin, 8,* 46–47.

Angell, J. R. (1936). James Rowland Angell. In C. Murchison (Ed.), *A history of psychology in autobiography* (Vol. 3, pp. 1–38). Worcester, MA: Clark University Press.

Angell, J. R., & Moore, A. W. (1896). Reaction time: A study in attention and habit. *Psychological Review, 3,* 245–258.

Anglin, J. M. (1973). Introduction. In J. S. Bruner, *Beyond the information given* (pp. xii–xxiv). New York: Norton & Company.

Ansbacher, H. L. (1959). The significance of the socio-economic status of the patients of Freud and of Adler. *American Journal of Psychotherapy, 13,* 376–382.

Ansbacher, H. L. (1971). Alfred Adler and G. Stanley Hall: Correspondence and general relationship. *Journal of the History of the Behavioral Sciences, 7,* 337–352.

Ansbacher, H. L. (1990). Alfred Adler's influence on the three leading cofounders of humanistic psychology. *Journal of Humanistic Psychology, 30,* 45–53.

Ansbacher, H. L. (1994). Alfred Adler (1870–1937). In R. J. Corsini (Ed.), *Encyclopedia of psychology* (2nd ed.) (Vol. 4, pp. 1–2). New York: John Wiley & Sons.

Ansbacher, H. L., & Ansbacher, R. R. (Eds.) (1956). *The Individual Psychology of Alfred Adler: A systematic presentation in selections from his writings.* New York: Basic Books, Inc.

Appleman, P. (Ed.) (1979). *Darwin: A Norton critical edition* (2nd ed.). New York: W. W. Norton & Company.

APS Observer. (1992). Computer and psychological scientist Allen Newell (1927–1992). *APS Observer, 5,* 27, 22.

Archer, R. L. (Ed.) (1964). *Jean Jacques Rousseau: His educational theories selected from Émile, Julie and other writings.* Woodbury, NY: Barron's Educational Series, Inc.

Arens, K. (1985). Mach's "psychology of investigation." *Journal of the History of the Behavioral Sciences, 21,* 151–168.

Armstrong, P. (1993). An ethologist aboard HMS *Beagle:* The young Darwin's observations on animal behavior. *Journal of the History of the Behavioral Sciences, 29,* 339–344.

Arnheim, R. (1969). *Visual thinking.* Berkeley, CA: University of California Press.

Arnheim, R. (1974). *Art and visual perception.* Berkeley, CA: University of California Press.

Arnheim, R. (1985). The other Gustav Theodor Fechner. In S. Koch & D. E. Leary (Eds.), *A century of psychology as a science* (pp. 856–865). New York: McGraw-Hill.

Arnheim, R. (1986a). The trouble with wholes and parts. *New Ideas in Psychology, 4,* 281–284.

Arnheim, R. (1986b). The two faces of Gestalt psychology. *American Psychologist, 41,* 820–824.

Asch, S. E. (1946a). Forming impressions of personality. *Journal of Abnormal and Social Psychology, 41,* 258–290.

Asch, S. E. (1946b). Max Wertheimer's contribution to modern psychology. *Social Research, 13,* 81–102.

Asch, S. E. (1956). Studies of independence and conformity: A minority of one against a unanimous majority. *Psychological Monographs, 70* (9, Whole No. 416).

Ash, M. G. (1989). Max Wertheimer's university career in Germany. *Psychological Research, 51,* 52–57.

Ash, M. G. (1992). Cultural contexts and scientific change in psychology: Kurt Lewin in Iowa. *American Psychologist, 47,* 198–207.

Atkinson, R. C., & Shiffrin, R. M. (1968). Human memory: A proposed system and its control processes. In K. W. Spence & J. T. Spence (Eds.), *The psychology of learning and motivation: Advances in research and theory* (Vol. 2, pp. 89–195). New York: Academic Press.

Augustine (1963). *Confessions.* New York: New American Library. (Original work published 400)

Augustine (1931). *The city of God* (Book VII). New York: E. P. Dutton & Co., Inc. (Original work published 412–427)

Averill, L. A. (1982). Recollections of Clark's G. Stanley Hall. *Journal of the History of the Behavioral Sciences, 18,* 341–346.

Axline, V. M. (1947). *Play therapy: The inner dynamics of childhood.* Boston: Houghton Mifflin.

Axtell, J. L. (Ed.) (1968). *The educational writings of John Locke.* Cambridge: University Press.

Ayllon, T., & Azrin, N. H. (1968). *The token economy: A motivational system for therapy and rehabilitation.* East Norwalk, CT: Appleton-Century-Crofts.

Babkin, B. P. (1949). *Pavlov: A biography.* Chicago: The University of Chicago Press.

Backe, A. (2001). John Dewey and early Chicago functionalism. *History of Psychology, 4,* 323–340.

Baddeley, A. (1994). The magical number seven: Still magic after all these years? *Psychological Review, 101,* 353–356.

Bagg, R. A. (1972). How do you spell Pawloff?: A note. *Journal of the History of the Behavioral Sciences, 8,* 387–388.

Bain, A. (1859). *The emotions and the will.* London: Parker & Son.

Bakan, D. (1952). The exponential growth function in Herbart and Hull. *American Journal of Psychology, 65,* 307–308.

Bakan, D. (1966). The influence of phrenology on American psychology. *Journal of the History of the Behavioral Sciences, 2,* 200–220.

Baker, D. B. (2002). Historical understanding and teaching in professional psychology. *History of Psychology, 5,* 219–223.

Baldwin, B. T. (Ed.) (1921). In memory of Wilhelm Wundt: By his American students. *Psychological Review, 28,* 153–188.

Baldwin, J. M. (1894). Psychology past and present. *Psychological Review, 1,* 363–391.

Baldwin, J. M. (1897). *Social and ethical interpretations in mental development.* New York: Macmillan.

Baldwin, J. M. (1898). On selective thinking. *Psychological Review, 5,* 1–24.

Baldwin, J. M. (1930). James Mark Baldwin. In C. Murchison (Ed.), *History of psychology in autobiography* (Vol. 1, pp. 1–30). Worcester, MA: Clark University Press.

Bandrés, J., & Llavona, R. (1992). Minds and machines in Renaissance Spain: Gómez Pereira's theory of animal behavior. *Journal of the History of the Behavioral Sciences, 28,* 158–168.

Bandura, A. (1973). *Aggression: A social learning analysis.* Englewood Cliffs, NJ: Prentice-Hall.

Bandura, A., Ross, D., & Ross, S. (1961). Transmission of aggression through imitation of aggressive models. *Journal of Abnormal and Social Psychology, 63,* 575–582.

Bandura, A., Ross, D., & Ross, S. (1963a). Imitation of film-mediated aggressive models. *Journal of Abnormal and Social Psychology, 66,* 3–11.

Bandura, A., Ross, D., & Ross, S. (1963b). A comparative test of the status envy, social power, and secondary reinforcement theories of identificatory learning. *Journal of Abnormal and Social Psychology, 67,* 527–534.

Banks, E. C. (2001). Ernst Mach and the episode of the monocular depth sensations. *Journal of the History of the Behavioral Sciences, 37,* 327–348.

Bare, J. K. (1998). Laurens Perseus Hickok: Philosopher, theologian, and psychologist. In G. A. Kimble & M. Wertheimer (Eds.), *Portraits of pioneers in psychology* (Vol. III, pp. 1–15). Mahwah, NJ: Lawrence Erlbaum Associates, Publishers.

Barker, R. G. (Ed.) (1963). *The stream of behavior.* New York: Appleton-Century-Crofts.

Barker, R. G. (1989). Roger G. Barker. In G. Lindzey (Ed.), *A history of psychology in autobiography* (Vol. 8, pp. 2–35). Stanford, CA: Stanford University Press.

Barker, R. G., Dembo, T., & Lewin, K. (1943). Frustration and regression. In R. G. Barker, J. S. Kounin, & H. F. Wright (Eds.), *Child behavior and development: A course of representative studies* (pp. 441–458). New York: McGraw-Hill.

Barker, R. G., & Wright, H. F. (1951). *One boy's day.* New York: Harper & Row.

Barlow, N. (Ed.) (1958). *The autobiography of Charles Darwin,* 1809–1882. New York: W. W. Norton. (Original work published as part of *Life and letters of Charles Darwin* in 1887)

Barnes, D. B. (1988). Psychiatrists psych out the future. *Science, 242,* 1013–1014.

Barsalou, L. W. (1985). Ideals, central tendency, and frequency of instantiation as determinants of graded structure in categories. *Journal of Experimental Psychology: Learning, Memory, and Cognition, 11,* 629–654.

Bartholow, R. (1874). Experimental investigations into the functions of the human brain. *The American Journal of the Medical Sciences, 67,* 305–313.

Bartlett, F. C. (1923). *Psychology and primitive culture.* Cambridge: Cambridge University Press.

Bartlett, F. C. (1932). *Remembering: A study in experimental and social psychology.* Cambridge: Cambridge University Press.

Bartlett, F. C. (1936). Frederic Charles Bartlett. In C. Murchison (Ed.), *A history of psychology in autobiography* (Vol. 3, pp. 39–52). Worcester, MA: Clark University Press.

Bauer, E. (1997). Parapsychology. In W. G. Bringmann, H. E. Lück, R. Miller, & C. E. Early (Eds.), *A pictorial history of psychology* (pp. 71–76). Chicago: Quintessence Publishing Co., Inc.

Baumgartner, E., & Baumgartner, W. (1997). Brentano: Psychology from an empirical standpoint. In W. G. Bringmann, H. E. Lück, R. Miller, & C. E. Early (Eds.), *A pictorial history of psychology* (pp. 61–65). Carol Stream, IL: Quintessence Publishing Co., Inc.

Baumrind, D. (1964). Some thoughts on ethics of research: After reading Milgram's "Behavioral study of obedience." *American Psychologist, 19,* 421–423.

Beach, F. A. (1950). The snark was a boojum. *American Psychologist, 5,* 115–124.

Beach, F. A. (1961). Karl Spencer Lashley: June 7, 1890–August 7, 1958. *Biographical Memoirs of the National Academy of Sciences, 35,* 162–204.

Beach, F. A. (1974). Frank A. Beach. In G. Lindzey (Ed.), *A history of psychology in autobiography* (Vol. 6, pp. 31–58). Englewood Cliffs, NJ: Prentice-Hall.

Beach, F. A. (1985). Conceptual issues in behavioral endocrinology. In R. Gandelman (Ed.), *Autobiographies in experimental psychology* (pp. 5–17). Hillsdale, NJ: Lawrence Erlbaum Associates, Publishers.

Beer, C. G. (1983). Darwin, instinct, and ethology. *Journal of the History of the Behavioral Sciences, 19,* 68–80.

Behrens, P. J. (1997). G. E. Müller: The third pillar of experimental psychology. In W. G. Bringmann, H. E. Lück, R. Miller, & C. E. Early (Eds.), *A pictorial history of psychology* (pp. 171–176). Carol Stream, IL: Quintessence Publishing Co., Inc.

Beier, E. G. (1991). Freud: 3 contributions. In G. A. Kimble, M. Wertheimer, & C. L. White (Eds.), *Portraits of pioneers in psychology* (pp. 43–55). Hillsdale, NJ: Lawrence Erlbaum Associates, Publishers.

Beit-Hallahmi, B. (1974). Psychology of religion 1880–1930: The rise and fall of a psychological movement. *Journal of the History of the Behavioral Sciences, 10,* 84–90.

Bell, C. (1948). Idea of a new anatomy of the brain. In W. Dennis (Ed.), *Readings in the history of psychology* (pp. 113–124). New York: Appleton-Century-Crofts, Inc. (Original work published 1811)

Benjamin, L. T., Jr. (1988). *A history of psychology: Original sources and contemporary research.* New York: McGraw-Hill Book Company.

Benjamin, L. T., Jr. (1993). *A history of psychology in letters.* Dubuque, IA: Wm. C. Brown.

Benjamin, L. T., Jr. (1996). Harry Hollingworth: Portrait of a generalist. In G. A. Kimble, C. A. Boneau, & M. Wertheimer (Eds.), *Portraits of pioneers in psychology* (Vol. II, pp. 119–135). Mahwah, NJ: Lawrence Erlbaum Associates, Publishers.

Benjamin, L. T., Jr. (1997). Wilhelm Wundt: The American connection. In W. G. Bringmann, H. E. Lück, R. Miller, & C. E. Early (Eds.), *A pictorial history of psychology* (pp. 140–147). Chicago: Quintessence Publishing Co., Inc.

Benjamin, L. T., Jr. (2000). Hugo Münsterberg: Portrait of an applied psychologist. In G. A. Kimble & M. Wertheimer (Eds.), *Portraits of pioneers in psychology* (Vol. IV, pp. 113–129). Mahwah, NJ: Lawrence Erlbaum Associates, Publishers.

Benjamin, L. T., Jr., Campbell, C., Luttrell, J., Bryant, W. H. M., & Holtz, C. (1997). Between *Psoriasis* and *Ptarmigan:* American encyclopedia portrayals of psychology, 1880–1940. *Review of General Psychology, 1,* 5–18.

Benjamin, L. T., Jr., Durkin, M., Link, M., Vestal, M., & Acord, J. (1992). Wundt's American doctoral students. *American Psychologist, 47,* 123–131.

Benjamin, L. T., Jr., & Nielsen Gammon, E. (1999). B. F. Skinner and psychotechnology: The case of the heir conditioner. *Review of General Psychology, 3,* 155–167.

Benjamin, L. T., Jr., Rogers, A. M., & Rosenbaum, A. (1991). Coca-Cola, caffeine, and mental deficiency: Harry Hollingworth and the Chattanooga trial of 1911. *Journal of the History of the Behavioral Sciences, 27,* 42–55.

Berger, P., & Luckmann, T. (1966). *The social construction of reality.* Garden City, NY: Anchor Books.

Bergmann, G. (1956). The contribution of John B. Watson. *Psychological Review, 63,* 265–276.

Bergström, J. A. (1894). [Review of *Experimentelle Beiträge zur Untersuchung des Gedächtnisses]. American Journal of Psychology, 6,* 299–301.

Berkeley, G. (1837). *The works of George Berkeley.* London: T. Tegg and Son. (Original works published 1709, 1710, 1713)

Bernard, L. L. (1921). The misuse of instinct in the social sciences. *Psychological Review, 28,* 96–119.

Bernard, L. L. (1924). *Instinct: A study in social psychology.* New York: Henry Holt & Co.

Bernard, W. (1972). Spinoza's influence on the rise of scientific psychology: A neglected chapter in the history of psychology. *Journal of the History of the Behavioral Sciences, 8,* 208–215.

Binet, A. (1905). Analyse de C. E. Spearman, "The proof and measurement of association between two things" et "General intelligence objectively determined and measured" [Analysis of C. E. Spearman, "The proof and measurement of association between two things" and "General intelligence objectively determined and measured"]. *L'Année psychologique, 17,* 145–201.

Bingham, W. V. D. (1952). Walter Van Dyke Bingham. In E. G. Boring, H. S. Langfeld, H. Werner, & R. M. Yerkes (Eds.), *A history of psychology in autobiography* (Vol. 4, pp. 1–26). Worcester, MA: Clark University Press.

Birch, H. G. (1945). The relation of previous experience to insightful problem-solving. *Journal of Comparative Psychology, 38,* 367–383.

Bjork, D. W. (1983). *The compromised scientist: William James in the development of American psychology.* New York: Columbia University Press.

Bjork, D. W. (1988). *William James: The center of his vision.* New York: Columbia University Press.

Bjork, D. W. (1993). *B. F. Skinner: A life.* New York: Basic Books.

Bjork, D. W. (1998). Burrhus Frederick Skinner: The contingencies of a life. In G. A. Kimble & M. Wertheimer (Eds.), *Portraits of pioneers in psychology* (Vol. III, pp. 261–275). Mahwah, NJ: Lawrence Erlbaum Associates, Inc.

Blakemore, C. (1977). *Mechanics of the mind.* New York: Cambridge University Press.

Blanshard, B., & Schneider, W. (Eds.) (1942). *In commemoration of William James.* New York: Columbia University Press.

Block, N., & Dworkin, G. (1976). *The IQ controversy.* New York: Pantheon.

Blowers, G. H. (2001). "To be a big shot or to be shot": Zing-Yang Kuo's other career. *History of Psychology, 4,* 367–387.

Blum, D. (2002). *Love at Goon Park: Harry Harlow and the science of affection.* Cambridge, MA: Perseus Books Group.

Blum, H. P. (1990). Freud, Fliess, and the parenthood of psychoanalysis. *Psychoanalytic Quarterly, 59,* 21–40.

Blumenthal, A. L. (1970). *Language and psychology: Historical aspects of psycholinguistics.* New York: Wiley.

Blumenthal, A. L. (1975). A reappraisal of Wilhelm Wundt. *American Psychologist, 30,* 1081–1088.

Blumenthal, A. L. (1979). The founding father we never knew. *Contemporary Psychology, 24,* 547–550.

Blumenthal, A. L. (1980). Wilhelm Wundt and early American psychology: A clash of cultures. In R. W. Rieber & K. Salzinger (Eds.), *Psychology: Theoretical-historical perspectives* (pp. 25–42). New York: Academic Press

Blumenthal, A. L. (1997). Wilhelm Wundt. In W. G. Bringmann, H. E. Lück, R. Miller, & C. E. Early (Eds.), *A pictorial history of psychology* (pp. 117–125). Chicago: Quintessence Publishing Co., Inc.

Blumenthal, A. L. (1998). Leipzig, Wilhelm Wundt, and psychology's gilded age. In G. A. Kimble & M. Wertheimer (Eds.), *Portraits of pioneers in psychology* (Vol. III, pp. 31–48). Mahwah, NJ: Lawrence Erlbaum Associates, Publishers.

Boakes, R. (1984). *From Darwin to behaviourism: Psychology and the minds of animals.* New York: Cambridge.

Bochenski, I. M. (1961). *A history of formal logic.* New York: Chelsea.

Boethius, A. M. S. (1981). De consolatione philosophiae *[The consolation of philosophy].* Millwood, NY: Kraus Reprint. (Original work published ca. 525)

Bohan, J. S. (1990). Contextual history: A framework for replacing women in the history of psychology. *Psychology of Women Quarterly, 14,* 213–227.

Bohan, J. S. (Ed.) (1992). *Replacing women in psychology: Readings toward a more inclusive history.* Dubuque, IA: Kendall/Hunt Publishing Co.

Bolles, R. C. (1993). *The story of psychology: A thematic history.* Pacific Grove, CA: Brooks/Cole Publishing Company.

Bondy, M. (1974). Psychiatric antecedents of psychological testing (before Binet). *Journal of the History of the Behavioral Sciences, 10,* 180–194.

Boneau, C. A. (1998). Hermann Ebbinghaus: On the road to progress or down the garden path? In G. A. Kimble & M. Wertheimer (Eds.), *Portraits of pioneers in psychology* (Vol. III, pp. 51–64). Mahwah, NJ: Lawrence Erlbaum Associates, Publishers.

Bordogna, F. (2001). The psychology and physiology of temperament: Pragmatism in context. *Journal of the History of the Behavioral Sciences, 37,* 3–25.

Boring, E. G. (1927). Edward Bradford Titchener: 1867–1927. *American Journal of Psychology, 38,* 488–506.

Boring, E. G. (1929). The psychology of controversy. *Psychological Review, 36,* 97–121.

Boring, E. G. (1935). Georg Elias Müller: 1850–1934. *American Journal of Psychology, 47,* 344–348.

Boring, E. G. (1950). *A history of experimental psychology* (2nd Ed.). New York: Appleton-Century-Crofts, Inc.

Boring, E. G. (1953). John Dewey: 1859–1952. *American Journal of Psychology, 67,* 145–147.

Boring, E. G. (1960). Lashley and cortical integration. In F. A. Beach, D. O. Hebb, C. T. Morgan, & H. W. Nissen (Eds.), *The neuropsychology of Lashley: Selected papers of K. S. Lashley* (pp. xi–xvi). New York: McGraw-Hill Book Company, Inc.

Boring, E. G. (1961). [Letter to the editor]. *Scientific American, 204*(6), 18–19.

Boring, E. G. (1965). On the subjectivity of important historical dates: Leipzig, 1879. *Journal of the History of the Behavioral Sciences, 1,* 5–9.

Boring, E. G. (1966). A note on the origin of the word psychology. *Journal of the History of the Behavioral Sciences, 2,* 167.

Boring, E. G. (1967). Titchener's Experimentalists. *Journal of the History of the Behavioral Sciences, 3,* 315–325.

Boring, E. G. (1969). Titchener, meaning and behaviorism. In D. L. Krantz (Ed.), *Schools of psychology: A symposium* (pp. 21–34). New York: Appleton-Century-Crofts.

Bos, J. (2003). A silent antipode: The making and breaking of psychoanalyst Wilhelm Stekel. *History of Psychology, 6,* 331–361.

Bottome, P. (1939). *Alfred Adler: A biography.* New York: Putnam's Sons.

Boudewijnse, G-J. A., Murray, D. J., & Bandomir, C. A. (1999). Herbart's mathematical psychology. *History of Psychology, 2,* 163–193.

Boudewijnse, G-J. A., Murray, D. J., & Bandomir, C. A. (2001). The fate of Herbart's mathematical psychology. *History of Psychology, 4,* 107–132.

Bousfield, W. A. (1953). The occurrence of clustering in the recall of randomly arranged associates. *Journal of General Psychology, 49,* 229–240.

Bower, G. H., & Hilgard, E. R. (1981). *Theories of learning* (5th ed.). Englewood Cliffs, NJ: Prentice-Hall, Inc.

Bowler, P. J. (1990). *Charles Darwin: The man and his influence.* Cambridge: Cambridge University Press.

Brainerd, C. J. (1996). Piaget: A centennial celebration. *Psychological Science, 7,* 191–195.

Brandon, S. (2002). Neal Miller—A scientist honored. *Psychological Science Agenda, 15,* 13.

Bransford, J. (1979). *Human cognition.* Belmont, CA: Wadsworth.

Brauns, H.-P. (1997). Ernst Heinrich Weber. In W. G. Bringmann, H. E. Lück, R. Miller, & C. E. Early (Eds.), *A pictorial history of psychology* (pp. 97–100). Chicago: Quintessence Publishing Co., Inc.

Brauns, H.-P. (1997). Hermann von Helmholtz. In W. G. Bringmann, H. E. Lück, R. Miller, & C. E. Early, *A pictorial history of psychology* (pp. 107–110). Chicago: Quintessence Publishing Co., Inc.

Breland, K., & Breland, M. (1966). *Animal behavior.* London: The Macmillan Company.

Bretherton, I. (2000). Mary Dinsmore Salter Ainsworth (1913–1999). *American Psychologist, 55,* 1148–1149.

Brewer, C. L. (1991). Perspectives on John B. Watson. In G. A. Kimble, M. Wertheimer, & C. White (Eds.), *Portraits of pioneers in psychology* (pp. 170–186). Hillsdale, NJ: Lawrence Erlbaum Associates, Publishers.

Bricke, J. (1974). Hume's associationist psychology. *Journal of the History of the Behavioral Sciences, 10,* 397–409.

Bridgman, P. W. (1927). *The logic of modern physics.* New York: Macmillan.

Bringmann, W. G., & Abresch, J. (1997). Clever Hans: Fact or fiction? In W. G. Bringmann, H. E. Lück, R. Miller, & C. E. Early (Eds.), *A pictorial history of psychology* (pp. 77–82). Carol Stream, IL: Quintessence Publishing Co., Inc.

Bringmann, W. G., Balance, W. D. G., & Evans, R. B. (1975). Wilhelm Wundt 1832–1920: A brief biographical sketch. *Journal of the History of the Behavioral Sciences, 11,* 287–297.

Bringmann, W. G., & Balk, M. M. (1992). Another look at Wilhelm Wundt's publication record. *History of Psychology Newsletter, 24,* 50–66.

Bringmann, W. G., Bringmann, M. W., & Early, C. E. (1992). G. Stanley Hall and the history of psychology. *American Psychologist, 47,* 281–289.

Bringmann, W. G., Bringmann, N. J., & Ungerer, G. A. (1980). The establishment of Wundt's laboratory: An archival and documentary study. In W. G. Bringmann & R. D. Tweney (Eds.), *Wundt studies: A centennial collection* (pp. 123–159). Toronto: C. J. Hogrefe.

Bringmann, W. G., Hewett, P., & Ungerer, G. A. (1997). An 18th-century baby biography. In W. G. Bringmann, H. E. Lück, R. Miller, & C. E. Early (Eds.), *A pictorial history of psychology* (pp. 37–41). Chicago: Quintessence Publishing Co., Inc.

Bringmann, W. G., Krichev, A., & Balance, W. (1970). Goethe as behavior therapist. *Journal of the History of the Behavioral Sciences, 6,* 151–155.

Bringmann, W. G., & Ungerer, G. A. (1980). The foundation of the Institute for Experimental Psychology at Leipzig University. *Psychological Research, 42,* 5–18.

Bringmann, W. G., Voss, U., & Balance, W. D. G. (1997). Goethe as an early behavior therapist. In W. G. Bringmann, H. E. Lück, R. Miller, & C. E. Early (Eds.), *A pictorial history of psychology* (pp. 35–36). Carol Stream, IL: Quintessence Publishing Co., Inc.

Bringmann, W. G., Voss, U., & Ungerer, G. A. (1997). Wundt's laboratories. In W. G. Bringmann, H. E. Lück, R. Miller, & C. E. Early (Eds.), *A pictorial history of psychology* (pp. 126–132). Chicago: Quintessence Publishing Co., Inc.

Broad, W. J. (1981). Sir Isaac Newton: Mad as a hatter. *Science, 213,* 1341–1342, 1344.

Broadbent, D. E. (1958). *Perception and communication.* London: Pergamon Press.

Brock, A. (1993). Something old, something new: The 'reappraisal' of Wilhelm Wundt in textbooks. *Theory & Psychology, 3,* 235–242.

Brooks, G. P. (1976). The faculty psychology of Thomas Reid. *Journal of the History of the Behavioral Sciences, 12,* 65–77.

Brown, R. (1958). *Words and things.* Glencoe, IL: Free Press.

Brown, R. (1965). *Social psychology.* New York: Free Press.

Brown, R. (1973). *A first language: The early stages.* Cambridge, MA: Harvard University Press.

Brown, R. (1989). Roger Brown. In G. Lindzey (Ed.), *A history of psychology in autobiography* (Vol. 8, pp. 36–60). Stanford, CA: Stanford University Press.

Brown, R., & Kulik, J. (1977). Flashbulb memories. *Cognition, 5,* 73–99.

Browne, J. (1995). *Charles Darwin: Voyaging.* New York: Alfred A. Knopf.

Brožek, J. (1989). Contributions to the history of psychology: LVI. J. E. Purkinje (1787–1869), "The Phenomenon" and beyond. *Perceptual and Motor Skills, 68,* 821–822.

Brožek, J. (1999). From "Psichiologia" to "Psychologia": A graphically documented archival study across three centuries. *Journal of the History of the Behavioral Sciences, 35,* 177– 180.

Brožek, J., & Hoskovec, J. (1997). Jan Evangelista Purkyne (Purkinje). In W. G. Bringmann, H. E. Lück, R. Miller, & C. E. Early (Eds.), *A pictorial history of psychology* (pp. 90–96). Carol Stream, IL: Quintessence Publishing Co., Inc.

Bruce, D. (1986). Lashley's shift from bacteriology to neuropsychology, 1910–1917, and the influence of Jennings, Watson, and Franz. *Journal of the History of the Behavioral Sciences, 22,* 27–44.

Bruce, D. (1991). Integrations of Lashley. In G. A. Kimble, M. Wertheimer, & C. L. White (Eds.), *Portraits of pioneers in psychology* (pp. 307–323). Hillsdale, NJ: Lawrence Erlbaum Associates, Publishers.

Bruce, D. (1998a). The Lashley-Hull debate revisited. *History of Psychology, 1,* 69–84.

Bruce, D. (1998b). Lashley's rejection of connectionism. *History of Psychology, 1,* 160–164.

Bruder-Bezzel, A., & Schiferer, R. (1997). Alfred Adler. In W. G. Bringmann, H. E. Lück, R. Miller, & C. E. Early (Eds.), *A pictorial history of psychology* (pp. 416–419). Carol Stream, IL: Quintessence Publishing Co., Inc.

Bruner, J. S. (1962). *On knowing: Essays for the left hand.* Cambridge, MA: Belknap Press.

Bruner, J. S. (1980). Jerome S. Bruner. In G. Lindzey (Ed.), *A history of psychology in autobiography* (Vol. 7, pp. 74–151). San Francisco: Freeman.

Bruner, J. S. (1986). *Actual minds, possible worlds.* Cambridge, MA: Harvard University Press.

Bruner, J. S., Goodnow, J. J., & Austin, G. A. (1956). *A study of thinking.* New York: Wiley.

Buber, M. (1970). *I and Thou* (W. Kaufmann, Trans.). New York: Charles Scribner's Sons. (Original work published 1923)

Buber, M. (1957). Guilt and guilt feelings. *Existential Psychiatry, 20,* 114–129.

Buchanan, R. D. (1994). The development of the Minnesota Multiphasic Personality Inventory. *Journal of the History of the Behavioral Sciences, 30,* 148–161.

Buchner, E. F. (1897). A study of Kant's psychology. *Psychological Review, 1* (Monogr. Suppl. 4).

Buckley, K. W. (1982). The selling of a psychologist: John Broadus Watson and the application of behavioral techniques to advertising. *Journal of the History of the Behavioral Sciences, 18,* 207–221.

Buckley, K. W. (1989). *Mechanical man: John Broadus Watson and the beginnings of behaviorism.* New York: The Guilford Press.

Bugental, J. F. T. (1996). Rollo May (1909–1994). *American Psychologist, 51,* 418–419.

Bühler, C. B. (1930). *The first year of life.* New York: Day.

Bühler, C. B. (1971). Basic theoretical concepts of humanistic psychology. *American Psychologist, 26,* 378–386.

Burghardt, G. M. (1985). Animal awareness: Current perceptions and historical perspective. *American Psychologist, 40,* 905–919.

Burkhardt, F. (Ed.) (1996). *Charles Darwin's letters: A selection.* Cambridge: Cambridge University Press.

Burnham, J. C. (1972). Thorndike's puzzle boxes. *Journal of the History of the Behavioral Sciences, 8,* 159–167.

Burt, C. (1952). Cyril Burt. In E. G. Boring, H. S. Langfeld, H. Werner, & R. M. Yerkes (Eds.), *A history of psychology in autobiography* (Vol. 4, pp. 53–73). Worcester, MA: Clark University Press.

Burton, G. (2001). The tenacity of historical misinformation: Titchener did not invent the Titchener illusion. *History of Psychology, 4,* 228–244.

Buss, A. R. (1976). Galton and the birth of differential psychology and eugenics: Social, political, and economic forces. *Journal of the History of the Behavioral Sciences, 12,* 47–58.

Butcher, J. N. (2000). Starke Rosecrans Hathaway: Biography of an empiricist. In G. A. Kimble & M. Wertheimer (Eds.), *Portraits of pioneers in psychology* (Vol. IV, pp. 235–250). Mahwah, NJ: Lawrence Erlbaum Associates, Publishers.

Buytendijk, F. J. J. (1959). *Phänomenologica 2: Husserl et la pensée moderne [Phenomenologica 2: Husserl and modern thought].* The Hague: Nijhoff.

Cadwallader, T. C. (1974). Charles S. Peirce (1839–1914): The first American experimental psychologist. *Journal of the History of the Behavioral Sciences, 10,* 291–298.

Calkins, M. W. (1894). Association. *Psychological Review, 1,* 476–483.

Calkins, M. W. (1906). A reconciliation between structural and functional psychology. *Psychological Review, 13,* 61–81.

Calkins, M. W. (1930). Mary Whiton Calkins. In C. Murchison (Ed.), *A history of psychology in autobiography* (Vol. 1, pp. 31–62). Worcester, MA: Clark University Press.

Candland, D. K. (1993). *Feral children and clever animals: Reflections on human nature.* New York: Oxford University Press.

Cannon, W. B. (1927). The James-Lange theory of emotions: A critical examination and an alternative. *American Journal of Psychology, 39,* 106–124.

Carlson, E. T. (1977). Benjamin Rush and mental health. In R. W. Rieber & K. Salzinger (Eds.), *The roots of American psychology: Historical influences and implications for the future* (pp. 94–103). New York: The New York Academy of Sciences.

Carlson, N. R. (1994). *Physiology of behavior* (5th ed.). Boston: Allyn and Bacon.

Carr, H. A. (1925). *Psychology: A study of mental activity.* New York: Longmans, Green.

Carr, H. A. (1936). Harvey A. Carr. In C. Murchison (Ed.), *A history of psychology in autobiography* (Vol. 3, pp. 69–82). Worcester, MA: Clark University Press.

Carr, H. A., & Watson, J. B. (1908). Orientation in the white rat. *The Journal of Comparative Neurology & Psychology, 18,* 27–44.

Carson, R. (1962). *Silent spring.* Boston: Houghton Mifflin.

Cartwright, D. (1947). Kurt Lewin: 1890–1947. *International Journal of Opinion and Attitude Research, 1,* 96–99.

Cartwright, D. (1979). Contemporary social psychology in historical perspective. *Social Psychology Quarterly, 42,* 82–93.

Cattell, J. M. (1890). Mental tests and measurements. *Mind, 15,* 373–381.

Cattell, J. M. (1928). Early psychological laboratories. *Science, 67,* 543–548.

Cattell, J. M. (1929). Psychology in America. *Science, 70,* 335–347.

Cattell, R. B. (1957). *Personality and motivation: Structure and measurement.* New York: World.

Cattell, R. B. (1963). Theory of crystallized intelligence: A critical experiment. *Journal of Educational Psychology, 54,* 1–22.

Cattell, R. B. (1973). Personality pinned down. *Psychology Today, 7,* 40–46.

Cattell, R. B. (1997). Open letter to the APA. Retrieved September 11, 2003, from http://www.cattell.net/devon/openletter.htm

Chisholm, R. (1981). Brentano's analysis of the consciousness of time. *Midwest Studies in Philosophy, 6,* 3–18.

Chomsky, N. (1957). *Syntactic structures.* The Hague: Mouton Publishers.

Chomsky, N. (1959). Review of Skinner's *Verbal behavior. Language, 35,* 26–58.

Chomsky, N. (1966). *Cartesian linguistics.* New York: Harper & Row.

Chomsky, N. (1980). *Rules and representations.* New York: Columbia University Press.

Chomsky, N., & Miller, G. (1958). Finite state languages. *Information and Control, 1,* 91–112.

Christie, R., & Geis, F. (1960). *Studies in Machiavellianism.* New York: Academic Press.

Churchland, P. (1984). *Matter and consciousness.* Cambridge, MA: MIT Press.

Clark, C. W. (1997). The witchcraze in 17th-century Europe. In W. G. Bringmann, H. E. Lück, R. Miller, & C. E. Early (Eds.), *A pictorial history of psychology* (pp. 23–29). Carol Stream, IL: Quintessence Publishing Co., Inc.

Clarke, E., & Jacyna, L. S. (1987). *Nineteenth-century origins of neuroscientific concepts.* Berkeley, CA: University of California Press.

Clements, R. D. (1967). Physiological–psychological thought in Juan Luis Vives. *Journal of the History of the Behavioral Sciences, 3,* 219–235.

Coan, R. W., & Zagona, S. (1962). Contemporary ratings of psychological theorists. *The Psychological Record, 12,* 315–322.

Cohen, J. (1962). The statistical power of abnormal-social psychological research: A review. *Journal of Abnormal and Social Psychology, 65,* 145–153.

Cohen, J. (1994). The earth is round ($p < .05$). *American Psychologist, 49,* 997–1003.

Cole, M. (1997). *Alexander Luria, cultural psychology and the resolution of the crisis in psychology.* Retrieved August 20, 2003, from University of California, San Diego, Laboratory of Comparative Human Cognition, Communication Department Web site: http:/lchc.ucsd.edu/People/Localz/MCole/luria.html

Coleman, S. R. (1997). B. F. Skinner: Maverick, inventor, behaviorist, critic. In W. G. Bringmann, H. E. Lück, R. Miller, & C. E. Early (Eds.), *A pictorial history of psychology* (pp. 206–213). Carol Stream, IL: Quintessence Publishing Co., Inc.

Coles, R. (1992). *Anna Freud: The dream of psychoanalysis.* Reading, MA: Addison-Wesley Publishing Co., Inc.

Commins, S. & Linscott, R. N. (Eds.) (1954). *Man & the universe: The philosophers of science.* New York: Pocket Books, Inc.

Conley, J. J. (1984). Not Galton, but Shakespeare: A note on the origin of the term "nature and nurture." *Journal of the History of the Behavioral Sciences, 20,* 184–185.

Cook, G. A. (1977). G. H. Mead's social behaviorism. *Journal of the History of the Behavioral Sciences, 13,* 307–316.

Cook, G. A. (1994). George Herbert Mead: An unpublished review of John Dewey's *Human nature and conduct. Journal of the History of the Behavioral Sciences, 30,* 374–379.

Coon, D. J. (1982). Eponymy, obscurity, Twitmyer, and Pavlov. *Journal of the History of the Behavioral Sciences, 18,* 255–262.

Coon, D. J. (1992). Testing the limits of sense and science: American experimental psychologists combat spiritualism, 1880–1920. *American Psychologist, 47,* 143–151.

Coon, D. J. (2000). Salvaging the self in a world without soul: William James's *The Principles of Psychology. History of Psychology, 3,* 83–103.

Copernicus, N. (1965). *De revolutionibus orbium coelestium [On the revolutions of the celestial spheres].* New York: Johnson Reprint Corp. (Original work published 1543)

Copleston, F. (1950). *A history of philosophy* (Vol. 2, Part 1). Westminster, MD: The Newman Press.

Coren, S., Ward, L. M., & Enns, J. T. (1994). *Sensation and perception* (4th ed.). Fort Worth, TX: Harcourt Brace College Publishers.

Costa, P. T., Jr., & McCrae, R. (1992). *Revised NEO Personality Inventory: NEO PI and NEO Five-Factor Inventory* (Professional Manual). Odessa, FL: Psychological Assessment Resources.

Costall, A. (1993). How Lloyd Morgan's Canon backfired. *Journal of the History of the Behavioral Sciences, 29,* 113–122.

Cowles, M. (2001). *Statistics in psychology: An historical perspective* (2nd ed.). Mahwah, NJ: Lawrence Erlbaum Associates, Publishers.

Cox, C. M. (1926). *Genetic studies of genius: Vol. 2. The early mental traits of three hundred geniuses.* Stanford, CA: Stanford University Press.

Craig, E. (1988). Introduction: *Daseinanalysis:* A quest for essentials. *Humanistic Psychologist, 16,* 1–21.

Crannell, C. W. (1970). Wolfgang Köhler. *Journal of the History of the Behavioral Sciences, 6,* 267–268.

Cravens, H. (1992). A scientific project locked in time: The Terman genetics studies of genius, 1920s–1950s. *American Psychologist, 47,* 183–189.

Crawford, M., & Unger, R. (2000). *Women and gender: A feminist psychology* (3rd ed.). Boston: McGraw-Hill Higher Education.

Creelan, P. G. (1974). Watsonian behaviorism and the Calvinist conscience. *Journal of the History of the Behavioral Sciences, 10,* 95–118.

Crews, F. (1996). The verdict on Freud. *Psychological Science, 7,* 63–68.

Croce, P. J. (1999). Physiology as the antechamber to metaphysics: The young William James's hope for a philosophical psychology. *History of Psychology, 2,* 302–323.

Cromer, W., & Anderson, P. (1970). Freud's visit to America: Newspaper coverage. *Journal of the History of the Behavioral Sciences, 6,* 349–353.

Cronbach, L. J. (1949). *Essentials of psychological testing.* New York: Harper & Row.

Cronbach, L. J. (1957). The two disciplines of scientific psychology. *American Psychologist, 12,* 671–684.

Cronbach, L. J., & Meehl, P. E. (1955). Construct validity in psychological tests. *Psychological Bulletin, 52,* 281–302.

Crovitz, H. (1970). *Galton's walk.* New York: Harper & Row.

Crowther-Heyck, H. (1999). George A. Miller, language, and the computer metaphor of mind. *History of Psychology, 2,* 37–64.

Cureton, E. E. (1950). Validity, reliability, and baloney. *Educational and Psychological Measurement, 10,* 94–96.

Dallenbach, K. M. (1959). Twitmyer and the conditioned response. *American Journal of Psychology, 72,* 633–638.

Damasio, A. R. (1994). *Descartes' error.* New York: Grosset/Putnam.

Damasio, H., Grabowski, T., Frank, R., Galaburda, A. M., & Damasio, A. R. (1994). The return of Phineas Gage: Clues about the brain from the skull of a famous patient. *Science, 264,* 1102–1105.

Danziger, K. (1979). The positivist repudiation of Wundt. *Journal of the History of the Behavioral Sciences, 15,* 205–230.

Danziger, K. (1980). The history of introspection reconsidered. *Journal of the History of the Behavioral Sciences, 16,* 241–262.

Darley, J. M., & Batson, C. D. (1973). From Jerusalem to Jericho: A study of situational and dispositional variables in helping behavior. *Journal of Personality and Social Psychology, 27,* 100–108.

Darley, J. M., & Latané, B. (1968). Bystander intervention in emergencies: Diffusion of responsibility. *Journal of Personality and Social Psychology, 8,* 377–383.

Darwin, C. (1958). *The origin of species, by means of natural selection or the preservation of favoured races in the struggle for life.* New York: New American Library. (Original work published 1859)

Darwin, C. (1979). *The expression of emotions in man and animals.* London: Julian Friedmann Publishers. (Original work published 1872)

Darwin, C. (1874). *The descent of man, and selection in relation to sex* (2nd ed.). New York: A. L. Burt, Publisher.

Darwin, F. (Ed.) (1898). *The life and letters of Charles Darwin* (Vol. 1). New York: D. Appleton and Company.

Deary, I. J. (1994). Sensory discrimination and intelligence: Postmodern or resurrection? *American Journal of Psychology, 107,* 95–115.

deCarvalho, R. J. (1989). Contributions to the history of psychology: LXII. Carl Rogers' naturalistic system of ethics. *Psychological Reports, 65,* 1155–1162.

deCarvalho, R. J. (1990). A history of the "third force" in psychology. *Journal of Humanistic Psychology, 30,* 22–44.

deCarvalho, R. J. (1990). Contributions to the history of psychology: LXIX. Gordon Allport on the problem of method in psychology. *Psychological Reports, 67,* 267–275.

deCarvalho, R. J. (1999). Otto Rank, the Rankian circle in Philadelphia, and the origins of Carl Rogers' person-centered psychotherapy. *History of Psychology, 2,* 132–148.

Decker, H. S. (1975). *The Interpretation of Dreams:* Early receptionby the educated German public. *Journal of the History of the Behavioral Sciences, 11,* 129–141.

Deese, J. (1965). *Structure of associations in language and thought.* Baltimore: Johns Hopkins Press.

Deese, J. (1970). *Psycholinguistics.* Boston: Allyn & Bacon.

Dennett, D. C. (1995). *Darwin's dangerous idea: Evolution and the meanings of life.* New York: Simon & Schuster.

Dennis, P. M. (2002). Psychology's public image in "Topics of the Times": Commentary from the editorial page of the *New York Times* between 1904 and 1947. *Journal of the History of the Behavioral Sciences, 38,* 371–392.

Dennis, W. (1948). *Readings in the history of psychology.* New York: Appleton-Century-Crofts, Inc.

Descartes, R. (1956). *Discourse on method* (L. J. Lafleur, Trans.). Indianapolis: Bobbs-Merrill. (Original work published 1637)

Desmond, A., & Moore, J. (1991). *Darwin.* New York: Warner Books.

de Villiers, J. G., & de Villiers, P. A. (1978). *Language acquisition.* Cambridge, MA: Harvard University Press.

Dewey, J. (1896). The reflex arc concept in psychology. *Psychological Review, 3,* 357–370.

Dewey, J. (1910). *How we think: A restatement of the relation of reflective thinking to the educative process.* Boston: Heath.

Dewey, J. (1917). The need for social psychology. *Psychological Review, 24,* 266–277.

Dewey, J. (1922). *Human nature and conduct: An introduction to social psychology.* New York: Holt.

Dews, P. B. (1981). Pavlov and psychiatry. *Journal of the History of the Behavioral Sciences, 17,* 246–250.

Dewsbury, D. A. (1990). Early interactions between animal psychologists and animal activists and the founding of the APA Committee on Precautions in Animal Experimentation. *American Psychologist, 45,* 315–327.

Dewsbury, D. A. (1992). Comparative psychology and ethology: A reassessment. *American Psychologist, 47,* 208–215.

Dewsbury, D. A. (1996). Robert M. Yerkes: A psychobiologist with a plan. In G. A. Kimble, C. A. Boneau, & M. Wertheimer (Eds.), *Portraits of pioneers in psychology* (Vol. II, pp. 87–105). Mahwah, NJ: Lawrence Erlbaum Associates, Publishers.

Dewsbury, D. A. (1997). In celebration of the centennial of Ivan P. Pavlov's (1897/1902) *The work of the diges-*

tive glands. American Psychologist, 52, 933–935.

Dewsbury, D. A. (1999). Molly Harrower (1906–1999). *Psychology of Women, 26,* 24, 27.

Dewsbury, D. A. (2000a). Frank A. Beach, master teacher. In G. A. Kimble & M. Wertheimer (Eds.), *Portraits of pioneers in psychology* (Vol. IV, pp. 269–283). Mahwah, NJ: Lawrence Erlbaum Associates, Publishers.

Dewsbury, D. A. (2000b). Molly R. Harrower (1906–1999). *American Psychologist, 55,* 1058.

Dewsbury, D. A. (2002a). The Chicago Five: A family group of integrative psychobiologists. *History of Psychology, 5,* 16–37.

Dewsbury, D. A. (2002b). Constructing representations of Karl Spencer Lashley. *Journal of the History of the Behavioral Sciences, 38,* 225–245.

Dewsbury, D. A. (2002c). The role of evidence in interpretations of the scientific work of Karl Lashley. *Journal of the History of the Behavioral Sciences, 38,* 255–257.

Diamond, S. (1971). Gestation of the instinct concept. *Journal of the History of the Behavioral Sciences, 7,* 323–336.

Diamond, S. (1980). Francis Galton and American psychology. In R. W. Rieber & K. Salzinger (Eds.), *Psychology: Theoretical-historical perspectives* (pp. 43–55). New York: Academic Press.

Diehl, L. A. (1986). The paradox of G. Stanley Hall: Foe of coeducation and educator of women. *American Psychologist, 41,* 868–878.

Dobson, V., & Bruce, D. (1972). The German university and the development of experimental psychology. *Journal of the History of the Behavioral Sciences, 8,* 204–207.

Dollard, J. C., Doob, L. W., Miller, N. E., Mowrer, O. H., & Sears, R. R. (1939). *Frustration and aggression.* New Haven, CT: Yale University Press.

Dollard, J. C., & Miller, N. E. (1950). *Personality and psychotherapy.* New York: McGraw-Hill.

Donnelly, M. (Ed.) (1992). *Reinterpreting the legacy of William James.* Washington, DC: American Psychological Association.

Dorfman, D. D. (1978). The Cyril Burt question: New findings. *Science, 201,* 1177–1186.

Doyle, K. O. (1974). Theory and practice of ability testing in Ancient Greece. *Journal of the History of the Behavioral Sciences, 10,* 202–212.

Drayton, H., & McNeill, J. (1879). *Brain and mind* (6th ed.). New York: Fowler & Wells Co., Publishers.

Dreyfus, H. (1982). *Husserl, intentionality, and cognitive science.* Cambridge, MA: MIT Press.

Dreyfus, H. L. (1972). *What computers can't do: The limits of artificial intelligence.* New York: Harper & Row.

Duke, C., Fried, S., Pliley, W., & Walker, D. (1989). Contributions to the history of psychology: Lix. Rosalie Rayner Watson: The mother of a behaviorist's sons. *Psychological Reports, 65,* 163–169.

Duncker, K. (1945). On problem-solving. *Psychological Monographs, 58* (5, Whole no. 270).

Dunlap, K. (1919). Are there any instincts? *Journal of Abnormal Psychology, 14,* 307–311.

Durant, W. (1939). *The life of Greece.* New York: Simon and Schuster.

Durant, W. (1944). *Caesar and Christ.* New York: Simon and Schuster.

Durant, W. (1950). *The age of faith.* New York: Simon and Schuster.

Durant, W. (1961). *The story of philosophy.* New York: Washington Square Press.

Durant, W., & Durant, A. (1963). *The age of Louis XIV.* New York: Simon & Schuster.

Durant, W., & Durant, A. (1975). *The age of Napoleon.* New York: MJF Books.

Early, C. E. (1994). Gustav Fechner and William James: A reassessment. *Revista de Historia de la Psicologia, 15,* 115–121.

Ebbinghaus, H. (1964). *Memory: A contribution to experimental psychology.* (H. A. Ruger & C. A. Bussenius, Trans.) New York: Dover. (Original work published 1885)

Ebbinghaus, H. (1910). *Abriss der Psychologie [A summary of psychology].* Leipzig: Veit.

Eco, U. (1983). *The name of the rose* (W. Weaver, Trans.). San Diego: Harcourt Brace Jovanovich.

Edie, J. (1987). *William James and phenomenology.* Bloomington, IN: University of Indiana Press.

Edman, I. (1955). *John Dewey: His contribution to the American tradition.* New York: Bobbs-Merrill.

Edwards, A. J. (1982). David Wechsler (1896–1981). *Journal of the History of the Behavioral Sciences, 18,* 78–79.

Eiermann, K. (1997–1999). *Penetrating Goethe* [On-line]. Available: wysiwyg://2/http://members.aol.com/ KatharenaE/private/Pweek/Goethe/goethe.html

Eiseley, L. (1961). *Darwin's century.* Garden City, NY: Anchor.

Elkind, D. (1985). Child development research. In S. Koch & D. E. Leary (Eds.), *A century of psychology as science* (pp. 472–489). New York: McGraw-Hill.

Ellenberger, H. F. (1972). The story of "Anna O": A critical review with new data. *Journal of the History of the Behavioral Sciences, 8,* 267–279.

Ellison, H. (1983). The whimper of whipped dogs. In H. Ellison, *Deathbird stories* (pp. 2–19). New York: Bluejay Books.

Ellsworth, P. C. (1994). William James and emotion: Is a century of fame worth a century of misunderstanding? *Psychological Review, 101,* 222–229.

Elwes, R. H. M. (1951). Introduction. In R. H. M. Elwes (Trans.), *The chief works of Benedict de Spinoza* (pp. v–xxxiii). New York: Dover Publications.

Eng, E. (1978). Looking back on Kurt Lewin: From field theory to action research. *Journal of the History of the Behavioral Sciences, 14,* 228–232.

Erdelyi, M. H. (1985). *Psychoanalysis: Freud's cognitive psychology.* New York: W. H. Freeman and Company.

Erikson, E. H. (1962). *Young man Luther.* New York: W. W. Norton & Company.

Erikson, E. H. (1963). *Childhood and society* (2nd ed.). New York: W. W. Norton & Company. (Original work published 1950)

Erikson, E. H. (1982). *The life cycle completed: A review.* New York: W. W. Norton & Company.

Esterson, A. (2002a). Misconceptions about Freud's seduction theory: Comment on Gleaves and Hernandez (1999). *History of Psychology, 5,* 85–91.

Esterson, A. (2002b). The myth of Freud's ostracism by the medical community in 1896–1905: Jeffrey Masson's assault on truth. *History of Psychology, 5,* 115–134.

Etaugh, C. A., & Bridges, J. S. (2004). *The psychology of women: A lifespan perspective* (2nd ed.). Boston: Pearson.

Evans, R. B. (1972). E. B. Titchener and his lost system. *Journal of the History of the Behavioral Sciences, 8,* 168–180.

Evans, R. B. (1990). William James and his *Principles.* In M. G. Johnson & T. B. Henley (Eds.), *Reflections on* The Principles of Psychology (pp. 11–31). Hillsdale, NJ: Lawrence Erlbaum Associates, Publishers.

Evans, R. B. (1991). E. B. Titchener on scientific psychology and technology. In G. A. Kimble, M. Wertheimer, & C. White, (Eds.) *Portraits of pioneers in psychology* (pp. 89–103). Hillsdale, NJ: Lawrence Erlbaum Associates, Publishers.

Evans, R. B., & Koelsch, W. A. (1985). Psychoanalysis arrives in America: The 1909 Psychology Conference at Clark University. *American Psychologist, 40,* 942–948.

Exner, J. E. (1974). *The Rorschach: A comprehensive system: Vol. 1.* New York: Wiley.

Exner, J. E. (1993). *The Rorschach: A comprehensive system: Vol. 1. Basic foundations* (3rd ed.). New York: Wiley.

Eysenck, H. J. (1980). Hans Jurgen Eysenck. In G. Lindzey (Ed.), *A history of psychology in autobiography* (Vol. 7, pp. 152–187). San Francisco: W. H. Freeman and Company.

Eysenck, H. J. (Ed.) (1982). *A model for intelligence.* New York: Springer-Verlag.

Eysenck, H. J., & Kamin, L. J. (1981). *The intelligence controversy: H. J. Eysenck versus Leon Kamin.* New York: Wiley.

Eysenck, H. J., & Rachman, S. (1965). *The causes and cure of neurosis.* San Diego: Knapp.

Faber, D. P. (1996). Suggestion: Metaphor and meaning. *Journal of the History of the Behavioral Sciences, 32,* 16–29.

Fancher, R. E. (1971). The neurological origin of Freud's dream theory. *Journal of the History of the Behavioral Sciences, 7,* 59–74.

Fancher, R. E. (1977). Brentano's *Psychology from an empirical standpoint* and Freud's early metapsychology. *Journal of the History of the Behavioral Sciences, 13,* 207–227.

Fancher, R. E. (1979). A note on the origin of the term "nature and nurture." *Journal of the History of the Behavioral Sciences, 15,* 321–322.

Fancher, R. E. (1984). Not Conley, but Burt and others: A reply. *Journal of the History of the Behavioral Sciences, 20,* 186.

Fancher, R. E. (1985). *The intelligence men.* New York: W. W. Norton & Company.

Fancher, R. E. (1987). Henry Goddard and the Kallikak family photographs: "Conscious skulduggery" or "Whig history"? *American Psychologist, 42,* 585–590.

Fancher, R. E. (1996). *Pioneers of psychology* (3rd ed.). New York: W. W. Norton & Company.

Fancher, R. E. (1997). Galton's hat and the invention of intelligence tests. In W. G. Bringmann, H. E. Lück, R. Miller, & C. E. Early (Eds.), *A pictorial history of psychology* (pp. 53–55). Chicago: Quintessence Publishing Co., Inc.

Fancher, R. E. (1998). Biography and psychodynamic theory: Some lessons from the life of Francis Galton. *History of Psychology, 1,* 99–115.

Fancher, R. E. (2000). Snapshots of Freud in America, 1899–1999. *American Psychologist, 55,* 1025–1028.

Farley, F. (2000). Hans J. Eysenck (1916–1997). *American Psychologist, 55,* 674–675.

Feather, S. (1996). Joseph Banks Rhine: A daughter's perspective. In G. A. Kimble, C. A. Boneau, & M. Wertheimer (Eds.), *Portraits of pioneers in psychology* (Vol. II, pp. 185–197). Mahwah, NJ: Lawrence Erlbaum Associates, Publishers.

Fechner, G. (1969). *The comparative anatomy of angels: A sketch by Dr. Mises* (H. Corbet & M. E. Marshall, Trans.). *Journal of the History of the Behavioral Sciences, 5,* 135–151. (Original work published 1825)

Fechner, G. (1966). *Elements of psychophysics* (Vol. 1) (H. E. Adler, Trans.). New York: Holt, Rinehart and Winston, Inc. (Original work published 1860)

Federn, E. (1997). Sigmund Freud A biographical sketch. In W. G. Bringmann, H. E. Lück, R. Miller, & C. E. Early (Eds.), *A pictorial history of psychology* (pp. 391–394). Carol Stream, IL: Quintessence Publishing Co., Inc.

Felleman, D. J., & van Essen, D. C. (1991). Distributed hierarchical processing in the primate cortex. *Cerebral Cortex, 1,* 1–47.

Ferster, C. B., & Skinner, B. F. (1957). *Schedules of reinforcement.* New York: Appleton-Century-Crofts, Inc.

Festinger, L. (1957). *A theory of cognitive dissonance.* Evanston, IL: Row, Peterson.

Festinger, L., & Carlsmith, J. M. (1959). Cognitive consequences of forced compliance. *Journal of Abnormal and Social Psychology, 68,* 359–366.

Festinger, L., Riecken, H., & Schachter, S. (1956). *When prophesy fails.* Minneapolis: University of Minnesota.

Feyerabend, P. K. (1975). *Against method.* London: New Left Books.

Fine, R. (1979). *A history of psychoanalysis.* New York: Columbia University Press.

Finger, S. (1988). *Brain injury and recovery: Theoretical and controversial issues.* New York: Plenum.

Finger, S. (1994). *Origins of neuroscience: A history of explorations into brain function.* New York: Oxford University Press.

Finger, S. (2000). *Minds behind the brains: A history of the pioneers and their discoveries.* New York: Oxford University Press, Inc.

Fischer, K. (1887). *Descartes and his school.* London: T. Fisher Unwin.

Fitzpatrick, J. F., & Bringmann, W. G. (1997). Charles Darwin and psychology. In W. G. Bringmann, H. E. Lück, R. Miller, & C. E. Early (Eds.), *A pictorial history of psychology* (pp. 51–52). Chicago: Quintessence Publishing Co., Inc.

Fletcher, R. (1991). *Science, ideology, and the media: The Cyril Burt scandal.* New Brunswick, NJ: Transaction Publishers.

Fodor, J. A. (1983). *The modularity of mind.* Cambridge, MA: MIT Press/Bradford Books.

Fodor, J. A., & Pylyshyn, Z. W. (1981). How direct is visual perception? Some reflections of Gibson's "ecological approach." *Cognition, 9,* 139–196.

Føllesdal, D. (1974). Phenomenology. In E. Carterette & M. Friedman (Eds.), *Handbook of perception: Vol. 1* (pp. 377–386). New York: Academic Press.

Fraisse, P. (1970). French origins of the psychology of behavior: The contribution of Henri Pieron. *Journal of the History of the Behavioral Sciences, 6,* 111–119.

Frank, J. D. (1978). Kurt Lewin in retrospect—a psychiatrist's view. *Journal of the History of the Behavioral Sciences, 14,* 223–227.

Frankl, V. E. (1959). *Man's search for meaning.* Boston: Beacon Press. (Original German edition published 1946 as *Ein Psycholog erlebt das Konzentrationslager*)

Frankl, V. E. (1994). Logotherapy. In R. J. Corsini (Ed.), *Encyclopedia of psychology* (2nd ed.) (Vol. 2, p. 350). New York: Wiley.

Franz, S. I. (1902). On the function of the cerebrum: The frontal lobes in relation to the production and retention of simple sensory motor habits. *American Journal of Physiology, 8,* 1–22.

Franz, S. I. (1932). Shepherd Ivory Franz. In C. Murchison (Ed.), *History of psychology in autobiography* (Vol. 2, pp. 89–113). Worcester, MA: Clark University Press.

Freeman, F. S. (1977). The beginnings of Gestalt psychology in the United States. *Journal of the History of the Behavioral Sciences, 13,* 352–353.

Freeman, W. (1949). Transorbital leucotomy: The deep frontal cut. *Proceedings of the Royal Society of Medicine, 42,* Supplement pp. 8–12.

Freud, A. (1937). *The ego and the mechanisms of defence.* London: The Hogarth Press Ltd.

Freud, E. L. (Ed.) (1992). *Letters of Sigmund Freud.* New York: Dover Publications.

Freud, S. (1910). The origin and development of psychoanalysis. *American Journal of Psychology, 21,* 181–218.

Freud, S. (1920). *A general introduction to psychoanalysis* (J. Riviere, Trans.). New York: Washington Square Press.

Freud, S. (1921). *Group psychology and the analysis of the ego.* London: Hogarth.

Freud, S. (1963). *An autobiographical study* (J. Strachey, Trans.). New York: Norton. (Original work published 1925)

Freud, S. (1938a). The history of the psychoanalytic movement. In A. A. Brill (Ed. and Trans.), *The basic writings of Sigmund Freud* (pp. 931–977). New York: The Modern Library.

Freud, S. (1938b). *The interpretation of dreams.* In A. A. Brill (Ed. and Trans.), *The basic writings of Sigmund Freud* (pp. 183–549). New York: The Modern Library.

Freud, S. (1938c). *Psychopathology of everyday life.* In A. A. Brill (Ed. and Trans.), *The basic writings of Sigmund Freud* (pp. 35–178). New York: The Modern Library.

Freud, S., & Breuer, J. (1966). Fräulein Anna O. (Breuer). In J. Strachey (Ed. and Trans.), *Studies on hysteria* (pp. 55–82). New York: Avon Books. (Original work published 1895)

Friedman, H. S., Tucker, J. S., Schwartz, J. E., Tomlinson-Keasey, C., Martin, L. R., Wingard, D. L., & Criqui, M. H. (1995). Psychosocial and behavioral predictors of longevity: The aging and death of the "Termites." *American Psychologist, 50,* 69–78.

Fuchs, A. H. (2000a). Contributions of American mental philosophers to psychology in the United States. *History of Psychology, 3,* 3–19.

Fuchs, A. H. (2000b). The psychology of Thomas Upham. In G. A. Kimble & M. Wertheimer (Eds.), *Portraits of pioneers in psychology* (Vol. IV, pp. 1–13). Mahwah, NJ: Lawrence Erlbaum Associates, Publishers.

Fuchs, A. H., & Viney, W. (2002). The course in the history of psychology: Present status and future concerns. *History of Psychology, 5,* 3–15.

Furumoto, L. (1979). Mary Whiton Calkins (1863–1930) fourteenth president of the American Psychological Association. *Journal of the History of the Behavioral Sciences, 15,* 346–356.

Furumoto, L. (1989). The new history of psychology. In I. S. Cohen (Ed.), *The G. Stanley Hall lecture series* (Vol. 9, pp. 5–34). Washington, DC: American Psychological Association.

Furumoto, L. (1991). From "paired associates" to a psychology of self: The intellectual odyssey of Mary Whiton Calkins. In G. A. Kimble, M. Wertheimer, & C. L. White (Eds.), *Portraits of pioneers in psychology* (pp. 57–72). Hillsdale, NJ: Lawrence Erlbaum Associates, Publishers.

Gallo, D. A., & Finger, S. (2000). The power of a musical instrument: Franklin, the Mozarts, Mesmer, and the glass armonica. *History of Psychology, 3,* 326–343.

Galton, F. (1971). *The narrative of an explorer in tropical South Africa.* New York: Johnson Reprint Corp. (Original work published 1853)

Galton, F. (1865). Hereditary talent and character. *Macmillan's Magazine, 12,* 157–166, 318–327.

Galton, F. (1874). *English men of science: Their nature and nurture.* London: Macmillan.

Galton, F. (1876). The history of twins, as a criterion of the relative powers of nature and nurture. *Journal of the Royal Anthropological Institute, 5,* 391–406.

Galton, F. (1892). *Hereditary genius: An inquiry into its laws and consequences* (2nd ed.). London: Watts & Co.

Garcia, J., Hankins, W. G., & Rusiniak, K. W. (1974). Behavioral regulation of the milieu internal in man and rat. *Science, 185,* 824–831.

Gardner, H. (1983). *Frames of mind: The theory of multiple intelligences.* New York: Basic Books.

Gardner, H. (1985). *The mind's new science: A history of the cognitive revolution.* New York: Basic Books.

Gardner, R. A., & Gardner, B. T. (1969). Teaching sign language to a chimpanzee. *Science, 165,* 664–672.

Garner, W. R. (1962). *Uncertainty and structure as psychological concepts.* New York: John Wiley & Sons.

Garrett, H. E. (1951). *Great experiments in psychology* (3rd ed.). New York: Appleton-Century-Crofts.

Gauld, A. (1992). *A history of hypnotism.* Cambridge: Cambridge University Press.

Gay, P. (1988). Freud: *A life for our time.* New York: W. W. Norton & Company.

Gazzaniga, M. S. (1967). The split brain in man. In *Progress in psychobiology: Readings from* Scientific American (pp. 369–374). San Francisco: W. H. Freeman and Company.

Gendlin, E. T. (1988). Carl Rogers (1902–1987). *American Psychologist, 43,* 127–128.

Gerard, D. L. (1997). Chiarugi and Pinel considered: Soul's brain/person's mind. *Journal of the History of the Behavioral Sciences, 33,* 381–403.

Gergen, K. J. (1994). *Toward transformation in social knowledge* (2nd ed.). New York: Springer-Verlag.

Gerow, J. R. (Ed.) (1988). *Time: Psychology 1923–1988.* Glenview, IL: Scott, Foresman and Company.

Gesell, A. (1952). Arnold Gesell. In E. G. Boring, H. S. Langfeld, H. Werner, & R. M. Yerkes (Eds.), *A history of psychology in autobiography* (Vol. 4, pp. 123–142). Worcester, MA: Clark University Press.

Gholson, B., & Barker, P. (1985). Kuhn, Lakatos, and Lauden. *American Psychologist, 40,* 755–769.

Gibbons, A. (1991). Déjà vu all over again: Chimp-language wars. *Science, 251,* 1561–1562.

Gibson, E. J. (1980). Eleanor J. Gibson. In G. Lindzey (Ed.), *A history of psychology in autobiography* (Vol. 7, pp. 238–269). San Francisco: W. H. Freeman and Company.

Gibson, J. J. (Ed.) (1947). Motion picture testing and research. *Aviation Psychology Research Reports,* No. 7 (Washington, DC: U.S. Government Printing Office).

Gibson, J. J. (1966a). James J. Gibson. In E. G. Boring & G. Lindzey (Eds.), *A history of psychology in autobiography* (Vol. 5, pp. 125–143). New York: Appleton-Century-Crofts.

Gibson, J. J. (1966b). *The senses considered as perceptual systems.* Boston: Houghton Mifflin.

Gibson, J. J. (1971). The legacies of Koffka's *Principles. Journal of the History of the Behavioral Sciences, 7,* 3–9.

Gibson, J. J. (1979). *The ecological approach to visual perception.* Boston: Houghton Mifflin.

Gibson, J. J. (1994). The visual perception of objective motion and subjective movement. *Psychological Review, 101,* 318–323. (Original work published 1954)

Gilbert, A. R. (1968). Franz Brentano in the perspective of existential psychology. *Journal of the History of the Behavioral Sciences, 4,* 249–253.

Gillham, N. W. (2001). *A life of Sir Francis Galton: From African exploration to the birth of eugenics.* New York: Oxford University Press.

Gilligan, C. F. (1982). *In a different voice.* Cambridge, MA: Harvard University Press.

Gilman, S. L. (1979). Darwin sees the insane. *Journal of the History of the Behavioral Sciences, 15,* 253–262.

Giorgi, A. (1970). *Psychology as a human science.* New York: Harper & Row.

Giorgi, A. (1989). Learning and memory from the perspective of phenomenological psychology. In R. S. Valle & S. Halling (Eds.), *Existential-phenomenological perspectives in psychology* (pp. 99–112). New York: Plenum Press.

Gleaves, D. H., & Hernandez, E. (1999). Recent reformulations of Freud's development and abandonment of his seduction theory: Historical/scientific clarification or a continued assault on truth? *History of Psychology, 2,* 324–354.

Gleaves, D. H., & Hernandez, E. (2002). Wethinks the author doth protest too much: A reply to Esterson (2002). *History of Psychology, 5,* 92–98.

Gleitman, H. (1991). Edward Chace Tolman: A life of scientific and social purpose. In G. A. Kimble, M. Wertheimer, & C. L. White (Eds.), *Portraits of pioneers in psychology* (pp. 226–241). Hillsdale, NJ: Lawrence Erlbaum Associates, Publishers.

Gleitman, H., Rozin, P., & Sabini, J. (1997). Solomon E. Asch (1907–1996). *American Psychologist, 52,* 984–985.

Glickman, S. E. (1996). Donald Olding Hebb: Returning the nervous system to psychology. In G. A. Kimble, C. A. Boneau, & M. Wertheimer (Eds.), *Portraits of pioneers in psychology* (Vol. II, pp. 227–244). Mahwah, NJ: Lawrence Erlbaum Associates, Publishers.

Glymour, C., Ford, K. M., & Hayes, P. J. (1995). The prehistory of android epistemology. In K. M. Ford, C. Glymour, & P. J. Hayes (Eds.), *Android epistemology* (pp. 3–21). Menlo Park, CA: AAAI Press/MIT Press.

Goddard, H. H. (1912). *The Kallikak family: A study in the heredity of feeble-mindedness.* New York: Macmillan.

Goethe, J. W. v. (1967) *Faust: A tragedy.* New York: Modern Library. (Original work published 1808, 1832)

Goffman, E. (1963). *Stigma.* Englewood Cliffs, NJ: Prentice-Hall.

Goffman, E. (1976). *Gender advertisements.* New York: Harper & Row.

Golden, C. J. (1978). *Diagnosis and rehabilitation in clinical neuropsychology.* Springfield, IL: Thomas.

Golden, C. J. (1994). Neuropsychology. In R. J. Corsini (Ed.), *Encyclopedia of psychology* (2nd ed.) (Vol. 2, pp. 478–483). New York: Wiley Interscience.

Golden, C. J., Hammeke, T. A., & Purisch, A. D. (1980). *The Luria-Nebraska Neuropsychological Battery: A manual for clinical and experimental uses.* Los Angeles: Western Psychological Services.

Goldman, B. D. (1999). The circadian timing system and reproduction in mammals. *Steroids, 64,* 679–685.

Goldstein, K. (1967). Kurt Goldstein. In E. G. Boring & G. Lindzey (Eds.), *A history of psychology in autobiography* (Vol. 5, pp. 147–166). New York: Appleton-Century-Crofts.

Goodwin, C. J. (1987). In Hall's shadow: Edmund Clark Sanford (1859–1924). *Journal of the History of the Behavioral Sciences, 23,* 153–168.

Götzl, H. (2003). Wolfgang Metzger: Perspectives on his life and work. In G. A. Kimble & M. Wertheimer (Eds.), *Portraits of pioneers in psychology* (Vol. V, pp. 177–191). Mahwah, NJ: Lawrence Erlbaum Associates, Publishers.

Gouaux, C. (1972). Kant's view on the nature of empirical psychology. *Journal of the History of the Behavioral Sciences,* 8, 237–242.

Gould, S. J. (1981). *The mismeasure of man.* New York: W. W. Norton & Company.

Graf-Nold, A. (1997). Carl Gustav Jung. In W. G. Bringmann, H. E. Lück, R. Miller, & C. E. Early (Eds.), *A pictorial history of psychology* (pp. 424–430). Carol Stream, IL: Quintessence Publishing Co., Inc.

Gravitz, M. A., & Gerton, M. I. (1981). Freud and hypnosis: Report of post-rejection use. *Journal of the History of the Behavioral Sciences, 17,* 68–74.

Gray, J. A. (1979). *Ivan Pavlov.* New York: Viking Press.

Green, B. F. (1992). Exposé or smear? The Burt affair. *Psychological Science, 3,* 328–331.

Green, M., & Rieber, R. W. (1980). The assimilation of psychoanalysis in America. In R. W. Rieber & K. Salzinger (Eds.), *Psychology: Theoretical-historical perspectives* (pp. 263–304). New York: Academic Press.

Greenwood, J. D. (1999). Understanding the "cognitive revolution" in psychology. *Journal of the History of the Behavioral Sciences, 35,* 1–22.

Greenwood, J. D. (2003). Wundt, *Völkerpsychologie,* and experimental social psychology. *History of Psychology, 6,* 70–88.

Greer, S. (2002). Freud's "bad conscience": The case of Nietzsche's *Genealogy. Journal of the History of the Behavioral Sciences, 38,* 303–315.

Gregory, R. L. (1966). *Eye and brain: The psychology of seeing.* New York: McGraw-Hill.

Grosskurth, P. (1991). *The secret ring.* Reading, MA: Addison-Wesley Publishing Company, Inc.

Gruber, H. E., & Wallace, D. B. (2001). Creative work: The case of Charles Darwin. *American Psychologist, 56,* 346–349.

Guilford, J. P. (1967a). *The nature of human intelligence.* New York: McGraw-Hill.

Guilford, J. P. (1967b). Joy Paul Guilford. In E. G. Boring & G. Lindzey (Eds.), *A history of psychology in autobiography* (Vol. 5, pp. 167–191). New York: Appleton-Century-Crofts.

Guilford, J. P. (1985). The structure of intellect model. In B. B. Wolman (Ed.), *Handbook of intelligence* (pp. 225–266). New York: Wiley.

Guthrie, E. R. (1930). Conditioning as a principle of learning. *Psychological Review, 37,* 412–428.

Guthrie, E. R. (1934a). Reward and punishment. *Psychological Review, 41,* 450–460.

Guthrie, E. R. (1934b). Pavlov's theory of conditioning. *Psychological Review, 41,* 199–206.

Guthrie, E. R. (1938). *The psychology of human conflict: The clash of motives within the individual.* New York: Harper & Brothers, Publishers.

Guthrie, E. R. (1939). The effect of outcome on learning. *Psychological Review, 46,* 480–484.

Guthrie, E. R. (1940). Association and the law of effect. *Psychological Review, 47,* 127–148.

Guthrie, E. R. (1952). *The psychology of learning* (Rev. ed.). New York: Harper & Brothers, Publishers.

Guthrie, E. R. (1959). Association by contiguity. In S. Koch, *Psychology: A study of a science* (Vol. 2, pp. 158–195). New York: McGraw-Hill Book Company, Inc.

Guthrie, E. R., & Horton, G. P. (1946). *Cats in a puzzle box.* New York: Rinehart.

Guthrie, R. V. (1998). *Even the rat was white: A historical view of psychology* (2nd ed.). Boston: Allyn and Bacon.

Guthrie, R. V. (2000). Francis Cecil Sumner: The first African American pioneer in psychology. In G. A. Kimble & M. Wertheimer (Eds.), *Portraits of pioneers in psychology* (Vol. IV, pp. 181–193). Mahwah, NJ: Lawrence Erlbaum Associates, Publishers.

Hale, N. G., Jr. (1995). *The rise and crisis of psychoanalysis in the United States.* New York: Oxford University Press.

Halford, G. S. (1989). Reflections on 25 years of Piagetian cognitive developmental psychology, 1963–1988. *Human Development, 32,* 325–357.

Hall, C. S. (1954). *A primer of Freudian psychology.* New York: Mentor.

Hall, G. S. (1883). The contents of children's minds. *Princeton Review, 11,* 249–272.

Hall, G. S. (1923). *Life and confessions of a psychologist.* New York: Appleton.

Hamilton, G. V. (1911). A study of trial-and-error reactions in mammals. *Journal of Animal Behavior, 1,* 33–66.

Hamilton, G. V. (1916). A study of perseverance reactions in primates and rodents. *Behavior Monographs, 3* (Serial No. 13).

Handel, S. (1989). *Listening: An introduction to the perception of auditory events.* Cambridge, MA: MIT Press.

Hannush, M. J. (1987). John B. Watson remembered: An interview with James B. Watson. *Journal of the History of the Behavioral Sciences, 23,* 137–152.

Harlow, H. F. (1951). Primate learning. In C. P. Stone (Ed.), *Comparative psychology* (pp. 183–238). Englewood Cliffs, NJ: Prentice-Hall.

Harlow, H. F. (1962). The heterosexual affectional system in monkeys. *American Psychologist, 17,* 1–9.

Harlow, H. F., & Harlow, M. K. (1965). The affectional systems. In A. M. Schrier, H. F. Harlow, & F. Stollnitz (Eds.), *Behavior of nonhuman primates: Mo-dern research trends* (Vol. 2, pp. 287–334). New York: Academic Press.

Harlow, J. M. (1868). Recovery from the passage of an iron bar through the head. *Massachusetts Medical Society Publication, 2,* 329–347.

Harms, E. (1972). America's first major psychologist: Laurens Perseus Hickok. *Journal of the History of the Behavioral Sciences, 8,* 120–123.

Harré, R., & Secord, P. F. (1973). *The explanation of social behavior.* Totowa, NJ: Littlefield, Adams & Company.

Harris, B. (1979). Whatever happened to Little Albert? *American Psychologist, 34,* 151–160.

Harris, C. S. (2001). Hans Wallach (1904–1998). *American Psychologist, 56,* 73–74.

Harrower, M. (1983). *Kurt Koffka: An unwitting self-portrait.* Gainesville, FL: University Presses of Florida.

Hartley, D. (1966). *Observations on man, his frame, his duty, and his expectations.* Gainesville, FL: Scholars' Facsimiles & Reprints. (Original work published 1749)

Hartley, M., & Commire, A. (1990). *Breaking the silence.* New York: Putnam's.

Hastorf, A., & Cantril, H. (1954). They saw a game: A case study. *Journal of Abnormal and Social Psychology, 49,* 129–134.

Hayes, B. (1993). Reading Darwin on disk. *American Scientist, 81,* 482.

Hayes, C. (1951). *The ape in our house.* New York: Harper.

Hays, R. (1962). Psychology of the scientist: III. Introduction to "passages from the 'idea books' of Clark L. Hull." *Perceptual and Motor Skills, 15,* 803–806.

Hearnshaw, L. S. (1979). *Cyril Burt, psychologist.* Ithaca, NY: Cornell University Press.

Hearst, E. (Ed.) (1979). *The first century of experimental psychology.* Hillsdale, NJ: Lawrence Erlbaum Associates, Publishers.

Hearst, E. (1999). After the puzzle boxes: Thorndike in the 20th century. *Journal of the Experimental Analysis of Behavior, 72,* 441–446.

Hebb, D. O. (1949). *The organization of behavior.* New York: Wiley.

Hebb, D. O. (1959). Karl Spencer Lashley: 1890–1958. *American Journal of Psychology, 72,* 142–150.

Hebb, D. O. (1963). Introduction to Dover edition. In K. S. Lashley, *Brain mechanisms and intelligence* (pp. v–xiii). New York: Dover Publications, Inc.

Hebb, D. O. (1980). D. O. Hebb. In G. Lindzey (Ed.), *A history of psychology in autobiography* (Vol. 7, pp. 272–303). San Francisco: W. H. Freeman and Company.

Hecht, J. M. (1997). A vigilant anthropology: Léonce Manouvrier and the disappearing numbers. *Journal of the History of the Behavioral Sciences, 33,* 221–240.

Heidbreder, E. (1933). *Seven psychologies.* New York: Appleton-Century-Crofts.

Heidbreder, E. (1972). Mary Whiton Calkins: A discussion. *Journal of the History of the Behavioral Sciences, 8,* 56–68.

Heidegger, M. (1962). *Being and time* (J. Macquarrie & E. Robinson, Trans.). New York: Harper & Row. (Original work published 1927)

Heider, F. (1958). *The psychology of interpersonal relations.* New York: Wiley.

Heider, F. (1970). Gestalt theory: Early history and reminiscences. *Journal of the History of the Behavioral Sciences, 6,* 131–139.

Heider, F. (1989). Fritz Heider. In G. Lindzey (Ed.), *A history of psychology in autobiography* (Vol. 8, pp. 126–155). Stanford, CA: Stanford University Press.

Heims, S. (1978). Kurt Lewin and social change. *Journal of the History of the Behavioral Sciences, 14,* 238–241.

Helson, H. (1933). The fundamental propositions of Gestalt psychology. *Psychological Review, 40,* 13–32.

Henle, M. (1961). *Documents of Gestalt psychology.* Berkeley, CA: University of California Press.

Henle, M. (1971). Did Titchener commit the stimulus error? The problem of meaning in structural psychology. *Journal of the History of the Behavioral Sciences, 7,* 279–282.

Henle, M. (1971). *The selected papers of Wolfgang Köhler.* New York: Liveright.

Henle, M. (1978a). One man against the Nazis: Wolfgang Köhler. *American Psychologist, 33,* 939–944.

Henle, M. (1978b). Kurt Lewin as metatheorist. *Journal of the History of the Behavioral Sciences, 14,* 233–237.

Henle, M. (1979). Phenomenology in Gestalt psychology. *Journal of Phenomenological Psychology, 10,* 1–17.

Henle, M. (1980). The influence of Gestalt psychology in America. In R. W. Rieber & K. Salzinger (Eds.), *Psychology: Theoretical-historical perspectives* (pp. 177–190). New York: Academic Press.

Henle, M. (1984). Robert M. Ogden and Gestalt psychology in America. *Journal of the History of the Behavioral Sciences, 20,* 9–19.

Henle, M. (1986). *1879 and all that: Essays in the theory and history of psychology.* New York: Columbia University Press.

Henle, M. (1987). Koffka's *Principles* after fifty years. *Journal of the History of the Behavioral Sciences, 23,* 14–21.

Henle, M. (1990). William James and Gestalt psychology. In M. Johnson & T. Henley (Eds.), *Reflections on* The Principles of Psychology: *William James after a century* (pp. 77–99). Hillsdale, NJ: Lawrence Erlbaum Associates, Publishers.

Henle, M. (1991). Systems as reconceptualizations: The work of Edna Heidbreder. In G. A. Kimble, M. Wertheimer, & C. L. White (Eds.), *Portraits of pioneers in psychology* (pp. 292–305). Hillsdale, NJ: Lawrence Erlbaum Associates, Publishers.

Henley, T. B. (1988). Beyond Husserl. *American Psychologist, 43,* 402–403.

Henley, T. B. (1989). Meehl revisited: A look at paradigms in psychology. *Theoretical and Philosophical Psychology, 9,* 30–36.

Henley, T. B. (1990). Natural problems and artificial intelligence. *Behavior and Philosophy, 18,* 43–56.

Henley, T. B., & Thorne, B. M. (1992). Eminent psychologists or psychological eminence? *American Psychologist, 47,* 1147–1148.

Henley, T. B., Johnson, M. G., Herzog, H. A., & Jones, E. M., (1989). Definitions of psychology. *The Psychological Record, 39,* 143–152.

Henry, L. C. (Ed.) (1955). *Best quotations for all occasions.* New York: Fawcett Premier.

Herrnstein, R. J. (1969). Behaviorism. In D. L. Krantz (Ed.), *Schools of psychology* (pp. 51–68). New York: Meredith Corp.

Herrnstein, R. J., & Murray, C. (1994). *The bell curve.* New York: The Free Press.

Heyd, T. (1989). Mill and Comte on psychology. *Journal of the History of the Behavioral Sciences, 25,* 125–138.

Hibbard, S., & Henley, T. (1994). Is psychology really 'The study of behavior'? A conceptual analysis of 'behavior' and some recommendations on the use of 'behavior' in psychology. *Theory & Psychology, 4,* 549–569.

Hilgard, E. R. (1939). Review of B. F. Skinner's *The Behavior of Organisms. Psychological Bulletin, 36,* 121–125.

Hilgard, E. R. (1957). Louis Madison Terman (1877–1956). *American Journal of Psychology, 70,* 472–479.

Hilgard, E. R. (1987). *Psychology in America: A historical survey.* San Diego: Harcourt Brace Jovanovich.

Hilgard, E. R. (1991). Harvey Carr and Chicago functionalism: A simulated interview. In G. A. Kimble, M. Wertheimer, & C. L. White (Eds.), *Portraits of pioneers in psychology* (pp. 120–136). Hillsdale, NJ: Lawrence Erlbaum Associates, Publishers.

Hilgard, E. R. (1993). Which psychologists prominent in the second half of this century made lasting contributions to psychological theory? *Psychological Science, 4,* 70–80.

Hilgard, E. R., Leary, D. E., & McGuire, G. R. (1991). The history of psychology: A survey and critical assessment. *Annual Review of Psychology, 42,* 79–107.

Hilgard, E. R., & Marquis, D. G. (1940). *Conditioning and learning.* New York: Appleton-Century-Crofts.

Hill, W. F. (1971). *Learning: A survey of psychological interpretations* (Rev. ed.). Scranton, PA: Chandler Publishing Co.

Hindeland, M. J. (1971). Edward Bradford Titchener: A pioneer in perception. *Journal of the History of the Behavioral Sciences, 7,* 23–28.

Hinkelman, E. A., & Aderman, M. (1968). Apparent theoretical parallels between G. Stanley Hall and Carl Jung. *Journal of the History of the Behavioral Sciences, 4,* 254–257.

Hirshbein, L. D. (2002). The senile mind: Psychology and old age in the 1930s and 1940s. *Journal of the History of the Behavioral Sciences, 38,* 43–56.

Hobbes, T. (1914). *Leviathan.* London: J. M. Dent & Sons Ltd. (Original work published 1651)

Hodos, W., & Campbell, C. B. G. (1969). *Scala naturae:* Why there is no theory in comparative psychology. *Psychological Review, 76,* 337–350.

Hoffeld, D. R. (1980). Mesmer's failure: Sex, politics, personality, and the zeitgeist. *Journal of the History of the Behavioral Sciences, 16,* 377–386.

Hoffert, S. D. (2003). *A history of gender in America: Essays, documents, and articles.* Upper Saddle River, NJ: Prentice Hall.

Hoffman, R. R., Bringmann, W., Bamberg, M., & Klein, R. (1987). Some historical observations on Ebbinghaus. In D. S. Gorfein & R. R. Hoffman (Eds.), *Memory and learning: The Ebbinghaus Centennial Conference* (pp. 57–75). Hillsdale, NJ: Erlbaum.

Hofstadter, D. R. (1979). *Gödel, Escher, Bach: An eternal golden braid.* New York: Basic Books.

Hogan, J. D. (2003). G. Stanley Hall: Educator, organizer, and pioneer developmental psychologist. In G. A. Kimble & M. Wertheimer (Eds.), *Portraits of pioneers in psychology* (Vol. V, pp. 19–36). Mahwah, NJ: Lawrence Erlbaum Associates, Publishers.

Hogan, J. D., & Broudy, M. S. (2000). June Etta Downey (1875–1932): Psychologist, poet, philosopher. *Psychology of Women, 27,* 25.

Hogan, J. D., Goshtasbpour, F., Laufer, M. R., & Haswell, E. (1998). Teaching the history of psychology: What's hot and what's not. *Teaching of Psychology, 25,* 206–208.

Hohman, G. W. (1966). Some effects of spinal cord lesions on experienced emotional feelings. *Psychophysiology, 3,* 143–156.

Hollingworth, L. S. (1913). The frequency of amentia as related to sex. *Medical Record, 84,* 753–756.

Hopkins, J. R. (1995). Erik Homburger Erikson (1902–1994). *American Psychologist, 50,* 796–797.

Horgan, J. (1999). The undiscovered mind: How the human brain defies replication, medication, and explanation. *Psychological Science, 10,* 470–474.

Horley, J. (2001). After "The Baltimore Affair": James Mark Baldwin's life and work, 1908–1934. *History of Psychology, 4,* 24–33.

Horn, J. (2001). Raymond Bernard Cattell (1905–1998). *American Psychologist, 56,* 71–72.

Horney, K. (1939). *New ways in psychoanalysis.* New York: W. W. Norton & Company.

Hornstein, G. A. (1992). The return of the repressed: Psychology's problematic relations with psychoanalysis, 1909–1960. *American Psychologist, 47,* 254–263.

Hovland, C. I. (1952). Clark Leonard Hull (1884–1952). *Psychological Review, 59,* 347–350.

Hovland, C. I., Janis, I. L., & Kelley, H. H. (1953). *Communication and persuasion.* New Haven, CT: Yale University Press.

Hovland, C. I., Lumsdaine, A. A., & Sheffield, F. D. (1949). *Experiments on mass communications.* Princeton, NJ: Princeton University Press.

Hovland, C. I., & Weiss, W. (1951). The influence of source credibility on communication effectiveness. *Public Opinion Quarterly, 15,* 635–650.

Howard, G. S. (1992). William James: Closet clinician. In M. Donnelly (Ed.), *Reinterpreting the legacy of William James* (pp. 313–322). Washington, DC: American Psychological Association.

Howes, E. P. (1929). The meaning of progress in the Woman Movement. *Annals of the American Academy of Political and Social Science, 143,* 14– 20.

Hsueh, Y. (2002). The Hawthorne experiments and the introduction of Jean Piaget in American industrial psychology, 1929–1932. *History of Psychology, 5,* 163–189.

Huguelet, T. L. (1966). Introduction. In D. Hartley, *Observations on man, his frame, his duty, and his expectations* (pp. v–xvi). Gainesville, FL: Scholars' Facsimiles & Reprints.

Hull, C. L. (1929). A functional interpretation of the conditioned reflex. *Psychological Review, 36,* 498–511.

Hull, C. L. (1930). Simple trial and error learning. *Psychological Review, 37,* 241–256.

Hull, C. L. (1937). Mind, mechanism, and adaptive behavior. *Psychological Review, 44,* 1–32.

Hull, C. L. (1943). *Principles of behavior: An introduction to behavior theory.* New York: Appleton-Century-Crofts, Inc.

Hull, C. L. (1952a). Clark L. Hull. In E. G. Boring, H. S. Langfeld, H. Werner, & R. M. Yerkes (Eds.), *A history of psychology in autobiography* (Vol. 4, pp. 143–162). Worcester, MA: Clark University Press.

Hull, C. L. (1952b). *A behavior system.* New Haven, CT: Yale University Press.

Hull, C. L. (1962). Psychology of the scientist: IV. Passages from the 'idea books' of Clark L. Hull. *Perceptual and Motor Skills, 15,* 807–882.

Hume, D. (1955). *An inquiry concerning human understanding.* Indianapolis, IN: Bobbs-Merrill. (Original work published 1748; "My own life," a brief autobiographical sketch, was originally published 1776)

Humphrey, N. (1983). *Consciousness regained.* Oxford, England: Oxford University Press.

Hunt, J. M. (1984). Orval Hobart Mowrer (1907–1982). *American Psychologist, 39,* 912–914.

Hunter, W. S. (1913). The delayed reaction in animals and children. *Behavior Monographs, 2* (No. 6).

Hunter, W. S. (1952). Walter S. Hunter. In E. G. Boring, H. S. Langfeld, H. Werner, & R. M. Yerkes (Eds.), *A history of psychology in autobiography* (Vol. 4, pp. 163–187). Worcester, MA: Clark University Press.

Hurvich, L. M., & Jameson, D. (1957). An opponent-process theory of color vision. *Psychological Review, 64,* 384–404.

Hurvich, L. M., & Jameson, D. (1974). Opponent processes as a model of neural organization. *American Psychologist, 29,* 88–102.

Husserl, E. (1931). *Ideas: General introduction to pure phenomenology* (W. R. B. Gibson, Trans.). New York: Macmillan. (Original work published 1913)

Ihde, D. (1979). *Experimental phenomenology.* New York: Paragon Books.

Inhelder, B. (1977). Genetic epistemology and developmental psychology. In R. W. Rieber & K. Salzinger (Eds.), *The roots of American psychology: Historical influences and implications for the future* (pp. 332–341). New York: The New York Academy of Sciences.

Inhelder, B. (1989). Bärbel Inhelder. In G. Lindzey (Ed.), *A history of psychology in autobiography* (Vol. 8, pp. 208–243). Stanford, CA: Stanford University Press.

Innes, J. M. (1969). A note on the usefulness of biographical material. *Journal of the History of the Behavioral Sciences, 5,* 268.

Innis, N. K. (1992). Tolman and Tryon: Early research on the inheritance of the ability to learn. *American Psychologist, 47,* 190–197.

Innis, N. K. (1997). A purposive behaviorist: Edward C. Tolman. In W. G. Bringmann, H. E. Lück, R. Miller, & C. E. Early (Eds.), *A pictorial history of psychology* (pp. 214–220). Carol Stream, IL: Quintessence Publishing Co., Inc.

Irvine, W. (1955). *Apes, angels, and Victorians.* Cleveland, OH: The World Publishing Co.

Irwin, F. W. (1943). Edwin Burket Twitmyer: 1873–1943. *American Journal of Psychology, 56,* 451–453.

Ivnik, R. J., Smith, G. E., Malec, J. F., Kokmen, E., & Tangalos, E. G. (1994). Mayo Cognitive Factor Scales: Distinguishing normal and clinical samples by profile variability. *Neuropsychology, 8,* 203–209.

Jackson, S. W. (1969). Galen—on mental disorders. *Journal of the History of the Behavioral Sciences, 5,* 365–384.

Jaeger, S. (1997). Wolfgang Köhler. In W. G. Bringmann, H. E. Lück, R. Miller, & C. E. Early (Eds.), *A pictorial history of psychology* (pp. 277–281). Carol Stream, IL: Quintessence Publishing Co., Inc.

Jaensch, E. R. (1909). Hermann Ebbinghaus. *Zeitschrift für Psychologie, 51,* i–vii.

Jahoda, G. (1997). Wilhelm Wundt's *"Völkerpsychologie."* In W. G. Bringmann, H. E. Lück, R. Miller, & C. E. Early (Eds.), *A pictorial history of psychology* (pp. 148–152). Chicago: Quintessence Publishing Co., Inc.

James, H., (Ed.) (1920). *The letters of William James.* Boston: The Atlantic Monthly Press.

James, W. (1890). *The principles of psychology* (Vols. 1–2). New York: Henry Holt.

James, W. (1894). The physical basis of emotion. *Psychological Review, 1,* 516–529.

Janet, P. (1930). Pierre Janet. In C. Murchison (Ed.), *History of psychology in autobiography* (Vol. 1, pp. 123–133). Worcester, MA: Clark University Press.

Janos, P. M., & Robinson, N. M. (1985). Psychosocial development in intellectually gifted children. In F. D. Horowitz & M. O'Brien (Eds.), *The gifted and talented: Developmental perspectives.* Washington, DC: American Psychological Association.

Jaspers, K. (1969). *Philosophy* (Vol. 1; E. B. Ashton, Trans.). Chicago: The University of Chicago Press. (Original work published 1932)

Jenkins, J. J. (1993). What counts as "behavior"? *The Journal of Mind and Behavior, 14,* 355–364.

Jennings, J. (1986). Husserl revisited: The forgotten distinction between psychology and phenomenology. *American Psychologist, 41,* 1231–1240.

Jensen, A. R. (1969). How much can we boost IQ and scholastic achievement? *Harvard Educational Review, 39,* 1–123.

Jensen, A. R. (1974). Kinship correlations reported by Sir Cyril Burt. *Behavior Genetics, 4,* 1–28.

Jensen, A. R. (1980). *Précis of Bias in Mental Testing. Behavioral and Brain Sciences, 3,* 325–372.

Jensen, A. R. (1981). *Straight talk about mental tests.* New York: The Free Press.

Jensen, A. R. (1982). The debunking of scientific fossils and straw persons. *Contemporary Education Review, 1,* 121–135.

Jensen, A. R. (1985). The nature of the black-white difference on various psychometric tests: Spearman's hypothesis. *Behavioral and Brain Sciences, 8,* 193–264.

Jensen, A. R. (2000). Hans Eysenck: Apostle of the London School. In G. A. Kimble & M. Wertheimer (Eds.), *Portraits of pioneers in psychology* (Vol. IV, pp. 339–357). Mahwah, NJ: Lawrence Erlbaum Associates, Publishers.

John, M., Eckardt, G., & Hiebsch, H. (1989). Kurt Lewin's early intentions (dedicated to his 100th birthday). *European Journal of Social Psychology, 19,* 163–169.

Johnson, D. F. (2000). Cultivating the field of psychology: Psychological journals at the turn of the century and beyond. *American Psychologist, 55,* 1144–1147.

Johnson, M. G., & Henley, T. B. (Eds.) (1990). *Reflections on* The Principles of Psychology. Hillsdale, NJ: Lawrence Erlbaum Associates, Publishers.

Johnson, M. G., & Henley, T. B. (1992). Finding meaning in random analogies. *Metaphor and Symbolic Activity, 7,* 55–75.

Johnson, R. C., McClearn, G. E., Yuen, S., Nagoshi, C. T., Ahern, F. M., & Cole, R. E. (1985). Galton's data a century later. *American Psychologist, 40,* 875–892.

Johnston, E. B. (2001). The repeated reproduction of Bartlett's *Remembering. History of Psychology, 4,* 341–366.

Johnston, T. D. (1995). The influence of Weismann's germ-plasm theory on the distinction between learned and innate behavior. *Journal of the History of the Behavioral Sciences, 31,* 115–128.

Johnston, T. D. (2002). An early manuscript in the history of American comparative psychology: Lewis Henry Morgan's "Animal Psychology" (1857). *History of Psychology, 5,* 323–355.

Jones, E. (1953). *The life and work of Sigmund Freud* (Vol. 1). New York: Basic Books, Inc.

Jones, E. (1955). *The life and work of Sigmund Freud* (Vol. 2). New York: Basic Books, Inc.

Jones, E. (1957). *The life and work of Sigmund Freud* (Vol. 3). New York: Basic Books, Inc.

Jones, E. E., & Davis, K. (1965). From acts to dispositions: The attribution process in person perception. In L. Berkowitz (Ed.), *Advances in experimental psychology* (Vol. 2, pp. 219–266). New York: Academic Press.

Jones, E. E., & Nisbett, R. E. (1972). The actor and the observer: Divergent perceptions of the causes of behavior. In E. E. Jones, D. E. Kanouse, H. H. Kelley, R. E. Nisbett, S. Valins, & B. Weiner (Eds.), *Attribution: Perceiving the causes of behavior* (pp. 79–94). Morristown, NJ: General Learning Press.

Jones, M. C. (1924a). A laboratory study of fear: The case of Peter. *Pedagogical Seminary, 31,* 308–315.

Jones, M. C. (1924b). The elimination of children's fears. *Journal of Experimental Psychology, 7,* 382–390.

Jones, M. C. (1974). Albert, Peter and John B. Watson. *American Psychologist, 29,* 581–583.

Jones, R. A. (1987). Psychology, history, and the press: The case of William McDougall and *The New York Times. American Psychologist, 42,* 931–940.

Jones, W. H. S. (1923). *Hippocrates* (Vol. 2). New York: Putnam.

Joravsky, D. (1988). L. S. Vygotskii: The muffled deity of Soviet psychology.

In M. G. Ash & W. R. Woodward (Eds.), *Psychology in twentieth-century thought and society* (pp. 189–211). Cambridge: Cambridge University Press.

Joynson, R. B. (1989). *The Burt affair.* London: Routledge.

Julien, R. M. (1995). *A primer of drug action* (7th ed.). New York: W. H. Freeman and Company.

Jung, C. G. (1923). *Psychological types or the psychology of individuation* (H. G. Baynes, Trans.). New York: Harcourt, Brace. (Original work published 1921)

Jung, C. G. (1933). *Modern man in search of a soul* (W. S. Dell & C. F. Baynes, Trans.). New York: Harcourt, Brace & World, Inc.

Jung, C. G. (1939). *The integration of the personality* (S. Dell, Trans.). New York: Farrar & Rinehart, Inc.

Jung, C. G. (1961). *Memories, dreams, reflections.* New York: Pantheon Books.

Jung, C. G. (1968). *Analytical psychology: Its theory and practice (The Tavistock Lectures).* New York: Pantheon Books.

Kahlbaugh, P. E. (1993). James Mark Baldwin: A bridge between social and cognitive theories of development. *The Journal for the Theory of Social Behavior, 23,* 79–103.

Kahneman, D., & Tversky, A. (1972). Subjective probability: A judgment of representativeness. *Cognitive Psychology, 3,* 430–454.

Kahneman, D., & Tversky, A. (1973). On the psychology of prediction. *Psychological Review, 80,* 237–251.

Kamin, L. J. (1974). *The science and politics of IQ.* Potomac, MD: Erlbaum Associates.

Kaminski, G. (1997). Roger Barker's ecological psychology. In W. G. Bringmann, H. E. Lück, R. Miller, & C. E. Early (Eds.), *A pictorial history of psychology* (pp. 288–292). Carol Stream, IL: Quintessence Publishing Co., Inc.

Kant, I. (1929). *Critique of pure reason* (N. K. Smith, Trans.). New York: St. Martin's Press. (Original work published 1787)

Kantor, J. R. (1929). *An outline of social psychology.* Chicago: Follett Publishing Company.

Kantor, J. R. (1936). *An objective psychology of grammar.* Bloomington, IN: Indiana University Publications.

Kaufman, W. (1956). *Existentialism from Dostoevsky to Sartre.* New York: World Publishing Company.

Kaufmann, W. (1974). *Nietzsche: Philosopher, psychologist, antichrist* (4th ed.). Princeton, NJ: Princeton University Press.

Keller, F. S. (1991). Burrhus Frederick Skinner (1904–1990). *Journal of the History of the Behavioral Sciences, 27,* 3–6.

Kelley, H. H. (1972). Attribution in social interaction. In E. E. Jones, D. E. Kanouse, H. H. Kelley, R. E. Nisbett, S. Valins, & B. Weiner (Eds.), *Attribution: Perceiving the causes of behavior* (pp. 151–174). Morristown, NJ: General Learning Press.

Kelly, G. A. (1955). *The psychology of personal constructs.* New York: W. W. Norton & Company.

Kemp, S. (1996). *Cognitive psychology in the Middle Ages.* Westport, CT: Greenwood Press.

Kemp, S. (1997). A medieval controversy about odor. *Journal of the History of the Behavioral Sciences, 33,* 211–219.

Kemp, S. (1998). Medieval theories of mental representation. *History of Psychology, 4,* 275–288.

Kendler, H. K. (2001). Subjective science and natural science. *History of Psychology, 4,* 195–197.

Kendler, H. K. (2002). A personal encounter with psychology (1937–2002). *History of Psychology, 5,* 52–84.

Kent, G. H., & Rosanoff, A. J. (1910). A study of association in insanity. *American Journal of Insanity, 67,* 37–96, 317–390.

Kernberg, O. F. (1976). *Object-relations theory and clinical psychoanalysis.* New York: Aronson.

Kimball, M. M. (2000). From "Anna O." to Bertha Pappenheim: Transforming private pain into public action. *History of Psychology, 3,* 20–43.

Kimble, G. A. (1990). A search for principles in *Principles of Psychology. Psychological Science, 1,* 151–155.

Kimble, G. A. (1991). Psychology from the standpoint of a mechanist: An appreciation of Clark L. Hull. In G. A. Kimble, M. Wertheimer, & C. L. White (Eds.), *Portraits of pioneers in psychology* (pp. 208–225). Hillsdale, NJ: Lawrence Erlbaum Associates, Publishers.

Kimble, G. A. (1994). A new formula for behaviorism. *Psychological Review, 101,* 254–258.

Kimble, G. A. (1996). Ivan Mikhailovich Sechenov: Pioneer in Russian reflexology. In G. A. Kimble, C. A. Boneau, & M. Wertheimer (Eds.), *Portraits of pioneers in psychology* (Vol. II, pp. 33–45). Mahwah, NJ: Lawrence Erlbaum Associates, Publishers.

Kimble, G. A. (1998). Kenneth W. Spence: Theorist with an empiricist conscience. In G. A. Kimble & M. Wertheimer (Eds.), *Portraits of pioneers in psychology* (Vol. III, pp. 277–292). Mahwah, NJ: Lawrence Erlbaum Associates, Inc.

Kimble, G. A. (2000). Behaviorism and unity in psychology. *Current Directions in Psychological Science, 9,* 208–212.

King, D. B. (2000). George Croom Robertson and *Mind:* The story of psychology's first editor. In G. A. Kimble & M. Wertheimer (Eds.), *Portraits of pioneers in psychology* (Vol. IV, pp. 33–48). Mahwah, NJ: Lawrence Erlbaum Associates, Publishers.

Kintsch, W. (1985). Reflections on Ebbinghaus. *Journal of Experimental Psychology: Learning, Memory, and Cognition, 11,* 461–463.

Kirk, G. S., Raven, J. E., & Schofield, M. (Eds.) (1983). *The Presocratic philosophers* (2nd ed.). Cambridge: Cambridge University Press.

Klein, S. B. (2002). *Learning: Principles and application* (4th ed.). New York: McGraw-Hill, Inc.

Kleinfeld, J. S. (2001). *Could it be a big world after all? The "six degrees of separation" myth.* Retrieved September 26, 2003, from http://www.uaf.edu/northern/big_world.html

Klopfer, W. G. (1973). The short history of projective techniques. *Journal of the History of the Behavioral Sciences, 9,* 60–65.

Knight, M. (Ed.) (1950). *William James.* Harmondsworth, England: Penguin Books.

Knowles. D. (1988). *The evolution of medieval thought* (2nd ed.). London: Longman Group UK Limited.

Koch, S. (1975). Language communities, search cells, and the psychological studies. *Nebraska Symposium on Motivation, 23,* 477–560.

Koch, S. (1992). Wundt's creature at age zero—and as centenarian: Some aspects of the institutionalization of the "new psychology." In S. Koch & D. E. Leary (Eds.), *A century of psychology as science* (pp. 7–35). Washington, DC: American Psychological Association.

Koelsch, W. A. (1990). The "magic decade" revisited: Clark psychology in the twenties and thirties. *Journal of the History of the Behavioral Sciences, 26,* 151–175.

Koenigsberger, L. (1965). *Hermann von Helmholtz* (F. A. Welby, Trans.). New York: Dover Publications, Inc. (Original work published 1906)

Koffka, K. (1922). Perception: An introduction to Gestalttheorie. *Psychological Bulletin, 19,* 531–585.

Koffka, K. (1924). *The growth of the mind* (R. M. Ogden, Trans.). New York: Harcourt.

Koffka, K. (1935). *Principles of Gestalt psychology.* New York: Harcourt.

Köhler, W. (1925). *The mentality of apes.* London: Routledge and Kegan Paul. (Original work published 1917)

Köhler, W. (1947). *Gestalt psychology: An introduction to new concepts in modern psychology.* New York: Liveright. (Original work published 1929)

Köhler, W. (1966). *The place of value in a world of facts.* New York: Liveright. (Original work published 1938)

Köhler, W. (1959). Gestalt psychology today. *American Psychologist, 14,* 727–734.

Kolb, B., & Whishaw, I. Q. (1996). *Fundamentals of human neuropsychology* (4th ed.). New York: W. H. Freeman and Company.

Konorski, J., & Miller, S. (1937). On two types of conditioned reflex. *Journal of General Psychology, 16,* 264–272.

Kopell, B. S. (1968). Pierre Janet's description of hypnotic sleep provoked from a distance. *Journal of the History of the Behavioral Sciences, 4,* 119–123.

Koshtoyants, K. S. (1957). Ivan Petrovich Pavlov and the significance of his works. In I. P. Pavlov, *Experimental psychology and other essays* (pp. 23–53). New York: Philosophical Library.

Kozulin, A. (1986). Vygotsky in context. In L. Vygotsky, *Thought and language* (pp. xi–lvi). Cambridge, MA: MIT Press.

Krantz, D. L., & Allen, D. (1967). The rise and fall of McDougall's instinct doctrine. *Journal of the History of the Behavioral Sciences, 3,* 326–338.

Krantz, D. L., Hall, R., & Allen, D. (1969). William McDougall and the problem of purpose. *Journal of the History of the Behavioral Sciences, 5,* 25–38.

Krech, D. (1967). Introduction to the second printing. In E. C. Tolman, *Purposive behavior in animals and men* (pp. xi–xvi). New York: Appleton-Century-Crofts.

Kreshel, P. J. (1990). John B. Watson at J. Walter Thompson: The legitimation of "science" in advertising. *Journal of Advertising, 19,* 49–59.

Kuhn, T. S. (1970). *The structure of scientific revolutions* (Rev. ed.). Chicago: University of Chicago Press.

Külpe, O. (1895). *Outlines of psychology* (E. B. Titchener, Trans.). New York: The Macmillan Co.

Kuna, D. P. (1978). One-sided portrayal of Münsterberg. *American Psychologist, 33,* 700.

Kuo, Z. Y. (1921). Giving up instincts in psychology. *The Journal of Philosophy, 18,* 645–664.

Kuo, Z. Y. (1922). The nature of unsuccessful acts and their order of elimination in animal learning. *Journal of Comparative Psychology, 2,* 1–27.

Kuo, Z. Y. (1929). The net result of the anti-heredity movement in psychology. *Psychological Review, 36,* 181–199.

Kuo, Z. Y. (1930). The genesis of the cat's responses to the rat. *Journal of Comparative Psychology, 11,* 1–35.

Laing, R. D. (1979, July 20). Round the bend. *New Statesman.*

Lakatos, I. (1978). History of science and its rational reconstructions. In J. Warrall & G. Currie (Eds.), *The methodology of scientific research programmes. Philosophical papers of Imre Lakatos* (Vol. 1, pp. 102–138). Cambridge: Cambridge University Press.

Lakoff, G. (1987). *Women, fire, and dangerous things: What categories reveal about the mind.* Chicago: University of Chicago Press.

Lakoff, G., & Johnson, M. (1980). *Metaphors we live by.* Chicago: University of Chicago Press.

Lamarck, J. B. (1914). *Zoological philosophy* (H. Elliot, Trans.). London: Macmillan. (Original work published 1809)

La Mettrie, J. O. d. (1912). *Man a machine* (M. W. Calkins, Trans.). La Salle, IL: Open Court. (Original work published 1748)

Lamiell, J. T. (1996). William Stern: More than the IQ guy. In G. A. Kimble, C. A. Boneau, & M. Wertheimer (Eds.), *Portraits of pioneers in psychology* (Vol. II, pp. 73–85). Mahwah, NJ: Lawrence Erlbaum Associates, Publishers.

Lander, H. J. (1997). Hermann Ebbinghaus. In W. G. Bringmann, H. E. Lück, R. Miller, & C. E. Early (Eds.), *A pictorial history of psychology* (pp. 167–170). Carol Stream, IL: Quintessence Publishing Co., Inc.

Lang, P. J. (1994). The varieties of emotional experience: A meditation on James-Lange theory. *Psychological Review, 101,* 211–221.

Langfeld, H. S. (1943). Jubilee of the *Psychological Review:* Fifty volumes of the *Psychological Review. Psychological Review, 50,* 143–155.

Langlois, J. H., & Roggman, L. A. (1990). Attractive faces are only average. *Psychological Science, 1,* 115–121.

LaPiere, R. T. (1934). Attitudes versus action. *Social Forces, 13,* 230–237.

Lapointe, F. H. (1970). The origin and evolution of the term "psychology." *American Psychologist, 25,* 640–646.

Lapointe, F. H. (1972). Who originated the term 'psychology'? *Journal of the History of the Behavioral Sciences, 8,* 328–335.

Larson, C. A. (1979). Highlights of Dr. John B. Watson's career in advertising. *The Industrial-Organizational Psychologist, 16,* 3–5.

Larson, C. A., & Sullivan, J. J. (1965). Watson's relation to Titchener. *Journal of the History of the Behavioral Sciences, 1,* 338–354.

Lashley, K. S. (1963). *Brain mechanisms and intelligence.* New York: Dover Publications, Inc. (Original work published 1929)

Lashley, K. S. (1950). In search of the engram. In Society for Experimental Biology (Great Britain), *Physiological mechanisms in animal behaviour* (pp. 454–482). Cambridge: University Press.

Latané, B., & Darley, J. M. (1970). *The unresponsive bystander: Why doesn't he help?* New York: Appleton-Century-Crofts.

Laudan, L. (1977). *Progress and its problems.* Berkeley: University of California Press.

Laver, A. B. (1972). Precursors of psychology in ancient Egypt. *Journal of the History of the Behavioral Sciences, 8,* 181–195.

Lavine, T. Z. (1984). *From Socrates to Sartre: The philosophic quest.* New York: Bantam Books.

Leahey, T. H. (1979). Something old, something new: Attention in Wundt and modern cognitive psychology. *Journal of the History of the Behavioral Sciences, 15,* 242–252.

Leahey, T. H. (1981). The mistaken mirror: On Wundt and Titchener's psychologies. *Journal of the History of the Behavioral Sciences, 17,* 273–282.

Leahey, T. H. (1992). The mythical revolutions of American psychology. *American Psychologist, 47,* 308–318.

Leahey, T. H. (1993). A history of behavior. *Journal of Mind and Behavior, 14,* 345–354.

Leary, D. E. (1978). The philosophical development of the conception of psychology in Germany, 1780–1850. *Journal of the History of the Behavioral Sciences, 14,* 113–121.

Leary, D. E. (1980). The historical foundations of Herbart's mathematization of psychology. *Journal of the History of the Behavioral Sciences, 16,* 150–163.

Leary, D. E. (1982). Kant and modern psychology. In W. Woodward & M. Asch (Eds.), *The problematic science: Psychology in nineteenth-century thought* (pp. 19–21). New York: Praeger.

Leary, D. E. (2002). Obituary: Ernest R. Hilgard (1904–2001). *History of Psychology, 5,* 310–314.

LeBon, G. (1960). *The crowd.* New York: Viking. (Original work published 1895)

Leibniz, G. W. (1949). *New essays concerning human understanding* (A. G. Langley, Trans.). La Salle, IL: Open Court. (Original work published 1765)

Lerner, M. (Ed.) (1961). *Essential works of John Stuart Mill.* New York: Bantam Books.

LeRoy, H. A., & Kimble, G. A. (2003). Harry Frederick Harlow: And one thing led to another . . . In G. A. Kimble & M. Wertheimer (Eds.), *Portraits of pioneers in psychology* (Vol. V, pp. 279–297). Mahwah, NJ: Lawrence Erlbaum Associates, Publishers.

Levin, G. (1975). *Sigmund Freud.* Boston: Twayne Publishers.

Levine, J. M. (1999). Solomon Asch's legacy for group research. *Personality and Social Psychology Review, 3,* 358–364.

Lewin, K. (1931). Environmental forces in child behavior and development. In C. Murchison (Ed.), *Handbook of child psychology* (pp. 94–127). Worcester, MA: Clark University Press.

Lewin, K. (1936). *Principles of topological psychology.* New York: McGraw-Hill.

Lewin, K. (1937). Carl Stumpf. *Psychological Review, 44,* 188–194.

Lewin, K., Dembo, T., Festinger, L., & Sears, P. S. (1944). Level of aspiration. In J. Hunt (Ed.), *Personality and the behavior disorders* (Vol. 1, pp. 333–378). New York: Ronald Press.

Lewin, K., Lippitt, R., & White, R. K. (1939). Patterns of aggressive behavior in experimentally created "social climates." *Journal of Social Psychology, 10,* 271–299.

Lewis, R. W. B. (1991). *The Jameses: A family narrative.* New York: Farrar, Straus and Giroux.

Ley, R. (1990). *A whisper of espionage.* Garden City Park, NY: Avery Publishing Group, Inc.

Leyens, J.-P., & Corneille, O. (1999). Asch's social psychology: Not as social as you think. *Personality and Social Psychology Review, 3,* 345–357.

Leys, R. (1984). Meyer, Watson, and the dangers of behaviorism. *Journal of the History of the Behavioral Sciences, 20,* 128–149.

Libbrecht, K., & Quackelbeen, J. (1995). On the early history of male hysteria and psychic trauma: Charcot's influence on Freudian thought. *Journal of the History of the Behavioral Sciences, 31,* 370–384.

Liebert, R. N., & Baron, R. A. (1972). Some immediate effects of televised violence on children's behavior. *Developmental Psychology, 6,* 469–475.

Likert, R. (1932). A technique for the measurement of attitudes. *Archives of Psychology* (No. 140).

Likert, R. (1947). Kurt Lewin: A pioneer in human relations research. *Human Relations, 1,* 131–139.

Lindenfeld, D. (1978). Oswald Külpe and the Würzburg School. *Journal of the History of the Behavioral Sciences, 14,* 132–141.

Lindsay, A. D. (1934). Introduction. In I. Kant, *Critique of pure reason* (J. M. D. Meiklejohn, Trans.; pp. vii–xx). London: J. M. Dent & Sons Ltd.

Lindzey, G., & Aronson, E. (Eds.) (1985). *The handbook of social psychology* (3rd ed., Vols. 1–2). New York: Random House.

Link, S. W. (1994). Rediscovering the past: Gustav Fechner and signal detection theory. *Psychological Science, 5,* 335–340.

Linschoten, J. (1968). *On the way towards a phenomenological psychology* (A. Giorgi, Trans.). Pittsburgh: Duquesne University Press.

Lippitt, R. (1947). Kurt Lewin, 1890–1947: Adventures in the exploration of interdependence. *Sociometry, 10,* 87–97.

Locke, J. (1964). *An essay concerning human understanding.* New York: New American Library. (Original work published 1690)

Locke, J. (1964). *Some thoughts concerning education* (F. W. Garforth, Ed.). Woodbury, NY: Barron's Educational Series. (Original work published 1693)

Loewi, O. (1960). An autobiographical sketch. *Perspectives in Biology and Medicine, 4,* 3–25.

Loftus, E. F. (1979). *Eyewitness testimony.* Cambridge, MA: Harvard University Press.

Loftus, E. F., & Palmer, J. C. (1974). Reconstruction of automobile destruction: An example of the interaction between language and memory. *Journal of Verbal Learning and Verbal Behavior, 13,* 585–589.

Logan, C. A. (1999). The altered rationale for the choice of a standard animal in experimental psychology: Henry H. Donaldson, Adolf Meyer, and "the" albino rat. *History of Psychology, 2,* 3–24.

Logan, C. A. (2002). When scientific knowledge becomes scientific discovery: The disappearance of classical conditioning before Pavlov. *Journal of the History of the Behavioral Sciences, 38,* 393–403.

Logue, A. W. (1985). Conditioned food aversion learning in humans. In N. S. Braveman & P. Bronstein (Eds.), *Experimental assessment and clinical applications of conditioned food aversions* (pp. 316–329). New York: Annals of the New York Academy of Sciences.

Loomis, L. R. (Ed.) (1942). *Plato: Five great dialogues.* Roslyn, NY: Walter J. Black, Inc.

Loomis, L. R. (Ed.) (1943). *Aristotle: On man in the universe.* Roslyn, NY: Walter J. Black, Inc.

Lorenz, K. (1966). *On aggression* (M. K. Wilson, Trans.). New York: Harcourt,

Brace & World, Inc. (Original work published 1963)

Lovejoy, A. O. (1936). *The great chain of being.* Cambridge, MA: Harvard University Press.

Lovie, A. D., & Lovie, P. (1993). Charles Spearman, Cyril Burt, and the origins of factor analysis. *Journal of the History of the Behavioral Sciences, 29,* 308–321.

Luboshitzky, R., & Lavie, P. (1999). Melatonin and sex hormone interrelationships—a review. *Journal of Pediatric Endocrinology & Metabolism, 12,* 355–362.

Lück, H. E. (1997). Kurt Lewin—Filmmaker. In W. G. Bringmann, H. E. Lück, R. Miller, & C. E. Early (Eds.), *A pictorial history of psychology* (pp. 282–287). Carol Stream, IL: Quintessence Publishing Co., Inc.

Lück, H. E., & Bringmann, W. G. (1997). Hugo Münsterberg: Pioneer of applied psychology. In W. G. Bringmann, H. E. Lück, R. Miller, & C. E. Early (Eds.), *A pictorial history of psychology* (pp. 471–475). Chicago: Quintessence Publishing Co., Inc.

Luria, A. R. (1932). *The nature of human conflict* (W. H. Gantt, Trans.). New York: Liveright.

Luria, A. R. (1968). *The mind of a mnemonist* (L. Solotaroff, Trans.). New York: Basic Books.

Luria, A. R. (1970). The functional organization of the brain. *Scientific American, 222,* 66–78.

Luria, A. R. (1973). *The working brain: An introduction to neuropsychology.* New York: Basic Books.

Luria, A. R. (1974). A. R. Luria. In G. Lindzey (Ed.), *A history of psychology in autobiography* (Vol. 6, pp. 251– 292). Englewood Cliffs, NJ: Prentice-Hall.

Lyman-Henley, L. P., & Henley, T. B. (2000). Some thoughts on the relationship between behaviorism, comparative psychology, and ethology. *Anthrozoos, 13,* 15–21.

Maccoby, E. E. (1989). Eleanor E. Maccoby. In G. Lindzey (Ed.), *A history of psychology in autobiography* (Vol. 8, pp. 290–335). Stanford, CA: Stanford University Press.

Maccoby, E. E., & Jacklin, C. N. (1974). *The psychology of sex differences.* Stanford, CA: Stanford University Press.

MacCorquodale, K., & Meehl, P. E. (1948). On a distinction between hypothetical constructs and intervening variables. *Psychological Review, 55,* 95–107.

MacCoun, R. (2002). Why a psychologist won the Nobel Prize in Economics. *APS Observer, 15,* 1, 8.

Mach, E. (1914). *Analysis of sensations.* La Salle, IL: Open Court. (Original work published 1886)

Machiavelli, N. (1891). *Il principe [The prince].* Oxford: The Clarendon Press. (Original work published 1532)

Mack, W. G. (1997). The Würzburg school of psychology. In W. G. Bringmann, H. E. Lück, R. Miller, & C. E. Early (Eds.), *A pictorial history of psychology* (pp. 177–181). Carol Stream, IL: Quintessence Publishing Co., Inc.

Mackenzie, B. D. (1972). Behaviourism and positivism. *Journal of the History of the Behavioral Sciences, 8,* 222–231.

MacLennan, B. (1995). *Word and flux.* Unpublished manuscript.

Macmillan, M. (2000). Nineteenth-century inhibitory theories of thinking: Bain, Ferrier, Freud (and Phineas Gage). *History of Psychology, 3,* 187–217.

MacNamara, J. (1993). Cognitive psychology and rejection of Brentano. *Journal for the Theory of Social Behaviour, 23,* 117–137.

Madigan, S., & O'Hara, R. (1992). Short-term memory at the turn of the century: Mary Whiton Calkins's memory research. *American Psychologist, 47,* 170–174.

Magner, L. N. (1992). *A history of medicine.* New York: Marcel Dekker, Inc.

Magoun, H. W. (1981). John B. Watson and the study of human sexual behavior. *The Journal of Sex Research, 17,* 368–378.

Maher, W. B., & Maher, B. A. (1985). Psychopathology: I. From ancient times to the eighteenth century. In G. A. Kimble & K. Schlesinger (Eds.), *Topics in the history of psychology* (Vol. 2). Hillsdale, NJ: Lawrence Erlbaum Associates, Publishers.

Maimonides, M. (1963). *The guide of the perplexed.* Chicago: University of Chicago Press. (Original work published 1190)

Malle, B. F., & Ickes, W. (2000). Fritz Heider: Philosopher and social psychologist. In G. A. Kimble & M. Wertheimer (Eds.), *Portraits of pioneers in psychology* (Vol. IV, pp. 195–213). Mahwah, NJ: Lawrence Erlbaum Associates, Publishers.

Malone, J. C. (1991). *Theories of learning: A historical approach.* Belmont, CA: Wadsworth Publishing Co.

Mandler, G. (2002a). Origins of the cognitive (r)evolution. *Journal of the History of the Behavioral Sciences, 38,* 339–353.

Mandler, G. (2002b). Psychologists and the National Socialist access to power. *History of Psychology, 5,* 190–200.

Maniou-Vakali, M. (1974). Some Aristotelian views on learning and memory. *Journal of the History of the Behavioral Sciences, 10,* 47–55.

Maratsos, M. (1983). Some current issues in the study of the acquisition of grammar. In J. H. Flavell & E. M. Markman (Eds.), *Cognitive development* (pp. 706–788). New York: Wiley.

Marbe, K. (1936). Karl Marbe. In C. Murchison (Ed.), *A history of psychology in autobiography* (Vol. 3, pp. 181–213). Worcester, MA: Clark University Press.

Marks, R. L. (1991). *Three men of the Beagle.* New York: Alfred A. Knopf.

Marshall, L. H., & Magoun, H. W. (1998). *Discoveries in the human brain.* Totowa, NJ: Humana Press.

Marshall, M. (1990). The theme of quantification and the hidden Weber in the early work of Gustav Theodor Fechner. *Canadian Psychology/Psychologie Canadienne, 31,* 45–53.

Marshall, M. E. (1969). Gustav Fechner, Dr. Mises, and The Comparative Anatomy of Angels. *Journal of the History of the Behavioral Sciences, 5,* 39–58.

Martindale, C. (2001). Oscillations and analogies: Thomas Young, MD, FRS, genius. *American Psychologist, 56,* 342–345.

Marx, J. L. (1975). Opiate receptors: Implications and applications. *Science, 189,* 708–710.

Marx, O. M. (1970). Morton Prince and the dissociation of a personality. *Journal of the History of the Behavioral Sciences, 6,* 120–130.

Maslow, A. H. (1936). The role of dominance in the social and sexual behavior of infrahuman primates: 1. Observations at Vilas Park Zoo. *Journal of Genetic Psychology, 48,* 261–277.

Maslow, A. H. (1966). *The psychology of science: A reconnaissance.* New York: Harpor & Row.

Masson, J. M. (1984). *The assault on truth: Freud's suppression of the seduction theory.* New York: Farrar, Straus, and Giroux.

Masterton, R. B. (1998). Charles Darwin: Father of evolutionary psychology. In G. A. Kimble & M. Wertheimer (Eds.), *Portraits of pioneers in psychology.* (Vol. III, pp. 17–29). Mahwah, NJ: Lawrence Erlbaum Associates, Publishers.

Matarazzo, J. D. (1979). *Wechsler's measurement and appraisal of adult intelligence* (5th ed.). New York: Oxford University Press.

Matarazzo, J. D. (1992). Psychological testing and assessment in the 21st century. *American Psychologist, 47,* 1007–1018.

May, R. (1950). *The meaning of anxiety.* New York: Ronald Press.

May, R. (Ed.) (1961). *Existential psychology.* New York: Random House.

Mayo, E. (1933). *The human problems of an industrial civilization.* New York: Macmillan.

Mayrhauser, R. T. von. (1989). Making intelligence functional: Walter Dill Scott and applied psychological testing in World War I. *Journal of the History of the Behavioral Sciences, 25,* 60–72.

Mazlish, B. (1975). *James and John Stuart Mill.* New York: Basic Books.

McCauley, C., & Rozin, P. (2003). Solomon Asch: Scientist and humanist. In G. A. Kimble & M. Wertheimer (Eds.), *Portraits of pioneers in psychology* (Vol. V, pp. 249–261). Mahwah, NJ: Lawrence Erlbaum Associates, Publishers.

McClearn, G. E. (1991). A transtime visit with Francis Galton. In G. A. Kimble, M. Wertheimer, & C. White (Eds.), *Portraits of pioneers in psychology* (pp. 1–11). Hillsdale, NJ: Lawrence Erlbaum Associates, Publishers.

McClelland, D. C. (1961). *The achieving society.* New York: Van Nostrand Company.

McClelland, D. C., Atkinson, J. W., Clark, R. A., & Lowell, E. L. (1953). *The achievement motive.* New York: Appleton-Century-Crofts.

McConnell, J. V., & Philipchalk, R. P. (1992). *Understanding human behavior* (7th ed.). Fort Worth, TX: Harcourt Brace Jovanovich College Publishers.

McCulloch, W., & Pitts, W. (1943). A logical calculus of the ideas immanent in nervous activity. *Bulletin of Mathematical Biophysics, 5,* 115–133.

McDougall, W. (1908). *An introduction to social psychology.* London: Methuen.

McDougall, W. (1921). The use and abuse of instinct in social psychology. *The Journal of Abnormal and Social Psychology, 16,* 285–333.

McDougall, W. (1930). William McDougall. In C. Murchison (Ed.), *A history of psychology in autobiography* (Vol. 1, pp. 191–223). Worcester, MA: Clark University Press.

McGeoch, J. A. (1933). The formal criteria of a systematic psychology. *Psychological Review, 40,* 1–12.

McKinney, F. (1978). Functionalism at Chicago—Memories of a graduate student: 1929–1931. *Journal of the History of the Behavioral Sciences, 14,* 142–148.

McLeod, R. (1969). *William James: Unfinished business.* Washington, DC: American Psychological Association.

McLynn, F. (1996). *Carl Gustav Jung.* New York: St. Martin's Press.

McNemar, Q. (1964). Lost: Our intelligence. Why? *American Psychologist, 19,* 871–882.

McNemar, Q. (1980). Quinn McNemar. In G. Lindzey (Ed.), *A history of psychology in autobiography* (Vol. 7, pp. 304–333). San Francisco: W. H. Freeman and Company.

McReynolds, P. (1996). Lightner Witmer: Father of clinical psychology. In G. A. Kimble, A. C. Boneau, & M. Wertheimer (Eds.), *Portraits of pioneers in psychology* (Vol. II, pp. 63–71). Mahwah, NJ: Lawrence Erlbaum Associates, Publishers.

McReynolds, P. (1997). *Lightner Witmer: His life and times.* Washington, DC: American Psychological Association.

McWhinnie, H. J. (1985). Carl Jung and Heinz Werner and implications for foundational studies in art education and art therapy. *Arts in Psychotherapy, 12,* 95–99.

McWhirter, P. T., & McWhirter, J. J. (1997). Lightner Witmer: Father and grandfather? *American Psychologist, 52,* 275.

Mead, G. H. (1934). *Mind, self and society from the standpoint of a social behaviorist* (C. W. Morris, Ed.). Chicago: University of Chicago Press.

Meehl, P. E. (1967). Theory-testing in psychology and physics: A methodological paradox. *Philosophy of Science, 34,* 103–115.

Meehl, P. E. (1978). Theoretical risks and tabular asterisks: Sir Karl, Sir Ronald, and the slow progress of soft psychology. *Journal of Consulting and Clinical Psychology, 46,* 806–834.

Meehl, P. E. (1989). Paul E. Meehl. In G. Lindzey (Ed.), *A history of psychology in autobiography* (Vol. 8, pp. 336–389). Stanford, CA: Stanford University Press.

Meehl, P. E. (1992). Factors and taxa, traits and types, differences of degree and differences in kind. *Journal of Personality, 60,* 117–174.

Meischner-Metge, A., & Meischner, W. (1997). Fechner and Lotze. In W. G. Bringmann, H. E. Lück, R. Miller, & C. E. Early (Eds.), *A pictorial history of psychology* (pp. 101–106). Carol Stream, IL: Quintessence Publishing Co., Inc.

Mendelson, E. (Ed.) (1976). *W. H. Auden: Collected poems.* New York: Random House.

Merenda, P. F. (1987). Toward a four-factor theory of temperament and/or personality. *Journal of Personality Assessment, 51,* 367–374.

Milar, K. S. (2000). The first generation of women psychologists and the psychology of women. *American Psychologist, 55,* 616–619.

Milgram, S. (1967). The small-world problem. *Psychology Today, 1,* 61–67.

Milgram, S. (1974). *Obedience to authority.* New York: Harper.

Milgram, S. (1992). *The individual in a social world* (2nd ed.). New York: McGraw-Hill.

Milite, G. A. (2001). Morgan, Christiana Drummond (1897–1967). *Gale Encyclopedia of Psychology* (2nd ed.). Retrieved September 25, 2003, from http://www.findarticles.com/cf_0/g2699/0005/2699000557/p1/article.jhtml

Mill, J. S. (1884). *A system of logic, ratiocinative and inductive, being a connected view of the principles of evidence and the methods of scientific investigation* (8th ed.). London: Longmans, Green, and Co.

Mill, J. S. (1967). *Analysis of the phenomena of the human mind* (2nd ed.). New York: Augustus M. Kelley, Publishers. (Original work published 1869)

Mill, J. S. (1969). *Autobiography.* Boston: Houghton Mifflin. (Original work published 1873)

Miller, E. F. (1971). Hume's contribution to behavioral science. *Journal of the History of the Behavioral Sciences, 7,* 154–168.

Miller, G., Galanter, E., & Pribram, K. (1960). *Plans and the structure of behavior.* New York: Adams-Bannister-Cox.

Miller, G. A. (1951). *Language and communication.* New York: McGraw-Hill.

Miller, G. A. (1956). The magical number seven plus or minus two: Some limits on our capacity for processing information. *Psychological Review, 63,* 81–97.

Miller, G. A. (1965). Some preliminaries to psycholinguistics. *American Psychologist, 20,* 15–20.

Miller, G. A. (1989). George Miller. In G. Lindzey (Ed.), *A history of psychology in autobiography* (Vol. 8, pp. 390–418). Stanford, CA: Stanford University Press.

Miller, G. A., & Johnson-Laird, P. N. (1976). *Language and perception.* Cambridge, MA: Harvard University Press.

Miller, N. E. (1948). Studies of fear as an acquirable drive: 1. Fear as motivation and fear reduction as reinforcement in the learning of new responses. *Journal of Experimental Psychology, 38,* 89–101.

Miller, N. E. (1958). Central stimulation and other new approaches to motivation and reward. *American Psychologist, 13,* 100–108.

Miller, N. E. (1969). Learning of visceral and glandular responses. *Science, 163,* 434–445.

Miller, N. E. (1978). Biofeedback and visceral learning. *Annual Review of Psychology, 29,* 373–404.

Miller, N. E., & Dollard, J. (1941). *Social learning and imitation.* New Haven, CT: Yale University Press.

Miller, N. E., & Dworkin, B. R. (1974). Visceral learning: Recent difficulties with curarized rats and significant problems for human research. In P. A. Obrist, A. H. Black, J. Brener, & L. V. Dicara (Eds.), *Cardiovascular physiology: Current issues in response mechanisms, biofeedback, and methodology* (pp. 312–331). Chicago: Aldine.

Mills, E. S. (1974). George Trumbull Ladd: The great textbook writer. *Journal of the History of the Behavioral Sciences, 10,* 299–303.

Mills, J. A. (1987). Thomas Brown on the philosophy and psychology of perception. *Journal of the History of the Behavioral Sciences, 23,* 37–49.

Mills, J. A. (1988). The genesis of Hull's *Principles* of behavior. *Journal of the History of the Behavioral Sciences, 24,* 392–401.

Mills, W. (1899). The nature of animal intelligence and the methods of investigating it. *Psychological Review, 6,* 262–274.

Milner, P. M. (1986). Donald Olding Hebb (1904–1985). *Trends in Neuroscience, 9,* 347–351.

Milner, P. M. (1993). The mind and Donald O. Hebb. *Scientific American, 268,* 124–129.

Minsky, M. (1985). *The society of mind.* New York: Simon & Schuster.

Minton, H. L. (1987). Lewis M. Terman and mental testing: In search of the democratic ideal. In M. M. Sokal (Ed.), *Psychological testing and American society 1890–1930* (pp. 95–112). New Brunswick, NJ: Rutgers University Press.

Minton, H. L. (2000). Psychology and gender at the turn of the century. *American Psychologist, 55,* 613–615.

Mischel, T. (1966). "Emotion" and "Motivation" in the development of English psychology: D. Hartley, James Mill, A. Bain. *Journal of the History of the Behavioral Sciences, 2,* 123–144.

Misiak, H., & Sexton, V. (1966). *History of psychology.* London: Grune & Stratton.

Moede, W. (1920). Einzel und gruppenarbeit [Individual and group work]. *Praktische Psychologie, 2,* 71–78, 108–115.

Montague, H., & Hollingworth, L. S. (1914). The comparative variability of the sexes at birth. *American Journal of Sociology, 20,* 335–370.

Moody, E. A. (1967). Medieval logic. In P. Edwards (Ed.), *The encyclopedia of philosophy* (Vol. 4, pp. 528–534). New York: The Free Press.

Moore, B. R., & Stuttard, S. (1979). Dr. Guthrie and *Felis domesticus* or: Tripping over the cat. *Science, 205,* 1031–1033.

Moorehead, A. (1969). *Darwin and the Beagle.* New York: Harper & Row.

Mora, G. (1975). The 1774 ordinance for the hospitalization of the mentally ill in Tuscany: A reassessment. *Journal of the History of the Behavioral Sciences, 11,* 246–256.

Morgan, C. L. (1894). *An introduction to comparative psychology.* London: Scott.

Morgan, C. L. (1932). C. Lloyd Morgan. In C. Murchison (Ed.), *A history of psychology in autobiography* (Vol. 2, pp. 237–264). Worcester, MA: Clark University Press.

Morgan, C. T. (1943). *Physiological psychology.* New York: McGraw-Hill.

Moskowitz, M. J. (1977). Hugo Münsterberg: A study in the history of applied psychology. *American Psychologist, 32,* 824–842.

Mountjoy, P. T., & Hansor, J. D. (1986). Jacob Robert Kantor (1888–1984). *American Psychologist, 41,* 1296–1297.

Mowrer, O. H. (1947). On the dual nature of learning—a reinterpretation of "conditioning" and "problem-solving." *Harvard Educational Review, 17,* 102–148.

Mowrer, O. H. (1960). *Learning theory and behavior.* New York: Wiley.

Mowrer, O. H. (1974). O. Hobart Mowrer. In G. Lindzey (Ed.), *A history of psychology in autobiography* (Vol. 6, pp. 327–364). Englewood Cliffs, NJ: Prentice-Hall.

Münsterberg, H. (1908). *On the witness stand.* New York: Clark Boardman Co.

Murphy, G., & Murphy, L. B. (1931). *Experimental social psychology.* New York: Harper.

Murphy, K. R., & Davidshofer, C. O. (1988). *Psychological testing: Principles and applications.* Englewood Cliffs, NJ: Prentice Hall.

Murphy, L. B. (1937). *Social behavior of young children: An exploratory study of some roots of sympathy.* New York: Columbia University Press.

Murphy, P. L. (1992). Applying a contextual analysis to the history of women in psychology. *Psychology of Women, 19,* 12, 17.

Murray, B. (2000). The degree that almost wasn't: The PsyD comes of age. *Monitor on Psychology, 31,* 52–54.

Murray, D. J. (1983). *A history of Western psychology.* Englewood Cliffs, NJ: Prentice Hall.

Murray, D. J. (1990). Fechner's later psychophysics. *Canadian Psychology/Psychologie Canadienne, 31,* 54–60.

Murray, H. A. (1938). *Explorations in personality.* New York: Oxford University Press.

Murray, H. A. (1956). Morton Prince. *Journal of Abnormal Psychology, 52,* 291–295.

Murray, H. A. (1967). Henry A. Murray. In E. G. Boring & G. Lindzey (Eds.), *A history of psychology in autobiography* (Vol. 5, pp. 283–310). New York: Appleton-Century-Crofts.

Myers, G. E. (1986). *William James: His life and thought.* New Haven, CT: Yale University Press.

Myers, I. B., McCaulley, M. H., Quenk, N. L., & Hammer, A. L. (1998). *MBTI Manual: A guide to the development and use of the Myers-Briggs Type Indicator* (3rd ed.). Palo Alto, CA: Consulting Psychologists Press.

Myers, R. E., & Sperry, R. W. (1953). Interocular transfer of a visual form discrimination habit in cats after section of the optic chiasma and corpus callosum. *American Association of Anatomists: Abstracts of Papers from Platform,* p. 351.

Nadler, S. (1999). *Spinoza: A life.* Cambridge: Cambridge University Press.

Nakayama, K. (1994). James J. Gibson—An appreciation. *Psychological Review, 101,* 329–335.

Nance, R. D. (1970). G. Stanley Hall and John B. Watson as child psychologists. *Journal of the History of the Behavioral Sciences, 6,* 303–316.

Neisser, U. (1967). *Cognitive psychology.* New York: Appleton.

Neisser, U. (1976). *Cognition and reality.* San Francisco: Freeman.

Neisser, U. (1981). John Dean's memory: A case study. *Cognition, 9,* 1–22.

Neisser, U. (1982). *Memory observed.* San Francisco: Freeman.

Neisser, U. (1987). *Concepts and conceptual development.* New York: Cambridge University Press.

Neisser, U. (1991). A case of misplaced nostalgia. *American Psychologist, 46,* 34–36.

Neisser, U., & Harsch, N. (1993). Phantom flashbulbs: False recollections of hearing the news about Challenger. In E. Winograd & U. Neisser (Eds.), *Affect and accuracy in recall: Studies of "flashbulb" memories* (pp. 9–31). New York: Cambridge University Press.

Nerlich, B., & Clarke, D. D. (1998). The linguistic repudiation of Wundt. *History of Psychology, 1,* 179–204.

Neuburger, M. (1981). *The historical development of experimental brain and spinal cord physiology before Flourens* (E. Clarke, Trans.). Baltimore, MD: The Johns Hopkins University Press. (Original work published 1897)

Neugebauer, R. (1978). Treatment of the mentally ill in medieval and early modern England: A reappraisal. *Journal of the History of the Behavioral Sciences, 14,* 158–169.

Newcomb, T. M. (1943). *Personality and social change.* New York: Dryden.

Newcomb, T. M. (1974). Theodore M. Newcomb. In G. Lindzey (Ed.), *A history of psychology in autobiography* (Vol. 6, pp. 367–391). Englewood Cliffs, NJ: Prentice-Hall.

Newell, A., & Simon, H. A. (1972). *Human problem solving.* Englewood Cliffs, NJ: Prentice-Hall.

Newton, I. (1972). *Philosophiae naturalis principia mathematica* (3rd ed.) *[Mathematical principles of natural philosophy].* Cambridge, MA: Harvard University Press. (Original work published 1726)

Nicholson, I. A. M. (1998). Gordon Allport, character, and the "Culture of Personality," 1897–1937. *History of Psychology, 1,* 52–68.

Nicolas, S., & Charvillat, A. (2001). Introducing psychology as an academic discipline in France: Théodule Ribot and the *Collège de France* (1888–1901). *Journal of the History of the Behavioral Sciences, 37,* 143–164.

Nicolas, S., & Ferrand, L. (1999). Wundt's laboratory at Leipzig in 1891. *History of Psychology, 2,* 194–203.

Nicolas, S., & Ferrand, L. (2002). Alfred Binet and higher education. *History of Psychology, 5,* 264–283.

Nicolas, S., & Murray, D. J. (1999). Théodule Ribot (1839–1916), founder of French psychology: A biographical introduction. *History of Psychology, 2,* 277–301.

Nicolas, S., Segui, J., & Ferrand, L. (2000). *L'Année Psychologique:* History of the founding of a 100-year-old French journal. *History of Psychology, 3,* 44–61.

Nietzsche, F. (1966). *Beyond good and evil* (W. Kaufmann, Trans.). New York: Vintage Books. (Original work published 1886)

Nietzsche, F. (1967). *On the genealogy of morals* (W. Kaufmann, Trans.). New York: Vintage Books. (Original work published 1887)

Nisbett, R. A. (2000). Stanley Schachter (1922–1997). *American Psychologist, 55,* 1505–1506.

Noel, P. S., & Carlson, E. T. (1973). The faculty psychology of Benjamin Rush. *Journal of the History of the Behavioral Sciences, 9,* 369–377.

Nordentoft, K. (1972). *Kierkegaard's psychology* (B. Kirmmse, Trans.). Pittsburgh: Duquesne University Press.

Norman, D. A. (1988). *The psychology of everyday things.* New York: Basic Books.

Nussbaum, M. C. (1998). Aristotle. In S. Hornblower & A. Spawforth, *The Oxford companion to classical civilization* (pp. 68–74). Oxford: Oxford University Press.

O'Donnell, J. M. (1979). The clinical psychology of Lightner Witmer: A case study of institutional innovation and intellectual change. *Journal of the History of the Behavioral Sciences, 15,* 3–17.

O'Donnell, J. M. (1985). *The origins of behaviorism: American psychology, 1870–1920.* New York: New York University Press.

Ogden, C. K., & Richards, I. A. (1923). *The meaning of meaning.* New York: Harcourt Brace Jovanovich.

Ogden, R. M. (1951). Oswald Külpe and the Würzburg school. *American Journal of Psychology, 64,* 4–19.

O'Neil, W. M. (1995). American behaviorism: A historical and critical analysis. *Theory and Psychology, 5,* 285–305.

O'Neil, W. M., & Landauer, A. A. (1966). The phi-phenomenon: Turning point or rallying point. *Journal of the History of the Behavioral Sciences, 2,* 335–340.

Orbach, J. (1982). The legacy of *Brain Mechanisms and Intelligence.* In J. Orbach (Ed.), *Neuropsychology after Lashley: Fifty years since the publication of* Brain Mechanisms and Intelligence (pp. 1–20). Hillsdale, NJ: Lawrence Erlbaum Associates, Publishers.

Orgler, H. (1963). *Alfred Adler: The man and his work.* New York: Mentor Books.

Osborne, R. T. (1994). The Burt collection. *Journal of the History of the Behavioral Sciences, 30,* 369–373.

Osgood, C. E., Suci, G. J., & Tannenbaum, P. H. (1957). *The measurement of meaning.* Urbana: University of Illinois Press.

Palermo, D. (1971). Is a scientific revolution taking place in psychology? *Science Studies, 1,* 135–155.

Parham, T. A., & Helms, J. E. (1985). Attitudes of racial identity and self-esteem of Black students: An exploratory investigation. *Journal of College Student Personnel, 26,* 143–147.

Paris, B. J. (2000). Karen Horney: The three phases of her thought. In G. A. Kimble & M. Wertheimer (Eds.), *Portraits of pioneers in psychology* (Vol. IV, pp. 163–179). Mahwah, NJ: Lawrence Erlbaum Associates, Publishers.

Pastore, N. (1978). The army intelligence tests and Walter Lippmann. *Journal of the History of the Behavioral Sciences, 14,* 316–327.

Pastore, N. (1991). Wittgenstein on Köhler and gestalt psychology: A critique. *Journal of the History of the Behavioral Sciences, 27,* 341–351.

Pauly, P. J. (1981). The Loeb-Jennings debate and the science of animal behavior. *Journal of the History of the Behavioral Sciences, 17,* 504–515.

Pavlov, I. P. (1960). *Conditioned reflexes: An investigation of the physiological activity of the cerebral cortex.* New York: Dover Publications, Inc. (Original work published 1927)

Pavlov, I. P. (1928). *Lectures on conditioned reflexes.* New York: International Publishers.

Pavlov, I. P. (1932). The reply of a physiologist to psychologists. *Psychological Review, 39,* 91–127.

Pavlov, I. P. (1957). Ivan Petrovich Pavlov: Autobiography. In I. P. Pavlov, *Experimental psychology and other essays* (pp. 57–62). New York: Philosophical Library.

Pearson, K. (1914–1930). *The life, letters and labours of Francis Galton* (Vols. 1–3). Cambridge, England: Cambridge University Press.

Peirce, C. S. (1878). How to make ideas clear. *Popular Science Monthly, 12,* 286–302.

Penfield, W. (1952). Memory mechanisms. *Archives of Neurology and Psychiatry, 67,* 178–198.

Penfield, W. (1958). Centrencephalic integrating system. *Brain, 81,* 231–234.

Perry, R. B. (1918). Docility and purposiveness. *Psychological Review, 25,* 1–20.

Perry, R. B. (1935). *The thought and character of William James* (Vols. 1–2). Boston: Little, Brown.

Perry, R. B. (1935). *The thought and character of William James: Briefer version.* New York: George Braziller, Publisher.

Petrina, S. (2001). The "never-to-be-forgotten investigation": Luella W. Cole, Sidney L. Pressey, and mental surveying in Indiana, 1917–1921. *History of Psychology, 4,* 245–271.

Petryszak, N. G. (1981). Tabula rasa—its origins and implications. *Journal of the History of the Behavioral Sciences, 17,* 15–27.

Pettijohn, T. F. (1998). *Psychology: A concise introduction* (4th ed.). Boston: Dushkin/McGraw-Hill.

Pfungst, O. (1965). *Clever Hans (The horse of Mr. von Osten).* New York: Holt, Rinehart and Winston, Inc. (Original work published 1911)

Piaget, J. (1952). Jean Piaget. In E. G. Boring, H. S. Langfeld, H. Werner, & R. M. Yerkes (Eds.), *A history of psychology in autobiography* (Vol. 4, pp. 237–256). Worcester, MA: Clark University Press.

Piaget, J., & Inhelder, B. (1941). *Le développement des quantités chez l'enfant [The child's construction of quantities].* Paris: Delachaux & Niestlé.

Piaget, J., & Inhelder, B. (1951). *La genèse de l'idée de hasard chez l'enfant [The origin of the idea of chance in children].* Paris: Presses Universitaires de France.

Pinker, S. (1984). *Language learnability and language development.* Cambridge, MA: Harvard University Press.

Pollio, H. R. (1982). *Behavior and existence.* Monterey, CA: Brooks/Cole Publishing Company.

Pollio, H. R. (1990). The stream of consciousness since James. In M. G. Johnson & T. B. Henley (Eds.), *Reflections on* The Principles of Psychology (pp. 271–294). Hillsdale, NJ: Lawrence Erlbaum Associates, Publishers.

Pollio, H. R., Henley, T. B., & Thompson, C. (1997). *The phenomenology of everyday life.* New York: Cambridge University Press.

Popplestone, J. A. (1983). Foreword. In M. Harrower, *Kurt Koffka: An unwitting self-portrait* (pp. vii–ix). Gainesville, FL: University Presses of Florida.

Popplestone, J. A., & McPherson, M. W. (1994). *An illustrated history of American psychology.* Madison, WI: Brown & Benchmark.

Posner, M. I. (1978). *Chronometric explorations of mind.* Hillsdale, NJ: Lawrence Erlbaum Associates, Publishers.

Post, D. (1980). Floyd H. Allport and the launching of modern social psychology. *Journal of the History of the Behavioral Sciences, 16,* 369–376.

Prenzel-Guthrie, P. (1996). Edwin Ray Guthrie: Pioneer learning theorist. In G. A. Kimble, C. A. Boneau, & M. Wertheimer (Eds.), *Portraits of pioneers in psychology* (Vol. II, pp. 137–149). Mahwah, NJ: Lawrence Erlbaum Associates, Publishers.

Pribram, K. H. (1960). A review of theory in physiological psychology. *Annual Review of Psychology, 11,* 1–40.

Pribram, K. H. (1971). *Languages of the brain: Experimental paradoxes and principles in neuropsychology.* Englewood Cliffs, NJ: Prentice-Hall.

Pribram, K. H. (1985). Brain, behavioral operants, cognitive operations, and holonomic transformations. In R. Gandelman (Ed.), *Autobiographics in experimental psychology* (pp. 63–97). Hillsdale, NJ: Lawrence Erlbaum Associates, Publishers.

Prilleltensky, I. (1994). On the social legacy of B. F. Skinner: Rhetoric of change, philosophy of adjustment. *Theory and Psychology, 4,* 125–137.

Pruette, L. (1926). *G. Stanley Hall: A biography of a mind.* Freeport, NY: Books for Libraries Press.

Puente, A. E. (2000). Roger W. Sperry: Nobel laureate, neuroscientist, and psychologist. In G. A. Kimble & M. Wertheimer (Eds.), *Portraits of pioneers in psychology* (Vol. IV, pp. 321–336). Mahwah, NJ: Lawrence Erlbaum Associates, Publishers.

Raby, P. (2001). *Alfred Russell Wallace.* Princeton, NJ: Princeton University Press.

Rachels, J. (1986). Darwin's moral lapse. *National Forum, 66,* 22–24.

Rachlin, H. (1970). *Introduction to modern behaviorism.* San Francisco: Freeman.

Rancurello, A. C. (1968). *A study of Franz Brentano: His psychological standpoint and his significance in the history of psychology.* New York: Academic Press.

Raphelson, A. C. (1973). The pre-Chicago association of the early functionalists. *Journal of the History of the Behavioral Sciences, 9,* 115–122.

Reed, E. S. (1996). James J. Gibson: Pioneer and iconoclast. In G. A. Kimble, C. A. Boneau, & M. Wertheimer (Eds.), *Portraits of pioneers in psychology* (Vol. II, pp. 247–261). Mahwah, NJ: Lawrence Erlbaum Associates, Publishers.

Reed, J. (1987). Robert M. Yerkes and the mental testing movement. In M. M. Sokal (Ed.), *Psychological testing and American society, 1890–1930* (pp. 75–94). New Brunswick, NJ: Rutgers University Press.

Reitan, R. M., & Wolfson, D. (1985). *The Halstead-Reitan neuropsychological test battery: Theory and clinical interpretation.* Tucson, AZ: Neuropsychology.

Restle, F. (1957). Discrimination of cues in mazes: A resolution of the "place-vs.-response" question. *Psychological Review, 64,* 217–228.

Richards, R. J. (1977). Lloyd Morgan's theory of instinct: From Darwinism to neo-Darwinism. *Journal of the History of the Behavioral Sciences, 13,* 12–32.

Richards, R. J. (1983). Why Darwin delayed, or interesting problems and models in the history of science. *Journal of the History of the Behavioral Sciences, 19,* 45–53.

Rieber, R. W. (1980). The Americanization of psychology before William James. In R. W. Rieber & K. Salzinger (Eds.), *Psychology: Theoretical-historical perspectives* (pp. 103–123). New York: Academic Press.

Rilling, M. (1996). The mystery of the vanished citations: James V. McConnell's forgotten 1960s quest for Planarian learning, a biochemical engram, and celebrity. *American Psychologist, 51,* 589–598.

Rilling, M. (2000). John Watson's paradoxical struggle to explain Freud. *American Psychologist, 55,* 301–312.

Risse, G. (1976). Vocational guidance during the Depression: Phrenology versus applied psychology. *Journal of the History of the Behavioral Sciences, 12,* 130–140.

Roazen, P. (1975). *Freud and his followers.* New York: Alfred A. Knopf.

Robinson, D. N. (1989). Thomas Reid and the Aberdeen years: Common sense at the Wise Club. *Journal of the History of the Behavioral Sciences, 25,* 154–162.

Robinson, D. N. (1993). Is there a Jamesian tradition in psychology? *American Psychologist, 48,* 638–643.

Robinson, D. N. (1995). *An intellectual history of psychology* (3rd ed.). Madison: University of Wisconsin Press.

Rock, I. (1957). The role of repetition in associative learning. *American Journal of Psychology, 70,* 186–193.

Roediger, H. L. III (2000). Sir Frederic Charles Bartlett: Experimental and applied psychologist. In G. A. Kimble & M. Wertheimer (Eds.), *Portraits of pioneers in psychology* (Vol. IV, pp. 149–161). Mahwah, NJ: Lawrence Erlbaum Associates, Publishers.

Rogers, C. R. (1951). *Client-centered therapy.* Boston: Houghton Mifflin.

Rogers, C. R. (1961). *On becoming a person.* Boston: Houghton Mifflin.

Rogers, C. R. (1967). Carl R. Rogers. In E. G. Boring & G. Lindzey (Eds.), *A history of psychology in autobiography* (Vol. 5, pp. 341–383). New York: Appleton-Century-Crofts.

Romanes, E. (1896). *The life and letters of George John Romanes.* London: Longmans, Green, and Co.

Romanes, G. J. (1895). *Animal intelligence.* New York: D. Appleton and Company. (Original work published 1881)

Rosch, E., & Mervis, C. (1975). Family resemblances: Studies in the internal structure of categories. *Cognitive Psychology, 7,* 573–605.

Rosch, E. H. (1978). Principles of categorization. In E. H. Rosch & B. Lloyd (Eds.), *Cognition and categorization* (pp. 27–48). Hillsdale, NJ: Lawrence Erlbaum Associates, Publishers.

Rosenzweig, M. R. (1959). Salivary conditioning before Pavlov. *American Journal of Psychology, 72,* 628–633.

Rosenzweig, S. (1987). The final tribute of E. G. Boring to G. T. Fechner: Concerning the date October 22, 1850. *American Psychologist, 42,* 787–790.

Rosenzweig, S. (1992). *Freud, Jung, and Hall the king-maker: The historic expedition to America (1909).* Seattle, WA: Hogrefe & Huber Publishers.

Rosenzweig, S. (1997). Freud's only visit to America. In W. G. Bringmann, H. E. Lück, R. Miller, & C. E. Early (Eds.), *A pictorial history of psychology* (pp. 395–398). Chicago: Quintessence Publishing Co., Inc.

Rosenzweig, S., & Fisher, S. L. (1997). "Idiographic" vis-à-vis "idiodynamic" in the historical perspective of personality theory: Remembering Gordon Allport, 1897–1997. *Journal of the History of the Behavioral Sciences, 33,* 405–419.

Ross, B. (1981). In memoriam: Robert I. Watson, Sr., 1909–1980. *Journal of the History of the Behavioral Sciences, 17,* 1–2.

Ross, B. (1991). William James: Spoiled child of American psychology. In G. A. Kimble, M. Wertheimer, & C. White (Eds.), *Portraits of pioneers in psychology* (pp. 13–25). Hillsdale, NJ: Lawrence Erlbaum Associates, Publishers.

Ross, D. (1972). *G. Stanley Hall: The psychologist as prophet.* Chicago: The University of Chicago Press.

Ross, E. A. (1908). *Social psychology: An outline and a sourcebook.* New York: Macmillan.

Rotter, J. B. (1966). Generalized expectancies for internal versus external control of reinforcement. *Psychological Monographs, 80* (Whole No. 609).

Rowe, F. B., & Murray, F. S. (1979). A note on the Titchener influence on the first psychology laboratory in the South. *Journal of the History of the Behavioral Sciences, 15,* 282–284.

Ruja, H. (1956). Productive psychologists. *American Psychologist, 11,* 148–149.

Rumbaugh, D. M. (1997). The psychology of Harry F. Harlow: A bridge from radical to rational behaviorism. *Philosophical Psychology, 10,* 197–210.

Rumelhart, D. E., McClelland, J. L., & the PDP Research Group (1986). *Parallel distributed processing: Explorations in the microstructure of cognition* (Vols. 1–2). Cambridge, MA: Cambridge University Press.

Runes, D. D. (1959). *Pictorial history of philosophy.* New York: Bramhall House.

Rushton, J. P., & Ankney, C. D. (1996). Brain size and cognitive ability: Correlations with age, sex, social class, and race. *Psychonomic Bulletin & Review, 3,* 21–36.

Russell, B. (1925). *Philosophy.* New York: W. W. Norton & Company.

Russell, B. (1937). *A critical exposition of the philosophy of Leibniz.* London: George Allen & Unwin Ltd.

Rutherford, A. (2000). Mary Cover Jones (1896–1987). *Psychology of Women, 27,* 22–23.

Rutherford, A. (2003). B. F. Skinner's technology of behavior in American life: From consumer culture to counterculture. *Journal of the History of the Behavioral Sciences, 39,* 1–23.

Rychlak, J. F. (1991). *Artificial intelligence and human reason: A teleological critique.* New York: Columbia University Press.

Ryle, G. (1949). *The concept of mind.* London: Hutchinson.

Sabini, J. (1986). Stanley Milgram (1933–1984). *American Psychologist, 41,* 1378–1379.

Sahakian, W. S. (Ed.) (1968). *History of psychology: A source book in systematic psychology.* Itasca, IL: F. E. Peacock Publishers, Inc.

Samelson, F. (1977). World War I intelligence testing and the development of psychology. *Journal of the History of the Behavioral Sciences, 13,* 274–282.

Samelson, F. (1980). J. B. Watson's Little Albert, Cyril Burt's twins, and the need for a critical science. *American Psychologist, 35,* 619–625.

Samelson, F. (1981). Struggle for scientific authority: The reception of Watson's behaviorism, 1913–1920. *Journal of the History of the Behavioral Sciences, 17,* 399–425.

Samelson, F. (1997). On the uses of history: The case of *The Bell Curve. Journal of the History of the Behavioral Sciences, 33,* 129–133.

Samelson, F. (1999). Assessing research in the history of psychology: Past, present, and future. *Journal of the History of the Behavioral Science, 35,* 247–255.

Sanford, E. C. (1924). Granville Stanley Hall 1846–1924. *American Journal of Psychology, 35,* 313–321.

Sarris, V. (1989). Max Wertheimer on seen motion: Theory and evidence. *Psychological Research, 51,* 58–68.

Sarris, V. (1997). Gestalt psychology at Frankfurt University. In W. G. Bringmann, H. E. Lück, R. Miller, & C. E. Early (Eds.), *A pictorial history of psychology* (pp. 273–276). Carol Stream, IL: Quintessence Publishing Co., Inc.

Sarton, G. (1954). *Galen of Pergamon.* Lawrence: University of Kansas Press.

Sartre, J.-P. (1938). *La nausée [Nausea].* Paris: Gallimard.

Sartre, J.-P. (1943). *L'être et le niant [Being and nothingness].* Paris: Gallimard.

Sartre, J.-P. (1947). *Huis clos [No exit].* Paris: Gallimard.

Savage-Rumbaugh, E. S., Murphy, J., Sevcik, R. A., Brakke, K. E., Williams, S. L., & Rumbaugh, D. M. (1993). Language comprehension in ape and child. *Monographs of the Society for Research in Child Development, 58* (3–4, Serial No. 233).

Sawyer, T. F. (2000). Francis Cecil Sumner: His views and influence on African American higher education. *History of Psychology, 3,* 122–141.

Scarborough, E. (1991). Continuity for women: Ethel Puffer's struggle. In G. A. Kimble, M. Wertheimer, & C. L. White (Eds.), *Portraits of pioneers in psychology* (pp. 104–119). Hillsdale, NJ: Lawrence Erlbaum Associates, Publishers.

Scarborough, E., & Furumoto, L. (1987). *Untold lives: The first generation of American women psychologists.* New York: Columbia University Press.

Scarr, S. (1985). Constructing psychology: Making facts and fables for our times. *American Psychologist, 40,* 499–512.

Scarr, S., & Weinberg, R. A. (1978). The influence of family background on intellectual attainment. *American Sociological Review, 43,* 674–692.

Schachter, S. (1989). Stanley Schachter. In G. Lindzey (Ed.), *A history of psychology in autobiography* (Vol. 8, pp. 448–470). Stanford, CA: Stanford University Press.

Schachter, S., & Singer, J. E. (1962). Cognitive, social, and physiological determinants of emotional state. *Psychological Review, 69,* 379–399.

Schaefer, C. S., & Anastasi, A. (1968). A biographical inventory for identifying creativity in adolescent boys. *Journal of Applied Psychology, 52,* 42–48.

Schank, R., & Abelson, R. (1977). *Scripts, plans, goals, and understanding: An inquiry into human knowledge structures.* Hillsdale, NJ: Lawrence Erlbaum Associates, Publishers.

Schank, R. C. (1972). Conceptual dependency: A theory of natural language understanding. *Cognitive Psychology, 3,* 552–631.

Schank, R. C. (1982). *Dynamic memory: A theory of reminding and learning in computers and people.* Cambridge, MA: Cambridge University Press.

Schlosberg, H. (1954). Three dimensions of emotion. *Psychological Review, 61,* 81–88.

Schlossman, S. L. (1973). G. Stanley Hall and the boys' club: Conservative applications of recapitulation theory. *Journal of the History of the Behavioral Sciences, 9,* 140–147.

Schmidt, J. (1985). *Maurice Merleau-Ponty: Between phenomenology and structuralism.* New York: St. Martin's Press.

Schneck, J. M. (1965). A reevaluation of Freud's abandonment of hypnosis. *Journal of the History of the Behavioral Sciences, 1,* 191–195.

Schneider, K. J. (1998). Toward a science of the heart: Romanticism and the revival of psychology. *American Psychologist, 53,* 277–289.

Schneider, W. H. (1992). After Binet: French intelligence testing, 1900–1950. *Journal of the History of the Behavioral Sciences, 28,* 111–132.

Schneidman, E. S. (2001). My visit with Christiana Morgan. *History of Psychology, 4,* 289–296.

Schönpflug, W. (1994). The road not taken: A false start for cognitive psychology. *Psychological Review, 101,* 237–242.

Schopenhauer, A. (1969). *The world as will and representation* (Vols. 1–2) (E. F. J. Payne, Trans.). New York: Dover Publications, Inc. (Original work published 1844)

Schusdek, A. (1966). Freud's "seduction theory": A reconstruction. *Journal of the History of the Behavioral Sciences, 2,* 159–166.

Schwartz, S. (1986). *Classic studies in psychology.* Palo Alto, CA: Mayfield.

Sdorow, L. (1990). *Psychology.* Dubuque, IA: Wm. C. Brown Publishers.

Seaman, J. D. (1984). On phi-phenomena. *Journal of the History of the Behavioral Sciences, 20,* 3–8.

Searle, J. (1983). *Intentionality.* New York: Cambridge.

Searle, J. R. (1980). Minds, brains, and programs. *Behavioral and Brain Sciences, 3,* 417–457.

Sears, R. R. (1980). Robert R. Sears. In G. Lindzey (Ed.), *A history of psychology in autobiography* (Vol. 7, pp. 394–433). San Francisco: W. H. Freeman and Company.

Sears, R. R. (1992). Psychoanalysis and behavior theory: 1907–1965. In S. Koch & D. E. Leary (Eds.), *A century of psychology as science* (pp. 208–220). Washington, DC: American Psychological Association.

Sears, R. R., Lapidus, D., & Cozzens, C. (1978). Content analysis of Mark Twain's novels and letters as a biographical method. *Poetics, 7,* 155–175.

Sears, R. R., Maccoby, E. E., & Levin, H. (1957). *Patterns of child rearing.* Stanford, CA: Stanford University Press.

Sedlmeier, P., & Gigerenzer, G. (1989). Do studies of statistical power have an effect on the power of studies? *Psychological Bulletin, 105,* 309–316.

Selfridge, O., & Neisser, U. (1960). Pattern recognition by machine. *Scientific American, 203,* 60–68.

Seligman, M. E. P. (1970). On the generality of the laws of learning. *Psychological Review, 77,* 406–418.

Seward, J. P. (1942). An experimental study of Guthrie's theory of reinforcement. *Journal of Experimental Psychology, 30,* 247–256.

Seward, J. P. (1954). Hull's system of behavior: An evaluation. *Psychological Review, 61,* 145–159.

Shakow, D. (1930). Hermann Ebbinghaus. *American Journal of Psychology, 17,* 504–518.

Shakow, D. (1969). Psychoanalysis. In D. L. Krantz (Ed.), *Schools of psychology: A symposium* (pp. 87–122). New York: Appleton-Century-Crofts.

Shannon, C. E. (1938). A symbolic analysis of relay and switching circuits. *Transactions of the American Institute of Electrical Engineers, 57,* 1–11.

Sharps, M. J., & Wertheimer, M. (2000). Gestalt perspectives on cognitive science and on experimental psychology. *Review of General Psychology, 4,* 315–336.

Sheffield, F. D. (1959). Edwin Ray Guthrie: 1886–1959. *American Journal of Psychology, 72,* 642–650.

Sheldon, H. D. (1946). Clark University, 1897–1900. *The Journal of Social Psychology, 24,* 227–247.

Shepard, R. N. (2000). Carl Iver Hovland: Statesman of psychology, sterling human being. In G. A. Kimble & M. Wertheimer (Eds.), *Portraits of pioneers in psychology* (Vol. IV, pp. 285–301). Mahwah, NJ: Lawrence Erlbaum Associates, Publishers.

Sherif, M. (1936). *The psychology of social norms.* New York: Harper & Row.

Sherif, M., & Cantril, H. (1947). *The psychology of ego involvements: Social attitudes and identifications.* New York: Wiley.

Sherif, M., Harvey, O. I., White, B., Hood, W., & Sherif, C. (1961). *Intergroup cooperation and competition: The Robbers Cave experiment.* Norman, OK: University Book Exchange.

Sherif, M., & Hovland, C. I. (1961). *Social judgement.* New Haven, CT: Yale University Press.

Sherrington, C. S. (1906). *The integrative action of the nervous system.* New Haven, CT: Yale University Press.

Shields, S. A. (1975). Ms. Pilgrim's progress: The contributions of Leta Stetter Hollingworth to the psychology of women. *American Psychologist, 30,* 852–857.

Shields, S. A. (1991). Leta Stetter Hollingworth: "Literature of opinion" and the study of individual differences. In G. A. Kimble, M. Wertheimer, & C. L. White (Eds.), *Portraits of pioneers in psychology* (pp. 243–256). Hillsdale, NJ: Lawrence Erlbaum Associates, Publishers.

Shiffrin, R. M. & Nosofsky, R. M. (1994). Seven plus or minus two: A commentary on capacity limitations. *Psychological Review, 101,* 357–361.

Shook, J. R. (1995). Wilhelm Wundt's contribution to John Dewey's functional psychology. *Journal of the History of the Behavioral Sciences, 31,* 347–369.

Shrout, P. E. (1997). Should significance tests be banned? Introduction to a special section exploring the pros and cons. *Psychological Science, 8,* 1–2.

Shrout, P. E. (2001). Jacob Cohen (1923–1998). *American Psychologist, 56,* 166.

Silverman, J. (1964). The problem of attention in research and theory in schizophrenia. *Psychological Review, 71,* 352–379.

Silverstein, B. (1989). Contributions to the history of psychology: LVIII. Freud's dualistic mind-body interactionism: Implications for the development of his psychology. *Psychological Reports, 64,* 1091–1097.

Simmel, M. L. (1966). Kurt Goldstein, 1878–1965. *Journal of the History of the Behavioral Sciences, 2,* 185–191.

Simon, H. A. (1980). Herbert A. Simon. In G. Lindzey (Ed.), *A history of psychology in autobiography* (Vol. 7, pp. 434–472). San Francisco: W. H. Freeman and Company.

Simon, H. A. (1992). What is an "explanation" of behavior? *Psychological Science, 3,* 150–161.

Simon, L. (1998). *Genuine reality: A life of William James.* New York: Harcourt Brace & Company.

Singer, J. E. (1998). Stanley Schacter [*sic*], scientist of distinction 1922–1997. *APS Observer, 11,* 46–48.

Skinner, B. F. (1935). Two types of conditioned reflex and a pseudo type. *Journal of General Psychology, 12,* 66–77.

Skinner, B. F. (1937). Two types of conditioned reflex: A reply to Konorski and Miller. *Journal of General Psychology, 16,* 272–279.

Skinner, B. F. (1938). *The behavior of organisms: An experimental analysis.* Englewood Cliffs, NJ: Prentice-Hall.

Skinner, B. F. (1948). *Walden two.* New York: The Macmillan Co.

Skinner, B. F. (1950). Are theories of learning necessary? *Psychological Review, 57,* 193–216.

Skinner, B. F. (1957). *Verbal behavior.* New York: Appleton-Century-Crofts.

Skinner, B. F. (1964). Behaviorism at fifty. In T. W. Wann (Ed.), *Behaviorism and phenomenology* (pp. 79–97). Chicago: University of Chicago Press.

Skinner, B. F. (1967). B. F. Skinner. In E. G. Boring & G. Lindzey, *A history of psychology in autobiography* (Vol. 5, pp. 385–413). New York: Appleton-Century-Crofts.

Skinner, B. F. (1971). *Beyond freedom and dignity.* New York: Alfred A. Knopf.

Skinner, B. F. (1974). *About behaviorism.* New York: Vintage Books.

Skinner, B. F. (1976). *Particulars of my life.* New York: Alfred A. Knopf.

Skinner, B. F. (1979). *The shaping of a behaviorist.* New York: Alfred A. Knopf.

Skinner, B. F. (1980). The experimental analysis of operant behavior: A history. In R. W. Rieber & K. Salzinger (Eds.), *Psychology: Theoretical-historical perspectives* (pp. 191–202). New York: Academic Press.

Skinner, B. F. (1981). Pavlov's influence on psychology in America. *Journal of the History of the Behavioral Sciences, 17,* 242–245.

Skinner, B. F. (1983). *A matter of consequences.* New York: Alfred A. Knopf.

Skinner, B. F. (1986). What is wrong with daily life in the Western world? *American Psychologist, 41,* 568–574.

Slamecka, N. J. (1985). Ebbinghaus: Some associations. *Journal of Experimental Psychology: Learning, Memory, and Cognition, 11,* 414–435.

Slobin, D. (Ed.) (1985). *The crosslinguistic study of language acquisition* (Vols. 1–2). Hillsdale, NJ: Lawrence Erlbaum Associates, Publishers.

Small, W. S. (1900). An experimental study of the mental processes of the rat. *American Journal of Psychology, 11,* 133–165.

Small, W. S. (1901). Experimental study of the mental processes of the rat. II. *American Journal of Psychology, 12,* 206–239.

Smith, A. H. (1995). Celestia Parrish. *Psychology of Women Newsletter, 22,* 10.

Smith, C. U. M. (1987). David Hartley's Newtonian neuropsychology. *Journal of the History of the Behavioral Sciences, 23,* 123–136.

Smith, L. D. (1990a). Metaphors of knowledge and behavior in the behaviorist tradition. In D. E. Leary (Ed.), *Metaphors in the history of psychology* (pp. 239–266). Cambridge, England: Cambridge University Press.

Smith, L. D. (1990b). Models, mechanisms, and explanation in behavior theory: The case of Hull versus Spence. *Behavior and Philosophy, 18,* 1–18.

Smith, L. D. (1992). On prediction and control: B. F. Skinner and the technological ideal of science. *American Psychologist, 47,* 216–223.

Snyderman, M., & Herrnstein, R. (1983). Intelligence tests and the Immigration Act of 1924. *American Psychologist, 38,* 986–995.

Sokal, M. M. (1971). The unpublished autobiography of James McKeen Cattell. *American Psychologist, 26,* 626–635.

Sokal, M. M. (1980). Science and James McKeen Cattell, 1894 to 1945. *Science, 209,* 43–52.

Sokal, M. M. (1987). James McKeen Cattell and mental anthropometry: Nineteenth-century science and reform and the origins of psychological testing. In M. M. Sokal (Ed.), *Psychological testing and American society 1890–1930* (pp. 21–45). New Brunswick, NJ: Rutgers University Press.

Sokal, M. M. (1990). G. Stanley Hall and the institutional character of psychology at Clark 1889–1920. *Journal of the History of the Behavioral Sciences, 26,* 114–124.

Sokal, M. M. (1992). Origins and early years of the American Psychological Association, 1890–1906. *American Psychologist, 47,* 111–122.

Sokal, M. M. (1994). James McKeen Cattell, the New York Academy of Sciences, and the American Psychological Association, 1891–1902. In H. E. Adler & R. W. Rieber (Eds.), *Aspects of the history of psychology in America: 1892–1992* (pp. 13–35). New York: Annals of the New York Academy of Sciences (Vol. 727).

Sommer, R. (1991). James V. McConnell (1925–1990). *American Psychologist, 46,* 650.

Southern, R. W. (1986). *Robert Grosseteste.* Oxford: Oxford University Press.

Spade, P. V. (1994). Medieval philosophy. In A. Kenny (Ed.), *The Oxford history of Western philosophy* (pp. 55–105). Oxford: Oxford University Press.

Spanos, N. P. (1978). Witchcraft in histories of psychiatry: A critical analysis and an alternative conceptualization. *Psychological Bulletin, 85,* 417–439.

Spearman, C. (1930). C. Spearman. In C. Murchison (Ed.), *A history of psychology in autobiography* (Vol. 1, pp. 299–333). Worcester, MA: Clark University Press.

Spearman, C. E. (1904). General intelligence objectively determined and measured. *American Journal of Psychology, 15,* 201–293.

Spence, J. T., & Helmreich, R. L. (1978). *Masculinity & femininity: Their psychological dimensions, correlates, & antecedents.* Austin: University of Texas Press.

Spence, J. T., Helmreich, R., & Stapp, J. (1974). The Personal Attributes Questionnaire: A measure of sex-role stereotypes and masculinity-femininity. *JSAS Catalog of Selected Documents in Psychology, 4,* 127.

Spence, K. W. (1937). The differential response in animals to stimuli varying within a single dimension. *Psychological Review, 44,* 430–444.

Spence, K. W. (1952). Clark Leonard Hull: 1884–1952. *American Journal of Psychology, 65,* 639–646.

Spence, K. W. (1960). *Behavior theory and learning: Selected papers.* Englewood Cliffs, NJ: Prentice-Hall, Inc.

Sperry, R. (1982). Some effects of disconnecting the cerebral hemispheres. *Science, 217,* 1223–1226.

Sperry, R. (1994). A powerful paradigm made stronger. *Psychological Science Agenda, 7,* 10–13.

Sperry, R. W. (1964). The great cerebral commissure. *Scientific American, 210,* 42–52.

Spiegelberg, H. (1960). *The phenomenological movement: A historical introduction.* The Hague: Nijhoff.

Spillmann, J., & Spillmann, L. (1993). The rise and fall of Hugo Münsterberg. *Journal of the History of the Behavioral Sciences, 29,* 322–338.

Spinoza, B. (1883). *Ethic demonstrated in geometrical order.* London: Trubner. (Original work published 1677)

Spreen, O., & Strauss, E. (1998). *A compendium of neuropsychological tests: Administration, norms, and commentary* (2nd ed.). New York: Oxford University Press.

Sprung, H. (1997). Carl Stumpf. In W. G. Bringmann, H. E. Lück, R. Miller, & C. E. Early (Eds.), *A pictorial history of psychology* (pp. 247–250). Carol Stream, IL: Quintessence Publishing Co., Inc.

Sprung, H., & Sprung, L. (2000a). Carl Stumpf: Experimenter, theoretician, musicologist, and promoter. In G. A. Kimble & M. Wertheimer (Eds.), *Portraits of pioneers in psychology* (Vol. IV, pp. 51–69). Mahwah, NJ: Lawrence Erlbaum Associates, Publishers.

Sprung, H., & Sprung, L. (2000b). Georg Elias Müller and the beginnings of modern psychology. In G. A. Kimble & M. Wertheimer (Eds.), *Portraits of pioneers in psychology* (Vol. IV, pp. 71–91). Mahwah, NJ: Lawrence Erlbaum Associates, Publishers.

Sprung, L., & Sprung, H. (1997). The Berlin school of Gestalt psychology. In W. G. Bringmann, H. E. Lück, R. Miller, & C. E. Early (Eds.), *A pictorial history of psychology* (pp. 268–272). Carol Stream, IL: Quintessence Publishing Co., Inc.

Stafford-Clark, D. (1965). *What Freud really said.* New York: Schocken Books.

Stagner, R. (1988). *A history of psychological theories.* New York: Macmillan Publishing Company.

Stanovich, K. E. (2001). *How to think straight about psychology* (6th ed.). Boston: Allyn and Bacon.

Stepansky, P. E. (1976). The empiricist as rebel: Jung, Freud, and the burdens of discipleship. *Journal of the History of the Behavioral Sciences, 12,* 216–239.

Sternberg, R. J. (1986). *Intelligence applied.* New York: Harcourt Brace Jovanovich.

Sternberg, R. J. (1995). For whom the bell curve tolls: A review of *The Bell Curve. Psychological Science, 6,* 257–261.

Sternburg, R. J. (2000). Cross-disciplinary verification of theories: The case of the triarchic theory. *History of Psychology, 3,* 177–179.

Stevens, R. (1974). *James and Husserl: The foundation of meaning.* The Hague: Nijhoff.

Stevens, S. S. (1935). The operational basis of psychology. *American Journal of Psychology, 47,* 323–330.

Stevens, S. S. (1956). The direct estimation of sensory magnitudes—loudness. *American Journal of Psychology, 69,* 1–25.

Stevens, S. S. (1961). To honor Fechner and repeal his law. *Science, 133,* 80–86.

Stierlin, H. (1974). Karl Jaspers' psychiatry in the light of his basic philosophic position. *Journal of the History of the Behavioral Sciences, 10,* 213–226.

Storr, A. (1973). *C. G. Jung.* New York: The Viking Press.

Stratton, G. M. (1917). *Theophrastus and the Greek physiological psychology before Aristotle.* New York: Macmillan.

Strunk, O., Jr. (1972). The self-psychology of Mary Whiton Calkins. *Journal of the History of the Behavioral Sciences, 8,* 196–203.

Stumpf, C. (1895). Hermann von Helmholtz and the new psychology. *Psychological Review, 2,* 1–12.

Stumpf, C. (1930). Carl Stumpf. In C. Murchison (Ed.), *A history of psychology in autobiography* (Vol. 1, pp. 389–441). Worcester, MA: Clark University Press.

Stumpf, S. E. (1989). *Philosophy: History and problems* (4th ed.). New York: McGraw-Hill.

Sullivan, H. S. (1970). *The psychiatric interview.* New York: W. W. Norton & Company, Inc. (Original work published 1954)

Svaetichin, G., & MacNichol, E. F., Jr. (1958). Retinal mechanisms for achromatic vision. *Annals of the New York Academy of Sciences, 74,* 385–404.

Sweet, J. J., Moberg, P. J., & Westergaard, C. K. (1996). Five year follow-up survey of practices and beliefs of clinical neuropsychologists. *The Clinical Neuropsychologist, 10,* 202–221.

Swets, J. A. (1961). Is there a sensory threshold? *Science, 134,* 168–177.

Szasz, T. (1974). *The myth of mental illness* (Rev. ed.). New York: Harper & Row. (Original work published 1961)

Tarde, G. (1903). *The laws of imitation* (E. C. Parsons, Trans.). New York: Henry Holt, Inc. (Original work published 1890)

Taylor, E. (1990). New light on the origin of William James's experimental psychology. In M. G. Johnson & T. B. Henley (Eds.), *Reflections on* The Principles of Psychology (pp. 33–61). Hillsdale, NJ: Lawrence Erlbaum Associates, Publishers.

Taylor, E. (1992). William James's contributions to experimental psychology. *History of Psychology Newsletter, 24,* 3–6.

Taylor, E. (2000). Psychotherapeutics and the problematic origins of clinical psychology in America. *American Psychologist, 55,* 1929–1033.

Teigen, K. H. (1984). A note on the origin of the term "nature and nurture": Not Shakespeare and Galton, but Mulcaster. *Journal of the History of the Behavioral Sciences, 20,* 363–364.

Teo, T. (2002). Friedrich Albert Lange on neo-Kantianism, socialist Darwinism, and a psychology without a soul. *Journal of the History of the Behavioral Sciences, 38,* 285–301.

Terman, L. M. (1916). *The measurement of intelligence.* Boston: Houghton Mifflin.

Terman, L. M. (1932). Lewis M. Terman. In C. Murchison (Ed.), *A history of psychology in autobiography* (Vol. 2, pp. 297–331). Worcester, MA: Clark University Press.

Terman, L. M. (1938). *Psychological factors in marital happiness.* New York: McGraw-Hill.

Terrace, H. S. (1979). *Nim: A chimpanzee who learned sign language.* New York: Alfred A. Knopf.

Teuber, M. L. (1994). The founding of the Primate Station, Tenerife, Canary Islands. *American Journal of Psychology, 107,* 551–581.

Thomas, R. K. (1997). Correcting some Pavloviana regarding "Pavlov's bell" and Pavlov's "mugging." *American Journal of Psychology, 110,* 115–125.

Thomas, R. K. (2003). *Shepherd Ivory Franz (1874–1933).* Retrieved May 13, 2003, from University of Georgia Web site: http://www.arches.uga.edu/~rkthomas/Franz.htm

Thompson, C., Locander, W., & Pollio, H. (1989). Putting the consumer back into consumer research. *Journal of Consumer Research, 16,* 133–146.

Thompson, R. (1978). *A behavioral atlas of the rat brain.* New York: Oxford University Press.

Thompson, R. (1993). Centrencephalic theory, the General Learning System, and subcortical dementia. In F. M. Crinella & J. Yu (Eds.), *Brain mechanisms: Papers in memory of Robert Thompson* (pp. 197–223). New York: The New York Academy of Sciences.

Thompson, R., & McConnell, J. (1955). Classical conditioning in the Planarian, *Dugesia dorotocephala. Journal of Comparative and Physiological Psychology, 48,* 54–68.

Thompson, R., Crinella, F. M., & Yu, J. (1990). *Brain mechanisms in problem solving and intelligence: A lesion survey of the rat brain.* New York: Plenum Press.

Thorndike, E. L. (1899). A reply to "The nature of animal intelligence and the methods of investigating it." *Psychological Review, 6,* 412–420.

Thorndike, E. L. (1911). *Animal intelligence.* New York: The Macmillan Co.

Thorndike, E. L. (1921). Measurement in education. *Teachers College Record, 22,* 371–379.

Thorndike, E. L. (1932). *The fundamentals of learning.* New York: Teachers College.

Thorndike, E. L. (1936). Edward Lee Thorndike. In C. Murchison (Ed.), *A history of psychology in autobiography* (Vol. 3, pp. 263–270). Worcester, MA: Clark University Press.

Thorndike, E. L. (1949). *Selected writings from a connectionist's psychology.* New York: Appleton-Century-Crofts.

Thorndike, E. L., Lay, W., & Dean, P. (1909). The relation of accuracy in sensory discrimination to general intelligence. *American Journal of Psychology, 20,* 364–369.

Thorndike, E. L., & Woodworth, R. S. (1901). The influence of improvement in one mental function upon the efficiency of other functions. *Psychological Review, 8,* 247–261.

Thorndike, R. L. (1991). Edward L. Thorndike: A professional and personal appreciation. In G. A. Kimble, M. Wertheimer, & C. L. White (Eds.), *Portraits of pioneers in psychology* (pp. 138–151). Hillsdale, NJ: Lawrence Erlbaum Associates, Publishers.

Thorne, B. M. (1995). Dr. Sheldon's penchant for measurement. *The Numismatist, 108,* 591–594, 619.

Thorne, B. M. (1995). Robert Thompson: Karl Lashley's heir? *Journal of the History of the Behavioral Sciences, 31,* 129–136.

Thorne, B. M. (1996). Edward Bradford Titchener: Numismatist. *The Numismatist, 109,* 833–836, 876–878.

Thorne, B. M. (1997). Can an ape learn a language? In W. G. Bringmann, H. E. Lueck, R. Miller, & C. E. Early (Eds.), *A pictorial history of psychology* (pp. 191–197). Carol Stream, IL: Quintessence Publishing Co., Inc.

Thorne, B. M. (1998). Contributions to the history of psychology: CXI. Factual errors and Watson's autobiographical essay. *Psychological Reports, 82,* 1147–1152.

Thorne, B. M., Rager, K., & Topping, J. S. (1976). DRL performance in rats following damage to the septal area, olfactory bulbs, or olfactory tubercle. *Physiological Psychology, 4,* 493–497.

Thorne, B. M., & Watson, J. B. (1999). When was Rosalie Rayner born? *Psychological Reports, 85,* 269–270.

Thurstone, L. L. (1928). Attitudes can be measured. *American Journal of Sociology, 19,* 441–453.

Thurstone, L. L. (1938). *Primary mental abilities.* Chicago: University of Chicago Press.

Thurstone, L. L. (1952). L. L. Thurstone. In E. G. Boring, H. S. Langfeld, H. Werner, & R. M. Yerkes (Eds.), *A history of psychology in autobiography* (Vol. 4, pp. 295–321). Worcester, MA: Clark University Press.

Thurstone, L. L., & Chave, E. J. (1929). *The measurement of attitude.* Chicago: University of Chicago Press.

Tibbetts, P. (1973). Historical note on Descartes' psychophysical dualism. *Journal of the History of the Behavioral Sciences, 9,* 162–165.

Tigner, R. B., & Tigner, S. S. (2000). Triarchic theories of intelligence: Aristotle and Sternberg. *History of Psychology, 3,* 168–176.

Timberlake, W., & Lucas, G. A. (1989). Behavior systems and learning: From misbehavior to general principles. In S. B. Klein & R. R. Mowrer (Eds.), *Contemporary learning theory: Instrumental conditioning theory and the impact of biological constraints on learning* (pp. 237–275). Hillsdale, NJ: Lawrence Erlbaum Associates, Publishers.

Tinbergen, N. (1969). *The study of instinct.* Oxford: Oxford University Press. (Original work published 1951)

Tinklepaugh, O. L. (1928). An experimental study of representative factors in monkeys. *Journal of Comparative Psychology, 8,* 197–236.

Titchener, E. B. (1898). The postulates of a structural psychology. *Philosophical Review, 7,* 449–465.

Titchener, E. B. (1901, 1905). *Experimental psychology: A manual of laboratory practice* (4 vols.). New York: Macmillan.

Titchener, E. B. (1910). *A textbook of psychology.* New York: Macmillan.

Titchener, E. B. (1912). The schema of introspection. *American Journal of Psychology, 23,* 485–508.

Titchener, E. B. (1915). *A beginner's psychology.* New York: Macmillan.

Titchener, E. B. (1921). Brentano and Wundt: Empirical and experimental psychology. *American Journal of Psychology, 32,* 108–120.

Titchener, E. B. (1921). Wilhelm Wundt. *American Journal of Psychology, 32,* 161–178.

Titchener, E. B. (1922). Functional psychology and the psychology of act: II. *American Journal of Psychology, 33,* 43–83.

Tolman, E. C. (1924). The inheritance of maze-learning ability in rats. *Journal of Comparative Psychology, 4,* 1–18.

Tolman, E. C. (1938). The determiners of behavior at a choice point. *Psychological Review, 45,* 1–41.

Tolman, E. C. (1951). Prediction of vicarious trial and error by means of the schematic sowbug. In E. C. Tolman (Ed.), *Collected papers in psychology* (pp. 190–206). Berkeley: University of California Press. (Original work published 1939)

Tolman, E. C. (1948). Cognitive maps in rats and men. *Psychological Review, 55,* 189–208.

Tolman, E. C. (1948). Kurt Lewin, 1890–1947. *Psychological Review, 55,* 1–4.

Tolman, E. C. (1952). Edward Chace Tolman. In E. G. Boring, H. S. Langfeld, H. Werner, & R. M. Yerkes (Eds.), *A history of psychology in autobiography* (Vol. 4, pp. 323–339). Worcester, MA: Clark University Press.

Tolman, E. C. (1959). Principles of purposive behavior. In S. Koch (Ed.), *Psychology: A study of a science* (Vol. 2, pp. 92–157). New York: McGraw-Hill Book Company, Inc.

Tolman, E. C. (1967). *Purposive behavior in animals and men.* New York: Meredith Publishing Co. (Original work published 1932)

Tolman, E. C., Ritchie, B. F., & Kalish, D. (1946). Studies in spatial learning. II. Place learning versus response learning. *Journal of Experimental Psychology, 36,* 221–229.

Tourney, G. (1965). Freud and the Greeks: A study of the influence of classical Greek mythology and philosophy upon the development of Freudian thought. *Journal of the History of the Behavioral Sciences, 1,* 67–85.

Townsend, K. (1996). *Manhood at Harvard: William James and others.* New York: W. W. Norton & Company.

Traxel, W. (1985). Hermann Ebbinghaus: In memoriam. *History of Psychology Newsletter, 17,* 37–41.

Triplet, R. G. (1982). The relationship of Clark L. Hull's hypnosis research to his later learning theory: The continuity of his life's work. *Journal of the History of the Behavioral Sciences, 18,* 22–31.

Triplet, R. G. (1992). Henry A. Murray: The making of a psychologist? *American Psychologist, 47,* 299–307.

Triplett, N. (1898). The dynamogenic factors in pacemaking and competition. *American Journal of Psychology, 9,* 507–533.

Trudeau, M. (1990). An introspective discussion with B. F. Skinner. *Science Agenda, 3,* 10–12.

Tryon, R. C. (1940). Genetic differences in maze-learning ability in rats. *Yearbook of the National Society for Studies in Education, 39,* 111–119.

Tsushima, W. T. (1994). Luria-Nebraska Neuropsychological Battery. In R. J. Corsini (Ed.), *Encyclopedia of psychology* (2nd ed.) (Vol. 2, pp. 355–356). New York: Wiley Interscience.

Tucker, W. H. (1994). Fact and fiction in the discovery of Sir Cyril Burt's flaws. *Journal of the History of the Behavioral Sciences, 30,* 335–347.

Tucker, W. H. (1997). Re-reconsidering Burt: Beyond a reasonable doubt. *Journal of the History of the Behavioral Sciences, 33,* 145–162.

Tulving, E. (1972). Episodic and semantic memory. In E. Tulving & W. Donaldson (Eds.), *Organization of memory* (pp. 381–403). New York: Academic Press.

Tulving, E. (1985a). How many memory systems are there? *American Psychologist, 40,* 385–398.

Tulving, E. (1985b). Ebbinghaus's memory: What did he learn and remember? *Journal of Experimental Psychology: Learning, Memory, and Cognition, 11,* 485–490.

Turing, A. M. (1950). Computing machinery and the mind. *Mind, 59,* 433–460.

Tversky, A., & Kahneman, D. (1973). Availability: A heuristic for judging frequency and probability. *Cognitive Psychology, 5,* 207–232.

Tweney, R. D. (1987). Programmatic research in experimental psychology: E. B. Titchener's laboratory investigations, 1891–1927. In M. G. Ash & W. R. Woodward (Eds.), *Psychology in twentieth-century thought and society* (pp. 34–57). Cambridge: Cambridge University Press.

Tweney, R. D. (1997). Edward Bradford Titchener (1867–1927). In W. G. Bringmann, H. E. Lück, R. Miller, & C. E. Early (Eds.), *A pictorial history of psychology* (pp. 153–161). Chicago: Quintessence Publishing Co., Inc.

Tweney, R. D. (1997). Jonathan Edwards and determinism. *Journal of the History of the Behavioral Sciences, 33,* 365–380.

Unger, R., & Crawford, M. (1992). *Women and gender: A feminist psychology.* Philadelphia: Temple University Press.

Ungerer, G. A., & Bringmann, W. G. (1997). Psichiologia [Psychology], Psychology. In W. G. Bringmann, H. E. Lück, R. Miller, & C. E. Early (Eds.), *A pictorial history of psychology* (pp. 13–18). Chicago: Quintessence Publishing Co., Inc.

Valenstein, E. S. (1973). *Brain control.* New York: Wiley.

Valentine, E. R. (1999). The founding of the Psychological Laboratory, University College London: "Dear Galton . . . Yours truly, J. Sully." *History of Psychology, 2,* 204–218.

Valle, R. S., & King, M. (1978). *Existential-phenomenological alternatives for psychology.* New York: Oxford.

Vande Kemp, H. (1992). G. Stanley Hall and the Clark School of Religious Psychology. *American Psychologist, 47,* 290–298.

Vande Kemp, H. (2002). Making the history of psychology clinically and philosophically relevant. *History of Psychology, 5,* 224–239.

Vanderploeg, R. D. (1994). Neuropsychological assessment. In R. J. Corsini (Ed.), *Encyclopedia of psychology* (2nd ed.) (Vol. 2, pp. 474–476). New York: Wiley Interscience.

Van Dijken, S., Van der Veer, R., Van Ijzendoorn, M., & Kuipers, H.-J. (1998). Bowlby before Bowlby: The sources of an intellectual departure in psychoanalysis and psychology. *Journal of the History of the Behavioral Sciences, 34,* 247–269.

van Leeuwen, C. (1989). PDP and Gestalt. An integration? *Psychological Research, 50,* 199–201.

Vernon, P. A. (Ed.) (1987). *Speed of information-processing and intelligence.* Norwood, NJ: Ablex.

Viner, R. (1996). Melanie Klein and Anna Freud: The discourse of the early dispute. *Journal of the History of the Behavioral Sciences, 32,* 4–15.

Viney, W. (1996). Dorothea Dix: An intellectual conscience for psychology. In G. A. Kimble, C. A. Boneau, & M. Wertheimer (Eds.), *Portraits of pioneers in psychology* (Vol. II, pp. 15–31). Mahwah, NJ: Lawrence Erlbaum Associates, Publishers.

Viteles, M. S. (1974). Industrial psychology: Reminiscences of an academic moonlighter. In T. S. Krawiec (Ed.), *The psychologists* (Vol. 2, pp. 441–500). New York: Oxford University Press.

Vives, J. L. (1963). *De anima et vita [Of soul and life].* Torino, Italy: Bottega d'Erasmo. (Original work published 1538)

von Békésy, G. (1960). *Experiments in hearing.* New York: McGraw-Hill.

Vygotsky, L. S. (1986). *Thought and language* (A. Kozulin, Trans.). Cambridge, MA: MIT Press. (Original work published 1934)

Vygotsky, L. S. (1978). *Mind in society: The development of higher psychological processes.* Cambridge, MA: Harvard University Press.

Wade, N. J., & Brozek, J. (2001). *Purkinje's vision: The dawning of neuroscience.* Mahwah, NJ: Lawrence Erlbaum Associates, Publishers.

Walsh, A. A. (1971). George Combe: A portrait of a heretofore generally unknown behaviorist. *Journal of the History of the Behavioral Sciences, 7,* 269–278.

Wann, T. W. (Ed.) (1964). *Behaviorism and phenomenology: Contrasting bases for modern psychology.* Chicago: University of Chicago Press.

Ware, M. E. (1993, March). *Science and fiction in psychology: Hall and Hollingworth.* Paper presented at the meeting of the Southeastern Psychological Association, Atlanta, GA.

Warren, H. C. (1919). *Human psychology.* Boston: Houghton Mifflin.

Washburn, M. F. (1932). Margaret Floy Washburn: Some recollections. In C. Murchison (Ed.), *A history of psychology in autobiography* (Vol. 2, pp. 333–358). Worcester, MA: Clark University Press.

Wassermann, I. (1958). Letter to the editor. *American Journal of Psychotherapy, 12,* 623–627.

Watkins, W. H. (1989, March). *Psychological prewarfare: A review of Hugo Münsterberg's dealings in international politics, 1897–1916.* Paper presented at the meeting of the Southeastern Psychological Association, Washington.

Watson, J. B. (1907). Kinaesthetic and organic sensations: Their role in the reactions of the white rat to the maze. *Psychological Monographs, 8*(33).

Watson, J. B. (1913). Psychology as the behaviorist views it. *Psychological Review, 20,* 158–177.

Watson, J. B. (1916). The place of the conditioned-reflex in psychology. *Psychological Review, 23,* 89–116.

Watson, J. B. (1919a). *Psychology from the standpoint of a behaviorist.* Philadelphia: Lippincott.

Watson, J. B. (1919b). A schematic outline of the emotions. *Psychological Review, 26,* 165–196.

Watson, J. B. (1970). *Behaviorism.* New York: W. W. Norton & Company. (Original work published 1924)

Watson, J. B. (1972). *Psychological care of infant and child.* New York: Arno Press. (Original work published 1928)

Watson, J. B. (1936). John Broadus Watson. In C. Murchison (Ed.), *A history of psychology in autobiography* (Vol. 3, pp. 271–281). Worcester, MA: Clark University Press.

Watson, J. B., & Morgan, J. J. B. (1917). Emotional reactions and psychological experimentation. *American Journal of Psychology, 28,* 163–174.

Watson, J. B., & Rayner, R. (1920). Conditioned emotional reactions. *Journal of Experimental Psychology, 3,* 1–14.

Watson, R. I. (1971). A prescriptive analysis of Descartes' psychological views. *Journal of the History of the Behavioral Sciences, 7,* 223–247.

Watson, R. I. (1979). *Basic writings in the history of psychology.* New York: Oxford University Press.

Webb, M. E. (1988). A new history of Hartley's *Observations on Man. Journal of the History of the Behavioral Sciences, 24,* 202–211.

Weidman, N. (1994). Mental testing and machine intelligence: The Lashley-Hull debate. *Journal of the History of the Behavioral Sciences, 30,* 162–180.

Weidman, N. (1997). Heredity, intelligence and neuropsychology; or, why *The Bell Curve* is good science. *Journal of the History of the Behavioral Sciences, 33,* 141–144.

Weidman, N. (1998). A response to Bruce (1998) on the Lashley-Hull debate. *History of Psychology, 1,* 156–159.

Weidman, N. (2002). The depoliticization of Karl Lashley: A response to Dewsbury. *Journal of the History of the Behavioral Sciences, 38,* 247–253.

Weidman, N. M. (1999). *Constructing scientific psychology: Karl Lashley's mind-brain debates.* Cambridge: Cambridge University Press.

Wells, F. L. (1944). James McKeen Cattell: 1860–1944. *American Journal of Psychology, 57,* 270–275.

Wells, G. L., & Loftus, E. F. (Eds.) (1984). *Eyewitness testimony: Psychological perspectives.* Cambridge, MA: Cambridge University Press.

Wells, M. (2002). BBC halts "prison experiment." *The Guardian.* Retrieved September 29, 2003, from http://www.guardian.co.uk/uk_news/story/0,3604,638243,00.html

Wendorf, C. A. (2001). History of American morality research, 1894–1932. *History of Psychology, 4,* 272–288.

Wentworth, P. A. (1999). The moral of her story: Exploring the philosophical and religious commitments in Mary Whiton Calkins' self-psychology. *History of Psychology, 2,* 119–131.

Wertheimer, Max (1968). Experimental studies on the seeing of motion. In W. S. Sahakian (Ed.), *History of psychology: A source book in systematic psychology* (pp. 418–422). Itasca, IL: Peacock. (Original work published 1912)

Wertheimer, Max (1945). *Productive thinking.* New York: Harper.

Wertheimer, Michael. (1965). Relativity and Gestalt: A note on Albert Einstein and Max Wertheimer. *Journal of the History of the Behavioral Sciences, 1,* 86–87.

Wertheimer, Michael (1980a). Gestalt theory of learning. In G. M. Gazda & R. J. Corsini (Eds.), *Theories of learning: A comparative approach* (pp. 208–251). Itasca, IL: Peacock.

Wertheimer, Michael. (1980b). Max Wertheimer, Gestalt prophet. *Gestalt Theory, 2,* 3–17.

Wertheimer, Michael. (1991). Max Wertheimer: Modern cognitive psychology and the Gestalt problem. In G. A. Kimble, M. Wertheimer, & C. White (Eds.), *Portraits of pioneers in psychology* (pp. 189–207). Hillsdale, NJ: Lawrence Erlbaum Associates, Publishers.

Wertheimer, Michael (1992, March). *Max Wertheimer in America.* Paper presented at the meeting of the Southeastern Psychological Association convention, Knoxville, TN.

Wertheimer, Michael. (2000). *A brief history of psychology* (4th ed.). Fort Worth, TX: Harcourt.

Wertheimer, Michael, & King, D. B. (1994). Max Wertheimer's American sojourn, 1933–1943. *History of Psychology Newsletter, 26,* 3–15.

Wertheimer, Michael, King, D. B., Peckler, M. A., Raney, S., & Schaef, R. W. (1992). Carl Jung and Max Wertheimer on a priority issue. *Journal of the History of the Behavioral Sciences, 28,* 45–56.

Wesley, F. (1968). Was Raehlmann the first behaviorist? *Journal of the History of the Behavioral Sciences, 4,* 161–162.

White, S. H. (1990). Child study at Clark University: 1894–1904. *Journal of the History of the Behavioral Sciences, 26,* 131–150.

Wilkening, H. E. (1973). *The psychology almanac.* Monterey, CA: Brooks/Cole.

Wills, G. (1999). *St. Augustine.* New York: Lipper/Viking.

Wilshire, B. (1968). *William James and phenomenology.* Bloomington: Indiana University Press.

Wilson, D. S., Near, D., & Miller, R. R. (1996). Machiavellianism: A synthesis of the evolutionary and psychological literatures. *Psychological Bulletin, 119,* 285–299.

Wilson, F. (1991). Mill and Comte on the method of introspection. *Journal of the History of the Behavioral Sciences, 27,* 107–129.

Wilson, M. D. (Ed.) (1969). *The essential Descartes.* New York: Mentor Books.

Windholz, G. (1983). Pavlov's position toward American behaviorism. *Journal of the History of the Behavioral Sciences, 19,* 394–407.

Windholz, G. (1984). Pavlov vs. Köhler: Pavlov's little-known primate research. *Pavlovian Journal of Biological Science, 19,* 23–31.

Windholz, G. (1986). A comparative analysis of the conditional reflex discoveries of Pavlov and Twitmyer, and the birth of a paradigm. *Pavlov Journal of Biological Science, 21,* 141–149.

Windholz, G. (1987). Pavlov as a psychologist: A reappraisal. *Pavlov Journal of Biological Science, 22,* 103–112.

Windholz, G. (1990). Pavlov and Pavlovians in the laboratory. *Journal of the History of the Behavioral Sciences, 26,* 64–74.

Windholz, G. (1996). Pavlov's conceptualization of the dynamic stereotype in the theory of higher nervous activity, *American Journal of Psychology, 109,* 287–295.

Windholz, G. (1997). The 1950 Joint Scientific Session: Pavlovians as the accusers and the accused. *Journal of the History of the Behavioral Sciences, 33,* 61–81.

Windholz, G., & Lamal, P. A. (1986). Pavlov and the concept of association. *Pavlov Journal of Biological Science, 21,* 12–15.

Winograd, T. (1972). *Understanding natural language.* New York: Academic Press.

Winston, A. S. (1990). Robert Sessions Woodworth and the "Columbia Bible": How the psychological experiment was redefined. *American Journal of Psychology, 103,* 391–401.

Wippel, J. F., & Wolter, A. B. (1969). *Medieval philosophy.* New York: Free Press.

Wiseman, D. B. (2000). Subjective science: Kenneth Spence's human learning research program. *History of Psychology, 3,* 262–283.

Wiseman, D. B. (2001). Two portraits of science. *History of Psychology, 4,* 198–200.

Witmer, L. (1907). Clinical psychology. *The Psychological Clinic, 1,* 1–9.

Wittgenstein, L. (1953). *Philosophical investigations* (G. E. M. Anscombe, Trans.). New York: Macmillan.

Wollheim, R. (1971). *Sigmund Freud.* New York: Viking Press.

Wolman, B. B. (1968). *The unconscious mind: The meaning of Freudian psychology.* Englewood Cliffs, NJ: Prentice-Hall, Inc.

Wood, J. M., Nezworski, M. T., & Stejskal, W. J. (1996). The comprehensive system for the Rorschach: A critical examination. *Psychological Science, 7,* 3–10.

Woodward, W. R. (1972). Fechner's panpsychism: A scientific solution to the mind-body problem. *Journal of the History of the Behavioral Sciences, 8,* 367–386.

Woodworth, R. S. (1909). Hermann Ebbinghaus. *The Journal of Philosophy, Psychology and Scientific Methods, 6,* 253–256.

Woodworth, R. S. (1978). A revision of imageless thought. In E. R. Hilgard (Ed.), *American psychology in historical perspective* (pp. 119–138). Washington, DC: American Psychological Association. (Original work published 1915)

Woodworth, R. S. (1921). *Psychology: A study of mental life.* New York: Henry Holt & Co.

Woodworth, R. S. (1932). Robert S. Woodworth. In C. Murchison (Ed.), *A history of psychology in autobiography* (Vol. 2, pp. 359–380). Worcester, MA: Clark University Press.

Woodworth, R. S. (1944). James McKeen Cattell (1860–1944). *Psychological Review, 51,* 201–209.

Woody, W. D. (1999). William James and Gestalt psychology. *The Journal of Mind and Behavior, 20,* 79–92.

Worcester, E. (1932). *Life's adventure: The story of a varied career.* New York: Scribner.

Wundt, W. (1862). *Die Geschwindigkeit des Gedankens* [The speed of thought]. *Gartenlaube,* 263–265.

Wundt, W. (1904). *Principles of physiological psychology* (5th ed., Vol. 1, E. B. Titchener, Trans.). New York: Macmillan. (Original work published 1902)

Yang, S.-Y., & Sternberg, R. J. (1997). Conceptions of intelligence in ancient Chinese philosophy. *Journal of Theoretical and Philosophical Psychology, 17,* 101–119.

Yates, A. J. (1980). *Biofeedback and modification of behavior.* New York: Plenum.

Yerkes, R. M. (Ed.) (1921). *Psychological examining in the U.S. Army.* Memoirs of the National Academy of Sciences (No. 15).

Yerkes, R. M. (1932). Robert Mearns Yerkes: Psychobiologist. In C. Murchison (Ed.), *A history of psychology in autobiography* (Vol. 2, pp. 381–407). Worcester, MA: Clark University Press.

Yerkes, R. M., & Dodson, J. D. (1908). The relation of strength of stimulus to rapidity of habit formation. *Journal of Comparative Neurology and Psychology, 18,* 459–482.

Yerkes, R. M., & Learned, B. W. (1925). *Chimpanzee intelligence and its vocal expressions.* Baltimore: Williams & Wilkins.

Yerkes, R. M., & Morgulis, S. (1909). The method of Pawlow in animal psychology. *Psychological Bulletin, 6,* 257–273.

Yerkes, R. M., & Yerkes, A. W. (1929). *The great apes: A study of anthropoid life.* New Haven, CT: Yale University Press.

Young, R. K. (1985). Ebbinghaus: Some consequences. *Journal of Experimental Psychology: Learning, Memory, and Cognition, 11,* 491–495.

Zajonc, R. B. (1965). Social facilitation. *Science, 149,* 269–274.

Zajonc, R. B., Murphy, S., & Ingelhart, M. (1989). Feeling and facial efference: Implications of the vascular theory of emotion. *Psychological Review, 96,* 395–416.

Zeigarnik, B. (1927). Über Behalten von erledigten und unerledigten Handlungen [On the retention of finished and unfinished acts]. *Psychologische Forschung, 9,* 1–85.

Zenderland, L. (1997). *The Bell Curve* and the shape of history. *Journal of the History of the Behavioral Sciences, 33,* 135–139.

Zilboorg, G. (1941). *A history of medical psychology.* New York: W. W. Norton & Company.

Zillmann, D. (1983). Transfer of excitation in emotional behavior. In J. T. Cacioppo & R. E. Petty (Eds.), *Social psychology: A sourcebook* (pp. 215–240). New York: Guilford Press.

Zillmann, D., Katcher, A. H., & Milavsky, B. (1972). Excitation transfer from physical exercise to subsequent aggressive behavior. *Journal of Experimental Social Psychology, 8,* 247–259.

Zimbardo, P. G. (1992). *Psychology and life* (13th ed.). New York: HarperCollins.

Zimbardo, P. G., Haney, C., Banks, W., & Jaffe, D. (1973, April 8). Pirandellian prison: The mind is a formidable jailor. *New York Times Magazine,* pp. 38–60.

Zinchenko, V. P. (1997). Russian psychology. In W. G. Bringmann, H. E. Lück, R. Miller, & C. E. Early (Eds.), *A pictorial history of psychology* (pp. 572–576). Carol Stream, IL: Quintessence Publishing Co., Inc.

Zusne, L. (1989). Contributions to the history of psychology: LV. Purkinje phenomenon: Original account and later definitions. *Perceptual and Motor Skills, 68,* 897–898.

Name Index

Bold numbers indicate pages containing the most complete biographical information.

Subject Index

Bold numbers indicate the page or pages on which the term is defined.

Psychology Begins

Wilhelm Wundt

Ivan Sechenov (1829–1905)
Wilhelm Wundt (1832–1920)

Franz Brentano (1838–1917)

William James (1842–1910)
G. Stanley Hall (1844–1924)
Carl Stumpf (1848–1936)
Ivan Pavlov (1849–1936)
Hermann Ebbinghaus (1850–1909)

Sigmund Freud (1856–1939)
Alfred Binet (1857–1911)
John Dewey (1859–1952)
James McKeen Cattell (1860–1944)
Oswald Külpe (1862–1915)
Hugo Münsterberg (1863–1916) Mary Calkins (1863–1930)
E. B. Titchener (1867–1927)

R. S. Woodworth (1869–1962) J. R. Angell (1869–1949)
Alfred Adler (1870–1937)
Edward Lee Thorndike (1874–1949)
Carl Jung (1875–1961)
John Watson (1878–1958)
Wundt's laboratory begins
Max Wertheimer (1880–1943)
Clark Hull (1884–1952)
Ebbinghaus publishes *Über das Gedächtnis* (1885)
Edwin Guthrie (1886–1959)
Edward Tolman (1886–1959) Kurt Koffka (1886–1941)
Wolfgang Köhler (1887–1967)
Karl Lashley (1890–1958) Kurt Lewin (1890–1947)
APA is founded
Dewey publishes "The Reflex Arc Concept in Psychology" (1896)
Jean Piaget (1896–1980)

Freud publishes *The Interpretation of Dreams* (1900)
Carl Rogers (1902–1987) D. O. Hebb (1904–1985)
B. F. Skinner (1904–1990) Kenneth Spence (1907–1967)
Abraham Maslow (1908–1970)
Neal Miller (1909–2002)

Watson publishes his "behaviorist manifesto" in 1913
Roger Sperry (1913–1994)
Herbert Simon (1916–2001)

Clark Conference

Noam Chomsky (1928–)

Representative Historical Events

1830 Typewriter patented
Goethe dies

1840 Auguste Comte gives sociology its name
U.S. Naval Academy opens

1850 California becomes a state

1860 Work begins on Suez Canal
Lee surrenders to Grant to end Civil War

1870 Darwin publishes *The Descent of Man* (1871)

1880 Helen Keller is born

1890 Cy Young begins his National League pitching career
Sherlock Holmes appears in *Strand* magazine
The X-ray is discovered

1900 H. G. Wells flourishes
Pavlov wins the Nobel Prize in medicine

1910 W. E. B. Du Bois founds NAACP

1920 World War I ends
Alexander Graham Bell dies

1930 Flashbulb photography begins